A Documentary History

of the

Jews in the United States

1654–1875

A Documentary History of the Jews in the United States *1654-1875*

Edited with notes and introductions by
MORRIS U. SCHAPPES

THIRD EDITION

SCHOCKEN BOOKS • NEW YORK

First SCHOCKEN EDITION 1971
Second Printing, 1976

Library of Congress Catalog Card No. 72–122332
Manufactured in the United States of America

TO THE MEMORY OF
MY FATHER AND MY MOTHER

INTRODUCTION TO THE 1971 EDITION

The heritage of the Jews and other immigrant groups in America has until recently been obscured by the dominance of the "melting pot" theory of the emergence of the unhyphenated "American" type. This theory was one manifestation of Anglo-Saxon, nativist, and racist assumptions of superiority. Objective conditions of anti-Semitic pressures and the assertion of Jewish identity in response to Nazism, the holocaust, and the creation of the State of Israel demonstrated the weakness of the melting-pot approach. Since about the turn of the century, Jewish and Negro historians, as well as historians of other groups, had begun to assemble data and to challenge omissions in American historiography acceptable to classical American historians and their followers among immigrant imitators and assimilationists. The gathering of data in American Jewish history in an organized manner has been in progress since the founding of the American Jewish Historical Society in 1892, but this book was the first attempt to fill the elementary need of a documentary history.

The settling of the first group of Jews in New Amsterdam in 1654 can be seen as an incident in the economic and political transformation of western Europe, in the conflict between the expanding capitalist states of England, France, and Holland (despite their own rivalries) on the one hand; on the other, the decaying feudalism of Spain and Portugal, whose hold on the Atlantic islands, on the gigantic mainlands of the southern parts of the hemisphere, on the trade routes, and on the African slave trade was weakened by the privateers, navies, and merchant adventurers of their rivals. The development of commerce and the piling up of stocks of capital were to stoke the fires of a later industrial capitalism, the struggle for citizenship based on equalitarian ideals, and the acquisition of overseas colonies based on the mercantilist principles that they would become sources of precious metals or raw materials, or both. These were also to compose the Old World background for New World history.

So in American Jewish history (which cannot be scientifically investigated except as a part of American history), the conditions of the New World spring from the crises, the disintegrations, and the social reintegrations of the Old. The "New World" is by no means a second "creation." The colonists had been formed in the Old World relations in which capitalist "free enterprise" was rising against, grappling with, and would eventually replace, feudalism. They brought with them, as part of their baggage, ideas, beliefs, work habits, skills, attitudes, superstitions, prejudices, fears, cultural patterns, and the resultant psychological traits. In so far as these colonists had had direct or indirect contact with Jews or the reputation of Jews, the content of their attitude to the Jews was conditioned by the old relations in the "old country." Thus the relationships that constitute the matter of the first chapters of American Jewish history are not relationships between a mythical New Jew and a mythical New non-Jew. Rather is it a contact between Jews and non-Jews, both of whom had old world baggage, but both of whom also were meeting each other under new conditions that were an extension, but at the same time a modification, of the old conditions.

Broadly speaking, the history of American Jewish life from colonial times on is a history of life under capitalism. Our country, essentially, has no history of feudalism, although certain reflections of feudalism continued to reveal themselves in American life even into the nineteenth century. Likewise, American Jewish life has no period of feudalism, and is thus distinguished from European Jewish history, which has a long feudal period. American Jewish history would obviously be much different had it worked itself out in part under pre-capitalist feudalism or post-capitalist socialism. Instead, Jewish life here has developed distinctively as a part of the economic, political, social, and cultural life of a nation developing under capitalist relations—with slavery and its aftermath of anti-Negro restrictions as the only pre-capitalist institution to play a major role in that development.

Certainly Jewish life in our country has never been independent of basic social relationships or self-sufficient even in the sense in which European Jewish ghetto-communities were autonomous. For Jews, this country has had no ghettoes. Yet the great historic democratic American promise of equality, which would have meant the complete integration of Jewish life into American life as a whole, has not been fulfilled. The economic machinery of our society necessarily gave to competition a priority it denied to social service and social cooperation. Such a society not only transatlantically transplanted feudal patterns of anti-Semitism but created new ones with new rationalizations and verbalizations. Bills of Rights and Constitutions federal and state may have proclaimed equality (and even some of these were defective until less than a century ago). Nevertheless, the use of anti-Semitism as a weapon to gain advantage over rivals or to divert bubbling social unrest has produced the result that to this day the Jewish people in the United States have not achieved full equality at *all* levels, economic, political, social, and cultural.

It may be a signal, sad, but illuminating value of these representative documents that they reveal for the first time that anti-Semitism in our country has a more ancient history, a more persistent continuity, and a wider dispersion than even liberal opponents of anti-Semitism have hitherto dreamed. The variety of anti-Semitic expressions, whose existence is barely suggested in this volume, can no longer be ignored. The types are many; we find official legal and political discrimination and abuse, as well as restrictions economic, social, and cultural. The rationalizations too are many. Anti-Semitica emerge phrased variously in the languages of piety, commercial spite, political billingsgate, or the gutter epithet with its roots in carefully preserved and designedly transmitted "folk-lore." The "reasons given" will include many things (and there is a *history* of reasons given and of the changing of reasons, which a full study of the history of anti-Semitism should explore). Among them are charges theological, esthetic, political, economic, racial, and "psychological," depending upon the specific situation and upon the people to whom the anti-Semitica are addressed. But the basic pattern is essentially the same. Stuyvesant wanted to oust the new Jewish immigrants from New Amsterdam because, he averred, the Jews were 1) usurers; 2) deceitful traders; 3) so poor they would be a burden on the community; 4) blasphemers of Jesus. There was no truth in these assertions, nor were they uttered for the good of the community. When Stuyvesant had to allow the Jews to stay, none of the evils he had conjured came to being; on the contrary, both the non-Jews and the Jews benefited. It is my judgment that the evidence points to a fundamental, irreducible cause of anti-Semitism: in any society so class-structured that a minority economically exploits, politically dominates, and culturally controls the majority, the usefulness of anti-Semitism in all its forms and verbalizations is assured and endless because it helps keep that minority in power.

In compiling this work, I did not seek artificially to limit or tendentiously to restrict the concept of Jews to any particular Jewish group or "community." The Jew outside the synagogue (and by the time we get to the last third of the period covered, most of them, it is generally admitted, were already outside) is as worthy of study as the Jew in the synagogue. The Jew who turns away from other Jews or even feels compelled to hide or deny his Jewish identity is responding to a particular situation in a way as distinctively Jewish as that of the pious Sabbath observer. For only a Jew could be compelled by social pressures to deny that he was a Jew. The historian is therefore obligated to be all-inclusive, to reveal the centrifugal as well as the centripetal forces in the group. Nor have I been bound by any theory that would include certain things done by Jews, such as those deeds that are by religious or cultural pattern or organizational affiliation "exclusively" Jewish, and exclude other things. To me it seemed that there is no Jewish life without Jews making a living. Therefore there has been considerable attention to the hitherto generally neglected field of the economic activities of Jews.

There is another tendency in the writing of Jewish history that is alert to the exclusion of Jews from any field, but dismisses as irrelevant their inclusion or acceptance. If a Jew is excluded from a certain industry or profession or residential section, the fact is regarded as pertinent; if accepted, he is taken as lost to Jewish interest, sucked as it were into the swamp of equality. Yet the Jew who fought without praying in the Union army is as much part of the Jewish American historical scene as the Jew who prayed without fighting. The integrative relations between Jew and non-Jew (for example, see the Index under business partnerships) are as relevant as anti-Semitic restrictions. Therefore some documents are included that are significant because of the simple fact that they are signed by Jews and non-Jews together. To this scope, then, nothing Jewish is alien, nothing done by Jews is irrelevant. But, unlike the indexer of a daily newspaper, to whom all facts are of equal import, I have given more representation and more weight to certain material and social facts all too often ignored or skirted.

The form of a documentary history also may require comment. The document has unquestionable authenticity; this is the record, in its original appearance and language, strained by no intervening "interpretation." This is how the Jews themselves spoke and lived and thought of themselves for two centuries in our country, and how their contemporary non-Jews thought and wrote of them.

With documents the writing of history must begin, but it must not end with them. For what people think of themselves is only one fact that the historical scientist takes into account. Consider for instance the vexed question of defining what the Jews are: a race, a religious group, a single nation, or a people. Reference to the Index (under "Jews, concepts of as") will show the number of times in the documents themselves the Jews thought of themselves (or were thought of by non-Jews) as a race, religious group, or single nation. (In Document No. 20, the Jews in Holland even speak of themselves as "merchants of the Portuguese nation" and as the "Jewish nation.") These facts provide clues, therefore, to the consciousness of the Jews, but is this evidence of what they *are?* Would a statistical count demonstrating that they thought of themselves more often as one thing than another be of any weight in objectively determining what they are? Useful as it is to have these facts, particularly for the history of the development of ideas and states of mind, the social scientist will look elsewhere for the facts from which he will derive his definition. Informed persons, for example, no longer regard the Jews as a race, and documentary proof (contained within) that Jews for a long time thought of themselves as such cannot stand up against the contrary finding of the scientific anthropologist.

This example has been given to illustrate the great value, and also one of the limitations, of a "documentary history." To prevent this limitation from becoming a confusing handicap, the editor has supplied his introductions and notes to each document, to help provide the objective setting in which it can best be appreciated and understood.

Another problem became apparent in the search for a balanced and representative selection from the mass of available material. Often the document testifying to an important event was so meager as to be unable to convey the meaning and the drama of what it was barely recording. Thus the decision, unprecedented perhaps in Jewish history, by which the majority of the Jews of New York City agreed to go into *voluntary* exile rather than stay and collaborate with the British and Hessian occupation of the city after its conquest in 1776, is recorded only in the bare-boned synagogue minutes. Instead of printing that, the editor chose briefly to refer to the event in introducing a document of quite the opposite import (No. 37), in which the minority of New York Jews who remained behind joined hundreds of non-Jews in a fulsome declaration of loyalty to the British crown and military authority. Then he represented Jewish participation in the American Revolution in other documents.

A third problem was what to do about "the short and simple annals of the poor," which he regards as more important than the brevity or simplicity would testify. Yet the scant newspaper notice of the suicide of an unemployed Jewish carpenter is voluble (No. 102), and the "philanthropist's" description of the living conditions of Jews in poverty (No. 90) is eloquent even though neither the suicide nor the poor left their own testaments to be reproduced as the real documents. The needy were many and miserable, and the philanthropy of which Jews have been so proud, and in comparison with other groups the pride may not be unjustified, was but a poultice. In the absence of statistics (since the studies to obtain even approximations have not yet been conducted) on the occupational distribution of the Jews, the interested reader will find the list of occupations in the Index as valuable as the list of congregations. The former list suggests the existence of a considerable number of Jewish workers, who made themselves felt, like most of the people, anonymously. Even the articulate and outstanding whose names recur in these pages owe their elevation to the anonymous mass of Jews. Surely this is true in the political as well as the economic arena. When an Emanuel B. Hart, taking over the mantle of M. M. Noah, Grand Sachem of Tammany Hall, is nominated for office (Document No. 100), we can recognize both his merit and the need of political bosses to give a certain degree of "representation" to the Jewish voters. Yet a voting list from Hart's district is not available because the formal registration of voters was not yet then required by law.

In this volume, then, the multitudes of working-class Jews that were later to become a great factor in Jewish life do not yet appear as an independent, organized, conscious shaping force. That was to come later, with the great migrations after 1875. But even towards the end of the period covered herein the beginnings are perceptible. Not only are there the harbingers in the utopian socialism of an Ernestine L. Rose and in the social-democratic theory of the 1850's advocated by a Sigismund Kaufmann. There is also evidence that the Jewish employers were becoming worried that workers, Jewish and non-Jewish, would enter the labor movement. In Document No. 146 there is a call from a group of far-sighted labor leaders for the unity of labor, "Jew or Gentile," Negro and white. Only a few months before this call was published, *The Jewish Messenger* (May 10, 1867) had expressed the point of view of the employers in an editorial, "The Labor Question." In terms hardly fresh even then, *The Jewish Mes-*

senger complained that workers are joining unions, and that therefore "capital is, practically, at the mercy of labor . . . and capital assumes a miserable, cringing, plebeian attitude." In denouncing "the most outrageous and unjustifiable demand" for the eight-hour day, the editor, whose periodical was genuinely devoted to "philanthropy," exclaimed in heartless horror: "Sixteen hours daily upon an ignorant man's hands! It is a deliberate wrong for society to permit such a dangerous waste of time." Thus we see the stage being prepared for the tremendous battles Jewish workers were to be compelled to wage against their employers, non-Jewish and Jewish.

A problem of judgment faces the Jewish historian concerned with both a people and the social issues and causes they upheld. Many a historian abdicates judgment by concluding that, since Jews are on both sides, the issue between them is of less importance than the paramount fact that Jews *are* on both sides. Another type of historian with a strong moral, social, or political commitment may conclude that all Jews should by rights (or by his lights) be on the proper side; the others are either not Jews, bad Jews, or at least Jews unworthy of inclusion in his history.

The former type, studying the relation of Jews to the wars our country has fought, from the wars against the Indians to the Civil War, strikes a superior attitude of "objectivity" (like the Jew in the anecdote on p. 469, Document No. 137), and blesses all sides of every conflict, leaving to other historians the necessary task of evaluating the issue. Since there were Jews on both sides of the War of the Revolution, the War of 1812, and the Civil War, such historians are content to chronicle events and "prove" that Jews can be loyal to all governments and all sides of basic social, political, and moral issues. Of course, such apologetics are often created by the need to offset anti-Semitic falsehoods. But the historian who never rises above this level, in providing a fillip to Jewish "national" pride or to a misbegotten concept of patriotism divorced from public morality, may be doing harm to history as a social science.

In order to serve the ends of historical objectivity the scholar is obligated to make his judgment on issues (these wars, for example) and on the basic values involved, knowingly or unknowingly, on each side. One may assume for the sake of the argument that the mass of soldiers of the line on both sides of the American Revolution thought they were doing the right or necessary thing, and were primed with words of noble ring, and believed some of them. But the historical fact is that the flags of the revolutionaries were the banners that, carried to victory, were to help the cause of progress not only in our country but also in England, in Hesse, and in France, and therefore the Jews in these countries too. Then the British or Hessian Jew, or the American Jewish Tory, who opposed the Revolution, must be seen objectively as having fought against the best interest of the Jews, which is linked to human progress. The same is true of the Civil War. The Jews of Shreveport, La., swore by what they called their "holy cause," and may have been piously honest in their protestations. But there is only minor merit in the honesty, and great condemnation in their blindness to the issue of slavery, a blindness that led them into the objective situation of fighting to perpetuate a vicious institution and an evil cause. Seeing this is not the same as seeing history shallowly in terms of good and bad, dastard and hero. The issue of complexity and of "good people on both sides" often diverts the historian from his professional duty of coping with all the complexity in order to reach the necessary judgment, short of which he abdicates his function and becomes a superficial chronicler. Such a chronicler, by his narrow "nationalistic" preoccupation with the Jews only, is not actually being Olympian and above the battleground on which issues must be settled; by failing to clarify issues, he is obscuring reality, and making more difficult the movement for progress.

But in displaying and analyzing the conduct of both sides, one encounters the objections of the second type of Jewish historian, who will be worried that Jews are found to have been on the unjust side of now settled, as well as some open, issues. Such historians confuse the true proposition that Jews have always, in their mass, tended to benefit from the march of historical progress, with the fond belief that all Jews have always been on the side of progress—the historical apologist's version of "the Chosen People." True, it can be said that, at least in our country, on every major issue there were always some Jews on the side of progress. At the same time there were Jews on the side of reaction. The reason can be missed only if one operates on the false and separatist theory that the attitudes of Jews are somehow shaped only by special causes and not by those that mold the conduct of the American people as a whole. On the issue of slavery and the biblical interpretation of it, American Jews were distinctive; no European Jewish community faced any such economic-socio-political-moral issue as slavery. Were the "people of the book" basically guided by Mosaic and biblical teachings on slavery? Did American Jews produce a uniform Jewish position on slavery? On the contrary. Pro-slavers and abolitionists used and abused their reading of Scripture to support, rationalize, and lubricate with piety positions determined by other factors. They divided along class, social, and political lines as did the remainder of the American population (most of whom also venerated the Bible). The consciousness of the Jews was determined and molded by the same forces that shaped the consciousness of the remainder of the people, by how they made a living, by their way of life, i.e., by their part in the technological processes and the relations of production of all material, social, intellectual, and spiritual goods and values, modified by political, legal, cultural, and moral factors, in the country and system they lived in.

To these forces, however, one has to add, for the Jews, their experience with anti-Semitic pressures and the effect of these on their way of making a living, on their aspirations and opportunities, on their psychology and culture. No theory of "sameness" should blur this difference, this distinctiveness.

To record these divisions in the past is to add historical depth to the existing divisions in Jewish life, and thus to shed light on them. One can understand the Jewish segregationist today for knowing the Jewish Confederate of yesterday. One can better understand the Jewish radical today for knowing of his antecedents in the colonials who "have distinguishedly suffered for their attachment to the revolution principles" (Document No. 43), in the Jeffersonians, and in the abolitionists. The problems of the Negro people in our country and of the Jews overlap, and there is continuing cooperation between them in combating discrimination. A glance at the Index will show how often the paths of Negroes and Jews have crossed, sometimes as opponents, sometimes as allies. There were slave traders, slave dealers, slave owners, and Confederates among the Jews, but there were democrats and abolitionists and thousands of soldiers in the Union army. In Reconstruction Tennessee the Ku Klux Klan lynched a Negro and a Jew simultaneously (Document No. 148), and a year earlier a labor manifesto called for the unity of Jew and non-Jew, Negro and white (Document No. 146). This history provides both a foundation for cooperative efforts today, and an understanding of why some oppose this cooperation.

In these pages are the names and activities of hundreds of Jews who, taken alone, are insignificant and would never appear in the pages of an ordinary history. Yet American life and American history are what they are because these Jews came and lived and worked and wrote and petitioned and prayed and sued and complained and fought and died and were, simply, Americans, Jewish Americans. They therefore deserve inclusion in the historical record. They not only shared but contributed to American democratic ideals. Jews and others can derive great inspiration from the work and utterances of an Asser Levy, a Solomon Simpson, a Benjamin Nones, a Rabbi David Einhorn, an Isidor Bush, an Ernestine L. Rose. In the words of Jacob De La Motta (Document No. 70), the Jews coming to our country "panted for Liberty and the enjoyment of equal rights." To this day, liberty and equality are still their need and, for most of them, their goal.

In so far as possible, the editor has striven to provide, if not a facsimile, at least a faithfully accurate reproduction of the texts of the documents. The original spelling, capitalization,and punctuation have been followed punctiliously, with these exceptions: the word Negro has been capitalized throughout, since the use of the small "n" is derogatory and properly resented; when raised letters (e.g., 24th) have had periods or other such markings underneath them, these have been eliminated for economic reasons. Editorial matter inserted into the text has been placed in square brackets: [ ]. The titles of the documents have in all cases, and the brief definition of their nature that follows each title in heavy type has in most cases, been supplied by the editor.

In the Notes, the following abbreviations have been used:

AJA —American Jewish Archives
AJHQ —American Jewish Historical Quarterly
AJHSP—American Jewish Historical Society Publications
JE —The Jewish Encyclopedia
UJE —The Universal Jewish Encyclopedia
DAB —The Dictionary of American Biography
DNB —The Dictionary of National Biography
DAH —Dictionary of American History
AJYB —American Jewish Year Book

The aim has been to make the documentation precise for the scholar, ample for the general reader, and suggestive for the student who may wish to explore a point further.

The Index is substantial but not exhaustive. It contains a *complete* listing of the following: Jews referred to in the documents and notes, their occupations, and the Jewish institutions and congregations mentioned. There is only a partial listing, because of space limitations, of non-Jews, of place names (countries, states, and cities), and of subjects. Only those authors are indexed, with references only to the pages on which each work used is first mentioned, who are so frequently cited that the reader would otherwise have had difficulty locating the item referred to by the overworked *op. cit.*

It would be futile to attempt here to record my thanks to the very many people who in so many ways helped to make this work possible, and to whom I have already otherwise expressed my deep appreciation. In my Notes I have cited extensively, but here I would emphasize the debt due those pioneers in American Jewish history who have delved laboriously in the field, and presented their findings in books and brochures, and in the *Publications* of the American Jewish Historical Society. I also wish gratefully to acknowledge the aid of the following:

Dr. Joshua Bloch (1890–1957), whose scrupulous reading of all the documents and the notes in galley-proof helped reduce the number of inaccuracies;

Dr. Philip S. Foner, who as historian, editor, and friend has been continually helpful;

Dr. Solomon Grayzel of Philadelphia, who encouragingly read more than half of the manuscript;

Rabbi Bertram W. Korn of Philadelphia, who offered useful suggestions and criticism on reading in galley-proof all the material dealing with slavery and the Civil War;

Professor Jacob R. Marcus, historian at the Hebrew Union College in Cincinnati, who read two-thirds of the manuscript and cordially made helpful detailed suggestions;

Dr. Herbert M. Morais (1905–1970), historian and friend, whose painstaking, judicious, and critical reading of the entire manuscript provided invaluable assistance;

Rabbi Emanuel Rackman of Far Rockaway, N. Y., who read most of the manuscript and critically evaluated important aspects of it;

Not least, to my wife, Sonya, who helped all the time in ways too many to detail.

Furthermore, I am immeasurably indebted to the hosts of archivists, librarians, and members of the staffs of the following institutions: the American Jewish Historical Society (Rabbi Isidore S. Meyer, librarian); the New York Public Library, the staffs of whose many divisions have been unfailingly cooperative, patient, and resourceful; the Library of Congress; the National Archives; the New-York Historical Society; the American Antiquarian Society; the Boston Public Library; the Chicago Public Library; the Columbia University Libraries; the Library of the College of Charleston, S. C.; the Library of the Dropsie College for Hebrew and Cognate Learning, Philadelphia; The Filson Club, Louisville, Ky.; the Georgia Historical Society; the Harvard University Library; the Howard University Library; the Henry E. Huntington Library, San Marino, California; the Jewish Theological Seminary of America; the Kansas Historical Society; the Kentucky Historical Society; the Lackawanna Historical Society, Scranton, Pa.; the La Crosse, Wisconsin, Historical Society; the Louisiana Historical Society; the Louisiana State Museum; the Maryland Hall of Records, Annapolis; the Massachusetts Historical Society; the Minnesota Historical Society; the Missouri Historical Society; the Newberry Library, Chicago; the New York City Hall of Records; the New York Society Library; the New York State Library; the North Carolina State Department of Archives and History, Raleigh; the North Carolina State Library; the Oklahoma Historical Society; the Historical Society of Pennsylvania; the Ridgway Branch of the Library Company of Philadelphia; the Historical Commission of South Carolina, Columbia, S. C.; the South Carolina Historical Society; the University of South Carolina Library; the Virginia Historical Society; the Western Reserve Union College Library; the Wisconsin State Historical Society.

For the revised edition, 1952, it was advisable to make only one important change: the last document in the first edition, which dealt with anti-Semitism in a Philadelphia courtroom, has been replaced by one describing the New York capmakers' general strike of 1874, in which hundreds of Jews took part. The substitution was made to meet in part the just criticism that the activity of Jewish workers had been underrepresented in the volume. Still uncompleted investigations have revealed that there were more Jews in the American labor movement at that time than had been noted.

Thus as far back as in the New York general tailors' strike of 1850, there were Jews involved and one, Morris Bernstein, was arrested for picketing. In 1852, there were German Jews in Wilhelm Weitling's Arbeiter-Bund in such cities as Cincinnati, Philadelphia, and Louisville. When the Communist Club of New York was founded late in October, 1857, its secretary was the young German Jew, Friedrich Jacoby (or Fritz Jacobi), who later enlisted in the Union Army as a private, rose in the ranks to become a First Lieutenant, and was killed in action at the Battle of Fredericksburg, December 13, 1862. In 1864, Samuel Gompers was joining the Cigar-Makers local in New York, and lists of Cigar union secretaries of 1867 and 1868 show there were Jews active in various parts of the country. In the 1870's, Adolph Strasser (1844–1939), a German-Hungarian Jew, helped Gompers reorganize the New York local, and both began to play roles that soon led them to the national leadership of the International Cigar-Makers' Union. In 1874, Strasser became national secretary of the Social Democratic Party of North America. The roster of Jewish workers in the American labor movement is sure to grow as more extensive researches are made. The substitution of the documents of the capmakers' strike is designed to reflect this increasingly important phase of Jewish life.

For this new edition, numerous textual corrections have been made, the Introduction revised, and the Index corrected. Textual changes are to be found on pp. 1, 24, 247, 325, 439, 481, 565, 566, 569, 571, 573, 576, 578, 580, 581, 583, 584, 586, 591, 597, 600, 611, 631, 646, 656, 671, 675, 676, 690, 700, 725, 734, 736–39.

Morris U. Schappes

New York
December 1970

CONTENTS

A Documentary History
of the
Jews in the United States
1654–1875

1. UNWELCOME

Extract from Letter of Peter Stuyvesant to the Amsterdam Chamber of the Dutch West India Company, Manhattan, September 22, 1654[1]

[Hostility, misunderstanding, and a request "in a friendly way" to depart confronted the first group of Jews to seek to colonize on what is now the continental United States. Although the Jews did not then face the persecution, imprisonment, and execution meted out to Quakers here, this letter of Stuyvesant's reveals the antagonism to be overcome before the Jewish refugees could remain here securely. In the first week of September, 1654, twenty three Jews had arrived in New Amsterdam on the *St. Catherine.* They were fleeing from the Portuguese, who by January, 1654 had recaptured from the Dutch certain colonies in Brazil. Having aided the Dutch in originally seizing the colonies from the Portuguese, the Jews now faced special severity from the Portuguese and their Inquisition, which had already been extended into the New World. In Holland's colonies the Jews expected to find the welcome they enjoyed in Holland itself. Instead they met the opposition of Stuyvesant (1592–1672), who, having been director of the West India Company's colony in Curaçao from 1634 to 1644, had come to New Amsterdam in 1647 as its director. The colony was small (in 1652 the population was about 750), but cosmopolitan in character, with men "of different sects and nations" speaking eighteen different languages.[2] Immigration was continual; 1132 arrivals were recorded from 1657 to 1664, when the British captured New Amsterdam and renamed it New York.[3] The Dutch West India Company controlling the colony had been formed June 3, 1621[4] as one means of achieving the supremacy of Dutch mercantile capitalism over the feudalism of Spain and Portugal. The Amsterdam Chamber, to which Stuyvesant addressed his letter, was the most important of the five chambers.]

. . . The Jews who have arrived would nearly all like to remain here, but learning that they (with their customary usury[5] and deceitful trading with the Christians) were very repugnant to the inferior magistrates,[6] as also to the people having the most affection for you; the Deaconry also fearing that owing to their present indigence[7] they might become a charge in the coming winter, we have, for the benefit of this weak and newly developing place and the land in general, deemed it useful to require them in a friendly way to depart; praying also most seriously in this connection, for ourselves as also for the general community of your worships, that the deceitful race,—such hateful enemies and blasphemers of the name of Christ,—be not allowed further to infect and trouble this new colony, to the detraction of your worships and the dissatisfaction of your worships' most affectionate subjects.

2. COOPERATION AND INFLUENCE

Petition of the Amsterdam Jews "To the Honorable Lords, Directors of the Chartered West India Company, Chamber of the City of Amsterdam," January 1655[1]

[This bold petition shows that the winning of a measure of equality by Jews in any one place helped them to advance the cause of equality for Jews elsewhere. The Amsterdam Jews assign four main reasons why Jews should be allowed to stay in New Amsterdam, despite Stuyvesant's objections: that they cannot go to Spain or Portugal because of the Inquisition; that they have risked "their possessions and their blood" to defend Dutch interests in Brazil; that the French and English allow Jews in their colonies; and that there are Jews who are "principal shareholders" (persons who had invested at least 6,000 guilders each) in the Dutch West India Company. Despite certain restrictions (on land ownership and the right to trade), the Jews in Holland at that time enjoyed a greater degree of equality than anywhere else in Europe. Since the arrival in Amsterdam of the first group of Jews escaping the Portuguese Inquisition in April 1593, the Jewish community had prospered and expanded. In this petition they are a reserve of strength for the insecure Jews of New Amsterdam.]

The merchants of the Portuguese Nation residing in this City respectfully remonstrate to your Honors that it has come to their knowledge that your Honors raise obstacles to the giving of permits or passports to the Portuguese Jews to travel and to go to reside in New Netherland, which if persisted in will result to the great disadvantage of the Jewish nation. It also can be of no advantage to the general Company but rather damaging.

Granted that they may reside and traffic, provided they shall not become a

There are many of the nation who have lost their

charge upon the deaconry or the Company. possessions at Pernambuco[2] and have arrived from there in great poverty, and part of them have been dispersed here and there. So that your petitioners had to expend large sums of money for their necessaries of life, and through lack of opportunity all cannot remain here to live. And as they cannot go to Spain or Portugal because of the Inquisition, a great part of the aforesaid people must in time be obliged to depart for other territories of their High Mightinesses the States-General and their Companies, in order there, through their labor and efforts, to be able to exist under the protection of the administrators of your Honorable Directors, observing and obeying your Honors' orders and commands.

It is well known to your Honors that the Jewish nation in Brazil have at all times been faithful and have striven to guard and maintain that place, risking for that purpose their possessions and their blood.

Yonder land is extensive and spacious. The more of loyal people that go to live there, the better it is in regard to the population of the country as in regard to the payment of various excises and taxes which may be imposed there, and in regard to the increase of trade, and also to the importation of all the necessaries that may be sent there.

Your Honors should also consider that the Honorable Lords, the Burgomasters of the City and the Honorable High Illustrious Mighty Lords, the States-General, have in political matters always protected and considered the Jewish nation as upon the same footing as all the inhabitants and burghers. Also it is conditioned in the treaty of perpetual peace with the King of Spain that the Jewish nation shall also enjoy the same liberty as all other inhabitants of these lands.[3]

Your Honors should also please consider that many of the Jewish nation are principal shareholders in the Company.[4] They having always striven their best for the Company, and many of their nation have lost immense and great capital in its shares and obligations.

The Company has by a general resolution consented that those who wish to populate the Colony shall enjoy certain districts of land gratis. Why should now certain subjects of this State not be allowed to travel thither and live there? The French consent that the Portuguese Jews may traffic and live in Martinique,[5] Christopher and others of their territories, whither also some have gone from here, as your Honors know. The English also consent at the present time that the Portuguese and Jewish nation may go from London and settle at Barbados,[6] whither also some have gone.

As foreign nations consent that the Jewish nation may go to live and trade in their territories, how can your Honors forbid the same and refuse transportation to this Portuguese nation who reside here and have been settled here well on to sixty years, many also being born here and confirmed burghers, and this to a land that needs people for its increase?

Therefore the petitioners request, for the reasons given above (as also others which they omit to avoid prolixity), that your Honors be pleased not to exclude but to grant the Jewish nation passage to and residence in that country; otherwise this would result in a great prejudice to their reputation. Also that by an Apostille and Act the Jewish nation be permitted, together with other inhabitants, to travel, live and traffic there, and with them enjoy liberty on condition of contributing like others, &c. Which doing, &c.

3. PERMISSION GRUDGINGLY GIVEN

Extract from Reply by the Amsterdam Chamber of the West India Company to Stuyvesant's letter, April 26, 1655[1]

[The reasoning in this document is particularly interesting. The loyalty of the Jews in Brazil and the capital investments of the Jews in Holland outweighed the fears and prejudices that the Dutch directors shared with Stuyvesant; the pressure of the Dutch Jews was effective. Stuyvesant later resorted to violations of the explicit instructions contained in this document.]

We would have liked to effectuate and fulfill your wishes and request that the new territories should no more be allowed to be infected by people of the Jewish nation, for we foresee therefrom the same difficulties which you fear,[2] but after having further weighed and considered the matter, we observe that this would be somewhat unreasonable and unfair, especially because of the considerable loss sustained by this nation, with others, in the taking of Brazil,[3] as also because of the large amount of capital which they still have invested in the shares of this company.[4] Therefore after many deliberations we have finally decided and resolved to apostille* upon a certain petition presented

* Apostille—an order written as a marginal notation—as in Doc. No. 2.—Ed.

by said Portuguese Jews that these people may travel and trade to and in New Netherland and live and remain there, provided the poor among them shall not become a burden to the company or to the community, but be supported by their own nation. You will now govern yourself accordingly.

4. NOT WANTED FOR DEFENSE

Resolution of Peter Stuyvesant and the New Amsterdam Council to exclude Jews from military service, August 28, 1655[1]

[The winning of equal rights for the Jews of New Amsterdam was a process every stage of which involved a specific struggle. This resolution indicates that even the right to defend the city was at first denied the Jews. Two reasons are given: "the disinclination and unwillingness" of the other militiamen, and the lack of precedent in Holland. It is noteworthy that precedents that favored the Jews were disregarded by Stuyvesant and his council, while those that worked against the Jews were considered binding. The Burgher Guard from which the Jews were excluded by this resolution consisted of two companies, with less than 200 men. In the spring of 1655 it was necessary to increase the Guard, since Stuyvesant was preparing an expedition to dislodge the Swedish colony on the Delaware (South) River which had been established when the Swedes captured Fort Casimir from the Dutch in 1654. The Council passed this resolution two weeks before the expedition left. Less than a week later, Indians attacked New Amsterdam, and killed many people before the Guard repulsed them. Note also the reasoning of the Council in the resolution: the denial of a civic right is combined with the imposition of a special tax![2]]

The Captains and officers of the trainbands of this city having asked the Director General and Council whether the Jewish people who reside in this city, should also train and mount guard with the citizens' bands, this was taken into consideration and deliberated upon; first the disinclination and unwillingness of these trainbands to be fellow-soldiers with the aforesaid nation and to be on guard with them in the same guard house, and on the other side, that the said nation was not admitted or counted among the citizens, as regards trainbands or common citizens' guards, neither in the illustrious City of Amsterdam nor (to our knowledge) in any city in Netherland; but in order that the said nation may honestly be taxed for their freedom in that respect, it is directed by the Director General and Council, to prevent further discontent, that the aforesaid nation shall, according to the usages of the renowned City of Amsterdam, remain exempt from the general training and guard duty, on condition that each male person over 16 and under 60 years contribute for the aforesaid freedom towards the relief of the general municipal taxes 65 stivers [$1.20] every month, and the military council of the citizens is hereby authorized and charged to carry this into effect until our further orders, and to collect, pursuant to the above, the aforesaid contribution once in every month, and in case of refusal to collect it by legal process. Thus done in Council at Fort Amsterdam, on the day as above.

Signed: P. Stuyvesant, Nicasius de Sille, Cornelis van Tienhoven.

5. ASSERTING THE RIGHT TO FIGHT

The Minute of the New Amsterdam Council on the Petition of Jacob Barsimson and Asser Levy to stand guard or be excused from tax, November 5, 1655[1]

[The preceding resolution is challenged as unfair by two Jews who "must earn their living by manual labor." Although this petition was denied, the right to stand guard was won later.]

Jacob Barsimson and Asser Levy[2] request to be permitted to keep guard with other burghers, or be free from the tax which others of their nation pay, as they must earn their living by manual labor.

After a vote, the answer was given: Director General and Council persist in the resolution passed, yet as the petitioners are of opinion that the result of this will be injurious to them, consent is hereby given to them to depart whenever and whither it pleases them.[3] Dated as above.

6. ENFORCING A RIGHT GRANTED

Petition to the Director General and Council of New Netherland for the right to travel and trade on the South (Delaware) River and at Fort Orange (now Albany), November 29, 1655[1]

[The clear instructions of the Directors of the Dutch West India Company were repeatedly contravened by Stuyvesant and the Council, and the Jews had to fight for the execution of these instructions. "With due reverence" the petitioners remind the officials of their rights. The summary of the discussion of the Council suggests the stubbornness with which the instructions were resisted, and the petition denied.]

TO THE HONORABLE DIRECTOR GENERAL AND COUNCIL OF NEW NETHERLAND:

With due reverence, Abraham deLucena, Salvador Dandrada and Jacob Cohen, for themselves and in the name of others of the Jewish nation, residing in this City, show how that under date of the 15th of February, 1655, the Honorable Lords Directors of the Chartered West India Company, Masters and Patrons of this Province, gave permission and consent to the petitioners, like the other inhabitants, to travel, reside and trade here, and enjoy the same liberties, as appears by the document here annexed. They therefore respectfully request that your Honorable Worships will not prevent or hinder them herein, but will allow and consent that, pursuant to the consent obtained by them, they may, with other inhabitants of this province, travel and trade on the South River of New Netherland, at Fort Orange and other places situate within the jurisdiction of this Government of New Netherland. Which doing, etc., the undersigned shall remain your Honorable Worships' Humble Servants:

Was signed, Abraham deLucena, Salvador Dandrada, Jacob Cohen[2]

The above request having been read to the meeting of the Director General and Council, it was resolved that each of the members of the Council shall give his opinion as to what apostille shall be placed thereon.

Here follow the opinions of the various members. Stuyvesant voted that the petition be denied for weighty reasons. LaMontagne gave a similar opinion. Nicasius deSille said that he did not like to act contrary to the order of the Lords Directors, but that as at present the Jews have put on board ship goods for the South River permission might be given to them, and further orders be awaited in answer to the last letter sent to the Lords Directors. Cornelis van Tienhoven was of the opinion that it would be injurious to the community and the population of the said places to grant the petition of the Jews, and that it should be denied for the coming winter, and ample report made thereon to the Lords Directors, but that for this time a young man of the nation be allowed to go to the South River with some goods, without thereby establishing a precedent.

Apostille granted upon the above request of the Jews: For weighty reasons, this request, made in such general terms, is declined; yet having been informed that suppliants have already shipped some goods, they are for the time being allowed to send one or two persons[3] to the South River in order to dispose of the same, which being done they are to return hither. Done as above.

7. DENIED THE RIGHT TO OWN A HOUSE

Petition to keep a house bought at auction, December 17, 1655. Denied, December 23, 1655[1]

[Even so elementary a right as that of owning a house was contested for "pregnant reasons" that the Council did not record. The house had been bought by Salvador Dandrada from one Teunis Cray for 1860 guilders (about $740 at that time). Denying Dandrada, the Jew, the right to buy also involved denying Cray, the Christian, the right to sell his house to the highest bidder. On January 13, 1656, Cray therefore petitioned that either the sale to Dandrada be authorized or the Council and Stuyvesant pay the promised purchase price. This petition was also denied.[2] On March 14, 1656, however, Cray, who was about to return to Holland, was awarded by the Council one-half of the difference between the price offered by Dandrada and that which Cray had been compelled to accept from a non-Jewish bidder.[3]]

TO THE HONORABLE WORSHIPFUL DIRECTOR GENERAL AND HIGH COUNCILLORS OF NEW NETHERLAND:

Salvador Dandradj, Jewish merchant here in this City, makes known, with submissive reverence, how that according to the authorization granted by the Honorable Lords Directors of the West India Company, Amsterdam Chamber, in Holland, to the Jewish nation, your petitioner has been conducting his business and trading here in this country, together with other merchants, and since his residence here has for this purpose rented and inhabited a house, and finally the said house and appurtenances were knocked down to him at a public sale by the secretary of the Noble Worships, held on the 14th of this month of December, and he has, pursuant to the same, come into the ownership thereof, according to the conditions under which the said house and appurtenances had been knocked down, an authentic copy of which is annexed;

And whereas your petitioner would like to enjoy his right to the same and to pay the purchase price stipulated, at the respective dates of maturity, he therefore submissively petitions that your Honorable Worships be pleased to permit and allow him so to do, expecting a favorable apostille regarding the same.

Will remain your Honorable Worships' Subject.

Was signed, Salvador Dandradj.

The above petition having been read, the following apostille was added to the same:

The conveyance of the premises mentioned herein is for pregnant reasons declined.

Done at a meeting on the above date.

8. LIST OF GRIEVANCES

Petition to the Honorable Director General and Council of New Netherlands, March 14, 1656, and the denial thereof[1]

[Not only had the preceding petitions been denied, but the authorities had even imposed special taxes on the Jews. The petitioners now ask "to enjoy the same liberty allowed to other burghers" with regard to trade and real estate ownership if they are to pay taxes. But Stuyvesant and the Council procrastinate and, refusing the request, suggest that the matter be raised again with the Lords Directors in Holland.]

TO THE HONORABLE DIRECTOR GENERAL AND COUNCIL OF NEW NETHERLANDS.

The undersigned suppliants remonstrate with due reverence to your Noble Honorable Lords that for themselves, as also in the name of the other Jews residing in this Province, they on the 29th of November last past exhibited to your Noble Honorable Lordships a certain Order of the Honorable Lords Directors of the Chartered West India Company, dated February 15, 1655, whereby permission and consent was given them, with other inhabitants, to travel, live and traffic here and to enjoy the same liberty, and following which they humbly requested that your Noble Honorable Lordships should be pleased not to hinder them but to permit and consent that they, like other inhabitants of this Province, may travel and trade to and upon the South River, Fort Orange and other places within the jurisdiction of this Government of New Netherland. Regarding which your Noble Honorable Worships were then pleased to apostille: For weighty reasons this request, made in such general terms, is declined; yet having been informed that the suppliants have already shipped some goods they are for the time being allowed to send one or two persons to the South River in order to dispose of the same, which being done they are to return hither. Also your Noble Honors were pleased, under date of December 23d following, to refuse the conveyance of a certain house and lot bid in by Salvador Dandrada at public auction, and as a consequence to forbid and annul the purchase, so that the said house was again offered for public sale anew on the 20th of January following, and sold to another. And whereas the Honorable Magistrates of this city have been pleased to demand, through their secretary and court messenger, of the undersigned suppliants, individually, the sum of one hundred guilders, towards the payment for the Works of this city, amounting alone for the undersigned, your Worships' suppliants, to the sum of f500,* aside from what the others of their nation have been ordered to contribute. Therefore your suppliants once more humbly request hereby that your Honors permit them if, like other burghers, they must and shall contribute, to enjoy the same liberty

* 500 florins.—Ed.

allowed to other burghers, as well in trading to all places within the jurisdiction of this Government as in the purchase of real estate, especially as this has already been consented to and permitted by the Honorable Lords Directors, as can be seen by the aforesaid Order shown to your Honors on November 29th. Then they are willing and ready, with other burghers and inhabitants, to contribute according to their means. Which doing, etc.

Below stood: Your Worships' Humble Servants:

Was signed: Abraham de Lucena, Jacob Cohen Henricque, Salvador Dandrada, Joseph d'Acosta, David Frera.[2]

The above request being read, the same, after consultation, was disposed of with the following apostille:

The subscription was requested by the Burgomasters and Schepens of this city and by the Director General and Council, for good reasons, for the benefit of this city and the further security of the persons and goods of the inhabitants, among whom the suppliants are also counted and included; therefore it is necessary that they, together with others, shall assist in bearing the burden occasioned thereby. In regard to the Order of the Lords Directors mentioned and exhibited, the Director General and Council are of opinion that pursuant to the same the Jewish Nation enjoy such liberty here in the city as the Order implies. Regarding the purchase and ownership of real estate, it is advised that the broad question be once again put to the Lords Directors, and pending the answer the last [request] is refused.

Thus done in our Assembly held at Fort Amsterdam, in New Netherland. Dated as above.

Was signed: P. Stuyvesant, Nicasius DeSille, LaMontagne.

9. STUYVESANT REBUKED

Extract from Letter of Directors of the Dutch West India Company to Stuyvesant, June 14, 1656[1]

[Stuyvesant's disregard for the orders he had received and the persistence of the Jews in asserting their rights, together perhaps with the addition of the name of Joseph D'Acosta, a principal shareholder in the Company, to the preceding petition, finally brought down upon Stuyvesant the "displeasure" of the Directors and a sharp request for "more respect" for their instructions.]

. . . We have here seen and learned with displeasure, that your Honors, against our apostille of the 15th of February, 1655, granted to the Jewish or Portuguese nation at their request, have forbidden them to trade at Fort Orange and South River, and also the purchase of real estate, which is allowed them here in this country without any difficulty, and we wish that this had not occurred but that your Honors had obeyed our orders which you must hereafter execute punctually and with more respect. Jews or Portuguese people, however, shall not be permitted to establish themselves as mechanics (which they are not allowed to do in this city), nor allowed to have open retail shops,[2] but they may quietly and peacefully carry on their business as heretofore and exercise in all quietness their religion within their houses, for which end they must without doubt endeavor to build their houses close together in a convenient place on one or the other side of New Amsterdam—at their choice—as they have done here.

10. WINNING THE LAST ROUND

Petition that Jews be admitted to the Burgher Right in New Amsterdam, April 20, 1657[1]

[Even after the rebuke already noted, obstacles continued to be placed in the way of the Jews, but their assiduity and the requirements of the economic situation finally prevailed. After more than two and a half years of repeated efforts, the Jews finally won the burgher right.]

TO THE NOBLE WORSHIPS, THE DIRECTOR GENERAL AND COUNCIL OF NEW NETHERLAND.

We, the undersigned, of the Jewish Nation here, make known, with due reverence, how that one[2] of our Nation repaired to the City Hall of this City and requested of the Noble Burgomasters that he might obtain his Burgher certificate, like other Burghers, which to our great surprise was declined and refused by the Noble Burgomasters, and whereas the Worshipful Lords consented under date of February 15, 1655, at the request of our Nation, that we should enjoy here the same freedom as other inhabitants of New Netherland enjoy, as appears from the petition here annexed; further that our Nation enjoys in the City of Amsterdam in Holland the Burgher right, and he who asks therefor receives a Burgher certificate there, as appears by the Burgher certificate hereto annexed; also that our Nation, as long as they have been here, have, with others, borne and paid, and still bear, all Burgher burdens: We, therefore, reverently request your Noble Worships to please not exclude nor shut us out from the Burgher right, but to notify the Noble Burgomasters that they should permit us, like other Burghers, to enjoy the Burgher right, and for this purpose to give us the customary Burgher certificate, in conformity with the order of the Worshipful Lords Directors above mentioned. Upon which, awaiting your Noble Worships' gracious and favorable apostille, we shall remain, as heretofore,

Below stood: Your Noble Worships' Humble Servants,

Salvador Dandrada, Jacob Cohen Henricques, Abraham deLucena, Joseph d'Acosta.

On the above petition is apostilled:

The Burgomasters of this City are hereby authorized and at the same time charged to admit the petitioners herein and their Nation to the Burghership, in due form. Dated as above.

P. Stuyvesant, Nicasius deSille, Pieter Tonneman.

11. CHARGED WITH BLASPHEMY

The Indictment of Dr. Jacob Lumbrozo in Maryland, February 23, 1658[1]

[How much worse was the plight of the Jew in Maryland in the mid-seventeenth century than it was in New Amsterdam then is seen in this document. The English fusion of church and state, a reflection of the feudal pattern still influential in England, affected the dominant forces in Maryland. The indictment against Lumbrozo was brought under "An Act Concerning Religion" (1649), which was improperly called "The Toleration Act," although it discriminated against Jews, Quakers and Socinians (Unitarians). Under this act, Lumbrozo faced death and confiscation of all his goods if convicted of a "denial of the doctrine of the Trinity." Fortunately Lumbrozo was never brought to trial, perhaps because Richard Cromwell, on succeeding his father Oliver as Lord Protector of the Commonwealth of England, issued a general amnesty on March 2, 1658.[2] In Maryland, disabilities against the Jews persist into contemporary times (see Document No. 74, Note 4)[3].]

At a Provincial Court, held at St. Mary's on Wednesday, this 23d February, 1658.

Present—Josias Fendall, Esq., Governor; Philip Calvert, Esq., Secretary; Mr. Robert Clarke; Mr. Baker Brooke; Dr. Luke Barber.

Was called afore the Board, Jacob Lumbrozo, and charged by his Lordship's Attorney for uttering words of blasphemy against our Blessed Saviour, Jesus Christ.

The deposition of John Hoffsett, aged 44 years, or thereabouts, sayeth this 19th day of February, 1658:—

That, about half a year since, this deponent being at ye house of Mr. Richard Preston, and there meeting with Jacob Lumbrozo, he, this deponent, and the said Lumbrozo falling into discourse concerning our Blessed Saviour, Christ, his resurrection, telling ye said Lumbrozo that he was more than man, as did appear by his resurrection. To which the said Lumbrozo answered, that his disciples stole him away. Then this deponent replied, yt no man ever did such miracles as he. To which ye said Lumbrozo answered, that such works might be done by necromancy or sorcery, or words to that purpose. And this deponent replied to ye said Lumbrozo, yt he supposed yt ye said Lumbrozo took Christ to be a necromancer. To which ye said Lumbrozo answered nothing, but laughed. And further this deponent sayeth not.

Jurat die et anno supradict. cor. me, Henry Coursey.

I, Richard Preston, jr., do testify yt, about June or July last past, coming from Thomas Thomas's, in company with Josias Cole and ye Jew Doctor, known by ye name of Jacob Lumbrozo, the said Josias Cole asked ye said Lumbrozo, whether ye Jews did look for a Messias? And ye said Lumbrozo answered, yes. Then ye said Cole asked him, what He was that was crucified at Jerusalem? And ye said Lumbrozo answered, He was a man. Then ye said Cole asked him, how He did do all His miracles? And ye said Lumbrozo answered, He did them by ye Art Magic. Then ye said Cole asked him, how His disciples did do ye same miracles, after He was crucified? And ye said Lumbrozo answered, that He taught them His art. And further saith not.

This was declared before me, as in the presence of God, that it is true, this 21st of February, 1658. Henry Coursey.

The said Lumbrozo saith, that he had some talk with those persons, and willed by them to declare his opinion, and by his profession, a Jew, he answered to some particular demands then urged. And as to that of miracles done by art magic, he declared what remains written concerning Moses and ye Magicians of Egypt. But said not anything scoffingly, or in derogation of Him Christians acknowledged for their Messias.

It is ordered, that ye said Lumbrozo remain in ye Sheriff's custody, until he put in security, body for body, to make answer to what shall be laid to his charge concerning those blasphemous words and speeches, at ye next Provincial Court; and yt the persons be then present to testify, *viva voce,* in Court.

Mittimus.—To ye Sheriff of St. Mary's County, according to the order *Supradict.*

12. BUSINESS PARTNERS

Application by Asser Levy for permission to build a slaughter-house, New York, January 8, 1677–8. Partnership confirmed, October 8, 1678[1]

[This document is one of the earliest records of a business partnership between a Jew and a non-Jew in the colonies on the continental mainland. After more than twenty years in the colony, Levy was a well known citizen. The operation of a slaughter house and the craft of butcher were regarded as semi-public functions; there were only six licensed butchers, each one of whom had to take an oath of office. Levy was a conscientious Jew, and "took the oath that Jews are accustomed to take" and not the oath on "the faith of a Christian." In 1660, he was granted permission "to be excused from killing hogs, as his religion does not allow him to do it."[2] His partner and he, of course, catered to the general population and not only to the Jews.]

Before Mr Steph[an]us Van Co^{rt}land $Mayo^{r}$; Mr John Inian Deputy May^{r}; Mr Joh[an]es De Peister, Mr Peter Jacobs, Mr Gylyne V: Planck, Aldermen

For Overseers of Chymnies or ffyres w^{th}in this Citty, John Cooly and John Derrickson Meyer. Co^{rt} Order to be Sworne till October next or ffurther Order, and that they once in Six Weekes Veiwe all Chimnies and fire hearths according to former Orders and Customes.

Ashur Levy then makeing his Addresse to the Court that hee might be admitted to build the Slaughter house mentioned in the order[3] dated (16th) of February 1676[-7] and to take in Garrett Janson Rose to be Partner with him therein, and that all persons should haue Liberty to kill & hang theire Meat there, paying for the same as formerly in other places

Whereupon hee building the said house according to his promise, Court grant and giue Libberty that the sayd Ashur Levy shall and may take in Garrett Johnson Rose to be his Partner therein, according to his Proposalls.

Before Stephanus van Cortlandt Mayor &c:

Ashur Levy came into the Court and affirmed that hee had built the Slaughter house and prayed the Court to confirme the same upon him and Garrett Johnson Rose Which the Court at his speciall instance & request doe confirme ye same according to former order.

13. AT THE DISPOSAL OF THE GOVERNOR

Petition to the Governor by New York city officials, November 9, 1683; the Governor "excepts the Jews," November 10, 1683 [1]

[In the absence of democratic government and rule by law, Jews were often at the mercy of the will of particular officials. In this petition, the city officials did not exclude the Jews from the "ancient customs, privileges and immunities" that they wanted reaffirmed by the new Governor, but the action of the Governor jeopardized the already hard-won right of the Jews in New York "to sell by retail or exercise any handicraft, trade or occupation." Rights the Jews had attained under the Dutch in New Amsterdam now had to be regained from the English. In England itself treatment of the Jews was for a long time to lag far behind that which they achieved in Holland.]

Petition presented to ye Governo^{r} in ye name of ye Mayo^{r} Aldermen & Comonalty of ye Citty ffor a Charter

> To the Right Honourable Coll Thomas Dongan Esqr Lieutenant & Governo^{r} & vice admirall vnd^{r} his Royall Highness James Duke of yorke & Albany &c of Newyorke and dependencyes in America

The Humble petition of ye Mayo^{r} Aldermen and Comonalty of ye Citty of Newyork

SHEWETH That this Citty hath had & enjoyed scucrall antient Customes priuiledges & Immunityes wch were Confirmed & granted to them by Coll Richd Nicholls late Governo^{r} of this Province by Authority vnd^{r} his Royall Highness Anno 1665 who Incorporated ye Inhabitants thereof New Harlem & all others Inhabiting on ye Island manhatan whereon this Citty standeth as one body pollitique and Corporate vnder ye Governm^{t} of a Mayo^{r} Aldermen & sheriffe in wch manner it hath Continued in practice euer since and hath had vsed and Injoyed ye Customes libertyes and priuiledges ffollowing, vizt, . . .

7th None were to be esteemed Freemen of the Citty but who were admitted by ye Magistrates afores^{d} & none before such admission to sell by Retayle or exercise any handycraft trade or occupation & euery Merch^{t} or shop keeper was to pay ffor ye publick vse of ye Citty 3 £ 12^{s} euery handy Craft man 1 £ 4^{s} an [on?] being made ffree . . .

All wch said Antient Customs priuiledges & lybertyes wee ye s^{d} Mayo^{r} & aldermen in behalfe of themselues & ye Citizens of ye s^{d} Citty do humbly present & make knowne to yor Honour humbly beseeching yor hono^{r} in their behalfe to Interceed & procure that ye same be Confirmed to them by Charter ffrom his Royall highnes. with these additions ffollowing . . .

Newyorke 9bre ye 9th 1683

> Some objections made by ye Governo^{r} & Councell to ye petition presented in ye name of ye Mayo^{r} Aldermen & comonalty with desire to be explained

Att a Councell held in Newyorke ye 10th 9^{ber} 1683

Present The Governo^{r}
Mr Frederick Phillips
Mr Lucas Sancton

A Petition from ye Deputy Mayo^{r} Aldermen and Comonalty of ye Citty of Newyorke being Read was concluded as ffollows

. . . And in ye seuenth article Jews are to be excepted who are left to ye disposall of ye Governo^{r}

By ord^{r} in Councell

John Spragg Secry

14. WHOLESALE ONLY

Saul Browne's petition for the right to sell at retail, New York, September 12, 1685 [1]

[The Council's exclusion of Jews from retail trade contributed to turning the Jews' attention to wholesale or foreign and intercolonial trade. Since foreign trade could not, by law, be conducted from towns outside New York, this restriction also tended to concentrate Jews in New York city.[2]]

. . . The Petition of Saul Browne Recomended by the Governor Was read, and the Councells opinion indorsed thereupon Was that noe Jew ought to Sell by Retaile within this Citty but may by whole Sale if the Governor think fitt to permitt the same

15. NOT IN PUBLIC

Denial of the right to worship in public, September 14, 1685 [1]

[In 1683 the New York Colonial Assembly had adopted a Charter of Liberties and Privileges granting immunity from persecution to all "who professed faith in God by Jesus Christ."[2] It was customary at that time to distinguish between the right of private worship in one's home and the right to hold a service in a public house of worship.]

. . . The Jews Petition to the Governor for Liberty to Exercise their Religion, Being by him Recommended to the Mayor and aldermen was read in Common Councell and they Returned their opinions thereupon That noe publique Worship is Tolerated by act of assembly, but to those that professe faith in Christ, and therefore the Jews Worship not to be allowed.

16. ELECTED CONSTABLES

Minutes of the New York Common Council, October 14, 1718 [1]

[The right and the power to enforce the law is a necessary part of the right to equality under the law. Here we notice that early in the eighteenth century Jews in New York were accepted and respected citizens whom their fellows entrusted with the power to enforce the laws even against themselves. The records of the New York Common Council have many references to the election of Jews as law-enforcement officers.[2]]

. . . Mr Nathan Simson & Mr Samuell Levy [3] were Sworn Constables of the South and North Wards and afterwards were Admitted to appoint their Deputies which were Dirck Cook & Isaac De Riemer Junr, to witt Dirck Cook for the North Ward & Isaac De Riemer Junr for the South Ward

17. DECLINES TO SERVE

Minutes of New York Common Council, October 14, 1719 [1]

[Long before Jews were being elected to office in European countries, they were beginning in New York to exercise their option of not serving even when elected. The Minutes show that it was not uncommon for persons elected to decline, and the law provided for such contingencies by imposing a fine. This document suggests that Jews did not necessarily seek office merely for the sake of office-holding.]

. . . Mr Moses Levy Merchant [2] who was Elected to Serve in the Office of Constable of the South Ward haveing refused to Serve in that Office & paid his fine of fifteen pounds into the hands of the Treasurer. It is *Order'd* Mr Mayor Issue his Warrant to the Alderman of that Ward for the Election of Another Sufficient Inhabitant of the Said Ward to Serve in that Office for the Year Ensueing & that the Election be made on Monday Next. . . .

18. EXECUTED FOR STEALING

Supreme Court Minutes in the case of *The King* vs *Moses Susman,* June 12 and 13, 1727; and Minutes of the New York City Common Council, June 20 and August 8, 1727 [1]

[The pathetic record published below dates back to the time when stealing was a major offense for which hanging was considered a fit punishment.[2] The record is all too brief: Moses Susman is hanged for stealing "Gold Silver money bag rings &c" from Moses Levy,[3] and Richard Noble is paid "the sum of two pounds Current Money of New York" for his expenses in erecting the gallows on which Susman was hanged. This is the first known colonial record of the execution of a Jew. Moses Susman's name has hitherto been unnoted in American Jewish history, and nothing else is known about him except what is herein recorded. The array of witnesses against him, which includes the Mayor, Robert Lurting, and several New York worthies of the time, seems extraordinary.]

Monday the 12th June 1727

Present

The Honble Lewis Morris Esqr, Chief Justice & Robert Walter Esqr, Second Justice

The Court opened . . .

On an Indictmt this day found by ye Grand Jury for Stealing Gold

Silver money bag rings &c of the goods and Chattles of Moses Levy the

The King
vs
Moses Susman

prisoner arraigned & pleades not guilty Mr Sideham being Sworn to interpret between ye Ct & prisoner. (he not understanding English) ye prisoner was ordered for tryall too morrow & being told thereof by his Interpreter had Nothing to alleadge agt it

[June 13, 1727]

On Tryall
The Jury Sworn

Evidences epte [ex parte] Dni [Domini] Regis
Nathan Levy,[4] Mr. Smith, Mr. Wenman, Mr. David Clarkson, Mr. Matthew Clarkson, Abraham Finchard, Joseph Webb, Col Lurting

The Jury not going from the bar find the Defendt guilty of the ffelony whereof he Stands indicted, but that he had no goods or Chattles Lands or Tenements to their knowledge at the time of the ffelony comitted or at any time Since

The prisoner being convicted was brot by order of the Court to the bar to receive his Sentence and being askt what he had to Say why Judgmt Should not pass agt him to dye according to Law, and having nothing to Say the Court gives Judgmt that he be taken hence to the place from whence he came, and thence to the place of Execution and that he be there hanged by the neck till he be dead, and that he be hanged on wednesday the twelfth of July between ye hours of ten and Eleven in the forenoon

City of New York } ss

Att A Common Council held at the City Hall of the Said City on Tuesday the twentieth day of June Anno Dom. 1727

... ORDER'D that Mr Mayor [Robert Lurting] or Mr Recorder [Francis Harison] and any two of the Aldermen of this Corporation have power and Authority at the Charge of this Corporation to Agree with and Appoint able and sufficient Persons to Watch the Prisons and Gaols of this City upon Such Occasions and Emergencies as they Shall Judge needfull during the Confinement of some Felons in the said Prisons & Gaols in Order to prevent Escapes therefrom.

No 429
Warrant Issued

ORDER'D the Mayor Issue his Warrant to the Treasurer to pay to Johannes Delamontagne Harman Bussing Robert Campbell Roeliff Van Mapelen Jacobus Delamontagne and Michael Cornelisse the Watch & Bellmen of this City, or to their Order the sum of Eight pounds Current Money of New York in full for their Extraordinary service for Watching and Guarding the Prisons and Gaols of this City for two Months Ending the twenty Second day of May last.

ORDER'D there be A Publick Gallows made and Erected upon the Common of this City at the usual place of Execution at the Charge of this Corporation.

City of New York } ss — At a Common Council held at the City Hall of the Said City on Tuesday the Eighth day of August Anno Domini 1727

No 431
Warrant Issued

ORDER'D the Mayor Issue his Warrant to the Treasurer to pay to Mr Richard Noble the sum of two pounds Current Money of New York for the like Sum by him Expended for making and Erecting A Publick Gallows on the Commons of this City for the Execution of Moses Sousman A Jew.

19. ADVERTISEMENT

***The New-York Gazette*, No. 205, September 29 to October 6, 1729**[1]

[Old advertisements tell us many things about the economic life of the Jews of the time, particularly about merchants who announced their wares. Lewis Gomez[2] was the patriarch of an important New York family of Jewish merchants. Lime, which he advertises here, continued to be one of his wares for many years, since on September 2, 1735 the Minutes of the Common Council record the issuing of an order to pay him £6, 5s for twenty five loads of lime he had sold to the city.[3]]

All Persons who shall have occasion for good Stone-Lime next Spring or Summer, may be supplyed with what Quantity they shall have occasion for, by Lewis Gomez in the City of New-York, at a reasonable Price.

20. PETITION FOR HONESTY IN TRADING

Petition to the New York Common Council, January 12, 1733 [1]

[Twenty-seven New York merchants, including two Jews, signed this petition to prevent the export from the city of flour "not merchantable" within the city. The struggle for fair trade practices has no national or religious boundaries. To maintain "the Credit of the Trade of this City" these merchants sought to restrain those who used sharp practices in business. The petition brought no immediate results: on March 31, 1735 a Committee of Aldermen was appointed to draft a law, and the Recorder was added to the committee on May 21, but after that the matter disappears from the record.[2]]

To the Worshipfull the Mayor Recorder Aldermen and Assistants of the City of New York

The Humble Petition of the subscribers being Merch[ts] Inhabiting and Residing in the said City

SHEWETH That many great Frauds and abuses for divers Years past have been and Still daily are Practised and Committed in this City in Vending selling and Buying for Exportation Flour not Merchantable whereby the Credit of the Trade of this City in one of its most Considerable Branches is Very much Lessened, and as your Petitioners have great Reason to apprehend will in a short time be wholy Ruin'd unless some Speedy Method be fallen upon to prevent such Frauds and Abuses for the future.

WHEREFORE Your Petitioners humbly pray that the same may be taken into Your Consideration and that some good wholsome and Effectual Law of this Corporation may be made to prevent the Selling Vending or Buying for Transportation any flour not Merchantable within this City all which is Nevertheless humbly Submitted by

Your Most Obedient Servants

Mord[y] Gomez, David Gomez.[3] [and 25 others]

21. COMING TO GEORGIA

Extracts from the Journal of the Transactions of the Trustees for Establishing the Colony of Georgia in America, December 22, 1733, etc [1]

[As in the case of New Amsterdam, influential Jews in the colonizing country helped the Jews become colonists in Georgia. The Georgia project was undertaken largely in order to create a buffer to protect Carolina from the Spanish and French in the Florida territory, and to provide certain raw materials for English merchants.[2] To supplement a parliamentary grant of funds, it was necessary to conduct a popular subscription. Among those empowered "to take subscriptions and collect money for the Purposes of the Charter" were Alvaro Lopez Suasso, Francis Salvador, and Anthony Da Costa, pillars of the London Sephardic Jewish community, and among the wealthiest men in England.[3] These three thus sought to use the opportunity in order to solve some of the problems of the increasing numbers of Jewish poor by helping a number of them to emigrate to distant Georgia.[4] Hearing about this plan, the Trustees of the Colony began to try to recover their Commissions, but met with resistance. While the Trustees insisted that all funds collected be turned over to them, Salvador, Suasso and Da Costa used the funds to finance the transportation of Jews to Georgia. Thus on July 11, 1733, 41 Jewish settlers arrived in Savannah, which at that time had only 275 inhabitants. Of the new arrivals, 32 were Sephardim and nine were Ashkenazim; 15 were female.[5] Despite the objection of the Trustees, whose views are set forth in these extracts, Governor Oglethorpe, although at first hostile, finally accepted the Jews and, since they found favor among the colonists, saw to it that they remained.[6]]

Palace Court, *Saturday, December* 22, 1733

At a meeting of Trustees, assembled by summons, Ordered That the Secretary do wait on Messrs Alvaro Lopez Suasso, Francis Salvador Junr and Anthony Da Costa with the following message in writing:

Whereas a message, dated Jany 31, 1732–3, was sent for the redelivery of their Commissions with which they did not think proper to comply, and which on the said Refusal were vacated by the Trustees: And Whereas the Trustees are inform'd that by monies rais'd by virtue of their commission (which monies ought to have been transmitted to the Trustees) certain Jews have been sent to Georgia contrary to the intentions of the Trustees, and which may be of ill consequence to the Colony; the Trustees do hereby require the said Mess[rs] Alvaro Lopez Suasso, Francis Salvador Jun[r], and Anthony Da Costa immediately to redeliver to M[r] [Benjamin] Martyn, their Secretary, the said Commissions and to render an account in writing to the Trustees of what monies have been raised by virtue thereof; and if they refuse to comply with this demand that then the Trustees will think themselves obliged not only to advertise the world of the demand and refusal of the said Commissions and Account, and of the misapplication before mentioned, in order to prevent any further impositions on his Majesty's Subjects under pretence of an authority granted by those vacated Commissions; but likewise to recover those commissions and demand an account of the monies collected in such manner as their Counsel shall devise.

Palace Court. *Saturday Janry* 5th, 1733–4

Ordered. That the Secretary do wait on Mess[rs] Alvaro Lopez Suasso, Francis Salvador Jun[r] and Anthony Da Costa with the following Message in writing:

The Trustees for establishing the Colony of Georgia in America having receiv'd a letter from Mess[rs] Alvaro Lopez Suasso, Francis Salvador Jun[r], and Anthony Da Costa, in answer to a message sent for their Commissions, which letter does not appear satisfactory to the said Trustees, they think themselves oblig'd not only to insist on the redelivery of their Commissions, but as they conceive the settling of Jews in Georgia will be prejudicial to the Colony, and as some have been sent without the knowledge of the Trustees, the Trustees do likewise require that the said Mess[rs] Alvaro Lopez Suasso, Francis Salvador Jr. and Anthony Da Costa, or whoever else may have been concerned in sending them over, do use their endeavors that the said Jews be removed from the Colony of Georgia, as the best and only satisfaction they can give to the Trustees for such an indignity offer'd to Gentlemen acting under his Majesty's Charter.

Palace Court. *Saturday, Janry* 19th, 1733–4

The Secretary acquainted the Board that pursuant to their order of Jan[ry] 5th instant he had waited on Mess[rs] Alvaro Lopez Suasso, Francis Salvador Jun[r], and Anthony Da Costa, and left with them the message of the Trustees in writing, and that he had receiv'd the Commissions formerly given to them; and then he delivered the said Commissions to the Board.

Resolved that the said Commissions be laid by, and the further consideration of this affair be postponed till Mr Oglethorpe comes home.

22. NATURALIZATION ALLOWED TO PROTESTANTS, JEWS, QUAKERS

An Act for naturalizing such foreign Protestants, and others therein mentioned, as are settled or shall settle, in any of his Majesty's Colonies in America. Anno 13 Geo. II [1740], Cap. VII [1]

[This act, admitting Jews to naturalization in the English colonies after seven years of residence, is a landmark in the history of Jewish emancipation. The act enables the Jews to omit the words, "upon the true Faith of a Christian," from the oath of abjuration. By 1740 the Jews in England, by participating actively in developing both foreign trade and domestic industries, had won sufficient favor among the commercial powers to make possible the passage of this act, which was designed in part to encourage Jews to continue to expand England's economic prowess. The previous history of the naturalization of Jews in England is uneven: up to 1610, individual Jews could be naturalized only by special acts of Parliament; from 1610 to 1675, only Christians could be naturalized; in 1675, this provision was modified to admit certain persons economically useful to the realm to naturalization without receiving the sacrament.[2] In the American colonies, before 1740 Jews had been naturalized by colonial action, legislative or gubernatorial. On December 4, 1753, a motion was introduced in the House of Commons to repeal this act, but it was defeated the same day by a vote of 208 to 88.[3] It should be noted that only Protestants, Jews and Quakers are provided for in this legislation; Catholics are excluded.]

Whereas the Increase of People is a Means of advancing with Wealth and Strength of any Nation or Country; And whereas many Foreigners and Strangers from the Lenity of our Government, the Purity of our Religion, the Benefit of our Laws, the Advantages of our Trade, and the Security of our Property, might be induced to come and settle in some of His Majesty's Colonies in America, if they were made Partakers of the Advantages and Privileges which the natural born Subjects of this Realm do enjoy; Be it therefore enacted by the King's Most Excellent Majesty, by and with the Advice and Consent of the Lords Spiritual and Temporal, and Commons, in this present Parliament assembled, and by the Authority of the same That from and after the first Day of June in the Year of our Lord One thousand seven hundred and forty, all persons born out of the Legiance of His Majesty, His Heirs or Successors, who have inhabited and resided, or shall inhabit or reside for the Space of seven Years or more, in any of His Majesty's Colonies in America, and shall not have been absent out of some of the said Colonies for a longer Space than two Months at any one time during the said seven Years, and shall take and subscribe the Oaths, and make, repeat and subscribe the Declaration appointed by an Act made in the first Year of the Reign of His late Majesty King George the First, intituled, An act for the further Security of His Majesty's Person and Government, and the Succession of the Crown in the Heirs of the late Princess Sophia, being Protestants; and for extinguishing the Hopes of the pretended Prince of Wales, his open and secret Abettors; or, being of the People called Quakers, shall make and subscribe the Declaration of Fidelity, and take and affirm the Effect of the Abjuration Oath, appointed and prescribed by an Act made in the eighth Year of the Reign of His said late Majesty, intituled, An Act for granting the People called Quakers, such Forms of Affirmation or Declaration, as may remove the Difficulties which many of them lie under; and also make and subscribe the Profession of his Christian Belief, appointed and subscribed by an Act made in the first Year of the Reign of their late Majesties King William and Queen Mary, intituled, An Act for exempting Their Majesties Protestant Subjects from the Penalties of certain Laws; before the Chief Judge, or other Judge of the Colony wherein such Persons respectively have so inhabited and resided, or shall so inhabit and reside, shall be deemed, adjudged and taken to be His Majesty's natural born Subjects of this Kingdom, to all Intents, Constructions and Purposes, as if they and every of them had been or were born within this Kingdom; which said Oath or Affirmation and Subscription of the said Declarations respectively, the Chief Judge or other Judge of every of the said Colonies is hereby enabled and impowered to administer and take; and the taking and subscribing of every such Oath or Affirmation, and the making, repeating and subscribing of every such Declaration, shall be before such Chief Judge or other Judge, in open Court, between the Hours of nine and twelve in the Forenoon; and shall be entered in the same Court, and also in the Secretary's Office of the Colony wherein such Person shall so inhabit and reside; and every Chief Judge or other Judges of every respective Colony, before whom such Oaths or Affirmation shall be taken and every such Declaration shall be made, repeated and subscribed as aforesaid, is hereby required to make a due and proper entry thereof in a Book to be kept for that Purpose in the said Court; for the doing whereof two Shillings and no more shall be paid at each respective place, under the Penalty and Forfeiture of ten Pounds of lawful Money of Great Britain for every Neglect or Omission: and in like manner every Secretary of the Colony wherein any Person shall so take the said Oaths or Affirmation, and make, repeat and subscribe the said Declarations respectively, as aforesaid, is hereby required to make a due and proper Entry thereof in a Book to be kept for that Purpose in his Office, upon Notification thereof to him by the Chief Judge or other Judges of the same Colony, under the like Penalty and Forfeiture for every such Neglect or Omission.

II. Provided always and be it enacted by the Authority aforesaid, That no Person, of what Quality, Condition or Place soever, other than and except such of the People called Quakers as shall qualify themselves and be naturalized by the ways and means hereinbefore mentioned, or such who profess the Jewish Religion, shall be naturalized by virtue of this Act, unless such persons shall have received the Sacrament of the Lord's Supper in some Protestant and Reformed Congregation within this Kingdom of Great Britain, or within some of the said Colonies in America, within three Months next before his taking and subscribing the said Oaths, and making, repeating and subscribing the said Declaration; and shall, at the time of his taking and subscribing the said Oaths, and making, repeating and subscribing the said Declaration, produce a Certificate signed by the Person administering the said Sacrament, and attested by two credible Witnesses, whereof an Entry shall be made in the Secretary's Office of the Colony, wherein such Person shall so inhabit and reside, as also in the Court where the said Oaths shall be so taken as aforesaid, without any Fee or Reward.

III. And whereas the following Words are contained in the latter Part of the Oath of Abjuration, *videlicet,* (upon the true Faith of a Christian): And whereas the People professing the Jewish Religion may thereby be prevented from receiving the Benefit of this Act: Be it further enacted by the Authority aforesaid, That whenever any Person professing the Jewish Religion shall present himself to take the said Oath of Abjuration in pursuance of this Act, the said Words (upon the true Faith of a Christian) shall be omitted out of the said Oath in administering the same to such Person, and the taking and subscribing the said Oath by such Person, professing the Jewish Religion, without the Words aforesaid, and the other Oaths appointed by the said Act in like manner as Jews were permitted to take the Oath of Abjuration, by an Act made in the tenth Year of Reign of His late Majesty King George the First, intituled, An Act for explaining and amending an Act of the last Session of Parliament, intituled, An Act to oblige all Persons, being Papists, in that part of Great Britain called Scotland, and all persons in Great Britain, refusing or neglecting to take the Oaths appointed for the Security of His Majesty's Person and Government, by several Acts herein mentioned, to register their Names and real Estates; and for enlarging the time for taking the said Oaths, and making such Registers, and for allowing further time for the Inrolment of Deeds or Wills made by Papists, which have been omitted to be inrolled pursuant to an Act of the third Year of His Majesty's Reign; and also for giving Relief to Protestant Lessees shall be deemed a sufficient taking of the said Oaths, in order to intitle such Person to the Benefit of being naturalized by virtue of this Act.

IV. And be it further enacted by the Authority aforesaid, That a Testimonial or Certificate under the Seal of any of the said Colonies, of any Persons having resided and inhabited for the Space of seven Years or more as aforesaid within the said Colonies or some of them, to be specified in such Certificate, together with the particular time of Residence in each of such respective Colonies (whereof the Colony under the Seal of which such Certificate shall be given to be one) and of his having taken and subscribed the said Oaths, and of his having made, repeated and subscribed the said Declaration, and in case of a Quaker of his having made and subscribed the Declaration of Fidelity, and of his having taken and affirmed the Effect of the Abjuration Oath as aforesaid, and in case of a Person professing the Jewish Religion, of his having taken the Oath of abjuration as aforesaid, within the same Colony, under the Seal whereof such Certificate shall be given as aforesaid, shall be deemed and taken to be a sufficient Testimony and Proof thereof, and of his being a natural born

Subject of Great Britain, to all Intents and Purposes whatsoever, and as such shall be allowed in every Court within the Kingdoms of Great Britain and Ireland, and also in the said Colonies in America. (Extended, 20 G. 2, c. 44, Sec. I.)

v. And be it further enacted by the Authority aforesaid, That every Secretary of the said respective Colonies for the time being, shall and is hereby directed and required at the End of every Year, to be computed from the said first Day of June in the Year of Our Lord One thousand seven hundred and forty, to transmit and send over to the Office of the Commissioners for Trade and Plantations kept in the City of London or Westminster, a true and perfect List of the Names of all and every Person and Persons who have in that Year intitled themselves to the Benefit of this Act, under the Penalty and Forfeiture of fifty Pounds of lawful Money of Great Britain for every Neglect or Omission: All which said lists to transmitted and sent over, shall, from Year to Year, be duly and regularly entered by the said Commissioners, in a Book or Books to be had and kept for that Purpose in the said Office, for publick View and Inspection as Occasion shall require.

vi. Provided always, and it is hereby further enacted, That no Person who shall become a natural born Subject of this Kingdom by virtue of this Act, shall be of the Privy Council, or a Member of either House of Parliament, or capable of taking, having or enjoying any Office or Place of Trust within the Kingdoms of Great Britain or Ireland, either civil or military, or of having, accepting or taking any Grant from the Crown to himself, or to any other in trust for him, of any Lands, Tenements or Hereditaments within the Kingdoms of Great Britain or Ireland; any Thing hereinbefore contained to the contrary thereof in any wise notwithstanding. (Extended, 20 G. 2, c. 44. Persons naturalized by this Act capable of Offices, etc., civil and military, 13 G. 3, c. 25.) [4]

23. APPRENTICED

Indenture of Apprenticeship of Salomon Marache to Isaac Hays of New York, May 15, 1749 [1]

[This contract affords us an insight into the conditions of life of a colonial apprentice. Of all the indentures in the New York Hall of Records, this is the only one in which the apprentice is to receive payment in money in addition to his training, food, and clothing.[2] Salomon Marache grew up to be a prosperous merchant in New York and, after the British occupied that city, in Philadelphia, where he was also active in congregational as well as civic and patriotic affairs.[3] The portions of the document printed in italics are handwritten additions to the standard printed form of the Indenture.]

THIS INDENTURE

Witnesseth, *That Salomon Morache, Son of Estter-Morache, Widow, of the City of New-York*.......Hath put himself, and by these Presents, *with the Advice and Consent, of his said Mother*....... doth voluntarily, and of his own free Will and Accord, put himself Apprentice to *Isaac Hays*[4] *of the said City of New-York, Merchant,* ....to learn the Art, Trade and Mystery of *a Merchant*........ and after the Manner of an Apprentice, to serve from the Day of the Date hereof, for, and during, and until the full End and Term of *Five years*........next ensuing, during all which Time, the said Apprentice his said Master faithfully shall serve, his Secrets keep, his lawful Commands every where readily obey. He shall do no Damage to his said Master, nor see it to be done by others without letting or giving Notice thereof to his said Master. He shall not waste his said Master's Goods, nor lend them unlawfully to any. He shall not commit Fornication, nor contract Matrimony within the said Term. At Cards, Dice, or any other unlawful Game, he shall not play, whereby his said Master may have Damage. With his own Goods, nor the Goods of others, without Licence from his said Master, he shall neither buy nor sell *without the consent of his mast^{r}*. He shall not absent himself Day nor Night from his said Master's Service, without his Leave: Nor haunt Ale-houses, Taverns, or Play-houses; but in all Things behave himself as a faithful Apprentice ought to do, during the said Term. And the said Master shall use the utmost of his Endeavour to teach, or cause to be taught or instructed, the said Apprentice in the Trade of Mystery of *a Merchant*.......and procure and provide for him sufficient Meat, Drink, *Apparel,*–Lodging and Washing, fitting for an Apprentice, during the said Term of *Five years, and shall give him Evening Schooling every Winter during the said Term: He shall also allow him Three Pounds, New-York Money, in the Second-year of the said Term:–Five Pounds in the third year; Seven Pounds in the Fourth: year, and Twelve Pounds in the last year; and at the Expiration thereof, if the said Apprentice goes to any of the West-India Islands, his said Master*

shall consign Ten Tons of Provisions to him, on his, the said Master's own Account,–
And for the true Performance of all and singular the Covenants and Agreements aforesaid, the said Parties bind themselves each unto the other firmly by these Presents. IN WITNESS thereof, the said Parties have interchangeably set their Hands and Seals hereunto. Dated the *Fifteenth* Day of *May*–in the *Twenty-Second.* Year of the Reign of our Sovereign Lord *George the Second*–King of GREAT BRITAIN, &c. ANNOQUE DOMINI One Thousand Seven Hundred and *Forty-Nine*–

Isaac Hays

Sealed and Delivered in the Presence of

her
Estter × *Marache*
mark
Dan[11] *Gomez*
Ash[r] *Myers*[5]

The master having left this city ordered that the apprentice be discharged from the Indtre of apprenticeship.

24. IMPORTED GOODS FOR SALE

Two advertisements from *The New-York Gazette Revived in the Weekly Post-Boy,* 1751

[The variety of goods advertised is an index to the extensive business of this prosperous importer. That imports into the colonies were always from England or its colonies was dictated by English mercantile policy.]

[January 7, 14, and 21, 1750–1]

Just imported from London, in the Brig Garland, Capt. Machet, and to be sold cheap by Benjamin Gomez,[1] at his Store, next Door to Mr. Isaac Gomez's,[2] in the Smith's-Fly; An Assortment of East India and European Goods; Also London Single Refin'd Sugar.

[June 3, 10, 17 and 24 and July 1, 1751]

Just imported, in the Mary, Capt. Badger from London, and to be Sold cheap by Benjamin Gomez, At his House opposite Col. Depuyster's, Treasurer; Broad and narrow Tandems, 3–4 Garlix, Prince's & Russia Linnens, Ozenbrigs, fine, coarse, flower'd & spotted lawns, fine Laces & Cambricks, Ducapes, Mantua Silks, Bandanoes, Muslins, Ginghams, Calicoes, Cotton & Silk Hollands, divers sorts of Checks, best hard and Common Pewter, Camblets, Starrets, Worsted Damasks, Calamincoes, Shalloons, Hangings, Stocking Breeches, Florets, gilt & silver'd Buttons, single refin'd Sugar; with sundry other Goods too tedious to mention.

25. FOR SALE: WHITE SERVANTS, ETC.

Advertisement in *The New-York Gazette Revived in the Weekly Post-Boy*, June 24 and July 1, 8, 15, and 22, 1751

[The selling of "White Servants" was common well into the nineteenth century, and both Jews and non-Jews were sold into indentured white labor servitude.[1] In the following advertisement, Abraham Van Horne, who is not a Jew, is in partnership with two Jews.]

Just imported from Liverpool, and to be sold on board the Snow Nancy, William Beekman Master, Several White Servants; also sundry sorts of Earthen Ware in Casks and Crates, Cheshire Cheese, Loaf Sugar, Cutlery Ware, Pewter, Grindstones, Coals, and sundry other Goods too tedious to mention: by Abraham Van Horne, Daniel & Isaac Gomez or said Master.

26. A CRAFTSMAN ADVERTISES

From *The New-York Gazette; or, the Weekly Post-Boy*, November 6, 1758

[There were artisans and craftsmen among the Jews of New York and other colonies, although the quantity and proportion are not known. This advertisement was inserted by one such craftsman.]

Levy Simons,[1] Embroiderer from London, informs the Ladies and Gentlemen, That, besides Gold and Silver, he works in

Silk and Worsted, Shading; likewise Robins and Facings, Shoes, &c. He Cleans Gold and Silver Lace, takes Spots out of Silk and Cloths, &c. &c. to be heard of at I. Abrahams,[2] near the Kings Arms.

27. SUPPLIES FOR THE FRENCH AND INDIAN WAR

King George's Warrant, August 4, 1760 [1]

[The syndicate of which Moses Franks was a part, and for whose benefit the King made out this warrant for £32,169 16s, did a very extensive business, and had contracts with the Crown for more than £764,000.[2] Partnerships between Jew and non-Jew, of which this syndicate is an example, were not uncommon in England or in the Colonies. Moses Franks himself, although born in New York and enrolled in that city's militia in 1738, removed to London thereafter and attained prominence as a merchant, shipowner, and speculator in the Western lands of the Illinois territory.[3] On the French side, the chief supplier and one of the leading figures in the organizing of the defense of the French territory in North America was the Jew, Abraham Gradis (c. 1699–1780). At the beginning of the war, he "equipped and sent twenty-six vessels carrying troops, ammunition and food," and later he helped recruit troops which he outfitted and transported.[4]]

Sir James Colebrooke, Bart. et al £32169 16 by way of further Advance for N° America

George R [signature]

Our Will and Pleasure is And We do hereby direct authorise and command that out of any monies in your hands that may be applied to this Service You do issue and pay unto Sir James Colebrooke Bart. Arnold Nesbitt George Colebrooke and Moses Franks Esqrs. (Contractors for victualling Our Forces in North America) or to their Assigns the sum of Thirty two thousand one hundred and sixty nine pounds sixteen shillings upon Account and by way of further Advance for carrying on that Service And this shall be as well to you for making such payment as to Our Auditors and all others concerned in passing your Accounts for allowing the same thereupon a sufficient Warrant Given at Our Court at Kensington this 4th day of August 1760 in the 34th year of Our Reign.

By his Majesty's Command

Holles Newcastle
H. B. Legge
James Oswald

Reverse Side.

To Our Right Trusty and Welbeloved Councillor Henry Fox Esqr Paymaster General of Our Guards Garrisons and Landforces

Sir James Colebrooke, Bart. et al £32169,,16,, by way of further Advance for No America.

[Signed] James Colebrooke
Arnold Nesbitt
G. Colebrooke
Moses Franks

28. NEWPORT SOCIAL CLUB

Rules of a Newport club of Jews, November 25, 1761 [1]

[Provision is made in these rules for suppers, wine, cards, and no talk "relating to Synagogue affairs." In 1761 there were only ten families with "56 souls of Jews" in Newport;[2] the seven families therefore represented by the nine members of this club probably constituted most of the adult males.]

Rules Necessary To Be Observed At The Club Viz:

FIRST.—The club to be held every Wednesday evening during the winter season. The members to be nine in number; and by the majority of votes a chairman to be elected to serve one month only.

SECOND.—After one month, or four club nights, a new chairman to be elected in the manner aforesaid.

THIRD.—No person to be admitted as a member of said club without approbation of the members.

FOURTH.—Each of the members shall have liberty to invite his friends to the club, well understood, one at a time only.

FIFTH.—The hours of club to be from 5 to 10, in the manner following: From 5 to 8 each member is at liberty to divert at cards, and in order to avoid the name of a gaming club, the following restrictions shall be strictly observed, viz.: That no member shall presume or offer to play for more than twenty shillings at whist, picquet or any other game besides his club; on proof of gaming for any more, the member or members so offending shall pay the value of four bottles good wines for the use and benefit of the ensuing club night.

SIXTH.—At eight of the clock the supper (if ready) to be brought in At ten the club to be adjusted and paid, and no cards or any other game shall be allowed after supper.

SEVENTH.—After supper if any of the members have any motion to make relating to the club he must wait till the chairman has just drank some loyal toast.

EIGHTH.—That none of the members shall . . . during . . . conversation relating to Synagogue affairs,[3] on the forfeit of the value of four bottles good wine for the use as aforesaid.

NINTH.—If any of the members should behave unruly, curse, swear or offer to fight,[4] the chairman shall lay such fine as he sees fit, not exceeding, for each offence, four bottles good wine for the use aforesaid.

TENTH.—If any of the members happen to be sick or absent, by acquainting Mr. Myer with the same, shall be exempt from paying anything towards the club, but if no notice given as aforesaid, shall pay his quota of the supper only.

ELEVENTH.—If any of the members does not meet at club nights, and can't offer sufficient reason for so doing, the chairman with the members shall determine if he or they are to pay the proportion of the whole club, or the quota of supper only.

TWELFTH.—If any of the members neglect coming to club three nights successively without being sick or absent, shall be deemed unwilling, consequently his name shall be erased from the list, not to be admitted during the season without the consent of the chairman and all the members.

THIRTEENTH.—Ever[y] member, after signing the articles, and not willing afterwards to conform to the same, his or their names shall be erased out of the list, and no more to be admitted during the season.

In witness whereof the members of said club have signed their respective names the day and year above written.

Moses Lopez, Isaac Polock, Jacob Isaacs, Abr'm Sarzedas, Nap't. Hart, Moses Levy, Issachar Polock, Naph't. Hart Jr., Jacob Rods. Rivera [5]

FOURTEENTH.—At a club held the 16th day of December, 1761, it is resolved and agreed by the chairman and the majority of all the members that these articles be inserted amongst the rules of said club, viz:

That in case the chairman is not at the club, the secretary, for the time being, shall take his place, and the same obedience shall be paid him as if the chairman was present, and to be invested with equal authority. As also the said secretary is hereby empowered to nominate with the concurrence of the members then present, a secretary to supply his place for the time being; and that every month a secretary shall be elected in the same manner and form as the chairman is elected.

29. NEWPORT SLAVE TRADE

Instructions to a Ship Captain, October 29, 1762 [1]

[Shocking as it may seem today, some of the "best people," including pious Christians and Jews, participated in the slave trade in the eighteenth and nineteenth centuries. This fact is additional evidence that the level of morality both of individuals and groups is determined not so much by any abstract religious or moral code as by the relations of production that govern the conduct of men in any given time and place. In the mid-eighteenth century, only a tiny minority in America was beginning to question the morality of the slave trade. In fact, Newport's pre-eminence then as an American port depended largely on two factors: the spermaceti (candle) industry and the African slave trade. When the latter declined, Newport lost its economic position. Noteworthy in this document is the matter-of-fact, business-like manner in which these two Jewish merchants give their instructions to the captain of their slave ship.]

Captain John Peck,

As you are at present master of the sloop *Prince George* with her Cargo on board and ready to sale you are to observe the following orders:

That you Imbrace the first fair wind and proceed to sea and make the best of your way to the windward part of the Coast of Affrica, and at your arrival there dispose of your Cargo for the most possible can be gotten, and Invest the neat proceeds into as many good merchantable young slaves as you can, and make all the Dispatch you possibly can. As soon as your Business there is Compleated make the best of your way from thence to the Island of New Providence and there dispose of your Slaves for Cash, if the Markets are not too dull: but if they should [be], make the Best of your way home to this port, take pilates and make proper protest where ever you find it necessary. You are further to observe that all the Rum on board your Sloop shall come upon an average in case of any Misfortune, and also all the slaves in general shall come upon an Average in case any Casualty or Misfortune happens, and that no Slaves shall be brought upon freight for any person, neither Direct nor Indirect.

And also we allow you for your Commission four Slaves upon the purchase of one hundred and four, and the priviledge of bringing home three slaves and your mate one.

Observe not neglect writing us by all opportunitys of every Transaction of your Voyage. Lastly be particular Carefull of your Vessell and Slaves, and be as frugal as possible in every expense relating to the voyage. So wish you a Good Voyage and are your Owners and humble Servants.

[No firm signature]

But further observe if you dispose of your Slaves in Providence lay out as much of your neat proceeds as will Load your Vessel in any Commodity of that Island that will be best for our advantage and the remainder of your Effects bring home in money.

Isaac Elizer
Samuel Moses [2]

30. MERCHANTS RESIST BRITAIN

The Non-Importation Agreement of Philadelphia, October 25, 1765 [1]

[There were nine Jews among the 375 merchants who signed this historic document protesting the "Restrictions, Prohibitions and ill advised Regulations" imposed upon the colonies by British mercantile policy. By limiting colonial exports and increasing the cost of their imports, the London merchants profited at the expense of the colonial merchants, who became ever more heavily indebted. The most effective economic weapon developed by the colonists in resistance against British domination was the non-importation agreement or boycott. The serious divisions on this issue that were evident among merchants in general were even more sharply reflected among the Jewish merchants.[2] That so many did participate in this preliminary struggle is a foreshadowing of the fact that most Jews were to play the role of patriots in the Revolution.]

The Merchants and Traders of the City of Philadelphia, taking into their consideration the Melancholy state of the North American Commerce in general, and the distressed situation of this Province of Pennsylvania in particular, do unanimously agree. That the many difficulties they now labour under as a trading people, are owing to the Restrictions, Prohibitions and ill advised Regulations, made in several Acts of the Parliament of Great Britain lately passed [3] to regulate the Colonies, which have limited the Exportation of some part of our Country Produce, increased the cost and expense of many Articles of our Importation, and cut off from us all means of supplying ourselves with Specie enough, even to pay the duties imposed on us, much less to serve as a Medium of our Trade. That this province is heavily in Debt to Great Britain for the Manufactures and other Importations from thence, which the Produce of our lands have been found unequal to pay for, when a free exportation of it to the best Markets was allowed of, and such trades open as supplied us with Cash and other Articles of immediate remittance to Great Britain.— That the late unconstitutional law, the Stamp Ac,[4] if carried into execution in this Province will further tend to prevent our making those Remittances to Great Britain for payment of old Debts, or purchase of more Goods, which the Faith subsisting between the Individuals trading with each other requires. And therefore, in justice to ourselves, to the Traders of Great Britain who usually give us Credit, and to the Consumers of British Manufactures in this Province: the Subscribers hereto have voluntarily and unanimously come into the following resolutions and agreements, in hopes that their Example will stimulate the good people of this Province, TO BE FRUGAL IN THEIR USE AND CONSUMPTION OF ALL MANUFACTURES EXCEPTING THOSE OF AMERICA,[5] and lawful goods coming directly from Ireland, manufactured there, whilst the necessities of our Country are such as to require it; and in hopes that their Brethren, the Merchants and Manufacturers of Great Britain will find their own interest so intimately connected with ours, that they will be spurred on to befriend us from that Motive, if no other should take place.

FIRST. It is unanimously resolved and agreed, that in all orders, any of the Subscribers to this Paper, may send to Great Britain for goods, they shall and will direct their Correspondents not to ship them until the Stamp Act is Repealed. SECONDLY. That all those amongst the subscribers that have already sent orders to Great Britain for goods, shall and will immediately countermand the same until the Stamp Act is Repealed. Except such Merchants as are owners of Vessels already gone or now cleared out for Great Britain, who are at liberty to being back in them on their own Accounts, Cotas, Casks of Earthenware, Grindstones, Pipes, Iron Pots, empty Bottles, and such other bulky Articles as owners usually fill up their Ships with, but NO DRY GOODS OF ANY KIND, EXCEPT SUCH KIND OF DYE STUFFS AND UTENSILS NECESSARY FOR CARRYING ON MANUFACTURES, that may be ordered by any person. THIRDLY. That none of the Subscribers hereto shall or will vend any Goods or Merchandize whatsoever, that shall be shipped them on Commission from Great Britain after the first day of January next, unless the Stamp Act be Repealed. FOURTHLY. That these resolves and Agreements shall be binding on all and each of us the Subscribers, who do hereby, each and every Person for himself, upon his WORD OF HONOUR, agree, that he will strictly and firmly adhere to, and abide by, every article from this time till the first day of May next, when a Meeting of Subscribers shall be called, to consider whether the further continuance of this obligation be then Necessary. FIFTHLY. It is agreed, that if goods of any kind do arrive from Great Britain, at such time or under such circumstances, as to render any signer of this Agreement suspected of having broken his Promise, the Committee now appointed shall enquire into the premises, and if such suspected person refuses, or cannot give them Satisfaction; the Subscribers hereto will unanimously take all prudent measures, to discountenance and prevent the Sale of such goods, until they are released from this agreement by mutual and general Consent. LASTLY. As it may be necessary that a Committee of the Subscribers be appointed to wait on the Traders of this City to get this present agreement universally subscribed, the following Gentlemen are appointed for that Purpose.—Thomas Willing & Samuel Mifflin, Esqrs. Thomas Montgomery, Samuel Howell, Samuel Wharton, John Rhea William Fisher, Joshua Fisher, Peter Chevalier, Benjamin Fuller & Abel James.

> [Then follow 375 signatures, including] Mathias Bush, Barnard Gratz, Michael Gratz, David Franks, Joseph Jacobs, Benjamin Levy, Hyman Levy Jr., Samson Levy, Abraham Mitchel, Moses Mordecai (his mark) [6]

31. A SHOEMAKER ELECTED TO OFFICE

Minutes of the New York Common Council, October, 1766 [1]

[The records of the election as constable of Isaac Moses, shoemaker, are unusual. After his first election, he was disqualified because he was not "a freeman nor freeholder." Confident of his support, he persisted, was qualified, and was promptly reelected at a special election. He was also elected constable in 1767, 1768, and 1769.[2] This Isaac Moses, whose name seems to be new to American Jewish history, is not to be confused with the much better known merchant of the same name.[3]]

At a Common Council held at the City Hall of the Said City on Tuesday the fourteenth day of October 1766.

. . . *Ordered* that there be a New Election of a Constable for the South ward in the room of Isaac Moses, who is neither a freeman nor freeholder; and that the Alderman of the said ward cause the said Election to be held on friday the twenty fourth of October Instant at Ten oClock in the forenoon. . . .

At a Common Councill held at the City Hall of the said City on Wednesday the 22[d] day of October Anno Dom 1766.

. . . Isaac Moses Cordwainer admitted and Sworn a freeman of this Corporation and *orderd* to be registred.

At a Common Councill held at the City Hall of the said City on Thursday the 30th day of October Anno Dom 1766.

. . . Alderman [Francis] Filkin reported that pursuant to an order of this Board he had Caused a New Election of a Constable for the South ward and that Isaac Moses [4] was Duly Elected a Constable for the said ward on the 24th of October Instant he the said Isaac Moses having been elected a Constable for the Said ward on the 29th of September last, and was then neither a freeman nor freeholder, but hath Since to witt the 22d day of this Instant October taken up his freedom, and was this day Sworn to Execute the said office accordingly.

32. PROPOSING TO HELP OPEN UP THE WEST

Letter from Michael Gratz of Philadelphia to his brother Barnard in London, July 6, 1770 [1]

[This letter, dealing with business, political, and personal affairs, is remarkable for its revelation of the extensiveness of the business interests and ventures of the Gratzes and their associates. They have dealings in England, Scotland, Maryland, New York, Rhode Island, Pennsylvania, and the great West. It was in relation to the West that the Gratzes played their most significant role. In association with David Franks, they were by 1770 already far on the way to replacing the monopoly of trade in the Illinois country that was held by the firm of Baynton, Wharton and Morgan. The successful completion of this process is due primarily to the greater influence of the Frankses and Gratzes at the London court.[2]]

Dear Barnard

I have wrote afew Lines Since the Failg of Daniel Wister who has not acted an honaust Part by his Crs [creditors] but as a villian, which is to tedious to mention, at Present only that am afraid Mr M. Franks [3] will be asufferer by him, for which am heartly Sorry for, tho must Say that is no ones Faulth, as he turnd out so bad aperson, no doubt Mr David Franks will be blamd much, but was not in his Power to Doe more than he & others thought Could be Don in the affairs, as had over Signd the Books, which Proved was Don to 2 & 3 different People in the Same maner, £21

Mr George Croghan has don nothing in his afair yet, so you may think the Disappointment with him & others, that Could wish I never Knew them, tho was informed that G. C. is gon up to Fort Pitt, where Mr Jos. Simon Followed him last monday, So hope on his return that there will be Something don towards his Promises, I should have gladly Sent you an Other Bill but is not in my Power,

So you must Try our Cousen Mr Solo. Henry,[4] as before mention who Shall be rememberd with Satisfaction in ashort time, what ever he may advance you and think the best way, if the acts not repealed, to goe with asmall Cargo to Marryland as mentiond to you before, with Such Goods as is allowd to import there, which is Caus [?] Goods & Linnens 1/6 Stg [sterling] p^{r} y^{d} Clothes from 4/ to 6/ p^{r} y^{d} Stuffes 18^{d} p^{r} y^{d} Blankets & Ruges 7/6 to 8/ p^{s} and other things as you have Seen by the newes Papers Sent you Some time Pass, in there salves [?]—

Find this Place is Determand of not importing[5] and realy Daingerus to attempd any Such thing, as there was one Capt. Spiere from Scottland who had Goods for n. York & this Place, which they would not Suffer to be tuch'd in either Place but reship'd to Scottland or England which was don from n. y & here, tho the Persons that had the Goods on Board have made & attampd to bring them up in Shallops from Lewistown & Down the river which was Found out, and where very glad to Diliver them up to the Committy, Ells their houses Goods & their lifes in Great dainger, on which they was oblige to make Great acknowledgement to the inhabattenes and made them selves out lyars don with Diffrand & [?] maner all to which is there names Signd too & at the Coffee house Bucks now, So is realy Daingerus, this way, but to Baltimore Marryland will Doe as agreed to all these Cans [?] Goods above mentiond in which is the Indian Good, So hope. you will not detain Long in England if the acts not repeald, and nothing advantageus offers, there, as hope Baltimore Marryland will answer the Purpose, to F. Pitt &c the Bucks County, Please God, the Rhode Island trade as yet Stop'd on acc^{t} the Dry Goods imported some time ago, tho Could wish had don with that Place & People, as Seem to be as tedious as G. C. or worse, or think not so safe, hope you have don Something in the 9050 acres[6] Land, to satisfaction as are very good & so nigh a Citty is very valuble, Expect they will fetch 2000£ Stg however you must know best, as on the spott, no more to add but that your Dear Rachel[7] & my Family thanks to God all well, who Janis [?] there Love to you & our Cousin, Solo. Henry, I remain My dear Barnard [,] Your Ever Lov'^{g} & Effec^{t} Brother

Michael Gratz.

M^{r} [Matthias] Bush & family all well My Compts to Miss R. Franks & br Charge the Postage of the Inclos to M^{r} M Hart[8] who has made us but Little Payment Since you left home. Bring afew Dimonds for the Poor man

33. KOSHER MEAT

Excerpts from the Minute Book of the Congregation Shearith Israel, New York, December 23 and 24, 1771 [1]

[A shohet "is Suspended till he is found Innocent," when charged with laxness in the execution of his duties properly to prepare, slaughter, examine and protect meat to be sold to the Jewish community. He was cleared of the charges.]

5532 on Monday 16th Tebeth [December 23, 1771]

The Parnas [Hayman Levy] and Assistants [Joseph Simson, Myer Myers, Sampson Simson, Asher Myers] being Assembled. Judah Jacobs appear'd before them, And Accused Moses Lazarus [2] our present שוחט [Shohet] with mixing at one time טרפה [Terefa] and כשר [Kasher] tongues together at another time he had killed four Oxen כשר [Kasher] and brought home only three tongues, when finding his mistake went back to the Slaughter House and brought home a tongue without a mark and made it כשר [Kasher] with his other tongues The said שוחט [Shohet] is also Accused of Sealing a lamb that was killed by a Butcher, which Can be proved against him The said שוחט [Shohet] was Order'd by the Parnas to appear at 3 OClock this Afternoon to Clear himself of the Above Accusations before he went to kill for the Congregation which Order he has not Comply'd with it is therefore resolved that he is Suspended till he is found Innocent.

5532 on Tuesday 17th of Tebeth [December 24, 1771]

At a meeting of the Parnas, and Assistants Moses Lazarus Appear'd, and Asked their Pardon for not Attending yesterday and in Answer to the Accusations against him he declared that Mr Manuel Myers had bought all his tongues the day before the mistake happen'd, and that the day after he told Mr Isaac Adolphus,[3] that he was very lucky in finding out a mistake he had made in taking home four טרפה [Terefa] Tongues and found it out and had Carried them to Michl: Varian a Butcher to sell for him and that he had no other tongues by him at the time, but say'd if he had had any, they must have been all טרפה [Terefa] Mr Adolphus and Mr Myers being present Confirm'd all he said in regard of the Tongues, and by examining said Evidences it appears in the Said שוחט [Shohet] favor and he therfore is Continued, on the following Conditions that if ever he makes any other mistakes in Regard to Killing בדיקה [Bedika] or Sealing or in any thing else belonging to his office that he then shall be dischargd from being שוחט [Shohet] to this Congregation

34. DEATH OF A PATRIOT

Letter from Major Andrew Williamson to the President of South Carolina, John Rutledge, August 4, 1776 [1]

[Before the news of the Declaration of Independence could reach him, Francis Salvador died a bloody death fighting a Cherokee Indian uprising instigated by the British and their Tory supporters. Major Williamson, in command of the American forces, found it necessary to include an account of Salvador's death and of the last words he uttered before expiring, since Salvador was well known to the leading patriots and officials in South Carolina. Born in London in 1747, Francis Salvador was the scion of a very wealthy English Jewish family. In December 1773, having lost most of an inheritance and a dowry that totaled £73,000 through the failure of the Dutch East India Company, the Lisbon earthquake, and other misadventures, he came to South Carolina to recoup his losses, leaving his wife and four children behind him. He was soon the owner of a plantation of 7000 acres and many slaves.[2] Active from the beginning in the struggle against British domination, he was elected a member of the First Provincial Congress of South Carolina on December 19, 1774, and also of the Second Congress, which transformed itself into the General Assembly of the new State on March 26, 1776. Salvador thus became the first Jew to hold State office. He also served on important committees and was an active advocate of independence.[3]]

Camp, two miles below Keowee,
August 4th, 1776.

Sir,

I received your Excellency's favours of the 26th and 27th ult. by express. In my last letter to your Excellency, of the 31st ult. I informed you of my spies, being returned with two white prisoners; who gave an account of [Alexander] Cameron's being arrived from over the Hills with twelve white men; and, that he, with the Seneca and other Indians, were encamped at Ocnore Creek, about thirty miles distant from Twenty-Three Mile Creek, where I then lay encamped. This intelligence induced me to march immediately to attack their camp, before they could receive any information of my being so far advanced.

I accordingly marched about six o'clock in the evening, with three hundred and thirty men on horseback; (taking the two prisoners with me, to show where the enemy were encamped; and told them before I set out, if I found they deceived me, I would order them instantly to be put to death;) intending to surround their camp, by day-break; and to leave our horses about two miles behind, with a party of men to guard them. The River Keowee lying in our route, and only passable at a ford at Seneca, obliged me, (though much against my inclination,) to take that road; the enemy either having discovered my march, or laid themselves in ambush, with a design to cut off any spies or party I had sent out, had taken possession of the first houses in Seneca; and posted themselves behind a long fence, on an eminence close to the road where we were to march. And, to prevent being discovered, had filled up the openings betwixt the rails, with twigs of trees, and corn-blades. They suffered the guides and advanced guard to pass; when, a gun from the house was discharged, (meant as I suppose, for a signal for those placed behind the fence;) who a few seconds after, poured in a heavy fire upon my men; which, being unexpected, staggered my advanced party.

Here, Mr. Salvador received three wounds; and, fell by my side: my horse was shot down under me, but I received no hurt. Lieutenant Farar of Captain Prince's company, immediately supplied me with his. I desired him, to take care of Mr. Salvador; but, before he could find him in the dark, the enemy unfortunately got his scalp: which, was the only one taken. Captain Smith, son of the late Captain Aaron Smith, saw the Indian; but thought it was his servant, taking care of his master, or, could have prevented it. He died, about half after two o'clock in the morning; forty-five minutes after he received the wounds, sensible to the last. When I came up to him, after dislodging the enemy, and speaking to him, he asked, whether I had beat the enemy? I told him yes. He said he was glad of it, and shook me by the hand—and bade me farewell—and said, he would die in a few minutes. Two men died in the morning; and six more, who were badly wounded, I have since sent down to the settlements; and given directions to Doctors Delahowe and Russell, to attend them.

I remained on the ground, till day-break, and burnt the houses on this side the river; and afterwards crossed the river the same day—reduced Seneca entirely to ashes. Knowing, that the Indians would carry immediate intelligence of my strength, to the place where Cameron lay encamped, who would directly move from thence; and having ordered the detachment from Colonels Neel's and Thomas' regiments to attack and destroy Estatoe, Qualhatchie, and Toxaway, and join me this day at Sugar Town, obliged me to march that way: which, this day a strong detachment consisting of four hundred men, has totally reduced to ashes. An old Indian, was found there; who said, the enemy had deserted the town four days ago; on hearing by a white man, that an army was advancing against them.

I am respectfully,

Your Excellency's most obt. servt.

A. Williamson.

His Excellency John Rutledge,
President of So. Carolina, Charlestown.

35. BUSINESS RIVALRY AND ANTI-SEMITISM

A business letter to Michael Gratz, from an agent in Virginia, September 6, 1776 [1]

[The American bourgeois-democratic revolution, although it laid the base for the formal emancipation of the Jews, did not of course destroy the social basis for anti-Semitic prejudice. Thus, in the very year of the revolution, a Virginia patriot reflects anti-Semitic attitudes when bested in a business matter.]

Port Royal, September 6, 1776.

Sir:—

Mr. Robert Johnstone of this place, who, it is reported, purchased half of the sloop Olive of the former owner, complains that he had no notice of the sale at Fredricksburg last Tuesday,—blusters much about it; says it is illegal; talks of setting it aside and says the Commissioners prefer Jews and Turks to him. That you may be able to judge of this matter yourself, you are to know that when the vessel was condemned, one half of her was British property and the other half the property of Henry (?) Leighburne, a native and resident in this county, and that the Convention ordered half the sales to be paid to the said Leighburne; that the said Leighburne was present at the sale and is to receive his part of the money, if he does not direct us to pay it to Johnstone. Thus you see we were under no greater obligations to give warning to Mr. Johstone than to you or the Grand Seignior. As a neighbor and acquaintance, we would have informed him, and thought he knew of the intended sale, it having been publicly mentioned in this place; but whether he was apprized of it or not is immaterial as to the legality of the proceedings, and you will act in the affair as you think proper. I am informed Mr. Johnstone will make you an offer of £23:0:0 for your bargain,[2] rather than contest the matter. I am, Sir,

Your Most Obedient

Fr'd Tennent.

Mr. Michael Gratz.

36. REVOLUTIONARY VIGILANCE IN CONNECTICUT

Petition to the Governor of Connecticut, New Haven, September 17, 1776 [1]

[Jews were active in many phases of the revolutionary war, including the exercise of vigilance against local tories, who acted as informers for the British. In Connecticut, the tories were stronger than in any other New England state, and worked in close collaboration with the British troops across the Sound on Long Island, as this petition clearly declares. Signed by 102 citizens of New Haven, two of whom were Jews, the petition names the persons suspected of loyalist sympathies and conduct and asks "that the aforementioned persons be removed to some interior part of the country," or that other steps be taken to render them harmless. New Haven was a particular target for the operations of British and tory raiding parties that burned haystacks and farm buildings, pilfered valuables, stole cows and hogs, and carried on a general guerrilla warfare against the patriots.[2]]

It stated, That the memorialists, from their maritime situation, are more exposed to the destructive measures of our internal enemies, than their brethren who live more remote from the sea coast; as the conveyance of intelligence to the British army, who are now in possession of the whole of Long Island, is liable to less interruption, than if there was a tract of inhabited country to travel through, before the camps of our enemies could be entered. These circumstances, added to a full persuasion and belief that there are persons, now residents in this town, who at least would rejoice at the loss of our liberties, and we fear, contribute their mite to the obtaining that end, induce us to approach your Honors on the present occasion. We should esteem ourselves very unfortunate, should we, in our zeal for the preservation of our liberties, entertain jealousies of any that are really friends to our country; but if an early disapprobation of Congressional measures; frequent assertions that we should certainly be overcome; that it was in vain to enter the lists against so potent a power as Great Britain, invariably treating, with singular marks of approbation the professed enemies of American liberty; in short, if an uniformity of conduct, the completion of which bears striking marks of their suspected character, will justify suspicion, we flatter ourselves we shall stand acquitted by your Honors of the imputation of feigning our fears.

Your Honors will permit us to point out the persons we have particularly in view: Abiather Camp, James Curgenven, William Glen, Edward Carrington, Ambrose Ward, and Ralph Isaacs [3] are the men we have in our eye; besides particular acts and expressions of these men, which will admit of no construction but what pronounces them unfriendly to the general cause; they have by the whole tenor of their conduct, evinced to us most clearly the same point.—We therefore consider their residence among us to be dangerous to our safety. We are every night exposed to be destroyed by our open enemies; we live on their borders, separated only by a few miles of water, the absolute command of which is in their hands; our internal enemies intimately acquainted with our harbors, and our defenceless situation can introduce them into our houses; can involve us, our property, our wives, and our little ones in ruin, before we apprehend their approach. The great law of self-preservation, therefore, calls upon us to leave no avenue unguarded—no measure that will procure our safety unessayed. As the laws of this State have not provided a remedy adequate to the evil, we are under the necessity of applying to your Honors, for your interposition in our behalf; praying that your Honors would order and decree, that the afore mentioned persons be removed to some interior part of the country; or that your Honors would in some other way make provisions for our security. This mode of procedure, we conceive, is not unprecedented among civilized nations; and, if we are rightly informed, was very recently adopted by a neighboring State, with regard to persons whose conduct had not afforded more grounds for jealousy than the conduct of those persons we have pointed out to your Honors. And your memorialists, as in duty bound, shall ever pray.

[Signed by] Jacob Pinto, Abraham Pinto [4] and 100 others

New Haven, September 17, 1776

37. JEWISH LOYALISTS

Address of Loyalty to the Conquerors, Admiral Richard Howe and General William Howe, New York, October 16, 1776 [1]

[Not all the Jews were patriots of the revolution, although the majority were. The loyalists were generally found among the rich merchants and landowners who put the class benefits they expected to derive from the continued connection with Britain above the national interests of the new state. While motivations involved factors such as abstract concepts of loyalty and personal and cultural ties with English life, the decisive factors lay deeper in the class relations, including especially fear of the democratic masses. When the British captured New York city, the majority of the Jewish community, under the leadership of its *hazzan* (reader), Gershom Mendez Seixas, left New York for Connecticut and Pennsylvania, refusing to stay behind and collaborate with the hostile government. Some of the richest Jews, however, did stay in New York; and Alexander Zuntz, a Hessian officer, became president of the congregation.[2] The British ruled oppressively, confiscating whig estates, and forcing some to take the oath of allegiance. At a mass meeting of loyalists this address was drawn up amid "loud acclamations and shouts of applause,"[3] and signed by the gentry, clergy, college faculty, and many others, to a total of 948 persons, including fifteen or sixteen Jews. The declaration is fulsome and abject, referring to "the tenderest emotions of Gratitude on this Instance of his Majesty's paternal goodness," and pledging "true allegiance to our Rightful Sovereign George the Third as well as warm affection to his sacred person Crown and Dignity."]

> To the Right Honorable, Richard, Lord Viscount Howe—of the Kingdom of Ireland—
>
> And to His Excellency the Honorable William Howe Esqr General of his Majesty's Forces in America; the King's Commissioners for restoring Peace to his Majestys Colonies in North America—

Your Excellencies, by your declaration, bearing date July 14th, 1776, having signified, that "the King is desirous to deliver his American Subjects from the Calamities of War and other Oppressions which they now undergo; and to restore the Colonies to his protection and peace"—and by a subsequent Declaration, dated Sepr 19th 1776, having also been pleased to express your desire "to Confer with his Majesty's well affected subjects, upon the means of restoring the public Tranquility and establishing a permanent union with every Colony, as a part of the British Empire."—We Therefore, whose names are hereunto Subscribed, Inhabitants of the City and County of New York, in the province of New York, reflecting with the tenderest emotions of Gratitude on this Instance of his Majesty's paternal Goodness; and encouraged by the Affectionate manner in which his Majestys gracious purpose hath been conveyed to us by your Excellencies, who have thereby evinced that Humanity, is inseparable from that true Magnanimity and those enlarged sentiments which form the most Shining Characters—beg leave to represent to your Excellencies—

That we bear true allegiance to our Rightful Sovereign George the Third as well as warm affection to his sacred person Crown and Dignity. That we Esteem the constitutional Supremacy of Great Britain, over these Colonies, and other depending parts of his Majestys dominions, as Essential to the Union, Security, and Welfare, of the whole Empire, and sincerely lament the Interruption of that Harmony, which formerly subsisted between the Parent State and these her Colonies—That many of the Loyal Citizens have been driven away by the Calamities of War and the Spirit of Persecution which lately prevailed; or sent to New England, and other distant Parts

We therefore hoping that the sufferings which our absent fellow citizens undergo for their Attachment to the Royal Cause may plead in their behalf; humbly pray that Your Excellencies would be pleased on these our dutiful representations to Restore this City & County to his Majesty's Protection and Peace—

[Signed by 948 names, including] Haob Aaron, Abm. J. Abramse, Abraham Gomez, Moses Gomez Jr., Barrak Hays, David Hays, Uriah Hendricks, Levy Israel, Aaron Keyser, David Levison, Henry Marx, Samuel Myers, David Nathan, Sam. Samuel, George Simpson, Isaac Solomons [4]

38. HAYM SALOMON OFFERS HIS SERVICES

His Memorial to the Continental Congress, Philadelphia, August 25, 1778 [1]

[In order to avoid being arrested a second time by the British occupation forces in New York, Haym Salomon had fled from the city, leaving his family and his growing fortune behind him. Penniless in Philadelphia, he addressed himself to the Continental Congress, recounting his services to the revolution, and asking for whatever public employment was available. This document, signed by Salomon himself, is the only reliable summary of Salomon's activity and trials during the first three years of the War for Independence.[2] When the Continental Congress ignored Salomon's application for employment, he busied himself with a brokerage business in Philadelphia, and soon became "the most successful of the war brokers."[3]]

To the Honorable the Continental Congress

The Memorial of Hyam Solomon late of the City of New York, Merchant.
humbly sheweth,

That Your Memorialist was some time before the Entry of the British Troops at the said City of New York,[4] and soon after taken up as a Spy and by General Robertson committed to the Provost [5]— That by the Interposition of Lieut. General Heister (who wanted him on account of his Knowledge in the French, polish, Russian

Italian &c[a] Languages) he was given over to the Hessian Commander [6] who appointed him in the Commissary Way as purveyor chiefly for the Officers—That being at New York he has been of great Service to the French & American prisoners and has assisted them with Money and helped them off to make their Escape [7]—That this and his close Connexions with such of the Hessian Officers as were inclined to resign and with Monsieur Samuel Demezes has rendred him at last so obnoxious to the British Head Quarters that he was already pursued by the Guards and on Tuesday the 11th inst. he made his happy Escape from thence [8]—This Monsieur Demezes is now most barbarously treated at the Provost's and is seemingly in danger of his Life And the Memorialist begs leave to cause him to be remembred to Congress for an Exchange

Your Memorialist has upon this Event most irrecoverably lost all his Effects and Credits to the Amount of Five or six thousand Pounds sterling and left his distressed Wife [9] and a Child of a Month old at New York waiting that they may soon have an Opportunity to come out from thence with empty hands—

In these Circumstances he most humbly prayeth to grant him any Employ in the Way of his Business whereby he may be enabled to support himself and family—And Your Memorialist as in duty bound &c[a].

Haym Salomon

Philad[a] Aug[t] 25th 1778.

39. SLANDER AND REPLY

Letter in *The South-Carolina and American General Gazette,* Charleston, December 3, 1778 [1]

[In this letter an American Jewish patriot defends the honor and reputation of his country and the Jewish people from the slanderous misrepresentation of both.]

MR. WELLS,[2]

On perusing Mrs. Crouch and Co's paper [3] of the 1st instant, I was extremely surprised to find, in a piece signed *An American,* a signature sufficient to lead every honest and judicious man to imagine, that whatever was said in so publick a manner, should be ingenuous and true, assertions directly contrary. Here are his words:

"Yesterday being by my business posted in a much frequented corner of this town, I observed, in a small space of time, a number of chairs and loaded horses belonging to those who journeyed, come into town.—Upon inspection of their faces and enquiry, I found them to be of the *Tribe of Israel*—who, after taking every advantage in trade the times admitted of in the State of Georgia, as soon as it was attacked by an enemy, fled here for an asylum, with their ill-got wealth—dastardly turning their backs upon the country when in danger, which gave them bread and protection—Thus it will be in this State if it should ever be assailed by our enemies—Let judgment take place."

I am apt to think, Mr. Printer, that the gentleman is either very blind, or he is willing to make himself so; for I am well convinced, had he taken the trouble of going closer to the chairs, he would have found that what he has thus publickly asserted was erroneous and a palpable mistake, as he might have been convinced they were of the female kind, with their dear babes, who had happily arrived at an asylum, where a tyrannical enemy was not at theirs or their dear offsprings heels. I do, therefore, in vindication of many a worthy Israelite now in Georgia, assert, that there is not, at this present hour, a single Georgia Israelite in Charles Town; and that so far to the contrary of that gentleman's assertion, I do declare to the Publick, that many merchants of that State were here on the 22d ult, and on being informed of the enemy landing, they instantly left this, as many a worthy Gentile knows, and proceeded post haste to Georgia, leaving all their concerns unsettled, and are now with their brother citizens in the field, doing that which every honest American should do.

The truth of this assertion will, in the course of a few days, be known to gentlemen of veracity, who are entitled to the appellation of Americans. The Charlestown Israelites, I bless Heaven, hitherto have behaved as staunch as any other citizens of this State, and I hope their further conduct will be such as will invalidate the malicious and designing fallacy of the author of the piece alluded to.

I am, Sir, Yours, etc,

A real AMERICAN, and True hearted ISRAELITE.

Charlestown, Wednesday, December 2, 1778.

40. PATRIOT CAPTURED

"Capture of Mordecai Sheftall, Deputy Commissary-General of Issues to the Continental Troops for the State of Georgia, viz., 1778, December 29th"[1]

[This exciting autobiographical account by one whom the British considered "a very great rebel" reveals the revolutionary spirit of its author, Mordecai Sheftall. So bold was his answer to the interrogation that he was ordered confined "amongst the drunken soldiers and Negroes," which both the British and Sheftall apparently considered a degradation. Sheftall (1735–1797), who was born and reared in Savannah, was Chairman of the Savannah Parochial Committee of resistance to British rule, and was denounced and proscribed by the British. A merchant, he joined the army when the Revolution broke out, became Commissary General for Georgia troops, then Deputy-Commissary of Issues for the Southern Department, and was captured, as herein described, at the fall of Savannah. He refused to enter British service and was finally paroled in September, 1780.[2]]

This day the British troops, consisting of about three thousand five hundred men, including two battalions of Hessians, under the command of Lieutenant-Colonel Archibald Campbell, of the 71st regiment of Highlanders, landed early in the morning at Brewton Hill, two miles below the town of Savannah, where they met with very little opposition before they gained the height. At about three o'clock, P.M., they entered, and took possession of the town of Savannah, when I endeavoured, with my son Sheftall,[3] to make our escape across Musgrove Creek, having first premised that an intrenchment had been thrown up there in order to cover a retreat, and upon seeing Colonel Samuel Elbert and Major James Habersham endeavour to make their escape that way; but on our arrival at the creek, after having sustained a very heavy fire of musketry from the light infantry under the command of Sir James Baird, during the time we were crossing the Common, without any injury to either of us, we found it high water; and my son, not knowing how to swim, and we, with about one hundred and eighty-six officers and privates, being caught, as it were, in a pen, and the Highlanders keeping up a constant fire on us, it was thought advisable to surrender ourselves prisoners, which we accordingly did, and which was no sooner done than the Highlanders plundered every one amongst us, except Major Low, myself and son, who, being foremost, had an opportunity to surrender ourselves to the British officer, namely, Lieutenant Peter Campbell, who disarmed as we came into the yard formerly occupied by Mr. Moses Nunes.[4] During this business, Sir James Baird was missing; but, on his coming into the yard, he mounted himself on the stepladder which was erected at the end of the house, and sounded his brass bugle-horn, which the Highlanders no sooner heard than they all got about him, when he addressed himself to them in Highland language, when they all dispersed, and finished plundering such of the officers and men as had been fortunate enough to escape their first search. This over, we were marched in files, guarded by the Highlanders and York Volunteers, who had come up before we were marched, when we were paraded before Mrs. Goffe's door, on the bay, where we saw the greatest part of the army drawn up. From there, after some time, we were all marched through the town to the course-house, which was very much crowded, the greatest part of the officers they had taken being here collected, and indiscriminately put together. I had been here about two hours, when an officer, who I afterwards learned to be Major Crystie, called for me by name, and ordered me to follow him, which I did, with my blanket and shirt under my arm, my clothing and my son's, which were in my saddle-bags, having been taken from my horse, so that my wardrobe consisted of what I had on my back.

On our way to the white guard-house we met with Colonel Campbell, who inquired of the Major who he had got there. On his naming me to him, he desired that I might be well guarded, as I was a very great rebel. The Major obeyed his orders, for, on lodging me in the guard-house, he ordered the sentry to guard me with a drawn bayonet, and not to suffer me to go without the reach of it; which orders were strictly complied with, until a Mr. Gild Busler, their Commissary-General, called for me, and ordered me to go with him to my stores, that he might get some provisions for our people, who, he said, were starving, not having eat anything for three days, which I contradicted, as I had victualled them that morning for the day. On our way to the office where I used to issue the provisions, he ordered me to give him information of what stores I had in town, and what I had sent out of town, and where. This I declined doing, which made him angry. He asked me if I knew that Charlestown was taken. I told him no. He then called us poor, deluded wretches, and said, "Good God! how are you deluded by your leaders!" When I inquired of him who had taken it, and when he said General Grant, with ten thousand men, and that it had been taken eight or ten days ago, I smiled, and told him it was not so, as I had a letter in my pocket that was wrote in Charlestown but three days ago by my brother. He replied, we had been misinformed. I then retorted that I found they could be misinformed by their leaders as well as we could be deluded by ours. This made him so angry, that when he returned me to the guardhouse, he ordered me to be confined amongst the drunken soldiers and Negroes, where I suffered a great deal of abuse, and was threatened to be run through the body, or, as they termed it, skivered by one of the York Volunteers; which threat he attempted to put into execution three times during the night, but was prevented by one Sergeant Campbell.

In this situation I remained two days without a morsel to eat, when a Hessian officer named Zaltman, finding I could talk his language, removed me to his room, and sympathized with me on my situation. He permitted me to send to Mrs. Minis,[5] who sent me some victuals. He also permitted me to go and see my son, and to let him come and stay with me. He introduced me to Captain Kappel, also a Hessian, who treated me very politely. In this situation I remained until Saturday morning, the 2d of January, 1779, when the commander, Colonel Innis, sent his orderly for me and son to his quarters, which was James Habersham's house, where, on the top of the step, I met with Captain Stanhope, of the Raven sloop of war, who treated me with the most illiberal abuse; and after charging me with having refused the supplying the King's ships with provisions, and of having shut the church door, together with many ill-natured things, ordered me on board the prison-ship, together with my son. I made a point of giving Mr. Stanhope suitable answers to his impertinent treatment, and then turned from him, and inquired for Colonel Innis. I got his leave to go to Mrs. Minis for a shirt she had taken to wash for me, as it was the only one I had left, except the one on my back, and that was given me by Captain Kappel, as the British soldiers had plundered both mine and my son's clothes. This favour he granted me under guard; after which I was conducted on board one of the flat-boats, and put on board the prison-ship Nancy, commanded by Captain Samuel Tait, when the first thing that presented itself to my view was one of our poor Continental soldiers laying on the ship's main deck in the agonies of death, and who expired in a few hours after. After being presented to the Captain with mine and the rest of the prisoners' names, I gave him in charge what paper money I had, and my watch. My son also gave him his money to take care of.

He appeared to be a little civiller after this confidence placed in him, and permitted us to sleep in a state-room—that is, the Rev. Moses Allen, myself and son. In the evening we were served with what was called our allowance, which consisted of two pints and a half and a half-gill of rice, and about seven ounces of boiled beef per man. We were permitted to choose our messmates, and I accordingly made choice of Captain Thomas Fineley, Rev. Mr. Allen, Mr. Moses Valentonge, Mr. Daniel Flaherty, myself and son, Sheftall Sheftall.

41. MERCHANT IN EXILE

Letter from Aaron Lopez to Joseph Anthony, Philadelphia, February 3, 1779 [1]

[From this letter one gets an intimate sense of the human problems and difficulties encountered by those, Jewish and non-Jewish, who were driven from their homes by the British during the war. When 8000 British and Hessian troops occupied Newport, destroying 480 houses, burning ships, devastating orchards and generally sacking the city, Aaron Lopez, his father-in-law, Jacob Rodriguez Rivera, and his son-in-law, Abraham Pereira Mendez, took their households to Leicester, Mass., where the families stayed until the war was over in 1783, "secured," as Aaron Lopez hoped, "from sudden Allarms and the Cruel Ravages of an enraged Enemy." Lopez (1731–1782) was a figure of considerable importance. "A biographical sketch of this Portuguese Jew almost epitomizes the commercial history of Newport in its golden age just before the American revolution."[2] He was outstanding as one of the merchants who developed inter-colonial and international trade, especially after 1770. He had an interest in or owned outright at least thirty ships. By 1757, he was heavily interested in the West Indian trade, and in the Guinea trade to Africa, to which he sent a slave ship about once a year. Because he did not join in the non-importation agreement, he was favored by the British, but he was not a tory, like Isaac Hart and a few other Newport Jews, and supported the revolution.[3] The mingling of business, politics, and personal "gossip" makes this letter interesting.]

My Dear and very worthy Friend,

How shall I express my gratitude to you for the satisfaction you have given me with the rec't of your friendly and obliging Favor of the

27th ulto. which this moment has been handed me by our mutual Friend Mr. Hewes, who telling me its Bearer returns again to Exeter tomorrow morning, I would not miss the opportunity of acknowledging its agreeable contents, and gratifying your wishes of hearing from me, from my family, and some thing from the distress'd Inhabitants of our once flourishing I[s]land; But before I render you this intelligence, permit me to tell you, that I am extreamly happy to learn, that the Almighty has been pleased to guide you and good Family to so safe an Asylum, and that *there* he has blest you with health, peace, and plenty arround you, during these times of publick and almost universal Callamity; But what I esteem still a greater Blessing, endowed you with a gratefull heart, susceptible of all those divine bounties, which I pray may be continued you with all the additional felicities this sublunary World is capable of affording. For my part I have the pleasure to acquaint my good Friend, that I consider myself under still greater obligations to Heaven; having hitherto enjoy'd every one of those inestimable Blessings you are pleased to tell me of, without the least Merit or Title to them; am therefore to acknowledge myself infinitely more thankfull for so mercifull Dispensations.

Since we left our Island my principal object was to look out for a Spot, where I could place my Family, secured from sudden Allarms and the Cruel Ravages of an enraged Enemy; Such a one I have hitherto found in the small inland Township of Leicester in the Massachusetts Bay, *where* I pitch'd my Tent, erecting a proportionable one to the extent of my numerous Family on the Sumit of an high healthy Hill, where we have experienc'd the civilities and hospitality of a kind Neighbourhood; and moved in the same Sphere of Business I have been used to follow, which, altho much more contracted, it has fully answer'd my wishes, and you know my Friend, when that is the case, it never fails of constituting real happiness: Add to this the satisfaction of having for a next door neighbour your truly well wishing Friend, my Father in Law Mr. Rivera, who with his Family I left in good health, spending in peace the fruits of his last summer's Labour on a small Farm. the Old Gentleman improves with much the same *Farming Faculties,* you tell me you cultivate yours; and I can farther inform you that while his hands have been imploy'd in that usefull Art, his agitated Mind has uniformly accompanied yours to poor Newport; where I do still hope we shall soon have the pleasure of meeting each other again and re-enjoy those injurd habitations, we have so long been deprived of, with all satisfaction.

By this Weeks Post Mrs. Lopez has informed me that the Widow Lee, who had the Liberty of going down from Providence in a Flag to Newport, after staying there some days, she had the indulgency of returning to Providence, and being engaged to nurse my Daughter Mrs. Mendez (who I have the consolation to tell you leaves [lives] also near me and next door to our good Neighbour Capt. Jno. Lyon formerly of Newport). This Mrs. Lee coming directly on her return into our Family inform'd Mrs. Lopez, that the poor Inhabitants of that Town, have been very much distress'd this Winter for the want of fewell and provisions, those Individuals of my Society in particular, who she said had not tasted any meat, but once in two months: Fish there was none at this Season of the Year, and they were reduced to the alternative of leaving upon Chocolate and Coffe. These and many other Callamities and Insults the wretched Inhabitants experience, ought to excite our thanks to that Great Being, who gave us resolution to exchange at so early a period that melancholy Spot for that we now are enjoying. Your Dweling house I understand has sufer'd much. Your Neighbour Augustus Johnson was found dead at his house. My Neighbour Gideon Sesson's Wife is crazy, and what I lament most, is, that the vertue of several of our Reputable Ladys has been attacked and sullied by our destructive Enemys,—so much for poor Newport. Capt. Benj. Wright continues at Jamaica. his zeallous wishes to put me in possession of some part of the large property I have had lock'd up in his hands since the commencement of this war, led him to address me with three Vessels loaded on my sole and proper account, all which have been taken by our American Cruizers; the first falling in honest hands was delivered up to me by a reference agreed to by the parties. The other two were libelled and contested, one of them was adjudged at Providence to be restored to me: the opposite party appealed to Congress. The third and most valuable was (contrary to the opinion and expectation of every spectator) condemn'd at a Connecticut Court of Admiralty. I appeald to Congress, which has brought me here in full hopes of obtaining redress.[4] Mrs. Wright was left porly at Newport, when Nurse Lee came away, which prevented Mrs. Wright coming off in the same Flagg, as she intended, but will do it soon, as she recovers.

I have oferd the poor distress'd Woman all the assistance in my power to grant her, as I esteeme her an object of real merit.

Now my Dear Friend I have only to add my sincere thanks for your kind invitation to spend a day or two with you at your habitation. I shall inform myself (not being acquainted where Exeter lays) and if I can anyways make it convenient to call on you, may expect to see me; meantime permit me to announce you and Mrs. Anthony every good wish pure esteem can suggest being very truly, Dear Sir, Your affectionate Friend and humble Servant.

[*Unsigned*]

42. PHILADELPHIA CITIZENS TO THE CONTINENTAL CONGRESS

The Address of the Citizens of Philadelphia and of the Liberties thereof—To his Excellency the President and Congress of the United States, July, 1783 [1]

[This address of loyalty to the revolutionary government, drafted by Thomas Paine,[2] was signed by 800 citizens, including about ten Jews. In it the signers pledge their support, and point to Philadelphia's record of activity in the revolution, in order to influence the Continental Congress to return to Philadelphia. In June, 1783, under unusual circumstances, the Congress had very hurriedly left Philadelphia and established itself at Princeton, N. J. The fighting in the revolution having ended, the soldiers were becoming increasingly discontented with the fact that they were not being paid and began to give expression to this and other grievances. In June, soldiers stationed near Philadelphia had mutinied and marched on the city to present their demands to the Congress itself. By leaving Philadelphia, the Congress was of course depriving the city of a considerable amount of business, and the merchants and other men of affairs began to consider ways and means of bringing the Congress back to Philadelphia. In the petition, the citizens proffer the government the financial support that it so badly needed, and that other states, perhaps less convinced of the prime necessity "to establish the National Character of America," were not so readily offering. Yet when the Congress left Princeton on November 4, 1783, it was only to remove to Annapolis, Md.]

Most Honble Sirs

From the Commencement of the late ever memorable contest for liberty and the honor and happiness of the human race, the Citizens of

Philadelphia, and of the Liberties thereof, have in an especial manner distinguished themselves by every exertion which principle could inspire or fortitude support.

Neither have they been free with their lives only as Militia but with their fortunes as Citizens. As instances of these we need only appeal to facts.

The progress of the War has fully confirmed the one and the monthly return of taxes from this State of which the City & Liberties form so great a part has not been exceeded by any and we wish they had been proportionally equaled by every State in the Union. To which we may add the establishment of the bank which has extended its usefulness to the public service, and acquired a permanency as effectual and in some instances superior to those of other nations.

The government of this State has, likewise, ever distinguished itself by adopting and passing and the Citizens by supporting all such laws recommended by Congress as were necessary to be passed throughout the Continent for bringing the War to a happy issue and for raising such monies as the expence of it required.

The Act for laying a duty of five Per Cent upon imported Articles tho' it would have found its richest mine in the Commerce and consumption of this City & State, yet struck with the propriety and equity of raising money from the Channel in which it most circulates and impressed with the Necessity as well as the bounden duty of maintaining the justice and honor of America we chearfully [sic] gave it our best support. And as we have ever been so we mean ever to continue to be among the foremost to establish the National Character of America as the firm basis of inviolable faith and sacred honor.

In thus expressing our minds to Congress we are likewise compelled to say, That from your residence among us We have been Witnesses to the uncommon difficulties you have had to struggle with. We have beheld them with concern and often times with heartfelt anxiety We have participated in Your Cares and partook of your burthens

While our chiefest consolation under them was that they did not arise from any unwillingness or backwardness in the Government of this State to adopt the proper measures for removing them or from any narrow views in the Citizens to counteract them—

We do not amuse the World with calling on Congress to do Justice to the army and to the creditors of America and yet withhold the means by which that Justice is to be fulfilled. On the contrary we freely offer ourselves to bear our share in any National measure to effect those purposes and to establish the character of America equal to her Rank.

We are now most solemnly to assure your Excellency and Congress that tho' we do not enter into the reasons or causes which might suggest to your Honorable Body the propriety of adjourning at the particular time you did adjourn from your long accustomed Residence in this city, Yet as a Testimony of the Affections of the Citizens to that Union which has so happily succeeded in accomplishing the freedom and independence of America, We beg leave to assure Congress that if either now or at any future time until the Residence of Congress shall be permanently established it should appear to your Hoñble Body that the situation of Philadelphia is convenient for transacting therein the concerns of the Nation that Congress may Repose the utmost confidence in its inhabitants, not only to prevent any Circumstance which may have a tendency to disturb their necessary deliberations but to aid in all measures to support the national honor and dignity.

[Signed by 800, including the following who are Jews] Moses Cohen, Isaac Franks, Seymour Hart, Isaac Levy, Moses Levy, Sol Marache, Isaac Moses, Jonas Phillips, Haym Salomon, Jacob Simpson [3]

43. PETITION FOR EQUAL RIGHTS

Extract from the Journal of the Council of Censors, Philadelphia, December 23, 1783, and a newspaper comment, January 21, 1784 [1]

[The fight for separation of Church and State, which men like Jefferson believed should be absolute, was waged in many ways, and is not yet complete. This petition, which is an incident in that historic battle, is remarkable for its vigor, clarity, and dignity. The petitioners express their opposition to the requirement that members of the General Assembly of Pennsylvania subscribe to a declaration of their belief in the divine inspiration of both the Old and New Testaments, and then proceed cogently to argue that such restrictions are liable to divert immigration to other States. The Jews' just pride in their services to the revolution is set forth ringingly as a reason for their enjoying equal rights.]

To the honourable the COUNCIL OF CENSORS,[2] assembled agreeable to the Constitution of the State of Pennsylvania.

The Memorial of Rabbi Ger. Seixas of the Synagogue of the Jews at Philadelphia, Simon Nathan their Parnass or President, Asher Myers, Bernard Gratz and Haym Salomon [3] the Mahamad, or Associates of their council, in behalf of themselves and their bretheren Jews, residing in Pennsylvania,

Most respectfully sheweth,

THAT by the tenth section of the Frame of Government of this Commonwealth,[4] it is ordered that each member of the general assembly of representatives of the freemen of Pennsylvania, before he takes his seat, shall make and subscribe a declaration, which ends in these words, "I do acknowledge the Scriptures of the old and new Testament to be given by divine inspiration," to which is added an assurance, that "no further or other religious test shall ever hereafter be required of any civil officer or magistrate in this state."

Your memorialists beg leave to observe, that this clause seems to limit the civil rights of your citizens to one very special article of the creed; whereas by the second paragraph of the declaration of the rights of the inhabitants, it is asserted without any other limitation than the professing the existence of God, in plain words, "that no man who acknowledge the being of a God can be justly deprived or abridged of any civil rights as a citizen, on account of his religious sentiments." But certainly this religious test deprives the Jews of the most eminent rights of freemen, solemnly ascertained to all men who are not professed Atheists.

May it please your Honors,

Although the Jews in Pennsylvania are but few in number, yet liberty of the people in one country, and the declaration of the government thereof, that these liberties are the rights of the people, may prove a powerful attractive to men, who live under restraints in another country. Holland and England have made valuable acquisitions of men who, for their religious sentiments, were distressed in their own countries.—And if Jews in Europe or elsewhere, should incline to transport themselves to America, and would, for reason of some certain advantage of the soil, climate, or the trade of Pennsylvania, rather become inhabitants thereof, than of any other state; yet the disability of Jews to take seat among the representatives of the people, as worded by the said religious test, might determine their free choice to go to New-York,[5] or to any other of the United States of America, where there is no such like restraint laid upon the nation and religion of the Jews, as in Pennsylvania.—Your memorialists cannot say that the Jews are particularly fond of being representatives of the people in assembly or civil officers and magistrates in the state; but with great submission they apprehend that a clause in the constitution, which disables them to be elected by their fellow citizens to represent them in assembly, as [is?] a stigma upon their nation and their religion, and it is inconsonant with the second paragraph of the said bill of rights; otherwise Jews are as fond of liberty as other religious societies can be, and it must create in them a displeasure, when they perceive that for their professed dissent to a doctrine, which is inconsistent with their religious sentiments, they should be excluded from the most important and honourable part of the rights of a free citizen.

Your memorialists beg farther leave to represent, that in the religious books of the Jews, which are or may be in every man's hands, there are no such doctrines or principles established, as are inconsistent with the safety and happiness of the people of Pennsylvania, and that the conduct and behaviour of the Jews in this and the neighbouring states, has always tallied with the great design of the revolution; that the Jews of Charlestown, New-York, New-Port and other posts, occupied by the British troops, have distinguishedly suffered for their attachment to the revolution principles; and their brethren at St. Eustatius,[6] for the same cause, experienced the most severe resentments of the British commanders. The Jews of Pennsylvania in proportion to the number of their members, can count with any religious society whatsoever, the whigs among either of them; they have served some of them in the continental army; some went out in the militia to fight the common enemy; all of them have chearfully contributed to the support of the militia, and of the government of this state; they have no inconsiderable property in lands and tenements, but particularly in the way of trade, some more, some less, for which they pay taxes; they have, upon every plan formed for public utility, been forward to contribute as much as their circumstances would admit of; and as a nation or a religious society, they stand unimpeached of any matter whatsoever, against the safety and happiness of the people.

And your memorialists humbly pray, that if your honours, from any other consideration than the subject of this address, should think proper to call a convention for revising the constitution, you would be pleased to recommend this to the notice of that convention.

The above was read and ordered to lie on the table.[7]

A correspondent says,[8] that he could wish, as a friend to the State of Pennsylvania, and as a friend to Christianity, that the religious test that should be required before the admission to any office whatever in the commonwealth, were, what the declaration of rights avows to be sufficient, simply this "I believe in one God, the creator and governor of the universe, the rewarder of the good and the punisher of the wicked."

He conceives that this abridgement of our religious test would be attended with the most beneficial consequences. It would benefit the state, by inviting hither a great number of Jews, who for their wealth, their information, and their attachment to the cause of liberty, might be of extensive and permanent service. It would tend to the propagation of Christianity, by impressing the minds of the Jews, from this generous treatment; with sentiments in favour of the gospel.

Our correspondent says, that we should consider that the Jews were once the darling people of the Almighty, that he 'bore them on eagles wings,' and that the sacred prophecies declare, he will again bless them after an appointed time of affliction. He says, that it would become the true disciples of Christ, to reflect upon what the Redeemer of Mankind uttered when he was extended on the cross, "Father forgive them, for they know not what they do."[9]

44. HOME AGAIN

Address of Israelites to Governor Clinton, signed and presented by Hayman Levy, Myer Myers and Isaac Moses, in January 1784, pursuant to a Resolution of Congregation Shearith Israel, December 9, 1783 [1]

["Lately returned from Exile," the Jews of New York pledge support to the revolutionary governor and the constitution. There is great drama implicit in the whole situation: the refusal of the majority of the congregation, in 1776, to accept British domination when New York city was captured, the exile chiefly in Philadelphia, the active support of the Revolution, and then the triumphant return to New York after the British withdrew in defeat, and "the Sacred Cause of America" was firmly established.]

To His Excellency George Clinton Esquire Governor Captain General and Commander in Chief of the Militia of the State of New York and Admiral of the Navy of the Same.—

May it Please Your Excellency.—

We the Members of the Antient Congregation of Israelites, lately returned from Exile, beg leave to Welcome Your Arrival in this City, with our Most Cordial Congratulations.—

Though the Society, we Belong to, is but small, when Compared with other Religious Societies, Yet, we flatter ourselves, that none has Manifested a more Zealous Attachment to the Sacred Cause of America, in the late War with Great Britain.—We derive therefore the Highest Satisfaction from reflecting, that it pleased the Almighty Arbiter of Events, to dispose us to take part with the Country we lived in; and we now look forward, with Pleasure to the happy days we expect to enjoy under a Constitution, Wisely framed to preserve the inestimable Blessings of Civil, and Religious Liberty.—

Taught by our Divine Legislator to Obey our Rulers,[2] and prompted thereto by the Dictates of our own Reason, it will be the Anxious endeavour of the Members of our Congregation to render themselves Worthy of these Blessings, by Discharging the Duties of Good Citizens and as an Inviolable regard to Justice and the Constitution, has ever distinguished your Administration, they rest Confident of receiving an equal Share of your patronage.—

May the Supreme Governor of the Universe take you under his Holy Protection, and may you long contine to Exercise the Dignified Office You now Possess, with Honor to Yourself, and advantage to your Constituents.—

We have the Honor to Be, with the greatest Respect,

In Behalf of the Antient Congregation of Israelites

Your Excellencys

Very Obedient Humble Servants [3]

45. FOR EQUALITY OF RELIGIOUS RIGHTS

Letter from Jonas Phillips to the Federal Constitutional Convention, September 7, 1787 [1]

[This petition is a vigorous and lofty expression of the Jews' interest in democracy and equality of religious expression. Phillips points to the contradictions in the Pennsylvania constitution as the basis for his fears that the Federal constitution would not adequately provide for religious equality. Since the convention met in secret, he did not know that on August 20, 1787, more than two weeks before he composed his letter, the convention had passed Article 6, stipulating that no religious test should be required of office-holders; the vote was eight to one, with North Carolina opposing it and the Maryland and Connecticut delegations divided. Even this provision, however, was considered insufficient; and on September 25, 1789 both houses of the first Congress agreed on the Bill of Rights, the first item of which declares that Congress shall make no law respecting an establishment of religion.]

To His Excellency the president and the Honourable Members of the Convention assembled:

Sires

With leave and submission I address myself To those in Whom there is wisdom understanding and knowledge, they are the honourable personages appointed and Made overseers of a part of the terrestrial globe of the Earth, Namely the 13 united states of america in Convention Assembled, the Lord preserve them amen—

I the subscriber being one of the people called Jews of the City of Philadelphia, a people scattered & dispersed among all nations do behold with Concern that among the laws in the Constitution of Pennsylvania, there is a Clause Sect 10 to viz—I do believe in one God the Creatur and governor of the universe and Rewarder of the good & the punisher of the wicked—and I do acknowledge the Scriptures of the old & New testiment to be given by divine inspiration—to swear & believe that the new testiment was given by divine inspiration is absolutely against the Religious principle of a Jew, and is against his Conscience to take any such oath—By the above law a Jew is deprived of holding any publick office or place of Government which is a Contridictory [sic] to the bill of Right Sec 2 viz

That all men have a natural & unalienable Right to worship almighty God according to the dictates of their own Conscience and understanding & that no man ought or of Right can be Compelled to attend any Religious Worship or Creed or support any place of worship or Maintain any minister contrary to or against his own free will and Consent, nor can any man who acknowledges the being of a God be Justly deprived or abridged of any Civil Right as a Citizen on account of his Religious sentiments or peculiar mode of Religious Worship, and that no authority can or ought to be vested in or assumed by any power whatever that shall in any case interfere or in any manner Controul the Right of Conscience in the free Exercise of Religious Worship.—

It is well known among all the Citizens of the 13 united states that the Jews have been true and faithful whigs, & during the late Contest with England they have been foremost in aiding and assisting the states with their lifes & fortunes, they have supported the cause, have bravely fought and bled for liberty which they can not Enjoy.—

Therefore if the honourable Convention shall in their Wisdom think fit and alter the said oath & leave out the words to viz—and I do acknowledge the scripture of the new testiment to be given by divine inspiration, then the Israelites will think themself happy to live under a government where all Religious societies are on an Equal footing—I solicit this favour for myself my children & posterity, & for the benefit of all the Israelites through the 13 united states of America.

My prayers is unto the Lord. May the people of this states Rise up as a great & young lion, May they prevail against their Enemies, may the degrees of honour of his Excellency the president of the Convention George Washington, be Exhalted & Raise up. May Everyone speak of his glorious Exploits.

May God prolong his days among us in this land of Liberty—May he lead the armies against his Enemys as he has done heruntofore. May God Extend peace unto the united states—May they get up to the highest Prosperitys—May God Extend peace to them & their seed after them so long as the sun & moon Endureth—and May the almighty God of our father Abraham Isaac & Jacob indue this Noble Assembly with wisdom Judgment & unanimity in their Counsells & may they have the satisfaction to see that their present toil & labour for the wellfair of the united states may be approved of Through all the world & particular by the united states of america, is the ardent prayer of Sires

Your most devoted obed. Servant

Jonas Phillips [2]

Philadelphia 24*th Ellul* 5547 or *Sepr 7th* 1787.

46. FOR A REPUBLIC, OLD TESTAMENT MODEL

Excerpt from Samuel Langdon, D. D., *The Republic of the Israelites an Example to the American States, A Sermon Preached at Concord, in the State of New-Hampshire; before the Honorable General Court at the Annual Election. June 5, 1788* (Exeter, 1788)

[The use of the Bible for revolutionary purposes, as this excerpt shows, continued from the Revolutionary War into the period when the form of the independent American government was a matter for debate between the advocates of a monarchy and of a republic. Among the people the Bible was then the most widely known of all books, and its authority was constantly invoked to justify all kinds of policies. Before and during the American Revolution the partisans of independence therefore had to counter the theory of the divine right of kings with the idea of the divine right of republics as demonstrated in the Old Testament. It has been widely noted that the bourgeois democratic revolutions against feudalism were popularly expressed in religious, Biblical terms. The revolutions were Protestant in form. Cromwell's soldiers sang Psalms in battle. Although Christian theology regarded both the Jewish Old Testament and the New Testament equally as parts of its Bible, these two testaments seem to have been invoked for different purposes.[1] It is unfortunate that the sermons of Jewish preachers in the American revolution have not come down to us. But the sermon of Langdon (1723–1797), former president of Harvard College (1774–1780), and a prominent revolutionary clergyman in New Hampshire, will exemplify how the experiences of the ancient Hebrews were interpreted for democratic purposes.[2]]

. . . When first the Israelites came out from the bondage of Egypt, they were a multitude without any other order than what had been kept up, very feebly, under the ancient patriarchal authority. They were suddenly collected into a body under the conduct of Moses, without any proper national or military regulation. Yet in the short space of about three months after they had passed the red sea, they were reduced into such civil and military order, blended together by the advice of Jethro, as was well adapted to their circumstances in the wilderness while destitute of property. Able men were chosen out of all their tribes, and made captains and rulers of thousands, hundreds, fifties and tens: and these commanded them as military officers, and acted as judges in matters of common controversy.

But the great thing wanting was a permanent constitution, which might keep the people peaceable and obedient while in the desert, and after they had gained possession of the promised land. Therefore, upon the complaint of Moses that the burden of government was too heavy for him, God commanded him to bring seventy men, chosen from among the elders and officers, and present them at the tabernacle; and there he endued them with the same spirit which was in Moses, that they might bear the burden with him. Thus a Senate was evidently constituted, as necessary for the future government of the nation, under a chief commander. And as to the choice of this Senate, doubtless the people were consulted, who appear to have had a voice in all public affairs from time to time, the whole congregation being called together on all important occasions: the government therefore was a proper republic.

And beside this general establishment, every tribe had elders and a prince according to the patriarchal order, with which Moses did not interfere; and these had an acknowledged right to meet and consult together, and with the consent of the congregation do whatever was necessary to preserve good order, and promote the common interest of the tribe. So that the government of each tribe was very similar to the general government. There was a President and Senate at the head of each, and the people assembled and gave their voice in all great matters: for in those ages the people in all republic's [sic] were entirely unacquainted with the way of appointing delegates to act for them, which is a very excellent modern improvement in the management of republics. . . .

. . . Now by the foregoing view of the general state of the nation during the time of the judges, we may plainly see the reason why, instead of rising to fame by the perfection of their polity, religion, and morals, their character sunk into contempt. But let us see whether they conducted better afterwards, under their kings.

It was their crime to demand such a king as was like the kings of other nations, *i. e.* a king with the same absolute power, to command all according to his own pleasure. In this view God only was their king, and the head of the nation was only to be his vicegerent. Therefore as they had implicitly rejected the divine government, God gave them a king in his anger;[3] the consequence of which was, the total loss of their republican form of government, and sad experience of the effects of despotic power. . . .

47. HEBREW TAUGHT

Advertisement in *The Pennsylvania Packet, and Daily Advertiser*, March 1, 4, 6, 9 and 11, 1790

[This is the first known public advertisement of a Jew offering to teach Hebrew. For the training of Christian clergymen, Hebrew was frequently included in the curriculum of colonial and early American colleges. Thus Judah Monis, a Jewish convert to Christianity, published the first Hebrew grammar in America in 1735, and was instructor in Hebrew at Harvard from 1722 to 1759. In Philadelphia, where this advertisement was published, Hebrew had been taught at the University of Pennsylvania from 1782 to 1784 by the Lutheran minister and scholar, John Christopher Kunze (1744–1807), who held the professorship of German and Oriental languages. When Kunze moved to New York in 1784, his successor at the University was Justus Henry Christian Helmuth (1745–1825), who seems, however, to have taught only German and not Hebrew. Kunze was a friend of Gershom Mendes Seixas.[1]]

Hebrew taught by Abraham Cohen, Son to the Rev'd JACOB COHEN [2]—For Particulars enquire at the above Rev'd JACOB COHEN'S, Cherry Alley, between Third and Fourth Streets.

N. B. Spanish also taught as above.

48. ANTI-SEMITISM, 1790

Letter from John Malcolm to General Horatio Gates, March 24, 1790 [1]

[The background against which the anti-Semitic verses quoted in this letter appeared is interesting. Early in the second session of the United States Congress in 1790, Alexander Hamilton had presented a plan to fund the domestic debt of about $60,000,000. Most of the paper money involved had passed from the original owners into the hands of speculators who had purchased it at from one-twentieth to one-sixth of its face value and who stood to profiteer tremendously if Hamilton's plan were approved by Congress. Popular opposition ran high, and sought not a repudiation of the debt "but to scale down the debt to something like its real value."[2] Shortly before this letter was written, Hamilton had, on March 4, 1790, presented a report proposing a series of high duties and taxes, the revenue from which would go "towards the payment of interest on the debts of the individual states."]

Dear General [3]

Since sealing the inclos'd a paper [4] has come to hand will shew you a specimen of the troubles the Ambitious undergo by diff^t writers—as follows—

"Tax on tax young Belcour cries,
More imposts, and a new excise.
A public debt's, a public blessing
Which 'tis of course a crime to lessen.
Each day a fresh report he broaches,
That Spies and Jews [5] may ride in coach[es].
Soldiers and Farmers dont dispair,
Untax'd as yet are Earth and Air.

This on the report of the Secretary of the Treasuary's to Congress to support public Credit.

I am Dear Sir

assuredly yours

Jno. Malcolm [6]

A Report prevails that the King of France has got out of Paris to the frontiers, and that the Clergy & his Army have join'd him.

49. BUSINESS, DEBTORS, LANDS, AFTER THE REVOLUTION

Michael Gratz in Philadelphia writes to his brother and partner Barnard in Richmond, May 30, 1790 [1]

[The variety and extent of the business of this important firm, and the methods used, are here again exemplified. In the post-war period, the land speculators came into continual conflict with veterans of the war who had received grants of land from the government for their services. These soldiers' warrants were frequently challenged by claims of the land-speculators, who used every means, economic and political, to have their way, even at the expense of the veterans.[2] Thomas Perkins Abernethy concludes a long and scholarly study with the judgment that "such settlers, not the speculators, were the real empire builders. Nevertheless, history has tended to transmute the vices of the land speculators into virtues, for they, too, played a part, regardless of the fact that their motive was pecuniary gain, in helping to open the way for the Westward moving caravan."[3] The Gratzes were prominent among these land-speculators.]

Philad^a May 30th 1790.

My dear Barnard

I have wrote you by one Mr Cooke, who left this monday last tho intended to go by post, but the mail being made up, troubled that Gentleman with it, who was in the Stage for Richmond & Petersburg, and promised to deliver it. So hope has Got safe to your hands. It is of consequence to Mr Jos: Simon, Your Self and us all, doubt not the one by Mr C. P. Howard has also reached you, where in mentiond to you Concerning the Snake in the Grass, S E from whom doubt not you was favord with a letter on a particular nature, which we all hope if minuetly Considerd, will not take place by you so easily, Especially after you hear Jos: Henry,[4] what has happend at Lancaster during his stay there, after his return from you, and hopes you will referr answering the letter till you See him, for my part have perplexitys enough, and this to add to it Can assure you I was for one week, so disturbed in my mind, that I knew not how to Contain my Self, however, as am Shure will make you uneasy Shall Say no more on this subject till we meet please God, which Expect will be Soon in next month unless money matters may delay you, which is much wanted here. At foot, you will see Situations of affairs, and how at present again pushed, since your last of the 17th Instant which Contents duly note and see those warrants are taken in Taxes pray take care of our Montgomery Lands and Ohio &C if any are sold, or Can be prevented infewter [in future] if you see any of those Shiref at Richmond that they may be Saved, hope ere this reaches you, have heard what is don in the case of Able Westfalls[5] if paid or have settled, if possable for you to Get a hundred pounds Sterling Bill, by a Good Safe Drawer or indorser on his Execution would beg you to do it, if even allowing something more than the interest on the Exchaing as would Serve to Stop the under mentiond affair of Russell & Smiths £21 it would make no odds if they are in Small bills, of Exch'g, of fifty, sixty or forty pound bills, as eather would be of Great Service, So See what can be don in, I should have bin happy to have afored you better news from here than I in generl have to acquaint you with, as for what I mentiond to you about bringing affairs to Crisis, was about the Settlement between S & E [Simon and Etting?] [6] with Creger & Mullet affair, and also about Mr Ashly, of ours with the Estate of late M. F., who tratened to proceed if nothing paid on. So you may judge what alife I lead, and had during Mr Jos. Simon & Etting, the Snakes Stay here, however as Showd him the letter wrote home, promisd to let it rest for the present, till he hears what directions Mr Cooper may Send by next packet or other opprty. So that must Shew now what Can be don with a Sale of any Lands to Rais money, which God only knows how it will be accomplish'd, am Glad to find Mr Hays [7] has recved his money which he told me you forward him abill for, J. Henry is oblige to you for the trouble you are at about his affair I have also wrote last week to Mr P. Bush, an answer to his letter Send you Coppy off, I see the opinion in regard of מו״מ [business] from those you consulted with, there remarks are just, pray, what think you of Williamsburg, if a Store would not answer there, by retail, aske Col. Jameson,[8] if nothing offers at Norfolk, we must see what to be don here after your return which I now wish for dayly, so let me hear in your next when to Expect you let me Know if those warrants Exchaingd for the present agregate fund will they be receivable for Taxes in Genrl, or are they better than the present ones in J. Hays & Dunlaps [9] name, have before mentiond if James Hays Could not be laid hold of by Law there as endorser have you made inquairy about it, is he worth anything, hope you will not forget about the division of Mr Hollingsworth and my land, of 1000 acres of Nixson with Hunters Executors for the Estate who holds 1000 acres in it, and if the return of Survey is come down to the office and how it is situated there with that we may not loose it and if we Can Get the pattents for them, is there any prospect of the next assembly doing anything in Colo. G. Croghans affair, and Indiana, what do you learn about it, as yet we hear no more about Illinois or Wabash Co.[10] affair as Congress to busy with other affair tho hope is in a good way, there is some Roomer about Congress removeing here, as the President has not his health at New York, if will take [place] is not yet known—

Now my dear Barnard shall not draw on you but pray see what you can possably do and Colact £21. הכל כסף אויש בית גאט ווייש אייב ווידרקומט[10a] So See what to be don, and urge home if no prospect doing anything there, as I will try the Boston affair Could wish you make inquiary in all parts of Virginia & Allixandria if there Can be no Effects found of Moses M. Hays [10b] of Boston to lay an attachment on, would sute well, I wrote you in my last that Mr Simon desire you to take Mr Lees Bills with an endorser on these Conditions, as to let the Execution rest till he hears of the bills paid and if that agreed to that you should higher horse to Goe and negotiat the business in your return for him which Expens he will pay you, so try to do it, as S. Etting [unclear Hebrew word] is not to Goe on that business as Expected at first, Mrs. Bell Cohen is arrived here on her way to Lancaster Miriam [11] Goes with her some day this week if the stage Comes with Mr and Mrs Salomon who Come to see the Family at Whitemarsh who we hear are well, have wrote again to Solo: Henry and Doctr J. Bush who are still in hopes will do something in the affair with Mr Cooper. Mr Moses Franks has got an appointment of Attorney Generall, at New providence, to which Island he is Expected dayly Mr Dd Franks is well desire his compts to you. I now conclude with Miriams, Rachl, Fanny, Simon, J. Henry and all the rest of Childrens best wishes, Love & affection to you, wishing this will reach you in perfect health, are the sincere wishes of

Dear Barnard

Your Ever affect Brother

Michl Gratz

Mrs. B. Cohen love to you hopes to see you here at her return from Lancaster which Expect will not be much before the 1st July

NB all my lawyers out of town Can not say what papers may be wanting to bring with you for T. Dunlaps tryall, but will let you know in my next please God soon—Exchaing of Stg bills Got up here to parr and 672 pr Ct for 100£ Stg

50. CORRESPONDENCE BETWEEN THE JEWS AND WASHINGTON

[These four sets of exchanges of greetings between the Jewish congregations and a Masonic Lodge, on the one hand, and George Washington as President, on the other, are of great historic interest as well as importance. In various ways, the Jews express their loyalty to the independent, democratic, and federal government of the United States of America for which they had fought on the field of battle as well as in the political arena. Washington, in his replies, eloquently declares the principles of equality of all religious denominations that he espoused. For a century and a half these declarations have been used to confound the enemy in the ceaseless struggle against those who would subvert American ideals through the propagation of anti-Semitism and other doctrines of bigotry.]

Ia. Address from the Hebrew Congregation of the City of Savannah to the President of the United States. May 6, 1789 [1]

Sir,

We have long been anxious of congratulating [2] you on your appointment by unanimous approbation to the Presidential dignity of this country, and of testifying our unbounded confidence in your integrity and unblemished virtue: Yet, however exalted the station you now fill, it is still not equal to the merit of your heroic services through an arduous and dangerous conflict, which has embosomed you in the hearts of her citizens.

Our eccentric situation added to a diffidence founded on the most profound respect has thus long prevented our address, yet the delay has realised anticipation, given us an opportunity of presenting our grateful acknowledgments for the benedictions of Heaven through the energy of federal influence, and the equity of your administration.

Your unexampled liberality and extensive philanthropy have dispelled that cloud of bigotry and superstition which has long, as a veil, shaded religion—unrivetted the fetters of enthusiasm—enfranchised us with all the privileges and immunities of free citizens, and initiated us into the grand mass of legislative mechanism. By example you have taught us to endure the ravages of war with manly fortitude, and to enjoy the blessings of peace with reverence to the Deity, and benignity and love to our fellow-creatures.

May the great Author of worlds grant you all happiness—an uninterrupted series of health—addition of years to the number of your days and a continuance of guardianship to that freedom, which, under the auspices of Heaven, your magnanimity and wisdom have given these States.

Levi Sheftal, President
in behalf of the Hebrew-Congregation.[3]

Ib. To the Hebrew-Congregation of the City of Savannah [4]

Gentlemen,

I thank you with great sincerity for your congratulations on my appointment to the office, which I have the honor to hold by the unanimous choice of my fellow-citizens: and especially for the expressions which you are pleased to use in testifying the confidence that is reposed in me by your congregation.

As the delay which has naturally intervened between my election and your address has afforded an opportunity for appreciating the merits of the federal-government, and for communicating your sentiments of its administration—I have rather to express my satisfaction than regret at a circumstance, which demonstrates (upon experiment) your attachment to the former as well as approbation of the latter.

I rejoice that a spirit of liberality and philanthropy is much more prevalent than it formerly was among the enlightened nations of the earth; and that your brethren will benefit thereby in proportion as it shall become still more extensive. Happily the people of the United States of America have, in many instances, exhibited examples worthy of imitation—the salutary influence of which will doubtless extend much farther, if gratefully enjoying those blessings of peace which (under favor of Heaven) have been obtained by fortitude in war, they shall conduct themselves with reverence to the Deity, and charity towards their fellow-creatures.

May the same wonder-working Deity, who long since delivering the Hebrews from their Egyptian Oppressors planted them in the promised land—whose providential agency has lately been conspicuous in establishing these United States as an independent nation—still continue to water them with the dews of Heaven and to make the inhabitants of every denomination participate in the temporal and spiritual blessings of that people whose God is Jehovah.

G Washington.

IIa. From the Newport Congregation to the President of the United States, August 17, 1790 [5]

[Observe that it was the Congregation and not Washington that first used the striking characterization of our government as one "which to bigotry gives no sanction, to persecution no assistance." In reply, Washington rejects the undemocratic concept of "toleration" for the democratic one of equality.]

Sir,

Permit the Children of the Stock of Abraham to approach you with the most cordial affection and esteem for your person and merits—and to join with our fellow-citizens [6] in welcoming you to New Port.

With pleasure we reflect on those days—those days of difficulty and danger, when the God of Israel, who delivered David from the peril of the sword—shielded your head in the day of battle:—and we rejoice to think that the same Spirit, who rested in the bosom of the greatly beloved Daniel, enabling him to preside over the Provinces of the Babylonish Empire, rests, and ever will rest upon you, enabling you to discharge the arduous duties of Chief Magistrate in these States.

Deprived as we have hitherto been of the invaluable rights of free citizens, we now, (with a deep sense of gratitude to the Almighty Disposer of all events) behold a Government, [(] erected by the Majesty of the People) a Government which to bigotry gives no sanction, to persecution no assistance—but generously affording to All liberty of conscience, and immunities of citizenship—deeming every one, of whatever nation, tongue, or language equal parts of the great governmental machine. This so ample and extensive federal union whose basis is Philanthropy, mutual confidence, and public virtue, we cannot but acknowledge to be the work of the Great God, who ruleth in the armies of Heaven, and among the inhabitants of the Earth, doing whatsoever seemeth him good.

For all the blessings of civil and religious liberty which we enjoy under an equal and benign administration we desire to send up our thanks to the Antient of days, the great Preserver of Men—beseeching him that the Angel who conducted our forefathers through the wilderness into the promised land, may graciously conduct you through all the dangers and difficulties of this mortal life—and when like Joshua full of days, and full of honor, you are gathered to your Fathers, may you be admitted into the heavenly Paradise to partake of the water of life and the tree of immortality.

Done and signed by order of the Hebrew Congregation in New Port Rhode Island August 17th, 1790.

Moses Sexias [sic][,] Warden.[7]

IIb. To the Hebrew Congregation in New Port, Rhode Island [8]

Gentlemen,

While I receive with much satisfaction your address replete with expressions of affection and esteem; I rejoice in the opportunity of assuring you that I shall always retain a grateful remembrance of the cordial welcome I experienced in my visit to New Port from all classes of Citizens.

The reflection on the days of difficulty and danger which are past is rendered the more sweet from a consciousness that they are succeeded by days of uncommon prosperity and security. If we have wisdom to make the best use of the advantages with which we are now favored, we cannot fail, under the just administration of a good government to become a great and a happy people.

The Citizens of the United States of America have a right to applaud themselves for having given to mankind examples of an enlarged and liberal policy, a policy worthy of imitation.

All possess alike liberty of conscience and immunities of citizenship. It is now no more that toleration is spoken of, as if it was by the indulgence of one class of people, that another enjoyed the exercise of their inherent natural rights. For happily the government of the United States, which gives to bigotry no sanction, to persecution no assistance, requires only that they who live under its protection should demean themselves as good citizens, in giving it on all occasions their effectual support.

It would be inconsistent with the frankness of my character not to avow that I am pleased with your favorable opinion of my administration, and fervent wishes for my felicity.

May the children of the Stock of Abraham, who dwell in this land, continue to merit and enjoy the good will of the other inhabitants, while every one shall sit in safety under his own vine and fig-tree, and there shall be none to make him afraid.

May the Father of all mercies scatter light and not darkness in our paths, and make us all in our several vocations useful here, and in his own due time and way everlastingly happy.

G Washington.

IIIa. King David's Lodge of Freemasons in Newport to Washington, August 17, 1790 [9]

[In the eighteenth and early nineteenth centuries, Free-Masonry was a progressive movement both in Europe and in our country. Here the Jews were significant participants in the Order.[10] Washington was himself a Mason, as this communication indicates.]

We the Master, Wardens, and Brethren of King David's Lodge in New Port Rhode Island with joyful hearts embrace this opportunity to greet you as a Brother, and to hail you welcome to Rhode Island. We exult in the thought that as Masonry has always been patronised by the wise, the good, and the great, so hath it stood and ever will stand, as its fixtures are on the immutable pillars of faith, hope, and charity.

With unspeakable pleasure we gratulate you as filling the presidential chair with the applause of a numerous and enlightened people

Whilst at the same time we felicitate ourselves in the honor done the brotherhood by your many exemplary virtues and emanations of goodness proceeding from a heart worthy of possessing the ancient mysteries of our craft; being persuaded that the wisdom and grace with which heaven has endowed you, will ever square all your thoughts words, and actions, by the eternal laws of honor, equity, and truth, so as to promote the advancement of all good works, your own happiness, and that of mankind.

Permit us then, illustrious Brother, cordially to salute you with three times three and to add our fervent supplications that the sovereign architect of the universe may always encompass you with his holy protection.

Moses Seixas[,] Master [11]
Hy [Henry] Sherburne } Comme [Committee]

New Port Augt 17. 1790.
By order Wm Littlefield Secy.

IIIb. To the Master, Wardens, and Brethren of King Davids Lodge in Newport Rhode Island [12]

Gentlemen,

I receive the welcome which you give me to Rhode-Island with pleasure, and I acknowledge my obligations for the flattering expressions of regard, contained in your address, with grateful sincerity.

Being persuaded that a just application of the principles, on which the masonic fraternity is founded, must be promotive of private virtue and public prosperity, I shall always be happy to advance the interests of the society, and to be considered by them as a deserving brother.

My best wishes, Gentlemen, are offered for your individual happiness.

G Washington.

IVa. The Address of the Hebrew-Congregations in the cities of Philadelphia, New York, Charleston, and Richmond. December 13, 1790 [13]

[Seeing the hand of God in the "late glorious revolution," these Congregations greet Washington, and elicit from him the proud assertion, in keeping with the fact that our government was then the most advanced in the world, that "the liberal sentiment towards each other which marks every political and religious denomination of men in this country stands unrivalled in the history of nations."]

Sir,

It is reserved for you to unite in affection for your character and Person, every political and religious denomination of men; and in this will the Hebrew Congregations aforesaid yield to no class of their fellow-citizens.

We have hitherto been prevented by various circumstances peculiar to our situation [14] from adding our congratulations to those which the rest of America have offered on your elevation to the chair of the federal government.

Deign then, illustrious Sir, to accept this our homage.

The wonders which the Lord of Hosts hath worked in the days of our forefathers, have taught us to observe the greatness of his wisdom and his might throughout the events of the late glorious revolution;

and while we humble ourselves at his footstool in thanksgiving and praise for the blessing of his deliverance; we acknowledge you the Leader of the American armies as his chosen and beloved servant; But not to your sword alone is our present happiness to be ascribed; That indeed opened the way to the reign of freedom, but never was it perfectly secure, till your hand gave birth to the federal constitution, and you renounced the joys of retirement to seal by your administration in peace, what you had atchieved [sic] in war.

To the eternal God who is thy refuge, we commit in our prayer the care of thy precious life, and when full of years, thou shalt be gathered unto the People "thy righteousness shall go before thee" and we shall remember, amidst our regret, that the Lord hath set apart the Godly for himself; whilst thy name and thy virtues will remain an indelible memorial on our minds.

Manuel Josephson.[15]

For and in behalf and under the authority of the several Congregations aforesaid.

IVb. To the Hebrew Congregations in the Cities of Philadelphia, New York, Charleston and Richmond [16]

Gentlemen,

The liberal sentiment towards each other which marks every political and religious denomination of men in this country stands unrivalled in the history of nations—The affection of such a people is a treasure beyond the reach of calculation; and the repeated proofs which my fellow citizens have given of their attachment to me, and approbation of my doings form the purest source of my temporal felicity—The affectionate expressions of your address again excite my gratitude, and receive my warmest acknowledgements.

The power and goodness of the Almighty were strongly manifested in the events of our late glorious revolution.—and his kind interposition in our behalf has been no less visible in the establishment of our present equal government—In war he directed the sword—and in peace he has ruled in our councils—my agency in both has been guided by the best intentions, and a sense of the duty which I owe my country: and as my exertions hitherto have been amply rewarded by the approbation of my fellow-citizens, I shall endeavor to deserve a continuance of it by my future conduct.

May the same temporal and eternal blessings which you implore for me, rest upon your congregations.

G. Washington.

51. ANTI-DEMOCRAT, ANTI-SEMITE

Preface to the American edition of *The Democrat*, published by James Rivington, New York, 1795 [1]

[The place of anti-Semitism in the pattern of reaction is exhibited in this preface to a tendentious novel opposing the American and French Revolutions written by Henry James Pye (1745–1813), poet laureate of England from 1790 to 1813. Of Pye's elevation to the laureate-ship for his political services to Pitt, Sidney Lee remarked that "no selection could have more effectually deprived the post of reputable literary associations."[2] The preface was written by James Rivington (1724–1802), the leading loyalist publisher in the American colonies, and "King's printer" from 1777. As editor of *Rivington's New-York Gazetteer,* he incurred the hatred of the revolutionary patriots; the Sons of Liberty attacked his print-shop on November 27, 1775. After the British evacuated New York, Rivington stayed on, continuing to incur the animosity of the patriotic forces. His sons, John and James, had received half-pay pensions for life from the King in 1783, on the recommendation of the British commander in New York. That Rivington neither changed his anti-democratic views nor desisted from expressing them is shown in this preface, in which he attributes American democratic views to the agitation of Paris agents and condemns democrats for their political association with Jews.[3]]

In the following work the public are presented with the life and adventures of a Democratic Missionary, sent from the Metropolitan See of Sedition and Murder at Paris, to propagate their principles in a neighbouring country. The reception he met with among the different orders of the people, and his awkward, though zealous endeavours in the cause of liberty and equality, will not fail of yielding the reader an abundance of amusement: but these adventures, besides being in themselves sufficiently diverting, have an additional claim to the attention of the American reader at this moment, when circumstances render them applicable to ourselves.

It is well known that the mother of our Democratic Clubs [4] established, long ago, a regular system of communication with all the "grumblers" in the United States; but this, upon experience, was, it seems, found inadequate to the grand design, and therefore they determined upon a mission *ad hoc,* as often as emergencies might require. In consequence of this resolution it was that one of their members was dispatched to Boston with a pack of treaties at his back, like a pedlar, loaded with the *justificatory pleadings* of Sir Bull-face Double-fee.

The success of these missions made them resolve upon an augmentation of their missionary corps; but, their *Louis d'ors* being all expended in pairs of gloves to Sir Bull-face, and in other items of corruption, they have been obliged to wait for a supply: when that arrives we may expect to see their enlightened crew sally forth, like *Jean Le Noir,* vested with unlimited powers for rousing the mob to a "holy insurrection."

This itinerant gang will easily be known by their physiognomy; they all seem to be, like their *Vice-President,*[5] of the tribe of Shylock: they have that leering underlook, and malicious grin, that seem to say to the honest man—*approach me* not. Did they not thus bear on their front the mark of their reprobation, the perusal of the Adventures of *Jean Le Noir* might enable the unwary to distinguish them. The political cant of *Le Noir,* and his propensity to equalize the property of every one whom he has any thing to do with, are so exactly of a piece with the talents of our democrats, that the reader finds himself in an embarrassment, something resembling that of Hudibras, to know whether *Jean Le Noir* be a type of them or they of *Jean Le Noir.*

52. DEMOCRATS ANSWER AN ANTI-SEMITE

Two replies to Rivington's Preface to *The Democrat,* December 17 and 19, 1795

[These two letters (anonymous, as was the custom of the time) indicate that the democratic patriots were not inclined to allow the generally reactionary sentiments and the anti-Semitic references in Rivington's preface to go unchallenged. In reprinting the letters in his *Journal,* Greenleaf displayed them on the front page, suggesting the importance he attached to them.]

a. To the WRITER of the PREFACE to DEMOCRAT [1]

It is a good maxim not to ridicule religion, or the natural defects of the human body. The first shews the depravity of the head, the latter the malignity of the heart. If this observation is just, we may conclude from the extraordinary preface, lately published by J-m-s R-v--gt-n to a novel entitled the Democrat, that the writer's head is as destitute of every liberal sentiment, as his heart is deficient in charity and compassion for the defects of his fellow-creatures, had such defects really existed.

I shall endeavour, in the course of a few observations, to place the preface in its proper point of view, but being unaccustomed to writing, the public are not to expect well-turned periods or elegance of diction, but in lieu thereof, I will endeavour to give them facts in plain and unadorned language; in doing this, I am in some measure under the disagreeable necessity of using a mode similar to that of the author of the preface, not indeed with a view of wounding the feelings of any person whatever, but merely to expose the absurdity ot the practice itself. I shall only take notice of such part of the preface as respects the Democrats, of whose Society I am a member, and leave those whom it concerns to notice the rest.

Speaking of the Democratic Society, it has the following words—*"This itinerant gang will be easily known by their phisiognomy,"* &c. The public will doubtless admire your sagacity, in discovering the Democrats to be a wandering *gang*. An abusive stile, Sir, is ever a very bad one; the word gang is made use of to denote ruffians and highway men.—Let us try how those elegant expressions will sound, when applied to other Societies—For instance, to the St. George's, St. Andrew's, St. Patrick, Tammany, Black Friars, or any other in this city. I believe, Sir, they will not be in a hurry to erect a statue to your memory, for the politeness of the expression, or the honour you meant to confér on them—*"They all seem, like their Vice-President, of the tribe of Shylock."*—Really, Sir, this is extremely sarcastic; the wits of the age ought to have your name wrote in letter of gold, for this brilliant proof of your satire. Perhaps some of the readers of your preface may be ignorant of the source from whence this pretty story took its rise; you ought to have the goodness to inform them, that by turning to Farneworth Pope Sixtus the Vth, page 401,[2] they would find it recorded at large; but this story, as erroneously represented by Shakespeare, could not be applied to the Vice-President, as it would not by any means suit his liberality of sentiment and general character (but might, with truth, be applied to a certain gentleman who commenced a suit against D-v-d C-m-b-ll for not allowing sufficient usury for his money) this will be evident to every person who is acquainted with the character of the Vice-President, and that of the late printer of the Royal Gazette. If, by the word Shylock, you mean a Jew, from my knowledge of the Vice-President, I dare say he would think himself honoured by the appellation, Judaism being his religious profession, as Democracy is his political creed.[3]

It is an old remark, that the great Author of the Universe has so beautifully variegated his works, that scarce any two things appear alike. To your inventive genius it was left to discover, that all the members of the largest Society in the state, look exactly like their Vice President—Go on, Sir, and convince the Philosophers of the age, that you have no equal.

With your permission I will make use of an old adage—It must be a bad rule that won't work both ways—let us try it. Your most gracious sovereign, for instance, was unfortunately inflicted with insanity; by a parity of reasoning, all his liege subjects must be mad men. Again, let it be said the Pr-si---t of the C--mb-r of C-mm-r-e [4] has a peculiar leer or cast of the eye, the S-c-et--y an underlook, ergo, the whole Chamber must have both a leer and an underlook. Once more, it is said that the great C-m-ll has something in his countenance resembling a Creole or African, ergo, all his adherents must be black. Do you not already see, Sir, the very great and essential service you have rendered your friends, by producing these elegant similies [sic], which never would have been thought of, or brought forward, but to expose your own absurdities; indeed, they ought to reward your zeal, though, like an unskilful counsellor, you have injured the cause you intended to promote.

Your enemies, as well as your friends, do you justice, and say you are no changeling; that you have acted, and still do act, consistently from your appointment of printer to his most gracious majesty to the present time. Courtier like, you have feared and flattered your superiors, and represented all those in the most ludicrous and false colouring, from whom you supposed you had nothing to fear.—While the British fleets and armies were wantonly burning our towns, and committing scenes that will scarcely at this day be believed, did not your zeal then, and does it not still continue to represent them as the bravest and most gallant people on the globe terrestrial? Did you not, on every occasion, represent the worthy and brave General Washington, and his army of heroes, as banditti, that could never stand before British troops? Did you not turn their well fought battles into so many defeats, and represent them as retreating with dismay over the Alleghany Mountains? Have you not, by your false and insidious publications, caused many brave Americans to be confined in the Provo, and Jersey prison-ship? Have you forgot your advertising the rebel N--- Cr-g-r being brought in prisoner within the British lines, and how handsomely that gentleman has since rewarded you for your trouble*?—I am bold to say, Sir, that the whole of the Democratic Society, from the President to the Door Keeper individually, would be pleased with an opportunity to serve you precisely in the same way: but rest assured, merit like yours will never fail to meet its due reward.

If I had a thousand mouths of brass, they would be inadequate to trumpet forth the many exploits you have made the bravest and most magnanimous people on the globe terrestial perform, and it would require as many more to represent the dastardly and dreadful situation in which you have uniformly placed the Americans, and do still some of their best friends.

To conclude, Sir, I deny the allegations as set forth in your preface, respecting the Democratic Society and their Vice-President, as untrue, but say the facts contained herein are true, and leave the decision to the impartial public.

SLOW AND EASY.

b. For the *New-York Journal,* &c [5]

To the Ci-Devant Printer of the *Royal Gazette.*[6]

Good Sir,

Qui caput ille facet,[7] is a sound old adage. If you have imprudently taken a share in affairs which ought not to concern you, you alone are to be answerable for all the evil consequences that may possibly attend your temerity. After the most lenient and indulgent treatment from a people, whom you had long been in the daily habit of calum-

* *Rewarded him with a good horse-whipping.* [Footnote in original.]

niating, it was to have been expected, that the return on your part would at least have been the observance of a respectful silence, if it had not inspired you with the more lively emotions of gratitude and esteem. Instead of this, sir, what have you done? let facts speak, let them, if possible, inspire a blush on a countenance, torpid to manly sensibility, and dead to shame. Unfortunately, old whigs of this country have become divided in their sentiments, upon a variety of important political subjects. Candor must induce us to believe, that the majority of them really wish to promote the prosperity of their native land—it cannot be otherwise—it is impossible that the great body of the people should will an injury to themselves;—but why sir, do you take an active part in their differences? What have you—what have the old tories done to entitle themselves to the confidence of the public? The preface that you have lately published to an American edition of a work entitled "the Democrat," is doubtless one of the most impudent performances that has ever appeared in any age, or country: the invidious and personal remarks that it contains, not only upon a worthy individual, but also upon a numerous class of citizens, who are certainly, at least, more sincere in their attachment to the interests of America than yourself, merits censure; and if repeated, may perhaps involve you in consequences, that may prove disagreeable, if not dangerous to yourself. The preface itself is not, nor are you, Mr. R—, entitled to any observation; it will not however, be amiss to conclude by advising you, in the most friendly manner, to abstain from a course of conduct that may prove injurious to yourself, and perhaps subject you to consequences, for which the writer of these remarks will not undertake to be answerable.

HORTENSIUS.

53. A DEMOCRATIC SERMON

Excerpts from *A Discourse, Delivered In the Synagogue In New-York, On The Ninth Of May, 1798,* by Gershom Mendez Seixas[1]

[President John Adams had set May 9, 1798 as a National Fast Day on which all religious institutions were to pray for peace with France, which was then engaged in a war of national defence against a reactionary monarchical coalition. The idea for the fast day had come from the Federalists, who held most of the government posts and wished to use the occasion to arouse public sentiment for their policy of war with France as allies of Great Britain. The Jeffersonian democratic forces, representing the deep popular desire for peace, opposed the presidential proclamation and the preparations for the observance of the Fast. The clergy, most of which was dominated or influenced by Federalist views, did use the occasion to turn the pulpits into forums for extravagant denunciations of French republicans and of all Americans who espoused democracy, whom the clergy attacked as French agents.[2] In the light of all the other sermons, this Discourse by Gershom Mendez Seixas, delivered to the Congregation Shearith Israel in New York, is exceptional. Seixas [3] himself had strong democratic leanings. Among his congregation there were leaders of the Democratic Society like Solomon Simpson, its president, and Naphtali Judah. The discourse was therefore printed by a democratic printer and published, as the title page indicates, for Naphtali Judah,[4] bookbinder and bookseller whose shop on Water Street was "at the Sign of Paine's Head" at a time when there was almost a price on Paine's head. When it was published, Seixas' sermon was advertised in two democratic newspapers, *The Time Piece* and the *Argus and Greenleaf's New Daily Advertiser,*[5] which were the constant targets of Federalist attacks and repression. The sermon pleased the Jeffersonians; it avoided the baiting of France and of American democrats, and adhered to its biblical text, "Behold how good and how pleasant it is for brethren to dwell together in unity" (Psalm 133).]

When the spirit of discord is extant, the imagination of man is filled with terrific ideas, and the apprehensions of evil arise from the most trifling causes; then it is that we fly for succour to our Maker, and we become more fully sensible of his almighty power. Let us then not delay imploring his divine protection at this time, when we are threatened with all the horrors of war by a great, a conquering nation; who but a few years past was looked upon to have been highly instrumental in procuring liberty and independence to the United States of America, when we were oppressed by the ravages and devastations of an enraged enemy, who sought to deprive us of our invaluable rights and privileges; when it pleased God to establish us in a state of freedom, independence, and peace, so that we became respectable among the nations of the earth. But, alas! how are we fallen! Our commerce is destroyed, our rulers are treated with indignity, and our envoys with contempt. I shall not take it upon me to enter into any civil or political discussion upon the subject, but shall confine myself entirely to the nature and consequence of such actions as are consistent with the true spirit and principles of religion . . .

When we consider the many various opinions that commonly exist in a society, either religious, or civil, composed of all ranks and descriptions of men, collected (perhaps) from different countries, each bringing with him the prejudices of the government he was brought up in, it would seem to require more than human means to form any kind of system to govern them, that would suit the genius, temper, and disposition of such a mixed body. Hence arises the question, how, or in what manner, is an union to be effected? The answer is plain; by strictly adhering to the grand principles of benevolence towards all our fellow creatures; and the only invariable rule is founded on the instructions given to us by our prophets, who received their knowledge of men and manners, from the fountain of all perfection. Attend to what is said by Moses, Lev. 6. 19th, [19:18] "thou shalt love thy neighbour as thyself." By following this rule in its general and extensive sense, you will have the means at all times within your power to promote unity in society, and you may with reason hope to accomplish whatever may be thought to produce an eventual benefit; nor is this so difficult a thing to be observed as many falsely imagine; for it only implies, do not unto another, what you would not have done unto yourself. . . .

"Depart from evil—and do good—seek peace—and pursue it": We come now to speak, thirdly, of seeking peace. In the 2d Book of Kings, we find, that the Lord gave Solomon his choice of three things, and he preferred wisdom; and in the subsequent relation of this circumstance we discover, that the Lord gave wisdom unto Solomon, and there was peace between Hiram and Solomon. From this passage, it appears as if peace was a natural consequence of wisdom; but the first leading principle thereto is the fear of the Lord, as it is expressed in the psalm: "The fear of the Lord is the beginning of wisdom;" and without we have this leading principle in our hearts, we never shall attain wisdom, nor its natural consequence, peace: But by accustoming yourselves to seek peace, you will acquire that fear of the Lord which is necessary to conduct you in the pursuit, which is the 4th lesson; and when once you have discerned the paths that lead to it, you must not leave anything undone in order to attain it: Try every thing and every mode within your power to effect this invaluable blessing, and pursue it through every stage of life until you have obtained it; then will you become worthy of being called those who fear the Lord, which is certainly one of the grandest appellatives that can be applied to the human race; and as King David says, in Psalm 112th, "Blessed is the man that feareth the Lord;" and in Malachi, it is said, "Then they that feared the Lord spake often one unto the other, and the Lord hearkened and heard it." . . .

It hath pleased God to have established us in this country where we possess every advantage that other citizens of these states enjoy, and which is as much as we could in reason expect in this captivity, for which let us humbly return thanks for his manifold mercies, and sincerely pray for a continuance of his divine protection: Let us not be deficient in acknowledging his power and his goodness, and with one heart supplicate him to promote the welfare of these states, the United States of America; to grant wisdom, knowledge and understanding to the rulers and administrators of the government, and enable them to persevere in the paths of rectitude, so as to procure peace and safety to the citizens, both in their persons and their properties; that every man may sit under his own vine and under his own fig-tree, when ye shall have beaten your swords into plough shares and your spears into pruning hooks. . . .

54. BENJAMIN NONES REPLIES

A Letter to the Printer of the *Gazette of the United States*, with a Covering Note to Mr. William Duane, editor of *The Philadelphia Aurora*, August 11, 1800 [1]

[This defense of the right of a Jew to be poor and a radical is one of the profoundest utterances made by an American Jew. The statement was evoked by a scurrilous letter slandering Benjamin Nones that had been published in the *Gazette of the United States, & Daily Advertiser,* a Federalist organ, on August 5, 1800; the letter exuded contempt for democratic ideals, for the Negroes, Jews, workingmen, and the poor in general. At the end of the anonymous letter, there was a note, explaining in mocking anti-Semitic terms why Nones did not contribute to the collection taken to pay for a room used for a meeting of the Democratic Society of Philadelphia held July 30, 1800: "*Citizen N—— the Jew.* I hopsh you will consider dat de monish ish very scarch, and besides you know I'sh just come out by de Insholvent

Law.—*Several.* Oh yes let N—— pass." When Caleb F. Wayne, printer of the *Gazette,* refused to publish Nones' reply, Nones turned to *The Philadelphia Aurora,* leading Republican organ, edited by William Duane (1760–1835), considered the most effective journalist of his time. Duane featured it.]

TO THE EDITOR.

Mr. Duane.

I enclose you an article which I deemed it but justice to my character to present for insertion in the Gazette of the United States, in reply to some illiberalities which were thrown out against me in common with many respectable citizens in that paper of the 5th inst. When I presented it to Mr. Wayne, he promised me in the presence of a third person, that he would publish it. I waited until this day, when finding it had not appeared, I called on him, when he informed me that he would not publish it. I tendered him payment if he should require it. His business appears to be to asperse and shut the door against justification. I need not say more:

I am &c.

B. Nones.[2]

Philadelphia Aug. 11, 1800.

TO THE PRINTER OF THE GAZETTE OF THE UNITED STATES.

Sir,

I HOPE, if you take the liberty of inserting calumnies against individuals, for the amusement of your readers, you will at least have so much regard to justice, as to permit the injured through the same channel that conveyed the slander, to appeal to the public in self defence.—I expect of you therefore, to insert this reply to your ironical reporter of the proceedings at the meeting of the republican citizens of Philadelphia, contained in your gazette of the fifth instant; so far as I am concerned in that statement.—I am no enemy Mr. Wayne to wit; nor do I think the political parties have much right to complain, if they enable the public to laugh at each others expence, provided it be managed with the same degree of ingenuity, and some attention to truth and candour. But your reporter of the proceedings at that meeting is as destitute of truth and candour, as he is of ingenuity, and I think, I can shew, that the want of prudence of this Mr. Marplot, in his slander upon me, is equally glaring with his want of wit, his want of veracity, his want of decency, and his want of humanity.

I am accused of being a *Jew;* of being a *Republican;* and of being *Poor.*

I *am* a *Jew.* I glory in belonging to that persuasion, which even its opponents, whether Christian, or Mahomedan, allow to be of divine origin—of that persuasion on which christianity itself was originally founded, and must ultimately rest—which has preserved its faith secure and undefiled, for near three thousand years—whose votaries have never murdered each other in religious wars, or cherished the theological hatred so general, so unextinguishable among those who revile them. A persuasion, whose, patient followers, have endured for ages the pious cruelties of Pagans, and of christians, and persevered in the unoffending practice of their rites and ceremonies, amidst poverties and privations—amidst pains, penalties, confiscations, banishments, tortures, and deaths, beyond the example of any other sect, which the page of history has hitherto recorded.

To be of such a persuasion, is to me no disgrace; though I well understand the inhuman language of bigotted contempt, in which your reporter by attempting to make me ridiculous, as a Jew, has made himself detestable, whatever religious persuasion may be dishonored by his adherence.

But I am a Jew. I am so—and so were Abraham, and Isaac, and Moses and the prophets, and so too were Christ and his apostles, I feel no disgrace in ranking with such society, however, it may be subject to the illiberal buffoonery of such men as your correspondents.

I am a *Republican!* Thank God, I have not been so heedless, and so ignorant of what has passed, and is now passing in the political world. I have not been so proud or so prejudiced as to renounce the cause for which I have *fought,*[3] as an American throughout the whole of the revolutionary war, in the militia of Charleston, and in Polafkey's legion, I fought in almost every action which took place in Carolina, and in the disastrous affair of Savannah, shared the hardships of that sanguinary day, and for three and twenty years I felt no disposition to change my political, any more than my religious principles.—And which in spite of the witling scribblers of aristocracy, I shall hold sacred until death as not to feel the ardour of republicanism.—Your correspondent, Mr. Wayne cannot have known what it is to serve his country from principle in time of danger and difficulties, at the expence of his health and his peace, of his pocket and his person, as I have done; or he would not be as he is, a pert reviler of those who have so done—as I do not suspect you Mr. Wayne, of being the author of the attack on me, I shall not enquire what share you or your relations had in establishing the liberties of your country. On religious grounds I am a republican. Kingly government was first conceded to the foolish complaints of the Jewish people, as a punishment and a curse; and so it was to them until their dispersion, and so it has been to every nation, who have been as foolishly tempted to submit to it. Great Britain has a king, and her enemies need not wish her the sword, the pestilence, and the famine.

In the history of the Jews, are contained the earliest warnings against kingly government, as any one may know who has read the fable of Abimelick, or the exhortations of Samuel. But I do not recommend them to your reporter, Mr. Wayne. To him the language of truth and soberness would be unintelligible.

I am a Jew, and if for no other reason, for that reason am I a republican. Among the pious priesthood of church establishments, we are compassionately ranked with Turks, Infidels and Heretics. In the *monarchies* of Europe, we are hunted from society—stigmatized as unworthy of common civility, thrust out as it were from the converse of men; objects of mockery and insult to froward children, the butts of vulgar wit, and low buffoonery, such as your correspondent Mr. Wayne is not ashamed to set us an example of. Among the nations of Europe we are inhabitants every where—but Citizens no where *unless in Republics.* Here, in France, and in the Batavian Republic alone, we are treated as men and as brethren. In republics we have *rights,* in monarchies we live but to experience *wrongs.* And why? because we and our forefathers have *not* sacrificed our principles to our interest, or earned an exemption from pain and poverty, by the direliction of our religious duties, no wonder we are objects of derision to those, who have no principles, moral or religious, to guide their conduct.

How then can a Jew but be a Republican? in America particularly. Unfeeling & ungrateful would he be, if he were callous to the glorious and benevolent cause of the difference between his situation in this land of freedom, and among the proud and privileged law givers of Europe.

But I am *poor,* I am so, my family also is large, but soberly and decently brought up. They have not been taught to revile a christian, because his religion is not *so old* as theirs. They have not been taught to mock even at the errors of good intention, and conscientious belief.

I hope they will always leave this to men as unlike themselves, as I hope I am to your scurrilous correspondent.

I know that to purse proud aristocracy poverty is a crime, but it may sometimes be accompanied with honesty even in a Jew. I was a bankrupt some years ago. I obtained my certificate and I was discharged from my debts. Having been more successful afterwards, I called my creditors together, and eight years afterwards unsolicited I discharged all my old debts, I offered interest which was refused by my creditors, and they gave me under their hands without any solicitations of mine, as a testimonial of the fact (to use their own language) as a tribute due to my honor and honesty. This testimonial was signed by Messrs. J. Ball, W. Wister, George Meade, J. Philips, C. G. Paleske, J. Bispham, J. Cohen, Robert Smith, J. H. Leuffer, A. Kuhn, John Stille, S. Pleasants, M. Woodhouse, Thomas Harrison, M. Boraef, E. Laskey, and Thomas Allibone, &c.

I was discharged by the insolvent act, true, because having the amount of my debts owing to me from the French Republic, the differences between France and America have prevented the recovery of what was due to me, in time to discharge what was due to my creditors. Hitherto it has been the fault of the political situation of the two countries, that my creditors are not paid; when peace shall enable me to receive what I am entitled to it will be my fault if they are not fully paid.

This is a long defence Mr. Wayne, but you have called it forth, and therefore, I hope you at least will not object to it. The Public will now judge who is the proper object of ridicule and contempt, your facetious reporter, or

Your Humble Servant,

BENJAMIN NONES.

55. DEFEATING THE FEDERALISTS, NEW YORK, 1800

Reminiscences of Mordecai Myers about the New York election of 1800 [1]

[This is a vivid autobiographical account of one of the decisive election campaigns in the history of the United States. The victory of the democratic-republicans in New York in the Spring of 1800 paved the way for the election of Jefferson to the presidency that fall. In what has been regarded as the first modern election campaign in this country, Mordecai Myers [2] took an active part as a canvasser and speaker.]

. . . I became an active politician just before the election of 1793,[3] which put a period to the despotic reign of John Adams (the elder) and placed Thomas Jefferson in the Presidential Chair in the following year. The Federal party was composed in part of the old Tories of the Revolution, and the rich merchants and traders, who boasted of having all the wealth, talent, and respectability of the American people. Congress, under the Federal Administration, had passed several oppressive laws, abridging the public rights. The Alien and Sedition Laws were particularly objected to by the Democratic party. The President had power to transport or imprison, without trial, any suspected person, and he actually did imprison many valuable citizens, for speaking disrespectfully of him as an individual. Several of these were editors.

The warm partisans of the dominant party would neither deal with or employ those who differed from them in politics. All the offices from highest to lowest were held exclusively by the Federal party. Many of the merchants stooped so low as to discharge clerks, cartmen, and others who differed with them in politics. The measure of wrongs was filled to overflowing. The parties, numerically, were nearly equal; but the wealth and patronage were against the Democrats.

One evening three gentlemen met at the house of Brockholst Livingstone, in Broadway—Mr. Livingstone, General Morgan Lewis, and Aaron Burr.[4] The wrongs of the people was the subject of conversation. Mr. Burr said, "We must, at the next election, put a period to this 'reign of terror.'" The others agreed that this was desirable, but saw no way to bring it about. Mr. Burr said, "We must carry the City, and that will give us the majority in the Legislature; and the State of New York being Democratic, will carry the Union, and transfer to the Democrats all the power and patronage of the government."[5]

The other gentlemen thought this a brilliant plan, but did not see how it would be possible to gain the ascendency in the City. Mr. Burr took pen and paper and made out an Assembly ticket, heading it with the names of Gov. George Clinton, Gen. Horatio Gates, Col. Willett, Henry Rutgers,[6] Brockholst Livingstone, Ezekiel Robbins, Aaron Burr, etc., making the whole ticket eleven members. Mr. Livingstone observed that many of these gentlemen would not agree to serve, and that, if they should, it would not be easy to get them nominated and elected.

Mr. Burr requested the gentlemen to discuss the question in a week from that night; but he said, "Mr. Livingston, you and I can agree at once: I will agree to serve my Country on this occasion, and I am sure that you will not refuse." He answered, "No; if the rest will serve." The party separated, feeling great ardor in the cause.

In the course of the week, Mr. Burr called on all the other gentlemen, and with his usual eloquence, and argumentative powers, induced them all to serve.[7] At the end of the week, the three gentlemen met according to agreement, and Mr. Burr reported the assent of all. He next proposed to call a general meeting at Tammany Hall,[8] and said, "As soon as the room begins to fill up, I will nominate Daniel Smith as chairman, and put the question quickly. Daniel being in the chair, you must each nominate one member. I will nominate one, and Fairley, Miller, Van Wyck, and others will nominate, and Daniel must put the question quickly on the names, and, in this way, we will get them nominated. We must then have some inspiring speeches, close the meeting, and retire. We must then have a caucus and invite some of our most active and patriotic Democrats, both young and old, appoint meetings in the different wards, select speakers to address each, and keep up frequent meetings at Tammany Hall until the election. We will put down the monster Federalism, and bring the country back to pure Democratic principles." The whole plan succeeded, and the civil revolution was brought about.

I give you an account of what took place at Mr. Livingstone's as it was related to me by Gen. Morgan Lewis, and of the after proceedings on my own authority—I being one of the actors. I accompanied Aaron Burr to several meetings which he addressed. I was one of those selected to address the people at Tammany Hall and in the wards. The general election was carried on with great energy by both parties.

Our organization was completed by dividing the city into small districts with a committee appointed to each, whose duty it was to canvass its district and ascertain the political opinion of each voter by going from house to house, seeing and conversing with as many as possible, and enquiring the politics of such as we could not see. The district committees reported their strength at the ward meetings, the names were called off with marginal notes stating whether good, bad, or doubtful, so that at the general meeting, we could determine very nearly what would be the result in the city; and the result of the election destroyed the hydra monster, Federalism.

After about sixty ballots taken in the House of Representatives, Thomas Jefferson and Aaron Burr had an equal vote. At that time, it was not customary to designate which should be President, and which Vice-President. The candidate having the greatest number of votes was chosen President, and the one having the next to the greatest vote, Vice-President. I think it was on the sixty-first ballot that Caesar Rodney, a Representative from Delaware, left his seat, and this gave Thomas Jefferson a majority of one vote.[9] Thus, Aaron Burr was elected Vice-President. . . .

56. MANUMISSION OF SLAVES

The Will of Isaiah Isaacs of Virginia, August 30, 1803 and January 8, 1806 [1]

[It was not uncommon for slave owners to provide for the freeing of their slaves in their wills, and at times even during their lifetime. In 1790, there were 59,527 free Negroes in the United States, most of whom had at one time been slaves. By 1860, the number of free Negroes, owing to natural increases and to manumissions, had grown to 488,070; from 1790 to 1860 the number of slaves, however, had increased from 697,897 to 3,950,531. The records show that Jews, like others, sometimes freed their slaves. In 1692, Arthur Levy's slave, Cresie, was thus freed in New York, and in 1761 Jacob Franks manumitted his slave, Cato.[2] Of special interest in the following Will of Isaiah Isaacs [3] is the declaration of his opinion that "all men are by nature equally free." This theory, however, did not impel him to the immediate freeing of his slaves; instead he sets a schedule covering some thirty years, which he modified in a codicil two years later.]

I, Isaiah Isaacs, of the town of Charlottesville and county of Albemarle, do make the following testamentary disposition of all my estate real and personal. It is my will that all my debts be paid and to enable my executors herein named to do the same. It is hereby directed that all the perishable part of my estate be sold as soon after my death as my executors can, with convenience and out of the money arriving therefrom, discharge such debts as I may owe at the time of my death, and the remaining surplus is to remain as an assisting fund in the hands of my executors for the maintenance of my children. It is my will that strict justice be done my children in the division of my estate. It is therefore my will, and I do hereby devise to Fanny Isaiah Isaacs, David Isaiah Isaacs, Patsy Isaiah Isaacs and Hayes Isaiah Isaacs, my four children by my dec'd wife Hetty Isaacs, formerly Hetty Hayes, all my estate both real and personal to them and their heirs forever. But as all my said children are in a state of infancy and incapable of acting for themselves, all the property aforesaid devised to them is hereby committed to the care of my executors until the youngest of my sd children shall *arrive* to the full age of twenty-one years. It is my will, and my executors are earnestly entreated so to manage my real estate, consisting partly in houses and Lots, as that it may at the period before prescribed for a division be delivered to my children unimpaired in its value; no part of my real estate is to be sold, but when my youngest child comes of age my executors are to exercise (cause) a just and fair valuation thereof to be made by disinterested commissioners to be appointed by the Court of that County where this will shall be recorded and divide the same into four parts, and allot one-fourth thereof to each of my said children, and as equality of division cannot be obtained in this manner those haveing [sic] the most valuable lots assigned to them are to make them of less value equal to the most valuable by paying the deficiency in money. It is my will that my tract of land in the County of Powhatan shall not be divided, but remain to my children and their heirs in common. It is my will that if any of my said children should die before he, she or they arrive at the age of twenty-one years, in that case the survivors or survivor shall enjoy the proportion of him, her or they who may die. But this clause of my will is to be so construed as only to take effect in case of such death or deaths without Issue; and the term of issue is meant to entitle any child or children that my daughters may have legitimate or illegitimate to their mother's proportion. It is my will that my children may be so educated as to make them useful citizens, they are therefore to be educated in such a manner as my executors may think their talents and capacities may justify, and to enable my executors to maintain and educate them the rents of my real estate are added to the surplus money arising from the sale of my Chattel Estate, and my executors are to place my children in the families of respectable *Jews* to the end that they may be brought up in the religion of their forefathers. Being of opinion that all men are by nature equally free and being possessed of some of those beings who are unfortunate doomed to slavery, as to them I must enjoin upon my executors a strict observance of the following clause in my will. My slaves hereafter named are to be and they are hereby manumitted and made free so that after the different periods hereafter mentioned they shall enjoy all the privileges and immunities of freed people. My slave Rachel is to go free and quit all manner of claim of servitude from and after the first day of January, which shall be in the year one thousand eight hundred and sixteen, James from and after the first day of January which shall be in the year one thousand eight hundred and twenty, Polly on the first day of January eighteen hundred and twenty-two, Henry on the first day of January which shall be in the year one thousand eight hundred and thirty, and William on the first day of January which shall be in the year one thousand eight hundred and thirty-four, and should either of my female slaves Rachel or Polly have a child or children before the time they become free such issue is to serve to the age of thirty-one and then to be discharged from servitude; the said slaves are not to be sold, but to remain the property of my children and to be divided in the same manner as directed as to the division of my real estate; each one of my slaves are to receive the value of twenty dollars in clothing on the day of their manumission. I constitute and appoint my friends Jacob I Cohen Adam Craig and Robert Mitchell and my brother David Isaacs [4] executors of this my last will and testament. In testimony whereof I have hereunto subscribed my name and affixed my seal this thirtieth day of August in the year one thousand eight hundred and three.

> Signed sealed and published as and for the last will and testament of Isaiah Isaacs in presence of us the said Isaac's [sic] signature being in the Hebrew language. John Carr, Thos. C. Fletcher, W. Wardlaw.

[*Hebrew Signature*] [Seal]

A Codicil to be annexed to this my last will

In as much as I have not been sufficiently explicit in that clause of my will which directs the course to be observed with respect the education of my children I have thought fit to add the following clause which is to be taken and considered as a part of this my will. It is my meaning and I do hereby request my executors before named to educate my sons for such professions as their talents may lead them to pursue and at proper ages to bind them to upright and discreet persons engaged in the professions their capacities may enable them to follow.

> Signed sealed and published as and for the last will and testament of Isaiah Isaac's [sic] in presence of us the signature of the said Isaacs being in Hebrew. John Carr, Thos. C. Fletcher, W. Wardlaw.

[*Hebrew Signature*] [*Seal*]

I Isaiah *Isaaks* being of sound mind have thought proper to make the following codicil to the within will to wit It is my will and desire that Joseph Marks [5] of the City of Richmond be added to the number of my executors heretofore appointed to the within will. It is my desire that my Negro woman Polly be free from and after the first day of January 1818 and whereas it is directed in my will that in case my female slaves Polly and Rachel should have children during their servitude the said children shall serve till their age of thirty-one—It is further my will that if the said children of my female slaves should have children during their servitude the said last mentioned Issue shall be free from their birth. It is also my will that if Mary the child of my Negro woman Rachel should have a child or children during her time of service that the sd child or children shall be free from the birth. It is also my will that Clement Washington the youngest child of Rachel shall be free from and after the first day of January 1836 and shall at his being free have same clothing given to him as in my will directed to be given to the others as witness my hand and seal this 8th day of January 1806.

[*Hebrew Signature*] [*Seal*]

> Teste Jas. Lewis, Thos. C. Fletcher, D. Carr.

An Instrument of writing purporting to be the last will and testament of Isaiah Isaacs deceased with a codicil thereto annexed were produced into Court and proved the will by the oaths of John Carr and Thos. C. Fletcher two of the witnesses thereto and the codicil by the oaths of Thos. C. Fletcher and Dabney Carr two of the witnesses thereto and by the Court ordered to be recorded.

> Teste Jno. Carr, C. C.
> A Copy Teste Alex'r. Garrett, C. C.
> A Copy Teste Wm. G. Pendleton, C.C.

57. CHARGING A JURY

Recorder Moses Levy's charge to the jury in the Philadelphia Cordwainers' Case, March 28, 1806 [1]

[In this first American labor case, in which eight shoemakers were found "guilty of a combination to raise their wages," Moses Levy,[2] presiding in the Mayor's Court, delivered a charge to the jury that was considered prejudiced in his own day by Jeffersonians and that is regarded as unsound by legal scholars today.[3] The case aroused high public interest at the time, revealed in the press and by the large number of spectators at the trial itself. It became the first of six criminal prosecutions against shoemakers for conspiracy, the last one being staged in Pittsburgh in 1815; the shoemakers lost four, won one, and compromised on another. The Philadelphia case arose out of a strike of the shoemakers in 1805 for the restoration of a 25% reduction in wage rates that they had been led to accept in the production of boots and shoes for consumption outside of Philadelphia. The prosecution based its case on the principles of English common law, which the Federalist judiciary had consistently applied against the interests of the American common people. The Jeffersonians almost succeeded in impeaching some of the worst judicial offenders, and sought a constitutional amendment to abolish the English common law from American court procedures. In the election of 1805, the common law was an important campaign issue, with the Jeffersonians losing in Pennsylvania to a small majority achieved by an alliance between Federalists and a minority faction that had split away from the Jeffersonians. The prosecution of the shoemakers was the first result of the election defeat of the Jeffersonians. Levy's conduct on the bench seems, on analysis, to have been biased;[4] his charge to the jury was in fact an argument for the prosecution: the defendants would cause a rise in the price of goods and thus take "an undue advantage of the public" and destroy all commerce; striking might lead workers to feed their wives and children "by burglary, larceny, or highway robbery"!; boots and shoes might go up to $50 a pair "at least for some time"; the law in his interpretation condemns a "conspiracy" to raise wages because it would benefit the workers themselves; it is tyranny to "compel" all shoemakers to join the union; most revealing of all: "If these evils were unprovided for by the law not existing, it would be necessary that laws should be made to restrain them."]

This laborious cause is now drawing to a close after a discussion of three days; during which we have had every information upon the facts and the law connected with them, that a careful investigation and industrious research have been able to produce. We are informed of the circumstance and ground of the complaints, and of the law applicable to them. It remains with the court and jury, to decide what the rule of law is;[5] and whether the defendants have, or have not violated it. In forming this decision, we cannot, we must not forget that the law of the land is the supreme, and only rule. We live in a country where the will of no individual ought to be, or is admitted, to be the rule of action. Where the will of an individual, or of any number of individuals, however distinguished by wealth, talents, or popular fame, ought not to affect or controul, in the least degree, the administration of justice. There is but one place in which to determine whether violation and abuses of the law have been committed. . . .[6] it is in our courts of justice: and there only after proof to the fact: and consideration of the principles of law connected with it.

The moment courts of justice lose their respectability, from that moment the security of persons and of property is gone. The moment courts of justice have their characters contaminated by a well founded suspicion, that they are governed by caprice, fear or favour; from that moment they will cease to be able to administer justice with effect, and redress wrongs of either a public or a private nature. Every consideration, therefore, calls upon us to maintain the character of courts and juries; and that can only be maintained by undeviating integrity, by an adhesion to the rules of law, and by deciding impartially in conformity to them.

Very able research has been made in this enquiry, and every principle necessary for your information has been laid before you. As far as the arguments of counsel apply to your understanding and judgment, they should have weight: but, if the appeal has been made to your passions, it ought not to be indulged. You ought to consider such appeals as an attack upon your integrity, as an attempt to enlist your passions against your judgment, and, therefore, listen to them with great distrust and caution. If this enquiry had been confined to its proper object and its merits, it need not have been extended to the length to which it has been drawn out, but many circumstances foreign to the case, have been brought into view. An attempt has been made to shew that the spirit of the revolution and the principle of the common law, are opposite in this case. That the common law, if applied in this case, would operate an attack upon the rights of man. The enquiry on that point, was unnecessary and improper. Nothing more was required than to ascertain what the law is. The law is the permanent rule, it is the will of the whole community. After that is discovered, whatever may be its spirit or tendency, it must be executed, and the most imperious duty demands our submission to it.

It is of no importance whether the journeymen or the masters be the prosecutors. What would it be to you if the thing was turned round, and the masters were the defendants instead of the journeymen? It is immaterial to our consideration whether the defendants are employers or employed; poor or rich. . . . Whether their numbers are diminutive or great. If they have done wrong, and were ten thousand strong, I should look upon myself guilty of a breach of my oath and of the law, if their numbers protected them from justice or prosecution, from plainly declaring my opinion, if I thought them guilty: while I set here, however distinguished for wealth, or talents, respectability, or numbers the defendants may be, if they have violated the law. . . . I trust I shall have firmness enough to say so, regardless of what the world may think of me or of popular abuse. This is the duty of the judge, and also of the jury. If they decide one way when one man is implicated, and another when twenty, the rights, the liberties and privileges of man in society, can no longer be protected within these hallowed walls. Numbers would decide all questions of duty and property, and causes would be hereafter adjudged, not by the weight of their reason, but according to the physical force of the parties charged. This jury will act without fear or favour; without partiality or hatred; regardless whether they make friends or enemies by their verdict . . . they will do their duty . . . they will, after the rule of law has been investigated and laid down by the court, find a verdict in conformity to the justice of the case.

If this, gentlemen, is your disposition, there are only two objects for your consideration.

First. . . . What the rule of law is on this subject?

Second. . . . Whether the defendants acted in such a manner as to bring them within that rule?

(Here the recorder referred to books of authority.)

No matter what their motives were, whether to resist the supposed oppression of their master, or to insist upon extravagant compensation. No matter whether this prosecution originated from motives of public good or private interest, the question is, whether the defendants are guilty of the offences charged against them? A great part of the crimes prosecuted to trial in this court, are brought forward, I believe, from improper motives: for example, the prosecutions against tippling houses are generally occasioned by a difference taking place between the buyer and the seller, when the one is nearly as much in fault as the other. In the case of the crime of treason, it is often one of the parties who impeaches the other, and a quarrel about the felonious booty often leads to the detection of the thief. If the defendants are guilty of the crime, no matter whether the prosecutor brings his action from motives of public good, or private resentment. The prosecutors are not on their trial, if they have proved the offence, alleged in the indictment, against the defendants; and if the defendants are guilty, will any man say, that they ought not to be convicted: because the prosecution was not founded in motives of patriotism? certainly the only question is, whether they are guilty or innocent? If they are guilty and were possessed of nine tenths of the soil of the whole United States, and the patronage of the union, it is the bounden duty of the jury to declare their guilt.

I am endeavouring to divest the case of what may prejudice its merits.

What are the offences alleged aginst them? They are contained in the charges of the indictment.

(Here he recited from the indictment the first and second counts.)[7]

These are the questions for our consideration, and it lies with you to determine how far the evidence supports the charges, and how the principles of the law bear upon them.

It is proper to consider, is such a combination consistent with the principles of our law, and injurious to the public welfare?

The usual means by which the prices of work are regulated, are the demand for the article and the excellence of its fabric. Where the work is well done, and the demand is considerable, the prices will necessarily be high. Where the work is ill done, and the demand is inconsiderable, they will unquestionably be low. If there are many to consume, and few to work, the price of the article will be high: but if there are few to consume, and many to work, the article must be low. Much will depend too, upon these circumstances, whether the materials are plenty or scarce; the price of the commodity, will in consequence be higher or lower. These are the means by which prices are regulated in the natural course of things. To make an artificial regulation, is not to regard the excellence of the work or quality of the material, but to fix a positive and arbitrary price, governed by no standard, controuled by no impartial person, but dependant on the will of the few who are interested; this is the unnatural way of raising the price of goods or work. This is independent of the number of customers, or of the quality of the material, or of the number who are to do the work. It is an unnatural, artificial mean of raising the price of work beyond its standard, and taking an undue advantage of the public. Is the rule of law bottomed upon such principles, as to permit or protect such conduct? Consider it on the footing of the general commerce of the city. Is there any man who can calculate (if this is tolerated) at what price he may safely contract to deliver articles, for which he may receive orders, if he is to be regulated by the journeymen in an arbitrary jump from one price to another? It renders it impossible for a man, making a contract for a large quantity of such goods, to know whether he shall lose or gain by it. If he makes a large contract for goods today, for delivery at three, six, or nine months hence, can he calculate what the prices will be then, if the journeymen in the intermediate time, are permitted to meet and raise their prices, according to their caprice or pleasure? Can he fix the price of his commodity for a future day? It is impossible that any man can carry on commerce in this way. There cannot be a large contract entered into, but what the contractor will make at his peril. He may be ruined by the difference of prices made by the journeymen in the intermediate time. What then is the operation of this kind of conduct upon the commerce of the city? It exposes it to inconveniences, if not to ruin; therefore, it is against the public welfare. How does it operate upon the defendants? We see that those who are in indigent circumstances, and who have families to maintain, and who get their bread by their daily labour, have declared here upon oath, that it was impossible for them to hold out; the masters might do it, but they could not: and it has been admitted by the witnesses for the defendants, that such persons, however sharp and pressing their necessities, were obliged to stand to the turn-out, or never afterwards to be employed. They were interdicted from all business in future, if they did not continue to persevere in the measures, taken by the journeymen shoemakers. Can such a regulation be just and proper? Does it not tend to involve necessitous men in the commission of crimes? If they are prevented from working for six weeks, it might induce those who are thus idle, and have not the means of maintenance, to take other courses for the support of their wives and children. It might lead them to procure it by crimes . . .

by burglary, larceny, or highway robbery! A father cannot stand by and see, without agony, his children suffer; if he does, he is an inhuman monster; he will be driven to seek bread for them, either by crime, by beggary, or a removal from the city. Consider these circumstances as they affect trade generally. Does this measure tend to make good workmen? No: It puts the botch incapable of doing justice to his work, on a level with the best tradesman. The master must give the same wages to each. Such a practice would take away all the excitement to excel in workmanship or industry. Consider the effect it would have upon the whole community. If the masters say they will not sell under certain prices, as the journeymen declare they will not work but at certain wages, they, if persisted in, would put the whole body of the people into their power. Shoes and boots are articles of the first necessity. If they could stand out three or four weeks in winter, they might raise the price of boots to thirty, forty, or fifty dollars a pair, at least for some time, and until a competent supply could be got from other places. In every point of view, this measure is pregnant with public mischief and private injury . . . tends to demoralize the workmen . . . destroy the trade of the city, and leaves the pockets of the whole community to the discretion of the concerned. If these evils were unprovided for by the law not existing, it would be necessary that laws should be made to restrain them.

What has been the conduct of the defendants in this instance? They belong to an association, the object of which is, that every person who follows the trade of a journeyman shoemaker, must be a member of their body. The apprentice immediately upon becoming free, and the journeyman who comes here from distant places, are all considered members of this institution. If they do not join the body, a term of reproach is fixed upon them. The members of the body will not work with them, and they refuse to board or lodge with them. The consequence is, that every one is compelled to join the society. It is in evidence, that the defendants in this action all took a part in the last attempt to raise their wages; . . . [George] Keimer was their secretary, and the others were employed in giving notice, and were of the tramping committee. If the purpose of the association is well understood, it will be found they leave no individual at liberty to join the society or reject it. They compel him to become a member. Is there any reason to suppose that the laws are not competent to redress an evil of this magnitude? The laws of this society are grievous to those not inclined to become members . . . they are injurious to the community, but they are not the laws of Pennsylvania. We live in a community, where the people in their collective capacity give the first momentum, and their representatives pass laws on circumstances, and occasions, which require their interference, as they arise.

But the acts of the legislature form but a small part of that code from which the citizen is to learn his duties, or the magistrate his power and rule of action. These temporary emanations of a body, the component members of which are subject to perpetual change, apply principally to the political exigencies of the day.

It is in the volumes of the common law we are to seek for information in the far greater number, as well as the most important causes that come before our tribunals. That invaluable code has ascertained and defined, with a critical precision, and with a consistency that no fluctuating political body could or can attain, not only the civil rights of property, but the nature of all crimes from treason to trespass, has pointed out the rules of evidence and the mode of proof, and has introduced and perpetuated, for their investigation, that admirable institution, the freeman's-boast, the trial by jury[.] its profound provisions grow up, not from the pressure of the only true foundations of all knowledge, long experience and practical observation at the moment, but from the common law matured into an elaborate connected system. Law is by the length of time, it has been in use and the able men who have administered it. Much abuse has of late teemed upon its valuable institutions. Its enemies do not attack it as a system: but they single out some detached branch of it, declare it absurd or [un]intelligible, without understanding it. To treat it justly they should be able to comprehend the whole. Those who understand it best entertain the highest opinion of its excellence. . . . No other persons are competent judges of it. As well might a circle of a thousand miles diameter be described by the man, whose eye could only see a single inch, as the common law be characterized by those who have not devoted years to its study. Those who know it, know that it regulates with a sound discretion most of our concerns in civil and social life. Its rules are the result of the wisdom of ages. It says there may be cases in which what one man may do with offence, many combined may not do with impunity. It distinguishes between the object so aimed at in different transactions. If the purpose to be obtained, be an object of individual interest, it may be fairly attempted by an individual. . . . Many are prohibited from combining for the attainment of it.

What is the case now before us? . . . A combination of workmen to raise their wages may be considered in a two fold point of view: one is to benefit themselves . . . the other is to injure those who do not join their society. The rule of law condemns both. If the rule be clear, we are bound to conform to it even though we do not comprehend the principle upon which it is founded. We are not to reject it because we do not see the reason of it. It is enough, that it is the will of the majority. It is law because it is their will . . . if it is law, there may be good reasons for it though we cannot find them out. But the rule in this case is pregnant with sound sense and all the authorities are clear upon the subject. Hawkins, the greatest authority [8] on the criminal law, has laid it down, that a combination to maintaining one another, carrying a particular object, whether true or false, is criminal . . . the authority cited from 8 Mod. rep. does not rest merely upon the reputation of that book. He gives you other authorities to which he refers. It is adopted by Blackstone, and laid down as the law by Lord Mansfield 1793, that an act innocent in an individual, is rendered criminal by a confederacy to effect it.

In the profound system of law, (if we may compare small things with great) as in the profound systems of Providence . . . there is often great reason for an institution, though a superficial observer may not be able to discover it. Obedience alone is required in the present case, the reason may be this. One man determin[e]s not to work under a certain price and it may be individually the opinion of all: in such a case it would be lawful in each to refuse to do so, for if each stands, alone, either may extract from his determination when he pleases[.] In the turn-out of last fall,[9] if each member of the body had stood alone, fettered by no promises to the rest, many of them might have changed their opinion as to the price of wages and gone to work; but it has been given to you in evidence, that they were bound down by their agreement, and pledged by mutual engagements, to persist in it, however contrary to their own judgment. . . . The continuance in improper conduct may therefore well be attributed to the combination. The good sense of those individuals was prevented by this agreement, from having its free exercise. Considering it in this point of view, let us take a look at the cases which have been compared to this by the defendants['] counsel. Is this like the formation of a society for the promotion of the general welfare of the community, such as to advance the interests of religion, or to accomplish acts of charity and benevolence? Is it like the society for extinguishing fires? or those for the promotion of literature and the fine arts, or the meeting of the city wards to nominate candidates for the legislature or the executive? These are for the benefit of third persons[,] the society in question to promote the selfish purposes of the members. The mere mention of them is an answer to all, that has been said on that point? There is no comparison between the two; they are as distinct as light and darkness. How can these cases be considered on an equal footing? The journeymen shoemakers have not asked an encreased price of work for an individual of their body: but they say that no one shall work, unless he recieves [sic] the wages they have fixed[.] They could not go farther than saying, no one should work unless they all got the wages demanded by the majority; is this freedom? Is it not restraining, instead of promoting, the spirit of '76 when men expected to have no law but the constitution, and laws adopted by it or enacted by the legislature in conformity to it? Was it the spirit of '79 [sic], that either masters or journeymen, in regulating the prices of their commodities should set up a rule contrary to the law of their country? General and individual liberty was the spirit of '76. It is our first blessing. It has been obtained and will be maintained . . . we will not leave it to follow an *ignus fatius* [sic], calculated only to mislead our judgment. It is not a question, whether we shall have an *imperium in imperio,* whether we shall have, besides our state legislature a new legislature consisting of journeymen shoemakers. It is of no consequence, whether the prosecutors are two or three, or whether the defendants are ten thousand, their numbers are not to prevent the execution of our laws . . . though we acknowledge it is the hard hand of labour that produces the wealth of a nation, though we acknowledge the usefulness of such a large body of tradesmen and agree they should have every thing to which they are legally entitled; yet we conceive they ought to ask nothing more. They should neither be the slaves nor the governors of the community.

I thought it necessary to say this much, as this trial appears to have excited a great deal of interest in the city. The numerous attendants that we have witnessed during the course of the trial, shews that numbers of our fellow citizens wait the result with anxious expectation. . . . It lays with you, gentlemen of the jury, to decide.

The sentiments of the court, not an individual of which is connected either with the masters or journeymen; all stand independent of both parties . . . are unanimous. They have given you the rule as they have found it in the book, and it is now for you to say, whether the defendants are guilty or not. The rule they consider as fixt, they cannot change it. It is now, therefore, left to you upon the law, and the evidence, to find the verdict. If you can reconcile it to your consciences, to find the defendants not guilty, you will do so; if not, the alternative that remains, is a verdict of guilty.[10]

58. BURYING THE DEAD

Letter from Joel Hart, Secretary of the Jerusalem Chapter No. 8, Royal Arch Masons of New York, March 14, 1808 [1]

[Membership of Jews in Masonic groups served to involve them in various public and civic activities. Here the Masons are seen cooperating with the then very progressive Tammany Society in a demonstrative political action connected with the interment of the bones of Americans who had died during the Revolutionary War on board the *Jersey,* a British prison-ship.[2]]

Sir,

I am desired by the presiding officers and members of Jerusalem Chapter [3] of Royal Arch Masons, to acknowledge the receipt of the letter you did them the honour to write in behalf of Tammany Society, and to express their pleasurable concurrence in the meritorious and patriotic intention of Tammany Society to inter the relics of those Citizens who perished in the glorious cause of liberty and independence on board the Jersey Prison Ship.

As most of the members composing Jerusalem Chapter are attached to the different lodges in the city, under the jurisdiction of the worshipful Grand Lodge, they will, with their respective Lodges, cheerfully co-operate in the measures to be adopted by their brothers.

I have the honour to be, with due consideration,

Your most obedient servant,

Joel Hart,

Secretary of Jerusalem Chapter.[4]

Robert Townsend, junr,[5] Secretary to the Committee of Tammany Society.

59. TALMUD TORAH, 1808

Constitution, Rules & Regulations, of the Talmud Torah. Established in the City of New-York on the First Day of Sivan, in the Year 5568, Corresponding with the 27th Day of May, 1808 [1]

[This constitution and set of rules are of historical interest for what they reveal of the intentions of the synagog leaders who drafted them and of their conception of pedagogical methods.[2] The institution itself has an interesting history. When Myer Polony died in New York city in 1801, he left $900 to the Congregation Shearith Israel, with the interest from which a Hebrew School was to be established. On Sunday, May 2, 1802, the Yeshibat Minhat Areb, which had been founded in 1731, was therefore renamed the Polonies Talmud Torah, and has borne the name ever since. The old Yeshibah had, since 1755, been teaching Spanish, English, writing and arithmetic in addition to Hebrew; the new Talmud Torah expanded its curriculum in 1804 to add the reading and writing of English; in 1818 geography was introduced, but in 1822 the secular subjects were dropped.[3] To "instruct the scholars, thoroughly, in the principles of religion and morality," which are regarded as necessarily related, the teacher "should, by the plainest arguments, unassisted by those obstruse speculations that generally tend to distract the judgment and injure the memory, impress on their minds the excellencies of our belief," and also inspire the "scholars with a sense of honor—a sense of shame—and above all, a sense of emulation."]

At a meeting of the Subscribers to the Hebrew and English School, the 15th of May, 1808.

Jacob Hart, Sen., Appointed Chairman
Isaac M. Gomez,[4] Secretary.

On motion resolved—That a committee of three subscribers be elected by ballot, who shall be empowered to co-operate with a committee of the trustees, to draft a plan, rules, and regulations, for the establishment of a Hebrew and English School, to contract with a suitable teacher or teachers, and to do every other thing requisite.

The meeting then proceeded to ballot, and Messrs. Gompert S. Gomperts, Judah Zuntz, and Dr. Joel Hart, were duly elected: the Board of Trustees appointed Messrs. I. B. Kursheedt, Moses L. Moses, and Mordicai [sic] Myers,[5] to co-operate with the above named gentlemen.—Meeting adjourned.

PREAMBLE

In the establishment of this institution, the following means are proper to be adopted for its accomplishment: firstly, to improve the understanding and to instruct the scholars, thoroughly, in the principles of religion and morality: and secondly, to have a strict attention paid to their actions, in order to make them conformable to the aforementioned requisites.

To accomplish the above object, the scholars are to be inspired with a sense of honor—a sense of shame—and above all, a sense of emulation.

As principles of religion generally accompany those of morality, an attention to the one insures the promotion of the other; their daily repetition of prayers can not alone constitute a strict adherence to religion; but it must be the knowledge of the Divine Origin of that religion, that can make them zealous adherents to every part of its tenets.

The task of informing their minds and maturing their judgment must necessarily devolve on the Teacher, who should by the plainest arguments, unassisted by those obstruse speculations that generally tend to distract the judgment and injure the memory, impress on their minds the excellencies of our *belief*. A certain time before or after the hours of study, should be appropriated to *devotion*, and the usual service ought to be performed by one of the scholars competent to the task. A sense of decorum during divine worship must be strongly inculcated, and a certain grade of punishment should be instituted for inattention to this observance.

The encouragement of a sense of emulation, should be the primary object of the teacher and superintendants [sic] of the school—to inspire it honestly in the breasts of all the scholars, would be the most certain means of insuring improvement in their studies—a favourable report to the inspectors of their assiduity and conduct—advancing them to the honourable post of monitor to the junior classes—removing them to a higher order of study—and the presentation of a medal at the annual public examination, are the rewards that should be held out to them as incentives to assiduous application.

Crimes or vices should, in every respect, be treated in a different manner from faults occasioned by idleness or neglect of studies; the punishment of the former should, at first, be by enjoining extraordinary tasks, and a degradation from the rank they hold in a class, to a lower one; when these methods prove ineffectual, and the scholar is found to be of an incorrigible nature, he certainly can be no longer a fit companion for the rest, and therefore should be reported to the inspectors, who may adjudge the punishment according to the crime, and, if the nature of it warrants the necessity, he should, for example sake, be publicly expelled [from] the school. Those faults occasioned by idleness or inattention, should be punished in a lesser degree, according to the discretion of the teacher.

It is also absolutely necessary, that the most profound respect should be paid to the preceptor, and a want of it should subject the delinquent to the severest penalty the rules can inflict.

The punishment of the scholars for appearing unclean in person and dress—the manner of conducting themselves—suppressing bad habits, &c. should rest entirely with the discretion of the teacher.

A strict and uniform adherance [sic] to the foregoing remarks, which are solely made with a view to benefit the institution, must ultimately tend towards promoting the chief end in contemplation, viz. To instill in the youthful mind a love of learning—a veneration for religion and morality—and an attainment of useful instruction—whilst all visionary and impracticable schemes should be rejected on the one hand—just and salutary maxims ought to be adopted on the other.

CONSTITUTION

Article I: That a school denominated *Polanies Talmude Torah,* be established for the purpose of teaching the *Hebrew* and *English* languages, in all their concomitant branches. That the said school be under the immediate care and direction of the board of Trustees, together with such inspectors as may be chosen—that a suitable teacher be provided and the establishment to go into operation the seventh of June ensuing.

Article II: There shall be three persons annually chosen by the subscribers after the expiration of the first year, to act as inspectors—and in case of the absence or resignation of either of them the trustees shall fill such vacancy by choice from their own body, or from the subscribers.

Article III: Persons subscribing to the amount of five dollars and upwards per annum, shall be entitled to vote on all occasions relative to the institution, and the members of the board of trustees for the time being, though not subscribers shall (*ex-officio*) have the privilege of voting.

Article IV: Every subscriber sending a scholar shall pay quarterly to the board of trustees the sum of six dollars and twenty-five cents, which scholar shall continue at least one year at the school—that the whole number of scholars shall not consist of more than *twenty-six,* out of which not exceeding *five* shall be admitted gratis.

Article V: That all additions, amendments, or alterations of this constitution shall be in the following manner:—on application of five subscribers in writing to the President of the Board of Trustees, stating the proposed addition or amendment, a written or printed notification shall be sent by him to each subscriber, requesting his attendance on a specified time—and stating the cause for the meeting—such addition, alteration or amendment shall only be effective if adopted by two thirds of the persons present.

RULES AND REGULATIONS

Article I: The school shall be opened daily, except certain times that will be specified hereafter. The mornings to be appropriated to the study of the *English* language, and the afternoon to the *Hebrew*. That from the first of May to the first of November, the hours of tuition shall be from eight o'clock in the morning till twelve, and from two in the afternoon till four, and from the first of November, till the first of May, at the usual school hours, say from nine till twelve, and from two till five.

Article II: No scholar of either sex, shall be admitted under the age of six years; and for the better regulation of study the scholars shall be divided into classes, in such manner as the teacher may think proper.

Article III: The duty of the inspectors shall be to visit the school at least once in every month, to observe the progress of the scholars, and report on the same to the board of trustees every six months. That the inspectors shall be judges of the qualifications of applicants, and shall have the power of receiving and discharging scholars, and to decide all differences that may arise between them and the teacher.

Article IV: That a public examination be annually held in the synagogue, and the *Parnas* for that purpose be requested by the inspectors, to cause a proclamation to be made in that place the preceding sabbath; that medals and other premiums, indicative of reward for improvement, be presented at the time of such examination, to those scholars who are adjudged deserving them.

Article V: That every scholar shall conduct himself toward the teacher with the most attentive respect, and if he be found guilty of any crime or vice, it shall be the duty of the said teacher to report him immediately to the inspectors, that they may act according as the nature of the case warrants.

Article VI: The expulsion of a scholar shall not exonerate the parent or guardian from the payment of the yearly subscription, neither can they supply the consequent vacancy by sending any other scholar for that year.

Article VII: That every scholar shall attend regularly at the stated hours of tuition, unless prevented by indisposition or some other cause, for which a cojent [sic] reason can be given, and that he attend the synagogue regularly at the time appointed by the teacher for prayer, and conduct himself with the strictest decorum.

Article VIII: That the teacher shall be particularly careful not to admit a scholar who is afflicted with any infectious disease: that he shall punish according to his discretion any scholar for appearing in school unclean in his person or dress, or who may be guilty of any improper act.

Article IX: Should any difference arise between the teacher and inspectors, the same shall be reported to the board of trustees, who shall decide, as the nature of the case may require.

Article X: The School will not be opened for the purpose of tuition on the following days: שבת - ראש השנה - כפור - סכות - פסח - שבועות - חנוכה - פורים - ערב - יום - טוב every Fast-Day—the 4th of July—the 25th of November—Friday afternoon, together with such other days as the Inspectors may direct.

Article XI: That all amendments, additions, or alterations, to these Rules and Regulations, shall be made in the same manner as before specified, relating to the Constitution.

At a meeting of the Joint Committee, on the 16th May, 1808. The foregoing Preamble, Constitution, Rules and Regulations, were unanimously approved of and adopted.

The choice of *three* inspectors for the first year devolving on the committee, they proceeded to ballot—and Messrs. Bernard Hart, Seixas Nathan,[6] & Joel Hart, Were duly elected to that office.

60. MANUMITTING SLAVES, 1806–1809

Excerpts from the Minutes of The Society for Promoting the Manumission of Slaves; and Protecting such of them as have been or may be Liberated, New York, 1806–1809 [1]

[This is a record of the first American Jew known to have participated in an organized manner in the early movements for the liberation of slaves, and the protection of free Negroes from being enslaved again. The record reveals that Moses Judah, a New York merchant,[2] served for two years on the Standing (executive) Committee of the New York Manumission Society, and was active on nine sub-committees that handled specific cases referred to them. The Society was founded on January 25, 1785 and continued its work until 1849. It was preceded only by the Pennsylvania Society for Promoting the Abolition of Slavery, founded in 1775. The New York society was established after attempts had been made in New York to seize several free Negroes and export them for sale. The purpose of the group, as stated in the preamble to its Constitution, was to help Negroes who, "destitute of friends and of knowledge; struggling with poverty; and, accustomed to submission, they are at great disadvantages in asserting their rights."[3] Between 1785 and 1813, the persons elected to membership numbered 340, but the dues paying membership in 1813 was 180, the remainder having died, resigned, or been dropped for inactivity or failure to pay the dues of $8 per year. Moses Judah was elected to the Society, after being nominated by Willet Seaman, on May 21, 1799; he was recommended for election to the Standing Committee on November 30, 1803, but not elected until November 11, 1806; he served until his term was up and he was replaced on January 10, 1809. While he was on it, the Standing Committee reported that through its efforts, it had effected the liberation of about fifty Negroes.[4] These brief minutes are full of human interest.]

January 2, 1807: Felicite a Black woman arrived at Norfolk, Virginia, from Cape Francois in 1793, where her master Delpiche found her, and by the assistance of a frenchman there had her sent to this City say about 1796—Her master took possession of her here & about 2 years after sold her to Mrs. Wise, opposite the North Church, who about One Year since sold her to Davie or David in W^m^ S^t^ who now holds her as a Slave—

Ref^d^ to Moses Judah
Jno. R. Willis

January 20, 1807: In the case of Felicity, no report—Committee Cont^d^ and [?] refer'd to the Councellors for directions

January 30, 1807: Isaac A. Van Hook was added to the Committee in the case of Felicity—

April 12, 1807: Elizabeth Freeman, Born about the Year 1788 in Monmouth County N. J. and when she was about 6 Years old she was sold to Anthony Fountain who brought her to Staten Island, and about the Year 1796 Fountain sold her to Gerritt Fountain his son for Life where she now lives.

Referd to M. Judah and
For Act of 22 Feb. 1788 J. R. Willis

June 10, 1807: Felicity v^s David, no report. . . . E. Freeman v^s Fountain, no report

June 23, 1807: Sam Joseph now in Jail was placed there by T. Cairon, it is alledg'd that C. has no legal right to this Boy, Joseph is about 33 Years of age—he is not Confined for debt; is from Cape Francois, was imported by Sophia Lovell more than a Year since.

Com^t Moses Judah
J. R. Willis

July 13, 1807: Sam Joseph now in Jail, no report

September 17, 1807: Elizabeth Freeman v^s Fontaine, no report . . . Sam Joseph now in Jail, no report . . . Felicity v^s David—& Woman reported free . . .

A. Garison was sold born in Kingston Esopus, Ulster Co. his Father & Mother were Slaves, his Father was Free some short time after he was born, the Boys Master Philip Newkirk bequeathed his Mother & him to his Son who sold the Mother when the boy was about 7 Yrs. old to Robt Gill of Poughkeepsie and *gave* the Boy to his Mother the Mother & Son liv'd with Gill and afterward left him the Boy is now taken up by Gills Son (Thos Gill) who lives as clerk to John Patrick who has lodged the Boy in Bridewell [prison], referd to

R. H. Bowne &
Moses Judah &
V. Hicks.

October 27, 1807: The Committee in the Case of Thomas Gill, or Garrison report that the Boy appears to be legally held, the Boy however is at large— . . .

Stella v^s V. Zandt. This Woman was the Slave of John Smith Esq of Perth Amboy, who during the War was in the British service and went away at the Peace, when his estate was confiscated, but she was not sold, with the rest of his property, after some Years Andrew Smith of this City Weighmaster took her daughter Stella and sold her to Peter Van Zandt (Chatham Street [)] for 12 Years, of which she has 4 Years yet to serve referd to

M. Judah &
Jacob Wood

December 27, 1807: Sam Joseph—Jacob Valentine added to this Committee [5]

April 2, 1808: The Com^e in the case of Stella v^s Van Zandt Report the Freedom of the Woman.

April 7, 1808: Flora was Born in the family of John Scuyler Bells Neck (N J) is now about 17 years of age, was sold to Mrs. Cortland about 1 year since who went to New Jersey and there purchased her

W Robins
J Wood

July 20, 1808: Phillis lives with Peter Van Allen Leonard St says that said Van Allen's wife purchased her in Jersey a few days before she came to New York, has lived here about Nine Months. Van Allen & his wife say she is owned in Jersey & as they showed a disposition to send her there the Committee met and after consulting Counsell agreed to replevy [bail] her which was done & she is now at liberty William F. Slocum [Chairman of the Standing Committee], & Charles Collins gave the Sheriff an indemnifying Bond. Referred to

Robert C. Cornell &
Moses Judah . . .

James Gotrand or Gohano states that he was brought from Jersey by John Turnbull in Nov. 1798 & was sold by him to George Caines in May 1803 as appears by Turnbulls Certificate; that said Caines having a Suit with some person gave Gotrand a Manumission Paper in order to make him a legal witness & took from Gotrand his Note for his time, Gotrand conceiving that he was intitled to his freedom when sold in this State wishes to be discharged from the Note. Referred to

Valentine Hicks &
Moses Judah . . .

In the Case of Flora vs Mrs. Courtland Jacob Wood one of the Committee to whom it was referred is released therefrom and Moses Judah is added

August 9, 1808: The Committee in the Case of Phillis report that a Writ of Replevin has been served on Peter Van Allen & that she is now at liberty

August 25, 1808: The Committees on the following Cases report their having paid due attention & find nothing requiring their aid, they are discharged therefrom & the Cases discontinued

. . . James Gotrand vs Geo: Caines
Flora vs Mrs. Courtland . . .

December 10, 1808: Jack Moore a black man states that he is entitled to his freedom in consequence of having served as a Soldier during the Revolution. Referred to Isaack A Van Hook, James Quackenbush & Moses Judah.

January 9, 1809: Committee in the Case of Phillis vs Van Allen report that she is in the enjoyment of her liberty; the case discontinued

January 10, 1809: [Report of the Standing Committee to the Society:] . . . There is one subject on which your Committee feels it peculiarly incumbent on them at this time to communicate. The Legislature of our State has interdicted the importation of Slaves under certain restrictions, but these restrictions are daily evaded, and hence our City becomes crouded [sic] with People of Colour. The mode practised to evade the Law is for the Slaves to be manumitted in a neighbouring State & immediately made or induced under the delusion of ultimately being free to bind himself or herself to the purchaser, and in many instances for a period which will carry them to old age, when behold they are helpless and either become the Subjects of the Clemency of our Charitable Institutions or are turned off to "beg their bread in other Climes;" a very large proportion of the attention of the Standing Committee is occupied in relation to cases of this nature, where the Subject has been clandestinely brought in upon us from the Jerseys. . . .

We offer for the consideration of the Society the names of the following Persons viz Silvanus Jenkins, William Collins, Wm S. Burling, R H Bowne & William Franklin out of whom to choose two to supply the places of Moses Judah & Isaac Sharpless who go off by rotation.

February 2, 1809: [Among the cases continued:] Jack Moore vs— Van Hook, Quack. & Judah

February 21, 1809: No reports being made on the other Cases the Committees are continued.

March 21, 1809: The Case of Jack Moore was dismissed [6]

61. JACOB HENRY SPEAKS FOR EQUALITY

An Address in the Committee of the Whole of the House of Commons of North Carolina, December 6, 1809 [1]

[This lofty address became justly celebrated and was widely reprinted soon after it was delivered. Challenging and eloquent, it argues "that the Conduct alone is the subject of human laws, and that man ought to suffer civil disqualification for what he does and not for what he thinks." The speech was delivered under trying circumstances. Jacob Henry [2] had represented Carteret County in the House of Commons of North Carolina in 1808, and was re-elected in 1809. Two weeks after the session of 1809 opened, Mr. Hugh C. Mills of Rockingham County moved that Henry's seat be vacated because, contrary to the Constitutional requirement, he "denies the divine authority of the New Testament, and refused to take the oath prescribed by law for his qualification."[3] The following day the House, as a Committee of the Whole, debated the question, and Henry delivered this impressive address; the same day the House concurred in the recommendation that the resolution be rejected. In the debate, Henry was aided by two prominent Catholics, William Gaston, then member of the House and later Chief Justice of the State Supreme Court, and John Louis Taylor, then the Attorney-General.[4] Jacob Henry retained his seat, but the victory was equivocal: the House had construed the constitutional provision as allowing Jews and Catholics to hold legislative office, but not executive or other office![5] Henry's speech was also used in furthering the struggle for equality in other states too: in Maryland, the address was quoted in debate in 1819 and 1822.]

To the Honble the Speaker,[6] and members of the House of Commons.

I must confess that the resolution against me yesterday was quite unexpected, as I had a right to expect, that the Gentleman who introduced it, would have had the politeness to have given me notice of it.

The Gentleman has stated that I deny the divine authority of the old and new Testament.

However Gentlemen, I know not the design of the declaration of Rights made by the people of this State in the year '76 and one day before the Constitution, if it was not to consecrate certain great and fundamental rights and Principles, which even the Constitution cannot impair: For the 44th section of the latter instrument declares that the declaration of rights ought never to be violated on any pretence whatever—If there is any apparent ~~discrepancy~~ difference between the two instruments they ought if possible be reconciled. But if there is a final repugnance between them, the declarition [sic] of Rights must be considered paramount: For I beleive [sic] that it is to the Constitution as the Constitution is to a Law; it controls and directs it absolutely and conclusively. If then a belief in the Protestant religion is required by the Constitution to qualify a man for a seat in this House and such qualification is dispensed with by the declaration of rights, the provission [sic] of the Constitution must be altogether inoperative, as the Language of the Bill of rights is that all men have a natural and unalienable right to worship Almighty God according to the dictates of their own Conscience. It is undoubtedly a natural right, and when it is declared to be an unalienable one, by the people in their sovereign and original capacity, any attempt to alienate it either by the Constitution or by Law, must be vain and fruitless. It is difficult to conceive how such a provission [sic] crept into the Constitution unless it was from the difficulty the human mind feels in suddenly emancipating itself from fetters by which it has long been enchained: And how adverse it is to the feelings and manners of the *people* of the present day every Gentleman may satisfy himself by glancing at the Religious beliefs of the persons who fill the various civil offices in this State—There are Presbyterians, Lutherians [sic], Calvinists, Menonists [sic], Baptists, Trinitarians & Unitarians. But as far as my observation extends, there are fewer Protestants in the strickt [sic] sense of the word used by the Convention than of any other persuasion; for I supposed that they meant by it the Prostentant [sic] religion as established by Law in England. For other persuasions we see houses of Worship in almost every part of the State, but very few for protestants; so few, that indeed I fear that the people of this State, would for some time, remain unrepresented in this House, if the clause of the Constitution is supposed to be in force. So far from beleiving [sic] in the truths of the 39 articles, I will venture to assert that a majority of the people have never read them. If a man should hold religious principles incompatible with the freedoom [sic] and safety of the State, I do not hesitate to pronounce that he should be excluded from the public Councils of the same; and I trust if I know myself no one would be more ready to aid and assist than myself. But I should really be at a loss to specify any known religious principles which are thus dangerous, it is surely a question between a man and his Maker, and requires more than human attributes to pronounce which of the numerous Sects prevailing in the world is most acceptable to the Deity. If a man fulfills the duties of that religion which his education or his Conscience has pointed to him as the true one; no person, I hold, in this our land of liberty, has a right to arraign him at the bar of any inquisition—And the day I trust is long past, when principles merely speculative were propagated by force, when the sincere and pious were made victims, and the light minded bribed into hypocrites.

The proud monuments of liberty knew that the purest homage man could render to the Almighty was in the sacrafice [sic] of his passions and in the performance of his duties; that the ruler of the universe would receive with equal benignity, the various offerings of mans adoration if they proceed from an humble spirit and sincere mind; that intolerance in matters of faith, had been from the earliest ages of the world, the severest torments by which mankind could be afflicted; and that governments were only concerned about the actions and conduct of man, and not his speculative notions. Who among us feels himself so exalted above his fellows, as to have a right to dictate to them their mode of belief? Shall this free Country set an example of Persecution, which even the returning reason of enslaved Europe would not submit to? Will you bind the Conscience in Chains, and fasten conviction upon the mind, in spite of the conclusions of reason, and of those ties and habitudes which are blended with every pulsation of the heart? Are you prepared to plunge at once from the sublime hieghts [sic] of moral legislation, into the dark and gloomy caverns of superstitious ignorance? Will you drive from your shores and from the shelter of your consti[tu]tions, all who do not lay their oblations on the same alter [sic], observe the same ritual, and subscribe to the same dogmas[?] If so which amongst the various sects into which we are divided, shall be the favored one? No Gentlemen, I should insult your understandings, to suppose it possible that you could ever assent to such absurdities. For you all know that persecution in all its shapes and modifications, is contrary to the Genius of our Government, and the sperit [sic] of our laws; and that it can never produce any other effect, than to render men hypocrites or martyrs. When Charles the fifth, Emperor of Germany, tired of the cares of Government, resigned his *Crown* to his son, he retired to a *monastery,* where he amused the evening of his life, in regulating the movements of watches, endeavouring to make a number keep the same time, but not being able to make any two go exactly alike, it led him to reflect upon the folly and crimes he had committed, in attempting the impossibility of making men think alike!!

Nothing is more easily demonstrated than that the Conduct alone is the subject of human laws, and that man ought to suffer civil disqualification for what he does and not for what he thinks. The mind can receive laws only from him, of whose divine essence it is a portion; he alone can punish disobedience; for who else can know its movements; or estimate their merits? The religion I profess, inculcates every duty which man owes to his fellow men; it enjoins upon its votaries, the practice of every virtue, and the detestation of every vice; it teaches them to hope for the favor of Heaven exactly in proportion as their lives are directed by just, honorable and beneficent maxims—This then Gentlemen is my Creed; it was impressed upon my infant mind, it has been the director of my youth, the monitor of my manhood, and will I trust be the Consolation of my old age. ~~Can this religion be founded upon the denial of the divine authority of the old and new Testament?~~ At any rates Gentlemen, I am sure that you cannot see, anything in this relegion [sic], to deprive me of my seat in this House. So far as relates to my life and conduct, the examination of these, I submit with cheerfulness to your candid and liberal construction. What may be the religion of those, who have made this objection against me, or whether they have any religion or not, I am unable to say. I have never considered it my duty to prye [sic] into the belief of my fellow citizens or neighbours, if their actions are upright and their conduct just, the rest is for their own consideration not for mine. I do not seek to make converts to my faith, whatever it may be esteemed in the eyes of my officious friend, nor do I exclude any man from my esteem or friendship, because he and I differ in that respect—The same charity therefore it is not unreasonable to expect will be extended to myself, because in all things that relate to the State and to the duties of civil life, I am bound by the same obligations, with my fellow citizens; nor does any man subscribe more sincerely than myself to the maxim, "Whatever ye would that men should do unto [ye], do ye so even unto them, for such is the Law and the Prophets.[”]

With the highest respect

I remain Gentlemen

yours respectfully

J. Henry

62. STATE AID TO PAROCHIAL SCHOOLS

Memorial of the Trustees of the Congregation Shearith Israel to the New York State Legislature, January 1811;[1] the Legislation passed

[At the time when the enforcement of the concept of the separation of Church and State had not yet led to the withdrawal of direct financial support from parochial schools, the Congregation fought for equality of treatment of its school. One memorial to the legislature having been unavailing, the Congregation succeeded in enlisting the aid of De Witt Clinton (1769–1828), then both Mayor of the city of New York and a State Senator, and the chief organizer of the Public School Society in 1805. Clinton drafted the memorial that is here reprinted, and presented it to the Legislature after it had been signed by the Trustees of the Congregation. This time the request was granted. The Trustees were slow to recognize the democratic necessity of the complete separation of church and state in the educational field. Thus on January 10, 1813, they memorialized the Legislature, protesting its allocation of funds only to the New-York Free School, and supporting the petition of the Presbyterian, Roman Catholic, Baptist and Methodist Churches for the assignment of public funds to their parochial charity schools. By 1825, the New York Common Council had ordered that Common School funds should not be given to religious societies. In 1840, when the Roman Catholics again asked for public funds for their schools, the Congregation joined in the petition, but both were unsuccessful.[2] The problem was basically resolved in 1842, when the Public School Society was replaced by the New York City Board of Education, and free public education was placed on a firm foundation. To this day, however, religious groups continue to press for public financial support for religious sectarian education, although Jews very seldom participate in these undemocratic movements.]

To the Honorable the Legislature of the State of New York. The petition of the trustees of the Congregation of Shearith Israel in the City of New York most respectfully represent:

That from the year 1793 a school has been supported from the funds of the said Congregation for the education of their indigent children. That on the 8th of April, 1801, certain school monies were distributed among seven charity schools of the said city, supported by religious societies. That the free school of the Roman Catholic church and that of your memorialists were overlooked in this benevolent distribution. That on the 21st of March, 1806, a law was passed placing the school of the former on the same footing as the others. That your memorialists also made application to the legislature, but did not succeed owing as they presume to the pressure of business. Your memorialists fully persuaded that the Legislature will look with an equal eye upon all occupations of people who conduct themselves as good and faithful citizens, and conscious that nothing has been omitted on their part to deserve the same countenance and encouragement which has been exhibited to others, do most respectfully pray your Honorable body to extend the same relief to their charity school which has been granted to all others in this city.

Chap. CCXLVI. An Act for the payment of certain officers of government, and for other purposes. Passed April 9, 1811. . . . [3]

Article XLIII. *And be it further enacted,* That it shall be lawful for the trustees of the congregation of Shearith Israel, in the city of New-York, the like sum as was paid to the other religious congregations respectively by virtue of the act entitled "An act directing certain monies to be applied to the use of free schools in the city of New-York," and the act entitled "An act respecting the free school of St. Peter's church in the city of New-York," the monies so paid to be applied according to the directions of the first mentioned act, and the treasurer of this state is hereby directed to pay to the said mayor, aldermen and commonalty of the city of New-York, the sum so paid by them out of the unappropriated money arising from the duties on sales at auction in the said city.[4]

63. FIGHTING THE BRITISH, 1813

Reminiscences of Mordecai Myers about the War of 1812 [1]

[Commissioned a Captain in the 13th United States Infantry on March 12, 1812, because of his previous military training, Mordecai Myers served through the war until his honorable discharge on June 15, 1815.[2] His detailed recollections of the battles on the Niagara frontier with Canada are lively first-hand accounts of the life of the camp and the field.]

. . . The barracks were, at length, completed, and were very comfortable. During the winter (1812–13), we were on the defensive, and, with the exception of many alarms, and the frequent marching of my company (1st or Grenadier of the 13th) and that of Captain [Lodowick] Morgan of the 12th to Buffalo and back, little or nothing worthy of note occurred. Marching to Buffalo so frequently was very severe duty. I occupied my quarters only one night after their completion; the remainder of the time I quartered in a tent either at Buffalo, or at the Cantonment.[3] I often encamped in the street in Buffalo, there being no quarters to be had. Finally I secured the Ball-room for my men and a shoemaker's shop by way of quarters for myself. Here, during the winter, many occurrences took place which were very amusing at the time, but they would not be interesting to read at this late period. As I before stated, the campaign of 1813 began with the affair of Little York.[4]

The troops remained there only two days. They took one or two schooners with stores, etc., burned a vessel on the stocks, and re-embarked and stood over for Fort Niagara.

Here the dead were buried and the wounded taken care of as well as circumstances would admit. Our squadron left Sackett's Harbor. General Smith's brigade, then at Williamsville encampment, was ordered to march to Fort Niagara. We descended the river in bateaux as far as the old French fort, one mile from Niagara Falls and just opposite to Chippeway. I was detached with two hundred men to take the boats back about two miles. We accomplished this with great difficulty, the current being so strong that we could barely stem it. After effecting our object, we set out on our return to Chippeway. The men shouldered their oars for convenience in carrying them. When we approached the garrison, the troops, seeing a body of men carrying arms fourteen feet long, feared an attack and beat to arms; but our long weapons were harmless. At reveille we proceeded in our march to Lewiston where we halted. There an order reached us directing General Smith to re-enforce Fort Niagara with our regiment of infantry; for an attack was expected from the enemy's troops at Fort George by way of retaliation for the affair of Little Rock. We were just pitching our tents to shelter our men from a snow storm, when the order came. Colonel [John] Christie [Chrystie], who was in command of our regiment, asked me if the regiment could move on immediately. Some of the other captains were consulted, and we finally started on the march without baggage.

The night was very dark, cold and stormy, and the roads were as bad as can be imagined. We commenced the march, left in front; so my company brought up the rear, a very unpleasant post, as those in the rear cannot go on until all stragglers have passed, when it is sometimes very difficult to catch up with the front. On arriving at the salt battery, Lieut. Col. [Peter Philip] Schuyler informed me that the field officers would go immediately to the fort, that I must halt and get shelter for the men, and, if it was necessary for us to come on, a rocket would be fired, in which case we must move down as quickly as possible. He gave me the parole and countersign. Our men took shelter such as they could find.

Captain [Samuel B.] Archer, of the light artillery, who was stationed in the battery, invited the officers to his quarters and ordered refreshments; but in less than half an hour the signal rocket was seen at the fort. I immediately formed as many men as I could collect, and left Captain [Hugh R.] Martin in command to follow as soon as possible, and to leave the same order to [John] Sprowl [Sproull] and the other captains. We groped along through Egyptian darkness, the rain fell in torrents, and the mud was ankle deep. When I arrived at the chain of sentinels I was obliged to advance slowly through the mud, slipping down now and then among the stumps and stones.

I answered the challenge, "a detachment of the 13th Infantry;" the answer was the discharge of a musket, and the fire was repeated all along the line of sentinels.

After some difficulty in exchanging countersign, etc., we gained admittance to the fort and found the garrison under arms, as they had thought, at first, that we were the enemy. Everything went on quietly for the remainder of the night, and at daylight the rear of our regiment arrived. We had no quarters, but tents were furnished and we encamped on the parade. The next night the wounded from Little York were landed, and the fort was then like a hospital. The mess house and the stairs leading to the mess room were all filled. We remained on duty in the fort for several days, and then the whole force, excepting the regular garrison, encamped on Snake Island. It was literally *Snake* Island, for it was full of snakes. The men frequently shook rattle snakes from their blankets in the morning, and at every drill or parade snakes were killed on the ground.

The inhabitants of the island said that the snakes came down from the mountains in the spring to get water at the lakes; but that before they reached the water they were harmless. None of the men were bitten by them, at all events. While at this encampment I was engaged as second in an affair of honor between Dr. James Bronaugh [5] and Major Stonard. Major Z. Taylor (late President of the U. S.)[6] was associated with me as friends to Major Stonard. Captain [Archibald C.] Randolph [of the 12th Infantry] and another gentleman were friends to the Doctor. The Major was shot in the thigh. He died of the wound in May, 1813. . . .

While at Snake Hill every preparation was made for taking Fort George. It was arranged that on the night before the landing, Fort Niagara, the salt battery, and a battery which I built one night assisted by Lieutenant Totten as engineer (now General Totten, U. S. A.)[7] should open fire of hot shot on Fort George and the batteries on that side, and at four o'clock, A. M., all the troops were to embark and wheel out by regiments. Lieut. Col. Winfield Scott commanded the left with his light artillery supported by infantry.

Next, on the right, was the 13th Regiment, commanded by Lieut.-Col. Christie; and the other regiments according to rank. Each regiment formed a line of boats and moved in silence at wheeling distance.

The companies were so arranged in each boat as to form line immediately on landing. It was a misty morning, and our fleet had taken up its position under cover of the fog to effect our landing. The cannonading on the right was very brisk and effectual; all the wooden buildings in Fort George were soon in flames, and the garrison marched out and formed on the plain ready to move in any direction. We had about five miles to row to the place of landing; as we neared the fleet the fog lifted, and a view was presented of our fleet at its moorings, and our full force approaching with flags displayed and our bands playing "Yankee Doodle." The garrisons of Forts George, Erie, and Chippeway, which had joined in the night, were in line near the bank. The firing now opened from the shore and shipping.

Lieutenant Trent, in the schooner "Julia," with one twenty-four pounder on a pivot, took a station opposite to a battery, furled his sails and moored his schooner for a "regular set to." Scott effected a landing, but did not succeed in advancing until reenforced. I commanded the in-shore boats of our regiment, and was rowing for my position when General [John Parke] Boyd, who was on shore, called out, "Wheel in my jolly snorters," (the sobriquet by which our regiment was known.) I immediately wheeled my boat when an order was passed from boat to boat "to keep on." I answered in the same way "Superior orders from shore." I landed and the remainder of the regiment followed, and Scott with all who were with him mounted the bank together. The contest was sharp, and soon ended. The British retreated, and were soon on a rapid march for "Twelve Mile" Creek. We advanced to Newark, but were annoyed by a fire of hot shot from a thirty-two pounder on a pivot in barbette in a block house. Colonel Christie was ordered to detach a force from his right and take it. I was ordered to take two companies from the right, and Lieutenant [Patrick] McDonough was to accompany me. Lieutenant [John Keyes] Paige commanded my second platoon or company.

When I approached the block house, I detached him to the rear to take prisoners if they attempted to jump over the parapet; for it was a battery on the water side, and a block house on the land. I entered through a sally-port five feet high and three feet wide. The garrison jumped over the parapet and ran. Paige had not gained his position, and I never saw Mr. McDonough or his twelve pounder. After taking this position, the army found nothing to obstruct its progress. There were a few reports to the effect that large quantities of ammunition had been placed in the public stores with trains of powder leading to them, but examinations proved them to be untrue. The whole body advanced as far as the public stores near the house of Mr. Black. Here the main body halted, and Lieut.-Col. Scott proceeded with his detachment to the ruins of Fort George. He found no troops to oppose him; all were on the march to the "Twelve Mile" Creek. The fired buildings were still burning. I was detached for main guard. The park of artillery was in the center, and the other troops were at the right and left facing south—the right near the road leading to the batteries. I was posted as main guard at about five hundred yards south of our line, and exactly in front of the park of artillery. I had occasion to go to Mrs. Black to instruct the family how far they could move without interruption. I took a glass of porter and some crackers and cheese with Mr. Black.

At about eight o'clock, Col. H[omer]. V[irgil]. Milton, as officer of the day, visited me and requested me to have fires made up. I complied, though to have fires on out post in the enemy's country was contrary to what I had been taught. He said that in case of an alarm I might withdraw my guards and place them between the fires and the line. At about eleven o'clock the sentinel on night guard fired. I sent a non-commissioned officer and a file of men to enquire the cause. It was reported to be a false alarm. I had retired as directed. The officer of the day then rode up and said that I had been in great danger. The artillery, supposing my guard to be the enemy had aprons off guns, the guns primed, and port-fire ready; and had he been five seconds later my guard would have been cut down by grape shot from the whole park. Thus, by the providence of God we were saved. There was no alarm during the remainder of the night. . . .

Our detachment under General Lewis marched from Fort George without baggage on the first day of June, 1813. It consisted of the 12th, 13th, and 14th Regiments of Infantry, Colonel Burns' regiment of Dragoons, and a strong detachment of Artillery, numbering in all, rank and file, about three thousand men. Our object was to attack the British in their entrenchments at Burlington Heights.

On the 2nd we halted to give the men a little rest at Crooks, twenty-two miles from the British lines. We had had a hard march of two days over bad roads obstructed by broken bridges and fallen trees placed in our way by the retreating enemy. Many of the officers took breakfast with Mr. Cook, a wealthy gentleman; and while I was enjoying the luxury of putting on a clean shirt, kindly lent me by Dr. J. Bronaugh with the injunction not to tell where I procured it, a party of Indians took possession of a high and almost perpendicular ridge of rocks in front of the house and commenced a heavy fire on the dragoon horses that were picketed in the door yard. Lieut. Joseph C. Eldridge, of my company, and adjutant of the regiment with the camp guard accomplished immediately, but with great difficulty, what seemed to be impracticable—he scaled the face of the rocks. At the same time, I was ordered to march to the rear of their retreat; but before I reached the top of the ridge they were all dispersed by Eldridge and had escaped.

We continued our march through mud and mire, it sometimes required six teams to drag our baggage wagons and artillery; the day was extremely warm, and we were obliged to repair several bridges before we could cross the streams. We halted in the evening at "Forty Mile" Creek. A detachment of boats with provisions and ammunition had followed our march. They were discovered by Commodore —— and we dispatched the schooners to destroy them.

As soon as we halted, Captain Archie of the artillery was ordered to the lake shore, supported by the 13th. Furnaces were erected and hot shot was soon prepared and used to such effect as to drive off the enemy. The remainder of our forces were bivouacked on either side of the road leading to the position of the enemy. Lieut. Van V—— commanded an advanced picket guard half a mile in advance on the road. This was the evening of the 3rd of June, and the 4th being the birthday of King George III, the enemy felt in good spirits, no doubt, and determined to precipitate our attack.

They moved their full force towards us in silence, bayoneted the advance sentinel, found the officer of the guard asleep, took the guard and marched straight into camp before they were discovered. Great confusion, of course, ensued. General [William H.] Winder and General [John] Chandler were taken prisoners while giving orders to the enemy, believing them to be their own troops, in consequence of one of our regiments having changed its position in the night to get better encamping ground. As soon as the firing was heard, Col. Christie moved our regiment along the beach with the intention to get in the rear of the enemy, take possession of the bridge over "Forty Mile" Creek, and cut off the retreat. We had nearly reached our point when an express came with orders to halt, and for the field officers to attend a council of war. General Lewis had been called back to Fort George, Gen. Winder and Gen. Chandler were prisoners and Christie thought that he ranked all the other officers. But, on going to the council, he found, much to his chagrin and mortification, that Col. Burns ranked by date of commission.

The question now was, shall we pursue or fall back? Our regiment was counter-marched over the field of battle after having taken twenty or thirty prisoners. When we arrived at the ground we found it strewed with dead and wounded of both parties to the number of four or five hundred. The troops on both sides were scattered. We buried the dead and stacked and burned the arms and baggage for want of transportation. We brought off the wounded and prepared to follow our retiring forces. I was informed that the British General S—— was lying among the dead. I sent an officer in search of him; he found a blanket and one of the General's pistols, but, like Lord G—— in the play, the General had carried off his own corpse. At noon we started after our retiring troops, and joined them at the "Forty Mile" Creek. Col. Schuyler asked permission to follow the retreating enemy with our regiment, but the Council of War would not consent. . . .[8]

64. A SLAVE PROMISED HIS FREEDOM

Legal paper promising freedom to George Roper from Jacob Levy, Jr., April 8, 1814 [1]

[An interesting relationship is here revealed between Jacob Levy, Jr. and his slave. Roper asked for his liberation, and was promised it in three years, depending upon his good behavior. Levy was obviously influenced by the New York Society for Promoting the Manumission of Slaves, in whose records this manuscript was found.]

Whereas my Slave George Roper has solicited me to give him his freedom at the expiration of three years from the thirteenth day of June next;[2] and in consideration thereof, he hath promised to serve me faithfully for the said term; Now I hereby agree to manumit & make free the said George Roper, at the expiration of the said term, of three years from the thirteenth day of June next; provided & upon the express condition that the said George Roper shall during that term well & faithfully serve me & my family as a Slave, & dutifully obey all my lawful commands.

[Signed] Jacob Levy Junr [3]

New York April 8th. 1814
Witnessed by Geo Brinckerhoff
Recorded 12th of 4 mo. 1814 by Nathan Comstock

65. ABOUT NAPOLEON

Editorial from the Charleston *Southern Patriot,* August 14, 1815, by Isaac Harby

[Contemporaneous reactions to Napoleon by American Jews are rare;[1] this editorial is therefore exceptionally interesting. Napoleon's relation to the Jews was both direct and indirect. Directly he convoked the famous Paris Sanhedrin of 1806–1807 in order to regulate the relation of the Jews of

France to the state;[2] indirectly, his aggressive foreign policy, by shaking up the feudal structures of European states, made what was up to that time the single greatest contribution to the emancipation of Jews from European feudal bonds. In his editorial, Harby asserts that Napoleon's "magnanimous and liberal policy as regards *Religion,* would alone embalm his memory to posterity." But Harby, as a Jeffersonian republican, also keenly notes the nature of the British-Austro-Prussian-Russian alliance against France when he states: "The war waged by the Allies, is not so much against Napoleon, not so much against France, as it is a war against the revival and dissemination of *Republicanism.*" Harby, during his short career, left his mark as a journalist, as a highly respected literary and dramatic critic, and as a leader of the Reformed Society of Israelites of Charleston.[3]]

THE GREAT NEWS

Which was received yesterday,[4] and which excited such emotions of surprize, such unbounded belief in some, and such flat infidelity in others—has not been backed with any thing like *confirmation,* by the additional articles we receive this day. If it be FALSE—why, there is an end to all reasoning or calculation with respect to its results; and it must be set down in company with many other wonderful offsprings of certain speculating and inventive geniuses.— But if it be TRUE, we confess we do not perceive what very great occasion the enemies of Buonaparte and of France have to rejoice.— Half of the great army under Wellington and Blucher have been put *hors de combat.* The English themselves acknowledge the loss of 40,000 men![5] And, if, with the restoration of a Republican Government—the enthusiasm of 1793 should preside in the bosoms of the French, we doubt not the powers, whoever they be, that dare to intermeddle with the internal concerns of France, or to threaten the invasion of her Frontiers, will be scattered like chaff before the tempest. As consistent lovers of freedom—as friends to the happiness and dignity of man wherever Heaven has placed him—we rejoice at the return of France to those sentiments whose operation wrought her Revolution—to that bourne and goal of political happiness, for which, with toils and treasures and blood, she has been so long contending.

We admire Buonaparte. We think, that in the worst of times, and under the most appalling circumstances, his GENIUS alone has reduced the chaos of faction into order and beauty—his valor and experience, have driven the charged clouds of invasion to be emptied on other shores.— His magnanimous and liberal policy as regards *Religion,* would alone embalm his memory to posterity.— But if France can be *free* and exist—if she can preserve that energy necessary to her salvation, and that liberty without which society is but a horde of slaves—no matter what personal sacrifices be made. Let the Buonapartes merge into private citizens—as the Bourbons have been already banished as traitors. So France is independent—the prayers of Freemen will go with her.— The abdication of Buonaparte, if unconditional—his resignation of the throne while the army is at his control—his taking the diadem from his brow, not to place it around the temples of another, but to cast it on the earth, where it might be trampled to atoms under the footsteps of Liberty—is the last and greatest sacrifice, which this great man can make to the happiness and dignity of his country.— His former relinquishment of imperial power,[6] though originating from a desire to save France from domestic bloodshed, was but to deliver her to another despotism, without brilliancy and without honor. But this last abdication is to restore her to Liberty, and to give up into the hands of the people, that sovereignty which they inherit from God and Nature.

It is evident, that these sentiments are predicated upon the supposition that the solitary fact of Buonaparte having abdicated the throne, *is true*—unaccompanied with the absurd and wild episodes which the imagination of the retailer has thrown around it.— *But that fact is highly doubtful.* It is highly doubtful, whether, at this moment, the wisdom and talents and *experience* of those men who preside in the councils of France, should be so suddenly obscured, as to agitate the question of abdication while the enemy was at their doors—and when all the energy and all the unity of thought and action, was necessary to repel invasion.— We think they could not have been so unseasonable, so impolitic.[7]

It may be asked, whether the dethronement of Buonaparte might not have been insisted on by the Allies, as a *sine qua non* of the alternative of peace? We think not. The war waged by the Allies, is not so much against Napoleon, not so much against France, as it is a war against the revival and dissemination of *Republicanism.*— And it may be confidently added, that imperial France, or even France under a limited Monarchy, does not present so dangerous an aspect to Priestcraft and despotism—as Republican France with all her energies united, and all her prerogatives of government rising and flourishing from the sovereignty of the people. As a Republic, therefore, France will have the same external obstacles to encounter and to destroy, as she had in the last years of the Eighteenth century.[8]

66. PERSONAL LETTER

From Rebecca Gratz of Philadelphia to Mrs. Ogden Hoffman of New York, October 20, 1817 [1]

[Family affairs, books and bookmen, and intermarriage of Jew and non-Jew are discussed in this intimate letter from a famous Jewish woman personality to a close friend.]

I have not written to you My dear Maria,[2] because I have been a good deal engaged, but my thoughts have often turned to you and I have talked about you, with friends who know & value you, so that my separation has not appeared as long as it really is.

last week John Myers & his parents left us. John had been at our house nearly four weeks, very sick, and as he was obliged to stay at home, my time was taken up, to keep him company. he came from Baltimore with the remains of a fever on him, which so affected his nerves as to alarm us, and induce us to write to his family to come up & visit him. this brought his Brother Saml [3] from Richmond & his Parents from Norfolk. Dr. Chapman attended him and recommended his going home, and if the symptoms did not soon disappear to put himself under a course of Mercury. his father however writes that he is better, but I hope they will be judicious and not, to avoid a severe remedy, permit a worse disease to take too deep root. he has been living in Baltimore two or three years keeps house, and in the solitariness of bachelors-hall, had no one to take proper care of him in his illness. accordingly he did many imprudent things while sick, and lastly traveled in the steamboat to Phil[a] with his fever unbroken. the first attack was some what similar to Jo's (from his account of it) a recuretting [?] bilious but being protracted, affected his nerves, which is always tedious and distressing. I hope however he will soon be well again. I have not seen the criticism of Washington [4] you mention, but confess myself very well satisfied with the Tale. I do not think she could have managed her fable better. there was a necessity for some sacrifice of religious principal [sic] and we are better pleased it should be kept out of view & have been made by the parents of Berenice than by either her or Washington. there is a strong instance too of religious tolerance in Monteveia's educating his daughter a Christian, and in the harmony of their affections towards each other, which contains the moral she would inculcate in her tale. I think however a more interesting & natural story might have been produced in making the characters of Jew & Christian associate, & assimilate in all the respective charities of social life, without bringing the passions into contact[.] I believe it is impossible to reconcile a matrimonial engagement between persons of so different a creed, without requiring one or the other to yield [sic] in all instances we have heard of in real life, this has been the case and where a family of children are to be brought up, it appears necessary that parents should agree on so important a subject. I have known many Jews marry Christian women, whose wives have become strict conformists to the rites of our religion —and Jewesses married to Christians who have entered the church, as in the instance of my Aunt Schuyler [5]—one instance similar to Monteveia I have heard of here—but the parties lived very unhappily —little jealousies were continually occurring, and at length when the husband died the widow & her daughters returned to her family & the synagogue while the son was put in the navy, and quite estranged from the family. The poor fellow is also dead, but had he survived the division of interests and sentiments would have broken up the harmony of feelings that should subsist between such near relations.

I saw our old friend James Paulding [6] in his way home, he appears to be agood [sic] deal out of health—and out of spirits—perhaps some feeling of sympathy for me may have occasioned his seriousness —he told me he had not seen you or Ann—he was but little in New York. I enquired for Gertrude he told me he had never seen her look better—I enquired no further—but when I asked when we should have a longer visit from him (he was only two days in town) he said he did not expect to be this way again until early in the summer, by which I conclude his affairs there are not in a very prosperous way, or at least not to be soon brought to a close—from the sensibility with which he spoke of his isolated manner of life at Washington—and the few persons who interested him there, I suspect were he in a situation to marry they would not delay. I think so highly of James, that notwithstanding former coquettry believe he would make an excellent husband, and agreeable domestic companion.

Maria & Sam[l] Nicholas are preparing for their removal to Savannah. they expect to sail next week, all the Southern folks are taking their departure from our city. Mrs. Minis [7] whom I beleive [sic] I mentioned to you, went last week, her little girl, who interested us all so much, is quite recovered. I think she has reason [to] be thankful that she was within reach of Dr. Physick, less skillful treatment might have cost the life of her child.

I am rejoiced My dear Friend, to recognise in your last letter, your own cheerful submission, God Grant you may long posess the blessings that console you for all your losses. I have seen so many this summer, suffering such evils, as have shorne us of much happiness—that I cannot fail to acknowledge that we but share the common lot, and humbly thank God for the support his holy love has afforded us in our trials—for Ah, My dear friend when they are smitten who have not been taught to raise their voice to Him who can sustain them, how ten-fold are their sufferings visited upon them—it is long since I have heard from the Ogdens, when you see them remember me to them, is Bella in N.Y?

Give my love to your husband & Ann, I hope Jo will be with you next week, and will bring me good news of you. take care of your health My Beloved friend, and thus restore cheerfulness & joy to your Husband, and comfort to the heart of your Affectionate RG. embrace the dear children for me—

67. FIGHT FOR EQUALITY IN MARYLAND

Legislation introduced in the Maryland House of Delegates, December 21, 1818 [1]

[One of the most protracted, bitter, exciting and instructive battles for equal civil rights for Jews took place in Maryland from 1797 [2] to 1826. One landmark in the struggle is this bill, which seeks to alter the State Constitution so that "no religious test" shall be required of a Jew for holding civil office, and so that a Jew may take his oath of office "on the five books of Moses." Until the final passage of such legislation in 1826, no Jew could hold any municipal or state office in Maryland, or even practice law, for the lawyer was an officer of the law. While the form of the struggle involved a religious question, the Jews as a whole, religious and non-religious, benefited from the victory.]

> AN ACT To extend to the sect of people professing the Jewish Religion, the same rights and privileges that are enjoyed by Christians.

WHEREAS, it is the acknowledged right of all men to worship God according to the dictates of their own conscience. And whereas, it is declared by the 36th Section of the bill of rights of this state, "That the manner of administering an oath to any person ought to be such as those of the religious persuasion, profession, or denomination of which such person is one, generally esteem the most effectual confirmation by the attestation of the divine Being." And whereas, religious tests for civil employment, though intended as a barrier against the depraved, frequently operate as a restraint upon the conscientious; and as the Constitution of the United States requires no religious qualification for civil office, therefore,

Sec. 1. Be it enacted, By the General Assembly of Maryland, that no religious test, declaration or subscription of opinion as to religion, shall be required from any person of the sect called Jews, as a qualification to hold or exercise any office or employment of profit or trust in this state.

Sec. 2. And be it enacted, That every oath to be administered to any person of the sect of people called Jews, shall be administered on the five books of Moses, agreeably to the religious education of that people, and not otherwise.

Sec. 3. And be it enacted, That if this act shall be confirmed by the General Assembly, after the next election, of delegates, in the first session after such new election, as the constitution and form of government direct; that in such case this act and the alteration and amendments of the constitution and form of government therein contained, shall be taken and considered, and shall constitute and be valid as part of the said constitution and form of government, to all intents and purposes, any thing in the declaration of rights, constitution and form of government contained, to the contrary notwithstanding.

Sec. 4. And be it enacted, That the several clauses and sections of the declaration of rights, constitution and form of government, and every part of any law of this state, contrary to the provisions of this act, so far as respects the sect of people aforesaid, shall be, and the same is hereby declared to be repealed and annulled on the confirmation hereof.[3]

68. INVITATION TO IMMIGRATION

Excerpt from *Memoir Addressed to Persons of the Jewish Religion in Europe, On the Subject of Emigration to, and Settlement in, One of the Most Eligible Parts of the United States of North America.* By W. D. Robinson, Citizen of the United States, London, October 20, 1819 [1]

[This "Plan for Establishing a Jewish Settlement in the United States" is an interesting example of the attitude of an American Christian to the Jews of Europe, and to the prospect of inducing them to come in greater numbers to this country.[2] The consolidation of European feudal-monarchic reaction after the defeat of Napoleon led to new anti-Semitic outbreaks that became widespread by 1819; in New York, Mordecai Manuel Noah conceived that year his abortive plan to found a Jewish state on Grand Island, N. Y. as a refuge for European Jews. It is noteworthy that Robinson regards the separation of the Jews of Europe from the soil as not in any sense due to innate qualities but to restrictions imposed upon the Jews. Nothing is yet known about the effect of the pamphlet even upon the Jews of London, although it is obvious that the plan as such never materialized. Charles P. Daly, author of the first history of the Jews in the United States, believes that any such attempt to "found a Jewish agricultural settlement, would have been a disastrous failure, like many analogous attempts in the early settlement of the United States."[3] The pamphlet soon became known in the United States, for Thomas Kennedy used it in his speech in the Maryland House of Delegates on January 29, 1820, in arguing for equal rights for the Jews.[4]

. . . It would not be possible to pourtray the benign influence of the spirit of universal toleration breathed throughout the American code. To be properly appreciated, it must be seen, but of its effects the United States stand as a proud and lasting monument. In any part of the American Union, the disciples of Jesus Christ, of Moses, and Mahomet, may come in contact with each other, without displaying the scowls of anger or jealousy; because each feels a perfect independence of the other, and all are equally secure of the protection of the laws, and of those who administer them. Under these circumstances, religious fanatics in the United States become perfectly harmless, and their influence is felt in a very limited sphere. However irrational their doctrines, or fantastic their customs and ceremonies, they only excite pity or laughter.

Among the immense variety and number of emigrants, who, by the pursuits of trade, or civil or religious dissentions, have been induced to leave Europe for the United States, very few have been of the Jewish persuasion. This circumstance has arisen from a variety of causes. The education and general habits of the Jews, throughout Europe, have fixed them in commercial cities and towns. Some few of them have acquired great wealth and live in luxurious magnificence, but even these few have been so much accustomed to manage the monied transactions of Europe, that they consider this the only proper theatre on which they can exist and flourish. A certain portion have, however, overcome this prejudice, and hence those Jews who have emigrated across the Atlantic, have in general been of the opulent class, and in the United States have been led to pursue the same occupations they did in the land from which they came. They are now the chief stock and money brokers in all the large cities, and their children, with very few exceptions, are educated in the same pursuits as their fathers: very rarely do we find an artisan among them, and still more rare is it to see any of them following the labours of agriculture, or rural occupations.

However wretched the situation of the poorer class of Jews in Europe, there we behold them carrying on the most menial operations in society to gain a livelihood, in preference to tilling the ground. This certainly cannot arise out of the consequences of impaired energies, or the incapabilities of individual exertion. Neither can it arise out of any inherent aversion to cultivate the soil, it rather seems to be the effect of the uncertainty of their social and political existence, and the consequent habits in which they are unfortunately reared. In addition to this, if a Jew should feel disposed to earn a competency or subsistence for himself and family, he is deterred from the pursuits of agriculture by many imperious difficulties. If he retires into the country, though surrounded by neighbours, he feels himself an isolated being, and, owing to the dominion of existing prejudices, cut off, as it were, from that social intercourse with his fellow species, which constitutes the chief felicity of man. All around him he beholds persons who pity or deride him, because he does not profess their religious tenets. He has no synagogue into which he can enter to adore his God according to Mosaic rites, consequently he is actuated by a constant anxiety to return to cities and towns, where he can associate with those of his own creed, and visit a temple of worship in which he can fulfil what he conscientiously believes to be his religious obligations. Under these circumstances, it is in vain to expect any important change in the character and condition of the Jews in Europe; but, if I mistake not, the plan I shall here suggest, would not only ameliorate the unfortunate state of this class of human beings who are enduring contumely and the greatest hardships, often under the vilest governments, but eventually elevate them to a rank in society which for many ages they have not enjoyed.

The only difficulty I anticipate in the realization of the present scheme, is, the habitual propensity of the Jews to follow other pursuits than those of agriculture. This I do not attribute to any want of physical or moral energy, but, as before stated, to their peculiar situation in the societies of Europe, and the political thraldom in which they are compelled to live. Surrounded by poverty and scorn, and constituting no one link of the general bond by which society is kept together, and uncertain also in the tenure of lands and the chance of reaping the precarious fruits of their own personal industry, they feel dejected, and are impelled by no stimulus to fixed habits of field-labour. Convey them, however, to a rich soil, a smiling country, and congenial climate, where every thing breathes content and plenty, and where they can eat of the fruit of the trees planted with their own hands, and the scene is changed; there a man is actuated by another soul, and is immediately stimulated to individual exertion. . . .

PLAN For Establishing A *Jewish Settlement in the United States.*

1. An association of wealthy and respectable Jews are to subscribe a fund, to as large an amount as may be practicable, for the purpose of purchasing a tract of land in the United States, adequate to the object in view.

2. This tract of land I recommend to be purchased in the Upper Mississippi and Missouri territory, in a climate particularly well adapted for European constitutions, and where the fertility of soil

is equal, if not superior, to any in North America. There are now for private sale, several large tracts contained in these two sections, and embracing several millions of acres, adjacent to the Mississippi and Missouri rivers, two of the most important navigable streams in the northern divisions of America, and destined, at no very remote period, to become the most populous and flourishing regions in the new world.

3. After the purchase of the necessary lands is effected by the company, they will then make known, through the medium of the chief papers in Europe, the most liberal conditions to all Jews desirous of emigrating to the settlement in question; offering in the first instance to each, a certain number of acres, on a credit of a specific number of years, giving particular encouragement to all such as take out their families; and, in the second place, pledging to convey them from Europe, free of expense, to New Orleans, and from thence, in steam boats, to their final destination. Agricultural implements of all descriptions are further to be provided by the company, and resold to the settlers on a credit, at a moderate profit; and all emigrants and settlers are to be subject to such rules and regulations as the company may determine on for the benefit and general interests of the settlement.

4. The government of the United States will feel every disposition to promote the views and prosperity of such a settlement, not only because it is conformable to the policy of their government, but also in strict accord with the interests and welfare of the country at large. In a more special manner will it excite the attention of the American government, on the principle of the object exhibiting a great example of philanthropy, in thus affording an asylum to an unfortunate and oppressed portion of the human race; nor do I entertain the least doubt, in case the company wishes to buy the public lands belonging to the United States, the government will readily make a sale of them, on the most liberal conditions.

5. I conceive that the company who subscribe to the fund in question, will not merely be rewarded with the grateful thanks of the emigrants and settlers, but for the investment of capital this will turn out to be an object of more magnitude and advantage than any other mode by which funds can at present be employed in Europe. Large fortunes have already been made by those who have invested their capitals in judicious purchases of land, and more especially by enterprizing individuals who have encouraged persons to settle on and

cultivate such purchased tracts, by giving them a credit of some years for small farms; because, in proportion as settlers are collected together, and cultivation spreads, the unoccupied lands adjacent increase in value and demand. It has not been uncommon, in several of the western States of America, for an individual to buy 4 or 500 acres of land on a credit of several years, and before the expiration of the time allowed for payment, by his mere personal labour, he has been enabled to pay the total value of the farm; so that from a state of absolute poverty, he has become an independent proprietor of the soil, and placed in a situation to sustain a numerous offspring with comfort. The holders of large tracts of land who have laid out their funds in the manner above stated, have uniformly become immensely rich, and beheld their late thickets and forests assume the aspect of culture, whilst villages, towns, and commerce, have sprung up as it were by the hand of magic. If, therefore, we reflect on the tide of emigration rolling to the west, the immense and valuable regions with which the Mississippi and Missouri are connected, and that they are now becoming the channel of communication, even with the shores of the Pacific; I am sincerely of opinion, that the company who become the proprietors of the tract of territory in which the Jewish settlement is to be established, will derive advantages, in point of interest and profit, superior to any other means that could now be devised for the investment of capital. Local regulations are, besides, to be established for the purpose of securing the reimbursement of the first sums expended, on terms not burdensome or cramping to the infant settlement.

6. I am of opinion, that not only among the opulent Jews, many men of liberal minds and generous hearts will be found to promote the plan, on the principles of philanthropy, but, among those of moderate fortune, numbers will cheerfully contribute their mite, and, by voluntary donations, increase the funds of the Company. Whenever the exercise of private benevolence is called for, three conditions are necessary, viz.:—that the end proposed is of such a kind as to be really desirable; secondly, that its attainment is within the reach of the effort to be made; and, lastly, that there is, from the peculiarity of the circumstances, a special need of interference: all these requisites will be found combined in the object in view, and its realization will always serve as a source of heartfelt gratification to those who have promoted it.

The plans proposed by individual adventurers, in emigrating and settling in a distant land, have frequently been destroyed by their going, on the principle of uncertainty, with their families, to a strange country, and before they have learned its habits, or selected and purchased a spot suitable for their undertaking, the funds brought out with them have been expended. Thus has their adventure failed for the want of an early helping-hand. But in the plan proposed, every thing is provided for them by a company, and their lands are measured and allotted before their arrival. Food, raiment, and all the necessary implements are laid in for them, till they are in a situation to meet their own wants. By this means, all misfortune and disappointment would be prevented, and plans might be formed, not only for the immediate assistance of the new emigrants and settlers, but also for the future encouragement of new branches of industry. The first settlers will, no doubt, feel a few temporary difficulties, and privations, but those who follow will always meet a directing friend to take them by the hand.

Whether, therefore, we consider the magnitude of the design, or the peculiar circumstances which, at the present moment, have led to its suggestion, the encouragement of the plan is worthy of the united efforts of every patriot and philanthropist. It must succeed, if only properly organized, because all its parts are clearly practicable. It requires nothing more than the aid and protection of the benevolent and powerful, on this side of the water; on the other, the scope is unbounded. By its realization both the political and moral situation of the Jews will be bettered, for they will enter on the enjoyment of civil rights, and to prevent crime, there is no safer means than to remedy misfortune. Much may be expected from the Jews when placed beyond the reach of want or persecution. They are an industrious, abstemious, and persevering race of people; and when urged by necessity, or animated by hope, they are, unquestionably, capable of making the same exertions as any other part of mankind. Where are the Jewish parents who would not feel delight in beholding their children pursuing the honourable and useful labours of agriculture, in preference to the wretched and menial occupations in which they are now generally engaged? Where is the individual of this class whose bosom would not throb with satisfaction, when he contemplates an establishment of his own brethren, in a country where all can enjoy the same privileges and blessings as the natives themselves? Can it be supposed, that if a prospect so interesting were unfolded to their view, they would be so blind as not to perceive its advantages? Would they not soon contrast their present degraded and persecuted situation with that which awaits them? No sooner would the first settlement be formed, and its benign effects made known by those who are partakers in it, than we should find thousands of distressed applicants praying to be removed from their hovels to the land of plenty and toleration. Even from the metropolis of the British empire, many families would emigrate, for, notwithstanding, by the laws of Great Britain, and the liberal spirit of British subjects, the Jews are there more secure and happy than in any other part of Europe, they are, nevertheless, excluded from certain political, as well as personal privileges, enjoyed by other classes in society. Besides these considerations, there exist a great number of Jews in London, in wretched condition, who find it difficult to earn a subsistence by occupations of the most degrading kind.

If a Jewish settlement should be established in the United States, on the enlarged scale here laid down, it does not require the gift of prophecy to foresee the result. In a very few years such a settlement would become known to the Jews in every quarter of the globe, and we should find thousands flocking to it, who never before dreamt that such an asylum could be procured in any part of the civilized world. We should behold Jewish agriculture spreading through the American forests; Jewish towns and villages adorning the banks of the Mississippi and Missouri, and the arts, commerce, and manufactures, would advance with the same rapidity in this new settlement, as has been exemplified in all the other agricultural regions of the United States.* Were I, indeed, to draw a picture of all the highly important consequences which suggest themselves to my mind on this subject, I fear I might be called a speculative enthusiast; but I flatter myself that the hints contained in this cursory memoir, will have a tendency to excite an impartial and serious investigation among that class of Jews whose liberal and benevolent minds will enable them to appreciate the merits of the plan proposed, and whose opulent circumstances give them the means to carry it into execution with promptitude, and on an extensive scale.

* Those of the Jews who escaped being burned in Portugal by the Inquisition, were driven from thence, and sought an asylum in Brazil; and these people, true there, as every where else, to their active and laborious disposition, were the first who began to cultivate the colony, which is indebted to them for its first harvest. The Portuguese, taught by the example of the Jews, began to feel the value of their new possession, and from that time the government applied themselves to it, and endeavoured to make it valuable.—DuPradt, on the Colonies, chap. 2.[5] [Note in the original.—Ed.]

69. ANOTHER PERSONAL LETTER

From Rebecca Gratz to Mrs. Hoffman, about 1820–1822 [1]

[Books, sermons, personalities, and the persecution of the Jews in Europe are the subjects of this characteristic letter.]

Has my long silence made me appear ungrateful for your last interesting letter, My Beloved friend? if it has remember appearances are decietful [sic] and believe it so in this instance, when I assure you how sincerely and greatly I am obliged to you for it—the interesting little sketches you give me from Washingtons letter renewed many affectionate recollections of that amiable & excellent young Man. We rarely find so much sensibility of heart in one whose varied destiny places them in situations to obliterate past events, and supply the loss of early friends, but I was prepared for such a state of feelings, by some pieces in his book, some passages in "the broken heart"—was a true deleniation [sic] of him-self, and I have no doubt he frequently indulges those bursts of sensibility—which cherishes the memory of her whose opening virtues elicited his first attachment. I hope the success of the sketch book,[2] will give him solid advantages, beside the reputation he gains by it, and that fortune will yet place him where he will be happiest—

I am glad your anxiety is relieved about Edward and hope he will enjoy health, and success in his new home, I was not surprised to hear of Mr Larneds marriage, as he appeared to be of a character likely to serve his own interest in any way, and an additional $1000 p annum was annexed to his salary on that condition, he is more over a vain man and has a good deal of susceptibility respecting his usefulness in the church. I think he is in the only situation, where that would be unequivocal—he is very eloquent and has a fine imagination, full of classical figures, and an enthusiasm of manner & expression that siezes [sic] the attention and charmes [sic] the senses—but among thinking, religious people, who would wish to have a solid commentary on the scripture text, and expect their pastor "to point to brighter worlds, & lead the way" Mr L. would not be so popular—he has not yet become indifferent to the pleasures of vanity. however, in New Orleans he will succeed better than a graver character, and may be excellent to prepare the way for a new view of religion in that licensuous [sic] community—

Have you heard from your Brother James since the dreadful fire at

Savannah? I have been very anxious to learn whether he had escaped injury—he has so often experienced the vicisitudes [sic] of fortune in his youth, that I suppose he has acquired more philosophy than falls to the lot of many of his years. Yet poor fellow, I should grieve if he were again arrested in his course of enterprising industry—

I thank you for thinking of me, when you were pleased with a good preacher—I should like to have heard the sermon—a liberal view of religion is a precious thing from the pulpit and if it were more common, would tend to bring much harmony & good will among men—it has always appeared strange to me, that intolerance should exist among Christian sects, where so little difference of doctrine is to be found—and I have always felt—that judgment belongeth to Him who ruleth, and not to his weak creatures—and therefore I have lived in universal charity with the whole world in religious matters—never the less, I love my own creed best, and am satisfied with it. The late persecutions of the jews in Europe [3] has greatly interested me in their fate—I wonder they do not come to America, if they could only bring enough with them, to feed & cloth [sic] them selves I should think they would be happier under such a government, than with the precarious wealth they accumulate under their oppressors—Mr. Noah is making some exertions to induce them, to such a measure,[4] and some gentlemen to the south have the same object in view—whether they have taken the wisest plans I know not—but methinks I would place foreigners in a more interior situation, both for their own security, and that of our own borders, in case of war—

I saw a letter from Bella, to her sister a few days ago, she is much pleased, and partakes of the hospitality of Charleston with more spirits than she has enjoyed for a long time—I hope the change of scene & feelings will dispell the gloom that has so long clung to her character, and provide her with a good stock of cheerfulness for her friends at home.

Mrs M. is gay as usual, and goes out [a] good deal this winter—she gives a party next Wednesday—[MSS torn: she sent?] me a piece of pleasantry from Mr. Verplancks [5] pen, the purloined box the other evening, and referred me to some others which I shall endeavour to procure—We have been amused with "Fanny" and the Croakers [6]—Your New York Wits are distinguishing themselves this winter. I understand the Croakers have been collected, and printed in a volume, which is not to be had here—if an opportunity offers I should thank you to procure & send it to me—

Another, heavy misfortune has fallen on the distressed family of Goodwin, in the death of poor Thomas, who went to Havanna to settle the affairs of his deceased brother-in-law, he fell a victim to the fever last summer, leaving a large & interesting family in reduced circumstances. With true brotherly affection Thos went to save the wreck of his property for his children—but a fatal destiny, seems to hover over their worldly concerns, and another excellent young man is cut off—What an overwhelming affliction to the poor Mother—one son, in a dungeon with the stain of blood upon his head—an other hurried into a premature grave in a foriegn [sic] land—I knew the family when they were among the most prosperous & happy people I ever saw—the sisters are all lovely interesting women, two of them married to wealthy men with fine families of children—The husbands of both were ruined in business within a few years, the younger recently a widow—and now doubly unfortunate in her brothers—I hope your husbands usual success will attend him, when he pleads the cause of his unhappy client. David B. is very sanguine also, he meant to visit the family, and give what consolations he dare hold out—but the account of Tho's death preceeded [sic] him one day and would perhaps prevent his seeing them—I am sorry Mr H. does not go to Washington this winter, as that would give me a chance of seeing him—My love to him & your dear children—let me hear from you soon again tho I have not deserved it—such charming letters as yours deserves a better return than I can make—but I pay in ardent affection, what I want in agreeableness, and am, my dearest Maria, most truly & devotedly your friend RG—We hear frequently from our Kentucky brothers. Ben [7] is at housekeeping there & very happy.

70. CONSECRATING A SYNAGOGUE

Excerpts from a Discourse by Dr. Jacob De La Motta in Savannah, Georgia, July 21, 1820,[1] with comments by James Madison and Thomas Jefferson

[This address reveals once more the consciousness on the part of the Jews of the measure of equality they enjoyed in the United States in contrast with the plight of "their brethren in foreign lands, writhing under the shackles of odious persecution, and wild fanatacism. [sic]" Jacob De La Motta (born, Savannah, 1789; died, Charleston, 1845) was a distinguished doctor who practised in several cities and was known both to the Jewish and general communities.[2] The comments on this discourse that he elicited from James Madison and Thomas Jefferson, which are here printed after the excerpts, are noteworthy as expressions of democratic policy by two of the greatest men of their time.]

. . . Unequal as I am, to this performance, the incentives to its completion are of no ordinary cast. The objects embraced in this celebration, are of the first magnitude to liberality and religious toleration—its effects beneficial to mankind. It discloses to the enlightened, the devoted state of a people, freed from the house of bondage, and willing to attest it, by an offering of the incense of gratitude, at the shrine of their God. A people! invigorated by the resplendent rays of their faith, would willingly undergo severer probations, than resign their trust. A people! dwelling in a land abounding with "milk and honey," and avowing in the utmost ardency of expression, the blessings they enjoy. A sect! exulting in the privileges guaranteed by the tutelar Goddess of Liberty, to worship God, according to the ritual of their ancestors. A Nation! whom, while appreciating the benefits granted by a spotless constitution, cast an eye to their brethren in foreign lands, writhing under the shackles of odious persecution, and wild fanatacism [sic]; with the fondest hope, the measure of their sufferings will be soon complete; that the gloom of bigotry will be displaced by the light of reason; and that a scattered race, may enjoy the privileges and immunities, *God* intended all should participate. A Nation! who have suffered for their transgressions, but never will be forsaken by *Him,* who appeared and led the way in a "cloud by day, and a pillar of fire by night."

Assembled as we are, to re-establish by commemoration,* the *Congregation* of this remnant, or small portion of the house of Isreal [sic]; your expectation of a brief sketch of our History, and particularly as connected with a primeval residence in this City, and for many years past, even down to our own time, shall be realized; and may I trust, it will not be uninteresting, as it will include the well known fact, that many Jews struggled, and sacrificed their dearest interest, for the independence of this country.

* . . . This day is the anniversary of the establishment of a building which was particularly appropriated as a place of worship, and in which the Jews congregatad [sic] for several years to offer up their prayers. [Footnote in original—Ed.]

* The emigration of Israelites to this City, from the best records and information, is traced to the earliest period of its settlement. The enterprising adventures, who accompanied the first Provincial Governor and Commander in Chief, James Edward Oglethorpe, had not long arrived within the River Savannah, when an additional number, including about twenty respectable Jew families, landed on our shores, on the 11th July, 1733, corresponding with the 16th *Tamus,* 5493, of the Hebrew Calender [sic].

Persecution sustained by bigotry, and strengthened by intollerance [sic], compelled many of our nation to abandon their precarious and gloomy abodes, in Spain and Portugal, and leave their possessions, families and friends. Threatened on all sides by a turbulent storm portentous of complete annihilation, no alternative was left, but flight, torture or death; and the most convenient port was their dernier refuge. Striken by contumely;—assailed by the keenest invectives—the aged and youthful driven from their home; were willing to engage in new adventures, that should promise security, tranquility and liberty. Uniting their destinies and common interest, with many respectable German Jews; they left Europe to sojourn in a foreign land; inspired by the benefits, that encouraging prospects, and a transatlantic clime, offered their migration. At this period the Government of Great Britain, under George 2nd, was transporting to the new country, many individuals, who were allured by proffered possessions in a rich soil, the luxuriant productions of which by proper cultivation, and a ready exportation, held out the means of amassing wealth; independent of the settlement and extension of a distant section of the habitable Globe. To effect this object, several under the munificence of their sovereign, were sent free of expense. Not so with the Jews. Their easy circumstances and high toned dispositions, placed them above the level of incumbents. They came unassisted by bounty.† The distribution of land to the new settlers, gave a portion to each, and certain tracts are still retained by the descendants of those, who possessed the original grants. For respectability—"even tenor of conduct"—correct deportment—and a zealous attachment to the prosperity of the country; the Jews stood on the same eminence with other sects, and by the privileges

* . . . From the want of sufficient *data,* I am unable to particularize the names of the different Israelites, who first arrived in this city; I am however credibly informed, that the most conspicuous of the number, were Benjamin Sheftall, Abram Minis, Dr. Samuel Nunez and Abraham Deleon. [Footnote in original—Ed.]

† . . . It is well known that the Jews paid their passage on their arrival, and refused to receive the king's bounty. [Footnote in original—Ed.]

extended to them in a* civil capacity; they were bound by no common ties, for the general weal. Thanks to the protectors of our liberties, *here* we still continue to boast, and enjoy the same rights. Many Jews removed to other places; several died; and those who remained, continued firm in their attachment. These gradually diminished in 1757 to three or four families, branches of whose posterity are within the sound of my voice; and have acquired as a legacy from their progenitors, that love for the soil, which can only cease with their existence, when the same soil shall have received their mortal remains. Those who deserved the appellation of inhabitants, were soon attached to a place, that from the inducements it afforded, altho' thinly settled, and the advantages to be derived, endeared it to their best regards. Participating alike with all Religions, those benefits the laws then in force enjoined—placed in such respective functions, as tended to elevate and dignify; a union of action kept pace, with a union of sentiment; and in order to strengthen the bonds of society, whose links were rivetted in one general chain; an association was formed, to keep alive the social compact; to extend the commiserating hand of Benevolence; and to evince those noble qualities of the heart, that exalt and adorn our species. A Society was at once established, now aged in years, as well as aged in the best of services, that enrolled as its founders,† an Episcopalian, a Catholic and a Jew. From such a union of opposites in mode of worship,‡ hence the name—but it was a union, predicated on preeminent virtues, and devoted to the best interest of humanity. From this institution, many have derived the substantial advantage of well cultivated minds—to laud that liberality, which disregarded particular tenets, when united for universal good.

The dawn of the Revolution, opened to their view, new scenes; and they revolved in their minds, the condition of their forefathers, who toiled and suffered under the yoke of servitude, during the reign of Pharoh. They saw in prospective, what would probably be their lot. They panted for Liberty and an enjoyment of equal rights, that "nature, and nature's God" intended they should partake. Resolving to separate from the standard of Tyranny, they united with freemen

* . . . At the time the American Revolution commenced, two distinct committees, and a council of safety, were constituted in this city. Mordecai Sheftall, esq. was appointed chairman of the Parochial committee, instituted for the internal regulation of the town and its environs. [Footnote in original—Ed.]

† 'An Episcopalian, a Catholic and a Jew'—Peter Tondee, John Milledge, and Benjamin Sheftall. [Footnote in original—Ed.]

‡ 'Hence the name,' Union Society, established April 23d, 1750. [Footnote in original—Ed.]

for the general good; contended for the independence of the states, and none were found more zealous, more active, more brave, and more patient, amidst the sufferings, that the fortune of war, the cravings of hunger, and the merciless breast, had daily subjected them. Their distresses and privations during the struggle for freedom, constituted conspicuous incidents. When the trump of war marshalled all classes to the tented field, Georgia produced her quota of Israelites, who were found equally as zealous, brave and enterprizing, as others of a different persuasion. The most stubborn inflexibility—the most unshaken integrity—the firmest attachment to American glory, acquired for the Jews the countenance, confidence and esteem of the General Government. Some obtained commissions, and others conspicuous appointments, that at once placed them on the same eminence with other nations; and there yet remains a few of those worthies, to testify their efforts in the general cause. They alike with others, were the theme of applause—the theme of admiration. . . .

. . . Turning from the review of degradation—casting the mantle of oblivion over the frailties and enormities bordering on proscription, that have darkened the path, and sullied the fair prospects, and successful advancement of the Israelites in distant climes; it must be inexpressibly pleasing to the Philanthropist, whose bosom is the receptacle for the generous feelings of humanity, to consider their present condition.

On what spot in this habitable Globe, does an Israelite enjoy more blessings, more privileges, or is more elevated in the sphere of preferment, and more conspicuously dignified in respectable stations? where can similar instances be noticed of the various appointments held by so great a majority of a few of the persuasion? Have we not ample cause to exult? but it is the exultation of grateful hearts, bounding by the impulsive action of transcendent feelings. Sensations of gratitude to Him, who rules the destinies of man, and compasionates the children of misfortune—Gratitude to Him, who has extended his protection to the* "gathering or hope of Israel."

Attentive to the admonition which exhort us to continue worthy of Divine favor, we must not forget those duties, which we owe society as well as ourselves. This is to be maintained, by a proper regard for, and attendance to this House of God; in which we are to render our-

* 'Gathering, or hope of Israel'—The translation of *Mikva Israel,* the name of the congregation. [Footnote in original—Ed.]

selves acceptable in his sight, and deserving his countenance. Were we not influenced by religious zeal, a decent respect to the custom of the community, in which we live, should actuate us to observe public worship. But we need no greater incentive, no stronger inducement, than the imperious mandate contained, and forcibly expressed in our sacred Decalogue. Remember the Sabbath Day—On that day the people of Israel should rest from their labors. Who can expect his soul to rest, who will not rest with his God? On the seventh day he ceased from his great work, and sanctified it; and it was promulgated to all nations of the earth. May it hereafter be perpetually observed: and may it be among this remnant of Israel, as a holy convocation.

In directing our attention to the privileges and benefits proffered to all in this country, and so strenuously aspirated by that palladium of our rights, the Constitution; we are led to forget those days of anarchy and bloodshed, which has stained the annals of other times. *Here,* a liberal and tollerant [sic] spirit, pervades every individual. *Here,* unbiased protection, and friendly co-operation, are alike extended, without consideration or reference to particular faith. *Here,* Justice presents her scale to public view, and guards its preponderance from the touch of illeberality [sic]. *Here,* a union of friendship and fellowship is promoted and encouraged. *Here,* the light of learning discloses the errors that mankind imperceptibly encounter; and it is by this light they are relieved from the vices and follies, incidental to weak-minded bigotry and blind superstition. It is *here,* that we are reasonably to expect the enjoyment of those rewards for our constancy and sufferings, as promised by the word of God, when he declared he would not forsake us. Be it then our care, to merit a continuance of that favor, which has already been extended—to insure a completion of his promise, by a rigid adherence to his commandments, and an undeviating pursuit of that path, which by his protection, leads to that eternal and exalted kingdom, the haven of benignity. . . .*

* . . . the present number of our congregation, including men, women, and children, is between 80 and 100. . . . The ceremony of consecration was according to the used custom, and accompanied with ocasional Hebrew tunes from a well toned organ, that gave fine effect to the Psalms selected; at the same time reviving an ancient custom, and now adopted in some synagogues in Europe, of having music on particular occasions. [Footnote in original—Ed. Although not altogether uncommon in West European synagogues, this is the first recorded instance in American Jewish life in which the organ was used in the synagogue service.]

Savannah, Georgia,[3]
August 7th 1820

Dear Sir,

The services of those who have acted well for their Country, can never be requited; and in a government like ours, the retirement of the first magistrate and relinquishment of his exalted station, does not lessen the respect that the people should at all times entertain for him. Under this impression, and believing that you have ever been, and still continue to be, liberal in your views of a once oppressed people; and confident that you would cheerfully receive any information, appertaining to the history of the Jews in this country; have been induced to solicit your acceptance of a Discourse, pronounced on the occasion of the consecration of the new Synagogue recently erected in our city. I am aware it contains nothing worthy attention, except a few facts in relation to the Jews. And I am imboldened to this act, not only from respect, but for the liberality you possess.

Allow me the honor of considering myself

very Respectfully

Your Ob^{t} Hum^{l} Servt

Jacob De La Motta

His Excellency James Madison &c.

Montpelier, August, 1820[4]

To Dr. De La Motta,

Sir.—I have received your letter of the 7th instant, with the Discourse delivered at the Consecration of the Hebrew Synagogue at Savannah, for which you will please accept my thanks.

The history of the Jews must forever be interesting. The modern part of it is at the same time so little generally known, that every ray of light on the subject has its value.

Among the features peculiar to the political system of the United States is the perfect equality of rights which it secures to every religious sect. And it is particularly pleasing to observe in the citizenship of such as have been most distrusted and oppressed elsewhere, a happy illustration of the safety and success of this experiment of a just and benignant policy. Equal laws, protecting equal rights, are found, as they ought to be presumed, the best guarantee of loyalty and love of country; as well as best calculated to cherish that mutual respect and good will among citizens of every religious denomination which are necessary to social harmony, and most favorable to the advancement of truth. The account you give of the Jews of your congregation brings them fully within the scope of these observations.

James Madison.

[September 1, 1820.][5]

Th. Jefferson returns his thanks to Dr. De La Motta for the eloquent discourse on the Consecration of the Synagogue of Savannah, which he had been so kind as to send him. It excites in him the gratifying reflection that his country has been the first to prove to the world two truths, the most salutary to human society, that man can govern himself, and that religious freedom is the most effectual anodyne against religious dissension: the maxim of civil government being reversed in that of religion, where its true form is "divided we stand, united, we fall." He is happy in the restoration of the Jews, particularly, to their social rights, and hopes they will be seen taking their seats on the benches of science as preparatory to their doing the same at the board of government. He salutes Dr. De La Motta with sentiments of great respect.

71. IMMIGRATION EDITORIALLY ENCOURAGED

Editorial from the *Commercial Advertiser*, New York, October 16, 1822

[It is noteworthy that this influential newspaper should be encouraging German Jews to immigrate to the United States in the hope that "the wealth and enterprize of the Jews would be a great auxiliary to the commercial and manufacturing" interests in our country. Significant also is the respect exhibited for M. M. Noah in this general newspaper.]

THE JEWS

We hastily mentioned some days ago that Mr. Noah had received an appointment from his European brethren. To prevent a construction being placed upon it which facts will not warrant, we took occasion to make inquiry of him relative to the report, and learn that it was a diploma from Berlin, constituting him extraordinary member and correspondent for the United States, of the society for the advancement of science and knowledge among the Jews [1]—which diploma was accompanied by a letter highly complimentary to this country. It seems, (as we are informed,) that the project originally started by Mr. Noah of bringing a colony of Jews to this country to settle in Grand Island, or some other part of the Union, has created a profound interest among this ancient and persecuted people. The conclusion of the continental war has brought back to their coffers an immense sum in cash with which the armies of Europe were supplied, and the same is now lying useless, or producing a very trifling interest. The agency which they exercised in those wars [2]—the importance and political weight of their great bankers—the wealth of the agriculturalists—are singularly contrasted with the national oppression under which they live; and as this people advance in the higher departments of knowledge, they cannot but turn their attention to this happy land, where perfect freedom awaits them.

The wealth and enterprize of the Jews would be a great auxiliary to the commercial and manufacturing, if not agricultural, interests of the United States. A new generation, born in more enlightened times, and having the benefit of education, would be free from those errors generally imputed to the Jews, and participating in the blessings of liberty, would have every inducement to become valuable members of society.—That toleration and mildness upon which the Christian religion is founded, will lend its influence to the neglected children of Israel, who, in the United States, can find a home undisturbed—land which they dare call their own—laws which they will assist in making—magistrates of which they may be of the number—protection, freedom, and as they comport themselves respect and consideration. We shall not be surprised if the views which shall be spread before them should lead to a valuable emigration of these people; and when they perceive one of their brethren honored with the highest executive office of the metropolis of the Union, and exercising a jurisdiction over Christians with Christian justice,[3] they will be satisfied of the practical utility of those institutions which proclaim equal freedom and privileges to all.

We have obtained a copy of the letter addressed to Mr. Noah, and herewith subjoin it.

Berlin, June 1, 1822[4]

Most Honourable Sir,

Amidst the general distress and public calamity under which a great part of the European Jews laboured some years ago, and still are seen to labour, it was indeed no small consolation to every one to whom the fate of our brethren would appear interesting, to hear the noble voice of a most excellent partaker o. our faith, animating the abject spirits of the members of an oppressed nation, by summoning them from an ungrateful and unjust country, to that part of our globe which they style the *new;* but would yet, with greater reason, name the better one.—It was you, honorable sir, that afforded us that sublime comfort. Since that period, the more enlightened and respectable portion of the European Jews, are looking with eager anxiety to the United States of North America—happy to exchange the miseries of their native soil for public freedom, which is there granted to every religion; and likewise, for that general happiness which not the adherents of a privileged faith alone, but every citizen is allowed to share.

The Society, who dare thus address you, united for the purpose of advancing science and knowledge amongst the members of our ancient and holy religion, penetrated in the meantime with the deepest feelings of gratitude for the pleasing prospect, which you have opened to our unhappy brethren, would have deemed itself failing in a most urgent duty, did we not acknowledge the full extent of your meritorious undertaking, by naming you Extraordinary Member and Correspondent General for the United States of North America. In conformity to which appointment, you will receive herewith enclosed, the patent of this nomination, with two accounts of the present state of our Society, which will perhaps, afford a better idea of our views and progress, than this short letter[.]

You would, most honorable sir, infinitely oblige us, if you would transmit every particular information relating to the state of the Jews in America—their progress in business and knowledge, and the rights allowed them in general, and by each State. But you would still more oblige us by proposing such a number of persons who may be able to be members of our society, and who under your Presidentship establishing a distinct society, would form a perpetual correspondence with us about the means of promoting the emigration of European Jews to the United States, and how such emigration may be connected with the welfare of those who may be disposed to leave a country where they have nothing to look for but endless slavery and oppression.

E. Gans, Dr. of Common Law, President; *Zuntz,* Dr[.] Philos. Vice President; *M. Maser* [Moser], Vice Secretary;[5] *Leo Wolf,* M. D. Hamburg, Corr'g Member.

To Mordacai [*sic*] *Manuel Noah,* Esq[.] New York.

72. FAVORABLE REPORT

Committee Report to the Maryland House of Delegates, December 18, 1822 [1]

[After the defeat in 1818 of the bill extending equal rights to Jews, Thomas Kennedy introduced similar bills in 1819, 1820, and 1821 without success. In 1822, however, the first breach was made, with the passage of a bill entitled, "An act to extend to the citizens of Maryland, the same civil rights and religious privileges that are enjoyed under the constitution of the United States." After prolonged debate, the bill was passed in the House of Delegates on January 23, 1823, by a vote of 40 to 33, and confirmed in the Senate on January 30, 1823. Kennedy (1776–1832), who had already for five years led the movement for equal rights for the Jews, was a Jeffersonian democratic-republican of high principle, persistence, and courage. A Scotch Presbyterian, he had come to this country in 1795; in 1817 he was elected to the House of Delegates from Washington County, a back-country Jeffersonian stronghold, and soon thereafter made the campaign for the "Jew Bill" his special interest. The victory achieved in 1822, however, was only the first round. In this report, Kennedy argues that Maryland is handicapped as a state because its unChristian intolerance denies to its citizens the full public use of their merit and ability.]

Mr. T. Kennedy delivers the following report:

The committee appointed to bring in a bill, entitled, "An act to extend to the citizens of Maryland the same civil rights and religious privileges that are enjoyed under the constitution of the United States," respectfully ask leave to report—That they have taken the subject into their serious consideration, and it is a subject of far greater importance than at the first glance may be imagined; it is a subject in which the honor, the character, the interest, and the future prosperity of the state, are all deeply interested.

Religious liberty does not exist in Maryland, for religious liberty cannot be said to exist under any government where men are not permitted to worship God in the manner most agreeable to the dictates of their own consciences, or what is the same thing, denied the enjoyment of civil rights, and rendered incapable of holding any office, civil, military or judicial, except they acknowledge their belief in a particular system of religion.

The constitution of Maryland was framed at an early period of the revolution, when ancient prejudices had a strong influence over the mind, when it was considered as going far in the work of reformation to declare, that there should be no established church in the state; and it certainly required great exertions to effectuate that object, for in Maryland, as well as in other states, even christian sects, catholics particularly, had formerly been proscribed, and we may at once see now [how] strongly these prejudices influenced the minds of the wise and worthy framers of the constitution, when in one breath they declared, (Declaration of Rights, 33d article) "that it is the duty of every man to worship God in such manner as he thinks most acceptable to him," and in the next, that it was only professing christians who were entitled to protection in their religious liberty.

When the revolutionary war was at an end, and the people of the United States had time to give to the principles of government, and of civil and religious liberty, a fair and full examination; when the immortal Washington, and his illustrious compeers, selected from every state in the union, met in convention to frame a constitution, which was ratified by the people of the United States, they unanimously declared, that "no religious test shall ever be required as a qualification to any office or public trust under the United States." Such a declaration, at such time, and from such an assemblage, comprising a greater share of talents, virtue and patriotism, than our own, or perhaps any other country will ever again exhibit, calls loudly for our admiration; they broke the last link of religious tyranny, and put an end to the dominion of superstition; the people, the free, sovereign and independent people of the United States, echoed, and re-echoed, the noble sentiment, "no religious test shall ever be required." Even Maryland joined in the general acclamation, and hailed the glad tidings with joy. And we find the names of a McHenry, a Jenifer, and a Carroll,[2] attached to that instrument, under which the United States have risen to glory and greatness.

The only state which imposes a restriction, in any degree similar to that of Maryland, is that of Massachusetts, which was also adopted during the revolutionary war; and even that is only applicable to a few offices. The state of Maine, which formed part of Massachusetts, and which was received into the union a few years past, has made it a part of her constitution, that no religious test shall ever be required as a qualification for office. The adjoining state of Delaware, was the first to follow the footsteps of Washington in this respect, and to use the same words in her constitution, as in that of the United States. Tennesse[e], Ohio, Illinois and Alabama, have all incorporated the same declarations in theirs; and all the other states have recognised religious liberty, as a "natural unalienable right" (Vide, constitutions of North-Carolina and New-Hampshire); as "an inestimable privilege" (New-Jersey); as a "right to be enjoyed" without discrimination or preference (New York and South-Carolina); "to cause no abridgement of civil rights" (Vermont); that "no human authority can in any case whatever, control or interfere with the right of conscience" (Pennsylvania); "that no person shall be denied the enjoyment of any civil right, merely on account of his religious principles" (Georgia); "that civil rights and privileges shall not be diminished or enlarged on account of religion" (Kentucky and Mississippi); and whenever they have not recognised the most perfect freedom in religious matters, they do not require, as a qualification for office, any other test than a simple oath. Maryland, therefore, stands alone in this respect. And your committee ask with confidence, why should Maryland continue to retain this feature in her constitution, since it has been virtually abolished by the constitution of the United States, and is at once inconsistent with the dictates of reason and common sense, and is not sanctioned by any authority human or divine. We have no right to interfere with the religious opinions of others; we have no right to punish or proscribe those who differ from us on religious subjects; we are all answerable in this respect to our great Creator; to God, and not Man.

Shall that religion, which was announced to humble shepherds on the plains of Bethlem, as the "glad tidings of great joy," as proclaiming "on earth, peace and good will toward men;" that religion which commands us to love our neighbors as ourselves; shall that religion be used any longer in Maryland as a political instrument to deprive worthy and virtuous citizens of their just rights? "Principles are eternal," and whether we proscribe from office ten, or ten thousand citizens, it amounts to the same thing, and is equally contrary to the law of God, which is written in every heart, and directly at variance with that precept which proceeded from the lips of our Divine Lord and Master: "Whatsoever you would that men should do unto you, do you even so to them;" and whosoever controverts this sacred command, may call himself a christian, may be a recorded christian, but he is not a christian in deed and in truth, he is not a real deciple [sic] of the meek and lowly Jesus, who declared that his kingdom was not of this world.

Situated as Maryland is, in the midst of large and powerful states, who have universally thrown open the doors of office and honor to all whose talents and merit entitle them to the confidence of the people, it becomes our interest, as well as our duty, to let the world know, that in Maryland, as well as in the other states, civil and religious liberty is enjoyed in its fullest extent, nor can we hope for prosperity as a state, until we do justice to all men.

Your committee will only further call the attention of the house to the inconsistency of retaining in the constitution a provision which is at war with the principles of civil and religious liberty, and remark, that the same citizen whom the people cannot choose to represent them in the state legislature, may be, by the same people, elected to congress; and may also be elected to the presidential chair; that he who cannot be a justice of the peace in Maryland, may be chief justice of the United States; and he who cannot be an ensign in the militia, may command the army of the nation.[3] Such inconsistency is too glaring, too ridiculous, to be longer tolerated by a free people.

This question has been presented to the consideration of former legislatures in another form. It is now presented to your consideration on what your committee think, is the true ground, on the ground of extending to all the citizens of Maryland, without distinction of sect or name, the same civil rights and religious privileges enjoyed under the constitution of the United States, and surely no danger can arise from our following the examples of our sister states, or from incorporating into the constitution of Maryland the language used in the constitution of the United States, and ask leave to report a bill to that effect. All which is respectfully submitted,

By order, J. COCKEY, Jr.Clk.

And a bill, entitled, An act to extend to the citizens of Maryland, the same civil rights and religious privileges that are enjoyed under the constitution of the United States; which were read.

73. DEFENCE AGAINST CONVERSION

The Preface to *The Jew; Being a Defense of Judaism against All Adversaries, and Particularly against the Insidious Attacks of ISRAEL'S ADVOCATE,* New York, 1823

[It is significant that the first American Jewish periodical [1] was devoted wholly to the attack on organized efforts to convert Jews to Christianity. These efforts were widespread, and the *Jewish Encyclopaedia* says of them: "Inspired undoubtedly by a genuine love for the Jewish nation . . . , 'societies for the promotion of Christianity among the Jews' were started at the beginning of the nineteenth century in Great Britain, and spread under various names over the whole earth, . . . [and they] have done great harm in endeavoring to uproot the faith of a race admired for its steadfast loyalty, . . . " Notable successes in conversion were achieved in Germany, where the semi-feudal oppressors after the Napoleonic wars were so dominant that many Jews decided on conversion as necessary to an economic or professional career; thus from 1822 to 1840, in the reign of Frederick William III, about 2,200 Jews in the larger cities were baptized. In the United States, where the Jews then had a greater degree of equality than anywhere else in the world, outright conversions of Jews to Christianity were few, despite many efforts.]

The right of defence,[2] when attacked, is considered a first law of nature: it is not only inherent in man, but exists with equal strength in the insect and the reptile; hence the adage, "tread on a worm and it will turn." Israel has long been a "worm, and no man;" and has borne (to call it by no harsher name) the gainsayings of the Gentiles.—It has indeed been a long day, "so that none is like it." The day of Jacob's trouble has now endured nearly eighteen centuries. And will it never have an end? will enlargement never come? Has it not in a great measure already come, or at least commenced? For our manifold transgression it has eventuated, as was foretold by Moses, (to whom is peace.) "And among these nations shalt thou find no ease, neither shall the sole of thy feet have rest: but the Lord shall give thee there a trembling heart, and failing of eyes, and sorrow of mind. And thy life shall hang in doubt before thee; and thou shalt fear day and night, and shalt have none assurance of thy life." [Deut. xxviii, 65.]

But is this all that has happened to us? Has not the Lord, blessed be his holy name, also turned our captivity, as he promised us? and may we not now with confidence look for the speedy fulfillment of his word to us:—"That then the Lord thy God will turn thy captivity, and will have compassion on thee, and will return and gather thee from all the nations whither the Lord thy God has scattered thee?" (Deut. xxx, 3.)

He has indeed turned our captivity, and the weight of the curse is taken off from us. We have enlargement; we have assurance of life: our life doth no longer hang in doubt; and we now, blessed be his name, find ease and rest to our feet. There is then no further occasion for the trembling heart, since, like other men, we are secured in life, and property; in short, in equal rights, among which are conceded the rights of conscience;—and, as other men, when our peculiar religious tenets, and our character, as a people, are attacked, we have the right of defence, and the guardianship of the laws, in common with them.

But we are told by our opponents, that "they, above all, have a right to demand that we should never forget the respect which we owe to that great body of men who are firm believers in . . . . . .ianity; who have adopted it after the most deliberate and satisfactory investigation." This language has heretofore been held in a religious controversy among themselves (Carey *v.* English.), and wherein Jews had no concern; and therefore, as we may expect that this, or a similar mode of reasoning will still be used against us, I will concisely consider the weight we ought to attach to it. When *all* enjoy *equal* rights, no party can demand a right ABOVE ALL; it would then be an exclusive right, derogating from the equal right of all; and although I can have no objection to concede the right demanded, I cannot concede it otherwise than a *general* right. Each party ought to be treated with respect, as well in regard to the subject discussed, as to the persons discussing it. The party departing from this course, ought to be apprised of it; but then his departure cannot derogate from the subject discussed, which should not, in any case, lose its right of being respectfully treated of; nor will it warrant or excuse the other party in assuming a like departure. The right of respect belongs to every party, whether consisting of a great body of men, or a smaller number. Numbers may indeed constitute power, but not right:—neither can we make any exclusive concession on account of the *"deliberate and satisfactory investigation;"* for in such a situation stands each and every party, and it is derogating from the respect due the opponents, to presume otherwise.

In questions of great interest and moment, wherein the parties differ so widely, plainness of speech is required, and indeed cannot be avoided. And as truth, and truth only, we are bound to presume, is the object of both parties, plain language should not occasion any soreness of feeling, but be charitably borne with by each. This soreness is the more to be guarded against, both because the plain language which occasions it, dare not be avoided, lest truth, the only legitimate end of controversy, should fail of being discovered by the neglect; and because it is the invariable resort of the unyielding convinced party.

And if any should blame an undertaking of this nature, either as a departure from the usual caution of our wisest men and rabbies, or because of the danger of the undertaking to our nation from ...... ians—I would ask of those to consider, that men as wise as any of our cautious rabbies have thought otherwise, and have victoriously defended Judaism against ......ians:—as the martyr Isaac Orobio, whose crown of martyrdom proves his victory. Rabbi Isaac, the son of Abraham; Rabbi Lipman; David Levy,[3] and Mr. Nicklesburger; of these five worthies, but one met danger, and that was personal only; two wrote in Hebrew, and the two last in English, in England, without damage or danger either to themselves or our community. It is paying a poor compliment to Americans, to suppose them less enlightened than Englishmen:—to such I would say, "The long agony is past!" caution is now fear, and instead of being a virtue, is in truth a weakness. In the present enlightened age, not to defend Judaism, would be considered a tacit acknowledgment that it was indefensible, or at least that we thought so. Not to defend our character as a people, as Jews, by repelling detraction, would be a deriliction [sic] of duty, and might be considered as a proof, either that we had not a character worth defending, or that we despised the good opinion of our fellow citizens, and of the world; and it is a vain expectation to presume that a concession not demanded will be granted: long established habits of uttering a hard and opprobrious language, when speaking of Jews, is considered as a warrantee of its fitness. We have long borne the grief, and carried the sorrowful load, insomuch that now our opponents, instead of charging themselves with speaking oppression, think they are justified, and pronounce us stricken, smitten, and afflicted of God:—and this is not confined to any particular sect, but is the erroneous, prejudiced usage of all Gentiles. Trinitarians, Unitarians, Deists, and even Materialists.—It is unpleasant to rehearse the unwarrantable language used; and we consider it the only unpleasant duty we have to perform; still calumnies must be repelled.

The American Society for Meliorating the Condition of the Jews, began its career under the name of the American Society for Evangelizing the Jews,[4] and only changed the word evangelizing to meliorating, in order to obtain a charter. This purpose answered, it can only be considered as a society instituted to evangelize Jews, that is, to convert them to ......ianity; for, as regards meliorating, nothing further can be done than to allow them equal rights when they become citizens, and which the law provides for, and the constitution guarantees; and we will not begin with a supposition that the intention is to insult Jews, by intimating that their condition is so bad as to want a temporal melioration.* Now, supposing the object of converting Jews to ......ianity to be legitimate—the only proper method must be to convince them of its truth; this done, they will be truly converted; and as it is not very likely Jews can be convinced of the truth of ......ianity till their objections against it are answered to their satisfaction, and since it is believed ......ians, or rather the American Society, are not acquainted with their objections, it is the purpose of this work to state them:—Who knoweth but good may be derived to one or other of the parties, or to both.

But hard, oppressive, and offensive language against Jews must be avoided, or rather entirely expunged, or the object is defeated. Neither persecution or detraction ever yet made a single convert. Men will not listen to arguments, when, with the same breath, they are charged with follies they despise, or with crimes they detest and abhor, as much at least as those who make the charges, and which they utterly deny: and so soon as it shall be ascertained that this object is not to be attained, we then shall know of a surety, that there is no longer any very great danger of the society's gaining many converts from among Jews. We shall then with pleasure leave that part of the field, and shall only, for the sake of our brethren and companions, continue the subject till it is exhausted.

That we may, in God's own way, be instrumental to bring many to righteousness, is the fervent prayer of

THE EDITOR.

* Are gentlemen aware that in all parts of the world Jews provide for the relief of their own poor? that there are, in most cities, societies for that particular purpose? and that such are in this city?[5] Their poor are not indeed enriched, neither are they suffered to want. [Footnote in original.—Ed.]

74. MARYLAND MEMORIAL

Memorial to the General Assembly of Maryland, presented January 8, 1824 [1]

[Since the disabilities to which the Jews of Maryland were subjected were provided for in the State Constitution, the Act which had been passed in 1823 needed to be confirmed by the next legislature. In the elections of 1823, however, this "Jew Bill" was made the main issue: a "Christian ticket" was put in the field that attacked Kennedy and those who had supported the bill as a "Jew ticket." Sixteen of those who had voted for the bill were defeated, including Kennedy himself. When the legislature convened, however, William F. Johnson of Baltimore County obtained leave on December 10, 1823 to bring in the confirmatory act, the management of which, however, was then taken over by Colonel William G. D. Worthington of the city of Baltimore, who had for many years worked for this legislation. The defeat of Kennedy and his associates apparently also stimulated the leading Jews of Baltimore to supporting activity on their own behalf. This memorial, signed by Solomon Etting, Levy Solomon and J. I. Cohen, Jr., and drafted by the latter,[2] was presented to the House by Colonel Worthington two days before the bill was scheduled to come up for debate. In moving terms it presents its argument for the separation of church and state and the equality of all religions. After long debate, nevertheless, the confirmatory act was defeated by a vote of 44 to 28, and the House proceeded to consider "the bill for the preservation of fish in Antietam creek . . . "[3]]

TO THE HONORABLE THE GENERAL ASSEMBLY OF MARYLAND. THE MEMORIAL OF THE SUBSCRIBERS, CITIZENS thereof, RESPECTFULLY REPRESENTS:

Your Memorialists are of that class of the Citizens of Maryland, long subjected to the pressure of political disqualifications, by the operation of a religious test in the Constitution of the State; and they approach your Honorable Body with this their prayer, that an Act passed the 29th of January 1823 "to extend to all the citizens of Maryland the same civil rights and religious privileges that are enjoyed under the Constitution of the United States," may be confirmed by the present session, becoming thereby part of the Constitution.

Your Memorialists, feeling it incumbent on them at this stage of the proceeding, address themselves on the subject, to your Honorable body, in the honest confidence, which the American is educated to entertain in his fellow citizens, and in the legislative guardians of his rights. It is not their wish to obtain from your honorable body, a grant of exclusive privilege; because such a privilege would be hostile, not only to the principles of our institutions, but to the express provisions of that charter which we have all alike, sworn to support; but it is equal rights which they petition; their voice is not raised in favor, but in opposition, to exclusive privilege; they ask an equality of rights with their fellow citizens. If the disqualifications under which they labor, were imposed as the penalty of law for civil delinquencies, for habits of social intemperance, or a disregard of the obligations of religion, they would blush to murmur; but it is, as they humbly apprehend, the retribution for a too honest perseverance in conscientious faith, unmindful of political disqualifications, of social inconvenience, and of individual contumely; and this same manly and virtuous constancy, which, exerted in the causes of their Country, would entitle them to be honored as patriots, exposes them to proscription, when exercised in the service of the acknowledged God. They firmly flatter themselves, and have at length some reason to believe, that your enlightened Councils will suffer no longer, those strange anomalies to endure—that the period has arrived at last, when conscience and reason, the peculiar gifts of an Omnipotent benevolence, will be respected, and persecutions be abandoned to the Inquisitor and the Bigot. Are their doctrines immoral? They are the foundation of the general faith. Are they dangerous? It is no part of them to work conversions. Are they new? Ancient as the revelation of Almighty truth. Your Memorialists, with all humility, are at a loss to understand what there is so peculiarly exceptionable in these their tenets, as to have induced a solitary, but persevering departure, from the sublime system of our American political jurisprudence: why even at this moment, when the whole American pulse throbs with indignation at the civil and religious proscriptions, renewed and asserted in the old world, the good people of Maryland alone, should find it necessary or expedient, to continue for a moment, the disqualification of any class of their fellow Citizens. Your Memorialists beg leave to remind your Honorable Body, that the honors of office in our happy Republic, are not assumed, but conferred; not usurped by guilty ambition, but bestowed directly or indirectly, by popular confidence; that to disqualify any class of your citizens, is for the people to disqualify themselves; can it be necessary, can it be wise or politic at this day, for the people to disqualify themselves on the score of opinion only, from consulting merit in the selection of their public servants?

Your Memorialists do not here propose, a voluminous discussion of the great principles involved in the question, which they desire to bring before you; because it is one, as they apprehend, at this day, almost universally understood. It is the same which has agitated like a tempest, the human family from its earliest existence; has armed the hands of men in wide and desolating wars; has strained nations and families with intestine crime; trampled the charities of life; and driven societies from their natural homes, to seek an asylum more hospitable, on the billows of the deep or amid the recesses of the desert: a question which, as it mainly contributed to populate this our common Country, was here first and fully understood: and one, the liberal and happy results of whose true nature, our own Maryland, though too long misled upon the subject, evinced at the last session of her Legislature, and as your Memorialists trust, will again prove to the world on the present occasion, are deeply felt and thoroughly appreciated.

America, instructed in the school of adversity and oppression, and warned by the calamities of nations, has attained the haven of political happiness, by the guide of political wisdom. Moderate in her might, she has never sought to find in power, the foundation of new rights, but metes out to the weak the same measure with the strong. It was reserved for her to discover, that true policy consists in Justice, which, whilst it secures the confidence and devotion of her own Sons, entitles her to the reciprocity of the stranger. Above all, America has been the first to respect opinion and the human mind, that mysterious and sacred relation of sublunary Man to Celestial Wisdom; nor has thought to control the measureless elasticity of that principle, which created for exclusive allegiance to the Omnipotent alone, is beyond the reach of temporal restraints. America has wisely relinquished it to the insidious policy of regal governments, to make an instrument of religion; she has forever sundered the spiritual from the temporal concerns of men, and convinced mankind that disqualifications and persecution are only fruitful of disunion and hate;—toleration and equal rights, of good will and peace on earth.

Your Memorialists humbly apprehend that a peculiar and most important crisis hath occurred in the political world, and in the history of man; and if in the eastern hemisphere, his struggles for civil and religious liberty, hitherto ineffectual, have been smothered in their birth, it is now particularly important that, successful throughout the west, no speck should endure upon the purity of that code, sublime in its nature, as in its origin, it is confessedly divine.

As fellow citizens of Maryland, as Brethren of the same human family; for the honor of the State, for the great interests of humanity; your Memorialists humbly pray at your hands, that the Bill before you may be confirmed.[4]

75. BEGINNINGS OF REFORM JUDAISM

Memorial to the President and Members of the Adjunta of Kaal Kadosh Beth Elohim of Charleston, South-Carolina, December 23, 1824 [1]

[This memorial, signed by forty-seven Jews of Charleston, is the first document specifically expressing the impulse to Reform Judaism in the United States. This impulse came from the needs of the rising Jewish middle class. These well-to-do business men attempted to adapt themselves as far as possible to the forms of life of the non-Jewish upper class with which they had or sought ever closer relations. Thus the emphasis was laid upon reducing the differences between Judaism and Christianity. The arbitrary rejection of this petition by the leaders of the Congregation Beth Elohim led to the founding of the Reformed Society of Israelites on January 16, 1825, under the leadership of Isaac Harby. Although the Society was disbanded on May 2, 1833, the Congregation Beth Elohim itself was reorganized in 1836, and elected a rabbi who followed the path of the Hamburg Reform Temple. The memorial itself notes an "apathy and neglect" on the part of the Jews of Charleston, then possibly the largest and wealthiest Jewish community in the country, and attributes this falling away to "certain defects which are apparent in the present system of worship." Seeking to check this decline in religious affiliation, the petitioners propose a "more rational means of worshipping the true God," by shortening the services, using English translations of the Hebrew prayers so that they may be comprehensible to the worshippers, abolishing the system of synagogue offerings, and instituting an "English discourse" on religious themes weekly. The text of the petition was drafted by Abraham Moise.[2]]

Gentlemen,

The memorial of the undersigned, showeth unto your honourable body, that they have witnessed with deep regret, the apathy and neglect which have been manifested towards our holy religion. As inheritors of the *true faith*, and always proud to be considered by the world as a portion of "God's chosen people," they have been pained to perceive the gradual decay of that system of worship, which, for ages past, *peculiarly* distinguished us from among the nations of the earth. Not unmindful, however, of the various causes which regulate human conduct; and at the same time, unwilling to shield themselves from any censure to which their actions may justly entitle them, they have ingenuously investigated the reasons which may have led them from the Synagogue, and are now seriously impressed with the belief, that certain defects which are apparent in the present system of worship, are the sole causes of the evils complained of.

In pointing out these defects, however, your memorialists seek no other end, than the future welfare and respectability of the nation. As members of the great family of Israel, they cannot consent to place before their children examples which are only calculated to darken the mind, and withhold from the rising generation the more rational means of worshipping the true God.

It is to this, therefore, your memorialists would, in the first place, invite the serious attention of your honourable body. By causing the Hasan, or reader, to repeat in English such part of the Hebrew prayers as may be deemed necessary, it is confidently believed that the congregation generally would be more forcibly impressed with the necessity of Divine Worship, and the moral obligations which they owe to themselves and their Creator; While such a course, would lead to more decency and decorum during the time they are engaged in the performance of religious duties. It is not every one who has the means, and many have not the time, to acquire a knowledge of the Hebrew language, and consequently to become enlightened in the principles of Judaism; What then is the course pursued in all religious societies for the purpose of disseminating the peculiar tenets of their faith among the poor and uninformed? The principles of their religion are expounded to them from the pulpit in the language that they understand; for instance, in the Catholic, the German and the French Protestant Churches: by this means the ignorant part of mankind attend their places of worship with some profit to their morals, and even improvement to their minds; they return from them with hearts turned to piety, and with feelings elevated by their sacred character. In this consists the beauty of religion,—when men are invoked by its divine spirit, to the practice of virtue and morality.

These results, it is respectfully submitted, would be sufficient of themselves to induce the alterations requested. But your memorialists cannot fail to impress upon the minds of your honourable body, the singular advantages this practice would produce upon the habits and attention of the younger branches of the congregation; besides the necessity of good behaviour, which the solemnity of the service should impose, they would become gradually better acquainted with the nature of our creed, the principal features which distinguish the Jew from every other religious denomination, and the meaning, and the reason, of our various forms and ceremonies. Believing, at the same time, that the above views of what is indispensable to the preservation of our faith, will meet with the approbation of every reflecting and liberal mind—they repeat, that they are actuated by no other motive, than to see our Synagogue in a better, a more wholesome, and a more respectable state of discipline; to see it elicit that regard from Jew and Gentile, which its great character deserves, and should always command; and finally, not to destroy long standing institutions, but to accommodate them to the progress of time, and change of situation and circumstances.

With regard to such parts of the service as it is desired should undergo this change, your memorialists would strenuously recommend that the most solemn portions be retained, and everything superfluous excluded; and that the principal parts, and if possible all that is read in *Hebrew,* should also be read in *English,* (that being the language of the country,) so as to enable every member of the congregation fully to understand each part of the service. In submitting this article of our memorial to the consideration of your honourable body, your memorialists are well aware of the difficulties with which they must contend, before they will be enabled to accomplish this desirable end; but while they would respectfully invite the attention of your honourable body to this part of their memorial, they desire to rest the propriety and expediency of such a measure, solely upon the *reason* by which it may be maintained. Your memorialists would further submit to your honourable body whether, in the history of the civilized world, there can be found a single parallel of a people, addressing the *Creator* in a language not understood *by that people?* It is indeed surprising, that heretofore no innovation has even been *attempted,* although it is readily admitted your honourable body may boast of many very enlightened, liberal and intelligent members.

Your memorialists would next call the particular attention of your honourable body to the absolute necessity of abridging the service generally. They have reflected seriously upon its present length, and are confident that this is one of the principal causes why so much of it is hastily and improperly hurried over. This must be evident to every reflecting mind, when it is seen, that notwithstanding the evil complained of, the service of the Sabbath, for instance, continues until *twelve* o'clock, although usually commencing at *nine*. It is therefore manifest, that, according to the prayer of your memorialists, should the service be in future conducted with due solemnity, and in a slow, distinct, and impressive tone, its length would certainly occupy the attention of the congregation, until two o'clock, if not later.

The *Offerings* will next command the attention of your honourable body; and upon this part of our memorial, we would respectfully crave the favour of a patient hearing, while we clearly set forth the entire uselessness and impropriety of this custom. In the first place, your memorialists earnestly protest against the unwise and absurd practice of rendering in the Spanish language, any offerings which may be intended to benefit the Synagogue, or which may be otherwise identified with our holy religion. Besides the free scope which the practice of offering in a language understood by few, affords to mischievous and designing men to pollute the holy altars by gratifying their evil intentions—we certainly think it highly inconsistent to select for this very purpose, the language of a people from whom we have suffered, and continue to suffer, so much persecution. But forgetting for a moment this consideration, your memorialists would further suggest to your honourable body, whether the arrangement recently made in the financial transactions of the congregation, would not altogether supercede the necessity of any offerings whatever? This is most seriously and strenuously desired by your memorialists, because they are prepared to show, by an act of your own body, that the practice of offering is not the result of any imperious necessity, but merely intended as an idle and absurd indulgence. By the 11th Article of the Constitution of your honourable body, it is provided, that such offerings as are made by any member of the congregation, shall, at the end of the year, be *deducted out of the amount of his annual subscription, as well as that of his wife, if he be a married man.* According to this part of the Constitution, a revenue is *created independent of the offerings which are subsequently made and deducted out of the amount of subscription at the end of the year.* Your memorialists would, therefore, inquire, wherein exists the necessity, under this arrangement, of any offerings whatever? How, and in what manner, the support of the congregation *depends* upon them? and, in a word, whether the above article is not a tacit admission by your Constitution, that so much of the offerings as may amount to the annual subscription of a member, was never intended as a means of supporting the congregation, inasmuch, as the whole amount is *already* anticipated long before a single offering is made! In fact, many persons, when their amount of assessment is exhausted in offerings, are induced to go out and remain in the Synagogue yard, to prevent being compelled to offer against their will,—a practice irregular, indecorous, and highly to be censured,—because it sets an ill example to our children, and draws upon us the eyes of strangers.

Your memorialists are aware, it may be said, that some few subscribers offer *more* than the amount of their annual subscription. But to this it may be answered, that it is certainly not difficult for the general body, in their wisdom and discretion, to devise some means equally profitable to the congregation, and at the same time, as well calculated to meet the views of the *liberal,* without resorting to a practice, which only interrupts the worship of God, and is productive of so little good. Your memorialists therefore respectfully suggest, that the addition in numbers to your body, which it is expected will shortly take place, will greatly aid in the funds, and serve as an additional reason why the offerings should be abolished; but as a further inducement for their entire abolishment, your memorialists would respectfully recommend, the propriety and expediency of addressing to the understanding of the people, and more particularly the younger branches of the congregation, appropriate discourses, *in the place and at the very time the offerings are usually made.*

According to the present mode of reading the Parasa,[3] it affords to the hearer neither instruction nor entertainment, unless he be competent to read as well as comprehend the Hebrew language. But if, like all other ministers, our reader would make a chapter or verse the subject of an English discourse once a week, at the expiration of the year the people would, at all events, know something of that religion which at present they so little regard.

It is also worthy of observation, that a number of Israelites, whom it should be the special care of your honourable body to bring back under your immediate protection and influence, are now wandering gradually from the true God, and daily losing those strong ties which bind every pious man to the faith of his fathers! In these individuals, your honourable body have fair subjects for the holy work of reformation; by moulding your present form of worship to suit their comprehensions, you will instantly receive them among you; they will collect under your especial care and guardianship; they will aid in the pecuniary resources of your holy institutions; and if, from among the whole number now scattered about our city and state, either through irreligion, through disabilities imposed, or any other cause, you are enabled to make but one convert, it will add much to those laudable ends which it should be the principal desire of your honourable body to accomplish. It should also be remembered that while other sects are extending the means of Divine Worship to the remotest quarters of the habitable globe—while they are making the most zealous efforts to bring together the scattered of their flock, offering the most flattering inducements to *all denominations*—we, who may be termed the mere remnant of a great nation, are totally disregarding the fairest opportunities of increasing our own numbers, and at the same time neglecting the brightest prospects of enlarging our resources, and effectually perpetuating our national character.

Your memorialists trust, that they have been perfectly understood by the foregoing observations, that they entirely disclaim any idea of wishing to abolish such ceremonies as are considered land-marks to distinguish the *Jew* from the *Gentile;* they are wholly influenced by a warm zeal to preserve and perpetuate the principles of Judaism in their utmost purity and vigour, and to see the present and the future generations of Israelites enlightened on the subject of their holy religion, so as by understanding, they may learn the nature of its Divine source, and appreciate its holy precepts; that they would not wish to shake the firmness of any man's faith, or take from his devotion towards it; that they will always fervently and zealously support it as the first and most ancient of religions.

The alterations above submitted, being all your memorialists can in reason and moderation require, they would beg leave, in concluding, to bring to the notice of your honourable body, the reformation which has been recently adopted by our brethren in Holland, Germany and Prussia.[4] The following is an extract from a German paper entitled the *"Frankfort Journal."*

"The functions relative to Divine Service, such as the rite of taking the Law out of the Ark, the promulgation of the Law, etc., shall no longer be sold by auction in the Synagogue. The Rabbis, and the Elders of the Synagogue, (the first in their discourses) must endeavor to put an end to the custom of *see-sawing* during the prayers, and to that of repeating the prayers in too loud a voice; all profane tunes during Divine Service are prohibited. The ceremony of striking the *impious Haman* at the festival of Purim, is most strictly prohibited. Children below the age of five years are not to be taken to the Synagogue. All unsuitable pleasantries, in which the young people sometimes indulge in the Synagogues on the eve of some festivals, or on the festivals themselves, as well as the distribution of sweetmeats by the women to each in the Synagogues, are strictly forbidden. Some of the religious ceremonies must be accompanied by a German discourse [that being the vernacular] on a Hebrew text, in which the meaning of these solemnities shall be *explained, and on the Sabbath a discourse shall be held in German* in every Synagogue after the reading of the prescribed passage of the Law, and a chapter of the Prophets."

Thus, from the above extract, it appears, that no climes, nor even tyranny itself, can forever fetter or control the human mind; and that even amidst the intolerance of Europe, our brethren have anticipated the free citizens of America in the glorious work of reformation; Let us then hasten to the task with harmony and good fellowship. We wish not to *overthrow,* but to *rebuild;* we wish not to *destroy,* but to *reform* and *revise* the evils complained of; we wish not to *abandon* the institutions of Moses, but to *understand and observe them;* in fine, we wish to worship God, not as *slaves of bigotry and priestcraft,* but as the enlightened descendants of that chosen race, whose blessings have been scattered throughout the land of Abraham, Isaac and Jacob.[5]

And your memorialists will ever pray.

Signed by forty-seven Israelites of the City of Charleston.[6]]

76. APPEAL FOR CONGREGATIONAL ASSISTANCE

The Hebrew Congregation in Cincinnati to the Elders of the Jewish Congregation at Charleston, July 3, 1825 [1]

[The struggle of Jews in frontier communities amid "the wilds of America" to maintain an organized Jewish religious life is depicted with human warmth in this letter. With other Americans, Jews had pushed west to "where a few years before nothing was heard but the howling of wild Beasts, . . ." Cincinnati then had the only congregation for hundreds of miles around.]

GENTLEMEN:—Being deputed by our Congregation [2] in this place, as their Committee to address you in behalf of our holy Religion, separated as we are and scattered through the wilds of America as children of the same family and faith, we consider it as our duty to apply to you for assistance in the erection of a House to worship the God of our forefathers, agreeably to the Jewish faith; we have always performed all in our power to promote Judaism and for the last four or five years, we have congregated where a few years before nothing was heard but the howling of wild Beasts, and the more hideous cry of savage man. We are well assured that many Jews are lost in this country from not being in the neighborhood of a congregation, they often marry with christians, and their posterity lose the true worship of God forever; we have, at this time, a room fitted up for a synagogue, two Manuscripts of the law, and a burying ground, in which we have already interred four persons, who, but for us would have lain among christians; one of our members also acts as שוחט. It will therefore be seen that nothing has been left undone, which could be performed by eighteen assessed and six unassessed members. Two of the deceased persons were poor strangers and buried at the expense of the congregation, one of whom was brought to be interred from Louisville a distance of near 200 miles.

To you Gentlemen we are mostly strangers, and have no further claim on you, than that of children of the same faith and family, requesting your pious and laudable assistance to promote the decrees of our holy Religion. Several of our members are however well known both in Philadelphia and New York—namely Mr. Samuel Joseph formerly of Philadelphia Messrs Moses & Jonas, and Mr. Joseph Jonas, the two Mr. Jonas's have both married daughters [3] of the late Rev[d] Gershom Mendes Seixas of New York. Therefore with confidence, we solicit your aid to this truly pious undertaking, we are unable to defray the whole expense, and have made application to you as well as the other principal congregations in America and England, and have no doubt of ultimate success.

It is also worthy of remark that there is not a congregation within 500 miles of this city and we presume it is well known how easy of access we are to New Orleans, and we are well informed that had we a

Synagogue here, hundreds from that City who now know and see nothing of their religion would frequently attend here during holidays.

With sentiments of respect & esteem

We are Gentlemen

Your obed[t] sev[ts]

S. Joseph Cha[n] [Hazzan], Joseph Jonas, D. I. Johnson, Phineas Moses [4]

I Certify the above is agreeable to a Resolution of the Hebrew Congregation in Cincinnati

Joseph Jonas. Parnas.[5]

77. NEW ORLEANS' FIRST CONGREGATION, 1828

An Act, To Incorporate a Society of Israelites, in New Orleans, March 25, 1828 [1]

[This charter of incorporation of the first congregation in Louisiana reflects the life of the Jews of New Orleans. The provision of the last article, that "no Israelite child shall be excluded either from the schools, from the temple or from the burrial ground, on account of the religion of the mother," suggests that intermarriage between Jewish men and non-Jewish women was not uncommon, but also that such intermarriage did not necessarily involve separation from Jewish life or the Jewish community. Jewish law required that the child take its faith or nationality from that of the mother; but this charter, to meet an existing situation apparently, alters the custom to make the nationality or religion of the father the determining factor. This congregation was organized at a rather late date, since there had been numbers of Jews in New Orleans from the beginning of the century. In 1824, twelve Jews gathered to organize a congregation, but did not complete the project.[2] When Jacob da Silva Solis, a member of the New York Congregation Shearith Israel, came to New Orleans on business in 1826, he found neither a *matzoth* bakery nor a congregation, and felt impelled to take the initiative to establish both.]

Incorporation of the society.

SECTION 1. *Be it enacted by the Senate and House of Representatives of the State of Louisiana, in General Assembly convened,* That Manis

Jacobs, Aaron Dainels, Isaac Philips, Plautz, S. S. Solis, Bernard junior, Souza senior,[3] and all other white Israelits [sic] living in this City,[4] who may desire to form a society, and their successors, are hereby constituted a body corporate under the name and title of "Shananreen Shosset of the Congregation of Israelites of New-Orleans," and under this title shall enjoy the right of perpetual succession for the space of twenty-five years,[5] and shall be capable in law of owning, purchasing receiving, accepting and holding, possessing and enjoying for them and their successors, all immoveables, lands, rents, inheritances, monies, moveables and effects, whatsoever, by means of all acts, contracts, deeds, purchase and transaction whatever, to receive all donations and cessions, whether intervivos or mortis causa; to accept or reject any legacies or successions; to sue and be sued, summon and be summoned, implead and be impleaded, in all suits and actions, generally whatever, and to enact and put in execution any regulations which may concern said Congregation, and may also have a seal, and may enact bye-laws and regulations for the better government of said society.

Pernassian and Gabaiin.

Sec. 2. *And be it further enacted,* That, said Congregation shall be represented by two Pernassien (wardens senior) and three Gabaiin (wardens junior) and who shall continue in office until others are appointed in their stead, and that no one can be appointed or elected, who shall not be twenty-five years of age, and domiciliated in this city: and *provided, moreover,* that at least one of the Pernassien and one of the Gabaiin shall be married and owner of real estate; and that they cannot continue in office more than five years, and that they shall appoint a keeper, who shall continue in office as long as they shall think proper.

Election.

Sec. 3. *And be it further enacted,* That the election shall take place every year on the eve of the festival of Houshanna Raba,[6] in the month of Tisre, (Corresponding to the month of September,) and the votes shall be given by ballot, in a general meeting called for that purpose, by a notice in two newspapers.

Secretary and Treasurer.

Sec. 4. *And be it further enacted,* That, a Secretary and a Treasurer shall be annually appointed to said society.

Places of worship not to be sold.

Sec. 4. *And be it further enacted,* That the members of said congregation shall not, either separately or collectively, under any pretext whatever, sell, cede, alienate, lease or rent, any of the places consecrated to public worship, or to the burrial of Israelites.

Election may be made at any time.

Sec. 6. *And be it further enacted,* That, in case an election should not take place on the day appointed for that purpose, said corporation shall not be deemed dissolved on that account, and any three members of the Congregation may call a meeting for said election.

Funds, how employed.

Sec. 7. *And be it further enacted,* That, the funds of said corporation shall be specially and exclusively appropriated and employed in erecting or repairing temples, relieving the unfortunate, and in establishing schools for the education of Israelites.

Israelite child not excluded on account of his mother.

Sec. 8. *And be it further enacted,* That, no Israelite child shall be excluded either from the schools, from the temple or from the burrial ground, on account of the religion of the mother.[7]

OCT. LABRANCHE,
Speaker of the House of Representatives.
Ad. BEAUVAIS,
President of the Senate.

Approved, March 25th, 1828: H. JOHNSON,
Governor of the State of Louisiana.

78. GREETING THE FRENCH REVOLUTION, 1830

Myer Moses' Introduction to an Account of the Celebration of the July Revolution, New York City, November 25, 1830 [1]

[The American people, triumphant in having elected Andrew Jackson to the presidency, rejoiced when the news of the July (28th to 30th) Revolution reached New York on September 3, 1830. The democratic Jacksonian press was jubilant. Meetings, parades, demonstrations and festivals were held, despite the hostility of the Whigs and the moneyed interests, in Richmond, Philadelphia, Washington (with the heads of the government participating), Baltimore, New York, and elsewhere. Our minister to France officially reported that he had witnessed "one of the most wonderful revolutions which have ever occurred in the history of the world," and our secretary of state, Martin Van Buren, instructed him to "explicitly state" that our people "are universally and enthusiastically in favor of the change." Of all the demonstrations, that in New York was called "the biggest fête ever held in the country," and thirty thousand came from nearby cities to see and take part in it.[2] Jews figured prominently in the organizing of this great democratic manifestation. When the Committee of Mechanics and Working Men met on November 8, to the original committee of fifteen sponsors there were added 256 names, including those of M. M. Noah, Joseph Dreyfous, Daniel Jackson, Mordecai Myers, Dr. Daniel L. M. Peixotto, Myer Moses,[3] and Lt. Uriah P. Levy of the Navy. The next meeting, on November 12, at Tammany Hall, was presided over by the venerable ex-president James Monroe, while Noah and Daniel Jackson were designated the two secretaries. Dr. Peixotto was placed on the Committee to receive "Deputations from Colleges and Public Schools," Joseph Dreyfous was assigned to the Music Committee, and Noah, Dreyfous and Daniel Jackson were among the 57 on the General Committee of Superintendence and Arrangements. Noah and Daniel Jackson were appointed by Samuel Swartwout, Marshal-in-Chief, as two of the twenty-one Marshals, and Noah, who, as Grand Sachem of Tammany, was especially prominent, was one of four Marshals that marched right behind the leading Squadron of Cavalry in the parade. Distinguished in the military aspect was also Captain John D. Jackson of the Scott Cadets, who mounted guard at Washington Square.[4] The introduction by Myer Moses reflects and exudes the deep democratic sentiments of international fraternity that inspired the American people at the time.]

If there be any event calculated to excite the noblest feelings of our nature it is that of a great nation successfully contending against tyranny and oppression. The struggles and sufferings of the Greeks in the cause of freedom, elicited our warmest sympathy. Their emancipation from Turkish slavery was hailed by us with a generous enthusiasm, commensurate only to the subsequent disappointment occasioned by the annihilation of the hopes we had formed of the establishment of freedom upon the ruins of despotism, in that land where a republic had once so gloriously flourished. The crowned despots, who, under the guise of humanity, interposed between the heroic Greeks and their Moslem oppressors, willed it otherwise; and the descendants of Lycurgus and of Aristides, of Xenophon and of Pericles, read their destiny in the fetters which they are doomed to wear, as the vassals of some crowned despot.

The recent glorious and unprecedented revolution in *France,* which the world beholds with amazement, and regards with admiration, presents to us a picture of a more cheering description. We behold a great nation majestically resume its rights, and severing in a moment the chains which a vile despotism attempted to fasten upon it. Tyranny, resistance, and victory followed in a space so brief, as to seem the effect of miracle. The revolution was effected: its consequences will be felt by all nations, and extend to future ages. No individual can claim the merit of having originated it. Austerlitz had its Napoleon—Waterloo had its Wellington; but the victory of Paris belongs alone to its heroic people. It has been achieved by the people, and for the people; and to them attaches an unrivalled glory, whose brightness shall serve as a guiding light to the world, until nations cease to exist.

During the twenty-five years which the *Bourbons* had been exiled (a period of regeneration and grandeur for France), the condition of society and government had been changed: the principles of equality had been introduced into the former, and that of liberty into the latter. Restored in 1814 by the enemies of vanquished France—the armies of all Europe combined—the *Bourbons* were incapable of appreciating those institutions, which had rendered France enlightened and great, and which had cost oceans of blood, and millions of treasure, to establish. Their first essay at innovation was to proscribe that flag whose variegated colours had, during one quarter of a century, shed a lustre over France, and led her sons to victory and to glory. As a substitute, they displayed that standard which had been so often covered by defeat and disgrace. They at once showed themselves to be the dynasty of the priests and emigrants,[5] and surrendered to their creatures the government, and all else that belonged to, and was dear to the people. It was impossible that liberal and enlightened France could long endure such a state of things. Between the nation changed by the revolution, and the dynasty of the Bourbons, there existed an incompatibility which placed reconciliation out of the question; a contest between the two flags, the white and the tri-coloured—between the two principles, despotism and liberty—between the emigrants and the mass of the nation, was unavoidable. It was necessary that the Bourbons should vanquish and enslave

France for ever, or that *France,* by a bold and determined blow, should exterminate the Bourbons from the land which they had disgraced. That great question has been decided: mistaking the moderation of the people for weakness, their patience for fear, the oppressors heaped wrong upon wrong, until the cup was filled to overflowing. The fire was now to kindle: the blaze was lighted by the *heroic Parisians,* and the three days of their brilliant illumination soon spread throughout regenerated France.[6] The king of France "by the grace of God," whose misrule had made him and his royal house exiles for ever from the land of their fathers, had ceased to govern; and the people, who had conquered for themselves, were fully competent to reflect, and to decide for themselves. *France,* beautiful France, now happy and free, illustrates the power vested in the *majesty of the people.*

It is not difficult to foretel the consequences which must result from this glorious event. A revolution in France is a revolution in Europe—her position constitutes her a centre of motion, and the slightest agitation which affects her, causes a vibration through every other part of the world. Belgium has already manifested its influence, in the successful accomplishment of her freedom and independence.[7] A few noble and patriotic souls have raised the shout of liberty in the now gloomy regions of Spain and Portugal, which will reverberate triumphantly through their vine-clad mountains and fertile valleys. Prussia will feel its effects in Poland,[8] and in its own dominions. Austria trembles for its consequences in Italy and Germany; and even in Great Britain the cause of reform will be advanced by it, in a manner the most effectual. *Russia,* remote as she is, with her extensive territory, her millions of population, her vassals, her lords, and her absolute government, swayed with a despot's power, yet has had scattered within her dominions sparks of the great fire wafted from revolutionary France; they will not become extinguished—some patriot hand will keep them alive.

In our own happy country, the sympathy which it has excited has been general and overwhelming. Statesmen, orators, poets, all contend in amicable rivalry for the honour of becoming its eulogists. The gallant veteran of our own glorious revolution, animated by the triumph of our ancient ally, grows young again in the recollection of his former achievements; with honest exultation he beholds his compatriot and fellow-soldier, the great and gallant Lafayette,[9] by the unanimous acclamation of his chivalric countrymen, exalted to that distinguished situation to which his godlike devotion in the sacred cause of liberty so pre-eminently entitles him. Our yeomanry, the zealous advocates of liberty, the defenders of the oppressed and persecuted of the regions of the earth, the *legitimate* possessors of feelings and principles by the right of heritage from patriot fathers; freemen, not because they are the offspring of the *Republic,* but because they are noble in mind and exalted in character—because they look far beyond their own happy country, and rejoice or regret as their fellow-man becomes unfettered of the chains of tyranny, or sinks the devoted victim of the oppressor's wrongs:—with such a race of men, how boundless the sympathy, how immeasurable the excitement in all that relates to France and to Frenchmen; to that beautiful land that rose from the ruins and devastation of long-protracted wars, and that replaced what the invader's hand had despoiled, with a brilliancy and lustre that bedazzled the admiring world—to that nation of men, identified for the last forty years with all the great political events of the world, and with the most glorious and warlike achievements that the annals of history can produce; looking back to the battle of *Jemmapes,* tracing the long chain of brilliant victories, and at last resting the finger upon that link which points to *Lutsen and Bautzen.*[10] These men, and the sons of these men, have, for themselves and for posterity, broken the sceptre of despotism: they now stand in the erect and noble position of *man.* What their magnanimity claimed from us, they have—our sympathies, our rejoicings. For their happiness and prosperity we offer up our wishes, our hopes, and our desires. For the perpetuity of their institutions based upon *liberal principles,* a solemn invocation to Almighty God. . . .[11]

79. DECLARATION ON POLITICS

Letter to *The Courier,* Charleston, S. C., October 1, 1832, by "Eighty-Four Israelites" [1]

[Even in the 1830s apparently the charge was being made that Jews vote as a unit and that there is "a Jewish vote." This communication, rejecting the accusation, sets forth a principle of the relation of Jews to political questions that has become classic, has frequently been repeated, and is here excellently stated. The Jews of Charleston who signed the proclamation "wholly disclaim any wish or intention to be represented as a peculiar community," and they "discountenance the idea of selecting any individual for office, either of profit or honor, upon the ground that such individual belongs to a particular sect, with the view of securing or of influencing the suffrages of such sect." It should be obvious that Jews in the United States do not vote or participate in political movements as a unit, since they are divided along class, economic, and social lines.]

The meeting of Israelites, held on Saturday night [September 29], was dissolved by an attempt to convert it into a meeting for party purposes. The subscribers unite to carry into effect the true object of said meeting.

WHEREAS, it is understood by the subscribers, belonging *to both parties,*[2] that an impression has been produced upon the minds of a portion of our fellow-citizens, that the Israelites of Charleston are desirous of being represented as a *religious sect* in our State Legislature; and moreover, that a list or petition was put into the hands of the Chairman of the Executive Committee of the Free Trade and State Rights Party, for a representation in the State Legislature.[3] A measure only to be known to be at once disclaimed and disavowed, as calculated to impair the confidence of the community in their independence, their personal pride and their sense of propriety. And, whereas, our political relations are identified in a common bond with our fellow-citizens, a sanction to such a course would indicate a desire on their part to impair the freedom of choice from among their fellow-citizens generally.—Therefore, we the subscribers agree to the following:

Resolved, We unite specially for the purpose of disclaiming, that the Israelites of Charleston have expressed a desire or intention to nominate any individual whatever.

Resolved, That we wholly disclaim any wish or intention to be represented as a peculiar community, and that we discountenance the idea of selecting any individual for office, either of profit or honor, upon the ground that such individual belongs to a particular sect, with the view of securing or of influencing the suffrages of such sect.

Resolved, That the perfect independence of the Israelites of Charleston, is beyond the control of any individual, it matters not to what sect or party he may be attached.

Resolved, That if any lists, from any motives whatever, have been drawn up, and handed about to secure the signatures of individuals, so as directly or indirectly to insist on, or to influence the nomination of any person from either party, such lists are neither sanctioned nor tolerated by us, and must have proceeded from persons not authorized by the will or wish of the undersigned.

Resolved, That while we are sensible there are gentlemen among us, who would do no discredit to any station public or private, we will not support any man for office who is not selected by the public for himself, his character and his talents.

Signed by EIGHTY-FOUR ISRAELITES.

The list is left at the *Mercury* Office, for the signatures of such gentlemen of the Hebrew persuasion as approve the objects expressed in the above.[4]

80. DEATH OF AN ATHEIST

a) "Charles C. C. Cohen," an obituary article in *The Free Enquirer,* Sunday, February 23, 1834 [1]

[This hitherto unnoted figure in American Jewish history seems to have been a man of courage and independent mind whose scientific training and studies led him to discard "the idea of an immaterial mind and the existence of a soul distinct from the laws and affections of matter." It is unfortunate that only the merest fragments of his thinking and writing have thus far been discovered. His death was gruesome: on Saturday, February 16, 1834, seven pounds of fulminating mercury exploded while he was preparing it, blowing off an arm that was never recovered, and killing him instantly.]

The lamentable death of this young but distinguished Chemist has produced considerable sympathy in the public mind, and in briefly presenting this sketch of his life we perform a duty, which, however painful in its exercise, his scientific attainments, his undaunted spirit of free inquiry, and private and social worth, require from us.

He was born in the year 1807 in the suburbs of London, of respectable and wealthy Jewish parents. His mother died in his infancy, and this bereavement operating on a weak constitution, threw his father into a state of insanity in which he died somewhere about the year 1824–5.

Previous, however, to these events he had been placed together with an elder brother, in a Hebrew seminary, at Highgate, conducted by Mr. Hurwitz, now professor at the London University.[2] The rapidity with which he acquired the ordinary exercises of the school, and especially the mathematical ones, was remarkable; but the system pursued excluded initiation in the higher branches of science or mathematics.

Two of his father's sisters became guardians to the children, and the subject of this memoir was removed to their residence; and as they were only distinguished for their rapacity and ignorance, the elements of his powerful mind were left uncultivated and unappreciated, to secure, amidst the formalities of Religion and the mental and moral degradation of his protectors, those sources of knowledge which few, with all the advantages of education, have so thoroughly and honestly explored.

At fourteen years of age he was apprenticed to an apothecary at Walworth; but so little caution was observed in investigating the character of this man, that, although a premium of $800 was given, twelve months had scarcely expired when he suddenly absconded.

From this period he contrived to live on money advanced from his patrimony by his aunts; but such was the confusion of his father's papers, and the nefarious policy of his guardians, that, when of age, he had scarcely sufficient to commence business as a druggist.

During his minority he read all works of literature or science with avidity. As his income afforded him the means of attending the lectures of Farraday [sic] and Brande at the London and Surrey Institutions,[3] he became familiar with the elements of Chemistry:—and pursuing the science under all imaginable disadvantages, he attained considerable proficiency before he was nineteen.

He married in the year 1829, and commenced business in the Islington North Road. But the location was so ill-chosen that he was compelled to wind up his affairs—sell off his stock, and, after remaining a few months with his wife's relatives, set off, in 1829, for New York, with about one hundred dollars in his possession. Saturated with theoretic but ignorant of practical and manufacturing chemistry, he continued under innumerable privations for nearly a year, with one room for a laboratory and a home.

By perseverance his prospects improved, and he became favourably known to the druggists of this city, from which time his circumstances were somewhat easier. His fondness, however, for the higher branches of his profession, and the absence of all worldly policy, exposed him to many difficulties, whilst the expenses attendant on the investigations he was constantly pursuing, straightened his circumstances.

For some years previous to his quitting England he had disengaged himself gradually from the peculiar customs and superstitions of the Jews, and had assimilated his opinions with those of Voltaire, Hume, d'Holbach, etc.[4] These impressions were strengthened by his attending the Lectures of the late Spurzheim,[5] who in vain attempted to weave the doctrines of Phrenology with those of Religion and immortality.

From examining the organization of the brain, its intellectual dependencies, the condition of man under different institutions and governments, and the structure and instincts of animals, he discarded the idea of an immaterial mind and the existence of a soul distinct from the laws and affections of matter.

Since his residence in New York, he connected himself with the Free Enquirers—giving lectures, on useful subjects of knowledge and investigation,[6] and occasionally writing for this publication.[7] The spirited and sensible rebuke given by Mr. Cohen, in our last number, to what he considered the pusilanimous and wavering conduct of Abner Kneeland, indicate at once that he professed honestly to maintain the conclusions of reason and free inquiry. It is not now our intention to defend his peculiar tenets, which are also our own; but his remarkable sincerity cannot but be the object of admiration. The nature of Mr. Cohen's accident prevented his expressing these opinions when about to resign life. However, his constant adherence to them in the vigour of life and intellect, are sufficiently satisfactory to us that superstitionists would have looked in vain for a recantion from him. That a man's opinions should be the most sincere and orthodox on a death-bed, while every impression of science or art is materially and evidently impaired, is a conception worthy only of fanatics, but will weigh little indeed with those who reflect on the operations of the mind in a state of health and disease. The believers in the almost numberless Religions of the earth die peaceably in the contemplation of their respective Deities, and why an Atheist should be conscience strickened when his body was shattered, is strange. However, if any should assert that Mr. Cohen was at once killed and converted by fulminating mercury, we ask for their statements and their names.

Having thus given a brief outline of the character of Mr. Cohen, we turn with regret to review the condition of his widow and three fatherless children now utterly destitute.

So seldom are the charities of Infidels invoked—so difficult is it from their want of organization to unite in concert on such an occasion—that we confidently intreat that the relic and offspring of a fearless champion of Infidelity may receive at the hands of our friends that assistance which bigotry will refuse. The whole christian world is employed in religious speculations, for which the canting voice of Priestcraft collects funds from the admonished flock. Millions are annually expended in Bible and Missionary and Tract societies:—and, exempt as Free Enquirers are from Theological taxes, when an object of humanity presents itself, and the widow and the fatherless plead for food and shelter, shall we remain indifferent, and allow the family of a highly gifted advocate of Infidelity to receive from the hands of christian charity [8] that assistance which we ourselves deny! Let our own union be in inverse ratio to our numbers, and let us show that benevolence may exist without Religion.

Our liberal friends in the country, should also, and it is to be hoped that they will, contribute their mite, not only in supplying the present wants of those who are now deprived of the protection of a husband and father, but in further providing for the education of the three helpless children who look only to public sympathy to befriend them.

Subscriptions will be gratefully received at our office,[9] *free of postage;* and the names or initials, with the sums subscribed for, will appear in the Free Enquirer.

b) Letter by C. C. C. Cohen, *The Free Enquirer,* February 16, 1834

[The subject of this letter, Abner Kneeland (1774–1844), was a Universalist minister who left the Universalist fellowship in 1829, went to Boston, founded the first Society of Free Enquirers and issued the *Boston Investigator,* the first Rationalist journal in our country. On December 20, 1833, Kneeland made the following statement in the *Investigator:* "Universalists believe in a God which I do not; but believe that their God, with all his moral attributes (aside from nature itself) is nothing more than a mere chimera of their own imagination." In January 1834, he was indicted for "blasphemy" and convicted, but his case was being appealed when Cohen wrote this letter in which he criticized Kneeland's line of defense.[10]]

To the Editor of the Free Enquirer.

MR. KNEELAND'S INCONSISTENCIES.

Dear Sir:—I hate cant of all descriptions, more especially in an avowed infidel, and consequently must hate that contained in Abner Kneeland's philosophical creed: for, is it not absurd for him to veil his real atheistic opinions under the jargon of "Hence I am not an atheist but a pantheist; that is, instead of believing there is no god I believe, in the abstract, that all is god, and that all power that is, is god, and that there is no power except that which proceeds from god"—at the same time giving us no rational definition of the word. For my own part I should say I can attach no idea to the word God, and cannot consequently believe in him. From matter proceeds all the phenomena of the universe, and without matter, no part of the universe could have existed, and therefore if God mean matter, or matter mean God, I shall not object to the term God being thus applied; but if God be not matter, then I assert that god cannot either act on or be acted upon by matter, and consequently, it cannot be of any importance to mankind either to admit or deny his existence. The axiom that no substance acts without being acted upon, must of course, be as applicable to God, as it is to the various kinds of matter in the universe; or, if god be excluded from being acted upon by matter, then neither is he capable of acting on it; such a supposition being perfectly absurd, that is to say, at variance with all observed and existing phenomena. Why do atheists shrink from the avowal of their opinions? Because they are ashamed of them? No!—but because they fear they will not make converts if they express their opinions freely. But, Mr. Editor, I would ask, is not silence far preferable to this hypocritical jargon? If Mr. Kneeland means anything peculiarly fine and recondite, let him in endeavouring to communicate his ideas to others, adopt that precept of Quintillian which directs an author to express himself not merely so that he may be understood, but in such a manner that it shall be impossible to misunderstand him; or if he shrinks from the open avowal of his opinions, let him change the name of his paper from *Investigator* to some other title more expressive of a desire to support than to examine into the pretensions of mystery.

I add my name to this, as an example to others of the same or of more orthodox opinions, (if such there be,) in order to induce my fellow man to be fearless in expressing clearly and definitely that which he deems the truth, and not hide his meaning so that his real purpose is totally mistaken. For my own part, I would not wish to make converts to my opinions by any deception; neither would I hesitate to express the result of my researches, and the arguments which led me to such results fearless of consequences; for Truth only is my object in investigation, and with truth as my pioneer, I will in the words of the Poet say, "Go on before I follow thee."

C. C. C. COHEN.

P.S. If Mr. Kneeland is ashamed of being an infidel, let him not any longer edit a paper which requires a fearless investigation careless of consequences. That he is so ashamed is evident from his quoting with approbation, and without comment, the assertion of his counsel, "that no man can be an atheist," at the time that he himself was editor of an avowed atheistic paper, altho' he now fears to admit that such was the fact. His remark, also, relative to obscenity and indecency, come with an ill-grace from one who so highly applauded the "Fruits of Philosophy," a work I cannot eulogise for its delicacy. If Abner Kneeland is disposed to chime in with his persecutors, let him, at least, forbear publishing direct falsehoods in his investigator, for it is certainly false that "no man can be an atheist," and Mr. Kneeland must have known this fact from original articles that have appeared in his paper. C.C.C.C.

c) Reprint of an article by M. M. Noah from his *New York Evening Star* in *The Free Enquirer*, March 16, 1834 [11]

[Noah sees the hand of a just, retributive Providence in the death of C. C. C. Cohen while he was working on the Sabbath and while his atheistic comment on Kneeland was being printed at the same time.]

DIVINE PROVIDENCE.

The untimely and melancholy death of C.C.C. Cohen, the chemist, produced a great sensation generally, but more particularly among those who knew him, and we are gratified to learn that the liberality of his friends will enable his widow and children to return with comfort to their home and family.

Mr. Cohen, though quite a young man, was an excellent practical chemist, and his readings generally were varied, scientific, and full of interest; but in matters of religion, he took a singular and extraordinary turn, and from being well educated in the Jewish faith, he became an *atheist;* and we think we can safely say, almost the only one of that persuasion [12] who, in any change of religion, utterly abandoned and surrendered all belief in a first great cause. Mr. Cohen joined the society of Free Inquirers, and preached atheistical doctrines, and was a correspondent and contributor to their paper; and we now notice this fact to relate a singular circumstance connected with his writings and death.

It is known that the Rev. Abner Kneeland was recently tried and convicted, in Boston, of atheism, and before sentence he published a kind of explanation of his creed, which in a great measure softened, if it did not entirely do away with the belief that he was an atheist. This recantation gave great offence to the Free Inquirers generally, but particularly to Mr. Cohen, who assailed him for so doing in the columns of the Free Enquirer, published in this city. The words of Mr. Kneeland were—

"Hence I am not an atheist but a pantheist; that is, instead of believing there is no god I believe, in the abstract, that all is god, and that all power, that is, is god, and that there is no power except that which proceeds from god."

In an article, which he signs with his name, Mr. Cohen assails such "jargon," as he called it, and makes this emphatic remark—*"For my own part, I should say, I can attach no idea to the word God, and cannot consequently believe in him."* This was printed on Saturday, February 16th, although the paper issues on Sunday; and Saturday, on the very day that such an avowal was made, under the deliberate sanction of his name, he was blown to pieces in his laboratory, while making fulminating powder. His head, we learn, by an understanding among the Free Inquirers, was given to the society for phrenological studies; his arm, which was blown off, has not since, as we are told, been found. Thus, his body has gone one way, his head another, and his limb another—scattered, we may say, to the winds.—Now, philosophers may smile, free-thinkers may laugh, and atheists may ridicule the idea of divine interposition or divine vengeance—all have a right to make their comment. We only state the fact, and, say what they may, it is a singular coincidence of profession and catastrophe. We never have applied the word infidel to an atheist;—he who does *not* believe, no matter in what rules of faith, is an infidel. We are all infidels in some things, but an atheist believes in nothing. Our laws, even in this free country, punish certain offences against religion, such as blasphemy, profanity, indecent railings—they punish, because these are offences against society—against public feeling—they are *contra bonos mores;*—but we assume the fact that no law should punish a man for being an atheist, because no human tribunal should assume the power of punishment on a point which belongs to God himself. Besides, if there is danger from infidelity—from open revilings of religion—there is none from atheism, for converts are seldom made to doctrines against which all Nature cries aloud. We intend no reflection on free inquirers by these observations. We know many of them personally, and know them as worthy men, whom we would trust, who have good feelings, and moral principles; and while we look with surprise and regret at their infatuation on this point, we would not abridge a single right which they possess, as citizens, to believe in what they please, so that society and good government are not thereby injured. Poor Cohen was a Jew, a well-educated Jew—of all nations on earth the last to renounce their God—his chosen and favoured people—he who brought them out of the land of Egypt—from captivity and bondage—who was their cloud by day, and their pillar of fire by night—who gave into their safe-keeping the great moral law which now governs every civilized nation—he who even now keeps them together as a distinct and separate nation for great objects hereafter. To disclaim, and renounce, and deny that God, is a most rare and extraordinary instance indeed! To so live without faith, and die without hope!—to openly deny the existence of God, and in the same moment, as it were, be hurried into his presence!

If men cannot believe, will not believe, let them be silent, and not proclaim to the world their heresy with the view of making converts.

We place the above article on a permanent record in our columns, as an impressive example of the effects of religious faith upon the human understanding; and we select it from among the common multitude of coincident examples with which the literature of the day abounds, because its value, as a philosophical lesson, is greatly enhanced by the celebrity and unquestionable energy of the writer's intellectual powers, and by the general candour and liberality of his character. . . .

81. AGRICULTURAL PROJECT

Address to the Jews of the Association Zeire Hazon (Tender Sheep), New York, Spring, 1837 [1]

[Prevented by feudal restrictions from becoming farmers in European countries, many of the Jews coming to the United States exhibited an active desire to acquire land and farm it. Under capitalist relations, however, in which the most honorific rewards are financial, better economic rewards were given to the urban than to the agricultural population. Especially for people without farming experience, it was easier to make a living in the city than on the farm. Immigrants who were poor, moreover, had that additional obstacle to interfere with any desire to settle on the land, since both land and implements required a capital outlay. Nevertheless, the Association Zeire Hazon, most of whose members had come from Germany "within the last three years," was eager to secure Jewish community support for the organizing of a settlement on the Western prairies both to solve their own economic problems and "to add so much lustre to the Jewish character." The year 1837, however, was a bad one for such an undertaking: the crop failure of 1835 had prevented many farmers from meeting their payments to land speculators and merchants; the panic of 1837 swept the land and by the end of May not a bank in the country was able to pay in specie; the sale of public land dropped from $20,000,000 in 1836 to $1,000,000 in 1841, in which year special Congressional legislation enabled 39,000 persons to cancel $441,000,000 worth of debt. The crisis lasted more than five years.[2]]

This Association, in accordance with a resolution adopted at the time of its organization address their brethren throughout the United States; in refference [sic] to the character of their association, and the purposes for which it was instituted. It is well known, that, every year, a greater or less number of Jewish Emigrants arrive in the different ports of this country; and that within the last two years their number has greatly increased; many of them, particularly those from Germany, are mechanics and agriculturists; and would do well, could they locate themselves, together, in some part of this country suitable for their purposes: but this, situated as they are, without the means necessary for such an undertaking, they are unable to do; [t]he result of which is, they are compelled to remain in the cities; where, in consequence of their being unable to compete with the native workmen, on account of the Sabbaths, and Holidays, and their ignorance of the language of the country, they are, from necessity, forced to engage in occupations of a triffling [sic] character, which tend to lessen their own respectability, and that of the society of which they are members. Under these circumstances, it is evident that something must be done to remedy the evil, both for these already here, and those who may hereafter arrive; the high price of rent, provisions, fuel, and other necessaries of life, the want of proper employment, and of fitting schools, to which they may send their children, to receive general and religious instruction; renders it necessary, that they should remove to some other location, where those difficulties may be obviated: As it is at present, all their time is employed in endeavouring to gain a support; and all the means that they can thus accumulate are spent in obtaining the bare necessaries of life; so that they are unable to lay up anything for their families, or to attend, properly, to the instruction of their children, who, if their situation should continue the same, must grow up destitute of that moral restraint so necessary to their becoming useful and intelligent members of society.

The members of this Association are mostly from Germany, and have arrived here within the last three years. Since their arrival, they have endeavoured to gain a livelihood by pursuing their different occupations, but owing to the difficulties with which they have had to contend, on account of their religion, and the high price of the necessaries of life, as already stated, are unable to lay up anything for their future support; in consequence of which, and the prospective misfortunes that must attend their families, should they remain where they are, they have organized themselves into an association, for the purpose of removing West, and settling on some part of the Public Lands, suitable for agricultural purposes. They are aware of the difficulties with which they will have, at first, to contend; and are prepared to meet them; as they are conscious they will last but for a short time, and that they will be soon enabled to command a competence; while, at the same time, they will be making a permanent provision for their children; those however are not the only benefits, which, in their opinion, will arise from this undertaking, but they will point out the way to others, and will, perhaps, be instrumental in founding an institution, which, in its future effects, may be productive of the most brilliant results.

That something should be done, to remedy the present state of things, is sufficiently evident, the number of Jewish Emigrants arriving in this country, continually increases, and owing to the arbitrary enactments which have recently been made in Hesse Cassell, and other states of Germany, a still greater number may be expected to arrive hereafter. The only way in which the evil resulting from such a rapid increase of population, in so short a time, can be averted, is by adopting the plan of our Association, and forming a settlement in some part of the Western Section of this country, when, what would otherwise have been an injury will become conducive to interests of the greatest importance.

To effect the object which this Association has in view, it is necessary, that they should be provided with the requisite means; the members of it depend, on their own labour for their support, as before stated; and consequently, are not possessed of an amount sufficient, to enable them, unaided, to carry so great an undertaking into effect; they are, therefore, compelled to have recourse to their brethren for assistance, trusting, that this appeal to their liberality, will not be in vain; and that an undertaking which promises to add so much lustre to the Jewish character may not fail for want of the trifling means necessary to ensure its success.—The means required, are for the purpose of enabling us to procure the different impliments [sic] of agriculture, the stock and materials necessary for farming purposes, and provisions, sufficient to last until a crop can be raised: The amount required for which purposes, is but triffling [sic], and which, if our brethren will but exhibit that liberality so conspicuous in their character heretofore, can easily be obtained.

The site which the Association intend locating on, will be some portion of the Government Lands in the west; this section of country being on account of its extreme fertility of soil, and mildness of climate, the best adapted to agricultural purposes, and in consequence of the immense quantity of rich, prairie land, which it contains, peculiarly fitted to a people, unacquainted with the labour of clearing a thickly timbered country; and who would be, in fact, inadequate to such a task.

One of the leading objects of this Association is the formation of a Congregation, wherever they may locate, for which purpose they will provide themselves with a שפר and ספר תורה besides there being several of their number duly qualified to act in the capacities of שחט and מול [sic].

The members of this association, are averse to removing separately into the country, as they have observed, with regret, that most Jews who do so, lose all respect for their religion, and by becoming blended with the general mass, not only forget their religion, but too often, those great moral precepts, and restraints which that religion inculcates. . . .

By Order of the Association

S. H. Jackson, President

Attest. T. W. Donovan, Secretary [3]

82. AID THE NEEDY IMMIGRANTS!

Circular addressed to Jews, New York, September 3, 1837 [1]

["Whereas a very great number of our nation, in very indigent circumstances," arrived in the city of New York, the Jewish community took steps to help at least the most needy. In 1836, it is estimated, there were about 2,000 Jews in the city connected with the synagogues; by 1840, the number increased to about 7,000, which implies a high rate of immigration. The percentage of synagogue-connected Jews in relation to the general population increased from .7% to 2.2%.[2]]

The undersigned have been appointed an Executive Committee, for the purpose of raising funds to aid and assist persons, recently arrived from foreign countries, and who may be in a destitute situation.

In addressing you, it is proper to state that a meeting was convened, of a number of the House of Israel, at the suggestion of the officers of the several Hebrew Benevolent Societies,[3] to take into consideration the distressed situation, of a great number of Israelites, lately arrived in this city from foreign countries. The funds of the different Societies having been nearly exhausted.

The gentlemen composing the meeting, having interchanged opinions, adopted the following Preamble, preceeding certain resolutions, one of which was as follows:—

"Resolved, that the Executive Committee be, and they are hereby impowered, under their hands and seals, to authorize such persons as they may think proper, to solicit Subscriptions in money, fuel, clothing, or such articles of food as the charitable and humane may be disposed to contribute."

PREAMBLE.

Whereas a great number of our nation, in very indigent circumstances, have arrived in this city, from different parts of Europe, and the probability of a number more shortly arriving the situation of most of them being such as to demand the attention and sympathy of every feeling heart; independent of the bounden duty we are under, as Yehudim, to assist each other in distress, and the bounden obligation by which we are commanded so to do, in Deuteronomy, Chap. 10, v. 19. ואהבתם את הגר כי גרים הייתם בארץ מצרים as read in Synagogue on the last Sabbath, *Love ye therefore the stranger: for ye were strangers in the land of Egypt.* And in Deut. XV. 11. פתח תפתח את ידיך לאחיך לעניך ולאביונך בארצך *"Open thy hand wide unto thy brother, to thy poor, and to thy needy, in thy land."*

And as the funds of the Congregations [4] and the different Societies, are not in a situation to afford relief to the great number that may absolutely require the same, and as the approaching cold weather may find them in a still more deplorable situation: the present season should not be suffered to pass without taking some measures to provide a fund, at least sufficient to supply the destitute, with the means to keep them from perishing.

The Executive Committee met on the evening of the 29th of August, and appointed Mr. Samuel N. Judah,[5] their Treasurer, and also, the following Gentlemen to hand round the subscription lists.

Messrs. SOLOMON J. JOSEPH, ABRAHAM MITCHELL. } No. 1.

Messrs. ELEAZER S. LAZARUS, MORLAND MICHOLL. } No. 2.

Messrs. T. I. TOBIAS, MYER LEVY. } No. 3.

In furtherance of this pressing business, you will be waited on by one of the above Committees and we trust and pray that this first call ever made in behalf of so great a number of strangers, will be answered by the usual liberality of our brethren.

The number already arrived is at least 3 or 400, and the probability that an equal number are now on their way to this country, and mostly bound to the port of New-York.

In addition to the duties of the Executive Committee, they will, as far as the funds admit, assist such persons as may be disposed to leave the city, and also endeavour to procure work for those who have trades.

An account of all donations will be duly entered on the minutes of the Committee, and a full and correct Journal kept of all proceedings, and which will always be open to the inspection of the contributors.

Relief in fuel, &c. will be delivered in preference to money, which will only be given under special circumstances of the applicant. The Committee, deem it quite unnecessary to make any appeal to the feelings of their brethren: satisfied as they are that they have never failed to answer the call of the distressed.

Constituting this Committee your almoners, will, in a great measure, relieve yourself from private calls.

We are respectfully

Your humble Servants,

Moses L. Moses, Abraham Mitchell, Solomon J. Joseph, Morland Micholl, Israel B. Kursheedt, T. I. Tobias, Eleazer S. Lazarus, Myer Levy, Naphtali Phillips.[6]

83. THE DAMASCUS BLOOD LIBEL

Consular Report to the Department of State, March 24, 1840 [1]

[The false and malicious accusation that Jews kill Christians in order to use their blood for ritual purposes at Passover is still being circulated, even in the United States.[2] The charge was first made against particular Jews in England in the twelfth century, and since then almost 200 cases are on record.[3] In the nineteenth century, even before the Damascus Affair of 1840, there were fifteen such cases in Romania, Poland, Russia, Italy, and Germany. That none of these preceding cases aroused the animated attention of both the Jews and non-Jews of several continents to the extent that the Damascus affair did is due to the interaction of two factors in the Damascus case: first, Damascus and its vicinity was in 1840 at the center of a vortex of imperial rivalry among Britain, France, Russia, Austria, and Prussia for the solution of the "Eastern Question," the name given to the process of the disruption of the Turkish empire; secondly, Jews had become increasingly influential in several countries. When, in February 1840, the Jews of Damascus were first imprisoned and tortured to make them confess to a ritual murder, almost all the consular officials in the area believed the charge, and, as is proved by the report of the American consul, published here for the first time, were sympathetic to the persecution of the Jews. With the exception of that taken by our own government, which then had no imperialist interests in the Middle East, the action of the Five Powers was determined primarily by the strategy of empire. In this particular situation, the relationship of forces was favorable to the cause of the Jews and justice.

The essential features of the situation are the following: Syria, in which Damascus is situated, was then controlled by Mehemet Ali (1769–1849), the Governor of Egypt, who had revolted against the Turkish Sultan in 1831 and conquered Syria in 1833; in the spring of 1839 the Sultan tried to reconquer Syria, but his army was defeated, and the Sultan died on June 20, 1839, to be succeeded by the sixteen year old Abdul-Mejid I. Mehemet Ali was now in a position to conquer all of Turkey and establish a new dynasty, but that plan for a new strong Turkish empire ran counter to the interests of England, Russia, Austria, and Prussia, which operated in such a manner that by October 1840 Mehemet Ali had been stripped of Syria and other territories and compelled to be content with Egypt alone. Russia, interested in the Straits, opposed the disruption of the Turkish empire because it preferred to conquer it as a unit, while also opposing Mehemet Ali's objective of unifying the Turkish empire because he might be strong enough to prevent the conquest by Russia.[4] Britain sought dominance in the area in order to guarantee its route to India, and regarded Russia as a threat to that aim. Austria, opposing Russia and particularly France, supported Britain. These rivalries were temporarily subordinated, all Four Powers regarding France as the greatest menace because French policy, with Thiers as foreign minister from February 20 to October 29, 1840, was aimed at securing its own dominance in the area by vigorously supporting Mehemet Ali. It took Four Power diplomacy and the Allied fleet to defeat France and Mehemet Ali.

In Syria itself, France was an important element because since 1535 it had enjoyed a "protectorate" over Christians in Turkey; it was the French consul who was the prime mover in the blood accusation; it was Thiers and the French Catholic and even some of the liberal press who backed up the consul. The Jews of England and France, although indignant at the charge of ritual murder and fearful of the consequences of not discrediting it, were slow to react in aid of their brethren because the leaders of the Jewish communities were not unmindful of the objectives of their own foreign offices.[5] Sympathy and fear were curbed by "tact," but when the British foreign office was ready, and the French foreign office was hopelessly opposed, an Anglo-French Jewish delegation finally went to Alexandria, Egypt. In the far off United States, action on the part of the Jewish community came even more slowly, and followed in the wake of London.

The following report of the American consul at Beyrout is a truly amazing document. Of the utmost significance, however, is the fact that the policy and conduct of our government were in direct contradiction to the views and sympathies expressed by our consul.]

United States Consulate
Beyrout 24th March 1840

Sir,

I have the Honor to relate briefly for Your Honours consideration some details of a most Barbarous secret, for a long time suspected in the Jewish Nation, which at last came to light in the City of Damascus, that of serving themselves of Christian Blood in their unleavened Bread at Easter, a Secret which in these 1840 Years must have made many unfortunate victims.

On the 5th of February last the Revd Capouchin Thomas [6] president of the Catholic Church of Damascus—together with his Servant having, all of a sudden disappeared from that City H. E. Sherif pashaw Governor General of Syria and the French Consul [7] of Damascus employed actively the pollice for making all strict inquiries after them, and some people having declared to have seen that priest and his servant enter on that evening in the Jews quarter, the suspitions of Government fall on the Jews, that they might have assassinated them.

On that day Revd Thomas had put up against the wall of a Jew Barbers shop, a written advertisement for some Articles to be sold by Auction, and was observed that the said advertisement had been removed from its place and put up again with different Wafers than those used by the priest. The Jew Barber was questioned and taken into prison, and after the application of some torments on his person he confessed that the Revd Thomas had been beheaded in the house of David Arari a rich Jew, by Seven of his coreligioners of Damascus,[8] and that, in order to take his Blood, it being ordered by their religion to make use of Christian Blood in their Unleavened Bread at Easter.

The Seven Jews thus accused, as well as all their high Priests; 64 Children, belonging to those families, and all their Butchers were immediately taken to prison, and after severe Tortures [9] and threats several of them confessed also the fact of the murder, adding that they had since cut the body in small pieces and threw it in a Canal, after collecting all the Blood in a large Bottle for religious purposes, which Bottle they had given to their high Priest. The Pashaw and the french Consul accompanied by Massons and a multitude of People went immediately to the spot, and having searched, they found in reality the Revd Thomas's body all cut in small bits, which were put in a Pinn Box and burried with a grand Prossession in the Church.[10]

The torments on the prisoners having continued, some of them confessed that the Servant also had been beheaded in the house of another jew, his Blood taken to the last drop, and his body cut in the same way like that of the Priest was thrown in another Canal. The Pashaw and the french Consul repared to the place and found that body also in pieces together with three sharp knives. The Murderers of this last are not yet arrested they having made their escape from Damascus, but the Pollice is after them actively employ'd. The Bottle of Blood neither has been found as yet.

The inquisition against the jews in that City (in which there may be 30000. Souls of that Nation) continues with much vigour and no jew can show his face out in the streets.

The french Consul is seizing all their religious Books with a hope of clearing that abominable secret. He found a Book printed in Latin, by "Lucio Ferrajo"[11] in which the passages are found taken from the Talmoud, which I have the honor to accompany in french.

Several of the prisoners in prison have died of the torments of the inquisition, and others turned Turks and the rest in number Seventy two are sentenced to be hanged, but the french Consul has requested to postpone their death in the hope of finding out through more torments the Bottle of Blood, which they pretend to have already distributed to their coreligioners in the different other City's.

In .the place where the Servants remains were found a quantity of other human Bons of old date in small bits have been discovered, which proves that they were accustomed in that house to such like umane sacrifices. A Doctor bribed by the Jews declared the Servants Bons to be those of some Beast but the Pashaw having since called a Commission of several Doctors they pronounced them to be umane.

I have the Honor to be with great respect, Sir,

Your Most Obedient Humble Servant

J. Chasseaud [12]

To The Honourable John Forsyth
Secretary of State, Washington

84. ENGLISH PUBLIC OPINION ON THE DAMASCUS AFFAIR

a) The Lord Mayor of London to the American Minister in England, July 8, 1840 [1]

[The report of our Consul given above was not received at our State Department until June 27, 1840. Meanwhile, the leaders of the Jewish communities of London and Paris had begun to act; on April 21, 1840, there was a meeting of the Jewish Board of Deputies at the home of Sir Moses Montefiore, and a delegation of eight was designated to wait upon Lord Palmerston, Secretary of State for Foreign Affairs. Palmerston received the delegation on April 30 and "promised to use his influence with Mohhammad Ali and the Turkish Government to put a stop to such atrocities."[2] Six weeks later, the Board of Deputies met again, this time with Crémieux [3] present, from Paris, as well as representatives of the English synagogues. There Sir Moses was asked to head a delegation that would go to Damascus and Alexandria; after a meeting at the London Great Synagogue repeated the request, Sir Moses agreed to go. By this time, Lord Palmerston was deep in the arrangements that finally led, on July 15, 1840, to a Four Power treaty between England, Russia, Austria and Prussia on one side and Turkey on the other, whereby the Powers undertook to compel Mehemet Ali to accept the Sultan's terms and restrict Mehemet Ali's power chiefly to Egypt and deprive him of Syria and other territories. When Sir Moses Montefiore and Baron Lionel de Rothschild visited Palmerston therefore on June 24, 1840, "Lord Palmerston was most friendly."[4] On July 3, 1840, public opinion was crystallized still further by a huge meeting called by the Lord Mayor of London, which passed the resolutions that are the subject of the correspondence that follows.]

Mansion House
July 8th 1840

Sir,

As the Chairman of the Great Public Meeting of the Merchants, Bankers and Traders of the City of London on the subject of the persecution of the Jews in the East. I have the honor to send herewith a copy of the Resolutions unanimously passed at that meeting requesting that your Excellency will be pleased to transmit such resolutions to your Government and in the confident expectation that that which has excited so deep an interest in England will ensure the Sympathy and support of the Government you represent.

I have the honor to be Sir

Your most obedient servant

[Signed] Chapman Marshall
Mayor

To his Excellency Andrew Stevenson [5]
32 Upper Grosvenor St[t]

b) The American Minister to the Lord Mayor of London, July 13, 1840

[Uninstructed by the State Department, Mr. Stevenson expressed his "deep sympathy in favor of these oppressed people."]

32 Upper Grosvenor Street
13th July 1840

My Lord,

I have the honor to acknowledge the receipt of your letter of the 8th instant, inclosing to me, for the purpose of transmission to my Government, the Resolutions, adopted at the meeting of the Merchants, Bankers, Traders and others of the City of Lonon, held at the Egyptian Hall on the 3[d] July, in relation to the cruelties practised towards the Jews in the East.—

I beg to assure your Lordship that I will take an early opportunity of transmitting these Resolutions to the President of the United States and I cannot do better Justice to my own feelings, or those which I feel confident will be entertained by the President and people of the United States, in relation to the subject of these resolutions, than to seize the occasion of expressing my deep sympathy in favor of these oppressed people.

I have the honor to be,

Your Lordships, Obedient Servant,

[Signed] A. Stevenson

To The Right Honorable The Lord Mayor

c) The American Minister to our Secretary of State, July 24, 1840

[Two weeks after receipt of the resolutions, Mr. Stevenson transmits them to the State Department.]

John Forsyth Esquire
Secretary of State, Washington.

Legation of the U. States.
London July 24. 1840.

Sir,

I transmit to you the inclosed Copies of Papers received a few days ago from the Foreign Office, respecting a Schooner called the 'Euphrates' equipped for the Slave Trade and having Papers as an American Vessell signed by the Vice Consul of the United States, at the Havanna. I simply acknowledged the receipt of the Papers with an assurance, that they would be forwarded for the information of my Government—

Papers of the Schooner 'Euphrates,' as a Slaver—

I also forward certain Resolutions of the Citizens of London upon the subject of the late persecution of the Jews in the East, with a Copy of the Lord Mayors letter, and my reply.

Resolutions of City London as to persecution of Jews—

I am Sir, very respectfully

Your obedient serv[t]

A. Stevenson

(d) The Resolutions Passed, July 3, 1840

[The meeting and the resolutions were very widely reported in the London and New York press.]

At a meeting of the Merchants, Bankers, Traders and others of the City of London, held in the Egyptian Hall, in the Mansion House the 3rd day of July 1840.—

WILLIAM THOMPSON Esquire M.P. and Alderman, at first in the Chair and afterwards The Right Honorable The Lord Mayor.—

It was moved by John Abel Smith Esq[re] M.P.[6] seconded by John Masterman Esq[re], and unanimously agreed to.—

1 That this meeting has heard with the deepest emotion and with the greatest horror the recital of the cruelties inflicted upon the Jews in the East and hereby expresses the deep sympathy of the Christian Public for the sufferers and its earnest hope that an immediate and impartial public investigation will take place so as to disprove in the face of the whole world the atrocious calumnies invented and propagated by their persecutors as a pretext for the infliction of cruelties almost unknown in the previous history of manking [sic].

It was moved by Sir Charles Forbes Bart, seconded by John Bowring Esqr L.L.[7] and unanimously agreed to.—

2 That this meeting deems it right thus publicly to declare its abhorrence of the use which has been made of torture for the purpose of extorting confessions from the unhappy persons accused its utter disbelief of the confessions thus obtained and its earnest hope that this relic of a barbarous age will be from henceforth abolished and that those just principles which have in European States secured to the accused a fair and impartial trial may be speedily extended to every Nation throughout the World.

It was moved by Samuel Gurney Esquire, seconded by James Morrison Esq: M.P.[8] and unanimously agreed to.—

3 That this Meeting expressed its deep regret that in this enlightened age a persecution should have arisen against our Jewish Brethren originating in ignorance and inflamed by Bigotry and it offers its anxious prayer that through the diffusion of sound principles of religion in every Country all Men may be considered as alike entitled to protection and to the benefit of just laws impartially administered.—

It was moved by Geo: De H. Larpent Esq:[9] seconded by Samuel James Capper Esq: and unanimously agreed to.—

4 That this meeting cannot separate without expressing its gratification that many persons of distinguished rank and station as well as the Government of this Country have testified their willingness to uphold and support the cause of suffering humanity and it hereby offers its thanks to The Right Honble Lord Palmerston Secretary of State for Foreign Affairs for his prompt interference and also to the Right Honble Sir Robert Peel [10] and other Members of the Legislature for the kind interest they have taken in this question.

It was moved by the Right Honble Lord Howden seconded by the Honble and Revd Baptist W: Noel [11] and unanimously agreed to

5 That the above resolutions be transmitted to her Majesty's Gov-

ernment and to the Representatives of the different powers resident at the English Court with a request that they will transmit them to their respective Governments.–

It was moved by Daniel O'Connell,[12] Esq. M.P. seconded by Wolverley Attwood Esq. M.P. and unanimously agreed to

6 That the Cordial thanks of this meeting be given to the Right Honorable The Lord Mayor for his readiness in calling the meeting and granting the use of his Hall and to Alderman Thompson M.P. for his kindness in taking the Chair for the ability with which he has presided over this meeting and for his general attention to the interests of this City.–

C. Marshall, Mayor

85. OUR STATE DEPARTMENT AND THE DAMASCUS AFFAIR

a) The Secretary of State to John Gliddon, our Consul at Alexandria, Egypt; Washington, August 14, 1840 [1]

[Minister Stevenson's letter and the Resolutions printed above were received at the Department of State on August 10, 1840. By that time, the Jewish delegations headed by Montefiore and Crémieux had arrived at Alexandria (August 4) and had the first interview with Mehemet Ali (August 5), who was then much more concerned with studying the Four Power ultimatum than with lesser matters. In addition to presenting a petition with reference to the Jews of Damascus, the delegation also transmitted the address of the London meeting of the Society for the Abolition of Slavery, which both Montefiore and Cremieux had attended in June, and Mehemet Ali, procrastinating, preferred to discuss the latter.[2] Of these developments, our State Department in those days of slow communication could not know. However, four days after the receipt of Minister Stevenson's despatches from London, the Department expressed its official views and instructions to our Consul at Alexandria, "to employ, should the occasion arise," his efforts in support of those already made by "several of the Christian Governments of Europe."]

Sir:– In common with all civilized nations, the people of the United States have learned with horror, the atrocious crimes imputed to the Jews of Damascus, and the cruelties of which they have been the victims. The President [3] fully participates in the public feeling, and he cannot refrain from expressing equal surprise and pain, that in this advanced age, such unnatural practices should be ascribed to any portion of the religious world, and such barbarous measures be resorted to, in order to compel the confession of imputed guilt; the offences with which these unfortunate people are charged, resemble too much those which, in less enlightened times, were made the pretexts of fanatical persecution or mercenary extortion, to permit a doubt that they are equally unfounded.

The President has witnessed, with the most lively satisfaction, the effort of several of the Christian Governments of Europe, to suppress or mitigate these horrors, and he has learned with no common gratification, their partial success. He is moreover anxious that the active sympathy and generous interposition of the Government of the United States should not be withheld from so benevolent an object, and he has accordingly directed me to instruct you to employ, should the occasion arise, all those good offices and efforts which are compatible with discretion and your official character, to the end that justice and humanity may be extended to those persecuted people, whose cry of distress has reached our shores. I am, sir,

Your obedient servant,

[Signed] John Forsyth.[4]

b) The Secretary of State to our Minister in Turkey, Washington, August 17, 1840 [5]

[Three days after the letter to our Consul at Alexandria, the Secretary of State wrote to our Minister at Constantinople "to prevent or mitigate these horrors." Of particular interest is the definition of the "distinctive characteristic of our government," that its "institutions, political and civil, place upon the same footing, the worshipper of God, of every faith and form, acknowledging no distinction between the Mahomedan, the Jews, and the Christian." None of the Four Powers with which the Sultan was then allied would even have claimed as much.]

David Porter Esq.[6]

Sir,

In common with the people of the U. States, the President has learned with profound feelings of surprise and pain, the atrocious cruelties which have been practised upon the Jews of Damascus and

Rhodes,[7] in consequence of charges extravagant, & strikingly similar to those, which, in less enlightened ages, were made pretexts for the persecution and spoliation of these unfortunate people. As the scenes of these barbarities are in the Mahomedan dominions, and as such inhuman practices are not of infrequent occurrence in the East the President has directed me to instruct you to do everything in your power with the Government of his Imperial Highness, the Sultan to whom you are accredited, consistent with discretion and your diplomatic character, to prevent or mitigate these horrors, the bare recital of which has caused a shudder throughout the civilised world; and, in an especial manner to direct your philanthropic efforts against the employment of torture in order to compel the confession of imputed guilt. The President is of opinion that from no one can such generous endeavors proceed with so much propriety and effect, as from the Representative of a friendly power, whose institutions, political and civil, place upon the same footing, the worshippers of God, of every faith and form, acknowledging no distinction between the Mahomedan, the Jews, and the Christian. Should you in carrying out these instructions find it necessary or proper to address yourself to any of the Turkish authorities you will refer to this distinctive characteristic of our government, as investing with a peculiar propriety and right the interposition of your good offices in behalf of an oppressed and persecuted race among whose kindred are found some of the most worthy and patriotic of our citizens. In communicating to you the wishes of the President I do not think it adviseable to give you more explicit and minute instructions, but earnestly commend to your zeal and discretion a subject which appeals so strongly to the universal sentiments of justice and humanity.

I am, sir, yr:obt: svt:

J. FORSYTH.

86. AMERICAN JEWS AND THE DAMASCUS AFFAIR

a) The Jews of New York to the President of the United States, August 24, 1840 [1]

[On August 19, 1840, the Jews of New York finally held a public meeting on the Damascus Affair, more than a week after our State Department had already sent its instructions to our Consul at Alexandria. It took another five days to dispatch the resolution adopted at the meeting to the President.[2]]

To His Excellency Martin Van Buren, *President of the United States.*

Sir:—At a meeting of Israelites of the City of New York, held on the 19th inst., for the purpose of uniting in an expression of sympathy for their brethren at Damascus, and of taking such steps as may be necessary to procure for them equal and impartial justice, the following resolution was unanimously adopted:

Resolved, That a letter be addressed to his Excellency, the President of the United States, respectfully requesting that he will direct the Consuls of the United States, in the Dominions of the Pacha of Egypt, to co-operate with the Consuls or other agents accredited to the Pacha,[3] to obtain a fair and impartial trial for our brethren at Damascus.

In transmitting the same to your Excellency, we beg leave to express what we are persuaded is the unanimous opinion of the Israelites throughout the Union, that you will cheerfully use every possible effort to induce the Pacha of Egypt to manifest more liberal treatment toward his Jewish subjects, not only from the dictates of humanity, but from the obvious policy and justice by which such a course is recommended by the intolerant spirit of the age in which we live. The liberal and enlightened views in relation to matters of faith, which have distinguished our Government from its very inception to the present time, have secured the sincere gratitude and kind regard of the members of all religious denominations, and we trust the efforts of your Excellency in this behalf will only serve to render more grateful and to impress more fully on the minds of the citizens of the United States, the kindness and liberality of that Government under which we live.

With the best wishes of those in whose behalf we address you—for your health and happiness, and for the glory and honor of our Common Country, we have the honor to be,

Your Excellency's obedient servants,

J. B. Kursheedt, Chairman.

Theodore J. Seixas, Secretary.[4]

b) The Reply of our Secretary of State, August 26, 1840 [5]

Washington, *August* 26, 1840.

Messrs. J. B. Kursheedt, *Chairman,* and Theodore J. Seixas, *Secretary.*

Gentlemen:—The President has referred to this Department your letter of the 24th inst., communicating a resolution unanimously adopted at a meeting of the Israelites in the City of New York, held for the purpose of uniting in an expression of sentiment on the subject of the persecution of their brethren in Damascus. By his direction I have the honor to inform you that the heart-rending scenes which took place at Damascus had previously been brought to the notice of the President by a communication from our Consul at that place, in consequence thereof, a letter of instructions was immediately [6] written to our Consul at Alexandria, a copy of which is herewith transmitted for your satisfaction.

About the same time our Charge d'Affairs at Constantinople,[7] was instructed to interpose his good offices in behalf of the oppressed and persecuted race of the Jews in the Ottoman Dominions, among whose kindred are found some of the most worthy and patriotic of our own citizens, and the whole subject, which appeals so strongly to the universal sentiment of justice and humanity, was earnestly recommended to his zeal and discretion. I have the honor to be, gentlemen,

Very respectfully,

Your obedient servant,

John Forsyth.

87. MINISTER'S REPORT ON THE DAMASCUS AFFAIR

a) Our Minister in Turkey to the Secretary of State, United States Legation, St. Steffano, October 17, 1840 [1]

[Having received his instructions, David Porter promises to comply with them "when necessary," and to be "on the alert" even when the "interest of my country" is "not immediately concerned."]

Sir,

I have the honor to acknowledge the receipt of your instructions of the 17th of August last, communicating to me the views of the President as to the course to be pursued by me in respect to the cruelties practiced upon the Jews of Damascus and Rhodes, and in all other cases where torture shall be employed in order to compel the confession of imputed guilt which, when necessary, shall be strictly complied with.—

The Hatti Schrieff [sic] of Gulhanah which His Highness the Sultan has sworn to support, copy of which I had the honor to send you on the 8th of November last,[2] will I hope prevent in future the necessity of my taking any steps when the interest of my country are [sic] not immediately concerned, but as I shall be always on the alert in every thing, when my interference will prevent humanity from being outraged, I shall be governed by the benevolent and philanthropic views of the President, as communicated in your instructions.—

The interest shown by Europe in the cruelties practiced under the Government of Mehemet Ali, for which His Highness the Sultan is not accountable, and the investigations and punishments which have been the consequence, will it is expected, deter others from the same practices in future.—

I have the honor to be With great respect

Your Ob^{t} Servt

[Signed] David Porter

b) Our Minister in Turkey to the Secretary of State, November 16, 1840 [3]

[Our Minister continues to reassure our government.]

Sir,

Jews of Damascus and Rhodes.

I have the honor to send you an Extract from a paper published by the authority of the Turkish Government,[4] by which you will perceive that it would be unnecessary that any further steps should be taken by me for the present in the affair of the persecution of the Jews at Damascus and Rhodes.—

I have the honor to be With great respect

Your obd^{t} serv^{t}

David Porter

c) Our Minister in Turkey to the Secretary of State, November 4, 1840 [5]

Sir,

I have the honor to send you an extract from a letter from Mr. Brown [6] the U.S. Dragoman of the Legation, with the copy of the Translation to which it refers.

Respecting the Jews of Rhodes and Damascus.

I have the honor to be With great respect

Your ob^t^ serv^t^

[Signed] David Porter

d) The Sultan of Turkey instructs the Judges of Constantinople, November 6, 1840 [7] (Translation)

[The Sultan declares that the blood accusation is "erroneous," that "it is fully proven" that Jews are not only "prohibited from using human blood but even that of animals in their sacrifices," and that "it is therefore evident that the accusations are false and pure calumnies." He ordered that "the Jewish people of my Empire . . . must in no manner be unjustly molested by any one, either in the performance of the ceremonies of their Church, or in their domestic quiet and tranquility."]

It having been heretofore currently believed by the public that Jews were in the habitual practice of sacrefizing [sic] a human being and making use of his blood at their fast of unleavened bread (Pasover); as a consequence of this erroneous belief, it has been brought to my Imperial knowledge, that some time ago several unfortunate individuals subjects of my Sublime Porte, resident in Damascus and the Island of Rhodes, have been calumniated and subjected to various vexations and tyranical persecutions.—

A short time only has elapsed since several Jews from the Island of Rhodes were brought to this Capital, and tried by the new regulations of justice and equity, and by the decision which was made after the trial, as also from the affidavits of several persons of talent and capacity who examined their secular books, it is fully proven that not only are they prohibited from using human blood but even that of animals in their sacrifices.—

It is therefore evident that the accusations brought against them are false and pure calumnies; and as the allegiance of the Jews to our authority is undoubted, they should in no wise be permitted to suffer from such absurd slanders, and moreover as by the protective principle which I entertain, and the Imperial Charter read at the Gul Khaneh, to the Jewish people are secured the same privileges and preemminencies which are given to the other subjects of my Empire, and they protected and defended accordingly. In consequence of this the Jewish people of my Empire being worthy of perfect protection and defense they must in no manner be unjustly molested by any one, either in the performance of the ceremonies of their Church, or in their domestic quiet and tranquility; for such is my Imperial will and determination, and to this purpose the present edict has been issued, signed with my Imperial sign manual, and given to said people.—

Now when this becomes known to you, who are Chief Judge, you will be careful to act in conformity to the above injunctions, and in order that nothing hereafter may be done contrary to this edict, you will register it in the Archives of the Tribunal, and deliver it to the Jewish people.—

Constantinople Ramazan 12: 1256.
November 6: 1840.

By your very ob^{t} serv^{t}

[Signed] John P. Brown.

Pera Nov:^{br} 21:1840.[8]

88. AN ART DEALER

Letter from Aaron Levy to M. M. Noah, August 10, 1842 [1]

[Whether or not Aaron Levy's establishment was, as he maintained, the "Only One of the Kind devoted to the fine Arts in the United States,"[2] this letter is of interest as the expression of one of the earliest art dealers in the nineteenth century.]

My dear Sir

My Object is to call the attention generally, and particularly to Strangers. to my present establishment,. having been established for many Years, and it being now the Only One of the Kind devoted to the fine Arts in the United States, it requires the aid of a good Doctor like yourself to renovate and bring it to a healthy Stand My collection of paintings. at present consists of an extensive number both modern and Ancient, amongst them are the works of *Cole, Shaw,. Wall* & *Vanderlyn*[3] justly celebrated for their works of Art, Also the Great picture by Whichelo[4] the destruction of Jerusalem 22 by 14 feet. a picture of Great & Sacred Interest, Also the Splendid painting. ordered by Prince Murat.[5] and Sold in his collection valued at $4000, when first bro^t^ to this country,. Christ & the Adultress & Charity two beautiful & masterly pieces by Guercino.[6] Holy family by Schidone[7] with numerous fine Cabinet & furniture pictures. with new varieties adding every Day. and which for the present are Offered at private Sale at very reduced prices, as you have the power of writing men into the presidential Chair[8] so well you can write A. Levys establishment 151 Broadway. into More Notice where Ladies & Gentlemen may pass an hour with much interest

Yours truly

A Levy[9]

89. FIRST FRATERNAL ORDER

Preamble to the Constitution of the Independent Order B'nai B'rith, 1843

[The first Jewish fraternal society in the world was founded in New York on October 13, 1843, when Henry Jones and eleven other German Jews organized the B'nai B'rith (Sons of the Covenant), today the largest, wealthiest, and most conservative of the fraternal orders. Among the founders were two shopkeepers, two jewellers, a tailor, a shoemaker, and a barber, and one hazzan and a synagogue clerk.[1] With eight congregations then operating in New York and very little unity among them, this group assumed "the mission of uniting Israelites in the work of promoting their highest interests and those of humanity . . . "[2] Since, however, as the preamble indicates, a few of the functions undertaken by the B'nai B'rith were such as had been fulfilled, in European countries, by the synagogue, some hostility was exhibited to it and to similar orders later for fear that they would divert

Jewish life from religious to secular preoccupations.[3] Yet it has not hitherto been noted by historians that the first lodge was organized after "a number of Israelites had, on account of their religion, been refused admittance in the Odd Fellows Lodges" of New York.[4]]

B'nai B'rith has taken upon itself the mission of uniting Israelites in the work of promoting their highest interests and those of humanity; of developing and elevating the mental and moral character of the people of our faith; of inculcating the purest principles of philanthropy, honor and patriotism; of supporting science and art; alleviating the wants of the poor and needy; visiting and attending the sick; coming to the rescue of victims of persecution; providing for, protecting and assisting the widow and orphan on the broadest principles of humanity.

90. POOR RELIEF

Report of the Committee of the Society for the Education of Poor Children and Relief of Indigent Persons of the Jewish Persuasion, New York, January 30, 1843 [1]

[Although records in which unemployed and impoverished Jews directly describe their struggles are not available for this period, some inkling of their condition is given in this report through the eyes of three wealthy Jews who were active in providing "relief." Thus we learn that "vast numbers of poor Jews are compelled to crowd into very small and unwholesome tenements, occupying but one or two small and uncomfortable rooms, and in many cases only one, and where the family consists of many individuals"; that rents are "enormous" and evictions frequent. Yet the capitalists who wrote the report could not forbear apologizing for the landlords by "explaining" that "the frequent default of payment renders it necessary that such prices should be exacted!" Nor is it amusing to read that one argument for building the projected "Shelter" for destitute and homeless Jewish families is that then "many of our charitable females" would be able to visit the poor, while "at *present* they are restrained from visiting the poor by the objectionable locations of their dwellings, driven as they are by their impoverished condition to seek such abodes." The face of this "charity" is not pleasant to behold.

The crisis of 1837–1843, however, was laying bare the fact that even then capitalism was not able permanently to supply the needs of the working masses. To palliate some of the most awful conditions, sections of the upper classes went in for philanthropy, and by 1840 there were more than thirty relief societies in New York city alone, but it was not until 1843 that the New York Association for Improving the Condition of the Poor was founded, with an apparatus that covered every ward in the city.[2] Among the Jews there were the following societies to aid the poor at the time this report was made: the Hebrew Benevolent Society, founded in 1822; the Society for the Education of Poor Children, etc., founded in 1827, and the New York Hebrew Assistance Society, founded in 1840.[3] The latter two bodies were organized by leaders of the Congregation Shearith Israel.

The signatories to the report were men of high economic standing: Benjamin Nathan (1813–1870) was a banker and member of the New York Stock Exchange; Henry Hendricks (1804–1861) was a member of the firm of Hendricks & Brothers, whose copper-rolling mill had been established in 1812; and Solomon I. Joseph was a senior member of a brokerage house.]

The Committee appointed at a meeting of the Society for the Education of Poor Children, &c., held on Sunday 8th January, 1843, to report forthwith upon "the expediency of extending the usefulness of this Society by a more permanent mode of extending relief to indigent persons of the Jewish persuasion, and to confer with the Hebrew Assistance Society for their co-operation therein, and such other matters connected therewith as may seem pertinent and appropriate to the objects here pointed out,

RESPECTFULLY REPORT:

That your Committee, fully impressed with the great importance of the subject submitted, have given to it their most serious reflection and deliberation, and are the more fully impressed with the many and undoubted advantages which must flow from the propositions they now submit, if carried into effect.

The Education Society was incorporated on the 11th April, 1831, for the following purposes, as by the 1st article of By-Laws:

I. Relief of the orphans and widows of deceased members.

II. Elementary and Religious Education and Trades to such orphans, and to the children of indigent Jews, giving a preference to those of indigent or deceased members. And in all cases, where evidence of superior talent in any child shall manifest itself, to extend, if practicable, a liberal education.

III. Aid to all Jews in distress, under such regulations as may hereafter be prescribed.

It is just as it is evident that the first claims on the assistance of the Society should be those of the widows and orphans of deceased members; and your Committee deem it even a matter of so much importance, as to suggest a By-Law more general in its character, and granting pensions to the widows of indigent deceased members, and which might induce many individuals to become members of the Society. Instances have occurred where widows and orphans have been largely, in fact, very essentialy benefited by reason of the membership of the husband or parent in such societies; and such are the vicissitudes of fortune that, in these cases, the members could have no presentiment that their survivors would require such aid.

The efforts of the Education Society to educate and bestow useful trades to orphans and children of indigent Jews, have unfortunately proved fruitless. Three boys were fed, clothed and educated, and severally bound to mechanics to acquire their trades, but none of them realized the wishes or intentions of the Society, and in no other instance has the Society succeeded in this branch of their duties. Your Committee deem the education of orphan children as one of the first principles of charity; but the system now adopted by the Society is so narrow in its action as to make it entirely useless. Again, the public schools in this city, now in existence, are so extensive, and the system of education adopted so liberal, that your Committee are of opinion that orphans placed in these schools can receive as good an education as from a school emanating from this board, while at the same time they can receive instruction in the Hebrew language from the Polonies Talmud Torah School, now in operation. Your Committee are, therefore, of opinion, that the 1st and 2d sections of article 1st should be more generally carried into effect. The 3d section of article 1st, to render it more useful and effectual, should be based upon the following system, which your Committee have no doubt will receive the support of the Hebrew Assistance Society. Your Committee having conferred with the board of managers of said society, herewith annex a series of resolutions passed at a meeting of the Board on 24th instant.[1]

It is first proposed that the Education Society and Assistance Society be merged into one institution, under such regulations and by-laws as may hereafter be agreed on, for the purpose of raising sufficient funds, by a joint contribution, for the erection of an asylum for the poor, the dispensing of charity, and the education of poor children.

Second, that a space of ground be purchased, and a building be erected, 100 feet long by 35 feet wide; that the building be three stories high, and each two rooms be connected by a door.—That a certain number of these rooms be rented out at a moderate rent to those who are able to pay, and others be disposed of, rent free, for a limited time to deserving objects.[5]

It is very evident that vast numbers of poor Jews are compelled to crowd into very small and unwholesome tenements, occupying but one or two small and uncomfortable rooms, and in many cases only one, and where the family consists of many individuals; for these rooms they are obliged to pay an enormous rent without the corresponding comfort which should attend them. Although frequently being unable to pay these rents, they are thrust into the street and forced by their destitution to seek a like tenement. The prices of these rents might appear to afford a large income to the landlord, but the frequent default of payment renders it necessary that such prices should be exacted. In numerous cases these poor families, if assisted with the means of paying their rents, are capable of earning an honest, though very scanty livelihood. It is a matter of every day's experience with the charitable societies that the principal (in most instances exclusive) wants of the poor are the means of defraying rent. It therefore becomes very desirable to afford the poor, but worthy Israelite in distress, the comforts of a shelter; and while every other denomination have built asylums and hospitals for the poor and sick, we Israelites have never attempted such an undertaking.

The funds of the Education Society now amount to ($7,000) Seven Thousand Dollars; and, by the second article of the By-Laws, one half of the interest of this amount, being ($245) two hundred and forty-five dollars, is dispersed in relieving the wants of the poor and educating poor children. Thus it appears, that during the existence of this Society, a period of 12 years, little more has been done than very gradually increasing its permanent fund. Its members have dwindled to sixteen, and a general apathy exists among them which destroys the little good they might otherwise accomplish, while the Hebrew Assistance Society has been only three years in existence, now numbers sixty members, and has distributed aid to one hundred families during the last year; and on comparison with its usefulness during this period, we find its course has been onward in its work of charity.

In the year 1840 its disbursements amounted to ..... $660 05.
In the year 1841, to .... $801 47.[6]
In the year 1842, rising .... $1,390 00.

It is true it has added nothing to a permanent fund, nor has it encroached on the legacy left it by the late Washington Hendricks,[7] amounting to Fifteen Hundred Dollars: your Committee therefore are of opinion that the union of these two Societies will infuse new life into the Education Society, and arouse its energies which now lie dormant and useless, and the influence of the Assistance Society towards the erection of an asylum will strengthen our ability to attempt its erection. Your Committee, therefore, strongly recommend the union, and suggest that the By-Laws be altered so as to meet the views of the Assistance Society, and tend to elevate this Society in the estimation of our brethren.

Various plans might be submitted for the payment of this building and the necessary grounds; but as the Assistance Society have appointed a Committee,[8] in conjunction with a like Committee from this Society, for this specific purpose, your Committee deem it improper to encroach on their duties; they are, however, of opinion, that if the two Societies are united, they can accomplish this most desirable object.

The trustees of the Congregation Shearith Israel expend annually to pensioners, for rent, $500, which is the interest at 7 per cent. per annum on ($7,000) Seven Thousand Dollars. Whether all this class of persons who receive this bounty would be willing to live in an asylum, is questionable; but your Committee are of opinion that many would gladly avail themselves of it: your Committee therefore think that the congregation would contribute, either by a donation or by yearly contributions, towards the erection of a building which would be a monument of the liberality of the Israelites of this city.

It is very evident, that for active and efficient charity, our own people will come forward and aid us, with a liberal hand, with the requisite means of benefiting our poor and unfortunate fellow-creatures. But, in order to make our appeals forcible and effectual, we must demonstrate to them the *practical* utility of our efforts and labors. When we spread a report of our doings, by their means, it inspires them with feelings proper to our cause; but if we are enabled to take them to a spot where we can point out a structure raised by their aid, and which shall afford shelter to numbers of our poor—if we can carry them through a clean and properly ventilated suite of rooms, we can thereby make a silent appeal to their charity far beyond any effort of tongue or pen. It will have the good effect of making manifest to the more prosperous of our people the situation and necessities of the poor. Many of our charitable females, whether members of societies or otherwise, would have opportunities of visiting and ministering to their health and wants. At *present* they are restrained from visiting the poor by the objectionable locations of their dwellings, driven as they are by their impoverished condition to seek such abodes. To those who are of opinion that charitable institutions increase pauperism,[9] we would say, come with us and visit the abode of the poor—see them with their baskets but poorly furnished with a few articles, whereby they can realize a few paltry cents. Follow them a day, through all kinds of weather, and watch their return at night, exhausted by their protracted journey through the city and country, with the proceeds of their work—look at their rooms, bare and unfurnished, without fuel, their children without clothing, and then ask if a few dollars given to them can increase their poverty or be ill bestowed. But there is still a higher object attained by charitable societies—it is, that by the assistance and encouragement afforded to well-directed industry, persons laboring under great temporary embarrassments, by a small amount granted them, are enabled to continue or resume their pursuits for a living, thereby rendering themselves independent of seeking further aid; and instances have occurred where such classes have refunded the amount given.

By the sixteenth article of the By-Laws, no alteration or amendment shall be made, unless proposed at a stated meeting, and agreed to at the next, by a vote of two-thirds. As the stated meeting of this Society will not take place before next July, your Committee have not considered what alterations in the By-Laws are necessary to carry their suggestions into effect, but are of opinion that many important amendments are necessary to carry out the spirit of the resolution appointing this Committee.

Your Committee have thus considered in what manner the usefulness of this Society might be extended, and submit their deliberations to the consideration of the Society.

Respectfully submitted,

BENJAMIN NATHAN,

HENRY HENDRICKS,

S. J. JOSEPH,

Committee of Education Society.

New-York, *Jan.* 30, 1843.

91. MOVING WESTWARD

The Jews in Ohio, by Joseph Jonas, an autobiographical account, December 25, 1843 [1]

[Frontier conditions of life hampered the development of certain religious sects, such as those, like the Presbyterians and Anglicans, requiring ordained ministers to conduct services. Others, like the Methodists and Baptists, flourished on the frontier because they encouraged lay preachers and were more democratic in their organization. Judaism, with its congregational worship, dietary laws, and so forth, was hardly adapted to frontier life.

In moving away from his Jewish neighbors and striking out into territories and cities where Jews had not yet settled, the religious Jew had special problems that the non-Jew did not face. Jonas reveals this and many other aspects of the life of the Jew in this personal account of the pioneer days of the Jews in Cincinnati. The problems of the isolated Jew, the struggle to build up a religious community, the tendency to modify ritual and custom, the debate as to the forms of Jewish education, and the relation to the non-Jews are all reflected here. About the latter point, especially interesting is the odd observation by Jonas that "many persons of the Nazarene faith residing from 50 to 100 miles from the city, hearing there were Jews living in Cincinnati, came into town for the special purpose of viewing and conversing with some of 'the children of Israel, the holy people of God,' as they termed us."

The motivation that led Jews out west was largely the same as that which attracted other middle-class elements: the desire to extend the capitalist market into new areas of consumption. Through past conditions over which the Jews had little control, there was not at that time in the United States a sizable Jewish working-class and farming population. Therefore there could be no Jewish farmers and workers moving westward to escape economic difficulties in the East, or to seek new and better opportunities in the West.]

Cincinnati, December 25th, 1843

REV. ISAAC LEESER,[2]

Dear Sir—In accordance with the request to furnish you "with a history of the settlement of the Jews in Ohio," with much pleasure I attend to that subject, and shall probably be more minute than many would consider necessary: you must indulge me in this my weakness, as every thing connected with the settlement of our nation, and the establishment of our holy religion in this city and state renews within me feelings of gratitude and veneration to the great Author of our being, who from a *single* individual, alone adoring his Unity, has in a few years assembled in this noble city two considerable congregations, numbering more than eighteen hundred souls.

It was in the month of October, 1816, that a young man arrived in New York from the shores of Great Britain, to seek a home and a residence in the New World. This individual's name was Joseph Jonas, from Plymouth, in England. He had read considerably concerning America, and was strongly impressed with the descriptions given of the Ohio river, and had therefore determined to settle himself on its banks, at Cincinnati. This he was encouraged in by a relative he met with in New York. On arriving at Philadelphia, he was persuaded to settle in that city, and took up his residence for a short time with the amiable family of the late Mr. Samuel Joseph, (peace be unto him.) He here became acquainted with the venerable Mr. Levi Philips, who took a great interest in him, using many persuasive arguments not to proceed to Ohio. One of them was frequently brought to his recollection: "In the wilds of America, and entirely amongst gentiles, you will forget your religion and your God."

But the fiat had gone forth, that a new resting place for the scattered sons of Israel should be commenced, and that a sanctuary should be erected in the Great West, dedicated to the Lord of hosts, to resound with praises to the ever-living God. The individual solemnly promised the venerable gentleman never to forget his religion nor forsake his God: he received his blessing, and taking leave of the kind friends with whom he had resided, departed for Pittsburg on the 2d of January, 1817. On his arrival, he found the navigation of the Ohio stopped by being frozen over. He procured profitable employment during the winter, being a mechanic, and at the breaking up of the ice was wafted on the bosom of this noble river to the then rising city of Cincinnati, where he arrived on the 8th day of March 1817. The city then contained about six thousand inhabitants, but the only Israelite was himself. With the assistance of the God of his ancestors, he soon became established in a lucrative and respectable business, and his constant prayer was, that he might be a nucleus around whom the first congregation might be formed, to worship the God of Israel in this great western territory. Solitary and alone he remained for more than two years; and at the solemn festivals of our holy religion, in solitude was he obliged to commune with his Maker. Some time in December, 1818, his heart was delighted with the arrival of his lamented and ever-valued friend, David Israel Johnson, (from Portsmouth, England,) with his wife and infant child. But they were bound for Brookville, Indiana, and again for a while solitude was his portion. In the month of June following, three members of our nation arrived, viz., Lewin Cohen, of London; Barnet Levi, of Liverpool; and Jonas Levy,[3] of Exeter, England; and the following ימים טובים were duly solemnized in Cincinnati, and probably in the western country, for the first time, my friend, D. I. Johnson, being summoned from Brookville, and joined us on the occasion. A few days afterwards the solitary sojourner was joyfully recompensed by the arrival of his brother, Abraham Jonas, his sister and her husband, Morris and Sarah Moses:[4] there also came with them Philip Symonds, his wife and child, all from Portsmouth, England. We began from this time to form a community of Israelites. In 1820 arrived Solomon Buckingham, Moses Nathan, and Solomon Minken,[5] all from Germany, and the ימים טובים of 1820 were solemnized in due form with the legal number and a Sepher Torah. In 1821 arrived Solomon Moses,[6] from Portsmouth, England. In 1822 arrived Phineas Moses, and Samuel Jonas, another brother of the solitary; and now were our hearts rejoiced, for the prospects of a permanent congregation were near at hand. During the ensuing year, 1823, arrived Simeon Moses, from Barbadoes, and Morris and Joseph Symonds, from Portsmouth, England.[7] We are now arrived on "terra firma," and have official records for reference. On the 4th of January, 1824, a majority of the Israelites in Cincinnati assembled at the residence of Morris Moses, who was called to the chair, and Joseph Jonas appointed secretary, when the following proceedings took place, and the subjoined preamble was adopted: "Whereas, it is the duty of every member of the Jewish persuasion, when separated from a congregation, to conform as near as possible to the worship and ceremonies of our holy religion, and as soon as a sufficient number can be assembled, to form ourselves into a congregation for the purpose of glorifying our God, and observing the fundamental principles of our faith, as developed in the laws of Moses:—with these impressions, the undernamed persons convened at the residence of Morris Moses, in the city of Cincinnati, state of Ohio, on the 4th day of January, 1824, corresponding to the 4th of Shebat, 5584."

"Present, Morris Moses, Joseph Jonas, David I. Johnson, Jonas Levy, Solomon Moses, Simeon Moses, Phineas Moses, Samuel Jonas, Solomon Buckingham, and Morris Symonds."

Sundry preparatory resolutions were adopted, a committee on constitution and by-laws appointed, and the chairman authorized to summon every member of the Jewish persuasion. We then find the following proceedings officially recorded:

"In accordance with a resolution of a convention which met at the residence of Morris Moses, in the city of Cincinnati, state of Ohio, on the 4th of January, 1824, corresponding with the 4th of Shebat 5584, a full convention of every male of the Jewish persuasion or nation was convened at the house of the aforesaid Morris Moses, in the said city and state, on the 18th of January, 1824, corresponding with the 18th day of Shebat, 5584.

"Present, Joseph Jonas, Morris Moses, David I. Johnson, Philip Symonds, Abraham Jonas, Jonas Levy, Solomon Buckingham, Solomon Minken, Solomon Moses, Phineas Moses, Samuel Jonas, Simeon Moses, Morris Symonds, Joseph Symonds. Morris Moses being in the chair, and Joseph Jonas secretary, a constitution and by-laws were adopted, and the following officers duly elected: Joseph Jonas, Parnass; Phineas Moses and Jonas Levy, vestrymen. Resolutions were then passed to procure a room, and to fit it up as a temporary place of worship.[”]

J.

II.

Before proceeding further, permit me to make a few remarks: from the period of the arrival of the first Israelite in Cincinnati to this date, the Israelites have been much esteemed and highly respected by their fellow-citizens, and a general interchange of civilities and friendships has taken place between them. Many persons of the Nazarene faith residing from 50 to 100 miles from the city, hearing there were Jews living in Cincinnati, came into town for the special purpose of viewing and conversing with some of "the children of Israel, the holy people of God," as they termed us. From the experience which we have derived by being the first settlers of our nation and religion in a new country, we arrive at the conclusion, that the Almighty will give his people favour in the eyes of all nations, if they only conduct themselves as good citizens in a moral and religious point of view; for it is already conceded to us by our neighbours that we have the fewest drunkards, vagrants, or individuals amenable to the laws, of any community, according to our numbers in this city or district of country; and we also appreciate the respect and esteem those individuals are held in, who duly conform to the principles of our religion, especially by a strict conformity to our holy Sabbath and festivals.

The original founders of our congregation were principally from Great Britain, and consequently their mode of worship was after the manner of the Polish and German Jews; but being all young people they were not so prejudiced in favour of old customs as more elderly people might have been, and especially as several of their wives had been brought up in Portuguese congregations. We therefore introduced considerable chorus singing into our worship, in which we were joined by the sweet voices of the fair daughters of Zion, and our Friday evening service was as well attended for many years as the Sabbath morning. At length, however, large emigrations of our German brethren settled amongst us; again our old customs have conquered, and the sweet voices of our ladies are seldom heard; but we have so far prevailed as to continue to this day, the following beautiful melodies, the 29th Psalm, מזמור לדוד which is chaunted as the procession slowly proceeds to deposit the Sepher Torah (Book of the Law) in the ark; also the אין כאלהינו and after the service is concluded none attempt to quit their seats until the beautiful hymn אדון עולם "Universal Lord! who the sceptre swayed," is finished, being sung by all the congregation in full chorus.

For several years we had no hazan (reader) and the service was read and chaunted in rotation by Messrs. David I. Johnson, Morris Moses, and Joseph Jonas. We had purchased a burial-ground about three years previous to our organization, and at that time Jonas Levy was our שוחט. Messrs Morris Moses and David I. Johnson were elected Parnass and Gabah for the year 5586; about which time Nicholas Longworth, Esq., gave the congregation a piece of land adjoining our burial-ground. During this year, a committee of correspondence was appointed to correspond with several congregations for the purpose of procuring aid from our brethren to build a Synagogue.[8] Applications at this time were responded to from Charleston, S.C., and a remittance forwarded to us of one hundred dollars, also fifty dollars from Benjamin Elkin, Esq[.], of Barbadoes, W.I.; the names of all the donors were duly recorded; twenty dollars were also received from Joseph Andrews, Esq., of Philadelphia. Some time in the year 5588 [1828], the corresponding building committee reported 16l. 2s. equal to $71 55 cents, received from the congregation of Portsmouth in England; the name of each donor was also recorded.

About this time we lost a worthy member of our congregation,

Samuel Joseph, Esq., late of Philadelphia, but originally from Plymouth, England. He lived respected and esteemed, and died regretted by every one, (peace be unto him;) also during the years 1826 and 1827, the God of our fathers thought proper to take to himself two amiable young women, sisters, and daughters of the late Rev. Gershom M. Seixas, of New York; lovely in their lives, both mental and personal, it may easily be supposed how deeply they were lamented by their bereaved husbands, Abraham and Joseph Jonas.[9]

During the year 5589 [1829], Messrs. Morris Moses and David I. Johnson were appointed a special committee to procure subscriptions towards building a Synagogue, from our brethren at New Orleans, and they reported 280 dollars collected; each individual's name was entered on record. About the same time Augustus Emden, Esq., gave us a donation of ten dollars.

During the month of July this year, the congregation purchased a suitable lot of ground on the east side of Broadway below Sixth Street, on which our present Synagogue is erected; thus far had the Lord prospered our way.

J.

III.

During the month of August, Messrs. Joseph Jonas, David I. Johnson and Phineas Moses were appointed a special committee to draft a constitution for the purpose of procuring a charter: and on the eighth of January 1830, "Morris Symonds, Jos. Jonas, Morris Moses, David I. Johnson, Solomon Moses, Jos. Symonds, Phineas Moses, Abraham Jonas, Saml. Jonas, Saml. J. DeYoung, Henry Hyman, Simon Block, David Lewis, Simon Symonds, Bernard Le Jeune, Lewis Levin, and Benjamin Silvers, and all other Israelites who may apply and be accepted into this congregation, and their successors," were, by an act of the General Assembly of the State of Ohio, declared to be "constituted a body corporate and politic, under the name and style of Kal Kodesh Beneh Israel, according to the form and mode of worship of the Polish and German Jews in Cincinnati;" and on the 5th of September following, corresponding with the 11th of Elul 5590 [1830], the requisitions of the charter were complied with, and the following named gentlemen were duly elected to the several offices attached to their names, which five officers form the vestry: Morris Moses, Parnass, (Warden Senior;) Bernard Le Jeune,[10] Gabah

Zedokah; Benjamin Silvers, Gabah Beth Hiam, (Wardens Junior;) Joseph Symonds, Treasurer; David G. Seixas, Secretary.

By the recorded names of the seat-holders at this date, our congregation seems to have consisted of thirty-two male, and twenty female adults.

On the 19th of October, 1832, departed this life, Simon Block, Esq., formerly of Richmond, Va. This venerable gentleman had filled the office of Parnass, and volunteered for a considerable time to be our שוחט without any emolument, the congregation not being able to procure one; he was also our only מוהל at that time. He was highly respected and lamented by the members. Being the oldest amongst us, we considered him as the father of the congregation, (peace be unto him.)

Nothing of interest took place, except a gradual increase of the congregation, until 1834, when Messrs. Joseph Jonas, Elias Mayer[11] and Phineas Moses were appointed a committee for building a Synagogue, with full powers to raise funds, collect materials, make contracts, &c.; and it is with considerable gratification we have to record the liberal donations given through the influence of the committee. Fifty-two gentlemen of the Christian faith, our fellow-citizens, gave us towards the building *twenty-five dollars each.* With very inefficient [sic] funds we commenced the good work; but during its progress, with the blessing of God, we were enabled to procure additional subscriptions. With these, and loans from the city banks, we were enabled to bring the holy work to its completion. On the 14th day of Sivan, 5595, corresponding to the 11th of June, 1835, the foundation stone was laid, with suitable enclosures and inscriptions; and with all due form and ceremony, attended with prayers to the supreme Eternal, it was solemnly deposited, in the presence of the building committee and many of the members, by the Rev. Joseph Samuels, our venerable pastor, (now no more.) During this year we received the following donations from our brethren abroad:—$100 from the late Harman Hendricks, Esq.,[12] of New York; $170 from a number of our brethren in Philadelphia and Baltimore, whose names we have duly recorded; among them we perceive Jacob I. Cohen, Jr., of Baltimore, $150; and the following from Philadelphia, viz.: John Moss, Esq.,[13] $50; Simpson Morris, Esq;, $40; R. & I. Phillips, Esqs., $40: H. Gratz, J. Gratz, and L. Allen, Esqs., $20 each; A. L. Hart, A. C. Peixotto, Frederick Samuel, A. Hart, P.S. Rowland, L. Bomeisler, and L. J. Levy, Esqs., $10 each; Mrs. E. Block, of Baltimore, and eleven gentlemen of Philadelphia, $5 each. Five large brass chandeliers were received from the Holy Congregation Shearith Israel, New York, with the condition attached, "that in case the congregation in Cincinnati at any future period should decline to use them, then to return them to the trustees of this congregation." They were originally used in the old Synagogue at New York, and were received by us with much pleasure. The original donor could have little dreamed at the time that his munificent gift would adorn and enlighten a temple erected to the service of the ever-living God in the far west.

The officers elected for 5586 [5596?–1836], the year the Synagogue was completed and consecrated were as follows:

Joseph Jonas, Parnass; Elias Mayer, Gabah Zedokah; Phineas Moses, Treasurer; Building Committee; Benjamin Moses, Gabah Beth Hiam; Morris B. Mann, Secretary.[14]

During the months of May, June and July, we sold seats in our new Synagogue to the amount of four thousand and five hundred dollars, which enabled us to finish the interior of the building in much superior style than we originally intended. The edifice is erected with a handsome Doric front, a flight of stone steps over the basement, with a portico supported by pillars. The building is eighty feet in length by thirty-three in breadth, including a vestibule of twelve feet. It has a very handsome dome in the centre, ornamented with panels and carved mouldings in stucco. On entering the building from the vestibule, the beholder is attracted by the chaste and beautiful appearance of the Ark situated at the east end; it is eighteen feet in front, surrounded by a neat low white balustrade, ornamented by four large brass candlesticks; it is ascended by a flight of steps handsomely carpeted; the entablature and frieze are composed of stucco work, supported by four large fluted pillars of the Corinthian order; the doors are in the flat, sliding into the sides; when opened, the interior appears richly decorated with crimson damask; the curtain is handsomely festooned in front of the doors; between the pillars on each side are two marble painted slabs containing the Decalogue in gold letters; the entablature and frieze contain suitable inscriptions; the whole is surmounted by a large vase in imitation of the pot of incense. Near the west end is the Taybah; it is a square surrounded on three sides by steps imitating marble, with seats enclosed for the Parnassim in front; it is handsomely painted, as well as all the seats, in imitation of maple: the balustrade of the Taybah is surmounted on the four corners by four large brass candlesticks; on the platform is the reader's desk, neatly covered, and supported by two small columns. The gallery, with a neat white front, is over the vestibule, supported by pillars, with six rows of seats. The seats in the area are placed four in a row, fronting the ark, on each side of the Taybah. The ceiling is handsomely finished, with five circles of stucco work, from which are suspended five large brass chandeliers. The edifice, when finished, was much admired, and the Building Committee received a vote of thanks from the congregation for their unremitted attentions in procuring the necessary funds and materials, and for the time and trouble bestowed by them in superintending the erection of the building. The 9th of September, 1836, corresponding to the 27th of Elul, 5596, was appointed for the consecration. The day having arrived, the crowd of our Christian friends was so great that we could not admit them all. We therefore selected the clergy, and the families of those gentlemen who so liberally had given donations towards the building. The members of the congregation assembled in the basement rooms, a procession was formed, with the Sepharim in front, (under a handsome canopy,) carried by Messrs. Joseph Jonas, Parnass; Elias Mayer, G.Z., and Phineas Moses, treasurer, (those gentlemen being also the Building Committee.) Mr. David I. Johnson officiated on the occasion, and chaunted the consecration service; he also led the choir of singers, supported by a band of music; the choir consisted of about twenty of the ladies and gentlemen of the congregation. Who did not enjoy supreme delight and heavenly pleasure, when the sweet voices of the daughters of Zion ascended on high in joyful praises to the great Architect of the universe on the glorious occasion of dedicating a temple to his worship and adoration? And what must have been the exciting feelings of the *founder* of this congregation, at the consecration of this first temple west of the Alleghany mountains, when on knocking thrice outside the inner door, he was addressed by the reader within—"It is the voice of my beloved that knocketh," and when he responded, "Open to me the gates of righteousness, I will go into them, and I will praise the Lord!" The consecration hymns and service were composed and selected by the Rev. Henry Harris. The ceremonies and service being concluded, an appropriate address was delivered by the Parnass, Mr. Joseph Jonas. The Sabbath evening service was then solemnly chaunted by Mr. David I. Johnson, in which he was again harmoniously supported by the vocal abilities of the ladies and gentlemen of the choir. The Sabbath of the Lord having commenced, the labours of man ceased, and the instrumental music was heard no more. The whole was concluded by one of the ladies leading in the splendid solo and chorus of "Yigdal," after which the numerous assemblage dispersed highly gratified.

IV.

Having passed this great epoch in our history, and established our congregation on a firm basis, and having returned thanks to the Giver of all good, for the protection afforded us, and for the prosperity, with His assistance, to which we have arrived at this period: let us now rest awhile, and view the Jewish horizon around us.—Alas! it is a bleak and dreary view; in the whole Mississippi Valley, from the Alleghany Mountains, to the city of New Orleans included, excepting Cincinnati, not a single community of Israelites is to be descried; numerous families and individuals were located in all directions; but not another attempt at union, and the worship of our God appeared to be dead in their hearts.

This with many might be considered a stopping-place to conclude our history; but not so, we are but in our infancy, only numbering at this time 62 members, and about 400 individuals of all ages. During the following year, 5597 [1837], Mr. Morris Moses being Parnass, we bought the adjoining lot of ground and added it to our cemetery, with a metaher house. A Hebrew school was established in the basement room of the Synagogue; Mr. David Goldsmith was appointed the first Rabbi or teacher.—I perceive on the records, Sept. 6, 1838, among the officers elected for the year 5599, Mr. David Mayer,[15] Parnass; Rev. Hertz Judah, Hazan and Rabbi,[16] and Mr. David Goldsmith, Shohet and Shamas.

Having received from the congregation at Charleston, S.C., the intelligence of the destruction of their Synagogue, we could not resist the appeal, and immediately $119 50, were subscribed by the members, and remitted with our sympathies to our Charleston brethren;—it must be recollected that at this period we were still indebted for the erection of our own building.

During 1838, "The Hebrew Beneficent Society of Cincinnati" was incorporated; they have a burial-ground attached to their institution. Their contributions are $3 per annum. At present they consist of near 140 members. If any of them are prevented from attending to their several avocations, through sickness or accidents, they are entitled to demand four dollars per week. At their annual meeting in Tishri, the following gentlemen were elected officers for the current year:—Morris Moses and Philip Symonds, Gabahim; Simon Crouse, Treasurer; Henry Hart, Secretary.[17] About the same period two other societies were instituted by the Jewish ladies, viz: "The Hebrew Ladies' Benevolent Society," and "The German Hebrew Ladies' Benevolent Society;" they are both in a prosperous condition, and were instituted for the purpose of assisting distressed widows and orphans. Their contributions are three dollars per annum.

The congregation K. K.B. I. rapidly increasing, it was found necessary, in 1841, to erect additional seats, and to enlarge the ladies' gallery, Mr. Moritz E. Moehring,[18] being Parnas. When completed, a number of the seats were sold for a sum much more considerable than the expense of the alterations. Also several additional Sepharim were procured and deposited in the ark, with the usual prayers and ceremonies. During this year the congregation "Benai Jeshurun" was founded, and at the ensuing session of the legislature was incorporated. They are in a very flourishing condition, occupying a large room fitted up as a Synagogue, and consist of about eighty members.—Some time near this period the first settlement of Jews, and the formation of a congregation commenced at Cleveland, Cuyahoga County, Ohio, situate on the shores of Lake Erie; this is likely to be a very thriving settlement, and is in a very wealthy portion of the State. The congregation was formed by considerable emigrations of our German brethren. Being at a great distance from them, and having very little correspondence, we are not able to give their numbers. Travellers inform us they are very numerous.[18a]

With the additional seats to our Synagogue we are now enabled to accommodate 250 gentlemen and 100 ladies. Mr. Elias Mayer was elected Parnass for the year 5602 [1842], the Hebrew school was reorganized, and Mr. David Barnard appointed teacher.

In the month of January, this year, we have to record the death of Mr. David I. Johnson, lamented by every one that knew him: truly may we say, "a good man has fallen in Israel." Peace be unto him. He was the second individual of our nation that arrived in Cincinnati; morally and religiously he laboured in the formation of our congregation.

On the 24th of April, 1842, a number of ladies of the congregation met at the vestry-room, and commenced the establishment of a Sunday

School, nominating Mrs. Louisa Symonds their first superintendent. Some time after, finding it interfered with other duties, she resigned her office, when, by a unanimous vote of the teachers, Mr. Joseph Jonas was requested to superintend the school, which since then has been under his direction. There were forty-six children in attendance, and still every appearance of increasing; the field is large, and the harvest has every appearance of being abundant. Considerable proficiency had been made by the children; but a blight appears to be moving over our prospects, from a source little to be expected—the *Rabbonim!* who ought to be the promoters, not the disturbers of a plan to forward the principles of our Holy Religion in the minds of youth; but perceiving that good might be done without their interference, the *craft* was in danger! and the school must be put down. It was consequently anathematized by them, for being held on *Sundays!* in consequence, the school is not increasing, and through their influence most of the German, and some English children, are prevented attending. The leader amongst these bigoted mischief-makers is Rabbi ——, a Talmid, or scholar of the Rev. Mr. R—— of B——.[19] I am well convinced that righteousness and true religion must prevail, and that the evil spirit of bigotry will be overwhelmed. We have endeavoured to reason and compromise with them, but to no purpose. Still whilst there are ten children in attendance, their teachers will not weary in superintending, knowing the benefits already done; we feel warm in the cause of the rising generation, and hope that this publication, sanctioned by some remarks in your useful periodical, may have some influence on their future conduct.

In the month of Heshvan, 5603 [1843], the Hebrew Benevolent Society of Cincinnati was instituted; its first President was Mr. Phineas Moses, under whom it flourished exceedingly; it now consists of seventy members, with every prospect of being much more numerous. Their anniversary dinner was well attended, and the voluntary contributions remarkably liberal. Mr. Joseph Jonas was elected Parnass for 5604 [1844]. The congregations in this city are continually increasing, their character stands high for morality, honesty and sobriety; sorry am I to say that I cannot state the same of many of them in a religious point of view. If only a *few* of the most able and respectable would commence *sincerely* keeping their Sabbaths and Festivals, it would have considerable influence on the minds of their erring brethren. But the "Solitary" is still thankful to the God of Israel, that he has been made the humble instrument in collecting near *two thousand* of his brethren of Israel, to worship the Lord of Hosts in this beautiful metropolis of the Great West.

J.

92. NON-SECTARIAN THANKSGIVING

Correspondence between the Jews of Charleston, S. C. and the Governor of South Carolina, and other documents, November 1844 [1]

[Another phase of the continuing struggle to establish an ever more complete separation of Church and State is revealed in the repeated efforts of Jewish communities in various states to persuade State Executives to issue Thanksgiving Day proclamations in a non-sectarian form, so that Jews too could properly participate in them.[2] Without going so far as Thomas Jefferson, who in his consistency meticulously refrained, during his terms as President, from issuing any such proclamations on the theory that they constituted a violation of the principle of separation of Church and State,[3] the Jews persistently sought to secure equality of treatment for the Jewish religion. Finding the governor's proclamation of 1844 offensive, the Jews of Charleston kept both their synagogues demonstratively closed on October 3rd, the day of Thanksgiving, and also gave at first private and then public utterance to their disapproval. The position of the Jews, however, was "erroneously construed and misstated in his reply;" at a subsequent public meeting, the Jews continued to maintain "that the state government, like that of the United States, is a government of *equal rights* in religious privileges, as in all other things, and not as his excellency infers, a *government of tolerance,* enabling rulers to give or to withhold." A few weeks later, when the succeeding governor, William Aiken, took office, he issued a proclamation the same day "in terms [which] gave up to the Jews the very point in controversy."[4]]

At a numerous meeting of Israelites, held at the Masonic Hall, on the 16th November, Michael Lazarus, Esq., was called to the Chair, and S. Valentine, Esq.,[5] requested to act as Secretary.

The Chairman explained the object of the meeting to be in consequence of the Governor's Proclamation of 9th September, the tenor of which excluded the Israelites of this city and State from his invitation to public prayer and thanksgiving. His excellency had been courteously addressed through a public and private source, calling his attention to the fact. *After the lapse of some time, he having declined to notice their complaint,* the following letter was transmitted to his excellency.

To his Excellency James H. Hammond, Governor of the State of South Carolina.

Sir,

The undersigned, Israelites of Charleston, deem it due to themselves as American freemen, sternly and solemnly to protest against the language and spirit of the Proclamation published by your excellency in the Charleston Mercury of the 13th ult. Their voice of firm remonstrance, would have long ere this been heard, but that you had been addressed on the subject by others of our citizens, and we desired to afford you ample time to respond. This you have failed to do; want of time cannot therefore be plead as an excuse, and the silence which courtesy prompted, must now be broken.

That no conflict of opinion may arise as to the precise language of your Proclamation, we here insert it, as it originally appeared,[6] over your official hand and seal.

Executive Department
Columbia 9th September 1844

By His Excellency James H. Hammond, Governor and Commander in Chief in and over the State of South Carolina.

Whereas, it becomes all christian nations to acknowledge, at stated periods, their dependence on Almighty God; to express their gradtitude [sic] for his past mercies, and humbly and devoutly to implore his blessings for the future. Now therefore, I, James H. Hammond, Governor of the State of South Carolina, do in conformity with the established usage of this State, appoint the first thursday in October next, to be observed as a day of thanksgiving, humiliation, and prayer, and invite and exhort our Citizens of all denominations to Assemble at their respective places of worship to offer up their devotions to God the Creator, and his Son Jesus Christ, the redeemer of the world, Given under my hand and the Seal of the State,

in Columbia, this ninth day of September in the year of our Lord One thousand eight hundred and forty four and in the Sixty ninth year of American Independence

J. H. Hammond

By the Governor
R. Q. Pinckney Secy of State
Recorded in Secy^{s} Office 13th Sep^{t} 1844

You have thus obviously excluded the Israelites of South Carolina from a participation in the religious observances of the occasion. To do this you have adopted a phraseology as *unusual* as it is offensive. No casuistry however subtle,—no constructions however ingenious, can bring the mind to any other conclusion. It is true, you "exhort our citizens of all denominations to assemble at their respective places of worship," and had you stopped there, you would have been clearly *within* the legitimate sphere of your official duty. But, sir, you go further; and state the particular creed upon which your excellency would have *"all these denominations"* to unite!—*all* are invited "to offer up their devotions to God, the Creator, AND his Son Jesus Christ, the Redeemer of the world." Now, it is scarcely necessary to remind one so profoundly skilled in logic, as well as ethics, as yourself, that to invite one to do that, which you know his conscience forbids, if not a mockery of his feelings, is certainly not far removed from an insult to his understanding; and yet you must, or should have known, that to a respectable portion of your constituents your invitation presented no other features.

Sir, the Israelites of Charleston, while they hold in all proper respect all other denominations of their fellow-citizens, profess themselves a God-serving and prayerful people. They cherish with unfaltering devotion their ancient and holy religion. They contemplate with veneration its sublime truths; and they rely with calm confidence upon its glorious and inspiring promises. They too, in common with all others of the human family, have bowed their heads in humble submission beneath the chastening rod of their Creator, and in their turn, have also had cause, gratefully to acknowledge bounteous blessings bestowed by His beneficent hand.

Judge then, sir, what must have been their emotions when they found themselved *excluded* by your Proclamation, from the general thanksgiving and prayer of the occasion!

So utterly repugnant to their feelings—so violative of their accustomed privileges—so widely variant from the ordinary language of such papers—so exclusive in its tone and spirit—did the Israelites of Charleston regard your Proclamation, that, although there are in the city two congregations of them, neither opened their doors for worship on the day you had appointed. Nor could they, with a proper reverence for the hallowed faith of their fathers, have acted otherwise.

Sir, it is not our purpose to enter with you into the discussion of doctrinal points; neither *your* orthodoxy, nor *ours* is now in question. We regard you in this issue *only* as the Governor of South Carolina, and we propose to test the position you have assumed, by that constitution, which you have sworn to support. From that alone do you derive your present authority. Thank God, sir, that noble instrument, together with the Constitution of the United States, presents a glorious panoply of defence against the encroachments of power, whether its designs be bold or insidious. Under its universal and protecting spirit, we do not sue for *toleration,* but we *demand our rights.* Let us refer to first principles. From the reference both the *Governor* and the *governed* may derive salutary instruction. What says then the *first section* of the *eighth article* of the Constitution of South Carolina? The words are these (1st Stat. at L. 191):

"The free exercise and enjoyment of religious profession and worship, *without discrimination or preference,* shall for ever hereafter be allowed within this state to all mankind."

Now, sir, we charge you with such obvious *discrimination and preference,* in the tenor of your proclamation, as amounted to utter exclusion of a portion of the people of South Carolina. It would seem (and we say it without irreverence) as if the finger of Providence had penned that section of the constitution, in prophetic anticipation of the case in point. From your perversion of it, what monstrous evils might arise? if your excellency could be justified in so framing your proclamations as to shut out the religious privileges of the Israelites, where are we to find the line of limitation? Instead of representing the *whole people* of the state in their various tenets and creeds, the governor would make *his own opinion* the standard of orthodoxy, be it what it may. Episcopacy and Presbytery would in turn exclude each other, as the views of the functionary who may happen to fill the chair might lead. *Individual* prejudice or prepossession would usurp the place of the constitution. An orthodox *Protestant* governor might exclude all who do not come up to his peculiar standard of faith; and the *Catholic,* the *Unitarian,* the Israelite, and numerous other sects, may find their privileges *discriminated* away, and their most cherished opinions crushed or slighted by a gubernatorial preference.

But, sir, while the constitution of our honoured State is cherished by our people, as it now is, the errors or misdeeds of those in authority cannot pass unnoticed, or unrebuked. It is a palladium that throws its broad and protecting influence over all who abide beneath it. It guarantees TO ALL, in its own expressive phrase, "without *discrimination or preference,*" the free and full enjoyment of every right, civil and religious; and we cherish its principles next to the Holy Testimonies of our God! It is a noble covenant of Liberty, won and consecrated by the blood of Heroes. The temple is pure and the shrine is sacred. If desecrated by the minister the fault shall not be ours. It is with hearts warmed by such memories, and minds kindling with such associations, that we now record this our solemn and emphatic protest against your proclamation, as unsanctioned by the letter or spirit of the Constitution, as offensive and unusual in language, as exclusive, arbitrary, and sectarian in its character.

In conclusion, sir, we would remind you that your term of office is about to expire. A few fleeting days, and the robe that you wear will grace the shoulders of your successor. We trust that for your own reputation you will, ere that period arrives, remove the impressions which the act in question has made upon the minds of a large portion of your constituents. We are, very respectfully,

Your obedient servants.

(The above letter was signed by upwards of one hundred Israelites,[7] and transmitted to his Excellency.)

The following reply was received from his Excellency.

Executive Department,
Silver Bluff, Nov. 4, 1844.

Gentlemen—I received to-day your memorial and protest against my Proclamation appointing the third day of October for Thanksgiving, which, in consequence of my allusion to "Jesus Christ the Redeemer" you denounce "as unsanctioned by the letter or spirit of the Constitution—as offensive and unusual in language, as exclusive, arbitrary and sectarian in its character." I have received heretofore several private communications on the subject, and a public letter addressed me through the columns of the Southern Patriot;[8] I made no reply to any of these, because I did not feel myself bound to notice them, and wished to avoid, if possible, a controversy of this nature. Your memorial and protest, however, signed as I perceive it is by over one hundred of the most respectable Israelites of Charleston, rebuking in no measured terms, and demanding, as I understand it, an apology, requires an answer. The simple truth is, that at the time of writing my Proclamation it did not occur to me, that there might be Israelites, Deists, Atheists, or any other class of persons in the State who denied the divinity of Jesus Christ. I could not therefore have intended to wound the feelings of such individuals or associations of them. But I am aware that forgetfulness can never justify a breach of public duty, I do not therefore urge it in the least. And as you force me to speak, it is due to candour to say, that had I been fully on my guard, I do not think I should have changed the language of my Proclamation! and that I have no apology to make for it now. Unhappily for myself I am not a professor of religion; nor am I specially attached by education or habit to any particular denomination, nor do I feel myself to be a fit and proper defender of the Christian faith. But I must say that up to this time, I have always thought it a settled matter that I lived in a Christian land![9] And that I was the temporary chief magistrate of a Christian people. That in such a country and among such a people I should be, publicly, called to an account, reprimanded and required to make amends for acknowledging Jesus Christ as the Redeemer of the world, I would not have believed possible, if it had not come to pass. I have not examined nor am I now able to refer to the Proclamations of my predecessors, to ascertain whether they have limited their fellow-citizens to address their devotions to the Father or the Son or to the Father only, nor could I verify the motives which might have influenced them to do the one or the other. But I am of opinion that a Proclamation for Thanksgiving which omits to unite the name of the Redeemer with that of the Creator is not a Christian Proclamation, and might justly give offence to the Christian People, whom it invited to worship. If in complaisance to the Israelites and Deists, his name must be excluded, the Atheists might as justly require that of the Creator to be omitted also; and the Mahometan or Mormon that others should be inserted. I feel myself upon the broad ground that this is a Christian community; and that as their chief magistrate it was my duty and my right in conformity with usage, to invite them to return thanks for the blessings they enjoy, to that Power from whence, and that Being through whose intercession they believe that they derive them. And whatever may be the language of Proclamation and of Constitution, I know that the civilization of the age is derived from Christianity, that the institutions of this country are instinct with the same spirit, and that it pervades the laws of the State as it does the manners and I trust the hearts of our people. Why do we observe the Sabbath instituted in honour of Christ? Why do our laws forbid labour on that day or the execution of civil process? it is because we are, and acknowledge ourselves, and wish to be considered a Christian people. You appeal to the Constitution as guaranteeing 'the free exercise and enjoyment of religious profession and worship without discrimination or preference to all mankind.' If the laws recognising the Christian Sabbath do not violate the Constitution, how can my Proclamation, which was compulsory on no one, do it? If both are unconstitutional, why have not the Israelites commenced by attacking these long-standing laws, and purifying our legislation? Do they deem it easier to intimidate one man, and extract from him a confession and an apology under the apprehension of their fierce and unrelenting hostility, than to reform the State? In whatever situation I have been placed, it has always been my aim to adhere strictly to the Constitution and uphold the Laws. I did not think, and do not now think, that I violated the Constitution of this State by my Proclamation. That forbids the legislature to pass any law restricting the most perfect toleration. I addressed to the Christian community, at their request, a Proclamation inviting them to worship in accordance with their faith; I had neither the power nor desire to compel any one to offer his devotions contrary to his faith, or to offer them at all. Those who did not choose to accept my invitation, were at full liberty to decline it, and if the Israelites refused to open their Synagogues, I had no complaint to make—no penalty to exact. Had they stopped at that, such a manifestation of their disapproval of my Proclamation would have been the more severely felt by me, because of its dignity and its consonance with true religious feelings as I apprehend them. But if, inheriting the same scorn for Jesus Christ which instigated their ancestors to crucify [10] him, they would have felt themselves degraded and disgraced in obeying my exhortation to worship their 'Creator,' because I had also recommended the adoration of his 'Son the Redeemer,' still I would not have hesitated to appoint for them, had it been requested, a special day of Thanksgiving according to their own creed. This, however, was not, I imagine, what the Israelites desired. They wished to be included in the same invitation to public devotion with the Christians! And to make that invitation acceptable to them, I must strike out the corner-stone of the Christian creed, and reduce the whole to entire conformity with that of the Israelites; I must exhort a Christian People to worship after the manner of the Jews. The Constitution forbids me to 'discriminate' in favour of the Christians; and I am denounced because I have not 'discriminated' in favour of the Israelites. This is the sum and substance of your charge. The terms of my Proclamation were broad enough to include all believers. You wished me to narrow it down to the exclusion of ninety-nine hundredths of my fellow-citizens. Neither the Constitution, nor my public duty, would allow me to do this, and they also forbid me to offer any apology for not having done it.

Many topics in your memorial and its vehement tone I pass over without comment, because I do not wish to go farther in this unpleasant discussion, than briefly to state the prominent grounds on which I justify my conduct. And I cannot but hope that when you come to look dispassionately at the matter, you will perceive that the warmth of your feelings has led you astray, that you have taken offence without sufficient cause, and that in fulminating your wrath at me, you have exhibited a temper which in the end may be more painful to yourselves than it can be to me. Not that I do not regret sincerely that I have so unexpectedly incurred your enmity, but because I suffer little when I am satisfied that I have done no wrong.

I have the honour to be

Very respectfully, your obedient servant,

J. H. Hammond.

All of which the chairman submitted to the consideration of the meeting.

Whereupon, it was, on motion,

Resolved, That the whole subject be referred to a committee, who, after due deliberation, submitted the following

REPORT.

It is evident to your committee, that, on the appearance of the governor's proclamation, the editor of the *Southern Patriot* brought the subject before the executive by stating through the columns of that journal, that the exclusion of the Israelites had given just cause of offence to many citizens of that persuasion. Some time after this, a gentleman, over his own signature, addressed a letter to his excellency, couched in the most respectful language. Had the governor been pleased to instruct his secretary to acknowledge either of these, simply declaring their exclusion an oversight, the matter would have been dropped at that point. But the courtesy usually extended in such cases was withheld on this occasion. His excellency did not, in his own language, "feel bound to answer," and accordingly he took no notice of either. This strange, and as we consider, discourteous course, prompted a large number of Israelites to address him, and his reply to them forms the subject of your committee's present report.

Your committee regret that the positions taken by the Israelites in their letter to his excellency, have been so erroneously construed and misstated in his reply. This of course they regard as unintentional on his part; but as an illustration of the remark, his excellency states in the very first paragraph, that his proclamation is denounced as unusual and offensive, in consequence of his allusion to "Jesus Christ the Redeemer." It will be perceived, by reference to the letter of the Israelites, that such construction cannot be maintained. The only correct interpretation of their language is, that in so framing his proclamation *they* were *entirely excluded* from "a participation in the religious observances of the occasion." That alone was their cause of complaint. Had his excellency, if he had even pleased *specially* to invite our Christian fellow-citizens, only gone a little farther, and extended it, as is customary, *to all other denominations,* no dissatisfaction, in the opinion of your committee, could possibly have existed among the Israelites. And was this an unreasonable expectation on their part? Or would it have been an extraordinary act on the part of his excellency? Assuredly not. He would have been but pursuing the course usual on such occasions—they but enjoying in common with other citizens an established privilege. His excellency states that he had not before him, when he wrote his proclamation, those "of his predecessors," to ascertain their mode of invitation. This your committee regret; for they believe he would have found that *usage* is against him. Of one thing they are assured; that it has been the pride of our governors to show their respect for the constitution, by the address with which they have on all occasions of this kind infused into its spirit what satisfies the most sensitive mind.

It is proper here to remark, that nothing is more common even in monarchical countries, having a state constitution, than for rulers to call on every denomination to offer up prayers at their respective places of worship. This practice prevails even in barbarous countries. If the Nile is tardy in rising, the pacha of a dominant mosque calls on persons of every sect to unite, but does not defeat the object by the mandate, and cry of Allah and Mahomet. Thus, if the governor was absolute, your committee cannot believe that a custom so general would be outraged against the followers of a particular faith. These comparisons, though rather mortifying to those constrained to make them, are nevertheless necessary. His excellency with a written constitution for his guide, has been pleased to act in direct contrast with this course. Your committee are too much in earnest on this subject to notice the sarcasm, temper, or taste of this letter from the "department of state." They decline to comment on these topics—nor is it their right to have been informed of his excellency's creed, any more than if he had been pleased to speak to us of his moral sentiments or private affairs. As citizens of the state, they are aware of the respect due the executive office, and shall not vary from the point of their rights. The feeling on their part is any thing but that of pride, that such a document should be filed among the annals of our state. With the miscellaneous remarks, theological, philosophical, they have as little to do; such views may suit ecclesiastical statesmen, and might form plausible reasons on their part, if efforts are ever made, to subvert the present constitution, and have one uniting church and state; but in the present form of the charter, it bears a far more liberal interpretation than his excellency has given it.

Neither can your committee, for the like reasons, and they are constrained to add in self-respect, properly notice the classification, in which you are included, of "Jews," "Atheists," "Mormons," &c. &c. except to expose the argument. The constitution has nothing to do with the relative numbers of the citizens—with popular or unpopular modes of faith. If either of these classes of citizens formed nine-tenths of the population, and the other tenth were Christians, with the present constitution, his excellency, under his view, must exclude the minority of Christians, and interpret Mormonism, or any other ism, as the religion of the state.

Your committee notice also in his excellency's letter, language which they deem calculated to excite the worst of feelings in our country. They cannot believe that it was penned with such intention, but it has been to them a source of much pain. They would notice particularly his allusion to the crucifixion of Christ, and deprecate it sincerely as tending to excite the prejudices of eighteen hundred years against a small portion of his constituents. They appeal, however, to their fellow-citizens of all denominations to support them in the declaration, that nothing is more common than for Israelites here and elsewhere to subscribe to the erection of churches consecrated to the numerous sectaries of Christianity;[11] and they trust to be found at their post, in defence of the humblest of them, should fanaticism, or outrage of any kind, (which Providence avert,) ever assail them.

But on the main point, your committee in seriousness, as citizens of this state, and of the United States, would be unworthy of the rights secured to them, in common with all others, if they did not protest against the principles set forth in the governor's letter, which if admitted, would form a base sufficient to measure away their rights, and the rights of others, for what affects you now, might at another time be fatal to the rights of other minorities. Such invasions silently creeping in, some future proclamation may make farther discriminations, expressing what the executive means by Christianity, and who are Christians. The worst species of wrong is the partial one that aims at the few; that abandons principles and strives to please numbers. Few or many, popular or otherwise, the Israelites hope to be found always upholding those principles, wherein as American citizens, they of right are at issue with the interpretation of the spirit of the laws as expressed by the governor. They maintain that the state government, like that of the United States, is a government of *equal rights* in religious privileges, as in all other things, and not as his excellency infers, a *government of tolerance,* enabling rulers to give or to withhold. It would be an outrage on the constitution, and on the character of the patriots who made it free and equal, and on our countrymen around us, if any contrivance should make it otherwise. The rights therein secured form the general sentiment of the people of this country, and when attempted to be tampered with, find confirmation from the Congress of the United States, in such manifestation, as in the celebrated report of the Hon. R. M. Johnson, on the petition to arrest the Sunday Mails.[12] To that noble exposition your committee would commend his excellency's attention.

There are numerous observations in the governor's letter, which however much they may have wounded your feelings as Israelites, we prefer with a view to the suppression of excitement to pass without notice here. Even that impeachment of the purity of your motives conveyed in his question "whether you found it easier to intimidate one man than to reform the state," your committee, while in justice they are compelled to disclaim and repel the insinuation, will also permit to pass without farther comment. They desire to assuage, not to exasperate—and they cannot but believe that much that is harsh and wounding in his excellency's letter, would not have been penned, but for the fact which he himself declares, "that he is not a professor of religion, and is not specially attached by habit or education to any particular denomination."

In conclusion, your committee cannot leave the whole matter with a safer guardian than the public opinion of the country.

After several animated addresses, the report was *unanimously* adopted.

On motion,

Resolved, That these proceedings be published in the public journals of this city, and of Columbia, S.C.[13]

MICHAEL LAZARUS, Chairman.

S. VALENTINE, Secretary.

Charleston Mercury.

93. ZIONISM: AMERICAN FORERUNNER

Excerpts from Mordecai Manuel Noah's *Discourse on the Restoration of the Jews,* New York, October 28 and December 2, 1844 [1]

[The traditional orthodox Jewish religious view of the restoration of the Jews to Palestine with the coming of the Messiah is here, for the first time in American history, given a political interpretation by Noah more than a half century before the first world Zionist congress was held at Basle in 1897. Addressing large audiences, including many clergymen, at the Broadway Tabernacle, Noah called upon the Christians to show less interest in fruitless attempts at the conversion of the Jews and more interest in helping the Jews return to Palestine. "The Jews are in a most favourable position to repossess themselves of the promised land, and organize a free and liberal government," he declared. And where, he asked, "can we commence this great work of regeneration with a better prospect of success than in a free country and a liberal government?" Of special interest is Noah's analysis of the conflicts among the Russian, British, French and Turkish empires from which he expected the Jews to benefit, with the "Christian powers" defeating the Mohammedan and Asian powers. Even then the strategy of "Zionism" was linked to that of imperial rivalry.

Noah (1785–1851) was a colorful and prominent figure as journalist, politician, American consul to Tunis, sheriff of New York, Grand Sachem of Tammany Hall, popular dramatist, and Jewish congregational leader.[2] His interest in the restoration of the Jews to Palestine goes back at least as far as 1818, when he referred to the matter in an address at the dedication of a synagogue of the Congregation Shearith Israel. From 1820 to 1825, however, he busied himself with a project of providing the Jews of the world with a territorial home on Grand Island, near Buffalo, N. Y. By 1834, however, he was again thinking of Palestine.[3] Similar interest was being exhibited in England, where Christian advocates of the Restoration frankly pointed to political advantages England would gain in the Levant by aiding the project.[4]]

. . . Where, I ask, can we commence this great work of regeneration with a better prospect of success than in a free country and a liberal government? Where can we plead the cause of independence for the children of Israel with greater confidence than in the cradle of American liberty? Where ask for toleration and kindness for the seed of Abraham, if we find it not among the descendants of the Pilgrims? Here we can unfurl the standard, and seventeen millions of people will say, "God is with you; we are with you: in his name, and in the name of civil and religious liberty, go forth and repossess the land of your fathers. We have advocated the independence of the South American republics, we have given a home to our red brethren beyond the Mississippi, we have combated for the independence of Greece, we have restored the African to his native land.[5] If these nations were entitled to our sympathies, how much more powerful and irrepressible are the claims of that beloved people, before whom the Almighty walked like a cloud by day and a pillar of fire by night; who spoke to them words of comfort and salvation, of promise, of hope, of consolation, and protection; who swore they should be *his* people, and he would be their God; who, for their special protection and final restoration, dispersed them among the nations of the earth, without confounding them with any!"

This, my countrymen, will be your judgment—your opinion—when asked to co-operate in giving freedom to the Jews. I am not required, on this occasion, to go over the history of the chosen people; you know it all; it is all recorded in that good Book which *we* have preserved for your comfort and consolation; that book which our fathers pressed to their hearts in traversing burning sands and the wide waste of waters, which famine, pestilence, and the sword could not wrest from them; which was the last cherished relic at night, and the first precious gift in the morning. You will find their history in the Bible. . . .

. . . On these unfulfilled predictions, my friends, rest the happiness of the human race; and you are heirs to this new covenant, partners in the compact, sharers in the glory. Understand these prophecies distinctly: they relate to the literal, and not to the spiritual restoration of the Jews, as many believe. Some think that these prophecies were fulfilled at the restoration from Babylon; but you will find in the eleventh of Isaiah, beginning at the eleventh verse, these words: "And it shall come to pass in that day, that the Lord shall set his hand *again* the *second* time to recover the remnant of his people, which will be left (not in Babylon, but) from Assyria, and from Egypt, and from Pathros, and from Cush, and from Elam, and from Shina, and from Hamath, and from the islands of the sea"—the whole world.

Above all, you that believe in the predictions of your apostles—you who believe in the second coming of the Son of Man—where is he to come to? By your own showing, to Jerusalem, to Zion, to the beloved city of hope and promise; He is, according to your own evangelists, to your own belief, to come to the Jews, and yet you would convert them *here;* you strive to evangelize them, in the face of all that is sacred in the promises of God and the predictions of his prophets, that they shall occupy their own land *as Jews.* In your zeal you forget the solemn, emphatic, brief declaration of your Redeemer, which you should remember as the shades of darkness draw around you, and the light of morning breaks upon your sight, *"Salvation is of the Jews."*

Within the last twenty-five years great revolutions have occurred in the East, affecting in a peculiar manner the future destiny of the followers of Mohammed, and distinctly marking the gradual advancement of the Christian power. Turkey has been deprived of Greece, after a fearful and sanguinary struggle, and the land of warriors and sages has become sovereign and independent. Egypt conquered and occupied Syria,[6] and her fierce pacha had thrown off allegiance to the sultan. Menaced, however, by the superior power of the Ottoman Porte, Mehemet Ali was compelled to submit to the commander of the faithful, reconveying Syria to Turkey, and was content to accept the hereditary possession of Egypt.

Russia has assailed the wandering hordes of the Caucasses. England has had various contests with the native princes of India, and has waged war with China.[7] The issue of these contests in Asia has been marked with singular success, and evidently indicate the progressive power of the Christian governments in that interesting quarter of the globe. France has carried its victorious arms through the north of Africa.[8] Russia, with a steady glance and firm step, approaches Turkey in Europe, and when her railroads are completed to the Black Sea, will pour in her Cossacks from the Don and the Vistula, and Constantinople will be occupied by the descendants of the Tartar dynasty, and all Turkey in Europe, united to Greece, will constitute either an independent empire, or be occupied by Russia, who, with one arm on the Mediterranean, and the other on the North Sea, will nearly embrace all Europe. The counterbalance of this gigantic power will be a firm and liberal union of Austria with all Italy and the Roman States, down to the borders of Gaul: but the revolution will not end here. England must possess Egypt, as affording the only secure route to her possessions in India through the Red Sea; then Palestine, thus placed between the Russian possessions and Egypt, reverts to its legitimate proprietors, and for the safety of the surrounding nations, a powerful, wealthy, independent, and enterprising people are placed there by and with the consent of the Christian powers,[9] and with their aid and agency the land of Israel passes once more into the possession of the descendants of Abraham. The ports of the Mediterranean will be again opened to the busy hum of commerce; the fields will again bear the fruitful harvest, and Christian and Jew will together, on Mount Zion, raise their voices in praise of Him whose covenant with Abraham was to endure forever, and in whose seed all the nations of the earth are to be blessed. This is our destiny. Every attempt to colonize the Jews in other countries has failed: their eye has steadily rested on their own beloved Jerusalem, and they have said, "The time will come, the promise will be fulfilled."

The Jews are in a most favourable position to repossess themselves of the promised land, and organize a free and liberal government; they are at this time zealously and strenuously engaged in advancing the cause of education. In Poland, Moldavia, Wallachia, on the Rhine and Danube, and wherever the liberality of the governments have not interposed obstacles, they are practical farmers. Agriculture was once their only natural employment; the land is now desolate, according to the prediction of the prophets, but it is full of hope and promise. The soil is rich, loamy, and everywhere indicates fruitfulness, and the magnificent cedars of Lebanon, show the strength of the soil on the highest elevations; the climate is mild and salubrious, and double crops in the low lands may be annually anticipated. Everything is produced in the greatest variety. Wheat, barley, rye, corn, oats, and the cotton plant in great abundance. The sugarcane is cultivated with success; tobacco grows plentifully on the mountains; indigo is produced in abundance on the banks of the Jordan; olives and olive oil are everywhere found; the mulberry almost grows wild, out of which the most beautiful silk is made; grapes of the largest kind flourish everywhere; cochineal is procured in abundance on the coast, and can be most profitably cultivated. The coffee-tree grows almost spontaneously; and oranges, figs, dates, pomegranates, peaches, apples, plums, nectarines, pineapples, and all the tropical fruits known to us, flourish everywhere throughout Syria. The several ports in the Mediterranean which formerly carried on a most valuable commerce can be advantageously reoccupied. Manufactures of wool, cotton, and silk could furnish all the Levant and the islands of the Mediterranean with useful fabrics. In a circumference within twenty days' travel of the Holy City, two millions of Jews reside. Of the two and a half tribes which removed east of the trans-Jordanic cities, Judah and Benjamin, and half Manasseh, I compute the number in every part of the world as exceeding six millions. Of the missing nine and a half tribes, part of which are in Turkey, China, Hindostan, Persia, and on this Continent, it is impossible to ascertain their numerical force. Many retain only the strict observance of the Mosaic laws, rejecting the Talmud and Commentaries. Others, in Syria, Egypt, and Turkey, are rigid observers of all the ceremonies. Reforms are in progress which correspond with the enlightened character of the age, without invading any of the cardinal principles of the religion. The whole sect are therefore in a position, as far as intelligence, education, industry, undivided enterprise, variety of pursuits, science, a love of the arts, political economy, and wealth could desire, to adopt the initiatory steps for the organization of a free government in Syria, as I have before said, by, and with the consent, and under the protection of the Christian powers. I propose, therefore, for all the Christian societies who take an interest in the fate of Israel, to assist in their restoration by aiding to colonize the Jews in Judea; the progress may be slow, but the result will be certain. The tree must be planted, and it will not want liberal and pious hands to water it, and in time it may flourish and produce fruit of hope and blessing.

The first step is to solicit from the Sultan of Turkey permission for the Jews to purchase and hold land; to build houses, and to follow any occupation they may desire, without molestation and in perfect security. There is no difficulty in securing this privilege for them. The moment the Christian powers feel an interest in behalf of the Jewish people, the Turkish government will secure and carry out their views, for it must always be remembered that the one hundred and twenty millions of Mussulmen are also the descendants of Abraham. There is but a single link that divides us, and they also are partners in the great compact. The Jews are, at this day, the most influential persons connected with the commerce and monetary affairs of Turkey, and enjoy important privileges, but hitherto they have had no protecting influence, no friendly hand stretched forth to aid them. The moment the sultan issues his *Hatti Scherif*, allowing the Jews to purchase and hold land in Syria, subject to the same laws and limitations which govern Mussulmen, the whole territory surrounding Jerusalem, including the villages Hebron, Safat, Tyre, also Beyroot, Jaffa, and other ports of the Mediterranean, will be occupied by enterprising Jews. The valleys of the Jordan will be filled by agriculturists from the north of Germany, Poland, and Russia. Merchants will occupy the seaports, and the commanding positions within the walls of Jerusalem will be purchased by the wealthy and pious of our brethren. Those who desire to reside in the Holy Land, and have not the means, may be aided by these societies to reach their desired haven of repose. Christians can thus give impetus to this important movement; and emigration flowing in, and actively engaged in every laudable pursuit, will soon become consolidated, and lay the foundation for the elements of government and the triumph of restoration. This, my friends, may be the glorious result of any liberal movement you may be disposed to make in promoting the final destiny of the chosen people.

The discovery and application of steam will be found to be a great auxiliary in the promotion of this interesting experiment. Steam packets to Alexandria leave England every fortnight; a line of packets are established between Marseilles and Constantinople, stopping at the Italian ports, and at Athens and Smyrna, thus bringing the Jewish people within a few days' travel of Jerusalem. Our Mediterranean and Levant trade, hitherto much neglected, will be revived, affording facilities to reach Palestine from this country direct.[10] . . .

94. DEMAGOGUE

Excerpts from Speech on the Naturalization Laws by Lewis C. Levin, House of Representatives, December 17–18, 1845[1]

[Rare indeed at that time was the American Jew who became an active leader of a movement directed against immigration and the foreign-born, yet it is instructive that at least one Jew succumbed to and contributed to this reactionary principle, which is fundamentally harmful to our democracy in general and to Jews in particular. This speech is permeated by demagogy and dangerous principle. "We stand now on the very verge of overthrow by the impetuous force of invading foreigners," we are told—in 1845. The remedy proposed included as its first point that immigrants should not be naturalized until they have been in this country for at least twenty-one years: since the American-born infant has to wait twenty-one years before he can vote, why should not the immigrant wait as long? "Why should he not, like our own sons, enjoy twenty-one years of infant freedom from political cares . . . ?" "Nativist" opposition to the foreign-born, which continues into the present day, has met its pithy and classic refutation in President Franklin D. Roosevelt's statement that "all of our people—except pure-blooded Indians—are immigrants or descendants of immigrants, including even those who came here on the Mayflower."[2]]

> On a motion for a Select Committee,[3] with instructions, to inquire whether any alterations were required in our present naturalization laws, for the protection of American institutions.

Mr. LEVIN [4] said: The gentleman who last occupied the floor has been anxious to proclaim the death of Native Americanism.[5] Sir, it is a principle that can never die. It is part and parcel of the country itself, and as natural to our soil as the mountains that rise in the clouds, or the rivers that water our plains. The principle which binds us together is one so irresistibly attractive, as to promise us a large majority of the people of these United States as friends and supporters—arrayed in the armor of truth, and inspired by the enthusiasm of patriotism. That principle, sir, is a living principle. It is no abstraction. It is an embodied vitality of all that is pure in life, lofty in patriotism, and sublime in achievement. It is identified with the birth of the Republic—the day-flash of our liberty—the maturity of our independence, and the establishment of our glorious Constitution. It is recognised as fame. It is consecrated as glory. The farmer at his plough feels its warmth in his heart. The boy at school, as his peach-bloom cheek flushes with pride, shoots a brighter glance from his eye, at the thought of the name, that is itself that principle, and which equally defies slander, repels calumny, conquers argument, and soars above scorn, contempt, and hatred. Is it necessary that I should mention the name, when there is but one that corresponds with the definition? And yet, so heavy have become the foreign mists that obscure men's minds, who lose all pride of the past in the selfishness of the present, that I find myself constrained to give breath to a charm that shall usher our adversaries into the very flood of noonday light. The name, sir, that embodies our principles is that of George Washington! If, then, any discredit can attach to being a Native American, I for one plead guilty, and fling myself upon the mercy of an age recreant to the principles of the Revolution, and dead to the claims of country. Will those who prefer to worship the Pagan idols of foreign altars (I speak politically) show mercy to one who claims the feelings and sympathies incident to a fellowship of birthright with George Washington—one who dare, without quailing before ridicule, or blushing at the ribald jest of the infidel scorner, lay his hand upon the Bible as the rock of his faith, and hold the Constitution to his heart as the monitor of his political duty—one who, whatever may be his fate on this stage of action, is content to abide by the verdict of a tribunal in which human frailty has no share.

As Native Americans, we desire to erect additional bulwarks for the protection of American institutions from foreign influence; and no sooner is the proposition made, than we are told that we are indebted to that very foreign influence for the birth of American freedom. The gentleman from Maryland [6] reminds us of a debt of gratitude we owe to France, for her friendly aid in achieving our independence! Has the gentleman forgotten that France has been paid some fifty millions of dollars for all her services, out of the spoliations of her cruisers on American commerce; that the brave Lafayette has been enriched by our bounty;[7] and that money and pensions have been liberally showered upon all foreigners worthy of that bounty? As far, then, as foreign aid contributed to our independence, it has been repaid with a generosity without a parallel in the history of nations, and to an extent that leaves not much for the parties to boast of on the score of disinterested chivalry or heroic love of freedom, so well paid for has been every blow struck by foreigners in the cause of our independence. When gratitude, then, is appealed to as a sentiment whose force ought to disarm justice, reverse the decisions of reason, and pervert the true American policy from the attitude of self-defence against foreign contamination, let us not forget that all its romance has vanished in the jingling purse that has so amply paid for what eventually resolved itself into a mercenary service. I now speak of France, and the foreign officers paid for their services. With no common pleasure do I record Lafayette as a glorious exception to the rule. With generous ardor did he sacrifice in the cause of American freedom; with generous ardor our proud Republic has repaid the voluntary homage of his virtuous devotion to the cause of human rights. What, then, is our debt of gratitude to foreigners for American independence? An account has been rendered, and the balance struck; a receipt in full has passed between us; and yet, after this plain mercantile transaction, we are often reminded of the debt of gratitude we owe to the Old World for American freedom. How monstrous the paradox, that the New World should be indebted to the Old World for American freedom! Let us look at this question in its actual relations.

The quarrel of the monarchs of Europe brought us France as an ally, not because her king could feel or fight for freedom, (for the idea is preposterous and absurd, that a king would prepare the elements of destruction for the overthrow of his own throne,) but because he did feel hatred of a rival monarchy (England) and sought to crush her. Who before has ever pretended that when France sent her armies to this country she so acted from love of liberty, instead of hatred of England? A boy at the first form would spurn the ridiculous idea that France, an absolute monarchy of feudal origin, would engage in our battles of freedom from love of those principles that must eventually undermine her own despotism. But it may be said that there is a sentiment of gratitude in every human breast, which, rising superior to all mercenary considerations, ennobles him who feels it. No doubt there is such a sentiment. Sacred be its throbs! But who will urge such a sentiment as an argument for the destruction of his country's independence, or the overthrow of the rights of man! Shall this sentiment urge us to the adoration of monarchy? Shall this sentiment wean us from the homage that every republican pays to freedom? On the contrary, the heart that swells with gratitude is the heart that burns with patriotism, leaps at the thought of freedom, and would sooner perish than yield one jot of that freedom to a foreign cabal.

Since our last national conflict with England, the monarchs of Europe have changed their tactics, not abandoned their object. Invulnerable as they have found us to be, to all their belligerent assaults by physical power, they have since resorted to a moral and political warfare, to compel our free institutions to conform to their feudal establishments. The conflict is the same; but the weapons used are new ones—the ballot-box, the naturalization law, and a class alien vote—all of which can achieve greater destruction than their armies or their navies. Am I asked, how is this manifested? I answer, in the moral impression made on the minds of the people who are hourly brought to sympathize with foreign monarchies, and to esteem the royalist, hot from the atmosphere of thrones as equal to—nay, as superior—to the native-born American, nursed in the lap and nourished from the bosom of Democratic institutions! Yes, superior—for that is the term made use of to the native; because, as the gentleman from Maryland had asserted, "the alien is a citizen from choice;" and choice implies preference of a Republic, which implies superior virtue and patriotism. Now, sir, are aliens citizens by choice? To make aliens "citizens by choice," they must have no motives of a compulsory character to drive them from their native homes to seek a foreign, strange, and remote land. Every circumstance of moral enjoyment and physical comfort must be equal to what they expect to find in this country, to constitute choice. What nation of Europe presents an equality with the United States, in any of the rational blessings of life? I know of none. The epicure of London, or gourmand of Paris, may prefer them for the delicacies of the table; and I am ready to confess that epicures do not swell the tide of foreign emigration at the present era of our history. The philosophers, antiquarians, and literati of Europe, may cling to their moss-covered Museums—to Eton, Cambridge, and Oxford —with reverential fondness; and, perhaps, in ancient lore and modern cookery, we may rank even inferior to France and Britain. But in all that ennobles the human mind—in all that sheds the halo of true glory around the brow of man, standing erect in all the god-like dignity of freedom, I challenge any country upon earth to show her claim to an equality with the United States of North America. But this is the feeblest point in the whole argument. Man must eat first, and think afterwards. Show me a nation of the face of the earth where mankind can obtain so abundantly all the comforts of life, at so little cost of labor as in the United States? Show me any nation of Europe where the mass of population do not suffer for want of subsistence? Here is the grand necessity which drives the swarms of Europe to our shores. Is not this necessity? The worst of all necessities—the physical force of famine. Can such men say they come here from "choice"— from love of freedom, or from love of bread? We may pity their destitution, but Heaven save us from lavishing ridiculous applause upon their patriotism for having chosen this country as their abode. In the time of Mr. Jefferson's administration, what was the general impulse that drove foreigners to emigrate from Europe to this country? It was not "choice," but political persecution. . . .

But we have been told that we belong to a party of "one idea." Is that a reason why we should not be privileged to bring this great subject in proper form to the full consideration of the House? The term conveys no disparagement; and if designed as a sarcasm, it has lost its point in the literal truth of the praise that lies enveloped in its meaning. All great achievements originate from "one idea." Our opponents may say we have but one. Shall we refer such charges to want of sense or want of candor? The attainment and preservation of national character is by no means "one idea." On the contrary, it is one of the most complex that man can conceive, and embraces a comprehension and variety of reforms, interests, principles, and measures, superior to all other parties. I thank the gentleman from Massachusetts for drawing the line so broad and deep between "Whigs" and "Native Americans."[8] I well knew that, notwithstanding the pathetic appeals so lately made to them in the city of Boston, no real sympathy existed, or could exist, between those who advocated THE RIGHTS OF THE PEOPLE and those who advocate THE INTERESTS OF A PARTY. Democracy is "one idea"—the popular element in the ascendant, though it be the foreign element. Whigism is "one idea"—an aristocracy of talent, or the conservatism of the moneyed interest. The two old parties are most emphatically based on "one idea." Not so, however, the Native American. Our great object is to attain to unity of national character; and as necessary to that end, we embrace every measure and policy decidedly American, or that can, in the most remote degree, contribute to establish the national character. We go for everything American in contradistinction to everything foreign. That, too, may be called "one idea;" but it is a glorious idea. For seven years Washington and his copatriots battled through blood, carnage, and intense suffering for "one idea;" and they at least accomplished the great achievement which gained us national independence, self-government, a free empire, religious and civil freedom, and the glorious fabric of an eternal Republic. These, sir, were the noble fruits to be reaped from sowing "one idea." I acknowledge that the Native Americans do cherish one idea of the character I have just described, that generates a thousand. A generative idea, sir, is the test of a great and growing party. Apply ours to any sound subject, and it will produce fruit gratifying to the heart of every American. If our national character is perfect, we shall want nothing to add to its lustre. If it be defective, we shall require every aid that patriotism can devise. Is our national character perfect? Are our free institutions placed beyond danger of corruption? Has Europe ceased to lust after our Government, or aim at our subjugation? Do the potentates of the Old World plot and conspire to influence our destiny as a nation? Are we certain that our children will inherit the blessings of freedom bequeathed to them by their fathers? Is our constitution placed above the danger of subversion by the influx of that horde of aliens, who combine to break down its barriers, that they may command in the citadel, or overrun the land? And do you propose to stifle inquiry on questions like these, and then, in justification of your anti-American course, tell us that we belong to a party of "one idea?" Yes, sir; we have one great leading idea on all great questions involving free institutions, as well as national policy, which, when traced to its roots, or followed out in all its ramifications, is found to enbrace the perfection of every science and principle, every art and scheme of life, that stamps man as an immortal and responsible being. Other parties, sir, may boast their ten thousand ideas of imbecility and corruption. We boast of but one; and that one, thank God, is honest, wise, benevolent, comprehensive; and last, not least, American. But, even on the supposition that we aimed at but one idea—the extension of the naturalization law to twenty-one years—[9] still that would not subject us to the imputation of one idea; for such a law involves more ideas than some of our opponents appear able to comprehend. Not that I am disposed, Mr. Speaker, to take the imputation as at all discreditable. When Newton felt the apple fall on his head, it struck him literally with "one idea;" and that led to the whole fabric of philosophy that bears the illustrious name of the discoverer, and has made us all familiar with the physical laws of nature.

Does not a naturalization law extend to the idea of the ballot-box? Does not that idea generate the idea of the good citizen, of the sound republican, of the glorious patriot? Never—oh, never say aught against the one idea, when it conducts us to so sublime a result, which clusters around us in one overpowering and resplendent halo all the brilliant renown of Athens and Lacedemon—of Venice in her palmy days, and Carthage in her pride of power. Never let the feeble voice of man be raised against "one idea," when he remembers the great conception that, at the fiat of Jehovah, ushered a universe into existence, and startled creation by the glittering image of its own beauty. . . .

The gentleman from Alabama has likened our cause to that of abolition.[10] Is this charge just? Is it true? Abolition seeks to overthrow an institution which exists under the Constitution, and which abolition is willing to overleap. Native Americanism seeks to defend every institution that exists under that glorious Constitution, which we venerate as the ark of our political covenant. Surely the gentleman from Alabama has not been made acquainted with the origin of the Native American movement in that State which I have the honor to represent in part. A foreign demagogue [11] addresses a political missive to a certain body of so-called American citizens, banded together as a distinct political organization, and tells them, "WHERE YOU HAVE THE ELECTIVE FRANCHISE, GIVE YOUR VOTES TO NONE BUT THOSE WHO WILL ASSIST YOU IN CARRYING OUT THE INTENTIONS"—of what? The

American Constitution? Oh, no! Of what? American freedom? Oh, no! But poll your votes to carry out the intentions of a foreign despot, who aims at the overthrow of American institutions. Was it a crime, sir, for Native Americans to repel this aggression, and proclaim to the world that no foreign potentate, or agent, or demagogue, should invade the constitutional rights of any portion of our American population? And now, sir, when we propose to erect bulwarks in defence of American rights, American institutions, and the American Constitution, a spurious appeal is made in behalf of the banded foreign legion, and we are asked to substitute the liberal spirit of the Declaration of American Independence for the venerated charter of our republican rights. This suggestion has long since been made by the demagogue of Europe to whom I have alluded, and I blush to find it re-echoed on our republican shores. By which document are we bound as citizens of these United States? The Declaration of American Indpendence is an exposition of the rights of man, which applies to the whole human family. The Constitution is a settled system of Government for the American people only. The cry raised here of natural rights, under an organized Government, is little better than the ravings of insanity. Natural rights are the offspring of revolution, that struggle through anarchy to settled system of law. Nations have a natural right to independence, but individuals under an organized Government can claim no rights not embraced in their legal institutions. Life, liberty, and the pursuit of happiness, are recognized, defined, and limited by the law. All such fallacies produce mischief, Mr. Speaker, and none more than that which supposes naturalization to be a right, a boon, or a favor granted to the alien. No alien has a right to naturalization; neither is it granted as a boon. We grant it in self-defence, as a protection to American institutions; it is one of the political fortifications of our free system of Government; it is a Bunker-Hill entrenchment to repel foreign assault. Exclusion is the original object of naturalization—not admission to citizenship; for, if that were the object, we should have no naturalization laws; in which case, all foreigners would become American citizens the moment they landed on our shores. To prevent this universal admission to citizenship, we frame naturalization laws, and prescribe forms that operate as a check upon the interference of foreigners in our institutions. At the epoch of the Federal convention, the broad line was drawn between native Americans and foreign emigrants. The Constitution, while it prescribed nativity as the qualification of our American rulers, also vested in Congress the power to pass uniform laws of naturalization as corresponding checks and supports of the precedence given to natives in the first and secondary offices of the Republic. Why, I ask, was this power vested in Congress? Certainly to protect American institutions from foreign influence—to secure Congress from foreign influence—to prevent aliens from filling the offices of the Republic—and to prevent the States from naturalizing aliens to suit the cupidity, ambition, and intrigue of local demagogues. . . .

But to return to the subject. Sir, when I ask the House for the passage of this resolution, it is not on the common grounds that relate to fraud, perjury, or evasion, or any other criminal corruption growing out of a general law. But the scope of the resolution, which I have the honor to offer, reaches to a higher point, and extends to a wider limit. It proposes an inquiry into the present relative influence of the population of Europe upon the institutions of this country, in comparison with those relations as they existed in times gone by—say forty years, or half a century ago; so that we may distinctly understand the position which the foreign population now bears to ours, and which the circumstances of this country now bear towards Europe. . . . With exceptions, too frivolous to merit consideration, Europe is under the universal sway of kings, who govern by a power superior to, and above, that of the people, and which imposes upon them the iron fetters of abject slavery, "divine right." Such marked and decided contrast of opinion could hardly fail to be attended by collision, both moral and physical. Nationally, we have seen this manifested in our wars with Europe. In a social relation, we have seen it displayed in the terrific riots that have deluged the streets of our cities in blood. This collision broke frightfully upon our senses when it scattered a peaceful meeting of American citizens, assembled at Philadelphia, under the aegis of the Constitution, to devise measures for the preservation of their rights. Drilled bands of armed foreigners rushed with impetuous fury upon native-born Americans, who carried no weapons but what equal rights had given them.[12] In the majesty of freemen, they stood armed only with moral power. The element opposing them was physical force. It was an important element—an European weapon—one peculiar only to the feudal institutions of the Old World, and one which never could have come in collision with the opinions of a free people, had not the barriers of their rights been rudely broken down by the inroads of foreign cabals. Observe the peculiar traits of this outrage. The citizens of a district in Kensington, in which they were born, call a public meeting in their own ward. It is broken up by an armed band—the followers and disciples of the demagogue to whom I have alluded, on the assumed ground that it was an Irish quarter, within whose limits no American dare to tread, except at the peril of his life. Here, then, you behold an "Irish quarter" in America —governed by Irish laws, Irish passions, and Irish prejudices—all inimical to freedom of speech—all combining to strangle freedom of thought. It is the same thing if you expunge the word "Irish," and substitute that of French, Spanish, or Italian. I speak to the principle involved in the argument, without appealing to the prejudices coiled up within a name. But that outrage is now a part of our history. It was an outrage of that foreign population, known as the followers of "Daniel O Connell," who had claimed the district for a series of years as an "Irish quarter," sacred from the intrusion of American laws, American sheriffs, and American institutions. Here, sir, I repeat, we come to history—the history of those collisions naturally incident to the unbridled passions of those foreigners; who, having been accustomed in the Old World to physical force, are strangers to constitutional rights, and ignorant of the moral power of opinion that gives sanctity to law without an appeal to the rifle, the musket, or the bayonet. Had an outrage of a similar character been committed on the deck of an American ship, by any of the Powers of Europe, who could have braced themselves to the damning act of treading under foot that flag that now floats in triumph over the dome of this Capitol, and of assassinating in cold blood ten American citizens, martyrs to freedom, would it not justly have provoked us into a war? As surely as that there throbs one pulsation of honor in an American heart! What, sir, would be just cause for war with a foreign Power, I repeat, is ample cause for inquiry into the character and tendency of foreign cabals, matured in the very heart of our country, to wage an exterminating war against American citizens, for the purpose of perpetuating in this country passions and feelings that have no natural affinity to our institutions.

I will not attempt to portray the burst of indignation that would have swept over this land of freedom if the outrage perpetrated in the "Irish quarter" had been committed on the deck of an American ship by any of the subjects of her Britannic Majesty. No language could convey an adequate idea of the popular fury that would have raged in the hearts of the American people; the fire of vengeance would have shot from every eye; every bosom would have heaved with indignation; every tongue would have evoked curses, loud and deep, on the wrong-doers, till the whole land, shaken by one wild cry, would have pierced the very skies with the flames of war. Why was all so calm—content? It happened to be on the eve of Presidential election, when both parties were equally anxious to seize upon this marketable commodity, which is now boasted of as the controlling vote of the Republic—the "balance of power" between the conflicting Whigs and Democrats.

In their eagerness to secure that banded foreign vote, they emulated each other in their efforts to misrepresent and distort the facts, in order that they might disease and poison the popular mind. The Democrats succeeded, it is true, in securing that vote, but it is still a marketable article; and, like the elephants of Pyrrhus of Epirus, that scattered desolation, not through the army of Curius Dentatus, but through his own,[13] so may this stupendous army of foreign voters, so sedulously guarded, and so proudly confided in, prove ultimately not the shield of their strength, but the very instrument of their destruction. . . .

I adduce these facts, not with the view of imbodying them into a report, but as just cause for inquiry. I am aware, sir, that various efforts have been made by our opponents to throw incidents into our cause which never were intended to form a part of our political creed, and which do not now. We have been denounced as sectarians—as fanatics and bigots. Can such a charge lie against us? If the blackened walls of St. Augustine and St. Michael's remain to tell of the outrages committed by a mob, there stands the church of St. Philip de Neri, a monument of the protective power of native-born Americans.[14] Who defended that church at the peril of their lives but native-born Americans, of Southwark, with Thomas D. Grover at their head, who determined to save the church or perish in the ruins? No, sir; we wage no war against freedom of conscience! It requires no demonstration to assure us of the importance of religion to all the secular interests and sensual passions of life. To the king on his throne, or the peasant at his plough—the miser on his money-bags, or the beggar gnawing his crust—the privilege to worship God after the dictate of our own heart is the most precious gift that humanity can enjoy. If the pages of history were not crowded with illustrations of the fact, the throbs of every immortal spirit that pants to enjoy a hereafter would alone be sufficient to attest the solemnity of the passion which clusters around the grave all the majesty of an eternal life, the passage to which must be obstructed by no human power—darkened by no superstitious shadow—taxed by no avaricious tyranny. Shake the crown from the brow of the king—hurl the throne from the emperor's feet—dash the sword from the warrior's grasp—take pomp from the proud, or pageantry from the powerful—blast love by perfidy, or poison friendship by deceit;—all these are trivial calamities that have their cure in life, or their balm in time: but there is no remedy for the frauds of religion—no balm for the wrongs of violated conscience. . . .

So far from interfering with freedom of conscience, sir, we will resist any sect that shall ever attempt to invade its sanctity—we will resist any sect that attempts to combine, as such, to accomplish a political object, whether that sect be Baptist, Methodist, Presbyterian, Episcopalian, or Roman Catholic. Let them attempt it when and where they may, and they will encounter from us the most determined hostility, the most unyielding resistance. If this be fanaticism, if this be bigotry, let gentlemen make the most of it.

Mr. Speaker, all that I have said has been drawn from me by the latitude that has been given to this debate, which ought to have been confined to the naked question of *reference*. I have avoided touching upon the merits of the main question, which we ask to bring in proper form to the consideration of the House, and which, I repeat, a select committee will alone enable us to accomplish. Will the House permit us to place before the nation such records, drawn from the proper departments, as will show that, unless some remedy be applied to this great and growing evil, THE DAY IS NOT FAR DISTANT WHEN THE AMERICAN-BORN VOTER WILL FIND HIMSELF IN A MINORITY IN HIS OWN LAND! Or will you continue to tell us that because we are not as liberal as we might be to foreign ignorance and foreign crime, you will shut out this appeal, which comes up to you in all its freshness from the hearts of the American people? . . .[15]

95. FIGHTING IN THE MEXICAN WAR

"The Mexican War. Reminiscences of a Volunteer," by Jacob Hirschorn [1846] [1]

[Even after more than fifty years Jacob Hirshorn (or Hirschorn) recalled vividly and with surprising accuracy his experiences as a soldier in the

Mexican War, in which he had enlisted as an immigrant boy of 16 in New York. Serving for almost two years, he participated in all the battles that led to the capture of the capital of Mexico, and was one of two hundred special volunteers that stormed the heights of Chapultepec by clambering up scaling ladders "under a terrible fire of artillery and muskets from the castle and wall." These reminiscences are told simply and modestly.

There was considerable opposition to the expansionist war of conquest from Whig and anti-slavery forces, who looked upon the war as an act of aggression against Mexico designed to add slaves states to strengthen the slaveowners' control of the government. The opposition expressed itself in many lengthy petitions to Congress to stop the war, and in denunciations of the war as unjust by literary men like Thoreau, Lowell and Emerson and by political figures like Senators Thomas L. Corwin, Charles Sumner and Daniel Webster and Congressman Abraham Lincoln. For his stand, Lincoln was denounced as "a second Benedict Arnold." In 1848, when Congress passed a resolution thanking the officers and soldiers who fought the war, the vote was only 82 to 81, and the resolution characterized the war as "unnecessarily and unconstitutionally begun by the President of the United States."[1a]]

In the latter part of the year 1846 I found myself in the city of New York, a boy sixteen years of age. My mother, a widow, and my only sister were still living at Fuerth, Bavaria, which was my native place. I, without an advisor or any relation, was left entirely to myself and I could do as I pleased. Being then without a position, after having scanned the New York Herald in the morning, I would generally visit the Cafe de Paris on Broadway, to sit down comfortably to read the *Courier des Etas* [sic] *Unis,* a French newspaper issued in New York. This cafe was the rendezvous of the best class of French and German, who came there regularly to drink their "verre de Cognac," which the proprietor imported directly from France.

After having visited the cafe three or four times, one day, I became acquainted with the French Count Gustave de Bougars,[2] a French nobleman of the old school, who was then an attache of the "Military Argus," an army paper. The count at once took an interest in me and engaged me in conversation, which of course was in French. He inquired into my past life and present doings. I frankly told him all about myself and he would express his satisfaction once in awhile saying, "Bon garcon, bon garcon!"

After having met him there regularly for a whole week, by his own appointments, he one day said to me, "Jaques, (Jacob) I have a proposition to make to you. I have no relatives, no family in this country,

I am all alone, come with me, as my protege. I hold a commission as captain of Company B., 1st Regiment, New York Volunteers, raised for the Mexican war. You will get a position in the army, you will fight for 'Uncle Sam,' and you will see a great deal of the world." All of that enthused me so much, that I consented. The next morning he went to Fort Hamilton with me, which was the headquarters of the First Regiment. Here, some difficulty arose. A boy, sixteen years of age, a minor, could not legally be mustered into the U. S. service. The count persisted, and somehow or other, I was accepted as a volunteer.[3] There I became acquainted with Lieutenant Reichart of Co. B. and the non commissioned officers and men of the company and regiment, Col. Ward B. Burnett, Lieut. Col. Charles Baxter, Mayor [Major] Burnham, Capt. Jarrett Dykeman and ever so many more.[4] After I was at the fort about two weeks, one day in December, a brigg came down from New York and dropped anchor in front of the fort. The next day we embarked on the good brigg "Montezuma" for Vera Cruz. We were on the ocean about a week or so, when we dropped anchor and landed on, as God-forsaken a place as I ever saw, called "Lobos Island," uninhabited, and situated about 200 miles from Vera Cruz. Our first skirmishes commenced here, with all the vile vermin, snakes etc., which could be conveniently collected on a small island.

Here the boys were drilled twice a day and exercised in shooting. Here they were made soldiers. After a sojourn of one week we embarked again and shortly afterwards we saw the city of Vera Cruz, and very prominently the castle of San Juan D'Ulloa. We also found quite a respectable fleet of U. S. warships.

The next day we disembarked about five or six miles below the city, which a few days afterwards was thoroughly invested[5] by the army in the shape of a half moon, on land, the other half being completed by the ships on the sea, fronting the city. Then the bombardment commenced by land and sea forces. So awful a sight, but still grand, I have never seen, especially at night, when one could follow the bombshells with the eye, as they were fired from the huge mortars on the frigates and line ships. The houses in the city began to burn, and after two days' bombardment, the castle and city, capitulated, the Mexican flag came down, and the "Stars and Stripes" were hoisted. This was celebrated by a salute from land and shore, deafening to a novice but nothing unusual to me after hearing that racket for two days and nights previous. Our encampment outside of Vera Cruz was a terribly trying one for the Northers as they blew in from the sea, over the sand hills in which we camped, caused immense suffering. The sand nearly blinded us. Our bodies, our food, our drinking water, all were covered with sand and dirt. Especially the water, which at best, was a little dirty warm mush obtained by digging into the sand about a foot or so. We were glad when orders arrived to strike tents and march inland towards Jalappa. At Cerro Gordo we found Santa Anna entrenched on the heights with 20,000 troops and any amount of artillery.[6] We had to pass there, no other way being passable, therefore general Scott,[7] ordered, the next day at sunrise, an assault on the fortified heights. Step by step we had to pull our guns up by ropes, 40 or 50 men, attached with one hand to the rope, and with the other hand getting a hold on some grass cactus or any other old thing, so as to keep a footing and not to roll down again, with gun and all, and the Mexicans, continually firing on us, from above. It was a terrible battle, but after six hours fighting .we conquered and the Mexicans fled "vamoosed" as they call it. There among a good many others who were wounded or killed, I saw General James Shields, who had been struck by a piece of shell, and I assisted in carrying him from the field to shelter.[8] We, at first, thought he was mortally wounded, but he recovered after three months. General Shields commanded our brigade, which consisted of the First Regiment New York Volunteers and the Palmetto regiment of South Carolina. Too soon did we enter Jalappa. There I became acquainted with General Worth, Twiggs, Quitman and a good many others.[9] When I say I became acquainted I do not mean intimately, for such a thing is not to be supposed of old stern martial regulars and a sixteen year old boy, but they were gentlemen all the same. Having rested up and seeing our wounded and sick comfortably housed in churches and convents fitted hastily as hospitals we left them at Jalappa under a guard, sufficiently strong to protect them and also to keep our communication with the sea open as we now were penetrating deeper into the enemies' country and if we should meet with a reverst and being over 3000 miles from home and cut off from the fleet, why the guerillas and regular troops could easily extinguish us. Annihilation comes nearer than anything. Orders now received were on to Pueblo de long [sic] Angelos [Puebla].[10] We had some skirmishes at Perote with some Mexican troops and after vanquishing them, by easy marches, we reached Pueblo. There we encamped for about three months. About half our force were invalids, some killed and wounded in battle and a great many sick at the hospitals as a result of eating the fruits of the country, which our boys could not stand. We had to wait for reinforcements, mail and supplies, before we could attempt to attack Santa Anna, entrenched in every conceivable shape, defending the city of Mexico.

Our situation in Pueblo became a very alarming one. Every day there were deaths and more sickness, for the able men had to do twice as much in the way of guard duties, scouting, foraging, &c. By reason of the sick not being able to attend to these duties, we were in desperate straights [sic]. Remember, we had to hold down a population of 75,000 or thereabouts, besides any amount of guerillas, swarming round the city, to pick up outposts, stragglers, or so, and we only had about 4 or 5 thousand men fit for duty. Finally one fine day we saw a wagon train approaching the city. They had only a few supplies, no re-enforcements, worth speaking of, but they had a mail and such a mail! When we got hold of the newspapers and we read of the proceedings in Congress, condemning the war with Mexico, hoping that the American army of invaders would meet with a hospitable grave at the hands of the Mexicans.[11] Then we began to despair. Aimless and desponding the boys walked about, thousands of miles away from home in the interior of the enemies' country, with thousands of sick and wounded comrades on hand, no supplies, no re-enforcements and forsaken at home by our own government.

Then we began to reason with each other. "We are not left by our government we are only betrayed by a portion of the whig party. The government still lives and they'll see us out"—and they did. About three or four days afterwards another wagon train of about 300 wagons, escorted by about 2600 men and plenty of supplies made their appearance [12] and then feasting would have commenced right then and there, if we had anything to feast on.

Being able to converse in English, German and French, I was from the start transferred to the quartermasters department. Because I was a minor, I could not get a regular commission in the army as an officer, but they would send me out in the country at the head of a company of dragoons or mounted riflemen and six or eight wagons, to scout and forage for anything eatable for man or beast. The country had a good many French and Swiss settlers, with whom I could converse, and so I always managed to bring in something. Of course I could not get enough to supply the whole army, but enough for the principal officers, and some for the convalescent in the hospitals. With the Peons or Indians I made short work. Anything they had in the way of corn for the horses and mules, hay, or in fact anything we could use, I pressed into the services [as] a military necessity, and gave them an order on quartermasters department, for payment. My friend Count Bougars resigned his captaincy, giving as the reason, that political affairs in France had taken such a turn, that it was of the greatest importance for him to return to France. Lieutenant Reichart commanded Company B now but only for a short time, for he also resigned shortly when Lieutenant M. Reid assumed command.[13] A more gentlemanly Englishman I have never met. We soon became very warm friends. He was of a very enthusiastic and sympathetic nature, a gifted author of an interesting book. After the war he returned to England and some years ago, he died. The second in command of Co. B. was a young highly educated young Frenchman, Hypolite Dardonvitte, thoroughly French, polite and brave.[14]

After a sojourn of about three months at Pueblo, the order was given to march and we moved on to the capital, the city of Mexico, with an army mustering about 12000 men fit for duty.

The first battle took place at Contreras,[15] where we encountered a part of the Mexican army under General Ampudia. We assaulted the fortified position about 4 o'clock a. m. after two hours of incessant firing. We carried the works, Ampudia and his men fell back about six miles and joined Santa Anna, heavily fortified and entrenched at Churubusco. About ten o'clock the same day, we attacked the enemy. Their strongest point was a bridge which our men would have to cross coming up from the main road. This bridge was strongly defended and the most vigorous defence was made by an Irish battery under Capt. Reilly, who had deserted the American army, at Monteroy [Monterey] with all accoutrement. They knew well what capture for them meant an ignominious, instant death. They fought bravely for their life and three times the regulars were repulsed under Worth and Twiggs.

My brigade then under the command of General Franklin Pierce consisting of the New York and South Carolina volunteers were ordered to attack. We formed in a Hacienda, about one and a half miles from the Mexican line fortifications in an open cornfield and at the first fire of the Mexicans about one per cent of the Palmetto boys and about the same number of our regiment fell, killed or wounded. There we lost our lieutenant Col. Chas. Baxter, for whom Baxter St. in New York is called. The Mexicans concentrated their fire on the center of our regiment, hence four different men carrying the colors, fell. Finally the dropping colors were taken up by Sergeant Paul von der Helm Rousayn of my company and he in turn fell pierced by five bullets. Seeing it was useless to stand up as a target in an open field we advanced on the enemy to attack them with cold steel.

We marched through the open field not minding their shots at all, reached a trench, which we filled with dead horses and mules, crossed over and attacked them with the bayonet. That was more than they could stand. They began to waver. Worth forced the bridge, Santa Anna ran for his life and his defeated army followed him pell-mell, and we after them to be revenged for our dead and wounded comrades. Oh! what a glorious sight it was to see Phil Kearney at the head of his dragoons, riding into them and the infantry following up.[16]

We would and could have entered the city of Mexico that same night, in glorious triumph, if we had not all of a sudden been stopped by an order from Commissioner Trist, a sort of political agent [17] who had been tricked by Santa Anna, to consent to a six week's truce, ostensibly to make peace, but in reality to collect his army again, fortify Chapultepec the west point of Mexico, Molina del Rey and the Garritas or gates of the city of Mexico. Enough we were stopped, camped on the conquered battle field, and looked to our wounded and dead. The next morning Reilly's battery was captured.[18] A court martial convened, tried them and in a few minutes, sentenced them to be hanged, which sentence was carried into execution next day, after they had dug their own graves, a long and deep trench, into which their corpses were flung. Their captain was reserved for a worse fate, to which I shall refer later on.

As I mentioned before General Scott commanded a halt. Our army encamped at a respectable distance from the city of Mexico and a six weeks' truce was proclaimed which was religiously kept by our army but which Santa Anna treacherously violated, by collecting his scattered army, building new fortifications and strengthening his position. The diplomatic "pour parle" having come to naught as was expected after the six months [weeks] expired, General Scott ordered an advance into the city of Mexico.

Molina del Rey an out work near Chapultepec was attacked first and carried.[19] Next Chapultepec, the west point of Mexico built on a steep hill and surrounded by a high wall, well defended by Mexicans and splendidly supported by the cadets, was to be assaulted. Here a call for volunteers from the different regiments was made to serve under the command of Major Twiggs (a brother of Gen. Twiggs) which command was called the "Forlorn Hope," because none of them ever expected to return alive.

We advanced two hundred strong. I omitted to say, that I volunteered to join.[20] Under a terrible fire of artillery and muskets from the castle and wall we approached the wall, raised our ladders, and began to climb up. It was a terrible sight to see our brave fellows drop from the ladders, shot. Finally we reached the top of the wall. The first man on top of the wall was Lieut. Sweeny of the First Regiment, New York volunteers (my regiment) for which he was promoted by Congress to a Lieutenancy in the regular army.[21]

As soon as the glorious "Stars and Stripes" floated from the wall the Mexican flag came down. The defenders became demoralized and vamoosed. It is unnecessary for me to mention here, that while the assault on the wall took place our siege guns, mortars and others poured shells and round shot into the castle, which, after awhile set the castle on fire. Then the complete route [sic] of that portion of the Mexican army took place. Having possession of the castle situated about three miles from the city, we advanced on the city. Our division [which] was to attack the garrita del Belen, were behind the breastworks. The Mexicans fought bravely, we forced them back however, and finally entered the city, opposed by the retreating enemy, who defended every foot of ground stubbornly and who were nobly assisted by hundreds of Mexican ladies, who from the tops of their houses (all flat tops) were pouring boiling water, boiling oil, rocks, anything they could lay their hands on, upon the very much exposed heads of our boys. Finally about four o'clock p. m. we reached the "Plaza," the principal square of the city, planted the American flag on top of the Halls of Montezuma the palace of Mexico and Gen. Scott established his headquarters therein.

Santa Anna and his army fled when we attacked. Our numerical strength was a trifle over 10,000 men. When we entered the city we had about 6,000 fit for duty the rest killed, wounded and on the sick list. To guard that city against the scattered forces and prowling guerillas, from the outside, to hold an inimical population of about 200,000 down, and to police the city beside with such a small force was no slight matter. Beside we had to establish hospitals for our sick and wounded and furnish our starving soldiers with food, as our wagon train had as usual been left behind about 25 miles. We found hospitals ready made and on hand, as the Mexican capital was well supplied with churches and convents of which we took possession at once.

We carried our wounded and sick in but had to lay them on the cold bare floor.

I was ordered to take a file of men and forage for anything I could get but was told General Scott had issued the strictest orders to respect private property, severe punishment to follow a violation of the order. While riding through one of the streets I read a sign over a shop "Brasserie allemana" (German Beershop.) That was enough for me. After repeated knocking with the butt end of our muskets, the door opened and a middle aged woman, stood tremblingly before me. I reassured her at once, in good German, told her she need not fear anything, we were not after her money or valuables, but that we must have something to eat and lots of beer. If she had any cigars or tobacco in the house, we would *buy* them. Well, we received substantial food, bottles of beer (the most wretched stuff I ever drank) made in Mexico and then she brought a box of Wheeling stogies, for which she charged me $10, about five times as much as her food, beer and cigars were worth. I did not complain, I took out my memorandum, tore out a leaf and very gracefully wrote out an order on the United States Treasury for ten dollars, gold. She was so elated over her business transaction, that she called her husband, who had been hiding upstairs. She introduced me to him as a landsman. We shook hands and I promised him to become his protector and influence our boys to do their drinking at his place. At the same time I wrote my address for him Regiment and all and told him that at any time that any of our boys should get drunk and cut up at his place to send for me. I then went into an adjoining room with him and after a little conversation, I had received a pointer, which enabled me to return to camp with a wagon-load of straw and ten barrels of flour. On leaving the beer shop, the old lady handed me a parcel to show her gratitude for my kind actions. Upon opening it in my tent that night, I found it to contain about a dozen slices of ham, four slices of rye bread and another bottle of that stuff called "beer." I called a few of my brother officers in, to partake of the feast. The ham and rye bread went well enough but when it came to the beer Lieut. Fitzgerald [22] suggested that it be improved upon and he pulled a bottle of whisky out of his pocket. (The Lord only knew how he got it.) He mixed the beer with the whisky in an old sauce pan, which was lying around loose and which had not been cleaned in six months, but soldiers don't mind such trifles.

The next day General Scott ordered the Alcade (mayor) and high officials to be brought up before him and made a requisition upon them for hundreds of mattresses, 600 barrels of flour, $500 in cash and a certain amount of forage for horses and mules. With a very polite but sickly assurance that this demand was impossible Mr. Alcade thought that was the end. But the general told them, equally polite but very firmly, that he would just give them three times twenty-four hours to comply with his demands, and in the meantime he would hold them as hostages of said request, and the goods were delivered on time. Our soldiers however, had an extremely hard time, with constant guard duties. Patrolling the city and outskirts a good many took sick which increased the hardships of those fit for duty. Finally one fine day a large wagon train from the United States carrying supplies of all sorts, escorted by 2600 new men entered the city.[23] Our army was deliriously delighted to get news from home. Letters and papers were in sight besides 2600 recruits on whose shoulders were shifted now the guard duties, patrolling etc., to give the old soldiers the needed rest.

Now a very interesting court martial was convened to try Captain Riley the commander of the deserted Artillery Co. who was captured at Churubusco. The sentence after having found Capt. Riley guilty of all the charges was as follows: Captain Riley fettered with chains and balls was to be taken to the place where all of our troops who could be spared were drawn up in a hollow square, the captain inside of the square to be attacked by the guard and (you may call him) the executioner, and a large D was to be branded with red hot iron on Capt. Riley's cheeks, D standing for deserter. From thence he was taken in irons, to the castle Chapultepec, kept prisoner there during the term that the war lasted and when peace was declared and the army marched back to Vera Cruz to embark for home, he had to walk on foot at the head of the troops dragging his chains and balls on each foot. On arrival at Vera Cruz, peace had been declared.[24] He was then shipped back to New Orleans with the rest of the army. After a five or six days sail, we arrived at the mouth of the Mississippi River went up to the city and were ordered to encamp at Carrolton.

A day or two after, we were ordered to the city to witness the final punishment of Capt. Riley who was mounted on a donkey (chains and balls had been taken off) facing the tail of the donkey. The said donkey was marched through the streets of New Orleans a drum and fife corps playing Rogues march and finally Capt. Riley was drummed out of the service of the U. S. What became of him afterwards I never learned, some said he committed suicide and others said he returned to Mexico. Here I took sick, with yellow fever, and had myself taken to the "La Charite" hospital, where I was tenderly cared for by the good sisters. An hour or so in the afternoons my nurse would read a little tract to me. I seemingly listened very attentively to her, but inwardly I muttered to myself: "Geh veg mit Deiner Schabbes Schmues."

In the meantime our Regiment was ordered to embark for Ft. Hamilton near New York City, where after recovering from my illness I joined my regiment. Here we were mustered out of the service of the U. S. and honorably discharged.[25] New York City gave us a splendid and very enthusiastic reception and a silver medal for each soldier. We left New York 1200 strong and we returned about 260.

St. Louis, Mo., July 1903.

96. IRISH FAMINE RELIEF

Address by Rev. J. J. Lyons, at a meeting in the Synagogue of the Congregation Shearith Israel, New York, March 8, 1847 [1]

[When the Irish potato crop failed in 1846 and the British government refused to prevent the absentee landlords in Ireland from exporting grain from that country, the suffering of the Irish population became acute, hundreds of thousands dying of starvation and the diseases born of hunger.[2] Especially in the United States, relief organizations became active. The fact that Jews participated in this relief movement evoked much public attention, including the long front-page account of the meeting from which this address is reprinted.

The first organized appeal for aid had been issued in New York, February 12, 1847, signed by sixty-two leading citizens, including the Jewish banker, August Belmont.[3] Responding promptly, the Trustees of Shearith Israel on February 21, 1847 called this meeting for March 8th.[4] The main address by Rev. Lyons is distinguished for its breadth of view and its explicit rejection of a narrow nationalism. "We are told," he stated, "that we have a large number of our own poor and destitute to take care of, that the charity which we dispense should be bestowed in this quarter, that the peculiar position of ourselves and our co-religionists demands it at our hand, that justice is a higher virtue than generosity, that self-preservation is a law and principle of our nature." But he replied that there was one "indestructible" and "all-powerful" link between the Irish sufferers and the Jews: "That link, my brethren, is HUMANITY!" Rev. Jacques Judah Lyons (1813–1877), born in Surinam of American parents, had come to the United States in 1837, after serving four years as Hazan of the Congregation Neve Shalom. From 1837 to 1839 he had been minister of the Congregation Beth Shalome, Richmond, Va., and then came to Shearith Israel in New York, serving until his death.]

BRETHREN: I address you on this occasion with feelings of diffidence and anxiety; diffidence caused by the novelty of the undertaking—anxiety by the importance, the interest, the solemnity of the subject which for a few moments I propose to dilate upon. That it is important and interesting is evinced by the unanimous and simultaneous action of the whole country, by the spontaneous assemblages of citizens to consider it, by its engrossing and all absorbing discussion. Its solemnity is graven in the heart of every intelligent and thinking individual. What is it, my brethren, that has thus affected us and others? Wherefore are the prejudices, the divisions, the hostility of all sects forgotten, and wherefore are found on the same platform men of all denominations, earnestly and zealously engaged in co-operating for a common object? Wherefore are the contests, the bickerings, the opinions of parties thrown aside to permit their respective partizans to act in unison for a single purpose? What great, what wonderful event in the progress of the world, has from a dormant state of toleration into recognition and fellowship called that people, chosen as His people by the God on high, but rejected, oppressed and persecuted by their fellow men? No devastating pestilence has invaded our shores; all with us is teeming with life and health. No dreadful blight has consumed our fields: all nature is smiling in beauty and abundance. No intestine commotions have threatened the permanency of our liberties, our rights, our government. Our national enemies have prevailed not against us. The elements themselves restrained and tempered by a merciful God have spared our cities, our villages and our plains, have only been ministers to our comforts, auxliaries to our happiness, our prosperity. Yet sadness and gloom pervade the land. A nation is in distress, a nation is starving. Numbers of our fellow-creatures have perished, *dreadfully, miserably* perished from hunger and starvation. Millions are threatened with the same horrid fate, the same dire calamity. The aged and the young, the strong and the feeble alike are prostrated. The heart of civilization is touched by the distress and wo of the sufferers. Relief, and if not relief at least alleviation, is the first sentiment to which utterance is given, and in obedience to that sentiment we are, my brethren, assembled this evening. When information was received in our country that great distress existed in unhappy Ireland, that her inhabitants, her peasantry and her laborers were suffering from the failure of the potato crop, that supplies must be drawn from this and other countries, the benefits we were to derive from such a state of affairs was the paramount consideration. That cases of individual suffering would ensue was admitted.—That the energies and capacities of the people would surmount their difficulties was confidently predicted, and it was not till the reality was made evident to us, not until we were absolutely horrified and heart-sickened by the accounts of the distress that measures were taken to prevent if possible the further ravages of the visitation. Our fellow-citizens have come forward with promptitude and generosity; contributions have poured in from all classes, from all sects. Aid and assistance to unhappy Ireland—raiment, food and *life* itself to her destitute people are now invoked at your hands. Each of you, I know, acknowledges the necessity of action, each feels that a state of affairs there exists, which it is the duty of society to change and improve. But while there is no diversity of opinion on these points, there is a great diversity of opinion as to what we should do in the premises. We are told that we have a large number of our own poor and destitute to take care of, that the charity which we dispense should be bestowed in this quarter, that the peculiar position of ourselves and our co-religionists demands it at our hand, that justice is a higher virtue than generosity, that self-preservation is a law and principle of our nature. Examine these objections for yourselves. Reflect upon them seriously and conscientiously; then ask yourselves whether they be forcible and true, or whether they are not in fact excuses which the lips utter, while they are rejected by the heart.—Ask yourselves if the contribution which this day you are requested to make will diminish in the smallest degree the other calls which you admit are imperative and binding; and if the responses be those which I anticipate, our meeting for this purpose will not have been in vain. It is true that there is but *one* connecting link between us and the sufferers; that while most others know only a political and geographical separation from them, we alone realize that formidable and eternal one which the hand of man made not. But thanks to the Lord *that* connecting link is strong enough, and long enough to withstand all attempts to make the separation complete and irreparable. Prejudice, bigotry, fanaticism with their attendant spirits, ignorance, intolerance, and persecution can not break it. Selfishness, avarice, cruelty in vain assist in the unholy work. Forged as it was, by religion, virtue and charity it is indestructible, it is all-powerful. That link, my brethren, is HUMANITY! Its appeal to the heart surmounts every obstacle. Clime, color, sect, are barriers which impede not its progress thither.—Reason at its approach deserts its strong places, its impregnable fortresses. Pride from its lofty seat and imperious throne leaps down to welcome its presence. It is lighted on its way by the divine spirit within us, and the halo and glory which accompanied it illumines its biding place long, long after its departure. It is this which has brought you here to-night, it is this and this only which will produce any result from this assemblage. Nothing that I can say, nothing that the more eloquent gentlemen who are to follow me can say (and I speak this with a full appreciation of their abilities and eloquence) can add one word which will make its action more prompt, its result more satisfactory. Its promptings enforce their own obedience, its commands require neither interpreter or assistant.

I have taken it for granted that you are all well acquainted with the present state of Ireland; that you are fully aware that the pursuit of its population is agriculture, that its land is chiefly owned by large proprietors, few of whom live on their estates; that it possesses no government of its own, and that its wants, its prosperity, its existence, depend upon the caprice of a minister, or the exigencies of a party; that the failure for two successive years of the staple article of food, and the withdrawal from its shores (even in such times) of its productions for the use of its absent landlords, have all tended to that end. I have also omitted all details of the sufferings of the people, though of thrilling interest, and affecting and persuasive for my purpose. Neither shall I dwell upon the position in which we are placed, as the first Israelite Congregation assembled for this purpose; that the eyes of the community are turned upon us, that their attention is directed to us, ought not, cannot, and will not affect us.[5] The ground on which we stand is holy ground. No evil thoughts, no base passions, no worldly considerations here actuate us. The better principles of our nature *here* exercise their beneficent and ennobling control. Our hearts turned to God and his glory, his goodness, his mercy, direct us to that path which his laws and his commandments teach us to be the true one. The guideposts to that path are numerous and distinct; and among the first and foremost placed before our eyes do we behold thee, *oh, Charity!* We recognize thy beautiful face, beaming with goodness and cheerfulness, and reflecting the joy and the happiness which thy practise brings with it. We neglect not thy precepts, and fail not at thy bidding. I have endeavored briefly, and I know imperfectly, to express the ideas which have presented themselves to me on this occasion. I have sought to impress them on you, not by texts drawn from our sacred writings; not by arguments based on our creed, our forms, our traditions, or our laws; not by appeals to your sympathies, your passions, or your pride. I have attempted only to express the *one* simple truth, that the sufferings of our fellow-men, wheresoever and howsoever situated, demand from us alleviation, assistance and relief. Grant it in *this* case, for it is a pressing one. Grant it mothers, for mothers once happy and blessed as ye are ask it of you for their own sakes and for the sakes of their suffering babes; they ask it of you by *that* bond of sympathy which nature has created between ye; they ask it of you with streaming eyes and outstretched hands, to save them from disease and starvation. *Grant it wives:* to save a famishing husband, a wife asks it of you, and what stronger claim can she present to you? *Grant it sisters:* in a brother's name, in the name of pure and holy love, is it asked of you, and you will not refuse. *Grant it brothers; grant it men:* in the name of God it is asked of you, and it is, *I know* it is granted.[6]

97. DRY GOODS AUCTIONS

"Auction Sales," article in the *Drygoods Reporter and Merchants' Gazette,* New York, September 25, 1847 [1]

[It would seem from this report that in a few years Jewish merchants in New York had become such a conspicuous factor in the dry goods market that the advent of an important Jewish holiday affected the market and lead to the postponement of auction sales of imported fabrics. It should be remembered that the dry goods importing trade had in 1846 but just recovered from the setback caused by the great Pearl Street fire of 1835, which blazed for several days and was not quelled until entire blocks with extensive warehouses were blown up by Navy gunpowder. Since there was then almost no system of insurance of property, many of the richest merchants were bankrupted through the loss of many millions of dollars worth of stock. Credit abroad was not restored fully until 1842, and it took several more years before the trade began to prosper again.[2] This situation may have helped Jewish merchants to enter this business and take root in it.]

From our week's report it will be perceived that our Auction houses are in full blast, and although we have heretofore expressed the opinion that the Auction business as at present conducted is an evil in the Dry Goods trade;[3] yet so long as they do exist, forming as they do one of the most important features in the business, it is politic to keep ourselves, and through the Reporter our subscribers, fully informed of the leading features that manifest themselves; as without doubt through the Auction room, the pulse of the market, beats strongly. We perceive that within a few years a new race of buyers have appeared at our auction markets. We allude to our Jewish population, who although their fame has been world wide as stock and exchange brokers, heretofore they have engaged very sparsely in Dry Goods.

At present we should think that full 25 per cent of the sales made in our auction rooms are to this class of buyers; as one heavy Auctioneer informed us a day or two since, their credit has risen vastly within *even* the last year. In fact, so important a class have they become that the importer arranges, in many instances, the time of his sale so as not to come on a Jewish holiday. When so many important sales are taking place around us, it may be invidious to distinguish, but some of them have been particularly heavy and well attended, although a Jewish holiday for the first of the week[4] caused some drooping in the prices of Shawls.

Tuesday, Sept. 21.

Austens & Spicer—Assorted catalogue of British, French and American goods.

Alpaccas—300 pieces plain, sold at low prices.

do —100 pieces Plaid and Figures. do.

Cloths—125 pieces sold at fair prices.

Linens—Consisting of Napkins, 7-4 Damask Barnsley, Sheetings, 7-4, 8-4 and 9-4, sold at good prices.

47 lots Burlaps, sold under the inspection of the Wardens of the Port,[5] at good prices. Purchasers in attendance nearly all Northern and Western men and our own city jobbers.

Foster & Livingston—Large sale of French goods, 667 lots.
Broche, Long and Square Shawls—1000 sold at fair prices.
Thibet Shawls—3000. do
Mouselin de Laine—500. do
Stradilla—300. do
Terkerri—100. do
Many heavy Shawl buyers were absent, it being a Jewish holiday; prices somewhat lower than last sale.

Catterfield & Topping [6]—Cash Auction. Assorted catalogue. Sale good—attendance large, but we miss (and no doubt the auctioneer did) the Jewish buyers; this house is much frequented by retailers and small jobbers who pick up many job lots here.

98. JEWS AND SUNDAY LAWS

Editorial article, "Sunday Laws," in *Sunday Times and Noah's Weekly Messenger,* February 13, 1848 [1]

[Whether the laws of a democratic United States, in which the separation of church and state is a professed ideal, are to compel Jews to observe *Sunday* as a day of rest is decided by a superior court in the affirmative in this Charleston case. This was not the first such instance to become an issue in Charleston. As far back as October 15, 1776, the matter of Jews' selling goods on Sunday had been the subject of a presentment of the Grand Jury.[2]

The basis of the 1848 case was this: on Sunday, December 21, 1845, Sol. A. Benjamin, in his shop on East Bay, sold a pair of gloves to W. C. Gatewood. Benjamin was then charged with violating a Charleston ordinance of May 2, 1801, forbidding the sale and exposure for sale of goods on Sunday, subject to a $20 fine for each offense. Benjamin admitted the sale, but denied that he had exposed his wares for sale.

Both before then and since then down to contemporary times the issue has been raised by Christian Seventh Day Adventists and by Jews. In the majority of cases the courts have ruled against those who protested that observers of Saturday as a day of rest could not constitutionally be required also to observe Sunday as such a day.[3]]

A very interesting case, involving the constitutionality of Sunday Laws, was argued before the Court of Errors in Charleston,

South Carolina, on an appeal from the decision of the recorder of the city, who decided that it was not unlawful for an Israelite to vend goods on the first day of the week called the Lord's day, and that the ordinence [sic] against it was in violation of the constitution of the United States and that of the state.[4] The case was argued with great ability on both sides, and, as a question of religious liberty, created great interest and attracted a crowded court. It was contended by the learned counsel for the city and the commonwealth, that this was not a constitutional question, or a question of conscience at all; that the state had conferred the power on the city council to pass such laws for order and good government as that body might see fit, and the proper observence [sic] of Sunday as a day of rest was supposed to be included in that power. The learned counsel maintained that Christianity was part and parcel of the common law—that the common law was the law in South Carolina, and had made the first day of the week a day of religious observence [sic] and rest from labor, as was equally binding on Jews as well as Christians. Col. Phillips for the respondents, made a very able and powerful argument, contending that the law was not binding on the Jews, and was in itself a violation of their rights under the constitution. He cited, in particular, that law which made it obligatory for the Jews to labor six days and rest on the seventh day, which was the Sabbath of the Lord; and that the Sunday law, compelling them to rest on two days, in effect violated the divine commandment to labor every day in the week excepting the seventh. He contended that the law of Sinai was equally binding on Christians as well as Jews; and that that law, so impressive and so holy, had been set aside by an ordinance of the city council. The learned counsel also contended that it violated the constitution of the state, which had secured liberty of conscience to all religious denominations. The argument on both sides was learned, luminous and interesting; but Judge O'Neal,[5] in a very able opinion, concurred in by the whole court, reversed the decision of the court below, sustaining the Sunday laws.

We entirely agree with the court in this opinion.[6] The question has nothing to do with liberty of conscience at all: it is a mere local or police regulation, which should be carried into effect by all religious denominations living in the city and protected by its government. The free exercise and enjoyment of religious opinions and worship secured by the constitution, is not molested by any ordinance requiring shops to be closed on Sunday: hence Sunday is recognized as a day set apart and devoted to rest and religious observence [sic]. Freedom of religion means a mere abolition of all religious disabilities. You are free to worship God in any manner you please; and this liberty of conscience cannot be violated. An ordinance for the better observance of Sunday is a mere prohibition of public employment in the way of labor, trade, and business. We cannot in this perceive how liberty of conscience is to be invaded. It does not say to the Hebrew, 'You shall not keep holy the seventh day;' but merely declares that you shall not disturb the Christian by business or labor on his Sabbath. We can see nothing wrong in this. If the Israelites possessed a government of their own, they would assuredly prohibit labor on the Sabbath day. It would be their duty to do so, enjoined by their own law. Why prohibit the Christians from enforcing the same regulations? The question ought not to have been raised. Respect to the laws of the land we live in, is the first duty of good citizens of all denominations.

99. INDIAN AGENT

a) Excerpt from "Recollections of Augusta Levy (Mrs. John M. Levy)," about the year 1848, La Crosse, Wisconsin [1]

[These reminiscences of the life of the trans-Mississippi pioneer a century ago are full of life and personality, as this description of an Indian Council held in her home will testify. Augusta Levy was a German girl living in St. Louis when she married John Meyer Levy. Son of Eve Worms and Meyer Levy, a London Hazan, he was born in 1820, educated in Amsterdam and Paris, and came to St. Louis in 1837. In 1845 he went from Prairie du Chien, Wisconsin, to La Crosse with his partner, Isaac Marks, and in the Spring of 1846 Levy brought his wife Augusta and his son Willie to La Crosse, where theirs was the fifth family to settle. He was a successful Indian trader until the Indians were removed from the region, and in 1848 he was a Squire (judge). He built up and grew with the town of La Crosse.[2]]

. . . In the spring there was a great excitement over the removal of the Indians and we lost a great many of our best settlers. Mr. [D. C.] White, Mr. Horton, and Mr. Marks went along with them.

They all found pretty good trading posts and did very well. They tried to coax my husband to go too. They promised him the best place for trading that there was, but he thought he had had enough of the Indians. He was very glad they were going, and said he would not follow them. The Indian traders were gone but most of the Indians were still scattered around in Minnesota. They liked this country so well they refused to leave till they were taken by force, which was done about the middle of May. They begged my husband to allow all the chiefs to meet at our house for a council. He allowed them to come but told them they must keep sober and behave themselves. They promised faithfully, and left satisfied. Next day about eleven o'clock, a beautiful, bright day, we could see a great way up and down the river, all at once we saw the greatest sight I ever saw. About fifty canoes appeared, filled with all the Indian chiefs, all of them dressed and painted, and with big bunches of feathers on their heads and tomahawks in their hands. They were dressed in their best, and glistened as if a procession all shining with gold and silver was coming down the river. I didn't know anything about their arrangements, so little Willie [3] and I were scared. We feared that they were coming to kill us all, I ran to shut all the windows and lock all the doors. We were alone in the house. Then we hid ourselves in a dark room. I couldn't keep myself in hiding. You know how it is with women, even if they think there is danger, they want to see everything. I saw the Indians had landed from their canoes, in front of our house, by the river bank. I marked them all as they landed safely and as they came marching directly up towards our house I became alarmed again, and ran back into my hiding place. They knocked and knocked but I would not open the door. Then I heard some one pounding and pounding, and kicking against the door. This noise was not by mocassins but by boots. Then some one tried to break in the door. Then I heard swearing, in English and German, but I wouldn't open the door. Finally my husband came around to the kitchen window and called my name. Then of course I thought I was all right, and quickly came out of my corner. I asked him if he didn't see the Indians around by the front door. They were all there, with their tomahawks, to kill us. He said "Open the doors quickly, in Heaven's name! What did you lock yourself in for?" Said I "Didn't you see the Indians at the front door to kill us?" Said he, "If you don't open the doors, quick, I'll kick them in!" So I opened the kitchen door to let him in and he went to the front door at once to let the Indians in, while I hastened back to my hiding place. If there was any scalping to be done, I thought they could take him first. But they all went very quietly into the dining room, sat down on the floor, had a smoke all around, and then they asked for some water. My husband called me to bring in a pail of water and a pint cup, that he would stay in sight. I told him to take the pint cup, and the Indians, and take them down to the river and water them down there. Our hired man made his appearance just then and he was sent to the river after the water, because we didn't have any well. After this I got up courage enough, as I didn't see any scalping done, to peep in. As I say, they sat all around the room, and there wasn't a clean spot to be seen anywhere. They had used it for a spittoon, continually. I felt mad enough now to go down to the river and get water enough to drown them all out. My husband saw I was excited, so he took me into the other room and told me to have patience. After the council was over and they had left, he would get a couple of men and have the room cleaned. They took a smoke all around again and then shook hands and departed. I wished them a pleasant journey, and never to return. They got my husband to write to Washington to ask the government to take the treaty back. They liked it so well here that they did not want to go to the new home the government had provided for them. They waited till my husband got an answer from Washington. They were in hopes that they could stay but were refused, and had to leave the country, mighty quick. It was very lonely in La Crosse after so many of our best settlers left.

By June the Indians had all left for St. Paul, and our neighbor woman's husband, after a big family quarrel, had also left, and gone below to enlist and be a soldier. . . .

b) Letter "To the President of the U. S. or To the Secratary [sic] of Indian Affairs," La Crosse, June 1, 1848 [4]

[Acting as agent for the Winnebago Indians, John M. Levy asks that they be not compelled to remove. According to a treaty signed on October 13, 1846 by the United States with the Winnebago Indians, a tribe of some 2500 known to have dwelt in Wisconsin since the seventeenth century, the Winnebagoes were to remove west of the Mississippi and northward into Minnesota on June 6, 1848, but when the time to move came the tribe was very reluctant, having "an almost fanatical attachment to the Great Father of Waters, and the woods and prairies convenient thereto . . ."[5] After the Council held in Levy's home, as described by Mrs. Levy, he despatched this appeal.]

To the President of the U.S. or
To the Secratary [sic] of Indian affairs

The undersigned agent for the Winnibago indians by their own and special desire announces to the Indian department the following to wit On the first day June the Head chief of the Winnibagoes together with 12 of the most respectable otherwise Chiefs of the same nation met in council with Wabashaw head chief of Sue nation together with the Head Chiefs of the same nation, and after due deliberation sold To the Winnibagoes the following described piece of land to wit. Commencing at a point on Root River thence up the stream about forty Miles from thence running north to the Bluffs of Wabashaw prairie to the Mississippi river.

The Winnebago Indians therefor beg that they be allowed to take possession of the same and not be compelled to remove to the purchase made last year, without being allowed to choose their Location,[6] they are willing to give possesion of their lands they have sold to the United States immediately and will forever stay from the stream and never molest any of the white citizens, and defend their property and lives from the intrusion of the indians, they have sworn brotherhood with the Sue nation below St Petres, who are willing to live in unity with them, and are ready to move with the same at any time the United States shall make a purchase from the Sues below St Petres, they are willing to conform, with such arrangements as the Government may seem proper to make for them and be forever governed by the President's wise consideration, this they most earnestly pray, and be ever ready to obey the command of the Government of the United States, they also wish that they may be allowed to come to Washington and state their grievences, and not have their words misrepresented by a few interested traders, hoping that they will have a speedy answer from the president they have the honor to remain your most obedient servants

John M. Levy

Agent express for the Winibago Indians[7]

LaCross Wisconsin June 1st 1848

100. ELECTION CIRCULAR

Circular, "To the Electors of the Fifth Ward," New York, Fall, 1848 [1]

[This circular presents Emanual B. Hart (1809–1897) in the early stages of a political career that extended from the election of Andrew Jackson in 1832 to the close of the second term of Grover Cleveland in 1897. During all this time Hart was a "regular" Democrat and during most of it he was closely associated with Tammany Hall, succeeding M. M. Noah as a Jewish leader in that institution. The 1848 elections saw the Democrats divided: the Free-Soilers nominated Martin Van Buren and Charles Francis Adams for President and Vice-President, and John A. Dix and Seth Gates for Governor and Lieutenant Governor, while the Hunkers, who opposed abolitionism and the agitation of the slavery issue, nominated the ticket named on this circular. The Whigs' candidates were Zachary Taylor and Millard Fillmore for President and Vice-President, and Hamilton Fish and George W. Patterson for Governor and Lieutenant-Governor. The Whig ticket carried the nation and the state, although the combined votes of Free-Soilers and Hunkers in New York was greater than the Whig vote. Hart went down to defeat with the remainder of this ticket.[2]]

The period has arrived for action. Those who desire the perpetuity of Republican Institutions in their original purity, will perform this duty intelligently. The Democratic Republican Party present the illustrious and eminent names of *Lewis Cass,* for President, and *William O. Butler* for Vice-President, on whom too [sic] lavish praise would be superfluous; their distinguished and eminent services in behalf of our common country is matter of record. For Governor and Lieutenant-Governor, we have chosen as our leaders, *Reuben H. Walworth* and *Charles O'Conor,*–the one the profound, enlightened and eminent Jurist, the other the emigrants' friend, and eloquent and patriotic advocate.[3]

For Congress we present for your suffrages, your own favorite, devoted, inflexible and vigilant champion, *Emanuel B. Hart,* a man whose services in the Common Council for two successive terms,[4] have proved useful in the highest degree to his fellow citizens; whose position in private and public life command the esteem of his fellow men, and who has performed with fidelity all the duties of a citizen, patriot, legislator and democrat. The electors of the Fifth Ward have too often testified their approbation of his worth to need any further comments in his behalf. The nomination of *Henry Arcularius, Jr.*, for Register, the poor man's friend, their indefatigable and eloquent champion, the warm-hearted soldier, and intrepid fireman, and *Nicholas Quackenbos,*[5] for Assembly, augments the responsibilities of the democracy of the Ward; and the nomination of such staunch, worthy and faithful democrats as *Shepherd* and *McMurray* deserves our warm and enthusiastic support.

One bold, earnest and strenuous effort, and victory will peach [perch?] on our banners.

The polls will be held in the following places:

1st District, 49 Leonard street
2d " 307 Washington street, corner of Duane street
3d " Marion House, 165 Chapel street
4th " 107 Hudson street
5th " 32 Vesey street

Francis Boss,
Chairman Fifth Ward Committee.

Samuel J. Webster }
Robert C. McIntire } Secretaries.[6]

101. JEWS NEED NOT APPLY

Editorial, New York Sun, March 17, 1849 [1]

[Interesting is not only the protest of a Jewish shade-painter against his exclusion from the right to equal opportunity in employment but the editor's distinction between institutional and personal discrimination.]

A Bohemian writes to ask us what we meant by saying in our article yesterday on the secret of success, that in this country *all are equally encouraged and protected;* for he says he is a Hebrew by race, though a naturalized citizen, and that certain persons, tradesmen, in advertising in a journal of this city for a number of shade painters, put in as an exception, 'No Jews wanted here.' Bohemian, being a Jew,[2] and a shade painter, thinks the doctrine of equal encouragement and protection don't work here. We did not expect any such interpretation. We meant simply that the *government and institutions* of this country hold out the same inducements and chances to every citizen—in thus much and thus far they are equally protected and encouraged. If individuals, or members of different races and clans will disagree and battle with each other, the quarrel is theirs, and the more pitiable and shameful is it, to him who draws the weapon first and uses it furthest. We apprehend the spirit of our institutions and government is often more liberal and generous than that of many individuals who enjoy its blessings and who ought to imitate its example.

102. SUICIDE IN BROOKLYN

News Item, *The Sun,* New York, May 7, 1849 [1]

[The short and simple annal of a Jewish worker.]

The body of a German named Marcus Cohen, was found in a remote part of Greenwood Cemetery on Friday last. It seems that on Wednesday last, in a fit of desperation on account of pecuniary embarrassments he with a hair trigger pistol terminated his existence. He was a carpenter by trade, and boarded at No. 74 Greenwich Street, New York.[2]

103. THE FIRST JEWISH WEEKLY

The Credo, March 30, 1849, and the Conclusion, June 29, 1849, of *Israels Herold,* New York [1]

[Although *The Occident* was then being published monthly in Philadelphia since 1843, the first Jewish weekly in this country was launched in New York in German by an editor who had very recently arrived as a refugee from the Austrian counter-revolution of 1848, Isidor Busch (or Bush as he later spelled it). The purpose of *Israels Herold* was "to bring about unity among Jews," regardless of religious, social, and political differences. Isidor Bush, one of the finest figures in American Jewish life of this period, was born in the Ghetto in Prague, then under Austrian domination, on January 15, 1822. In 1837, his father, Jacob I. Bush, withdrew from the cotton trade in which he had made his wealth, and became a partner in the great publishing house of Von Schmidt, in Vienna; in December 1839, Isidor Bush became a member of the firm. From 1842 to 1847, Bush edited the *Kalender und Jahrbuch für Israeliten,* the first German periodical in Austria devoted to the new scientific study of Judaism. During the 1848 revolution in Austria, he published and edited the *Oesterreichisches Central-Organ für Glaubensfreiheit, Kultur, Geschichte und Literatur der Juden,* forty-nine numbers appearing between April 4 and October 25, 1848. In both magazines, Bush sought to help unify the Jewish community in behalf of religious and political liberty. The presses that printed the *Central-Organ* also printed revolutionary papers. Finally, Isidor Bush, together with his wife, Theresa Taussig Bush, and his only son, Raphael, left for the United States, landing at New York, January 4, 1849. Within less than three months after his arrival, Bush had begun to issue *Israels Herold.*[2]

In its brief career, this periodical reported on and stimulated various Jewish organizations, such as: the *Verein der Lichtfreunde,* which furthered the Reform movement, a Jewish Emigration Aid Society, a Society for the Promotion of Industrial and Agricultural Pursuits among Israelites, and a Jewish Ladies Penny Society for the maintenance of a Lying-In Hospital. *Israels Herold* also published the first attempts to write the history of the Jews of New York. One reason perhaps for the lack of support for the periodical was that, although it sought unity, it tended to reflect the views and report the addresses more of the spokesmen for Reform than any others. Not long after the discontinuation of publication, Bush and his family migrated to St. Louis, where he became a leader of the German-American and Jewish American communities, as we shall see in later documents.]

Credo

God has placed in every human breast the divine urge for truth, but truth in its *full* compass is supreme knowledge, the omniscience of God. This man cannot and should not attain on earth. The Creator in his infinite goodness has given man a ray, a reflection of His spirit —sufficient for man to *strive* to resemble God; sufficient for mankind always to make progress in this ceaseless striving; sufficient for our joy and happiness; but too weak for us to attain the goal of this aspiration and yet be secure against error. But in order that man, in the knowledge of the most important and noblest truths that have the greatest influence on his earthly and eternal well-being, and which constitute the most fervent wishes and hopes of his heart, be not subject to such errors, God gave His revealed laws, His teaching. He gave them first to us, and through us to all the rest of humanity.

Every word of this teaching is eternal truth. But divine wisdom, which follows a single plan in everything, has, in giving this teaching to man, not cut him off from further striving after knowledge, from the search by his spirit after these highest truths; has not made this either unnecessary or impossible for him. On the contrary, this very searching has been made his sacred duty; the Torah is to be only a guide to those who stray. Guided by it we are to search night and day. With confidence we are to march on in the knowledge of God, the fountainhead of all truth, until that blessed day, "when even the learned do not stray" (Isaiah, 35.8); "when the earth is full of the knowledge of God, as the waters cover the bottom of the sea." (Isaiah, 11.9).

But how can we approach this goal if we do not impart that which we have found to be truth along the way of such meditation? We feel its weight, it resolves our former doubts, it strengthens our courage, and our trust in God, or it urges us to virtue or gives us solace or comfort, and these are always the tokens of truth. Shall we not hope and wish that it also become truth and conviction for others? Are we to refuse to hearken because it might perhaps rob us of errors which through long usage have become endeared or even venerable to us?—Believe not that truth can be pernicious; only error is harmful! To be sure, even truth must not be imposed upon us by force; and errors in matters of faith, upon which thousands have often built a part of their moral philosophy, should not be torn down before those thousands have recognized the truth. Indeed, one man often considers worthless, nay, ridiculous what to another is inviolable, venerable, and dear. Thus it is quite understandable that readers and colleagues ask us what path we intend to tread, to what party we belong.

We have already declared in our prospectus [3] that we serve no color, that we shall be impartial and further only the interchange of ideas, and that *our* individual opinions are of no consideration. But for many that is not sufficient. They say, "Some will give themselves the appearance of impartiality and protest with passionate zeal and in bitter tones that they serve truth. Others, instead of giving reasons and proof for their opinion, will only hurl jeers and jibes against the old."

Well, such persons you will grant little credence. And we can readily see whether they change their conviction in the next attempt to gain advantage, favor, and places of honor. Fear not, dear brothers. Just allow the various opinions and convictions to express themselves and truth must emerge from the struggle of the contending parties as gold separates itself in the fire from the base metals.

We have declared in our prospectus that it shall be our most zealous endeavor to bring about unity among Jews. Now some ask: shall we direct this zeal toward the end that all observe the same religious forms and practises in life and in the divine service; or that we eliminate them all?

Neither, my brothers, but we shall work toward the end that you see that differences in this matter must not and should not divide us; that agreement here is not possible, and if it were—is not good. Just as no face is exactly like another, neither is any way of thinking. And yet, in spite of this difference, and in part perhaps because of it, men can and should love one another fervently; and likewise in spite of the most varied forms, they can honor God in truth and in the right way. It is not religious indifferentism, not half-heartedness of belief, that causes us to speak thus. It is our innermost conviction and the teaching that we have received from our prophets. "Is the Eternal well pleased with thousands of rams, with myriad streams of oil? No! He has made known to you, O man, what is good and what the Eternal demands: Justice, Love, and Humility." [Micah, 6. 7–8] Toward that we shall strive, in it be united, for it strengthen ourselves, and to this endeavor I dedicate these columns with all my soul.

Isidor Busch

Conclusion

"It is premature!" This is today's fateful theme. There has been too little cooperation given this enterprise and the subscription solicited in the last number (Number 12) has had such a weak response, that I prefer to give up the paper entirely rather than win for it an artificial, forced existence based on begging and the like.—I am so little vain that I say quite frankly that my paper has not pleased sufficiently; it has satisfied but few. To be sure, literary support here has been very weak, and in Europe too today special interest cannot be looked for or expected. Indeed, parties oppose one another so bitterly that they desire no reconciliation and understanding—yet, let that not excuse me or deter others. I believe and hope that someone else will soon publish such an organ with more skill and better luck.[4] Yet this first attempt cannot be denied the praise that it was indeed the first German publication here of its kind, that it stimulated much that was good, helped lay the cornerstone of many a benevolent organization, that it kept itself entirely free of malicious personalities, scandal, etc. (of which more contributions were submitted for publication than of any other kind), and even of kow-towing to parties; and finally that it has not enriched my pocket.—On the contrary, I have sacrificed many a dollar to the undertaking. Nevertheless, those who have paid for more than three months may without delay obtain the remainder from me on the presentation of their receipt. And may I be permitted the request that those gentlemen who have not yet paid their subscription at seventy-five cents (and there are more than sixty) no longer withhold this trifling sum.

To all those who have aided me in this difficult task through subscription, articles, etc., who have given the undertaking cooperation, forbearance, and favor—heartfelt thanks from

The Publisher.

New York—9th Tammuz 5609 [June 29, 1849]

104. TEMPERANCE

Letter to *The Experiment,* Portchester, Westchester County, New York, June 16, 1849 [1]

[This anonymous correspondence appears as the leading article on the front page of this rare small-town newspaper edited by Abraham G. Levy, in the only issue known to be in existence. That Levy was interested in the temperance movement may be inferred from this item elsewhere in the issue:

"THE EXPERIMENT, at Portchester, is down on the rum-selling Post-Master at that place, with a perfect tornado. Give it to him, Abraham; get the Post Office out of the rum-hole.—*N. Y. Washingtonian.*

"We have succeeded. The Postmaster is removed. We rest content."

But Levy's views did not prevent him from printing the advertisements of two New York City establishments offering "Champaignes, Brandies, Wines, Ale, Porter and Segars."]

Out of local beginnings in 1789 and 1804, the temperance movement had brought forth the first national organization in the United States in 1826, when the American Society for the Promotion of Temperance was established in Boston; in 1833, at a delegated convention in Philadelphia, the Society was converted into the American Temperance Union.[2]]

MR. EDITOR.

It gave me great pleasure to see in the last number of your paper, an advertisement of a Temperance Meeting, to be held in this place. The truth is, such a meeting should be no rarity in this community. There should be such a living interest in the glorious work of saving men from disgrace and ruin, as would make a Temperance Meeting a thing of frequent occurrence, and not only so, but the actual state of the community imperatively *demands* that energy and constancy of action on the part of the friends of the cause, which are the sure precursors of most triumphant success. As long as the liquor traffic is spreading itself, unmolested by law,[3] and unchecked by the morality of the people; as long as the Youth of our community are bound down in cruel bondage by a tyrant appetite; as long as old men tottle about our streets, with withered forms and hopeless souls, the living monuments of Rum's destroying hand; as long as the popular voice is silent in its condemnation of a system of moral, intellectual and physical destruction, unequalled in the annals of cruelty and oppression, so long will the *necessities of the case* call loudly upon us for unremitted and energetic action in the Temperance movement.

I would, Sir, that it might be your high privilege, through the medium of your paper, to set so fully before the community the awful ravages of Intemperance, as to warm into new life those generous and philanthropic emotions, which, developed into manly action, would cause the bold face of Intemperance, in this community, to wear the frown of despair, and would set in new motion, the now sluggish stream of Reform. Sluggishness and discouragement, on our part, is just what our opponents desire to see; for as long as the friends of the drunkard will neglect to spread the Truth, the contented venders will smile complacently at their indifference, and feast on the fruits of their pernicious traffic.

I ardently hope, Sir, that notices of Temperance Meetings will so frequently appear in your columns, as to be a source of great-uneasiness to those in our midst, who, worse than the wreckers on some unfriendly coast, live upon the shattered remnants of blasted hopes and withered joys. I hope it may be my privilege again to contribute my mite, to the advancement of the Temperance movement, through the medium of your paper;—meanwhile I remain

Yours truly

ALPHA.

105. AN OUTRAGE

Newspaper Clipping, "Outrage on the Living and the Dead," New York, August 12, 1849 [1]

[A bit of American social history is recorded in this account of how German-Americans in Brooklyn prevented Jewish-Americans from burying their dead.]

There are some 12 or 14,000 persons of the Jewish persuasion in this city, and finding it difficult to obtain burial grounds within the city limits, they have purchased land on Long Island and in other places. A German congregation purchased a burying ground near East New York, and one day last week, having occasion to bury an aged member, the German population of that place, with stones, guns, and clubs, dispersed the members, ordered them off, wounded several persons severely, and compelled them to deposit the body in the Cypress Hills Cemetery.[2] Complaint was made of the outrage to the authorities of Brooklyn, and we presume the parties will be arrested and made to answer for their conduct. These German emigrants imagine that a free country means the privilege of doing what they please, and violating law and order whenever it suits their purpose. A lesson or two will let them understand in what their rights consist.

106. OPPOSING SLAVE IMMIGRATION

A Communication On The Subject Of Slave Immigration, Addressed To Hon. Reuben Chapman, Governor of Alabama, By S. Heydenfeldt, Esq. Montgomery: . . . 1849

[Hitherto known only by its title, this document is here located and reprinted for the first time.[1] Speculation based upon the title has led to the misconception that Solomon Heydenfeldt was an early Southern Jewish abolitionist. In this pamphlet, however, Heydenfeldt complains of the "unjust and bitter crusades of the Northern Abolitionists," and it is known that when he went to California in the spring of 1850 his Southern pro-slavery principles involved him in conflicts with the California Democrats, led him to oppose the Union, and finally to denounce Lincoln's policy in 1861 as "tyranny." Yet this man who was later to be known as a "passionate secessionist"[2] opposed the importation of slaves into Alabama in 1849 on very interesting *economic* grounds: "I insist that the unproductiveness of slave labor, and its gradual, but certain, impoverishment of our State, is a sufficient reason for limiting its farther propagation among us." He is concerned because, on account of the slave system, "the State of Alabama is now poorer than she was fifteen years ago," and he fears that other Southern states, as they realize the uneconomic character of slave labor, will dump their slaves upon Alabama. He would, with slave importation limited, prefer to see "the employment of capital in other pursuits which never have been less profitable than cotton planting, and which, at the present prices of cotton, are so infinitely superior as to require no detailed examination." Finally, he answers those who are afraid that free laborers will lead to sharp struggles against capital with the argument that intelligent social legislation can mitigate these conflicts!]

TO HIS EXCELLENCY REUBEN CHAPMAN,
Governor of the State of Alabama:

Sir—Under the constitution it becomes your duty to recommend to the Legislature the enactment of such measures as you may deem best to promote the public welfare. For this reason I take the liberty of proposing for your consideration the question of prohibiting the further immigration of slaves into the State of Alabama, and a copy of the Bill to be brought into the next Legislature to amend the Constitution so as to effect that purpose. A measure somewhat similar, but more limited in its character, has been heretofore proposed. I allude to the attempt to prohibit slaves from being brought in for sale.[3] That scheme failed, I think for two reasons—first, because the public mind was not prepared for it; and, second, because the measure itself was too impotent to effect the good it aimed at. It was evident that such a law could be too easily evaded, and therefore did not strike at the root of the evil.

The State of Mississippi, I am informed, once had a similar law, and to provide against evasions, enacted that no slave brought into the State for the ostensible purpose of settlement should be sold or offered for sale within twelve months.

The result was that the slave dealers established plantations, stocked them with full supplies of Negroes, and at the end of the required twelve months' residence sold out, and replenished again from abroad, and thus went through the same formula each succeeding year. The only probable advantage which that law conferred, enured to the Negro dealer. It taught him that he could carry on his businčss more profitably and at less expence by having a farm, and raising his supplies of necessaries, in the centre of the slave market.

The measure here contemplated is more extensive in its operation. It is to prevent the future immigration of slaves for any purpose whatsoever, and to be so framed as to vindicate itself by the forfeiture of the slave introduced contrary to its provisions, and the still further punishment of the law-breaker as a felon.

This, and this only, is deemed of sufficient severity to ensure to the State that self-protection which her situation demands—the reasons for which I will now proceed to give.

It is very evident to any one, who is not [a] careless observer, that a restless and uneasy state of public feeling exists in the slave States North of us upon the subject of slavery. Maryland, Virginia, North Carolina, Tennessee, Kentucky [4] and Missouri, are pervaded with a feeling of hostility to the institution, which is only suspended from open exhibition and action by the dread of pecuniary loss, and the hope of finally shifting their slave population for value received upon the Southwestern States. This last alternative will doubtless be accelerated by the enactment of prospective emancipation laws, which means simply what it has ever meant by the States which have already abolished slavery—that is, that their citizens may have time enough to sell us their slaves, and having pocketed the price, to unite against us in the unjust and bitter crusades of the Northern Abolitionists.

It will then be easy to foresee that the Gulf States must become the St. Domingo of the Continent, or rush into a war of extermination, to the utter prostration of their capital.

The States above mentioned comprise more than half of the political strength of the slave States. It is therefore wise to endeavor to preserve our strength by keeping them on our side, and united with us in the same interest. This must be the result of the measure here advocated, not merely from the money value which these States affix to their slave population, but from the necessity of keeping in the only proper mode of subjection a class which otherwise will become a fearful nuisance. Or, if they be sincere in their ideas of Abolition, if they are actuated by sickly sympathy for the condition of the slave, then at least we force them to turn their slaves loose upon their respective domains, and thus keep their own nuisances and submit to their own loss. But, it may be safely said, that this latter alternative need not be apprehended. They dare not turn them loose.

But a stronger reason for immediate action upon this question lies nearer at home, and may be a startling assertion to those who have never investigated the subject. We have in our midst the germ of an anti-slavery party—not in the Northern sense of the term—not men who sympathise with the slave, and would therefore turn them loose upon society; but composed of those who are wearied with the struggle of unproductive labor; those who deem of slavery that it has produced pecuniarily nought but barrenness, and politically nought but bitterness; those who desire more populous white communities for the purposes of trade and education; and of those who regard the slave as their rival in production. This combination of opinion against slavery [5] has prodigiously increased within a few years, and is now increasing among us at a rapid pace. Numbers are every day added to those who long for the exodus of the slave; and unless we adopt, as a conservative measure, the plan here proposed, the time will come when we will see our capital in this species of property prostrated at a blow, and when, unprepared for such a change by any of the steps which a prudent foresight always adopts in mitigation, we will be in the same condition of poverty and embarrassment, without hope, which the misrule of Great Britain upon this same question has inflicted upon her West Indian dependencies. Upon this subject we cannot take the past as any indication for the security of the future. We can now, for the first time, see, within a short travel of us, the practical as well as political limitation of slave territory, whilst the business of slave breeding has extended in almost the same ratio as the productiveness of slave labor has diminished.

Some may think this an imprudent exposition under the present aspect of the relations existing between the North and South. I humbly conceive that those relations create a still stronger reason why the eyes of the South should be opened to the truth upon the question of extending slavery into the new territories.[6] If there is anything which can unite the South in a firm and determined attitude to resist any deprivation of her rights of emigration and occupation, it is the fact that she is already over-supplied with a laboring population not sufficiently productive to remunerate her, and about the future fate of which she is compelled to entertain just and reasonable apprehensions.

Thus far the argument has been exclusively on the ground of self-defence; I propose now to consider it in its other aspects, and to answer some of the objections I have met with.

I insist that the unproductiveness of slave labor, and its gradual, but certain, impoverishment of our State, is a sufficient reason for limiting its farther propagation among us. Cotton and Sugar are the only staples to which slave labor is reasonably fitted, and as but a small proportion of the slaves in the Union would soon fill up the lands profitably suited for the sugar culture, we are driven to assume that the cultivation of cotton is the only thing which can afford regular employment to the great mass of this population. In our State, upon an average calculation, cotton at its present price, will hardly pay the expense of producing it, and it is only in the fertile valleys of the Southwestern rivers that it can be profitably raised—and there, even, at lower prices.

To these valleys the slave emigration of the non-cotton producing States is rapidly tending, and we are beset with the fear of over-production as well from that source as from the natural propagation of those now among us.— That the number of cotton laborers is constantly and rapidly increasing here and in the best producing portion of the South, no one will contest, whilst, upon the other hand, we have no safe data upon which we can calculate for the increase of consumption beyond the natural increase of the populations of those countries which consume it, to which may be added a small increased consumption usually attendant upon the lowness of price; all of which, we may safely assert, cannot keep pace with the present increasing production. This, alone, must finally depreciate the value of slaves among us, until their transfer will become a mere nominal consideration.

One of the effects which the measure I propose would have upon our State, would be at once felt not only in curtailing the increasing supply of cotton, but in what is a natural corollary, the employment of capital in other pursuits which never have been less profitable than cotton planting, and which, at the present prices of cotton, are so infinitely superior as to require no detailed examination.

It may be asked whether the views here presented are not sufficient to impel our planters into the various other enterprises which are alluded to, by the considerations of their own interest, without the adoption of a measure which at first blush may revolt our feelings by its exclusiveness? I answer, No! The habit of a pursuit is as strong as any other kind of habit. Our people are accustomed to what they conceive are old and safe investment. If they make but little money directly by the production of labor, or merely pay expenses, they nevertheless suppose that they make a reasonable profit by the natural increase of their slaves, and do not reflect that, in a national point of view, if the workers are unproductive, so must be their issue.

Again, they know nothing about other pursuits, and as long as, with their surplus cash, they can purchase slaves, this habit, amounting to a constitutional indolence, will prevent their entering upon any investigation of other employments. To that investigation, and its consequent expectant fruits, they can only be driven by an unbending necessity.– Our immense water power–our coal, iron, lead, marble, granite, lumber, turpentine–our capacity to produce wool and silk and hemp–to build railways, and to carry on commerce, may all, in turn, be presented to their minds in liveliest colors, and will produce but a barren assent. The State of Alabama is now poorer than she was fifteen years ago–notwithstanding that, within that period of time, there has been expended within her limits nearly ten millions of foreign capital, and for which a heavy State debt is now hanging over her prople, at the same time that her resources for taxation are every day diminishing; and while a question of fearful domestic import is agitated for her destruction, her political strength is yielding to the rottenness of a system which must finally reduce it to a cypher. The statistics of population exhibit, that as slaves increase, the white population decrease. This seems to be a law of population. With us in the agregate [sic], it is undeniable, that slaves continue to increase, and if this is permitted to progress, with the consequent diminution of white population,[7] the far future of the South presents a picture, which, although now but "seen through a glass darkly," is of sufficient gloom to arouse into action her best energies, and prevent her from quiescently transmitting to posterity a problem, the solution of which seems so dreary a task.

I have been met with the objection, that as slaves form the principal feature in our system of taxation, the increase of that resource will be defeated, and taxes must fall heavier upon other property. I have already shown that the prospect of their future depreciation is so great as would scarcely leave them available for revenue purposes if the present system remains unchecked. This sufficiently answers the objection—while, again, the exclusion of their further introduction will, to a certain extent, appreciate the value of those remaining in the State. And it must be borne in mind, that of absolute necessity, the entire surplus production of the State which is now annually represented by investment in slaves, must be forthwith engaged in many of those other pursuits, which, yielding comparatively immense profits, will add materially to the wealth of the State, build up sources of taxation, and create ability to pay, infinitely superior to that which is produced by slave labor.

Another objection is, that it would diminish the value of our lands. This is utterly untenable. As long as good lands can be purchased in the Southwest at the government minimum, we have an established scale which must regulate the value of lands throughout the cotton region. Improved lands will only sell for as much as the improvements are valued at aside from the land. If this rule is seen to be occasionally violated, it will be found to depend on some peculiarity of local condition, or upon private circumstances surrounding the individual purchaser. The result is, that our lands may be now rated at their lowest possible depreciation. On the other hand, the probabilities are that, following the enactment proposed, a healthy white immigration would soon commence, which would appreciate the price of lands, from the fact that the very cause which would then induce this kind of immigration exists no where in the Southwest, nor elsewhere on the Continent, with the same attractive condition of climate, soil or natural resources.—Even admitting, for the sake of the argument, that a depreciation would ensue, that of itself would be an inducement to a more immediate immigration, which would soon restore prices.

Some have asked whether the proposed restriction would not be an infringement of our obligations under the Federal Constitution? This is already *res judicata*. The whole subject came under review by the Supreme Court of the United States in the case of Groves et al. vs. Slaughter,[8] reported in 15th Peters, p. 449, and the able opinion there delivered has settled the question in favor of the right and power of the States.

But, it may be inquired, why put restrictions upon the growth of an institution which has received the high praise of being conservative? for although it be less productive than other species of labor, is it not also less dangerous? That it is conservative, to a limited extent, I will not undertake to deny; but beyond this limit, as this whole argument proves, it must be disorganizing from its very impoverishing tendency. I have also sincere doubts whether this phase of the question of social conservatism has or ever will have any real merits in this country, whatever its importance in older and more populous ones. It is supposed that our slaves, representing as they do the laboring class of other countries, are so absolutely controlled as to remove any fears of the untutored radicalism which seems to threaten the peace of those communities. If such an argument be good at all, it would, as a consectary, lead to the social enslavement, or the extinction, of every free laboring population, as to ensure the conservation of order, and prevent the much feared peril of a conflict between labor and capital. But the fear of such a conflict with us, however distant, is, in my opinion, the result of a want of proper perception of the improving spirit and political economy of the age. We have yet to acquire the population to be feared, and it may safely be assumed that the great poverty leading to the debasement of any class has been well attributed to unequal and unjust laws, resulting from partial and ignorant legislation. There is enough in the world to supply every mouth, and this can be easily done, with a little more attention to the equity of distribution. True, we cannot destroy the distinction between wealth and poverty, which is necessary, and must always exist as long as men are created with unequal intellectual and physical proportions; but by the enactment of many just and wholesome laws, and the abrogation of the errors and inequalities of a legislation which yet shadows boldly its feudal descent, we may so mitigate the distinction as to prevent that amount of poverty and ignorance which, combined, produce the mob. And this, in the present enlightened and progressive phase of society, we have reason to expect and to hope.

In the limits which I have assigned myself, I am unable to do full justice to the subject to which I have called your attention, or to give the full scope and strength of the reasoning which sustains it. Born and reared at the South, I feel that I owe her my first duty and my best thoughts. This has induced me to venture, unaided, upon a task from which stronger hands have shrunk. What I have attempted has been with a pure devotion to the interests and prosperity of a country blessed beyond all others in her natural condition, but the development of whose resources are so far behind the civilization of the world as makes her seem to lack the Genius of Humanity.

With the highest consideration,

I am your excellency's [9]

Obedient servant,

S. HEYDENFELDT.

107. CONTRASTING EDUCATIONAL SYSTEMS

Letter from Dr. Joseph Goldmark to Professor Gabriel Gustav Valentin in Bern, Switzerland, dated New York, September 6, 1850 [1]

[This witty and intelligent letter records the first impressions of a refugee from the defeated 1848 Revolution in Vienna in contrasting the status of American education, especially in the medical field, with his experience in Vienna and Switzerland. Dr. Goldmark notes pointedly the low standards of instruction, the insecurity and small salaries of the professors, the scarcity of highly qualified professional men, and the growing receptivity to European scientists. The sum is a vivid picture of the material conditions of intellectual life in our country. If the portrait is negative and not flattering, it should be remembered that Dr. Goldmark's appreciation of the relative freedom of the American intellectual climate had already been expressed in a preceding letter, in which he had concluded: "The man of European culture who has fled from the old world in its ossification and decay, is alienated by the still unformed, uncultivated conditions of the new. Only in its new principles, in the brilliant promise of its vigorous youth does he find hope of a new and better organization of society. The important factor in this new order I find in American family life and the system of education, so totally opposed to the European."[2]

Dr. Goldmark (1819–1881) was a physician, chemist, and bourgeois-democratic leader in the March 1848 revolution in Vienna. Born in Poland, and educated in Hungary and at the University of Vienna, he was an assistant physician in the Vienna General Hospital when the revolution was maturing and winning adherents particularly in the medical school. He became a captain in the Academic Legion, served in important positions on the leading committees of the revolutionary movement, and was one of five Jews elected to the new Reichstag, which voted to abolish the feudal land system and all special taxes and residence restrictions on Jews. He was on the committee that drafted the democratic Kremsier Constitution. When the Minister of War was killed in the workers' uprising of October 6, 1848, and the white terror led to the triumph of counter-revolution and the dissolution of the Reichstag by Francis Joseph on March 6, 1849, Goldmark was accused of complicity in the killing of Minister Latour, although he had actually tried to protect him. With other revolutionary leaders, he had to escape from the country, and arrived in New York on July 29, 1850. Democratic circles in the German and general communities, as well as the Jewish community, welcomed his arrival.[3]]

New York, September 6, 1850

Dear Friend,[4]

I have just come from New Haven, where, because of the meeting of the American Association for the Advancement of Science, I had a favorable opportunity to see Prof. Agassiz[5] sooner than would have been the case if I had gone to Cambridge, which I should probably have been able to visit next month. New Haven is a very friendly, quiet university town situated on Long Island Sound, inhabited by pious Puritans, where theaters are banned by law as irreligious institutions and where Sunday boredom has set up headquarters. If I were a European reactionary and C. Vogt[6] fell into my hands, his death sentence would be exile for a Sunday to New Haven; to be sure Vogt would be right in saying that the punishment would be more easily bearable in my company, but that would not be part of the plan. If I spoke of the appearance of a university town, you must not imagine the venerable picture of a German alma mater. Except for the noise of the students and the Philistinism, the schools here have nothing in common with the German ones. The position of the teachers, the manner of instruction are as different as day and night. In all of the United States there are no real state universities.[7] All such institutions are private. Only a few receive occasional grants from their particular states. Most are established by the endowments of rich private individuals and are supported in addition by student fees. Many are simply private business enterprises, such as Crosby College[8] here. Several professors, licensed by the state. provide the necessary buildings and apparatus and open classes. Every newly entering professor contributes his quota to the common capital, and any one leaving takes his share out. Pensions and appointments for life are quite unknown in the United States. Agassiz is appointed for only *five* years. But as a rule the professors remain until advanced old age because the prosperity of the institution is bound up with their fame and learning. At the endowed universities there are regular salaries that are not very high. Thus Agassiz himself has an annual salary of only $1500. At many others, income is dependent on the number of students; at Crosby College here that would amount to about $2000. In addition, the more famous professors have a considerable and easy source of income from their public lectures, which are very well attended. You see, it is customary throughout the Union for the more notable scholars to visit the larger cities and give popular scientific lectures, both at the invitation of the numerous scientific societies and clubs, as well as on their own. Thus Agassiz when he came here gave six lectures that brought in $2000. His annual income is increased by such lectures to $4000. A third very considerable source of income for the medical professors is their practise as consulting physicians, which takes little time and is very lucrative, if one has acquired some reputation. Instruction itself is extremely superficial. The first introduction consists in visiting patients at the side of a practicing physician. Then the student, who usually has had no previous scientific training, takes a two semester course, of four months[9] each, in anatomy, chemistry, pharmacy, therapy, and surgery, and after an easy examination gets his doctor's degree, which, however, is not necessary for practising, since any one, without the slightest medical knowledge, may assume the title of doctor and begin practising. Here in New York there are three medical schools: the medical faculty of the university, where the professor of chemistry will now lecture on physiology too;[10] Crosby College, where so far as I know physiology is not yet taught at all;[11] and the recently established New York Medical College, from the program of which you will see that there is already talk of physiology, organic chemistry, and microscopy, but whether much of that is taught seems very doubtful.[12] Nevertheless there are very capable specialists: for example, the anatomist Knight in New Haven, the operating surgeon Mott here, who was the first one to tie up the anonyma, and the outstanding mineralogist Dana. These men, however, acquired their knowledge in Europe.[13] There is precious little to be found in the way of thorough general scientific, not to speak of philosophical, education. All philosophy here consists of theological controversies, which are quite the equal in absurdity of the old Talmudic *midrashim,* and with which Agassiz had to contend on account of his attacks on the Biblical story of creation. On the other hand, there are in most states very well organized secondary schools—"free schools, free academies"—supported at public expense, where the students are provided free of charge with all necessary books and writing materials.

In regard to appointment to higher academic positions, there prevail here, as in Europe, private considerations, family connections, and national pride. The direct invitation of European teachers, without their previous personal presence, is something quite rare. Nevertheless, European and particularly German science is being more and more recognized here, and its representatives are highly regarded and very welcome, because the American knows very well that the rapid growth of the country can only be ascribed to intellectual activity. Therefore he respects every intellectual power and seeks to acquire it for his advantage. I am firmly convinced that Liebig,[14] who according to the local papers is to come here to give lectures, will receive the most splendid offers, while it would be unlikely that an invitation would be sent to him in Europe. So to form any judgment from these facts in regard to your request, it would be about as follows: it is true, as Agassiz told me too, that you cannot expect an immediate *direct* invitation, still less an advance appointment with pay; however, that you will quite certainly find a very fine position, when you have become personally known to the professors and influential men here, and to the lay public through the press and some lectures. In my opinion it would thus be best to continue your study of English through the winter, finish the next summer semester as early as possible, and come here immediately, alone. By steam ship these days it is a pleasure trip of eleven days, and from Bern to this country in the first cabin the cost is no more than $200, at the rate of two florins, 30 kreuzer. During the two vacation months you will then have time to become acquainted with the country and its conditions, to give lectures in several large cities, to become acquainted with the academic world at the meeting of American natural scientists which will take place next spring in Cincinnati and in Albany in the fall, and to determine, after some choice, the place of your professional activity, which will not be at all difficult, in view of the considerable number of medical schools.[15] The pecuniary advantages will probably be the same everywhere, consisting of an annual income of at least $4000 from courses and lectures, which could be considerably raised by a consultation practise (and I can see no real reason for its being less), while household expenses here in New York would amount to $1500 or at most $1800, for food is cheaper here than in Vienna and only rooms and clothing are more expensive. A decent place to live costs from $300 to $350.

In regard to your future position and effectiveness, I feel I must not hide the fact that you will have to descend quite far to the students' level of comprehension in order to raise it gradually, as Agassiz had to also; but that you will find a very wide field of activity and without doubt every recognition. There is not a single important physiologist in America, and very few biologists. The difficulties of lecturing in a foreign language are soon overcome after a short sojourn in the country. Agassiz read his first lectures here out of notebooks and even after having been here four years he speaks very correctly, to be sure, but still with an obvious German accent. However, this has only made his lectures all the more piquant and popular. Agassiz was indeed the center of this year's meeting; he towered far above all other members, he was tirelessly engaged all day as a member of nearly every committee of the conference, yet he gave several lectures at every session, always in free, fluent language. He is known and highly regarded throughout the Union partly for his lectures and partly through the exceedingly powerful press. From his experience, it is evident that one can expect the usually meagre resources for scientific work to become more adequate. He was asked why he did not use the university library. When he answered that there was nothing usable in it, the librarian [16] asked him for a list of desirable books. Agassiz refused, with the comment that he would prepare the list as soon as the necessary money was made available; whereupon the bookdealer was ordered immediately to supply $3000 worth of books of Prof. Agassiz's selection. There is quite a lack of scientific periodicals and inexpensive instruments. The analytical laboratory in New Haven gets all its pure chemicals and its apparatus from Europe.

There is nothing to report about the scientific or intellectual life in general of the Germans here (New York numbers 80,000 of them, and about 25,000 Jews). There is a society of German doctors, the purpose of which is supposed to be the furthering of science; its accomplishments up to now, however, have been nil. In its meetings the members exchange their practical experiences as to the native disposition, (*genius epid.*) and its possible gastric-catarrhic-bilious pathological character. In Philadelphia at present a German medical periodical is being published, whose main weakness is its lack of competent collaborators.

About the bonds of the United States I can tell you only what I have learned from the papers. There are United States bonds and bonds of the individual states. Both yield 6 percent and have a definite date of maturity, at the end of which they are redeemed at their face value. Those are higher which have a later date of maturity. Those that fall due in 1868 are now 116–116½ and are very much desired in Europe because they are more secure than all the European issues. In case you want to buy any, one of my acquaintances has offered to buy them and to send them to his banker in Paris, where you can get them. But he wants a guaranty that you will be certain to take them in Paris.

I should have liked very much to enclose a clipping on the death of poor Prof. Webster, but the weight of the letter makes it impossible. He admitted the murder but to the very end denied premeditation.[17]

Finally, one request with which I burden you because I see in the note from Agassiz the possibility of its rapid realization. The acquisition of European scientific publications is made difficult here for private individuals through tariff, slow transportation, and high prices. (Institutions do not have to pay import duties.) It would therefore be very desirable if you would kindly send me Oesterlein's "Manual of Materia Medica," 3rd edition, and Wunderlich's "Special Pathology and Therapy," so far as it has appeared, through H. Major of Neufchatel, whom Prof. Agassiz is expecting here at the end of October.[18]

And now adieu, with best wishes for your health and happiness, let me know any questions of detail that you still want answered by your friend

Goldmark.[19]

108. EARLY CHICAGO DAYS

Recollections of Chicago in 1850–1851, by Leopold Mayer [1]

[These personal reminiscences provide significant detail about the life of Jews in Chicago when that city, incorporated in 1837, had only some 30,000 inhabitants in 1850. Mayer recalls facts about the religious, educational, economic, social, political and family life that help vivify the century-old setting. Leopold Mayer (1827–1903), born in Abendheim, Germany, had two older brothers in Chicago, who had been there four and six years respectively, when Leopold arrived in 1850. In addition to engaging in the activities he records in these reminiscences, he became president, in 1858, of the Jüdische Reformverein, which led to the establishment of the Sinai Congregation, of which Mayer was an incorporator, July 20, 1861.[2]]

Leopold Mayer, whose half-century of residence in Chicago is all but complete, spoke before the Council of Jewish Women at Sinai temple [3] yesterday afternoon on Jews and Jewish life in Chicago in the early '50s.

Mr. Mayer began his career here as a teacher of secular and religious learning to his compatriots in Chicago, who then numbered 200.

Today he is a banker, the firm being Leopold Mayer & Son, and holds a foremost place in the social and religious life which centers at Sinai temple.

Mr. Mayer said, in passing: "I relate what I remember, and offer my reminiscences as a slight but perhaps not entirely valueless contribution to the history of the beginnings and progress of our people in Chicago."

He began with his departure from Germany:

"Fifty years ago, on the 19th day of this month, on a cold, rainy morning, at about 5 a.m., with my sister and sainted father, I boarded a Rhine steamer. After some delay I reached Antwerp, and here, I saw for the first time, a Jewish burial from the synagogue, instead of from the home. The funeral was that of the president of the congregation, chief of the branch house of the Rothschilds; otherwise, the rites would have been of the same character as in my home, a small town in the interior of Germany.

"Finally, after a stormy voyage of 65 days, I arrived on Friday, Feb. 15, 1850, in New York. I gave my first exhibition of 'greenness' during the ride in an omnibus to the home of my friend. I was astonished to see so much twist bread, used in Germany, only for the Sabbath, and I remarked that Jews must be numerous, as Sabbath bread was so in evidence.

Freedom at Last

"How happy I was when I reached the promised land of freedom, where the laws, at least, are the same for Jews as for non-Jews.

"At that time, the stigma of inequality burned in me like a fiery coal, because I felt its sting and suffered its pangs. In New York, my best friend and former teacher, known to many of you, Moses Spiegel, took me to the first Jewish Reform temple I had ever visited; situated in Christie street, Dr. Me[r]zbacher was its rabbi.[4] There I found the male attendants divided, one class composed of those with hats, the other of those with caps. The women were then still in a separate part of the temple, but whether they, also, were classified as to headgear, I can not say. From the observations of later years, I might say 'yes.' Reform Judaism deserves credit for the redemption of the women from separation during the divine service. In Chicago, Sinai con[gre]gation granted equality to the women from its inception.

"April 23, 1850, when I came to Chicago, the Jews numbered possibly 200. The congregation had 28 contributing members, and on the very first day I was introduced to most of them, including the president and minister.[5] The congregation provided for a reader, a chasen, and a shachet—a man able to kill cattle and fowl according to Jewish rites. The German arrangement of prayers was in vogue, but it was so diversified that it often depended on the reader what prayer was read, and the addition or omission of a prayer was an infringement upon the religion, and so I remember that as late as 1858 the omission of a certain prayer created a row in the synagogue.

"The duties of a minister were manifold. He was the reader, he had to perform the marriage ceremony, he had to be present at funerals and read the prayer there as well as in the house of mourning, he had to act as shachet—that is, to kill cattle and fowl according to Jewish rite and custom.

"Instruction in both the tenets and the morals of Judaism were lacking. Every Jew was his own teacher and rabbi. A religious school for children was not necessary, as there were but few children of school age here.

Sorrows of the Colony

"The two previous years, 1848–9, had been trying for the Jewish colony, on account of the cholera, which not only bore away several of its members, but left the survivors in constant dread of its return. A burial ground had been purchased from the city as early as 1846.[6] It is remarkable how anxious the Jews are to provide a resting place for their dead, when, as yet, they have scarcely a foothold for the living; this is noticeable through all their history. To the praise of the Jews then here, I must say that they clung together in sorrow and in joy. The good fortune of one was the happiness of the other, while the gloom of one cast a shadow over all. Thus, on my first Friday night in Chicago, I watched, with one of my brothers, at the bedside of the sick child of a friend.

"The place of worship was then located on the southwest corner of Lake street and what is now Fifth avenue, on the third floor. The narrow, uninviting entrance was unpleasantly obstructed by the goods of an auctioneer, who occupied the store floor below. Already at this period the Sabbath was more or less violated. It is true that most of the women and many of the men were regular attendants, but the latter, as a usual thing, left hur[r]iedly for their places of business. Many stores were already open, and the younger men, engaged as clerks, were invisible in the synagogue. The younger women, likewise, were few, and of children under 15 there were scarcely any.

Educational Needs Faced

"During the fall of 1850 I tried to organize a religious school from the few scholars I already had and the few more I might gather round me. To show the necessity for this, one incident will suffice. To make known my purpose, I went to the president of the congregation to ask leave to post on the door of the synagogue a notice to the effect that I would open a school to teach religion. In all seriousness he, the president, asked me what I intended to teach, and I found that my first lesson must be given to the head of the congregation.[7]

"The year 1851 was important in the religious development of Jewish life. In June the first Chicago synagogue, on Clark street, between Adams and Quincy, was dedicated by Mr. Isaacs of New York.[8] The exercises were well described by Mr. Elias[s]of in his history of K. A. M.[9] Mr. Isaacs, in his Saturday morning sermon, charged the congregation with neglect of the purity laws, and then declared that the punishment of God was visible in the death of young married women, several of whom had recently died. To the credit of the president be it said that he at once left the synagogue.

"Let us now turn to the social and political life. Our people were far from being a political unit. Some were hard-shell democrats and some were ardent whigs; free-soilers, there were hardly any. My first political knowledge came from the free-soilers, and I readily adopted their doctrines, as they coincided closely with the ideas of liberty I had imbibed in Germany during the stormy times of '48.[10]

Relations Between Jews and Non-Jews

"The relations between Jews and non-Jews were cordial, and many of the former not only belonged to the various political and fraternal organizations, but also held offices therein. Numbers belonged to the volunteer fire department, and Henry Greenebaum [11] was captain of engine company, No. 6, when he was scarcely 21 years old. The balls and festivities given by the non-Jews were often attended by the Jews, who were never in the least looked upon as undesirable. The Germans, Jews, and non-Jews were one, and the prejudices from the fatherland, if not dead, were at least hidden. For myself, I must say that I was made welcome in every American household in which I had scholars or where I had been introduced. I was invited to all the parties given by the young people of my acquaintance, and it was to an American lady that I owed my success.

"Among the Jews themselves social entertainments gradually increased in number as the number of young men and women grew. Engagements were still few, but the young folks longed for diversion. In summer, carriage rides and joint walks in the fields, and in winter, sleigh-rides were in order; sometimes there were even theatre parties given.

"The visiting day was Sunday, and it was always prearranged at whose house the following Sunday should be spent. There were no whist nor poker parties—as yet, the ladies did not play cards. Dances, today called balls, were difficult to arrange; but we had them.

Jewish Business Beginnings

"Now, a word to the commercial and financial condition of the Jews. Ladies, please remember that most were German im[m]igrants and that rich people seldom emigrate. Hence, in comparison with their standing in the fatherland, the Jews in Chicago were fairly well situated. They were already engaged in the various branches of commerce. Some had dry goods, others clothing stores; many were engaged in the cigar and tobacco business, and there were already a plumber and joiner, and even a carpenter, here. Some—loading their goods upon a wagon, others upon their shoulders—followed the honorable vocation of peddling. Honor to them! They were respected and liked by their customers, who every season awaited their arrival before laying in a stock of necessary goods. Whether or not to compare them to the renowned Yankee peddler, I leave to you. At all events, they made a good living for their families, and while gathering money, at the same time established a business that grew with the country. At that time there were no millionaires among the Jews, but all felt independent. The words and acts of the charity of today were not then in vogue, for each lived by his own exertion.

Life in the Home

"In order to give my picture tone and color, I must take up one more subject, the last but not the least—the home. What had the Jews preserved of the old home traditions of the fatherland, so often lauded and cited as the greatest cause of the preservation of the Jews in spite of centuries of persecution? The home was the cement which bound child to parent and parent to child. The bond between brother and sister. We might call it a three-stranded thread which could not be torn asunder. If the Englishman called his house his castle, the Jew could with justice call his home his religion, his comfort, and his delight.

"To give you an idea of the Jewish home in Germany, let me lead you into one. We will make our visit on neither a festive day nor a Friday evening, for of these you have doubtless heard or read very often.

"Let us step over the threshold silently, lest we disturb the inmates. We enter a gloomy room with but one light on the so-called Sabbath lamp, just bright enough to bring out the darkness.

"Our first glance discloses a man of about 45 years, sitting at the table and surrounded by his children. His face and the silence and tears of the children, all express dismal grief and sorrow. A closer inspection reveals the cause of the gloom. On the bed lies a sick woman, emaciated by the dread disease, consumption. The body is nothing but skin and bones. Disturbed by our entrance, she turns to the light, her eyes still bright. In a hushed voice, scarcely audible, she asks for her boy; he is not only her nurse, but her angel, and in her suffering her comfort. She desires him to commence his usual vocation during the long, dreary nights, to read to her. There, my friends, you see a Jewish home in distress. The oldest child, the staff and support of his sick mother, reading to her night after night to while away the dreary, dreary hours, when sleep does not come to relieve the patient sufferer whom the angel of death has already marked for its victim. Such devotion, such filial love, you found among the Jews of the fatherland, and it is not remarkable that with such memories to spur them on the Jewish pioneers in America, to some degree, at least, emulated their parents.

Homes Humble but Happy

"The houses in which we lived in those days in Chicago were modest one or two story frame dwellings. Samuel Cole was the only one occupying a brick home, though Mr. Schubert lived over his brick store.[12] The dietary laws were strictly observed and the Sabbath and festivals were celebrated with Jewish rites. Business houses were at no great distance from the homes and the men were generally to be found with their families after business hours. The women occupied themselves with needlework, household duties, and reading. The children were reared to honor and obey their parents. The father had not yet attained to the dignity of 'governor,' nor was the mother mentioned as the 'old woman.' If the Jewish home was not quite what it was in Germany, it was still founded on filial love and respect."

At the conclusion of the lecture a vote of thanks was tendered Mr. Mayer.

109. THE FUGITIVE SLAVE LAW

Editorial, "The Higher Law," from *The Asmonean*,[1] January 10, 1851

[The Fugitive Slave Law of 1850, described as "one of the most barbarous pieces of legislation ever enacted by a civilized country,"[2] strengthened the ineffective law of 1793. The new legislation provided that United States Commissioners as well as the courts could decide to issue a warrant for the seizure of a fugitive slave; that the claimant's assertion or his agent's was enough to establish ownership of the accused Negro; that punishment for violations included $1000 fine, six months imprisonment, and liability to damages of $1000 for each slave lost; that all citizens must aid in executing the law; that commissioners be paid $10 for issuing a warrant but only $5 for setting a Negro free from his captors; that United States marshals refusing to execute the law were subject to $1000 fine or payment of the value of the slave. It is this law that is here upheld.

It should be noted, however, that some Jews, as well as non-Jews, opposed the law, and even aided fugitive slaves in defiance of the law. Thus in Chicago, in 1853, Michael Greenebaum led a crowd of citizens against a United States marshal who had arrested a Negro, and freed him; "the same evening a big meeting was held to ratify this act."[3]]

Congress, by a most emphatic vote, has refused to revive the discussion upon the Fugitive Slave Bill; and its determination to allay the excitement roused by wrangling on so fertile a theme, deserves the approbation of all well-meaning men. We have at various times been favored with comments from correspondents, upon the view to be taken of the law of Moses, regulating slavery; and with but one exception (Asmonean, No. 1, Vol. 3)[4] we have passed them by, as being partial and futile. Not that we deem it wrong to set up the Bible for a rule of action in modern times,[5] but that those exponents seize hold of a clause which apparently bears up their views upon a particular topic: and, disregarding how the clause has been construed by the people to whom the law was given; overlooking [t]he various difficulties incidental to the vast change in the position of things since the law was enunciated; considering a police regulation to be a religious ordinance or construeing [sic] a religious ordinance by the rules of political economy; they hurry to a conclusion and claim for the cited passage an indisputable authority—an authority over and beyond that of laws made by man; thus demanding and seeking to enforce a succumbing of the laws of the land to the laws given to the Israelites. The difficulties in which such a mode of reasoning involves Christians are manifold; even its advocates cannot be blind to the shock, the enforcement of the principle would give to the stability of the church of which they are members. Urged by the desire to place around their sentiments a marble shield, they eagerly adopt principles, and quote as author[it]ative the ordinances, of a people on whom they have showered bitter scorn for remaining stedfast thereto. This fealty real, or assumed, may be thought congenial to our feelings as Hebrews; it is not so: The laws of Moses need no forced interpretation or strained application. They were given to the tribes at Sinai, to be propagated among the nations of the world, to day, as well as when the people stood at the foot of the mount. They contain words of wisdom and of holiness, are fraught with precepts of unparallelled excellency, abounding with principles productive of love and happiness: Yet we demur to the application of an isolated clause without reference to the mode in which our ancestors understood and administered it.

When we look to the Bible for precedents in the matter of a fugitive slave, we find that it is not without proof of the presence and exercise by the Hebrews of the principle of the American law; and if our friends, so ready with the text of Deuteronomy,[6] had gone further to the palmy days of Israel, when the probability is that the laws of Moses were as well comprehended and as rigidly adhered to as they ever have been, even in Jerusalem; the principle of reclaiming the absconded slave was proven and acknowledged. For upon the accession of Solomon to the throne, in rewarding and punishing the friends and enemies of his departed sire, he enjoined a Benjam[in]ite, one Shimei [7] the son of, Gera, on the peril of his life, not to depart the walls, not to cross the brook Kidron, to which the latter assented, but failed therein; and for greater accuracy we cite the passage, 1 Kings 11 v 39 and 40.

39 And it came to pass, at the end of three years, that two of the servants of Shimei ran away unto Achish son of Maachah king of Gath: and they told Shimei, saying, Behold thy servants *be* in Gath.

40 And Shimei arose, and saddled his ass, and went to Gath to Achish to seek his servants: and Shimei went, and brought his servants from Gath.

It is unnecessary to recite the arguments which able commentators have raised upon this episode in the life of Solomon; some having impeached the justice and clemency of the wise monarch, asserting, that the restricting Shimei within the walls was virtually a sentence of death: as the inspired knowledge of the King must have foreknown, that the workings of man[']s spirit would induce a violation of so simple a restriction; yet the cause for the infraction is given as a legitimate reason why Shimei left the city; hence the claiming and the restoration of the fugitive was not contrary to the law.

Turning from the books held to be scriptural by the Hebrew, let us regard what the canons of Christianity contain in reference to this subject. The epistle of Paul to Philemon is written to save Onesimus [8] a fugitive slave from punishment; and the writer after stating that he might enjoin what was convenient by "their brotherhood in faith" says:

"Yet, for love's sake, I rather beseech *thee,* being such a one as Paul the aged.

10 I beseech thee for my son Onesimus, whom I have begotten in my bonds.

11 Which in time past was to thee unprofitable, but now profitable to thee and to me:

12 Whom I have sent again: thou therefore receive him, that is, mine own bowels.

15 For perhaps he therefore departed for a season: that thou shouldest receive him forever:

18 If he hath wronged thee, or oweth *thee* aught, put that on mine account.

19 I Paul have written *it* with mine own hand, I will repay *it*.

Having shown the practical operation of the law at periods when it may be assumed the code did not want for zealous defenders, it cannot be necessary to press the point further, or, to go back and argue the general principles which dictated its enactment. To do this, it would be essential that an agreement should exist, to regard the laws as an entirety, retaining full force, binding upon all. Will the opposers of the Fugitive Slave Bill assent to such a proposition?[9]

110. STATES' RIGHTS VS EQUALITY ABROAD

a) Letter from Joseph Abraham and other Jews of Cincinnati to Secretary of State Daniel Webster, February 25, 1851 [1]

["Having been taught that when religious persecution commences its end cannot be foretold," twenty four American Jews asked that the Treaty of Friendship, Commerce, and Extradition negotiated with the Swiss Confederation on November 25, 1850 be rejected because, the petitioners maintained, the Treaty declared that "Christians alone are entitled to the enjoyment of the privileges guaranteed by the present article in the Swiss cantons." That such a stipulation could even have been included in any draft presented to the Senate is startling in itself, and can be understood only in terms of the theory of the supremacy of states' over federal rights that then prevailed in government circles in this country and in Switzerland. To such theorists, the Swiss defense that their federal government could not interfere with the anti-Semitic provisions and practices of the several Cantons was plausible, since in the United States the same reasoning was being used to defend a state's right to perpetuate slavery against federal action.

A. Dudley Mann (1801–1889), the special agent who negotiated the Treaty, was a Virginian advocate of states' rights, and later a secessionist and Confederate special agent in Europe; when the Confederacy was defeated, Mann did not return to the United States, and he died in Paris. Now Mann was "a convinced democrat [who] viewed the rise and sweep of the revolutionary movement [in Europe] with unbounded enthusiasm," and he was eager to negotiate this treaty because he feared the Tsar and his counter-revolutionary allies would dominate the Swiss.[2] But the Instructions Mann had received from Secretary of State John M. Clayton of Delaware (1796–1856) defined two motives for negotiating the treaty: "At this period when the reactionary movement of continental Europe seems to threaten the obliteration of liberal political institutions we owe it to the character of our own free government, as well as to the commercial interests of our country, to strengthen, by all the means at our disposal, the ties, which bind us to the Swiss confederation, which like our own happy land is the home of the free." Then Clayton very specifically defined the economic interest of the Southern plantation owners in this treaty: ". . . Switzerland with a population of something less than two millions and a half, is reckoned to be the consumer of 150,000 bales of American cotton as well as much of our tobacco, rice and other products. The Swiss duties on tobacco are merely nominal, as they are upon the other products of the United States. Were the confederation even now to enter the Deutsche Zollverein, the heavy duties amounting to 3.35 pr cwt. on tobacco would add to the oppression of the regié, and enormous duties in other countries already so deeply affecting that American staple. . . ."[3] Thus Southern export interests dovetailed with states' rights to make the equal rights of Jews, as we shall see, secondary.

The Senate ratified the Treaty, after amending it, on March 7, 1851, and President Millard Fillmore endorsed it on March 12, 1851. On September 25, 1851, Webster, sending the revised Treaty to Mann with instructions to present it to the Swiss government, wrote: "The President hopes, that these amendments will not prove a fatal objection on the part of the Swiss Confederation." Replying from Berne, November 23, 1851, Mann wrote to Webster: "It is not easy of arrangement solely on account of the Constitutional difficulty relative to the Israelites." Then, in extenuation of his having even presented the original unpalatable draft, he concluded: "I may remark that I yielded with extreme reluctance to a departure from the first Article; and I distinctly informed the Swiss Plenipotentiaries at the time of my doing so, that I could give them no assurance whatever that the Article, as changed [to exclude Jews], would meet with the approval of either branch of our Treaty-making power."[4] That Mann's conduct was not held against him is indicated by the fact that, from 1853 to 1856, Mann served as Assistant Secretary of State.

In this conflict between Southern interests and states' rights and the rights of the Jews to equal treatment before the law, the latter were sacrificed until the Civil War decided that states' rights are subordinate to the federal power. In this fundamental sense, progress in the struggle for equal rights for Jews was related to the issues of slavery and Union. American Jews who supported the states' rights point of view and yet agitated for equal rights in the Swiss Treaty were inevitably frustrating their efforts by failing to see the contradiction in their position.[5]]

Cincinnati 25 Feby 1851

Hon.ble D. Webster, Secy of State

Sir

Allow me respectfully to call your attention to a treaty recently made by the accredited agent of our government & the authorities of Switzerland. the said treaty excluding from its benefits a vast portion of loyal citizens of this republic, and being partial should not in my estimation be ratified by the treaty making power of this government; the treaty referrd [sic] to grants privileges exclusively to christian citizens of the United States.

The amendment to the Constitution adopted March 4th 1789 part of which is as follows "Congress shall make no law respecting an establishment of religion or prohibiting the free exercise thereof" would appear to exclude the right or power of the Senate to ratify any treaty confering [sic] exclusive rights to any religious denomination, apart from this it is contrary to the whole spirit of our institutions.

As a member of the Jewish Church and one of the proscribed do I venture [6] to draw your notice to the subject.—It may appear inviduous [sic] in one of our nation specially noticing this matter when *all* but those of the christian faith are excluded from the participation of the benifits [sic] of this treaty. But Sir we constitute a large portion of the integral parts of this republic, we are law abiding citizens, jealous of our rights as such, & having for centuries been under the ban of persecution, watch with a vigilant eye encroachments on our rights, having been taught that when religious persecution commences its end cannot be foretold. We diligently observe all laws, we serve our country in the legislative hall, in the judicial forum, or in the battle field, as the archives of the war office will fully testify, & why I would ask should we be deprived of any right granted to our fellow citizens.—What would be the fate of a treaty made by any agent [of] this country with a foreign power giving any peculiar rights to the citizens of Louisiana or any other such State and not to the whole republic. It would and very properly be not entertained for a moment. Where then is the difference, if the privileged class be confined by geographical limits or by religious tests?

I will not however add argument to one whose sense of justice, & judgment of right is as proverbial as your own I trust Sir the matter may be laid before the President as well as the Senate in its proper light. In the mean while it would be a source of satisfaction to myself as well as a large number of our coreligionists to know the views you entertain on this to us momentous question—I am

Respectfully yours

Joseph Abraham [7]

Please address me to care

Hon B Stover

We members of the Jewish persuasion fully concur & coincide in the within

Simon A. Wolf, Mosely Ezekiel, Morris A. Levin, M. B. Mann, M. Bettman, M. Klaw, S. Katzenberger, J. Seasongood, Nathan Malzer, Henry Lenz, Lewis S. Rosenstiel, Ph. Heidelbach, J. Goldberg, Adolph Ancker, A. Harris, David Mayer, F. Harris, Eli M. Ancker, Elias Mayer, Phineas Moses, Lewis Abraham, A. Lorenz, A. A. Mayer.[8]

b) Reply by Daniel Webster, Washington, March 5, 1851 [9]

Department of State,
Washington, 5th March, 1851.[10]

Joseph Abraham, Esquire,
And other citizens of the Jewish persuasion, Cincinnati.

Gentlemen,

I have the honor to acknowledge the receipt of your communication, of the 25th ultimo, and to acquaint you, in reply, that the objections, to certain stipulations of the Swiss Convention, to which you refer, were duly pointed out by the Executive, at the time of submitting the Convention to the Senate.

You do me, gentlemen, no more than justice in expressing the belief, that I would not approve of any measure, which might infringe the rights and privileges of any class of our fellow citizens.

I am, Gentlemen, very respectfully,

Your obedient servant,

Daniel Webster.[11]

c) Circular, New York, March, 1854 [12]

[While A. Dudley Mann was waiting for the Swiss government to decide whether it would accept the United States Senate's amendments, new repressions against the Jews of Switzerland were undertaken in several Cantons, particularly in Basle, from which most of the Jews were ordered to leave. From Albany, N. Y., Isaac Mayer Wise issued a call for "protest against the illegal, inhuman and degrading laws," and proposed a national conference, a petition to Congress, and resolutions.[13] In the summer of 1852, disturbing rumors also began to appear to the effect that the Swiss treaty would still allow discrimination against Jews.[14] On February 7, 1853, President Fillmore transmitted the new draft to the Senate with a statement that the Swiss Government's modifications of the Senate amendments were "not inconsistent with the object and spirit of those amendments."[15] With this reassurance, the Jews seem to have been content, for discussion of the issue disappears from *The Asmonean* and *The Occident,* while the Senate debate in the Committee of the Whole begins on March 15 and is still unconcluded when Congress recesses. When debate is again resumed on February 4, 1854, however, the Jews have had reason to begin to feel alarmed and agitation begins in New York for a national petition campaign. This Circular was the instrument for organizing this campaign.]

Sir,

We have the honor to hand you herewith, a petition to the Senate of the United States, which has been prepared for circulation and signature among our Jewish brethren. You are aware that a great effort is now making, to induce despotic and illiberal governments, to concede to our citizens of all denominations, visiting the countries under their sway, that full enjoyment of religious liberty, which is accorded to their subjects on our soil.[16] The importance of active and zealous participation in this effort, is self-evident: and the annexed letter of General Cass, to Jonas P. Levy, Esq., intimates the propriety of its receiving our support.[17] We ask your co-operation, and would urge your uniting in the expression of those sentiments of humanity and liberality, which history shows we have ever cherished. Early attention is requested, as none can venture to predict how soon this matter may again come under discussion; and we recommend that you transmit the petition, with as many signatures as can be obtained, to the Senators of your State at Washington.

With assurances of regard and esteem, yours.[18]

David Samson, E.M. Swart, Jacob I. Moses, B. Benrimo, Albert Priest, M. Myers, H. B. Herts, Jr., Henry Goldsmith, Jonas P. Levy, Mark Levy, Geo.S. Mawson, P.J. Joachimsen

Jacob Pecare, Hon. Secretary Alexander Kursheedt, Chairman.

d) Petition to the United States Senate, Philadelphia, April 11, 1854 [19]

To the Honorable the Senate of the United States.

The petition of the undersigned respectfully shows: that they are citizens of the United States professing the Jewish religion, and that their brethern [sic] in faith and fellow Citizens are often necessarily absent in Foreign lands. That when so absent, they are in very many instances deprived of most of their civil and religious rights, while the Citizens and subjects of the lands thus intolerant, enjoy under our laws, equal privileges with our Citizens.

Your petitioners therefore pray, that the attention of Government [20] may be directed to this want of reciprocity in the rights accorded to Foreigners among us, and those extended to our Citizens in other Countries, and that in its wisdom it will endeavour to obtain for every American Citizen abroad, of every creed, a just degree of civil and religious freedom.

And your petitioners will ever pray, &c.

Jo Gratz
Isaac Hays
Hor Etting
Benj Etting
Jac. Gratz
Hyman Gratz [21]

Philadelphia April 11th 1854

e) Memorial presented to President James Buchanan, October 31, 1857 [22]

[Despite the petitions and public protests, the insufficiently revised Treaty was ratified by President Franklin Pierce on November 6, 1854, the two governments exchanged ratifications on November 8, 1855, and the Treaty was proclaimed the following day. The Washington *Union,* in publishing the Presidential proclamation on November 14, 1855, commented: "The very first article of this compact contains a flagrant violation of the privileges secured by the constitution to a certain denomination of our citizens—we mean the Israelites of the United States."[23] However, with the Jewish leaders of New York and Philadelphia timid and hesitant, leadership in the public agitation finally was assumed by Isaac Mayer Wise (1819–1900), then the vigorous editor of *The Israelite,* lively Reform journal in Cincinnati, in an editorial call, August 7, 1857, headed: "AGITATE. CALL MEETINGS. ENGAGE THE PRESS IN YOUR FAVOR." Indignation meetings were, in the next two months, held in Indianapolis, Easton, Cincinnati, Rock Island, Illinois, Pittsburgh, Baltimore, Washington, D. C., St. Louis, Cleveland, Nashville, Chicago and Milwaukee. Editorial comment in support of equal rights for the Jews appeared in the Chicago *Press* and *Daily Journal,* Louisville *Banner,* Shelbyville *Republican Banner,* Vincennes *Gazette,* Charleston *Evening News, Courier,* and *Mercury,* Milwaukee *Daily American,* Indianapolis *The Daily Sentinel* and *The Daily Journal,* Philadelphia *Press,* Richmond *Daily Dispatch,* Cincinnati *Daily Enquirer* and *Reporter,* Baltimore *Patriot* and Providence *Journal.* But the Washington, D. C., *Star* and the Dubuque *Express and Herald* editorially supported the discriminatory treaty. At the same time, it became known that an American Jew, A. H. Gootman, had in 1853 and 1854 been subject to difficulties with the Swiss authorities when he sought to establish residence in the canton of Neuchatel.[24] That one of the points repeated by the Swiss was the American application of the theory of states' rights to slavery is seen from Rev. Isaac Leeser's lame rejoinder in *The Occident:* ". . . the miserable pretext, that should there be a citizen of that republic who is of African descent, he would not be admitted even as a stranger into some of the southern states of America, is too shallow to stand the test of a candid criticism, since there are not many colored people in Europe."[25] This was not to be the last time that major contradictions in our American practice of democracy were to lessen our moral-political influence and position abroad.]

This Memorial, Of the undersigned, Delegates of the Israelites from various States of the Union, to his Excellency the President of the United States,

Respectfully represents:

That a Convention was concluded on the 25th of November, 1850, and proclaimed on the 9th of November, 1855, between the United States of America and the Swiss Confederation, "for friendship, reciprocal establishments, commerce, and for the surrender of fugitive criminals."

The first clause of the first Article of said Convention, reads as follows:

"The citizens of the United States of America and the citizens of Switzerland shall be admitted and treated upon a footing of reciprocal equality in the two countries, *where such admission and treatment shall not conflict with the constitutional* [or legal] *provisions as well Federal as State and Cantonal of the contracting parties.*"

It so happens that certain Cantons of the Swiss Confederation among which [are] Basle and others have laws prohibiting Israelites from sojourning temporarily, domiciliating or establishing themselves permanently. These laws being Cantonal Laws of the Swiss Confederation have been construed to come within the Saving Clause of the above quoted Article of Convention, and in their operation, affect those citizens of the United States who belong to the Israelitish persuasion.

Your memorialists have been elected at general meetings of Israelites of different States, as delegates to lay their grievances before your Excellency, and to pray for that remedy, to which they deem themselves entitled as citizens of the United States. They humbly submit the following suggestions:

The Constitution of the United States.—emphatically declares that "no religious test shall ever be required as a qualification to any office or public trust under the United States." and again in Article I, of the amendments to the constitution, "Congress shall make no law respecting an establishment of religion or prohibiting the free exercise thereof."

Ever since the adoption of the Constitution, this government has with a broad and liberal construction of the constitution acted upon those enlightened principles, which have secured the blessings of liberty upon all citizens of the United States without religious distinction. This government disclaiming all religious distinction as to the political rights of its citizens at home can not consistently recognize such distinction abroad. If conventions between different governments are made for any purpose they are made in furtherance of public justice, and more particularly for the purpose of extending the rights of citizens which they enjoy at home, into such other countries. The treaty in question has clearly failed in that object; for when we attempt to enjoy the extension of those rights, we are met by a dark-aged proscriptive law, declaring us unworthy of participating in the rights of our fellow citizens, on account of our professing the Israelitish religion. As citizens of the United States, we can not but consider such a construction antagonistic to the progressive, liberal policy of our government, and unworthy of the philanthropic fame which that policy has achieved; and as Israelites, we must feel mortified, should our government sanction Switzerland's slander upon religion.

Treaties, being laws of the land, must, as to their justness and validity, be tested by the application of principles governing her conduct; and will this treaty stand such a test?

It has been argued, that the commercial advantages this country derives from that treaty, would justify a slight sacrifice of principle; and while your memorialists are satisfied that such are not your Excellency's sentiments, they nevertheless respond, that if such were the policy of our government, Europe's despots would soon ask us mockingly: what is the price of all your liberties? Pecuniary considerations should certainly, least of all, induce a departure from principle.

Your memorialists further represent, that the clause referred to above, conferring reciprocal equality upon the citizens of the two countries, is directly contradicted, if that attempted construction be carried out; because, while it confers equal rights upon all citizens of the respective countries, it contradicts itself, by restrictions under Cantonal laws. But, more than this, there is a strange clashing of the rights of the two governments, as to the effect of their respective constructions of that clause. If it is against the *Cantonal* laws of Swtizerland that those citizens of the United States, who are Israelites, come within the benefits of that treaty, then it is at least as clearly against the constitutional laws of the United States, that those citizens be excluded, and yet both Cantonal and constitutional laws of the contracting governments are guarded against a conflict with the articles of convention. The whole subjects [sic] seems thus reduced to the question: Which of the two governments shall yield, and waive its equal right of construction? This pliant clause, then, must refer to such laws only, as do not effect the general purposes of the treaty, and if a choice as to the construction is to be made, that side must be chosen, which has humanity, reason, consistency and the voice of an enlightened, progressive age for its support, and a great and magnanimous republic to proclaim it. While your memorialists take pleasure in expressing in behalf of themselves and of their constituents their implicit confidence in your Excellency's wisdom as to the remedy, and in the firmness to enforce it, they nevertheless humbly suggest, that a construction in accordance with these views, communicated to the Swiss confederation, would be followed by those salutary results, for whose obtention your memorialists are so solicitous. Such action would send a thrill of gratitude through the thousands of Israelitish citizens of the United States—it would be hailed as a timely act of national justice by the people generally, and will engraft itself upon the hearts of your memorialists, never to be effaced.

We beg leave to subscribe ourselves,

Very respectfully,

Your Excellency's most obed't serv'ts.

M.I. COHEN, Maryland.	REV. DR. ISAAC M. WISE, Ohio.
REV. DR. H. HOCHHEIMER, do.	MARTIN BIJUR, Kentucky.
PH. HERZBERG, do.	M.M. GERSTLEY, Illinois.
	LEWIS F. LEOPOLD, Ohio.[26]

Done in Convention, at Baltimore, this 29th day of October, 1857.[27]

111. EQUAL RIGHTS FOR WOMEN

Speeches by Ernestine L. Rose at the third National Woman's Rights Convention, Syracuse, N. Y., September 8–10, 1852[1]

[Speaking as "a daughter of poor, crushed Poland, and the down-trodden and persecuted people called the Jews, 'a child of Israel,'" Ernestine L. Rose continued her pleas "for the equal rights of her sex." Already known in a score of states and a hundred cities as "the Queen of the Platform," Mrs. Rose was then reaching the height of her powers of eloquence, wit, and persuasion, evoking enthusiasm from her supporters and respect from even rowdy opponents, to many of whom the sight of any woman speaking in public was a flout and a provocation. Contemporaries described her as "beautiful"; a scoffer wrote of "such foreign propagandists as the ringleted, glove-handed exotic, Ernestine L. Rose."[2]

Her development and career had been extraordinary. Ernestine Louise Siismondi Potowski (born, Piotrkow, Russian Poland, 1810; died Brighton, England, 1892) was the daughter of a rabbi. As a child she studied the Scriptures and was observant in her practice of Judaism, but at fourteen she had accumulated so many doubts that she revolted against her religion, and later became an active atheist. Her mother died when Ernestine was sixteen. After pleading and winning her own case in a lawsuit involving her right to certain inherited properties—a rare feat for a young girl—she left her home, and spent the following five years traveling in Poland, Russia, Germany, Holland, Belgium, and France, often intervening with audacity and success in the fight for human rights. In 1832, she arrived in England, and fell under the powerful intellectual influence of the Utopian Socialist, Robert Owen (1771–1858). Owen was then beginning to break with the trade union movement with which he had been actively associated. On May 1, 1835, she presided at a conference called by Owen that reorganized several Owenite bodies into the Association of All Classes of All Nations, "a name eloquent of the founder's departure from all thoughts of a struggle of classes as the means of achieving his ideal."[3] But while Owen was abandoning the fight for immediate changes in favor of preaching his New Moral Order, Ernestine and her husband, William Ella Rose (a non-Jewish watchmaker, Owenite and atheist whom she married in 1835 in a civil ceremony), came to New York in the spring of 1836. A few months later, Mrs. Rose was already leading the campaign for woman's rights;[4] in subsequent years she lectured widely on "The Science of Government," on atheism, on the evils of slavery, on education for women and the whole range of woman's rights, including political equality. From 1850 on she attended every national woman's rights convention, and innumerable state and county conventions in various parts of the country. In this work she was closely associated not only with the other main leaders of the woman's rights movement but with outstanding public figures like William Lloyd Garrison, Wendell Phillips, Frederick Douglass, the ex-slave abolitionist leader, William Henry Channing, and Thomas Wentworth Higginson, most of whom have recorded their admiration of her ability and work.

Although some of the rights for which Ernestine L. Rose fought for fifty years have been partially won, the vitality of her speeches has not ebbed.]

ERNESTINE L. ROSE, being introduced as a Polish lady, and educated in the Jewish faith, said—

It is of very little importance in what geographical position a person is born, but it is important whether his ideas are based upon facts that can stand the test of reason, and his acts are conducive to the happiness of society. Yet, being a foreigner, I hope you will have some charity on account of speaking in a foreign language. Yes, I am an example of the universality of our claims; for not American women only, but a daughter of poor, crushed Poland, and the down-trodden and persecuted people called the Jews, "a child of Israel," pleads for the equal rights of her sex. I perfectly agree with the resolution, that if woman is insensible to her wrongs, it proves the depth of her degradation. It is a melancholy fact, that woman has worn her chains so long that they have almost become necessary to her nature—like the poor inebriate, whose system is so diseased that he cannot do without the intoxicating draft, or those who are guilty of the pernicious and ungentlemanly practice of using tobacco until they cannot dispense with the injurious stimulant. Woman is in a torpid condition, whose nerves have become so paralyzed that she knows not she is sick, she feels no pain, and if this proves the depth of her degradation, it also proves the great wrong and violence done to her nature. * * *

Woman is a slave, from the cradle to the grave. Father, guardian, husband—master still. One conveys her, like a piece of property, over to the other. She is said to have been created only for man's benefit, not for her own. This falsehood is the main cause of her inferior education and position. Man has arrogated to himself the right to her person, her property, and her children; and so vitiated is public opinion, that if a husband is rational and just enough to acknowledge the influence of his wife, he is called "hen-pecked." The term is not very elegant, but it is not of my coining; it is yours, and I suppose you know what it means; I don't. But it is high time these irrationalities are done away, for the whole race suffers by it. In claiming our rights, we claim the rights of humanity; it is not for the interest of woman only, but for the interest of all. The interest of the sexes cannot be separated—together they must enjoy or suffer—both are one in the race.[5] * * *

II

If the able Theologian[6] who has just spoken had been in Indiana when the Constitution was revised, she might have had a chance to give her definitions on the Bible argument, to some effect. At that Convention, Robert Dale Owen[7] introduced a clause to give to a married woman the right to her property. The clause had passed, but by the influence of a minister was recalled; and by his appealing to the superstition of the members, and bringing the whole force of Bible argument to bear against the right of woman to her property, it was lost. Had Miss Brown been there, she might have beaten him with his own weapons. For my part, I see no need to appeal to any written authority, particularly when it is so obscure and indefinite as to admit of different interpretations. When the inhabitants of Boston converted their harbor into a tea-pot, rather than submit to unjust taxes, they did not go to the Bible for their authority; for if they had, they would have been told from the same authority to "give unto Cesar [sic] what belonged to Cesar." Had the people, when they rose in the might of their right to throw off the British yoke, appealed to the Bible for authority, it would have answered them, "submit to the powers that be, for they are from God." No! on Human Rights and Freedom on a subject that is as self-evident as that two and two make four, there is no need of any written authority. But this is not what I intended to speak upon. I wish to introduce a resolution, and leave it to the action of the Convention:

Resolved, That we ask not for our rights as a gift of charity, but as an act of justice. For it is in accordance with the principles of republicanism that, as woman has to pay taxes to maintain government, she has a right to participate in the formation and administration of it. That as she is amenable to the laws of her country, she is entitled to a voice in their enactment, and to all the protective advantages they can bestow; and as she is as liable as man to all the vicissitudes of life, she ought to enjoy the same social rights and privileges. And any difference, therefore, in political, civil and social rights, on account of sex, is in direct violation of the principles of justice and humanity, and as such ought to be held up to the contempt and derision of every lover of human freedom.

* * * But we call upon the law-makers and law-breakers of the nation, to defend themselves for violating the fundamental principles of the Republic, or disprove their validity. Yes! they stand arrayed before the bar, not only of injured womanhood, but before the bar of moral consistency; for this question is awakening an interest abroad, as well as at home. Wherever human rights are claimed for man, moral consistency points to the equal rights of woman; but statesmen dare not openly face the subject, knowing well they cannot confute it, and they have not moral courage enough to admit it; and hence, all they can do is to shelter themselves under a subterfuge which, though solidi-

fied by age, ignorance and prejudice, is transparent enough for the most benighted vision to penetrate. A strong evidence of this, is given in a reply of Mr. Roebuck,[8] member of Parliament, at a meeting of electors, in Sheffield, England. Mr. R., who advocated the extension of the franchise to the occupants of five pound tenements, was asked whether he would favor the extension of the same to women who pay an equal amount of rent? That was a simple, straight-forward question of justice; one worthy to be asked even in our Republican Legislative Halls. But what was the honorable gentleman's reply? Did he meet it openly and fairly? Oh, no! but hear him, and I hope the ladies will pay particular attention; for the greater part of the reply contains the draught, poor, deluded woman has been accustomed to swallow—FLATTERY: "There is no man who owes more than I do to woman. My education was formed by one whose very recollections at this moment make me tremble. There is nothing which, for the honor of the sex, I would not do—the happiness of my life is bound up with it—Mother, Wife, Daughter, Woman, to me have been the Oasis of the desert of life, and, I have to ask myself, would it conduce to the happiness of society to bring woman more distinctly than she now is brought, into the arena of politics? Honestly I confess to you I believe not. I will tell you why. All their influences, if I may so term it, are gentle influences. In the rude battle and business of life, we come home to find a nook and shelter of quiet comfort, after the hard and severe, and I may say, the sharp ire and the disputes of the House of Commons. I hie me home, knowing that I shall there find personal solicitude and anxiety. My head rests upon a bosom throbbing with emotion for me and our child; and I feel a more hearty man in the cause of my country, the next day, because of the perfect, soothing, gentle peace which a mind sullied by politics is unable to feel. Oh! I cannot rob myself of that inexpressible benefit, and therefore I say, NO."

Well, this is certainly a nice, little, romantic bit of Parliamentary declamation. What a pity that he should give up all these enjoyments, to give woman a vote. Poor man! his happiness must be balanced on the very verge of a precipice, when the simple act of depositing a vote by the hand of woman, would overthrow and destroy it forever. I don't doubt the Honorable gentleman meant what he said, particularly the last part of it, for such are the views of the unthinking, unreflecting mass of the public, here as well as there. But like a true politician, he commenced very patriotically, for the happiness of society, and finished by describing his own individual interests. His reply is a curious mixture of truth, political sophistry, false assumption and blind selfishness. But he was placed in a dilemma, and got himself out as he could. In advocating the franchise to five pound tenement-holders, it did not occur to him that woman may possess the same qualification that man has, and in justice, therefore, ought to have the same rights; and when the simple question was put to him, (simple questions are very troublesome to statesmen,) having too much sense not to see the justness of it, and too little moral courage to admit it, he entered into quite an interesting account of what a delightful little creature woman is, provided only she is kept quietly at home, waiting for the arrival of her lord and master—ready to administer a dose of purification, "which his politically sullied mind is unable to feel." Well! I have no desire to dispute the necessity of it, nor that he owes to woman all that makes life desirable—comforts, happiness, aye, and common sense too, for it is a well-known fact, that smart mothers always have smart sons, unless they take after their father. But what of that? Are the benefits woman is capable of bestowing on man, reasons why she must pay the same amount of rent and taxes, without enjoying the same rights that man does. But the justice of the case was not considered. The Honorable gentleman was only concerned about the "happiness of society." Society? what does the term mean? As a foreigner, I understand by it a collection, or union of human beings: men, women, and children, under one general government, and for mutual interest. But Mr. Roebuck, being a native of Briton and a member of Parliament, gave us a Parliamentary definition, namely: society means the male sex only; for in his solicitude to consult "the happiness of society," he enumerated the benefits man enjoys from keeping woman from her rights, without even dreaming that woman was at all considered in it; and this is the true Parliamentary definition, for statesmen never include woman in their solicitude for the happiness of society. Oh, no! she is not yet recognized as belonging to the honorable body, unless taxes are required for its benefit, or the penalties of the law have to be enforced for its security. Thus, being either unwilling or afraid to do woman justice, he first flattered her, then, in his ignorance of the true nature of woman, he assumed, that if she has her rights equal with man, she would cease to be woman—forsake the partner of her existence, the child of her bosom, dry up her sympathies, stifle her affections, turn recreant to her own nature. Then his blind selfishness took the alarm, lest, if woman were more independent, she might not be willing to be the obedient, servile tool, implicitly to obey and minister to the passions and follies of man; "and as he could not rob himself of these inexpressible benefits, therefore he said, No."

Such are the lofty views of statesmen on woman, that equality of rights, the only and sure means to enlighten and elevate man, would degrade and corrupt woman. The genial rays of the sun of freedom, that vivify, cheer and ennoble him, would chill the heart and destroy the affections in her, and therefore it is inexpedient to give her her rights, "to bring her more distinctly into the political arena." Oh, yes! the Turk deems it inexpedient (for the happiness of society,) to give woman any personal freedom, therefore he encloses her in a harem. It is a well-known characteristic of tyrants and cowards, when they dare not face a question of right, to shelter themselves under expediency. It was inexpedient for Nicholas of Russia [9] to allow Hungary to free herself from Austrian oppression, therefore he sent his infernal machines to prevent it. It was expedient for Louis Napoleon [10] to destroy the Roman Republic, and inexpedient to await the issue of another election, and therefore he violated his oath, and, with bayonet in one hand and musket in the other, compelled his re-election. The bright and noble spirits of France were inexpedient to his treachery, so he incarcerated them, or banished them from the country—all these are measures of expediency. Thus in the more despotic countries of Europe, it is expedient for the rulers to deprive the people of every vestige of freedom. In constitutional England, it is already expedient to advocate (and I hope they soon will obtain it) the extension of the elective franchise to every man who pays five pounds rent, but it is yet inexpedient to give woman the same privilege. And here, in this glorious land of freedom, a Republic that has proclaimed equality of rights—that has written on its banners universal suffrage—even here it is yet deemed by the wiseacres of the nation, expedient to exclude half of its population from that universality. And do you know, my friends, the reasons given for all these measures of tyranny and oppression? Why, the happiness of society. But the question we ask, is not whether woman shall forsake her household, like man, to intrigue in politics, fight at elections, marshall armies, or direct navies. The question at issue is whether woman, as a being amenable to the laws under which she lives, shall have a voice in their enactment—as a member of the social compact, shall participate and control those institutions to which she is made subject? Or shall man, in his assumption of power, continue to deprive her of her natural and inalienable rights, prescribe her sphere of action within the least possible limits, restrict her education, and the development of her powers to the lowest degree, cripple her physical, mental and moral energies, that he may have a docile, obedient slave to do his bidding? These are questions not of expediency, but of right; not of charity, but of justice. And yet, though we might well leave the issue of our cause on its own merits, I would be perfectly willing to meet the opposers of our claims on their own grounds, and convince them that even on the question of expediency they have not an atom of ground to stand upon. The greatest objection I have yet heard, in public or private, against woman's political rights, is the corruption of the present state of party politics. It is represented to be in so low and degraded a condition, that no one can enter the political arena without contamination, and therefore woman must be kept from its very atmosphere. Now, without disputing the validity of the testimony, as humiliating confessions come mostly from gentlemen belonging to these honorable bodies, I would ask, what is to be done? Leave forever our Legislative Halls, the Stygian pools, as the honorable Horace Mann [11] calls them, that they now are? For what rational hope have we that they will ever become purified unless woman takes them in hand, seeing that man has had the exclusive possession of them so long, and they only seem to grow worse. No! no! something must be done. Expediency, "the benefit of society," calls for woman's "purifying influence," for "the perfect, soothing, gentle peace which the politically sullied minds" of our legislators, seeing how they fight in Congress, "are unable to feel." Let woman then, be with him wherever duty calls her, and she will soon cleanse the Legislative Halls, as she has cleansed and purified the festive board of the excess that existed there.

" 'Tis not well for man to be alone"—Mother, Sister, Wife, Daughter, woman must be with him, to keep him in his proper sphere. Do you doubt it? Then look at exclusive assemblies of men, and even among the best you will perceive the rude, uncultivated nature of Adam, before mother Eve civilized him, by making him partake of the Tree of Knowledge. Expediency, therefore, as well as justice, demands that woman should have her political, civil and social rights, that she may be better able to "soothe, quiet," and aid man, abroad as well as at home. And the beneficial effects to society will soon be apparent; for as she will be better educated, have all her powers developed, her judgment expanded, she will be more competent to fulfil the various duties devolving upon her—as mother, to train her sons (aye, and her daughters, too,) in the way they should go, from which, when they grow old, they will not depart; as wife, more truly affectionate, so that when the husband's head will rest on her throbbing bosom, she would be able to give him counsel and courage, as well as rest; and though at the marriage ceremony she might not be willing to say "Obey," she will substitute the far better word, Assist. As a companion, she would be more interesting and instructive, and as a member of society, more useful, honorable and happy.[12]

112. ABOLITIONISTS REPORT

From *The Thirteenth Annual Report of the American & Foreign Anti-Slavery Society, Presented at New-York, May 11, 1853* [1]

[This section of the report summarizes what those who had been active in the organized abolitionist movement for more than twenty years knew and thought of the extent of the participation of Jews in that movement up to 1853. Noteworthy is the disappointment so poignantly expressed in the last sentence of this excerpt. This section on the Jews is the last one in the portion of the report dealing with the views, attitudes and activities of some twenty religious organizations. The conclusion reached is that "it will be seen that slavery has steadily increased within the pale of the Christian denominations during the last half century, as it has within the limits of our political organizations."[2]]

The Jews

The Jews of the United States have never taken any steps whatever with regard to the Slavery question. As citizens, they deem it their policy "to have every one choose which ever side he may deem best to promote his own interests and the welfare of his country."[3] They have no organization of an ecclesiastical body to represent their general views; no General Assembly, or its equivalent. The American Jews have two newspapers,[4] but they do not interfere in any discussion which is not material to their religion. It cannot be said that the Jews have formed any denominational opinion on the subject of American slavery. Some of the Jews, who reside in slave States, have refused to have any property in man, or even to have any slaves about them.[5] They do not believe that any thing analogous to slavery, as it exists in this country, ever prevailed among the ancient Israelites. But they profess to believe that "the belief of Abraham, enlarged by Moses, and now acknowledged by the Jews, is one of purity and morality, and one which presents the strongest possible supports for civil society, *especially a government based upon principles of equality and liberty of the person!* They believe that the coming of the King Messiah will be the signal for universal peace, UNIVERSAL FREEDOM, universal knowledge, and universal worship of the One Eternal."

The objects of so much mean prejudice and unrighteous oppression as the Jews have been for ages, surely they, it would seem, more than any other denomination, ought to be the enemies of CASTE, and the friends of UNIVERSAL FREEDOM.

113. JUDAH TOURO'S WILL

Text of Will, dated New Orleans, January 6, 1854[1]

[This will, together with many other benefactions made during his life, has made Judah Touro (1775–1854) one of the best known names in American Jewish history. The two latest instances of national governmental recognition of his name are: the launching of the Liberty tanker, *Judah Touro,* in New Orleans, December 4, 1943;[2] and the dedication of the Touro Synagogue in Newport as a National Religious Shrine, August 31, 1947.

One of the earliest of prominent American philanthropists, Touro in this will bequeathed $387,000 to various Jewish and non-Jewish institutions and causes, $38,000 to personal friends, $30,000 to the executors of his estate, and the remainder, perhaps $750,000, to the man who had saved his life and was his chief executor. Negro institutions and causes, perhaps needing assistance most, were not among Touro's beneficiaries. In 1854, however, "philanthropy" was in its infancy in our country. The development of laissez-faire economics and capitalist expansion in Touro's lifetime had brought riches to some, and acute and sudden poverty to many. Public social welfare being undeveloped, Charity appeared to bridge a little of the wide gap. Since the rich who give, however, are preferable to those who only take, Touro's example made a sensation at the time, and added new honors to a name that had already won renown by generous gifts to the fund for building the Bunker Hill Monument in Boston, to the relief of victims of the many yellow fever epidemics in New Orleans and of the great fire in Mobile, Alabama, to the founding and support of libraries, to the aid of Jews in Palestine and China, and to needy Jewish and Christian congregations in the United States.[3]

Born in Newport, Rhode Island and raised in Boston, Judah Touro spent more than fifty years of his life in New Orleans and amassed his wealth there as an enterprising merchant, ship-owner, and real-estate owner, contributing considerably to the commercial expansion of that city and growing with it. His will constitutes almost a catalogue of important institutions of the time in Jewish life, as well as in the general life of New Orleans, Newport, and Boston.]

JUDAH TOURO

UNITED STATES OF AMERICA

State of Louisiana, City of New Orleans

Be it Known that on this Sixth day of January, in the year of our Lord One Thousand, Eight Hundred and Fifty Four, and of the Independence of the United States of America the Seventy Eighth at a quarter before Ten O'Clock A.M.

Before me, Thomas Layton, a notary Public, in and for the city of New Orleans, aforesaid duly commissioned and sworn, and in Presence of Messieurs, Jonathan Montgomery, Henry Shepherd Jr. and George Washington Lee [4] competent witnesses residing in said city and hereto expressly required

Personally appeared Mr Judah Touro of this City, Merchant, whom, I the said Notary and said witnesses found setting in a room at his residence N° 128, Canal Street, Sick of body, but sound in mind, memory and Judgment as did appear to me, the said Notary and to said witnesses. And the said Judah Touro requested me, the notary, to receive his last will or Testament, which he dictated to me, Notary, as follows, to wit & in presence of said witnesses.

1st I declare that I have no forced heirs.

2^d I desire that my mortal remains be buried in the Jewish Cemetery in New Port Rhode Island,[5] as soon as practicable after my decease.

3^d I nominate and appoint my trusty and Esteemed friends Rezin Davis Shepherd [6] of Virginia, Aaron Keppel Josephs of New Orleans, Gershom Kursheedt of New Orleans, and Pierre Andre Destrac Cazenave of New Orleans, my Testamentary Executors and the detainers of my Estate, making, however, the following distinction between my said Executors, to wit: to the said Aaron Keppel Josephs, Gershom Kursheedt and Pierre Andre Destrac Cazenave, I give and bequeath to each one separately the sum of Ten Thousand dollars, which legacies, I intend respectively not only as tokens of remembrance of those esteemed friends, but also as in consideration of all Services they may have hitherto rendered me, and in lieu of the commissions to which they would be entitled hereafter in the capacity of Testamentary Executors as aforesaid. And as regards my other designated Executors, say my dear old and devoted friend the said Rezin Davis Shepherd to whom, under Divine Providence, I was greatly indebted for the preservation of my life, when I was wounded on the 1st of January 1815, I hereby appoint and institute him, the said Rezin Davis Shepherd, after the payment of my particular legacies and the debts of my succession, the Universal Legatee of the rest and residue of my estate, moveable and immoveable.

In case of the death, absence, or inhability [sic] to act of one or more of my said Executors, I hereby empower the remaining Executor or Executors to act in carrying out the provisions of this my last Will; and in the event or default of any one or more of my said Executors before my own demise, then and in that case, it is my intention that the heirs or legal representatives of those who may depart this life before my own death, Shall inherit in their Stead the legacies hereinabove respectively made to them.

4th I desire that all leases of my property and which may be in force at the time of my demise, Shall be faithfully executed until the Same Shall have expired.

5th I desire that all the Estate Real, Personal and mixed, of which I may die possessed, Shall be disposed of in the manner directed by this my last will or Testament

6th I give and bequeath to the Hebrew Congregation the ["]Dispersed of Judah" of the City of New Orleans,[7] all that certain property situated in Bourbon Street immediately adjoining their Synagogue, being the present School house and the residence of the Said Mr Gershom Kursheedt, the same purchased by me from the Bank of Louisiana; and also to the said Hebrew Congregation, the Two adjoining brick Houses purchased from the Heirs of David Urquhart, the revenue of said property to be applied to the founding and support of the Hebrew School connected, with Said congregation, as well to the defraying of the Salary of their Reader or Minister, Said Property to be conveyed accordingly by my said Executors to said congregation, with all necessary restrictions.

7th I give and bequeath to found the ["]Hebrew Hospital of New Orleans"[8] The entire property purchased for me, at the succession sale of the late C. Paulding upon which property the Building now Known as the "Touro Infirmary" is situated: The said contemplated Hospital to be organized according to law, as a charitable Institution for the relief of the Indigent Sick, by my Executors and such other persons as they may associate with them conformably with the laws of Louisiana.

8th I give and bequeath to the Hebrew Benevolent Association of New Orleans [9] Five Thousand Dollars.

9th I give and bequeath to the Hebrew Congregation "Shangarar Chased" of New Orleans [10] Five Thousand Dollars.

10th I give and bequeath to the Ladies Benevolent Society of New Orleans,[11] the Sum of Five Thousand dollars.

11th I give and bequeath to the Hebrew Foreign Mission Society of New Orleans,[12] Five Thousand Dollars

12th I give and bequeath to the Orphans Home Asylum of New Orleans,[13] the sum of Five Thousand Dollars.

13th I give and bequeath to the Society for the relief of Destitute Orphan Boys in the Fourth District,[14] Five Thousand Dollars.

14th I give and bequeath to the St Anna's Asylum for the relief of destitute females and children,[15] the sum of Five Thousand Dollars.

15th I give and bequeath to the New Orleans Female Orphan Asylum at the corner of Camp & Prytania Streets,[16] Five Thousand Dollars.

16th I give and bequeath to the St Mary's Catholic Boys Asylum [17] of which my old & esteemed friend Mr Anthony Rasch is chairman of its Executive Committee, the sum of Five Thousand Dollars.

17th I give and bequeath to the Milne Asylum of New Orleans,[18] Five Thousand Dollars.

18th I give and bequeath to the Fireman's charitable Association of New Orleans,[19] Four Thousand Dollars.

19th I give and bequeath to the Seamen's Home in the First District of New Orleans [20] Five Thousand Dollars

20th I give and bequeath for the purpose of establishing an Alms House, in the City of New Orleans,[21] and with the view of contributing as far as possible to the prevention of mendicity in said city, the sum of Eighty Thousand Dollars (say $80,000.); and I desire that The Alms House, thus contemplated, shall be organized according to law; and further it is my desire that after my Executors Shall have legally organized & established said contemplated Alms House and appointed proper persons to administer and controll the direction of its affairs, then such persons legally so appointed and their successors in office, conjointly with the Mayor of the City of New Orleans and his successors in office shall have the perpetual direction and controll thereof

21st I give and bequeath to the City of New Port in the State of Rhode Island, the Sum of Ten Thousand Dollars, on condition that the said sum be expended in the purchase and improvement of the property in Said City, Known as the "Old Stone Mill["][22] to be Kept as a public Park or Promenade ground

22d I give and bequeath to the Red Wood library of New Port [23] aforesaid, for Books & Repairs Three Thousand Dollars

23. I give and bequeath to the Hebrew Congregation Oharbay Shalome of Boston Massachusetts [24] Five Thousand dollars.

24. I give and bequeath to the Hebrew Congregation of Hartford Connecticut [25] Five Thousand dollars.

25. I give and bequeath to the Hebrew Congregation of New Haven Connecticut [26] Five Thousand dollars.

26. I give and bequeath to the North American Relief Society for the Indigent Jews. of Jerusalem Palestine of the City and State of New York [27] (Sir Moses Montefiore of London, their agent) Ten Thousand Dollars, Say ($10,000.)

27. It being my earnest wish to co-operate with the said Sir Moses Montefiore of London, Great Britain, in endevouring [sic] to ameliorate the condition of our unfortunate Jewish brethern [sic] in the Holy Land,[28] and to secure to them the inestimable privilege of worshipping the Almighty according to our Religion, without molestation, I therefore give and bequeath the sum of Fifty Thousand Dollars to be paid by my Executors for said object through the said Sir Moses Montefiore, in such manner as he may advise as best calculated to promote the aforesaid objects, and in case of any legal or other difficulty or impediment in the way of carrying said bequest into effect, according to my intentions, then and in that case, I desire that the said sum of Fifty Thousand dollars be invested by my Executors

in the foundation of a Society in the City of New Orleans Similar in its objects to the North American Relief Society for the Indigent Jews of Jerusalem, Palestine, of the City of New York, to which I have before referred in this my last Will.

28. It is my wish and desire that the Institutions to which I have already alluded in making this Will, as well as those to which in the further course of making this Will, I shall refer, Shall not be disqualified from inheriting my legacies to them respectively made for reason of not being Incorporated & thereby qualified to inherit by law, but on the contrary, I desire that the parties interested in such Institutions and my Executors Shall facilitate their Organization as soon after my decease as possible, & thus render them duly qualified by law to inherit in the premises according to my wishes.

29. I give and bequeath to the Jews Hospital Society of the City and State of New York [29] Twenty Thousand Dollars

30. I give and bequeath to the Hebrew Benevolent Society Mashebat Nafesh of New York,[30] Five Thouand dollars.

31. I give and bequeath to the Hebrew Benevolent Society Gimelet Chased of New York [31] Five Thousand Dollars.

32. I give and bequeath to the Talmueh [sic] Torah School fund attached to the Hebrew Congregation Sheareth Israel of the City of New York [32] and to said Congregation Thirteen Thousand Dollars.

33. I give and bequeath to the Educational Institute of the Hebrew Congregation Briai Jeshurum [sic] of the City of New York [33] the sum of Three Thousand Dollars.

34. I give and bequeath to the Hebrew Congregation Shangarai Tefila of New York [34] Three Thousand Dollars.

35. I give and bequeath to the Ladies Benevolent Society of the City of New York,[35] the same of which Mrs Richey Levy was a directress at the time of her death, and of which Mistress I. B. Kursheedt was first Directress in 1850, Three Thousand Dollars.

36. I give and bequeath to the Female Hebrew Benevolent [Society] of Philadelphia [36] (Miss Gratz Secretary) Three Thousand Dollars.

37. I give and bequeath to the Hebrew Education Society of Philadelphia (Pennsylvania)[37] Twenty Thousand Dollars.

38. I give to the United Hebrew Benevolent Society of Philadelphia [38] aforesaid Three Thousand Dollars.

39. I give and bequeath to the Hebrew Congregation Ashabat Israel of Fells Point Baltimore,[39] Three Thousand Dollars.

40. I give and bequeath to the Hebrew Congregation Beth Shalome of Richmond [40] Virginia, Five Thousand dollars.

41. I give and bequeath to the Hebrew Congregation Sheareth Israel of Charleston South Carolina [41] the sum of Five Thousand Dollars.

42. I give and bequeath to the Hebrew Congregation Shangarai Shamoyen of Mobile Alabama [42] Two Thousand Dollars.

43. I give and bequeath to the Hebrew Congregation Mikve Israel of Savannah Georgia [43] Five Thousand Dollars.

44. I give and bequeath to the Hebrew Congregation of Montgomery Albama [44] Two Thousand dollars say ($2000).

45. I give and bequeath to the Hebrew Congregation of Memphis Tennessee [45] Two Thousand dollars.

46. I give and bequeath to the Hebrew Congregation Adas Israel of Louisville Kentucky [46] Three Thousand Dollars

47. I give and bequeath to the Hebrew Congregation Briai Israel [sic] of Cincinnati Ohio [47] Three Thousand Dollars.

48. I give and bequeath to the Hebrew School Talmud Jeladin of Cincinnati Ohio [48] Five Thousand Dollars.

49. I give and bequeath to the Jews Hospital of Cincinnati Ohio [49] Five Thousand Dollars.

50. I give and bequeath to the Hebrew Congregation Tifareth Israel of Cleveland Ohio,[50] Three Thousand Dollars.

51. I give and bequeath to the Hebrew Congregation Briai El [sic] of St Louis Missouri [51] Three Thousand dollars.

52. I give and bequeath to the Hebrew Congregation of Beth El of Buffalo New York [52] Three Thousand dollars (say Three Thousand Dollars.)

53. I give and bequeath to the Hebrew Congregation of Beth El of Albany New York [53] Three Thousand Dollars.

54. I give and bequeath to the three following Institutions named in the Will of my greatly beloved brother the late Abraham Touro of Boston,[54] the following Sums.

First, To the Asylum for Orphan Boys in Boston Massachusetts, Five Thousand dollars.

Second, To the Female Orphan Asylum of Boston aforesaid, Five Thousand Dollars.

Third, And to the Massachusetts General Hospital Ten Thousand Dollars.

55. I give and bequeath Ten Thousand dollars for the purpose of

paying the salary of a Reader or Minister to officiate at the Jewish Synagogue of New Port Rhode Island [55] and to endow the Ministry of the same as well as to keep in repair and embellish the Jewish Cemetary [sic] in New Port aforesaid; the said amount to be appropriated and paid or invested for that purpose in such manner, as my Executors may determine Concurrently with the Corporation of New Port aforesaid, if necessary; And it is my wish and desire that David Gould and Nathan H. Gould sons of my Esteemed friend the late Isaac Gould Esq of New Port aforesaid, should continue to oversee the Improvements in said Cemetary and direct the same, and as a testimony of my regard and in consideration of Services rendered by their Said Father, I give and bequeath the Sum of Two Thousand Dollars to be equally divided between them, the said David and said Nathan H. Gould.

56. I give and bequeath Five Thousand Dollars to Miss Catherine Hays now of Richmond Virginia,[56] as an expression of the Kind remembrance in which that esteemed friend is held by me.

57. I give and bequeath to the Misses Catherine, Harriet and Julia Myers, the three daughters of M[r] Moses. M. Myers of Richmond Virginia [57] the Sum of Seven Thousand Dollars to be equally divided between them.

58. I give and bequeath the Sum of Seven Thousand dollars to the Surviving Children of the late Samuel Myers of Richmond Virginia,[58] to be equally divided between them in token of my remembrance.

59. I give and bequeath to my Friend M[r] Supply Clapp Thwing of Boston Massachusetts,[59] the sum of Five Thousand Dollars as a token of my esteem and Kind remembrance.

60. I give and bequeath the sum of Three Thousand Dollars to my respected friend the Rev[d] Isaac Leeser [60] of Philadelphia as a token of my regard

61. I give and bequeath the Sum of Three Thousand Dollars to my friends the Rev[d] Moses N Nathan,[61] now of London and his wife to be equally divided between them.

62. I give and bequeath the Sum of Three Thousand dollars to my friend the Rev[d] Theodore Clapp of New Orleans,[62] in token of my remembrance.

63. To Mistress Ellen Brooks, Wife of Gorham Brooks Esquire of Boston Massachusetts and daughter of my friend & Executor Rezin Davis Shepherd, I give the sum of Five Thousand dollars, the same

to be employed by my Executor in the purchase of a suitable Memorial to be presented to her as an earnest of my very Kind regard

64. I give and bequeath the sum of Twenty Five Hundred dollars to be employed by my executors in the purchase of a suitable Memorial of my esteem to be presented to Mrs M. D. Josephs wife of my friend Aaron K. Josephs Esquire of this City.

65. I give and bequeath the Sum of Twenty Five Hundred dollars to be employed by my Executors in the purchase of a suitable Memorial of my esteem for Mistress Rebecca Kursheedt wife of Mr Benjamin Florance of New Orleans.

66. I revoke all other Wills or Testaments which I may have made previously to these presents.

Thus it was that this Testament or last Will was dictated to me, the notary, by the said Testator in presence of the witnesses hereinabove named and undersigned and I have written the same such as it was dictated to me, by the Testator, in my own proper hand in presence of Said Witnesses; and having read this Testament in a loud and audible voice to the Said Testator, in presence of Said Witnesses, he, the Said Testator, declared in the same presence that he well understood the Same and persisted therein.

All of which was done at one time, without interruption or turning aside to other acts.

Thus Done and passed at the said City of New Orleans at the Said residence of the said Mr Judah Touro, the day, month and year first before written in the presence of Messieurs Jonathan Montgomery, Henry Shepherd Jr and George Washington Lee, all three being the Witnesses as aforesaid, who with the Said Testator, and me, the Said Notary have hereunto Signed their names.

"Signed" J. Touro—J. Montgomery—Henry Shepherd—Geo. W. Lee—Thos Layton, Not: Pub:

I Certify the foregoing to be a true copy of the original act, on file and of Record in my office.

In faith whereof I grant these presents, under my signature, and the impress of my Seal of office, at the City of New Orleans, this Twenty First day of January 1854.

Signed

Thos Layton Not: Pub:

114. ATTITUDES TO JEWS

a) Editorial, "The Jews, As Citizens," in *Washington Sentinel,* Washington, D. C., May 21, 1854

b) Editorial, "Characteristic Traits of the Jews," in *Sunday Dispatch,* New York, N. Y., May 28, 1854 [1]

[The views expressed in these two editorials are of value not because they are in any sense a profound evaluation of Jewish character but because they reveal what some non-Jewish editors thought of the Jews a century ago.]

The Jews, As Citizens.

"Not a Single Jew Requiring Temporary Relief."—

Such is the report of the missionaries and colporteurs appointed by the New York Society for the Amelioration of the Condition of the Jews [2] in that city.—*Exchange paper.*

Such would be the report in almost every city in the United States —we might say in the world. This ancient race can boast that there are among them fewer paupers and fewer criminals than any other race can exhibit. When the history of the Jews is considered; when the hardships, trials, and persecutions to which they have been subjected are borne in mind, it is indeed wonderful that they should have retained most of those better traits that dignify and adorn civilized man. Oppressed by rigorous laws in every country, defrauded, insulted, beaten, and spit upon by every people, it is surprising that they have not been rendered fierce, resentful, and malignant. It is surprising too, that they should have retained their elasticity and their business capacity.

Denied citizenship in most of the countries of Christendom, debarred from the pursuits of ambition, incapable of holding offices of honor and profit, kicked and cuffed by all mankind, they have bent all their energies to one object, and that the accumulation of money. But even money, when obtained, attracted to them a more rigorous persecution. That persecution, which broke their spirit and destroyed their manliness, served at the same time to quicken their wits, sharpen their sagacity, and drive them into a closer and firmer brotherhood. With no friends in the wide world, they learned to cling with affectionate tenacity to one another. The wit that under their persecutions enabled them to accumulate money, also enabled them to conceal their treasures from the vigilant eyes of their enemies. Many of them, even in the dark ages, were princes in wealth, but very babies in spirit and in helplessness.

But, happily for this ancient race—this, the oldest and the purest of earth's aristocracy, for they are descended from the kings, prophets, and nobles of Israel—happily for them, as the world became enlightened and christianized, persecution relaxed its iron hand, and privileges were accorded to them.

Now, in this golden age, they are allowed to come and go as they will. They can choose their abiding-places as inclination may dictate. But the liberal institutions of this favored land induce many to live amongst us. The Jew here has the same privileges, social, religious, and political, that any other class enjoys. He exercises the right of suffrage. He is eligible to office. All the professions that ambition delights in, all the pursuits that the love of gain inclines to, are open to the Jew as to any other man.

The habit of acquisitiveness which seems to be natural, but which may be the result of oppression, still clings to them. They seldom enter the professions. They seldom turn their attention to politics. They seldom till the soil. They seem to prefer trade and commerce.

Yet some of the finest lawyers and orators that this country can boast of belong to the ancient Jewish race. We did not, however, design writing an essay on this subject. That would be better adapted to a review, than a journal like ours. We only intended to call attention to the fact developed in the statistics of the country, that the Jews are among our best citizens. If we enter a penitentiary or prison of any description, the marked face of the Israelite is rarely to be seen within its walls. Such a thing as a Jew in a poor-house was hardly ever known. Jews seldom commit murder or any of those crimes and offences that are marked by violence and passion. The offences committed by them, and they are of rare occurrence, are frauds, and small larcenies. A Jewish beggar is a thing almost unknown.

But they are generally regarded as a close and cold-hearted race. That they are so towards the outside world, is perhaps true; for their bounties, their charities, and benevolence are rarely extended beyond their race and brotherhood. But none can deny that they take care of their poor, comfort their afflicted, and relieve their distressed. In this they set an example worthy of all imitation. They are among the best, most orderly, well-disposed of our citizens.

Characteristic Traits Of The Jews.

In looking over the statistics of New York for the past year, we find that, among the numerous applicants for city aid, there was not one application from that large class in our midst of the tribe of Levi.

No race of people that exist are marked by a more distinctive individuality than the Jews. Mingling for centuries in close relations, commercially and politically—and speaking also the same language—with the Christians and other sects of America, Europe and Asia, still, with that deathless tenacity of purpose which marks their whole character, they have preserved their own peculiar distinctiveness of character and organization untarnished by the tenets of any other faith, or by the crossing, physiologically, with any other nation.

A little anecdote, culled from an article entitled "Wanderings in Servia," in the *Dublin University Magazine,* for May, will illustrate that trait of the character of the sons of Levi which keeps them always above the want that stoops to the asking for charity from others. It also alludes to the unjust oppression which this race has always received, east or west, the world over. The [anonymous] author, from whom we extract, is reviewing a book entitled "Sud Slavische Wanderingen in Sommer 1850" ("Wanderings in Southern Sclavonia in the Summer of 1850"), the year immediately succeeding the unhappy war in Hungary, in which the Sclavonians had taken a part. The following scene will give also some idea of the miseries which war inflicts:—

"The steamer lay to a somewhat desolate spot, near Neusatz, opposite to Peterwarde[i]n. I had been advised to take up my abode at the 'White Boat' inn, and a little Jewish boy, who seized upon my carpet-bag as I stepped out of the vessel, offered to be my guide.

" 'Are you strong enough to carry it?' I said to the lad, whose dress consisted of an old military cap, a worn-out Honved's [3] jacket patched in all directions, and trowsers picked up from the rejected wardrobe of a huzzar, as its tatters clearly indicated.

" 'Why not?' asked the boy, in accent which left no doubt of his Jewish extraction. 'And even if I were not strong enough I must still do it, or starve.'

" 'Have you no parents to take care of you?'

" 'Parents?' replied the lad, shouldering the carpet-bag, and leading the way, 'my mother is alive, but they killed my father about a year ago.'

" 'Who killed him?'

" 'God only knows! he went out early one day, and was found dead in the evening, just outside of the town, and it was no one's business then to look after the murderer. When a Hungarian met a Jew, he slew him for being a Servian, and when a Servian met a Jew, he slew him for being a Magyar. My mother was at her wit's end to support me and my little brothers and sisters; and she fell ill of want and sorrow. Then came the fire; the house we lived in was burnt to the ground, with nearly all that we possessed; what was saved from the fire the soldiers took. I do not know if they were Servians or Magyars, and when we opened our eyes next morning, we had not even a crust of bread left! Since then my mother has been too ill to work; she lives with the little children in a little village hard by. I go every day to the steamer, and give her what I earn.'

" 'And do you earn something every day?' said I to this young supporter of a household.

" 'I *must*, sir,' was the answer, 'otherwise we should all starve; when I get no job at the steamer, I manage to earn something by selling cigars up at the castle; I make four kreutzers by every packet, and I generally sell at least four packets every day.'

" 'And is that enough for you to live upon?'

" 'We must make it do; we *have* lived upon it, and more over, since New Years' day, I have laid by three florins; with these I shall buy pipe sticks and lucifer matches; and if I have any money left over and above, I shall buy laces, thread and handkerchiefs, and things will be better with us then.'

"The barefooted Jew boy was a true type of his whole race—*so often bent but never broken*. Crushed by misfortune, the Jew loses all but his untiring energy; he is ever ready to begin life again; he never loses patience, *but turns a stone into a farthing and a farthing into a florin*."

The Jews have been stigmatized the world over as usurers, as a nation treacherous, as a nation so fond of money that it would sell its own mother and its own soul for a dime.

But look into the aggregate character, and we find a nation devoted in kindness to the members of its own individual family, and one, if it attempts to overreach in trade outside nations, it acts but in accordance with the letter of its own code of laws—"an eye for an eye," &c., repaying some part only of the interest it owes for long back persecutions, and revilings, and despiteful usings.

Surely the spirit of pride that keeps all the members of so large and so diffused a family above want and charity is worthy of praise.

115. JEWS AND FARMING

"A call to establish a Hebrew Agricultural Society, to encourage agriculture amongst the Israelites of America," by Dr. Sigismund Waterman, New York, May, 1855 [1]

[Freed from feudal restrictions against owning and tilling land, Jews concerned with the status of their people began to conceive plans to settle Jews on land. They were stimulated in part by the fact that, as this Call declares, "The exclusive pursuit of commerce and its cognate branches by our people, is often used as a reproach and it must be confessed with some good show of reason." But the reproach is based upon a fundamental confusion: that in an economic system distribution is less socially useful than production. Thus commerce and those engaged in it are blamed for evils that result not from the exchange of goods but from the capitalist system of production and exchange as a whole. Failure to comprehend the nature of our capitalist economy led both to the "reproach" and to an apologetic defense against it. In the history of American economic life, the trend of population shift has been continually from the rural into the urban community. Americans were increasingly leaving the farm and going to town to work in expanding manufacture and industry or to find places in trade and commerce. When the tide is toward the city, because of greater opportunities and rewards there, repeated attempts [2] to turn immigrant urban Jews into agricultural workers in significant numbers necessarily proved futile under capitalism. Anti-Semitism cannot be fought by asking of some Jews what is required of no other group, that it go counter to the main lines of economic development. This document, and the discussion it aroused, present the problem in essence.]

Sir!

The necessity to direct the attention of the Israelites of America to agriculture has long been felt. The exclusive pursuit of commerce and its cognate branches by our people, is often used as a reproach and it must be confessed with some good show of reason. The mechanical arts have found few representatives amongst us in this country,[3] a few trades having been entirely monopolized, whilst many of the more elevated, requiring higher manual skill and technical perfection are in vain sought for. The agriculturist however is entirely wanting. It is on this account that we are looked upon as transitory inhabitants, having neither the desire nor the capacity to settle as permanent citizens.

This view erroneous in itself is nevertheless justified by the exclusive pursuit of commerce, which permits the accumulation of wealth without the acquirement of permanent interest in the soil of the land which constitutes the real title to citizenship and to the full enjoyment of civic rights.

In a sound national economy, in which all are benefited by one and one by all, an undue preponderance of any particular interest, must work injuriously upon the wellfare [sic] of the whole. If then, we as a Jewish community push exclusively the commercial interest, it is clear we pursue a course inimical to the wellfare [sic] of our country.

In order then to change this undesirable state of affairs, in order to create a taste for and encourage agriculture amongst our people, a calling so honorable and ensuring the greatest degree of independance [sic] and happiness and finally in order to employ the newly arrived emigrants, and the working man generally in want of employment and to give them a chance to gain by honesty and industry a comparatively happy living and to wean them from beggary and from becoming a burden to our charitable institutions, it is proposed to organize an association under the title "American Hebrew Agricultural and Horticultural Association" to be chartered under the general act of the legislature of the state of New York, passed April 1848, and governed according to a constitution, to be accepted by the society in proper time, best calculated to ensure the desired object.

It is proposed to have the society consist of share holders, of an indefinite number, each share to the amount of $12, one Dollar to be paid in monthly.

As soon as circumstances will permit the Association will purchase a tract of land. If said land can be purchased in the neighborhood of New York it would be advisable to turn first to Horticulture, Botanic, i.e. the raising of vegetables, of flowers, to the culture of wool and silk, the raising &c. of cattle poultry, the making of cheese and butter and so forth, because these branches pay better within the reach of this metropolis, and will form a more agreeable transition from other trades to that of agriculture.

There shall be a competent and reliable manager to superintend the whole property of the Association, who shall give ample security and into whose hands is to be confided the management of the soil, the division of labour, but being bound to give strict account of every transaction.

A person applying to be sent there must be of proper age and of good character. He shall receive all the necessaries of life in consideration of his diligent and honest labour. He shall be well treated, used according to his capacities, and instructed in Horticulture and Agriculture theoretically and practically. If his labours are more worth than his board and keeping, a due credit shall be given him monthly and said surplus paid in as shares, at the usual rate of $12 per share. He will thus become materially interested in the soil upon which he works.

The yearly net profits shall be laid out in Dividents [sic] and every share receive an equal amount of said Dividend, which it is supposed will more than tripple [sic] the original sum invested.

A certain sum, shall be applied annually to the building of new houses, schools, houses of worship and learning, to the purchase of cattle, seed, implements and general improvements, so as to enlarge from year to year the sphere of action and usefulness of the Association.

Thus it will be possible to establish as it were a school for those desirous to turn agriculturist, it will create a taste for it in those whom poverty and want of employment has driven there. It will repay the outlays of the shareholders and be an honour to us and a great benefit to our country.

We submit this outline to you, relying upon your hearty co-operation. We have the liveliest conviction that the plan is good and practicable and that it wants only for its fullest realization a generous support, a decided, hearty good will, "a pull, a strong pull and a pull together."

You are therefore respectfully invited to attend a mass meeting, where this subject will be considered, on the 13th inst. 8 o'clock P.M.

at No. 56 Orchard str. in the room of the Maimonides Library Association where several distinguished speakers are invited to address the meeting.[4]

Respectfully yours

B. Rothshild, J. Rosenbourgh, Dr. S. Waterman, Henry American, Maurice Werner, Samuel Trechet, Gottlieb Rosenblatt, H. Hildburghauser, S. Kimmelstiel, A. Asch, E. Buchstein, S. Engel, Hyman Gutman, J. Sulzberger, S. Straus, Ch. Northschild, S. Rothschild, H. Straus, Henry Kling, J. Muhlhauser, A. Chailly.[5]

116. JOINING A THIRD PARTY

Three letters from Jonathan Nathan to Hamilton Fish, New York, April and June, 1856 [1]

[These letters are a partial record of a close personal friendship that lasted about forty years between Jonathan Nathan (1811–1863) and Hamilton Fish (1808–1893). The intimacy began before they entered Columbia College, from which both were graduated in 1827, continued in the law-office in which they were fellow-students, and endured until Jonathan Nathan died. When Fish became an important political figure and Governor of New York, he took counsel from Whig party elders like Thurlow Weed, but "he leaned still more heavily for advice upon his classmate Jonathan Nathan . . ."[2] Nathan generally subordinated his own desires for political office or appointment to the needs of Fish, on one occasion refusing Fish's offer to appoint him reporter to the Court of Appeals because he believed that Fish would be harmed by making the appointment.[3]

For more than twenty years, Nathan and Fish were Whigs together; these letters of 1856 mark the transition that led them to become Republicans together. In the spring of 1856, Kansas had become a bloody battlefield between the anti-slavery settlers and the pro-slavery Missourians who crossed the border at election times to out-vote the settlers. President Franklin Pierce, in his Message to Congress, January 24, 1856, had sided with the Missouri "border ruffians." Renewed violence and bloodshed was being reported daily for the next few months. Nathan and Fish, reluctant to admit that the conservative, upper-class Whig party, which was born in the struggle against Jacksonian democracy, was dying, were finally impelled, with thousands of others, to build a third party to save the nation and democracy from the aggressive slave power.]

Friday [April 25, 1856]

My dear Gov.[4]

I have your two favors of 24th. I think you over-rate the strength of the niggerism [5] in the letter—It did not strike me as ultra antislavery. The great difficulty in our position arises from the fact that the only issue between parties is *slavery*—there is no other dividing line no other practical question—Whig and Democrat so far as principles are concerned are in my opinion convertible terms—We dont want a Tariff—we dont want a Bank—we like the sub Treasury—We and they profess to go for an honest and Economical administration of the Government—for submission to nothing wrong & demand of only the right &c &c— (and we both in fact belie our professions in practice—) and therefore with these views do I contend that we must be either Democratic or Republican—Now if Republicanism means abolition I aint there—but if the choice be presented to me of Abolition or Slavery extension and Southern principles and predominance I ask you which must I take—What republicanism means will be determined by its candidate—Before then it cant well be seen or understood—Shall you wait—You have not been heard on the Kansas question [6]—Is not this a fair & proper opportunity to have your opinion known—Prune or alter (or destroy) the draft sent you so as to convey your honest sentiments reserving expressly the right of leaving the company when you find their designs either unreasonable or not in accordance with your own views—I am sorry you are sick—I wont weary you more—I am troubled with a giddy head—and dont see clear—

Ever yours

J N

Saturday [April 26, 1856]

My dear Gov—

I have yours of yesterday—I have carefully studied it—differing from you on some points I yet agree in the main with your determination not to send the document[7] *provided* you will take some other opportunity of declaring your adhesion to the Northern side of the Kansas question—I have been anxious for the letter for this purpose solely and when I urged its preparation I did not anticipate that our friend would have been so thorough and ultra—Its greatest defect is that it forces you to do ungracefully (if you please) what might & will be all right on proper occasion and at a proper time—I will give you my views of the state of politics at another time—I am now going home—

Yours ever

J

P. S. I want to be early on record with the Pittsburg ticket

Fremont P.
Moses H. G.[rinnell].[8] V President—

Thursday [June 26, 1856]

My dear Gov.

There is treason in my camp at home—my wife has been so much with the Blairs & "Jessie"[9] as to have become a violent red republican and she insisted on my going to see what kind of a meeting there was last night. I went as far as the door of the Tabernacle—it was crowded to excess & there were a couple of outside meetings—there is a good deal of excitement here growing out of the desperate efforts of Fillmores friends to make him appear popular & strong—It dont work—his reception was (I am told) a failure in point of numbers—enthusiasm & pageantry &c &c—[10] There is a growing enthusiasm for Fremont—Jessie will give tens of thousands of votes to him—She is made to appear the brave, heroic self-sacrificing—feminine character which excites the gallant & chivalrous natures of the bhoys—She is immensely popular—and where 3 cheers are given to him 6 are called for Jessie—[11] I have no news to send you—weather again hot close damp sultry oppressive &c &c.

When will you be in for the 4th

Ever yours,

J.

117. WITH JOHN BROWN IN BLEEDING KANSAS

Reminiscences by August Bondi of the Border War in Kansas, May-June, 1856 [1]

[To keep the Territory of Kansas from becoming a slave-state was a necessary objective of the militant abolitionists and of all others who opposed the expansion of slavery. The violence of the pro-slavery settlers and the "Border Ruffians" who poured across the border from Missouri was met by the guerrilla warfare of the anti-slavery settlers, led by figures like John Brown. August Bondi's autobiographical account of his participation in this cause, while it may not be fully accurate [2] in some details which undoubtedly became blurred in the twenty-five years that passed before he set them down, still conveys the tension, the spirit, the methods, and the purposes of the Free-State party. His attitude toward slavery had been shaped in part by his observation of Negro slaves on a plantation near New Orleans when he arrived in the United States in 1848 and by instances of the brutal treatment of slaves that he witnessed in Galveston, Texas in 1851. He was in fact deterred from marrying a southern "woman with slaves" because he "felt that my father's son was not to be a slave-driver."[3]

The excerpt begins here shortly after the Pottawatomie massacre of five pro-slavery men on May 24, 1856 by a party of eight led by John Brown, in retaliation for the sacking of Lawrence, Kansas, by pro-slavery forces and in rejoinder to threats to drive free-state men from Kansas. Expressive of the stern ethics of guerilla warfare is Bondi's judgment of the Pottawatomie killings: "John Brown and his handful of men only executed upon those scoundrels a just sentence of death for the benefit of many unprotected families."[4]]

Chapter V: Border War

On the 26th of May, 1856, at an early hour in the morning, our little crowd rode on to the claim of John Brown, Jr., on Vine Branch, one mile and a half from Middle Creek bottom. About 5 o'clock that afternoon Carpenter,[5] from near Prairie City, joined us and reported that he had come at the instance of his neighbors to request Capt. Brown's assistance against the Border Ruffians, who, in spite of all proclamations, continued to harass the settlers. It was Carpenter's mission to beg Capt. Brown's assistance in behalf of the settlers of the southern part of Douglas County against these marauders organizing under territorial laws and armed with guns furnished by the government. Capt. Brown declared his readiness to go at once, and sent one of his sons [6] to tell Mrs. Jason Brown to send any enquiring friend who wished to join us to come to Carpenter, near Prairie City. We started after dark, eleven in number. Capt. Brown carried a sabre and a largest size revolver. His sons and Thompson [7] had a revolver, cutlass and a squirrel rifle each. Townsley [8] an old musket. Wiener [9] a double-barrelled shot gun. Carpenter one revolver; myself a flint lock musket of 1812 pattern. About 4 o'clock on the morning of the 27th of May, we reached the hiding place on Taway Creek which Carpenter had picked out for us. Brown inspected the surroundings, put out guards and appointed reliefs. After a while Carpenter brought in some corn for our horses and a small sack of coarse flour, and Capt. Brown began to prepare breakfast. We staid here until Sunday, June 1st; during these few days I learned to appreciate the exalted character of my old friend. He showed at all times the most affectionate care for each of us. On the morning of the 28th of May, Ben. Cochrane,[10] a settler and member of the Pottawatomie Rifles, joined us. He related that in the last raid the ruffians had burned my cabin, stolen my cattle and plundered Wiener's store;[11] all this had happened in the presence of the U. S. troops, under their commanding officer. Capt. Cook, Company F, 2d U. S. Dragoons,[12] was asked by the settlers to interfere. He refused, saying he had no orders to that effect, but ordered the leader of the Border Ruffian militia to surrender all his prisoners to the U. S. troops. In the afternoon of that day, Carpenter brought Charles Kaiser, a native of Bavaria, and an old soldier of the Revolution of '49, to our camp. He was extremely well pleased to find in me a member of the old Vienna Legion.

On the 29th of May, Capt. Shore of Prairie City Rifles and Dr. Westfall,[14] a neighbor of Carpenter, came into camp and told us that many horses and other property had been stolen near Willow Springs, about 10 or 15 miles distant, and asked old Brown what he calculated to do. Brown replied with the question, "Capt. Shore, how many men can you furnish me?" Shore answered that his men were just now very unwilling to leave home. Brown said, "Why did you send Carpenter after us? I am unwilling to sacrifice my men without some hope of accomplishing something." On the evening of the 29th of May, Capt. Shore visited us again and brought us some flour. Brown told him that if his men continued unwilling to turn out we would not stay there, as the enemy would soon find our retreat. Shore asked him to wait yet a few days. He felt that the Missourians suspected that Brown was not far from Prairie City and fear of him had protected the neighborhood from raids. Brown gave him until Sunday to gather the settlers, that with combined force we might hunt for the militia and offer them battle wherever we might find them. Shore promised to do his best. On the morning of the 31st, Capt. Shore informed us that a large company of Missouri militia had gone into camp on the Santa Fe road, near Black Jack (Spring);[15] that a few hours ago a house in Palmyra had been raided, the men disarmed and their weapons carried off. Rumors had been sent through the settlement summoning everybody to appear at Prairie City at 10 o'clock next forenoon. Capt. Shore concluded with the words: "We expect you with us." Capt. Brown grabbed Capt. Shore's hand and answered, "We will be with you." It was near midnight when our visitors left us. Next morning, June 1st, Capt. Brown had breakfast by sun up and when shortly afterwards Capt. Shore arrived to pilot us, we shouted with a will. Carpenter, Kaiser and Townsley assisted Wiener to empty his bottle. Capt. Brown called out, "Ready, forward march," and we were on the road. After a short ride we arrived at Prairie City. We found about a dozen settlers gathered around the principal building, a hewed log house, 18x24 feet. After picketing our horses we joined those present and were told that a circuit preacher had made an appointment for the day. Soon numbers arrived and the service began at noon. The prayers were hardly finished, when three men with guns across their saddles were seen galloping towards the village. They came within 50 yards and halted. The two Moore brothers,[16] armed with carbines, and four or five others mounted and went out to meet the strangers who turned and put spurs to their horses; but racing down the first hill, one of their horses fell, when they surrendered to their pursuers. When brought before Capt. Brown they acknowledged they were from the camp of the Kansas Militia at Black Jack, on the Santa Fe road, commanded by H. Clay Pate,[17] from Westport. Their company numbered about 80 men, all well armed with rifles and revolvers. One of the prisoners owned up that he was one of the three who had raided Palmyra the evening before, and that, not knowing of the Free State meeting, they had come to Prairie City for a like purpose. These prisoners and their arms were turned over to Capt. Shore, who detailed seven of his men as guard. The prisoners also told us that they had several Free State prisoners in their camp, one of them, an old man, a preacher, named Moore, whom they had picked up near Westport and taken along for their special fun. The Moore brothers at once knew this to be their father and begged us to start at once, but Capt. Brown declared we should not start before night had set in, and attack the enemy at daybreak, to which plan all agreed. After supper about forty men, Prairie City Rifles, put themselves under the leadership of Capt. Shore. Carpenter, the two Moores and Dr. Westfall asked permission to face next day's dangers in his company, which was freely granted. On unanimous request Capt. Brown accepted the command-in-chief. After sundown the order to saddle up was given, but it was already night when our force of 60 men left Prairie City. At midnight we halted in a post-oak grove, two miles from the enemy. All hands rested near their horses. That night it was agreed to leave the horses with a small guard, to move on foot up to within a mile of the enemy, Capt. Brown's company in advance and center, Capt. Shore's men thrown out as skirmishers on each flank, all together, without firing a shot, to charge upon the Border Ruffian camp, Monday, June 2d, 1856.

Capt. Shore detailed five men as guard with the horses; Capt. Brown prevailed upon his son, Fred, to stay with them. At first streak of day we started, Brown's company ahead, consisting of Capt. Brown and his sons, Owen, Solomon [Salmon] and Oliver, Henry Thompson, Charles Kaiser, Theo. Wiener, Carpenter, the three Moores, Dr. Westfall, Benj. Cochrane, August Bondi and James Townsley. After a march of a mile and a half we reached the summit of a hill, and saw before us, about a mile distant, the hostile camp, in the midst of a small grove. Capt. Brown called out, "Now follow me!" and down the hill he and his company started on a run. We had not made half the hill, when we were greeted with the shots of the Missouri pickets, at the same time we heard the guns of Shore's men replying behind us. Soon the Missourians sent whole volleys against us, but Brown's company charged right on. When we arrived at the foot of the hill we saw before us the old Santa Fe road with its oldest wagon trail which in many places had been washed out some two or three feet wide and about two feet deep. Beyond, within about two hundred yards, was the Missouri camp.

Capt. Brown jumped into the old washed out trail and commanded, "Halt, down!" His companions followed his example, and now we saw that not a man of Capt. Shore's company, except Capt. Shore himself, had followed down hill; most of them had already disappeared, a few yet on the brow of the hill wasting ammunition, and very soon these also retired in the direction of their comrades. So, right in the beginning of the fight Brown's forces had been reduced to his own men.

He scattered them all along that old trail, and using it as a rifle pit, we opened fire, to which the enemy replied with continuous firing. Wiener and myself were posted on the extreme left flank. Capt. Brown passed continually up and down the line, sometimes using his spy glass to inspect the enemy's position and repeatedly cautioning his men against wasting ammunition. About a quarter of an hour after we had reached the old trail, Henry Thompson was shot through the lungs and was led away by Dr. Westfall; shortly after Carpenter was shot through the upper arm and had to retire. Then Capt. Shore squatted himself on the ground and said to Capt. Brown, "I am very hungry." Brown never answered and went on his way to see that the gaps, caused by the absence of Thompson, Carpenter and Westfall, be filled as well as possible. Capt. Shore then spoke up: "Boys, I have to leave you to hunt up some breakfast." And the hero of that day–according to Mr. Utter [18]–got up and dusted. After the lapse of another half hour Townsley asked Capt. Brown for permission to go for ammunition. Capt. Brown did not reply, and Townsley left. Neither he nor Capt. Shore returned to us till after H. C. Pate's surrender, when they came to us following behind the Lawrence Stubbs.[19] It might have been about nine o'clock in the forenoon when Captain Brown stopped near Wiener and me and, having looked through his spy glass for some time, said, "It seems the Missourians have also suffered from our fire; they are leaving one by one; we must never allow that. We must try to surround them; we must compel them to surrender." He then walked down our line, spoke with some of the men, and returned with the Moore boys to where Wiener and myself were posted and beckoned us to follow him. We five, Capt. Brown, the two Moores, Wiener and myself, ran up a hill south of the Missouri camp. As soon as we had gained a commanding position within two hundred yards of the enemy, Capt. Brown ordered the two Moores to aim with their carbines at horses and mules exclusively, and not to shoot at any men at this time, if it could be avoided, as he wanted to take as many prisoners as possible. The Moore boys, with four shots, killed two mules and two horses, which we could perceive created a great consternation in the Missouri camp, and we saw several leaving. Now Capt. Brown drew and cocked his revolver and declared that he should advance some twenty yards by himself and if then he should wave his hat, we were to follow; Wiener and me ahead; the Moores to come up more slowly that, if necessary, they could cover our retreat with their carbines.

According to previous agreement our comrades along the Sante Fe road were to run to us as soon as they saw his signal with the hat. Capt. Brown advanced but about twenty steps when he stood, waved his hat and we joined him. Then the Captain and we four behind him, together with the seven along the Sante Fe road, charged against the Missouri camp. Capt. Pate stepped out in front of his men and waved a white handkerchief and called out to Capt. Brown that he was ready to leave. Capt. Brown kept on until within five feet of Capt. Pate, and, covering the hostile commander with his revolver, called out, "Unconditional surrender." The rifles slipped from the grasp of the Ruffians and Pate surrendered his sword. Twenty-four well armed cut-throats laid down their arms; some thirty had run off during the engagement; seven, more or less seriously wounded, lay on the ground. The booty of the day consisted of thirty stands of U. S. rifles and accoutrements, as many revolvers, thirty saddle horses and equipments, two wagons with their teams, and a large amount of provisions, ammunition and camp equipage.[20] Capt. Pate surrendered his sword and revolver and I, being right by, asked him for the powder flask he carried, and gave it to me. I kept the old 1812 musket I carried at Black Jack with that powder flask like a sacred relic. They burned up in the old claim-shanty on my father's place, near Greeley, while I was in the military service.[21] I found, afterwards, the flintlock in the debris. It is now in the collection of the Historical Society in Topeka.

While Capt. Brown was giving orders concerning the guarding of the prisoners, we discovered two riders, one behind the other, charging down the Santa Fe road towards us. The first was Fred Brown, who introduced the other as Mr. Phillips,[22] the correspondent of the New York *Tribune*. They informed us that the Lawrence Stubbs were right behind them. Now the three prisoners of the Border Ruffians appeared and words fail to describe the joy and gratitude shown by these men. Their treatment had been most barbarous. Now came up the Lawrence Stubbs with Major Abbott, Luke Parsons and Hoyt [23] in the lead. Capt. Shore and Townsley came up behind them. After a few minutes, Capt. Brown succeeded in bringing into order the general turmoil, and with the prisoners in our midst we started for Prairie City.

On our arrival at Prairie City with prisoners and booty, Capt. Brown ordered our squad who had fought and won to continue guarding the prisoners and he would find some women to bake bread and fry some meat to prepare a meal for us and the prisoners from the captured supplies. We obeyed and staid with the prisoners and it was seven o'clock before supper for the prisoners was ready. Capt. Brown first saw that the wounded prisoners were well taken care of—Dr. Westfall was with them—then he ordered that the thirty-six well prisoners eat first, after which we would be served, as he had in the meantime prevailed on the Lawrence Stubbs, Capt. Shore and MaWhinney [McWhinney] [24] to prevail with their crowd to relieve us, guarding while we ate our supper. None of our crowd had tasted food or drink since the preceding day about four or five o'clock p. m., and were almost faint. At last we had our supper, at which time immense stacks of biscuits and meat just disappeared. After supper, twilight lasting, we marched to a grove on Tawny [Taway] Creek, where we, the men with Brown, and the Lawrence Stubbs made camp, the prisoners in the center, organized some reliefs for the night and rested as best we could. That night, June 2nd, everything portable of the Brown outfit and what we had captured was made away with and stolen by the settlers around the country. Wiener and I lost one pair of heavy Mackinaw blankets; Capt. Brown lost most of the blankets used by himself and his boys and a valuable pair of saddle-bags containing a complete set of surgical instruments and we had all we could do to save our horses and equipments and a few blankets.[25]

Next morning, June 3rd, we organized messes, the mess wagons of the captured Pate company furnishing the provisions, reorganized companies, elected commissioned and non-commissioned officers, and John Brown commenced to entrench, using the high banks of the Creek for breastworks wherever possible, and digging rifle-pits at other places. We fortified this Camp Brown to withstand the attack of any force without artillery.

By noon of the third day of June we were about 125 to 150 men, reasonably well organized. A beef was brought in and killed and other like meat supplies were provided for the following days.

Several of the Stubbs, Shores and MaWhinney's companies joined the John Brown company. Special mention of Luke I. Parsons, who joined Brown's company. He was just my age and was peculiarly attractive to me; we bunked together more or less during the campaigns of 1856. In the afternoon of June 3rd, we held council how to improve our exterior, the Brown outfit being altogether in rags. Capt. Brown selected five men to ride to the store of a pro-slavery man, Menard,[26] of Westport, who kept at Centrapolis to "impress" for our use some clothing. Fred and Oliver Brown and three of the Stubbs went and soon returned with some palm leaf hats, check shirts, linen coats, a few linen pants and bandanna handkerchiefs. I was on camp guard when they returned. Fred Brown, however, kept for me a check shirt, a palm leaf hat and a bandanna handkerchief, and one of Stubbs gave me a pair of jean pants, so I was well fitted out, only that I regretted that my toes showed too much for their good and stubbed continually on roots in the timber.

The work of entrenching went on and by evening it was fairly well completed, only artillery could have dislodged us.

We had elected a settler by the name of Walker [27] for corporal, he claiming to be a Mexican war veteran. About four a. m., June 4th, I was on outlying camp guard when one of our prisoners made his appearance, coming from Prairie City. I halted him and called for the corporal of the guard, Walker. The prisoner related that he and Walker had been neighbors in Missouri, and Walker had sent him during the night for a quart of whisky, which he had now with him. The loud talk attracted Capt. Brown, who after information, confiscated the booze and handed it to Wiener, who was by. He reduced Walker to the ranks and sent the prisoner to his place with the other captives of war. Wiener and Kaiser took each a big drink to Walker's health.

About 10 o'clock the morning of June 4th, Brackett,[28] the 1st lieutenant of the captive Border Ruffian company, got into some altercation with me. I cannot remember how it started. The dispute waxed loud; he used the expression, "What does a d---d Dutchman know of liberty?" Wiener mixed with it; Brackett challenged Wiener to a duel, and Wiener accepted at once, when Capt. Brown, attracted by the rumpus, came up, ordered Brackett and Wiener to their quarters and the noise stopped at once. This Brackett figured for years in many midnight forays of Missouri robberies on Kansas farmers in Bourbon and Linn Counties. He commanded the Ruffians in the Indian Post massacre and many other outrages. He was taken prisoner November, 1861, by a company of the 6th Kansas, court-martialed and executed.

Now that we boys were well fed, clothed and idle, of course we must be up to some scheme. So, after supper, June 3rd, Solomon [Salmon] and Oliver Brown, Luke Parsons and I discussed a plan to have the free state men secede Kansas from the U. S., raise a lone star flag and declare independence. We were very enthusiastic; but when John Brown was informed of our project he soon cooled our fervor by his cool, simple words, "Boys, no nonsense."

On Thursday, June 5th, about 9 o'clock a. m., Col. Sumner,[29] in command of the 2nd U. S. Dragoons, with his regiment, came up to our camp, halted within a mile and proceeded with some of his officers and a U. S. deputy marshal to our camp. When halted by our guard, he sent word to Capt. Brown demanding an interview. Capt. Brown met the Colonel at once, accompanied by me. Brown and Sumner stepped aside and held a quite spirited conversation for some ten minutes; of course, I heard nothing of their conversation nor did any one else. I caught Sumner's last words, however. "I have no orders for your arrest, but he has," and I supposed that by "he," Sumner meant the U. S. marshal.[30]

By noon, within one hour of the interview between Sumner and Brown, the grove was vacated; Camp Brown had ceased to exist. . . .

The raids of the Missourians continued in a peculiar manner; some half dozen would steal into a settlement and drive off a lot of cattle and horses, rush them ten miles off, then sometimes divide into two or three parties, always herd the stolen stock in some out of the way place during the first day following the raid and drive them to Missouri the second night. Some efforts were made to steal our herd and also to steal Brown's herd of Devons. We, Brown, Benjamin and I put our cattle together and with all the families, moved them to David Garrison's,[31] who had a large corral, into which we put them at nights under guard. The Mannes boy staid with us. This boy, John Bean Mannes,[32] was afterwards of my company, K, 5th cavalry. We made this move about August 10th. A day or two before this move I was called upon to assist in the protection of an old German settler, on South Pottawatomie, "Schutte";[33] a few Missourians had been seen lurking around his place. He had six or seven of the best horses in the country. Henry Kilbourn,[34] Point Dexter, Mannes [Poindexter Mannes], Ben Cochrane and I staid around Schutte's two days, scouted through the timber, found signs of a late camp in a ravine, but no Missourians, so we left Schutte's. Mind, we were always afoot, and after we had traveled a few miles towards Kilbourn's, we met a runner sent from Osawatomie to get, at least, twenty men to assist in defending the town, as a body of Border Ruffians had reached Paola bent on plunder. We four marched to Osawatomie, reached the town tired, slept on the floor of some house there. By morning the news came in that the Missouri company at Paola had retreated, not considering themselves strong enough to raid Osawatomie. We were about to leave the town, after a scant breakfast, when an old man came to us and asked about the locality of our claims and informed us that four yoke of pro-slavery work cattle, formerly owned by the New Georgia colony,[35] were with his cows. The New Georgia men had stolen his four horses before we routed them and he was afraid that when some of them might return for these four yokes they would drive his cows with them. There was yet a large Santa Fe wagon without box on the old site of New Georgia, and some log chains and yokes close by in a hollow. He wished that we would take away oxen, wagon, yokes and chains. He lived five miles from Osawatomie. We went with him at once. Arrived at his place we hid in the timber all day and at sunset came out, ate a hearty supper at our friend's house, hitched up the four yoke to the wagon and drove to the Mosquito Branch, arriving there by morning. We took the wagon to Kilbourn's timber and the eight oxen were put with the Bondi and Benjamin cattle and with them moved to Garrison's. These four yoke staid with our cattle until late in October, then we put them out to winter with a man named Saunders, on North Middle Creek. In the Spring we divided the spoils. To Kilbourn and Mannes, the best two yoke of oxen; to Benjamin and me, the two smaller yoke, the wagon and chains.

About the middle of August, a band of Free State boys, thirty in number, commanded by Capt. Cline, came on the Pottawatomie Creek; most of them had, with their captain, lately come from Iowa.[36] They had some teams and provisions along. All of them were well mounted on horses captured from pro-slavery men. They had several brushes with Border Ruffians and as yet had always routed them. Their last raid had been on the Rev. Martin White's place (a Baptist minister from Missouri); here they had captured eleven good horses.[37]

About August 20th, ('56) old John Brown reached Osawatomie with a spick and span four-mule team, the wagon loaded with provisions, besides he was well supplied with money—all contributed by northern friends of the Kansas Free State men, like Thad Hyatt.[38] With Brown had come some thirty men from near Topeka and Lawrence—mostly of the Stubbs—amongst them Luke I. [F.] Parsons and Charles Kaiser.

Old Brown told me and some of the neighbors, who had come to greet him, that he intended to invade the pro-slavery settlements of Linn and Bourbon counties, to give them a taste of the treatment their Missouri friends would not cease to extend to the free state settlements up the Marais des Cygnes and Pottawatomie. As he saw that I was not mounted, he ordered some of his men to capture all of Dutch Henry's horses; and when they were brought in, I received a four-year-old fine bay horse (steed) for my mount. I was furnished my own equipments from some new saddlery goods of the old store which had been hidden in the brush for safety. Old John Brown rode a fine blooded bay.

The Capt. Cline Company joined us and we moved from Osawatomie about August 24th. Benjamin and my brother-in-law [39] remained with Mrs. Benjamin [40] and the cattle at Garrison's, and it was agreed before I started with the Brown command that in case of an attack on the settlement, Benjamin should turn out; but my brother-in-law should under all circumstances remain with Mrs. Benjamin and the cattle. The boy, Mannes, too, was to continue to assist herding the entire bunch.

When Brown's company started from Osawatomie, a few men of the neighborhood joined the command and a few joined Capt. Cline's. I can recall some of those who joined Brown's command: Evander Light, Whitney Wood, J. M. Anthony (Susan's brother),[41] and Cyrus Tator, afterwards probate judge of Miami County, elected in the fall of 1857, and in July, 1860, he was lynched on the overland Pike's peak route for highway robbery and murder.

Ben Cochrane and Point Dexter Maness joined Cline's command; James Holmes,[42] afterwards secretary of the Territory of New Mexico, was with Cline, also.

Brown's company was about thirty-five strong; Cline's about forty-five. Cline and most of his men were Free State Yankees, deteriorated into free booters.

Both companies, Brown's and Cline's, started from Osawatomie August 24th. When camped for dinner rest, Capt. Brown made a talk to us of his company. He wished us all to understand that we must not molest women nor children, not take nor capture anything useless to us or Free State people; further, never destroy any kind of property wantonly nor burn any buildings, as Free State people could use them after the pro-slavery people had been driven out. Never consider captured horses or cattle as anything else than common property of the Free State army. The horses for military use, the cattle for food for our soldiers and settlers. He ordered also that we should keep some distance in camp from the Cline company, as they were too riotous. Whenever he could he would hire out meals, as he had ample means to pay for them. He then made arrangement with Capt. Cline that the two companies should daily exchange places on the March. One day, Brown's in advance, the next day, Cline's; the teams with the provisions always in the center during the march and in the rear during a fight.

We camped the first evening near a small Quaker settlement of three families, near Sugar Creek, Linn County. Capt. Brown had them prepare supper and breakfast for us. We there received information that a large pro-slavery force of about 500, among them the Bourbon County Rangers, with a red flag ornamented with skull and cross-bones, were raiding the Free State settlers of Linn and Bourbon Counties; that a man, Montgomery,[43] by name, and his neighbors had been compelled to flee and had all moved to Lawrence a day or two ago. Capt. Brown also learned the names and the residences of the local pro-slavery leaders.

When we broke camp on the morning of August 25th, '56, the Cline company had the advance. By 10 o'clock a. m., we came on the fresh tracks of the pro-slavery raiders and quickened our pace. By noon we received information of their camping on South Middle Creek and hastened to surprise them, the Cline company in advance. On the last hills, overlooking the valley two miles wide, the pro-slavery camp was in full view; and the Bourbon County Rangers and their Border Ruffian auxiliaries, outnumbering us five or six to one, immediately upon sighting us, galloping down the hill, turned and fled, leaving the camp teams, many horses, provisions, tents and their red flag with the skull and cross-bones; yea, some who had been enjoying a noon siesta, left their clothes, hats, shoes and boots. I found a pair of boots which were just the fit, and as mine were in favor of keeping my feet aired, I was not long in changing. I also found a hat which I appropriated; my palm leaf of Camp Brown memory was used up. I still wore the pants and coat which had been apportioned me, the pants hardly holding together. In vain I looked for a pair amongst the plunder.

Capt. Cline saw Capt. Brown about the division of the spoils; he claimed the larger share because his men were in advance. Capt. Brown remarked, "My men do not fight for plunder; keep it all," and so Cline kept almost the whole spoils. This was the "Battle of South Middle Creek." We made camp on the ground deserted by the enemy, and rested there until morning. The Cline outfit quarreled till midnight about the division of the spoils.

The morning of the 26th we started to raid the pro-slavery settlement on Sugar Creek (Linn County). Brown's company had the advance. About 10 o'clock a. m., we stopped on the place of a "Capt.

Brown";[44] he was captain of the pro-slavery or Shannon Militia. We took his cattle, about fifty head, and while searching the house for clothing, a young woman, his daughter, just berated the abolitionists for all out. Amongst her other remarks, I caught this one: "No Yankee abolitionist can ever kiss a Missouri girl." As she uttered these words, I spied a litter of hound pups in the corner of the kitchen. I picked up one and said, "I would kiss a hound pup before I would kiss a Missouri girl," and I kissed the pup. While rummaging around I found a couple of empty nail kegs and a box marked B, as my kegs and boxes had been marked, and this Capt. Brown had been in the raid on Wienersville. I opened a trunk, no doubt belonging to Capt. B., and found there a new pair of jean pants, about five sizes too large for me; nevertheless I exchanged my nether garments. The newly acquired breeches reached nearly up to my arm pits, but were quite comfortable.

We returned from our raid to Osawatomie on the afternoon of the 28th of August, bringing along some 150 head of fat cattle.[45] Of these Capt. Brown had four killed at once to feed the hungry settlers around. Early next morning Brown and Cline divided the captured stock, each taking one-half. Capt. B. charging to his share the four killed the previous evening, and he ordered four more killed for the settlers. The eight hides he gave to a poor widow who had given us six bushels of corn to feed our horses. . . .[46]

118. EXPLORING THE WEST WITH FREMONT

Selections from a book of travels by Solomon Nunes Carvalho, 1857 [1]

[Fascinating is Carvalho's account of one of the great adventures of nineteenth century far western exploration. Born in Charleston, S. C., in 1815, Carvalho was an artist and photographer who practised in Philadelphia and Baltimore before he came to New York. In 1852 he was awarded a diploma and silver medal from the South Carolina Institute for his painting, "The Intercession of Moses for Israel."[2] An admirer of John Charles Fremont, a man of his own age but already famous as an explorer, a conqueror of California, and an anti-Slavery senator from that State, Carvalho accepted Fremont's invitation on August 22, 1853 to accompany him on his fifth expedition across the Rocky

Mountains. Secretary of War Jefferson Davis having exhibited his preference for the southernmost route to California as the path for a projected railway, and having sent out other expeditions to demonstrate the practicability of his plan, Fremont, privately financed by Senator Thomas Hart Benton of Missouri and his own funds, determined to prove that a central route was also practicable and more desirable. Carvalho was engaged to make daguerreotype photographs, and thus became the first official photographer ever to accompany a scientific expedition. After a couple of months spent painting portraits in Salt Lake City, which he reached on March 1, 1854, Carvalho started for California on May 6, 1854 in the wake of a group of Mormon missionaries, arriving over the mountains at San Bernardino on June 9, 1854. He was probably the second Jew to cross the Rockies into California.[3] His book is the chief surviving source of information about the expedition. He speaks simply but effectively of the hardships of twenty-two men crossing the Rockies on foot in winter across uncharted territory.]

When we left the Utah village, we travelled a long day's journey, and camped on the Grand River, thirty miles from the last camp; my pony behaved admirably well on the road, and I would not have parted with him on any account.

While at supper, the guard on the look-out gave the alarm that mounted Indians were approaching, the word was given to arm and prepare to receive them.

About fifty or sixty mounted Utah Indians, all armed with rifles, and bows and arrows, displaying their powder horns and cartouch boxes most conspicuously, their horses full of mettle, and gaily caparisoned, came galloping and tearing into camp.

They had also come to be compensated for the horse we had paid for the night before;[4] they insisted that the horse did not belong to the woman, but to one of the men then present, and threatened, if we did not pay them a great deal of red cloth, blankets, vermilion, knives, and gunpowder, they would fall upon us and massacre the whole party.

On these occasions, Col. Fremont never showed himself, which caused the Indians to have considerable more respect for the "Great Captain," as they usually called him; nor did he ever communicate directly with them, which gave him time to deliberate, and lent a mysterious importance to his messages. Very much alarmed, I entered Col. Fremont's lodge, and told him their errand and their threats. He at once expressed his determination not to submit to such imposition, and at the same time, laughed at their threats; I could not comprehend his calmness. I deemed our position most alarming, surrounded as we were by armed savages, and I evidently betrayed my alarm in my countenance. Col. Fremont without apparently noticing my nervous state, remarked that he knew the Indian character perfectly, and he did not hesitate to state, that there was not sufficient powder to load a single rifle in the possession of the whole tribe of Utahs. "If," continued he, "they had any ammunition, they would have surrounded and massacred us, and stolen what they now demand, and are parleying for."

I at once saw that it was a most sensible deduction, and gathered fresh courage. The general aspect of the enemy was at once changed, and I listened to his directions with a different frame of mind than when I first entered.

He tore a leaf from his journal, and handing it to me, said: here take this, and place it against a tree, and at a distance near enough to hit it every time, discharge your Colt's Navy six shooters, fire at intervals of from ten to fifteen seconds—and call the attention of the Indians to the fact, that it is not necessary for white men to load their arms.

I did so; after the first shot, they pointed to their own rifles, as much as to say they could do the same, (if they had happened to have the powder), I, without lowering my arm, fired a second shot, this startled them.

I discharged it a third time—their curiosity and amazement were increased: the fourth time, I placed the pistol in the hands of the chief and told him to discharge it, which he did, hitting the paper and making another impression of the bullet.

The fifth and sixth times two other Indians discharged it, and the whole six barrels being now fired it was time to replace it in my belt.

I had another one already loaded, which I dexterously substituted, and scared them into an acknowledgment that they were all at our mercy, and we could kill them as fast as we liked, if we were so disposed.

After this exhibition, they forgot their first demand, and proposed to exchange some of their horses for blankets, etc.

We effected a trade for three or four apparently sound, strong animals; "Moses," one of the Delaware chiefs, also traded for one, but in a few days they all proved lame and utterly useless as roadsters, and we had to kill them for food.

The Indians with the consent of Col. Fremont, remained in camp all night; they had ridden thirty miles that day, and were tired. On this occasion, eleven men, fully armed, were on guard at one time.

The Indians who no doubt waited in camp to run our horses off during the night, were much disappointed in not having an opportunity. They quietly departed the next morning, while our whole camp listened to the energetic exclamation of Col. Fremont, that the "price of safety is eternal vigilance."

The crossing of the Grand River, the eastern fork of the Colorado, was attended with much difficulty and more danger. The weather was excessively cold, the ice on the margin of either side of the river was over eighteen inches thick; the force of the stream always kept the passage in the centre open; the distance between the ice, was at our crossing, about two hundred yards. I supposed the current in the river to run at the rate of six miles an hour. The animals could scarcely keep their footing on the ice, although the men had been engaged for half an hour in strewing it with sand. The river was about six feet deep, making it necessary to swim our animals across; the greatest difficulty was in persuading them to make the abrupt leap from the ice to the roaring gulph, and there was much danger from drowning in attempting to get on the sharp ice on the other side, the water being beyond the depth of the animals, nothing but their heads were above water, consequently the greater portion of their riders' bodies were also immersed in the freezing current.

To arrive at a given point, affording the most facilities for getting upon the ice, it was necessary to swim your horse in a different direction to allow for the powerful current. I think I must have been in the water, at least a quarter of an hour. The awful plunge from the ice into the water, I never shall have the ambition to try again; the weight of my body on the horse, naturally made him go under head and all; I held on as fast as a cabin boy to a main-stay in a gale of wind. If I had lost my balance it is most probable I should have been drowned. I was nearly drowned as it was, and my clothes froze stiff upon me when I came out of it. Some of the Delawares crossed first and built a large fire on the other side, at which we all dried our clothes standing in them.

It is most singular, that with all the exposure that I was subjected to on this journey, I never took the slightest cold, either in my head or on my chest; I do not recollect ever sneezing. While at home, I ever was most susceptible to cold.

The whole party crossed without any accident; Col. Fremont was the first of our party to leap his horse into the angry flood, inspiring his men, by his fearless example to follow.

"Julius Caesar crossed the Rubicon with an immense army; streams of blood followed in his path through the countries he subdued, to his arrival at the Eternal City, where he was declared dictator and consul."

On a former expedition, Col. Fremont crossed the Grand River with a handful of men; but no desolation followed in his path. With the flag of his country in one hand and the genius of Liberty resting on his brow, he penetrated through an enemy's country, converting all hearts as he journeyed, conquering a country of greater extent than Caesar's whole empire, until he arrived at San Francisco, where he became military commandant and governor in chief of California, by the simple will of the people.[5] Fremont's name and deeds, will become as imperishable as Caesar's.

At last we are drawn to the necessity of killing our brave horses for food. The sacrifice of my own pony that had carried me so bravely in my first buffalo hunt,[6] was made; he had been running loose for a week unable to bear even a bundle of blankets. It was a solemn event with me, and rendered more so by the impressive scene which followed.

Col. Fremont came out to us, and after referring to the dreadful necessities to which we were reduced, said "a detachment of men whom he had sent for succor on a former expedition, had been guilty of eating one of their own number." He expressed his abhorrence of the act, and proposed that we should not under any circumstances whatever, kill our companions to prey upon them. "If we are to die, let us die together like men." He then threatened to shoot the first man that made or hinted at such a proposition.

It was a solemn and impressive sight to see a body of white men, Indians, and Mexicans, on a snowy mountain, at night, some with bare head and clasped hands entering into this solemn compact. I never until that moment realized the awful situation in which I, one of the actors in this scene, was placed.

I remembered the words of the sacred Psalmist (Psalm cvii. 4–7) and felt perfectly assured of my final deliverance.—"They *wandered* in the *wilderness* in a solitary way: They found no city to dwell in.

"*Hungry* and *thirsty* their souls fainted within them. Then they cried unto the Lord in their trouble, and he *delivered them* out of their distresses.

"And he led them forth by the *right way* that they might go to a *city of habitation.*

"Oh, that *men* would *praise the Lord* for his goodness, and for his wonderful works to the children of men." . . .

Four days before we entered the Little Salt Lake Valley, we were surrounded by very deep snows; but as it was necessary to proceed, the whole party started, to penetrate through what appeared to be a pass, on the Warsatch Mountains. The opening to this depression was favorable, and we continued our journey, until the mountains seemed to close around us, the snow in the cañon got deeper, and further progress on our present course was impossible.

It was during this night, while encamped in this desolate spot, that Col. Fremont called a council of Capt. Wolff and Solomon of the Delawares—they had been sent by Col. Fremont to survey the cañon, and surrounding mountains, to see if a passage could be forced. On their return, this council was held; Capt. Wolff reported it impossible to proceed, as the animals sank over their heads in snow, and he could see no passage out. The mountains which intercepted our path, were covered with snow four feet deep. The ascent bore an angle of forty-five degrees, and was at least one thousand feet from base to summit. Over this, Captain Wolff said it was also impossible to go. "That is not the point," replied Col. Fremont, "we must cross, the question is, which is most practicable—and how we can do it."

I was acting as assistant astronomer at this time. After the council, Col. Fremont told me there would be an occultation that night, and he wanted me to assist in making observations. I selected a level spot on the snow, and prepared the artificial horizon. The thermometer indicated a very great degree of cold; and standing almost up to our middle in snow, Col. Fremont remained for hours making observations, first with one star, then with another, until the occultation took place. Our lantern was illuminated with a piece of sperm candle, which I saved from my pandora box, before we buried it;[7] of my six sperm candles this was the last one. I take some praise to myself for providing some articles which were found most necessary. These candles, for instance, I produced when they were most required, and Col. Fremont little thought where they were procured.

The next morning, Col. Fremont told me that Parowan, a small settlement of Mormons, forty rods square, in the Little Salt Lake Valley, was distant so many miles in a certain direction, immediately over this great mountain of snow; that in three days he hoped to be in the settlement, and that he intended to go over the mountain, at all hazards.

We commenced the ascent of this tremendous mountain, covered as it were, with an icy pall of death, Col. Fremont leading and breaking a path; the ascent was so steep and difficult, that it was impossible to keep on our animals; consequently, we had to lead them, and travel on foot—each man placed his foot in the tracks of the one that preceded him; the snow was up to the bellies of the animals. In this manner, alternately toiling and resting, we reached the summit, over which our Delawares, who were accustomed to mountain travel, would not of themselves have ventured. When I surveyed the distance, I saw nothing but continued ranges of mountains of everlasting snow, and for the first time, my heart failed me—not that I had lost confidence in our noble leader, but that I felt myself physically unable to overcome the difficulties which appeared before me, and Capt. Wolff himself told me, that he did not think we could force a passage. We none of us had shoes, boots it was impossible to wear. Some of the men had raw hide strapped round their feet, while others were half covered with worn out stockings and moccasins; Col. Fremont's moccasins were worn out, and he was no better off than any of us.

After we were all rested, Col. Fremont took out his pocket compass, and pointing with his hand in a certain direction, commenced the descent. I could see no mode of extrication, but silently followed the party, winding round the base of one hill, over the side of another, through defiles, and, to all appearance, impassable cañons, until the mountains, which were perfectly bare of vegetation, gradually became interspersed with trees. Every half hour, a new snow scape presented itself, and as we overcame each separate mountain, the trees increased in number.

By noon, we were in a defile of the mountains, through which was a dry bed of a creek. We followed its winding course, and camped at about two o'clock in a valley, with plenty of grass. Deer tracks were visible over the snow, which gave fresh life to the men. The Delawares sallied out to find some. Col. Fremont promised them, as an incentive to renewed exertions, that he would present to the successful hunter, who brought in a deer, a superior rifle.

They were out several hours, and Weluchas was seen approaching, with a fine buck across his saddle.

He received his reward, and we again participated in a dish of wholesome food.

We had now triumphantly overcome the immense mountain, which I do not believe human foot, whether civilized or Indian, had ever before attempted, from its inaccessibility; and on the very day and hour previously indicated by Col. Fremont, he conducted us to the small settlement of Parowan, in Little Salt Lake Valley, which could not be distinguished two miles off, thus proving himself a most correct astronomer and geometrician. . . .

Col. Fremont's lodge, at meal time, when we had good, wholesome buffalo and deer meat presented quite a picturesque appearance. A fire was always burning in the centre; around it cedar bushes were strewn on which buffalo robes were placed. Sitting around, all of us on our hams, cross-legged, with our tin plates and cups at each side of us, we awaited patiently the entrance of our several courses; first came the camp kettle, with buffalo soup, thickened with meat-biscuit, our respective tin plates were filled and replenished as often as required. Then came the roast or fry, and sometimes both; the roast was served on sticks, one end of which was stuck in the ground, from it we each in rotation cut off a piece. Then the fried venison. In those days we lived well, and I always looked forward to this social gathering, as the happiest and most intellectually spent hour during the day. Col. Fremont would often entertain us with his adventures on different expeditions; and we each tried to make ourselves agreeable.

Although on the mountains, and away from civilization, Col. Fremont's lodge was sacred from all and every thing that was immodest, light or trivial; each and all of us entertained the highest regard for him. The greatest etiquette and deference were always paid to him, although he never ostensibly required it. Yet his reserved and unexceptionable deportment, demanded from us the same respect with which we were always treated, and which we ever took pleasure in reciprocating.

The death of Mr. Fuller filled our camp with deep gloom; almost at the very hour he passed away, succor was at hand. Our party was met by some Utah Indians, under the chieftainship of Ammon, a brother of the celebrated Wakara, (anglicized Walker) who conducted us into the camp on Red Creek Cañon. At this spot our camp was informed by Mr. Egloffstien,[8] that our companion in joy and in sorrow, was left to sleep his last sleep on the snows. The announcement took some of us by surprise, although I was prepared for his death at any moment. I assisted him on his mule that morning, and roasted the prickles from some cactus leaves, which we dug from the snow, for his breakfast; he told me that he was sure he would not survive, and did not want to leave camp. . . .

I was riding side by side with Egloffstien after Mr. Fuller's death, sad and dejected. Turning my eyes on the waste of snow before me, I remarked to my companion that I thought we had struck a travelled road. He shook his head despondingly, replying "that the marks I observed, were the trails from Col. Fremont's lodge poles." Feeling satisfied that I saw certain indications, I stopped my mule, and with very great difficulty alighted, and thrust my hand into the snow, when to my great delight I distinctly felt the ruts caused by wagon wheels. I was then perfectly satisfied that we were "saved!" The great revulsion of feeling from intense despair to a reasonable hope, is impossible to be described; from that moment, however, my strength perceptibly left me, and I felt myself gradually breaking up. The nearer I approached the settlement, the less energy I had at my command; and I felt so totally incapable of continuing, that I told Col. Fremont, half an hour before we reached Parowan, that he would have to leave me there; when I was actually in the town, and surrounded with white men, women and children, paroxysms of tears followed each other, and I fell down on the snow perfectly overcome.

I was conducted by a Mr. Heap to his dwelling, where I was treated hospitably. I was mistaken for an Indian by the people of Parowan. My hair was long, and had not known a comb for a month, my face was unwashed, and ground in with the collected dirt of a similar period. Emaciated to a degree, my eyes sunken, and clothes all torn into tatters from hunting our animals through the brush. My hands were in a dreadful state; my fingers were frost-bitten, and split at every joint; and suffering at the same time from diarrhoea, and symptoms of scurvy, which broke out on me at Salt Lake City afterwards. I was in a situation truly to be pitied, and I do not wonder that the sympathies of the Mormons were excited in our favor, for my personal appearance being but a reflection of the whole party, we were indeed legitimate subjects for the exercise of the finer feelings of nature. When I entered Mr. Heap's house I saw three beautiful children. I covered my eyes and wept for joy to think I might yet be restored to embrace my own.[9] . . .

119. FIRST NEW YORK RUSSIAN-JEWISH CONGREGATION

Appeal for the support of the *Beth Hamidrash,* by Rabbi Abraham Joseph Ash, New York, March, 1857 [1]

[Founded June 4, 1852 by recently arrived immigrants from Russia, the *Beth Hamidrash* constituted the first Russian-Jewish congregation to be established in the United States and soon became the center of religious orthodoxy and defense against the encroachments of Reform Judaism. The twelve founders first met for worship and study in a garret at 83 Bayard Street, but by the time this appeal was made, the congregation had moved four times and was now quartered at 78 Allen Street.[2] The *Beth Hamidrash* has been called the only institution in the country at the time where religious studies were pursued according to the traditional East-European pattern. The scholars thus developed were, during this period, frequently called upon to provide authoritative answers to questions about religious law and practice.[3] This appeal, written in Hebrew by Rabbi Ash and translated probably by Isaac Leeser, contains a summary of the aims and methods of the Beth Hamidrash.]

The following is an account of the founding of the Beth Hammidrash, and the views of its originators, whom our God may remember for good.

This institution, which is at present situated in New York, is like a lily in the country of America—alone yet, pleasant as the dawn, and trusting for support from the Friend of all good.

1. It is one that awakens the heart of every man of Israel, saying, "Rouse thee from thy sleep, get thee ready, and return to thy God ere thy light be quenched; perhaps He may receive thee graciously."
2. It has drawn to itself these five years, from the day of its founding till the present, morning and evening, every man in whom the spirit of the Almighty is active, to pray in the assembly of the faithful.
3. It is open all the day for all who may watch at its doors, and for every one whose mind may spur him on to quench his thirst in the study of the law.
4. There are found therein at this day students of the law, many

of whom know how to decide for the people correctly in matters of religious duty.

5. There is daily a portion of law expounded publicly, from its founding until now, every evening, when the people rest from their daily task, to teach them the law, that they may know the God of their fathers, and the deeds which they should do in his service, and to warn them that they may not be caught in the snare of transgression.

6. Besides this, there are persons who study the law for themselves, either in pairs or singly.

7. The house is full to overflowing, on Sabbaths and festivals, in the evening and morning, to pray in common before they put food or drink into their mouths.

8. It is well calculated to excite the heart of every Israelite who enters into this house to pray, to incite him to make ready his heart to appear before his Maker with the fire of religious fervor and devotion.

9. It is filled with all sorts of holy books, several sets of the Babylonian and Jerusalem Talmuds, the Turim, Rambam, Rif, Shulchan Aruch, Rabbinical opinions, Bibles, commentaries, books of devotion and instruction, Midrashim, Kabbalah, and it has many Sepharim in the Hechal, so that every one who seeks may obtain pleasant instruction for his soul.[4]

10. It is the only institution in the land, that is otherwise a waste, as regards religious knowledge, which laughs to scorn every scorner, him who goes astray, and the ignorant who walks in the self-will of his heart, and departs from the ways of the Lord and his laws; and it bids defiance to every unbeliever and infidel, who endeavors to mislead the multitude of Israel through the strength of his tongue, with his abundance of vain prattle without end, devoid of knowledge and devoid of faith, only to find favor by his tongue, in the eyes of the blinded Hebrews, and to make lighter for them the yoke of the service of the Lord and his commandments, in order that they may be snared and caught in the net of the times, and snatched from among the remnant, as though this were the whole duty of man.

The Beth Hammidrash as it were calls aloud on all, that whoever longs for eternal life, who desires to cause his soul to escape from perdition, should flee to it; for there is the refuge which will rescue him, to make even his path, that he may believe in God, his law and his commandments; so that after his death he may inherit his portion among the association of those who listen to the voice of our Father, to find delight in the pleasantness of the Lord, and to inquire in his sanctuary. And that he may shine in the light of life, to find pleasure in the splendor of the Almighty, in the midst of the souls of our holy fathers, let him turn his steps hither, and not have regard to the false words of those who speak calumny against the righteous with pride and contempt.

Its founders were few, and they established it in poverty and the want of all; in affliction, deprivation, and straightness they watched over its early rise, for which may they be always remembered before the Lord; who, because He saw that their intention was for the cause of truth, showered gradually his mercy on them, so that one by one, daily, men of Israel united with them, until they have become a numerous flock, and now it is supported by about eighty men of Israel. And though our members are poor in money, they are prominent with a liberal spirit; they labor hard for their daily bread, and yet set aside from their limited means a portion for the holy offering, to support the might of the Law. Until now God has aided us, thus far, that we have saved one thousand dollars,[5] to erect for us a permanent house on a sure foundation; and we pray that the good work of the Lord may prosper in our hands, that we may not be behind the flocks of our fellow-Israelites. "And now aid us to found a school for the instruction of children:" this is our call to every one of a liberal spirit, who may be inclined to assist us; and may the favor of the Lord our God be upon us, and may He establish the work of our hands for us: yea, may He establish the work of our hands for his sake. May God exalt it on high, until the horn of Israel be lifted up at the coming of the founder of our righteousness, speedily and in our days; and may the intelligent shine with the brightness of the expanse, and like the stars for evermore. *Amen.*

120. NAVAL HERO VINDICATED

From the *Defence of Uriah P. Levy, Before the Court of Inquiry, Held at Washington City, November and December, 1857* [1]

[Today the United States Navy officially recognizes Captain Uriah Phillips Levy (1792–1862) as one of the heroes of American naval history; on March

28, 1943 the Navy launched a destroyer named after him. Yet a review of his career and the discrimination he faced in our navy for more than forty years led one writer in 1899 to designate Levy "an American forerunner of Dreyfus."[2]

Levy ran away from home in Philadelphia at the age of ten to serve as a cabin boy. At eighteen he was already the second-mate of a brig, and at twenty he was captain of a ship he partly owned. Appointed a sailing Master in the War of 1812, he served on the famous *Argus* (but was not in the great battle with the British *Pelican*), was captured aboard a prize-ship of which he had been put in charge, and spent at least sixteen months in the notorious Dartmoor prison. In 1817 he began his career as an officer in the Navy, when he was commissioned a Lieutenant; he became a Commander in 1837, and a Captain in 1844. His life was full of adventure, and some of his many exploits are connected with his readiness to resent insults aimed at the United States and at his being a Jew.[3] Appalled by the practise of flogging used in the Navy, Levy played a great role in agitation that led to the abolition of the practise, and considered that his most important contribution to the Navy. In the last years of his life, he published at his own expense a *Manual of Rules for Men-Of-War* which went into several editions, and in which he set forth his more humane and modern ideas of punishment.[4] Nevertheless, because he was a Jew, Levy faced ostracism, insult, six courts martial in which he was always found guilty and usually given excessive punishments, dismissal—and then, through persistent defence, he achieved vindication, restoration of rank, and new honors. In 1855, he was one of 200 officers dismissed "to improve the efficiency of the Navy." Public protest led to the appointment of a Court of Inquiry to review the dismissals; about one third were reinstated.[5] It was before this Court of Inquiry that Levy made the defence that follows. He was reinstated on January 29, 1858, given command (his first in fifteen years) of the USS *Macedonian* on April 16, 1859, sailed with her in the Mediterranean, and became the commander of the Mediterranean squadron on February 21, 1860. (As such, he was officially considered a Commodore and addressed by that title, although the Commission of Commodore was not created until after Levy's death.)[6]

The entire Defence is a stirring one, both in its recital of the facts in the many cases of the court-martialing of Levy, and in its eloquent insistence on the right of the Jew in the Navy to equality of treatment not only for the sake of the Jew but for the security of the service and the welfare of the country.]

. . . My parents were Israelites, and I was nurtured in the faith of my ancestors. In deciding to adhere to it, I have but exercised a right, guaranteed to me by the constitution of my native State, and of the United States—a right given to all men by their Maker—a right more precious to each of us than life itself. But, while claiming and exercising this freedom of conscience, I have never failed to acknowledge and respect the like freedom in others. I might safely defy the citation of a single act, in the whole course of my official career, injurious to the religious rights of any other person. Remembering always that the great mass of my fellow-citizens were Christians; profoundly grateful to the Christian founders of our republic, for their justice and liberality to my long persecuted race; I have earnestly endeavored, in all places and circumstances, to act up to the wise and tolerant spirit of our political institutions. I have therefore been careful to treat every Christian, and especially every Christian under my command, with exemplary justice and ungrudging liberality. Of this, you have had clear proof, so far as my command of the Vandalia [7] is concerned, from the lips of Lieutenants [Edmund] Lanier and [John N.] Maffit. They testify to the observance, on board that ship, under the standing rules and regulations prescribed by me, of the Christian Sabbath, and to the scrupulous regard paid by me on all occasions, to the religious rights and feelings of the officers and men.

I have to complain—more in sorrow than in anger do I say it—that in my official experience I have met with little to encourage, though with much to frustrate, these conciliatory efforts. At an early day, and especially from the time when it became known to the officers of my age and grade, that I aspired to a lieutenancy, and still more, after I had gained it, I was forced to encounter a large share of the prejudice and hostility by which, for so many ages, the Jew has been pursued. I need not speak to you of the incompatibility of these sentiments with the genius of Christianity, or the precepts of its author. You should know this far better than I; but I may ask you to unite with the wisest and best men of our own country and of Europe, in denouncing them, not merely as injurious to the peace and welfare of the community, but as repugnant to every dictate of reason, humanity and justice.

In February, 1818, I was transferred, by Commodore [Charles] Stewart, from his ship, the Franklin, 74, to the frigate United States, under the command of Captain [William M.] Crane. Under the influence of the double prejudice to which I have alluded, a conspiracy was formed among certain officers of this frigate to prevent my reception in her. Commodore [T.A.C.] Jones, in answer to the eighth interrogatory on my part, gives a full account of it. He says:

"Lieutenant Levy, for several months, was fourth, and I first lieutenant, of the frigate United States, where he discharged his duty satisfactorily to the captain as well as to the first lieutenant, notwithstanding his advent into our ship was attended with such novel and discouraging circumstances as, in justice to captain Levy, renders it necessary here to record them.

"On the arrival of the Franklin, of 74 guns, at Syracuse, in 1818, bearing the broad pennant of commodore Charles Stewart, to relieve commodore [John S.] Chauncey, then in command of the Mediterranean squadron, it was understood that lieutenant Levy, a supernumerary on board of the Franklin, was to be ordered to the frigate United States, then short of her complement of lieutenants. Whereupon, the *ward-room mess,* without consulting me, determined to remonstrate against Levy's coming aboard. I was called on by a member of the mess to communicate their wishes to Captain Crane and ask his interference.

"Astonished at such a proposition, I inquired as to the cause, when I was answered, that he was a Jew, and not an agreeable person, and they did not want to be brought in contact with him in our then very pleasant and harmonious mess of some eight or nine persons; and, moreover, that he was an interloper, having entered the navy as *master,* to the prejudice of the older midshipmen, &c.,&c. Such was the reply, in substance, to my inquiry. I then asked the relator if he, or any member of our mess, knew anything, of his own knowledge, derogatory to lieutenant Levy, as an officer and as a gentleman. The answer was *no,* but they had heard thus and so, &c., &c. I endeavored to point out the difficulties that might result from a procedure so much at variance with military subordination, and the justice due to a brother officer, against whom they had nothing but vague and ill-defined rumors; but my counsel then did not prevail. The remonstrance was made directly to captain Crane, and by captain Crane to commodore Stewart. Levy soon after reported on board the frigate United States, for duty. When Lieutenant Levy came on board, he asked a private interview with me, wishing my advice as the proper course he ought to pursue under such embarrassing circumstances. I gave it freely and simply, to the effect, viz.: do your duty as an officer and a gentleman, be civil to all, however reserved you may choose to be to any, and the first man who observes a different course towards you, call him to a strict and prompt account. Our messmates were gentlemen, and having perceived their error before lieutenant Levy got on board, had, in accordance with my previous advice, determined to receive lieutenant Levy as a gentleman and a brother officer, and to respect and treat him as such, till by his conduct he should prove himself unworthy. I continued a few months longer on board the frigate United States, as her first lieutenant, during the whole of which time Lieutenant Levy's conduct and deportment was altogether unexceptionable, and I know that, perhaps with a single exception, those who opposed his joining our mess, not only relented, but deeply regretted the false step they had incautiously taken."

During the few months that Commodore Jones remained in the ship United States, his wise and just counsels had the effect he describes. After he left her, I am sorry to be obliged to say, the old prejudices revived in the breasts of too many of my associates.

In December, 1824, a conspiracy of the same kind was formed among the junior officers of the ward-room mess, on board the North Carolina. She was about to sail for the Mediterranean to join the squadron in that sea; and I was ordered to take passage in her, and to report myself to Commodore Creighton, the commander-in-chief of the squadron. Commodore Isaac Mayo, one of the witnesses produced by me, gives a full account of this cabal, and of his refusal to join it. His testimony will be referred to hereafter, in another connexion. . . .

In 1844, the President [John Tyler] nominated me to the Senate for promotion as captain. This nomination was confirmed on the [31st] day of May, 1844,—my appointment to take rank from the 29th March, 1844. The circumstances attending this appointment were of peculiar interest to me; and it is most important that they should be fully understood by the Court. Attempts were made, outside the Senate, by certain officers of the Navy, to induce that body to reject my nomination. The naval Committee of the Senate, to whom the nomination had been referred, were approached by officers hostile to or prejudiced against me; and such objections were made to my appointment, that the committee felt it proper to call on the Secretary of the Navy for all papers on file relating to my official conduct. The archives of the Department were ransacked; charges preferred against me during my service as sailing-master, lieutenant and commander, growing (with a single exception) out of those petty altercations and personal quarrels unfortunately too common in our profession, were raked up; and the records of all the courts martial before which, in the course of thirty years, I had been brought, were laid before the committee. These documents having been thoroughly examined by them, they reported in favor of the nomination; and on their report it was unanimously confirmed. . . .

When, in 1855, I complained to Secretary [of the Navy, James C.] Dobbin of "some unseen influence" seeking "through unmerited prejudice to injure me with the Department," and to prevent it from according to me my just rights, I stated what I then fully believed, and what I had long before suspected to be the fact. I was driven to this conclusion by the persistent refusal of the several secretaries to employ me, in the face of all the proofs of my fitness, in the records of the Department, and of the recommendations and support of so many distinguished men, in support of my applications. I could draw, from the circumstances, no other inference; nor do I think that any other can be drawn by you. But the fact is not now left to inference merely. You have, in the deposition of the Secretary, Mr. [George] Bancroft,[8] direct evidence of the fact. In answer to the ninth interrogatory on my part, he says:

"When Secretary of the Navy, I never had cause to doubt, and never doubted, Captain Levy's competence to serve the United States in the grade of captain. I did not find myself able to give him a command, for three reasons:

1st. The excessive number of officers of his grade made it impossible to employ all of them who were fit.

2d. The good of the service, moreover, seemed to require bringing forward officers less advanced in years than most of the captains, and the law sanctioned that course.

3d. I perceived a strong prejudice in the service against Captain Levy, which seemed to me, in a considerable part, attributable to his being of the Jewish persuasion; and while I, as an executive officer, had the same liberal views which guided the President and Senate in commissioning him as a captain, I always endeavored in fitting out ships to have some reference to that harmonious co-operation which is essential to the highest effectiveness."

To the first of these reasons no exception can be taken. The second is founded on a favorite theory of Mr. Bancroft, while Secretary, to which, were it impartially carried out, I should be as little disposed to object as any other officer of my rank and age.

The third reason assigned by Mr. Bancroft, though last in order, is not least in importance.

The fact that it is assigned by him as one of the reasons for not giving me a command, justified the inference that the first two reasons would not have been sufficient to produce that result without the addition of the third.

From what source, or in what manner, Mr. Bancroft perceived the strong prejudice in the service against me, of which he speaks, he does not state. But it is easy to trace it to its origin. He had never been officially connected with the Navy until he came to Washington in 1845, as head of the Department. He was then brought into intercourse with such officers of the Navy as were enabled, by their rank, their connection with bureaux, or their social position, to cultivate the acquaintance, and get the ear of the secretary. It was only by means of such intercourse, that it was possible for him to become acquainted with the prejudices which existed in the service against any of its members. It was only in this way that he could learn that any such prejudice existed against me. Among the officers of the Navy to whom the secretary was thus peculiarly accessible, there were some who were friendly to me; but there were others who were not only unfriendly, but also active and bitter in their hostility against me. How else than through intercourse with those who had the motive, and took the pains, to force it upon him, was it possible for Mr. Bancroft to know that any prejudice existed against me in the Navy; and how could he form any estimate as to its strength, except from the frequency and rancour with which it was obtruded upon his notice?

From the same source which informed him of the prejudice, he learned its nature and grounds—the chief, if not the sole ground, being my peculiar religious faith—my "being of the Jewish persuasion." Doubtless, those who could make such a fact the pretext for a prejudice against a brother officer, so inveterate and unyielding, as to compel the head of the department reluctantly to recognise and admit as—to some extent at least—an element of his official action, would not scruple to disparage and traduce, in other respects, the object of their aversion. But even their efforts failed to awaken, for a moment, in the mind of the secretary, a solitary doubt as to my *competence*. This he tells us in the most emphatic terms.

In the satisfaction which this avowal gives me—in the gratitude I owe, and shall ever cherish, to one who, in spite of such efforts, retained towards me an opinion so favorable—I could almost pass over, without remark, the injury done me—most unwittingly, I am sure—by his allowing to such an objection any weight whatever. Had it then come to my knowledge, I could have shown him, just as I have now shown to you, from the records of the department, that during my year's command of the Vandalia, my religious faith never impaired the efficiency of my ship; that I never permitted it to interfere with the rights, or to wound the feelings, of my Christian officers and men; and that I did what I could, and all that they desired, to respect and satisfy those rights and feelings. I might have shown to him, as I have shown to you, by the evidence of the many officers, who, in this investigation, have testified in my behalf, that the prejudice to which he was constrainted to give such serious effect against me, was far from being so general or so strong as he was led to believe;—that officers, more in number than my traducers, and far better qualified to judge, were untainted by it—treated it with contempt, and denounced it as inconsistent with the spirit of our institutions—unworthy of the present age, and degrading to the honor of the naval service. And I might thus, perhaps, have afforded him the opportunity, which, I doubt not, he would gladly have seized, not only from a sense of justice to myself, but in accordance with his own liberal and enlightened convictions, of setting his face, like a flint, against the double-headed hydra of personal prejudice and religious bigotry, and of driving it forever from the councils of his department. The benefit of such an act to myself would have been insignificant, in comparison with the vindication it would have furnished of the dignity and justice of our Government, and its faithful conservation of the most sacred of our public and private rights. . . .

Mr. President and Gentlemen of the Court:

My defence, so far as it depends on the examination of the evidence, is before you; and here, perhaps, I ought to stop. But the peculiarities of my case—the importance and far-reaching interest of the principles it involves—requires, what I hope you will allow me, a few additional remarks.

That the allegation of unfitness for the naval service, made against me by the Government, was wholly unsupported by evidence; and that I have made out a complete defence against the attempt to justify my dismissal, and an affirmative title to restoration, by the proofs on my part; these I regard as undeniable propositions. And yet there are those connected with the navy, who, notwithstanding all the proofs I have produced, are hostile to my restoration. This, it would be vain to deny to others, or to conceal from myself. Should any one of these dare to obtrude upon you the opinion or the wish, that I should not be restored; or, being restored, should not be placed upon the active list; you have only to refer him to the oath which you have taken, to silence and rebuke him. Permit me—not that I suppose you can have forgotten its terms, but because of their peculiar pertinency to my case—to quote the closing words of this oath. It not only requires you, as before remarked "well and truly to examine and inquire, according to the evidence, into the matter now before you;" but, to do this, "without partiality or prejudice." This oath, although exceedingly brief, is exceedingly comprehensive and precise. The lawmakers who framed it well knew the special dangers to which Courts of Inquiry are exposed—partiality towards influential prosecutors and accusers, and prejudice against the accused. Against these, the oath solemnly warns you; and if ever there was a case in which such a warning was right and seasonable, this is that case.

The Government, with its vast power and influence, is, in name at least, my prosecutor. Men in high places, who have once done me grievous wrong, are interested to prevent the remedying of that wrong. There are others, not without their influence, who, by their activity in support of the wrong, and in opposition to the remedy, have a common interest with my prosecutors.

Never, on the other hand, was there a man, in the ranks of our profession, against whom, in the breasts of certain members of that profession, prejudices so unjust and yet so strong, have so long and so incessantly rankled. Such, too, are the origin and character of these prejudices, as to make them, of all others, the most inveterate and unyielding. The prejudice felt by men of little minds, who think themselves, by the accidental circumstances of wealth or ancestry, better than the less favored of their fellows; the prejudice of *caste,* which looks down on the man who, by honest toil, is the maker of his own fortunes; this prejudice is stubborn as well as bitter, and of this I have had, as you have seen by the proofs, my full share. But this is placable and transient compared with that generated and nourished by religious intolerance and bigotry.

The first article of the amendments to the Constitution of the United States, specially declares, in its first clause, that "Congress shall make no law respecting an establishment of religion, or prohibiting the free exercise thereof;" thus showing by its place, no less than by its language, how highly freedom of conscience was valued by the founders of our Republic. In the constitutions of the several States, now in force, the like provision is contained. Our liberality and justice, in this regard, have been honored by the friends of liberty and human rights throughout the world. An eminent British writer, about thirty years ago, in the ablest of their reviews, used, in reference to this point, the following language:

"They have fairly and completely, and probably forever, extinguished that spirit of religious persecution which has been the employment and the curse of mankind, for four or five centuries; not only that persecution which imprisons and scourges for religious opinions, but the tyranny of incapacitation, which by disqualifying from civil offices, and cutting a man off from the lawful objects of ambition, endeavors to strangle religious freedom in silence, and to enjoy all the advantages, without the blood, and noise, and fire of persecution. * * * * * * * * * In this particular, the Americans are at the head of all the nations of the world.*"

Little did the author of this generous tribute to our country suspect, that even while he was penning it, there were those in the American navy, with whom it was a question whether a Jew should be tolerated in the service? Still less did he dream, that at the very moment when, in his own country, a representative of the illustrious house of RUSSELL,[9] eminent by his services in the cause of freedom, of education, and of justice, is about giving himself, with the full assent of his government, to the work of Jewish emancipation, a spectacle like the present should be witnessed in this land of equality and freedom. For with those who would now deny to me, because of my religious faith, the restoration, to which, by half a century of witnesses, I have proved myself entitled, what is it but an attempt to place the professors of this faith under the ban of incapacitation?

This is the case before you; and, in this view, its importance cannot be overrated. It is the case of every Israelite in the Union. I need not speak to you of their number. They are unsurpassed by any portion of our people in loyalty to the Constitution and to the Union; in their quiet obedience to the laws; and in the cheerfulness with which they contribute to the public burthens. Many of them have been distinguished by their liberal donations to the general interests of education and of charity; in some cases, too—of which the name of JUDAH TOURO will remind you—to charities controlled by Christians. And of all my brethren in this land—as well those of foreign birth as of American descent—how rarely does any one of them become a

* Sydney Smith, in Edinburgh Review, July, 1824, [p. 429].

charge on your State or municipal treasuries! How largely do they all contribute to the activities of trade; to the interests of commerce; to the stock of public wealth! Are all these to be proscribed? And is this to be done while we retain in our Constitution the language I have quoted? Is this language to be spoken to the ear, but broken to the hope, of my race? Are the thousands of Judah and the ten thousands of Israel, in their dispersions throughout the earth, who look to America, as a land bright with promise—are they now to learn, to their sorrow and dismay, that we, too, have sunk into the mire of religious intolerance and bigotry? And are American Christians now to begin the persecution of the Jews? Of the Jews, who stand among them the representatives of the patriarchs and prophets;—the Jews, to whom were committed the oracles of God;—the Jews, from whom these oracles have been received, and who are the living witnesses of their truth;—the Jews, from whom came the founder of Christianity; —the Jews, to whom, as Christians themselves believe, have been made promises of greatness and of glory, in whose fulfilment are bound up the hopes, not merely of the remnant of Israel, but of all the races of men? And think not, if you once enter on this career, that it can be limited to the Jew. What is my case to-day, if you yield to this injustice, may to-morrow be that of the Roman Catholic or the Unitarian; the Episcopalian or the Methodist; the Presbyterian or the Baptist. There is but one safeguard; and this is to be found in an honest, whole-hearted, inflexible support of the wise, the just, the impartial guarantee of the Constitution. I have the fullest confidence that you will faithfully adhere to this guarantee; and, therefore, with like confidence, I leave my destiny in your hands.

U. P. LEVY.

121. THE MORTARA CASE

Rev. Isaac Leeser, in the Philadelphia *Public Ledger*, November 25, 1858 [1]

[Edgar Mortara was born in Bologna on August 27, 1851, son of Girolamo Mortara Levi and Marianna Padovani Levi. When he was about a year old, the child endured what the parents considered a minor illness, but the Catholic nurse was persuaded by a neighboring druggist secretly to baptise the Jewish child lest he die a heathen. The nurse kept the baptism secret until 1858, when the Holy Office (the Inquisition) was informed of the baptism. The Archbishop of Bologna, Michele Viale Prelà (1799–1860), with a reputation for "exaggerated fanaticism," immediately ordered the child taken from its home; an officer of the Inquisition, accompanied by gendarmes, on June 23, 1858, informed the distraught parents of the decision, and the following evening took Edgar by force from his parental home to the House of the Catechumini in Rome, an institution for the education of converts.[2] When the facts of the abduction became public, an international outcry developed in Europe (England, France, Russia, Germany, Holland, Austria) and the United States.[3] Between October 30, 1858 and January 27, 1859, indignation meetings were held, in the order given, in Cincinnati, Philadelphia and St. Louis, Boston, Richmond, Baltimore, Charleston, New York, Syracuse, Chicago, New Orleans, Mobile, Indianapolis, Albany, San Francisco, Detroit, Rochester, and Memphis, the largest meetings being in New York (2000 present) and San Francisco (3000 present).

Most of the non-Catholic American press was critical of the abduction and of the Pope, Pius IX, for endorsing the action, with only the Boston *Courier* and the *New York Herald,* later, opposing the protests.[4] Although there was some Catholic dissent in Europe, the American Catholic press unanimously upheld the abduction. Typical was the article in *Brownson's Quarterly Review,* which wrote: "The case entirely turns on this point, that the child had received baptism, which makes him a Christian and entitles him to the privileges of Christian citizenship, which the State guaranties and guards, by insisting on his Christian education. . . . But whatever was the object of the law, the elder Mortara, by hiring a Christian nurse, was its violator and exposed himself to fines which the government forbore inflicting. If she used an opportunity to baptize the child, he must blame himself for employing her. . . . The Jews have shown great want of moderation and prudence in this affair. . . . The wisdom of the President in refusing to interfere even by way of friendly remonstrance is manifest. . . . Our own 'domestic institutions' are quite as unintelligible to those of other countries, and far more liable to become the matter of censure . . ."[5] In this instance, as in the case of the Swiss Treaty, the domestic institution of American slavery was used at home and abroad by supporters of the abduction to embarrass those who protested. The American government's refusal to take any kind of action was openly stated to be based on a desire to avoid foreign official criticism of our peculiar institution.[6] Almost as active as the Jews in the protests were the American Protestants; many of the meetings were attended by Jews and Christians, and many of the speakers were not Jewish. In certain instances, the American nativist Know-Nothing movement, with its rabid anti-alien and anti-Catholic propaganda, seized upon the issue in its own unprincipled way, and the American Jews and Protestants interested in religious liberty found themselves in unwholesome company.[7]

In the letter that follows, Leeser sharply but temperately rebukes an anonymous Catholic who had publicly proposed the suppression of the Jewish religion and its holy books and the destruction of the synagogues.]

THE MORTARA CASE.—TO THE AMERICAN PUBLIC.

There are constantly occurring, in the course of human events, transactions which, from their nature, are calculated to arouse and fix the attention of the friends of freedom and mental progress. It need not be precisely an occurrence of vast magnitude; a battle, where nations immolate each other on the ensanguined field of slaughter, nor one where mighty fleets destroy each other, to satisfy the insatiable ambition of rival tyrants, contending for the empire over the earth; but it may be a wrong inflicted on an humble, before unknown individual, which, from its atrocity and strangeness, may bid the mind to reflect whether indeed it were safe to let such an act pass unheeded, and not provide the means against its recurrence.

Such an act is that which was lately committed in Bologna, a city under the immediate dominion of the Roman Pontiff, who, from his position, claims to be the head of Christendom, and, in this quality, the chief of all mankind—who, by rights, as his followers assert, ought to be subjected to the control of the universal Church, deriving, as the Pope professes, his power immediately, by regular succession, from the founder of Christianity. A claim so universal, based on the assumption of an uncircumscribed religious power—having for its supporters empires, kingdoms, and republics—taught in thousands of schools and colleges, enforced from pulpits all over the world, and propagated by millions of devoted and highly educated ministers, who all have a personal interest in the success of their cause—a claim so universal, I would say, appears almost irresistible. For, while all other religious societies are comparatively small, and goverend [sic] by deliberative bodies, more or less independent, the Church of Rome knows of but one head, one will, which governs and shapes all the vast machinery composed by its countless hierarchy, members of which are met with in every distant settlement wherein the foot of civilization can penetrate, no less than in almost every hospital, and in many schools, either as open or secret emissaries, so that *kindness* may pave the way before force can be resorted to, in order to acquire an entrance for the tenets of Catholicism.

It is a quality attendant on the possession of power, that it regards all it holds as justly belonging to it, no matter how it was acquired.

This is true in political history, where men have been arraigned and punished as traitors for daring to defend their country's wrongs against oppressors or usurpers. It not being my purpose to indite an historical essay, it will not be required of me to prove by examples what every well read person will undoubtedly know without this aid. But religious power is not less oblivious of *original* rights, when it surveys its acquired authority as a whole, from which it will not yield the least, unless compelled to submit to superior force. A case in point, is the Mortara affair, of which I spoke in the beginning. The facts of the occurrence are very simple and will not be disputed. A child, about a year old, was, when sick, secretly baptized, or rather sprinkled, with what is called holy water, by a Roman Catholic nurse-maid. No one was present to witness the deed. Nothing was said of it at the time it took place; but when, after the lapse of about five years, the thing came to the knowledge of the person who is called the Inquisitor of the city of Bologna, he despatched, on the evening of the 23d of June last, a messenger of the self-styled Holy Office (Santo Ufficio), with a sufficient escort of police officers, to seize the child, Edgar Mortara, under the pretext that baptism had been administered by some one, at some time, under some circumstances; the official messenger declined giving particulars. But the unhappy parents showed such distress, were so near despairing, which is easily understood, when one reflects on the tenacity with which pious, or even careless Israelites cling to their religion, the suddenness of the misfortune was so overwhelming, that the messenger consented to leave the child for that night under the parental roof, taking, however, the precaution to place there a sufficient guard to prevent its being carried away out of the jurisdiction of the tribunal whose deputy he was. Next day, the father made all the interest possible, and went to the Inquisitor in person; but he, too, was as brief as his messenger, and simply told the distracted parent that the Holy Office having made the decree, could not be expected to make any alteration in it; his child was a Christian, according to his view of the case, and he could not be permitted to keep it to educate it as an Israelite. One account says that the mother hastened to Modena, where her parents reside, to see what she could effect there, leaving six young children at home; it is also said that grief caused her to be taken seriously ill while there. It is possible that this part of the story may be an embellishment, though there is no reason to doubt it, as it would be perfectly natural, without a great stretch of the imagination. Be this, however, as it may, the emissaries of the

Inquisition, (I will call them no hard names, and only say, they were emissaries worthy of their calling to act as kidnappers,) came with a carriage at the hour of ten o'clock at night, and seizing on Edgar with force, snatched him out of his father's arms, placed him into the vehicle, which was then driven off, surrounded by a military force. This latter precaution was surely useless; for the spirit of the Italian Israelite, except those who have the happiness to live in Sardinia, where a Constitutional government prevails, is so broken, that a pigmy armed with a straw could frighten them from even defending themselves, much less making an aggressive attack on others. The sequel is briefly told, the child was taken to the convent of the Catechumens at Rome, and is there detained to be educated as a Catholic. It is even said that the Pope himself will pay the expenses of his education. The father has been permitted to see him; but when asking for his restoration, he received the hint to keep his peace, for fear of meeting with worse consequences.

In the above, the American people have an unvarnished tale of an occurrence calculated to arouse an anchorite to phrenzy. What wonder, then, that the Israelites of Sardinia met in general conference at Alessandria, sometime in August, and sent memorials to their fellows in faith in England and France to urge them to co-operation?[8] Nor need it excite any astonishment that we, residing in the United States, should move in the matter the moment sufficiently reliable information had been received, to guard us against taking any false step, or accusing any one wrongfully. Some people have, indeed, imagined that the members of the Catholic church in America would disavow this act, and that it would stand out as a deed of barbarity, committed in a country where the principles of freedom are not understood. But in so judging, one would deceive himself. The transaction, on the contrary, is approved of and defended in the official organ of Bishop Neuman,[9] the *Catholic Herald and Visitor,* of November 20th; and also by a writer of a communication in the *Public Ledger,* on November 23d, so that it appears that *the ministers of the Romish community would think themselves bound* to resort to similar measures under a parity of circumstances, and that their not doing it is not owing to any want of inclination, but to the simple *absence of power.* What security this country can have against violence, should ever the Catholics obtain the power to legislate religiously and civilly for the people, may be freely left to every candid person to elucidate for himself; the hand that can write a defence for robbing Mr. Mortara of his child, under the flimsy pretext now offered, would not hesitate to snatch from your bosom, Oh American matron! the nursling that nestles there, if he were told that it had been made a Catholic through the sacrament of baptism, so that you, its heretic Protestant mother, might not deprive *the Church* of one of its acquired members.

But the whole plea of *"Plures in Unum,"* the author of the communication in the *Ledger,* is based on the assumption that the whole world is bound to regard as binding, what Catholicity has established as dogmas for its own followers. I may hereafter, let me say in passing, pay my respects to the Bishop's organ; let it wait awhile, as it was printed before the resolutions passed at the town meeting of Israelites on the 18th inst.,[10] and of which I may own myself the author, were made public. But *Plures, &c.,* (will he have the kindness to write his name, should he reply to me, as I use my own signature?) steps forward to correct the misapprehension of the Israelites, under the impression that they did not understand the subject of which they were speaking; he, therefore, merits a prompt and full reply. It would, indeed, have displayed more good sense than he shows, not to have called the attention of Americans to his doctrines, even if the Israelites had not fully comprehended them; the public indignation is sufficiently aroused already to the Roman iniquity not to need any fresh fuel; hundreds of non-Israelites in the city are ready to sign the memorial to the President, asking his good offices in the case; but, as he chooses to enlighten our ignorance, let us see what he has to allege. It is no business of mine to apologize for Luther, nor to defend the conduct of Protestants, if it be true that they surreptitiously educate Catholic children in their various creeds; since I am no follower of Luther, and have no greater inclination for Protestantism of all kinds, than for the Romish Church. "I am a Hebrew, and worship the Lord, the God of heaven, who has made the sea and the dry land." Educated partly in a Catholic college, and having enjoyed, though then but a boy, the kindness and instruction of several clergymen of that religion,[11] it would be strange were I to have any prejudice against it. Its tenets, properly carried out, will make men, no doubt, as good as Protestantism. But it would be folly in me, or any one else, to shut my eyes against the baseless assumptions of the teachers and ecclesiastics of that Church—to admit which would be the downfall of all freedom, both religious and civil.

"Plures" tells us, that "baptism is a sacrament which effaces original sin, and makes the recipient a child of God and of the Church." He therefore assumes, or his Church for him, that without this rite or sacrament *all* are not children of God, and that with it they belong to the Church. But does he not see, that he has to prove the truth of this assumption before he can impose it on Israelites especially, who do not believe in any sacrament? How can he demonstrate to Mortara, for instance, that following, as he has done, the Law of Moses, and *circumcising* his child at the age of eight days, he left him in a condition not to be a child of God? And granting that the baptism afterwards administered without the parents' consent or knowledge, should have conferred on Edgar an additional divine favor not before existing, who gave to the Church the power to seize on him and abduct him away from a father's and a mother's care, even to confer on him the rights and privileges of Christianity, which Israelites are debarred from under the papal dominion—paternal though it is alleged to be? It is not now the question what Church Councils teach; for no doubt they have laid down a canon, that if a Jew is found having in his possession a child baptized by a nurse, he shall be compelled, though he is the father, to give it up to the myrmidons of the Inquisition, or the messenger of an Abbot, a Bishop, a Cardinal, or of the Pope himself. No doubt that the Mortara case comes under this category. But, I demand in the name of freedom of conscience, who authorized the Council of Trent, or any of its predecessors, to decide on the rights of mankind who do not profess to be Catholics? Can "Plures" show any authority derived from the Christian Gospels, even, which would satisfy any man, no matter how high or low his capacity? I will not mention the Old Testament, or, as I would call it, the Bible; for no such power can be derived from that. Hence the whole right is based merely on what Catholics themselves have decreed; and against this all honest men must protest, as a cruel and unwarranted interference in the conscientious convictions of other men. Mortara's child has rights independent of the Pontiff's favor; he was born of parents who owe him no religious allegiance; and it is hence time enough when he growes to man's estate, if even then, to inform him of the great boon *the* Church has conferred upon him when he was a yearling baby, through a nurse fourteen years old.[12] If this baptism had really made any mental impression on him, he would rejoice in the revelation thus brought home to him, and fly for protection to *the* Church from the damnation which he would earn when remaining attached to Judaism. But it appears "Plures" would not be willing any more than Pio Nono,[13] to trust to the miraculous effect of infant baptism; but he says it was right to steal Edgar, and to prevent his losing the advantage which he had already obtained by being made a member of the Church. So, then, the ineffaceable impression of baptism does not amount to much, and the civil arm has to come to its aid to make it of any avail. There is some absurdity in all this, and on the same plea *the* Church might make any act of barbarity legal, provided it be safe to enforce it, so only that its power and numbers may be thereby extended. It is against this we, as Israelites, complain; it is against such tyranny that we invoke the aid of the President, and of all liberal governments, and it is against this assumption of a never-conferred power that we ask the co-operation of all liberal persons, who dread, by anticipation, to feel the iron heel of *the* Church, should it ever become dominant again.

I have yet much more to say, but must break off at present, as my remarks are, I fear, too long for any paper.

ISAAC LEESER,
Minister Cong. Beth-El-Emeth.[14]

Philadelphia, November 23d, 1858.

122. KEEPING THE SABBATH

Resolution Regarding Sabbath Observance, adopted in Cincinnati, October 6, 1859 [1]

[Innumerable and, in the long run, unavailing were the efforts of religious leaders to organize and enforce the cessation of work and business among Jews on Saturday. With the economic activities of the Jews so extensively interconnected with those of non-Jews, it became virtually impossible for any but the most pious and abstemious to observe the Sabbath in the traditional manner. The contradiction between the requirements of religion and the economic and political pressures (Sunday laws) was too great for the majority of Jews.[2] It was not until the five-day working-week became wide-spread in production that workers could easily observe the Sabbath if they wished to do so; in merchandising, however, the six-day week still prevails and confronts the observant Jew with a special problem. Even this resolution of 1859 tries to meet the factor of economic competition by specifying that it will go into effect only if a certain number of Jewish merchants agree to suspend business on the Sabbath. The Rev. Isaac Leeser objected to this condition, and sharply inquired whether any individual Jew was relieved from obeying one of the Commandments by the failure of others to keep it.[3]]

Whereas the observation of the Sabbath is a fundamental doctrine of our religion; and

Whereas a strict observation of the Sabbath is only then practicable among merchants, if business is entirely suspended on that day, and all unite on it as a day of rest; and furthermore,

Whereas the merchants of Cincinnati professing the creed of Israel, now occupy such a position in business that they are capable of effecting this purpose[4]—therefore be it

Resolved, That this meeting recommends to all business men of this city, professing the Jewish creed, to keep their places of business closed during the Sabbath.

Resolved, That we will unite our influence to persuade all business men of our creed in this city, to observe the Sabbath by abstaining from all business transactions.

Resolved, That we in signing our names to these Preamble and Resolutions, declare that we pledge our word and honor to each other and to all, to keep our places of business closed during every Sabbath of ours; to transact no business ourselves, nor allow any of our clerks, book keepers, or any other person in our employment to transact business for us on that day on our premises.

Resolved, That a committee of five be appointed whose special duty it shall be to call on every business house of this city, if the members thereof profess our creed, and solicit the consent and signature of all of them to these Preamble and Resolutions.

Resolved, That the members of those firms, who now observe the Sabbath, by keeping closed their places of business, shall also be requested to place their signatures under these Preamble and Resolutions.

Resolved, That the third resolution of this series shall take effect immediately after Twenty-Five wholesale houses, besides those who now keep their places of business closed on Sabbath—shall have given their consent to these Preamble and Resolutions.

Signatures: S. Kuhn,[5] Marcus Fechheimer, Stadler, Brother & Co., G. Simon & Son, Jacob Netter, B. Bischof, S. March, S. Stricker, Heidelbach, Wertheimer & Co., A. & J. Wolf & Co., J. L. Mack, Friedman & Miller, Ch Thurnauer, B. Simon & Co., S. Shohl, Menderson & Frohman, J. H.

Wertheimer, Lewis Eichberg & Co., D. Marks, Goodhart & Grabfield, Mack & Worms, M. Steiner & Bier, Weiler & Trost, Lehman Hollstein, Lazarus Katzenberger, Henry J. Lauer & Co., Hyman & Brother, Mack & Brothers, Rosenfeld & Kaufman, Zeiller & Wise, Mack & Krouse, A. & M. J. Mack, Shloss & Goetz, Stix, Krause & Co., Friedman, Hirsch & Eichberg, Simon & Cohen, H. J. Amburgh & Brother.

The Committee of Five: Dr. Max Lilienthal, Dr. I. M. Wise, A. Aub, Jacob Netter, —— Simon.[6]

123. HELPING ELECT LINCOLN

Excerpts from Abram J. Dittenhoefer, *How We Elected Lincoln—Personal Recollections of Lincoln and Men of His Time,*[1]—1860

[In the first of these selections, Dittenhoefer explains intimately how difficult it was, in the overwhelmingly Democratic pro-slavery atmosphere of New York City, for a young Jewish college graduate with political ambitions to become an opponent of slavery and an active Republican. His account of what motivated his decision that a Jew particularly should be anti-slavery is notable.[2] In the second selection, we have a vivid recollection of the horrors of the Draft Riots of 1863. Abram Jesse Dittenhoefer, son of Isaac and Babetta Dittenhoefer, was born in Charleston, S. C. on March 17, 1836, and was brought to New York at the age of four. He served one term as the Magistrate of a City Court, but distinguished himself especially as a lawyer and political figure. In 1864, he was one of the New York Electors on the Lincoln ticket, and he acted as chairman of the General Republican Central Committee for twelve terms. In his legal practise, he was counsel to large corporations and several important banks, but he made his most important contribution as a specialist in the copyright law of the theater. He died in New York, February 23, 1919.[3]]

Circumstances brought to me personal knowledge of Mr. Lincoln for nearly four years. I had frequent interviews with him, and so was able to form a well-considered estimate of the great Emancipator's character and personality.

Born in Charleston, South Carolina, of Democratic pro-slavery parents, I was brought in early youth to New York; and although imbued with the sentiments and antipathies of my Southern environment, I soon became known as a Southerner with Northern principles. At that time there were many Northern men with Southern principles.

The city of New York, as I discovered upon reaching the age of observation, was virtually an annex of the South, the New York merchants having extensive and very profitable business relations with the merchants south of the Mason and Dixon line.[4]

The South was the best customer of New York. I often said in those days, "our merchants have for sale on their shelves their principles, together with their merchandise."

An amusing incident occurred to my knowledge which aptly illustrates the condition of things in this pro-slavery city. A Southerner came to a New York merchant, who was a dealer in brushes and toilet articles, and offered him a large order for combs. The New York merchant, as it happened, was a Quaker, but this was not known to the Southerner. The latter made it a condition, in giving this large order, that the Quaker merchant should exert all his influence in favor of the South. The Southerner wished to do something to offset the great agitation headed by the abolitionists which had been going on for years in the North for the extinction of slavery in the South. The Quaker merchant coolly replied that the South would have to go lousy for a long time before he would sell his combs to them under any such conditions.

Another occurrence that took place at an earlier period still further illumines this intense pro-slavery feeling. When Wendell Phillips, to my mind one of the greatest orators of America, delivered a radical and brilliant anti-slavery speech at the old Tabernacle, situated in Broadway below Canal Street, the hall was filled with pro-slavery shouters; they rotten-egged Phillips in the course of his address. With some friends I was present and witnessed this performance.

At nineteen I was wavering in my fidelity to the principles of the Democratic party, which, in the city of New York, was largely in favor of slavery.

I had just graduated from Columbia College,[5] which was then situated in what is now known as College Place, between Chambers and Murray streets. At that time many of our prominent and wealthy families lived in Chambers, Murray, and Warren streets, and I frequently attended festivities held by the parents of the college boys in the old-fashioned mansions which lined those thoroughfares.

Soon after leaving college I became a student in the law office of Benedict & Boardman, occupying offices in Dey Street, near Broadway. At that time the late John E. Parsons, a distinguished member of the New York bar, was the managing clerk; and Charles O'Conor,[6] the head of the New York bar in that generation, and who, in later years, ran as an Independent candidate for the Presidency, was connected with that firm as counsel.

Sitting one day at my desk, I took up a newspaper, and the debate between Judah P. Benjamin, the rabid but eloquent pro-slavery Senator from Louisiana, and Benjamin F. Wade, the free-soil Senator from Ohio, attracted my attention.

Benjamin had made a strong address in defense of slavery when Wade arose and replied. He began his reply with some bitter and memorable words, words which completely changed my political views.

"I have listened with intense interest," said he, "as I always do to the eloquent speech of my friend, the Senator from Louisiana—an Israelite with Egyptian principles."[7]

My father, who was a prominent merchant of New York in those days, and very influential with the German population,[8] had urged me to become a Democrat, warning me that a public career, if I joined the Republican party, would be impossible in the city of New York. I felt that he was right in that view, as the party was in a hopeless minority, without apparent prospect of ever being able to elect its candidates.

This was absolutely plain from the fact that Tammany Hall controlled the entire election machinery in this city, there being no law at that time which required the registration of voters before Election Day. Moreover, the inspectors of election were Tammany heelers, without any Republican representation on the election boards. In consequence, fraudulent voting prevailed to a large extent.

And yet my convictions were irrevocably changed by the reading of Wade's speech in answer to Benjamin. It struck me with great force that the Israelite Benjamin, whose ancestors were enslaved in Egypt, ought not to uphold slavery in free America, and could not do so without bringing disgrace upon himself.

Having convinced my father that slavery should no longer be tolerated, he abandoned his old political associations, cast his vote for Lincoln and Hamlin, and remained a Republican until his death.[9]

Several years later, if I may anticipate, William M. Tweed,[10] who had not yet become "Boss," but who had great and powerful influence in Tammany Hall, besought me to join Tammany, calling my attention to the fact that the power of the Democratic party was supreme in the city of New York, and that the organization needed some one to influence the German element.

He gave me his assurance that if I came into Tammany Hall I should receive prompt recognition, and in a few years undoubtedly would become judge of the Supreme Court; later on I might go still higher up. I thanked Mr. Tweed for his friendly interest in me, but told him that no political preferment could induce me to abandon my convictions and lead me to support slavery.

When Tweed became the absolute "Boss" of Tammany, some years later, he renewed his request that I should join Tammany Hall. Recurring to his previous promise, he again urged me to become a member of his organization; again I refused.

One can hardly appreciate to-day what it meant to me, a young man beginning his career in New York, to ally myself with the Republican party. By doing so, not only did I cast aside all apparent hope of public preferment, but I also subjected myself to obloquy from and ostracism by my acquaintances, my clients, and even members of my own family.

I was about twenty years of age when the first Republican convention met at Pittsburg. . . .

* * *

The relief experienced through General Lee's defeat at Gettysburg and his retreat across Maryland into Virginia was followed,[11] ten days later (July, 1863), by the draft riots in New York.

The horrors of those three days have never been fully described.[12] Led and encouraged by Southern sympathizers, who had retained the feelings they held before the war, the rabble of the city surged through the streets, destroying property, burning a Negro orphan-asylum, and killing black men. Nominally a protest against enforced enlistment, the riots were really an uprising of the dangerous element that existed in the city at the time.

I lived in Thirty-fourth Street, near Eighth Avenue, and had been a persistent speaker against the extension of slavery and in favor of the Federal cause. The day before the riots began, an anonymous note was received by my family, stating that our home would be attacked and that we had best leave the city. We did not heed the warning.

On the first day of the riots, July 13, 1863, a crowd gathered in front of my house, shouting: "Down with the abolitionists!" "Death to

Dittenhoefer!" I sent a messenger for the police, and a squad arrived as the leaders of the mob were preparing to break in my door. Active club work dispersed the crowd, and by order of the captain of the precinct several policemen were kept on guard until the end of the riots.

It was at this time that I met Mrs. Carson, the daughter of the only Union man in South Carolina, who, with her father, was compelled, after the firing on Fort Sumter, to leave South Carolina, while his property was confiscated.[13] I had been anxious to sell my house in Thirty-fourth Street. Noticing a "For Sale" sign on the property, Mrs. Carson called on me and expressed a willingness to buy the house at the price named, asking me to see Samuel Blatchford, who in later years became a Supreme Court Judge of the United States, and who, she said, was the head of an association raising funds for her support in New York. I saw Judge Blatchford,[14] and a contract was signed for the sale. Later, in consequence of the serious illness of my wife, I was obliged to ask Judge Blatchford to cancel the contract, saying that, by way of making up for the disappointment, I would gladly contribute a sum of money to the fund for Mrs. Carson. The contract was accordingly canceled. I never saw Mrs. Carson afterward. About a year before the close of the rebellion, Mr. Lincoln offered to appoint me judge of the district court of South Carolina, my native State, but my increasing business in the city of New York and the disinclination of my wife [15] to move to South Carolina compelled me to decline the honor.

A little while before the offer of the Carolina judgeship was made me by the President I received a letter signed by Mrs. Carson, in which the writer said that the President had asked her to recommend a man for the position, and, remembering what I had done years before, she had suggested my name to him. . . .

124. PROPAGANDA FOR SLAVERY

Letter by Edwin De Leon from Alexandria, Egypt, June 30, 1860 [1]

[It was "incompatible with [his] principles and opinions" for Edwin De Leon to accept the invitation of the Institut d'Afrique at Paris to become an honorary officer of that anti-slavery organization. Speaking for those "who live under the system" by which *others* are enslaved, he considered those who opposed slavery as guided by "a mistaken philanthropy" and a disregard for "Providence" and "God." Some two years after he had written this letter, De Leon published it as part of a pamphlet that he caused to be printed in discharge of his duties as one of the chief European propaganda agents of the Confederacy, sent abroad by Jefferson Davis and Judah P. Benjamin on a secret mission for the special purpose of helping to persuade Britain, France, and other countries to grant diplomatic recognition to the Confederacy. He served from April 1862 to February 1864, spending a "slush fund"[2] of some $30,000, but his mission failed. Because the masses of England and France were unalterably opposed to slavery, the efforts of Confederate agents to exploit the fears of the ruling circles of those countries that the United States would grow too strong if it won the war could not move the British and French governments to risk recognition of the Confederacy. To De Leon, abolitionism was not the sole evil; not only did he consider Lincoln's Administration as despotic as that of the Tsar of the Russian Empire,[3] but he was prepared to fight the "radical democracy" that he expected to arise in the Confederacy after it won the war.[4]

Edwin De Leon was born in Charleston, S. C. in 1818, was graduated from the South Carolina College at Columbia, S. C. in 1837, and admitted to the bar there in 1840. He became a contributor to Southern journals, writing on domestic politics and foreign affairs. In 1845, in an address before the South Carolina College, De Leon welded together an exaggerated sectional consciousness with the European ideal of young nationhood (expressed in movements like Young Germany and Young England) and joined this mixture to the concept of American expansionism. Significant political contributions to the Democratic party as a journalist and editor in Columbia, S. C. and then in Washington, D. C. won for him the appointment by Pierce (later renewed by Buchanan) as United States Consul-General at Alexandria, Egypt, in which position he served from his arrival there in March, 1853 until he resigned, November 30, 1861, and ran the blockade to Richmond, Va. to offer his diplomatic talents to the Confederacy. After the war, De Leon did not avail himself of the amnesty and preferred to live for more than thirty years in Europe. Shortly before his death, he came to this country with his wife (Ellen Mary Nowlan, of Rothgar, near Dublin, whom he had married at Sortwood Chapel, Somerset, England, on August 25, 1858), for a lecture tour which bad health terminated, November 30, 1891. He was buried from St. Francis Xavier's Church, New York city, in the Calvary Cemetery (Catholic), but it is not clear whether he was converted in his last year or whether he arranged to be buried in Calvary Cemetery so that his wife might rest with him.[5]]

To the Chevalier Hippolyte de St Anthonie,
Secretary General,
African Institute, 22, Place Vendôme, Paris.

Sir,

Since the receipt of your letter of April 30, announcing my nomination as Honorary Vice-President of the "Institut d'Afrique"[6] of Paris, founded in 1838 by many noble and distinguished persons of all countries, for the abolition of the slave trade and slavery, I have carefully examined the statutes of that association, and am compelled to decline the proffered honour as incompatible with my principles and opinions. At the same time, I must beg you to tender the Committee of Presentation, who have paid me this unmerited compliment, the assurances of my grateful regard; and I pray you, also, sir, to accept for yourself my acknowledgments for the letter to which I now respond. In my own country my name has been much connected with this very subject,[7] but always in opposition to a mistaken philanthropy, which, in my judgment, has assumed to be wiser than Providence—stronger than God—and which, wherever triumphant, has brought forth weeds, ashes, and blood as its only fruits; as witness the emancipation of St. Domingo and the British West Indies, and the horrors of the coolie traffic in red skins to substitute for the black.[8] It is no reproach to the eminent names that figure in your association to say that we, who live under the system, must comprehend it better than those who either draw upon their imaginations for their facts, or accept them from the poisoned lips and pens of our native traducers, themselves equally ignorant or heedless of the truth.

Let them reflect whether any large community would willingly and cheerfully live in and die for the permanence of an institution which really was at once a misfortune and a crime, and a clinging curse to themselves and their children. Even now the spectacle is presented to the world of eight millions of white freemen deliberately discussing the disruption of a beloved confederacy, as an alternative to be preferred to the abolition of slavery in the Southern States of the American Union. This alone should convince foreign philanthropists of the hopelessness of the task they have undertaken, in imitation of the benevolent ladies in *Æsop's Fables*—"to scrub the Ethiop white"—even did not all previous experience teach the same lesson. Nor are these sentiments strange as coming from an American citizen. The fathers of our Republic refused to recognize either an equal or a citizen in the Negro.[9] They left him to that condition which he has ever occupied since the hieroglyphics were engraved upon the rock tablets of Egypt—(where he figures ever as a bearer of burdens; never as a conqueror or a king)—down to the present day, when France seeks "apprentices," and America retains slaves, in his descendants. With regard to the slave trade, America first declared it piracy,[10] and at this moment her vessels are busy in suppressing the traffic. Should not an American prefer to follow in the footsteps of the sages and patriots of the Revolution, rather than in those of a faction, which in his own country has as its chief prophets an elderly female romancer,[11] and a male "Belisarius,"[12] who have paraded their "stars" and their "stripes" over Europe for the disgrace and defamation of their native land? From these reasons, which I might, but will not, multiply, you will perceive, sir, that I could not, consistently or honourably, either accept or be silent under the embarrassing circumstances in which your communication placed me. But, while responding with perfect frankness, I have sought to do so with all respect to gentlemen whose motives I do not question;—and remain, with sentiments of high consideration, your obedient servant,

EDWIN DE LEON.

Agency and Consulate General of the United States of America in Egypt.

Alexandria, June 30, 1860.

125. SUMMARY, 1860

Editorial, "The Jews in 1860," in *The Journal of Commerce,* New York, October 17, 1860 [1]

[This editorial was described by a contemporary Jewish periodical as "a strange compound of facts and fiction, praise and abuse, based upon a limited knowledge of the Hebrews."[2] For all that, the article seems well-intended and reveals significantly the attitude toward Jews of an important section of the non-Jewish business world in that American city which then had the largest Jewish population in the country.]

The Jewish year 5621 has just been ushered in, and we have passed through its opening solemnities. The Hebrews of the metropolis, throwing aside for the moment all worldly cares, join faithfully in the ceremonies peculiar to the people, which have been so perseveringly celebrated and so carefully transmitted through the many generations that have lived since the destruction of Jerusalem and the banishment of its inhabitants. Not the least wonderful, even of the many wonderful things of our day, and a living proof of the truth of Christianity, is the distinct and separate preservation, without the least shadow of a national abode, of a people numbering millions of individuals, scattered throughout every division and district of the world, possessing talent sufficient, not only for self-government, but for the general advancement of civilization, successful in any branch of science or of art to which they devote themselves, exhibiting a fortitude in suffering and an energy in favorable circumstances that have excited the amazement, if not the admiration of all classes. They mingle continually with the business men of different nations, aid in the formation and support of various governments, render their assistance almost whenever and wherever required, and yet remain completely isolated, maintaining a pride of origin that almost forbids sympathy or pity. In this city, and generally throughout this country, where their rights are never invaded, they live so quietly that unless one goes into their quarters, he seldom meets with them. Few of our citizens know them socially, and all are too willing to believe Shylock their true type. But although, as a whole, the Jews have neglected education, and comparatively few have accepted the means of mental improvement placed within their reach by the governments under which they live, some have stepped forth from the ranks, and braving the Christian prejudices that have been accumulating for ages, have drawn the attention of mankind, and left their names on the page of history. Such instances are not very common, because the Jews, for the most part, are so content to live quietly and unostentatiously, and those who are remarkable for their intellectual powers are so inclined to give their undivided attention to the study of ancient records and commentaries. Still the Jews in Europe frequently make valuable contributions to literature and art, and it is not unusual on the continent to find them holding professorships.[3] Such names as Rothschild, Disraeli, Beethoven, Mendelssohn, and Rachel,[4] illustrate the variety of their talents and the greatness of their capacity, and there is no reason to doubt that, under favorable circumstances, and with such incentives as a fixed national habitation only could furnish, they would develop the same genius that was manifested by their early lawgivers, generals, and historians.

In this city their number, at present, is about 40,000, of whom the majority are rather indigent,[5] and either because they begin the battle of life while very young, or are disinclined to social intercourse with others, (having no distinct literary institutions of their own,) or both, they remain uneducated.[6] Their national studies, even if generally pursued, could not give that knowledge of the sciences without which it is impossible to keep pace with the rapid strides of civilization in our day. The minds of such students may be cultivated, but they are not enlightened.

There are seventeen synagogues in New York.[7] The first was erected in Mill St., now South William St., in 1729, where the congregation worshiped for more than a century. Some twenty-five years ago or more they removed to Crosby St., and recently have dedicated a new synagogue in West Ninteenth St.,[8] said to be more imposing in appearance than any other in the United States. It is built of Nova Scotia stone, in a style combining two orders of architecture—the Ionic and Corinthian. The entire cost of the structure and its site, was about $110,000.

This city, also, contains a hospital, supported at the expense of the Jews, and as a proof of liberality really existing among them, for which they are rarely credited, it may be mentioned that two years ago they raised $10,000 as the net proceeds of a ball given to sustain it.[9] Preparations are making to repeat the experiment. Six months ago $20,000 was raised by the Jews of this country, numbering but 150,000, for their brethren in Morocco, who were suffering from the war then raging.[10]

In Philadelphia, 15,000 members have established seven Hebrew congregations, two educational and eleven charitable associations, and a publication society.[11]

The Jews are scattered over the whole country, but are more numerous in commercial cities and towns. Throughout the West, especially, wherever there is a chance for profitable trade, they have insinuated themselves. Two synagogues were recently dedicated in Cincinnati. Wherever they go, their institutions accompany them as invariably as the household gods went with the ancient Romans.

Since the commencement of the present month, the Jews in this city have been almost constantly occupied in the observance of various solemnities. The Feast of Tabernacles, the Feast of Palms, and the Feast of the Law, have followed each other in quick succession. In a few weeks they will be called on to observe the Feast of the Dedication of the Temple and then a Fast commemorative of the Destruction of Jerusalem. What a world of emotion the celebration of these revered ceremonies must excite! How must the Jew mourn over the departed glories of a nation once so powerful and renowned, now weak and fallen! [12] Is it after all very wonderful that men who can trace their lineage to such an origin, should cling with tenacious vigor to their rites and refuse to blend with others of the race? Is it strange that they wish to preserve pure in their veins the blood of Moses, of David, of Solomon, and the Prophets?

Jerusalem was taken by Titus on the 8th of September, A. D. 70. Ninety-seven thousand prisoners were captured during the siege, and eleven thousand died of starvation. The loss of the Jews in killed, wounded and missing, during the war, is computed in round numbers at 1,400,000. The Emperor Vespasian disposed of the Jewish lands for his own use, compelled the conquered people to pay into his treasury the usual tribute of the sanctuary, and cut off the branches of the House of Judah that he might forever deprive them of the hope of deliverance from a coming Messiah. Broken hearted, they left the land they loved so well, never since to return. They have wandered over Africa and settled on its Eastern and Northern coasts, have traveled far into Asia, within the walls of China,[13] have sought the frozen regions of Russia, the beautiful lands of Spain and Italy, and the wild mountains of Switzerland, have taken up their abode in Germany and Holland, in France, England, Sweden, Norway,—in fact, in every land under the sun,—everywhere abused and persecuted with a severity and malignity that know no parallel in history. During the past century, however, one government after another has made concessions in their favor, and under this milder treatment they have rapidly increased in numbers and in influence. Even Russia has acknowledged their importance as citizens, and 2,000,000 of them dwell within her empire. In Germany they are very numerous; the chief magistrate of Hamburg is a Jew.[14] Poland is their stronghold; within its former limits 1,000,000 of them may be counted. Nearly half a million are in Morocco; 90,000 in Constantinople; 70,000 in Italy; 40,000 in England. The whole number on the globe is variously estimated at from 6,000,000 to 12,000,000: the probable number is 8,000,000. Of course no pretensions to accuracy can be made in such a computation: there are tribes said to be running wild in the interior of Africa.

A movement has been initiated at Paris, with the knowledge, and possibly at the instance of the Emperor Napoleon, for the purpose of organizing the whole people into associations, and establishing communication among them.[15] They have long cherished the expectation of return to the Holy Land. May some of them not think that their restoration draws near? The signs of the times encourage the hope. The Turkish Empire is falling in pieces, and the occupation of the ancient Canaan by an essentially trading people,[16] when the Suez canal shall have been opened, will add to the commercial facilities and wealth of the world. It is said that Baron Rothschild is intimate with the Emperor, and, ambitious to distinguish himself in the service of his nation, keeps the project constantly before him.

126. THE SLAVEHOLDERS' BIBLE

"Bible View of Slavery," a Discourse by Rabbi Morris Jacob Raphall before Congregation Bnai Jeshurun, New York, on the National Fast Day, January 4, 1861 [1]

[In 1700 an anti-slavery pamphlet published in the Massachusetts colony invoked the Old Testament to support its case; in 1701 a pro-slavery reply likewise proved its case from both the Old and New Testaments. For a century and a half afterwards, in an increasing flood that reached its crest in the decade before the Civil War, the dispute continued as to whether the Bible did or did not sanction and justify slavery. For the slaveowners, the theory that the Bible approved their peculiar institution was a great comfort and became "the cornerstone" of their argument in religious and political debate, and was used more frequently than any other.[2] Since the Bible still exerted a weighty influence on the minds of the people, the opponents of slavery argued that slavery was not only an economic, political and social evil but also a moral sin, condemned by the Bible. Thus a scholar in *The Journal of Southern History* concludes: "The North usually appealed to the teachings of the New Testament, the South to verses of the Old. The North used what might be described as a liberal, modernistic interpretation; the South denied the existence of any authority in religious matters other than the Bible, and it insisted on word for word literalism."[3] Who won this war of Biblical citations cannot be determined, since "methods of biblical interpretation were such that neither side could lose."[4] The issue was settled not in the pulpits but in economic, political and military arenas. But even as an ideological debate the method was fruitless. Both sides ignored the historical method, which would have shown that slavery in antiquity was not restricted to the Jews and developed from economic and social conditions and class relations before the treatment of slaves was codified in law secular or "divine," and that in the history of class oppression slavery in antiquity marked a step forward in the organization of the labor process and therefore in the development of civilization.[5]

To the controversy as it had been waged for more than a century by Christian ministers, Rabbi Raphall's sermon added nothing of substance. If his views became the special target of praise and censure, it was not because they were unusual, but because they were uttered by a prominent Rabbi, and therefore, said Rev. Hugh Brown in East Salem, N. Y., "the impression on the minds of some is, that he must know the Hebrew of the Bible so profoundly that it is absolutely impossible for him to be mistaken on the subject of slavery; and that what he affirms respecting it, is as true almost as the word of God itself."[6] Supporters of slavery passed over many a pro-slavery sermon preached that very same day, and seized upon the new, the Jewish ally, who had appeared in their midst. Pro-Southern New York Democrats asked Rabbi Raphall to repeat his discourse orally, and it was reprinted in newspapers, pamphlets and book form.[7] His theories obviously did not surprise his followers, for he remarks that he had been asked to deliver his sermon by prominent non-Jews, his subject was announced in advance, and among his audience in the Synagogue there were non-Jewish Southern ladies in the gallery and gentlemen on the main floor, who were among the first and heartiest in their congratulations.[8] The reason is that, as Rabbi Raphall said late in his discourse, "I find I am delivering a pro-slavery discourse."[9] His mild and brief distinction between Southern slavery and Biblical slavery did not change the total effect, which was useful to the slaveowners. Thus the *Richmond Daily Dispatch* declared that the sermon "receives the praise of the press as the most powerful argument delivered" in the controversy, and a member of the Virginia House of Delegates, speaking in support of his resolution that a Richmond rabbi be invited to give one of the daily invocations in the House, referred to Raphall's "vindication of that social institution in which our peace and welfare are vitally involved."[10]

Raphall had already achieved prominence because on February 1, 1860, he had become the first Jew to open a session of the House of Representatives with prayer. When the Civil War broke out, he supported the Union; his son, Alfred, joined the Army, became a major and lost an arm at the Battle of Gettysburg.[11]]

"The people of Nineveh believed in God, proclaimed a fast, and put on sackcloth from the greatest of them even to the least of them. For the matter reached the King of Nineveh, and he arose from his throne, laid aside his robe, covered himself with sackcloth, and seated himself in ashes. And he caused it to be proclaimed and published through Nineveh, by decree of the King and his magnates, saying: Let neither man nor beast, herd nor flock, taste anything; let them not feed nor drink any water. But let man and beast be covered with sackcloth, and cry with all their strength unto God; and let them turn every individual from his evil way and from the violence that is in their hands. Who knoweth but God may turn and relent; yea, turn away from his fierce anger, that we perish not. And God saw their works, that they turned from their evil way: and God relented of the evil which he had said that he would inflict upon them; and he did it not."—Jonah iii. 5–10.

My Friends—We meet here this day under circumstances not unlike those described in my text. Not many weeks ago, on the invitation of the Governor of this State, we joined in thanksgiving for the manifold mercies the Lord had vouchsafed to bestow upon us during the past year. But "coming events cast their shadows before," and our thanks were tinctured by the foreboding of danger impending over our country. The evil we then dreaded has now come home to us. As the cry of the prophet [*Jonah,* iii, 4], "Yet forty days and Nineveh shall be overthrown," alarmed that people, so the proclamation [of South Carolina on December 20, 1860], "the Union is dissolved," has startled the inhabitants of the United States. The President—the chief officer placed at the helm to guide the vessel of the commonwealth on its course—stands aghast at the signs of the times. He sees the black clouds gathering overhead, he hears the fierce howl of the tornado, and the hoarse roar of the breakers all around him. An aged man, his great experience has taught him that "man's extremity is God's opportunity;" and conscious of his own inability to weather the storm without help from on high, he calls upon every individual "to feel a personal responsibility towards God," even as the King of Nineveh desired all persons "to cry unto God with all their strength"—and it is in compliance with this call of the Chief Magistrate of these United States that we, like the many millions of our fellow-citizens, devote this day to public prayer and humiliation.[12] The President, more polished, though less plain-spoken than the King of Nineveh, does not in direct terms require everyone to turn from his "evil way, and from the violence that is in their hands." But to me these two expressions seem in a most signal manner to describe our difficulty, and to apply to the actual condition of things both North and South. The "violence in their hands" is the great reproach we must address to the sturdy fire-eater who in the hearing of an indignant world proclaims "Cotton is King."[13] King indeed, and a most righteous and merciful one, no doubt, in his own conceit; since he only tars and feathers the wretches who fall in his power and whom he suspects of not being sufficiently loyal and obedient to his sovereignty. And the "evil of his ways" is the reproach we must address to the sleek rhetorician who in the hearing of a God-fearing world declares "Thought is King." King indeed, and a most mighty and magnanimous one—no doubt—in his own conceit; all-powerful to foment and augment the strife, though powerless to allay it. Of all the fallacies coined in the North, the arrogant assertion that "Thought is King" is the very last with which, at this present crisis, the patience of a reflecting people should have been abused. For in fact, the material greatness of the United States seems to have completely outgrown the grasp of our most gifted minds; so that urgent as is our need, pressing as is the occasion, no man or set of men have yet come forward capable of rising above the narrow horizon of sectional influences and prejudices, and with views enlightened, just, and beneficent, to embrace the entirety of the Union and to secure its prosperity and preservation. No, my friends, "Cotton" is not King, and "Human thought" is not King. *Adonai Meleck.* The Lord alone is King! *Umalkootho Bakol Mashala,* and His royalty reigneth over all. This very day of humiliation and prayer—what is it but the recognition of His supremacy, the confession of His power and of our own weakness, the supplications which our distress addresses to His mercy? But in order that these supplications may be graciously received, that His supreme protection may be vouchsafed unto our Country, it is necessary that we should begin as the people of Nineveh did; we must "believe in God." And when I say "WE," I do not mean merely us handful of peaceable Union-loving Hebrews, but I mean the whole of the people throughout the United States: the President and his Cabinet, the President elect [Lincoln] and his advisers, the leaders of public opinion, North and South. If they truly and honestly desire to save our country, let them believe in God and in His Holy Word; and then when the authority of the Constitution is to be set aside for a higher Law,[14] they will be able to appeal to the highest Law of all, the revealed Law and Word of God, which affords its supreme sanction to the Constitution. There can be no doubt, my friends, that however much of personal ambition, selfishness, pride, and obstinacy, there may enter into the present unhappy quarrel between the two great sections of the Commonwealth—I say it is certain that the origin of the quarrel itself is the difference of opinion respecting slaveholding, which the one section denounces as sinful—aye, as the most heinous of sins—while the other section upholds it as perfectly lawful. It is the province of statesmen to examine the circumstances under which the Constitution of the United States recognizes the legality of slaveholding; and under what circumstances, if any, it becomes a crime against the law of the land. But the question whether slaveholding is a sin before God, is one that belongs to the theologian. I have been requested by prominent citizens of other denominations, that I should on this day examine the Bible view of slavery, as the religious mind of the country requires to be enlightened on the subject.

In compliance with that request, and after humbly praying that the Father of Truth and of Mercy may enlighten my mind, and direct my words for good, I am about to solicit your earnest attention, my friends, to this serious subject. My discourse will, I fear, take up more of your time than I am in the habit of exacting from you; but this is a day of penitence, and the having to listen to a long and sober discourse must be accounted as a penitential infliction.

The subject of my investigation falls into three parts:—

First, How far back can we trace the existence of slavery?

Secondly, Is slaveholding condemned as a sin in sacred Scripture?

Thirdly, What was the condition of the slave in Biblical times, and among the Hebrews; and saying with our Father Jacob, "for Thy help, I hope, O Lord!" I proceed to examine the question, how far back can we trace the existence of slavery?

1. It is generally admitted, that slavery had its origin in war, public or private. The victor having it in his power to take the life of his vanquished enemy, prefers to let him live, and reduces him to bondage. The life he has spared, the body he might have mutilated or destroyed, becomes his absolute property. He may dispose of it in any way he pleases. Such was, and through a great part of the world still is, the brutal law of force. When this state of things first began, it is next to impossible to decide. If we consult Sacred Scripture, the oldest and most truthful collection of records now or at any time in existence, we find the word *Ngebed* "slave," which the

English version renders "servant," first used by Noah, who, in Genesis ix, 25, curses the descendants of his son, Ham, by saying they should be *Ngebed Ngabadim,* the "meanest of slaves," or as the English version has it "servant of servants." The question naturally arises how came Noah to use the expression? How came he to know anything of slavery? There existed not at that time any human being on earth except Noah and his family of three sons, apparently by one mother, born free and equal, with their wives and children. Noah had no slaves. From the time that he quitted the ark he could have none. It therefore becomes evident that Noah's acquaintance with the word slave and the nature of slavery must date from before the Flood, and existed in his memory only until the crime of Ham called it forth. You and I may regret that in his anger Noah should from beneath the waters of wrath again have fished up the idea and practice of slavery; but that he did so is a fact which rests on the authority of Scripture. I am therefore justified when tracing slavery as far back as it can be traced, I arrive at the conclusion, that next to the domestic relations of husband and wife, parents and children, the oldest relation of society with which we are acquainted is that of master and slave.

Let us for an instant stop at this curse by Noah with which slavery after the Flood is recalled into existence. Among the many prophecies contained in the Bible and having reference to particular times, persons, and events, there are three singular predictions referring to three distinct races or peoples, which seem to be intended for all times, and accordingly remain in full force to this day. The first of these is the doom of Ham's descendants, the African race, pronounced upwards of 4,000 years ago. The second is the character of the descendants of Ishmael, the Arabs, pronounced nearly 4,000 years ago; and the third and last is the promise of continued and indestructible nationality promised to us, Israelites, full 2,500 years ago. It has been said that the knowledge that a particular prophecy exists, helps to work out its fulfilment, and I am quite willing to allow that with us, Israelites, such is the fact. The knowledge we have of God's gracious promises renders us imperishable, even though the greatest and most powerful nations of the olden time have utterly perished. It may be doubted whether the fanatic Arab of the desert [15] ever heard of the prophecy that he is to be a "wild man, his hand against every man, and every man's hand against him." (Gen. xvi. 12.) But you and I, and all men of ordinary education, know that this prediction at all times has been, and is now, literally fulfilled, and that it has never been interrupted. Not even when the followers of Mahomet rushed forth to spread his doctrines,[16] the Koran in one hand and the sword in the other, and when Arab conquest rendered the fairest portion of the Old World subject to the empire of their Caliph, did the descendants of Ishmael renounce their characteristics. Even the boasted civilization of the present century, and frequent intercourse with Western travelers, still leave the Arab a wild man, "his hand against everybody, and every man's hand against him," a most convincing and durable proof that the Word of God is true, and that the prophecies of the Bible were dictated by the Spirit of the Most High. But though, in the case of the Arab, it is barely possible that he may be acquainted with the prediction made to Hagar, yet we may be sure that the fetish-serving, benighted African[17] has no knowledge of Noah's prediction; which, however, is nowhere more fully or more atrociously carried out than in the native home of the African. Witness the horrid fact, that the King of Dahomy is, at this time, filling a large and deep trench with human blood, sufficient to float a good-sized boat; that the victims are innocent men, murdered to satisfy some freak of what he calls his religion; and that this monstrous and most fiendish act has met with no opposition, either from the pious indignation of Great Britain, or from the zealous humanity of our country.[18]

Now I am well aware that the Biblical critics called Rationalists,[19] who deny the possibility of prophecy, have taken upon themselves to assert, that the prediction of which I have spoken was never uttered by Noah, but was made up many centuries after him by the Hebrew writer of the Bible, in order to smooth over the extermination of the Canaanites, whose land was conquered by the Israelites. With superhuman knowledge like that of the Rationalists, who claim to sit in judgment on the Word of God, I do not think it worth while to argue. But I would ask you how is it that a prediction, manufactured for a purpose—a fraud in short, and that a most base and unholy one, should nevertheless continue in force, and be carried out during four, or three, or even two thousand years; for a thousand years more or less can here make no difference. Noah, on the occasion in question, bestows on his son Shem a spiritual blessing: "Blessed be the Lord, the God of Shem," and to this day it remains a fact which cannot be denied, that whatever knowledge of God and of religious truth is possessed by the human race, has been promulgated by the descendants of Shem. Noah bestows upon his son Japheth a blessing, chiefly temporal, but partaking also of spiritual good. "May God enlarge Japheth, and may he dwell in the tents of Shem," and to this day it remains a fact which cannot be denied, that the descendants of Japheth (Europeans and their offspring) have been enlarged so that they possess dominion in every part of the earth; while, at the same time, they share in that knowledge of religious truth which the descendants of Shem were the first to promulgate. Noah did not bestow any blessing on his son Ham, but uttered a bitter curse against his descendants, and to this day it remains a fact which cannot be gainsaid that in his own native home, and generally throughout the world, the unfortunate Negro is indeed the meanest of slaves. Much had been said respecting the inferiority of his intellectual powers, and that no man of his race has ever inscribed his name on the Pantheon of human excellence, either mental or moral.[20] But this is a subject I will not discuss. I do not attempt to build up a theory, nor yet to defend the moral government of Providence. I state facts; and having done so, I remind you that our own fathers were slaves in Egypt, and afflicted four hundred years; and then I bid you reflect on the words of inspired Isaiah (lv. 8), "My thoughts are not your thoughts, neither are your ways my ways, saith the Lord."

II. Having thus, on the authority of the sacred Scripture, traced slavery back to the remotest period, I next request your attention to the question, "Is slaveholding condemned as a sin in sacred Scripture?" How this question can at all arise in the mind of any man that has received a religious education, and is acquainted with the history of the Bible, is a phenomenon I cannot explain to myself, and which fifty years ago no man dreamed of. But we live in times when we must not be surprised at anything. Last Sunday an eminent preacher is reported to have declared from the pulpit, "That the Old Testament requirements served their purpose during the physical and social development of mankind, and were rendered no longer necessary now when we were to be guided by the superior doctrines of the New in the moral instruction of the race."[21] I had always thought that in the "moral instruction of the race," the requirements of Jewish Scriptures and Christian Scriptures were identically the same; that to abstain from murder, theft, adultery, that "to do justice, to love mercy, and to walk humbly with God," were "requirements" equally imperative in the one course of instruction as in the other. But it appears I was mistaken. "We have altered all that now," says this eminent divine, in happy imitation of Molière's physician, whose new theory removed the heart from the left side of the human body to the right.[22] But when I remember that the "now" refers to a period of which you all, though no very aged men, witnessed the rise; when moreover, I remember that the "WE" the reverend preacher speaks of, is limited to a few impulsive declaimers, gifted with great zeal, but little knowledge; more eloquent than learned; better able to excite our passions than to satisfy our reason; and when, lastly, I remember the scorn with which sacred Scripture (Deut. xxxii. 18) speaks of "new-fangled notions, lately sprung up, which your fathers esteemed not;" when I consider all this, I think you and I had rather continue to take our "requirements for moral instruction" from Moses and the Prophets than from the preacher of Brooklyn. But as that reverend gentleman takes a lead among those who most loudly and most vehemently denounce slaveholding as a sin, I wished to convince myself whether he had any Scripture warranty for so doing; and whether such denunciation was one of those "requirements for moral instruction" advanced by the New Testament. I have accordingly examined the various books of Christian Scripture, and find that they afford the reverend gentleman and his compeers no authority whatever for his and their declamations. The New Testament nowhere, directly or indirectly, condemns slaveholding, which, indeed, is proved by the universal practice of all Christian nations during many centuries. Receiving slavery as one of the conditions of society, the New Testament nowhere interferes with or contradicts the slave code of Moses; it even preserves a letter written by one of the most eminent Christian teachers to a slave-owner on sending back to him his runaway slave. And when we next refer to the history and "requirements" of our own sacred Scriptures, we find that on the most solemn occasion therein recorded, when God gave the Ten Commandments on Mount Sinai—

> There where His finger scorched, the tablet shone;
> There where His shadow on his people shone
> His glory, shrouded in its garb of fire,
> Himself no eye might see and not expire.

Even on that most solemn and most holy occasion, slaveholding is not only recognized and sanctioned as an integral part of the social structure, when it is commanded that the Sabbath of the Lord is to bring rest to *Ngabdecha ve Amathecha,* "Thy male slave and thy female slave" (Exod. xx. 10; Deut. v. 14). But the property in slaves is placed under the same protection as any other species of lawful property, when it is said, "Thou shalt not covet thy neighbor's house, or his field, or his male slave, or his female slave, or his ox, or his ass, or aught that belongeth to thy neighbor" (Ibid. xx. 17; v. 21). That the male slave and female slave here spoken of do not designate the Hebrew bondman, but the heathen slave, I shall presently show you. That the Ten Commandments are the word of God, and as such, of the very highest authority, is acknowledged by Christians as well as by Jews. I would therefore ask the reverend gentleman of Brooklyn and his compeers—How dare you, in the face of the sanction and protection afforded to slave property in the Ten Commandments—how dare you denounce slaveholding as a sin? When you remember that Abraham, Isaac, Jacob, Job—the men with whom the Almighty conversed, with whose names he emphatically connects his own most holy name, and to whom He vouchsafed to give the character of "perfect, upright, fearing God and eschewing evil" (Job i. 8)—that all these men were slaveholders, does it not strike you that you are guilty of something very little short of blasphemy? And if you answer me, "Oh, in their time slaveholding was lawful, but now it has become a sin," I in my turn ask you, "When and by what authority you draw the line? Tell us the precise time when slaveholding ceased to be permitted, and became sinful?" When we remember the mischief which this inventing a new sin, not known to the Bible, is causing; how it has exasperated the feelings of the South, and alarmed the conscience of the North, to a degree that men who should be brothers are on the point of embruing their hands in each other's blood, are we not entitled to ask the reverend preacher of Brooklyn, "What right have you to insult and exasperate thousands of God-fearing, law-abiding citizens, whose moral worth and patriotism, whose purity of conscience and of life, are fully equal to your own? What right have you to place yonder grey-headed philanthropist on a level with a murderer, or yonder virtuous mother of a family on a line with an adulteress, or yonder honorable and honest man in one rank with a thief, and all this solely because they exercise a right which your own fathers and progenitors, during many generations, held and exercised without reproach or compunction? You profess to frame your 'moral instruction of the race' according to the 'requirements' of the New Testament—but tell us where and by whom it was said, "Whatsoever shall say to his neighbor, *Raca* (worthless sinner), shall be in danger of the council; but whosoever shall say, thou fool, shall be in danger of the judgment." My friends, I find, and I am sorry to find, that I am delivering a pro-slavery discourse. I am no friend to slavery in the abstract, and still less friendly to the practical working of slavery. But I stand here as a teacher in Israel; not to place before you my own feelings and opinions, but to propound to you the word of God, the Bible view of slavery. With a due sense of my responsibility, I must state to you the truth and nothing but the truth, however unpalatable or unpopular that truth may be.

III. It remains for me to examine what was the condition of the slave in Biblical times and among the Hebrews. And here at once we must distinguish between the Hebrew bondman and the heathen slave. The former could only be reduced to bondage from two causes. If he had committed theft and had not wherewithal to make full restitution, he was "sold for his theft." (Exod. xxii. 3.) Or if he became so miserably poor that he could not sustain life except by begging, he had permission to "sell" or bind himself in servitude. (Levit. xxv. 39 *et seq.*) But in either case his servitude was limited in duration and character. "Six years shall he serve, and in the seventh he shall go out free for nothing" (Exod. xxi. 2). And if even the bondman preferred bondage to freedom, he could not, under any circumstances, be held to servitude longer than the jubilee then next coming. At that period the estate which had originally belonged to his father, or remoter ancestor, reverted to his possession, so that he went forth at once a freeman and a landed proprietor. As his privilege of Hebrew citizen was thus only suspended, and the law, in permitting him to be sold, contemplated his restoration to his full rights, it took care that during his servitude his mind should not be crushed to the abject and cringing condition of a slave. "Ye shall not rule over one another with rigor," is the provision of the law. (Lev. xxv. 46.) Thus he is fenced round with protection against any abuse of power on the part of his employer; and tradition so strictly interpreted the letter of the law in his favor, that it was a common saying of Biblical times and homes, which Maimonides has preserved to us, that "he who buys an Hebrew bondman gets himself a master."[23] Though in servitude, this Hebrew was in nowise exempt from his religious duties. Therefore it is not for him or his that the Ten Commandments stipulated for rest on the Sabbath of the Lord; for his employer could not compel him to work on that day; and if he did work of his own accord, he became guilty of death, like any other Sabbath-breaker. Neither does the prohibition, "thou shalt not covet the property of thy neighbor," apply to him, for he was not the property of his employer. In fact, between the Hebrew bondman and the Southern slave there is no point of resemblance. There were, however, slaves among the Hebrews, whose general condition was analogous to that of their Southern fellow sufferers. That was the heathen slave, who was to be bought "from the heathens that were round about the land of Israel, or from the heathen strangers that sojourned in the land; they should be a possession, to be bequeathed as an inheritance to the owner's children, after his death, for ever," (Levit. xxv. 44–46.) Over these heathen slaves the owners' property was absolute; he could put them to hard labor, to the utmost extent of their physical strength; he could inflict on them any degree of chastisement short of injury to life and limb. If his heathen slave ran away or strayed from home, every Israelite was bound to bring or send him back, so he would have to do with any other portion of his neighbor's property that had been lost or strayed. (Deut. xxii. 3.)

Now, you may, perhaps, ask me how I can reconcile this statement with the text of Scripture so frequently quoted against the Fugitive Slave Law, "Thou shalt not surrender unto his master the slave who has escaped from his master unto thee" (Deut. xxiii. 16).[24] I answer you that, according to all legists, this text applies to a heathen slave, who, from any foreign country escapes from his master, even though that master be an Hebrew, residing out of the land of Israel. Such a slave—but such a slave only—is to find a permanent asylum in any part of the country he may choose. This interpretation is fully borne out by the words of the precept. The pronoun "thou," is not here used in the same sense as in the Ten Commandments. There it designates every soul in Israel individually; since every one has it in his power, and is in duty bound to obey the commandments. But as the security and protection to be bestowed on the runaway slaves are beyond the power of any individual and require the consent and concurrence of the whole community, the pronoun "thou" here means the whole of the people, and not one portion in opposition to any other portion of the people. And as the expression remains the same throughout the precept, "With thee he shall dwell, even among ye, in the place he shall choose in one of thy gates where it liketh him best," it plainly shows that the whole of the land was open to him, and the whole of the people were to protect the fugitive, which could not have been carried out if it had applied to the slave who escaped from one tribe into the territory of another. Had the precept been expounded in any other than its strictly literal sense, it would have caused great confusion, since it would have nullified two other precepts of God's law; that which directs that "slaves, like lands and houses, were to be inherited for ever," and that which commands "property, lost or strayed, to be restored to the owner." Any other interpretation would, moreover, have caused heartburning and strife between the tribes, for men were as tenacious of their rights and property in those days as they are now. But no second opinion was ever entertained; the slave who ran away from Dan to Beersheba had to be given up, even as the runaway from South Carolina has to be given up by Massachusetts; whilst the runaway from Edom, or from Syria, found an asylum in the land of Israel, as the runaway slave from Cuba or Brazil would find in New York. Accordingly, Shimei reclaimed and recovered his runaway slaves from Achish, king of Gath, at that time a vassal of Israel (Kings ii. 39, 40). And Saul of Tarsus sent back the runaway slave, Onesimus, unto his owner Philemon. But to surrender to a ruthless, lawless heathen, the wretched slave who had escaped from his cruelty, would have been to give up the fugitive to certain death, or at least to tortures repugnant to the spirit of God's law, the tender care of which protected the bird in its nest, the beast at the plough, and the slave in his degradation. Accordingly, the extradition was not permitted in Palestine any more than it is in Canada.[25] While thus the owner possessed full right over and security for his property, the exercise of that power was confined within certain limits which he could not outstep. His female slave was not to be the tool or castaway toy of his sensuality, nor could he sell her, but was bound to "let her go free," "because he had humbled her" (Deut. xxi. 14). His male slave was protected against excessive punishment; for if the master in any way mutilated his slave, even to knock a single tooth out of his head, the slave became free (Exod. xxi. 26, 27). And while thus two of the worst passions of human nature, lust and cruelty, were kept under due restraint, the third bad passion, cupidity, was not permitted free scope; for the law of God secured to the slave his Sabbaths and days of rest; while public opinion, which in a country so densely peopled as Palestine must have been all-powerful, would not allow any slave-owner to impose heavier tasks on his slaves, or to feed them worse than his neighbors did. This, indeed, is the great distinction which the Bible view of slavery derives from its divine source. The slave is a *person* in whom the dignity of human nature is to be respected; *he has rights.* Whereas, the heathen view of slavery which prevailed at Rome, and which, I am sorry to say, is adopted in the South, reduces the slave to a *thing,* and a thing can have no rights. The result to which the Bible view of slavery leads us, is—1st. That slavery has existed since the earliest time; 2d. That slaveholding is no sin, and that slave property is expressly placed under the protection of the Ten Commandments; 3d. That the slave is a person, and has rights not conflicting with the lawful exercise of the rights of his owner. If our Northern fellow-citizens, content with following the word of God, would not insist on being "righteous overmuch," or denouncing "sin" which the Bible knows not, but which is plainly taught by the precepts of men—they would entertain more equity and less ill feeling towards their Southern brethren. And if our Southern fellow-citizens would adopt the Bible view of slavery, and discard that heathen slave code, which permits a few bad men to indulge in an abuse of power that throws a stigma and disgrace on the whole body of slaveholders—if both North and South would do what is right, then "God would see their works and that they turned from the evil of their ways;" and in their case, as in that of the people of Nineveh, would mercifully avert the impending evil, for with Him alone is the power to do so.

127. ABOLITIONISTS' BIBLE

Michael Heilprin replies to Dr. Raphall, the *New-York Daily Tribune,* January 15, 1861 [1]

[Horace Greeley's *Tribune* had already published two editorials attacking Raphall's sermon [2] when Heilprin's scholarly and indignant retort was received. Printing it promptly, the editor called special attention to it as "an able and most conclusive reply" by "a learned Jew of this city, who, in historical, philological, and biblical knowledge, has few living equals. . . ."[3] Although it was not the only rejoinder to Raphall written by a Jew,[4] it was the only one that reached a substantial newspaper audience. Heilprin expressed trenchantly the special resentment that the Jewish abolitionist felt whenever a Jew appeared as a supporter of slavery. "Must the stigma of Egyptian principles be fastened on the people of Israel by Israelitish lips themselves?" Yet *The Jewish Messenger,* which had liberally given space to a long summary of Raphall's sermon, rejected the request that it reprint Heilprin's answer, "as we have no desire to take part in a controversy of this nature."[5]

Michael Heilprin (1823–1888), born in Piotrkow, Poland, fled to Hungary in 1842 to escape Polish oppression, and took an active part in the 1848 Hungarian revolution led by Kossuth. Heilprin was secretary of the literary bureau of the revolutionary government. When the counter-revolution triumphed, he escaped to France, and made his way to the United States in 1856, soon becoming interested in American politics and the anti-slavery cause. From 1858, he worked for the *New American Cyclopaedia,* where his vast knowledge and mastery of twelve languages quickly established his reputation for learning, the diversity and modernity of which are revealed in this reply to Raphall.]

The Rev. Rabbi Raphall, on the 4th of this month, preached a sermon on Slavery and the Bible, "having been requested, by prominent citizens of other denominations, that he should on that day examine the Bible view of Slavery, as the religious mind of the country requires to be enlightened on this subject." I have perused it, and find that the Rabbi arrives at the conclusion that Slavery is not sinful in the eyes of the God of Israel, the God of Moses and the Prophets. It is true, he is "no friend to Slavery in the abstract, and still less friendly to the practical working of Slavery." He is "sorry to find that" he is "delivering a pro-Slavery discourse." He distinguishes between Slavery as practised by the Hebrews, which was "confined within certain limits," and according to which a "slave was a person in whom the dignity of human nature was to be respected," and "who had rights," and the heathen system of Slavery, "which," he is "sorry to say, is adopted in the South," "which reduces the slave to a thing," and makes him a prey to "two of the worst passions of human nature, lust and cruelty." Still, "after humbly praying to the Father of Truth and of Mercy," he regards it as his duty to proclaim from the pulpit that it is a sin—to preach against Slavery in the South! I had read similar nonsense hundreds of times before; I knew that the Father of Truth and Mercy was daily invoked in hundreds of pulpits in this country for a Divine sanction of falsehood and barbarism; still, being a Jew myself, I felt exceedingly humbled, I may say outraged, by the sacrilegious words of the Rabbi. Have we not had enough of the "reproach of Egypt?" Must the stigma of Egyptian principles be fastened on the people of Israel by Israelitish lips themselves?[6] Shall the enlightened and humane of this country ask each other, "Are these the people of God, who have come from his land?" I hoped, however, that, amid the flood of scum that is now turned up by the turbulent waves of this stormy time, the words of the Rabbi would soon disappear, like so many other bubbles, and the blasphemous teachings of a synagogue find no longer echoes than those of Christian Churches. But I am grievously mistaken. Day after day brings hosannahs to the Hebrew defamer of the law of his nation; and his words are trumpeted through the land as if he were the messenger of a new salvation. So depraved is the moral sense of our Pro-Slavery demagogues, so debauched the mind of their mammon-worshiping followers, so dense the Egyptian darkness which covers their horizon, that, all other false lights being exhausted, a spark of Hebrew Pro-Slavery rhetoric is hailed as a new lightning from Sinai, as a new light from Zion, sent to guide the people of the United States safely through the dark tempests that threaten to destroy their ship of State. Down with conscience, humanity, reason, experience! Just listen to the angelic Hebrew sounds of the God-sent Rabbi! He has scrutinized the Hebrew Scriptures and their commentaries, the Mishna, the Gemara, the mediaeval Rabbis, perhaps also the Cabalists. If he has not discovered truth, nobody will. And what a stupendous knowledge of profane history, from antediluvian times down to the day when the Rev. H. W. Beecher last preached in Plymouth Church! All this, I trust, will convert few rational Jews or Christians to the infamous doctrines of Slavery, but, on the other hand, it may induce many people to believe that the God of the Jews was or is, after all, a God of Slavery. Allow me, therefore, to show both Christian and Jewish readers of *The Tribune* the real value of the Rabbi's biblical scholarship and, if space permits, also of his logic. "Because of Zion I will not be silent."

Of course, he commences with Noah, and tells us how it came that that man, who first planted a grapevine, &c.,&c., was acquainted with the condition of an *'ebed* (or *ngebed,* as the Rabbi spells it), which he translates by "slave," and not like the English version, by "servant," and arrives "at the conclusion that, next to the domestic relation of husband and wife, parents and children, the oldest relation of society with which we are acquainted is that of master and slave." A fine discovery, which must have been charming to the ears of the Southern part of his hearers! The peculiar domestic institution almost as old as the fratricide of Cain, and certainly as old as the time when the earth was full of violence, and the Lord, repenting that he had made man, determined to destroy him from the face of the earth (Gen. vi.)! Thus biblical criticism, a blessed instrument in the hands of a competent scholar, traces everything to its origin, and naturally links together the brother of Abel with the late Preston S. Brooks, Lamech with Rhett,[7] and perhaps even sister Carolina's going out of the Union, with mother Eve's going out of Paradise! Who the serpent was, has long been discussed. It remains only to be proved that the tree of knowledge was the first full grown palmetto.[8]

But let us go back to Noah, whose utterances, after having tasted the juice of the vine, are believed to contain the true solution of the great problem now before the statesmen and people of America. Now, by my Jewish brethren, I am sorry to say, the first planter of the grape vine has never been regarded as a saint, and distinguished Rabbis have been bold enough to explain the word *bedorothav* (in his generations), which is attached to the enumeration of his virtues, to his disparagement, meaning that he was eminently pious only as compared with others at a time when the earth was all corrupt, full of violence, and deserving of destruction. Our learned Rabbi knows this well enough, but he prefers to canonize Noah because of his curse on Ham, and he also prefers the word "slave" as translation of the Hebrew *'ebed,* which Noah used on that occasion, to the "servant" of the English version. Our people's appreciation of Noah's personal merits, of course, can have but little historical or practical value, but the word *'ebed* is a point upon which the information of a Hebrew is of decisive importance.

Now, being a Hebrew myself, and pretending to an equal knowledge of the beautiful tongue of my ancestors with the Rev. gentleman, I must tell you, statesmen of these United States, that if you undertake to reconstruct the shattered Constitution of your Great Republic on the basis of the learned Rabbi's translation of that word,[9] you will find yourselves woefully mistaken. I doubt if there be one Jewish authority in favor of the Rabbi's preference, but certainly for every one there are ten against him. Moses Mendelssohn in his celebrated German translation of the Pentateuch[10] has *Knecht* (servant), and not *Sklave;* Dr. Zunz's German Bible,[11] the most favorably received Jewish version of our age, has *Knecht!* Rabbi Raphall prefers the "meanest of slaves" for *'ebed 'abadim* to "the servant of servants" of the English version; Mendelssohn renders it: *ein Knecht wie alle Knechte,* and Zunz's Bible: *ein Knecht der Knechte!* Now let me also tell the same gentlemen and all others concerned, challenging a refutation, that the word is used in so many places and with so manifold meanings in the Hebrew Scriptures, that it would certainly be no less a task to make the great lights of biblical criticism and theology agree upon a harmonious translation of it in all passages, than to bring about a similar harmony regarding the construction of the United States Constitution in all its parts, between Senators Seward and Bigler, Wade and Iverson, Sumner and Davis, Wilson and Toombs,[12] &c. The word which is believed to bear freedom and slavery, peace and civil war, union and disruption in its mysterious significance, the Hebrew *'ebed* (pl. *'abadim,* spelled by Rabbi Raphall *ngabadim*), a derivative of the verb *'abod,* which signifies to work, to toil, to cultivate, to serve, to administer, to officiate, to worship, &c., is used not only of servants, subjects, serfs, bondsmen, slaves, hirelings, and soldiers, but also of officers of the court (those of Pharaoh, for instance), of satraps (those of the great King of Assyria), of royal ambassadors (that of David to the Court of Ammon), of worshipers, messengers, and other instruments of the Divinity, including patriarchs, prophets, kings, and nations. Abraham is called the *'ebed* of God; so are Moses, Job, Isaiah, Cyrus, Jacob or Israel, as a nation! *'Abadai hannebiim* is frequently used of the prophets collectively. Now for Noah's blessings and curse.

The Rabbi tells us sundry things about Shem and Japheth, destined to strengthen the belief of his hearers in prophecy, which I may be allowed to pass by without scrutiny (observing, by the by, that the only interesting part, that concerning the Arabs, is taken from the Hebrew writings of the late Italian scholar Reggio),[13] our principal object here being the third son of Noah, the cursed one, the darling of Pro-Slavery theologians, Ham, the Negro in the Bible![14] "There are three predictions," says our Rabbi, "which seem intended for all times, and accordingly remain in force to this present day. The first of these is the doom of Ham's descendants, the African race, pronounced upward of four thousand years ago." A few words, but full of falsehood, nonsense, and blasphemy!

The doom of the descendants of Ham, of the Hamites, in the predictions? Where? Ham's fourth son, Canaan, alone is mentioned. Where is the slightest authority for the doom of his other sons, or his race? Noah, awakening from his drunkenness, curses, in punishment of an insult, a son of the offender, and a race is to be "doomed for all times!" Doomed by whom, "preacher in Israel?" By the God whom you teach our people to worship, the God of Mercy, whom our lawgiver proclaims to extend his rewards to the thousandth generation, and his punishment of crimes only to the fourth? Doomed to be punished for the crime of their antediluvian progenitor for all times by the rod of man, whom our law, the law of Moses, prohibits from inflicting any punishment on a son for the crime even of a father? And all this uttered by a Jew whose very race was but of late generally believed to be cursed forever for one ancient crime! And what inspires your blasphemous assertions? Teacher in Israel, is it the trivial, vulgar notion of your Pro-Slavery patrons, or the text of the Scriptures? Open your book! Where is there a word confirming your absurdities? Noah cursed, but did God? History shows it, you say. Compare Ham, the African race, and our Negro! What a strange mixture! Where is the identity? South Carolina and Dahomey, Alabama and Timbuctoo, have more features of resemblance than the biblical Hamites and your Negroes.

Ham, the "meanest of slaves" in biblical history? No, preacher in Israel; on the contrary, the conquering race *par excellence!* Whom do you find among the descendants of Ham in Genesis (x.)? There is Cush, or the Ethiopians, with their Meroë, which by many distinguished scholars is still believed to have been the cradle of all civilization this side of India. There is Misraim, or the Egyptians (the Ham proper of the Scriptures), of whose wisdom and power the Scriptures are full, the teachers of Chaldea and Greece, the builders of the most stupendous works of antiquity, the enslavers of our Semitic ancestors, the conquerors at many times of Western Asia, the circumnavigators of Africa. There is Nimrod, the founder of Babylon, the learned and profligate mistress of the Asian world, whose iron rod, so long endured by our Semitic ancestors, appears broken only on the last pages of our Scriptural history. There is Ashur, or the Assyrians of Nineveh, the powerful rival of the city on the Euphrates, whose conquering sword scattered over the world and nationally destroyed ten of the twelve tribes of Semitic Israel. There is Sheba, or the Sabaeans, the masters of the gold and spice region of Arabia Felix, whose queen came to Jerusalem to vie in wisdom with our King Solomon. There is Caphtor, supposed by the best critics to mean the Cretans, whose Minos was renowned for power as for wisdom and justice, the constructors of the Cnossian labyrinth, the masters of the Grecian seas, to whom the city of Minerva was tributary. There are the Philistines, who so long disputed with our Semitic ancestors the possession of the land which the Greeks finally named after them. There is Sidon, and other Phoenician tribes, whose glorious cities and unrivaled commerce, over sea and land, with all the nations of the ancient globe, are described in such glowing words by our prophet Ezekiel. There are

Dedan and Raama, Seba, and Havilah, tribes, like Sheba, settled on the shores of the Arabian seas, and rich by their traffic in gold, spices, and other precious things with the equally Hamitic Tyre (Ezekiel xxvii.). There are the Ludim and other Libyans, masters of the northern margins of Africa, but of Caucasian race. There are some few others, of whom we must say with Josephus (Ant. Book I, Chap. 6): "We know nothing of them beside their names," and among whom I allow you, learned Rabbi, to look for your Negro. But where is the Hamites' doom to be the "meanest of slaves" confirmed in biblical history? King Solomon married Hamite women (Egyptian, Sidonian, &c.). Other kings of Israel did the same. But they were wicked, you say. Our lawgiver, Moses himself, married a Hamite (Cushite) woman (Num. xii.), and his brother and sister, who gainsayed it, were reprimanded for so doing. The cursed son of Ham, Canaan, had nothing to do with the African race. The ethnological chapter of Genesis (x.) fixes the boundaries of the abode of his descendants, which did not extend beyond the limits of Syria, and even hardly beyond those of Palestine.

The same historical accuracy is evinced by our Rabbi in regard to later periods. In one sweeping passage he makes "Abraham, Isaac, Jacob, Job"—"the men with whom the Almighty communed, with whose names he emphatically connects his most holy name"—all slaveholders! Teacher in Israel, speaking thus before the descendants of those men, in a temple dedicated to that God, on a day of prayer and humiliation destined to avert the horrors of a civil war from this once glorious Republic, but now threatened to become reputed like the United States of Sodom and Gomorrah, Admah and Zeboim,[15] under the dictates of a slave-breeding, slave-trading, slave-hunting faction—"does it not strike you that you are guilty of something very little short of blasphemy?" And of what absurdity! Peaceable, unwarlike, nomadic patriarchs, "migrating from people to people, and from land to land," with their wives, children, and flocks, and a few attendants, mostly through half-settled regions, and beyond the borders of other societies, in order to escape the contagion of heathen iniquities, continually surrounded by dangers and enemies, unable to defend the honor here of a wife, there of a child, robbed here of a well, and there concluding a treaty under oath about another—are represented to have been slaveholders! How did they guard their slaves, wise Rabbi, on their grazing places between Haran and the River of Egypt, in the valley of the lower or upper Jordan, in the surroundings of

Hebron, Shechem, Gomorrah, or Gerar? Had they concluded anti-fugitive slave treaties with the Hittites, Amorites, and other Hamites of Canaan, with the roving and slave-trading Midianites, or with the strictly law-observing magistrates of Sodom? Just think of Abraham hastening with his trained men to the rescue of his friends from the invasion of the Kings of Elam, Shinar, &c., and leaving his Sarah and Hagar (by the by, also a Hamitic woman) under the protection of his slaves! Or that younger slaveholder, Jacob, stealing away from the regulation of his father-in-law, Laban, with his wives, children, flocks, and slaves! Did the slaves carry the children, or the children guard the slaves, on their flight from Haran in Mesopotamia, across the Euphrates, to the hill in Gilead, where they erected a monument? Just imagine the Hon. Robert Toombs running away with his chattels before the vengeance of a reactionary mob in the Republic of Georgia, and first breathing freely when calling the roll of his slaves on Bunker Hill, at the foot of the monument! And while speaking of that monument which Jacob called Gal'ed, could not the learned Rabbi tell us who were the "brethren" of that patriarch, who gathered stones for him (Gen. xxxi., 46)? "Brethren?" Yes, *ehav,* "his brethren," and he had but one brother, who was absent. "Brethren," Rabbi, is another term for the *'abadim* of Jacob! And "the eldest of his house (*zekan betho*), who ruled over all he had," is another designation of an *'ebed* of Abraham (Gen. xxiv., 2). Whether acquired by persuasion, according to the explanation of the word *'asu* (Gen. xii., 5) by the Rabbis, or hired (*sakhir*) as Jacob was by Laban, or brought (*miknath kesef*), either from themselves, or from their parents, as wives were at that time, in order to make the mutual agreement morally more binding, the attendants and servants of the patriarchs, whom our Rabbi persists in calling slaves, were but their voluntary followers, their pupils and friends, enjoying all the privileges of free persons, the advantages of mutual protection and assistance, and the blessings of a wise rule.

Or does the learned Rabbi mean to say that they were bought from pirates or slave-traders, as were Joseph, Plato, Cervantes, and Arago,[16] and that he who denounces the slave-trade is also "guilty of something a little short of blasphemy?" And does he mean to say that the female followers of the patriarchs were bound to serve in their harems (the concubines of Abraham are mentioned in Gen. xxv. 6) whether they agreed or not, and that a denunciation of similar relations in Louisiana or Mississippi would be blasphemy?

For, if the Rabbi proves anything, he proves strange things. He proves bigamy, polygamy, concubinage, Semitic (not African) Slavery, the traffic in Semitic flesh—all these and many similar things to be protected forever by the sanction of a divine law. I say Semitic and not African, because the passage which he quotes as allowing the Hebrews to buy slaves from the heathens distinctly designates those that were round about, or in the land of Israel (Lev. xxv. 44), where, as the Rabbi well knows, no Negroes dwelt or sojourned, while some of the principal next neighbors of the Hebrews were not only Semites, as the Syrians (Aram) of Damascus, to whom, also, Abraham's *'ebed* Eliezer belonged, but Semites of the same branch with the Hebrews, as the Ammonites and Moabites, and even descendants of Abraham himself, as the Edomites and Ishmaelites.

If Moses allowed the buying of slaves, he distinctly excluded the Negroes, believing, perhaps, with our Rabbi, that "the unfortunate Negro is the meanest of slaves;" or knowing something of what "has been said respecting the inferiority of his intellectual powers." Accordingly, the people of Hayti could not be gainsayed for the importation of Hebrew slaves, from Morocco, for instance, who might contribute to the amelioration of the moral condition of their country, while the people of the Cotton States could be denounced without incurring the guilt of blasphemy for Africanizing their region by their unsanctioned practices, and for dooming their posterity to the fate of the whites of St. Domingo.

Again, according to the Rabbi, should the people of Utah, before or after their admission into the Union as a sovereign State (on which occasion they would, no doubt, avail themselves of the precedent of the Cotton States, immediately to secede from the Union), establish certain peculiar domestic institutions of an incestuous character, "the eloquent preacher of Brooklyn" could not speak against it without incurring the guilt of blasphemy, Jacob having married two sisters, and our Rabbi being unable to discover "the precise time when" an act that was permitted to a patriarch and prohibited by Moses only to the Hebrews, "ceased to be permitted and became sinful" to all others.

"But after all," the Rabbi may say, "have I not proved, by numerous quotations, that Moses allowed Slavery to our people?" Not at all, Rabbi; firstly, because you substitute "slave" for "servant" or "bondman" without authority; secondly, because one of your quotations (Deut. xxii. 3) is obviously fallacious; thirdly, because two others, those from the Ten Commandments, are as ridiculous as they are sacrilegious; fourthly, because the strongest of all (Lev. xxv. 44–46) can prove no more than the so rigorously limited allowance of buying the life-long service of a free person, and the right of inheriting the claims to the same personal service, as the word *le'olam,* which you render "forever," is admitted by yourself to mean "for life" in another passage on the same subject (Exod. xxi. 6); and lastly, because if there be anything apparently favoring your view in these or other passages, that would not be sufficient to fasten "the reproach of Egypt" (*herpath Mitzraim*) on the law of the great fugitive slave, who inaugurated his divine mission as liberator of a people of slaves by slaying one of their overseers, and who, to the end of his career repeated, and over again repeated: "Forget not that ye have been slaves in Egypt!" "An eye for an eye" is written in the plainest words in the same law; still you hold with all the Talmudists, that this is not to be understood literally.

For those Rabbis wisely understood that there are numerous things to be explained, or explained away in our Scriptures, which, though pervaded by a divine spirit of truth, justice, and mercy, they found to contain much that may be called contradictory, unjust, and even barbarous. And they also knew that much was yielded by the law of Moses to the stubborn passions of man, of his people of freed slaves, and of his time. You know the Talmudical: *Lo dibberah torah keneged yetzer hara'*—"the law does not ignore the evil instinct." There is a passage to be explained away even in the very text of your sermon, which you preferred to that passage of Isaiah (lviii. 6), which is read on the great fast day of atonement in all the Synagogues of Israel, and which was obviously most appropriate for the occasion: "Is not this the fast that I have chosen? to loose the bands of wickedness, to undo the heavy burdens, and to let the oppressed go free, and that ye break *every* yoke?" Are not those words in your text (Jonah iii. 10): "And God repented of the evil," &c., as well as those others: "And the Lord repented that he had made Saul king over Israel" (I Sam. xv. 35), in flagrant contradiction with another passage contained in the same chapter with the preceding, "the Strength of Israel will not lie nor repent: for He is not a man, that He should repent?" And as regards concessions in the Mosaic law, does it not allow and sanction in Deuteronomy (xvii. 14–20) what Samuel, in the name of God, repeatedly declares to be the greatest of sins (I Sam. viii. x., and xii.), I mean the desire to have a king? Rabbi, do you know the precise time when it had become sinful?

But I almost forgot our above-mentioned friend Job, the noblest conception of Hebrew poetry (at least according to the Talmudical: *Iyob lo hayah velo nibra,* "Job never existed"), whom you also stigmatize as a slaveholder, him, who utters those noble words—speaking of his *'ebed* (xxxi. 15), "Did not He that made me in the womb make him? and did not One fashion us in the womb?" If your assertion needs a refutation you can find it in the concluding passages of the Book of Job, in which you will find how the martyr was rewarded for his constancy, all his former possessions being restored double, his sheep, his camels, his oxen, and his she asses—but is there a word of slaves? So much for your proofs from passages of the Scriptures.

Another ample and general refutation of our Rabbi's view can be found in the history of the Hebrews as a nation, a history of fifteen centuries, full of wars, revolutions, civil strifes, and catastrophes, but without a mention of a single slave rising, or a single similar event. And how often do the Helots figure in Spartan history! how often slaves in the history of Rome! The history of this country, alas! has scarcely a page on which is not written the black word "Slavery." Shall its history be so continued? Answer, statesmen and people of America!

And you, Rev. Rabbi Raphall, make your Bible, by some process of reasoning, to be pure, just, and humane, if you want to have it regarded as divine; or reject it as full of human frailty, if you dare! *Shalom!*

M. HEILPRIN.[17]

New-York, Jan. 11, 1861.

128. FAREWELL TO THE UNITED STATES

Address by Judah P. Benjamin in the United States Senate, February 4, 1861 [1]

[Refusing to abide by the election of Lincoln, the slave and plantation owners who dominated the southern states began their attempt to disrupt the Union. South Carolina headed the secession parade on December 20, 1860; by February 1, 1861, Mississippi, Florida, Alabama, Georgia, Louisiana and Texas had fallen into line. Judah P. Benjamin, "a leader of the extreme Southern party in the Senate" and "one of the ablest and most eloquent defenders of the

Southern point of view on slavery and States' Rights,"[2] had already delivered an influential address in the Senate, advocating secession, on December 31, 1860, and had joined in a letter to a special Louisiana convention, urging immediate secession,[3] which was voted on January 26, 1861. On February 4th, the senior Senator from Louisiana, John Slidell, delivered a bristling farewell speech in which he explained, among other things, that the southern states could not assent to the inauguration of Lincoln and remain in the Union because their slaves would have regarded March 4th "as the day of their emancipation" and "servile insurrection" would have confronted the slave-owners. After Slidell, Benjamin rose to make the speech universally acclaimed by his supporters and often reprinted since then. In defense of slavery and secession, Benjamin speaks much of freedom, but that was the habit of Confederate oratory, and it must be remembered that the assassin of Lincoln accompanied his fatal shot with the demagogic cry, "Sic semper tyrannis!" Benjamin's final appeal to the verdict of history makes ironic reading, for history has found Benjamin guilty and his cause evil.

Judah Philip Benjamin (1811–1884), born in the British West Indies, was brought up in Charleston, educated at Fayetteville, N. C. and for a while at Yale, and arrived in New Orleans in 1828. He won eminence as a lawyer, Louisiana legislator, plantation and slaveowner, and United States Senator. Representing the interests of planters as well as of the commercial bourgeoisie, he "was a symbol of the union of interests which dominated Louisiana," according to Dr. Roger W. Shugg. It is the judgment of Benjamin's biographer, Professor Robert Douthat Meade, that when he delivered this farewell address Benjamin "had proved himself to be one of those politicians who followed rather than directed opinions and events," but that "his ability to foresee political change enabled him to appear to lead when he was really drifting with the current"; "he had not yet attained the proportions of a statesman" that he acquired later as Attorney-General, Secretary of War, Secretary of State of the Confederacy and confidential adviser to Jefferson Davis.[4]

His career taken as a whole is that of an opportunist of extensive abilities which were never linked with devotion to any great principle or cause.

His interest in Jewish life and his contact with the Jewish community were negligible; nevertheless, during the war, anti-Semites in the Confederacy and even in the Union used the fact that Benjamin was a Jew as a club with which to beat the Jews.]

MR. PRESIDENT, if we were engaged in the performance of our accustomed legislative duties, I might well rest content with the simple statement of my concurrence in the remarks just made by my colleague [Mr. Slidell]. Deeply impressed, however, with the solemnity of the occasion, I cannot remain insensible to the duty of recording, amongst the authentic reports of your proceedings, the expression of my conviction that the State of Louisiana has judged and acted well and wisely in this crisis of her destiny.[5]

Sir, it has been urged, on more than one occasion, in the discussions here and elsewhere, that Louisiana stands on an exceptional footing. It has been said that whatever may be the rights of the States that were original parties to the Constitution,—even granting *their* right to resume, for sufficient cause, those restricted powers which they delegated to the General Government in trust for their own use and benefit—still Louisiana can have no such right, because *she* was acquired by purchase. Gentlemen have not hesitated to speak of the sovereign States formed out of the territory ceded by France as property bought with the money of the United States, belonging to them as purchasers; and, although they have not carried their doctrine to its legitimate results, I must conclude that they also mean to assert, on the same principle, *the right of selling for a price that which for a price was bought.*

I shall not pause to comment on this repulsive dogma of a party which asserts the right of property in free-born white men, in order to reach its cherished object of destroying the right of property in slave-born black men—still less shall I detain the Senate in pointing out how shadowy the distinction between the condition of the servile African and that to which the white freeman of my State would be reduced, if it indeed be true that they are bound to this Government by ties that cannot be legitimately dissevered, without the consent of that very majority which wields its powers for their oppression. I simply deny the fact on which the argument is founded. I deny that the province of Louisiana, or the people of Louisiana, were ever conveyed to the United States for a price as property that could be bought or sold at will. Without entering into the details of the negotiation, the archives of our State Department show the fact to be, that although the domain, the public lands, and other property of France in the ceded province, were conveyed by absolute title to the United States, *the sovereignty was not conveyed otherwise than in trust.*

A hundred fold, sir, has the Government of the United States been reimbursed by the sales of public property, of public lands, for the price of the acquisition; but not with the fidelity of the honest trustee has it discharged the obligations as regards the sovereignty.

I have said that the Government assumed to act as trustee or guardian of the people of the ceded province, and covenanted to transfer to them the sovereignty thus held in trust for their use and benefit, as soon as they were capable of exercising it. What is the express language of the treaty?

"The inhabitants of the ceded territory *shall be incorporated in the Union* of the United States, and admitted *as soon as possible,* according to the principles of the Federal Constitution, to the enjoyment of *all* the rights, advantages, and immunities of citizens of the United States; and in the mean time they shall be maintained and *protected* in the enjoyment of their liberty, *property,* and the religion which they profess."

And, sir, as if to mark the true nature of the cession in a manner too significant to admit of misconstruction, the treaty stipulates no price; and the sole consideration for the conveyance, as stated on its face, is the desire to afford a strong proof of the friendship of France for the United States. By the terms of a separate convention stipulating the payment of a sum of money, the precaution is again observed of stating that the payment is to be made, not as a consideration or a price or a condition precedent of the cession, but it is carefully distinguished as being a consequence of the cession.[6] It was by words thus studiously chosen, sir, that James Monroe and Thomas Jefferson marked their understanding of a contract now misconstrued as being a bargain and sale of sovereignty over freemen. With what indignant scorn would those stanch advocates of the inherent right of self-government have repudiated the slavish doctrine now deduced from their action!

How were the obligations of this treaty fulfilled? That Louisiana at that date contained slaves held as property by her people through the whole length of the Mississippi Valley—that those people had an unrestricted right of settlement with their slaves under legal protection throughout the entire ceded province—no man has ever yet had the hardihood to deny. Here is a treaty promise to *protect* that property—that *slave property,* in that *Territory, before* it should become a State. That this promise was openly violated, in the adjustment forced upon the South at the time of the admission of Missouri,[7] is matter of recorded history. The perspicuous and unanswerable exposition of Mr. Justice Catron, in the opinion delivered by him in the Dred Scott case,[8] will remain through all time as an ample vindication of this assertion.

If then, sir, the people of Louisiana had a right, which Congress could not deny, of the admission into the Union with *all* the rights of *all* the citizens of the United States, it is in vain that the partisans of the right of the majority to govern the minority with despotic control, attempt to establish a distinction, to her prejudice, between her rights and those of any other State. The only distinction which really exists is this: that she can point to a breach of treaty stipulations expressly guarantying her rights, as a wrong superadded to those which have impelled a number of her sister States to the assertion of their independence.

The rights of Louisiana as a sovereign State, are those of Virginia; no more, no less. Let those who deny her right to resume delegated powers, successfully refute the claim of Virginia to the same right, in spite of her express reservation made and notified to her sister States when she consented to enter the Union. And, sir, permit me to say that, of all the causes which justify the action of the Southern States, I know none of greater gravity and more alarming magnitude than that now developed of the denial of the right of secession. A pretension so monstrous as that which perverts a restricted agency, constituted by sovereign States for common purposes, into the unlimited despotism of the majority, and denies all legitimate escape from such despotism, when powers not delegated are usurped, converts the whole constitutional fabric into the secure abode of lawless tyranny, and degrades sovereign States into provincial dependencies.

It is said that the right of secession, if conceded, makes of our Government a mere rope of sand; that to assert its existence imputes to the framers of the Constitution the folly of planting the seeds of death in that which was designed for perpetual existence. If this imputation were true, sir, it would merely prove that their offspring was not exempt from that mortality which is the common lot of all that is not created by higher than human power. But it is not so, sir. Let facts answer theory. For two thirds of a century this right has been known by many of the States to be, at all times, within their power. Yet, up to the present period, when its exercise has become indispensable to a people menaced with absolute extermination, there have been but two instances in which it has been even threatened seriously: the first, when Massachusetts led the New England States in an attempt to escape from the dangers of our last war with Great Britain; the second, when the same State proposed to secede on account of the admission of Texas as a new State into the Union.[9]

Sir, in the language of our declaration of secession from Great Britain it is stated, as an established truth, that "all experience has shown that mankind are more disposed to suffer while evils are sufferable, than to right themselves by abolishing the forms to which they have been accustomed." And nothing can be more obvious to the calm and candid observer of passing events than that the disruption of the Confederacy has been due, in great measure, not to the existence, but to the denial of this right. Few candid men would refuse to admit that the Republicans of the North would have been checked in their mad career, had they been convinced of the existence of this right, and the intention to assert it. The very knowledge of its existence, by preventing occurrences which alone could prompt its exercise, would have rendered it a most efficient instrument in the preservation of the Union. But, sir, if the fact were otherwise—if all the teachings of experience were reversed—better, far better, a rope of sand, ay, the flimsiest gossamer that ever glistened in the morning dew, than chains of iron and shackles of steel; better the wildest anarchy, with the hope, the chance, of one hour's inspiration of the glorious breath of freedom, than ages of the hopeless bondage and oppression to which our enemies would reduce us.

We are told that the laws must be enforced; that the revenues must be collected;[10] that the South is in rebellion without cause, and that her citizens are traitors.

Rebellion! The very word is a confession; an avowal of tyranny, outrage, and oppression. It is taken from the despot's code, and has no terror for other than slavish souls. When, sir, did millions of people, as a single man, rise in organized, deliberate, unimpassioned rebellion against justice, truth, and honor? Well did a great Englishman exclaim on a similar occasion:

"You might as well tell me that they rebelled against the light of heaven; that they rejected the fruits of the earth. Men do not war against their benefactors; they are not mad enough to repel the instincts of self-preservation. I pronounce fearlessly that no intelligent people ever rose, or ever will rise, against a sincere, rational, and benevolent authority. No people were ever born blind. Infatuation is not a law of human nature. When there is a revolt by a free people, with the common consent of all classes of society, there must be a *criminal* against whom that revolt is aimed."

Traitors! Treason! Ay, sir, the people of the South imitate and glory in just such treason as glowed in the soul of Hampden;[11] just such treason as leaped in living flame from the impassioned lips of [Patrick] Henry; just such treason as encircles with a sacred halo the undying name of Washington!

You will enforce the laws. You want to know if we have a Government; if you have any authority to collect revenue; to wring tribute from an unwilling people? Sir, humanity desponds, and all the inspiring hopes of her progressive improvement vanish into empty air at the reflections which crowd on the mind at hearing repeated, with aggravated enormity, the sentiments against which a Chatham launched his indignant thunders nearly a century ago. The very words of Lord North and his royal master are repeated here in debate, not as quotations, but as the spontaneous outpourings of a spirit the counterpart of theirs.

In Lord North's speech, on the destruction of the tea in Boston harbor, he said:

"We are no longer to dispute between legislation and taxation; *we are now only to consider whether or not we have any authority there*. It is very clear we have none, if we suffer the property of our subjects to be destroyed. We must punish, control, or yield to them."[12]

And thereupon he proposed to close the port of Boston, just as the Representatives of Massachusetts now propose to close the port of Charleston, *in order to determine whether or not you have any authority there*. It is thus that, in 1861, Boston is to pay her debt of gratitude to Charleston, which, in the days of her struggle, proclaimed the generous sentiment that "the cause of Boston was the cause of Charleston."[13] Who, after this, will say that Republics are ungrateful? Well, sir, the statesmen of Great Britain answered to Lord North's appeal, "yield." The courtiers and the politicians said, "punish," "control." The result is known. History gives you the lesson. Profit by its teachings.

So, sir, in the address sent under the royal sign-manual to Parliament, it was invoked to take measures "for better securing the execution of the laws," and acquiesced in the suggestion. Just as now, a senile Executive, under the sinister influence of insane counsels, is proposing, with your assent, "to secure the better execution of the laws," by blockading ports and turning upon the people of the States the artillery which they provided at their own expense for their own defense, and intrusted to you and to him for that and for no other purpose. Nay, even in States that are now exercising the undoubted and most precious rights of a free people; where there is no secession; where the citizens are assembling to hold peaceful elections for considering what course of action is demanded in this dread crisis by a due regard for their own safety and their own liberty; ay, even in Virginia herself, the people are to cast their suffrages beneath the undisguised menaces of a frowning fortress. Cannon are brought to bear on their homes, and parricidal hands are preparing weapons for rending the bosom of the mother of Washington.

Sir, when Great Britain proposed to exact tribute from your fathers against their will, Lord Chatham said:

"Whatever is a man's own is absolutely his own; no man has a right to take it from him without his consent. Whoever attempts to do it, attempts an injury. Whoever does it, commits a robbery. You have no right to tax America. I rejoice that America has resisted. . . .

"Let the sovereign authority of this country over the colonies be asserted in as strong terms as can be devised, and be made to extend to every point of legislation whatever, so that we may bind their trade, confine their manufactures, and exercise every power, *except that of taking money out of their own pockets without their consent.*"[14]

It was reserved for the latter half of the nineteenth century, and for the Congress of a Republic of freemen, to witness the willing abnegation of all power, save that of exacting tribute. What imperial Britain, with the haughtiest pretensions of unlimited power over dependent colonies, could not even attempt without the vehement protest of her greatest statesmen, is to be enforced in aggravated form, if you can enforce it, against independent States.

Good God! sir, since when has the necessity arisen of recalling to American legislators the lessons of freedom taught in lisping childhood by loving mothers; that pervade the atmosphere we have breathed from infancy; that so form part of our very being, that in their absence we would lose the consciousness of our own identity? Heaven be praised that all have not forgotten them; that when we shall have left these familiar Halls, and when force bills,[15] blockades, armies, navies, and all the accustomed coercive appliances of despots shall be proposed and advocated, voices shall be heard from this side of the Chamber that will make its very roof resound with the indignant clamor of outraged freedom. Methinks I still hear ringing in my ears the appeal of the eloquent Representative [Hon. George H. Pendleton, of Ohio], whose Northern home looks down on Kentucky's fertile borders: *"Armies, money, blood, cannot maintain this Union; justice, reason, peace, may."*[16]

And now to you, Mr. President [John C. Breckinridge of Kentucky], and to my brother Senators, on all sides of this Chamber, I bid a respectful farewell; with many of those from whom I have been radically separated in political sentiment, my personal relations have been kindly, and have inspired me with a respect and esteem that I shall not willingly forget; with those around me from the southern States, I part as men part from brothers on the eve of a temporary absence, with a cordial pressure of the hand and a smiling assurance of the speedy renewal of sweet intercourse around the family hearth. But to you, noble and generous friends, who, born beneath other skies, possess hearts that beat in sympathy with ours; to you, who, solicited and assailed by motives the most powerful that could appeal to selfish natures, have nobly spurned them all; to you who, in our behalf, have bared your breasts to the fierce beatings of the storm, and made willing sacrifice of life's most glittering prizes in your devotion to constitutional liberty; to you, who have made our cause your cause, and from many of whom I feel I part forever, what shall I, can I say? Nought, I know and feel, is needed for myself; but this I will say for the people in whose name I speak to-day: whether prosperous or adverse fortunes await you, one priceless treasure is yours—the assurance that an entire people honor your names, and hold them in grateful and affectionate memory. But with still sweeter and more touching return shall your unselfish devotion be rewarded. When, in after days, the story of the present shall be written; when history shall have passed her stern sentence on the erring men who have driven their unoffending brethren from the shelter of their common home, your names will derive fresh luster from the contrast; and when your children shall hear repeated the familiar tale, it will be with glowing cheek and kindling eye; their very souls will stand a-tiptoe as their sires are named, and they will glory in their lineage from men of spirit as generous and of patriotism as high-hearted as ever illustrated or adorned the American Senate.[17]

129. STANDING BY THE UNION

Editorial, "Stand by the Flag!" in *The Jewish Messenger*, New York, April 26, 1861

[On April 12, 1861, the Confederacy had fired on Fort Sumter; on April 14, the Fort surrendered. The following day Lincoln issued his call for volunteers to repel the aggression and preserve the Union. This editorial unequivocally supports that call. Although the majority of the voters of New York had not voted for Lincoln, and although New York was going to emerge more and more as a center of Copperheadism and of appeasement of the slaveholders, the first response was one of indignation at the attack and of support of the Union. *The Jewish Messenger* had already on January 25, 1861, editorially declared that "Israelites, as Israelites, have *no* politics. We exercise the high privileges of American citizens, and, as such, entertain, each for himself, what we may conceive just views on the questions of the day . . . Whatever betide, we are *for the Union* . . ." Now it reaffirmed its loyalty to the "*Union* and the *Constitution*" not because the editor understood that the democratic rights of the Jewish people, as of the country as a whole, would be undermined by a victory of the slaveowners, but on the general grounds of "patriotism." That the Jews had a particular stake in the defeat of slavery and the advance of industrial capitalism is at best only hinted at in the comment that the Union "extends its hearty invitation to the oppressed of all nations," including the Jews, and that the Constitution is "guaranteeing to all, the free exercise of their religious opinions."

The Jewish Messenger was the only Jewish periodical that wholeheartedly supported the Union. Its editor was Rev. Samuel Meyer Isaacs (1804–1878); born in Holland, he had lived for twenty-five years in England before coming to New York in 1839 as preacher and Hazan of Congregation B'nai Jeshurun. In 1847, when the Congregation split, Rev. Isaacs went with the new Orthodox Congregation Shaaray Tefilah. In 1857, he had founded *The Jewish Messenger,* and when *The Asmonean* ceased publication in 1858 the *Messenger* remained as the only weekly Jewish publication in the East and soon achieved a national circulation.

The *Messenger's* outspoken defense of the Union attracted favorable general attention, *The Independent,* an abolitionist weekly, for instance, recommending that it "might well be imitated by certain professedly Christian Editors, who . . . by continually discoursing the evil of war, passively sympathize with those who would overthrow the union."[1]]

It is almost a work of supererogation for us to call upon our readers to be loyal to the Union, which protects them. It is needless for us to say anything, to induce them to proclaim their devotion to the land in which they live. But we desire our voice, too, to be heard at this time, joining in the hearty and spontaneous shout ascending from the whole American people, to stand by the stars and stripes!

Already we hear of many of our young friends taking up arms in defence of their country,[2] pledging themselves to assist in maintaining inviolate its integrity, and ready to respond, if need be, with their lives, to the call of the constituted authorities, in the cause of law and order.

The time is past for forbearance and temporizing. We are now to *act,* and sure we are, that those whom these words may reach, will not be backward in realizing the duty that is incumbent upon them—to rally as one man for the *Union* and the *Constitution.* The Union—which binds together, by so many sacred ties, millions of freemen—which extends its hearty invitation to the oppressed of all nations, to come and be sheltered beneath its protecting wings—shall it be severed, destroyed, or even impaired? Shall those, whom we once called our brethren, be permitted to overthrow the fabric reared by the noble patriots of the revolution, and cemented with their blood?

And the Constitution—guaranteeing to all, the free exercise of their religious opinions—extending to all, liberty, justice, and equality—the pride of Americans, the admiration of the world—shall that Constitution be subverted, and anarchy usurp the place of a sound, safe, and stable government, deriving its authority from the consent of the American people?

The voice of millions yet unborn, cries out, "forbid it, Heaven!" The voice of the American people declares, in tones not to be misunderstood, "it shall not be!"

Then stand by the flag! What death can be so glorious as that of the patriot, surrendering up life in defense of his country,—pouring forth his blood on the battlefield—to live for ever in the hearts of a grateful people? Stand by the flag! Whether native or foreign born, Christian or Israelite, stand by it, and you are doing your duty, and acting well your part on the side of liberty and justice!

We know full well, that our young men, who have left their homes to respond to the call of their country, will, on their return, render a good account of themselves. We have no fears for their bravery and patriotism. Our prayers are with them. God speed them on the work which they have volunteered to perform!

And if they fall—if, fighting in defence of that flag, they meet a glorious and honorable death, their last moments will be cheered by the consciousness, that they have done their duty, and grateful America will not forget her sons, who have yielded up their spirit in her behalf.

And as for us, who do not accompany them on their noble journey, our duty, too, is plain. We are to pray to Heaven that He may restore them soon again to our midst, after having assisted in vindicating the honor and integrity of the flag they have sworn to defend; and we are to pledge ourselves to assume for them, should they fall in their country's cause, the obligation of supporting those, whom their departure leaves unprotected. Such is our duty. Let them, and all of us, renew our solemn oath that, whatever may betide, we will be true to the Union and the Constitution, and

Stand By The Flag!

130. THE CONFEDERATE "HOLY CAUSE"

Resolution of the Hebrew congregation, Shreveport, La., May, 1861 [1]

[In reply to *The Jewish Messenger's* editorial appeal for support of the Union, the Jews of Shreveport, La. resolved to "scorn and repel" the advice, affirmed their devotion to "our holy cause," and denounced the *Messenger* as "a black republican paper" and its editor as "an enemy to our interest and welfare" inciting them to treason. The Shreveport congregation, made up chiefly of German Jews, had been formed in 1857, although as early as 1848 there were about a dozen Jewish families in the city, most of them probably merchants and storekeepers whose economic ties were with the dominant plantation economy.[2] The Reverend Julius Lewin was the leader of the congregation.

The reaction of Southern subscribers to the *Messenger* who cancelled their subscriptions created serious financial difficulties for the periodical, which for a time changed from weekly to fortnightly publication, but Rev. S. M. Isaacs refused to change his course. Referring to the different policy of *The Israelite,* Isaacs wrote: "We are not disposed, like our Cincinnati contemporary, to seek to 'harmonise conflicting interests, and be neutral, so as not to injure our business connection in either section.' We conceive, there is no neutral ground, just now, and the loss of a portion of our subscribers shall not induce us to passively sympathise with those who would overthrow the UNION, which we love." To the Shreveporters' charge that he had abandoned religion for politics, Rev. Isaacs had replied: "We have always avoided politics. Nor shall we now give up our paper to political discussions. But this is not a political question. . . . We are not citizens of the North or of the South, we are not republicans or democrats, but loyal citizens of that great republic, which has ever extended a welcome to the oppressed, and has ever protected Israel."[3]]

Whereas, we received the "Jewish Messenger" of the 26th of April, a paper published in New York, in which an appeal has been made to all, whether native or foreign born, Christian or Israelite. An article headed "Stand by the Flag!" in which the editor makes an appeal to support the stars and stripes, and to rally as one man for the Union and the Constitution. Therefore be it

Resolved, That we, the Hebrew congregation of Shreveport, scorn and repel your advice, although we might be called Southern rebels; still, as law-abiding citizens, we solemnly pledge ourselves to stand by, protect, and honor the flag, with its stars and stripes, the Union and Constitution of the Southern Confederacy with our lives, liberty, and all that is dear to us.

Resolved, That we, the members of said congregation, bind ourselves to discontinue the subscription of the "Jewish Messenger,"[4] and all Northern papers opposed to our holy cause, and also to use all honorable means in having said paper banished from our beloved country.

Resolved, That while we mistook your paper for a religious one, which ought to be strictly neutral in politics, we shall from this out treat it with scorn, as a black republican paper, and not worthy of Southern patronage; and that, according to our understanding, church and politics ought never to be mingled, as it has been the ruination of any country captivated by the enticing words of preachers.

Resolved, That we, the members of said congregation, have lost all confidence and regard to the Rev. S. M. Isaacs, Editor and Proprietor of the "Jewish Messenger," and see in him an enemy to our interest and welfare, and believe it to be more unjust for one who preaches the Word of God, and to advise us to act as traitors and renegades to our adopted country, and raise hatred and dissatisfaction in our midst, and assisting to start a bloody civil war amongst us.

Resolved, That we believe like the Druids of old, the duties of those who preach the Holy Word to be first in the line of battle, and to cheer up those fighting for liberty against their oppressors, in place of those who are proclaiming now from their pulpits, words to encourage an excited people, and praying for bloody vengeance against us. Brutus, while kissing Caesar, plunged the dagger to his heart.

Resolved, That a copy of these resolutions be sent to the editor of the "Jewish Messenger."

Resolved, That papers friendly to the Southern cause, are politely requested to publish the foregoing resolutions.

M. Baer, *President.*

Ed. Eberstadt, *Secretary, pro tem.*

131. JEWISH BUSINESS INTERESTS IN CALIFORNIA

Article by Henry J. Labatt, in the *True Pacific Messenger,* San Francisco, May 24, 1861 [1]

[The Gold Rush having swept Jews too into its tide, Jewish groups and congregations appeared all over California in the 1850s, in the mining camps as well as the cities. San Francisco, San Diego, Sacramento and Stockton developed Jewish communities, and they were to be found in mining camps in Coloma, Eldorado County, Sonora, Marysville, Jesu Maria, Nevada City, Jackson, Grass Valley, Fiddletown, Shasta, and Folsom. The largest community was in San Francisco, in which the Jewish middle class expanded rapidly and consolidated its position. Henry J. Labatt, himself a lawyer and a commissioner of deeds for Louisiana (several Labatts had moved to San Francisco from New Orleans in 1849 and the early 1850s), ascribes this rise in commercial prominence to the ability of the Jewish merchants to work hard themselves, dispensing with clerks, to avoid ostentatious display, and especially to the practise of the theory that a rapid turnover even with a small profit per item will in the long run lead to substantial profits.

The exact status of the Jewish business interests in San Francisco at that time has not yet been described, but it may be suggestive that on February 1, 1861, when the *California* sailed east with a shipment of gold, among the 26 shippers were three Jewish firms, Ben Davidson (agent for the Rothschilds of London), sending $128,000, Levi Strauss & Co., clothing jobbers, sending $59,732.34, and J. Seligman & Co., clothing jobbers, sending $43,700.[2] More significant is an 1865 list of heavy tax-payers that includes the tax-assessments of Jewish firms in the following pattern: one firm with an assessment of over $300,000; one, over $150,000; one, over $100,000; one, over $80,000; three, over $70,000; three, over $60,000; two, over $50,000; eight, over $40,000; nine, over $30,000; eight, over $20,000; twenty, over $10,000. The firms named in this list were in the following lines of business: 15 dry goods jobbers, 7 clothing jobbers, 5 cigar and tobacco jobbers, 4 jewelry and watch jobbers, 3 gents' furnishing jobbers, 2 hat and cap jobbers, 2 carpet and upholstery jobbers, 2 in boots and shoes, 2 wholesale grocers, 2 insurance men, 2 merchants, one real-estate man, one banker, one mining-stock broker, one wholesale stationer, one hides and wools jobber, one crockery and glassware dealer, one willow-ware merchant.[3]

Labatt's belief that the expanding position of the Jewish bourgeoisie would lead to the disappearance of anti-Semitism was of course Utopian, since the very conditions of capitalist life were breeding anti-Semitism.]

On a first arrival in our city, it becomes a matter of astonishment to all who see the large number of mercantile houses conducted by Israelites, being much greater, in proportion to the commerce, than in any other city in America. Every line of business is engaged in by them, with credit to themselves and honor to the community.

Among the largest importers, rank foremost many Jewish firms, the prosperity of whose engagements is evident in the large returns which are made on every steamer day.

The influence they command upon the trade in the State, the weight of their transactions, and the generality of their mercantile callings, may well class them among the most useful, beneficial, and respectable merchants.

Each mining town and city has a large representation, and everywhere you hear of their success and prosperity, which in turn they devote to the improvement of the place, by erecting substantial buildings and warehouses for the increase of their business, caused by industry, economy, and attention.

In all the great fires which have devastated the settlements of California, they have been great sufferers.[4] Year after year, have they seen the hard earnings of their labor swept away by the ruthless conflagration, and yet, with the indomitable energy of their race, have they toiled on to regain what they thus were deprived of by misfortune. Often, indeed, would they not only lose what they had accumulated, but become reduced by being brought into debt by the destruction of their stock. Even this would not deter them.—The previous character which prudence and honesty had stamped upon them, created unmistakable confidence and sympathy, and they soon rose above these accidents.

Every where they seemed anxious to guard against this great affliction of our country and, by erecting substantial tenements, avoid another calamity.

In all commercial enterprises they keep pace with the marked improvements of the day, and, as merchants, are courted, admired—nay, even sometimes envied.

The almost universal success of the Jews, as merchants, in California, must be attributed to some peculiar reasons; for while many of all nations have succeeded in this State, yet, as a general thing, no class of people who began with so small a capital, have accumulated the same amount of fortune. Any close observer will find that their individual industry dispenses with the necessity for extra clerks, who, at the exorbitant rates necessary for their support, soon make sad inroads upon the monthly profit. They seldom pay unwarrantable rents, being willing to submit to many inconveniences rather than indulge in extravagance. They eschew all display of brilliant fixtures, or other unnecessary expenses, but study economy in every department of their business. Yet, after years of success, when they are conscious of their ability to display their wares and merchandise, then you may find a few who indulge in such outlays.

Their method of conducting business is also worthy of consideration. They seem anxious to dispose of their stock in a short time, and at little profit, and you will generally find throughout the country, that their stores are known as the "cheap stores." This is a great secret of trade; and when once that reputation is acquired, the custom will seek that store. For the most part, they first seek this enviable notoriety for their establishment, and then, by courtesy and a determination to give satisfaction, success seems inevitable; and what is thereby gained, economy secures.

Their quick perception gives them an insight into the requirements of every branch of trade, and when they once embark in it they are determined to call to their assistance every available faculty; and the natural sympathy of, and connection with, the other members of their faith, incite them to an emulation, the result of which is a high commercial position in the community.

Merchandise, from the time it is freighted on the clipper ships until it is consumed, passes principally through the hands of the Jewish merchants. As importers, jobbers, and retailers, they seem to monopolize most of the trade, and our business streets are thickly studded with their warehouses, shops, and stores. Their commercial position is high indeed, and without them now, trade would almost become stagnated in the State. The Express Companies of the interior depend mainly upon them for support, and the freight and package lists continually abound with their names. This position they have not acquired without great attention, honesty, industry, and personal sacrifice, and by unremitted prudence and civility; and they seem determined to add to it dignity and wealth.

This has had much influence in banishing the shameful prejudices otherwise existing against the Israelites, as a sordid and cunning race.[5] Practice and experience in California have taught our neighbors the falsity of these opinions. Nowhere in America is the Jew so well understood, and so readily appreciated, as in this State; and nowhere does he more deserve the respect and esteem of his fellow citizens. May it always be so. May this abandonment of those prejudices be as lasting as it is just; and the Jew, as he is just and honest, ever merit that esteem and regard which has been so long withheld from his nation, and which always the liberty of America, and the honesty of California, is willing to accord to his enterprise, civility, forbearance, and capability.

132. ABOLITIONIST FORCED TO FLEE

Rev. Dr. David Einhorn, "The Publisher's Departure from Baltimore," Philadelphia, June, 1861 [1]

[Courage and steadfast adherence to democratic principles are revealed in this personal account of how an active abolitionist and Reform rabbi was driven out of Baltimore by the threats of a pro-slavery mob. David Einhorn (1809–1879) had felt the whip of Austrian absolutism before he came to the United States, not only seeking his own freedom but enlisting at once in the cause for the extension of freedom to the slaves. Born in Bavaria and trained in a Talmudical academy, Einhorn early became a religious radical and leader of Reform Judaism in Central Europe. The counter-revolution that crushed the 1848 revolution also arrested Dr. Einhorn on the charge of preaching a political sermon in Pesth, Hungary, against Austrian oppression, in October, 1849. The government closed his office again in 1851. Finally, in 1855, he accepted a call to Baltimore and took charge of the Har Sinai Temple and Congregation, which he made into an outstanding Reform institution. At the same time, right in the heart of a slave state and in a city in which one-tenth of the population consisted of slaves, Dr. Einhorn at once proclaimed himself an abolitionist, and in the German-language monthly, *Sinai,* which he founded in February, 1856, repeatedly advocated emancipation. He hailed the birth of the "so-called Black Republican Party" and backed Fremont in 1856 as the best way to fight "the cancer of the Union," slavery. The supporters and appeasers of slavery among his own congregation found no comfort in his forthright sermons or articles. As he says towards the end of this account, he continually "defied the thick-headed, arrogant pride of money with deep contempt." After escaping from Baltimore, he continued his anti-slavery work in Philadelphia, for which he was elected an honorary member of the abolitionist Union League Club.[2]]

Though I am not so presumptuous as to claim any right to direct public attention to my personal affairs, it seems to me nevertheless appropriate to say a few words of explanation about the abovementioned move, for the nature of my work requires that I show the fundamental facts in their true light and combat the hateful distortions of the hostile press. At the very beginning of the present political ferment, I became keenly aware that the air of Baltimore had become too sultry for men who had moved to America in order to be able to speak and write freely, and to escape the rule of the lash. Truths which were only slightly related to the burning question of slavery lost their former harmless quality and began, whether expressed orally or in print, to frighten people, or even to be regarded as criminal. The bare mention of slavery in a sense not expressing southern views was looked upon as completely unheard of audacity that bordered on madness. With deepest sorrow I gradually became aware that even a part of my own congregation was infected with this fever—and to their honor it must be noted specifically that they were worried not merely about their own persons, but above all about the safety of their preacher or editor and the fellow members of the congregation. In fact, owing to the mortal enmity that certain persons in that city bore towards me, the worst was to be feared. It so happened that at that time the New York *Evening Post,* immediately after the appearance of Raphael's libel, printed, without my knowing it, an excerpt from a sermon published a short time before in *Sinai,* in which, without alluding to the political situation, I sharply emphasized that all men had been created in the image of God without distinction as to origin.[3] An attempt was then made to goad several Jews into a public declaration "that they did not belong to the congregation of this abolitionist preacher"; this attempt was all the more shameful because this New York paper is hardly read in Baltimore, and therefore at the bottom of this declaration there lay not so much fear as the malicious intention to direct public attention to my anti-slavery views and bring down a mob upon my neck! However, I was not frightened by this malevolence. Instead, in the February issue of this monthly,[4] I took upon myself the dreadful crime of presenting Judaism as unsullied by the brand of shame that the great Rabbi of New York had stamped upon it, to the delight of Jewish slaveowners and stockholders, when, with truly jesuitical zeal, he proclaimed the God of Israel as the God of slavery and denounced convictions about the unholiness of the southern institution as so much heresy. I was well aware that this would incite the utmost rage of my personal enemies, and was not at all surprised to hear that in the presence of a member of my congregation the following accusation was made about my rejoinder: "Only a guttersnipe could write that way!" However, I could not and would not keep silent in the face of such a defamation of Judaism, no matter what might follow. Therefore, at every available opportunity, I continued, both in *Sinai* and from the pulpit, to demonstrate the moral grandeur of the Mosaic *Principle* on this issue too, and also to show up the immorality of those "black-paint artists" who are masters of the art of "blackening" even the pure light of God. I felt particularly compelled to do so because in my own congregation there were some individuals who spoke enthusiastically about "Southern rights," who condemned the "Black Republicans" to the lowest depths of hell and exalted the "Black-dyers" to heaven. That my procedure, without in any way compromising with the truth, was also marked by circumspection, will be clear to the unprejudiced from these two facts: the way in which the aforementioned criticism of Raphael's speech defined the perilous question of the day, and the way I decisively rejected the offer of a New York friend to have the criticism appear in English in the "Tribune," although admission to the pages of the then pro-southern "Herald" would indeed have been welcome. On the other hand, in the presence of friends and acquaintances I openly declared my conviction that if Maryland left the Union [5] I should have no other choice than to lay down my post in Baltimore, for there would be more tolerance shown free speech even in Russia and Austria than in a seceded slave-state. Thus matters stood when the revolution broke out in Baltimore on the 19th of April, and the city was suddenly subjected to the reign of terror of an inflamed and raging mob, which immediately set to work to murder, pillage and burn at will, to sack unpopular establishments and presses, and to put out of the way citizens who were suspect because of their love for the Union or even because of "black-republican" sympathies.[6] I immediately resolved to take my family and possessions to Philadelphia within four or five days, but to return at once to my post and await the further course of events, or even, if I could find a reliable person to accompany my wife and children, not to leave the city at all. On the following day two leading members of my congregation came to my house; without being able to conceal their great anxiety, they urged me to leave the city with all possible speed, for I had been personally threatened, since I was already identified as the editor of a "black-republican" paper whose press had in fact been destroyed that same day.[7] When I replied that I could not possibly desert my post in this manner, I was assured that my congregation begged me to go away for the present and that they would recall me at the proper time. Later a soldier transmitted the same urgent warning to me several times, and on the evening of the 21st of April several friendly young men came to my house, armed, in order to protect my family and myself as much as possible against any attack during the night, since they had heard that my name was underscored on the proscribed list. Under these circumstances I believed I owed it not merely to my family, which was greatly upset, and also to my congregation to yield to the pleas for my withdrawal, especially since from all that had occured I could not help being convinced that under the prevailing conditions a considerable part of the congregation would receive my sermons with fear and trembling for their own safety as well as for mine. Therefore on the afternoon of the 22d of April, I started with my family on the journey to Philadelphia. From this city, a few days after my arrival I informed the president [8] of the Har-Sinai Congregation by letter of my intention to return to Baltimore as soon as I was recalled. Later I learned, from published reports as well as from private communications from the president of the Congregation and various other friends that orderly conditions again prevailed in Baltimore, but I desired an official answer in order to feel certain that my congregation too was again prepared fearlessly to receive the true doctrine from the lips of their teacher. Only the compulsion not to leave my congregation without a sermon during the Feast of Weeks, which had in the meantime drawn near,[9] caused me to suppress this desire and make arrangements for my return. However, רבות מחשבות בלב איש ועצת י׳ תקום. [Prov. xix, 21: "There are many devices in a man's heart; but the counsel of the Lord, that shall stand."] I became ill and, despite the best of intentions, I had to put the trip off. Then on the day before the Feast of Weeks I received the following reply:

Baltimore, May 12, 1861.

Rev. Dr. Einhorn, Philadelphia.

Dear Doctor: At the meeting of the Congregation this morning, called to lay before it your esteemed communication of the 30th of the month (received only on the 4th because of the irregularity of the mails) and to inform you of the result of our deliberations, we were directed in the name of the congregation to inform you as follows: that for several weeks peace and order have prevailed here, and everything is quiet now; that the majority of the congregation, as you may well believe without specific assurance, both mourn your absence and long for your return. To be sure, in these days, when sections are ranged against one another in a spirit of hostile preparedness, no one knows what change a single day and an unforeseen event may bring to pass here too, and much as the congregation might like to, it does not feel justified in speaking of the future with assurance. At the same time we have been directed in behalf of the congregation, dear Doctor, most respectfully to propose to you that it would be very desirable, both for the sake of your own safety and out of regard for that of the members of the congregation, if in the future you will avoid everything in the pulpit that touches upon the explosive questions of the day, and we beg you to attribute this observation only to our unhappy condition. Finally we beg you, dear Doctor, to be so kind as to accept the assurance of our complete respect and esteem.

(There follow the signatures of the secretary and president of the congregation.)

P. S. Please inform us when we may expect you.

After receiving this communication I could not for one moment doubt what course to take. According to the view of the congregation therein proclaimed, I as their minister had to choose between doing injury to the truth and capitulating to the security of the members. I did not hesitate to choose a third course: the immediate relinquishing of a post that carried lifelong tenure. On the 16th of May my resignation, to take effect at the end of the month, was sent to Baltimore, although I had not had the slightest premonition of the telegraphic communication, delivered a few hours later, wherein a braver congregation unanimously and in the most respectful manner called me to be their Rabbi.[10] Under these circumstances I was compelled to forego directing even so much as a single word of farewell to my congregation. It is painful to be forced to depart under such conditions from a post occupied for almost six consecutive years, a post in which I encountered not only much hate but much love; nevertheless, I leave with the pleasant consciousness of having brought to a conclusion in no unworthy manner a significant period of effectiveness in office that brought me hatred and love only in consequence of honest struggle for the welfare of my congregation and the honor of Israel, that permitted me to sow many a seed that some day will bear fruit and that also succeeded in winning in other congregations a recognition of my efforts that expressed itself brilliantly in these very last few days.

No one will expect me to waste so much as a word over the nonsense of a pious children's magazine appearing in New York that was sent me a few weeks ago by a good-natured friend. This paper chants notes of joy over the circumstance that a heretic who had protested against the Board of Delegates had, because of his political sermons, been dismissed by the citizens of Baltimore with only a few hours notice and now was wandering about (probably in the woods) in the vicinity of Philadelphia.[11] A sinner may be compelled קול עלה נדף [Lev. xxvi, 36: "and the sound of a driven leaf shall chase them"] to tremble at the sound of a rustling leaf but never at that of a driveling leaflet or ignorant little Hazan. Only in reference to the statement, "that the Jews of Baltimore will rejoice in the banishment of the heretic," let it be noted that it makes little difference to me if a part of the same are glad to be rid of one who denounced the orthodox consecration of incestuous marriage, who scourged the sabbath-profaning Jekum-Purkan-heroes,[12] who beat back unprovoked villainous attacks upon himself and his congregation with devastating effectiveness, and defied the thick-headed, arrogant pride of money with deep contempt. On the other hand, whether I at any time sought personal strife with anyone, whether I did not completely ignore many shocking occurrences in the camp of the enemy that other papers triumphantly seized upon, as well as suffer in silence all too many personal affronts out of consideration for mutually beneficial institutions—in all this I can confidently allow the better part of the Jews of Baltimore, in and out of my congregation, to judge.

Philadelphia, May 1861.

The Publisher.

133. AIDING SOLDIERS' FAMILIES

Letter, "Assist the Families of our Soldiers!" Washington, D. C., June 23, 1861 [1]

[The anonymous writer of this letter proposes the establishment of a fund to aid the families of Jewish soldiers who had enlisted in Washington, D. C. How many such persons there were, he does not state,[2] but he describes the volunteers as mostly "mechanics . . . earning for themselves and families a comfortable living," but their families are now "in abject want." Since the base pay of the private was then $11 per month, the need for additional aid was obvious. Even when the pay was increased on August 6, 1861 to $13 per month, $2 was retained until the enlistment ended, to ensure the good conduct of the volunteer![3]

The Jewish congregation in Washington, founded in 1852 with twenty-one families affiliated, had grown to 55 by 1855, and was described by the same correspondent as "large and rapidly increasing" in the fall of 1861.[4] What results the appeal brought are not known; the matter is not again mentioned in the *Messenger* for that year.]

Editors of the "Jewish Messenger."

When the first alarm was sounded in this city, there were a number of our co-religionists belonging to the organized military companies, who immediately responded to the call, and were sworn in for the war. Most of them are mechanics, and were earning for themselves and families a comfortable living. They felt a patriotic pride, *as Jews,* to sustain the government they had sworn allegiance to, and in their enthusiasm did not weigh the chances, as possibly they should have done, of how, and by what means their families were to be supported during their enlistment. The danger to our city was too imminent to be weighed in a scale with mere dollars and cents for the balance, and hence, with pride be it said, *they* at least were not influenced by any sordid motive. Unlike you in New York, we have no fund to support the families of poor soldiers, and the unhappy consequence is, the wives and the children of these poor men are in *abject want.* The very few here, who are disposed to give, have done all that lies in their power, but the limited relief afforded has done but little to alleviate their sufferings.

The men, like true soldiers, say, they willingly undergo every and any deprivation, but they feel it hard, indeed, as only our people *can* feel, to see those they love, and who have a right to look to them for their support, suffer for the *necessaries of life*. Those who have small families will be able to eke out a scanty living, as soon as the Government pay them their pittance, but a majority of them have large families, who are in want, and must *continue* to want, unless the large-souled liberality of your people come forward to relieve them. And that they *will* come forward, my past experience assures me.

They cannot well give to a better cause, and they may rest assured, every dollar will be frugally and well expended.

The Editors of the *Messenger* have kindly consented to forward donations, and acknowledge the same in their paper, and will guarantee a faithful disposition of the monies so forwarded.

Let the response to this reluctant appeal be immediate, and worthy of the proverbial liberality of the great City of New York.

SEMI-OCCASIONAL.

Washington, D. C. June 23rd, 1861.

134. INFLUENCING BRITISH OPINION

a) Letter from August Belmont in New York to Baron Lionel de Rothschild, M. P., in London, May 21, 1861 [1]

[During the Civil War, the main strategic objective of the Lincoln administration in its foreign policy was to keep the British government, and hence other European governments, from supporting the Confederacy, and to persuade European capitalists not to lend monies to the Confederacy. Although in England it was the loyal support of the Union by the working-class that was decisive in shaping the Government's policy, other factors contributed to the result. One of these was the influence exerted by August Belmont upon the Rothschilds, and through them upon public opinion and the Government. The *Dictionary of American Biography* estimates that Belmont's "most valuable service, perhaps, was a constant correspondence with influential friends in Europe, the Rothschilds and others, in which he set forth forcibly the Northern side in the great conflict. . . . His influence upon public opinion in financial and political circles, both in England and throughout Continental Europe, was of value to Lincoln and his advisers."[2]

By 1861, August Belmont (1816–1890) had already made his mark in banking, politics, and diplomacy. Born into the family of a wealthy landowner in the Rhine-Hesse, Germany, he had entered the employ of the Rothschilds in Frankfurt as a boy. He came to New York during the crisis of 1837, and set up his own firm, August Belmont and Company, but continued to act as Rothschild's American agent. By 1844, he was active in the Democratic Party, and soon became one of its heavy financial backers. Between 1845 and 1855 his estimated capital doubled, from $100,000 to $200,000. In 1845, he became the Provisional Consul General of Austria in New York, Pennsylvania, New Jersey, Delaware, Maryland, Virginia, and the District of Columbia, and in 1848 he was made Consul General for these states. He resigned in 1850, in protest against the Austrian government's terror against the 1848 revolutionaries and particularly against Kossuth. For political services rendered in the election of President Franklin Pierce, Belmont sought a diplomatic post in Naples, where he believed his connections with the Rothschilds would help the administration take over Cuba; instead, Pierce commissioned him Chargé d'Affaires at the Hague on May 24, 1853, and advanced him to the rank of Minister Resident, June 29, 1854, in which post Belmont served until September 22, 1857. As a leading Democratic political backer, Belmont actively supported the Democratic administrations from Polk to Buchanan, each of which, according to Professor Roy Franklin Nichols, "sought to offset the negative qualities of their laissez-faire, do-nothing views on domestic issues with a swashbuckling spread-eagle foreign policy." In 1847, Belmont had, as an agent for the Rothschilds, helped finance the war of aggression against Mexico. He was for annexation of Cuba and expansion into Latin America. His funds were ever-ready to aid Buchanan follow an expansionist policy. In 1860, he was therefore elected Chairman of the Democratic National Committee, and served in that capacity until 1872. On the issue of slavery, he opposed the abolitionists, supported Douglas against Lincoln, and even, as he explained in this letter to Lionel de Rothschild, advocated allowing the Confederacy to secede. Belmont's efforts at this early period of the war in behalf of the Lincoln administration therefore reflect the pressure of the tremendous and unified mass support that rallied to Lincoln at the firing on Fort Sumter.[3]

Belmont's connection with Jewish affairs was negligible, but he did serve as a target for those who sought to spice their opposition to his politics with the sauce of anti-Semitism. In 1849, he had married Caroline Slidell Perry, niece of John Slidell, Democratic leader from Louisiana, and daughter of the Commodore Perry who was then opening up Japan for American trade. Miss Perry was an Episcopalian. In 1853, when he was appointed to his post in Holland, nativist Whigs attacked the selection because Belmont was foreign-born and a Jew. To one such attack, *The Asmonean* could find no better response than to deny that Belmont was a Jew because he had intermarried! On other occasions, however, when Belmont appeared in the press in a favorable light, other Jewish periodicals claimed him for their own.[4]

This letter of Belmont's is a forceful and telling exposition of the Union's stand on the civil war, and an able refutation of Confederate arguments, especially as they were advanced by their agents in England. When the political leader Thurlow Weed sent a copy of the letter to Secretary of State William H. Seward, the latter was so impressed with it that he showed it to Lincoln, whom it also pleased. On May 27, 1861, Seward wrote to Belmont, thanking him for having written to Rothschild; Seward added that he had taken the liberty of copying the letter, because "it contains some suggestions which may prove useful to me in the discussion of the subject you have so ably treated."]

To Baron LIONEL de ROTHSCHILD, M.P.,[5]
London.

New York, May 21, 1861.

DEAR BARON,—The telegraphic report of Lord John Russell's declaration in Parliament, on the 6th inst., concerning Southern privateers,[6] has created a painful surprise and disappointment throughout the whole North.

In placing them upon the footing of *belligerents,* the English government takes an initiative step toward recognizing the Southern Confederacy, because the letters of marque of an unauthorized and unrecognized government, in rebellion against the constituted authorities, can, under the law of nations, only be regarded by every maritime power as pirates, and treated accordingly.

If Ireland or Scotland should revolt against the British crown, or Canada attempt to dissolve her allegiance to the mother country, would the United States be justified in recognizing the privateers fitted out by the rebels, as belligerents? I am sure that our government would not assume such an unfriendly position, and give so material a support to a rebellious province, in endangering the trade of its allies, and of the world at large.

With the blockade of the Southern ports,[7] which before a fortnight can have elapsed will be an effective one, from the Chesapeake to the Rio Grande, the privateers of Jeff. Davis would have soon disappeared from the ocean, even if they ever made their appearance, had the declaration of Lord John not opened to them the British ports in the West Indies, Canada, and Great Britain.

It may be that the British government will not condemn any prizes brought by the privateers into its ports, but the fact of their being allowed to run in for supplies and coal, and to escape into the many ports and inlets of the West Indies, where our ships of war cannot follow them, will attract numerous lawless adventurers under the piratical flag of the Southern rebels.

The position which your government seems inclined to take in the contest, is, in my opinion, a very unfortunate one. It will complicate matters, must prolong the struggle, and result in a very bitter feeling between this country and England.

The whole North, without distinction of party, is determined not to allow our government and our Union to be destroyed, and I am sure the sword will never be laid down until the American flag floats again from Maine to the Mississippi. The people feel that they are fighting for their national existence, and that no sacrifice can be too great in order to maintain and preserve that boon.

What the South claims now is for us to give up every port, from the Chesapeake to the Mississippi, to a foreign power, which has shown sufficiently within the last few months how far public and private property and obligations are to be respected by it.[8]

In the struggle which is before us we had hoped for the sympathy of Europe, and particularly of England. Your statesmen and your press have at all times taken the most violent and uncompromising stand against slavery, and it is more than strange to see the British government now give its moral countenance to a power which, under the declaration of its Vice-President (Alex. Stephens) is based upon *slavery* as its principal fundamental strength.[9] That basis will most probably require the reopening of the slave trade, as soon as England shall have recognized the Confederacy, and should in that event the sympathy of the British cabinet stop short, and not allow the *cotton-growers* to strengthen the foundations of their government, then Mr. Jeff. Davis will of course put an embargo upon the export of cotton,[10] in order to compel England to consent to the nefarious traffic in human flesh. He could certainly not be charged with a want of logic, by reasoning that the same power which induced England to throw her weight into the scale of a rebellious slave power, trying to overthrow our free institutions, would also be sufficiently potent to compel her to consent to the Confederacy drawing its supplies from Africa, of an element which the founders of that Confederacy had openly declared to the civilized world to be the basis of this young creation, claiming rank among the civilized nations of the world.

Some few months back there were many conservative men at the North, and I was among the number, who, when all attempts at compromise had failed against the blind ultraism of both sections, advocated a peaceable separation of the *cotton States.*[11] This was, however, to be confined to them alone, and was then considered the surest means of an early reconstruction, when the Union feeling in the misguided States would have had time and opportunity to develop itself, by showing to the people of those States how fatally they were mistaken in their hopes of prosperity outside of the Union.

Things have, however, changed very materially since. The attack upon Fort Sumter, the lawless acts of the Southern Confederacy, the treason in Virginia and Tennessee,[12] have placed every loyal citizen to the choice between a firm and manful support of our government, or a disgraceful drifting of our nationality into a state of anarchy and dissolution, similar to the fate of Mexico and Central America.

Lord John Russell draws an analogy of the Southern rebellion to the struggle for independence by Greece, and asserts that because England recognized Greece then as a belligerent, the South has to be recognized now by her in the same character. Greece was a conquered and enslaved *province* of a semi-barbarous despotism, and had never been completely subjugated. It was a Christian people, tyrannized by fanatical Moslemism, and had the warm and active sympathy of the whole civilized world on its side.

The Southern States, who are now in a state of rebellion against the Federal government, were free and voluntary parties to a compact of union, which was declared to be perpetual. They cannot point to a single right guaranteed to them by the Constitution, which has been violated, and the only ground upon which they justify their rebellion, is the *fear* that their peculiar institution of slavery may hereafter be interfered with by the party which put Mr. Lincoln into power.

I am free to say that the simile of Lord John is as unfortunate as the position which he has initiated for his government in this crisis. The British cabinet will, if this course should be persisted in, commit the fatal error of losing the good will of the party *which in the end must be successful,* in order to gain the friendship of those whose defeat can only be a question of time. We have three times as large a population, as united and brave as theirs; we have a navy, we have money and credit, in which latter they are most sadly and justly deficient.

Already, Davis is again in the market with a loan of fifty millions of dollars.[12a] Who will loan a dollar to a confederacy of States, of which four have already repudiated their debts, while the remaining five will in less than three months be in default of their semi-annual dividends, unless it be that the name of Jeff. Davis, notwithstanding his advocacy of repudiation in his own State, Mississippi, should have a sweeter sound to European capitalists, than I think he will ever acquire. In less than a year the Confederate States will pay their obligations in treasury warrants, which will have the same ultimate value as the French "assignats."

You know that I have never been in favor of the party which is now at the head of our government, and my convictions on this point have in no way been changed. I am, however, convinced that the whole North, to a man, will stand by the administration in the present struggle, and that *come what may,* the integrity of the Union, and the inviolability of our territory, will be maintained to the bitter end.

Civil war is now upon us; no human power can prevent it. A vigorous and gigantic effort, on the part of the North, may, and I am confident will, shorten its horrors and disastrous results. An interference or one-sided neutrality, such as is foreshadowed by Lord John Russell's speech, can only prolong the fratricidal war, and entail ruin, not only upon both sections of our country, but upon the material interests and commerce of the world.

[August Belmont]

b) Letter from August Belmont, in Germany, to Secretary of the Treasury Salmon P. Chase in Washington, D. C., August 15, 1861 [13]

[On July 17, 1861, Belmont had sailed for England, ostensibly only to join his wife and family for a few months in Europe, but also on certain unofficial missions for the Lincoln Administration. On a visit to Washington in the middle of June, Belmont had had an interview with Secretary of State William H. Seward and perhaps also with Secretary of the Treasury Chase. In a letter to Chase on July 3, 1861, Belmont had offered secretly to undertake to negotiate a loan in Europe. Arriving in London on July 28, 1861, Belmont had an hour's interview the following evening with Lord Palmerston, the British Prime Minister, and on July 30, Belmont sent a lengthy account of his conversation to Seward. Then Belmont went to the Continent, first to Paris and Frankfort, and then to Schlangenbad, in the area of his birth, from which he wrote this letter to Chase, reporting his estimate both of political and financial attitudes to the Union. Chase's reply of September 13, 1861 indicates what close attention he gave to some of Belmont's views, but also reflects Chase's satisfaction with the success of his domestic bond issues, so that he can write that "the condition of the foreign market possesses less interest than it would in a different condition of affairs." Belmont's opinion about the effect of the protectionist high tariff on European capitalist opinion, Chase as a confirmed Republican ignored.[14]]

Private August Belmont
Schlangenbad (By Nassau) [Germany]
August 15: 1861

My dear Sir:

I arrived here a few days ago after having passed a few days in London, Paris & Frankfort AM in all of which places I saw several leading political & financial representative men with whom I had opportunities to confer freely on the all absorbing state of our affairs. In a letter from London I communicated to Governor Seward the substance of a very long conversation I had with Lord Palmerston & I cannot but repeat here the conviction, which that interview left upon my mind, viz: that it was absolutely necessary for our Government, that we should with all possible dispatch render the blockade of our southern ports *in the strictest sense of the word "effective"*. From the manifold questions, objections & quibbles of the British Premier I am convinced that England will seize the first chance in order to justify by some shallow excuse the forcing of our blockade, and I am sorry to say that the French Government [15] under the influence of the Cotton interest & I fear also of the reports of its diplomatic agents in America is very much inclined the same way, at least for the present. Our last high tariff has also a good deal to do with this state of feeling on the part of the great powers of Western Europe. One of the closing remarks of Lord Palmerston to me was: "We do not like Slavery, but we want Cotton & and we do not like your tariff."[16]

A good deal of mischief has also been done of late in England by the sensation articles of the New York Herald, advocating a war with

England & the taking of Canada. The articles alienate the sympathies of a good many, the Herald's influence being very much exaggerated in Europe, and they are used by the London Times as a welcome excuse for onslaughts against our Government & people.[17] I think the influence of the Administration might be very profitably exerted toward preventing the publication of such hostile articles against European Governments, which in our present position can only produce mischief.

I am very glad to see that some of our leading papers have contradicted the mischievous rumors spread by the New York Daily News [18] that I had been sent on by your Department for the purpose of negociating a large Government loan abroad. These rumors had found their way to England & upon my arrival there I found myself assailed by questions on all sides. Lord Palmerston among others asked me, where the U. S. Government expected to get all the money necessary for the prosecution of the war to which I replied that I supposed we would do like all other borrowers & try to get it where it could be obtained cheapest, but that apart from that consideration there seemed to me a strong inclination on the part of our people to avoid if possible foreign loans. The time & prospect for a negociation in London are not at all propitious–the English seem delighted with the position of neutrality assigned to them by the Queen & think also that by withholding their funds they may force us into a compromise & a consent to a separation. The British cabinet undoubtedly would like to see the latter whatever the antislavery proclivities of the majority of the English people may be.[19] In France & Germany [20] the feeling for the justice of the North & the maintenance of the Union is very general, and I have yet to meet the first person, who entertains an unfriendly sentiment to the Federal Government. If our army & navy shall be placed upon a more efficient footing & the supremacy of our strength in any way demonstrated, which I have no doubt it will soon be, there will be no difficulty in negociating very large amounts of our Securities on the Continent of Europe. A 5 or 6% stock payable in France or England will however find at a proportionate rate more favor with European Capitalists than a 7% stock. There is an immense deal of floating capital now in Europe & the subscriptions latterly opened for loans in the way, which I suggested to you, in case of a foreign negociation, by my letter from Newport,[21] have given the most unprecedented results. The french Government for a call of 5% stock to the amount of fr 150 Millions for the consolidation of its Railways received the extraordinary amount of fr *2000* Millions, say abt 14 times the sum required, subscribed for—the New Kingdom of Italy, not yet recognized by several of the Continental Governments [22] & threatened still by complications of all Kind, opened subscriptions for a 5% loan of fr 500 Millions at about 7% at which rate, barely more than 1% below the quotations of the 5% Piemontese Rente, over fr 1000 Millions were subscribed for in Italy, France, England & Germany. Any successful movement of our Navy & Army on any of the Southern ports such as Savannah, Charleston or New Orleans, besides probably disorganizing to a certain extent the large Rebel force in Virginia, would tend to restore our lost prestige [23] in Europe & facilitate very much any financial negociation which you may contemplate hereafter.

I intend to return to Paris very shortly, and if you have any thing to communicate your letters addressed to the care of de Rothschild Brothers [24] there will reach me.

Yours: very truly

August Belmont

To the Honble S. P. Chase
Washington

135. AID TO THE POOR

Annual Report to the Ladies' Hebrew Relief Sewing Association of Philadelphia, by the Recording Secretary, Isaac M. Long, December 3, 1861 [1]

[One evening a week the members of this Relief Sewing Association met in a room in the synagogue of Congregation Rodeph Shalom in order to sew garments for the poor and to make bandages for the war wounded. The membership of over 300 women made possible the distribution in the course of the year of only about $800 in cash, but to this was added about 1,000 articles of clothing and a couple of thousand yards of cloth, as well as some free medical attention. Thus did those who came from "happy homes and cheerful firesides" seek vainly through private charity to meet the great public evil of poverty in our social system.]

To the Hon. President, and the Members of the Ladies' Hebrew Relief Sewing Association:

The following report is most respectfully submitted:

Our Association has passed the first year of its existence.[2] We are assembled for purposes concerning its welfare, and I am pleased to announce the triumphant success which our organization has attained, especially as we have labored under many difficulties. The year which has just ended, is without parallel in the history of want and suffering, and the worst of calamities, a civil war pervades our land; it has thrown distress and want in our midst, and we have experienced a wide field, in which to spread the welcome hand of aid and comfort. Our co-religionists have also increased largely, and among them distress has left a bitter mark.[3]

You who enjoy pleasant homes and cheerful firesides cannot realize the existing want and suffering, which surround you. The earth is like a sea, many being thrown upon the tumultuous billows of life, without a mite for their comfort. To be kind and charitable are attributes of our national character; thus inspired were all those, who so cheerfully responded to the call for the formation of our society, and beyond expectations have we been successful.

Our weekly meetings have been invariably well attended, while a spirit of ardor and cheerfulness prevailed. A large amount of work had been prepared—the same distributed to the deserving poor by competent visiting committees. Patriotism has also found its way among us. Having kind remembrances for those brave ones, we have sacrificed all for their country's honor, extra meetings have been held and a large quantity of lint and bandages manufactured for the sick and wounded of those regiments which have been the recipients of the same.

Especially would I call your attention to the untiring efforts of the "Committee on Donations", who spared no pains in accumulating as large an amount as possible, which, in these stringent times, has been a fact, bordering on impossibility. We reside in a country, where religious persecution is unknown, and thankful to those who have lent us a helping hand, even persons not of our persuasion, have received what aid we found it in our power to bestow.

Your Board of Directors [4] have used every effort for the promotion and welfare of the Society. Several vacancies having occurred by resignations, the same have been filled by regular elections—and in all particulars the utmost discretion has been adopted. Nothing has been done conflicting with similar institutions, but a spirit of co-operation has always been advised with the kindred feeling that in UNION there is power.

The resignation of the President, *Mrs. S. Sternberger,* is to be regretted. It is evident that it was her desire to see the Society prosper, and to that end she exerted herself with a zeal seldom manifested. She well merits the kindest wishes and thanks of the Association.

The Association, under the supervision of your Board of Directors, have distributed the following to the deserving poor of the city:—856 finished Garments, 150 pairs of Shoes, 75 pairs of Hose,[5] 20 heavy blankets, 2,283 yards of Calico, Flannel &c., and 12 entire suits of Boys' Clothes.

This will be found a very flattering result for a Society having but just reached the end of the first year. It is also proper to state that the greatest care has been taken, in order to avoid any deception on the part of applicants while at the same time all who were actually in need, received plentifully.

Dr. J. Solis Cohen[6] kindly tendered his professional services; he attended to many poor invalids. He deserves the hearty thanks and approbation of the Association. The receipts for regular dues have reached the amount of $551—this would have been somewhat more had not several delinquencies occured on the part of members failing to pay their regular dues.

The amount of Donations received in cash was $455, besides a large amount of Merchandise. This, it is evident, has been a helping hand to our Association, and it is to be hoped, that the success will be equally as great in the forthcoming year.

The entire outlay during the year has been $844 55, leaving a balance on hand of $151 45.

Our members at present number three hundred and nine. The accessions to the roll have been quite numerous during the year, and it is to be hoped that the same will not be diminished. All should exert themselves to the utmost, and in no instance should the payment of dues be neglected. It is to be hoped that every member will assist in increasing the numerical strength of our Association.

Compare your happy homes and cheerful firesides, to the dreary and unprotected homes of the poor. You, who have not witnessed the ravages of that stern agent "want", cannot realize the horrors of destitution. The object of our Association is a noble one—*"to alleviate in part the suffering surrounding us."* We should be infinitely thankful to an almighty power, for placing in our hands the means of doing good. We have been successful, and our labors have merited the most flattering results. How many homes (for years the scene of poverty and degradation) have been revived and made cheerful through our agency. After witnessing such scenes can any one hesitate in offering up his mite on the great altar of charity! We must obey a high ordeal, let us do it cheerfully.

Our Association is about to enter a new period of its existence. Let us hope that success may light its path, and that it may yet rank first among the Jewish Charitable Institutions of the country.

ISAAC M. LONG,

Recording Secretary.

136. JEWISH CHAPLAINS IN THE UNION ARMY

Statement submitted to the United States Senate Committee on Military Affairs and the Militia, by Rev. Dr. Arnold Fischel, December, 1861 [1]

[When Congress on July 22 and August 3, 1861 legislated for the appointment of Chaplains in the Union Army, the law contained the unfortunate sectarian provision that the Chaplain "must be a regular ordained minister of some Christian denomination." When, in debate on July 12, Representative Clement L. Vallandigham of Ohio, an obstreperous opponent of the war and later the leader of the "copperhead" sabotage of the war effort, pointed out that Congress would be discriminating against the Jews in this measure, no attention was paid to his objection.[2] Two lines of conduct developed in the Jewish community. Those like Rev. Dr. Isaac Mayer Wise of Cincinnati, who opposed the war, at first did very little about changing this legislation because they could then agitate it as an additional "reason" for discouraging Jewish support of the war.[3] Those loyal to the Union and the war, however, speedily set about bringing pressure to bear on Congress to abolish the discrimination, and quickly succeeded. It should also be noted that the Confederate Congress, while in theory the comparable legislation did not exclude Jews from the Chaplaincy, in practice never included Jews in this post—and the Jews of the Confederacy never publicly raised the issue.[4] The result was that there were no Jewish Chaplains in the Confederate Army, while they were appointed to the Union Army.

In this statement to the Senate Committee, Dr. Fischel was acting as the agent of the Board of Delegates of American Israelites, which had on December 4th designated him to lobby for a change in the law. But Dr. Fischel also had a personal interest in the problem. In October, the officers of the 65th Regiment of the 5th Pennsylvania Cavalry, known as "Cameron's Dragoons" after Simon Cameron, Secretary of War, had elected Dr. Fischel their Chaplain; but Dr. Fischel's formal application for the position had been rejected by Cameron because of the Congressional limitation on his choice.[5] Fischel arrived in Washington on December 10, 1861; the following day he secured an interview with Lincoln, who promptly agreed to seek to change the legislation; on December 13, Lincoln placed the matter before the Cabinet, and on the 14th he wrote to Fischel, "I shall try to have a new law broad enough to cover what is desired by you in behalf of the Israelites."[6] Meantime petitions, inspired by *The Israelite* and the Board of Delegates, began to arrive in Congress, which had convened on December 2, 1861: On December 9, Senator Charles Sumner of Massachusetts presented three memorials from Jews; on December 12, Senator Lyman Trumbull of Illinois presented a petition from a rabbi; on December 16, Senator James W. Grimes of Iowa presented one from citizens of Iowa, Senator Sumner offered another signed by the Mayor and "the leading editors" of Boston, and Senator Ira Harris of New York presented the memorial of the Board of Delegates itself. All these were referred to the Committee on Military Affairs. In the House on December 20, William S. Holman of Indiana secured the passage of a resolution requiring the House Committee on Military Affairs to "inquire into the expediency" of changing the law. On March 12, 1862, the Senate passed legislation that abolished the discrimination; there was a delay of a few months in the House, but the measure finally became law on July 17, 1862.[7]]

TO THE CHAIRMAN OF THE MILITARY COMMITTEE.[8]

SIR, Jewish ministers being by law excluded from the office of Chaplain in the Army, the Board of Delegates of American Israelites have, at their own expense, appointed me to attend to the spiritual welfare of the Jewish soldiers in the Camps and Hospitals of the Army of the Potomac, and have, at the same time, deputed me to submit to the proper authorities the injustice inflicted by that law on the Jewish community, who cannot help viewing the same as a violation of the principle of religious equality, guaranteed to all American citizens by the Constitution. With this view, I beg most respectfully to submit to your consideration, the propriety of having erased from the said act of Congress, the words *"of a Christian denomination,"* leaving the religion of the Chaplain to be determined by election, in such a manner as shall fairly represent the sentiments of the volunteers in this respect. Such an amendment would not only be most in accordance with the Constitution, which requires no religious tests as qualification for offices held in the service of the U.S., but it is the only one that can protect the Jewish Community from unjust legislation, the only one that can ensure to them the full benefits of that Constitution, for the maintenance of which they are now freely and lavishly pouring out their blood and treasure. The Israelites have always looked with special affection on this Government, because it was the first to guarantee to them equal political rights with citizens of other religious denominations, and they are, therefore, the more anxious to keep this precious boon inviolate, fearing that this, the first step towards their exclusion from office, may be used as a precedent for further restrictions on future occasions, and finally lead to such oppressive laws as will deprive them of the full privileges enjoyed by other citizens. This subject is of no less interest to the nation in general, than to the Israelites, since history conclusively shows that the union of Church and State [9] owed its origin less to direct legislation than to the gradual encroachment on the principle of religious liberty, which at first affected only a small minority, but eventually extended its baneful influence on all religious denominations that had not the power of controlling the Government of the country, leading to interminable interference with religious matters, to endless struggles for civil power on the part of the oppressed, and finally to fierce strife between the privileged and excluded churches.

Exclusive legislation, which, in this instance, affects the Jews only, may be used as a precedent for the oppression of other religious societies, and we, therefore, consider it to be as much the interest of the nation as of the Israelites, to have no religion specified in the Act of Congress providing for the appointment of Chaplains. Should it be desired by the Military Committee that I present myself before them, to explain more fully the sentiments of the Israelites on this subject, it will afford me great pleasure to comply with their wishes, in the hope that a just request, hitherto not in vain addressed to your august legislative body, may also, in this instance be readily acceded to,[10] especially as it involves the constitutional rights of a large, influential and loyal class of citizens.

137. UNION SOLDIER'S CORRESPONDENCE

"Sketches from the Seat of War," by "a Jewish Soldier," with the Army of the Potomac in Virginia, February, 1862

[This anonymous letter from an army camp reflects in many ways the thinking of a conscious Jew confronted with problems of military life among associates most of whom are not Jewish. Some hesitate to disclose their Jewish identity for fear of annoyance. Some deeply religious Jews find and create ways of unobtrusively performing their rituals. One such soldier, unaware of or indifferent to the precedent presumably set in the wars of the Maccabees—that one may fight on the Sabbath because the Sabbath is made for man and not man for the Sabbath—, engages in battle on Yom Kippur morning without breaking his fast. Noteworthy also is the writer's rejection as impracticable of the idea of having separate Jewish detachments, and his conclusion that "we are quite satisfied to fight with our Christian comrades for one cause, one country, and THE UNION." That there was anti-Semitism in the army was not due to the just cause for which the men were fighting, but to the social system which put a premium on competition in a framework of scarcity, and thus bred antagonism.]

Mr. Russell, L.L.D.,[2] in one of his letters to the *London Times,* speaks of the Jewish element in the federal army, as consisting of a "slight sprinkling of Jews in the Cameron Dragoons," and adds that their application for a Jewish Chaplain was nothing but "a hoax of imperceptible fun and tendency."[3] I happen to know the father[4] of this itinerant reporter, who is quite a respectable clerk in a fancy store, and being a plain-spoken Irishman, would express my views in something like the following phrases: "My son! hero of three wars, and a dozen battles! have the many dangers thou hast encountered affected thy reason, or have the wicked Yankees corrupted thy morals? I will not complain of thy costume which gives thee the appearance of a London Alderman, after his return from Paris, but why, O why didst thou allow, on thy arrival in Yankeedom, a set of political loafers and secessionists to pounce upon thee, who, hoping to secure through thy pen, the influence of *The Times,* did indulge thee in thy favorite enjoyments, such as wine, *early* hours and other things? Why didst thou permit cute ladies to administer to thee such wholesale doses of flattering compliments, to pay thee homage with such servility as would suffice to gratify the vanity of a monarch, but has alas! created in thy mind the hallucination that in thee the power of prophecy has been revived, and lo! thou writest to *The Times,* all that is going to happen one or two months hence, which is published just in time to be belied by the facts recorded in the news column? By all the fancy things in my master's store, tell me, my dear Bill, what art thou about?" To which the hero of three wars, and a dozen battles would reply in language more polished than I could express, that he does not condescend to look down from the pinnacle of his glory, to notice the criticisms of men who are neither heroes nor prophets. Knowing this to be your humble opinion, Mr. Bill, I do not expect you to correct your statements about the Jews and their Chaplain, but assure you by Jefferson Brick,[5] and all other names sacred in the eyes of war correspondents, that you draw your assertions from your imagination, and not from actual observation and inquiry.

A friend of mine, who has special facilities for ascertaining the extent of the Jewish element in the army, and has devoted considerable time to that inquiry, informs me, that, although it is extremely difficult to obtain correct statistics, yet he believes that there are no less than five thousand Jews in our army.[6] He attempted, by a twofold process, to arrive at a correct estimate of their member [sic—number?], first by requesting the Quartermasters of each regiment, to ascertain how many Jews there were in each company, and secondly, by calling upon the Jewish soldiers in general, to send in their names to his address, in both of which, he signally failed. This want of success on his part may be traced to various causes, but principally to the fact that few people feel disposed to give an account of their religious principles, when no practical object is to be attained, and inquiries of this nature are generally regarded as unbecoming, and even insulting. As a general rule, the Jews do not care to make their religion a matter of notoriety, as it would at once involve them in an intricate controversial disquisition with the Christian Chaplains, for which they do not always feel themselves qualified, and which, of course can, under no circumstance, afford them any thing but annoyance. Some of our brethren fear that, were they known as Hebrews, it would expose them to the taunts and sneers of those among their comrades who have been in the habit of associating with the name of Jew, everything that is mean and contemptible; but I must say, and it redounds much to the credit of the army, that in the course of my experience in the camps, which has been considerable, I have heard but of a single instance in which a Jew was wantonly insulted on account of his religion, and that was by a drunken Scotchman,[7] who commenced damning in every variety of language and motion, when he learned that he was addressing an Israelite, declaring them all to be cheats and thieves. His wrath was, however, of short duration, for the soldiers who were present, finding him incorrigible, after having repeatedly warned him to desist, at last resolved to inflict summary punishment, and collectively flung him into a certain capacious receptacle for liquid matter, from which, let us hope, he emerged a wiser and a cooler man.

My friends found [friend founds] his estimate of the number of Jewish soldiers on the fact, that according to his observation, at least, one in every hundred soldiers is a Jew, and supposing the army to consist of half a million of men, the Jews must number at least five thousand. This estimate, he believes to be supported by other calculations, for, supposing the Jews to have enlisted in the same proportion as the rest of the population, which is two and a half per cent. this would make them reach the above figure, as it is generally supposed that there are two hundred thousand Jews in this country. Without, however, insisting on the accuracy of this estimate, we may safely assert, that they are largely represented in the army, not only among the privates, but also among the commissioned officers. There are at least five Jewish colonels, as many lieutenant colonels and majors, and quite a host of captains, lieutenants, and quartermasters among the volunteer regiments,[8] but in the regular army I know of no Jew holding a higher rank than that of captain. Some of the Jewish officers and privates told me that they had taken part in the Crimean, Hungarian and Italian wars, and that they followed the profession of arms from inclination, but not liking the dull routine of a soldier's life in times of peace, they eagerly avail themselves of every opportunity to return to their tents and the battlefield. This was the first time I had ever heard of the existence of such a class of military adventurers among our people.

Most people take it for granted, that every soldier is an infidel, and that no sooner does he enter on active duty, than he banishes all idea of religion from his mind. This is a great mistake, at least as far as the Jews are concerned. My own observation has convinced me that military life does not injuriously affect their ideas of duty and devotion, but that, on the contrary, in well disciplined minds it evokes religious feelings of the most sterling character. It is quite common for Jewish soldiers belonging to the same company, to meet together for worship on Sabbath, in some secluded spot, and I know a young soldier, who was on Kippore morning, ordered to take part in a skirmish, near Harper's Ferry, which he had to go through, without having tasted food, and as soon as the enemy retreated, he retired to the woods, where he remained until sunset, reading his prayers. The character of these devotions is not the less interesting from the fact, that they are always performed in solemn silence, and in some secluded spot, where the noise of the camp cannot penetrate. When looking on those groups, I cannot help reflecting on the remarkable history of our race. Here are the descendants of the Hebrew patriarch who smote the confederated kings near Damascus,[9] the descendants of those who overthrew the colossal hosts of proud Egypt, and conquered the powerful nations of Philistea, who, under the Maccabees, triumphed over the Syrian despot, the survivors of all ancient dynasties, the participants in every remarkable event of history, behold them now in the New World, shedding their blood for the maintenance of the liberties secured to them by this Republic. Whilst thus reflecting, I feel most solemnly impressed by hearing in these Virginian forests my brethren, utter the *Shymang Israel,* which first our great lawgiver proclaimed in the plains of Arabia.

It is with no little satisfaction that I hear from all quarters, the most favorable accounts of their conduct, and, in fact, not a single instance has come to my knowledge of neglect of duty or insubordination on their part. Not only do the military authorities speak well of their conduct in camp, but also in the performance of active duty, many of our brethren have evinced, on various occasions great bravery,[10] and I am quite sure, that when we move forward, our people at home will have no occasion to be ashamed of us. In promising as much, I do not claim any special merit for ourselves, since bravery is to be found among all nations that have a glorious history to sustain, much more so among ancient nations, and therefore especially among the Hebrews, who have a history of more than three thousand years to back them.

A few months since, some Jewish soldiers suggested the idea of organising all the Jewish soldiers in the army, into distinct regiments, with Hebrew banners, etc., so that both our food and religious services may be more consonant with our habits and ideas, and we may have the pleasure of associating with our own brethren. I was further informed that such was actually the custom among the Dutch Jews [11] when they entered on active duty, and many curious stories were told of the orders being given in Hebrew, of prayers before the battle, and of *Tephillies* in the knapsacks. One of these soldiers, related by informant, was very religious, and whenever he fired off his gun, he cried out *Shma Israel.* This was at the battle of Waterloo. On being asked, why he said it so often, he replied that "it may be some Yehudee gets killed by him, and he could never pardon himself, if any one of his brethren should, through him, go out of the world without *Shemos.*" I well remember, having read in one of the English Cyclopaedies, that a Jewish regiment was among those who most distinguished themselves at the battle of Waterloo.[12] General Chasse,[13] on being asked his opinion about Jewish soldiers, replied, that "were he to go again on active duty he would wish nothing better than to have an army of such Jews as fought under him in Antwerp." The suggestion of my friends to form themselves into separate regiments was, however, disapproved of by wiser heads, which was altogether unnecessary, as it is at present impracticable, and we are quite satisfied to fight with our Christian comrades for one cause, one country, and THE UNION.

It may be interesting to you to learn, that the great stronghold behind which the enemy is entrenched in front of us, derives its name from a Jew. In these mountain passes there once stood a small lodging house, where the travellers used to pass some hours, or tarry over night on their journey to Richmond, or to Winchester, and as its location was central it—because [?became] quite a famous place in the days of stage coaches. The proprietor was called Menasseh, hence, on inquiring whether there was a place halfway to stop at, you would be told: "Yes at Manasseh's." Thence the junction has retained that name, though it is now spelled Manassas.[14] I say, Old Manasseh, you can get a million of dollars and more, if you would just admit us to your place this evening. At all events, old boy, immortality has been thrust upon thee!

138. COMPANY C, 82ND ILLINOIS INFANTRY

Report in the *Chicago Journal,* August 14, 1862 [1]

[With Lincoln's call of July 6, 1862 for 300,000 volunteers meeting with but a slow response, special efforts were undertaken to mobilize this force. Among these was the project of the Jews of Chicago to recruit a Jewish infantry company of 100 men. For the first time since the organization of the Jewish community in Chicago in 1847, the Jews gathered as Jews to plan a secular action, "for the purpose of making a united effort in support of a vigorous prosecution of the war." The Jewish population of Chicago was then only about 1,000,[2] but in two days time 96 men had enrolled in the Concordia Guards, $11,000 had been raised in order to provide each enlisted man with a bonus of $100, and the Jewish women had made the regimental flag. The Chicago *Tribune* exclaimed, "Can any town, city or state in the North show an equally good two days' work?"[3]

This unit, officially known as "the Israelite Company," became Company C of the 82nd Illinois Infantry, a regiment chiefly of German-Americans, with the exception of Company I, composed of Scandinavians. The Regiment of 1,000 men fought in many engagements before it was mustered out, June 9, 1865 with only some 300 men left. It distinguished itself particularly at the battles of Chancellorsville, May, 1863, and Gettysburg, July, 1863, and also won special commendation for its part in the Atlanta campaign, accompanying Sherman on his decisive strategic march through Georgia to the sea.[4] Although most of the Jews in the Regiment were in Company C, there were other Jews in all but two of the ten companies, including the Scandinavian, which ended its service with a Jewish captain, Joseph Gottlob. Another Jewish captain was Joseph B. Greenhut of Company K. The highest-ranking Jewish officer in the Regiment was Edward S. Salomon, who was the lieutenant-colonel when the regiment was organized, succeeded Colonel Frederick Hecker to the command when the latter resigned, March 21, 1864, and was brevetted brigadier-general, March 13, 1865, when he was only twenty-eight years of age.[5]]

An enthusiastic meeting of Jewish citizens was held last evening at Concordia Hall, 151 South Dearborn street, to devise ways and means for the purpose of raising a company of volunteers under the auspices of the good and patriotic Israelites of Chicago. On motion Mr. M. M. Gerstley was elected President of the meeting; the following gentlemen as Vice Presidents: B. Shoeneman, Jacob Rosenberg, M. A. Meyer, Henry Greenebaum, S. Hyman, I. L. Stettheimer; as Secretaries, Joseph Frank and S. Flersheim.

The following gentlemen were appointed to draft resolutions; F. Greenebaum, M. Selz, G. Shoyer, S. Cole and B. Shoeneman.[6]

The committee on resolutions reported the following:

Whereas, The present crisis in the affairs of our nation directly appeals to every citizen enjoying the inestimable blessing of American freedom to exert himself to his utmost in assisting the Government in its effort to maintain the integrity of the Union and the crushing out of the rebellion, which must and shall be done, a number of Israelites of this city, for the first time since their residence here, have met together as such, to act upon any public matter whatever, and this time for the purpose of making a united effort in support of a vigorous prosecution of the war. It is hereby

Resolved, That as Israelites we disclaim towards each other any and all relation aside on [sic] one common religious belief, except such as should exist among citizens. In all questions of a political nature the Israelite is untrammelled and free to act for himself, and does exercise his individual judgment and discretion.

Resolved, That having contributed individually heretofore, whenever called upon, in support of the war, we are impelled only by the deepest sense of patriotism and a sincere attachment to this land of our choice and love, to make an united effort in behalf of our country.

Resolved, That we will raise the sum of $10,000, or more, among the Israelites of this city, for the purpose of immediately recruiting and organizing a company for active service in the war.

Resolved, That an Executive Committee of seven be appointed by the chairman of the meeting to carry out the object of these resolutions.

Resolved, That the Jewish company will join the new Hecker regiment.[7]

The resolutions were carried unanimously.

The following gentlemen form the Executive Committee: B. Shoeneman, M. Selz, Henry Greenebaum, N. Eisendraht, Jacob Rosenberg, M. M. Gerstley, M. A. Meyer, S. Harris and G. Shoyer.[8]

Near six thousand dollars were subscribed in less than fifteen minutes. The call for the meeting was made at noon, and it was altogether an almost spontaneous outburst, true patriotism being there evinced.

The most of the subscribers to the fund have heretofore contributed liberally to the Board of Trade fund and others.[9]

The company is to be attached to the Hecker Regiment, Mr. J. Lasalle, a former Prussian officer, to be Captain, and M. Frank, First Lieutenant. There have been a dozen names placed on the muster roll since twelve o'clock last night.[10]

139. REVOKING GENERAL GRANT'S ORDER NO. 11

a) Letter to Pres. Abraham Lincoln, from Jews in Paducah, Ky., December 29, 1862
b) Newspaper report of a Delegation to Pres. Lincoln, by Rev. Isaac Mayer Wise, Washington, D. C., January 8, 1863 [1]

[On October 25, 1862, Major-General U. S. Grant assumed command of the Department of the Tennessee, which included northern Mississippi and the parts of Kentucky and Tennessee west of the Tennessee River, and immediately began to prepare for the siege of the strategically important Confederate stronghold of Vicksburg. One of his problems was to limit the trade with the Confederacy. Regarding "any trade whatever" as contributing to the military strength of the Confederacy, Grant opposed all commercial traffic, but he had to yield to the Treasury Department policy, responsive to mercantile clamor, of attempting to regulate the trade. Hordes of speculators swarmed into the Department of the Tennessee, seeking and making enormous profits out of buying cotton, and paying gold for it. (Cotton had jumped from 10 cents a pound in December, 1860 to 68 cents in December, 1862, and was to continue rising rapidly.) On August 28, 1862, Secretary of the Treasury Salmon P. Chase tightened the regulations by forbidding transportation of goods or bullion into the Confederacy, but the speculators continued to operate, corrupting many army officers through bribery and partnerships in the illegal enterprises.[2] A portion of these speculators was Jewish. Grant, however, identified the entire traffic with the Jews as such! On November 9 and 10, 1862, he issued two specific orders to officers in Jackson, Tenn., to forbid travel south of Jackson to all persons, "the Israelites especially," because they were "such an intolerable nuisance."[3] Then he received a rebuke from Washington for his failure to solve the problem. On December 17, 1862 he responded in two ways: He wrote to C. P. Wolcott, Assistant Secretary of War, explaining that the Treasury regulations were being violated "mostly by Jews and other unprincipled traders," and proposing that the only real solution was that the Government purchase "all the cotton at a fixed rate" and send it elsewhere to be sold, thus enabling him to expel *all* traders from the Department of the Tennessee. At the same time Grant issued his General Orders, No. 11: "The Jews, as a class violating every regulation of trade established by the Treasury Department and also department orders, are hereby expelled from the department within twenty-four hours from the receipt of this order. . . ."[4] Although, as will be seen from the documents that follow, Lincoln ordered this harsh and discriminatory edict revoked as soon as he was convinced it had really been issued, that portion of the Jewish press that was not fully supporting the war and that in fact had copperhead leanings sought to magnify the issue. It professed it would not be content till "the lineal descendant of Haman," General Grant, was hanged or at least removed from the army, and even rejoiced in his early defeats at Vicksburg.[5] Those Jews who supported the war, however, rejoiced that this official act of injustice against the Jews had been so speedily and decisively corrected.[6] In the general press, editorials critical of Grant's Order appeared in the Cincinnati *Volksfreund* and *Enquirer,* January 3, 1863, in the Philadelphia *Public Ledger and Daily Transcript,* January 13, 1863, and in *The New-York Times,* January 18, 1863, the latter declaring the expulsion of the Jews as a class as "contrary to common sense and common justice—contrary to Republicanism and Christianity."[7]]

Paducah, Ky., *December* 29, 1862.

Hon. Abraham Lincoln,

President of the United States:

General Orders, No. 11, issued by General Grant at Oxford, Miss., December the 17th, commands all post commanders to expel all Jews, without distinction, within twenty-four hours, from his entire department. The undersigned, good and loyal citizens of the United States and residents of this town for many years, engaged in legitimate business as merchants,[8] feel greatly insulted and outraged by this inhuman order, the carrying out of which would be the grossest violation of the Constitution and our rights as good citizens under it, and would place us, besides a large number of other Jewish families of this town, as outlaws before the whole world. We respectfully ask your immediate attention to this enormous outrage on all law and humanity, and pray for your effectual and immediate interposition. We would respectfully refer you to the post commander and post adjutant as to our loyalty, and to all respectable citizens of this community as to our standing as citizens and merchants. We respectfully ask for immediate instructions to be sent to the commander of this post.

D. WOLFF & BROS.
C. F. KASKEL.
J. W. KASKEL.[9]

Washington, D. C., Jan. 8. [1863]

The history of General Grant's order and its revocation forms quite an interesting chapter in the annals of the day. Gentlemen from Paducah, Ky., telegraphed to the President, who informed General Halleck instantly; we wrote immediately to Secretary [of War] Stanton; but neither the former nor the latter believed that Gen. Grant could have issued an order so absurd and ridiculous, and, therefore, did not do anything in the matter. When Mr. Kaskel came to Washington, January 3, and was introduced to the President, by Mr. Gurley of Cincinnati, the President at once gave order to Gen. Halleck to revoke said order.[10] General Halleck would not believe in the existence of such order, till Mr. Kaskel showed him the official copy. General Halleck instantly and peremptorily revoked the order and telegraphed to Gen. Grant to inform all post commanders instantly, of the will of the government in this matter.[11] The Cincinnati and Louisville delegation came too late.[12]—The order was rescinded. Still we thought proper to see the President and express our thanks for his promptness in this matter.—Mark, however, how democratic things look in Washington. We arrived from Baltimore about 5 P. M. on Wednesday [January 6], arrived in the hotel without changing clothes. Rev. Dr. Lilienthal inquired and was informed that Mr. Gurley was in the same house, but was not in at present. Meanwhile, Mr. Bijur and myself went to Mr. Pendleton of Cincinnati and talked half an hour to him.

On returning to our hotel we met Mr. Gurley, who without bestowing any consideration on our traveling garbs, went with us to the White House and before 8 P. M. we were introduced to the President, who being all alone, received us with that frank cordiality, which, though usually neglected, becomes men high in office so well.[13] Having expressed our thanks for the promptness and dispatch in revoking Gen. Grant's order, the President gave utterance to his surprise that Gen. Grant should have issued so ridiculous an order, and added—"to condemn a class is, to say the least, to wrong the good with the bad. I do not like to hear a class or nationality condemned on account of a few sinners." The President, we must confess, fully illustrated to us and convinced us that he knows of no distinction between Jew and Gentile, that he feels no prejudice against any nationality, and that he by no means will allow that a citizen in any wise be wronged on account of his place of birth or religious confession. He illustrated this point to us in a very happy manner, of which we can only give the substance at present, and promise to give particulars on another occasion. Now then, in our traveling habiliments, we spoke about half an hour to the President of the U. S. in an open and frank manner, and were dismissed in the same simple style.

Sorry we are to say that Congress did not think proper to be as just as the President is.[14] Congress is not now the people's legislative body, it belongs to a party. Senator Powel[l] of Kentucky, as noted elsewhere, introduced a resolution condemning the unjust order of Gen. Grant, to inform others that orders of this kind must not be issued; but the resolution was tabled to be killed, when called up again. Mr. Pendleton of Cincinnati, attempted in vain on Monday and Tuesday to bring the following resolution before the house. He finally succeeded on Wednesday (yesterday) to propose the following:

Mr. Pendleton offered a preamble setting forth that Major General Grant, on the 17th of December, as the commander of the Department of the Tennessee, did issue an order stating that the Jews, as a class, had violated every regulation of trade established in that department, and for this were to be expelled from the department within twenty-four hours, &c., and as in the pursuance of the order General Grant caused many peaceful citizens to be expelled within twenty-four hours without allegation of misconduct, and with no other proof than that they were members of a certain religious denomination; and whereas said sweeping order makes no discrimination between the innocent and the guilty, and is illegal, unjust, tyrannical and cruel, therefore

Resolved, That the said order deserves the sternest condemnation of the House and of the President of the United States as Commander-in-Chief of the Army and Navy.

Mr. PENDLETON moved the previous question on the passage of this proposition.

Mr. WASHBURNE (R) moved that it be laid upon the table; and this was agreed to—yeas 56, nays 53.

On motion of Mr. Washburne, the everlasting Mr. Washburne,[15] the resolution was tabled by a vote of 56 yeas to 53 nays. If the Hebrew citizens of the United States were "gentlemen of color," Mr. Washburne would certainly have made a brilliant effort to vindicate their rights and expose a general who committed a gross outrage on them. But being only white men, it would not pay.[16] Partisan legislation, that is all we have to expect of this congress. Mr. Pendleton said Washburne's motive was that of friendship for Grant, whom to defend in congress he had several times taken upon himself; but Republican members openly say, it is a rule of the House to vote down every thing coming from the other side, viz: the democratic. How do you like this remarkable impartiality?

Having to see a good many things to-day, we must conclude this, to say more to-morrow.[17]

THE EDITOR.

[Isaac Mayer Wise]

140. MISSOURI EMANCIPATIONIST

Address by Isidor Bush favoring immediate Emancipation, at the Missouri State Convention, Jefferson City, Missouri, June 29, 1863 [1]

[The provisions of Lincoln's Proclamation of Emancipation of slaves in the seceded states had not changed the legal status of slaves in the border states, including Missouri. Despite strong opposition by pro-slavery forces, however, Missouri became the first state to emancipate its slaves during the Civil War. Early in 1861, the Missouri government had actually made an unsuccessful attempt to take Missouri out of the Union, but a new administration, created on July 31, 1861 by a constitutional convention, had been charged with full support to the Union. This pro-Union course was determined basically by the recent development of railroad connections between Missouri and the eastern markets, which made it less dependent upon Missouri and Mississippi River trade with the southern states, and which stimulated the commercial and manufacturing middle classes to grasp the value of Union with the East.[2] The struggle for emancipation legislation had begun at the June, 1862 session of the state constitutional convention, before Lincoln's Proclamation was issued, and was waged until it succeeded in January, 1865. Among those most active in promoting the cause not only of Union but of abolitionism was Isidor Bush, a Jewish leader of the large German-American community in St. Louis.

At the Missouri state convention that had decided that Missouri would remain loyal to the Union, Bush had on March 20, 1861 "made the most clean cut, unconditional union speech in the whole convention."[3] At the 1862 session, his abolitionist views were so outstanding that he was elected, when the convention reassembled June 15, 1863, to the important Committee on Emancipation, consisting of nine members. When the majority of that committee agreed on a report proposing emancipation in 1876, Bush on June 23 presented a minority report of one, proposing emancipation to go into effect on January 1, 1864.[4] The address here published not only argues the desirability of speedy emancipation but also closes tellingly with a factual refutation of the common slanders that free Negroes would rape and murder the white population. Bush concludes: "It is not enough that you hold them in bondage, toys of your whim and your lust, but you must charge them with crimes they never committed and never dreamt of. I pray you have pity for yourselves, *not* for the Negro."]

Mr. Bush. Mr. President, I have listened for days [5] to the gentlemen speaking on the subject of emancipation, and I now bespeak their attention for a few minutes.

The one said "slavery" and the other "anti-slavery" is the cause of this war. I say it is part of that everlasting war between Ormuzd and Ariman, between light and darkness, between right and wrong; it is that irrepressible conflict between free labor and slave labor. The South wanted to put down abolitionism with fire and sword, establishing and extending a great empire of slave aristocracy. The North will now, and must in self-defence, put down slavery. It matters not whether the President of the United States, much less whether you or I, have any such desire and intention or not; it is the inevitable logic, the necessary consequence of events, stronger than the will of the President, the decrees of courts, or the acts of Congress. The people of this State have to take a stand on one side or the other. To place ourselves on the middle ground between the contending parties is to be destroyed by both fires. When they decided to stay in the Union, to fight with the North in this struggle to maintain our national existence, this question was virtually decided. You had only to draft the deed and to acknowledge it. You ought to have declared simply that we will *cheerfully* sacrifice the institution of slavery, whose value *has already been destroyed, by this rebellion,* to our country, and the people would execute the deed; thus showing to the South, as well as the North, on which side Missouri will forever stand. The great majority of the people are in favor of emancipation. Most of those even who were opposed to it, a short time ago, acknowledge that we cannot avoid it even if we would; that emancipation is an unavoidable necessity of this war.[6] I might almost say, in the Lincolnian style, that "as we cannot remove anti-slavery, we must remove slavery." *Still you hesitate.*

Much has been said about the right and power of this Convention to pass an ordinance of emancipation, and whether it should be submitted to the people for its ratification or rejection. Many of you, and among these some learned jurists and judges, have argued that we have that right, and that even without the sanction of the people it would have full force. They urge, indeed, that we should not submit it to them. While I have no pretension to such learning, I am but expressing the unmistaken and unmistakable voice of the people in saying, that, if you should refuse to submit your action on this subject to the popular vote, you would exercise a doubtful, an unjust, and a very improper authority; the more so, as you assume to exercise it twenty-eight months after you were elected, and elected on no such issue; after you have once declared to the people and to Congress that you do *not* feel authorized to act *at all* on this subject; after a new Legislature has come duly into existence, fresh from the people![7] With the same propriety you could perpetuate yourselves, and, if a majority of this body were in opposition to a majority of the Legislature, might nullify every act passed by that Legislature. And yet gentlemen undertake to say "we must take the responsibility." And why? To avoid agitation.

Now, gentlemen, the "let alone" policy—to use a common but expressive phrase—the "let alone" policy is played out. The very call of this Convention,[8] for purposes which one year ago you decided to "let alone" by an overwhelming majority, is but one of the many proofs of the fallacy of your system. An early decision by the people at the ballot-box is the only way to close agitation, is the only means to give any action of yours force and stability. But while many of you boldly assume that we have the unlimited right and power to pass an ordinance of emancipation, and care little about the consent of the sovereign people, some of you have yet one serious objection, namely, that emancipation without compensation to loyal owners is unjust—some call it robbery. This objection is not without weight with me. I would favor any reasonable and practicable plan of compensation, and am opposed only to such plans as would have no practical results except to defeat any emancipation ordinance. Members of the committee, and some other gentlemen here, are aware that I myself suggested a plan of compensation—that the various railroad companies should issue stock to the amount of aid received from the State, (over $20,000,000,) which stock might be used for the purpose of such compensation, without increasing the State debt, thus giving to the slave owners an interest in the one great institution (railroads)[9] in exchange for the other (slavery)—an exchange by which, in my opinion, all parties would gain. I soon found out, however, that all slave owners scorn such a compensation. On the other hand, I find, from the admission of loyal slaveholders themselves, that the value of slaves has been destroyed by the rebels; and while they are chargeable with the loss, it is not for the loyal people, who did nothing to damage it, to compensate the owners for the same. If another throws down this tumbler (the glass of water) from this desk, breaking it to pieces, and I afterwards remove the worthless, injurious fragments, am I to pay you the damage? Moreover, it has not been proposed by any one that the slave owner should lose the right to the labor of his servant for some years. I voted, all the friends of speedy emancipation voted, for long terms of continued servitude,[10] depriving you only of the right to sell a human being, a right which you never had under the Constitution of the United States, as you contend; but, whether you have it or not, which you cannot exercise, as there is no market, and God grant never will be, for this traffic any more.

It is further a fact, established by proof and experience, which cannot be denied, that the wealth and general prosperity of the State would be so much increased, that it is not only proper that the interest of the individual should give way to the interest of the whole, but that it must also benefit the former slave owner. He, the slave owner, is at the same time, almost without exception, also a land owner; and it is admitted that the *plus value* of lands cultivated by free labor exceeds the capital represented by slaves. The gentleman from Pike himself calculated that the difference in the increased value of personal property and real estate in Missouri, at the ratio of the last ten years here and in Illinois, would amount during ten years to come to $200,000,000; and, singularly enough, he is still in favor of keeping Missouri ten years longer a slave State.[11]

Now, sir, as the abolishment of slavery in Missouri cannot be avoided, as you believe you have the right and power to do it, and as it would be to the great advantage of Missouri in general, while it would prove but a small loss to the slaveholder, the question seems to be now only whether slavery shall cease in 1876 or in 1866. But even this is by no means, in reality, a question. Does any gentleman on this floor really believe that, in the present state of our national affairs, slavery can exist until 1876, or even 1870? The gentleman from Livingston (Mr. Woolfolk), pro-slavery man as he is, has well and honestly stated that every plan of emancipation in 1870, or any such prospective period, will only invite and offer a premium to the Negroes to run away from their owners.[12]

You will admit, Mr. President [Gen. Robert Wilson], that slavery is rapidly disappearing, and no one will deny, I think, that it is now in fact, though not in law, a mere voluntary servitude.[13] Such is the present. Now look to the future; look to history as it will be transmitted to your children and children's children. On the one hand, the humiliation, that we would not consent to free ourselves from the institution of slavery until the slave freed himself; that, worthless as the institution has become, we would not sacrifice the peculiar institution to the maintenance of our Union, to the peace and safety of the State. On the other hand, the proud and glorious record, that this was the first State that, by the free and voluntary action of its own people, and without compensation, nobly sacrificed and blotted out that peculiar institution. Which are you inclined to choose? The majority report of your Select Committee on Emancipation shows it; your vote on the amendment for 1864, and then on the amendment for 1866, shows it; your vote on the amendment for 1868 shows it—for even if I and twelve others, true friends of emancipation, the Radicals, as you call them, had voted for it, it would still have failed; but, above all, your vote on submitting your ordinance to the people in November, 1863, shows it.[14] I think it is enough. You voted them all down; let us go home. Do not deceive yourselves; and do not believe you can settle this matter for the people. They do not want us.

Mr. President, I desire to notice but one point more before I close. Some of the gentlemen, members of this Convention, have drawn so horrible a picture of the evils resulting from emancipating the Negroes and leaving them afterwards free among us, that they and their misguided hearers inevitably come to the conclusion that emancipation without deportation would ruin this State. They tell us that the Negroes would be but one great band of idlers and vagabonds, robbers, murderers, and thieves. If this be true, I ask these gentlemen, "Are these the boasted blessings of Christianity, which you, the advocates of slavery, have ever and always claimed to have given to these poor Africans, in return for their freedom?" But it is not true, and you cannot help knowing it to be false. Look at Delaware—I do not ask you to go for information to Jamaica, or the other West India Islands—look at Delaware, I say. The census of 1860, now before you on your tables, will show you that 19,829 free Negroes live in that little State of our Union—a State not larger than three of our counties; and you pretend to say that Missouri, thirty-two times as large as Delaware, would be ruined by a comparatively small number of her Negro population, if free! New Jersey has 25,318 free Negroes, on an area only one-eighth that of Missouri; and where is the murder, the rapine, and other crimes, committed by that class? Three cases of murder, and two of homicide, are all that occurred in New Jersey in 1860, against twenty-one cases of murder, and twenty-six of homicide, during the same period in Missouri. I have no words for such slanders against poor human beings, so much sinned against. It is not enough that you hold them in bondage, toys of your whim and your lust, but you must charge them with crimes they never committed and never dreamt of. I pray you have pity for yourselves, *not* for the Negro. Slavery demoralizes, slavery fanaticism blinds you; it has arrayed brother against brother, son against father; it has destroyed God's noblest work—a free and happy people.

I am done, Mr. President, and I now renew the motion of the gentleman from Buchanan:

Resolved, That the Convention now adjourn *sine die*.[15]

141. CONFEDERATE DIARY

Excerpts from the War Diary of Lewis Leon of North Carolina, April, 1861 to April, 1865 [1]

[Lewis Leon (1841–1919) was not yet seventeen when he left his home on Norfolk Street on the lower East Side of New York in 1858, and went south to Charlotte, North Carolina, to become a dry goods clerk.[2] Within three years he thoroughly absorbed the point of view of the reactionary classes in the South, and he volunteered to fight for the Confederacy even before North Carolina, the tenth of eleven states to secede from the Union, formally declared its secession on May 21, 1861. He served for three and one half years, became a sharpshooter, took part in many battles, including Gettysburg, remembered the Jewish holidays well enough to record them but not to observe them, was captured and imprisoned, finally "took the cursed oath" of allegiance to the United States of America, and closed his Diary with the sentiment, "I still say our Cause was just, nor do I regret one thing that I have done to cripple the North." There is not a mention of slavery in the entire Diary, so little did the fundamental cause of the war impress itself upon the consciousness of this Jewish rank-and-file private.]

April 25, 1861—I belong to the Charlotte Grays, Company C, First North Carolina Regiment.[3] We left home for Raleigh. . . .

We enlisted for six months. . . .

A few days after that a squad of us were sent out to cut down trees, and, by George! they gave me an axe and told me to go to work. Well, I cut all over my tree until the lieutenant commanding, seeing how nice I was marking it, asked me what I had done before I became a soldier. I told him I was a clerk in a dry-goods store. He said he thought so from the way I was cutting timber. He relieved me—but what insults are put on us who came to fight the Yankees! Why, he gave me two buckets and told me to carry water to the men that could cut. . . .

We changed camp a number of times, made fortifications all around Yorktown, and when our six months were over we were disbanded, and returned home. So my experience as a soldier was over.

I stayed home five months, when I again took arms for the Old North State, and joined a company raised by Capt. Harvey White, of Charlotte, and left our home on April 23, 1862, at 6.30 P. M. I stayed in Salisbury until next night, when I, with several others, took the train for Raleigh, where our company was. We went to the insane asylum to see Langfreid, who wanted to go home by telegraph to see his cotton and tobacco. . . .

June 21, [1862]—We reached Petersburg, Va., this morning at half-past two, and had barely laid down with a brick wall for my pillow when breakfast was announced in the shape of Mack Sample, who told us where we could get it. I ran the blockade with Katz, and went to see Mike Etlinger. He was not at home. Afterward we met [Henry] Wortheim, and we all went again and got something good to eat. We then returned to our regiment, which is the 53d North Carolina Regiment, infantry, Col. William Owens, commander. We are enlisted for three years, or the war. . . .[4]

July 27—Had a few friends visit us from home, and moved camp twice. To-night we were ordered to fall in line. Went to Petersburg, and there took the cars for Weldon. On the road a dreadful accident occurred. On the flat car that we were on, a captain of the navy with us had his leg cut off by a sheet of iron flying off the flat. Lieutenant [W. M.] McMatthews, Henry Wortheim and myself were knocked down, but not badly hurt. The captain died two days after. . . .

August 20—Left here at 6 P. M. and arrived at Petersburg at 3 o'clock in the morning. Took the same bed that I had the last time

—the sidewalk—and the wall for my pillow. Katz, Hugh Sample, 'Bat' Harry, Lieutenant [S. E.] Belk and some others were left behind, sick. . . .[5]

August 22—Sam Oppenheim, of the 44th North Carolina Regiment, an old comrade of the 1st North Carolina Regiment, came to see me. He is stationed on the other side of the city [Richmond].

August 23—Went uptown to see my brother, Morris, of the 44th Georgia Regiment; but his regiment had already gone to Gordonsville, so I returned to camp. . . .[6]

September 1—Wortheim and myself went to Halfway Station, to get a box that was sent to us from home, but it did not come. . . .

September 23—Left here this morning at 10 o'clock and got to our old camp at 4 o'clock this evening. This expedition was to strengthen Longstreet's forces near Suffolk. We got there after he was relieved and the siege of Suffolk abandoned.

September 27—Up to to-day nothing new, only to-day is my New Year (the Jewish New Year).[7]

October—this month passed off with nothing new, except Katz returned on the 7th, and Donau [8] was discharged. We are still in our camp.

November 5—There is nothing for me to write. To-day Wortheim and myself went to Petersburg to get a box that was sent from home, and while there we had a very good time. . . .

December 3—Katz and myself went to Petersburg to-day. We met with friends, and the consequence you can imagine. The headache we had next day was caused by too much whiskey.

December 8—My birthday to-day. I am a man twenty-one years old, but I must say that I have been doing a man's duty before I was twenty-one, providing a soldier's duty is a man's. I spent to-day in bringing mud to a palace for a fireplace. . . .

December 21—I went to the creek to wash my clothing and myself, and when I got back the water had frozen on my head so that I was obliged to hold my head by the fire so as to thaw it out. Wortheim's eyes are so bad that he can hardly see. Sam Wilson broke his shoulder blade.

December 25—There is nothing new up to to-day, Christmas. We moved out camp a little piece. Eigenbrun came to see us to-day from home, and brought me a splendid cake from Miss Clara Phile. . . .

February 6, [1863]—Nothing to eat yet. Wortheim, W. Engle [9] and myself went out foraging, to buy something to eat. . . .

February 8—Wortheim and myself went uptown to get something to eat. We got corn bread and bacon. . . .

February 25—Henry Wortheim was sent home on a sick furlough, as he is very bad off. . . .

March 16—A picket came in this morning and reported the enemy advancing. We were put in line of battle to receive them, and after marching one mile up the road to get to our brigade we were put at the extreme left of our line, and made breastworks out of rotten logs. Stayed here one hour, when another picket came and reported them ten miles away. So we resumed our march for camp and got there at 7 o'clock—twenty-one miles to-day. Tom Notter,[10] Aaron Katz and myself pressed into service to-day a donkey and a cart with a Negro, who took us to Kinston. . . .

March 20—Katz went home to-day on a furlough. Nothing new up to the 23d.

March 23—We had a man whipped to-day in our regiment for desertion. . . .[11]

April 3—Little Washington is on Tar River, and as one of the Yankee gunboats was trying to get in, one of our cannon gave them a ball, which caused heavy firing all day, and, in fact, the shells came very close to our flag, which made us dodge pretty smart. We have Washington besieged. . . .

April 4—Firing at intervals all day. The reserve was sent to the river to support our artillery. The colors went with them. It is raining hard. We laid in line two and a half hours in an old field. It is very cold. The Yankees are firing all the time. Then the 43d Regiment came and relieved us. Katz came in to-day and reported Henry Wortheim dead—he died Monday, March 30 [1863].

April 8—This morning Tom Trotter, Katz and myself went with Captain [Harvey] White to meet three Yankees with a flag of truce; but they would not come half way, so Colonel Owens ordered us back. . . .

April 24—This morning I was detailed by Colonel Owens to go to Wilson, N. C., to get the baggage for our officers. Left at 3 A. M., got to Tarboro at 7 P. M. This is a very pretty town. Stayed here until 3 and took the cars to Rocky Mount. Got there at 5, left at 7, and got to Wilson at 8 on the morning of the 25th. Got my baggage and left at 3 P. M. Arrived at Rocky Mount at 4. Saw some fun with a girl and an old woman. The young one had stole a petticoat from the old one, and was compelled to take it off and return it in the presence of at least fifty men. Left at 8, got to Tarboro at a quarter after nine. . . .

May 17—Up to to-day nothing. But this morning at 4 we were ordered to cook up all our rations, and be ready to march in one hour. We left Kinston by rail at 12 M. Got to Goldsboro at 3, went through to Weldon, left here at 5 P. M., and got to Petersburg, Va., on the morning of the 18th; left there at 6 P. M. Katz and myself went uptown—ate two suppers. Had a very good time while in town. . . . May 26 and 27, [1863]—Rested. I went to see my brother Morris, who belongs to Dowles' [Doles'] Brigade, 44th Georgia Regiment [near Fredericksburg]. Did not see him, as he was on picket.

May 28—Morris came to see me to-day. We are both in the same division and corps. Our corps is commanded by [Lieutenant-] General [Richard S.] Ewell. . . .

June 3—Saw my brother Morris several times. . . .

July 1—We left camp at 6 A. M., passed through Heidelsburg and Middleton. At the latter place we heard firing in the direction of Gettysburg. We were pushed forward after letting the wagon trains get in our rear. We got to Gettysburg at 1 P. M., 15 miles. We were drawn up in line of battle about one mile south of town, and a little to the left of the Lutheran Seminary. We then advanced to the enemy's line of battle in double quick time. We had not gotten more than 50 Paces when Norman of our company fell dead by my side. Katz was going to pick him up. I stopped him, as it is strictly forbidden for anyone to help take the dead or wounded off the field except the ambulance corps. We then crossed over a rail fence, where our Lieutenant McMatthews and [M. E.] Alexander were both wounded. That left us with a captain and one lieutenant. After this we got into battle in earnest, and lost in our company very heavily, both killed and wounded. This fight lasted four hours and a half, when at last we drove them clear out of town, and took at least 3,000 prisoners. They also lost very heavily in killed and wounded, which all fell into our hands. . . . After we had them all put up in a pen we went to our regiment and rested. Major [James Johnston] Iredell, of our regiment, came to me and shook my hand, and also complimented me for action in the fight.[12] At dusk I was about to hunt up my brother Morris, when he came to me. Thank God, we are both safe as yet. We laid all night among the dead Yankees, but they did not disturb our peaceful slumbers.

July 2—Our division was in reserve until dark, but our regiment was supporting a battery all way [day?]. . . . Just at dark we were sent to the front under terrible cannonading. Still, it was certainly a beautiful sight. It being dark, we could see the cannon vomit forth fire. Our company had to cross a rail fence. It gave way and several of our boys were hurt by others walking over them. We laid down here a short time, in fact no longer than 10 minutes, when I positively fell asleep. The cannonading did not disturb me. One of the boys shook me and told me Katz was wounded by a piece of shell striking him on the side, and he was sent to the rear. We went on to the Baltimore Turnpike until 3 in the morning of the 3d.

July 3—When under a very heavy fire, we were ordered on Culps Hill, to the support of [Major-] Gen. A. [? Edward] Johnson. Here we stayed all day—no, here, I may say, we melted away. We were on the brow of one hill, the enemy on the brow of another. We charged on them several times, but of course, running down our hill, and then to get to them was impossible, and every time we attempted it we came back leaving some of our comrades behind. Here our Leitenant [sic] Belk lost his arm. We have now in our company a captain. All of our lieutenants are wounded. We fought here until 7 P. M., when what was left of us was withdrawn and taken to the first day's battlefield. At the commencement of this fight our Brigade was the strongest in our division, but she is not now. We lost the most men, for we were in the fight all the time, and I have it from Colonel Owens that our regiment lost the most in the Brigade. I know that our company went in the fight with 60 men. When we left Culps Hill there were 16 of us that answered to the roll call. The balance were all killed and wounded. There were 12 sharpshooters in our company and now John Cochran and myself are the only ones that are left.[13] This day none will forget, that participated in the fight. It was truly awful how fast, how very fast, did our poor boys fall by our sides—almost as fast as the leaves that fell as cannon and musket balls hit them, as they flew on their deadly errand. You could see one with his head shot off, others cut in two, then one with his brain oozing out, one with his leg off, others shot through the heart. Then you could hear some poor friend or foe crying for water, or for 'God's sake' to kill him. . . .

July 4—We laid on the battlefield of the first day, this the fourth day of July. No fighting to-day, but we are burying the dead. They have been lying on the field in the sun since the first day's fight; it being dusty and hot, the dead smell terribly. The funny part of it is, the Yankees have all turned black. Several of our company, wounded, have died. Katz is getting along all right. The battle is over, and although we did not succeed in pushing the enemy out of their strong position, I am sure they have not anything to boast about. They have lost at least as many in killed and wounded as we have.[14] We have taken more prisoners from them than they have from us. If that is not the case, why did they lay still all to-day and see our army going to the rear? An army that has gained a great victory follows it up while its enemy is badly crippled; but [Major General George Gordon] Meade, their commander, knows he has had as much as he gave, at least, if not more. As yet I have not heard a word from my brother Morris since the first day's fight.

July 5—Left this morning at 5 o'clock. Only marched ten miles to-day. The enemy being in our rear, and skirmishing very strong. . . .

July 8—We are resting, and, goodness knows, we need it very much. . . . Our three lieutenants are all wounded and prisoners. Katz is also a prisoner. Nothing further up to the 10th. . . .

July 14—The roads are so bad that it is hard work to trudge along. . . . We are now, thank God, on Confederate soil, but oh, how many of our dear comrades have we left behind. We can never forget this campaign. We had hard marching, hard fighting, suffered hunger and privation, but our general officers were always with us, to help the weary soldier carry his gun, or let him ride. In a fight they were with us to encourage. Many a general have I seen walk and a poor sick private riding his horse, and our father, Lee, was scarcely ever out of sight when there was danger We could not feel gloomy when we saw his old gray head uncovered as he would pass us on the march, or be with us in a fight. I care not how weary or hungry we were, when we saw him we gave that Rebel yell, and hunger and wounds would be forgotten. . . .

August 24—Was on guard this morning, but Sergeant Hugh Reid sent for me, and detailed me, with some men out of every regiment in our brigade, to hunt deserters. Si Wolf and myself, out of our company.[15] We left camp at 3 this evening, marched two miles up the railroad, and took the cars to Gordonsville. Got there at 4. It is a small place, but one of importance, as all our supplies for the army from Richmond come from this station. . . .

September 1—To-day we went on a general hunt in full force. We went into a house where we suspected there was a deserter. We hunted through all the out-houses, then went to the house, and the lady strongly denied there being any one there, but would not give us permission to look. We then searched the house, but found no one. I then proposed that we go in the loft. She objected again. But of course we were determined. It was pitch-dark in the loft. We called in, but no answer came. I then proposed, in a loud voice, so that if any one was there they could hear me, that we fix bayonets and stick around and satisfy ourselves that no one was there. Still no answer. I then got in the loft, took my gun and commenced sticking around. At last an answer came from the far corner that he would surrender. The way I got into the loft was, I being a little fellow, and Si Wolf a tall man, they put me on his shoulder, and in that way I crawled in. We then left for camp, passed a church, and was in time to see a wedding. We drilled for the ladies, and had a good time.

September 2—On a hunt to-day several of my comrades with myself came to a house, and the first thing we heard was, "Is there a Jew in your detachment that caught a deserter yesterday?" They would like to see him, etc. At last one of the boys told them that I was the Jew. After that I had a very good time there, and in fact wherever I went I was received very kindly, and was very sorry to see on the 4th that orders came for us to return to our brigade. . . .

September 15—Still some firing in front. We are in reserve. I went to see the fight. I saw the enemy very plainly, and thus I spent my New Year's Day.

September 16—To-day there was a man shot for desertion. . . .

September 23—Day of Atonement to-day. Nothing more up to the 26th. . . .

September 29—All quiet to-day. Brother Morris returned from Richmond yesterday, where he has been for ten days on a furlough. Before our Jewish New Year there was an order read out from General Lee granting a furlough to each Israelite to go to Richmond for the holidays if he so desires.[16] I did not care to go. . . .

April 3, [1864]—As I have not heard from my parents since the war, they living in New York, I thought I would send a personal advertisement to a New York paper to let them know that my brother and myself are well, and for them to send an answer through the Richmond paper. I gave this to a Yankee picket, who promised me he would send it to New York. . . .[17]

May 5—Moved this morning, feeling for the enemy, and came up to them at noon, five miles from the Run, in the Wilderness. It certainly is a wilderness; it is almost impossible for a man to walk, as the woods are thick with an underbrush growth and all kinds of shrubbery, old logs, grapevines, and goodness knows what. My corps of sharpshooters was ordered to the front.[18] We formed in line and advanced to the enemy. We fought them very hard for three hours, they falling back all the time. Our sharpshooters' line got mixed up with [Major General John B.] Gordon's Brigade, and fought with them. In one charge we got to the most elevated place in the Wilderness. We looked back for our brigade, but saw it not. Just then a Yankee officer came up and we took him prisoner. Some of Gordon's men took him to the rear. Six of our regiment, sharpshooters, myself included, went to the right to join our regiment, but were picked up by the Yankees and made prisoners. We were run back in their line on the double quick. When we got to their rear we found about 300 of our men were already prisoners. The Yankees lost very heavily in this fight, more than we did. Although we lost heavy enough, but, my Heavens! what an army they have got. It seems to me that there is ten of them to one of us. . . .

May 6— . . . Several of our boys came in as prisoners to-day, with them Engle of our company. They think I was killed, so does my brother, but as yet the bullet has not done its last work for your humble servant. . . .

May 11—This morning about 800 more prisoners came in. Most of them were from my brigade, as well as from Dole's Georgians. I was surprised to see my brother with them. He was taken yesterday, but before he surrendered he sent two of the enemy to their long home with his bayonet. . . .

May 14—We are still camped here. Have been prisoners since the 5th of this month, and have drawn three and a half days' rations. On that kind of a diet I am not getting very fat. . . .

May 16—Left this morning at 11 in a tugboat, and from here packed into the Steamer S. R. Spaulding. We are now on our way to a regular prison. We got there at 8 o'clock to-night, and found it to be Point Lookout, Md., fifty miles from Belle Plain. It is in St. Mary's County. . . .

May 20—Three years ago to-day the Old North State left the Union, and we went to the front full of hopes to speedily show the Yankee Government that the South had a right to leave the Union; but to-day, how dark it looks!

May 21—I heard to-day that my brother Morris was a prisoner at Fort Delaware, Pa. [? Del.] I asked for a parole to-day to go and see my parents in New York, but they could not see it. . . .

May 25—Engle received a letter from his father to-day, who told him they had seen my parents, and I would hear from them soon. This is the first time that I have heard about my parents since the commencement of the war. Thank God, my parents, as well as my sisters and brothers, are well.

May 26—Received two letters to-day, one from home and one from my brother Pincus, who went to Washington on his way to visit Morris and myself, as he has to get a pass from headquarters before he can see us. He was refused and returned home. . . .

June 8—There is nothing new up to to-day, when I received a box of eatables, one or two shirts, and one pair of pants from home. The only way we can pass our time off is playing cards and chess. . . .

June 27—Received money to-day from home, but they gave me sutler's checks for it, as we were not allowed any money, for fear we would bribe the sentinels and make our escape.

July 4—Four hundred prisoners left here for some other prison, as there were too many here.

July 8—Engle, Riter, and myself received boxes from New York to-day, but as Riter has gone to the other prison with the 400 we have made away with his box.

July 23—Three hundred more were sent from here to the new prison, which is in Elmira, N. Y., myself with them.

July 25—Left Point Lookout at 8 o'clock this evening in the frigate Victor for New York. There are 700 prisoners on board.

July 26—To-day on the ocean a great many of our boys were seasick, but not I. I was promised a guard to take me to see my parents in New York for thirty minutes.

July 27—We see the Jersey shore this morning. Our vessel was racing with another. We had too much steam up; the consequence was a fire on board, but we soon had it out. We landed at Jersey City at 12 M., and were immediately put in cars, and the officers that promised to send me to my parents refused to do so. We left here at 1, got to Elmira at 8 in the evening. . . .[19]

April, [1865]—I suppose the end is near, for there is no more hope for the South to gain her independence. On the 10th of this month we were told by an officer that all those who wished to get out of prison by taking the oath of allegiance to the United States could do so in a very few days. There was quite a consultation among the prisoners. On the morning of the 12th we heard that Lee had surrendered on the 9th, and about 400, myself with them, took the cursed oath and were given transportation to wherever we wanted to go. I took mine to New York City to my parents, whom I have not seen since 1858. Our cause is lost; our comrades who have given their lives for the independence of the South have died in vain; that is, the cause for which they gave their lives is lost, but they positively did not give their lives in vain. They gave it for a most righteous cause, even if the Cause was lost. . . . I shall now close this diary in sorrow, but to the last I will say that, although but a private, I still say our Cause was just, nor do I regret one thing that I have done to cripple the North.

142. WOMEN AID THE SOLDIERS

Letter from Myer S. Isaacs to Rev. H. W. Bellows, President, New York Sanitary Commission, New York, November 19, 1863 [1]

[This hitherto unpublished letter asks that "there should be no discrimination as to creed, in selecting the ladies to be honored with the duty of aiding" the Committee organizing the great "Metropolitan Fair" that was to be held in New York in the Spring of 1864 to raise funds for the care of sick and wounded soldiers and their families, which constituted the chief functions of the Sanitary Commission.[2] Rev. Bellows gave assurance that there would be no discrimination, and when the working committees were announced they contained the names of several members of Jewish business circles.[3] At first *The Jewish Messenger* happily declared that there would be a separate booth or stand, tended by "pretty Jewesses," but objections by a correspondent to the *Messenger* and editorially in *The Jewish Record* suggested reconsideration of this plan, unless other religious groups had their own stands. The result was that there was no Jewish booth or table, although the Episcopalian, Lutheran, Baptist, Methodist, Presbyterian and Dutch Reformed Churches, and the German Turnverein and the Welsh National

Society all had tables of their own at which they sold their wares.[4] Thus the Jewish middle class's interpretation of equality had led to effacement.]

150 Nassau Street,
New York, Nov. 19. 1863.

Rev. H. W. Bellows;
Pres[t] N.Y. Sanitary Commission:

Rev. & Dear Sir,

I observe that a "Metropolitan Fair" is to be given in this city, under the auspices & for the benefit of your noble organization. Feeling a deep interest in the success of such a measure for the benefit of our soldiers, facing danger for *our* sakes, fighting *our* battles—I am satisfied you will pardon the liberty I take in offering a suggestion intended to assist the cause.

The Hebrew ladies of this city possess many organizations, by means of which they extend judicious and liberal relief to their indigent coreligionists. At the breaking out of the war, several of these associations were converted into Soldiers' Aid Societies and undertook the duty of cooperating in the good work proposed by the Commission. These same societies would, I am convinced, esteem it an agreeable and congenial occupation to prepare and solicit articles to be exhibited at the projected Fair; and it is certainly meet that there should be no discrimination as to creed, in selecting the ladies to be honored with the duty of aiding your Committee, when Christian and Israelite are working zealously side by side on the battle field, disregarding the difference of religious belief, and remembering that they are Americans.

Should you judge this suggestion worthy of consideration, I should be proud to cooperate in any way in which I could be of service and should cheerfully throw open the pages of our paper, the "Jewish Messenger" for the benefit of the cause. If you desire it, I could furnish you with the names of two or three prominent ladies in the Ladies' Hebrew Benevolent Society of "Shaaray Tefila," the Aid Associations of "Shearith Israel" and "Emanuel",[5] which have heretofore contributed to the cause, and in this way a Committee of Hebrew Ladies could be formed embracing the most influential of our community; and it is needless to say, their record at the Fair would be inferior to that of no other cooperating body.

Pardon the liberty I take in addressing you on the subject, but the earnest interest I feel in it will, I am assured, be my best justification.

Awaiting your reply, I am, honored sir,

Yours Respectfully,

Myer S. Isaacs.[6]

Editor "Jewish Messenger"

143. ANTI-SEMITISM IN THE RANKS

Letter from Private Max Glass to Major General Benjamin F. Butler, Norfolk Jail, Virginia, April 12, 1864 [1]

[This unpublished letter tells pathetically of the misadventures, at the hands of swindlers, anti-Semites, and negligent officers, of a veteran of European armies who had come to New York to join the Union forces. In his faulty English, Max Glass describes the mistreatment that brought him finally into a prison charged with desertion, and he implores the Commanding Officer to transfer him to another regiment, because he would be "more useful in the field than in prison." After investigation, General Butler pardoned Glass, but instead of transferring him returned him to his old regiment.[2] A few days later Glass took part in the battle of Cold Harbor, Va., on June 1, 1864, and was apparently wounded, for on July 22 he was admitted to Mower General Hospital in Philadelphia. Again returned to his regiment, Glass deserted on December 2, 1864, this time with no record of the circumstances.[3]]

Norfolk Jail 12th April. [1864]

To B. F. Butler
Maj. Genl Comdg.

General

I hope you will excuse the liberty I thus take in addressing a letter to you. My name is Max Glass, I served honorabl in the Italien and Austrian arme. After Asperemonte [Aspromonte] wher Garibaldy was woundet [4] I resigned. Last year I succidet in coming to America, and to offer my service for the country. I arived 12th August in N.Y. My intention was to remain a few days in the city, and then to present myself befor the Govenor, show him my papers, and to offer him my service. Unfortunate after being three days in the City I made an acquaintance with a man dressed in a capt: uniform, and as he spoke German I questioned him, wath I would have to do in such a case. He advised me not to go to the Govenor, becaus every one who desired a comition has to help to recruit a company, and that would need a great deal of money, and as I dont speak English my way would be useless, but if I wanted to join the service I must give him my papers which he would show his Colonel, and assured me after being in service a short time that I would recievd a comition and the benefit of a bounty, he said he belonged to the 12th N.Y. Cavl: and that I should go with him to Norwich wher his Regt. was recruiting. As I had no money and faith in the word of an officer I followed him to that place wher we arrived the next morning. After taking my papers he left me and returned with a citizien and told me to go with the citizien, and that all was right. I was carried to an office wher I was told to sign my name, after doing this I was carried befor a doctor and sworn in. I was astonished to be brought in a room wher I was guarded; I questioned but no one understood me. Later I found a man in the clothing office who spok the French language and to my surprise I found that I had been decieved. I was brought as a substitut,[5] and the man who brought me was no Capt. but a N.Y. Swindler. Without frind being in America 5 days, I had no aide. I was sent to New Haven and ther I complained me to colonel commanding, but he said as I now [know] not the man who brought me he could do nothing, but detaild me for Prof. guard duty, wich duty I have done faithfull. As I later desired to be sent for the enemy, I was sent to the 8th Con. V. Arrived at the regt: I was abused for reason that I never understand. It may have been, becaus I did not make them my companions in drinking, or as I am a Jew. If I went in the street or any wher I was called Jew. Christh killer & such names. I also had stones, dirt thrown at me. I complained me to the comp. office & the Colonel, begged to be transferred, that no man that had feeling could stand such treatment; but no one would investigate. I wnt to General Heckman [6] but could get no hearing. Five weeks ago we had a skirmish drill. A part of the Regiment only was going through drill, and we were reposing, as usual many of them began to abuse me by throing mud at me & calling me some of the most infamous names. The officie. in charge 1t Lt. Radburn [Rathbun] acted not as was his duty by not stoping the abusement, and as my feeling was very much moritified I started to the camp in order to report it to the comander of the regt., but as I made about twenty pases the named offic. cried after me halt Dutchman, and as that was no way to order a soldier I kept on, and the offic: sent after me a corp. with the tow men who had abused me, they caught me by the collar & draged me back., befor the whole company of man so they could make fun of me. After finishing drill I reported the whole affair to the comd. of the regt. Capt. Hoyt,[7] demanded a court-marshal for the offence and myself, I waited some time but no court marshal was given to me and I was still abused. After seeking in every way for Justice & not recieving it I resolved to go to Norfolk and stay eight days and reported myself as a deserter in order to get a courtmarshal. Arrived at Norfolk I learned that man were wanted in the navy & I entlisted for a Gun Boat, thinking I was doing no wrong. I was arested ther by an offic. of my regmt; and brought to this prison.

General! I hope you will take this into your kind consideration, and I beg you heartily concerning this that I was decieved, il treated, no justice given to me and therefor needed to leave the regiment; that you shall not find me guilty to suffer now in prison.

I cant be called a deserter from the service of the U.S. I cant be called a bounty jumper,[8] I never recieved a bounty. As I would be more useful in the field than in prison I emplore you to transfer me from my Regt. to another taking again 3. years service without any bounty. Closing this I have no more to say, that all that I said I cane prove by witnesses officer or privates.[9] In hope of your pity for unfortunate man whose intention are the best.

I remain your humble servent

Max Glass.

144. GEORGIA RECOLLECTIONS

Civil War Recollections of Isaac Hermann, of Sandersville, Washington County, Georgia, 1861–1866 [1]

[Isaac Hermann at the age of twenty-one had arrived at Castle Garden in the Port of New York in a four-masted schooner in the fall of 1859, coming from Alsace-Lorraine in France. With his cousin Abram, he found his way to Davisboro and then to Fenn's Bridge, Georgia. How much of the ideology of the dominant class in Georgia he had soaked up by 1861 is not clear from these reminiscences, since they were written down some fifty years after the events. The value of these passages is different from that of a contemporaneous diary, since we have here an exposition of attitudes and opinions that have been crystallized in the passage of time. Of interest are not only his encounter with J. P. Benjamin, but particularly his reflections and frame of mind at the end of the war. After returning from the Confederate army in the fall of 1865, he became a small merchant in Sandersville, raised a family of six sons and one daughter, served on the local board of education, and wrote his memoirs.[2] The title of "Captain" he acquired not in the Confederate army, but shortly after the war when he was elected Captain of a volunteer artillery company that he initiated in order to "defend" the county's white population against the freed Negroes! [3]]

. . . The writer being a Frenchman, a rather scarce article in those days in this country, elicited no little curiosity among the members of the First Georgia Regiment.[4] . . .

In getting my transportation the Quartermaster asked me to deliver a package to General [Pierre G. T.] Beauregard as I would pass via Manassas Junction. When I arrived I inquired for his quarters, when I was informed that he had left for Centreville, I followed to that place, when I was told he had left for Richmond. Arriving at Richmond I went at once to the Executive Department in quest of him and should I fail to find him, would leave my package there, which I did. This was on Saturday evening, I had not a copper in money with me, but I had my pay roll; going at once to the Treasury Department, to my utter consternation, I found it closed. A very affable gentleman informed me that the office was closed until Monday morning. I said, "What am I to do, I have not a cent of money in my pocket and no baggage," for at that time hotels had adopted a rule that guests without baggage would have to pay in advance. I remarked that I could not stay out in the streets, so the gentleman pulled a $10.00 bill out of his pocket and handed it to me saying, "Will that do you until Monday morning, 8 o'clock? When the office will be open, everything will be all right." I thanked him very kindly. Monday I presented my bill which was over six months in arrears. They paid it at once in Alabama State bills, a twenty-five cent silver and two cents coppers. I did not question the correctness of their calculation. I took the money and went in quest of my friend who so kindly advanced me the $10.00. I found him sitting at a desk. He was very busy. I handed him a $10.00 bill and again thanked him for his kindness; he refused it saying: "Never mind, you are a long ways from home and may need it." I replied that I had enough to make out without it, I said that I appreciated it, but didn't like to take presents from strangers; he said, "We are no strangers, my name is Juda P. Benjamin." Mr. Benjamin was at that time Secretary of the Treasury of the Confederate States. He was an eminent lawyer from the State of Louisiana, he became later Secretary of War, and when Lee surrendered he escaped to England to avoid the wrath of the Federal Officials who offered a premium for his capture. He became Queen's Consul [Counsel] in England and his reputation became international. No American who was stranded ever appealed to him in vain, especially those from the South. It is said of him that he gave away fortunes in charity. . . .

New edicts appeared from time to time from Washington, D. C., Congress promulgated laws to suit their motives, and notwithstanding the agreement between General Lee and General Grant at Appomattox that the men should return, build up their waste places and not again to take up arms until properly exchanged and they should not be molested as long as they should attend to their daily avocations, Congress established what was then known as the Freedmen's Bureau,[5] seemingly for the protection of the Negroes, as if they needed any, as their devotion to their master and their behavior at home while every white man able to bear arms was at the front fighting for their homes and firesides, leaving their families in the hands of their slaves whose devotion was exemplary, was not that a sufficient guarantee of the relationship between slaves and masters? The attachment was of the tenderest kind and a white man would have freely offered his life for the protection of his servants; but that condition did not suit our adversaries. . . .

The garrisons were gradually withdrawn; the carpet baggers remained and ruled; Negroes formed themselves into clubs and organizations under their leadership, when as an avalanche all over the Southern states appeared the K. K. K.'s, called the Ku Klux Klan, or the Boys Who Had Died at Manassas, who have come back to regulate matters. Terror struck into the ranks of the guilty and of the would be organizers and the country soon resumed its normal state, Governor fled and Legislators took to the bush. . . .[6]

I had rented the store house from Mr. Billy Smith where he and

Slade had done business before the war, in Sandersville, and opened up business in heavy and family groceries. In the meantime my team was making the trip between Sandersville and the Central terminal, which had not considerably advanced, owing to the demoralized condition of labor, so I concluded at this particular time it would accelerate matters by hauling a load of merchandise with my team; hence I drove through all the way to Savannah. While there, on passing Congress street, I met an old friend named Abe Einstein, of the firm of Einstein and Erkman [sic: Eckman], wholesale drygoods merchants.[7] He was speaking to one Mr. Cohen from New York, who had just arrived by steamer with a cargo of drygoods. He wanted to locate in Augusta,[8] but owing to the Federals having torn up that branch of the railroad at Millen the Augusta trains run no further than Waynesboro. Hence he was trying to fill in the gap with teams. Mr. Einstein told him that I had a splendid team and that I would be a good man for him to employ. So he asked me if I would haul a load for him. I replied I would if he would pay me enough for it. He said, How much can you pull at a load? I said, My mules can pull all that the wagon can hold up. What do you ask? Four hundred dollars. Whiz, I did not want to buy your team, I only wanted to hire it. I said to him, Well, that is my price. I said, You fellows up North tore up the road, you ought to be able to pay for such accomodations as you can get. He studied over the situation a little. Turning to Mr. Einstein, Do you know this man; can I rely on him? Mr. Einstein replied, Perfectly reliable, I stand sponsor. He said, I tell you what I'll do, I'll pay you down $200.00 and Mr. Einstein will pay you $200.00 when you return. . . .

145. ON THE ASSASSINATION OF LINCOLN

Funeral Oration by Dr. Max Lilienthal at the Broadway Synagogue, Congregation Bene Israel, Cincinnati, April 19, 1865 [1]

[Those of us who personally experienced and shared the national grief at the death of President Franklin D. Roosevelt can have a direct inkling of the emotions aroused by the assassination of Lincoln. On April 14, 1865

(Good Friday) there was high jubilation, and victory sermons and addresses were being delivered to celebrate Lee's surrender to Grant at Appomatox on April 9. On April 11 (which happened to be the first day of Passover), Lincoln had addressed a joyous throng from the White House, stressing the responsibilities of reunification and reconstruction. While the victory sermons were still being delivered and published, John Wilkes Booth shot Lincoln at about 10 P. M. in Ford's Theater in Washington. Expressing the Confederate slogan that the Federal Government was tyrannical in frustrating secession, Booth had shouted the murderous and demagogic motto, *"sic semper tyrannis!"* Lincoln died early Saturday morning. Wrath, gloom, and grief rocked the Union. On Wednesday, April 19, at noon, funeral services were held in Washington, and simultaneously in numberless cities and towns. This address by Dr. Max Lilienthal (1815–1882) was one of many thus delivered.[2] It is both a tribute to "the first laborer-President" and the Union, and an appeal that "justice and no vengeance" should govern our attitude to the defeated Confederacy.[3] Dr. Lilienthal's was an influential voice in Cincinnati, to which he had come in 1855 to assume the ministry of the Reform congregation, Bene Israel. Since 1860 he had been a member of the Cincinnati Board of Education. On the eve of the Civil War he had vigorously advocated preservation of the Union, and he privately favored the Union during the course of the war, although he "remained singularly silent" in public, perhaps under the influence of Dr. I. M. Wise, on whose *The Israelite* Dr. Lilienthal was an editor.[4] With the murder of Lincoln, Dr. Lilienthal eloquently broke his silence.]

Brethren, is this the same flag which a grateful and victorious people but a few days ago was greeting with the intensest national pride and national joy? Why is it drooping to-day its brilliant stars, its mighty stripes? Why is it draped in mourning? And this bust, crowned but a few days ago with the laurel-wreath of fresh and decisive victories, why does it look pale? Why, too, is it craped and hidden? Why are we ashamed and frightened to-day to look up to its mild and good features?

Alas, this is a gloomy day! From the dawn of American history up to this mournful hour, such an assemblage has never been convened. We have buried our Washington and our Jefferson, our Franklin and our Jackson, but such a meeting has never been witnessed. These patriots were full of years and full of honors; their task had been finished, and, resigned to the stern laws of nature, a grateful people accompanied them quietly to their resting place. But to-day the feelings of the nation are aroused as never before; a new crime has made its way into the land of our Republic, and murder! murder! is the agonizing cry that echoes from the Atlantic to the shores of the Pacific.

Oh, on the fatal Saturday morning that brought us such gloomy tidings, when receiving our morning papers, we were only prepared to read of the festivities of the nation, and to enjoy once more the jubilee of the past day. We hurried to the telegraphic dispatches—what letters are these? What do they mean? We were unwilling to trust our senses; we thought in the dizziness of yesterday's feast we had forgotten our letters, had unlearned our spelling; we could at first not realize the stern truth. But when we recovered from our first shock—when we became convinced of the terrible reality—then the heart of the nation stood still, breathless, lifeless, paralyzed! And when tears began to relieve our stupification, the lips were quivering and shivering with the heart-rending exclamation: O, God, our good President has been assassinated!

That was a terrible morning, indeed! People were running to and fro, restless, comfortless, pursued in all streets by the same bewildering uneasiness, void of speech, void of thought—for we had not yet learned to read and to understand a page of American history, written by the dagger [6] of an Assassin.

Indeed, a great man has fallen in Israel! There never sat in the Presidential chair of this country a man, who, by his life, as well as by his death, so fully demonstrated the progress of modern ideas and the greatness and glory of our institutions. Disregarding the sterling virtues of the individual man, it seems as if it had been his manifest destiny to impress upon the people the invaluable privilege of our laws and our institutions. The nation feels this, and hence, at the shrine of the assassinated body, offers prayers and thanks for having witnessed the example of such a man's life; thinks herself especially indebted to him and to his memory, and mourns so much the deeper for his loss.

Who was Abraham Lincoln? The first laborer-President! Of his antecedents nothing could be said, but that he had risen by his own energies from the lowest sphere of life. He had battled with all kind of personal difficulties, and had overcome them; he had struggled against all obstacles, and had conquered them; and by his sagacity, energy and unsophisticated honesty, had succeeded to be elected to fill the greatest office in the hands of the people. And thus his election proved, for the first time, the full meaning of American liberty and equality.

The people, the laboring classes, all over the world, were now emancipated indeed; their rights were not a mere dead letter, they were now sealed and signed by the majestic hand of history, they were, in Abraham Lincoln, the workman, raised to the full acquisition of the infinite rights of man. Do not give up the work, says his example, because you are born in an obscure station; do not get disheartened, because you have to wrestle with the disadvantages of a want of education—life is the best school, energy and perseverance the best teacher, honesty of purpose the best means for obtaining success; follow his example, and we shall finally, and in fact, establish the equality of mankind. He has achieved this triumph, and a whole world stands there, first amazed and then admiring the man, who, by his own indomitable energy, proved the greatness and glory of our institutions.

But not this fact alone endears him to the American heart and the liberty-loving people all over the world. Still faster he took hold on our affections by being the truest representative of our unlimited and invincible love for the Union and our flag. There lives no man in this country in whom the people had more implicit confidence that he would not surrender the Union cost what it may. There his kindness was at an end, there he would hear of no party cry; the Union must, and shall, be saved was the unwavering motto of his administration. Union first. In the North he tried all means to reconcile the party spirit. He called to his aid every man of the Democratic party in whose loyalty he could put his trust; Stanton, and Grant, and Sherman, and a host of other Democrats, were called to the most important offices of the Government; let the party spirit be silent, was his request, till the Union is saved; for Heaven's sake, put the country above the party. And towards the South? Lay down your arms, reconstruct the Union, and I am ready to receive you with open arms, was his prayer, the words of his proclaimed amnesty.[6] He was the true interpreter of our feelings toward the South. We did love her, in spite of all her crimes, and he did love her too. We wanted to extend pardon to every repentant rebel, and he was ready to grant it in the fullness of the executive power. We were willing to forget the hecatombs of blood and treasure, provided the old flag were acknowledged again all over the insurgent States; he too, though weeping with the widow and mourning with the orphan, was willing to cover treason and rebellion with the mantle of love and clemency. But for the Union he stood, immovable as the North Star, and hence the confidence of the people in his integrity, in his constancy. He was re-elected for the second term, not by politicians, not by the wire-pulling of hungry office seekers, but by the stern voice of the people, who knew that in his hands their wishes for the South, and for the safety of the Union were the best cared for; his sincerity, the simplicity of his heart, and the homely shrewdness of his mind were, to the people, the best guarantees against the intrigues of diplomacy, or the connivances of party passions. And the Union was saved under his Administration—established upon a platform broader and finer than under either Washington or Jackson. Not a Union half free and half slave; not a Union of semi-independent sovereignties; not a Union of Mason and Dixon's line; not a Union floating on the border ruffianism of a Missouri Compromise; but a Union one and indivisible, free from north to south, and east to west; a supreme power enhanced over all state sovereignties. The dangers which Washington predicted passed; the threats which Jackson uttered fulfilled; and over a redeemed and newborn country floated the star-spangled banner, stained yet with the fresh blood of its heroes, but with the stripes in all their grandeur, the thirty-six stars in all their splendor. What wonder that we began to look on him as the incarnation of our Union? We revered him, we loved him, we regarded him as a man of superior destiny, and intrusted willingly and thankfully to him the helm of our ship.

But what his life could not accomplish, to make him the full representative of our great institutions, and the true interpreter of the character of our people, fell to the lot of his death. If he had lingered on his sickbed, and died a natural death, the calamity then, too, would have been a national one, but it would not have taught us a new and important lesson. In the midst of civil warfare, in the midst of still living party passions, to fall by the dagger of an assassin, suddenly, unexpectedly, and with no revolution, no anarchy, no outbreak, but everywhere respect for the law, willing submission to the constituted authority, the machinery of Government neither interrupted nor out of order, that lesson fills us with new reverence for our almost superhuman institutions; makes the Republic still more precious, in our estimation, than ever before. And this lesson we profited by the death of our lamented President; his blood was the great seal that was affixed to republican government and republican institutions. Who, henceforth, will contest the vitality, the possibility, the efficiency, of free institutions? Who, hereafter, will deny that the history of this nation outshines all other nations in respect for law and order?

The hand of death hallows every human corpse, enshrines every death-bed with a sanctifying halo; but how much more the coffin of our illustrious martyr! We stand with feelings of awe and reverence at the side of such a martyr, and such a sacrifice. But the sight is too overwhelming; the meaning of such a life and death overawes our innermost soul. We turn away, and our heart longs for the object to whom our love and our affection were devoted. We gaze no longer at the hero and patriot, we look at the man and the friend. And what a change! This man, without pride and ostentation, with a smile for everyone and everything, with the welcoming grasp and winning word—is that the man who is identified with the nation's terrible struggle and its deliverance?[7] Yes, this man is Lincoln; behind this homely appearance beats a heart full of faith, love and charity; within this heart thrones an integrity that escaped suspicion in the most corrupt time. All the foul slanders of his enemies and his opponents could excite in him neither anger, nor hatred; his good humor assists him in overcoming the onerous duties of his office, or the malice of his assailants; he often enlivens the consultation by an apt anecdote; he indulges in sallies of wit, but they leave no sting behind. His heart is as good as his conscience is just and clear. He can do no harm; he can not mistrust; he can not punish; he can only love and forgive; he is only bent on grace and reconciliation. Stern to himself, he is lenient toward others; faithful to his trust and his duties, he can not mistrust others; knowing the obstacles he himself has to overcome, he has an excuse for the tardiness and the shortcoming of others; when every one points to faults and mistakes, he is still hopeful and waits for improvement; when everyone desponds and despairs, he has still faith in the sacred cause of his mission; and then, and only then, when the success of his sacred charge is at stake, then he strikes the blow, which others would have dealt long ago. What wonder that such amiableness won him the love and respect of all those who knew him, who had spoken to him; what wonder that this faithfulness to his charge at last won for him the respect even of the rebel press in Richmond; what wonder that this combination of firm, unselfish patriotism with such a kindliness of heart and shrewdness of mind obtained for him the admiration of Europe. His last inaugural address [8] raised him to the pinnacle of admiring acknowledgment; he was on the point of being compared, by the impartial press of England, with Washington, Hampden [9] and Cromwell. The nation began to feel proud of him; the country began to feel assured of a happy termination of this terrible struggle, with a harvest full of peace, and the blessings of reconciliation; the nations were looking for a new birth-day of human liberty; inaugurated by the laborer-President; and his words became as full of influence as any of the sovereigns of the great powers.

And these hopes were blighted by foul premeditated assassination! these anticipations were frustrated by the dagger of a murderer! Brethren, the first, wild excitement, that so justly aroused all, has passed away; consideration, stern, calm and impassionate, takes its place, and now we do not know which shall we more condemn—the atrocity of the crime, or the folly and madness of the murder. Whom?—what did they slaughter? Was Lincoln a Julius Caesar, whose ambition, military genius and indomitable energy represented and supported a new order of things? Was Lincoln a man like Louis XIV, who declared—I am the State? Lincoln was no Caesar, no Henry IV, no William of Orange, no Louis XIV. He was neither the military genius of this war, that by his death our armies were deprived of their leader; nor was he a pioneer, standing alone and aloof in his age; nor did he represent a concentrated power like Louis XIV; he was nothing but the exponent of the sovereign will of the people; nothing but the elected executive of the people's Government; nothing but the representative of the idea [of] universal freedom, as enunciated in 1860, and indorsed by an overwhelming majority of the people in 1864.[10] You may kill a man, but you can not kill a nation. You may kill the temporary Executive, but you can not assassinate the Government. In the hour of defeat and surrender, in the hour of hopeless prostration at the feet of your conqueror, you murder him, who alone was able to save you; who, invested by the people with the sovereign power of pardon and clemency, was willing to forgive and to pardon you; who, seeing still in the rebel foe only a prodigal son of the Union, was willing to receive you back with loving arms. Madman, stop; you strike your best, your truest friend! In vain the victim falls and reels in his blood!

God help the South, exclaimed a rebel Major in Washington when he heard the stunning tidings; that is the severest blow the South has yet received, cried out Colonel Ould.[11] The hour of mercy is past; the day of bloody retaliation is dawning. Oh! God, why dost thou allow our brethren in the South to be so shockingly misled by their leaders? Why must they empty the cup of sin and crime to its very last dregs? Was the rebellion not enough that brought mourning to every hearthstone and misery to every fireside; that robbed the cradle and grave and swept with ruin and desolation throughout the land—why yet that villainous crime of assassination? There she stands now, disgraced before the world; the Cain's mark on the dejected brow; all sympathy is lost for her, all pity with the vanquished is gone for her; the assassin is shunned, given up to law's bloody vengeance. The nations despise her; the princes will hate her for having given such an example; her Negroes will exult in having obtained license for murder and assassination. May the Lord have mercy on your poor souls!

But no, brethren, we are assembled to do homage to his memory; we have come to do honor to his great and good name; let us not desecrate this solemn hour by thoughts of vengeance and outbursts of indignation, becoming the first moment of wild and inconsiderate excitement, but not befitting the calm and magnanimous character of a great, free, and victorious nation. Do you wish to honor his memory indeed; do you intend to hand down to posterity his name in all its grandeur and glory, unstained by passions and untarnished by violence!—consider the legacy he has left you, execute it in the sense he was willing to finish his great work. To finish the work he has begun; to do it with that spirit of justice and firmness he has taught and shown us; to perform our duties with that sincere aspiration for universal happiness, without any desire of satisfying a momentary passion or impulse, however justifiable it may be—this is the only way in which we can honor the departed, and celebrate this hour in a manner becoming the great man who is gathered to his predecessors.

Be men, before, and above all, cool, calm, and dispassionate. He has set us the example, and by following his teachings, we will honor his memory. His disposition was not turned to passion by the bloodiness of the time. Obliged to make his way privately through a slave State to escape a plot to assassinate him on his way to the Capitol to assume his office;[12] ridiculed for his precautions by those who desired his death; made the object of abuse so foul and malignant, that it would have aroused implacable animosity in any man of ordinary human feelings—he retained his moderation of temper, his self-command, sound judgment, rectitude of intention, and kind disposition. He closed his life with an act of unexampled magnanimity and clemency, by dismissing the armed leaders of the rebellion to their homes,[13] and to return to peace and equal rights in the country they had deluged with blood. Let us profit by his almost divine example. The arm of the law is strong; the eye of justice is sharp and watchful; the constituted authorities will do their duty fully and solemnly, to bring the criminals and their abettors to light, and to the bar of punishment. Let us not take justice into our hands. No mob and no anarchy!

I know, the suspicion of a wide spread conspiracy is aroused in many a mind; we think ourselves justified in tracing the root of the atrocious crime to other men than those, who committed the bloody deed. This may be; but leave it to the proper hands, they will find the guilty ones. We have stood the trial of rebellion and we have broken it, we stood the horrors of the battle-fields and their agonies, and we have conquered; let us stand the trial of this gloomy hour, too, and all danger will soon have vanished.

The world, which we have taught, that a free people is able to support and to defend its Government, must also learn, that a free people considers liberty to be respect for the law under any, even the most stirring trials, and that anarchy has nothing in common with the spirit of true freedom. Hence, be cool, calm, and dispassionate.

This remark, of course, does not imply that the sword of justice shall be sheathed—that treason shall receive an homage of mercy—that arson, and pillage, and murder shall go unpunished, and that all will be forgotten if only the Union be restored. No, brethren, it means only: Justice but no vengeance! It was the only fault of our lamented President, and he had to pay for it with his precious life, that he believed, by pardon and mercy, he could reconcile the bitter enemies of this country, and win them over to the sacred cause of our united Republic. To allow a man like Booth—a man who, on the stage of New Orleans, trampled upon our flag, spat at it and disgraced it—to allow such a man to go about free and unmolested in our capital, was a fatal error, a disastrous mistake, and the whole country has to suffer and to mourn for it. No! the days of leniency with rebel leaders are gone—the days of indulgence with open conspirators, and their aiders and abettors, are past; crime must be punished: the majesty of the law must be vindicated. We owe that to our self-preservation; we are prompted to do it from motives of mere self-defense. Secessionists in our midst must be silenced, rebel sympathizers must be hushed down, let them beware to arouse the fury of the insulted and afflicted nation. Yes, justice must be met; whosoever sheds man's blood, his will be shed; but brethren, let this be done by the proper authorities; let it be done with the stern calmness and majesty of the law—justice and no vengeance. Vengeance strikes the guilty and the innocent one; vengeance would tarnish our victory, disgrace our history, and miss the aim of our endeavors to reconstruct our country. There are thousands in the South who abhor the crime committed in our midst, there are thousands waiting eagerly for an opportunity of renewing their allegiance to our Constitution; shall we estrange them to our cause, by unmerited punishment? Shall we drive them to despair, and a second rebellion, by coupling the repentant sinner with the guilty criminal and leader? No, brethren; justice and no vengeance must henceforth be our motto, justice and no vengeance must be the sacred pledge and vow of this day, by which we will honor the memory of the departed, and assist in carrying out the work to which his virtuous and noble life was devoted.

Thirdly, in this solemn and mournful hour, by the grave of the assassinated President, let us renew our own promise, that neither life nor treasure shall be spared until the Union will be restored in all its majesty and integrity. If the murder was not the mere result of passionate madness; if it was not the mere offspring of personal hatred, inconsiderate vengeance and gratification, if, in the counsel of those who projected it, planned it, and, may be, paid for it, this foul crime had some meaning: it was the intent to paralyze the strong arm of the nation, and to wrest from us, in the final hour of victory, the palm of success and glory. Let us prove to them, that as futile as were their calculations about the weakness and the division of sentiment in the North at the outbreak of this wicked rebellion, so false and absurd were their estimates at the planning and the execution of this murder. Let us show them that the strength of the Republic lies in the integrity of the people, which no assassin can destroy. Let them understand that it was even strengthened by the dastardly act which took the life of Abraham Lincoln. Let them learn that this calamity binds us closer to our country; that to a considerable extent it has already healed divisions, and that in this hour, this flag, redeemed from rebellion and treason appears to us more precious than ever. Let us rally around our banner, and do our duty manfully and thoroughly. Let us rally round the man who now holds the responsible and honorous [onerous?] office of Chief Magistrate, and let him have our hearty and undivided support. Let a mistake, though displayed under circumstances which caused National mortification, not undermine our confidence in the man;[14] his past life, his martyrdom for the sacred cause of the Union, is the best guarantee that he will prove himself worthy of the high office. Let him have our best wishes, our most fervent prayers. Being a Southern man himself, he knows better than any man in the North, how to distinguish between the Southern people and their leaders. With stern justice in the right hand, he will move forward, tempering it with mercy, and offering the olive branch of pardon and peace. Let us be confident that the executive office is safe in his hands, and that we [he?] will carry out the wishes of the loyal people in closing up the rebellion. And when that day will come, on which he will lay down on the grave of our murdered chief, as a tribute of the people, the flag of the country, no star missing, no star darkened, all redeemed in their brightest glory, all shining in one glorious constellation, when he then will say: The work thou hast begun, is done and finished; the Union is now a Union in reality, the people are now an undivided nation in sentiment and institutions; and this end was attained by the hearty support of the people, and by their implicit confidence in their Government. Brethren, then we will have honored the memory of the departed; then we will have celebrated this hour in a manner becoming the principles he has proclaimed; then we may erect him a monument with the epitaph: A free, united, and grateful nation, to Abraham Lincoln, the preserver of the Union.

Yes, illustrious martyr, this is the vow we make, swearing on the blood of thy wounds; these are the resolutions we are forming in this solemn hour of national grief and national mourning. Thou shalt not have lived, thou shalt not have toiled and labored, to no purpose; we take up thy legacy, and will execute [it] faithfully and thoroughly; we will cleanse this land from treason and rebellion; that the country shall not be deluged again with the life-blood of its children. We will forgive, as his example has taught us, the repentant sinner. Over the fresh grave of our hero, we will take him back to our heart, sharing with him our blessings and our rights. We will, as thou hast admonished us, co-operate in regenerating the Southern half of our Union, and repay the misery she has brought to our homes, with unlimited love and mercy. We will stand firm to our Government and our flag, till the work thou hast so gloriously begun shall be brought to a still more glorious end. Smile on! they can not bury the principles thou hast bequeathed us; thy name shall be as immortal as the truth of thy teaching. Abraham Lincoln, friend of the people, the poor and the slave, farewell! We will cherish and revere thy memory forever; for thou wast great, because thou wast good, and thou wast good, because thou wast great. Farewell, till God grants us a meeting in eternity.

146. WORKERS, JEW AND GENTILE

Excerpt from *The Address of the National Labor Congress to the Workingmen of the United States,* by A. C. Cameron, *Chicago, July, 1867* [1]

[This *Address,* an important landmark in American labor history, contains the first discovered reference to the fact that the trade union movement wants Jewish workers to join the ranks of organized labor. The passage affirms the elementary fact that "the interests of labor are one; that there should be no distinction of race or nationality; no classification of Jew or Gentile, Christian or Infidel; that there is but one dividing line—that which separates mankind into two great classes, the class that labors and the class that lives by others' labors." The records are obscure as to what portion of the then still small Jewish working class belonged to trade unions, but it is known that by 1864 there were Jews in the cigar-makers' union, and probably in the tailors' unions.

The National Labor Congress, which founded the National Labor Union, had opened in Baltimore on August 20, 1866, with 60 delegates from the majority of states in the Union. A Committee headed by Andrew Carr Cameron (1834–1890), a Chicago printer and labor editor of Scottish descent, was instructed to draft the document. The *Address,* which was widely distributed in leaflet form, dealt with every important issue confronting the workers: the eight-hour day, independent labor political action, the rights of women workers, and particularly, as in the excerpt given, the need to organize Negro workers into the general trade unions.[2]

It should be observed that it was while emphasizing the need for unity in the trade unions of Negro and white workers that the *Address* included reference to the need for unity of Jew and Gentile in the unions.]

. . . The first thing to be accomplished before we can hope for any great results is the thorough organization of all the departments of labor. This work, although its beginning is of such recent date, has progressed with amazing rapidity. Leagues, societies and associations exist in all the large towns and cities, and in many villages and country districts. There are central organizations in many of the states, and one national labor congress, the result of whose deliberation on the future welfare of the country can scarcely be overestimated. In this connection we cannot overlook the important position now assigned to the colored race in this contest. Unpalatable as the truth may be to many, it is needless to disguise the fact that they are destined to occupy a different position in the future, to what they have in the past; that they must necessarily become in their new relationship an element of strength or an element of weakness, and it is for the workingmen of America to say which that shall be.

The systematic organization and consolidation of labor must henceforth become the watchword of the true reformer. To accomplish this the co-operation of the African race in America must be secured. If those most directly interested fail to perform this duty, others will avail themselves of it to their injury. Indeed a practical illustration of this was afforded in the recent importation of colored caulkers from Portsmouth, Va., to Boston, Mass., during the struggle on the eight hour question. What is wanted then, is for every union to help inculcate the grand, ennobling idea that the interests of labor are one; that there should be no distinction of race or nationality; no classification of Jew or Gentile, Christian or Infidel; that there is but one dividing line—that which separates mankind into two great classes, the class that labors and the class that lives by others' labors. This, in our judgment, is the true course for us as workingmen. The interest of all on our side of the line is the same, and should we be so far misled by prejudice or passion as to refuse to aid the spread of union principles among any of our fellow toilers, we would be untrue to them, untrue to ourselves and to the great cause we profess to have at heart. If these general principles be correct, we must seek the co-operation of the African race in America. . . .

147. EXCLUDING JEWS FROM INSURANCE

Editorial, "The Insurance Companies and the Jews," *Sunday Disptach,* Philadelphia, April 21, 1867 [1]

[Early in 1867, the long-standing and wide-spread practise of fire insurance companies in New York and elsewhere of discriminating against small Jewish merchants was brought into the open and became a public issue. In general, the fire insurance companies had had three bad years, with 1866, the worst, bringing "ruin and disaster to many."[2] In New York city, 23 of 104 companies omitted their annual dividends, while others had to declare smaller ones than usual.[3] Of course, the insurance rates went up, but some of the companies sought to reduce the risks by general orders to their agents not to insure Jews or to insure them only under special circumstances that did not apply to others.

The first signs of the discriminatory practice were noted in *The Israelite* of December 7, 1866 and February 8, 1867, in which attention was called to the anti-Semitic instructions issued by the Hartford Fire Insurance Company of Hartford, Conn. and the Manhattan Fire Insurance Company of New York. The Jews did not begin to rouse themselves, however, until *The Israelite* of March 1, 1867,[4] followed by *The Jewish Messenger* a week later, published the full texts of a "Special Circular" sent out by Alexander Stoddart, General Agent of the Underwriters' Agency in New York. This Agency coordinated the insurance business in southern and western states of four New York companies, the Germania, Hanover, Niagara, and Republic.[5] The circular, together with his correspondence with agents, left no room for doubt that he was discriminating against Jews as a whole. Then resolutions, indignation meetings, boycotts and cancellations of policies were organized in Cincinnati, Indianapolis, St. Louis, Richmond, Va., Louisville, Ky., Chicago, Memphis, Evansville, Ind., Cleveland, Ligonier, Ind., New Haven, Conn., Quincy, Ill., and Philadelphia.[6] There was public discussion of the possibility that Jews would organize their own insurance company if driven to do so, but nothing came of that idea.[7] In the general press, the discriminatory practice was supported, justified or explained away in the *Wall Street Underwriter, The Insurance Monitor and Wall Street Review,* the *Baltimore Underwriter,* the New York *Herald,* the *Cincinnati Commercial,* and *The Nation.* Opposition to the unjust discrimination was expressed in the Baltimore *Telegram,* the New York *Handels Zeitung,* the *New-York Tribune,* the *Petersburg* (Va.) *Daily Examiner,* the Nashville *Press and Times,* the New York *Round Table,* the Philadelphia *Evening Telegraph,* and the *Banking and Insurance Chronicle* of Chicago. *The New York Times* equivocated.[8] At least one cartoon, replete with "hook-noses" and "Jewish accent," appeared in a "comic" magazine.[9]

The editorial that follows hints at the fundamental cause when it notes that capitalism stimulates sharp practices without regard to race, nationality, or religion: "It is an undeniable fact that in their business relations the Jews stand as high as any other class in the community. They have a proverbial reputation for close dealing, but the generality of Christian merchants are fully as ready to drive a hard bargain whenever they have an opportunity as any of their Hebrew neighbors."

That the issue is still not closed can be seen from the report of November,

1949, in the *Personal ADL Letter* of the Denver office of the Anti-Defamation League of B'nai Brith, that the Farmers Alliance Insurance Company of McPherson, Kansas had "cancelled all contracts with Jewish policyholders in Denver."]

For some time past the Jews have been very much excited on account of the action of certain insurance companies, who decline to take risks from individuals of that religious belief. Much indignation has been expressed, not only among the Jews, but among citizens of all classes, and the illiberal conduct of the companies has generally been condemned by the better class of business men. The difficulty was first started by the Underwriters' Agency of New York city, an organization representing the Niagara, Republic, Hanover and Germania companies. The agents of this association were instructed to refuse making any insurance on property belonging to Jews. Other companies followed the lead of the Underwriters' Agency; and the Jewish merchants, very properly considering the matter not merely an insult to their religion, but as a reflection of the most serious kind on their integrity as business men, held a meeting to take some action in regard to it. A committee was appointed to consult with the insurance companies, and a circular was issued asking each of them whether they approved of the proscriptive movement.[10] To this a large number of replies were received, all of them written in respectful terms except those from the Home and Metropolitan companies.[11] Others did not reply, and it was consequently concluded that they endorsed the action of the Underwriters' Agency. The committee who had the matter in charge recently made a report to a large meeting of Jewish merchants, who assembled in the synagogue on Nineteenth street in New York,[12] and they offered the following preamble and resolutions, which were unanimously adopted:

WHEREAS, Unjust discriminations have been adopted by certain insurance companies between citizens professing the Jewish religion and those of other denominations:

And whereas, This course is calculated to deepen prejudices unworthy the age and country; therefore

Resolved, That duty and self-respect alike demand that we, as Israelites, should cease all connection with such institutions.

Resolved, That the following insurance companies—the Merchants', Croton, Exchange, Firemen's, American Exchange, Howard, National,

St. Nicholas, International, Humboldt, Indemnity, Lafayette, Arctic, Commercial, Corn Exchange, Commerce, Fulton, New Amsterdam, United States, St. Mark's, Hanover, Niagara, Connecticut, Long Island, Montauk (of Brooklyn), Jersey City, Enterprise, Firemen's Trust, Peter Cooper,[13] Washington and North River Companies—having failed to reply to the circular of the committee, they recommend that until satisfactory replies are received, our co-religionists do not insure in either of those companies.

Resolved, That the Jewish citizens throughout the United States be requested not to insure in the Home or Metropolitan Companies until the insulting letters sent to the committee be retracted; and finally,

Resolved, That the proceedings of the meeting be published in pamphlet form for distribution throughout the United States.[14]

The Jews say that the dishonesty of one or two persons, even if proved, is no reason why the whole body of Hebrew citizens should be proscribed, and they denounce the action of these insurance companies as nothing more nor less than an attempt at persecution, and as utterly unworthy of the present age and country. It is an undeniable fact that in their business relations the Jews stand as high as any other class in the community. They have a proverbial reputation for close dealing, but the generality of Christian merchants are fully as ready to drive a hard bargain whenever they have an opportunity as any of their Hebrew neighbors. There is this much to be said, however, that when the Jews do conclude a bargain they almost invariably stick to it, and when they undertake to do a thing they seldom fail to carry it out.

During the past nineteen years we have had numerous dealings with Jews, and they have uniformly been of the most satisfactory character. Among them are some of our best friends, and we can bear testimony to their general good conduct as citizens, to their integrity as merchants, to their liberality in religious sentiment, and to their general refinement and intelligence. In all of these respects they are fully the peers of any other religious sect in the country. We seldom or never hear of the failure of a Jewish merchant; Jews are very rarely accused or convicted of crimes, and the community is not charged with the support of Hebrew vagabonds and paupers in our almshouses and prisons. All of these facts speak very highly for the Jews, and show them to be orderly and well-behaved citizens. Besides this they are an unusually well-read and intelligent people, and it is a well known fact that they have among them some of the most learned men of the day. Several years ago there was published in the columns of the *Dispatch* a "Post-Biblical History of the Jews," by the celebrated Rabbi Raphael [Raphall] of New York.[15] This work was afterward issued in book form, and was commented upon in favorable terms by the press generally. The London *Athenaeum*—a journal well qualified to speak in the matter—pronounced it the best work of the kind ever written.

The peculiarities of the Hebrew religion have a tendency to keep those who adhere to its ancient forms in a measure separated from other citizens, and many persons who have but little to do with them know nothing about their good or bad qualities, and consequently would be likely to take this unjust action of the insurance companies as indicative of a general untrustworthiness on the part of all classes of Jews. Those who are best acquainted with them, and who have had most frequent dealings with them, know that the implied charge against their character is without the slightest foundation.[16]

The Jews are numerous and wealthy enough to organize insurance companies among themselves, and they could readily dispense with assistance of that kind from outsiders; but it is contrary to the interests of the country and to the proper business spirit that any such course should be adopted. The tendency to clannishness among persons of particular nationalities or religious beliefs should be discouraged as inimical to our republican institutions. That such conduct as that of the insurance companies will have the effect to draw the line between the Jewish and Christian religious sects broader and more distinct than it has ever been before must be evident to every one, and the Jews would not certainly be to blame if they were to retaliate by refusing to patronize any insurance companies in which the stock is not held by themselves. We hope that the good sense of our merchants will cause them to look at this matter in the proper light, and to condemn in the strongest terms the insulting action of a portion of the New York insurance companies. If the principle that any set of men are to be proscribed because they are members of a particular religious sect is once admitted there is no telling where it may end and it will be a subject of infinite vexation and annoyance in the future.[17]

148. DOUBLE–LYNCHING OF A JEW AND A NEGRO

News-story, "The Franklin, Tenn., Double Murder," *The Israelite,* Cincinnati, Ohio, August 28, 1868 [1]

[It was in Tennessee that the Ku Klux Klan was first organized in 1866, to become an instrument for the terrorizing of Negro and white supporters of the Radical Reconstruction government in the state, to keep the enfranchised Negroes away from the polls, and to restore economic and political power to the class that had led Tennessee into the Confederacy.[2] Disfranchised former Confederate Army generals were its state-wide leaders.

In the town of Franklin, the seat of Williamson county in Central Tennessee, S. A. Bierfield,[3] a young Russian Jew operating a dry-goods store, was known as a Radical Republican. He was friendly with the Negro population, employed a Negro as a clerk, and attracted a good number of Negroes as customers.[4] With the presidential elections approaching, the Klan terror intensified in the spring and summer of 1868, and a special session of the State Legislature convened on July 27 to cope with the problem by reconstituting an armed militia of Negro and white volunteers. On the night of August 15th, while Bierfield and his clerk, Lawrence Bowman, and a second Negro named Henry Morton were eating watermelon in the store, a masked lynch-mob broke in, and only Henry Morton escaped alive, to tell his story later to an official investigator.

Reports of the outrage appeared not only in the Tennessee press, but in the New York *Times* (front-page) as well as in newspapers in Philadelphia, Cincinnati, and elsewhere. After carrying the account printed below, *The Israelite* took no further notice of the event. In a few years, the Klan and the elements it represented succeeded in re-establishing the oppression of the Negro through minority rule.]

The deliberate and fiendish murder of Mr. Bierfeld, an Israelite, and a gentleman of good standing and character, as also the murder at about the same time a Negro in Bierfeld's [sic] employ, has been reported a week ago by telegraph, but so vaguely, that we refrained from mentioning the dark affair until the receipt of a more reliable account. This we find in the Nashville *Republican* of the 19th inst., sent us by a friend, and we reproduce the same below. The hands of the Ku Klux are, doubtless, red with guilt in the sad premises, and their real grounds consisted of but the fact, that Bierfeld was an intelligent advocate of the present reconstruction policy of Congress,[5] and a friend to the freedmen of his neighborhood, among whom—he being a merchant—he commanded quite a trade, and perhaps found it expedient to keep one from among their number in his employ, who shared the fate of his employer at the same hands.

The scarce less detestable creatures who apologized for the hounds in human guise on the surmise that Bierfeld was accessory to the murder of a young man a few days previous,[6] are liars inferentially we are safe to say, since no member of the Jewish race in this country, if in the world, at the present day would be accessory to a foul murder, and that, too, in a locality where he lives in peace, and prospers as a merchant. We let the aforesaid journal speak, display lines and all:

TERRIBLE MURDERS.

Two Men Killed in Franklin by a Lot of Armed Horsemen.

The *Press and Times*[7] of a late issue contains the following: At eleven or twelve o'clock on Saturday night, as great crowds of people were going to their homes after leaving Robinson's circus, a troop of horsemen dashed into town, yelling frightfully, and telling the crowd which they passed to get into their houses as quickly as possible. In a few moments every one was in doors, and a dead silence reigned around, save when heavy sounds were borne on the night from the dry-goods store of one Bierfeld, an Israelite, who carried on a little business in that line, and had a Negro man employed selling goods for him. The horsemen were breaking in his house. They dragged the Israelite out. They were about to hang him when he escaped and ran some hundred yards away from his house and took refuge in a livery stable. His enemies were upon him immediately, pistol in hand. They shot four balls into him, from the effects of which he died almost instantly. The colored man remained in the store, where they found and shot him through the body. He died yesterday morning.[8]

The cause of the intense enmity which could ripen into so fearful a crime is not definitely known. Our informants, Dr. Cliffe and N. J. Nichol, said it was thought that Bierfeld had something to do with the murder of young Ezell, some two or three weeks ago. He is the same man that was driven out of Pulaski[9] some months since by the same sort of fellows.

There is no apparent cause for the murder of the colored man.

When the fiendish outrage had been committed, the squad of troopers rode furiously out of town, whooping and hallooing frightfully.

* * *

Since the above was in type, we have received the following statement from a gentleman from Franklin:

"On Saturday night, the 15th inst., about eleven o'clock, Mr. Bierfeld, an Israelite, who was engaged in trading, fled from his store scared by men in disguise who had entered his place of business and attempted to conceal himself in Mr. Bostick's stable, but was pursued by the said disguised parties, and violently and forcibly dragged into the streets. While pleading for his life, and begging them to spare him for his mother's sake, he was shot four times in the breast. This happened in the streets of Franklin, near Mr. Briggs' store. If any one offered to intercede for him, it is not known. The parties who say they know the reason why he was killed by the men in disguise, alledge [sic] that he was in some way connected with the killing of Ezell, and that the foul deed was done in retaliation. Six or eight witnesses will testify that Mr. Bierfeld, on the night of the killing of Ezell, slept in the house of Mr. Colby. The good citizens condemn the atrocious act, while others attempt to justify the crime by saying that it was done in retaliation. Mr. Bierfeld was an active and prominent Republican, having considerable influence with the colored people."

Our informant says that was his only crime. A clerk of Mr. Bierfeld, whose name we can not learn, was killed at the same time, and by the same parties. Mr. Bierfeld's body was brought to Nashville [10] yesterday for interment.

149. "THE JEWS HAVE IT"

Extract from Editorial in the Los Angeles, California, *Daily News,* January 22, 1869 [1]

[Within the first month of its existence, the first daily newspaper in Los Angeles, then a city of only 5,000 population, felt it necessary to speak out against the "filthy way some persons have of classifying an individual with the nation or people from which he sprung, and seeking to involve him in the prejudice that may exist against that people and nation." The Census of 1850, the year in which Los Angeles was first incorporated, found six Jewish names in that city; the number grew slowly, so that in 1862, when the Congregation B'nai Berith was founded, it had thirty members, most of them immigrants from Germany and France. The anti-Semitic talk that the editor rebuked was compounded of what was even then already the stereotype that the Jews were rich, greedy, cautious, and "don't build houses," that is, they are transient. The editor argues against each of these "charges." It should be noted that he also touches on the taunting of the Irish; there were then very few Chinese in the area, although they later became the main target of abuse.]

We fell in conversation, the other day, with a stranger: "You have a good climate here," said he, "and all that; and your town looks thriving enough, but, my dear fellow, the Jews have it." It is no matter repeating our response, but the recollection of the stranger's remark provokes the present comments. And we will say at the outset that it is a filthy way some persons have of classifying an individual with the nation or people from which he sprung, and seeking to involve him in the prejudice that may exist against that people and nation. It is the part of an undiscriminating blackguard. "O, he's an Irishman." And because in certain circles it is allowable to speak tauntingly and depreciatingly of the Irish, it must be inferred that there's no polish or gentility among the Irish.

If the Jewish people were savages elsewhere, steeped in all grossness and villainy, yet if the portion of our population of that class were estimable citizens, it is the dictate of common decency to base an opinion in regard to them upon scrutiny.

Now we venture the assertion that the males and females of Los Angeles appertaining to the Israelitish persuasion, are among the most deserving of our people. We will say that the men are peculiarly marked for their sobriety and the women for their chaste and decorous demeanor and the freedom from the fearful scandal to which their Anglo-American sisters are so freely addicted. You will never witness a dissection of character or any indecent curiosity about neighbor's affairs among the Jewish ladies of Los Angeles.

It is Shakspeare['']s Shylock and Scott's Isaac of York, both wretchedly imitated by Dickens' Fagin,[2] that feed fat the old unfounded prejudice against the Jews in the English and American mind.

With one exception of a vagabond straggler, we will venture the assertion that there has not been a criminal prosecution against a Jew since the organization of the city. Mercilessly and remorselessly have confiding Californians been plucked of their substance in this section; but it is not the Jew, under guise of favor and friendship, that has wrested from them their fair and hereditary possessions by extortionate rates of interest—rates that have absorbed valuable ranches in a year or two. As a class, they have been punctiliously honorable in their commercial dealings. If any one of their number strays into sharpness that savors of commercial fraud, he at once becomes an object of obloquy and open disparagement with his fellow-Israelites; but let any one of their class fall into pecuniary misfortune, and they run to his relief as so many Samaritans. "He is a Jew and of course is getting rich;" and so would you, if you pursued his honorable course. He accumulates by living within his means, and avoiding modes of dissipation that cancer the heart and disease the body and eat into worldly substance and paralyze energy. The secret of the Jews' thrift is economy and abstinence from small vices, and earnest attention to his calling. Who is so ready as the descendants of Jacob in our midst to respond with heartiness to every charitable appeal? It was a Sister of Charity that told us that the Jews of Los Angelos ever met their merciful advances with encouraging words and open purses. If the Jew here has greed, the Gentile far outstrips him in grasping avarice. He is cautious, because educated to commerce, but not backward in public enterprises; he devotes himself to his business, and interferes not with his neighbor's concerns. You say he don't build houses. "The fool builds houses, the wise occupy them.["] If Jew or Gentile can attain the same comfort in a rented domicile, at less expense than in one of his own construction, what business is it to either Jews or Gentiles?

It is not in a spirit of praise or exaggeration that we commend our citizens of Israelitish extraction. We commend them for their general business and personal probity. We applaud them for their commercial integrity and their studied isolation from the prevalent vices of gambling, lechery, and inebriation, for their individual and class benevolence and for their courteous demeanor. They are among our very best citizens, and the city suffers nothing in their hands. The Patriarch of the race, whose accomplished daughters have mated with our worthiest and wealthiest citizens [3]—who is held in higher esteem? His urbanity and purity are the delicious comment and pride of the town. It would be well if our Gentile population would imitate his revered example. If such as he "had" the city of Los Angelos, it would be well with us.

* * *

The "Patriarch" so kindly alluded to, is Mr. Joseph Newmark, formerly an honored resident of this city. If we had a few more such men living in our various cities, the Jews generally would be benefited. Newspapers and others would then entertain better opinions concerning the Jews.[4]

150. SEPARATING RELIGION FROM PUBLIC SCHOOLS

a) The Board of Education of Cincinnati, Defendant, Answers John D. Minor *et al.*, Plaintiff, in the Superior Court of Cincinnati, November 26, 1869 [1]

[This historic case, which dragged through the courts from 1869 to 1873, when the Ohio Supreme Court ruled on it and upheld the Board of Education in Cincinnati against a lower court decision, marked the first victory in the United States of those who believe in a rigorous separation of the church from the state in the field of public education. Test cases in Maine in 1854 and Massachusetts in 1866 had been lost; the Cincinnati Board scored the first defeat of the hitherto prevailing practice.[2]

The Board of Education consisted of forty members, two elected from each ward. Of these, eighteen were Protestants, ten Catholics, two Jews, and ten "others," including Unitarians, Hicksite Quakers, Atheists, etc. At that time, the public schools had some 19,000 pupils, while the Catholic parochial schools, about 100 in number, had some 12,000 students.[3] The Jewish population of over 10,000 sent its children to the public schools, with after-school religious education supplied in special institutions. On September 6, 1869 a motion was made at the meeting of the Board to suspend the practise of reading daily from the King James, Protestant, version of the Bible. One Catholic member of the Board also moved that the Catholic Church be invited to unite its parochial schools with the public schools. While this latter invitation was being rejected by the hierarchy in Cincinnati, a public campaign of pressure was exerted on the Board to defeat the motion to discontinue the reading of the Protestant Bible. In two weeks, petitions with some 10,000 signatures were presented, mass meetings were staged, and large audiences attended the meetings of the Board itself.[4] Nevertheless, on November 1, 1869, by a majority of 23 to 15, the Board passed the resolution. The following day, Protestants filed suit in the Superior Court in Cincinnati for an injunction to restrain the board from carrying out its decision. The reply by the Board clearly enunciates the sound principles on which the majority based their action. The minority of the Board filed a separate reply disclaiming responsibility for the action of the majority. Of the two Jewish members of the Board, one, Edgar M. Johnson, was with the majority, while the other, Henry Mack, was with the minority.[5]]

Superior Court of Cincinnati.

John D. Minor et al.,
Plaintiffs,
v.
The Board of Education of the City of Cincinnati et al.,
Defendants.

The Board of Education of the City of Cincinnati, the City of Cincinnati and W. J. O'Neil, J. H. Brunsman, J. W. B. Kelley, Edgar M. Johnson, Benjamin J. Ricking, D. J. Mullaney, Henry W. Poor, Joseph P. Carbery, F. Macke, H. P. Seibel, C. F. Bruckner, Stephen Wagner, Joseph Kramer, F. W. Rauch, Thos. Vickers, A. Theurkauf, John Sweeney, George D. Temple, John P. Story, Samuel A. Miller, Herman Eckel, J. F. Wisnewski and H. L. Wehmer,[6] defendants in the above entitled action, in answer to the petition say: That it is true that on the 1st day of November, 1869, said Board of Education passed the resolutions [7] in said petition set forth; that these defendants also believe it to be true that the rule abrogated by said resolutions was adopted by the Board of Trustees and Visitors of the Common Schools in 1852; that it is also true that the version of the Bible generally in use in the common schools of Cincinnati is that known as King James' Version; that these defendants are not informed as to the truth of the allegation in the petition respecting the action of the School Board in 1842, but that if said allegation be true the rule claimed in the petition to have been adopted in 1842[8] has long since ceased to be acted upon or to be recognized as of binding force, the same not being found among the standing rules published and promulgated by the School Board, or Board of Education, during the last twenty-five years; that the sole version of the Bible which has been read in the common schools at any time within the knowledge of the defendants is that known and described in the petition as the King James' Version; that it is true that there are books other than the Bible now in use in the common schools of Cincinnati, which contain passages and selections from the Bible, and from writings inculcating truths which by many persons are designated as religious truths, but that such books are not religious books, and are not used for the purpose of conveying religious instruction; that these defendants believe it to be true that a number of children, who are educated in the common schools, receive no religious instruction or knowledge of the Bible except that communicated in said schools: that while the defendants do not deny that religious instruction is necessary and indispensable to fit said children to be good citizens of the State of Ohio, and of the United States, they deny that such instruction can or ought to be imparted in the schools established by the State; and these defendants say that it is true that the individuals named as defendants, are, with the exception of W. F. Hurlbut, members of said Board of Education, duly elected and qualified, and that said W. F. Hurlbut is clerk of said board, and that his duties are correctly described in the petition; and these defendants deny each and every other allegation of the petition which is not hereinbefore admitted.

And said defendants further answering, say that the citizens of Cincinnati, who are taxed for the support of the schools under the management of said Board of Education, and all of whom are equally entitled to the benefits thereof by having their children instructed therein, are very much divided in opinion and practice upon matters connected with religious belief, worship and education; that a considerable number thereof are Israelites who reject the Christian religion altogether, and believe only in the inspired truth of what is known as the Old Testament, and this only in the original Hebrew tongue, and such other religious truths and worship as are perpetuated in their body by tradition; that also, many of said citizens do not believe the writings embraced in the Bible to be entitled to be considered as containing an authoritative declaration of religious truth; that a still greater number of said citizens together with their children are members of the Roman Catholic Church, and conscientiously believe in its doctrines, faith and forms of worship, and that by said church the version of the scriptures referred to in the petition, is taught and believed to be incorrect as a translation and incomplete by reason of its omission of a part of the books held by such church to be an integral portion of the inspired canon; and furthermore, that the scriptures ought not to be read indiscriminately, in as much as said church has divine authority as the only infallible teacher and interpreter of the same, and that the reading of the same without note or comment, and without being properly expounded by the only authorized teachers and interpreters thereof, is not only not beneficial to the children in said schools, but likely to lead to the adoption of dangerous errors, irreligious faith, practice and worship, and that by reason thereof the practice of reading the King James' version of the Bible, commonly and only received as inspired and true by the Protestant religious sects, in the presence and hearing of Roman Catholic children, is regarded by the members of the Roman Catholic Church as contrary to their rights of conscience, and that such practice as heretofore pursued has had the necessary effect to prevent the attendance of large numbers of children of those who are members of said church, who, in consequence thereof have erected, and now maintain, separate schools at their own expense, in which there are enrolled and taught a number, about two-thirds of the number of those who are enrolled and taught in the schools under the management of said Board of Education; that also there are other religious sects and denominations and bodies of citizens who either do not regard the Bible as the authoritative source of religious truth, or who regard themselves as possessed of the only true sense thereof; that furthermore, a large number of persons in this community who are ready and qualified to act as teachers in said public schools object to the reading of the Bible in the version in use (or, indeed, in any version without note or comment) on conscientious grounds, and are thereby precluded from employment as teachers in said schools; that in consideration of these facts said Board of Education has concluded that it was not possible for it to take upon itself any instruction in religion, and that it is neither right nor expedient to continue in use in said public schools the reading of any version of the

Bible as a religious exercise, or any other religious exercise whatever, and therefore has passed the resolutions now complained of by the plaintiffs.

These defendants pray to be dismissed with their costs.

WALKER & CONNER,

Solicitors for City.

S. & S. R. MATTHEWS,

GEO. HOADLY,

STALLO & KITTREDGE,[9]

Attorneys for other Defendants.

b) Excerpt from the Argument in behalf of the Board of Education by J. B. Stallo, December, 1869 [10]

[Stallo spoke directly after the first counsel for the Plaintiffs had opened the argument. Stallo maintained that the King James Bible is a sectarian book, unacceptable to some Christians and certainly to Jews and free-thinkers. He also challenged the theory that Christianity is in any way a part of the American common law, in part demonstrating his thesis by pointing to the rights enjoyed by the Jews in the United States. In view of the fact that he had been both a student and a teacher in Catholic institutions, Stallo's vigorous advocacy of the complete separation of Church and State was particularly impressive. Interest in the subject, moreover, was not restricted to the school issue, for since 1864 a campaign had been in progress, initiated by the Presbyterians, to achieve "national recognition of God the Lord Jesus Christ, and the Holy Scriptures," by a suitable amendment to the federal constitution.[11]]

. . . To show how idle it is to assert that the reading of the Bible in the schools ought not to be offensive to reasonable Catholics and others, let me suppose a case. It is entirely possible that the time is not far distant, when the Catholics in this city will be in the majority. Now up to the days of the reformation, every Christian, from time immemorial, symbolized his faith in the doctrine of redemption, by making the sign of the cross, before and after every secular act of his life, after rising and before going to sleep, before and after meals, etc. This practice is commemorated by innumerable authorities, some of which are not wholly spurned, even by Protestants. "Ad omnem promotum," says Tertullian (*De Cor. Mil.* III) "ad omnem progressum, ad omnem aditum et exitum, ad vestitum, ad calceatum, ad lavacra, ad mensas, ad lumina, ad cubicula, ad sedilia, quandocunque nos conversatio exercet, frontem crucis signaculo terimus." Similarly Cyril (*Hieros. Catech. IV.*). "Fac hoc signum, sive edas, sive bibas, sive sedeas, sive stes, sive loquaris, sive ambules, sive in omni negotio, et seq."[12] The cross is the sacred symbol of Christianity, and the making of the sign an inveterate practice, for the refusal to renounce which many of the early professors of the faith have suffered the death of martyrdom. What would the Protestants say if a Catholic majority in the School Board should enjoin this practice upon the teachers and children in the public schools? Would they listen to the plea that no believer in the death of the Redeemer on the cross could reasonably object to the emblem of universal salvation? Would not their instant reply be: It is enough for us to know that the sign of the cross is now the peculiar symbol of Catholicism, and it can not be tolerated in the schools established by and for Protestants and Catholics alike? And has not the Catholic the right, for the same reason, to say: reading the Bible without comment is the peculiar symbol of Protestantism, and it is not to be tolerated in the schools established by Catholics and Protestants alike?

Thus far I have considered the main question at issue on the hypothesis that the theory of our opponents, according to which the equality of all forms of belief before the law is applicable only to Christian beliefs, is tenable. I have argued the question as it stands between the various Christian denominations, leaving out of account the large body of citizens who are not Christians, the Jews, and those persons whose faith is not formulated in the writings and professions of any of the Christian sects, those who have lately been indiscriminately denounced as atheists and infidels. That as against the belief or non-belief of these citizens, and in view of the presence of their children in the public schools, the Bible, embracing the Old and New Testament, is not a sectarian book, can not, I am sure, be seriously contended. If they have equal civil rights with the orthodox Christians, the Bible must of necessity be excluded from the State schools, and sent to the Christian houses, Sunday schools and churches. The objection of the Israelites and free-thinkers to the reading of the Bible in schools, which they have helped to erect and still help to maintain equally with orthodox Catholics and Protestants, can be successfully met only by the assertion, which I understand to be distinctly made on the other side, that Christianity is part of the fundamental law of the State and that the Bible is an organic instrument behind the Constitution, for the reason, that both our social life and our political institutions rest upon the broad substratum of Christian civilization.

The doctrine thus seriously (and in view of the exigencies of their case *necessarily*) broached by our opponents, that Christianity is part of the common law of our State, because this law has its roots in Christian civilization, is a momentous doctrine. It is pregnant with the most serious consequences. It draws in question the civil rights, as I believe, of nearly one-half of our citizens. I propose to examine it therefore candidly, fearlessly, and as far as I may thoroughly. If this is a Christian country, in the sense that the non-Christians have no rights which the Christians are bound to respect, or in the narrower sense, that the Christians enjoy rights and privileges, which the law denies to the non Christians, the time has come for the refluence of the wave which has brought so many millions of European thinkers and laborers to the shores of the new Western world.

While entering upon the inquiry into the truth or falsity of this great fundamental theory of our opponents, I am puzzled *in limine* [at the beginning] to understand, what is meant by the sounding phrase, that Christianity is part of the common law of the State. The law—positive civil law—either imposes duties or it confers rights. If Christianity is part of the law of the State, then, there must be certain duties enjoined upon the citizens, which are peculiarly Christian, or certain rights, which none but Christians possess. Now the duties enforced by the State, the duty to respect your neighbor's life, his person, his property, his good name, to refrain from murder, robbery, theft, defamation, etc., are not peculiarly Christian duties; they are enforced or at least enjoined by all States, whose citizens are civilized in any modern sense. They are enjoined and enforced because their observance is essential to the very existence and good order of society, and not because they are Christian virtues. I know of no duty which the State recognizes as a merely Christian duty. Similarly I know of no civil right which the Christian holds in preference over the professors of another creed or of no creed. The Jew for instance, can hold property. He can acquire it by inheritance, or by devise, or by purchase. He can sue and be sued. There are the same remedies, civil and criminal, for wrongs inflicted upon a Jew, as for those done to a Christian. The Jew can be a witness in a court of justice, for the

Constitution provides, that "no person shall be incompetent to be a witness on account of his religious belief." The Jew has the right to vote. He can hold any office, for again the Constitution provides, "That no religious tests shall be required as a qualification for office." A Jew may sit upon the bench, and administer justice *"without respect of persons,"* between Christians, as a Jew now sits upon the bench in New York.[13] A Jew may not only administer the law, but help to make it. A Jew sat last winter, in the Ohio Legislature,[14] and there is nothing in the Constitution to hinder that the majority of the Legislature may be Jews—a case which, according to the theory of the plaintiffs, would present the remarkable anomaly of a body of Jews making Christian laws. A Jew was recently appointed, by this Court, commissioner of the Southern railroad.[15] Jews have sat in both Houses of Congress. A Jew may be President of the United States, if he has the requisite other qualifications and can obtain the requisite number of electoral votes. A Jewish temple or synagogue is exempt from taxation no less than a Christian church. I might proceed indefinitely with this enumeration of rights, but I have gone far enough to show, that there is no particular, definite civil right, which Jews, Christians and non-believers do not share in common. And in view of this I am not able to see the force of the assertion so frequently and so confidently made, that Christianity is part of the law of the State. It is strange, that any one should at this day refer to the nebulous deliverances of Judge Story in his *Commentaries of the Constitution* (secs. 1870–1879), and seek to discredit as an *obiter dictum* the emphatic language of our own Supreme Court in the case of *Bloom v. Richards,* 2 Ohio State Reports, 387 [390–391], which I now beg leave to quote.[16]

"The Constitution of Ohio," says Judge Thurman, in deciding that case, "having declared that all men have a natural and indefeasible right to worship Almighty God according to the dictates of conscience; that no man shall be compelled to attend, erect or support any place of worship, or to maintain any ministry against his consent; and that no preference shall ever be given by law to any religious society or mode or worship, and no religious test shall be required as a qualification to any office of trust or profit, it follows that neither Christianity or any other system of religion is a part of the law of this State. We sometimes hear it said that all religions are tolerated in Ohio, but the expression is not strictly accurate. Much less accurate is it to say that one religion is a part of the law, and all others only tolerated.

It is not by mere toleration that every individual here is protected in his belief or disbelief. He reposes not upon the leniency of Government or the liberality of any class or sect of men, but upon his natural, indefeasible rights of conscience, which, in the language of the Constitution, are beyond the control or interference of any human authority. We have no union of Church and State, nor has our Government ever been vested with authority to enforce any religious observance, simply because it is religious." . . .

c) Excerpts from the dissenting opinion of Judge Alphonso Taft, Superior Court of Cincinnati, February 15, 1870 [17]

[Two of the three judges, M. B. Hagans and Bellamy Storer, ruled against the Board of Education and an injunction was issued permanently restraining the Board from carrying out its resolutions to suspend the reading of the King James Bible in the schools. Judge Storer had been President of the School Board from 1850 to 1854, and since then had served continually on the Superior Court; in his younger days he had been a member of the "Flying Artillery," a zealous group that went from town to town promoting religious revivals.[18] Alphonso Taft (1810–1891), a radical Unitarian, wrote a courageous dissenting opinion which was later "sustained in every point" by the Ohio Supreme Court, but which was also used on two occasions to prevent his being nominated as Governor of Ohio. Judge Taft, father of the later President of the United States, did however serve as Attorney-General of the United States in Grant's cabinet. At the time of this case, the most important to come before him on that bench, Taft had had some experience in school matters too, having been on the Union Board of Cincinnati High Schools.[19]

To the widespread outcry in the press and pulpit that the Board of Education by its resolutions had shown itself hostile to the Bible, to Protestantism and to religion in general, Judge Taft wisely replied: "The Bible is not banished, nor is religion degraded or abused. The Board have simply aimed to free the common schools from any just conscientious objections, by confining them to secular instruction, and moral and intellectual training. This, in my opinion, was, under the circumstances, just, and under the Constitution of Ohio, a duty which they could not omit without violating the rights of conscience of those who, on conscientious grounds, objected to the practice under the old rule."]

I regret to find myself in a minority on this question. Nothing but a sense of duty has induced me to prepare a dissenting opinion.

The action in this case is brought to enjoin the Board of Education of the City of Cincinnati, from acting under the two following resolutions, which were adopted Nov. 1, 1869, viz.:

"*Resolved,* That religious instruction and the reading of religious books, including the Holy Bible, are prohibited in the common schools of Cincinnati, it being the true object and interest of this rule, to allow the children of the parents of all sects and opinions, in matters of faith and worship, to enjoy alike the benefit of the common school fund."

"*Resolved,* That so much of the regulations on the course of study and text-books in intermediate and district schools (p. 213, Annual Reports), as reads as follows: 'The opening exercises in every department shall commence by reading a portion of the Bible by, or under, the direction of the teachers, and appropriate singing by the pupils,' be repealed."

The injunction is sought against both resolutions, but on grounds which apply mainly, if not exclusively, to the first.

I propose to consider them separately, and in the order in which they were adopted. The object of this resolution is sufficiently indicated by its language, "it being the true object and intent of this rule, to allow the children of parents of all sects and opinions in matters of faith and worship, to enjoy alike the benefit of the common school fund."

I see no reason to suppose, the Board of Education intended anything more or less, than it has thus expressed. Its opinion evidently was, as the majority have said by their answer, that in the great diversity of religious faiths which exists among us, true conformity to the spirit and language of our Constitution could be best secured, by confining the instruction in the common schools which are supported by general taxation, to secular knowledge and moral and intellectual culture, leaving what is commonly understood by religious and doctrinal teachings, to other and more appropriate instrumentalities. By the words "religious instruction" as used in this rule, I understand special or formal religious teaching, such as would be in conformity to the views of some one, or more, of the numerous religious sects, and by consequence, would be offensive to some one, or more, of the other religious sects. The Board would probably have used the word sectarian, in connection with, or instead of "religious" instruction, but for the dispute that would have arisen, as to what was sectarian, each sect being likely to suppose its own views free from that objection. But, that its purpose might not be misunderstood, the explanatory clause is added, that the object and intent of the rule was, "to allow the children of parents of all sects and opinions in matters of faith and worship, to enjoy alike the benefit of the common school fund." Whether this policy may or may not require any changes in the school books now used, beyond the omission of the reading from King James' version of the Bible, and the singing of hymns, can not now be determined, and if it could, would not in my judgment be material in the decision of the present case. But this first resolution does undoubtedly pledge the Board of Education as at present constituted, to all parents, that no religious doctrines shall be taught in the common schools, and no form of religious worship used, so far as it is practicable to avoid it, which is offensive to the religious convictions of any. . . .

. . . The authority of the Archbishop of Cincinnati was, however, used in this connection, to show that these resolutions, if carried out, would not be effectual to gather the children of Catholics into the public schools, which they, in common with other tax-payers, support.[20] It appears that the Archbishop, like the plaintiffs, is not satisfied with secular education in the schools. In principle, he stands where they do, with the exception that they are in possession. Being out of possession, he would prefer to get out of the public treasury the share of the school fund, proportioned to the Catholic population, and apply it to the support of the parochial schools with Catholic religious instruction. If the Catholics were in possession, as the plaintiffs are, with the Douay version and Catholic forms of worship, perhaps he might still be willing to divide the money, and perhaps not, in which latter case he would occupy about the same position now occupied by the plaintiffs in this suit.

It is said that the Catholic clergy demand their share of the fund, to be used in carrying on schools under their control. That can not be done under the Constitution. But this affords no reason why the Board of Education should not grant to the Catholic people, what the Bill of Rights guarantees to every sect, that their rights of conscience shall not be violated, and that they shall not be compelled to attend any form of worship, or to maintain it against their consent, or be compelled to submit to religious preferences, shown by the government to other religious societies.

It is not for a court to anticipate, before judgment, that any party will not be satisfied with what the law gives him, nor are courts accustomed to withhold what is due because something else is asked.

Another numerous class of heavy tax-payers, the Jews, object to the old rule. But it is claimed on behalf of the plaintiffs, that the Jews have met with something like a conversion, and have become reconciled to the New Testament. That they held out for a while, but afterward came in, and there was no further difficulty with them, and that their case need not to have been further regarded. There is too much evidence of dissent on their part, from the old rule, to permit us to conclude that they have ever intended to waive their rights of conscience and of religious liberty. Like the majority of us, the Jews have received their faith from their ancestors, and according to that historic faith, the assertion in the New Testament that Jesus of Nazareth is God, is blasphemy against the God of Israel. If a Protestant Christian would object to have the common schools daily opened with the forms of worship peculiar to the Catholic Church, which worships the same triune God with him, how much more serious must be the objection of the Jew, to be compelled to attend, or support, the worship of a being as God, whose divinity and supernatural history he denies?

The truth in this matter undoubtedly is, that the Jews, like many others, have found out that our common schools are munificently endowed, and, in general, well conducted, so that the privilege of attending them is inestimable, and they have wisely concluded to secure for their children the secular education of the common schools, and attend to their religious nurture at home and in their own organizations. A faith which had survived so much persecution, through so many centuries, they may well have risked in the common schools of Cincinnati, though at some cost of religious feeling.

It is in vain to attempt to escape the force of the clauses of the Bill of Rights by assuming that the Protestant Christian religion was intended in the Bill of Rights, and that the sects of Protestant Christians *only* were, therefore, entitled to Protection. Between all forms of religious belief the State knows no difference, provided they do not transgress its civil regulations—a mighty contrast to some times and some countries, which have boasted of their religious liberality, because the ruling sects have tolerated the dissenting minority, as a nuisance, which they have magnanimously forborne to abate. . . .

. . . Each sect feels a comfortable assurance that it is not mistaken in its faith, and must be excused, if it can not appreciate the faith, or want of faith, in others.

But nevertheless, the idea, that a man has less conscience because he is a Rationalist, or a Spiritualist, or even an Atheist, than the believer in any one of the accepted forms of faith, may be current, but it is not a constitutional idea, in the State of Ohio.

No sect can, because it includes a majority of a community or a majority of the citizens of the State, claim any preference whatever. It can not claim that its mode of worship or its religion shall prevail in the common schools. Nor does it make the case any better, if several sects agree in a certain degree and kind of religious instruction and worship, among themselves, though together forming a large majority of the community or State. So long as there are any, who do not believe in or approve of their mode of religious worship or instruction, they can not insist that it is not sectarian, or that any non-believing taxpayer shall be compelled to submit to it in the common schools.

While the Court will take cognizance of the existence of the Christian religion and of the Protestant religion, it is only for the purpose of preserving civil peace and order, and the welfare of the State; and for the same purpose, it will take cognizance of the existence of every sect. The State protects every religious denomination in the quiet enjoyment of its own mode of public worship. It protects them from blasphemy, when the public peace and order require it.

It is, therefore, an entire mistake, in my opinion, to assert, that the Protestant Christian religion has been so identified with the history and government of our State or country, that it is not to be regarded as sectarian under our Constitution; or, that, when the Bill of Rights says that "religion, morality and knowledge being essential to good government," it means the Protestant Christian religion. That would be a preference, which the same section expressly disclaims, and emphatically forbids.

To hold otherwise, and that Protestant Christians are entitled to any control in the schools, to which other sects are not equally entitled, or that they are entitled to have their mode of worship and their Bible used in the common schools, against the will of the Board of Education, the proper trustees and managers of the schools, is to hold to the union of Church and State, however we may repudiate and reproach the name. Nor is it to be presumed, that the cause of genuine religion, or of the Bible, can be permanently advanced by a struggle for this kind of supremacy. The government is neutral, and, while protecting all, it prefers none, and it *disparages* none. The State, while it does not profess to be Christian, exercises a truly Christian charity toward all. Its impartial charity extends to all kinds of Protestants, Roman Catholics, Jews, and Rationalists alike, and covers them with its mantle of protection and encouragement; and no one of them, however numerous, can boast of peculiar favor with the State.

Nothing but the severest experiences of religious persecution in other countries, and in other times, could have planted liberty of religious opinion so deeply and so ineradicably in the American State governments. It was not realized under the Colonial government, which, though far removed from, were still closely allied to, the laws and religious institutions of the mother country. Roger Williams was greatly in advance of his time, and seemed to comprehend the principle of religious liberty. But even he dared not to claim its full realization, and what he claimed was not allowed.

"There goes many a ship to sea," said he, "with many hundred souls in one ship, whose weal and woe is common, and is a true picture of a commonwealth, or human combination, or society. It hath fallen out sometimes, that both Papists and Protestants, Jews and Turks may be embarked in one ship; upon which supposal, I affirm that all the liberty of conscience I ever pleaded for, turns upon these two hinges, that none of the Papists, Protestants, Jews or Turks be forced to come to the ship's prayers or worship, nor compelled from their own particular prayers or worship, if they practice any."[21]

There is no more striking evidence of the advance which has been made in religious liberty, since the time of Roger Williams, than is to be found in the American State Constitutions of the present day, and in the most intelligent comments upon them by approved writers and jurists. The ideal is absolute equality before the law, of all religious opinions and sects, provided they do not infringe the laws enacted purely for civil government, with no symbols of the superiority of any faith over others, upheld by the power of the State. If this ideal has not been practically reached in all the older States, it may be ascribed to the fact that in several of them, as in Massachusetts and Connecticut, an established church was preserved till a comparatively recent period. And it is to be borne in mind that the adjudications of the Courts in a State with a church establishment maintained by law, are not applicable to the condition of religious equality existing in Ohio.

Mr. Cooley, in his valuable work, recently published, on Constitutional Limitations,[22] discusses, with great intelligence and force, the subject of religious liberty and the rights of conscience, under the American State Constitutions. His opinion is strongly expressed in favor of secular instruction in the schools. In the course of the discussion of the American Constitutions on this subject, and of the adjudication thereunder, he makes an interesting statement of things not permitted under American Constitutions, in the interest of religious liberty and rights of conscience. He says:

"Those things which are not lawful under any of the American Constitutions may be stated thus:

"1. Any law respecting an establishment of religion. The Legislatures have not been left at liberty to effect a union of Church and State, or to establish preferences by law in favor of any one religious denomination or mode of worship. There is no religious liberty where any one sect is favored by the State and given an advantage by law over other sects. Whatever establishes a distinction against one class or sect is, to the extent to which the distinction operates unfavorably, a persecution; and if based on religious grounds, is religious persecution.

"It is not toleration which is established in our system, but religious equality.

"2. Compulsory support, by taxation or otherwise, of religious instruction. Not only is no one denomination to be favored at the expense of the rest, but all support of religious instruction must be entirely voluntary."

This great principle of equality in the enjoyment of religious liberty, and the faithful preservation of the rights of each individual conscience is important in itself, and is essential to religious peace and temporal prosperity, in any country under a free government. But in a city and State whose people have been drawn from the four quarters of the world, with a great diversity of inherited religious opinions, it is indispensable. When the Board of Education, therefore, which represents the civil power of the State in the schools, finds objection made to the use of the Protestant Bible and Protestant singing of Protestant hymns, on conscientious grounds, and concludes to dispense with the practice in the schools, it is no just ground to charge on the Board hostility to the Bible, or to the Protestant religion, or to religion in general. The Bible is not banished, nor is religion degraded or abused. The Board have simply aimed to free the common schools from any just conscientious objections, by confining them to secular instruction, and moral and intellectual training. This, in my opinion, was, under the circumstances, just, and, under the Constitution of Ohio, a duty which they could not omit without violating the rights of conscience of those who, on conscientious grounds, objected to the practice under the old rule. . . .

d) Excerpt from the Decision of the Supreme Court of Ohio, 1873 [23]

[Unanimously the five judges of the Supreme Court reversed the decision of the Superior Court of Cincinnati and sustained the opinion of Judge Taft's dissent. Judge John Welch, who wrote the Supreme Court opinion, denied that Christianity is part of the law of the United States: "True Christianity asks no aid from the sword of civil authority. It began without the sword, and wherever it has taken the sword it has perished by the sword. To depend on civil authority for its enforcement is to acknowledge its own weakness, which it can never afford to do." The Board of Education of Cincinnati was therefore accorded the right to enforce its own resolutions on the matter of Bible-reading in the schools. In 1895, however, when the Court of Common Pleas was asked to rule whether the new School Board could legally require the reading of the King James Bible, the Court ruled that the Board could do so, and the reading was reinstituted. In 1933, about 85% of the schools in Ohio had such Bible-reading, by decision of the local school boards. In the country as a whole, in that year 12 states legally required such Bible-reading, 7 states specifically permitted it by state law, 11 states prohibited it, and 18 states made the choice optional on the part of school boards.[24]]

. . . This opinion might well end here. Were the subject of controversy any other branch of instructions in the schools than religion, I have no doubt it might safely end here, and the unanimous opinion of the court thus rendered be satisfactory to all. The case is of peculiar importance, however, in the fact that it touches our religious convictions and prejudices, and threatens to disturb the harmonious working of the state government, and particularly of the public schools of the state. I deem it not improper, therefore, to consider briefly some of the points and matters so ably and elaborately argued by counsel, although really lying outside of the case proper, or only bearing on it remotely.

The real claim here is, that by "religion," in this clause of the constitution, is meant, "Christian religion," and that by "religious denomination" in the same clause is meant "Christian denomination." If this claim is well founded, I do not see how we can consistently avoid giving a like meaning to the same words and their cognates, "worship," "Religious society," "sect," "conscience," "religious belief," throughout the entire section. To do so, it will readily be seen, would be to withdraw from every person not of Christian belief the guaranties therein vouchsafed, and to withdraw many of them from Christians themselves. In that sense the clause of section 7 in question would read as follows:

"Christianity, morality, and knowledge, however, being essential to good government, it shall be the duty of the general assembly to pass suitable laws to protect every *Christian* denomination in the peaceable enjoyment of its own mode of public worship, and to encourage schools and the means of instruction."

Nor can I see why, in order to be consistent, the concluding clause of section 2, article 6, should not read as follows: . . . "But no *Christian,* or other sect or sects, shall ever have any exclusive right to or control of any part of the school funds of the state; *but Christians, as a body, including all their sects, may have control of said funds.*"

I do not say that such a reading of the sections in question is literally contended for; and yet I see no fair escape from it, if the word "Christianity," or the words "Christian religion," or "the religion of the Bible," are to be interpolated, or substituted for the word "religion," at the place indicated.

If, by this generic word "religion," was really meant "the Christian religion," or "Bible religion," why was it not plainly so written? Surely the subject was of importance enough to justify the pains, and surely it was of interest enough to exclude the supposition that it was written in haste, or thoughtlessly slurred over. At the time of adopting our present constitution, this word "religion" had had a place in our old constitution for half a century, which was surely ample time for studying its meaning and effect, in order to make the necessary correction or alteration, so as to render its true meaning definite and certain. The same word "religion," and in much the same connection, is found in the constitution of the United States. The latter constitution, at least, if not our own also, in a sense, speaks to *mankind,* and speaks of the rights of *man.* Neither the word "Christianity," "Christian," nor "Bible," is to be found in either.

When they speak of "religion," they must mean the religion of man, and not the religion of any *class* of men. When they speak of "all men" having certain rights, they can not mean merely "all Christian men." Some of the very men who helped to frame these constitutions were themselves not Christian men.

We are told that this word "religion" must mean "Christian religion," because "Christianity is a part of the common law of this country," lying behind and above its constitutions. Those who make this assertion can hardly be serious, and intend the real import of their language. If Christianity is a *law* of the state, like every other law, it must have a *sanction*. Adequate penalties must be provided to enforce obedience to all its requirements and precepts. No one seriously contends for any such doctrine in this country, or, I might almost say, in this age of the world. The only foundation—rather, the only excuse—for the proposition, that Christianity is part of the law of this country, is the fact that it is a Christian country, and that its constitutions and laws are made by a Christian people. And is not the very fact that those laws do *not* attempt to *enforce* Christianity, or to place it upon exceptional or vantage ground, itself a strong evidence that they *are* the laws of a Christian people, and that their religion is the best and purest of religions? It is strong evidence that their religion is indeed a religion "without partiality," and *therefore* a religion "without hyprocrisy." True Christianity asks no aid from the sword of civil authority. It began without the sword, and wherever it has taken the sword it has perished by the sword. To depend on civil authority for its enforcement is to acknowledge its own weakness, which it can never afford to do. It is able to fight its own battles. Its weapons are moral and spiritual, and not carnal. Armed with these, and these alone, it is not afraid nor "ashamed" to be compared with other religions, and to withstand them single-handed. And the very reason why it is not so afraid or "ashamed" is, that it is not the "power of *man*," but "the power of God," on which it depends. True Christianity never shields itself behind majorities. Nero, and the other persecuting Roman emperors, were amply supported by majorities; and yet the pure and peaceable religion of Christ in the end triumphed over them all; and it was only when it attempted itself to enforce religion by the arm of authority, that it began to wane. A form of religion that can not live under equal and impartial laws ought to die, and sooner or later must die.

151. AID TO RUSSIAN REFUGEES

Circular to Hebrew Congregations and Charitable Societies in New York and Vicinity, April 27, 1870 [1]

[This call is the first to be issued in behalf of East European immigrant Jews. On March 19, 1870, "114 grown persons and 22 children" were shipped out of Hamburg to the United States, some of them "upon direct invitation of their husbands or relatives already in America."[2] The emigrants were sent out by the Central Frontier Committee in Koenigsberg, Prussia, established in October, 1869 by the heads of the German Jewish communities and the Alliance Israélite Universelle, with the latter financing the emigration.[3] The spokesmen for the well-to-do Jews who headed the Board of Delegates of American Israelites, as well as the New York Jewish weeklies, had opposed this immigration and advised against it, but the Koenigsberg Committee decided not to wait, hoping that the actual arrival of the group would stimulate practical aid. The immigrants arrived in New York on April 19, 1870.

The urgency of the emigration at this moment had both its immediate and fundamental causes. Famine had swept Lithuania and parts of Poland from 1867 to 1869, and the cholera epidemic of 1868 in those regions compounded the distress. These afflictions were added to what the Alliance called the "ancient and deep-rooted causes": the impoverishment of the country; exclusion of Jews from agriculture; absence of large factories and decrease in commerce; heavy taxation; and the legal restrictions on Jews moving outside the Pale of Settlement, as sorely afflicted non-Jews were doing.[4] It was hoped that tens of thousands of Jews would be aided to migrate to the United States, but the resistance of the Board of Delegates of American Israelites was so effective that only 528, according to its own figures, were sent over in 1870 and 1871, and these were carefully screened, so that only the young, strong, and the skilled in craft or trade were encouraged to come.[5]

The Jews of course constituted only a small part of the swelling tide of immigration. From January 1 to April 27, 1870, for instance, 44,257 persons entered through the immigration station at Castle Garden, New York.[6] Only about one-half of one per cent of these were Jews.]

Office of the Executive Committee,
New York, April 27, 1870 [7]

To The President:—Notwithstanding our urgent remonstrances against indiscriminate emigration from West Russia,[8] hundreds of Israelites are here, despatched by the Koenigsberg committee, and utterly penniless. We cannot see them starve or sent to Ward's

Island. Something must be done for them. The Charity Committee of the Hebrew Benevolent Society have already sent twenty-two West to their friends, and the following gentlemen have consented to take the matter in charge and to distribute, in the most effective way, the means placed at their disposal for the benefit of the immigrants:— Messrs. Myer Stern, P. W. Frank and S. Solomon, of the Hebrew Benevolent Society; H. S. Allen of the Hebrew Relief Society; E. Japha, President of the Henry street Synagogue; N. Cowen, of the Chrystie street Synagogue; A. Baum, of the East Broadway Synagogue, with L. Cohn, A. S. Saroni, E. Joseph and T. H. Keesing, of the committee.[9] Please take up a collection among your members at once, as we need a large amount to give temporary relief to those here and soon to arrive, to send them West or South,[10] or enable them to earn a livelihood. Please send the sum collected to A. S. Saroni, Treasurer, 83 Leonard street. Yours, respectfully,

L. Cohn, Chairman.

M. S. Isaacs, Secretary.

152. WHAT ARE THE JEWS?

Two Editorials, "Can a Man Be a Jew and an Irishman?", *The Sun,* New York, September 16 and 19, 1870 [1]

[At first with wit and levity, but then in all seriousness, *The Sun* posed a question that in substance meant, "can a man be a Jew and an American?" One answer was given by the Jew who explained that of course a Jew could be an American (or an Irishman or a German, and so forth) because to be a Jew was merely to have a certain religious faith. While seeming to accept this reply, the editorial writer was not quite content, for it seemed to him that the Jews were something more or other than a religious group. That something else he called, in the loose and unscientific vernacular of his day, and even of our own, a "race." The helpful term, "people," had not yet come into use to describe the Jews.]

I

The Republican Convention, trying to get German votes, have nominated the Hon. Sigismund Kaufmann of Kings County for

Lieutenant-Governor.[2] He is a good fellow and a good citizen, but the question has been raised whether he is a Teuton or a Hebrew.

For our own part, we don't care much; though if we must vote for any man from considerations of nationality, we say frankly that we would sooner vote for a Jew than a Teuton. Such considerations have no proper place in our politics. The right question is whether a man is capable and honest, and all the rest is trash. And as Germans are many and Jews comparatively few, we should, if forced to decide upon reasons of genealogy and birth, certainly vote for a Jew against a Teuton, supposing the two to be set up in opposition to each other. Besides, the Jews, with their fine and powerful intelligence, and their stern adherence to the moral law, are generally much better politicians than the Teutons.

But this is not now the issue. Have the Republican Convention made a mistake or not? Have they nominated a Teuton supposing they were nominating a Jew, or the contrary? That is what is in dispute. Some people who have written us letters on the subject maintain that there is no difference between the two, and that a man may be both a Jew and a German. We do not so understand it; and to make the subject clear, we will put a question in our turn. Is a man of Hebrew descent, who is born in Ireland, an Irishman? And would his nomination be a good way of getting Irish votes?

We do not deny that Mr. Kaufmann may be a Teuton and not a Jew. That is a point about which we have no information. He is a good man, besides being handsome, and we like him, and have no doubt that he would preside with dignity over the Senate of New York. But though the question is of little consequence, we are sorry not to have it settled. Is he a Teuton or is he a Jew? Or does he really claim to be both, just as a Jew born in Dublin might claim to be an Irishman? At any rate, why doesn't he or somebody for him answer the question, since it has been asked? Is he unwilling to have the truth stated? We don't believe it. It has not been our fortune to be born of Hebrew parents; but if we were, we should be proud of it.

II

We are glad to say that we have at last received a lucid explanation of the difficulty involved in this curious problem. It is contained in the following communication sent to us by a Jewish gentleman of great intelligence and perspicacity:

"The word 'Jew' is not the name for the once great nation of Palestine, but it merely describes their faith of belief. If you should ask me what religion I have, my answer would be, 'I am a Jew.' Ask my nationality—my answer, 'I am a German.' The same as a Protestant can be an Irishman, as well as a Catholic can be a German, or a Jew can be a Frenchman. Mr. *Sig. Kaufmann* is a German by nationality and a Jew by religion; and if a Jew is born in Dublin, he is as well an Irishman as a German born in New York is an American. I don't believe there is a Jew living on the globe that could trace his descent; for, when the emigration from Asia to Europe took place, Jews and Gentiles went there as well as Jews and Gentiles came to America. You have attended Jewish weddings and funerals as well as Catholic, and both were Germans. Can a Jew be a Teuton or can a Lutheran be an American, are both the same question. The Jewish religion is taught all over the globe."

In regard to the point upon which this discussion has been raised, our correspondent's statements are perfectly conclusive. Mr. *Kaufmann* was born in Germany of Hebrew parents. As our correspondent expresses it, he is a German by nationality and a Jew by religion. If this be a sound view of the question, the Republican Convention, in nominating him to get German votes, have done better than they knew; for he will bring to their ticket the support of Jewish as well as Teutonic electors.

But we think that our respected correspondent overlooks one important element of the puzzle. The Jews are not merely a church; they are a race, and as such they are altogether distinct from the Teutons. They belong to that branch of mankind which is described by ethnologists as the Semitic family, while the Teutons or Germans are members of the Aryan [3] or Indo-European family. Among all the divisions of humanity none is more profound or more distinctly defined than that of these two races. It extends to physical constitution, language, religion, and all intellectual qualities. The Jewish race is one of the most tenacious and strongly marked in all the history of man. The great idea of the unity of the Divine Being was first manifested among the Jews, while the Teutons and all other offshoots of the Aryan family were still lost in fantastic beliefs in many gods. To the Jews also belongs the glory of being the oldest distinct race in existence, and of maintaining an unbroken, indestructible continuity through calamities and persecutions unexampled in severity which have beset them for thousands of years.

In modern times, and under the influences first brought into the world by the Founder of Christianity, there is a remarkable tendency to the commingling of all the families and races of men, and to the removal of the antagonism between the Semitic, the Aryan, the Mongolian, the aboriginal American, and so forth,[4] by the extinction of some and the amalgamation of the others into one common brotherhood of man. A striking evidence of this tendency is seen in the cessation of that hostility toward the Jews which they have endured with such patience and heroic perseverance. Instead of being regarded as strangers among the Aryan nations with which their lot has been cast, they have, in several countries, been admitted to an equality of political and social rights. This is a great step, and it looks forward to the establishment of genuine political and social unity all over the globe. But as yet this great movement is only in its inception. The races of men, though beginning to be fused together, still preserve their individuality. A Jew is a Jew, a Celt is a Celt, a Teuton is a Teuton. This is true even in this country, where no political or social advantage is attributed peculiarly to any race, and where individuals belonging to any of them can truly and proudly declare that they are American citizens.

This beneficient process of fusion, however, is considerably hindered by the intrigues of the politicians. A specimen of those intrigues is the nomination of Mr. *Kaufmann* for Lieutenant-Governor, not because his talents, his political services, his power of performing the duties of the office are so eminent that they justify such an honor, but simply because it is believed that he can get some German votes which would not otherwise be given to a Republican candidate. This we condemn. It is unworthy of the Republican party; it is opposed to the spirit of American institutions; and it will fail of its object. Let every candidate be nominated because he is fit, and not because he is a Jew or a Gentile, a Celt or a Teuton, a Catholic or a Protestant. All these distinctions are foreign to our political system. The Republican Convention erred gravely in fishing for German votes by the nomination of Mr. *Kaufmann,* and before long the Republican party will find it out.[5]

153. ROUMANIAN JEWS

a) From the Proceedings of the United States Senate, June 3, 1870 [1]

[On June 1 and 2, 1870, many American newspapers published a cable purporting to come from Constantinople announcing the cold-blooded massacre of "thousands" of Jewish men, women, and children in Roumania.[2] While uncorroborated, these horrendous accounts were readily believed both by Jews and non-Jews because for three or four years previously there had been frequent and verified reports of the imposition of restrictions, discriminations, and other hardships upon the approximately 250,000 Jews in Roumania.[3] Although still under Turkish rule, the provinces of Moldavia and Wallachia had in 1866, through the machinations of Tsarist Russia, been organized as the principality of Roumania, with the Hohenzollern Prince Charles (later Carol I) as the head. Jews had lived in those territories for centuries. Toward the end of the eighteenth century, Jewish merchants and traders had in fact been encouraged to migrate from Poland and Russia into Roumania, and another similar wave of immigration was welcomed after 1829, when by the Treaty of Adrianople the Danube was first declared open to freedom of shipping. By 1870, the Jews were thus playing "an active role in transforming the old feudal system into a modern capitalistic economy."[4] In performing this useful function, however, the Jews encountered the hostility of two kinds of forces: those feudalistic land-owning classes, and their government and clerical exponents, who opposed the rise of the capitalist middle class; and those sections of the non-Jewish Roumanian middle class that regarded the Jews as their capitalist competitors and wished to curb and eliminate them. "Roumanian anti-Semitism in modern times always was directed from the top," and did not originate among the peasants or working-men.[5]

The response of American public opinion to the newspaper reports of the anti-Semitic attacks was prompt and generous.]

Mr. *Morton*.[6] I ask unanimous consent to submit certain resolutions in the nature of a memorial at this time.

The *Vice President* [Schuyler Colfax]. The Chair will receive them if there be no objection.

PERSECUTION OF JEWS.

Mr. *Morton*. I present resolutions adopted at a meeting of Israelites in Indianapolis yesterday;[7] and I ask to have them read and referred to the Committee on Foreign Relations.

The Chief Clerk read the resolutions, as follows:

Indianapolis, Indiana, June 2, 1870.

At a meeting of Israelites of this city, held this evening, the following resolutions were unanimously adopted:

Whereas the harrowing news of the terrible massacre of the Jews in the province of Roumania has reached us: Therefore,

Be it resolved, That our hearts are filled with sorrow and anguish at this dreadful act of barbarism committed in a country and by a people said to be civilized and professing the Christian religion.

Resolved, That our Senators and Representatives in Congress be requested to present this subject to the President, and urge him to immediately interpose in behalf of this persecuted and outraged people, and to use all influence and power at his command without delay to shield them from further outrages and alleviate their sufferings.

Resolved, That we call upon the whole civilized world, and the people of this country in particular, to arise and proclaim in living words their abhorrence of this unheard-of massacre, and in the name of civil and religious liberty and common humanity demand of our Government to put forth its strong arm to stay the fearful effusion of more innocent blood.

Please give this matter your immediate attention.

S. H. Bamberger,[8]
Sol. Moritz,
A. J. Landaur.

The *Vice President.* The resolutions will be referred to the Committee on Foreign Relations.

Mr. *Sumner.*[9] In connection with that subject I offer the following resolution:

> *Resolved,* That the President of the United States be requested to communicate to the Senate, if in his opinion not incompatible with the public interest, any information in the possession of the Department of State[10] concerning the reported persecution and massacre of Israelites in Roumania.

By unanimous consent, the Senate proceeded to consider the resolution.

Mr. *Sumner.* I will remark that the news we have from Roumania is so absolutely horrible that it is difficult to believe—it is incredible.

One is disposed to believe that there is at least some gross exaggeration in the report.[11] It is important, however, it seems to me, in the interest of humanity, and in that guardianship of humanity which belongs to the great Republic, that we should possess ourselves at once of all the information attainable on the subject.

Mr. *Morton.* I desire to state that the names attached to those resolutions are names of gentlemen of the highest respectability and position, and they represent a very large and numerous class of people in Indianapolis and in Indiana.

Mr. *Sprague.* In my opinion, an examination of this subject will result in establishing these facts: the Jews in this principality had obtained possession of the whole of the trade, a great portion of the lands, and about all of the business connected with the affairs of that people. There was then exhibited on one side a population poor, without occupation or business, and on the other side a rich, trading, monopolizing class. It was that condition of affairs that has brought these Jews to the condition which to-day the world is called upon to contemplate and to sorrow over. There is food for reflection for us, Mr. President and Senators, in the condition of things occurring every day in this country, while we are contemplating the occurrences that have taken place in Roumania.[12]

Mr. *Stewart.* I do not know but that it would be rather a dangerous rule to establish that a man when he gets rich shall be killed. (Laughter.) I do not think it would agree very well with some of us.[13]

The *Vice President.* The question is on the adoption of the resolution offered by the Senator from Massachusetts [Sumner].

The resolution was adopted.[14]

b) Editorial, *The Nation,* New York, October 10, 1872 [15]

[Restrictions against and attacks upon the Jews in Roumania continued, and reached a new peak in the winter of 1871–1872. In Ismail, a city of 20,000 with some 2,000 Jews, a pogrom began on December 24, 1871 (January 5, 1872, New Style) and lasted for several days, with hundreds of Jews beaten, their homes pillaged, their synagogues desecrated; the rioting was then spread to the towns of Vilcovu and Cabul with similar results. The rioters, when arrested, were promptly acquitted, while innocent Jews falsely accused were sentenced to several years in prison.[16]

Among those who attempted, with only superficial success, to aid the Jews was the American Consul at Bucharest, Benjamin Franklin Peixotto (1834–

1890). Following the pogroms reported in the American press in the summer of 1870, Peixotto had been appointed as consul at a city in which the United States had no real consular business to transact, but at which our Government wanted him to execute the special mission of ameliorating the condition of the Jews in Roumania. Not remunerated by the Federal Treasury, Peixotto was sustained and his work financed by wealthy American Jews, from whom he won support for his mission by explaining that his objects would be to improve the Roumanian public opinion of the Jews, primarily by exercising "a powerful influence among and over them to get them to abandon their ancient long gowns, (more generally) their three-cornered hats and other badges now creating and keeping alive invidious distinctions, and so bring them to adopt the apparel of Western Europe, of Paris and London, and by degrees to become Roumanians, citizens in fact . . . "[17] Jesse Seligman, the New York banker who helped provide the funds for the Peixotto mission, publicly declared that he was glad to aid such an emissary to "those bigoted and demi-civilized heathens, our co-religionists in Roumania."[18] With such an outlook, Peixotto could obviously have no effect upon the cause or course of anti-Semitism in Roumania, even though he could, and occasionally did, mitigate the sufferings of the victims. When he saw that the "Ku-Klux of Roumania," as he called it in his dispatch to Secretary of State Hamilton Fish on May 5, 1872, was continuing its work, Peixotto began to contemplate emigration as a solution, as this editorial indicates.]

The Jewish question has taken an almost amusing turn in Roumania. As we have several times explained in these columns,[19] the Jews of that region, not over 200,000 in all, are almost the sole traders and bankers, and in short form the only approach to a middle class the country possesses.[20] They are consequently nearly everybody's creditor, and the Roumanians delight in being debtors, so that to the traditional hatred of the Jew by the Christian is added the animosity of the average man towards people who lend him money and want it back when he cannot pay it. The result is the persecutions and outrages of which we have been hearing so much for the last two or three years. But now Mr. Peixotto has proposed the emigration of the Jews of Roumania to the United States, and the Roumanian Government has taken up the scheme with almost frantic delight, and has issued a circular giving the Jews full leave to go, and many private persons offer subscriptions in aid of the enterprise.[21] There is not much chance that the Christians will be gratified by any such exodus, but if it took place it would have an effect on Roumania not unlike the emigration of the Huguenot from France or of the Moors from Spain; indeed worse, for they would leave behind them nothing but an ignorant peasantry and an idle and licentious aristocracy.[22] Usury would probably come to an end, but so would industry.

c) Letter to Columbus Delano, Secretary of the Interior, from A. Wellington Hart, New York, October 24, 1872 [23]

[This unpublished manuscript suggests the contemplation of a hitherto unnoted large-scale colonization project for some 40,000 "Roumanian & Continental Jews." Whether the company mentioned by Hart, with its capital of 250,000 to 500,000 pounds sterling, was already in existence or was planned, is not yet ascertained.]

53 Beaver St.
New York 24 Oct. 1872

Hon Columbus Delano [24]
Secy of Interior

Sir

The Israelites of Europe are moving in the matter of settling a Colony of Roumanian & Continental Jews in America.

Can I ask you if the Government has the power to concede to a Company possessing a paid up Capital of £250 000 c £500 000 Sterling say 250 000 acres of land for the purpose of *Eventually locating thereon* some 8000 families comprizing 40 000 persons[.] This immigration will cover a term of years the first year they propose to settle 250 families & 500 in Successive years if habitations can be Erected for them in the time.

As some of the leading Capitalists in Europe are interested in promoting the Company I hope the US Government will add its sympathy by Extending to the Company a title to the land conditionally that so many families shall be located annually[.]

Your Early reply for transcription to London will oblige

A. Wellington Hart.
(formerly of Int. Revenue Bureau)[25]

The desire is to have but *one large settlement.*

d) Letter to Secretary Columbus Delano from W. W. Curtis, Acting Commissioner of the General Land Office, Washington, D. C., October 28, 1872 [26]

[This unpublished letter makes clear that "there is no law providing for disposing of public lands in the manner proposed" by Hart and the company on behalf of which he had made his inquiry. Homesteading was on an individual basis, with no large-scale colonization or settlement envisioned.]

Washington, D.C. October 28 1872.

Hon. C. Delano,
Secretary of the Interior.

Sir,

I have the honor to return herewith the letter addressed to the Secretary by A. Wellington Hart, Esq., dated at N° 53 Beaver street, New York, the 24th inst., and referred to this office for report on the 25th—Mr. Hart therein states that "the Israelites of Europe are moving in the matter of settling a colony of Roumanian and Continental Jews in America;" that there is "a company possessing a paid up capital of 250,000 to 300,000 pounds sterling" which contemplates settling in this country "some 8,000 families, comprising 40,000 persons," and the question is presented whether the United States Government will "extend to the company a title to the land" required, "say 250,000 acres," conditionally "that so many families shall be located annually," it being the desire "to have but *one large settlement.*"

In reference to the subject, I have to report that there is no law providing for disposing of public lands in the manner proposed in Mr. Hart's enclosed letter—The laws in favor of actual settlers deal directly with the individual, not with companies or colonies, allowing to each settler, if a citizen of the United States, or if he has declared his intention of becoming such, according to the provisions of the naturalization laws, a quantity of land not exceeding 160 acres, as a homestead, the fee simple title to which is conveyed to him on the legal conditions being fully complied with, requiring five years' continuous settlement and cultivation of the land, or, if he should prefer it, he may pay the legal price for the land, making proof of his settlement and cultivation for a shorter period, not less than six months, and so acquire title to the land, being allowed a pre-emption right to the same.

Although the land desired by the company, supposing so large an area of unappropriated land should be found in one body, could not be given, for the purpose, under existing laws, and to do so would require further legislation, yet the heads of families for whom it proposes to act may individually avail themselves of the provisions of the law in favor of actual settlers, if they should take the required steps for becoming citizens, and otherwise fulfill the legal conditions, as indicated in official circular of August 30, 1872, and the "Brief description of the public lands," prepared by this office under date of October 1, 1871, of each of which a copy is herewith enclosed.

Very respectfully,

Your obt. servant,

W. W. Curtis
Acting Commissioner.

e) Editorial, "A New Exodus," *The Philadelphia Inquirer,* April 24, 1873 [27]

[A "warm welcome" to "our national brotherhood" is extended in this editorial to an expected sizable immigration of Roumanian Jews that really did not, at that time, materialize. Whatever ideas Peixotto may have had about mass emigration from Roumania were decisively vetoed at the first international Jewish conference held in modern times. While the discussion of Peixotto's inquiry and the Roumanian government's proposal to issue free passports was at its height, the prominent Berlin banker and financial counselor to Bismarck, (Gerson von) Julius Bleichroeder, issued a call on September 19, 1872 for a conference to be held in Brussels on October 29 and 30, 1872. Forty-five Jews from England, France, Germany, Belgium, Holland, Austria-Hungary, Roumania and the United States (represented by Peixotto and Isaac Seligman of London) met at the home of the Belgian banker, Jonathan Raphael Bischoffsheim. In addition to the bankers, there were political leaders, scholars, and writers in attendance, twenty-one of the forty-five having been knighted and decorated. They unanimously rejected the idea of organized emigration, and decided instead to memorialize the Roumanian government for the granting of full civic and political equality for the Jews. The Vienna *Neue Freie Presse* thought this decision "speaks better of numerous illusions than of practical sense."[28]

Nevertheless, individually and in very small groups, Roumanian Jews did emigrate, and by August, 1873, some 150 had arrived, according to the figure of Leopold Bamberger, president of the Roumanian Emigration Society in New York.[29]]

We are accustomed to complacently congratulate ourselves, in reading of the horrors wrought by religious fanaticism in the bigoted and intolerant past, upon the fact of the greater enlightenment of the age in which we live. Persecution, for conscience sake, we would fain regard as banished with the superstitions and tyrannies belonging to a lower civilization than our own. Especially is it difficult for us to realize, in the broad freedom of our young Republic, the cruelties perpetrated in the name of religion, with which the traditions of the Old World are filled. Yet we are about to witness, on our own free shores, a most extraordinary meeting of extremes, in the arrival of the victims of a persecution, inspired solely by the spirit of religious bigotry as savage and atrocious as any to be found in the history of the world. Several wealthy Roumanian Hebrews have already arrived in this country to make arrangements for the reception of their oppressed co-religionists, who, to the number it is said, of fifty thousand, desire to seek a refuge in our broad, free land. For years they have been absolutely without protection of life or property in the land of their birth, and the recent and constantly occurring outrages perpetrated upon them, and against which they have no redress, has made their existence so intolerable that they propose to forever exchange barbarous Roumania for free America. It is expected that they will fix upon a settlement in Nebraska, and even if the number of actual emigrants falls short of the present estimate, there is little doubt but that we shall receive a large accession to our population by the arrival of these unfortunate people. They will engage largely in agricultural pursuits, to which many of them have been accustomed at home, and will be assured of a warm welcome, not only out of sympathy with their misfortunes, but as being, by their peaceable and industrious habits, a valuable addition to our national brotherhood.

154. ON BEHALF OF IMMIGRANT WORKERS

A Call to a Public Meeting, issued by J. K. Buchner, New York, January 4, 1871 [1]

[The aim of this meeting was to establish an institution "whereby every one of our number is to be enabled to learn a trade," thus becoming "more

ON RABBINICAL EDUCATION

Editorial, "Hebrew Rabbinical Education," *The New York Herald*, July 22, 1872 [1]

interest of the general community in Jewish affairs is reflected in this ial, published in the newspaper with the largest circulation in the polis. Reprinting it, *The Jewish Messenger* on July 26 called it "one most important, suggestive, and accurate statements of the necessities Jewish community we have seen in the secular press" and hoped it "arouse the Hebrews of the United States to a keen sense of their table neglect of duty." The editorial calls attention to "the great need glish speaking rabbies and preachers," on the ground that "to maintain sm in America something more than a mere recitation of prayers in w and German is necessary." The promise is held out that "give them ewish youth] religious as well as secular instruction in their vernacular, here will not be much cause to complain of empty pews and neglected gues." The *Herald*, expressing the point of view of the American mid-ass, tended to encourage the Reform movement in Judaism.]

The HERALD some time ago was the first to call the atten-f the Israelites of this city and of the country to their great need glish speaking rabbies and preachers. The Jewish press took notice of our article at the time and commented upon it—some bly and some otherwise.[2] The editors and their patrons thought were pretty well off because three of their largest and finest gues and most wealthy and flourishing congregations in this ere supplied with English preaching. They rested there, and h more than a year has elapsed nothing has been done and no has been made to supply this want any further. But the leaven een working ever since, and now, when an emergency has d, the Jewish press re-echoes our cry of need, and the *Messenger* t week has a couple of doleful articles on the subject.[3] The ading synagogues of the city, and indeed of the country, are to be, and one is certain to be, deprived of English preaching he end of this year. The Rev. Dr. Gutheim has resigned his n as English preacher in the Temple Emanuel, Fifth avenue, as re-engaged with the congregation whom he served in New s before he came to New York.[4] The Temple congregation been advertising for a successor for a couple of months past; s yet, have not found one. And now the Congregation B'nai

civilized" and joining the ranks of those "who are useful members of the world of industry." So equipped, the rapidly increasing numbers of East-European Jewish immigrants would not have to resort to "that dirty peddling" or the semi-skilled work, to which many newly arrived immigrants took, of an itinerant glazier. Moreover, they will be helped to observe the Sabbath.

Although unsuccessful, the attempt itself, and the ideas it reveals, were significant, because it was along the road of productivization and of the development of a large Jewish working class that the immigrant masses finally did move.]

115 East Broadway, New York,
January 4, 1871.

To the Editor of the Hebrew Leader:

Sir:—The position of the poor Jews and especially the Jewish emigrants in this country is such which requires a certain help, through the existence of the Emigrants Society, erected in this city a short time ago.[2] The bad situation of emigrants is mostly grounded on these facts: Hereto they have kept the Sabbath-day, but now having come to this country, they must, if they want to look for an employment in any factory, turn from it at once, wherefore peddling or glazing is taken refuge to without delay; I therefore am working since several months for their cause,[3] trying to raise an institution, whereby every one of our number is to be enabled to learn a trade. This would not only prevent them from being obliged to get their livelihood by that dirty peddling, etc., which inclines them to lose all confidence in truthfulness, but also they will be enabled to keep the Sabbath-day, and instead of lowering their character, which at the same time becomes unprofitable to all the Jews, they will by the means of getting acquainted with a trade have the opportunity to get connected with different classes of people and become more civilized by it, and also it may be the means of once seeing our Jewish brethren amongst those who are useful members of the world of industry. There will be held a public meeting for this cause on Sunday next (afternoon)[4] at 3 o'clock, in Harris Hotel, 115 East Broadway. I should be glad to see you present on that occasion, and I hope that you will assist this undertaking with an article in your paper of this week.

I remain sir, yours,

J. K. Buchner.

We attach great importance to this subject, especially because the above letter emanates from a gentleman who stands in close relation to the unfortunate Russo-Polish emigrants. If before the date of the projected meeting in their interest, we have somewhat recovered from the heavy trial that has befallen us, we shall comply with the wish expressed to us.

[Editor.][5]

155. ATTEMPTS AT CONVERSION

Editorial, "The Conversion of the Jews," *Sunday Dispatch*, Philadelphia, May 28, 1871 [1]

[The non-Jewish editors of this general newspaper had no patience with efforts of missionaries to convert the Jews to Christianity. Such efforts were made repeatedly in this country from the beginning of the nineteenth century, with but little success. One such missionary's attempt to compute the number of Jewish converts in the entire century in the United States produced the estimate of 1,267, but most of these were by missions established in the last decade of the century,[2] and even these figures are unverified and untested. Outside religious sectarian circles, these missionary efforts met with little public sympathy. *The Jewish Messenger* was thankful for this editorial.[3]]

One of the most curious things connected with the recent crop of religious anniversaries in New York city [4] is the report of the board of managers of the "Society for the Promotion of Christianity among the Jews." This association has been in existence for some years, and, although it has occasionally claimed credit for the conversion of a Jew to Christianity during a cycle of three or five years, the aggregate shows a miserable return, and might perhaps show the conversion of a sixth of a Jew per annum. At the last anniversary the Rev. L. C. Newman,[5] who is supported by the funds contributed by over-zealous Christians as the missionary of this society, made a report of his work. He has been rotating around the Union searching for susceptible Hebrews and persuading them to apostolize from the faith of their fathers. The candor of Mr. Newman incites him to say that he does not even claim the conversion of a fraction of a Jew as the evangelical work of the year 1870. He avers that he traveled about

through the United States more than four thous
had sought "the good of the natural children of
had discovered one Israelite who was already a wo
copal church, whose conversion therefore, he cou
where he was not able to do much. In New Yo
synagogues [6] and one hundred thousand Jews, he w
so little interest was taken by the Christian comm
of his labors that they would not contribute a si
the support of a missionary. This fact, which Mr. N
disgraceful to New York Christianity, is probably
common sense. New Yorkers know how to spend m
anything is to be gained in exchange. They even
their money away; but, in that case, the matter
excites their folly, claims their sympathies, or aw
siasm. New Yorkers know that there can be no
to convert Jews to Christianity as long as they f
is an untrue doctrine. The Jews, in fact, believe
an imposture. They believe in the coming of C
believe that he is yet to come.[7] With these opin
otherwise than consider Christianity as a delusion;
they may respect the motives of honorable men w
are doing right, they could not allow their judg
by their zealousness.

Mr. Newman was therefore compelled to fall
tion that he was held in high esteem by the Je
accounts of his interviews with rabbis, and sta
argued with them in Hebrew upon the Messiah,
the Trinity,[8] and quoted to them confoundin
Scriptures, the Mishnah, Talmud, Targum, an
displays of learning, he averred, secured him t
Jews. On the whole, not much of a satisfactory
from this report of the Hebrew Conversion Soci
is to be found, with all the importance of a po
letter, just as the end of the report: "The con
financially, is satisfactory, *and the board were h*
increase the salary of their indefatigable missio
fore, as the Rev. Mr. Newman finds that his sala
and can even have it increased, it may be expect
drearily about the country, seeking for impo
never expects to convert.

156.

[The
edito
metro
of th
of th
woul
lamer
of En
Judai
Hebr
[the J
and t
synag
dle c

tion
of E
some
favor
they
synag
city
thoug
effort
has b
arrive
for la
two l
liable
after
positi
and h
Orlea
have
but, a

Jeshurun in Thirty-fourth street, second only to the Temple in size, numbers and influence, are looking for a preacher to succeed the eloquent Dr. Vidaver.[5] And where are those congregations to look for the men they need? Not to America, for they are not here. The *Jewish Messenger* utters the sad lamentation that "there is not a single Jewish pulpit in America occupied by a minister instructed on our soil." And should Dr. Vidaver leave the city there would then be but one English speaking rabbi left among us—namely, Rev. S. M. Isaacs, of Forty-fourth street synagogue.[6]

Nor can the congregations look to England for the supply which they so greatly need, since the *Messenger*, which ought to be good authority, asserts that "there is no seminary in Europe which can furnish ministers capable of supplying the American Jewish pulpit." And yet the Israelites of this country have known, or they might have known these many years, that just such a time as the present would come upon them, but they made comparatively no provision against it. A few years ago, it is true, they established the Maimonides College in Philadelphia; but it has never received any support worthy of the cause or of American Hebrew wealth, and to-day it is reported in a languishing condition, with just three students in it.[7] And the extremity becomes more alarming when we consider that this is the only Jewish rabbinical college in the country.

Looking away from our own metropolis, which can command at best but three English speaking rabbies, how many do we find elsewhere in the United States? In Cincinnati there are Drs. [Isaac Mayer] Wise and [Max] Lilienthal, radical reformers; in Philadelphia there is Rev. Mr. Jacobs, and in New Orleans his brother, Canadians, and consequently speaking English fluently enough;[8] and in Evansville, Ind., Rev. George Brown, who has given up the professions of law and medicine and taken to the pulpit.[9] These, so far as we can ascertain, are all the English speaking rabbis in the United States.[10] But what are they among so many? The difficulty hitherto has been in supposing that American Jews would remain forever content to study Hebrew and German for the sake of worshipping God in those languages. It was a great mistake, and its fruits are but just appearing. Far easier would it have been to have educated one hundred ministers in English than one hundred thousand people in German and Hebrew. Israelites born on American soil cannot be expected to have as much sympathy as their fathers with those languages, nor with European nationalities and ideas; and to maintain Judaism in

America something more than a mere recitation of prayers in Hebrew and German is necessary. The people now are much more intelligent than they were a century or half a century ago, and any religious system that keeps not up with the progressive spirit of the age must expect to meet just such crises as this in which the Jewish Church in America now finds itself. The rising generations demand a form of religion which their hearts can appreciate and hold fast to, though they ask for no change in the true spirit of religion at all; and it is the attempt to confine them within the iron bands of the systems of bygone ages that has produced that result which the Hebrew press so generally and so frequently lament—namely, that the young Israelites do not manifest that love for the synagogue which their fathers and forefathers showed.[11] Rightly understood this very religious indisposition is a sign of progress which calls loudly and earnestly on the Jewish Church to furnish such spiritual food as young American souls can digest. Give them religious as well as secular instruction in their vernacular, and there will not be much cause to complain of empty pews and neglected synagogues. We make no such mistakes anywhere as in religion, and nowhere so frequently as there; and yet there is nothing so important for a people or a nation as religious instruction brought within their comprehension, and designed in its precepts and practice to ennoble and elevate them.

The synagogues of this city that have the largest and best congregations at all times are those that have English preaching. In the matter of architecture the Jews are leading all other religionists here, but in ritual, and in religious instruction in English they have not kept equal pace with others. It would be a great loss to New York if Drs. Gutheim and Vidaver should both leave us. Their ministrations, as we have shown, cannot be easily supplied, and their services should be correspondingly appreciated.

But why do not those rabbies who have sons, and who feel and express the great need of which we write, train up some of those sons for the ministry? Drs. Wise and Lilienthal and Mr. Isaacs have sons, but not one of them has taken to his father's profession.[12] There is not money enough in it to compensate for the amount of study and labor required, and hence they take to law and medicine and journalism in preference. Dr. Adler, of the Temple, has a son now in Europe studying for the ministry—a young man born in America and to whom English is his native tongue.[13] He may, perhaps, step into Dr. Gutheim's place by and by, and ultimately, perhaps, into that of his father's. Seeing that Jewish rabbies themselves do not advance the ministry of their own faith in this regard it can hardly be blameworthy in others to follow their example. Let them ponder over these things and seek a remedy in the future if they desire or hope to preserve Judaism intact in America.[14]

157. IN PRAISE OF THE JEWS

Editorial, "The Jew As A Citizen," *The Evening Telegraph,* Philadelphia, Saturday, October 19, 1872 [1]

[This editorial, occasioned by a Jewish hospital project and appearing in the afternoon newspaper claiming the largest circulation in the country, is of interest because it concedes to them all the middle-class virtues which the Jews have claimed for themselves under capitalism, and also mentions the middle-class vices of which the Jews are most frequently "accused." Thus the Jews are seen as an asset to a developing capitalism because they have "enterprise and energy" and wealth; the Jew takes care of himself and of his own, and he never applies for charity except to Jews; "a Jewish beggar is almost unknown" and Jews are law-abiding and are seldom seen in the criminal courts; and the Jew is generous, both to his own people and to the community at large. On the other hand, "he is perhaps more inoculated with the love of money-getting than is the average Christian, and hence a little keener and closer in his business transactions," but then again, taken as a whole, "Jews, if sharp, are to the full as honorable in their dealings as any other body of business men." And the Jew "is essentially a trader" and "does not take to manual toil nor mechanical occupations." As the observations of a well-intentioned and influential non-Jewish metropolitan editor, these are useful as summing up the benevolent stereotype of the Jews, which was already being widely challenged by the anti-Semitic stereotype.[2]

When the hospital was finally constructed, it contained an inscription over the main entrance even more liberal than the editor foresaw, for it read: "This Hospital was erected by the voluntary contributions of the Israelites of Philadelphia, and is dedicated to the relief of the sick and wounded, without regard to creed, *color,* or nationality . . . "[3]]

WHEREVER there is a chance for enterprise and energy the Jew is to be found. Go to whatever land and into whatever city you may, and he will be met with. In this country he has made strong footing. The peculiar advantages it offers to his characteristic abilities render America his favorite home. And Americans should be glad that such is the case, for the Jew as a citizen is to be highly esteemed. He brings into every community wealth and qualities which materially assist to strengthen and consolidate its polity. He never causes anxiety or apprehension. He takes care of himself and his own. A Jew is never an applicant for public or private charity outside of Judaism, neither will he ever allow one of his race to be. In the history of our public institutions, scarcely an instance occurs of a Jew availing himself of their advantages, although he is frequently a generous supporter of them. Should he require assistance, his fellow-believers extend it, and should he fall sick and become needy or incapacitated from earning his living, they make him their special charge. It is a matter of principle and pride with them to take care of each other. As a consequence a Jewish beggar is almost unknown. The Jew is also law-abiding. No other element in the community is so orderly in character and so observant of the law. A Jew is seldom or never seen in our courts on a criminal charge. Now and again those who represent themselves as Jews get into trouble with the authorities, but an investigation into their case would almost certainly show that they are renegades, or that for ill-doing they have been thrust without the pale. He is perhaps more inoculated with the love of money-getting than is the average Christian, and hence a little keener and closer in his business transactions, but he can also be open-handed, and his liberality is generally well directed. He is sober and industrious, although singularly enough he does not take to manual toil nor mechanical occupations. He is essentially a trader, and is most in his element as a "middle-man." There are those who delight in overreaching, but as a class Jews, if sharp, are to the full as honorable in their dealings as any other body of business men. Indeed, from whatever standpoint they may be viewed, no candid observer can fail to perceive that they form a good element in society, and it is remarkable that at this advanced day any country should be so short-sighted as to oppress them.

These observations are suggested by the recent illustration of Jewish benevolence afforded in the laying of the corner-stone of their new hospital on the Olney road, near the York pike. The institution, which has grown from small beginnings, is designed for the relief of the sick and as an asylum for the aged and infirm.[4] A noble site, comprising fifteen acres, has been secured, and the building itself will cover about a quarter of an acre. The accommodations will be extensive, and will be, as those of the present establishment have ever been, open to the sick, the aged, and infirm of all nationalities and creeds. While taking a justifiable pride in its purely Jewish origin, the founders, with a broad and cosmopolitan charity worthy of all admiration and emulation, declare that its mission of kindness and love would be incomplete did it not embrace suffering humanity irrespective of all distinctions. Charity such as this is the crowning virtue of a citizen.

158. ANTI-SEMITISM IN THE ARMED FORCES

a) Letter to the Editor, *The Jewish Times,* New York, October 25, 1872, by B. F. Waterman
b) Letter to the Editor, *The New York Herald,* December 17, 1872, by N. M. Davis of Memphis, Tenn.

[Mr. Waterman justly complains of an "outrage on American rights and privileges" that had been committed against him when, after having been duly elected and sworn into a militia company, he was compelled to withdraw his application because of the existence of a Company regulation barring from membership either foreign-born or native American Jews. Following the publication of this letter, the "Military Gossip" column of *The New-York Times* reported on November 3, 1872 that "some amount of excitement has existed in military circles during the past week" because of this incident. On November 8, *The Jewish Messenger* reprinted the item from the *Times* with an indignant comment. Governor John T. Hoffman presumably ordered an investigation, but his term expired with the end of the year, and nothing was heard of the matter after that.[1] A month later, from distant Memphis, a voice was lifted in protest, but the New York press, both Jewish and general, having forgotten about the issue, it disappeared from public attention.]

To the Editor of the "Jewish Times":

DEAR SIR: I was not aware that those prejudicial sectarian feelings, which we hoped were long since eradicated in this "free country," are still harbored and so fanaticised, that one inspired with the true feelings of justice and honor could not fail to shudder at. Let me communicate to you a nice example of it. A few weeks ago, I enlisted in *A* Company, 22d Regiment, N. G. S. N. Y., to properly serve as soldier in defence of my State. I was ballotted for, elected, and duly took the oath of allegiance, as prescribed by law. A day or two ago, I was informed by the captain [2] of my company, that a law was passed three years ago (in said company) prohibiting from admission in the company any person, either of foreign or American birth, who should be of the Jewish persuasion; and was also informed by him, that in the name of *A* Company he was requested to inform me to withdraw my name, as they would under no circumstances deviate from that law.

Is this liberty! Is this right and justice! Is this to be tolerated in a country that has shed torrents of blood in vindication of human equality, and expended millions of treasure in defence of equality before the law! I am an American, and I am proud of it, but I am of Jewish parentage, of which I am prouder still. Dear sir, it is not solely my own grievance for which I plead, but in rebuke of the gross insult offered to our co-religionists. There are many young men who have found themselves in the same predicament, and who were too unambitious to expose to the public the internal complications of some of our military organizations. I ask it of you, and hope I am not unreasonable in my demand, to prominently place this outrage on American rights and privileges before a just and honor-loving public.

Very respectfully,

B. F. Waterman.

To the Editor of the Herald:—Not having seen any notice of a certain outrageous proceeding that lately transpired in your city, and being interested in the matter, I beg to call your attention to it, feeling assured you will give it the attention it merits. A young man named Waterman was elected a member of Company A, Twenty-second regiment New York Militia, and after a short time the Captain informed him that he must resign, as they did not permit Jews as members of their company. What think you of this in a country of equal rights? What think you of this in the face of the respectable position of your New York Jewish merchants, lawyers and bankers? Have you the courage to bring this matter before the community in its true light? Are you the champion of oppression, come it in what shape it may? I don't know your opinion of a class of men who would ostracise a gentleman on account of his religious faith;

but I don't think much comment is necessary. What I'd like to get at is their muster roll. Being a merchant[3] I might perchance be brought in contact with them, or some of them, and the opportunity might be a mutual advantage. I feel very much like applying some adjectives to these gentlemen; but I leave it to you—you who, I feel, are charged with so sacred a trust—the columns of the most influential journal in the land.

Respectfully,

N. M. Davis

159. CAPMAKERS ON STRIKE, 1874

a) Statement of Principal Manufacturers, issued by Marks Bros. & Thompson, New York, February 4, 1874

[This would seem to be the first strike in which it is known that hundreds of Jewish workers took part. Of the 1,500 to 2,000 strikers, about one-third were women and girls, most of them Irish immigrants, some American born and some German immigrants. Most of the men, however, were German immigrants, of which the great majority were German Jews.[2] It is also significant that the strike headquarters was in Covenant Hall, 56 Orchard Street, owned and operated by B'nai Brith.[3]

The strike was called when the Crisis of 1873, precipitated in September by the bankruptcy of Jay Cooke and Company, was ravaging the people. By the end of 1873, fully one-fourth of the workers in New York were unemployed.[4] The *Herald* editorially called both the cigarmakers and capmakers "foolish" for striking at such a time,[5] but the capmakers, in their reply to their employers, stated the ample provocation that compelled them to strike. For by "cruel and oppressive use" of "their power" the employers had cut wages by more than half in the past couple of years. Furthermore, said the strikers, "our craftsmen work, not like Christians or Jews, but like heathens, seven days in the week," and at that, twelve, fifteen or even twenty hours a day.[6]

Preparations for the strike began on January 10, when the Hat and Cap Makers' Protective Association was organized, which later expanded into the Central Union of Capmakers, with the following officers: President, William C. Ober; Secretary, M. Weiner; Vice-President, H. Benjamin; Treasurer, —— Bromberg.[7] The workers were organized on a shop basis, with a "president" in each shop who also served on the central council of the Union, which constituted the strike leadership. Daily mass meetings were held at Covenant Hall, attended by 700 to 1,200 workers, men and women.[8] The economic demands were simple: an increase of 20% to 40% in the prices paid. The workers also demanded acceptance of the Union rules and regulations: that no worker could hire more than one girl assistant; that work be restricted to ten hours a day; that no worker be discharged without the consent of the shop president; that employers' books be open to examination on payday to guarantee accurate wage accounting; that all strikers be rehired; that scabs be either discharged or compelled to join the Union and pay a fine.[9]

The strike began January 29. On February 4, led by Marks Bros. & Thompson, the largest firm and the first to cut wages, the big manufacturers locked out their 800 workers, while some of the small manufacturers began to accede to the Union terms. The same day, the Union appealed to the capmakers of Philadelphia, Boston and other cities to support their strike by adopting the same demands; in New York, the struggle expanded when the blockers joined the Union and entered the strike, greatly strengthening the finishers and operators. When the cutters organized and joined the Union in a body, the strike was solid, and the manufacturers were compelled to begin negotiations on February 9. The first offer of the employers, in which some prices were even lower than before the strike, was indignantly rejected. On February 11, the big manufacturers publicly threatened to close their factories, and bound one another to forfeit $5,000 if any of them separately signed an agreement. On February 16, the Union offered a compromise price-list, which, with modifications, was accepted by the big manufacturers on February 20. While most workers went back to work on February 24, having gained an average of 15% increase, some of the big manufacturers held out, refusing to accept the Union rules, particularly the one requiring the discharge of scabs. On March 3, Marks Bros. & Thompson even had three workers arrested for picketing, but the charges were dismissed. On March 9 the Union withdrew its insistence on some rules, and the strike ended.[10] The *Arbeiter-Zeitung* congratulated the capmakers on the victory they won despite the unfavorable circumstances.]

[February 4, 1874][11]

A meeting of the principal hat and cap manufacturers has been held in the office of Marks Bros. & Thompson, Nos. 80 and 82 Greene Street, the unanimous sense of which was to resist the demand of their operatives, who are now on strike, for an advance in the scale of prices. The following houses were represented: Marks Bros. & Thompson, L. J. Phillips & Co., W. J. Willis & Co., Isidor & Hein, Charles Fox's Sons & Co., and the Chairman.[12] After an animated discussion, in the course of which it was stated that the demand for an advance of price was 125 per cent., it was unanimously resolved that it is inconsistent with the interests of the trade to accede to the rate of prices adopted by the United Capmakers' Association. These houses employ about

800 men, who are thus locked out,[13] with no prospect of a reinstatement unless their demands are lowered.

[Signed] Marks Bros. & Thompson.

b) Reply by the Strikers, issued by the Central Union of Capmakers [1]

We deny that we have asked 125 per cent. more than we received for the same kind of work formerly. When we made the new price-schedule, our object was, and still is, to fix the prices for work as high only as we received three years ago. Since that time rent has not become cheaper; food, clothing, and all other indispensable necessaries of life have remained almost stationary. But since two years back, business has been rather dull in the cap line, and the consequence was that the manufacturers, all eager and anxious to sell goods, tried everything in their power to gain this desirable object. Among the many methods to make the goods up cheap, the cutting down of wages was the most prominent, and of this method our manufacturers made such liberal use that now all the work, without exception, brings, on an average, 50 per cent. less than its real value. We are striking for a fair day's wages for a fair day's work only, notwithstanding all assertions to the contrary; and if our demands are now 125 per cent. higher than the manufacturers paid during the last two years, it merely shows what cruel and oppressive use they have made of their power.

It will be said that there was a general decline of wages during the past two years. We have been living too fast. All this is true; but to cut down wages 125 per cent. is a little too much of a good thing. This strike was provoked by our employers, and they alone are accountable for the consequences of it. There is not a more peaceable fraternity on the globe than the capmakers, and this appears to be why they have been taken advantage of.

Our craftsmen work, not like Christians or Jews, but like heathens, seven days in the week; and if they don't work more, it is simply because there are no days left. Still they manage to work nine days in the week by working twelve, fifteen, and, in some instances, twenty hours out of twenty-four. This is the reason why some can show you $20 and $25 as the week's earnings. Let the capmaker work for ten hours only, without help, and let him be ever so smart, he will not be able to earn more than $15, even at our new price-schedule, on the average.[14]

GLOSSARY

Adjunta: governing council of a Sephardic congregation
Bedika: examination of an animal or fowl before ritual slaughter
Gabay: a synagogue treasurer; a trustee
Hazan or *Chasan:* a cantor or reader who conducts the service; in American Sephardic congregations, a minister
Kahal: autonomous organization of the Jewish community
Kahal Kadosh: the holy community or congregation
Kosher or *Kasher:* conforming to Jewish dietary laws
Mahamad: trustees of a Sephardic congregation, elected by members
Metaher house: place for the ritual washing of a corpse
Minhag: a Jewish social or religious custom
Mohel: one who performs the rite of circumcision according to Jewish law
Parnas: the president of a congregation or kahal
Sefer: a book, often referring to a *Sefer Torah*
Sefer Torah: Scroll of the Law (Pentateuch)
Shamas or *Shammash:* a beadle or sexton of a synagogue
Shema or *Shemang:* first word of the Jewish profession of faith, *Shema Yisroel . . .* (Hear, O Israel, the Lord our God is One)
Shohet: a Jewish ritual slaughterer
Shofar: ram's horn blown in the synagogue during the penitential season at the turn of the Jewish calendar year
Shomre Shabas: observers of the Sabbath; promoters of the observance of the Sabbath
Talmud Torah: an elementary Jewish religious school
Taybah: lectern at the side of the Ark in a synagogue
Tephillin: phylacteries
Yeshiva or *Yeshibah:* advanced school for study of Jewish law and lore
Yigdal: first word of hymn used in daily prayer, based on the Thirteen Creeds of Maimonides

Notes

1. Unwelcome

1. Oppenheim, *AJHSP,* XVIII (1909), 4–5.
2. Father Isaac Jogues, cited in A. B. Hart, ed.: *Source Book of American History,* New York, 1925, p. 42.
3. Daniel Van Pelt, *Leslie's History of the Greater New York,* New York, 1896, Vol. 1, pp. 50, 55.
4. "The Dutch West India Company," *Enc. Brit.,* 1947 ed., VII, 780–781.
5. The cry of usury against the Jews was commonplace, yet it was a Dutch ideologist who had established the capitalist theory of interest (usury) under which Holland was prospering. W. E. H. Lecky, impressed with the irony of this charge, and contemptuous of it, writes: ". . . the author to whom the first unequivocal assertion of the modern doctrine of interest is due seems to be Saumaise [Salmasius], who, between 1638 and 1640, published three books in its defense. His view was speedily but almost silently adopted by most Protestants, and the change produced no difficulty or hostility to Christianity." (*History of the Rise and Influence of the Spirit of Rationalism in Europe,* London, 1897, Vol. 2, p. 266.)
6. The Schout (Sheriff), Burgomasters (Mayors) and Schepens (Aldermen) had been constituted on February 26, 1654 as the Inferior Court of Justice.
7. For the journey, the twenty three Jews owed the captain, Jacques de la Motte, 1567 florins. Their goods were sold to pay the debt, but 495 guilders still being due, David Israel and Mose Lumbroso, two of the arrivals, were placed under civil arrest. Finally the creditor agreed to wait until the Jews received funds from Holland.

2. Cooperation and Influence

1. Oppenheim, *op. cit.,* 9–11.
2. Pernambuco (Recife), capital of Dutch Brazil, had a Jewish community of about 5000 when the Portuguese reconquered it. By the capitulation agreement of January 25, 1654, Dutch citizens were amnestied and given three months to leave, or to stay as Portuguese subjects or as aliens (*ibid.,* 37ff.).
3. Treaty of Münster, 1648, in which the Jews are not mentioned, but under which they claimed full rights as Dutch subjects. In 1657 the Dutch States-General asserted the right of Dutch Jews to trade in Spain.
4. Jews had been among the founders of the Dutch West India Company, contributing about one per cent of the capital supplied in Amsterdam. The extent of their influence in the Company may be inferred from these data: in 1656, four per cent of the principal shareholders were Jewish; in 1658, six to seven per cent; in 1671, about five per cent: in 1674, about ten per cent. The amount of their holdings is not known. (Herbert I. Bloom, *The Economic Activities of the Jews of Amsterdam in the Seventeenth and Eighteenth Centuries,* Williamsport, Pa., 1937, pp. 125–126.)
5. There were Jews in Martinique when the French took possession in 1635. In 1658, a few years after this example was cited in the petition, the right of the

Jews to trade in Martinique was contested by French Jesuits and a long struggle ensued. ("Martinique," *JE,* VIII, 353.)

6. Jews had first settled in the Barbadoes in 1628; six families came there about 1654. (Oppenheim, *op. cit.,* 16.)

3. Permission Grudgingly Given

1. Oppenheim, *op. cit.,* 8.
2. On April 4, 1652, the directors of the Dutch West India Company, writing to Stuyvesant, then in Curaçao, that they have granted a colonizing privilege to a Jew for the second time, expressed the opinion that "Time must show whether we shall succeed well with this nation; they are a crafty and generally treacherous people in whom therefore not too much confidence must be placed." (Cone, *AJHSP,* X, 1902, p. 147.)
3. The records of the Spanish Inquisition reveal how influential the Jews were considered to have been in the taking of Brazil and in the wars of Holland against Portugal and Spain. When the Dutch fleet moved against Brazil in 1623, it was guided by information about the situation in Brazil provided by Jews living there; the Jews also aided in the Dutch conquest of Bahia in 1624. When the Portuguese recaptured Bahia eleven months later, they executed five Jews for helping the Dutch. (Adler, *AJHSP,* XVII, 1909, 45–51; Kohler, *AJHSP,* I, 1893, 42–44; George Alexander Kohut, "Sketches of Jewish Loyalty, Bravery and Patriotism in the South American Colonies and the West Indies," in Simon Wolf, *The American Jew as Patriot, Soldier and Citizen,* Philadelphia, 1895, pp. 443–459.
4. For details about this investment, see Note 4 to the preceding document.

4. Not Wanted For Defense

1. Oppenheim, *ibid.,* 24n–25n.
2. L. D. Scisco, "The Burgher Guard of New Amsterdam," *The American Historical Register,* II (1895), 743–745.

5. Asserting the Right to Fight

1. Oppenheim, *ibid.,* 25.
2. Barsimson and Salomon Pietersen, the first Jews in New Amsterdam, arrived on August 22, 1654 from Holland. Barsimson had left with a passport from the Directors of the Dutch West India Company. (Oppenheim, *AJHSP,* XXIX, 1925, pp. 39ff.) Later, in 1658, Barsimson was to win the right not to have to testify in court on his Sabbath.

   Asser Levy, who had come with the first group of Jews on the *St. Catherine,* began as a manual laborer, but became a licensed butcher, a tavern-keeper, real estate operator, trader, and civic figure. He became the first Jew to achieve citizenship on the American mainland. When he died in 1681, he was the richest Jew in New York, with an estate valued at over £2000. (Huhner, *AJHSP,* VIII, 1900, pp. 9–23.)
3. The meaning of this "permission to leave" is not entirely clear. Oppenheim (*ibid.,* 52) points out that ten days before this matter came before the Council, an order had been issued restricting depopulation by forbidding emigration from the colony to anyone who had been there less than one year. The purpose of this order was to prevent persons from coming to the colony only for the trading season, during which they could make profits without adding to the

wealth of the community, and then leaving New Amsterdam to spend their money elsewhere. Barsimson and Levy, however, had both been in New Amsterdam for more than one year, and the consent to depart may therefore be barbed.

6. Enforcing a Right Granted

1. Oppenheim, *AJHSP,* XVIII (1909), 27–28.
2. Abraham De Lucena, merchant, had come to New Amsterdam from Holland in February, 1655. He took part in several struggles for equality, including the right to trade and travel, to establish a Jewish burial ground, to own real estate, and to become a citizen.

   Salvador Dandrada, a very wealthy merchant and tobacco importer, was also a participant in several civil rights contests.

   Jacob Cohen (Henriques) was later, April 11, 1657, denied the right to bake and sell bread at retail by action of the Council (*ibid.,* 35n). That Cohen was quick to resent an insult to his people is recorded in the Court Minutes of August 20 and 27, 1658: Joannes Vervelen, accusing Cohen of having short-weighted a keg of nails, proceeded to say, "You are a Jew, you are all cheats together." In Court, Vervelen denied having made the slur; and the official Weigher, on oath, testified that Cohen's weight had been honest. (Berthold Fernow, ed., *The Records of New Amsterdam,* New York, 1897, II, 419, 424.)
3. The two persons actually sent were Isaac Israel and Benjamin Cardoso (Oppenheim, *op. cit.,* 28).

7. Denied the Right To Own a House

1. Oppenheim, *ibid.,* 29–30.
2. *Ibid.*
3. Ellis Lawrence Raesly, *Portrait of New Netherland,* New York, 1945, p. 161. Dr. Raesly calls attention to the fact that in contrast to the denial of the right to hold real estate to the Jews, whose competition New Amsterdamers feared, they had accorded this right to free Negroes as far back as 1643.

8. List of Grievances

1. Oppenheim, *ibid.,* 31–32.
2. The first three petitioners we have met in earlier documents. Joseph D'Acosta (brother of Uriel D'Acosta, the famous rebel against formal Judaism), had come to New Amsterdam in 1655. He had been a leading merchant in Amsterdam and was a principal shareholder of the Dutch West India Company (Oppenheim, *AJHSP,* XXIX, 1925, p. 49).

   David Frera (or De Ferera) arrived in New Amsterdam in the spring of 1655, leased a house and became a merchant, acting also as agent for Moses da Silva, an Amsterdam merchant. An extensive record of a legal case in which he was imprisoned and fined for offending a bailiff, and finally saved from the severity of the punishment by arbitration arranged by Stuyvesant, makes interesting reading (Oppenheim, *AJHSP,* XVIII, 1909, pp. 54–58, 77–86).

9. Stuyvesant Rebuked

1. Oppenheim, *ibid.,* 33.
2. That the Dutch should have encouraged Jewish merchants to participate in

international, wholesale trade but prevented them from entering the retail field is significant. This restriction dates back to an ordinance of the Burgomasters of Amsterdam, March 29, 1632 (Bloom, *op. cit.*, 23, 136, 142–143). Apparently activities in which the Jews helped to increase the economic weight of Holland in relation to its competitors, England, Spain, and Portugal, were welcomed more than local enterprise. In New Amsterdam, however, the Jews soon won the right to open retail shops (Oppenheim, *op. cit.*, 34). Dr. Raesly sees the clash between the Directors and Stuyvesant as a reflection of the conflict between "the practical business philosophy of bourgeois Holland" and the "medieval contempt" for Jews that Stuyvesant had (*op. cit.*, 215). The bourgeoisie, however, never completely rid itself of some of its "medieval" attitudes.

10. Winning the Last Round

1. Oppenheim, *op. cit.*, 36.
2. It was Asser Levy who, on April 11, 1657, had presented his claim and been denied. He had done so in response to the proclamation of the Burgomasters and Schepens on April 9, 1657 that all claimants of that right must present their names that week. The "small burgher right" was open to "all those who have resided and kept fire and light within the City one year and six weeks," to native born, and to the husbands of native born women ("The Burghers of New Amsterdam and the Freemen of New York, 1675–1866," *Collections of the New-York Historical Society for the Year 1885*, 7–19). Any one who wished to open a retail store had to buy this small burgher right for twenty guilders (about $4). The right to election to office, however, was restricted to those who held the Great Burgher Right.

11. Charged with Blasphemy

1. *Records of the Provincial Court* (Maryland), Lib. S. 1658 to 1662, *Judgments*, pp. 159–160, as cited in George Lynn-Lachlan Davis, *The Day-Star of American Freedom; . . .* New York, 1855, 66–67.
2. Jacob Lumbrozo (born in Portugal; died, Maryland, 1665–1666) came to the colony before 1656 and soon achieved prominence as a doctor, trader, and money-lender. After experiencing this indictment, Lumbrozo married a Christian in 1662. To obtain the limited form of citizenship known as denization, he took the oath "on the true faith of a Christian" on September 10, 1663. This action enabled him, the following day, to acquire the 200 acres of land, free of cost, that was allowed to himself and his wife "for transportation." (B. H. Hartogensis, "Ye Jew Doctor and Maryland," *The Jewish Exponent*, December 2, 1927, pp. 1, 10. Mr. Hartogensis also shows that Lumbrozo's later career brought him into disrepute in the community.)
3. In 1927, Mr. Hartogensis wrote: "The present criminal Code of Maryland prescribes as the penalty for denying the divinity of Christ or of any of the three persons of the Trinity, fine and imprisonment or both . . ." (*Ibid.*, 1.)

12. Business Partners

1. Herbert L. Osgood, ed., *Minutes of the Common Council of the City of New York, 1675–1776*, New York, 1905, I, 67–68.
2. Huhner, *AJHSP*, VIII (1900), 15, 19.
3. This order of February 16th is not in the Minutes as published.

13. At the Disposal of the Governor

1. Osgood, *op. cit.,* I, 102–103, 105.

14. Wholesale Only

1. Osgood, *op. cit.,* I, 169. Saul Brown's original name was Pardo (Spanish for "gray"), a family of Dutch and before that Spanish ancestry. In 1677 he was a merchant in Newport, R. I. There on March 31, 1685 Saul Brown and six other Jews had successfully defended themselves against a suit charging them with illegally conducting an export and import trade. Shortly thereafter Brown moved to New York, where he became a well-to-do general merchant and householder. By 1695 he was also the first minister (Hazan) of the Shearith Israel congregation. He died in 1702 or 1703, leaving his wife, Esther, and two children. (Abram Vossen Goodman, *American Overture, Jewish Rights in Colonial Times,* Philadelphia, 1947, pp. 41–42, 105; D. de Sola Pool, in *Occident and Orient,* London, 1936, pp. 68, 72.)
2. Kohler, *AJHSP,* VI (1897), 96–97. Stella H. Sutherland, *Population Distribution in Colonial America,* New York, 1936, p. 14, states: "Possibly to discourage Jews, aliens were forbidden to sell at retail in Connecticut" and (p. 156) "Property-holding restrictions in the Colonies generally compelled the Jews to live in towns, even had they desired to dwell in the country and to till the soil." Rabbi Goodman remarks that this denial to the Jews of the right of retail trade by the English authorities "represented a severe setback for the civil rights of the Jews," who, under the Dutch, had begun to exercise that right (*op. cit.,* 105–106).

15. Not in Public

1. Osgood, *op. cit.,* I, 169.
2. Kohler, *op. cit.,* 94–95. For a sharp comment on the effect of the British on religious freedom at that time, see Dyer, *AJHSP,* VIII (1900), 27–28.

16. Elected Constables

1. Osgood, *op. cit.,* III, 183, 186.
2. *Ibid.,* IV, 71, 74, 346, 351. For the duties of the constable, see Arthur Everett Peterson, *New York as an Eighteenth Century Municipality Prior to 1731,* New York, 1917, pp. 33, 159–162, 167–168.
3. Nathan Simson was a prominent merchant in New York, 1706–1722, when he went to London, dying there in 1725 (Oppenheim, *AJHSP,* XXV, 1917, pp. 87–91).

   Samuel Levy engaged in trade and owned shares in several vessels; he died in office in the spring of 1719, naming Nathan Simson as an executor of his will (Friedman, *AJHSP,* XXIII, 1915, p. 150. For the Council action ordering an election to replace Levy, see Osgood, *op. cit.,* III, 204).

17. Declines to Serve

1. Osgood, *op. cit.,* III, 213–214. Notice of his election appears in III, 210.
2. Born in Germany in 1665, he went to London, becoming a merchant and shipowner "engaged in the trade with the north of Africa." About 1705, he came to New York, prospered here, and was for several years President of the Congre-

gation Shearith Israel, dying in office, June 14, 1728 (Phillips, *AJHSP,* IV, 1896, 189–191).

18. Executed for Stealing

1. *Minute Book of the Supreme Court of Judicature, June 4, 1727,* New York City Hall of Records, pp. 271, 273, 275, 282; Osgood, *op. cit.,* III, 412–414.
2. While Peterson, *op. cit.,* makes no mention of capital punishment in his chapter on "correction" in New York before 1731, George William Edwards writes, "The number of criminals hanged in the city was appalling, for the old English penal code with its numerous capital offences lost little of its severity as enforced in the colony." (*New York as an Eighteenth Century Municipality, 1731–1776,* New York, 1917, p. 108.)
3. Probably the Moses Levy (1665–1728) who was then president of the Congregation Shearith Israel (see Note 2, Document 17). In 1711 he had been one of seven Jews who had contributed to a fund to build the steeple of Trinity Church. There was also a son, however, named Moses Levy (1704–1792) who may be the one referred to above. (Phillips, *op. cit.*)
4. Another son of the elder Moses Levy, Nathan Levy (1704–1753), lived in New York until he removed to Philadelphia in 1730 (Phillips, *AJHSP,* VI, 1897, p. 127; Sabato Morais, *AJHSP,* I, 1893, p. 20).

19. Advertisement

1. I am informed by Mrs. Viola Cole Galpert that this advertisement was repeated in the issues of October 6–13, 13–20, Oct. 27–Nov. 3, Nov. 3–10, 1729.
2. Lewis Gomez (born, Madrid, 1654; died, New York, March 31, 1740) came here from London about 1705, bearing special letters of denization. The Gomez family engaged both in foreign and retail trade, dealing in wheat, wines, and Negro slaves, the slave trade then being a staple among colonial merchants (Kohler, *AJHSP,* V, 1897, pp. 137–155; Solis, *AJHSP,* XI, 1903, pp. 141–142).
3. Osgood, *op. cit.,* IV, 277.

20. Petition for Honesty in Trading

1. Osgood, *op. cit.,* IV, 169–170.
2. *Ibid.,* IV, 251–252. Dr. Edwards believes that the municipal authorities took no action because they were "mindful of provincial prerogative." Continued pressure on the Albany legislature finally led first to the registration of all bolters of flour in 1751 and then to "regulations regarding the quality of flour." Since flour was the greatest single article of export from New York, the city had incurred a bad reputation, being considered by West India importers, for example, as nothing less than "cheats." (*Op. cit.,* 65–67.)
3. Mordecai, eldest son of Lewis Gomez, had become a freeman of New York on February 7, 1714, and was declared elected the Collector for the East Ward on September 30, 1723. He died in New York in November, 1750 (Solis, *op. cit.*, 143; Osgood, *op. cit.,* III, 327; the date of his death is variously given by Pool, *AJHSP,* XX, 1911, p. 163, and *AJHSP,* XXVII, 1920, p. 291).

   David, a brother of Mordecai, was born August 14, 1697 and died in New York, July 15, 1769 (Phillips, *AJHSP,* XVII, 1909, p. 198).

21. Coming to Georgia

1. Charles C. Jones, Jr., *History of Savannah, Ga.*, Syracuse, N. Y., 1890, pp. 52–53.

2. Reba Carolyn Strickland, *Religion and the State in Georgia in the Eighteenth Century*, New York, 1939, pp. 13–15.

3. Abrahams, *AJHSP*, XVII (1909), 167n–169n.

4. Cecil Roth, *A History of the Jews in England*, Oxford, 1941, p. 201; Huhner, *AJHSP*, X (1902), 69; Goodman, *op. cit.*, 172ff.
5. M. H. Stern, "New Light on the Jewish Settlement of Savannah," *AJHQ*, LII (1963), 175–177.
6. Huhner, *op. cit.*; James Edward Oglethorpe(1696–1785) wanted to send the Jews back, but when one of them turned out to be a physician who stopped an epidemic after a score of settlers had died before his appearance on the scene, Oglethorpe changed his view. To persuade the Trustees that the Jews would be useful, he reported the feat of the physician, Dr. Samuel Nunez Ribiero, and also "tactfully took the opportunity . . . to let them know that one Jew had decided to become a Christian." (Leslie F. Church, *Oglethorpe: A Study of Philanthropy in England and Georgia*, London, 1932, pp. 234–235.) That the settlers were friendly to the Jews is shown by W. Guenther Plaut, "Two Notes on the History of the Jews in America. I, Early Settlement in Georgia," *Hebrew Union College Annual*, XIV (1939), 579. Catholics, incidentally, had been excluded for fear they would become spies for the Spanish and French.

   Very outspoken in his hostility to Jewish colonization in Georgia was the Trustee, Thomas Coram (1688?–1751), who in a letter to the Trustees dated March 27, 1734 expressed the fear that Georgia "will soon become a *Jewish* colony," with only those Christians remaining in it whom the Jews will "find most necessary and useful," such as "Carpenters, Sawyers, Smiths, &c." ([Thomas Stephens]: *A Brief Account of the Causes That have retarded the Progress of the Colony of Georgia, in America* . . . London, 1743, pp. 16–17.)

22. Naturalization Allowed to Protestants, Jews, Quakers

1. Rosendale, *AJHSP*, I (1893), 94–98.

2. Hollander, *AJHSP*, V (1897), 104.

3. *Ibid.*, 107–109. It is important to observe that within a few days after this reaffirmation of the Act of 1740, the House of Commons unanimously repealed the Act of 1753 extending naturalization to Jews in England (Roth, *op. cit.*, 212–220).

4. From 1740 to 1770 altogether about 200 Jews are known to have been naturalized under the provisions of this Act, three-fourths of them in Jamaica, thirty-four of them in New York and the remainder in Pennsylvania, Maryland, and South Carolina (Huhner, *AJHSP*, XIII, 1905, pp. 1–6, which adds to and corrects some of the figures and spellings of names as given by Hollander, *op. cit.*, 110). Dr. Strickland calls attention to the relation between the British colonial naturalization policy and the strategy of empire, thus: "If England had applied the system of France and Spain, she would, indeed, have achieved uniformity; but the enormous strengthening of the colonies by the influx of dissenters and European Protestants would have been lost and the development of the British Empire seriously retarded." (*Op. cit.*, 29.) This point helps explain why Jews faced fewer restrictions in the colonies than in Great Britain itself.

23. Apprenticed

1. From the original in the New York City Hall of Records, File No. PL–1754–1837 A 307.
2. Marcus Wilson Jernegan, *Laboring and Dependent Classes in Colonial America, 1607–1783*, Chicago, 1931, makes no mention of apprentices receiving any financial payment, nor does Samuel McKee, Jr., *Labor in Colonial New York, 1664–1776,* New York, 1935. But Richard B. Morris, *Government and Labor in Early America,* New York, 1946, p. 383, states, "Traditionally apprentices received no wages," and then cites four known exceptions, including the case of Marache, who received "an unusually generous treatment."
3. Huhner, *AJHSP,* XXIII (1915), 172; Phillips, *AJHSP,* II (1894), 57.
4. Hays is probably the merchant who advertised "A Choice Assortment of Cutlery Ware, good Scotch Snuff and dry Goods" in *The New-York Gazette Revived in the Weekly Post-Boy,* November 4 and 11 and December 2, 1751. In 1747 and 1748 there was an Isaac Hays in New York who was a "tallow-chandler" but it is not known whether both are identical.
5. Daniel Gomez (born, June 23, 1695; died, 1780) was a son of Lewis Gomez and a New York merchant with a very extensive trade. He became a freeman of New York on November 21, 1727, was naturalized under the Act of 1740, and was active in the affairs of the Congregation Shearith Israel (*AJHSP,* XXVII, 1920, pp. 244–250, and *passim*).

   Asher Myers was a brazier in New York and an active figure in Philadelphia during the revolution (Kohler, *AJHSP,* VI, 1897, 102).

24. Imported Goods for Sale

1. Another son of Lewis Gomez; Benjamin was born in 1711, and died in 1772.
2. Isaac, his brother, was born in 1705, and died in 1770.

25. For Sale: White Servants, etc.

1. Kisch, *AJHSP,* XXXIV (1937), 11–49.

26. A Craftsman Advertises

1. A Levy Simons is listed on the rolls of the Congregation Shearith Israel for 1783 (*AJHSP,* XXI, 1913, p. 142).
2. In 1747, there was an Israel Abrahams on the same rolls (*ibid.,* 55).

27. Supplies for the French and Indian War

1. MS in the American Jewish Historical Society. A similar warrant, dated April 7, 1762 and made out to the same syndicate, orders payment of £6514, 15s, 4d for provisions for the garrison at Louisburg (*Emmet Collection,* Box Great Britain, MSS Division, New York Public Library). That Jews were suppliers for the Crown also in the early and European stage of the war can be seen from the contract "for furnishing a Number of Bread-Waggons for the Use of the Hessian Troops in the Pay of Great Britain" signed in Hanover, April 27, 1757, by Colonel Jeffery Amherst and David Mendes da Costa (*Theodorus B. Myers Collection,* No. 234, MSS Division, N. Y. P. L.; Roth, *op. cit.,* 184, 284).

2. M[ax]. J. K[ohler]., "The Franks Family as British Army Contractors," *AJHSP,* XI (1903), 182.

3. Max J. Kohler, "Phases of Jewish Life in New York before 1800," *AJHSP,* II (1894), 92; Samuel Oppenheim, "Jewish Owners of Ships Registered at the Port of Philadelphia, 1730–1775," *AJHSP,* XXVI (1918), 236; Henry Necarsulmer, "The Early Jewish Settlement at Lancaster, Pa.," *AJHSP,* IX (1901), 33.

4. Benjamin G. Sack, *History of the Jews in Canada,* I, Montreal, 1945, pp. 33–35.

28. Newport Social Club

1. *The Newport Historical Magazine,* IV (1883), 58–60.

2. Morris Jastrow, Jr., "References to Jews in the Diary of Ezra Stiles," *AJHSP,* X (1902), 9. The estimate is that of Moses Levy, one of the members of the club.

3. Ground for the synagogue of the Congregation Jeshuat Israel had been broken August 1, 1759, but the dedication did not take place until December 2, 1763. All the members of the club figured in the work connected with building and financing the synagogue. Naphtali Hart was the President of the Congregation in 1761; Jacob Rodriguez Rivera had been President in 1760; Moses Lopez became President in 1762.

4. A similar injunction against disharmony is to be found in Article X of the rules and order of The Fellowship Club, organized in Newport on December 5, 1752 and chartered by the General Assembly, June 15, 1754, whose membership contained no Jews (*The Newport Historical Magazine,* IV, 1883, 165).

5. Moses Lopez (died 1767, aged 61) had been naturalized in 1740; in 1753 the General Assembly had given him a licence to make potash. He was a brother of Aaron Lopez. (Morris A. Gutstein, *The Story of the Jews of Newport,* New York, 1936, pp. 55, 306.)

   Isaac Polock died in 1764, aged 63; both Issachar and he were merchants. (*Ibid.,* 54, 306.)

   Jacob Isaacs (died 1798) was a shopkeeper, broker, and inventor.

   Abraham Sarzedas was a merchant who had become a freeman of New York in 1753 (Max J. Kohler, "Civil Status of the Jews in Colonial New York," *AJHSP,* VI, 1897, p. 102).

   Moses Levy (died 1792, aged 88) was a prominent merchant (Gutstein, *op. cit.,* 319).

   Jacob Rodriguez Rivera (c. 1717–1789) is said to have introduced the manufacture of spermaceti candles into the country, and together with "Naph Hart & Co, Aaron Lopez & Co" and others formed a monopoly combination on November 5, 1761 (*Mass. Hist. Soc. Collections,* 7 Ser., IX, *Commerce of Rhode Island, 1726–1800,* I, 88–92, 97–100; Goodman, *op. cit.,* 50).

29. Newport Slave Trade

1. *Massachusetts Historical Society Collections,* 7 Ser., IX, *Commerce of Rhode Island, 1726–1774,* I, 96–97.

2. Isaac Elizer was a merchant and an active figure in the Newport Congregation. On March 11, 1762, shortly before this document was written, Aaron Lopez and he had been denied the right of naturalization by the Superior Court of Newport on the equivocal grounds that the colony was already full and that only Christians could be naturalized. (Max J. Kohler, "The Jews in Newport," *AJHSP,* VI, 1897, p. 71; Goodman, *op. cit.,* 53–59; *AJHSP,* XXVII, 1920, *passim.*)

Very little is known about Samuel Moses. For a letter by Moses and Elizer connected with this voyage, sent to Christopher Champlin, merchant in New Providence, Bahamas, asking him to send the slave cargo on the *Prince George* to Charlestown, S. C., if the prices of slaves are too low in the Bahamas, see Elizabeth Donnan, ed., *Documents Illustrative of the History of the Slave Trade to America,* Washington, 1930–1935, III, 189–190.

30. Merchants Resist Britain

1. Facsimile, *Emmet Collection,* No. 230, Manuscript Division, N.Y.P.L.
2. Albert M. Friedenberg, " 'Some New York Jewish Patriots,' " *AJHSP,* XXVI (1918), 237–239, in which he corrects the errors in Max J. Kohler, "Incidents Illustrative of American Jewish Patriotism," *AJHSP,* IV (1896), 89.
3. The new Sugar Act of 1764, designed both as a revenue measure and to end smuggling in molasses, gave British sugar planters a monopoly of the market; among other obnoxious features, this act also cut into the profits of the food and fish ships in the Mediterranean trade by imposing, for the first time, a duty on Madeira wine. In the same year, Britain added to the long list of enumerated commodities, export of which was restricted, the following: coffee, pimento, cacao, hides and skins, whale fins, raw silk, pot and pearl ashes, iron and lumber. Colonial merchants were directly affected and distressed. In April, 1765, Parliament had also passed the Quartering Act, requiring the colonies to quarter British troops in barracks, taverns, barns or houses.
4. The Stamp Act, passed in March, 1765, called for taxes on periodicals, pamphlets, and all legal and commercial documents. On October 5, 1765, the Stamp Act Congress in New York, at which there gathered representatives from nine colonies, petitioned for repeal of the Stamp Act and the annulment of acts interfering with American commerce, including the Sugar Act. The non-importation agreements were supplementary weapons.
5. "By the end of 1765 about £700,000 worth of American orders was lost to British businessmen." (Herbert M. Morais, *The Struggle for American Freedom,* New York, 1944, p. 167.)
6. Mathias Bush was a prominent merchant and landowner (in Pennsylvania and Virginia); in 1749 he was naturalized in Philadelphia.

   Barnard Gratz (1738–1801) and Michael Gratz (c. 1733–1811) were very distinguished merchants whose especial importance lies in their Western land speculations and in their outstanding contribution to the opening of the West. By 1765 they had already begun to develop their ocean trade and had also established themselves in the coast-wise trade from New Orleans to Quebec. After their signing the non-importation agreements they had to turn their attention more to the West. (William Vincent Byars, *B. and M. Gratz, Merchants in Philadelphia, 1754–1798,* Jefferson City, Mo., 1916, p. 14.) For the date of birth of Michael Gratz, see Sidney M. Fish, "The Ancestral Background and the Early Youth of Barnard and Michael Gratz," paper presented at Annual Meeting, American Jewish Historical Society, Feb. 22, 1948.

   David Franks (1720–1793), who later became a Tory, was also a well-known merchant, participating in many partnerships both with Jewish and non-Jewish "merchant venturers."

   About Joseph Jacobs and Hyman Levy, Jr. nothing further is known. The latter is not to be confused with Hayman Levy, the New York merchant (Samuel Oppenheim, "The Jewish Signers of the Non-Importation Agreement of 1765," *AJHSP,* XXVI, 1918, p. 236).

Benjamin Levy (1720–after 1793) was an active patriot.

Samson Levy was a brother of Benjamin.

Abraham Mitchell was a partner in the firm of (Joseph) Simon and Mitchell, fur traders since before 1762, but his Jewish identity has not been established.

Moses Mordecai is known in only one other connection: some time before the Declaration of Independence, he, together with David Franks, Solomon Marache, and others, had signed an agreement to accept colonial paper money instead of gold and silver (Hyman Polock Rosenbach, *The Jews in Philadelphia, Prior to 1800,* Philadelphia, 1883, pp. 12–13).

31. A Shoemaker Elected to Office

1. Osgood, *op. cit.,* VII, 40, 42, 43, 44. 45. For the declaration of his first election, see VII, 34.
2. *Ibid.,* VII, 82, 86, 127, 132, 183, 186. Moses was not present at the swearing in on October 14, 1769. Whether his absence is due to the fact that the day was Saturday is not known. The minutes contain no further record of his having been sworn in, nor of his having been replaced.
3. The records show that from 1795 on there were two persons named Isaac Moses in New York, one a shoemaker, one a merchant. Whether the shoemaker of 1795 is the same as the shoemaker of 1766 is not known. (William Duncan, *The New-York Directory, and Register, for the Year 1795,* New York, 1795, p. 153; John Low, *The New-York Directory, and Register, for the Year 1796,* New York, 1796, p. 130; *Longworth's American Almanack, New-York Register, and City Directory,* New York, 1797, pp. 253–254). In the first attempt at a city directory in 1786, David Franks (not a Jew) listed Isaac Moses, auctioneer, but no shoemaker; likewise in 1787 there is Isaac Moses, the merchant, but not the shoemaker (*The New-York Directory for 1786,* New York, 1786, p. 40; *ibid.,* 1787, p. 26).
4. Through an error, the name is given in the text as Samuel Moses when it should obviously be Isaac.

32. Proposing to Help Open Up the West

1. McAlister MSS, The Library Company of Philadelphia, Ridgway Branch; the text in Byars, *op. cit.,* 111–112 is not only modernized in spelling, punctuation and grammar but is often inaccurately read.
2. Charles M. Thomas, "Successful and Unsuccessful Merchants in the Illinois Country," *The Illinois State Historical Society Journal,* XXX (1938), 430, 440.
3. Probably Moses, brother of David, Franks, and the merchant already noted as part of a syndicate that had crown contracts for supplying the British troops.
4. Croghan had been an Indian trader since 1741; in 1756 he became Deputy Superintendent of Indian Affairs. The Gratzes and their partners became associated with him in tremendous land speculations involving millions of acres of Western lands.

   Joseph Simon (1711–1804) was a pioneer merchant and Indian trader on the frontier in Lancaster, Pa., from 1742; his daughter, Miriam, married Michael Gratz, author of this letter.

   Solomon Henry was a prominent London merchant related to the Gratz family.
5. The non-importation agreements of 1765, signed by the Gratzes, had helped effect the repeal of the Stamp Act and the Sugar Act, and then had been

abandoned, their purpose having been partially fulfilled. But when the oppressive Townshend Acts were passed in 1767, new non-importation agreements were signed in Boston and New York in 1768, and in Philadelphia in March 1769. Whether the Gratzes signed the latter is not known. But from this letter it is clear that while they will not attempt to import into Philadelphia because the enforcement of the agreement is too effective, the Gratzes are planning to import into other colonies which are not so well policed by the people.

6. This large tract of land in the Mohawk valley, near Albany, had been bought from George Croghan as a speculative venture, and was being offered for sale in London (Byars, *op. cit.,* 112–113).
7. Rachel Gratz (1764–1790) was Barnard's daughter.
8. Richa Franks was a sister of David; in 1769, after the death of her father, Jacob, she had gone to London to join two other brothers, Naphtali and Moses.

   Myer Hart, a founder of Easton, Pa., was one of its richest merchants and a business associate of David Franks (Joshua Trachtenberg, *Consider the Years, the Story of the Jewish Community of Easton, 1752–1942,* Easton, 1944, pp. 55–67).

33. Kosher Meat

1. *Lyons Collection I, AJHSP,* XXI (1913), 112–113.
2. Joseph Simson, who was known "by the title of Rabbi" in the Congregation, had been its president in 1748, 1755, and 1762. He had arrived from Germany in 1718 and become a substantial merchant and Jewish community leader. Sampson Simson was a son of his. (N. Taylor Phillips, "Items Relating to the History of the Jews of New York," *AJHSP,* XI, 1903, p. 155; *AJHSP,* XXI, 1913, 211.)

   Myer Myers (1723–1795) had been president of the Congregation in 1759 and 1770. He was a famous silversmith. (*Ibid.;* Phillips, *op. cit.,* 155; "A New York Jewish Silversmith of the Eighteenth Century," *AJHSP,* XXVIII, 1922, 237.

   Asher Myers had been president of the Congregation in 1765 and 1771, up to the time when Hayman Levy was elected.

   Moses Lazarus was shohet for the Congregation from 1771 to 1773. On August 11, 1771, he had applied for an increased salary. (*AJHSP,* XXI, 1913, p. 109.)
3. Manuel Myers had been president of the Congregation in 1769 and was to serve eight more terms before he died in 1799 (*ibid.,* 211).

   Isaac Adolphus had been president of the Congregation in 1767 (*ibid.*).

34. Death of a Patriot

1. John Drayton, *Memoirs of the American Revolution, from its commencement to the year 1776, inclusive; as relating to The State of South-Carolina: and occasionally refering to the States of North-Carolina and Georgia,* Charleston, 1821, II, 369–371. The memoirs are those of Chief Justice William Henry Drayton of South Carolina, with whom Salvador corresponded.
2. *Ibid.,* 348.
3. Barnett A. Elzas, *The Jews of South Carolina,* Philadelphia, 1905, 69ff.

35. Business Rivalry and Anti-Semitism

1. Byars, *op. cit.,* 161.
2. The Gratzes were interested, among other things, in shipping, and, during the Revolutionary War, in privateering.

36. Revolutionary Vigilance in Connecticut

1. Royal Ralph Hinman, ed., *A Historical Collection, from Official Records, Files, &c., of the Part Sustained by Connecticut, during the War of the Revolution*, Hartford, 1842, pp. 566–567. For a listing of numerous other petitions from 1777 to 1781 which included Jewish signers, see Jacob Rader Marcus, "Light on Early Connecticut Jewry," *American Jewish Archives*, I, No. 2, Jan., 1949, pp. 18n–20n.
2. Lorenzo Sabine, *Biographical Sketches of Loyalists of the American Revolution*, Boston, 1864, I, 27; Lloyd A. Brown, *Loyalist Operations at New Haven*, Ann Arbor, Mich., 1938.
3. Ralph Isaacs, a notorious Tory, was not a Jew. (Marcus, *op. cit.*, 20n–21n.)
4. Jacob Pinto had lived in New Haven since about 1755; as resistance to British oppression grew, he was active in the movement. On October 2, 1775 he was one of a committee of four that exacted from Abiathar Camp, one of the loyalists named in this petition, a confession that he had violated the Committee of Inspection's order not to send his vessels out under the Restraining Act, and that he thereafter would abide by decisions of the Continental Congress. (For the text of this confession and Pinto's attest, see John Warner Barber, ed., *Connecticut Historical Collections*, Second Edition, New Haven, 1837, p. 176.) Jacob Pinto "apparently joined the Congregational Church" and married a Gentile (Marcus, *op. cit.*, 27).

   Abraham Pinto, son of Jacob, was later wounded, together with his brother Solomon, in the defense of New Haven against the British attack, July 5–6, 1779.

37. Jewish Loyalists

1. *New York City During the American Revolution. Being a Collection of Original papers (Now First Published) from the Manuscripts in the Possession of The Mercantile Library Association, of New York City*, New York, 1861, 117–119.
2. Hyman B. Grinstein, *The Rise of The Jewish Community of New York, 1654–1860*, Philadelphia, 1946, p. 69; Morris U. Schappes, "Themes for the People's Artist," *Jewish Life*, New York, II, No. 1, November, 1947, Supplement.
3. Alexander Clarence Flick, *Loyalism in New York During the American Revolution*, New York, 1901, pp. 96–97.
4. Of Haob Aaron, Aaron Keyser, David Levison, David Nathan, Sam. Samuel and George Simpson nothing further is known. The Jewish identity of some is therefore in doubt, although they are listed as Jews by Max J. Kohler, "Phases of Jewish Life in New York Before 1800, II," *AJHSP*, III (1895), 83.

   Abraham I. Abrahams was well known as a *mohel*, teacher, and community leader in the New York congregation (*AJHSP*, XXI and XXVII, *passim*).

   Abraham Gomez (c. 1742–1808) was a son of Mordecai Gomez.

   Moses Gomez, Jr. was probably a brother of Abraham.

   Barrak (Baruch) Hays was listed as a "Vendue Master" when he became a freeman of New York on August 3, 1768 (Max J. Kohler, "Civil Status of the Jews in Colonial New York," *AJHSP*, VI, 1897, p. 102).

   David Hays, merchant, became a freeman of New York on September 16, 1735, and was president of the Congregation Shearith Israel in 1751. He is not to be confused with the David Hays of Westchester County, who was an active patriot during the Revolution, but was born in March 1732 (Solomon Solis-Cohen, "Note Concerning David Hays and Esther Etting His Wife, and Michael

Hays and Reuben Etting, their Brothers, Patriots of the Revolution," *AJHSP,* II, 1894, p. 71).

Uriah Hendricks (1737–1798) came from London in 1755, established a metal business in 1764 which is still operative, and was "very assiduous" in 1770 in fighting the Non-Importation agreement (Albert M. Friedenberg, "'Some New York Jewish Patriots,'" *AJHSP,* XXVI, 1918, p. 238).

Levy Israel was *shammash* (sexton) of the Congregation Shearith Israel, 1759–1783.

Samuel Myers, a shopkeeper, and president of the Congregation in 1744, must have left New York after signing this address, for he was in Philadelphia in 1782 (*AJHSP,* XXVII, 1920, pp. 211, 468).

Isaac Solomons had supported the Non-Importation agreement in 1770, but chose to stay in New York in 1776 (Friedenberg, *op. cit.,* 239). A fervid New York Jewish supporter of the King whose name does not appear on this address was Abraham Wagg (1719–1803) who, in 1778, when the British cause began to seem hopeless, advocated that the Crown grant the colonies their independence in order that England could secure an alliance with America against the main enemies, France and Spain. In 1782, having returned to England, Wagg sought to influence the Prime Minister to thwart the more democratic forces in America by negotiating a separate peace, splitting America away from her ally France, and encouraging the conservative, pro-British American forces to come to power. (Cecil Roth, "A Jewish Voice for Peace in the War of American Independence," *AJHSP,* XXXI, 1928, pp. 33–75, and "Some Jewish Loyalists in the War of American Independence," *AJHSP,* XXXVIII, 1948, pp. 81–107; Mr. Roth's interpretation, however, is dominated not by an interest in international democracy but in the expansion of the British Empire.)

A second petition, signed by more than 700 loyalists, was presented November 28, 1776; the Jewish signatories were Uriah Hendricks, Abraham Gomez, Barrak Hays, Abraham I. Abrahams and Abraham Wagg, and possibly Haenry [sic] Solomon and William Miers, who are otherwise not identified (MS in The New-York Historical Society; R. W. G. Vail, "The Loyalist Declaration of Dependence of November 28, 1776," *The New-York Historical Society Quarterly,* XXXI, 1947, pp. 68–71; I am indebted to Mr. Vail for permitting me to inspect this manuscript). The following Jews are also listed as loyalists in another source: Haob Aaron, Abraham J. Abrahams, Aaron Cohn, Abraham Gomez, Moses Gomez, Jr., Lion Hart, Barrack Hays, David Hays, Levy Israel, Uriah Hendricks, Samuel Levy, Samuel Myers, M. Noah, Isaac Solomons, Abraham Wagg and Alexander Zuntz (William Kelby, ed., *Orderly Book of the Three Battalions of Loyalists Commanded by Brigadier-General Oliver De Lancey, 1776–1778,* New York, 1917, pp. 115, 118, 120, 121, 122, 123, 126, 127, 128, 130, 131).

38. Haym Salomon Offers His Services

1. *Papers of the Continental Congress,* IX, No. 41, pp. 58–59, The Library of Congress.

2. In his pamphlet, *Haym Salomon, the Patriot Broker of the Revolution, His Real Achievements and their Exaggeration,* New York, 1931, Max Kohler revolutionized the status of knowledge about Haym Salomon and for the first time put it upon a historically scientific basis. Kohler used the extensive original research done in the field by the scrupulous and thorough Samuel Oppenheim and his assistants, which Oppenheim was prevented from publishing by his death. My examination of the Oppenheim Papers at the American

Jewish Historical Society led me to make additional investigations, which have in all cases corroborated the conclusions of Kohler. All books and articles that preceded the work of Oppenheim and Kohler therefore seem to me untrustworthy and discredited. The legends and falsifications, however, die hard, and even after the publication of Kohler's work innumerable writers, including those for the *Dictionary of American Biography* and the *Universal Jewish Encyclopedia,* continue to perpetuate unsubstantiatable statements about Salomon's career for which Haym Salomon himself is in no way responsible. To be used with special precautions is the one biography of Salomon, Charles Edward Russell, *Haym Salomon and the Revolution*, New York, 1930, which Kohler subjects to a keen analysis. Kohler and Oppenheim demonstrated first that Salomon, although an energetic, patriotic broker selling government securities, did not himself lend money to the government, and never claimed he did. In 1781 and 1782, Salomon sold about $200,000 worth of government securities, and was paid a broker's fee for his valuable services. Salomon did lend money to delegates to the Continental Congress like James Madison and Edmond Randolph, often charging no interest, and to prominent Pennsylvanians. Oppenheim and Kohler also showed, among other things, that Salomon had no connections with Pulaski and Kosciusko, and did not take part in the Polish Revolution of 1770; nor is there any evidence that Salomon was a member of the New York Liberty Boys. In their work, Oppenheim and Kohler do not question any statements about Salomon or his services or activities made by Haym Salomon himself; they do eliminate from serious historical consideration false claims and myths built up about Salomon, chiefly by his son, Haym M. Salomon. The most widely known of these myths is that Salomon "financed the revolution" by lending vast sums of money to the government.

3. Robert A. East, *Business Enterprise in the American Revolutionary Era*, New York, 1938, pp. 157–158, 258. By 1781, when Salomon first began to do business with the Office of Finance, he was already known for his work as "Broker of the Consul-General of France and to the Treasurer of the French Army." His exact relations to the Office of Finance emerge clearly from an examination of the official *Diaries in the Office of Finance, 1781–1784,* in *The Robert Morris Papers,* Library of Congress, in which there are 114 references to Haym Salomon, 26 to Major David S. Franks, 12 to Manuel Josephson, 5 to Isaac Moses, 3 to the Sheftalls, and 2 to Moses Michael Hays. (Schappes, "References to Haym Salomon and other Jews in Robert Morris' 'Diaries in Office of Finance, 1781–1784'," paper presented at the Annual Meeting, American Jewish Historical Society, February 12, 1950.)

4. Haym Salomon was born in Lissa, Poland, about 1740. When he came to New York is not known exactly, but the earliest possible evidence places him there in 1764 (Korn, *AJHSP,* XXVIII, 1922, pp. 225–226). On June 12, 1776, the prominent New York merchant, Leonard Gansevoort, recommended Salomon to Major-General Philip Schuyler, in command of the Northern Department in New York. In support of Salomon's desire "to go suttling to Lake George," that is, to be permitted to sell provisions to our troops stationed there, Gansevoort wrote: "I can inform the General that M[r] Solomon has hitherto sustained the Character of being warmly attached to America." (*Schuyler Papers,* MSS Div., N. Y. P. L.) By the time the British occupied New York City on September 15, 1776, Salomon had returned from Lake George, and was arrested.

5. Notice that Salomon himself does not say he was sentenced to death; it is

others who have felt it necessary to embroider and falsify the story. General James Robertson (c.1720–1788) had been designated Commandant of the conquered city. The "Provost" was the old prison, erected in 1759, and was in charge of William Cunningham, a brutal and disreputable Englishman who was hanged for forgery in England in 1791; the newly erected prison, the Bridewell, was reserved for the "better class of prisoners" (Wilbur C. Abbott, *New York in the American Revolution,* New York and London, 1929, p. 208).

6. Lt.-Gen. Leopold Philipp von Heister (c. 1716–1778) had arrived off New York August 12, 1776 with his Hessian mercenaries in a fleet of 107 vessels, and helped capture the city. (Max von Eelking, *The German Allied Troops in the North American War of Independence, 1776–1783,* Albany, N. Y., 1893, p. 283; Thomas Jefferson Wertenbaker, *Father Knickerbocker Rebels,* New York and London, 1948, p.88.)
7. As interpreter and commissary, Salomon apparently had the freedom of the city, continuing in business as a merchant and marrying (*Thomas Witter, Receipt Book, 1759–1786,* MSS at N. Y. H. S., receipts signed by Salomon dated November 19 and 26, 1777; advertisements of "Ship Bread," "Fresh Rice" or "new Rice," *The Royal American Gazette,* January 1, 1778, and *The New-York Gazette: And The Weekly Mercury,* January 12 and 19, 1778, and of "White Wine and common Vinegar," *The Royal American Gazette,* June 18, 1778).
8. Unlike his biographers, Salomon does not say he escaped from the "Provost." Evidently he avoided re-arrest and fled the city.
9. On July 6, 1777 Salomon had married Rachel Franks, daughter of the rich merchant Moses Franks, who had refused to join the majority of the Congregation in its voluntary exodus from the city to avoid serving the British. The Hebrew date of the marriage is the first of Tammuz, 5537, and not the second of Tebeth, or January 2, as it has hitherto been given (the original *ketubah* or marriage contract is in the American Jewish Historical Society). Later Salomon's wife and child joined him in Philadelphia.

39. Slander and Reply

1. From Barnett A. Elzas, *The Jews of South Carolina,* Philadelphia, 1905, pp. 88–89.
2. John Wells, Jr., publisher of the periodical. His father, Robert Wells, had issued the periodical before him, but, as a loyalist, had left the country in May 1775. John Wells was a supporter of the American cause when he printed this letter. In 1779, when the British invaded Charleston, John Wells espoused the side of the British and in 1781 the periodical became *The Royal Gazette.* (Clarence S. Brigham, *History and Bibliography of American Newspapers, 1690–1820,* Worcester, Mass., 1947, pp. 1036–1037.)
3. Mary Crouch and Company published *The Charlestown Gazette,* beginning in August, 1778. The issue of December 1st, in which the offensive article appeared, is not known to be extant. The political complexion of this periodical is not known. (*Ibid.,* 1032–1033.)

40. Patriot Captured

1. George White, *Historical Collections of Georgia,* third edition, New York, 1855, pp. 340–342. (*AJHSP,* XVII, 1909, 176–178.)

2. Edmund H. Abrahams, "Some Notes on the Early History of the Sheftalls of Georgia," *AJHSP,* XVII (1909), 174–184; Barnett A. Elzas, *op. cit.,* 84n.

3. Sheftall Sheftall (1762–1847) was assistant-deputy to his father when they were both captured.

4. Moses Nunes, a loyalist, was Searcher of the Port of Savannah from 1768 to 1774; in 1779 he was an Indian interpreter for the British. He was one of the very few loyalists among the forty Jewish families in Georgia.

5. Mrs. Philip Minis and her sister-in-law Judith were confined to their dwelling when the British captured Savannah, so well known were they as "Great Whigs," and later they were ordered out of town.

41. Merchant in Exile

1. *Massachusetts Historial Society Collections, Seventh Series,* X, *Commerce of Rhode Island, 1775–1800,* II, pp. 50–54.

2. Bruce M. Bigelow, "Aaron Lopez: Colonial Merchant of Newport," *The New England Quarterly,* IV (1931), 757.

3. Donnan, *op. cit.,* III, 211–213, 264–265, 269–270; Morris Jastrow, Jr., "References to Jews in the Diary of Ezra Stiles," *AJHSP,* X (1902), 14–16.

4. Lopez had considerable difficulty getting the Continental Congress to acknowledge his claims, which it finally did on April 10, 1779; but even then he had to resort to the courts for the enforcement of his claim, and the case was not closed until September, 1783 (Lee M. Friedman, *Pilgrims in a New Land,* Philadelphia, 1948, pp. 47–57). Although he was a wealthy merchant before the revolution, Lopez suffered many setbacks during the course of the war. Despite the fact that he increased the prices of his goods four to six times, his losses in general were too heavy, and he died insolvent (*Mass. Hist. Soc. Coll., op. cit.,* 66; Harold Korn, "Documents Relative to the Estate of Aaron Lopez," in *AJHSP,* XXXV, 1939, p. 139).

42. Philadelphia Citizens to the Continental Congress

1. Varnum Lansing Collins, *The Continental Congress at Princeton,* Princeton, 1908, pp. 87–89, 263ff.

2. Philip S. Foner, ed., *The Complete Writings of Thomas Paine,* (New York, 1945) II, 263–265, 1219–1220.

3. With one exception the names are those selected by Leon Huhner, "Jewish Signers to a Patriotic Address to Congress in 1783," *AJHSP,* XXII (1914), 196–197. Joseph Israel, whom Mr. Huhner includes in his list, was the brother of Israel Israel, and probably not a Jew (Henry S. Morais, *The Jews of Philadelphia,* Philadelphia, 1894, pp. 32–34).

   Moses Cohen opened an Intelligence Office in Philadelphia in 1782 (see his advertisements in *The Pennsylvania Packet, or The General Advertiser,* May 28, June 4, 13, 25, July 2, 11, 18, 25, 1782).

   Isaac Franks (1759–1822) had arrived in Philadelphia in the summer of 1782, opened a Broker's Office and become a keen competitor of Haym Salomon. While serving in Colonel Lesher's Volunteer New York Regiment, he had been taken prisoner on September 15, 1776, when the British captured New York. After three months, he escaped, rejoined the army near West Point, was commissioned an Ensign on February 22, 1781 and held his post until he resigned on the advice of the Regimental Surgeon in June 1782.

(Herbert Friedenwald, "Some Newspaper Advertisements of the Eighteenth Century," *AJHSP,* VI, 1897, pp. 50, 54–56; Morris Jastrow, Jr., "Documents Relating to the Career of Colonel Isaac Franks," *AJHSP,* V, 1897, pp. 7–34.)

Seymour Hart and Jacob Simpson are not otherwise identified as Jews.

Isaac Levy was a Philadelphia merchant from the late 1750s, and also interested in shipping (Samuel Oppenheim, "A Philadelphia Jewish Merchant's Day-Book, 1755–1761," *AJHSP,* XXVI, 1918, p. 233, and "Jewish Owners of Ships Registered at the Port of Philadelphia, 1730–1775," *ibid.,* 236).

Moses Levy was either the prominent lawyer and judge (Morais, *op. cit.,* 431) or the merchant of Moses Levy and Company who, in 1780, with Robert Morris, owned the six gun Pennsylvania schooner, the *Havannah* (Leon Huhner, "Jews Interested in Privateering in America during the Eighteenth Century," *AJHSP,* XXIII, 1915, p. 172).

See Index for further references.

43. Petition for Equal Rights

1. *The Freeman's Journal: Or, The North-American Intelligencer,* January 21, 1784, pp. 2–3. The text is innacurately given by Charles Edward Russell, *Haym Salomon and the Revolution,* New York, 1930, pp. 301–303. December 23, 1783 is not the date of the filing of the petition but of its consideration by the Council of Censors.
2. The Council of Censors, a unique body created by the Pennsylvania Constitution of 1776, consisted of two delegates from each city and county "to enquire whether the constitution has been preserved inviolate in every part" and whether the legislature is doing its duty. (J. Paul Selsam, *The Pennsylvania Constitution of 1776, A Study in Revolutionary Democracy,* Philadelphia, 1936, pp. 199–201.) The Council met only once, and, being permanently split by twelve to ten votes, made no recommendations for constitutional change. The changes proposed by the majority were sharply criticized by the minority as uniformly undemocratic, creating an upper house, strengthening the appointive power of the Governor, and limiting the power of the people (*The Freeman's Journal,* January 14, 28, 1784).
3. Gershom Mendes Seixas had come to Philadelphia from Stratford, Conn., in 1780 to head the Congregation Mikveh Israel.

   Simon Nathan (born, Frome, England; died, Philadelphia, 1822) had left New York when the British captured it.

   For other references to these three, see the Index.
4. When the State Constitution was finally adopted on September 28, 1776, the clause on the religious test, undemocratic though it still was, did mark an advance over previous restrictions, which had banned Catholics from office. The new clause was therefore vigorously attacked from the reactionary side as subjecting Christians to "Jews, Turks, Spinozists, Deists, perverted naturalists" (Selsam, *op. cit.,* 216–221). In respect to religious equality the Pennsylvania Constitution was more democratic than most other state constitutions of the time.
5. Refers to Article 38 of the New York State Constitution of 1777, which extended equality to all religious groups.
6. In 1781 the British captured the Dutch island of St. Eustatius in the West Indies and, among other depredations, vented their wrath upon the wealthy Jewish community on that island, driving a large number of the Jews from

their homes (N. Taylor Phillips, "Items Relating to the History of the Jews of New York," *AJHSP,* XI, 1903, pp. 151–152).

7. On January 19, 1784, the Council of Censors acted on the clause that this petition challenges, but made no change. See Note 2 above.

8. What follows is a form of editorial comment on the petition.

9. It has not hitherto been noted that this Memorial was printed also in *The Independent Gazetteer, Or, The Chronicle Of Freedom* (Philadelphia), on January 17, 1784, p. 3 (with insignificant textual variations from the text given here). At the end of the first paragraph, Eleazer Oswald and Daniel Humphreys, the publishers, placed an asterisk calling attention to the following highly principled editorial footnote: "This inconsistency in the frame of government is the more singularly striking and conspicuous, as Pennsylvania has hitherto been distinguished for liberality of sentiment; and all her sister states make no political distinction whatever between Jews and Christians. The Jews on this continent have ever demeaned themselves as good and worthy subjects, and have been peculiarly firm and united in the great cause of America; and therefore are, of right, entitled to all the privileges and immunities of her mild and equal government, in common with every other order of people: And it is an absurdity, too glaring and inconsistent to find a single advocate, to say a man, or a society, is Free, without possessing and exercising a right to elect and to be elected." The same issue contained advertisements from the following Jewish brokers: Haym Salomon, Lazarus Barnett, Lyon Moses, Benjamin Nones & Co., and Moses Cohen; but lest this factor be considered to have swayed editorial judgment, it should be understood that in *The Freeman's Journal,* which was equally favorable, there was no advertising by Jews.

44. Home Again

1. *AJHSP,* XXVII (1920), 33–34.

2. The Talmudic precept, *dina d'malchuta dina* (the law of the land is the law), had not been so understood by the Jews in 1776 as to lead them to support British rule. For a discussion of this principle in the light of the necessity to resist unjust rule, see Bernard J. Bamberger, "Individual Rights and the Demands of the State: the Position of Classical Judaism," in *Yearbook, Central Conference of American Rabbis,* LIV (1944), 204–206.

3. Hayman Levy (1721–1789) was the largest fur trader in colonial times, active in support of the non-importation agreements, and, like the others, one of those who went to Philadelphia in 1776. Myer Myers (1723–1795) had been prominent both in the New York and Philadelphia congregations. Isaac Moses (1742–1818) was a wealthy merchant, owner or part owner of some eight or ten privateers, a financial supporter of the revolutionary government, and, when he returned to New York, one of those who advocated expropriation of the loyalists and the use of public lands to aid the patriots (Leon Huhner, "Jews Interested in Privateering in America during the Eighteenth Century," *AJHSP,* XXIII, 1915, pp. 171–174; Max J. Kohler, "Phases of Jewish Life in New York before 1800," *AJHSP,* II, 1894, pp. 86–87; David T. Valentine, *Manual of the Corporation of the City of New-York for 1858,* New York, 1858, pp. 639–641).

45. For Equality of Religious Rights

1. Herbert Friedenwald, "A Letter of Jonas Phillips to the Federal Convention," in *AJHSP,* II (1894), 108–110.

Also in Max Farrand, ed., *The Records of the Federal Convention of 1787,* New York and London, 1911, III, 78–79; Anson Phelps Stokes states that this letter by Phillips was the only one sent to the convention "by any individual petitioner on the subject of religious freedom" (*Church and State in the United States,* New York, 1950, I, 528).

2. Phillips (born, Germany, 1736; died, Philadelphia, January 29, 1803) came from London to Charleston in 1756, later lived in Albany and New York, and then in Philadelphia from 1773, to which he moved before the general exodus of the Jews in 1776 (see his advertisement, *Pennsylvania Packet and General Advertiser,* September 11, 1775, p. 3). In New York he had served as *shohet* from 1765 to 1770, and had signed the non-importation agreement of 1770 (*AJHSP,* XXI, 1913, p. 90, 106). In Philadelphia he enlisted in the militia in 1778, and was president of the congregation in 1782. That he was a man of staunch principle may be derived from the fact that when, on Saturday, April 5, 1793, he was called as a witness in a court of law, he refused to be sworn on his Sabbath and was therefore fined £10 by the Court (John Samuel, "Some Cases in Pennsylvania Wherein Rights Claimed by Jews Are Affected," *AJHSP,* V, 1897, p. 35).

46. For a Republic, Old Testament Model

1. Generalizing the European experience, W. E. H. Lecky, *History of the Rise and Influence of the Spirit of Rationalism in Europe,* London, 1897, new ed., II, 172, states: "it is at least an historical fact that in the great majority of instances the early Protestant defenders of civil liberty derived their political principles from the Old Testament, and the defenders of despotism from the New. The rebellions that were so frequent in Jewish history formed the favourite topic of the one—the unreserved submission inculcated by St. Paul, of the other." In a pioneer work, Oscar S. Straus showed that the American clergy supporting independence tended to challenge the monarchic idea by arguments and examples from the Old Testament (*The Origin of the Republican Form of Government in the United States of America,* New York, 1885). Louis I. Newman and Richard B. Morris draw a distinction between the democratic and undemocratic influences of the Mosaic code on early New England legislation, but conclude that "In the growth of republican principles during the eighteenth century [Scripture] played a dominant role; and prior to and during the Revolution it gained a new ascendancy . . ." ("The Jewish Tradition at the Birth of America," *The American Hebrew,* September 30, 1921, p. 527). See also Isidore S. Meyer, "A Fount of American Democracy," in *The Menorah Journal,* XXVII (Oct.–Dec. 1929), p. 250. Alice M. Baldwin, *The New England Clergy and the American Revolution,* Durham, N. C., 1928, attempts no evaluation of the main uses to which the two Testaments were put, although examples she quotes indicate that the New Testament was also on occasion used to justify revolution.

2. Later in 1788, Langdon was a delegate to the state Constitutional Convention that ratified the Federal Constitution, but not without proposing a Bill of Rights.

3. Not only the clergy but Tom Paine, most popular propagandist of the revolution, used the words of Hosea, xiii, 2 "I gave them a king in mine anger." ("The Forester's Letters, No. 3," *Pennsylvania Journal,* April 24, 1776, in Philip S. Foner, ed., *The Complete Works of Thomas Paine,* New York, 1945, II, 78.) In *Common Sense,* published January 10, 1776, widely read by soldier and civilian, Paine asserted that "Monarchy is ranked in scripture as

one of the sins of the Jews," and then summarized Samuel's outline of what kings would do to the people (I Sam. viii) (Foner, *ibid.*, I, 9–12). In 1792, in England, appealing to the English people to overthrow their monarchy, Paine again used the story of Samuel ("Letter Addressed to the Addressers on the Late Proclamation," *ibid.*, II, 475–476). Paine evidently knew the force of this argument among the people, although he was himself hardly devout.

47. Hebrew Taught

1. For the study of Hebrew at Harvard, see Meyer, *AJHSP*, XXXV (1939), 145–170; about the University of Pennsylvania, see Edward Potts Cheyney, *History of the University of Pennsylvania, 1740–1940*, Philadelphia, 1940, pp. 133–134, and *DAB* articles on Kunze and Helmuth.

2. Abraham Cohen was the second *Shamash* (Sexton) of the Congregation Mikve Israel in Philadelphia (Morais, *op. cit.*, 45).

   Reverend Jacob Raphael Cohen had been minister of the Jewish congregations in Montreal and New York before he came to Philadelphia in 1784 to take charge of the Congregation Mikve Israel on the occasion of Gershom Mendes Seixas' return to New York (*ibid.*, 18; Sack, *op. cit.*, 62).

48. Anti-Semitism, 1790

1. *Horatio Gates Papers*, New York Public Library, Manuscript Division. The letter was sent from Monckton Park, near Bristol, Bucks County, Pa., and was addressed to Gates "at his Seat—/Travellers-rest/ Berkley County—/Virginia" (now West Virginia).

2. Charles A. Beard, *Economic Origins of Jeffersonian Democracy*, (New York, 1915) p. 141.

3. Horatio Gates (1727–1806) had commanded the Northern army that defeated General Burgoyne in 1777, but had then commanded the Southern army that suffered the debacle at Camden, S. C. in 1780. He was a man of pronounced democratic and liberal views, but his reaction to this letter and the poem is not known. (Samuel White Patterson, *Horatio Gates, Defender of American Liberties*, New York, 1941.)

4. *The Pennsylvania Gazette*, March 17, 1790, p. 3, col. 3.

5. *The Daily Advertiser*, New York, February 13, 1790, p. 3, col. 3, implied that if Hamilton's plan succeeded, Robert Morris would profit $18,000,000, Jeremiah Wadsworth, $9,000,000, and Governor George Clinton, $5,000,000. None of those mentioned was Jewish.

6. John Malcolm had been an officer from 1777 to 1779 in a New York regiment.

49. Business, Debtors, Lands, After the Revolution

1. McAlister MSS, Ridgway Branch, Library Company of Philadelphia; also Byars, *op. cit.*, 236–238, but his text is inaccurate and omits words in Hebrew script. The letter was addressed to Barnard, care of the firm, Messrs. [Jacob I.] Cohen and [Isaiah] Isaacs, of Richmond, Va., which operated in business from 1781 to 1792.

2. Abernethy, *Western Lands and the American Revolution*, New York and London, 1937, pp. 263–264.

3. *Ibid.*, 368–369.

4. Joseph Henry (d. 1793) was a nephew of the Gratz brothers, and a successful merchant (Byars, *op. cit.*, 28, 252).

5. "The case of Abel Westfall" is interesting: Michael Gratz had contracted with Westfall to move the Hampshire county, Virginia, hemp crop, with Michael supplying the money. When Hampshire county citizens rebelled against the enormous war taxes, Westfall responded to the call for volunteers to put down the rebellion. But after he had succeeded, he was no longer able to buy the hemp from the suppressed and resentful citizens. Gratz sued Westfall, who argued that it was his civic duty to suppress rebellion, hemp or no hemp; the court decided in favor of Gratz (*ibid.*, 22).

6. Solomon Etting (1764–1847) was a partner of Joseph Simon in Lancaster, Pa.

7. This Mr. Hays cannot be further identified.

   This J. Henry is not to be confused with Jacob Henry, cousin of the Gratzes, who died in the 1760s (*ibid.*, 8, 60).

8. Colonel John Jameson was a merchant in York, Va. (*ibid.*, 234).

9. John Dunlap was a merchant in Philadelphia (*ibid.*, 141).

10. The Illinois and Wabash Company was a merger of two land companies, effected March 26, 1779. Barnard Gratz had been its secretary; its membership included Robert Morris, Silas Deane, John Holker, Ferdinand Grand, the Paris banker, Conrad Gerard, the French Minister, and other prominent "merchant venturers." Its activities lasted only until 1784, when Virginia turned her western lands over to the Federal government, but litigation about these lands continued (Abernethy, *op. cit.*, 234).

10a. This Yiddish passage, for the reading of which I am indebted to Mr. M. Lutzki of The Jewish Theological Seminary of America, is translatable as: all the money in (of) the house, but God knows if it will ever return.

10b. Moses Michael Hays (1739–1805) was a prominent Jewish merchant in Newport and then Boston.

11. Bell (Bilah, Belah) Cohen was a daughter of Joseph Simon who had married Solomon Cohen, and was therefore related to Michael Gratz, who had married her sister, Miriam.

12. Solomon Henry of London was a cousin of the Gratzes.

    This Moses Franks was a son of David and Margaret Evans Franks, and should not be confused with the brother of David Franks by the same name (see Doc. No. 27) who had died April 2, 1789, a year before this letter was written. (Solomons, *AJHSP*, XVIII, 1909, p. 214.)

    New Providence is in the Bahamas, British West Indies.

    David Franks died in Philadelphia, October 1793. In 1748 he had been a member of a dancing and gaming Assembly; during the revolutionary war he sided with the British; the Americans imprisoned him for a short time, and confiscated his property. (Morais, *op. cit.*, 34; Solomons, *loc. cit.*, 214.)

50. Correspondence Between the Jews and Washington

1. This correspondence has frequently been reprinted, but in varying texts. The texts used herein are copies of the manuscripts in the *Washington Papers*, Library of Congress; this first item is in the "Letter Book," pp. 129–130. The date is given in the original manuscript as described in Edmund H. Abrahams, "Some Notes on the Early History of the Sheftalls of Georgia," *AJHSP*, XVII (1909), 185. Washington had taken the oath of office on April 30, 1789.

2. It is noteworthy that the Hebrew Congregation was the only religious group in Savannah that sent such congratulations to Washington (Adelaide Wilson, *Historic and Picturesque Savannah,* Boston, 1889, p. 95).

3. Levi Sheftall was the eldest son of Benjamin Sheftall and the older brother of Mordecai Sheftall. Born in 1739, he became a merchant, and a supporter of the revolution. He died on January 26, 1809 (*Republican and Savannah Evening Ledger,* January 26, 1809, citation supplied by the Georgia Historical Society, July 31, 1946).

4. *Washington Papers,* 131–132.

5. *Washington Papers,* 17–18. Why sixteen months elapsed between the addresses sent by the Savannah and Newport congregations is obscure. The plan was to have one memorial from all the congregations in the country. As the oldest, the Congregation Shearith Israel of New York was to draw up the document. On June 20, 1790, when it began to organize the joint address, the Congregation blamed the "local situation" for the delay and expressed resentment at the fact that the Savannah congregation had "officiously" acted independently. The Newport congregation in its reply justified the action of the Georgians. (*AJHSP,* XXVII, 1920, pp. 217–220.)

6. On August 17, 1790, when Washington arrived at Newport, he received similar addresses of welcome from various groups, including the clergy of Newport. Because of the smallness of the Newport Congregation, it had informed the New York Congregation Shearith Israel that it hesitated to subscribe to a joint congregational letter to Washington before other groups in Rhode Island had sent their addresses (*Lyons Collection II,* in *AJHSP,* XXVII, 1920, pp. 218–220). Rhode Island, it should be noted, had rejected the Federal Constitution at the first state convention in June 1788, and had ratified the Constitution at a second convention on May 24, 1790 by a vote of only thirty four to thirty two (Edward Frank Humphrey, *Nationalism and Religion in America, 1774–1789,* Boston, 1924, pp. 469–470). With the community so divided, the Jews seemed diffident of expressing themselves until Washington himself, in the company of Jefferson and others, visited Newport in order to consolidate the position of the new government.

7. Moses Seixas (1744–1809) was an elder brother of Gershom Mendez Seixas and a prominent merchant. When the British occupied Newport on December 8, 1776 and sacked the city, Moses Seixas chose not to leave the city with the patriots who fled the British occupation. (N. Taylor Phillips, "The Levy and Seixas Families of Newport and New York," *AJHSP,* IV, 1896, pp. 201–203; Morris Jastrow, Jr., "References to Jews in the Diary of Ezra Stiles," *AJHSP,* X, 1902, p. 13; John C. Miller, *Triumph of Freedom, 1775–1783,* Boston, 1948, p. 144.)

8. *Washington Papers,* 19–20.
   The original letter was on the "Freedom Train" that toured the country in 1947.

9. *Washington Papers,* 27–28.

10. Samuel Oppenheim, "The Jews and Masonry in the United States before 1810," *AJHSP,* XIX (1910), 1–94.

11. Moses Seixas became Senior Warden of King David's Lodge on June 7, 1780, and Master in 1783; later he became the Grand Master of Rhode Island. This address, although dated August 17th, was not presented until the following day (*ibid.,* 21–23).

12. *Washington Papers,* 29.

13. *Washington Papers,* 30–31. The address was presented in Philadelphia, the new capital (N. Taylor Phillips, "Items Relating to the History of the Jews of New York," *AJHSP,* XI, 1903, pp. 156–157).

14. The difficulties attending the attempt to get a joint statement by all the congregations were many, and it took more than seven months before these four congregations acted in concert. On July 15, 1790, Jacob Cohen drafted an address for the Charleston congregation, the text of which has been frequently reprinted as one sent to Washington. However, the address was not sent to Washington, but to Isaac Moses of the Congregation Shearith Israel, in response to a letter from that Congregation, dated June 20, 1790, asking for the submission of such drafts. In a letter dated November 20, 1790, representatives of the Charleston Congregation, Beth Elohim, complain that they have received no reply from Moses, do not know whether an address has been presented, and now do not wish to be included "as we think it has been too tardy in the delivery." (*AJHSP,* XXVII, 1920, p. 221.) When Philadelphia's congregation informed Shearith Israel that it was planning to present its own address on the occasion of the removal of the capital to Philadelphia, Solomon Simson, president of the New York congregation, sent Isaac M. Gomez to Philadelphia with a letter proposing that the Philadelphia Congregation draft the address and present it in the name of all four congregations (Phillips, *op. cit.*).

15. President of the Congregation Mikve Israel, Manuel Josephson (1729–1796) had been a merchant in New York until the British occupation began. He had provided certain "guns, cutlasses and bayonets" to the revolutionary army (*Journal of the Assembly of the State of New-York,* 1792, p. 162, and 1795, pp. 21, 48).

16. *Washington Papers,* 32–33.

51. Anti-Democrat, Anti-Semite

1. The full title is: *The Democrat; or Intrigues and Adventures of Jean Le Noir, From his Inlistment as a Drummer in General Rochembeau's Army, and arrival at Boston, to his being driven from England in 1795, after having borne a conspicuous part in the French Revolution, and after a great variety of Enterprises, Hazards and Escapes during his stay in England, where he was sent in quality of Democratic Missionary. In Two Volumes. . . . New York: Printed for James Rivington, No. 156 Pearl-street. 1795.*

2. *DNB,* XVI, 511–513.

3. Morris U. Schappes, "Reaction and Anti-Semitism, 1795–1800," *AJHSP,* XXXVIII, 1948, pp. 109–137.

4. The Democratic Society had been formed in New York in 1794 (Eugene Perry Link, *Democratic-Republican Societies, 1790–1800,* New York, 1942, p. 14).

5. The Vice-President of the Society in New York, and one of its founders, was Solomon Simpson (or Simson) (1738–1801), a Jewish merchant. In 1794, when the Society was established, he was the Second Vice-President, in 1795 and 1796 he was First Vice-President, and in 1797 he became President. In 1794 and 1795 Simpson also held the elected office of Assessor in the Second Ward. When the British had occupied New York, he left the city for Connecticut, but returned by 1786. He was president of the Congregation Shearith Israel in 1773, 1776, 1787, 1790, and 1791. (Phillips, *op. cit.,* 155 and Iyda R. Hirsh, "The Mears Family and Their Connections, 1696–1824," *AJHSP,* XXXIII, 1934, p. 202; William Duncan, *The New-York Directory, and Register for the Year*

1794, pp. 280, 238; ibid., 1795, pp. 323, 280; John Low, *The New-York Directory, and Register for the Year 1796,* p. 57 of the Register; *Longworth's American Almanac, New York Register, and City Directory,* 1797, p. 84; David Franks, *The New-York Directory 1786,* p. 47.)

52. Democrats Answer an Anti-Semite

1. *The Argus, or Greenleaf's New Daily Advertiser,* December 17, 1795. My attention to this letter was called by Link, *op. cit.,* 51n, where, however, he misrepresents "Slow and Easy" by calling him anti-Semitic! Thomas Greenleaf (1755–1798) was a democratic printer and owner of the *New York Journal* since 1787. Federalists had wrecked his printing press because he opposed ratification of the Constitution as insufficiently democratic. He was a member of the New York Democratic Society, which Rivington had attacked in his preface. (Frank Luther Mott, *American Journalism,* New York, 1941, p. 119.)
2. Gregorio Leti, *The Life of Pope Sixtus V,* translated by Ellis Farneworth, London, 1754; in this edition, on pages 293–295, is told a story similar to that in *The Merchant of Venice,* but with the characters inverted, that is, a Christian is to cut a pound of flesh from the Jew. Sixtus the Fifth was pope from 1585 to 1590. Whether this story reached England about that time and was known to Shakespeare has not been established.
3. See note on Solomon Simpson in connection with the preceding document.
4. Comfort Sands was President of the Chamber of Commerce, 1794–1798; Nicholas Cruger is listed as a merchant and David Campbell as an attorney in the New York Directory for 1795.
5. *Greenleaf's New York Journal, & Patriotic Register,* December 19, 1795.
6. At one time the name of Rivington's periodical.
7. [illegible], "he who is the head will act, or will call the tune."

53. A Democratic Sermon

1. The title-page reads: *A Discourse, Delivered In the Synagogue In New-York, On The Ninth Of May, 1798, Observed As A Day Of Humiliation. &c. &c. Conformably to a Recommendation Of The President of the United States of America. By Rev. G. Seixas. . . . New-York: Printed by William A. Davis & Co. for Naphtali Judah, Bookseller and Stationer, No. 47 Water street. 1798.* There is only one other sermon by Seixas published during his lifetime: *Religious Discourse, Delivered In The Synagogue In This City, On Thursday The 26th November, 1789. . . .,* which was a Thanksgiving Day sermon. Of a third sermon, delivered during the War of 1812, appealing for funds to aid those in the Northwest Territory who had suffered at the hands of British and Indian enemies, excerpts appear in Leon Huhner, "The Patriot Jewish Minister of the American Revolution," in *Jewish Comment,* Baltimore, January 10, 1902, pp. 4–5, but the full text of the manuscript, which Mr. Huhner found in the archives of the Congregation Shearith Israel, is now reported missing.
2. For titles of nineteen other sermons examined and a fuller discussion of the National Fast Day, see Morris U. Schappes, "Anti-Semitism and Reaction, 1795–1800," *AJHSP,* XXXVIII, 1948, pp. 122n–123n.
3. The Reverend Gershom Mendes Seixas (1745–1816) was undoubtedly one of the most important figures in the American Jewish community. Hazan (reader)

of the New York congregation from June 16, 1768 to his death (except for the seven years spent in voluntary exile from New York during the British occupation), he transformed the position into that of a spiritual and social leader of the Jewish community, and also became a prominent public figure in the general life of the city. In 1776, when Solomon Simpson was president of the Congregation, Seixas helped persuade the majority of the Jews to leave New York rather than collaborate with the British. He went to his father's home in Stratford, Conn., remaining there until 1780, when he moved to Philadelphia to become the leader of the Mikveh Israel Congregation. On March 23, 1784, he returned to New York, together with many other Jews who had left in 1776. On May 1, 1784, by act of the State Legislature changing King's College into a University of the State of New York, he became one of the Regents of the University, representing the Jewish congregation; on May 4, 1784, he attended the first meeting of the Regents. When the Legislature, on April 13, 1787, reorganized the government of Columbia College, he was named one of the Trustees; he attended his first meeting as a Trustee on May 8, 1787, and served until his resignation in 1815. In 1796, he was a Trustee of the Humane Society in New York (founded in 1794), which was, among other things, "intended for general improvement in the medical profession, so as to embrace every subject which is connected with the public health, and the safety of individuals." (John Low, *The New York Directory, and Register for the Year 1796,* p. 56 of the Register; Grinstein, *op. cit., passim; AJHSP,* XXVII, 1920, pp. 136, 367, and *passim; A History of Columbia University, 1754–1904,* New York, 1904, pp. 59–60; *Laws of the State of New York, 1785–1788,* Ch. 82, 524–531; *Trustees Minutes,* Typewritten copy of MSS in Columbiana Collection, Seth Low Memorial Library, Columbia University, II, Part 1, pp. 1, 73, and *passim;* D. de Sola Pool, "Gershom Mendes Seixas' Letters, 1813–1815, to His Daught[illegible] Seixas- Kursheedt and Son-In-Law Israel Baer Kursheedt," *AJ*[illegible] 1939, pp. 189–205.)

4. Naphtali Judah, also a vital figure, was a Trustee of the Congrega[illegible] Shearith Israel for ten terms beginning in 1797, President for four terms, and Treasurer in 1808. In 1798 he was a member of the General Society of Mechanics and Tradesmen of the City of New York, and also of the Tammany Society, of which he served as a Sachem from 1803 to 1818. In 1825, he was among the group that left Shearith Israel to establish the Congregation B'nai Jeshurun, but he remained a member of Shearith Israel, and when he died at the age of 82 on September 16, 1855, he was buried in its cemetery. (*AJHSP,* XXI, 1913, pp. 168, 212, 169; *The Charter and Bye-Laws Of The General Society of Mechanics & Tradesmen Of The City Of New-York. Also, The Rules And Orders With A Catalogue Of Names Of The Members. . . .* New York, 1798; *New York City. Society of Tammany or Columbian Order,* MSS Division, New York Public Library, List of Signers of the original constitution, August 10, 1789, p. 50 col. 2, and *ibid., Grand Council Minutes, May 24, 1802 to May 24, 1819;* Israel Goldstein, *A Century of Judaism in New York,* New York, 1930, pp. 53, 383, Records of the Congregation Shearith Israel.)

Naphtali Judah was one of 12 children of Samuel Judah (1728–1781) and Jessie Jones Judah. Naphtali married Hetty Hendricks, November 11, 1801. The commission and importing business from the West Indies in which he engaged with his older brothers was ruined by the War of 1812 and the embargo that preceded it; later he became an auctioneer, and then a lottery broker. He was also on the first board of directors of the Mechanics (National) Bank, and a Mason for more than 50 years. (Robert W. Reid, *Washington Lodge No. 21, F. & A. M. and Some of its Members,* New York, 1911, pp. 173–174.)

5. In *The Time Piece* on May 30 and June 1, 6, 8, 11, 13, 15 and 18, 1798; on August 30, 1798 *The Time Piece* ceased publication because the government turned the newly passed sedition law against it. The same advertisement appeared in the *Argus and Greenleaf's New Daily Advertiser* on June 15, 19, 20 and 21, 1798.

54. Benjamin Nones Replies

1. *The Philadelphia Aurora,* August 13, 1800. The letter to Duane is republished here for the first time. The date of Nones' letter to Wayne is not, as is usually thought, August 11th but a date shortly after August 5th, when the *Gazette* appeared. The text of the main letter corrects minor errors that appeared in Cyrus Adler, "A Political Document of the Year 1800," *AJHSP,* I (1893), 111–115.
2. Nones (born, Bordeaux, France, 1753; died, Philadelphia, 1826) had come from France to this country in 1777 (or 1772?). The Jews of Bordeaux in 1782 collected a fund to buy a warship for the American navy (Sack, *op. cit.,* 43).
3. Nones served long and bravely in the revolutionary war. At the Siege of Savannah (September-October 1779) he served with conspicuous gallantry as a private in Pulaski's Legion in what proved to be a disastrous defeat for the American and French forces, and was rewarded with a high commendation from his Captain, Verdier (Morais, *op. cit.,* 26). He fought at the Battle of Camden, S. C., August 16, 1780, where the American forces were again routed. It is unnecessary, as some have done, to exaggerate his military feats, to ascribe to him posts of command of which there is no evidence. [illegible] to perpetuate the legend that even one of his own sons believed, that No[illegible] helped to carry General De Kalb wounded from the field of battle at [illegible] It is known that De Kalb was captured by the British and died in their hand[illegible] while Nones was not one of those captured (J. Spear Smith, "Memoir of the Baron de Kalb," in *Maryland Historical Society, Publications No. 24,* 1858, pp. 25–26). This letter by Nones to the *Gazette* in defense of his principles outweighs any other single act of his.

55. Defeating the Federalists, New York, 1800

1. *Reminiscences 1780 to 1814 Including Incidents in the War of 1812–1814 Letters Pertaining to His Early Life Written by Major Myers, 13th Infantry, U. S. Army to His Son,* Washington, 1900, pp. 10–12. The letter is dated Schenectady, New York, February 21, 1853.
2. Mordecai Myers (1776–1871) was the son of a Hungarian Jewish father and an Austrian Jewish mother who had come to New York in 1750. Mordecai was born in Newport. His father dying in November 1776, his mother stayed on in Newport until the British evacuated it in 1780, when she went to New York, then under British occupation. She left the city again in 1783, returning in 1787, then removing to Richmond, where Mordecai first began his military service in a company under Colonel John Marshall (*ibid.,* 6ff); here he also became a founder of the Congregation Beth Shalome (Ezekiel and Lichtenstein, *op. cit.,* 240). Back in New York, Mordecai Myers became active

in the Congregation Shearith Israel (he was a Trustee in 1800, 1801, 1802, 1803 and 1808), in the Society of Tammany, and in the New York Society for the Manumission of Slaves (*AJHSP*, XXI, 1913, p. 168; *New York City, Society of Tammany or Columbian Order, Constitution and Roll of Members, 1789–1816,* p. 52; *Manumission Society, New York City, Minutes,* IX, Dec. 7, 1802, MS., New-York Historical Society).

3. Written some fifty years after the events, these reminiscences contain some slight errors and confusion of dates. From Myers' further description, he is here referring obviously to the campaign of 1800.

4. Henry Brockholst Livingston (1757–1823) had risen to the rank of lieutenant-colonel in the Revolutionary War. Although the Federalist John Jay was his brother-in-law, and he had been closely associated with him, Livingston broke with the Federalists and joined the Jeffersonians. In 1800 he headed a group, however, that was having its inner-political differences with the state leadership of the Jeffersonians headed by George Clinton.

   Morgan Lewis (1754–1844), deputy Quarter Master General in the Revolutionary War, was then a judge of the New York State Supreme Court.

   Aaron Burr (1756–1836) was the brilliant political manager of this campaign.

5. For election, a presidential nominee needed 70 votes in the Electoral College. Outside New York state, the Jeffersonians and anti-Federalists could count on 61 votes. New York was entitled to 12 votes, and could therefore be decisive. New York City elected 13 Assemblymen to the State Legislature, which chose the electors; the New York city delegation therefore could determine whether the 12 electoral votes would all go to the Federalists or the Democratic-Republicans.

6. George Clinton (1739–1812) had served six successive terms as Governor, 1777 to 1795; he was re-elected in this election of 1800. He had distinguished himself for his defense of Alexander McDougall, head of the Liberty Boys, and for his severity against the Loyalists.

   Marinus Willett (1740–1830) had been a Liberty Boy, a radical leader, a lieutenant-colonel in the Revolutionary War, and several times Sheriff of New York City.

   Henry Rutgers (1745–1830), a Liberty Boy and a captain in the Revolutionary War, had already served in the State Assembly in 1784.

7. Achieving this unity of all the anti-Federalist tendencies in the city was a great factor in the election victory.

8. Tammany was at that time a very progressive democratic society, but was drawn into election campaigning for the first time now. Its members were chiefly artisans and workers; its one-story Wigwam was contemptuously called The Pig-Pen by the Federalists. Because of the property qualifications for voting, most Tammany members were disfranchised. Burr worked out a way, however, of circumventing the undemocratic law: by pooling their small resources, Tammany members could buy land as joint tenants, enabling all the partners to vote. (Nathan Schachner, *Aaron Burr, A Biography,* New York, 1937, p. 175.) The Republicans in New York city achieved an average majority of 490, despite great odds: restrictions of franchise, no secret balloting, and threats of economic reprisals by merchants and employers against their workers unless they voted Federalist (*ibid.,* 165, 168, 177).

9. The New York elections were held from April 29 to May 2, 1800. The balloting in the Electoral College took place from January 11 to January 17, 1801. (Claude G. Bowers, *Jefferson and Hamilton,* Boston, 1925, pp. 502ff.) After

being defeated in New York, Hamilton tried to cancel the election results by asking Governor John Jay to call a special session of the then existing legislature to take away from the State Legislature its right to choose the national electors in order to "prevent an atheist in religion and a fanatic in politics from getting possession of the helm of state." Jay refused (*ibid.*, 454).

56. Manumission of Slaves

1. *Will Book 13,* p. 486, Chancery Court of Richmond, Va. Ezekiel and Lichtenstein, *The History of the Jews of Richmond,* Richmond, 1917, pp. 327–330, garbles a passage.
2. Samuel McKee, Jr., *Labor in Colonial New York, 1664–1776,* New York, 1935, pp. 133–134.
3. Isaiah Isaacs (1747–1806) was the first Jew in Richmond, Va., where he settled before the revolution. On June 11, 1783, he was one of those signing a petition calling upon the State Legislature to deprive of the rights of citizenship those who had sided with the British during the war. He was a tax assessor, twice elected to the Common Hall of Richmond, and a founder of the Congregation Beth Shalome (Ezekiel and Lichtenstein, *op. cit.*, 14–16, 32, 63–64, 240, 326–327). In 1799, he freed one of his female slaves, Lucy.
4. Jacob I. Cohen (c.1744–1823) was the partner of Isaacs from 1781 to 1792; in his own will, January 10, 1816, Cohen provides for the freeing of his own slaves immediately on his death (*ibid.*, 18, 19, 330–335).
5. Joseph Marx, a Richmond Jew, died in 1840 in his 69th year (*ibid.*, 303).
   Isaiah's younger brother, David Isaacs, had been born in Frankfort on the Main, 1760; he died in Richmond, 1837 (*ibid.*, 297).

57. Charging a Jury

1. *The Trial of the Boot & Shoemakers of Philadelphia, on an Indictment for a Combination and Conspiracy to Raise Their Wages. Taken in Short-Hand, By Thomas Lloyd,* Philadelphia, 1806, pp. 140–149; the full text of the stenogram of the trial can be found in John R. Commons, Eugene A. Gilmore, and associates, *A Documentary History of American Industrial Society,* Cleveland, 1910, III, 59–248.
2. Moses Levy (1757–1826) attained prominence as a lawyer, before he became Recorder in 1802, serving until 1822. He was at one time himself a Jeffersonian, and elicited an anti-Semitic attack from the Federalist, William Cobbett (Schappes, *op. cit.*, 129–130, 133). Later he was a judge in the District Court of Philadelphia. "The success at the bar of the brothers Moses and Sampson Levy was in the teeth of racial and caste obstacles which at that time were substantial. Both became Episcopalians." (Nelles, 172n, as cited in Note 3.)
3. The Jeffersonian *General Advertiser* (*Aurora*), March 31, 1806, said of Levy: "A man, who did not know the purposes for which the law contemplated the appointment of a *recorder* to preside in the mayor's court, would unquestionably have concluded that Mr. Recorder Levy had been paid by the master shoe-makers for his discourse in the mayor's court on Friday last —never did we hear a charge to the jury delivered in a more prejudiced and partial manner—from such courts, recorders and juries, good lord deliver us." The conservative *New-York Evening Post,* April 2, 1806 and the *New-York Gazette & General Advertiser,* April 3, 1806 both said: "The Recorder

Moses Levy, esq. in a very clear, forcible and eloquent address to the jury, expounded the law and detailed the evidence. . . . His charge was direct and decisive against the defendants— . . . This trial has established a principle of the utmost importance to the manufacturing interest of this flourishing city— . . ." For a legal scholar's unflattering analysis of Levy's hostile conduct and prejudicial charge to the jury, see Walter Nelles, "The First American Labor Case," *Yale Law Journal,* XLI, 1931, pp. 165–200. In 1888, New York State Commissioner Charles F. Peck wrote of Levy's charge to the jury: "[it] reads like a lecture on political economy. . . . His reputation [as an eminent lawyer], probably, does not rest on this case. The charge was most improper. It was an argument, not a summary of the law . . . he drew on his imagination for most of his law. . . ." (*Fifth Annual Report of the Bureau of Statistics of Labor of the State of New York, for the year 1887,* Albany, 1888, pp. 675–677.)

4. John R. Commons, David J. Saposs, and associates, *History of Labor in the United States,* New York, 1918, I, 151–152.

5. Today a jury would have the authority to decide only the facts; at that time the jury in theory decided both on the facts and the law.

6. The ellipses (. . .) here and elsewhere in this text occur in the original stenogram and do not signify omissions by this editor.

7. The first indictment accused the shoemakers of "contriving unjustly and oppressively to augment the prices usually paid to them . . ." The second charged "conspiring and agreeing to endeavor to prevent by threats and other unlawful means" other shoemakers from working for lower wages. The third and last stated that the shoemakers "did assemble and combine, and did conspire and agree" not to work for less pay after November 1805. (*General Advertiser* (*Aurora*), March 31, 1806.)

8. For a legal and historical analysis of the inconsequential weight of these authorities, see Nelles, *op. cit.,* 193–199.

9. The strike was broken by the arrest of the eight leaders on the charges of conspiracy; when the strike failed, forty members, almost one third of the total, left the society (*ibid.,* 168). After the conviction, the shoemakers opened a warehouse of their own, and appealed for customers to save them from "abject poverty." (John Bach McMaster, *A History of the People of the United States,* New York, 1891, III, 512.)

10. The jury returned a verdict: "We find the defendants guilty of a combination to raise their wages." (For the possible significance of this formulation, see Nelles, *op. cit.,* 192–193.) To persuade the jury to reach a verdict of guilty, the prosecution had assured the jurymen that "no men will be more ready than the prosecution to shield the journeymen from any disagreeable consequences from a conviction." (Commons and Saposs, *op. cit.,* 148–149.) Each of the defendants was therefore given a sentence of only an eight dollar fine, but the evil principle had been established. Public resentment against the decision was high. In the elections in the fall of 1806, the Jeffersonians gained a small majority in both houses of the State legislature. Dr. Michael Leib, who had resigned from Congress in order to conduct the Jeffersonian battle in the State legislature, together with his aid, James Engle, began a campaign for the impeachment of Governor Thomas McKean. As part of this campaign there was introduced, on December 13, 1806, a bill to prevent the Recorder of Philadelphia (Moses Levy) from practising in any court of law, thereby depriving him of his main source of income. On February 21, 1807, the bill passed the House, 40 to 31; on March 5 it passed the Senate, 11 to 8. On March 25,

1807, McKean vetoed the bill, and the Jeffersonians were unable to muster the two-thirds majorities required to override the veto. The charges of impeachment against McKean, which were almost successful, contained an accusation that he had used his veto-power irresponsibly. (*Journal of the Seventeenth House of Representatives of the Commonwealth of Pennsylvania,* Lancaster, 1806, pp. 58, 443, 682–4, 747–8; *Journal of the Senate of the Commonwealth of Pennsylvania,* Lancaster, 1806, pp. 230, 267, 274, 339, 367–9; James Hedley Peeling, "Governor McKean and the Pennsylvania Jacobins, 1799–1808," *The Pennsylvania Magazine of History and Biography,* LIV, 1930, pp. 343–349.) Of the legal effect of Levy's rulings, Nelles declared that popular Jeffersonian "counter-pressures sufficed to assure that prosecutions of labor unions would for long be rare; that the rule of law, in spite of Recorder Levy, would not be felt as clear and settled; and that the Recorder's doctrine would not, without verbal qualification, be adopted in later cases" (*op. cit.,* 200). Formally, Levy's ruling was superseded by Chief Justice Shaw of Massachusetts in 1842 in Commonwealth v. Hunt (Walter Nelles, "Commonwealth v. Hunt," *Columbia Law Review,* XXXII, 1932, pp. 1128–1169).

58. Burying the Dead

1. *An Account of the Interment of the Remains of 11,500 American Seamen, Soldiers and Citizens, Who Fell Victims to the Cruelties of the British, on Board their Prison Ships at the Wallabout. . . .* New York, 1808, pp. 39–40.
2. The *Jersey* prison-ship, perhaps best remembered now because of Philip Freneau's poem of that name, was one of several old British men-of-war used to hold prisoners in the Wallabout, now the site of the Brooklyn Navy Yard. In 1803 Tammany for the first time began to agitate for a public burial of the heaps of human bones that had been turned up in the process of digging the foundations for the Navy Yard. In 1808, Tammany finally organized an impressive parade and public interment in which there participated the State militia, the mayor and governor and their staffs, the Mechanics Society, shipwrights, tailors, coopers, hatters, Hibernians, the Masons, and of course the thirteen tribes of Tammany. A pro-British Federalist paper like the *New-York Evening Post* sneered at the parade as "the shabbiest ever exhibited in this city by daylight" (May 27, 1808) and laughed at the Tammany Indians with tails where their heads ought to be, but reflected that "since Mr. Jefferson had been in power nature had entirely changed, and that the tail governed, instead of the head . . ." (May 26, 1808). Naphtali Judah, as Sachem of the Fox Tribe, probably took part in the event.
3. Among the members there were the following, in addition to Hart, who were Jews: Isaac Gedalia, Gompert S. Gomperts, William Hays, Naphtali Judah, Moses Monsanto, Seixas Nathan, and Moses L. M. Peixotto (Oppenheim, *AJHSP*, XIX, 1910, p. 33).
4. Joel Hart (1784–1842) was the only son of Ephraim Hart, wealthy New York stock-broker and State Senator in 1810. Joel Hart obtained a medical degree in London, and was a charter member of the Medical Society of New York County. On the recommendation of Sachem Napthali Judah, he was admitted to membership in the Tammany Society of New York on March 23, 1807; the same year he joined Jerusalem Chapter No. 8, R. A. M., and in 1812 he became Chapter High Priest and in 1815 Chapter Scribe. He was United States consul at Leith, Scotland, from 1817 to 1832. (*New York City. Society of Tammany or Columbian Order. Minutes March 4, 1799 to Feb. 1, 1808,* MSS Division, New York Public Library; Charles Victor Twiss, *The Centennial History of*

Jerusalem Chapter No. 8 of Royal Arch Masons of New York, 1799–1899, New York, 1899, pp. 49, 316–320.)

5. Robert Townsend, Jr. was a carpenter.

59. Talmud Torah, 1808

1. I am indebted to Mr. Eugene L. Schwaab of Brookline, Mass. for calling my attention to this hitherto unnoted item in the New York Society Library. Although a hundred copies were ordered printed (*AJHSP,* XXI, 1913, p. 162), not even the archives of the Congregation itself now contain a copy (letter from Mr. Victor Tarry, Executive Secretary of the Congregation, May 20, 1946).

2. Alexander M. Dushkin, *Jewish Education in New York City,* New York, 1918, p. 44, expresses the judgment that "this school did not play a significant part in the development of Jewish education."

3. Hartstein, *AJHSP,* XXXIV (1937), 123, 130; D. de Sola Pool, "The Earliest Jewish Religious School in America," *The Jewish Teacher,* I (1917), 162.

4. Jacob Hart (born, Germany, 1746, di^d, 1822) came to this country in 1775, was a patriotic merchant in the Revolution in Baltimore, and held the post of treasurer and president in the Congregation.

   Isaac M. Gomez (1768–1831) was a merchant and ship-owner; he was Clerk of the Congregation for many years and a Trustee in 1795.

5. Gompert S. Gomperts was a member of Jerusalem Chapter No. 8, Royal Arch Masons of New York.

   Judah Zuntz (c. 1783–1829) was active in the congregation.

   About Joel Hart see Note 4 to Document No. 58.

   Israel Baer Kursheedt (born, Germany, 1766, died, 1852) came to the United States from Prussia in 1796, where he had been an army contractor. He was president of the Congregation Shearith Israel in 1810 and 1811, but after returning from a twelve year stay in Richmond, Va., he affiliated with the newly established German Congregation B'nai Jeshurun in 1825. While in Virginia, Kursheedt was an acquaintance of Jefferson's and visited him at Monticello. Kursheedt's wife was Sarah Abigail Seixas, daughter of Gershom Mendes Seixas. (Reid, *op. cit.,* 165.)

   Moses L. Moses, a son of Isaac Moses, was president of the Congregation Shearith Israel twelve times between 1827 and 1842.

   About Mordecai Myers consult the Index.

6. Bernard Hart (born, England, 1764, died, 1855) came to New York in 1780 from Canada, and became a merchant and stock-broker; he succeeded Jacob Isaacs as Secretary of the New York Stock Exchange in 1831 and held the post until 1853. In the Congregation he held, at various times, the posts of Clerk, Treasurer, Trustee, and President.

   Seixas Nathan (1785–1852) was a merhant and stock-broker, and president of the Congregation in 1811 and 1812; he was a member of Jerusalem Chapter No. 8.

60. Manumitting Slaves, 1806–1809

1. *Manumission Society of New York City. Minutes, May 18, 1791–Feb. 13, 1807,* MSS Minutes, Vol. 7, and *Minutes, March 11, 1807–July 8, 1817,* Vol. 10, at the New-York Historical Society.

2. His genealogy has not yet been established, but the following is certain: from 1796 to 1800, as a young man, he was a partner in the firm of Dunlap and

Judah operating a "looking-glass and hardware store" (*Diary of William Dunlap, 1766–1839,* New York, 1929–1931, *passim:* New York City Directories, 1796–1800). He is not to be confused with the much older Moses Judah (1735–1822), who seems to have been a lawyer (*The New-York Evening Post,* September 27, 1822). In April 1798 the young Judah was compelled to marry a Miss Peck because she was then already pregnant by him (Dunlap, *op. cit.,* 317–319). Between 1804 and 1815, Moses Judah was in business as a merchant at 253 and then 263 Pearl Street, his address while he was on the Standing Committee of the Manumission Society; from 1818 to 1831 he was in partnership with Thomas L. Callender of North Carolina at 269½ Pearl Street (New York City Directories, 1801–1832; Dunlap, *op. cit.,* 522).

3. *Constitution of the Society for Promoting the Manumission of Slaves, and Protecting such of them as Have Been, or May Be Liberated,* New York, 1796, pp. 1–2.

4. *Minutes, Jan. 16, 1798–Dec. 12, 1814,* Vol. 9, *passim; Minutes of Meetings, Reports From Committees 1785–1822,* Vol. 5, *passim; ibid.,* Vol. 10, *passim.*

5. I have not been able to find any disposition of the case of Sam Joseph in the minutes.

6. Judah seems to have continued as a member of the Society, since his name does not appear on any of the lists of persons resigned or dropped. Another Jew who was a member of the Society was Mordecai Myers, who was proposed for membership by Christopher M. Slocum and elected on January 18, 1803 (*Minutes, op. cit.,* Vol. 9). *The Minutes* (Vols. 8 and 10) also contain accounts of six instances between 1812 and 1831 in which the Society proceeded in the defense of Negroes against Jewish masters. Thus the Society acted against "Solomon a Jew;" Moses Gomez; a Mrs. Judah, the wife either of Aaron or Carey Judah, merchants and brothers living at 1 Old-slip in 1814; Jacob Levy; Simon Moses; and Levi Hyman, whose identity has not otherwise been established.

61. Jacob Henry Speaks for Equality

1. The MS is in the State Legislative Records, State Department of Archives and History, Raleigh, N. C., and is fuller than that usually given, as for example in Huhner, *AJHSP,* XVI (1907), 68–71.

2. Jacob Henry is not, as Mr. Huhner guessed him to be (*ibid.,* 47), a brother of Michael Gratz who changed his name to Jacob Henry. He is the son of Joel Henry and his wife, Amelia, of Beaufort, Carteret County, N.C. (Will of Joel Henry, December 8, 1803, *Carteret County Records, Wills, Inventories, Sales and Settlements of Estates 1741–1887,* Vol. VI, 44; and Will of Amelia Henry, December 2, 1806, *ibid.,* A–Z, p. 54; both in the State Department of Archives and History). On February 9, 1801, Jacob Henry had applied for a license to marry Esther Whithurst (*Carteret County Marriage Bonds, H*). In 1807, he is also listed as a Mason in Beaufort County (Oppenheim, *op. cit.,* 75), and perhaps the same Jacob Henry is named as a Mason in Newbern, N. C. in 1812. He died in 1847, aged 72–73 (*AJA,* XXII, No. 2 [November, 1970], 120).

3. *Journal of the House of Commons of the State of North-Carolina, First Session . . .* 1809, pp. 27–28.

4. John H. Wheeler even reports that the speech is "said to be the production of . . . Taylor . . ." (*Historical Sketches of North Carolina, from 1584 to 1851,* Philadelphia, 1851, II, 74).

5. Huhner, *op. cit.*, 52: "As a matter of fact, the test was more firmly implanted than ever." The problem came up again at the North Carolina State Constitutional Convention in 1835, but after much debate the only change made was to substitute "Christian" for "Protestant," thus admitting Catholics but still excluding Jews. It was not until the Reconstruction Convention of 1868 that Jews gained their equal rights (Huhner, *ibid.*, 68).
6. Thomas Davis of Fayetteville.

62. State Aid to Parochial Schools

1. Minutes of the Congregation, January 3, 1811, Dushkin, *op. cit.*, 452.
2. *AJHSP,* XXVII, 1920, pp. 92–95; Dushkin, *op. cit.*, 44.
3. *Laws of the State of New York . . . 1811,* p. 462. The text in Dushkin, *op. cit.*, 453, is garbled.
4. The amount received was $1565.78 (*ibid.*).

63. Fighting the British, 1813

1. Myers, *op. cit.*, 26–33.
2. Francis B. Heitman, *Historical Register and Dictionary of the United States Army, . . . 1789 . . . 1903,* Washington, D. C., 1903, I, 740; Huhner, *AJHSP,* XXVI (1918), 174.
3. The Cantonment Williamsville was eleven miles from Buffalo. For an interesting letter writter by Myers to Naphtali Phillips from this Cantonment, March 31, 1813, see *AJHSP,* XXVII (1920), 396–397.
4. Then a village of 900 on the north shore of Lake Ontario, Little York is now the city of Toronto, Ontario. The 1813 American plan of campaign included pushing the war into Canadian territory. Itself unimportant, Little York had been the site of the construction of several war-ships, and Commodore Isaac Chauncey decided to capture it in order to achieve command of Lake Ontario. The victory, on April 27, 1813, was costly in casualties (about 70 killed and some 225 wounded), but accomplished the capture of a couple of hundred British soldiers. Four days after the surrender, the American troops re-embarked to move on Fort George. (Henry Adams, *The War of 1812,* Washington, Infantry Journal ed., 1944, p. 83; Benson J. Lossing, *The Pictorial Field-Book of the War of 1812,* New York, 1869, pp. 586–591.)
5. Dr. James C. Bronaugh, a Virginian, was the Surgeon of the 12th United States Infantry. He continued in the Army after the War until 1821, and died the following year (Heitman, *op. cit.*, I, 247).
6. Zachary Taylor (1784–1850), twelfth President of the United States, died in office in 1850, three years before these reminiscences were written.
7. Joseph Gilbert Totten (1788–1864) had already been promoted to a captaincy on July 31, 1812, and was later promoted several times for exceptional service in the War of 1812. For his conduct at the siege of Vera Cruz in the War with Mexico he was made a Brigadier General on March 29, 1847. (*Ibid.*, I, 966.)
8. Later that year, on November 11, 1813, leading his company in an attack on British troops near Williamsburg, Upper Canada, Myers was seriously wounded in an arm and disabled for four months. Twenty-three of the eighty-nine men in his company were killed in that engagement. At the end of the War he was pensioned on half pay. While recuperating from his wound, Myers met Char-

lotte Bailey, daughter of Judge William Bailey of Plattsburg, and married her in March, 1814. Mr. Leon Huhner states that "after his marriage, Myers became estranged from the Jewish community." (*Op. cit.*, p. 177.) Myers became separated from the synagogue and his children were brought up in the Christian religion, but to the end of his life he maintained contact with Jewish life, answering appeals to the Sons of Israel to contribute to Zion College, the Jewish Hospital and Talmid Yelodim Institute in Cincinnati, the Orphan Asylum in New York, and other institutions, and subscribing to *The Jewish Messenger* and *The Israelite.* As late as 1860, he was active in a movement to persuade the twenty-five or thirty Jewish storekeepers in Schenectady to close their shops on the Sabbath. (*The Israelite,* II, Jan. 25, 1856, p. 237; V, Jan. 7, 1859, p. 214; VII, Dec. 7, 1860, p. 182; *The Jewish Messenger,* VIII, Oct. 19, 1860, p. 117 and Oct. 26, 1860, p. 125; Dec. 27, 1861.) After the War of 1812, Myers became active in business and politics. From 1831 to 1834 he served as a State Assemblyman from New York City; in 1851 and 1854 he was Mayor of Schenectady, N. Y. (Huhner, *op. cit.*) In 1841 he sought but failed to obtain the post of Commissary General (Letter by Silas Wright to Major M. Myers, Washington, December 5, 1841, *Theodorus B. Myers Collection,* No. 154, New York Public Library, MSS Division).

64. A Slave Promised His Freedom

1. *Manumission Society, New York City, Indentures, 1809–1829,* III, 75 (New-York Historical Society).
2. On June 30, 1817, in accordance with this agreement, Roper was set free. The legal document manumitting him is in *ibid., Register of Manumission of Slaves, New York City, 1816–1818,* II, 81. On March 5, 1817, Jacob Levy, Jr. had also liberated his slave Mary Mundy; on March 6, 1817, he freed John Jackson, Samuel Spures, Edwin Jackson, Elizabeth Jackson, and James Jackson, (*ibid.,* 51, 50, 52). Ephraim Hart (1747–1825) liberated his slave Silvia on January 30, 1818 (*ibid.,* 110); Haym M. Solomon liberated his slave Anna, "now aged ten years & two months or thereabouts," (*ibid., Indentures, 1809–1829,* p. 64). The quantity of manumissions in 1817 may have been influenced by the fact that early that year the New York State Legislature passed a complete abolition act to take effect on July 4, 1827, on which day 10,000 slaves were freed. The Manumission Society was instrumental in achieving these results (Alice Dana Adams, *The Neglected Period of Anti-Slavery in America, 1808–1831,* Boston and London, 1908, pp. 89–90).
3. Jacob Levy, Jr. (died 1837) was active in the Congregation Shearith Israel, and was connected with prominent Jewish families: his daughter Judith married Moses B. Seixas; another daughter, Abby, was the wife of Moses I. (or J.) Hays; a third daughter married Joseph L. Joseph. George Brinckerhoff, who is the witness for the promise of freedom to George Roper, was also a witness when Jacob Levy, Jr., "Gentleman," wrote his will on March 25, 1837 (*New York City Hall of Records, Record of Wills, Surrogate's Court,* Lib. 76, pp. 299–304).

65. About Napoleon

1. For another reference, see an excerpt from a sermon by Gershom Mendes Seixas, January 11, 1807, *AJHSP,* XXVII (1920), 140–141.
2. For a current evaluation of the effect of Napoleon on the Jews, see Salo Baron, *A Social and Religious History of the Jews,* 1937, Vols. 2 and 3, *passim;* for

the contemporary documents about the Paris Sanhedrin, see M. Diogene Tama, *Transactions of the Parisian Sanhedrim, . . .* London, 1807.

3. L. C. Moise, *Biography of Isaac Harby with an account of The Reformed Society of Israelites of Charleston, S. C., 1824–1833,* Columbia, S. C., 1931.

4. News of the Battle of Waterloo, at which Napoleon's forces were decisively defeated on June 18, 1815, and of Napoleon's second abdication from the throne on June 22, 1815.

5. Arthur Wellesley, first Duke of Wellington, commanded the English, Dutch, Belgian, and Hanoverian forces of about 94,000 men; Field Marshal Gebhard Leberecht von Blücher commanded the Prussian, Saxon and other German forces of 121,000 men. Napoleon's army consisted of 128,000 men. The losses cited by Harby are exaggerated. The official figures of the Allies give 22,428. The French lost over 31,000. The rout was unmistakable.

6. Napoleon's first abdication, on April 11, 1814, led to the restoration of the Bourbon Louis XVIII.

7. The abdication, although unpopular with the French masses, was welcomed by "those men who preside in the councils." Eugene Tarlé writes: "The bourgeoisie far more easily reconciled itself to the prospect of a foreign invasion of the capital than to the political interference, apparently just beginning, of the Parisian workers, who desired to resist the entry of the Allies." (*Bonaparte,* New York, 1937, p. 393.)

8. Later Harby, in reviewing Byron's "Ode to Napoleon Buonaparte" (written on his first abdication), defends Napoleon against Byron's excessive strictures. Harby sees Napoleon "as the scourge of his country and of Europe" but also as "a counterpoise and check to the cupidity and tyranny of England . . ." (Henry L. Pinckney and Abraham Moise, *A Selection from the Miscellaneous Writings of the Late Isaac Harby, Esq.,* Charleston, 1829, p. 240.)

66. Personal Letter

1. MS in *Rebecca Gratz Letters, Folder G,* American Jewish Historical Society. David Philipson, ed., *Letters of Rebecca Gratz,* Philadelphia, 1929, contains less than about half of the manuscript letters available. Rebecca Gratz (1781–1869), daughter of Michael Gratz and Miriam Simon Gratz, for almost three quarters of a century was a well-known figure in Philadelphian social and benevolent circles, both in the Jewish community and outside of it. In 1801, she was Secretary of the Female Association for the Relief of Women and Children in Reduced Circumstances; in 1815, she helped to found the Philadelphia Orphan Society, and served as its Secretary from 1819 to 1859; in 1838 she established the Hebrew Sunday School Society, the first of its kind in the United States, and was its secretary until 1864.

2. Maria Fenno Hoffman was the second wife of Judge Josiah Ogden Hoffman (1776–1837) of New York.

3. Any one of three persons might be referred to here: the Samuel Myers who died in Richmond, August 22, 1836 at the age of 82; the Samuel Myers, born at Norfolk, February 24, 1790, who died at Richmond in 1829; or the Samuel Hays Myers, born January 1, 1799, who died at Richmond, October 2, 1849 (Ezekiel and Lichtenstein *op. cit.,* 307). John Myers (1787–1830) was the son of Moses Myers (1752–1835) of Norfolk, Va.

4. Washington Irving (1783–1859) was a friend of the Hoffmans and Rebecca Gratz became acquainted with him at the Hoffman home. Meeting Walter

Scott in Europe in 1817, Irving had occasion to give him such a pen-portrait of Rebecca Gratz that Scott apparently modeled his figure of Rebecca in *Ivanhoe* after it (Philipson, *op. cit.*, pp. xix–xx; Jacobs, *AJHSP,* XXII, 1914, p. 60; Coleman, *AJHSP,* XXXV, 1939, pp. 235–237).

5. Shinah Simon, sister of Rebecca Gratz's mother, had married Dr. Nicholas Schuyler of Troy, New York, despite the opposition of her father, Joseph Simon. In 1804, when Joseph Simon, in his ninety-second year, was dying, Rebecca Gratz persuaded him to forgive Shinah. She arrived at the Simon household on January 23, 1804, received her father's blessing, and held him in her arms when he died the following day. (Rollin G. Osterweis, *Rebecca Gratz, A Study in Charm,* New York and London, 1935, pp. 73–75.)

6. James Kirke Paulding (1779–1860) was a writer and politician.

7. Mrs. Minis is Divina Cohen Minis of Georgetown, S. C. (1787–1874), wife of Isaac Minis (1780–1856). One of their thirteen children was named Rebecca Gratz Minis.

67. Fight for Equality in Maryland

1. E. Milton Altfeld, *The Jew's Struggle for Religious and Civil Liberty in Maryland,* Baltimore, 1924, pp. 77–78. The bill was drafted by William Pinkney (Hartogensis, *AJHSP,* XXV, 1917, p. 95), and introduced by Thomas Kennedy. This great struggle for democratic rights has been ignored by all American historians except McMaster, *op. cit.,* V, 390–392.

2. December 13, 1797, the long battle began with the following action in the House of Delegates: "A petition from Solomon Etting, and others, stating, that they are a sect of people called Jews, and thereby deprived of many of the invaluable rights of citizenship, and praying to be placed upon the same footing with other good citizens, was preferred, read, and referred to Mr. [James B.] Robins [Worcester County], Mr. [Edward] Hall [Anne-Arundel County] and Mr. [James] Carroll [Baltimore County], to consider and report thereon. . . .

   "Mr. Robins, from the committee, brings in and delivers to the speaker the following report:

   "The committee to whom was referred the petition of Bernard Gratz, and others, professing the Jewish religion, in the state of Maryland, report, that they have taken the same into consideration, and conceive the prayer of the petition is reasonable, but as it involves a constitutional question of considerable importance, they submit to the house the propriety of taking the same into consideration at this advanced stage of the session." (*Votes and Proceedings of the House of Delegates of the State of Maryland, November Session 1797. Being the First Session of this Assembly,* 69, 71–72.) The session lasted from November 8, 1797 to January 21, 1798. Petitions and bills were introduced in 1801, 1802, 1803, 1804 and 1805, but with no success. The struggle was resumed again in 1816, and was waged continually thereafter until it was successful. The number of Jews in Maryland was very small: about 100 in 1817, and about 200 in 1826. No complete and accurate account of this chapter in American history has yet been written; Mr. Altfeld's, the most extensive, is confused in organization and too often inaccurate. A good short account, fresh in interpretation but not free from error, is given by Joseph L. Blau, "The Maryland 'Jew Bill:' A Footnote to Thomas Jefferson's Work for Freedom of Religion," *The Review of Religion,* March, 1944, pp. 227–239.

3. The bill was defeated by a vote of 50 to 24 on January 22, 1819. Supporters of

the bill placed this political interpretation on the result: "Whether there were any political arrangement or *caucussing* on the question we know not, but it is a remarkable fact that only two Federalists in the whole House voted for the bill . . ." (*Sketch of Proceedings in the Legislature of Maryland, December Session, 1818, On What Is Commonly Called The Jew Bill;* . . . Baltimore, 1819, p. 68n.) Editorial opinion in the South compared Maryland's treatment of the Jews with persecutions of Jews in Turkey (Natchez, Miss., *Independent Press*), in Russia and Austria (Danville *Virginia Republican*), in Germany (Charleston *Southern Patriot* and Winchester, Va., *Genius of Liberty*). (*Ibid.*, 71–78.)

68. Invitation to Immigration

1. *Lyons Pamphlets, II,* No. 2, at American Jewish Historical Society.
   About Robinson, of whom nothing, not even his full name, has been known to American Jewish historiography, this much is ascertainable: William Davis Robinson was born in Philadelphia, October 15, 1774, and baptized in the Second Presbyterian Church on December 25, 1774. He was a merchant interested especially in South American trade, and connected with firms both in London and Baltimore. In January 1815, during the War of 1812, he published a pamphlet in Georgetown, D. C.: *A Cursory View of Spanish America,* suggesting that 15,000 to 20,000 Kentucky and Tennessee volunteers could help free Mexico from Spanish domination and also defeat British plans for South American control, that we should support Simon Bolivar's revolutionary movements, and that it would be desirable and possible to cut a canal through the Isthmus of Panama. In 1816, he entered Mexico from New Orleans, commissioned by a New York firm to sell 10,000 guns to Mexican revolutionaries. He was captured by the Spaniards, imprisoned for more than a year, was sent to Cadiz, and finally made his way back to the United States probably in April, 1819. His *Memoirs of the Mexican Revolution,* 1820, was reprinted in London in 1821, in Dutch in Haarlem in 1823, in Spanish in London in 1824. What led to his interest in 1819 in the Jewish agricultural settlement is a matter for further investigation. (*A Catalogue of Books Represented by Library of Congress Printed Cards,* Vol. 127, p. 103; Eduardo Enrique Rios, *El Historiador Davis Robinson y su Aventura en Nueva España,* frontispiece and p. 11; *British Museum Catalogue of Printed Books; The National Cyclopaedia of American Biography,* XVIII, 185–186, which is inaccurate in some respects but indicates he died "sometime before 1823"; Lee M. Friedman, *Pilgrims in a New Land,* Philadelphia, 1948, pp. 233ff.)
2. For the characteristic attitude of the time welcoming immigration, see Henry Pratt Fairchild, *Immigration,* New York, 1913, pp. 53–60. It is significant that in 1819 in Stuttgart, capital of Wuerttemberg, there was an emigration society named the *Nordamerikanische Kolonisationsgesellschaft* (Kisch, *AJHSP,* XXXIV, 1937, pp. 26–27).
3. *The Settlement of the Jews in North America,* New York, 1893, pp. 93–94.
4. Altfeld, *op. cit.,* 130, 133.
5. Dominique Dufour de Pradt (1759–1837), member of the Constituent Assembly in France and Archbishop of Mechlin, in *Les Trois Ages Des Colonies, Ou De Leur État Passé, Présent Et A Venir,* Paris, 1801, I, 52–53. In 1817, de Pradt issued a new volume, based on the earlier one, entitled *Des Colonies, Et De La Révolution Actuelle De L'Amerique,* but the passage Robinson quoted no longer appears there, nor in the English translation of it published in London in 1817.

69. Another Personal Letter

1. MS in *Rebecca Gratz Letters, Folder B* (*1822*), American Jewish Historical Society. Although this letter is placed in the 1822 folder, some of the references in it suggest that it may have been written as early as 1820.
2. Washington Irving's *The Sketch Book,* in which is found the story, "The Broken Heart," was published in New York in 1819 and in London in 1820.
3. With Napoleon's Waterloo in 1815, the reactionary Holy Alliance triumphed in Europe. For the Jews that meant often the re-establishment of the ghettoes and the withdrawal of civil rights won in the preceding quarter-century. The authorities organized, encouraged, or condoned attacks on the Jews in Würzburg, Bamberg, Carlsruhe, Frankfort, Hamburg, Mannheim, and Heidelberg, and Jews were killed, robbed, and burned in both German and Danish cities. In 1819, the murderous cry of "Hep, hep," was raised in Würzburg: HEP being the initial letters of *Hierosolyma est perdita,* Latin for "Jerusalem is destroyed." (Kohler, *AJHSP,* XXVI, 1918, pp. 33–125.)
4. On January 19, 1820, Mordecai Manuel Noah's memorial to the New York State Assembly asking for authorization to buy Grand Island in the Niagara River as a home for the Jews was referred to a Committee which reported favorably on it on January 24, 1820. The Committee report speaks of "the recent persecution of the Jews in various parts of Europe." (Isaac Goldberg, *Major Noah,* Philadelphia, 1938, p. 149.)
5. Gulian Crommelin Verplanck (1776–1870) was a prominent man of letters.
6. *Fanny,* a Byronic poem by Fitz-Greene Halleck (1790–1867), had been published in 1819 and was very popular; the Croakers were Joseph Rodman Drake (1795–1820) and Halleck, who in 1819 published witty topical anonymous verse in *The New-York Evening Post* that "caught the provincial ear of polite society" (Parrington, *op. cit.,* II, 200).
7. Benjamin Gratz married Maria Cecil Gist, who was not Jewish, on November 24, 1819; they lived in Lexington, Kentucky.

70. Consecrating a Synagogue

1. *Discourse, Delivered At The Consecration Of The Synagogue, Of The Hebrew Congregation, Mikva Israel, In The City of Savannah, Georgia, On Friday, the 10 of Ab, 5580; Corresponding With The 21st of July, 1820. By Jacob De La Motta, M. D. Savannah: . . . 1820,* pp. 6–9, 16–17.
2. Elzas, *op. cit.,* 179, 318. In 1810, De La Motta published a pamphlet in Philadelphia entitled *An investigation of the properties and effects, of the Spriraea trifoliata of Linnaeus, or Indian physic.* During the War of 1812, he served as a surgeon in the South Carolina Second Artillery from May 1, 1812 to June 1, 1814 (Heitman, *op. cit.,* I, 365). On July 2, 1816 his stature was recognized when he was called upon to deliver the funeral oration over Gershom Mendes Seixas in New York, the text later being published in pamphlet form. In 1818 he was serving as Surgeon of the Third Brigade of the New York State Infantry, 51st Regiment (*AJHSP,* XXVII, 1920, p. 398). On January 1, 1820, shortly before this discourse was delivered, he addressed the Georgia Medical Society at its anniversary meeting, presenting *An oration, on the causes of the mortality among strangers, during the late summer and fall,* which was also published as a pamphlet. He was later active in public life, holding the elected office of a Commissioner of the Poor House (1831) and acting as Assistant Commissioner of Health (1837) in Charleston.

3. MS, *The Papers of James Madison,* Vol. 67, Library of Congress.
4. Kohler, *AJHSP,* IV (1896), 219–220.
5. Kohler, *AJHSP,* XX (1911), 21. The MS of De La Motta's letter to Jefferson, which was in the possession of the American Jewish Historical Society, is now reported missing.

71. Immigration Editorially Encouraged

1. The Verein für Kultur und Wissenschaft der Juden was founded in Berlin on November 27, 1819 "to improve the social position of the Jews and to check the conversions to Christianity which at that time had alarmingly increased in the Berlin community" (*JE,* XII, 419–420). Some fifty intellectuals joined in Berlin, including Heine, and about 20 in Hamburg. In 1822–1823 the Society issued three numbers of its *Zeitschrift für die Wissenschaft des Judenthums,* edited by Leopold Zunz, but the group stopped functioning in 1823.
2. Among the most prominent financiers of the Napoleonic Wars was Nathan Mayer Rothschild (1777–1836), leader of the London Stock Exchange. Having staked vast sums on the fortunes of the reactionary Holy Alliance, Rothschild was disturbed by Napoleon's return from Elba. Napoleon's defeat at Waterloo boosted the family fortunes and opened new avenues for financial success. Turning to the foreign loan market, Rothschild and his sons, from 1816 to 1822, advanced huge sums to Prussia, France, Austria, Naples, and Russia, gaining interest as high as nine and ten per cent. Egon Caesar Corti, *The Rise of the House of Rothschild,* New York, 1928, pp. 137, 158, 187ff. The Jewish people, however, suffered renewed repressions by the Holy Alliance.
3. In 1822 Noah had been appointed Sheriff of the City of New York. To those who objected that this appointment would enable a Jew to hang a Christian sentenced to death, Noah retorted that it was a pretty poor sort of Christian who would require hanging (Goldberg, *op. cit.,* pp. 156–160). The office however having become elective, Noah was defeated because of a factional division in Tammany; to comfort him, Martin Van Buren had Noah made Grand Sachem of Tammany.
4. On October 4, 1825, this letter was printed again, in a different translation, in the Albany *Daily Advertiser,* and there it is dated January 1, 1822. (Oppenheim, *AJHSP,* XX, 1911, pp. 147–149. Oppenheim's inference, which is accepted by Goldberg, that Noah *first* released the letter to the press three years after receiving it in order to combat criticism of his Grand Island project is negated by the fact that he had already had it published in 1822.)
5. Eduard Gans (1798–1839) was a German jurist then a docent at the University of Berlin. In 1825, despite his previous hostility to apostasy, he became a Christian and rose rapidly thereafter to a full professorship at the University.

   Leopold Zunz (1794–1886) became a great figure in the renaissance of the study of Jewish history and culture that developed in the nineteenth century.

   Moses Moser (1796–1838) was a German merchant and bank cashier with an interest in mathematics and philology; he corresponded at length with his friend Heine.

72. Favorable Report

1. *Votes and Proceedings of the General Assembly of the State of Maryland, at December Session, 1822,* Annapolis, 1822, pp. 34–36. On Kennedy's motion of December 3, 1822, the following committee had been appointed to bring in the

bill: Kennedy, John L. Millard of Saint Mary's County and Henry E. Wright of Queen Anne's County.

2. James McHenry (1753–1816), Daniel of St. Thomas Jenifer (c. 1723–1790), and Daniel Carroll (1756–1829) had been three of Maryland's five delegates to the Federal Constitutional Convention, and were prominent Maryland statesmen.

3. In 1801, President Thomas Jefferson had appointed Reuben Etting (1762–1848) a United States Marshal in Maryland, thereby underlining the contradiction that a Jewish citizen of Maryland who could not hold state office could hold federal office, the duties of which were to be executed in that state.

73. Defence Against Conversion

1. This periodical appeared monthly from March, 1823 to March, 1825. At the end of Volume 1, Number 1 it is stated that "Communications, Intelligence, and Subscriptions, are respectfully solicited, and will be received by the Rev. Rabbi Mosha Chiem Mapurga, Beaver-street." In July 1822, a sum of $163.50 was given to Moses Haim Morpurgo, apparently a new arrival from Surinam, and the trustees of Shearith Israel agreed to engage him as a teacher, *AJHSP*, XXI, 1913, p. 166 and XXVII, 1920, p. 107. At the end of the second number, the name of the person to whom inquiries are to be addressed is given as Lewis Emanuel, then of 342 Pearl Street and later of 265 Broadway. Emanuel was a member of the Congregation Shearith Israel until 1825, when he became a charter member of Congregation B'nai Jeshurun (Goldstein, *op. cit.*, p. 412). The editor of *The Jew* was Solomon Henry Jackson. Born in England, Jackson had come to the United States about 1787, settled in Pike County, Pennsylvania, and married Helen Miller, daughter of a Presbyterian minister. After the death of his wife, Jackson came to New York City, where he established himself in the 1820s as the first Jewish printer in the city, handling almost all of the synagogue printing. He raised his five children as Jews; four married Jews, the fifth, Eliza, marrying Dr. Peter Donovan, who embraced Judaism. In addition to editing *The Jew,* Jackson translated and published an English and Hebrew Prayer Book in 1826 and issued the first American edition of the Passover *Hagada* in English and Hebrew in 1837. He was one of those seceding from Shearith Israel to establish B'nai Jeshurun in 1825, and he was active in forming Anshe Chesed in 1828 and Shaarey Zedek in 1839. He died about 1847. (*UJE*, VI, 4; Grinstein, *op. cit.*, 218.)

2. In 1820 there had been published *Israel Vindicated; Being A Refutation Of The Calumnies Propagated Respecting The Jewish Nation: In Which The Objects And Views Of The American Society for Ameliorating the Condition of the Jews, Are Investigated. By An Israelite.* New-York: Published by Abraham Collins. Library card catalogues give the author's name as George Houston (who in 1822 became the editor of the literary weekly, *The Minerva*). Among other things, Houston quotes M. M. Noah's discourse at the consecration of the new synagogue of Shearith Israel, April 18, 1818, in which Noah objected to pulpit attacks on Jews and attempts at conversion. Jackson's periodical, *The Jew,* is the second known Jewish reaction to the American Society for Ameliorating the Condition of the Jews, and was evoked particularly by the appearance, in January 1823, of its organ, *Israel's Advocate; Or The Restoration Of The Jews Contemplated And Urged,* as a monthly magazine. *Israel's Advocate* continued until 1827. Collins later became a charter member of B'nai Jeshurun.

3. Isaac Orobio (c. 1620–1687) was born in Portugal of Marrano parents, became

a teacher of metaphysics at the University of Salamanca and then practised medicine in Seville. Denounced to the Inquisition as a Jew, he spent three years in a dungeon and was subjected to torture; denying the charges, he was released and exiled from Spain. He migrated to Toulouse, where he became professor of medicine at the University, but in 1666 he went to Amsterdam and openly professed Judaism. He conducted public discussion on Christianity with the Dutch preacher Philipp von Limborch, and published a work attacking Spinoza's ethics in 1684.

Yom-Tob ben Solomon Lipmann-Mülhausen was imprisoned together with several other Jews on August 16, 1399 in Austria on the charge of a convert to Christianity named Peter that they had insulted Christianity in their writings. The accusations were refuted but, on August 22, 1400, 77 of the Jews were killed, and three more were executed on September 11, 1400. Lipmann alone escaped execution. He was an active controversialist, having mastered Latin and studied the New Testament, which was unusual for Jewish Talmudists at the time. Christians published several works in reply to his.

David Levi (1742–1801) was an English Hebraist, shoemaker, hatter, printer, and synagogue poet, who translated the Hebrew prayers into English (1789–1793), published a Hebrew dictionary and grammar, and answered pamphlets on the Jews written by the English scientist and philosopher, Joseph Priestley, as well as Paine's "Age of Reason."

4. On December 30, 1816, The American Society for Evangelizing the Jews was formed. When Joseph S. C. F. Frey (1771–1850), a German-Jewish convert and missionary, went to Albany to obtain a charter for the organization, objection was made to the words "colonizing and evangelizing" and Frey substituted "meliorating" for them. The charter was granted April 15, 1820. Some very distinguished Americans were officers of the Society, including Elias Boudinot (1740–1821), formerly president of the Continental Congress, John Quincy Adams, then Secretary of State, William Phillips, Lieutenant Governor of Pennsylvania, and Rev. Dr. Jeremiah Day, President of Yale College. Levi Lincoln, Jefferson's Attorney-General, was president of the Worcester County Auxiliary in 1824. In that year, there were more than 200 branches from Maine to Georgia. Yet the Society succeeded in making very few converts in several decades. (*Constitution Of The American Society For Ameliorating The Condition Of The Jews; With An Address From The Hon. Elias Boudinot,* New York, 1820; *The First Report Of . . . ,* New York, 1823; Lee M. Friedman, *The American Society for Meliorating the Condition of the Jews, and Joseph S. C. F. Frey, Its Missionary,* Boston, 1925; but note that Mr. Friedman errs in stating that *Israel's Advocate,* the Society's organ, had a circulation of 20,000, for the figure should be 2,000, according to *The Second Report of . . . ,* Princeton, 1824, p. 20.)
5. In 1822, "Ashkenazic immigrant members of Shearith Israel" had founded the Hebrew Benevolent Society, *Meshibat Nefesh* (Grinstein, *op. cit.,* p. 145).

74. Maryland Memorial

1. Aaron Baroway, "The Cohens of Maryland," *Maryland Historical Magazine,* XVIII (1923), 366–369. The text in Altfeld (*op. cit.,* 28–31) differs only insignificantly with reference to six marks of punctuation, although Blau strangely calls it a "somewhat garbled version" (*op. cit.,* 233n).
2. *Votes and Proceedings of the General Assembly of the State of Maryland, at December Session, 1823,* Annapolis, 49. Baroway, *op. cit.,* 366, ascribed the drafting of the petition to Cohen, although Hartogensis, *AJHSP,* XXV, 1917,

p. 95n, names Solomon Etting as the author of all the petitions presented to the legislature, and regards him as the "moving spirit" in the struggle. Baroway asserts that Jacob I. Cohen, Jr. (1789–1869) "led the movement" (*op. cit.,* 365). Soon after the final passage of the act in 1826, both Solomon Etting and Jacob I. Cohen, Jr. were elected to the First Branch of the City Council of Baltimore.

3. *Votes and Proceedings . . . 1823,* p. 85.

4. The subsequent history of the legislation is short but exciting: in 1824, Kennedy was re-elected to the House, and again took up the issue. On the last day of the session, February 26, 1825, the bill passed by a vote of 26 to 25, with more than one third of the delegates absent; on January 5, 1826, the confirmatory act was passed by 45 to 32 (Blau, *op. cit.,* 238). As finally passed, the law required a person "professing the Jewish religion" to take a special oath subscribing "to a belief in a future state of rewards and punishments." Hartogensis makes this pointed comment on the limitations on religious freedom still operative even under the new law: "Citizens unwilling to avow a belief in Christianity, or being Jews, unwilling to subscribe to a belief in a hereafter; non-conforming Christians and Jews, unwilling to submit or subscribe to the test, deists (like Thomas Jefferson), atheists, Pantheists, Moslems, Buddhists, and Brahmins were excluded from office. This is still the law of Maryland [in 1917]." (*Op. cit.,* 98–99.) He also points out that the law preventing a Negro from testifying against a white Christian was amended on January 23, 1847, at the instance of Dr. Joshua I. Cohen, so as to apply to all white persons, including Jews (*ibid.,* 101). Thus the Jew gained a right, but the Negro lost one. Elsewhere Hartogensis has noted that it was not until 1927 that Jews could in full legality be married "outside of the Christian Church," that the Blasphemy Act of 1924 provides six months' imprisonment and $100 fine or both for anyone denying the divinity of Christ and the Holy Trinity, and that many other discriminations on account of religion persist ("Wherein Maryland Is Not a Free State," *The Debunker,* IX, Jan. 1929, pp. 81–83).

75. Beginnings of Reform Judaism

1. Moise, *op. cit.,* 52–59. This volume contains all the pertinent major documents connected with the history of this Charleston Reform movement.

2. Abraham Moise (1799–1869) was very active in the Reform movement, Vice-President of the Society in 1827 and President from 1828 to 1832. That he drafted the memorial is noted in his own handwriting, "written by Abraham Moise," in his own copy of the rare volume, *The Constitution of the Reformed Society of Israelites, for Promoting True Principles of Judaism according to Its Purity and Spirit. Founded in Charleston, South-Carolina, 16th of January, 1825. Charleston: Printed by B. Levy, a member of the Society. 1825.* The Appendix contains the Memorial and the notation of authorship. I am indebted to Mr. L. C. Moise for making this volume available to me.

3. Sections of the Pentateuch read in regular order each Sabbath during the course of the year.

4. It is significant that this Charleston movement was directly influenced by the beginnings of Reform Judaism in Europe, where it was one of the results among the Jewish middle classes of the tide of emancipation from feudal restrictions that rose with the egalitarian ideals of the French Revolution. In Holland, in 1796, the Amsterdam congregation Adath Jeshurun shortened its

services and introduced sermons in Dutch. During the Napoleonic occupation of Westphalia, the first Reform temple was dedicated at Seesen, July 17, 1810, under the leadership of Israel Jacobson. When the occupation ended, he transferred his activities to Berlin, where he established a private Reform temple in 1815; conflict with the orthodox rabbis ensued, and led to a victory for the rabbis when the Prussian government outlawed such services in a decree, December 9, 1823. The Hamburg Reform Temple was dedicated October 18, 1818, and a branch was opened in Leipsic in 1820.

5. In the prayer book that the Society developed, there were omitted the declaration of belief in a personal Messiah, in the bodily resurrection, in the restoration of the sacrificial cult, and in the return to Palestine. (Barnett A. Elzas, ed., *The Sabbath Service and Miscellaneous Prayers, Adopted by the Reform Society of Israelites, . . .* , New York, 1916; David Philipson, *The Reform Movement in Judaism,* rev. ed., New York, 1931, p. 331; Kaufman Kohler, "A Revaluation of Reform Judaism," *Yearbook, Central Conference of American Rabbis,* XXXIV, 1924, p. 225; Beryl Harold Levy, *Reform Judaism in America. A Study in Religious Adaptation,* New York, 1933, p. 5.)

6. The list of names of the forty-seven signers is not extant. The names of forty-four members of the Society appended to the Constitution are given in Moise, *op. cit.,* 71–72.

76. Appeal for Congregational Assistance

1. Philipson, *AJHSP,* X (1902), 98–99.

2. The Congregation had been definitely organized on January 18, 1824, almost seven years after Joseph Jonas, the first Jew known to have settled in Cincinnati, came there on March 8, 1817.

3. Samuel Joseph (born, England, died, 1826) was a "Distiller of Cordials" in Cincinnati, to which he came in 1822.

   Joseph Jonas (born May 5, 1792, Exeter, England; died May 4, 1869, Spring Hill, near Mobile, Ala.) was a watchmaker and silversmith. He founded the congregation and served it for many years, being president as late as 1843–1844 and 1847–1848. In 1860–1861 he was a Democratic member of the Ohio Senate and "placed himself on the side of slavery" when the Civil War began (Barnett R. Brickner, *The Jewish Community of Cincinnati,* unpublished dissertation, University of Cincinnati, 1933, p. 351).

   In New York, Joseph Jonas had married Rachel Seixas, while his brother Abraham had married Lucia Orah Seixas, who died June 17, 1825, shortly before this letter was written (Philipson, *AJHSP,* VIII, 1900, p. 48).

4. David Israel Johnson (born, England, died, 1842) came to this country in 1818, went to Indiana, and settled permanently in Cincinnati in 1820; he founded a family active in Ohio civil affairs for three generations.

   Phineas Moses (born, England, c. 1798; died, June 21, 1896) followed his brother Solomon from England to Cincinnati in 1822; the brothers were partners as merchants. When the Congregation was established, Phineas Moses was elected one of the two Gabayim. (David Philipson, *The Oldest Jewish Congregation in the West, Bene Israel, Cincinnati,* Cincinnati, 1924, p. 10n.)

5. Financial contributions came from the congregations in Charleston and Philadelphia, from individual Jews in New Orleans and Barbados, W. I., and from 52 Christians in Cincinnati who each contributed $25.

77. New Orleans' First Congregation, 1828

1. *Acts Passed At the Second Session Of The Eighth Legislature Of The State Of Louisiana*, New Orleans, 1828, No. 84, parallel texts in English and French, pp. 162–165.

2. *The Asmonean*, August 2, 1850, Vol. 2, p. 118.

3. Either the State Printer or the Legislative Clerk allowed certain errors in the names to appear: Dainels should be *Daniels*, Plautz should be *Plotz*, S. S. Solis should be *J. S. Solis*, Bernard junior should be *Bernard LeJeune* (*The Constitution and Bye-Laws, of the Israelite Congregation, of Shanarai-Chasset, (Gates of Mercy,) of the City of New-Orleans, State of Louisiana. Founded February 2d, A. M. 5588, By Jacob S. Solis, of the State of New-York, December 20th, 1827. New-Orleans: Printed By F. Delaup, Printer of the Congregation. 1828.* Parallel texts in English and French.) Bernard LeJeune, on January 8, 1830, was one of the incorporators of the Cincinnati Congregation Bene Israel (David Philipson, "The Jewish Pioneers of the Ohio Valley," in *AJHSP*, VIII, 1900, p. 51). Jacob da Silva Solis (1780–1829) came to the United States from his birthplace, England, in 1803, and was engaged in business with his brother Daniel (1784–1867) in New York City, Wilmington, Delaware, and elsewhere. In addition to helping to found the New Orleans congregation, he was an authorized solicitor of funds for the Cincinnati congregation Bene Israel (his credential is in the American Jewish Historical Society, and for permission to cite it I am indebted to Miss Emily Solis-Cohen).

4. The restriction of the congregation to "white Israelites" does not necessarily imply that there were Negro Jews in New Orleans. The restriction seems to be conventional for the time and place: thus "An act to incorporate a French Evangelical Church Society in the city of New Orleans," passed March 21, 1828, names the incorporators, and adds, "their associates, and all such free white persons . . ." The list of the members of the congregation, as given in *The Constitution and Bye-Laws* . . . is here reproduced for the first time, together with the list of Jewish and non-Jewish contributors. The officers were: Manis (Menahem) Jacobs, president; Aaron Daniels, vice-president; A. Plotz, Junior Warden; A. Green, Junior Warden; A. Philips, Junior Warden; Isaac Philips, treasurer; A. Audler, secretary. There were 28 members: Jacob S. Solis, Bernard Lejeune, Jacob Myers, L. S. Levy, David Lewis, Moses J. Hart, Ralph Jacobs, A. P. Levy, Myers J. Ellis, J. La Salle, Solomon Hunt, L. Jones, Joseph Solomons, E. Stern, Abs. Goldsmith, Nathan. Hart, A. H. Dejong, A. S. Emmonny, Samuel Jacobs, Marx Myers, Levy Prince, Solomon Ferth, Lewis Kokernot, Marton P. Levy, Charles Myers, Aaron Kirkham, Abr. Block, Doct. Z. Florance. There are 33 "Israelite Donors" who are not members: Judah Turo, Daniel Goodman, Edward Gottschalk, Jacobs L. Workum, Souza, sen., Souza, jnr., Hyam Harris, A. H. Harris, Moses Harris, Jacob L. Florance, Wm. Florance, H. Florance, L. Jacobs, Bendict [sic] Solomons, L. Solomons, Joseph De Pass, Samuel De Pass, William Hardcastle, M. Joseph, D. Kokernot, Israel Solomons, L. B. Baruck, Daniel Depass, John Marks, L. Morange, L. Jacobs, jr., S. Sacerdote, Edward Engelhart, S. Silverberger, A. Lange, Isaac Lyons, M. Milone, Myer Barnett, senior. (L. Jacobs, Joseph De Pass and Samuel De Pass appear among the incorporators in the charter of the second New Orleans congregation, The Dispersed of Judah, dated June 4, 1847.) Some of the Israelite donors apparently did not live in New Orleans (Letter from Manis Jacobs, June 4, 1828, to Jacob S. Solis, Louisville, Ky., in the American Jewish Historical Society, in which Solis is asked to give copies of the Con-

stitution and Bye-laws to some of these donors, "near Louisville.") There were also donors "not Israelites": George W. Morgan, W. M. F. Saul, J. H. Holland, J. J. Mercier, J. Peillon, Jno. R. Grymes, L. Pilié, Joshua Lewis, John Woolfolk, John M. Baity, Carlile Pollock. It should be noted that of the seven persons named in the charter itself, none appears in John Adems Paxton, *The New-Orleans Directory and Register* for 1822. That the list of members and donors given above does not exhaust the Jews then living in New Orleans is suggested by the fact that this directory was printed by Benjamin Levy & Co., Levy having lived in New Orleans since at least 1811, when he was operating a bookstore there.

5. On March 5, 1853, "the congregation reincorporated by enrollment of a perpetual charter," the first charter having been for only twenty-five years (*Inventory of the Church and Synagogue Archives of Louisiana; Jewish Congregations and Organizations.* Prepared by the Louisiana Historical Records Survey, Division of Community Service Programs, Works Projects Administration, La., 1941, p. 19.)

6. Seventh and concluding day of Sukkot (Feast of Tabernacles), marking the culmination of the celebrations.

7. The Bye-Laws contain the following articles bearing upon burial: Article 19: "All deluded women (*femmes perverties*) that have not reformed previous to their death, shall be buried in a place appropriated for that purpose, together with persons that have committed suicide." Article 21: "Any Israelite member being married to a strange [non-Jewish] woman, shall have the privilege of enterring the said wife in the walls of the burial ground, in a section of ground situated on the south-west corner, . . . It is to be well understood, and forcibly regarded (*observer soigneusement*), that they shall be buried after the Israelite custom." Article 22: "There shall be no service administered in the said burial ground, that varies from the Israelite order and all prayers offered shall be after the custom of the Portuguese Israelites." (This article contradicts the frequently repeated notion that this congregation followed the German ritual.) Article 23: "All children born of an Israelite, and not having abjured the religion of the father, shall be entitled to burial." Article 31: "All adultresses shall be buried apart; all Israelites [sic] females married or have been married to strange men, and have not acknowledged a religion opposed to that of the Israelites, at their request can be admitted in our burial ground, provided they pay a sum demanded (*fixée*) by a committee for that purpose." Article 35: "Members married to strange women, having a desire to be buried next to their wives or children, the request, in all cases, shall be granted, by informing the President of the same in writing, who shall have full power to act on all occasions."

78. Greeting the French Revolution, 1830

1. Myer Moses, *Full Account of the Celebration of the Revolution in France, in the City of New-York, on the 25th November, 1830: Being the Forty-Seventh Anniversary of an Event that Restored our Citizens to their Homes and to the Enjoyment of their Rights and Liberties,* [New York, 1830], pp. 3–6. November 25th is the anniversary of the British evacuation of New York in 1783.

2. Elizabeth Brett White, *American Opinion of France,* New York, 1927, pp. 85ff.

3. Joseph Dreyfous, an importer, was a charter member of B'nai Jeshurun in 1825 (Goldstein, *op. cit.*, p. 412; [Thomas] *Longworth's American Almanac, New-York Register, and City Directory . . . 1830,* p. 239).

There were two Daniel Jacksons in New York in 1830, but it was the Daniel Jackson of the First Ward who is meant here. He was a merchant, first president of the Hebrew Benevolent Society in 1822, and helped establish B'nai Jeshurun in 1825. (*Ibid.*, 347; Grinstein, *op. cit.*, 146; Goldstein, *op. cit.*, 52–55, 384.) His daughter, Rebecca Esther Jackson, married M. M. Noah on November 28, 1827. Solomon Henry Jackson was Daniel Jackson's son. (Goldberg, *op. cit.*, 219.)

Dr. Peixotto, born in Amsterdam, son of Rev. Moses L. M. Peixotto, was graduated from Columbia College in 1816, and became a prominent physician and community leader; he died in 1843.

Myer Moses (1779–1833) of Charleston had been a member of the South Carolina Society for the Promotion of Domestic Arts and Manufactories in 1809, a member of the State Legislature in 1810, a Commissioner of Free Schools in 1811, a Director of the Planters and Mechanics' Bank the same year, a captain of state troops in the War of 1812, a Commissioner of Public Schools in 1823, and a merchant throughout. About 1825, when Charleston was declining in economic importance, he left for New York, where he also achieved distinction both in Jewish and general community affairs. (Elzas, *The Jews of South Carolina*, 143–144; *AJHSP*, XXVII, 1920, p. 311.)

4. John D. Jackson, who operated a lottery-office, was a charter member of B'nai Jeshurun and clerk of the congregation, 1830–1831 (*Longworth, op. cit.*, 348; Goldstein, *op. cit.*, 382, 384; Moses, *op. cit.*, 7–11, 12, 15, 16, 18, 51, 55, 137, 144, 145).

5. The Bourbon émigrés were allied with the Catholic priests. During the course of the 1830 Revolution, when the supporters of the Bourbon Charles X used the Church of Saint-Germain l'Auxerrois for their political ends, the people sacked the church (*Encyclopaedia Britannica,* 1947 ed., IX, 646).

6. "The workers, driven to the barricades by the deliberate closing of the workshops," fought the troops for three days and won (*ibid.*). But despite the republican desires of the workers, the liberal bourgeoisie installed a young Bourbon, Louis Philippe, as king, and he crushed the workers' movements until the 1848 revolution led to the Second Republic.

7. The Belgian movement for independence from Holland, to which England had delivered it in 1815 as a bulwark against France, was stimulated by the July Revolution. The revolution in Brussels, which began on August 25, 1830, was supported by the provinces, and led to the proclamation of independence on October 4, 1830.

8. On November 29, 1830, four days after the New York demonstration, the Polish insurrection began, and war between Poland and Russia lasted until September 1831 before the Poles were defeated. The insurrection, however, interfered with the plans of Czar Nicholas I to use Polish troops against the French and Belgian revolutions.

9. Lafayette (1757–1834), when he revisited our country, July 1824 to September 1825, created an occasion for the expression of American democratic hostility to the Bourbons and support to the oppressed people of France (White, *op. cit.*, 79–85). Lafayette was active in the July Revolution and took command of the National Guard. Louis Philippe later turned the National Guard into the force that suppressed the workers.

10. It was at Jemappes that the French Revolutionary Army, on November 6, 1792, defeated the Austrian invaders and won great prestige. The battle of Lützen, in Saxony, was fought during the Thirty Years War, on November 16, 1632; Gustavus Adolphus led his Swedish army to victory over the Austrians under

Wallenstein. At Bautzen, in Saxony, on May 20–21, 1813, Napoleon I had defeated the armies of the Russians and Prussians.

11. The contradiction between democratic ideals of equality, expressed in the most sweeping fashion, and the slave system in the United States was apparent then only to the opponents of slavery and the abolitionists. Otherwise, Southern slave-owners hailed revolutions elsewhere with indifference to logical contradictions. In Charleston, for instance, Myer Moses had been one of the democratic, forward-looking civic leaders. Yet he was a slave-dealer. The following is the full text of an advertisement of his in *The Southern Patriot,* Charleston, August 14, 1815:

Sales at Auction by Myer Moses

On TUESDAY, 22d August, at 10 o'clock, will be exposed to public sale, at the North side of the Exchange, the following

VALUABLE PROPERTY.

That well settled FARM, on Charleston Neck, situated but one mile from the Lines, fronting on King and Russel-streets. On the premises is a comfortable Farm House, two very convenient Negro Houses, containing eight Rooms, with fire places, Carriage and Cart House, Stables, Seed House, an excellent Dairy, and a Well of superior Water, completely covered in. The Farm is in the highest state of Cultivation, and contains Eight Acres.—The growing value of property so near the City and situated on the King-street Road, would render this purchase an object to any one, who would hold it for a few years.

Should a Sale not be effected of the Farm entire, a part of it will then be divided into Lots, in manner following, and sold seperately [sic]:—say Eight LOTS, fronting on King street, of 53 feet front, and 200 feet deep; and a FARM fronting on Russell street, (with all the Buildings, &c as above mentioned) of 613 feet deep on the South line, and 463 feet on the north line, by 368 feet front. With the Farm will be given, two good CARTS and TACKLE, Carpenters TOOLS, and Farming Utensils, consisting of every necessary Article.

At the same time will be Sold, THE FOLLOWING VALUABLE SLAVES

BOOMA, (an African) about 22 years of age, an excellent jobbing carpenter, and a prime field hand, has been employ'd several years as a market man, in selling vegetables, &c.

MARIA, (a country born) about 22 or 23 years old, an excellent market wench, speaks French remarkably well, is a plain cook and tolerable washer, but prefers the attendance of market, or working in the field, and is a prime field hand.

SARAH, (a country born) about 20 years old, a prime field hand.

BEN, (an African) about 18 years old, a prime field hand and a good boatman.

ANDREW, (an African) age unknown, a prime field hand, possesses an uncommon good disposition.

And a Family, consisting of,

PHILLIS, (a country born) a cook, washer, ironer, &c.

JOHN, (ditto) her son, a mullatto boy, about 16 or 17 years old, a smart house servant, understands the management of horses, drives a chair, &c.

ROBERT, (ditto) her son, a mullatto boy, about 5 years old.

This Family will be sold together or seperate [sic].

Conditions—For the Lots and Farm, one half cash, balance payable in 12 months, by Note with two approved endorsers; for the Negroes, cash, or Notes with two approved endorsers, at 60 days, with discount added.

☞ Indisputable titles will be given, and the Negroes warranted sound and agreeable to description.

August 3.

79. Declaration on Politics

1. The names of the signers are not known.
2. The Union and State Rights Party and the Free Trade and State Rights Party, generally called the Union Party and the State Rights Party because of the difference of emphasis, were engaged in a sharp struggle when this letter was printed. The issue was the high protective tariff schedule adopted in 1828 and amended in 1832. The agricultural south, in which the development of manufactures was being limited by slavery, opposed protective tariffs. The Union Party wanted to fight the tariff by constitutional methods; the State Rights Party pressed for a declaration of Nullification by South Carolina and other states, thereby making federal law inoperative unless implemented by state approval. Early in September, 1832, the State Rights ticket had won the Charleston city elections by a majority of 160, but not without using dubious and rough means. The state elections occurred early in October. It was in connection with these elections that this statement was issued. Jews were active in both parties. In the Union Party there were such figures as Nathan Hart, Chapman Levy (1787–1850), Franklin J. Moses, Abraham Moise, Jacob De La Motta, Joshua Lazarus, and M. C. Myers of Georgetown. A leader in the State Rights Party was Myer M. Cohen, who served as Secretary of the State Rights and Free Trade Convention, held in Charleston, February 22 and 25, 1832, which came out expressly for nullification. (Also present at this convention were Myer Jacobs of Beaufort, Aaron Lopez of Winyaw, and Benjamin Hart of Lexington, the Jewish identity of the last two being uncertain.) (Chauncey Samuel Boucher, *The Nullification Controversy in South Carolina,* Chicago, 1916, pp. 67, 78–79, 202, 204, 205n–206n; Elzas, *op. cit.,* 206; *Proceedings of the State Rights & Free Trade Convention . . . ,* Charleston, 1832, pp. 3, 4, 11.)
3. Whatever the reason for his selection, Philip Cohen, who was prominent in the State Rights Party, was elected to the State Legislature from Charleston in the October 1832 elections. Philip Cohen had been a member of the Charleston Board of Health, 1819–1823, and had served as Commissioner of the Marine Hospital since 1826. (Elzas, *op. cit.,* 143, 189; *Legislative Proceedings, General Assembly, South Carolina,* Columbia, 1832–1833, *passim.)*
4. The State Rights Party won the elections in the State by a popular vote of about 23,000 to 17,000. On October 22, 1832, a special session of the newly elected legislature called a state convention for November 19, 1832 to act on the tariff issue. At this Nullification Convention, there were four Jews: Philip Cohen from Charleston, Myer Jacobs from Beaufort, Chapman Levy from Kershaw and Philip Phillips (1807–1884) from Chesterfield. The vote in favor of Nullification was 136 to 26. Cohen and Jacobs voted for nullification; Levy and Phillips voted against it. (*Journal of the Convention of the People of South Carolina: Assembled at Columbia on the 19th November, 1832, and again, on the 11th March, 1833.* Columbia, 1833, pp. 4, 5, 21, 23–24; for votes on later developments, see pp. 103–104, 117, 119, 120.) President Andrew Jackson's firm statement that he would use force if necessary to maintain the law, and the compromise tariff of 1833, which provided for biennial reductions until 1842, temporarily averted the crisis.

80. Death of an Atheist

1. This obituary takes up almost the entire first page, which is heavily bordered in black. *The Free Enquirer, Third Series* was owned and edited, beginning with the issue of January 5, 1833, by H. D. Robinson, who was simultaneously

editing another freethinking periodical, *The Comet,* and who was to publish his translation of D'Holbach's *The System of Nature* in 1835. Cohen's full name was Charles Cleomenes Coleman Cohen (*The Free Enquirer,* March 9, 1834), although the New York City Directory listed him as Cleomenes C. C. Cohen, "analytical and manufacturing chemist, 34 Hamilton," living at 72 Catharine Street. I am indebted to Mr. Eugene L. Schwaab of Brookline, Mass., for calling this obituary to my attention, and to the New-York Historical Society for permission to reproduce these items.

2. Hyman Hurwitz (1770–1844), a Polish Talmudist who had come to England, had established The Highgate Academy, "a seminary for Jewish youth," in 1799. In the 1820's he became professor of Hebrew in University College, London. (*JE,* VI, 507.)

3. Michael Faraday (1791–1867), the great English chemist and physicist, and William Thomas Brande (1788–1866), "the leading chemist of the metropolis" in the 1820's, lectured together in 1825 at the Royal Institution in London. Brande's "A Manual of Chemistry" was an authoritative work for a long time. (*DNB,* II, 1124–1126.)

4. Voltaire (1694–1778) and Paul Henri Thiry D'Holbach (1723–1789) were French rationalists and materialists. D'Holbach was a militant atheist. David Hume (1711–1776), the Scottish philosopher, challenged the traditional religious bases of morality by developing, in ethics, a social utilitarianism that judged conduct in terms of the welfare of society.

5. Johann Gaspar Spurzheim (1776–1832) was a follower of and collaborator with Franz Joseph Gall (1758–1828), the founder of phrenology. In 1826, Spurzheim published, in London, *The Anatomy of the Brain* and *Phrenology, in Connection with the Study of Physiognomy,* followed later by other works. In 1832 and thereafter several of his books were published in the United States. Early phrenological investigations were incorrectly attacked as materialist because of their emphasis on the material brain, and some were "prohibited as subversive of religion and morality." (*Encyclopaedia of Social Sciences,* "Gall," by A. A. Roback, VI, 548.)

6. On December 9, 1832, he was to lecture at Concert Hall "on the Definition and History of Chemistry" (*The Free Enquirer,* December 8, 1832). On November 24, 1833, he was one of four men (George Houston was another) who debated at Tammany Hall on the subject, "Are the events of the world controuled [sic] by an overruling Providence, or are they the effects of inherent natural principles?" A summary of Cohen's remarks is in *ibid.,* December 8, 1833.

7. Probably some of the writings were anonymous; the only signed item identified is the one on Abner Kneeland (for which see the next document). In *The Free Enquirer* for June 29 and October 5, 1833, there are two articles, "Religion of the Jews," of which the anonymous author states that "much information [was] furnished us by our friend C. C. Cohen."

8. Both Christian and Jewish charity were regarded with suspicion, since Cohen's associates in atheism did not want his children to "be educated in the principles of Jews or Gentiles." Two meetings were held to raise funds, one at Concert Hall and one at Tammany Hall. The editor of *The Free Enquirer* noted: "It is intended to apply the amount collected in establishing Mrs. Cohen in a respectable business with which she is familiar, where we trust the friends of the deceased and Liberals in general will extend their patronage. By this means it is hoped she will be released from the necessity of returning to the Jewish members of her family, in which event her offspring would be inevitably

educated with the ridiculous prejudices and doctrines of that persuasion." (March 9, 1834.)

9. In the issue of February 23, 1834, the names of twelve apothecaries are listed, with their addresses, as a committee appealing for donations. Of the list, the name of Lewis Feuchtwanger, 377 Broadway, may be that of a Jew, but I have not been able to establish that identity.

10. After two juries disagreed, Kneeland's conviction was upheld finally in 1838, and he had to serve sixty days in prison. After serving his sentence, Kneeland left Massachusetts for Iowa, where he founded Salubria, a Free Enquirers' colony. Despite the equivocation that Cohen points to, Kneeland's name is still highly honored by historians of free thought.

11. February 28, 1834, p. 2, col. 3. The article is unsigned, but the paper was edited by Noah and there is no reason to doubt the ascription of the piece to him.

12. In commenting on this statement, *The Free Enquirer* later in the same article declared: "We, on the contrary, know, in this country alone, at least five or six most intelligent men, originally Jews, 'well-educated in the Jewish faith,' who are now professed and fearless Atheists, and who cannot believe in 'a first great cause,' because they well know that this belief involves the contradiction of a cause existing *before the first*. In other countries, we have known many more; and altho' our acquaintance with persons of the Hebrew faith has never been extensive, we have reason to believe that as many of that persuasion have become Atheists as of any other. . . ."

81. Agricultural Project

1. *Address and Articles of the Association* צעירי הצאן *to their Brethren in the United States. New-York. 5597. Lyons Scrapbook I,* item 130c. In addition to the address, there is a Preamble and twenty articles, which are adequately summarized in Grinstein, *op. cit.*, 116–119, except for his omission of the provision that the proceedings are to be kept in "English and in Jewish German" (Yiddish). This project is not mentioned in the otherwise extensive treatment by Leo Shpall, "Jewish Agricultural Colonies in the United States," *Agricultural History,* XXIV, July, 1950, pp. 120–146.

2. Harold Underwood Faulkner, *American Economic History,* New York, 1943, fifth edition, 168.

3. T. W. Donovan was the Clerk of Anshe Chesed; the Treasurer of the Association Zeire Hazon was W. Frank, and the Managers were Simon Cohen and P. Americk. Donovan, Cohen, and Americk are not in the New York city directory for 1837; there is a William Frank, "saddler, 263 Rivington," but whether he is the W. Frank of this association has not yet been ascertained. When the Address was received by Anshe Chesed, the trustees invited the congregations Shearith Israel and B'nai Jeshurun to a meeting of the trustees of the three synagogues. The former did not reply to the invitation; the latter accepted, but did not come to the meeting. (Grinstein, *op. cit.*)

82. Aid the Needy Immigrants!

1. *Lyons' Scrapbook III,* item 129, American Jewish Historical Society.

2. Grinstein, *op. cit.*, 469.

3. The Hebrew Benevolent Society (*Meshibat Nefesh*), founded in 1822, and the

Hebrew Mutual Benefit Society (*Hebrah Gemilut Hesed*), founded in 1826 and still in existence.

4. At that time there were three Congregations in the city: Shearith Israel, B'nai Jeshurun (founded 1825), and Anshe Chesed (founded 1828). (*Ibid.*, 472.)
5. Samuel N. Judah (died, 1849) had been a Trustee of Shearith Israel in 1834 and 1835, and was active in the Society for the Education of Poor Children and the Relief of Indigent Persons of the Jewish Persuasion (*Hebrah Hinukh Nearim Veezrat Evyonim*), founded in 1827. (*Ibid.*, 148–149, 552.)
6. Moses L. Moses was then President of Shearith Israel, an office he held twelve times (*AJHSP,* XXI, 1913, p. 212). He was also active in *Hebra Hased Vaamet* (founded 1802), a burial society for the poor (Grinstein, *op. cit.*, 547). He was a broker at 52 Wall Street (Longworth, *op. cit.*, 1837, pp. 450–451).

   Abraham Mitchell, a merchant, was then President of B'nai Jeshurun, an office he held for many terms. He had served in the War of 1812, and had been active in the Hebrew Benevolent Society. He died in 1856. (*Ibid.*, 440; Goldstein, *op. cit.*, 384, 90; Grinstein, *op. cit.*, 552.)

   Solomon J. Joseph is not in the City Directory, nor on the lists of members of Shearith Israel or B'nai Jeshurun.

   Morland Micholl, who sold hosiery and gloves at 291 Broadway, was then Treasurer of B'nai Jeshurun and a leader in the Hebrew Benevolent Society (Longworth, *op. cit.*, 434; Goldstein, *op. cit.*, 384, 70).

   For Israel B. Kursheedt, see the Index.

   Tobias I. Tobias, a merchant, was an active figure in Shearith Israel, in the *Hebra Hased Vaamet* and in the Society for the Education of Poor Children (Longworth, *op. cit.*, 612, *AJHSP,* XXI, 1913, p. 168; Grinstein, *op. cit.*, 547, 552).

   Eleazer S. Lazarus, a distiller, was a leader in Shearith Israel (Longworth, *op. cit.*, 377; *AJHSP,* XXI, 1913, pp. 168, 212).

   Myer Levy, of Shearith Israel, had an office at 55 Wall Street (*ibid.*, 214; Longworth, *op. cit.*, 382).

   Naphtali Phillips (1773–1870), a revenue officer, was then the Clerk of Shearith Israel, after having served fourteen times as President and five times as Trustee of the Congregation. He had helped found the *Hebra Hased Vaamet.* (*Ibid.*, 492; Grinstein, *op. cit.*, 78, 542, 547; *AJHSP,* XXI, 1913, pp. 212, 168.)

83. The Damascus Blood Libel

1. *General Records of the Department of State. Consular Despatches, Beirut, volume 1.* The National Archives, Washington, D. C. I am greatly indebted to Mr. Roscoe R. Hill, Chief, Division of State Department Archives, for locating these documents for me and for supplying me with valuable information about the American consul at Beirut.
2. In April 1947 the Pioneer News Service, P. O. Box 435, Chicago, Ill. was selling a pamphlet by Arnold S. Leese, formerly published in London in 1938, in which the blood libel is repeated and the Damascus case is invoked as "evidence." (Moshe Backal, "Anti-Semites in America Spread the Vile Blood-Libel," in Yiddish, *Morning Freiheit,* April 5, 1947, p. 5.) On September 23, 1928, in Massena, St. Lawrence County, New York, Rabbi Berel Brennglass was interrogated at the suggestion of Mayor W. Gilbert Hawes by state trooper Corporal H. M. McCann, as to what the Jews of Massena knew about four year old Barbara Griffith, who had disappeared the preceding afternoon, and who, it was implied, might have been sacrificed by the Jews on the eve of the Day of

Atonement. (*AJYB*, 5690, 1929–30, pp. 348–352; *The New York Times*, October 3, 5, 6, 7, 8, 1928.) In June, 1935 in New York City, Raymond J. Healy and Ernest F. Elmhurst were found guilty of distributing a tract with a falsified quotation from the Talmud about ritual murder of gentiles; Dr. Joshua Bloch, Chief, Jewish Division of the New York Public Library, testified that a correct translation described the proper kosher slaughter of chickens and food animals. (*The New York Times*, June 8, 1935; interview with Dr. Bloch, April 2, 1947.) German anti-Semitism made continual use of the blood libel and of the Damascus case: see August Rohling, *Meine Antworten an die Rabbiner oder Fünf Briefe über den Talmudismus und das Blut-Ritual der Juden*, Prag, 1883; *Der Mord Zu Damaskus*, Marburg (Hessen), 1888. A century after the event, the Nazis were spreading wide the eleventh edition of Gerhard Utikal, *Der jüdische Ritualmord*, Berlin, 1941, with a chapter on Damascus. Utikal asserts that his original contribution to the theory on the question lies in his connecting Jewish individual ritual murders with such Jewish-Bolshevik "mass-murder" as was revealed in the French Revolution of 1789 and the Russian Revolution of 1917!

3. Originally, the Romans had accused the early Christians of drinking the blood of pagan children as part of a Christian religious ritual (Edward Gibbon, *The Decline and Fall of the Roman Empire*, Modern Library Edition, New York, 1932?, I, 452). Helpful background material on the blood accusation against Jews can be found in the article by Joseph Jacobs, *JE*, III, 260–267, by Anatol Safanov, *UJE*, II, 407–410, and in Cecil Roth, ed., *The Ritual Murder Libel and the Jew. The Report by Cardinal Lorenzo Ganganelli (Pope Clement XIV)*, London, 1934.

4. *The New-York Tribune*, July 25, 1853, letter by Karl Marx, reprinted in *The Eastern Question*, London, 1897, p. 62. Other useful background material will be found in the *Encyclopaedia Britannica* articles on "The Eastern Question," "Louis Adolphe Thiers," "Metternich," "Turkey," "Mehemet Ali," "Egypt," and "Syria." A vivid summary of the Damascus Affair is included in H. Graetz, *History of the Jews*, Philadelphia, 1895, Vol. 5; see also R. R. Madden, *Egypt and Mohammed Ali*, London, 1841, pp. 212–253; Frederick Stanley Rodkey, "Lord Palmerston and the Rejuvenation of Turkey, 1830–41," *The Journal of Modern History*, II, 1930, pp. 193, 214; Salo W. Baron, "The Jewish Question in the Nineteenth Century," *ibid.*, X, 1938, p. 62; Albert M. Hyamson, ed., *The British Consulate in Jerusalem in relation to the Jews of Palestine, 1838–1914*, London, 1939, pp. xxxvi, 2, 31–35; James Parkes, *A History of Palestine*, London, 1949, pp. 210–218.

5. Jacobs, *AJHSP*, X (1902), 120–121.

6. Thomas de Camangiano, a Sardinian, known as *il padre Tomaso*, more than sixty years old, had lived in Damascus for thirty years and was widely known as an ecclesiastic and as a practitioner of medicine. Madden (*op. cit.*, 219) states that the head of the Capuchin order did not believe the charges against the Jews and opposed the proceedings; Graetz (*op. cit.*, V, 650) reports that the missionary who replaced Father Tomaso objected to the incomprehensible tortures of the Jews.

7. All accounts agree that the French Consul, Ratti Menton, was the chief instigator of the blood libel charge, and the main propagandist of it, as well as the prime inquisitor. A French citizen of Italian birth, Ratti Menton had been in Damascus only a brief time before Father Tomaso disappeared. He had been a merchant and French consul in Sicily, which he left because of his unpopularity; when he came to Tiflis as French Consul, the Russian government

demanded his withdrawal. He was a Bourbon and "Legitimatist of the oldest and worst school." (Clipping, perhaps from the London *Times* of May 18, 1840, dated Paris, May 12, in *Lyons Scrapbook,* III, Item 6; Graetz, *op. cit.,* V, 633; S. Posener, *Adolphe Crémieux, A Biography,* Philadelphia, 1940, p. 90.) The English Consul, Wherry, accepted the blood libel and supported Ratti Menton (David Salomons, *An Account of the Recent Persecution of the Jews at Damascus* . . . London, 1840, pp. 46, 54). Only the Austrian Consul at Damascus, Merlato, after some time, denounced the activities of Ratti Menton in despatches that Metternich allowed to receive wide publication. Thirty years later, another English consul at Damascus, Sir Richard Francis Burton (1821–1890), the Orientalist and literary figure, was to accept and progagate the blood accusation and revive the Damascus libel (*The Jew The Gypsy and El Islam,* London, 1898, pp. vii, 128).

8. Those named and arrested were David Arari, his brothers and his son, Moses Abulafia, Moses Saloniki, and Joseph Laniado. Laniado died under torture; Abulafia became a convert to Mohammedanism to escape further torture. In 1840 Damascus had a Jewish community of about 10,000. So many fled that even by 1848 there were only 4,000 and by 1860 only 6,000.

9. G. M. Pieritz, a Jewish convert to Christianity who investigated the situation at Damascus itself from March 30 to the beginning of May, 1840, reported that "the tortures employed were—1st. Flogging. 2d. Soaking persons in large tanks of cold water, in their clothes. 3d. The head machine, by which the eyes are pressed out of their sockets. 4th. Tying up the tender parts, and ordering soldiers to twist and horribly dispose them into such contortions that the poor sufferers grew almost mad from pain. 5th. Standing upright for three days, without being allowed any other posture, not even to lean against the walls; and when they would fall down, are aroused up by the by-standing sentinels with their bayonets. 6th. Being dragged about in a large court by their ears, until the blood gushed out. 7th. Having thorns driven in between their nails and the flesh of fingers and toes. 8th. Having fire set to their beards, till their faces are singed." (Salomon, *op. cit.,* 46–47.)

10. Efforts on the part of Sir Moses Montefiore to have the Pope and the Vatican official in charge of the Capuchin order effect the removal of the plaque over the tomb in the Damascus Church which blamed the Jews for the killing of Tomaso were unavailing, and the plaque remained until the Church itself was burned down in anti-Christian riots in 1860.

11. Chasseaud's accompanying translation described "Lucio Ferrajo" as having lived in "the ninth century of the Christian era," and Graetz declares that the book was a three volume work in Latin, which Ratti Menton had had translated into Arabic so that Sherif Pasha, governor of Damascus, could circulate it among the Mohammedan population (*op. cit.,* V, 639). However, the author and his book are given as Lucio Ferrario and *Bibliotheca prompta* in L. H. Loewenstein, *Damascia,* Rödelheim, 1840, p. 174, and as Lucius Ferrari and *La Prompta Bibliotheca* in Áchille Laurent, *Relation Historique des Affaires de Syrie depuis 1840 jusqu'en 1842,* Paris, 1846, II, 394–398. Laurent prints what purports to be "Ferrari's" Latin translation of the Talmud with a French version accompanying each section. The facts are these: Lucio Ferraris (1687–1763), Italian ecclesiastical scholar of the Franciscan Order, published *Prompta Bibliotheca Canonica,* an eight volume canonical encyclopedia in Latin, in Bologna, 1746; this work was frequently reprinted, the latest edition being in Rome, 1895–1899. Vol. 4, p. 179 (Paris ed., 1860) contains the passage transmitted by Chasseaud; Ferraris explains that the data are taken from the work

of Sixtus of Siena. This Sixtus (1520–1569) was a Jewish convert to Christianity who became an anti-Talmudic agitator, and in 1559 helped organize the burning of some 10,000 copies of the Talmud gathered in Cremona, after having incited pogroms against Jews in various parts of Italy. The alleged excerpts from the Talmud cited by Ferraris, incidentally, do not mention the use of blood, but purport to show that the Talmud is simply an anti-Christian work. (Dr. Meyer Reinhold of Brooklyn, N. Y. helped me locate the text in Ferraris; *Enciclopedia Italiana,* Milan, 1932, XV, 57; *The Catholic Encyclopedia,* VI, 48–49; *JE,* XI, 399.)

12. Jasper Chasseaud, our Consul, was not an American citizen, but a Macedonian. He had been commissioned our Consul at Beirut on March 3, 1835 and served from March 25, 1835 to December 1840, when war suspended his operations. Re-commissioned on August 6, 1842, he served from September 6, 1842 to July 1850, when he was dismissed because the law then required that American consuls be American citizens. I am informed that "only a routine acknowledgement to his report was made by the Department of State." (Letters to this editor by Mr. Roscoe R. Hill of the National Archives, December 6, 1945 and July 16, 1946.)

84. English Public Opinion on the Damascus Affair

1. This correspondence, published for the first time, is from the *General Records of the Department of State. Diplomatic Despatches, Great Britain,* Volume 47. These interventions marked a "turning-point in Jewish history, the beginnings of the concerted effort to make the Jewish cause wherever attacked the concern of all Jews without distinction." (Paul Goodman, introduction to "The Damascus Affair, Diary of Dr. Louis Loewe, July–November 1840," *Yehudith,* Ramsgate, England, I, No. 3, p. 4.)

2. L. Loewe, ed., *Diaries of Sir Moses and Lady Montefiore . . . 1812 to 1883 . . . ,* (London, 1890) I, 214.

3. Crémieux, the outstanding Jewish statesman in France, finally entered the case when "A well known Jewish journalist, A. Créhenge, published an open letter to Crémieux urging him to undertake a campaign in behalf of the victims." (Posener, *op. cit.,* 95.) Heine, then Paris correspondent for the *Allgemeine Augsburger Zeitung* (*ibid.,* 90), was particularly "caustic" in describing the slowness with which the Jewish community of Paris reacted to the needs of their brethren and especially sharp with the Jewish bankers in Paris (Francois Fejto, *Heine, A Biography,* London, 1946, pp. 213–215). Unlike the English Jews, however, the French Jews had to oppose the policy of their government in order to aid the Jews of Damascus.

4. Loewe, *op. cit.,* I, 215.

   Goodman, as well as Zionist historians, see this action of Britain in 1840 as the beginning of the policy that led to the Balfour Declaration in 1917 (*Op. cit.,* 8).

5. Andrew Stevenson (1784–1857) was a Virginian supporter of Jackson and had been influential in keeping Virginia from following South Carolina's nullification policies. In 1834 the Senate refused to confirm Jackson's nomination of Stevenson as Minister to Great Britain, but Jackson persisted, made no appointment, and in 1836 Stevenson was accepted by the Senate. He served as Minister until the Whigs triumphed in 1841.

6. John Abel Smith (1801–1871) had been an active promoter of the Reform Bill of 1832 and an advocate of the admission of Jews into Parliament.

7. Sir Charles Forbes (1774–1849), although a tory opponent of the Reform Bill, had supported Catholic emancipation and women suffrage.

   John Bowring (1792–1872) was a radical journalist, linguist, and traveller who had spent the years 1837–1838 in Egypt, Syria, and Turkey.

8. Samuel Gurney (1786–1856) was a prison reformer, philanthropist, and head of the world's greatest discounting house.

   James Morrison (1790–1857) was a very rich merchant and liberal politician who had supported the Reform Bill.

9. Sir George Gerard De Hochepied Larpent (1786–1855) had made his fortune in East India and was a Whig politician.

10. On June 22, 1840, on the interpellation of Sir Robert Peel (1788–1850), Lord Palmerston had announced in the House of Commons that he had unofficially warned Mehemet Ali of British opposition to the persecution of the Jews in Damascus. (*Hansard's Parliamentary Debates,* LIV, 1383–1386.)

11. Sir John Hobart Caradoc, Lord Howden (1799–1873) was a diplomat who in 1827 had been assigned to Egypt to try to keep Mehemet Ali from helping the Turkish Sultan put down the Greek revolution, which the Powers were then supporting.

    Baptist Wriothesley Noel (1798–1873) was a very prominent London preacher and reformer.

12. Daniel O'Connell (1775–1847), the Irish leader of the struggle for Catholic emancipation in England, was also an advocate of Jewish emancipation. On June 22, 1840, when both Peel and Palmerston promised aid to the Jews, O'Connell said in the House of Commons: "The statement which had been that night made, though it came from a most respectable quarter, would have been much more forcible if it had proceeded from a Hebrew gentleman in that House." In reply to O'Connell's inquiry whether the Government would introduce a bill for the emancipation of the Jews, Lord Russell said no. (Hansard, *op. cit.,* 1386.) At the meeting on July 3, 1840, there was slight hissing when O'Connell rose to speak but he was cheered at the end (for text of his remarks, see *Lyons Scrapbook,* III, Item 14). O'Connell was a friend of Isaac Lyon Goldsmid, the London bullion broker (Bernard Shillman, *A Short History of the Jews in Ireland,* Dublin, 1945, p. 75).

85. Our State Department and the Damascus Affair

1. Ezekiel, *AJHSP,* VIII (1900), 143–144. John Gliddon served as Consul from 1835 to his death in 1844. This letter was ineffectual, for it "arrived after all practicable amends had been obtained through other channels" (John Gliddon, despatch to the Department of State from Cairo, February 12, 1841, in which he reports receiving the instruction in January, 1841; information supplied by Mr. Almon R. Wright, head of Executive and Foreign Affairs Branch of The National Archives, April 23, 1947).
2. Loewe, *op. cit.,* I, 225–226.
3. Martin Van Buren (1782–1862) was President from 1837 to 1841.
4. John Forsyth (1780–1841) was a Virginian, a supporter of Madison and Jackson, and a leader of the opposition to the nullificationists that kept Georgia, to which he had moved, from following South Carolina. In June 1834, Jackson had appointed Forsyth his Secretary of State, in which post he continued during Van Buren's administration.

5. *General Records of the Department of State. Diplomatic Instructions, Turkey,* Volume 1.
6. David Porter (1780–1843) had been a naval officer from 1798 to 1826, achieving the rank of Commodore. Resentful of what he regarded as an unfair court-martial, he resigned, and in 1830 entered the diplomatic service, first as consul-general to the Barbary States, then as chargé d'affaires at Constantinople, as minister resident, and in 1839 as minister. In 1835 there was published a two volume work of his in New York, *Constantinople and Its Environs. In a Series of Letters, Exhibiting the Actual State of the Manners, Customs, and Habits of the Turks, Armenians, Jews, and Greeks, as Modified by the Policy of Sultan Mahmoud.* The Chapter on the Jews is a letter dated August 15, 1833, and had already been published in the "New-York Monthly Magazine." Having described the Jews as "everywhere a persecuted people," (II, 160) Porter finds their way of living and manners distasteful. Pertinent to the blood libel charge which the Secretary of State was asking Porter to defend the Jews against is this passage: "It cannot be doubted that the hatred of the Jews towards the Christians is inveterate in the extreme, and opportunities only are wanted to make this manifest. An occasion offered, where the venerable Greek patriarch was hanged by the Turks at the commencement of the Greek revolution. The Jews volunteered their services to cast his body into the sea; their services were accepted, and his corpse was dragged through the streets by them with gratuitous insult.

   "This circumstance, with others of a similar nature, so exasperated the Greeks, that during the revolution they revenged themselves on every Jew that fell into their hands with the most dreadful retaliation. These mutual prejudices are so strong, that they give rise to many accusations and recriminations, with which they assail each other.

   "The Jews accuse the Christians of being eaters of human flesh, while the Christians charge them with crucifying adults on Good Friday, in mockery of the crucifixion of Christ; and with purloining children, and sacrificing them as paschal lambs at their passover. These things, however, are scarcely worth repeating, and I mention them, not because I believe them, but because they are too generally believed here." (II, 177.)
7. In May, 1840, a blood accusation stimulated by the Damascus affair was made on the Island of Rhodes, then belonging to Turkey. A ten year old Greek boy having hanged himself, the Jews were accused of a ritual murder, and a persecution began which was abetted by the Consuls of England, France, and Sweden, who pressed Jussuf Pasha, governor of Rhodes, for action. Jewish deputies from Rhodes and also Nathaniel de Rothschild interceded with the Sultan, who ordered an inquiry that led to the dismissal of Jussuf Pasha as governor and the acquittal of the Jews charged with the murder, at the end of July. At that time the Jews of Damascus were still imprisoned. (Graetz, *op. cit.,* V, 640, 647.) In March 1840, in Jülich, Rhenish Prussia, the blood libel was raised when a nine-year old girl accused Jews of stabbing her and of killing an old man. A judicial investigation led to the finding of the old man and to evidence that the girl had not been stabbed at all. (*Ibid.,* V, 642.)

86. American Jews and the Damascus Affair

1. Ezekiel, *op. cit.,* pp. 141–142.
2. Following the one in New York, there were meetings in other cities. On August 27, 1840, there was a meeting called by the Congregation Mikveh Israel in Philadelphia, and on August 31, 1840 a Committee addressed a letter to Presi-

dent Van Buren (Jacobs, *op. cit.*, 126–128). On August 31, 1840, a meeting was held by the Congregation Beni Israel in Cincinnati (undated, unidentified clipping, *Lyons Scrapbook,* III, item 17). On September 3, 1840, a meeting was held in Savannah, Georgia, called by the Mayor of Savannah (undated, unidentified clipping, *ibid.*, item 18). On September 4, 1840, in Richmond, Virginia, a Committee of Jews considered a communication received from Kursheedt and Seixas in New York, and addressed a letter of appreciation to President Van Buren (Ezekiel, *op. cit.,* 144–145). In Richmond, also, the Rev. Dr. L. Magoon, Baptist minister, preached a sermon on the Damascus Affair (*The Press,* Philadelphia, December 1, 1882, *Philadelphia Scrapbook,* II, p. 912, American Jewish Historical Society). On November 2, 1840, a meeting was held at the "New Synagogue of Congregation Beth Israel," Philadelphia, to help raise funds for the Jews of Damascus (undated, unidentified clipping, *Lyons Scrapbook,* III, item 19b).

3. It is reported that our Consul at Alexandria, late in August, 1840, and before he could have received the instruction addressed to him by Secretary John Forsyth on August 14th, joined with the Consuls of England, Prussia, Russia, Spain, and Tuscany in signing a petition to Mehemet Ali, Pasha of Egypt, requesting the liberation of the imprisoned Damascenes. (Posener, *op. cit.,* 116.) It is not clear whether the petition was actually presented to the Pasha (Loewe, *op. cit.,* I, 248–249), but apparently the Pasha learned of it and decided not to seem to yield to obvious pressure by appearing to act independently, and on August 28, 1840 he issued an order that the imprisoned Jews be freed; the order was carried out on September 6th (Posener, *op. cit.,* 118). On September 16, 1840, Sir Moses Montefiore visited Mehemet Ali to thank him for his action. By that time Syria was in revolt against Mehemet Ali, and the British fleet had begun to bombard Beirut. Sir Moses records in his Diary that when, after thanking Mehemet Ali, he rose to leave, Mehemet Ali "motioned me to remain. . . . He then said that he frequently gave orders for ships, guns, and other things to be sent from England, that six months elapsed before they were ready to be shipped, and that as I was going there he would like to make some arrangement with me to guarantee the parties, and said that I should always have the money before the things were shipped. . . . I told His Highness that I would consult with my friends in England, and would write to him as soon as I got back to London; he expressed his satisfaction, and we retired." (Loewe, *op. cit.,* I, 261; there is no further mention of the matter in the published diaries.) It should perhaps be noted that Sir Moses had, on another trip to Egypt, had an interview with Mehemet Ali, July 13, 1839 in which, after asking that the Jews of Safed, Tiberias, and Hebron be admitted as witnesses in courts, "I then spoke of establishing joint stock banks with a capital of £1,000,000 sterling, with power to increase it, if necessary. His eyes sparkled at this; he appeared delighted, and assured me the bank should have his protection, and he should be happy to see it established. I mentioned the branches: Alexandria, Beyrout, Damascus, Jaffa, Jerusalem, and Cairo." (*Ibid.,* I, 199–200.)

4. Theodore J. Seixas, a son of Gershom Mendes Seixas, was born in 1803, and married Anne, the daughter of Naphtali Judah, November 1, 1843.

5. Ezekiel, *op. cit.,* 142–143.

6. This statement does not quite correspond to the facts as revealed in the documents themselves: our Consul at Damascus sent his report on March 24th; it was received at our State Department on June 27th; the instructions to our Consul at Alexandria are dated August 14th; in the meantime, on August 10th,

the State Department had received the communications from London printed above.

7. David Porter, to whom the letter was addressed, was no longer Chargé d'Affaires but our Minister to Turkey.

87. Minister's Report on the Damascus Affair

1. *General Records of the Department of State. Diplomatic Despatches, Turkey,* volume 9. This dispatch was received at the State Department on January 8, 1841.

2. On November 3, 1839, at an Assembly at Gulhana, the new Sultan had read a Hatti Scheriff (imperial order or decree). Minister Porter had enclosed a French translation of this document with his despatch of November 8, 1839 (*ibid.*); a manuscript notation on the copy in the State Department reads, "Translation published in the Globe January 1840". The following paragraphs from this Hatti Scheriff are relevant: "Therefore the case of all prisoners will henceforth be judged publicly after inquiry and examination, in conformity with our divine laws, and as long as a regular judgment has not been declared, no one will be able to let another person perish secretly or publicly from poison or any other torment. . . . These important concessions will be extended to all our subjects regardless of their religion or sect and they shall benefit from them without exceptions. Complete security shall therefore be granted by us to all our subjects as to their lives, their honor, and their property as required by the sacred text of our laws." (For this translation of the document from the French I am indebted to Dr. Francine Bradley.)

3. *Ibid.* This dispatch was received at the State Department, January 14, 1841.

4. This clipping from a French newspaper contains the French translation of the Firman of the Sultan issued on November 6, 1840.

   The Sultan's Firman of 1840 was invoked in aid of the Jews as recently as March, 1931 when a Christian Arab newspaper in Jaffa revived the blood libel (F. H. Kisch, *Palestine Diary,* London, 1938, pp. 390–391).

5. *Ibid.* This dispatch was also received at the State Department, January 14, 1841.

6. John P. Brown, son of Minister Porter's sister, Mrs. Mary Brown, became dragoman (interpreter of Arabic) to our Legation in 1836 and continued in the consular service until his death in 1871 (David D. Porter, *Memoir of Commodore David Porter of the United States Navy,* Albany, 1875, p. 406).

7. *General Records of the Department of State, op. cit.*

8. That the Damascus affair made a deep impression upon members of the Jewish community in our country may be inferred from a notation made in his scrapbook by the Rev. J. J. Lyons of the Congregation Shearith Israel, New York. In 1848, noticing an item in a newspaper about the disappearance of a man employed in a Jewish home, this American minister expressed his uneasiness that the "Blood question" might be involved if it were near Passover! Both the newspaper item and the comment in the handwriting of the Rev. Lyons (*Lyons Scrapbook,* I, p. 7) are here given in full:

   "New York Tribune January 10, 1848"

   Missing.—A colored man named *Peter Williams,* about 35 years of age, 6 feet high, rather bald, has been missing since the 27th of December last— He was supposed to be living in Broadway with a Jewish family in the capacity of waiter. He was a man of good habits, and fears are entertained that some evil may have befallen him. Any information in regard to him will be thankfully received by his wife, who lives at 75 Second-Avenue, or any information will be communicated to her if left at 33 Ann-street.

[*In Lyons' handwriting:*] Who is Peter Williams? And what is the name of the Jewish Family here alluded to? The compiler can not answer; his object in preserving this notice, is to ascertain if possible, whether it is true that such a man is missing, otherwise the motive is palpable, that of calumny; fortunately it is not near the pasover [sic] or the Blood question might be re [MS worn away at corner].

88. An Art Dealer

1. *Duyckinck Papers, Literary Correspondence, Noah Folder,* MSS Div., New York Public Library. I am indebted to Mr. Jay Leyda for calling this item to my attention.
2. In 1842, in New York, the following were also listed as art dealers: John B. Glover, Royal Gurley, and Henry E. Riell & Jacob S. Arcularius (Harold Lancour, *American Art Auction Catalogues, 1785–1942, A Union List,* New York, 1944, pp. 30–31).
3. Thomas Cole (1801–1848) was the English-born painter of American landscapes who was elected to our National Academy in 1826. Joshua Shaw (1776–1860), also born in England, was a landscape painter who came to Philadelphia in 1817 and painted there for many years. William G. Wall (born 1792) came to New York in 1818, became prominent as a painter of views of the Hudson, and was elected to the National Academy in 1826. John Vanderlyn (1775–1852), an American painter of portraits and historical subjects, won many honors at the Paris Salons. (Mantle Fielding, *Dictionary of American Painters, Sculptors and Engravers,* Philadelphia, 1926, pp. 71, 329, 390, 380–381.)
4. C. John M. Whichelo (before 1800–1865) was an English artist best known as a landscape and marine painter (E. Bénézit, *Dictionnaire Critique Et Documentaire des Peintres, Sculpteurs Dessinateurs & Graveurs,* Paris, 1924, Vol. 3, p. 1058).
5. Joachim Murat (1771–1815), Marshal of France, was King of Naples, 1808–1815.
6. Giovanni Francesco Barbiere, Il Guercino (1591–1661) was an Italian master. (Ralph N. James, *Painters and Their Works,* London, 1896, Vol. 1, pp. 497–498.)
7. Bartolomeo Schidone (1570?–1615), of Modena, painted many Holy Families, examples of which hang in the Uffizi Gallery in Florence and the Hermitage in Leningrad. (John D. Champlin, Jr. and Charles C. Perkins, *Cyclopaedia of Painters and Painting,* New York, 1887, Vol. 4, p. 131.)
8. Noah had just recently begun to edit *The Union* (July 23, 1842), the official organ of the Whig party. He had been appointed editor of the paper at the suggestion of President John Tyler, whom he had supported for the presidency. (Goldberg, *op. cit.,* 251). The paper lasted only until March, 1843. Copies for the period covered by Levy's letter cannot be located.
9. Aaron Levy (1771–1852) was a son of Hayman Levy and a son-in-law of Isaac Moses. From 1797 (possibly even from 1793) until 1849 he was a merchant and auctioneer in New York. (New York City Directories from 1793 to 1850, *passim.*) When he was commissioned an auctioneer in 1830, he moved his place of business from his home to an establishment at 128 Broadway. In 1839, he is at 151 Broadway, the address given in this letter. From 1834 on he was frequently an art auctioneer. He issued catalogues of art collections that he offered for sale in 1838, 1839, 1840, 1841, 1843, 1844, and 1845. (Lancour, *op. cit.,*

21.) In 1844, he was also associated in this line of business with a dentist, S. Spooner, with whom one of the catalogues is issued. From 1800 to 1819 he served in various capacities in the New York State Artillery, rising to the rank of Lieutenant Colonel; in the War of 1812 he was a Captain. (*AJHSP*, XXVII, 1920, p. 338.) For fifty years he was very active and held several offices in the Congregation Shearith Israel (*ibid., passim*).

89. First Fraternal Order

1. Henry Jones was the Clerk of Anshe Chesed, one of the four German congregations in New York. His associates were: Henry Anspacher; Isaac Dittenhoefer, who sold drygoods at 414 Grand Street; Rev. Jonas Hecht, hazzan at Anshe Chesed, 1838 1857; Hirsch Heineman, who sold "fancygoods" at 172 West Broadway; Henry Kling, a tailor at 471 Grand Street; Valentine Koon (1810–1889), "boot & shoemaker" at 48 Hubert Street, who had come to New York in 1842; William Renau, "haircutter & segars" at 47 Norfolk Street; Reuben M. Roadacher, a member of Anshe Chesed; Isaac Rosenbourgh, a jeweller at 420 Grand Street; Samuel Schafer, who dealt in watches across the way at 419 Grand Street; Michael Schwab, a member of Anshe Chesed. It is reported that Jones first discussed the project in the shop of Aaron Sinsheimer, shoemaker and later owner of a "porterhouse" at 60 Essex Street. (*Doggett's New-York City and Co-Partnership Directory, 1843 & 1844, passim*, and *ibid., 1844 and 1845;* Grinstein, *op. cit.*, cf. his index; Bernard Postal, *This Is B'nai B'rith*, Washington, 1946, p. 6, *The Menorah*, January, 1890, pp. 48–49.) German was the official language until 1850.
2. It is interesting that Hirsch Heineman became a founder of a rival organization, the Independent Order Free Sons of Israel, in 1849; he was the first president of the original lodge and later Grand Master of the Order (Grinstein, *op. cit.*, 112).
3. For such fears expressed as late as the fiftieth anniversary of the founding of the Order, see *The Jewish Messenger*, October 13, 1893, "The B'nai B'rith."
4. Dr. S. Waterman, "Sketch of the History of the Order," *The Hebrew Leader*, X, No. 3, April 19, 1867, cols. 1–2, reports that in September, 1843, Reuben Roadacher visited Henry Jones, an official of the Odd Fellows, to inform him of the exclusion and to propose the establishment of a separate Odd Fellows lodge of Jews. "Mr. Jones answered that such a grant would certainly not be given, because the O. of O. F. did not recognize any confessional religious difference . . ." But Jones did offer to help Roadacher to organize a new society with a Jewish ritual "framed in a manner as to be equally unobjectionable to the Orthodox as to the Reformers . . ." William Renau helped draw up the ritual.

90. Poor Relief

1. *Lyons Scrapbook II, item 35c.* The report is printed as a 12-page pamphlet.
2. Stuart Alfred Queen, *Social Work in the Light of History*, Philadelphia and London, 1922, p. 109; David M. Schneider, *The History of Public Welfare in New York State, 1609–1866*, Chicago, 1938, p. 265.
3. Grinstein, *op. cit.*, 144ff, although he dates the founding of the New York Hebrew Assistance Society as 1839, which is contradicted by a Circular of the Society (*Lyons Scrapbook II, item 19c*), which gives the date as February 23, 1840.

4. These resolutions indicate that the Hebrew Assistance Society was prepared to accept the recommendations contained in this report. The proposed merger did not take place, for both societies were still extant in the 1850s. It is difficult to understand why the fusion did not go through, since Benjamin Nathan was also President of the Hebrew Assistance Society and Joseph and Hendricks were on its Board of Managers.
5. As far back as 1806, the *Kalfe Zedakah Matan Beseter* (society for the anonymous bestowal of charity) had issued a circular projecting the building of a poorhouse and hospital when $5000 had been accumulated, but nothing came of the plan. (Grinstein, *op. cit.*, 145.)
6. In 1841 the Hebrew Benevolent Society also reported it had helped 195 persons with an expenditure of $1,763 (*ibid.*, 146). There were approximately 7,000 Jews in New York at this time (*Lyons Scrapbook II, item 19c*).
7. Washington Hendricks, of the copper-processing firm, had died in 1841.
8. By the aforementioned resolutions of January 24, 1843, the Hebrew Assistance Society had appointed Henry Hendricks, Solomon I. Joseph and Asher Kursheedt as a committee to report on the building plans. Asher Kursheedt was a Wall Street broker. (Joseph's name is sometimes carelessly given as Solomon J. Joseph.)
9. As the crisis-bred poverty of the masses grew deeper and the relief-methods were glaringly inadequate, there were found voices in the upper class to challenge the whole idea of relief! "It was the opinion of many influential citizens that the aid given the poor during the course of the depression served to break down their morale and was responsible for the increase of mendicancy and able-bodied pauperism." (Schneider, *op. cit.*, 265.) One consequence was the formation, in 1843, of the New York Association for Improving the Condition of the Poor, whose primary emphasis was on "moral assistance" to the poor rather than material aid (*ibid.*, 266).

91. Moving Westward

1. *The Occident,* February 1844, pp. 547–550; April 1844, pp. 29–31; June 1844, pp. 143–147. For the identity of the author, see Philipson, *AJHSP,* VIII (1900), 44.
2. Isaac Leeser (1806–1868) was editor of *The Occident,* 1843–1868. He was outstanding as a Jewish scholar, minister, and writer, expounding and defending the Conservative viewpoint. Among his achievements is a translation of the Bible into English in 1853.
3. Jonas Levy is listed as a watchmaker and silversmith in the 1825 Cincinnati Directory and as a jeweler in 1830; in 1839 he was one of the seceders from Bene Israel who founded the Reform congregation Bene Yeshurun.
4. Morris Moses was President of Bene Israel in 1826–1827, 1836–1838, 1840–1841, 1845–1846.
5. The 1830 Directory lists Solomon and Simon Menken as dry-goods merchants.
6. Solomon Moses is listed as a merchant in the 1825 Directory.
7. Simeon Moses became a Trustee of Bene Israel; Morris Symonds was a merchant in 1825.
8. See Document No. 77.
9. See Document No. 77, note 4.

10. Bernard Le Jeune, whose father Isaac was a native of Amsterdam, died in 1843 at the age of thirty-two.

11. Elias Mayer was Vice-President of Bene Israel in 1835–1836 and 1851–1853, and President in 1842–1843 and 1854–1855.

12. Harmon Hendricks (1771–1838), of the distinguished family that contributed to developing the metal industry in this country, established the first copper-rolling mill in the United States in 1812 with his partner and brother-in-law, Solomon I. Isaacs, and subscribed $40,000 to a government loan. He was President of Shearith Israel in New York, 1824–1826.

13. John Moss (born, London, 1771, died, Philadelphia, 1847) was a merchant, ship-owner, railroad director and business executive who retired from business in 1823 and devoted himself to civic affairs. He was a member of the Philadelphia City Council and a supporter of Andrew Jackson, as well as a Trustee of Congregation Mickve Israel.

14. Morris B. Mann also served as secretary in 1841–1842 and 1843–1844.

15. David Mayer had served as Vice-President in 1837–1838; he was President again in 1848–1850.

16. Rev. Hertz (Hart) Judah served until 1855, when Rev. Max Lilienthal succeeded him.

17. Henry Hart also held the following offices: Vice-President, 1836–1837, 1840–1841; President, 1839–1840; Secretary, 1842–1843, 1854–1855.

18. Moritz E. Moehring had served as secretary, 1838–1839; he was President again, 1844–1845, and Treasurer, 1847–1848. In 1850, together with Hyman Moses and others, he founded the second Jewish hospital in the United States a year after the cholera plague swept Cincinnati (Brickner, *op. cit.*, 183–184).

18a. The first Jew to settle in Cleveland, in 1837, was Simson Thorman of Bavaria; in 1839, there arrived the first Jewish family, that of Samuel Hoffman (Hopferman). That year, 20 Jews founded the first congregation, the Israelitische Society, with Isaac Hoffman as rabbi, cantor and mohel. In 1842, a Reform group seceded, led by Asher Lehman, who had been associated with Reform in Neustadt on Dessen, where he had operated a slaughter-house. The first Jews in Cleveland were peddlers of clothing and cooking utensils, butchers, bakers, and drygoods store keepers. (Moses J. Gries, *The Jewish Community of Cleveland*, Cleveland, c. 1910; *UJE,* III, 320.)

19. Rabbi Abraham Rice of Baltimore was the first rabbi of Congregation Nidche Israel, serving from 1840 to 1849 and exerting much influence. To whom Jonas is referring as the Cincinnati rabbi who led the attack on the Sunday school is unclear, since neither congregation had an ordained rabbi. However, the reader (hazan) of Bene Israel was Hart Judah, of Bene Yeshurun, Simon Bamberger.

92. Non-Secretarian Thanksgiving

1. *The Occident,* January 1845, pp. 500–510.

2. The first recorded dispute took place in 1812 in South Carolina; other instances occurred throughout the century (Kohler, *AJHSP,* XIII, 1905, pp. 19–23, 33–36; Hackenburg, *AJHSP,* XX, 1911, pp. 133–135).

3. Letter to Rev. Samuel Miller, Jan. 23, 1808 (P. L. Ford, ed., *The Writings of Thomas Jefferson,* New York, 1898, IX, 174–176).

4. Elizabeth Merritt, *James Henry Hammond, 1807–1864,* Baltimore, 1923, p. 63.

5. Michael Lazarus represented the Congregation Beth Elohim, and S. Valentine the Congregation Sheyreth Israel.
6. Since there are slight differences between the original text and that given in *The Occident,* I am using the original text as kindly supplied to me by A. S. Salley, State Historian of South Carolina (*Miscellaneous Book O,* p. 190).
7. The only one of the signatories known is A. Moise, Jr. (Merritt, *op. cit.,* 62–63); the list of signatories is not known to be extant.
8. At this time the editor and owner of *The Southern Patriot* was the Jewish writer and journalist, Jacob Newton Cardozo (1786–1873).
9. Whether ours is a "Christian nation" has been subject to much discussion. That this is a "Christian nation" was expressly denied in our Treaty with Tripoli in 1797. For a lawyer's treatment of "how religious beliefs of the dominant Christians in the United States are allowed effectually to control our every day affairs," see B. H. Hartogensis, "Denial of Equal Rights to Religious Minorities and Non-Believers in the United States," *Yale Law Journal,* XXXIX, March, 1930, pp. 659–681.
10. This outrageous allegation naturally aroused the resentment of the Jews. For modern scientific investigation of the unsubstantiated charge that the Jews crucified Jesus, see Solomon Zeitlin, *Who Crucified Jesus?,* New York, 1942, Max Radin, *The Trial of Jesus of Nazareth,* Chicago, 1931, and Hyman E. Goldin, *The Case of the Nazarene Reopened,* New York, 1948.
11. In 1711, seven New York Jews had contributed to the funds then being collected to build the steeple of Trinity Church. More recently, Judah Touro's benefactions to a church in New Orleans from 1822 on had become known.
12. Richard Mentor Johnson (1780–1850), United States Senator from Kentucky, and chairman of the Senate Committee on the Post Office and Post Roads, was a staunch Jeffersonian. His report on the problem of whether the mails should be carried on Sundays, which had been agitated in Congress since about 1811, was delivered on January 19, 1829 (*Senate Documents, 20th Congress, 2d Session, Report No. 46*). In an able analysis, he defends the principle of separation of Church and State, and opposes changing the practice of carrying mails on Sundays. In the House, on the same day, Samuel McKean, chairman of the corresponding committee, made a report advocating stopping the delivery of mails on Sundays. The proposed legislation was defeated.
13. In 1847, this protest of the Jews was used by Sir Robert Harry Inglis, Bart., when, representing the University of Oxford, he delivered a speech in the House of Commons opposing equal rights for Jews in England. An article on the issue, summarizing the documents not without bias, which had appeared in the *New York Courier,* November 30, 1844, is reprinted in Sir Robert Harry Inglis, Bart., *The Jew Bill . . . ,* London, 1848, pp. 30–32.

93. Zionism: American Forerunner

1. *Discourse on the Restoration of the Jews: Delivered at the Tabernacle Oct. 28 and Dec. 2, 1844, by M. M. Noah, With a Map of the Land of Israel,* New York, 1845, pp. 10–11, 32–39. Keen Christian interest in the approaching restoration of the Jews to Palestine is evidenced in a pamphlet like that of the professor of Hebrew at New York University, George Bush, *The Valley of Vision; or The Dry Bones of Ezekiel Revived,* New York, 1844, in which he was confident "that the most accurate researches in prophetic chronology, as well as the pregnant signs of the times, afford abundant warrant for the belief, that

we are now just upon the borders of that sublime crisis in Providence of which the restoration of the Jews to Syria, and the ingathering into the church, is to be one of the prominent features." (P. iv.) Spencer H. Cone also issued a Circular Letter of the New York Baptist Association on "The Restoration of the Jews" in 1844.

2. Isaac Goldberg, *Major Noah: American-Jewish Pioneer,* Philadelphia, 1936, is a valuable biography.

3. *AJHSP,* XXI (1913), 200.

4. Hyamson, *AJHSP,* XXVI (1918), 132–144.

5. The Latin American revolutions against Spain had evoked much popular sympathy and support in the United States, and somewhat more cautious approval by our government until the cession of Florida by Spain. In 1822, our government entered into diplomatic relations with Colombia, Argentina, Chile, Mexico, Brazil, and Central America.

The federal Treaties of St. Louis (1823), Prairie du Chien (1830), Fort Armstrong (1832), and the Sac and Fox Agency (1842) had recognized the rights of Osage, Kansas, Sac, Fox, Sioux, and other Indian tribes to lands west of the Mississippi in Missouri, Kansas, Oklahoma, Iowa, and Minnesota.

The Greek War of Independence from Turkey (1821–1827) led to the establishment of a Greek kingdom under the protection of Great Britain, France and Russia. Americans expressed much sympathy with the Greeks. Noah himself wrote *The Grecian Captive; or The Fall of Athens,* which was produced in New York in 1822. In 1837, the United States concluded a commercial treaty with Greece.

Between 1822 and 1832 our government and the American Society for the Colonization of the Free People of Color of the United States founded several settlements of free Negroes, and of Negroes taken on slave-smuggling ships, on a strip of land at Cape Mesurado purchased from the natives. The colonization was not successful. The Republic of Liberia was not established until 1847, *after* Noah's reference to restoring "the African to his native land." Noah, as journalist, judge, and politician was an active supporter of American slavery, and was frequently denounced for his views and activities by abolitionists like William Lloyd Garrison in *The Liberator. The Freedom's Journal,* first Negro periodical in the country, was launched in 1827 partially in order to combat the anti-Negro propaganda of Noah (I. Garland Penn, *The Afro-American Press,* Springfield, Mass., 1891, p. 28).

6. Egypt, in the First Syrian War, which ended in 1832, extended its territory at the expense of Turkey's empire. Ibrahim Pasha, the successful Egyptian general, was finally stopped by European intervention. The Second Syrian War of 1839 was also a triumph for Egypt, under its governor, Mehamet Ali.

7. The process of Russian conquest of the Caucasus from Persia and Turkey began with Peter I in 1722 and continued into the nineteenth century. Between 1801 and 1839 most of the Caucasian territories were conquered, despite fierce opposition which persisted into the 1860's.

Between 1803 and 1843, British armies conquered large sections of central India, Burma, Assam, Sind, and other areas. The first Afghan War, 1837 to 1842, was unsuccessful.

The Treaty of Nanking, August 29, 1842, ended the "Opium War" between England and China arising from Chinese opposition to British importation of opium into China. The treaty ceded Hong Kong to Britain, and made other important concessions. In 1843 another treaty gave Britain most favored nation status and laid the basis for extraterritoriality "rights." In 1844, the United States and France obtained similar treaties.

8. After a three years' war ending July 5, 1830, France occupied Algiers. In 1844, France was at war with Morocco.

9. It is startling to note how this forerunner of Zionism accepts the manifest imperialist destiny of Great Britain as the condition for the restoration of the Jews to Palestine. Isaac Leeser, however, commenting on Noah's plan, rejected it chiefly because he did not trust the imperialist powers; he recalled that these powers had taken half of Turkey, partitioned Poland, pillaged India and seized Algiers, and he had no hopes that they would not use the Jews in Palestine for their own imperialist purposes (*The Occident,* March, 1845, p. 600).

10. For a sketch of the reaction to Noah's Discourse, see Goldberg, *op. cit.*, 257–263. Nathaniel Peabody Rogers (1794–1846), in his abolitionist paper, *Herald of Freedom,* Concord, N. H., April 25, 1845, did not think the restoration to Palestine practicable and offered instead to help Noah fight persecution of the Jews in the United States. In 1849 Noah reasserted his thesis at a public meeting in New York called to raise funds to build a synagog in Jerusalem (Grinstein, *op. cit.*, 459).

94. Demagogue

1. *The Congressional Globe,* 29 Cong., 1 Sess., Appendix, 46–50.

2. B. D. Zevin, ed., *Nothing to Fear: Selected Addresses of Franklin Delano Roosevelt,* Boston, 1946, p. 431, speech in Boston, November 4, 1944. Roosevelt had stated the same idea on October 5, 1944: Philip S. Foner, ed., *Franklin Delano Roosevelt, Selections from His Writings,* New York, 1947, pp. 34–35, and in a famous address to the Daughters of the American Revolution, in which he reminded them pointedly that "all of us, and you and I especially, are descended from immigrants and revolutionists." (*The Public Papers and Addresses of Franklin D. Roosevelt,* 1938 volume, New York, 1941, p. 259.)

3. The occasion for the speech was the following: on December 15, 1845, two weeks after the opening of the 29th Congress, Representative Robert C. Winthrop, a Whig from Massachusetts, presented certain resolutions of the Massachusetts legislature proposing the investigation of "gross frauds" in elections and, if necessary, "amendments to the naturalization laws." (*Cong. Globe, loc. cit.*, 52, 67.) Richard Brodhead (Pa., Dem.), moved the resolutions be referred to the Committee on the Judiciary; Levin, fearing lack of sympathy for the resolutions in that committee, promptly countered with the proposal that a special "select" committee be created for the purpose, and announced his intention of debating the issue. Although the problem was ostensibly the technical matter of reference to committee, the debate actually dealt with the substance of the matter of the relation of immigration to the country.

4. Lewis Charles Levin was born in Charleston, S. C. in 1808, and was graduated from the South Carolina College there. About 1828 he was in Woodville, Miss., teaching school; there he was also badly wounded in a duel in which Jefferson Davis was his second. Turning to law, he practiced in Maryland, Louisiana, and Kentucky, marrying Ann Hays in the latter state. About 1838, he settled in Philadelphia, continued the practise of law, and became a temperance speaker. In 1842–1843 he was editor of *The Temperance Advocate.* In 1843 he also became one of the leading figures in the Philadelphia Native American movement, and editor of one of its organs, *The Daily Sun,* 1844–1846. Playing

a prominent part in the Philadelphia riots of 1844, he was elected to Congress as a Native American, and served for three terms, from 1845 to 1850, during which time "he preached nativism with almost fanatical zeal." One contemporary describes him as "a brilliant adventurer" and "one of the most brilliant and unscrupulous orators" of his day. After being defeated for re-election in 1850, he retired to private practise. His wife having died, he married Julia Gist, a widow. In the 1856 presidential campaign, he emerged again to support Millard Fillmore against John Fremont and James Buchanan, using nativistic arguments and denouncing the "Black Republicans" and abolitionists as agents of the Pope! When he died in 1860, he was insane; he was buried in the non-denominational Laurel Hill Cemetery. While most Philadelphia and New York general newspapers took note of his death, remembering him as one of the main figures in the Native American movement, no mention of his decease was made in *The Jewish Messenger, The Occident,* and *The Israelite,* although in 1858 Levin is listed in the latter as a Jew who had been in Congress (September 10, 1858, p. 78). (Morais, *op. cit.,* 395–396; *DAB;* A. K. McClure, *Old Time Notes of Pennsylvania,* Philadelphia, 1905, I, 89–90; *The Press,* Philadelphia, March 15, 1860, p. 2, col. 5; letter to this editor by William J. Proud, Superintendent, Laurel Hill Cemetery Company.)

5. The previous speaker, Frederick Perry Stanton, Tennessee Democrat, had favored referring the resolutions to a select committee although he opposed Native Americanism. Candidates elected as Native Americans were pledged to two main aims: the passage of legislation requiring twenty-one years of residence for naturalization, and opposition to attempts "of any religious or sectarian body . . . to influence or modify the civil or governmental institutions of the country . . ." (*American Republican Association. Report of a committee to draft a delegate system for Philadelphia.* Adopted July 19, 1844, New York Public Library, MSS Division.) The first point also included restricting all office-holding to native Americans; the second included the insistence that the Protestant Bible was a non-sectarian book, and that Catholics, who had expressed objection to having Catholic children compelled to read the Protestant Bible in the public schools and asked for the right to have them read the Catholic Bible, were thereby undermining the separation of church and state. The extreme anti-Catholic bias of the Native Americans comes out perhaps most clearly in the continual misrepresentation of the Catholic view as somehow an invasion of the rights of Protestants. Native Americanism was also marked by fierce hostility to the foreign-born, especially the Irish and German Catholics, whom it denounced as agents of Papal subversion of the United States. In New York City, Native Americanism was temporarily allied with civic reform and good government forces hostile to Tammany corruption (Gustavus Myers, *The History of Tammany Hall,* New York, 1917, pp. 124–125ff) and sometimes expressed in distorted form the fear of workers that competition from unorganized immigrants would reduce their wages, but in Philadelphia and elsewhere these elements seem to be absent and they do not occur in Levin's many addresses. At the first Native American National Convention in Harrisburg, Pa., July 5 and 7, 1845 there were delegates from fourteen states. In the 29th Congress (1845), the Native Americans had six members, four from New York and two from Pennsylvania. Their decline was continual, however; the similar Know-Nothing movement of the 1850's also did not last long. It should be noted that these movements were directly harmful to Jews as well as other immigrants. Isidor Bush reports that the Jews of St. Louis were intimidated to keep out of public affairs by nativist agitation ("Historical Sketches. The Jews of St. Louis," *The Jewish Tribune,* December

21, 1883). Jonathan Nathan, writing to his friend, Governor Hamilton Fish of New York on December 21, 1853, states that although "generally cold & unexcitable, I am particularly sensitive on Native Americanism & religious intolerance," and that he expects the "fermentation" soon to "explode to somebody's damage." (*Hamilton Fish Papers, Letters from Jonathan Nathan,* MSS in Columbiana Collection, Columbia University.) Isaac Mayer Wise preached against nativism in 1855 and reports that he had to face attacks from Jewish "American aristocrats" (*Reminiscences,* Cincinnati, 1901, pp. 310–311), which he apparently answered effectively. (See also John Hancock Lee, *The Origin and Progress of the American Party in Politics,* Philadelphia, 1855, written by a Native American; Max Berger, "The Irish Emigrant and American Nativism as Seen by British Visitors, 1836–1860," *The Pennsylvania Magazine,* Vol. 70, 1946, pp. 146–160; Joseph Jackson, *Encyclopedia of Philadelphia,* Harrisburg, 1932, III, 926–927.)

6. William Fell Giles, Maryland Democrat, had defended the immigrants against the allegations of fraud, and favored referring the resolutions to the Judiciary Committee.

7. The fact is that by about 1838 France had completed payment *to the United States* of $5,558,108 in settlement of a claim for $12,000,000 that our government had made on account of French seizure of American ships and cargoes by Napoleonic decrees. As for Lafayette, during his triumphal tour of the United States in 1824 and 1825, on the invitation of President James Monroe, he had been presented with $200,000 in cash and a township of land by Congress.

8. Robert C. Winthrop, Massachusetts Whig, had sought to disassociate the Whigs from the Native Americans, although in some instances in various places temporary political alliances had been formed. The Whig party, founded in 1834, was dominated in the north by manufacturing, financial, and commercial interests and was frequently hostile to the foreign-born. The party disintegrated after losing the elections in 1852.

9. To extend the period of residence before naturalization to twenty-one years was the main and best known aim of the Native Americans. It had been agitated continually since at least 1838, with groups of citizens and even the Louisiana House of Representatives petitioning Congress for the necessary legislation. In the Congress preceding the one to which Levin was elected, there were about thirty-five petitions in the Senate and House for the twenty-one year residence requirement. (Frank George Franklin, *The Legislative History of Naturalization in the United States, From the Revolutionary War to 1861,* Chicago, 1906, pp. 191–278; Ray Allen Billington, *The Protestant Crusade 1800–1860,* New York, 1938, pp. 206–218.)

10. William Lowndes Yancey, Alabama Democrat and planter, in his talk had favored Levin's amendment for a select committee. Himself pro-slavery, Levin sought support for his Nativism from Southern slaveowners by frequently denouncing anti-slavery tendencies as inspired by the Pope and his agents (*Speech of Mr. L. C. Levin, of Penn., on the Proposed Mission to Rome,* Delivered in the House of Representatives . . . March 2, 1848, Washington, 1848). Nevertheless, the Catholic Church in the United States was not distinguished for its opposition to slavery.

11. Daniel O'Connell, the Irish liberator, was continually being attacked by Levin for having stimulated the founding in the United States of Repeal Clubs of Irish-Americans who supported Ireland's desire to repeal the Union with Britain. Levin asserted that the Irish should free themselves from the greater

evil of Catholic domination before they sought freedom from Britain (*A Lecture on Irish Repeal, in Elucidation of the Fallacy of Its Principles, and in Proof of its Pernicious Tendency, in its Moral, Religious, and Political Aspects,* Philadelphia, 1844). Since O'Connell was also anti-Slavery, Levin blamed the Irish in America for abolitionism.

12. Levin's account of the Philadelphia Riots hardly corresponds to the essential facts. The first riot was in the Kensington quarter in Philadelphia, largely inhabited by Irish immigrants, on May 6, 7 and 8, 1844. Seven were killed and about fifty wounded. Two Catholic churches, a female seminary and about thirty dwellings were burned to the ground by the Nativist mob, and some 200 families were rendered homeless, before order was restored. The second occurred on July 7, 1844, in the Southwark district; here the fighting was chiefly between the Nativist rioters and the military forces, artillery being used on both sides. The casualties were two soldiers killed and eighteen wounded, with thirteen killed and twenty-six wounded among "rioters and bystanders." Examination of the reports in the Philadelphia contemporary press leads to the conclusion that the important thing is not who fired the first shot (the immigrants or the Nativists), since the evidence is quite contradictory, but wherein lay the main responsibility. The anti-alien, anti-Irish, and anti-Catholic sentiment whipped up by the Nativist papers examined, was founded on prejudice and appealed to base feelings that became uncontrollable when the physical conflict began. (Jackson, *op. cit.*, I, 87–90; Billington, *op. cit.*, 221–233; the longest account of the riots, written by a Nativist, is in Lee, *op. cit.*, in which he is not above the imputation that the Catholics burned their own churches as a provocation; also influenced by the fact that Thompson Westcott was a Nativist leader is J. Thomas Scharf and Thompson Westcott, *History of Philadelphia. 1609–1884,* Philadelphia, 1884, pp. 663–673; the Catholic view is in John Gilmary Shea, *A History of the Catholic Church within the Limits of the United States,* New York, 1892, III, 46–54; a contemporary Irish account is in Thomas D'Arcy McGee, *A History of the Irish Settlers in North America . . . to . . . 1850,* Boston, 1852, pp. 142–147, in which he incorrectly describes "Levins" as "an English Jew.")

13. Pyrrhus, King of Epirus, famous for his Pyrrhic victories over the Romans in 281 B. C., was completely defeated by the Roman general and consul, Manius Curius Dentatus in 275 B. C. near Beneventium.

14. Levin was himself the speaker when the Kensington riot began on May 6, 1844. On the afternoon of May 8th, St. Michael's Church was burned and in the evening St. Augustine's. On May 11th, writing editorially in his paper, *The Daily Sun,* which during the course of the riots had been issuing extras in which the main emphasis was not on discipline and order but on the alleged responsibility of the immigrants for the deaths that had occurred, Levin wrote: "Next to the terrific calamity of loss of life, the most horrible of evils at all times, is the burning of churches and destruction of property—a crime so fiendish, that few men with human hearts in their bosoms, would dream of the atrocity; and still fewer who would not sacrifice everything, short of life, to avert them." Between May and July, however, such warnings against church-burnings were not so effective as the anti-alien sentiments that received the main stress. In the July riot, therefore, St. Philip de Neri's Church became a target for the nativist mob, which attacked it with battering ram and cannon. In this case, when the mob got into the church, Levin, Thomas D. Grover, a vice-president of the Native Americans, and others addressed the crowd and prevented it from sacking the church. Levin also helped persuade one gang from firing its cannon a second time against the church. (Lee, *op. cit.*, 169, 191.)

15. After the long debate, the House decided, without even a roll-call vote, to refer the resolution to the Judiciary Committee, which reported on February 10, 1845 against any extension of the residence requirement. Levin continued his advocacy, however, and as late as January 23, 1850 he gave notice of a bill for twenty-one-years' residence and a tax on immigrants. (Franklin, *op. cit.*, 278.)

95. Fighting in the Mexican War

1. *The American Israelite*, Vol. 50, No. 3, July 16, 1903, pp. 1, 4–5, *The St. Louis City Directory*, 1903, lists a Jacob Hirshorn as residing at 4056 Laclede Avenue, together with Abraham S. Hirshorn, a clerk, and probably a son. Jacob Hirshorn died in 1905, for the 1906 Directory lists only Mary Hirshorn, widow of Jacob, at the aforementioned address.

1a. Justin H. Smith, *The War with Mexico*, New York, 1919, II, 272ff; McMaster, *op. cit.*, VII, 475–500; Carl Sandburg, *Abraham Lincoln, The Prairie Years*, New York, 1926, I, 371–372. Valuable data on the relation of slavery and anti-slavery attitudes to the war are given in John Douglas Pitts Fuller, *The Movement for the Asquisition of all Mexico, 1846–1848*, Baltimore, 1936. Robert Selph Henry, *The Story of the Mexican War*, Indianapolis, 1950, strangely slights the active opposition to the war.

2. A Gustave De Bongar is listed in Heitman, *op. cit.*, II, 49, as a captain in the first New York Infantry, volunteers. *The Military Argus and Naval Chronicle* was a New York weekly then appearing in about its seventh year.

3. By December 1846 the New York volunteers included about 800, of whom 300 were American born, and the others Dutch, Irish, French, English, Poles, Swedes, Chinese and Indians. Apparently there were several boys under age; one witness described the surgeon as "rejecting a number of boys unable to carry a musket . . . but they were soon thrust into line again by our magnanimous officers." (*The 'High Private,' with a Full and Exciting History of the New-York Volunteers, . . .* by a "Corporal of the Guard," New York, 1848, p. 9.) Max J. Kohler infers from the records of the New York volunteers that there were 17 Jews among them, including Hirshorn, but the Jewish identity of some of those named has not been carefully established (*The American Hebrew*, February 9, 1894, p. 433). It is interesting that Hirshorn makes no mention of other Jews in the regiment.

4. Lt. Reichart is not listed in Heitman's register. Colonel Ward Benjamin Burnett (1811–1884) was in command of the Second New York Volunteers, and was seriously wounded at the battle of Churubusco. Lt. Col. Charles Baxter (1814–1847) was very popular with his men, was mortally wounded at Chapultepec and died in Mexico City on September 18, 1847. Major James C. Burnham (c. 1820–1866) fought in all the engagements from Vera Cruz to Mexico City and assumed command of the regiment at the gates of Mexico City when Burnett and Baxter were both disabled. Capt. Garret Dyckman is listed in Heitman's register.

5. The siege of Vera Cruz began about March 10, 1847 and lasted until the city surrendered on March 29. The Northers mentioned blew on March 12 and 13, March 23 and 24, and March 26, 1847. (R. S. Ripley, *The War with Mexico*, New York, 1849, II, 24–42.)

6. At the battle of Cerro Gordo (April 18–19, 1847), Santa Anna had about 13,000 men and the Americans 9,000 with which to storm an entrenched position. Our troops lost 431 officers and men killed and wounded. (*Ibid.*, 60–67.)

7. When Taylor was seen to be making but little headway on the drive to Mexico City southward from the Rio Grande, General Winfield Scott (1786–1866) was ordered on November 23, 1846 to attempt the southern route from Vera Cruz inland to the capital.

8. Brigadier-General James Shields (1806–1879) was brevetted major-general for his gallant conduct at Cerro Gordo. Born in Ireland, he had come to our country in 1826, and was a legislator and judge in Illinois before the war.

9. Major-General William Jenkins Worth (1794–1849) was a New Yorker who had fought well with Taylor at the victories at Palo Alto and Resaca de la Palma, and been transferred to Scott when the Southern expedition was ordered. Major-General David Emanuel Twiggs (1790–1862) had also served with Taylor in the north, as had Major-General John Anthony Quitman (1798–1858).

10. American troops occupied Puebla on May 15, 1847, and stayed there until August 7th, when they resumed the march forward.

11. On February 11, 1847, Senator Thomas Corwin of Ohio (1794–1865) delivered a speech in which the following passage occurred: "But the Senator from Michigan [Lewis Cass] says we will be two hundred millions in a few years, and we want room. If I were a Mexican I would tell you, 'Have you not room in your own country to bury your dead men? If you come into mine we will greet you with bloody hands, and welcome you to hospitable graves.'" He also accurately predicted the civil war that would develop from the acquisition of new territory into which slavery would strive to extend, but the locution about the "hospitable graves" was seized upon and became the occasion for sharp denunciation and even petitions for his expulsion from the Senate. Our soldiers in Mexico burned Corwin in effigy.

12. Brigadier-General Franklin Pierce (1804–1869) reached Puebla on August 6, 1847 with 2429 men, providing the reinforcements necessary to move forward. Pierce had already been a congressman and senator, and later became president (1853–1857).

13. Second Lieutenant Mayne Reid (1818–1883), the Irish writer, who later wrote some ninety novels and adventure stories, had not yet published a book when Jacob Hirshorn knew him in the army, although he had contributed a chapter to Philip Kearny's *Service with the French Troops in Africa,* New York, 1844. Reid was severely wounded at the battle of Chapultepec on September 13, 1847, and was promoted to First Lieutenant on September 16th.

14. Heitman's register lists a Hippolyte Dardonville as a Second Lieutenant in the first New York Infantry.

15. The Battle of Contreras was fought August 19–20, 1847, and the Battle of Churubusco followed it immediately on August 20th, with the Americans losing 133 killed, 905 wounded and missing, while the Mexicans are estimated to have suffered 6000 casualties. General Shields's brigade of New York and South Carolina volunteers lost 240 killed and wounded at Churubusco (*Report of the Proceedings of the Joint Committee Appointed to Make Suitable Arrangements for Bringing on the Bodies of the Officers of the New York Regiment of Volunteers, from Mexico,* New York, 1848, pp. 37–38).

16. Philip Kearny (1814–1862) was a very wealthy and dashing New York cavalry leader who became General Scott's bodyguard on the advance on Mexico City. While heading the charge against the retreating Mexicans that Hirshorn describes, Kearny had his left arm shattered so that it required amputation.

Yet he was reported to be the first American to enter the conquered city of Mexico a few days later.

17. Nicholas Philip Trist (1800–1874) had been sent as a special agent to General Scott to negotiate a peace treaty, but did not succeed until after the fall of the capital of Mexico.

18. Sgt. John Riley, Reilly or O'Reily of Co. K, 5th U. S. Infantry was said to have been a sergeant in the 66th Regiment of the British army in Canada, from which he had deserted. Before war against Mexico was officially declared, he deserted to the Mexican Army, perhaps attracted by the appeals of Mexican catholic priests to American catholics and by the offers of 320 acres of land and citizenship. With other deserters, a Battalion of San Patricio was organized which fought throughout the war until 87 were captured at Churubusco. The court martial of the first 29 was conducted by Colonel Bennet Riley, and sentenced all of them to hang. General Scott commuted the sentence of seven to a public lashing, branding on the cheek with a D, hard labor for six months, and dishonorable discharge, and pardoned two who proved they had been captured and compelled to fight. Reilly was not executed because he had deserted before the declaration of war. Altogether 70 of the 87 were hanged. (Edward S. Wallace, "Deserters in the Mexican War," *The Hispanic American Historical Review,* XV, 1935, pp. 374–383.) William W. Sweeny asserts that the loyal Irish soldiers in the American army were especially pleased by the measures taken ("The Irish Soldier in the War with Mexico," *The Journal of the American Irish Historical Society,* XXVI, 1927, p. 255); but James Reilly, "An Artilleryman's Story," *Journal of the Military Service Institution of the United States,* XXXII, 1903, p. 443, in his reminiscences of the occasion, calls the court martial a "farce" and describes the general who executed the orders as "a military martinet." Ripley (*op. cit.,* 355–356) argues that since Mexico City still had to be captured, stern measures were necessary to enforce discipline.

19. The Battle of Molino del Rey, "the hardest contested battle of the whole war," (Ripley, *op. cit.,* 381–382) was fought September 8, 1847; of the 4,000 Americans engaged, 787 were killed and wounded.

20. Major Levi Twiggs of the Marines, who led the assault for which Hirshorn volunteered, was killed in the charge (Edward W. Callahan, *List of Officers of the United States and of the Marine Corps from 1775 to 1900,* New York, 1901, p. 699).

21. Thomas William Sweeny (b. Ireland, d. 1892) was transferred from the volunteers to the regular army on March 3, 1848 (Heitman, *op. cit.,* I, 939). To remember so accurately details of this sort Hirshorn must have had either an amazing memory, a diary, or research assistance in re-creating the picture of the times.

22. Lt. Edward H. Fitzgerald (d. 1860) of the quartermaster's department became a captain on August 5, 1847 and was brevetted major on September 13, 1847 for gallantry and meritorious conduct at Chapultepec (Heitman, *op. cit.,* I, 422).

23. These reinforcements arrived at Mexico City about December 17, 1847.

24. The peace treaty was negotiated by Trist on February 2, 1848, ratified by the Senate March 10, and the ratifications exchanged May 30, 1848.

25. The regiment was disbanded August 1, 1848. What Hirshorn did after that has not yet been recorded.

96. Irish Famine Relief

1. *New-York Daily Globe,* March 10, 1847, p. 1, cols. 6–7; also in *Lyons Scrapbook II,* pp. 30, 30b, 31a. The *New-York Daily Globe* was an organ of Tammany Hall, in which M. M. Noah, a speaker at this meeting, was then very prominent; other New York newspapers, however, also gave this meeting notice, even if not such extensive coverage.
2. A. L. Morton, *A People's History of England,* London, 1938, pp. 441–442; *Encyclopaedia Britannica,* 1947 ed., XII, 612; McGee, *op. cit.,* 136–141.
3. Belmont became one of the seventy-four members of the official General Standing Committee for the Relief of Famishing Poor in Ireland and contributed $500 (*Report of the General Relief Committee of the City of New York . . .* New York, 1848, pp. 147, 17, 162).
4. The *Globe* reported that "a large and respectable assembly" was present, and elected the following to preside: as chairman, Samuel Lazarus, President of the Congregation; as vice-president, Isaac Phillips (1812–1889), an employee in the customs-house; as secretary, Samuel J. Jacobs, listed in the city directory for that year as a clerk.
5. Later the Rev. Lyons was to learn that on February 22, 1847, in Charleston, at the laying of the corner-stone of a new synagogue, "after the conclusion of the ceremony, a collection was made for the relief of the Irish." (*Lyons Scrapbook II,* p. 31b, clipping identified by a manuscript notation in Lyons' handwriting as from "the New Orleans Commercial Times of March . . .") A few days after the meeting at Shearith Israel, Rev. Samuel Meyer Isaacs, Hazan and Lecturer at Shaarey Tefilah, held a similar meeting and raised $80 (*Report of the General Relief Committee,* p. 40). Moreover, on February 20, 1847, Captain Uriah P. Levy of the United States Navy had written to the Secretary of the Navy, J. Y. Mason, offering his services as commander of a vessel to transport supplies to Ireland, his pay to go to the relief fund. His offer was not accepted, although the navy supplied two vessels for this purpose. (*Defense of Uriah P. Levy . . .* New York, 1858, p. 18.)
6. The *Globe* reports that after Lyons, the following spoke: Uriah H. Judah, a merchant; Jonas B. Phillips (1805–1869), dramatist, lawyer, and then an Assistant District Attorney in New York; M. M. Noah. $175 was turned in to the Relief Committee as the proceeds of the collection (*Report . . .* p. 37).

97. Dry Goods Auctions

1. *Lyons Scrapbook II,* p. 15. No copy of this weekly is known to be extant; the clipping is therefore identified only by a manuscript notation in the hand of Rev. J. J. Lyons, who, however, errs in recording the date as Saturday, September 25, 1845: the periodical did not begin to appear until 1846, and Saturday, September 25 fell in 1847 and not in 1845. His note also states that the *Reporter* was published in New York, Boston and Philadelphia, and was edited by Robert R. Boyd. The Office of original publication, however, was at 38 William Street, New York, from which it was probably distributed to the other cities. (*Dogget's New-York City Directory for 1847 & 1848,* p. 130.)
2. *The Dry Goods Economist, Jubilee Number, Fiftieth Anniversary, 1846–1896,* New York, 1896, p. 13.
3. Criticism of the auction system of wholesale selling was common and had led to state and federal legislation to correct outstanding abuses (Roy B. Wester-

field, "Early History of American Auctions," *Transactions, Connecticut Academy of Arts and Sciences,* XXIII, 1920, pp. 165ff). In 1851, in New York, $7,500,000 worth of dry goods, foreign and domestic, was auctioned off; yet by 1897 the standardization of market techniques and prices had led to the abandonment of the auction system, which now plays only a marginal role in the distribution of standard merchandise (Paul D. Converse, *Marketing, Methods and Policies,* New York, 2d ed., 1924, pp. 178–179).

4. Yom Kippur, the Day of Atonement, fell on Monday, September 20, 1847.
5. The Port Wardens, appointed by the Governor and Senate of the State, consisted of one Master Warden, five deputies, and a clerk.
6. Austens & Spicer at 24 William Street, Fosters & Livingston at 53 Beaver, and Catterfield & Topping at 39 William were among the most prominent auction houses in New York.

98. Jews and Sunday Laws

1. This newspaper was owned by Noah, Deans & Howard and was edited by M. M. Noah from 1843, when he merged his *Noah's Weekly Messenger* with the *Sunday Times,* until his death in 1851. In all probability, Noah himself wrote the editorial, and it is therefore of special interest as expressing the viewpoint of one of the most prominent Jews of his time.
2. Friedenwald, *AJHSP,* V, 1897, p. 202. A comprehensive description and analysis of the history of the question is given by Jacob Ben Lightman, *A Study of Reported Judicial Opinions of the American Courts Regarding the Status of Jews with Respect to the Sunday Laws,* unpublished Master's Thesis, Graduate School for Jewish Social Work, New York, 1933, in which the case discussed in this editorial is presented on pages 76, 81–84, 160–165. A summary of this thesis is available in print in *Jewish Social Service Quarterly,* Vol. 11 (1934–1935), pp. 223–228, 269–276.
3. In the fall of 1950, a test of the constitutionality of the Sunday laws of New York, instituted by the American Jewish Congress, will be argued in the State Court of Appeals by Mr. Leo Pfeffer of the legal staff of the Congress. This case involves Sam Friedman, 16 Jackson Street and Sam Praska, 46 Jefferson Street, two New York east side butcher-shopkeepers who were convicted of selling meat on Sundays and fined $10 each despite the fact that they keep their stores closed on the Jewish Sabbath. Supported by the Rabbinical Board of Greater New York, the Union of Orthodox Rabbis of the United States and Canada, the Mizrachi Organization of America, the Agudath Israel, and Young Israel, the American Jewish Congress took the case to the Appellate Division. In a powerful brief, Mr. Pfeffer argued in part that if the state law under which the defendants were convicted does not exempt Sabbath-observing Jews, it is unconstitutional, since it violates the first and fourteenth amendments to the United States constitution and sections three and eleven of the state constitution. The Appellate Division upheld the conviction, without writing an opinion. The Court of Appeals, however, accepted the case for review. (American Jewish Congress, Brief by Leo Pfeffer, December 30, 1949.)

   Another type of case that has recently developed, and that has already been argued in more than twenty states, arises from the administration of unemployment insurance codes. Such cases involve Jews or others who, observing Saturday as a day of rest, refuse to accept employment that would require their working on Saturdays, and apply for unemployment compensation. In

May, 1950, the American Jewish Congress, with Mr. Pfeffer as counsel, won such a case for Miss Adele Scheinwald of New York. The similar case of Mary Jane Heisler was pending in the Court of Common Pleas, Mahoning County (Youngstown), Ohio in June, 1950; Mr. Pfeffer co-operated with local counsel in writing the brief, filed April 19, 1950. (American Jewish Congress, *Press Release,* May 10, 1950; Brief by Schermer, Goldstein & Millstone and Leo Pfeffer.)

4. The case was argued in the 1846 Term of the City Court. The Judge, Recorder William Rice, ruled in favor of Benjamin, and in his opinion stated: "in a community where there is a complete severance between Church and State, and where entire freedom of religious faith and worship is guarantied to all its citizens alike, *without discrimination or preference,* the observance of any particular day, in a religious sense, is a matter of mere ecclesiastical or religious discipline and authority, and in no way pertaining to the civil power or legislative authority of the State . . . Is it no discrimination or preference, to select by the civil law of the State, the day considered sacred in a religious sense by the Christian, and to compel the Jew to unite externally, at least, in its observance; to protect from possible disturbance those who worship on that day, by requiring all others to abstain from every species of labour and employment, while the Jewish Sabbath is protected by no similar regulation? In the view of the constitution, are not the Jewish Sabbath and the Christian Sunday precisely equal, and those who worship God upon one or the other day, entitled to a perfect equality of immunity and privileges? . . ." (The full text of Rice's statement is in *The Occident,* IV, March, 1847, pp. 588–595.) It should be noted that in the same year, 1846, the court ruled in favor of the Jewish defendant in the case of *The City of Cincinnati vs. Jacob Rice* (Lightman, *op. cit.,* 77).

5. Judge John Belton O'Neall (1793–1863), of Quaker parentage, had been president of the Newberry Baptist Society since 1837. He had been active in South Carolina politics since 1816, and a judge since 1828. (*Cyclopaedia of Eminent and Representative Men of the Carolinas of the Nineteenth Century,* Madison, 1892, pp. 668–671.) In his decision (full text in *The Occident,* V, March, 1848, pp. 594–599), Judge O'Neall argued that Christianity is part of the common law and underlies the State Constitution, and declared that only a police power and not a constitutional question was involved. "If the Legislature, or the City of Charleston were to declare that all shops within the State or City should be closed . . . on the 4th of July or 8th of January in each year, would any one believe such a law was unconstitutional. It could not be pretended religion had anything to do with that! What has religion to do with a similar regulation for Sunday? It is in a political and social point of view a mere day of rest. Its observance, as such, is a mere question of expediency. . . ." The importance of this opinion lies in the fact that it has usually been quoted by other courts down to 1929 (Lightman, *op. cit.,* 164n–165n, lists the cases in which O'Neall's opinion is cited).

6. Jewish leaders were divided on the question. Opposing Noah's views was Isaac Leeser, editor of *The Occident,* and two of his contributors: VI, April, 1848, pp. 36–39, in which a lawyer signing himself "An Hebrew" calls Judge O'Neall "unquestionably a fanatic;" VI, July, 1848, pp. 186–193, in which "An American Jew" challenges O'Neall's statement that Christianity is the only standard of good morals; VI, September, 1848, p. 302, in which Judge O'Neall explains that he included the Old Testament in his concept of Christianity; and VI, October, 1848, pp. 367–368, in which "An American Jew" finds O'Neall's explanation unsatisfactory.

99. Indian Agent

1. Wisconsin State Historical Society, MSS Division. Mrs. Levy's reminiscences were first written in German, then crudely translated into English with the aid of a ten year old grand-daughter; the present version is edited by Ellis B. Usher, pp. 22–24 of the typescript, from pp. 18–20 of the English manuscript. A very short and dry edition of the entire work has been edited by Albert H. Sanford and published in the *Proceedings of the State Historical Society of Wisconsin,* Vol. 59, 1911, pp. 201–215. I am indebted to Mr. Sanford, now director of the La Crosse Historical Society, for considerable assistance in the compilation of many of the facts given herein.

2. When sheer building was primary, he was well-known for his enterprise, building the first hotel, the first wharf-boat, the first dock, and so forth. He was Mayor of La Crosse in 1860, 1866 and 1867, and an alderman eight times, as well as an Assessor in 1862 and director of the Board of Trade in 1871. Economically, he became an unsuccessful banker, his enterprise collapsing in the crisis of 1857; later he was a grocer and real estate operator. In his last years, he was impoverished and was supported by old friends. In the 1870's he was an officer of the Cremieux Lodge, No. 138, of B'nai B'rith, and a lecturer in the congregational Sunday School. When he died, April 20, 1910, flags were lowered to half mast by official proclamation and the city offices were closed on the afternoon of his funeral, at which Rev. J. S. Lower of St. Paul's Universalist Church officiated. (*The La Crosse Tribune,* April 21, 1910; *History of La Crosse County, Wisconsin* . . . Chicago, 1881, pp. 453–455; Charles Seymour, *The Northwestern Centennial Celebration, in La Crosse, Wisconsin, Tuesday, July 4th, 1876,* La Crosse, 1877, p. 20; *LaCrosse Tribune and Leader-Press,* December 6 and 14, 1941; *The American Israelite,* January 23, 1874, January 29, 1875, July 16, 1875, May 19, 1876; correspondence with Mr. Albert H. Sanford.)

3. Willie was killed when a horse accidentally stepped on his head the following spring; he died on April 7, 1849, aged seven (p. 41 of these "Recollections").

4. The National Archives. *Records of the Office of Indian Affairs. Letters Received, 1848, Winnebago, P–193.*

5. *Annual Report of the Commissioner of Indian Affairs, 1848–1849,* Washington, 1850, from Report of Alexander Ramsey, Superintendent of Indian Affairs, Minnesota Territory, October 13, 1849, p. 88; Frederick Webb Hodge, ed., *Handbook of American Indians North of Mexico,* Washington, 1910, Part 2, pp. 958–959.

6. The location had been chosen not by the Indians but by Henry M. Rice, later United States Senator from Minnesota ([Reuben S. Thwaites]: "The Wisconsin Winnebagoes. An Interview with Moses Paquette," *Collections of the State Historical Society of Wisconsin,* XII, 1892, p. 407. Paquette was an agent engaged by Rice to help effect the removal of the Indians. He reports the removal was not completed until November, while Augusta Levy gave the date as July.)

7. To this letter a reply was sent, dated Office Indian Affairs, June 24, 1848, and signed W. M. The letter was peremptory, declared that "no such measure can be countenanced for a moment," and warned Levy against interfering in any way with the scheduled removal, subject to the punishment of the law (The National Archives. *Records of the Office of Indian Affairs. Record Copies of Letters Sent, Volume 41, p. 49*). The removal was finally effected after troops were called into play (Edward Duffield Neill, *The History of Minnesota,* . . .

4th edition, Minneapolis, 1882, pp. 484–485). Nevertheless, the Indians refused to stay in Minnesota, despite the fact that Ramsey called in troops to keep them there (*Annual Report, loc. cit.*, 91). Paquette, who helped in the removal, states, "It always seemed to me that the removal was unnecessary, and involved useless hardships," while Henry M. Rice wrote to Reuben G. Thwaites, October 14, 1887: "Wisconsin was always the region they desired, and it is doubtful if the generation of that day would have ever been content elsewhere." ("The Wisconsin Winnebagoes," *loc. cit.*, 409, 407n.) They finally had to retire to Omaha, Nebraska.

100. Election Circular

1. *Lyons Scrapbook I*, item 75b, American Jewish Historical Society.
2. In 1849, after his defeat in this election, Hart became Chairman of the Tammany General Committee, and he was one of the Sachems in 1857, 1858, 1867, 1868, 1870, 1871, and 1872, the latter period including the piratical reign of "Boss" William M. Tweed. Hart held many political offices and appointments, both municipal and federal: Alderman, 1845, 1846, 1871; Representative in Congress, 1851–1853; Surveyor of the Port of New York, 1857–1862, during which term he helped reform abuses in the New York Custom House; a Commissioner of Immigration, 1870–1873; a New York Excise Commissioner, 1880–1883; Disbursing Agent at the New York Custom House, 1885–1889; Cashier in the New York County Sheriff's Office, 1889–1893; an Officer in the Internal Revenue Department, 1893–1897. In 1884, as a supporter of Cleveland, he was active in a movement to reform the New York Democracy. In his early days, he was a stock and bond broker, and later, when not holding office, a merchant; in 1878 he was connected with the Texas and Pacific Railway Company. At various times he was president of Mount Sinai Hospital and of the Home for the Aged and Infirm, and Treasurer of the Society for Relief of Poor Hebrews. (*Lamb's Biographical Dictionary of the United States*, Boston, 1900, III, 566; *The National Cyclopedia of American Biography*, New York, 1893, III, 391; *The Biographical Directory of the American Congress, 1774–1927*, p. 1069; [Robert B. Roosevelt:] *The New York Democracy*, New York, 1884, p. 5; Letter to Hon. Rufus E. Cowing, November 20, 1878, on stationery of Texas and Pacific Railway Company, 50 Exchange Place, New York, in New-York Historical Society, Misc. MSS; Tammany printed circulars and clippings in *Tammany Scrapbooks*, 3 vols., New York Public Library; Henry L. Clinton, *Speeches of, The Tammany Ring Exposed and Denounced*, New York, 1872, p. 17.)
3. For Lewis Cass, see the Index for other references.

   William Orlando Butler (1791–1880), who had played a prominent part in the attack on Mexico and was in chief command when the war ended, had been nominated to offset Taylor's Mexican War record, and partly because as a Kentuckian he would appeal to southern votes.

   Reuben Hyde Walworth (1788–1867) had been a county and state judge before he became Chancellor of New York State, serving from 1828 to 1848, when the new constitution abolished that position.

   Charles O'Conor (1804–1884) was a leader of the Friends of Ireland and a vigorous opponent of the anti-slavery movement.
4. After two terms as Alderman, Hart had refused renomination. During his first term he was subjected to a contemptible and foully phrased anti-Semitic onslaught in *The Subterranean*, January 3, 1846, p. 2, col. 1. This weekly was edited by Michael ("Mike") Walsh (1810–1859), a colorful and rambunctious

democratic politician who often gave voice to the real needs of the masses without contributing anything substantial to their satisfaction. For a while he fought Tammany Hall on the issue of patronage until he made his peace with it and was elected to the State Assembly and later to Congress. His periodical often foamed with anti-Semitic diatribes in connection with M. M. Noah, Hart, and other Jews. (J. Fairfax McLaughlin, *The Life and Times of John Kelly,* New York, 1885, pp. 146–153; James O'Meara, *Broderick and Gwin,* San Francisco, 1881, pp. 7–10; Mario Emilio Cosenza, *The Establishment of the College of the City of New York . . .* New York, 1925, pp. 131–142, 212–214; *Speech of Mike Walsh, of New York, on the Kansas and Nebraska Bill,* Washington, D. C., 1854.)

5. Henry Arcularius, Jr. was employed in the Register's office, and Nicholas Quackenbos was a lawyer (*Doggett's New York City Directory . . . 1848–1849,* pp. 29, 333).
6. A Francis Bos is in the Directory, but the others are not.

101. Jews Need Not Apply

1. *Lyons Scrapbook I,* p. 99.
2. By 1846, there were a sufficient number of Bohemian Jews in New York city for them to establish their own society, *Böhmischer Verein,* out of which there grew in 1848 the Bohemian congregation, Ahabat Chesed (Grinstein, *op. cit.,* 476). In 1849 there were some 80 members in the congregation (Guido Kisch, *In Search of Freedom, A History of American Jews from Czechoslovakia,* London, 1949, p. 299).

102. Suicide in Brooklyn

1. *Lyons Scrapbook I,* p. 148, American Jewish Historical Society.
2. The *New-York Daily Tribune,* May 7, 1849, p. 3, col. 1, reported that the body had been found "with his brains blown out and a pistol lying near him," but gave neither name, trade, nor residence.

103. The First Jewish Weekly

1. For access to the complete file, March 30 to June 15, 1849, of this rare periodical I am indebted to Mrs. and Rabbi Stephen S. Wise. The translations from the German are by Mr. Harold Kirshner, German Department, Long Island University, New York. For an analysis of the contents, see Guido Kisch, "*Israels Herold:* The First Jewish Weekly in New York," *Historia Judaica,* II, 1940, pp. 65–84.
2. James A. Wax, "Isidor Bush, American Patriot and Abolitionist," *Historia Judaica,* V, 1943, pp. 183–203; Salvatore Sabbadini, "Relazione epistolari fra I. S. Reggio e Isidoro Busch," *Festschrift Armand Kaminka zum Siebzigsten Geburtstage,* Vienna, 1937, pp. 121–22; *The Menorah,* June, 1889, p. 328; Kisch, *op. cit.,* 68–69; *The Menorah,* September, 1898, p. 140.
3. This two-page prospectus (*Lyons Scrapbook I, item 128b*) is dated March, 1849, and contains endorsements in German by Dr. H. Felsenheld, New York; I. G. Gutheim, Cincinnati; Dr. A. Günsburg, Baltimore; P. J. Joachimssen, New York; Dr. I. Kohlmeyer, New Orleans; Dr. Lilienthal, New York; Dr. L. Merzbacher, New York, and Dr. Wise, Albany, N. Y. In English there are endorsements by M. M. Noah and S. M. Isaacs. For Bush to have in such short time won such diversified support for his project speaks both for his energy and for

the need for a liberal Jewish magazine. Julius Bien asserts that *Israels Herold* was the first organ of B'nai B'rith (*The Menorah*, April, 1887, pp. 161–163), but Dr. Kisch concludes that "it is not known if the periodical received financial support from B'nai B'rith (*op. cit.*, 67), and Rabbi Wax states that Bush did not join B'nai B'rith until July, 1849, after the periodical was discontinued (*op. cit.*, 186). My examination of the file showed no evidence that it could be considered an organ of B'nai B'rith.

4. *The Asmonean* began to appear, in English, on October 26, 1849 and lasted until its editor died in 1858.

104. Temperance

1. By courtesy of the Henry E. Huntington Library, San Marino, California. This four page weekly, 11¼ by 15 inches, appeared from August 12, 1848 to August 25, 1849, when its owner and editor, Abraham G. Levy, abandoned it and went to Ossining, N. Y., where he purchased *The Hudson River Chronicle*, which he operated until he sold it in 1851 (J. Thomas Scharf, *History of Westchester County, New York*, Philadelphia, 1886, II, 699, 354). No further information about Levy is available. The only item of specific Jewish interest in this issue occurs among the more than two pages of advertisements, which include one from P. J. Joachimssen (1817–1890), then Assistant Corporation Attorney of New York City.
2. *Standard Encyclopaedia of the Alcohol Problem*, Westerville, Ohio, 1930, VI, 2721–2722.
3. In 1845, the New York State Legislature had enacted legislation providing for elections the following May, in all towns and cities outside New York City, to determine locally what should be done about the sale of intoxicating liquor, but the Law had been repealed in 1847 (Ernest H. Cherrington, *The Evolution of Prohibition in the United States of America*, Westerville, Ohio, 1920, pp. 128, 130).

105. An Outrage

1. From the *Sunday Times and Noah's Weekly and Messenger*, August 12, 1849, edited by M. M. Noah; clipping in *Lyons Scrapbook I*, p. 144.
2. This non-sectarian cemetery had been dedicated November 21, 1848, after the New York legislature in 1847 had passed a law permitting voluntary associations to establish rural cemeteries (*The Cypress Hills Cemetery*, New York, 1858, pp. 5, 19).

106. Opposing Slave Immigration

1. Friedenberg, *AJHSP*, X, 1902, 130n–131n; and A. S. W. Rosenbach, *An American Jewish Bibliography, AJHSP*, XXX, 1926, No. 648. The original is in the Historical Society of Pennsylvania.
2. Friedenberg, *op. cit.*, 138n. Heydenfeldt, born in Charleston in 1816, moved to Alabama in 1837 and practised law; in 1840 he was a judge in the County Court in Tallapoosa, Ala. In 1850, when he went to California, he became active in politics, and served on the Supreme Court bench from 1852 to 1857. In 1862, he suspended his practise as a lawyer because, as a Southerner, he refused to take the oath of loyalty to the Union; later he became a wealthy advisory counsel without arguing cases in court. He died in 1890.

3. In 1827, James G. Birney (1792–1857), a Kentucky abolitionist born into a rich slave-holding family, had persuaded the Alabama legislature to forbid the importation of slaves into Alabama for sale or hire. In 1832, this provision was written into the State constitution, and enforced by legislation in 1837 (when Heydenfeldt came to Alabama), but the legislation was repealed in 1846. (Jesse Macy, *The Anti-Slavery Crusade,* New Haven, 1921, pp. 33–35.)
4. In 1849, Henry Clay (1777–1852) proposed that Kentucky provide for gradual emancipation of its slaves, arousing much opposition.
5. For a sketch of the anti-Slavery sentiment existing in the South, see Alice Dana Adams, *The Neglected Period of Anti-Slavery in America, (1808–1831),* Boston, 1908, pp. 30–45, and Macy, *op. cit.,* 62–65, describing the anti-Slavery debates in the Virginia legislature in 1831. In Alabama there had been considerable hostility to slavery. In January 1848 the *Tuscaloosa Monitor* wrote: "We believe that the Southern States themselves would be better off without this institution than with it. We feel confident that, if it had no present existence with us, a large majority of the Southern people would be found opposed to its introduction." (Albert Burton Moore, *History of Alabama and Her People,* Chicago and New York, 1927, I, 471.)
6. The Wilmot Proviso, banning slavery from the Territories, had been repeatedly passed in the House of Representatives from 1846 to 1849, but had been defeated in the Senate.
7. In 1830, Alabama had 117,549 slaves, equalling 38% of the total population. In 1820, the slaves had constituted 32% of the total. From 1830 to 1860, the white population increased 171%, the slave population by 270.1%. In 1860, the slaves were 45% of the total population in Alabama. (*Ibid.,* I, 447–448.)
8. The issue in the case of Groves v. Slaughter was this: the Mississippi constitution of 1832 declared that from May 1, 1833 the importation of slaves for sale was prohibited, while new settlers could bring them in only for their individual use. Since no legislation had been enacted, a suit developed in Mississippi, Louisiana, and ultimately in the United States Supreme Court testing whether the constitutional provision was sufficient or required legislative reinforcement. The Supreme Court in 1841 ruled that legislation was necessary. (Helen Tunncliff Catterall, ed., *Judicial Cases concerning American Slavery and the Negro,* Washington, D. C., 1926–1937, III, 277–279.)
9. Reuben Chapman (1799–1882) was not renominated for Governor. His successor, referring in his inaugural address to Congressional bills banning slavery in new States, declared, "Alabama, at the last session of the General Assembly, with entire unanimity, took ground with Virginia, and pledged herself to act in concert with the other slaveholding States for the defense of the institution of slavery; that such is her unalterable determination I cannot doubt." (*Inaugural of Gov. Henry W. Collier, delivered before the two houses of the General Assembly of the State of Alabama, at its Second Biennial Session, November 17, 1849,* Montgomery, 1849, p. 9.) Collier represented the more conservative elements in Alabama.

107. Contrasting Educational Systems

1. This letter, translated and published in full for the first time, was kindly made available to me by Miss Josephine Goldmark, a daughter of Dr. Goldmark. Excerpts from it appear in Miss Goldmark's *Pilgrims of '48,* New Haven, 1930, pp. 253–257. The translation is by Mr. Harold Kirshner.

2. Goldmark, *op. cit.*, 248–252.
3. *Ibid.*, *passim; The Asmonean*, II, September 6, 1850, p. 156.
4. Professor Gabriel Gustav Valentin (1810–1883), professor of physiology at Bern University, was a distinguished Jewish savant at whose home Goldmark found refuge until the efforts of the Austrian government to extradite him compelled him to leave Switzerland. Professor Valentin gave Goldmark letters of introduction to friends in Strassburg and also to Louis Agassiz at Harvard.
5. Jean Louis Rodolphe Agassiz (1807–1873), the great Swiss naturalist, had come to the United States in 1846 and been appointed professor of zoology and geology at the newly organized Lawrence Scientific School at Harvard University in 1847. An important influence in the scientific world, he was also popular as a lecturer; in 1848 and 1849 the Boston *Evening Traveller* printed the full texts of his local lectures the day after their delivery, and then issued them in pamphlet form.
6. Carl Vogt (1817–1895) had in 1847 been dismissed from his post as professor of zoology at the University of Giessen because of his revolutionary views. He had been a student of Agassiz's. "A thorough-going materialist," he later became a "champion of Darwinism." (*Chambers's Biographical Dictionary*, London and Philadelphia, 1935, p. 946.)
7. Having been in this country only six weeks, Goldmark had not yet learned that there were then in existence fifteen state universities in fourteen states (Paul Monroe, ed., *A Cyclopaedia of Education*, New York, 1913, V, 681).
8. No institution by that name is known; Dr. Goldmark probably was referring to the College of Physicians and Surgeons, located since 1837 at 67 Crosby Street, New York. Founded in 1807, it had merged with the Columbia College Faculty of Physic in 1813, and been reorganized in 1826. (William Frederick Norwood, *Medical Education in the United States Before the Civil War*, Philadelphia, 1944, pp. 109ff.)
9. The length of the semester was an issue on which the founding convention of the American Medical Association in 1847 strongly expressed itself, recommending an extension to six months. Abraham Jacobi declares that none of the existing schools adopted this recommendation ("The New York Medical College 1782–1906," *Annals of Medical History*, N. S. I, 1917, pp. 369ff) but N. S. Davis states that the College of Physicians and Surgeons added one month to its regular term and also a preliminary course, the total exceeding "the six months required by the convention" (*History of Medical Education and Institutions in the United States . . . to the Year 1850*, Chicago, 1851, p. 135). Davis concedes, however, that this instance was exceptional, and Dr. Goldmark's observation is therefore accurate.
10. The Medical Department of the University of the City of New York (now New York University) had been opened in 1841. Its graduates "were authorized by charter to practise in the state without the formality of receiving a license from the state or county societies." (Norwood, *op. cit.*, 136.) The professor of chemistry was the great John William Draper (1811–1882), who had helped to organize the medical department in 1841; his outstanding contribution, however, was made in 1852, with the publication of his *History of the Intellectual Development of Europe*, which was speedily translated into French, German, Italian, Polish, and Russian.
11. It had escaped Dr. Goldmark's notice that since 1848 the chair of physiology and pathology had been filled by Dr. Alonzo Clark (1807–1887). (James J. Walsh, *History of Medicine in New York*, New York, 1919, IV, 22.)

12. This institution had been chartered on April 8, 1850, the cornerstone had been laid in July, 1850, but it did not open until October 16, 1850, more than a month *after* Dr. Goldmark's letter. The new college was a courageous and remarkable attempt to reform medical education along the lines suggested by the American Medical Association. (Jacobi, *op. cit.,* 369.) Walsh calls it "a veritable oasis in the desert of low grade medical education in America at this time." (*Op. cit.,* II, 375.)

13. Jonathan Knight (1789–1864), anatomist and physiologist, was then professor of surgery at the Yale Medical School.

Valentine Mott (1785–1865) had an international reputation as a surgeon; having been professor of surgery at the College of Physicians and Surgeons, he had later helped to found the Medical Department of N. Y. U., at which he was the professor of surgery and surgical anatomy until 1850, when he resigned and revisited Europe. In 1818, he had been the first to tie the innominate artery (anonyma).

James Dwight Dana (1813–1895) was the mineralogist appointed to the United States exploring expedition to the South Seas in 1837. Except for a cruise in the Mediterranean in 1833 as an instructor in the navy, Dana did not visit Europe until 1860, and did not therefore, as Dr. Goldmark states, receive his training in Europe. Goldmark had been in a party with Dana that took a little geological excursion while attending the New Haven meeting of the A. A. A. S. (Goldmark, *op. cit.,* 253).

14. Justus von Liebig (1803–1873), then professor of chemistry at Giessen, was "one of the most illustrious chemists of his age" (*Chambers's Biographical Dictionary,* 590). If he did come to this country, he did not remain long, for in 1852 he became professor of chemistry at the University of Munich.

15. For unknown reasons, Professor Valentin did not come to this country (Goldmark, *op. cit.,* 257).

16. Thaddeus William Harris, M. D. (1795–1856), librarian at Harvard from 1831 to his death, was also a distinguished scientist and is known as the father of American economic entomology.

17. John White Webster (1793–1850), professor of chemistry at Harvard, was hanged in Boston on August 30, 1850 "before an immense assembly." (*The Asmonean,* II, September 6, 1850, p. 157.) Driven by a low salary and extravagant living into a considerable debt to Dr. George Parkman, he killed Dr. Parkman on November 23, 1849, and dismembered and burned the body. Convicted on circumstantial evidence, he protested his innocence and aroused much public sympathy, but in a final plea for clemency he confessed the murder while disclaiming premeditation. The case is famous in the history of American murder.

18. Friedrich Oesterlen (1812–1877) had published his *Handbuch der Heilmittellehre* in a second revised edition in 1847 in Stuttgart and Tuebingen. The *Handbuch d. Pathologie u. Theraphie* by Karl Reinhold August Wunderlich (1815–1877) was published in eighteen instalments in Stuttgart from 1846–1854. Agassiz's two daughters arrived from Neufchatel, in the custody of his cousin, Auguste Mayor, at the end of August (Jules Marcou, *Life, Letters, and Works of Louis Agassiz,* New York and London, 1896, II, 36). They would seem to have arrived sooner than Agassiz expected.

19. Goldmark's life in the United States is interesting. He began to practise as a physician specializing in skin diseases. In March 1856, the absolutist Austrian government convicted him *in absentia* of treason and of complicity in

the killing of Minister Latour, and hanged him in effigy (obituary, *New Yorker Zeitung,* April 18, 1881). In 1859 he began to manufacture percussion caps and cartridges in Brooklyn and then in Bayonne, N. J., according to a formula he had patented in 1857. During the Civil War he was one of the large suppliers for the Federal government, turning down special bids from the Confederacy. The Draft Rioters in July 1863 fired on the Goldmark factory in Brooklyn and a detachment of soldiers was detailed to protect the premises. Amnestied in 1867 by Francis Joseph, he insisted on returning to stand trial on the murder charge, was triumphantly exculpated, and honored by the University of Vienna and the Austrian Reichstag. Rejecting offers to build branches of his plant near Vienna and Budapest, he preferred to return to the more democratic environment of the United States. He was a charter member of the Chemical Society, a member of the Society of German-American Physicians, and a founder of the Republican party before the Civil War in Kings County (Brooklyn), New York. (Goldmark, *op. cit., passim.* This valuable book is an account of the related Goldmark, Wehle, and Brandeis families.)

108. Early Chicago Days

1. *Chicago Journal,* Tuesday, November 14, 1899, p. 5.
2. Hyman L. Meites, *The History of the Jews of Chicago,* Chicago, 1924, p. 64; *The Sunday Times-Herald,* Chicago, June 9, 1895, p. 20, interview with Mayer in "German Pioneers of Chicago."
3. The National Council of Jewish Women had been founded in 1893 in Chicago at the Congress of Religions held at the World's Fair. The Sinai Congregation was the third in Chicago, having been preceded by the Kehillath Anshe Maarab, 1846, and B'nai Sholom, 1852. (Morris A. Gutstein, "The Founding of K. A. M. in Chicago," paper presented at meeting of the American Jewish Historical Society, February 20, 1949.)
4. From 1847 to 1854, Temple Emanu-El was at 56 Chrystie Street. Leo Merzbacher (1810–1856) had come to New York in 1842, had served at Rodeph Shalom and at Anshe Chesed until 1844, and in 1845 had become the rabbi at Emanu-El, holding the post until his death. (Grinstein, *op. cit.,* 473, 486; "Obituary," *The Israelite,* October 31, 1856, p. 129, which says of Merzbacher, "He was the first in the United States who could scientifically substantiate the principles and projects of reform . . .") Moses Spiegel was the father of the famous Col. Marcus M. Spiegel (1829–1864), killed in the Civil War (Meites, *op. cit.,* 91).
5. The president of the Kehillath Anshe Maarab was Morris L. Leopold (1821–1889) who had been born in Laubheim, Württemberg. The first minister, who served from 1847 to 1853, was Ignatz Kunreuther (1811–1884), born in Gelnhausen, near Frankfort am Main.
6. The date is given as 1845 by Eliassof, *AJHSP,* XI, 1903, pp. 120–121.
7. It was not until 1853 that the congregation established a day-school in which Hebrew, as well as the general common school curriculum, was taught.
8. Samuel Meyer Isaacs (1804–1878) was then the Hazan and Lecturer at Shaarey Tefilah in New York (Grinstein, *op. cit.,* 486).
9. This history, by Dr. B. Felsenthal and Herman Eliassof (1849–1918), was published in Chicago, 1897.
10. When the first official call for a German mass meeting to join the Republican Party was issued in the *Staats Zeitung,* Leopold Mayer was one of the five signers (*The Sunday Times-Herald, loc. cit.*).

11. Henry Greenebaum (1833–1914) had arrived in Chicago in 1848, had been an alderman in 1856 (*The Israelite,* March 28, 1856, p. 307), the first president of the Hebrew Relief Association in 1859, a presidential elector on the Douglas Democratic ticket in 1860, and a leading figure in congregational life for several decades (Eliassof, *op. cit.,* 127–128).

12. Samuel Cole had come to Chicago in 1845 or 1846, was one of the signers of the constitution of Kehillath Anshe Maarab, and was an early leader of the Reform movement in Chicago.

    Benedict Schubert (c. 1812–1853) had arrived in Chicago in 1841, became the first merchant-tailor in the city, and built the first brick house in Chicago. (*Ibid.,* 118, 119, 121; Meites, *op. cit.,* 63, 37.)

109. The Fugitive Slave Law

1. *The Asmonean* (1849–1858), an orthodox Jewish weekly published in New York, was edited by Robert Lyon, an English Jew (1810–1858) who came to the United States in 1844, and edited the *Mercantile Journal,* a trade paper, at the same time that he issued *The Asmonean* (for a useful sketch of the periodical, see Hyman B. Grinstein, "The 'Asmonean': The First Jewish Weekly in New York," *Journal of Jewish Bibliography,* I, 1939, pp. 67–71; it later became known that the *first* Jewish weekly was Isidor Bush's *Israels Herold*).

2. Macy, *op. cit.,* 109.

3. *The Sunday Times-Herald,* Chicago, June 9, 1895, p. 20; also cited by Simon Wolf, *The American Jew As Patriot, Soldier and Citizen,* Philadelphia, 1895, pp. 425–426. Greenebaum (1824–1894) had come to Chicago from Germany in 1846, worked as a tinsmith and plumber, was in 1851 the founder of the Hebrew Benevolent Association, and later was an active Republican.

4. This article, "The Fugitive Slave Bill," was signed M. R. M. (*The Asmonean,* October 25, 1850, p. 6). The editor disclaimed responsibility for the correspondent's views, but added this footnote: "The Fugitive Bill is now the law of the land, and as such entitled to the highest and fullest observance. It may be regretted that the framers of the law made its retrospective action unlimited. Ex post facto laws are invariably oppressive, and this is more than ordinar[i]ly so from the liability of the fugitive of long standing, having acquired new relations (wife and children) which to tear asunder violates man's best nature. Had the operation been restricted to six months before the passing of the act, the greater portion of its severity would be destroyed and its opponents deprived of their strongest arguments for its repeal."

5. Between 1788 and 1851 at least 10 pamphlets, in addition to numerous periodical and newspaper articles, had been published discussing whether the Bible sanctioned or opposed slavery.

6. Probably refers to *Deut.,* xxiii, 16–17 (which had been discussed by M. R. M., see footnote 3 above): "Thou shalt not deliver unto his master a bondman that is escaped from his master unto thee; he shall dwell with thee, in the midst of thee, in the place which he shall choose within one of thy gates, where it liketh him best; thou shalt not wrong him." (Jewish Publication Society translation.)

7. The opponents of slavery did not regard the example of Shimei as convincing, in view of the fact that Shimei is described as a liar, hypocrite and blasphemer in ii Samuel xvi, 5–8, and i Kings ii, 8–9 (Rev. Hugh Brown, *Review of Rev. Dr. Raphael's Disco'rse* . . . North White Creek, N. Y., 1861, p. 34).

8. The instance of Paul and Onesimus had been several times refuted before this editorial appeared (see Rev. La Roy Sunderland, *The Testimony Of God Against Slavery . . .* ,New York, 1836, p. 136 and James Duncan, *A Treatise On Slavery . . .* , Vevay, Ind., 1824, pp. 102–103).

9. In *The Asmonean,* June 5, 1851, p. 53, Dr. S. Waterman had an article, "The Jews and the Union," in which he pleaded for unity on the ground that the Bible had "decided the question for you—'Thou shalt return the slave to his owner.' " When this article was reprinted in the *Allgemeine Zeitung des Judenthums,* Leipzig, June 30, 1851, pp. 311–312, an editorial note was appended taking issue with Dr. Waterman's view and citing against it *Deut.,* xxiii, 16.

110. States' Rights vs. Equality Abroad

1. MS in *Record Group No. 59, General Records of the Department of State. Miscellaneous Letters, February 1851,* The National Archives. A version with some interesting differences appeared in the *Cincinnati Commercial,* April 4, 1851, and is reprinted in *AJHSP,* XXVII, 1920, pp. 507–508.

2. Henry Merritt Wriston, *Executive Agents in American Foreign Relations,* Baltimore, 1929, pp. 347–348. Important light on the relation of states' rights to the Swiss treaty is to be found in a work not at all concerned with the discrimination against the Jews: Ralston Hayden, "The States' Rights Doctrine and the Treaty-Making Power," *The American Historical Review,* XXII, 1917, pp. 566, 571–580.

3. Clayton to Mann, June 15, 1850, MS, *Record Group No. 59, . . . Special Missions,* I, 310, 311–312.

4. *Ibid., Special Missions,* I, 339; Mann to Webster, *Special Agents, German State, Hungary,* No. 12 by Mann.

5. Thus Robert Lyon, denouncing the treaty in an article in his *The Asmonean,* January 24, 1851, p. 108, objected only to the explicit exclusion of American Jews from the benefits of the treaty and asserted that an American Jew in Switzerland should ask for no right that a Swiss Jew did not have: "it is clear that the citizenship of America would not entitle a man to reside there, no more than under this Treaty, the coloured Christian born in Switzerland, could go unmolested into South Carolina, under the cover of his character as a Swiss citizen," since an American free Negro could not enter South Carolina. The Swiss Consul in New York, Ls. Ph. De Luze, in a letter in *The New York Herald,* Aug. 10, 1857, objecting to an article on the Treaty, protested that the Swiss Cantons "are sovereign States, as well as the several States of the American Union" and pointed to the American doctrine of state's rights. In *The Charleston Daily Courier,* Aug. 25, 1857, "A Jew" argued in a similar vein: "There are two Federal Republics—one of them has Cantons in which laws exist precluding Jews from domicil; the other has States in which laws exist precluding persons of color from domicil. The largest and most powerful nation says to her weaker sister, abolish your anti-jewish laws; the weaker power replies, I cannot, they are not under my control any more than your anti-african laws are under yours. Then says the powerful nation, I will not meddle with my States' rights, but you *shall* meddle with yours, or I will not treat with you. Suppose the Swiss government had yielded; would that be a triumph of justice and humanity? It seems to me more like the good old rule, that 'he who has the power should take.' " (Clipping, Swiss Treaty Folder, Rosenbach Collection, American Jewish Historical Society.)

6. Agitation against the Treaty among the Jews was begun in New York by Dr. Sigmund Waterman with a proposal that "An Address signed by every Jew in the land should be drawn up and sent to the President" (*The Asmonean,* January 24, 1851, p. 110). On January 25, John Samuel of Philadelphia wrote to Webster and received a reassuring reply (*ibid.,* February 7, 1851, p. 125). February 14, *The Asmonean* published an appeal addressed to Rev. Dr. Lilienthal, expressing the hope that American Jews will help prevent the ratification of the Treaty. The same issue carried a call to action from a Savannah Jew. On February 13, 1851, President Millard Fillmore, in his Message to the Senate, specifically requested that the draft of the treaty be amended to exclude the obnoxious clause. Nevertheless, the public pressure continued.

7. Joseph Abraham (1817–1894), born in England, had lived in Jamaica, New York and Philadelphia before he settled in Cincinnati in the 1830s. First a clothier, then a notary public, he later became a well-known lawyer. In 1851 he was secretary of the Congregation Bene Israel and active in the B'nai B'rith. (*The Menorah,* XVII, 1894, pp. 246–48; *Williams' Cincinnati Directory for 1849–50,* p. 17, for *1851–52,* p. 10, and for *1864,* p. 25; David Philipson, *The Oldest Jewish Congregation in the West,* Cincinnati, 1924, pp. 59–60.)

   Bellamy Stover (1796–1875) had been a congressman and presidential elector; Joseph Abraham studied law with him. (George Irving Reed, ed., *Bench and Bar of Ohio,* Chicago, 1897, I, 113–14.)

8. A Morris Levin is listed in the 1849–50 Directory as a clerk.

   Morris Bettman, a dry-goods merchant, was a Trustee of Bene Israel (Directory for 1851–52, p. 27; Philipson, *op. cit.,* 61).

   Solomon Katzenberger was a member of the German congregation, Bene Yeshurun (*The History of the K. K. Bene Yeshurun,* Cincinnati, 1892). With his brother Lazarus, he was a partner in the firm of Katzenberger, Straus & Co., clothing and drygoods (Directory for 1849–50, p. 159).

   Nathan Malzer was a clothier, and active in Bene Israel.

   Lewis S. Rosenstiel, also active in Bene Israel, was in dry goods.

   The Directories list both a Jacob Goldberg and a Joseph Goldberg, as well as a James Goldberg.

   Abraham Harris, a clothier, had been Treasurer of Bene Israel in 1848–49.

   Elias Mayer was a merchant tailor (Directory for 1851–52, p. 174).

   Lewis Abraham (1825–1903) was then dealing in wholesale liquors, wines and cigars; he had been secretary of Bene Israel in 1848–49. Later he married Hetty Mayer, daughter of Elias Mayer. He became a prominent writer for the *American Israelite* under the pseudonym of *Sopher* and a distinguished lawyer specializing in patent law. (Directory for 1851–52, p. 10; *The American Israelite,* January 7, 1904, p. 4.)

   Adolphus A. Mayer son of Elias Mayer, had been in the clothing business with his father.

   Mosely Ezekiel, an "inspector of liquors," had been secretary of Bene Israel from 1844 to 1848 (Directory for 1849–50, p. 95).

   Morris B. Mann was a book-keeper.

   Michael Klaw was then vice-president of Bene Israel; he was in the clothing business.

   Jacob Seasongood, then treasurer of Bene Israel, was with Philip Heidelbach a member of Heidelbach, Seasongood & Co., "one of the largest and most extensive cloth jobbing and clothing concerns in the West" (*The Biographical Cyclopaedia and Portrait Gallery with an Historical Sketch of the State of Ohio,* Cincinnati, 1884, II, 560–62). After the Civil War he became a banker.

Born in Bavaria in 1814, he came to New York in 1837 and soon left for Ohio (Armin Tenner, *Cincinnati Sonst und Jetzt,* Cincinnati, 1878, pp. 248–50).

Philip Heidelbach was then president of Bene Israel.

Adolph Ancker was a salesman.

David Mayer had been a merchant tailor but was now a broker (Directories for 1849–50, p. 194 and 1851–52, p. 174).

9. MS, *Record Group No. 59, General Rec. of Dept. of State. Domestic Letters, XXXVIII.*

10. On the same day, the Senate received, and laid on the table, memorials protesting the provisions of the treaty from "Joseph Jonas and others, Israelites, of Cincinnati" and from "M. M. Noah and others, Israelites, of New York" *Journal of the Executive Proceeding of the Senate . . . 1848 to . . . 1852,* Washington, 1887, p. 311). Noah, incidentally, died on March 22, 1851.

11. For similar replies by Webster and for the first historical treatment of the subject, see Stroock, *AJHSP,* XI 1903, pp. 7–52.

12. *Lyons Scrapbook I,* item 180m. The circular was reprinted in *The Asmonean,* IX, March 31, 1854, p. 190 and in *The Occident,* XII, May, 1854, p. 99.

13. *The Asmonean,* May 28, 1852, p. 44. The following week, Robert Lyon, the editor, declared that "we do not agree with the measures proposed" and suggested instead that the problem be solved by bringing the Jews of Europe to the United States (June 4, 1852, p. 52). For action in accordance with Wise's call, see the issues of June 4, 12 (sic), and 18, 1852.

14. On July 27, 1852, Representative Emanuel B. Hart wrote to the State Department inquiring about the status of the treaty, and followed this with an interview with the Acting Secretary of State, who told him that no treaty had yet been concluded (*ibid.,* August 13, 152, p. 149).

15. *Journal of the Executive Proceedings of the Senate of the United States of America . . .* 1852 . . . 1855, Washington, 1887, Vol. 9, p. 25. To trace the bare record of the debate, see pp. 57, 69, 102, 116, 146, 181, 216, 234, 320, 330, 331.

16. In 1852, evidence of discrimination against American Protestants by European Catholic governments had led to the presentation of many petitions. As a result the Committee on Foreign Relations on February 17, 1853 had presented a report proposing that our government, in future treaties, "if practicable," secure to all American citizens residing abroad the right to worship and to purchase burial grounds (*32 Cong., 2 Sess., Senate Report No. 418*).

17. On February 28, 1854, Senator Lewis Cass of Michigan wrote to Levy, welcomeing the possibility of a petition from the Jews (the text was also published in *The Asmonean,* March 31, 1854, p. 190, and *The Occident,* May, 1854, pp. 98–99). That such an inquiry should have been needed and the reply used as justification suggests timidity and perhaps even opposition on the part of some Jews.

18. The initiative for this petition seems to have come from only one congregation, B'nai Jeshurun. Every one of the names listed was a signatory of the invitation to attend a dinner for the B'nai Jeshurun Educational Institute on March 23, 1854, while Swart and Goldsmith were on the Board of Directors and the latter taught Hebrew at the Institute (*AJHSP,* XXVII, 1920, pp. 514–15; Grinstein, *op. cit.,* 232; Israel Goldstein, *A Century of Judaism in New York, B'nai Jeshurun, 1825–1925,* p. 139, understates the case when he writes that "two-thirds of the Committee of signatories, were members of B'nai Jeshurun"). The occupations of the signers, as given in *Trow's New York City Directory,*

1854/55, are: David Samson, grocer; Jacob I. Moses (c. 1804–1854, *The Occident,* XII, 1855, pp. 531–32), merchant; Henry B. Herts, Jr., stationer (and president of the Young Men's Hebrew Benevolent and Fuel Association, Grinstein, *op. cit.,* 150); Jonas P. Levy (1807–1883), brother of Uriah P. Levy, was a sea-captain who had commanded the *America* when it transported American troops to Vera Cruz in the Mexican War; George S. Mawson, merchant; Emanuel M. Swart was in "whalebone"; Barrow Benrimo was in "segars"; Michael Myers (not Mordecai Myers) operated a "mourningstore" (*Trow's Directory, 1853/54*); Henry Goldsmith was in "segars" at 60 Fulton Street with Emanuel L. Goldsmith; Mark Levy was an importer and a Trustee of B'nai Jeshurun, and died in July, 1854 (*The Occident,* XII, 1854, pp. 322–23; the Directory lists four other Mark Levys that year!); Philip J. Joachimsen was a lawyer; Jacob Pecare was an "agent"; Alexander Kursheedt was a lawyer. Goldsmith, Mark Levy, Mawson and Pecare were active in the Hebrew Benevolent Society, and Swart, Pecare and Benrimo in the Bachelors' Hebrew Benevolent Loan Association (Grinstein, *op. cit.,* 552, 553).

19. MS, *Records of the United States Senate, 33rd Congress 1st Session,* The National Archives. On the back of this copy is noted the fact that Senator Lewis Cass presented the petition on April 18, 1854, and that it was referred to the Committee on Foreign Relations. The Senator's brief remarks on the occasion are in the *Congressional Globe,* 33 Cong. 1 Sess. Vol. 28, part 2, p. 929.

20. In Stroock, *op. cit.,* 20 and in *AJHSP,* XXXVI, 1943, p. 301, this phrase is incorrectly given as "of these Governments."

21. All six signatories are members of the Gratz family. Joseph Gratz, brother of Rebecca Gratz, was a merchant. Dr. Isaac Hays (1796–1879), a nephew of Rebecca Gratz, was a well-known ophthalmologist, and editor of *The Medical News* and the *American Journal of the Medical Sciences.* Horatio and Benjamin Etting, brothers, were merchants, and also nephews of Rebecca Gratz. Jacob Gratz (1788–1856), her brother, was a merchant and had served in the Pennsylvania State Senate. Hyman Gratz (1776–1857) is the merchant and philanthropist after whom Gratz College, Philadelphia, is named. In 1854 he was President of the Pennsylvania Company for Insurances on Lives and Granting Annuities, Treasurer of the Pennsylvania Academy for Fine Arts, and Treasurer of the Congregation Mikveh Israel. Dr. Hays and Joseph and Jacob Gratz were also active in the same Congregation.

It should be noted that this is the only copy of the petition circulated by the New York committee that is now extant in The National Archives. Much has been made of the importance of this "Cass petition," but the small number of names signed to it perhaps indicates why it was not effective in preventing the Senate from ratifying the Treaty on May 29, 1854, with the obnoxious clause still in it. Article 1 of the Treaty guaranteed reciprocity of treatment only where such "treatment shall not conflict with the constitutional or legal provisions, as well federal as State and cantonal, of the contracting parties." That the United States government was as eager to have this protection of State's rights as the Swiss government is indicated clearly in the despatch of Secretary of State William L. Marcy (1786–1857) to Theodore S. Fay (1807–1898), our Minister Resident in Switzerland, on June 8, 1854. Instructing him in the matter of securing Swiss assent to the draft, Marcy informs Fay that the stipulation concerning the right of Swiss citizens to reside in the United States will be restricted because the Federal government "has not the power to carry the stipulation practically into effect in such States, the number having been reduced it is believed to three or four, as withhold their assent to such a procedure." (MS, *Diplomatic Instructions, Switzerland,* Vol. 1, No. 12, pp. 16–17.) Marcy does not mention the Jews, but a minister so instructed could not well object to the Swiss application of the theory of cantonal rights to the exclusion of Jews. Fay had been confirmed by the Senate as Minister Resident on March 16, 1853, having been nominated specifically to effect conclusion of the treaty (*Journal of the Executive Proceedings of the Senate . . .*, IX, 25, 72).

22. *The Israelite,* November 6, 1857, p. 142, cols. 2–3. The Memorial was drafted by Martin Bijur, a lawyer from Louisville, Ky., and was accepted "after due consideration . . . almost as reported by Mr. Bijur" (*ibid.*). The Conference that accepted the Memorial convened in Baltimore on October 28 in response to a call issued by Wise in *The Israelite* on October 9. Disunity among the Jews themselves kept the attendance down (Rev. David Einhorn of Baltimore did not attend), but those who came went on with their work. Bijur represented Louisville in the State Legislature, 1865–1867 (Lewis Collins and Richard H. Collins, *History of Kentucky,* Covington, Ky., 1874, II, 357).

23. Cited in the *Charleston News,* December 29, 1855, and quoted in *The Israelite,* January 18, 1856, p. 227, cols. 2–3.

24. The meetings and press statements are culled chiefly from *The Israelite,* August 7 to November 6, 1857. The Gootman Case is mentioned for the first time in this connection in Einhorn's *Sinai,* September 1857, pp. 662–664, and October 1857, pp. 683–686; in the latter it is included in the Text of another Memorial, signed by 200 residents of Charleston, that was presented to President Buchanan by Captain Jonas P. Levy, on October 31, 1857, the same day that the Baltimore conference delegation visited Buchanan. Levy also presented a Memorial from Washington, D. C. The disunity was thus emphasized. (*The Occident,* December 1857, p. 435.) For the Gootman case see also *AJHSP,* XXXVI, (1943), pp. 303–305.

25. *The Occident,* October, 1857, pp. 350–351.

26. Mendes I. Cohen of Baltimore (1796–1879) had served at Fort McHenry in the War of 1812; entered the banking firm of his oldest brother, Jacob I. Cohen; toured Europe and Egypt, being reported to be the first American to go up the cataracts of the Nile, and collecting antiquities he later bestowed upon Johns Hopkins University; and sat in the Maryland House of Delegates, 1847–1848.

Rev. Dr. Henry Hochheimer (1818–1912) had been compelled to leave Germany because of revolutionary articles he had written in 1849, and was then the rabbi of the Baltimore Hebrew Congregation (Nidche Israel).

Philip Hertzberg had come to Baltimore in 1840 from Bavaria, where he had been born in 1822; he became a clothing manufacturer and merchant, and an active communal leader.

M. M. Gerstley of Chicago (1812–1893), had come to Pennsylvania in 1839 from Bavaria and moved to Chicago in 1848 (Eliassof, *AJHSP,* XI, 1903, p. 124).

Lewis F. Leopold of Cleveland had been established with his family at Mackinac Island, Michigan, in 1845 (Heineman, *AJHSP,* XIII, 1905, p. 58).

27. The delegation was introduced to the President by the well-known Jewish lawyer and former Representative of Alabama in Congress, 1853–1855, Philip Phillips (1807–1884), whose address is in *The Israelite,* November 6, 1857, p. 142, col. 4. According to the official report of the delegation, Buchanan "unequivocally promised a speedy and energetic course of action with a view

to a remedy, not inconsistent with international faith." Therefore the delegation urged "implicit confidence in the Executive" and concluded "with the request to our co-religionists, to abstain from further agitation on the subject." (*Ibid.*) With this complacent recommendation, both Leeser in *The Occident* and Einhorn in *Sinai* disagreed. Leeser advised "all congregations, that have not yet acted," to send memorials to Buchanan (December 1857, p. 435); and Einhorn even a year later was mocking the delegation for having interpreted defeat as victory (September 1858, pp. 1023–1028). In 1859, Leeser, reporting on a delegation to Buchanan on the Mortara Affair, noted that a memorial on the Swiss Treaty had also been handed to Secretary of State Lewis Cass (*The Occident,* February 1859, p. 539). Meanwhile our Minister in Switzerland, Theodore S. Fay, who was very sensitive to the sensitivity of the Swiss on this subject (*The Jewish Messenger,* October 18, 1861, p. 59, citing correspondence between Fay and Cass of 1857 and 1858) had for a year and a half been gathering material for a "Note" to the Swiss government, which he finally presented in May 1859 (*AJHSP,* XXXVI, 1943, pp. 319–321), and issued also in German and French translation so as to influence public opinion. In 1861, Lincoln's Secretary of State, William H. Seward, appointed as Minister to Switzerland the New Hampshire Republican, George Gilman Fogg (1813–1881). Fogg analyzed the problem more realistically: on April 16, 1864, he wrote to Seward that the Swiss justify their discrimination against the Jews by using "South Carolina's theory of State sovereignty and no rights to freed Negroes." (Stroock, *op. cit.,* 49.) During this period, the governments of Holland, Belgium and France were delaying their renewals and negotiations about various treaties with Switzerland pending the outcome of the struggle for equality for Jews coming to Switzerland from those countries (*The Jewish Record,* New York, April 24, 1863, p. 2, cols. 1–2; May 22, 1863, p. 2, col. 5; July 10, 1863, p. 1, col. 5). On June 30, 1864, however, the situation was somewhat improved when the Swiss signed a treaty with France agreeing to treat French citizens "without distinction of creed" just as they did "Christians" (Lucien Wolf, *Notes on the Diplomatic History of the Jewish Question,* London, 1919, p. 67). This precedent did not yet, however, have a direct effect on the Swiss-American problem. But on January 14, 1866, shortly after the defeat of the Confederacy, a referendum on the discriminatory articles in the Swiss Constitution led to a partial victory for equal rights to the Jews by a slim majority (Achilles Nordmann, *Geschichte der Juden in Basel . . . 1397–1875,* Basle, c. 1915, p. 154). It was not until May 29, 1874, when the new constitution was adopted, that the Jews won legal equality in Switzerland. That the problem of the relation between treaties signed by a federal government and states' rights is still current can be seen from the fact that the United States Senate, in ratifying the Charter of the United Nations, obligated the government to the observation and enforcement of Article 55-c, which provides for "universal respect for, and observance of, human rights, and fundamental freedoms for all without distinction as to race, sex, language, and religion." This Article is widely violated in many states of the Union, and waits for enforcement upon proper test cases before the Supreme Court; one such case was that arising in the Westminster school district in Orange County, California, which segregated children of Mexican-Americans (Carey McWilliams, "Is Your Name Gonzales?," *The Nation,* March 15, 1947, pp. 302–303); unfortunately, the school boards dropped the case when the Ninth Circuit Court of Appeals ruled against the discriminatory practise, and the definitiveness of a Supreme Court decision was avoided.

111. Equal Rights for Women

1. *The Proceedings of the Woman's Rights Convention, Held at Syracuse, September 8th, 9th & 10th, 1852,* Syracuse, 1852, pp. 63–64, 68–74. Mrs. Rose was very active at this convention, serving as head of the Nominating Committee, as a member of the Business (resolutions) Committee, and being re-elected to the Central Committee for the ensuing year. The second speech given herein was also printed as Woman's Rights Tracts, No. 9. Among those particularly inspired by Mrs. Rose's speech was Susan B. Anthony (1820–1906), then attending her first woman's rights convention, and later one of the great leaders of the woman suffrage movement (Rheta Childe Dorr, *Susan B. Anthony,* New York, 1928, p. 70.)
2. *Albany Daily State Register,* March 7, 1854, cited in Elizabeth Cady Stanton, Susan B. Anthony, and Matilda Joslyn Gage, *History of Woman Suffrage,* 2d ed., Rochester, 1889, I, 608.
3. G. D. H. Cole, *Robert Owen,* 2d ed., London, 1930, p. 295. The Association aimed "to effect peaceably, and by reason alone, an entire change in the character and condition of mankind, by establishing over the world, in principle and practise, the religion of charity for the opinions, feelings, and conduct of all individuals, without distinction of sex, class, sect, party, country, or colour, combined with a well-devised, equitable, and natural system of united property" (*Manual of the Association of . . . ,* No. 2, London, 1836, p. 30), and in a few years Owen built up a membership of about 100,000 (Arthur John Booth, *Robert Owen,* London, 1869, p. 188).

   Most of the information about Mrs. Rose's life before she came to the United States is based on an important biographical sketch by L. E. Barnard in *The Liberator,* May 16, 1856, p. 80, which was later expanded in the *History of Woman Suffrage,* I, 95–98. For other data, see Schappes, "Ernestine Rose, Queen of the Platform," *Jewish Life,* March, 1949.

   Since Mrs. Rose tried to correct misstatements about her in the press (see her letter to the *Albany Daily State Register,* denying that she had had to flee from Poland, *History of Woman Suffrage,* I, 610), statements made in her own lifetime and in places to which she had ready access, and left unchallenged by her may be credited.
4. Mrs. Rose was prominent in the agitation from 1836 to 1848 that led the New York State Legislature to pass the first Married Woman's Property Act in the country. In a letter to Susan B. Anthony from London, January 8, 1877, Mrs. Rose wrote: "I sent the first petition to the New York Legislature to give a married woman the right to hold real estate in her own name, in the winter of 1836 and '37, to which after a good deal of trouble I obtained five signatures. . . . I continued sending petitions with increased numbers of signatures until 1848 and '49, when the Legislature enacted the law . . . During the eleven years from 1837 to 1848, I addressed the New York Legislature five times . . ." (*Ibid.,* I, 99–100.) Elizabeth Cady Stanton, herself active in that campaign, points out that the bill had the support of "the leaders of the Dutch aristocracy, who desired to see their life-long accumulation descend to their daughters and grandchildren rather than pass into the hands of dissipated, thriftless sons-in-law." (*Eighty Years and More, 1815–1897, Reminiscences,* New York, 1898, p. 150.)
5. The omissions indicated by these asterisks are in the original proceedings.
6. This address was delivered at the Evening Session. The previous speaker was

Antoinette Louisa Brown (1825–1921), known as the first American woman minister, who had recently begun her first pastorate in a Congregational Church in South Butler, N. Y. The Indiana Constitutional Convention was held in 1850.

7. Robert Dale Owen (1801–1877), son of Robert Owen, had settled in the United States in the 1830's and become an active reformer in Indiana, serving in its State Legislature and representing it in Congress. In 1844, Mrs. Rose had lectured in Richmond, Indiana (Stanton, Anthony and Gage, *op. cit.*, I, 99).
8. John Arthur Roebuck (1801–1879) had been an independent radical in Parliament from 1832 on, first representing Bath and, after 1849, Sheffield. He became generally conservative in the 1850's and ended by supporting Austrian domination of Italy and the Confederacy in the Civil War.
9. Nicholas I (1796–1855), a pillar of the Holy Alliance and known as the Iron Tsar, sent in troops in 1849 at the request of Francis Joseph to crush the Hungarian revolution and restore the country to Habsburg rule.
10. Louis Napoleon (1808–1873), elected President of the Republic on December 10, 1848, helped destroy the Roman republic in March 1849, stamped out civil liberties and popular opposition in France, and a few months after Mrs. Rose's speech was formally proclaimed Emperor on December 2, 1852.
11. Horace Mann (1796–1859) was a great educational reformer.
12. Mrs. Rose's resolution was adopted.

112. Abolitionists Report

1. Pp. 114–115. See also Kohler, *AJHSP,* V, 1897, 143–144.
2. P. 66 of the Report. Evidence to show that the disappointment expressed by the Report was based on ignorance of the record of Jewish anti-slavery activity is listed by Maxwell Whiteman, introduction to *The Kidnapped and the Ransomed,* Philadelphia, 1970, pp. 25ff.
3. The source of the two quotations from Jewish sources is unknown.
4. *The Occident,* Philadelphia monthly, edited by Rev. Isaac Leeser, 1843–1868, and *The Asmonean,* New York weekly, edited by Robert Lyon. For material in *The Asmonean* published before this report, see Document No. 109. Had the abolitionists known of Lyon's views, their disappointment might have been even greater.
5. For instances of Southern Jews who manumitted their slaves, see Doc. No. 60.

113. Judah Touro's Will

1. Since many reprintings of this Will have been carelessly transcribed, this text is copied from the original in the Civil District Court, Parish of Orleans, Louisiana, Will Book Vol. 9, Folio 488–496.
2. The vessel was renamed USS MINK while in service in the Navy for two years, according to a letter to this writer from the Office of Public Information, Navy Department, April 16, 1947.
3. A complete list of Touro's benefactions will be found in Leon Huhner, *The Life of Judah Touro 1775–1854,* Philadelphia, 1946, the only available biography. For a critical evaluation of the serious shortcomings of this work, as well as for a comment on the social meaning of philanthropy, see Schappes, "Towards the Biography of Judah Touro," *Jewish Life* (published by the Morning Freiheit Association, New York), April, 1947, pp. 21–24.
4. Jonathan Montgomery had for many years been one of the three executors of the Fund for philanthropic purposes created by Stephen Henderson in his

will of August 1, 1837 (John Smith Kendall, *History of New Orleans,* Chicago and New York, 1922, II, 636).

5. Judah Touro died January 18, 1854 in New Orleans; on June 6, 1854 he was interred in the Newport Cemetery, the deed to which dates back to February 28, 1677.

6. "A notable event in the life of Mr. Touro occurred just two weeks before his death. One of the newspapers printed a lengthy editorial which went on to say that Mr. R. D. Shepherd had saved the life of Mr. Judah Touro. The consequence of this was that a contemplated will which had been made, but not signed, was altered, . . ." (*Historical Sketch Book and Guide to New Orleans and Environs,* New York, 1885, p. 306). The *Providence Journal,* June 8, 1854, estimated that Mr. Shepherd received three-quarters of a million dollars (cited in *The Israelite,* July 21, 1854, p. 10). Shepherd saved Touro's life in the following way: Touro, having volunteered for the militia to defend New Orleans against the British, although he was already in his fortieth year, was engaged in the hazardous task of bringing ammunition up to the front lines under heavy British artillery fire when "he was struck on the thigh by a twelve-pound shot, which produced a ghastly and dangerous wound, tearing off a large mass of flesh. . . . He was in charge of Dr. David C. Ker, who had dressed his wound but who, shaking his head, declared that there was no hope for him. Mr. Shepherd [who had accidentally found him], with the devotion of true friendship, determined to make every effort to save his old companion. He procured a cart and, lifting the wounded man into it, drove to the city. . . ." (Alexander Walker, *Jackson and New Orleans,* New York, 1856, cited by Stanley Clisby Arthur, *The Story of the Battle of New Orleans,* New Orleans, 1915, pp. 170–171.)

7. This Congregation, *Nefuzoth Yehudah* (Dispersed of Judah), was incorporated in 1846 with Gershom Kursheedt as President and Benjamin Florance as Vice-President, and followed the Sephardic ritual. Touro had already provided it with a synagogue building. In 1881, the group amalgamated with the Congregation Gates of Mercy and was renamed the Touro Synagogue; it is now a Reform congregation.

8. In connection with one of the yellow-fever epidemics, Touro had established a hospital that became known as the Touro Infirmary; in 1852, he bought the Paulding estate for $8,000, remodelled it for hospital use and gave it to the Touro Infirmary. This institution is still in existence and is non-sectarian with regard to the religion of its patients; Negroes, however, are admitted to the clinic but not to hospital bed facilities (letter to this writer by Dr. Lewis E. Jarrett, the Director, February 7, 1947).

9. The Hebrew Benevolent Society had been organized in 1844; in 1869 it amalgamated with the Touro Infirmary.

10. This Congregation, Gates of Mercy, had been incorporated in 1828, and was the first in New Orleans.

11. The Ladies' Hebrew Benevolent Society was started in 1847 (Max. Heller, *Jubilee Souvenir of Temple Sinai, 1872–1922,* New Orleans, 1922, p. 8).

12. This Society had been founded in 1853 in response to appeals for help to the Jews of China, and was started off by a contribution by Touro (Huhner, *op. cit.,* 172).

13. This was not a Jewish institution.

14. This non-Jewish institution had gone into operation in 1824 and was incor-

porated in 1825 (*Norman's New Orleans and Environs*, New Orleans, 1845, p. 113).

15. Information about this institution has proved inaccessible.

16. Established in 1836, this institution was caring for about 160 children in 1845 (*ibid.*, 111).

17. See Note 15 above.

18. Endowed in 1839 by Alexander Milne, a Scotsman, the Asylum took in children of both sexes (*ibid.*, 116).

19. When the Association was founded in 1834, Abraham C. Labatt, a Jew, was elected secretary. The Henderson Fund, of which Jonathan Montgomery was one of the Executors, had provided a cemetery for the Association in 1838. (Thomas O'Connor, *History of the Fire Department of New Orleans*, New Orleans, 1895, pp. 63, 69.)

20. As a ship-owner, Touro was interested in this institution, of which F. Rickert was superintendent (*Cohen's New Orleans Directory . . . for 1854*, p. 216).

21. It was not until 1882 that the Touro-Shakespeare Almshouse was established; it still exists. By 1862 a building was ready, paid for by Touro's bequest, accretions to it made by careful investments by R. D. Shepherd, and $60,000 of Shepherd's own; but it was occupied by Federal troops during the Civil War and accidentally burned down on August 31, 1865, when fire spread from an oven in which the soldiers were baking beans (Kendall, *op. cit.*, II, 645). When Mayor Joseph A. Shakespeare obtained city funds to supplement those still in the hands of the Touro trustees, the institution was finally completed in 1882.

22. The Old Stone Mill, also known as the Newport Tower, is supposed to have been built by Norsemen in the eleventh century, and is now called Touro Park (Huhner, *op. cit.*, 79).

23. This Library, chartered August 24, 1747, was supported by important Newport Jews from the very beginning. On November 17, 1843, the Library Company elected Touro an Honorary Member; in accepting the honor, Touro sent a check for $1000 to repair the portico and offered to pay the cost of other repairs. Touro had a considerable interest in books: in 1807 he had brought into New Orleans 750 volumes of the latest novels (Roger Philip McCutcheon, "Books and Booksellers in New Orleans, 1730–1830," *The Louisiana Historical Quarterly*, XX, 1937, p. 611); in 1824, Touro was the chief founder of the Touro Free Library Society, whose collection, kept in the Presbyterian Church until 1838, was open to the public (McCutcheon, "Libraries in New Orleans, 1771–1833," *ibid.*, 157).

24. This Congregation, organized in 1843, had been preceded in New England only by the Newport congregation; it had built the first synagogue in Boston in 1852. The correct spelling is *Ohabei Shalom*.

25. The Hartford Congregation, *Beth Israel*, was chartered in 1843; the Touro bequest helped it built its first synagogue, which was named Touro Hall. The Congregation is still in existence. At this point the following comment of Rev. Isaac Leeser is pertinent: "And it is a pleasing reflection that in making his will, Mr. Touro remembered nearly all the objects of public beneficence which we had brought to his notice as editor during the last ten years . . ." This statement helps explain, perhaps, Touro's selection of institutions for bequests.

26. The Congregation *Mishkan Israel* of New Haven was founded in 1840. With the Touro bequest it bought a building for a Synagogue in 1856; the Congregation is still in existence.

27. The Society was founded in 1853 by Sampson Simson (1780–1857) and still exists, with Mr. Leon Huhner as President.

28. The Judah Touro Almshouses were established at Jerusalem in 1855 on a trip made by Sir Moses Montefiore and Gershom Kursheedt. Touro's bequest proving insufficient, Sir Moses added £5,000 for maintenance (Huhner, *op. cit.*, 123). In 1875 it was reported that the Touro Almshouses in Jerusalem had fallen on evil days, and are used by well-to-do persons who rent their own homes out and live in the institution in idleness; Touro's name is forgotten, and the institution is called after Montefiore. (*The Jewish Messenger*, November 19, 1875, p. 5, cols. 1–2.)

29. In 1852 Sampson Simson, after many communal attempts had failed, organized the Jews' Hospital, and the cornerstone was laid Thanksgiving Day, 1853. Since 1866 the name has been Mount Sinai Hospital. (Grinstein, *op. cit.*, 157.)

30. The Hebrew Benevolent Society was founded in 1822 by Ashkenazic immigrant members of the Congregation Shearith Israel, and in the 1840's and 1850's became the "outstanding Jewish philanthropic group" in the city (*ibid.*, 145–146). It is noteworthy that Touro's bequest of $5,000 was more than enough to cover the disbursements of the Society for an average year.

31. The Hebrew Mutual Benefit Society had been organized in 1826 as a burial society by members of the newly seceded Congregation Bnai Jeshurun, which had left Shearith Israel in 1825. The Society is still in existence. (*Ibid.*, 106.)

32. This was the Polonies Talmud Torah; see the Index for other references.

33. In 1853, Bnai Jeshurun had established an all-day Jewish parochial school with a separate building, as Congregation Emanu-el had done in 1850 (*ibid.*, 238–239).

34. This congregation had been established in 1845, chiefly by English Jews (*ibid.*, 473).

35. The Female Hebrew Benevolent Society, founded in 1820, is reputed to be the "first recorded Jewish women's society," and was directed by Richa Levy (*ibid.*, 152, 553).

36. This society was founded in November 1819 and incorporated in 1837.

37. This society was founded in 1847 through the efforts of Rev. Isaac Leeser, incorporated in 1849, and opened its first sessions in 1851.

38. The United Hebrew Beneficent Society had been organized in 1822 (Morais, *op. cit.*, 143).

39. The Fell's Point Hebrew Fellowship Congregation, the second one in Baltimore, had been organized in 1838; it dissolved in 1904.

40. This first congregation in Richmond was already well established in 1791, and followed the Sephardic ritual; it dissolved in 1898.

41. In 1843, when the majority of the Congregation Beth Elohim voted to build an organ in their synagogue, a minority seceded to form Shearith Israel (Elzas, *op. cit.*, 213).

42. This was the first congregation in Alabama, founded in 1844 with 52 members.

43. Probably first organized in 1733, when Jews began to settle in Georgia, it

dissolved in 1740 when most of the Jews left the colony, was reorganized in 1750, and chartered in 1790.

44. The Kahl Montgomery was incorporated in 1852.

45. This first congregation of Memphis, Children of Israel, had just been organized in 1853.

46. Established in 1836 and chartered in 1843, this congregation had dedicated its first synagogue in 1849, and is still in existence. In 1851 a congregation of Polish Jews, House of Israel, was chartered.

47. For other references to this congregation, see the Index.

48. The Talmud Yelodim Institute of the Congregation B'ne Yeshurun opened in October 1849 with 56 pupils and was chartered in 1851. Touro's bequest, made at the suggestion of Rabbi James K. Gutheim, who had left B'ne Yeshurun in 1850 to become the minister of the New Orleans Congregation Shangarai Chased, was used to help acquire a new building. (Barnett R. Brickner, *The Jewish Community of Cincinnati . . . 1817–1933,* University of Cincinnati Doctoral Dissertation, unpublished, pp. 136–137, 140.)

49. Founded in 1845, this institution is described as "the first Jewish hospital in the United States supported by Jewish funds which did not limit its clientele to Jewish patients exclusively" (*UJE,* V, 470).

50. In 1850 a Reform group had seceded from Ansche Chesed to found this congregation.

51. This second St. Louis congregation was founded in 1840, reorganized in 1852, and is still in existence.

52. Polish Jews founded this congregation in 1847 as an Orthodox institution; it still exists as a Conservative congregation.

53. Organized in 1838 as an orthodox congregation, it had Isaac Mayer Wise as its minister from 1847 to 1850, when Wise led a secession that established the Reform Congregation Anshe Emeth; Beth El remained orthodox until on December 1, 1865 it united with Anshe Emeth to form the Congregation Beth Emeth.

54. Abraham Touro (1774–1822), Judah's older brother, had bequeathed some $50,000 to various institutions. He had also left $100,000 to Judah, who, however, "refused to touch a penny of it, permitting it to accumulate for charitable purposes" (Huhner, *op. cit.,* 66). The Boston Asylum had been formed in 1814, the Boston Female Asylum in 1800, and the Massachusetts General Hospital in 1799 (*Bacon's Dictionary of Boston,* Boston and New York, 1886, pp. 48, 54, 241).

55. The famous Jewish Synagogue of Newport had been dedicated on December 2, 1763.

56. Catherine Hays, his cousin, was born in Boston in 1776 and died in Richmond, January 2, 1854. Certain traditions have arisen that Touro was in love with Catherine Hays and left Boston because her father was opposed to the marriage (see Huhner, *op. cit., passim,* for the latest restatement of the legend, and Schappes' review for an analysis of Mr. Huhner's sources). Another version is given by Caroline Cohen, *Records of the Myers, Hays and Mordecai Families from 1707 to 1913,* privately printed, no date, p. 10: "There was one great sorrow, the death in August, 1802, at the age of thirty-three, of Rebecca Hays, the eldest daughter, whose love affair with her cousin, Judah Touro, disapproved of by her father and home circle, caused, no doubt, much painful

friction. Her two unmarried sisters, Catharine and Sally, were for some reason unknown to me, violently opposed to the match." According to the inscription on her tombstone, Rebekah Hays died July 22, 1802, "aged 33 years 5 months" (Gutstein, *op. cit.*, 315). The fact that she was some six years older than Touro may have been a cause for opposition to the marriage, that is, if there is anything in this tradition. This version was also given by Rev. M. J. Michelbacher of Richmond in *The Jewish Messenger*, December 31, 1869, p. 5; it is unexplained why Rev. Michelbacher waited for fifteen years after the death of Catherine Hays to make his statement, especially since the newspapers of 1854 that mentioned a romance in Touro's life tended generally to name Catherine and not Rebecca Hays as the one he loved.

57. Moses M. Myers (1771–1860); Catharine Hays Myers (1798–1874); Harriet Myers (1800–1882); Julia Myers (1803–1883) (Ezekiel and Lichtenstein, *op. cit.*, 306–307). Caroline Cohen, *op. cit.*, 16, writes: "When Miss Slowey Hays died [October 19, 1836] her sister Catharine moved into her own house, next door to the Monumental Church, where, with failing mind, she lived, cared for by her Boston housekeeper, Miss Excey Gill, and some valuable Negro servants, the Forresters, and in turn, by her nieces, Catharine, Harriet and Julia, who spent some weary years in this way . . . [until] the death of their aunt Catharine Hays, January 1854, when they inherited what was then a large fortune of about one hundred thousand dollars, by her will made by her sister Slowey . . ."

58. Samuel Myers died in 1836 at the age of 82; his surviving children were Rebecca Hays Myers (1803–1877) and Ella C. Myers (1808–1892) (Ezekiel and Lichtenstein, *op. cit.*).

59. Supply Clap Thwing (1798–1877) had since 1831 been Touro's agent in Boston (Walter Eliot Thwing, *Thwing: A Genelogical, Biographical and Historical Account of the Family*, Boston, 1883, pp. 86–89).

60. See the index for further reference to Rev. Isaac Leeser.

61. From February 1850 to the end of 1853, Rev. Moses N. Nathan (1807–1883) had served as Hazan of the Congregation Nefutzoth Yehuda (Dispersed of Judah). When Rev. Nathan was brought to New Orleans from St. Thomas, West Indies, Touro had agreed to pay his salary of $2500 a year for two years. When that period expired, the congregation failed to meet his salary, and Rev. Nathan resigned, to be succeeded in January 1854 by Rev. James K. Gutheim (1817–1886). (*The Jewish Chronicle*, London, May 18, 1883, pp. 9–10.)

62. Rev. Theodore Clapp (born, Easthampton, Mass., 1792; died, Louisville, Ky., 1866) was a Presbyterian minister who came to New Orleans in 1822. In 1833 he was deposed by the Presbytery for heretical views that "were substantially those held at that period by the Universalists and Unitarians." Touro and Clapp became close friends, and Touro gave him directly at least $20,000, as well as twice, in 1822 and 1851, supplying Rev. Clapp with a church in which to conduct services. On the latter occasion, Rev. Clapp's church having burnt down, "no other church in the city would open its doors to Clapp and his congregation for fear of seeming to countenance heresy, but again the noble-hearted Jew, Touro, came to the rescue. He purchased a small chapel on St. Charles Street for the congregation to use without charge, until an adequate new structure could be erected . . ." (Henry Wilder Foote, "Theodore Clapp," *Unitarian Historical Society, The Proceedings of*, III, Part 2, 1934, pp. 13, 20, 28, 33, 36.) Touro's action of 1822 received such attention that it was cited in the debate in the Maryland House of Delegates on December 18 as an argument for abolishing the disabilities against the Jews.

63. During the next twenty-five years after Touro's death, other important philanthropic bequests by Jews were made by Rosanna Ostermann of Galveston, Texas, who died in 1866, leaving to Jewish and non-Jewish institutions (some of which had been beneficiaries of Touro) $31,500 in cash and the dividends on over 1000 shares of stock and income from real estate holdings (Cohen, *AJHSP*, II, 1894, pp. 153–156); and by Michael Reese of California, who died in 1878 while on a trip to Europe, leaving $50,000 to the University of California and more than $100,000 to various Jewish and non-Jewish charities.

114. Attitudes to Jews

1. Both clippings are in *Lyons Scrapbook I,* p. 168. The *Washington Sentinel* was edited by William M. Overton, Charles Maurice Smith, and Beverley Tucker. *The Sunday Dispatch* was owned and edited by Amor J. Williamson, who was also an Alderman from the Second Ward in 1854. (*Trow's New York City Directory, 1854–55,* p. 797 and App. p. 38.)
2. The American Society for Ameliorating the Condition of the Jews, founded in 1820, had the following officers in 1854: Rev. John Forsyth of Newburgh, N. Y., president; Rev. E. R. McGregor of the Bible House, New York, corresponding secretary; William Libby, treasurer. Its work in converting Jews to Christianity had been markedly unsuccessful. By 1853 it was in low repute: Rev. Robert Burns, in "The Jewish Society of New York arraigned at the Bar of Public Opinion," Toronto, 1853, wrote: "In the meantime I may add that the society is not in very good odour. It has been discarded by all the old school Presbyterian churches and the only agents of any worth which it had are now laboring in connection with the Home Mission Board of that church. It gets little support in New York where its facts and its history are best known." (Quoted by Lee M. Friedman, *The American Society for Meliorating the Condition of the Jews, . . . ,* Boston, 1925, p. 17n.)
3. The Honved was the Hungarian army in the revolutionary war of 1848–1849.

115. Jews and Farming

1. Circular, *Lyons Scrapbook I,* item 192b, American Jewish Historical Society. The same call, with some minor editorial variations, appeared in *The Asmonean,* May 4, 1855, p. 22. That Dr. Waterman wrote the call is revealed in *ibid.,* May 18, 1855, pp. 36–37. Dr. Waterman had discussed the idea with members of Lebanon Lodge No. 9, I. O. B. B. (*ibid.,* May 4, 1855, p. 22, letter by Dr. Waterman), a committee of which was appointed to draw up this plan.
2. A useful survey is that by Benjamin Steinberg, but it must be taken cautiously in so far as he sometimes does not distinguish between projects to settle Jews on the land and the projects of Jews to promote settlement by non-Jews: "Geschichte fun Agrarizatsia fun Idn in America (biz 1880), "*Yorbuch fun Amopteil,* New York, 1938, pp. 60–90. Noteworthy before the date of this Call are the projects of Noah in the 1820's; of the colony of Shalom, settled by some twelve Jewish families from New York from 1837 to 1842, in the township of Warwarsing, Ulster County, N. Y. (Moses Klein, *Migdal Zophim, The Watch Tower*, Philadelphia, 1889, pp. 38–39); of the proposal of Julius Stern, Philadelphia merchant, that there be founded a colony "in one of the Western territories" that could ultimately become a Jewish State in the Union (*The Occident*, April, 1843, p. 31–32; also The *Sun,* New York, February 24, 1849). Robert Lyon, editor of *The Asmonean,* remarked that "we have been for three or four years past requested to draw attention to this subject by friends in the

interior" but considered the suggestions premature (April 20, 1855, p. 4, leading editorial, "Agricultural Societies"). In 1853, Simon Berman (c. 1820–1884) had presented a plan to a meeting attended by Rabbi Raphall, Rev. Isaac Leeser, Dr. Waterman and others, but Dr. Waterman then felt the time was not yet ripe (Menashe Unger, "Shimon Berman un zein proyect tsu Colonizirn Idn in America," *Yorbuch fun Amopteil,* 1938, p. 101).

3. Whether this was true was disputed at the time. An unsigned letter commenting on the Call directly after its appearance in *The Asmonean,* declared that there are more Jewish farmers in New York, New Jersey, and the Western states than Dr. Waterman assumes, and that in New York City "there are abundant tailors, shoemakers, tin and locksmiths, carpenters, joiners, butchers, bakers, masons, architects, and manufacturers of all kinds" who are Jews (May 11, 1855, p. 30, "Agricultural Societies"). D. E. M. De Lara argued that Dr. Waterman's circular "is nearly a verbal repetition of the charges brought against the Jews by their bitterest enemies and most cruel persecutors during the middle ages; . . . but that such a charge should be brought against them in the middle of the nineteenth century,—that the pursuit of commerce should be cast in the face of the Jews as a pursuit inimical to their country," and that the charge should be made by a Jew, was shocking (*ibid.,* May 25, 1855, p. 46). In reply, Dr. Waterman maintained he had criticized only the "*exclusive* pursuit of commerce," and that while there were a few Jewish tailors, carpenters, segar makers and glaziers, they were conspicuously absent as steam engine manufacturers, telegraph workers, cotton spinners, weavers, navigators, workers in iron, brass, glass, metals, ship carpenters, millers, miners, chemists, carvers, and agriculturists (*ibid.,* June 8, 1855, pp. 61–62). But De Lara then testified that to his own knowledge there are Jewish statuaries, bakers, paper-hangers, book-binders, pocket-book makers, trunk-makers, surgical instrument makers, piano makers, cabinet makers, machine makers, silversmiths, goldsmiths, jewellers, diamond cutters, tin-plate workers, gold-lace weavers, mechanical dentists, engineers, machinists, designers, umbrella and whale-bone makers, printers, compositors, shoe and bootmakers, hatters, papier-mache makers, basket makers, portrait painters, sailors, mates and captains of merchant ships, police officers, book-keepers, doctors, lawyers, magistrates, messengers, and teachers (*ibid.,* June 22, 1855, pp. 76–77). If the dispute produced no definitive answer, it at least provided us with the best available list of pursuits of the Jews of New York City. De Lara also called attention to difficulties that keep more Jews from becoming workers: Sabbath observance; "the decided objection" of Christian workers to working with Jews; lack of training; lack of capital to become masters; the greater ease and profitability of commerce and trading. With reference to the latter, De Lara observed that Jews, like all people, prefer the easier to the harder way of making a living. In the course of this discussion, De Lara came closest to an understanding that the problem is not abstract but presents itself concretely under capitalist relations, and that Jews have a democratic right to choose their economic pursuits without special criticism.

4. The Maimonides Library Association had been founded in 1850 by several lodges of the Bnai Brith; in 1855 it had 150 members and 800 volumes (Grinstein, *op. cit.,* 203).

The meeting was very well attended. Dr. Waterman was Chairman. Rabbi Morris Jacob Raphall and the Rev. H. A. Henry spoke in favor of the plan. Henry Jones supported the aim, but disagreed with the specific plan. De Lara severely criticized the call. Dr. Waterman's refutation of the critics was "warmly applauded" and it was agreed to proceed with the project (*The Asmonean,* May 18, 1855, pp. 36–37). More than a year later, the Association had not yet succeeded in raising $3,000 with which to open its "school of Practical Agriculture," to train Jewish farmers, although the Association had been finally organized on October 5, 1855 and later chartered by the State. Robert Lyon commented editorially: "It is to be regretted, in a community so wealthy and so enterprising as this, that an undertaking promising so many benefits should be permitted to creep a weary, lengthened course before it receives public attention." (*Ibid.*, August 15, 1856, p. 140.) The failure of this project did not prevent similar attempts, a few of them somewhat more successful, from being made.

5. Unless otherwise noted, the data about the signers are derived from *Trow's New York City Directory*, 1855/56, and Grinstein, *op. cit., passim*, according to index: Henry American was a teacher, and active in the Mutual Benefit and Burial Society of Shaarey Tefilah; A. Asch was active in the Hebrah Gemilut Hesed Veemet of Congregation Shaarey Zedek, but is not in the Directory (however, Abel Ash and Abraham Ash, tailors, are listed); Emanuel Buchstein was an accountant; Alexander Chailly was in "fancygoods," and Vice-President of the Maimonides Library Association; Simon Engel was a grocer; Hyman Gutman is not in the Directory, but a Hermann Gutman of 285 Grand Street was in "upholstery"; Hyman Hildburghauser was in "stoves"; Samuel Kimmelstiel was a baker; Henry Kling, a tailor, was one of the founders of Bnai Brith; Jacob Muhlhauser was probably the printer and not the cutter or smith also listed in the Directory; Gottlieb Rosenblatt was in "fancygoods," and active in the German Hebrew Benevolent Society; Isaac Rosenbourgh, a jeweler, was also a founder of Bnai Brith and, in 1845, Treasurer of Congregation Emanu-El (Myer Stern, *The Rise and Progress of Reform Judaism*, New York, 1895, p. 18); Baruch Rothschild was in "fancygoods" and active in the German Hebrew Benevolent Society and in Congregation Emanu-El; of S. Rothschilds there are the following: Samuel, a policeman, and Samuel, in "shirts," Seligman, a tailor, and Simon J., in "millinery"; Henry Straus was in "liquors"; of S. Strauses, there are Salomon, in clothing, Samuel, a carrier, Selig, in "segars," Solomon, the pedler, and Solomon, the "segar maker"; Joseph Sulzberger was a clerk; Dr. Waterman, a physician, was a religious reformer and an outstanding German-Jewish intellectual in the city; Maurice Werner was in "millinery," and active in the Young Men's Hebrew Benevolent and Fuel Association; Ch. Northschild and Samuel Trechet are not in the Directory.

116. Joining a Third Party

1. *Hamilton Fish Papers, Letters from Jonathan Nathan. 1847–1857,* Low Memorial Library, Columbia University. Most of the letters are accurately dated by virtue of the fact that the recipient usually marked the date received.
2. Allan Nevins, *Hamilton Fish,* New York, 1937, pp. 30–31.
3. Nathan to Fish, December 20, 1850. Fish's estimate of Nathan's qualities may be inferred from Fish's letter to President Lincoln, March 4, 1861, recommending Nathan unsuccessfully for the post of Naval Officer of the Port of New York, in which he speaks of Nathan as "a Lawyer by education & profession—A Gentleman of rare intelligence, & high culture, with habits of business, & of strict integrity—. . . For upwards of twenty years he was among the wisest and most efficient in the ranks of the Whig party—latterly an earnest Republican . . ." (*Hamilton Fish Papers,* Library of Congress, Letterbook "R," pp. 151–152.) Nathan held the office of Master in Chancery, 1840–1845 (Milton Halsey Thomas, *Columbia University Officers and Alumni, 1754–1857,* New

York, 1936), and was a Commissioner of Records in 1862. He was Parnas of the Congregation Shearith Israel from July 1, 1861 to October 10, 1863 (*AJHSP*, XXI, 1913, p. 213); he continued the intimate association with that congregation of his parents, Isaac Mendez Seixas Nathan and Sara Seixas (*AJHSP*, XXVII, 1920, p. 166).

4. Before Fish became Governor (1848–1850), Nathan used to address him as "My dear Ham;" later he used "My dear Gov." even after Fish became United States Senator in 1851.

5. "Niggerism" was one of the objectionable terms used by opponents of the abolitionist movement to describe their activity. The letter referred to was a draft that Nathan had sent Fish on April 22, 1856, prepared by his law associate, Alexander W. Bradford, and himself. Fish had been invited to a meeting at the Tabernacle in New York on April 29, 1856 to hear a report from the New York delegates to the Pittsburgh Convention of the Republican Party, held February 22, 23, 1856. Fish was considering sending a reply to the invitation; Nathan's draft was presented for his judgment; as is clear from the second letter, Fish decided not to reply at all, apparently being not yet ready to commit himself to the Republican Party. When the Call to the meeting was printed in the *New-York Daily Tribune*, April 29, 1856, among the 2500 names appended were those of Jonathan Nathan's younger brother, Gershon (Gershom) Nathan, Jacob Levy, Simon Levy, Abrm. Levy, H. Cohen, Philip Aaron, Saul Solomon and others that may be Jewish. For background, see Philip S. Foner, *Business and Slavery*, Chapel Hill, 1941, pp. 116–125.

6. In his draft, Nathan had written: ". . . I would fail in justice to myself were I to refrain on this & every appropriate occasion from expressing my deep & earnest Sympathy with every struggle of freedom, and especially with all just & proper effort to bring the territory of Kansas into the Union as a free State—. . ." Fish agreed with the position but still hesitated publicly to make such a statement.

7. In a letter dated Wednesday, April 30, 1856, Nathan reported that the "papers are full of the great meeting," and of Fish's decision not to send the document he said, "B[radford] takes it kindly—he appreciates your position and laughs at your scruples."

8. Nathan was a bad prophet. When the Republican Nominating Convention met in Philadelphia on June 17, 1856, as had been agreed on at Pittsburgh, Fremont was selected as the Presidential candidate, but it was not Moses H. Grinnell, the wealthy New York merchant and shipowner, who was chosen as his running mate but William L. Dayton of N. J.

9. Francis Preston Blair (1791–1876) was one of the main organizers of the Republican Party but rejoined the Democrats after the Civil War; his eldest son, Montgomery Blair (1813–1883), who had been the counsel for Dred Scott, was a Free-Soiler who joined the Republicans when the American (Nativist) Party was silent on the slavery issue; another son, Francis Preston Blair, Jr. (1821–1875) was an active Missouri Republican. Jessie Benton Fremont (1824–1902) was the candidate's very popular wife.

10. Millard Fillmore (1800–1872), who had been President, 1850–1852, was now the candidate of the Native American Party. Mayor Fernando Wood and the New York City Council staged an official reception for him when he returned from England; the *New-York Daily Tribune* estimated that the procession "by actual count numbered 710 persons" (June 25, 1856). In the elections, Buchanan and the Democratic Party won, the Native Americans and Whigs were practically

eliminated, while the Republicans carried all of New England, New York, Michigan, Wisconsin.

11. "Jessie played only a slighter part in the campaign than her husband, and 'Fremont and Jessie' seemed to constitute the Republican ticket rather than Fremont and Dayton." (Allan Nevins, *Fremont, the West's Greatest Adventurer,* New York and London, 1928, Vol. 2, pp. 496–497.) The "bhoys" was a disparaging term used by the Whigs and others to describe the masses of Irish immigrants who flocked to the banner of Tammany Hall in New York.

117. With John Brown in Bleeding Kansas

1. From *Autobiography of August Bondi, 1833–1907,* Published by His Sons and Daughters for Its Preservation, Galesburg, Ill., 1910, pp. 49–54, 60–63. Bondi first set down these reminiscences, however, in 1884, when they were published in the Salina, Kansas, *Herald* (August Bondi, "With John Brown in Kansas," *Transactions of the Kansas State Historical Society, 1903–1904,* VIII, pp. 275–89).
2. James C. Malin, *John Brown and the Legend of Fifty-Six,* Philadelphia, 1942, pp. 424, 475, 737n. Professor Malin, however, setting out to prove that John Brown was little more than a common murderer and horse-thief, is harsh with all those, like Bondi, whose view was the contrary; moreover, Professor Malin is not without bias against Bondi, whom he incorrectly labels "a Jewish speculator" (p. 678). The period of this chapter of Bondi's *Autobiography* is covered in greater detail in Oswald Garrison Villard, *John Brown 1800–1859,* New York, 1943 ed., pp. 189–224, and in Malin, pp. 589–592.
3. *Autobiography,* pp. 24, 30–31. August (Anshl) Bondi (1833–1907) was born in Vienna; in 1843 he was admitted to the academic *Gymnasium* in Vienna, managed then, as were all such institutions, by Piarist monks. Although not yet fifteen, he was accepted into the Academic Legion that took part in the March, 1848 Revolution in Vienna. To escape the counter-revolution, his family and he left Vienna on September 6, 1848 on a journey that brought them to New Orleans in November. By January 8, 1849, he was already attending political rallies in St. Louis that opposed slavery extension. For a time he clerked in a dry goods store, served as a printer's apprentice, held a partnership in a tavern, and taught school. In 1851, he enlisted in an expedition to liberate Cuba, but the outfit never moved from its base; going to New Orleans, he tried to join Perry's Japanese Expedition, but found recruiting had already ended. In 1855, reading an editorial in the *New-York Daily Tribune* "appealing to the freedom loving men of the states to rush to Kansas and save it from the curse of slavery," Bondi left St. Louis on March 26, and settled on the Mosquito branch of the Pottawatomie creek in the middle of May, together with another Jew, Jacob Benjamin (1827–1870), for whom Bondi had worked as a clerk in St. Louis in September 1854. Later a third Jew, Theodore Weiner (or Wiener), joined them, and an attempt was made to form a general merchandising business as an adjunct to tilling the soil. All three served with John Brown in Kansas. (*Autobiography,* 1–42; also Huhner, *AJHSP,* XXIII, 1915, 55–78.)
4. *Autobiography,* 48. John Brown, Jr., the eldest son of John Brown, had not been with his father at the Pottawatomie raid, but he was arrested by "Border Ruffians," brutally maltreated and driven temporarily insane, and then held on a charge of treason until released on bail on September 10, 1856 (Villard, *op. cit.,* 193ff, 254).

5. O. A. Carpenter and his brother Howard were free-soil settlers.

6. John Brown had six sons: John Jr., Jason (died, 1912), Owen (1824–1899), Frederick (1830–1856), murdered on August 30, 1856 by Rev. Martin White, Oliver (1839–1859), who died at Harper's Ferry, and Salmon Brown, who lived to be over eighty. On the expedition that Bondi describes here, John Jr. and Jason were not present.

7. Henry Thompson (1822–1911) of Lewis, N. Y., was John Brown's son-in-law, having married his daughter Ruth.

8. James Townsley (1815–1890) of Maryland was a painter before he became a farmer in Kansas; he served in the Union army in the Civil War (Malin, *op. cit.*, 617, 683).

9. Theodore Weiner (1820–1906) was a Polish Jew, born in Posen (then part of Prussia). After living "for a long time in Texas and Louisiana," Weiner came to Kansas, writes Bondi, "to trade and to make money" and he "was in politics as late as the spring of 1855, a rank pro-slavery man. He was a thorough Douglas-squatter-sovereignty democrat and considered all free state reports regarding invasions of the Border Ruffians from Missouri as fakes and lies." But when the pro-slavery Dutch Bill Sherman, 6 feet 3 inches tall and weighing 250 pounds, came to Weiner to beat him up, Weiner, who also weighed 250 pounds but was only 5 feet 10 inches tall, thrashed Dutch Bill and "after that Weiner acknowledged himself Free State." (Bondi, *op. cit.*, 45.) He was with John Brown at Pottawatomie.

10. Benjamin Cochran[e] is one of the eight listed by John Brown as having stayed through the battle of Black Jack until the enemy surrendered (Villard, *op. cit.*, 614).

11. In 1859, an investigating commission of the Kansas Territorial Legislature awarded Bondi $1,000 in damages but rejected Weiner's claim for $4,500 "on the ground that he was not a resident of Kansas" (Malin, *op. cit.*, 391).

12. Bondi probably meant the commanding officer of the 2d U. S. Dragoons, Lt. Col. Philip St. George Cooke (1809–1895), a Virginian who later served in the Union army although his son was a Confederate general and his daughter married Confederate General J. E. B. Stuart (*The National Cyclopaedia of American Biography*, New York, 1897, IV, 189–190).

13. Kaiser was captured by Border Ruffians at the Battle of Osawatomie, August 30, 1856, and shot by them on September 1st.

14. Samuel T. Shore had come to Kansas from Missouri (William Phillips, *The Conquest of Kansas*, Boston, 1856, p. 334), but nothing more is ascertainable about him or Dr. Westfall.

15. On Route US-50, three miles east of Baldwin, Douglas county, Kansas, the "marker" placed there by the Kansas Historical Society reads as follows: "Battle of Black Jack. This 'Battle' was part of the struggle to make Kansas a free state. In May, 1856, Proslavery men destroyed buildings and newspaper presses in Lawrence, Free-State Headquarters. John Brown's company then killed five Proslavery men on Pottawatomie Creek not far from this spot. In retaliation Henry C. Pate raided near-by Palmyra and took three prisoners. Early on the morning of June 2 Brown attacked Pate's camp in a grove of Black Jack oaks about ¼ mile south of this sign. Both sides had several wounded and numerous desertions before Pate and 28 men surrendered, Brown claiming he had only 15 men left. As evidence of Civil War this fight received much publicity and

excited both the North and South." ("Kansas Historical Markers," *The Kansas Historical Quarterly,* X, 1941, p. 354.)

16. The only available identification of members of the Moore family is that of Captain Silas Moore, listed by John Brown as having taken part in the Black Jack engagement (Villard, *op. cit.,* 614).

17. Henry Clay Pate (1832–1864), a Virginian, was the Kansas correspondent of the Westport, Mo., *Missouri Republican,* and had taken part in the sack of Lawrence (Phillips, *op. cit.,* 331); he was later a cavalry officer in the Confederate army and died in service (Villard, *op. cit.,* 201).

18. Rev. David N. Utter (1844–1926), a Unitarian minister, had written that "the real hero of Black Jack was Captain Shore" in an article seeking to discredit John Brown in *The North American Review,* Vol. 137, November, 1883, p. 445; Rev. Utter thought Brown's "principles were those of the Russian nihilists" and therefore "not a proper hero for the youth of our country to worship, . . ." It was in reply to Utter that Bondi first wrote the articles in the Salina *Herald* cited above in Note 1. Malin's chapter, "The Utter Controversy, 1883–84," should be read with great care because of Malin's own predilections (*op. cit.,* 405–428).

19. The Lawrence "Stubbs" were a Free-State company from Lawrence, Kan.

20. For John Brown's own account of the surrender, written shortly after the event, see Villard, *op. cit.,* 205–206; in many details it differs from Bondi's later reminiscences.

21. In November, 1861, Bondi enlisted in the Union army: "My mother said that as a Jehudi I had a duty to perform, to defend the institutions which gave equal rights to all beliefs." He became First Sergeant of Company K of the 5th Kansas Volunteer Cavalry, was dangerously wounded September 11, 1864 and discharged December 2, 1864. While he was away, his mother took care of his wife and child. (*Autobiography,* 72, 133.)

22. William Addison Phillips (1824–1893), born in Paisley, Scotland, came to Illinois with his parents, and thence to Kansas, where he settled; after rising to the rank of Colonel in the Union army, he became a writer on economic and political subjects and a Republican Congressman. His book does not mention Bondi and Weiner in its account of the Black Jack engagement (pp. 334–342) but it corresponds to Bondi's account in essential matters.

23. Captain James B. Abbott (1818–1879) of Connecticut had arrived in Lawrence in October 1854 and had helped defend the city against sacking (William E. Connelley, *A Standard History of Kansas and Kansans,* Chicago and New York, 1918, III, 1291–1292). Luke F. Parsons (1833–1926) later agreed to accompany John Brown on the Harper's Ferry raid, but pulled out at the last minute (Villard, *op. cit.,* 344). David Starr Hoyt (1821–1856) had come to Kansas from Deerfield, Mass.; he was killed by Border Ruffians about August 12, 1856 (Letter to the writer from Miss Helen M. McFarland, librarian of the Kansas State Historical Society, February 9, 1949; Villard, *op. cit.,* 215).

24. Brown's roster of those who took part in the Black Jack fight includes Hugh and John McWhinney, Hugh being one of those to whom the surrender was made.

25. About this pilfering, John Brown made the bitter comment: "After the fight, numerous Free State men who could not be got out before were on hand; and some of them I am ashamed to add, were very busy not only with the plunder of our enemies, but with our private effects, leaving us, while guarding

our prisoners and providing in regard to them, much poorer than before the battle." (Quoted by Villard, *ibid.*, 208.)

26. Bondi must mean Joab M. Bernard, who estimated his losses from this raid at $4,000 (Malin, *op. cit.*, 590–591); in 1859 Bernard was awarded $9,524.91 for losses incurred on this raid and on a later raid in September, 1856 (Villard, *op. cit.*, 614).

27. Samuel Walker (1822–1893) of Pennsylvania and Ohio was a cabinetmaker before settling in Kansas in April 1855; during the Civil War he became a Major in the 5th Kansas Cavalry in which Bondi served (Connelley, *op. cit.*, III, 1223).

28. Bondi must mean Lt. W. B. Brocket.

29. Col. Edwin Vose Sumner (1797–1863) was then in command not of the 2d U. S. Dragoons but of Fort Leavenworth. His attempts to preserve order in Kansas by dispersing armed bands on both sides met with the disapproval of Secretary of War Jefferson Davis, who relieved him of his command (Villard, *op.* cit., 219).

30. Villard, like Bondi, regarded William J. Preston as a United States Deputy Marshal (*ibid.*, 210); Malin scouts the idea, and asserts that he was only a Deputy Sheriff appointed by the Governor of the Territory to accompany Colonel Sumner (*op. cit.*, 591).

31. David Garrison (1826–1856) was shot down on August 30, 1856 by Border Ruffians while he was unarmed (Villard, *op. cit.*, 181; letter by Miss McFarland, cited).

32. John Bean Mannes (or Manes) was then eleven years old. His father was Poindexter Mannes, mentioned below.

33. According to the land records, there was a Zachariah Schutte, Jr. in the vicinity (Malin, *op. cit.*, 762).

34. Henry Kilbourn (or Kilburn) had come to Kansas from Ohio with his two brothers, Sam and William, and was only fourteen years old in 1856 (*ibid.*, 237, 197).

35. About 150 Georgians had been brought in to settle near Osawatomie to help make Kansas a slave state (*ibid.*, 122); they came under the command of Major Jefferson Buford as a military organization (Villard, *op. cit.*, 137).

36. Malin states that James B. Cline was from Milwaukee, Wisconsin (*op. cit.*, 212–213).

37. Martin White had come to Kansas from Illinois, where he had served in the State Legislature; in an affidavit explaining his murder of Frederick Brown, Martin described the raid on his home, maintaining that seven horses and other property to the value of $1,000 had been taken (*ibid.*, 532, 136).

38. Thaddeus Hyatt (1816–1901) of New York was President of the National Kansas Committee organized at Buffalo in July, 1856, to aid anti-slavery settlement in Kansas. After Harper's Ferry, he was imprisoned for three months for refusing to testify before a Senate Investigating Committee "for the sake of the principle involved" (Villard, *op. cit.*, 227, 582–583).

39. In 1854, his sister had married her cousin, Emanuel Bondi, in Louisville, Ky. (*Autobiography*, 32.)

40. "Mrs. Benjamin died in confinement about the middle of October [1857]; her

child, a son, died soon after. . . . Benjamin married again in January, 1857, a daughter of Maness, her first name was Elizabeth." (*Autobiography,* 66.)

41. Jacob Merritt Anthony (1834–1900), brother of the famous Susan B. Anthony, was the youngest of the six Anthony children; he later served in the Union army, 1861–65 (Ida Husted Harper, *The Life and Work of Susan B. Anthony,* Indianapolis, 1908, p. 1217).

42. James H. Holmes (1833–1907) of Tompkins county, New York, a student of agricultural chemistry, had originally come to Kansas to join a vegetarian colony and conduct soil experiments, but finding the colony disbanded, he went to Lawrence (Malin, *op. cit.,* 610; letter by Miss McFarland, cited.)

43. James Montgomery (1814–1871) of Ohio and Kentucky was a leader of the free-state forces in Linn county, Kansas, where he had settled; in the Civil War, he was the colonel of a Kansas volunteer infantry regiment and then in 1863, as colonel of the 2d South Carolina Negro Regiment, he took part in the raiding of Georgia ([Alfred Theodore Andreas], *History of the State of Kansas,* Chicago, 1883, p. 302).

44. John E. Brown was the Sheriff of Linn county (Malin, *op. cit.,* 614).

45. Malin estimates the number as "about seventy-five" (*ibid.,* 617).

46. Bondi achieved local prominence in various ways after the days of bloody Kansas, and held several local offices: township trustee, probate judge, register's clerk in the federal land office, and clerk in his school district. In 1860, he married Henrietta Einstein, with whom he had two sons and eight daughters. As a Kansas farmer he withstood cyclones and grasshoppers alike. At 70, he wrote: "I do not regret a single step or instance in my long life to further and to assist the realization of my devout wishes that tyranny and despotism may perish, and bigotry and fanaticism may be wiped from the face of the earth. Never orthodox but a consistent Jew nevertheless; I believed in the continuance and upholding of all the ceremonial laws. . . ." (*Autobiography,* 133.)

118. Exploring the West with Fremont

1. *Incidents of Travel and Adventure in the Far West; with Col. Fremont's Last Expedition Across the Rocky Mountains: Including Three Months' Residence in Utah, and a Perilous Trip Across the Great American Desert, to the Pacific,* New York, 1857, pp. 96–103, 128–138. Carvalho's preface is dated Baltimore, September 1856, and the volume may have been planned to appear in time to influence the 1856 elections in which Fremont was a candidate for President, but the title-page bears the date 1857. However, excerpts from Carvalho's diaries were published in John Bigelow, *Memoir of the Life and Public Services of John Charles Fremont,* . . . New York, 1856, pp. 430–442, which appeared in time for the elections and was published by Derby & Jackson, who later issued Carvalho's volume.

2. *Catalogue of the Twenty-Sixth Annual Exhibition of the Pennsylvania Academy of the Fine Arts* . . . 1849, p. 6; *The Occident,* January, 1853, pp. 503–504; *Trow's New-York City Directory, for 1853–1854,* p. 121.)

3. Emanuel Lazarus had been one of a party of seventeen led by Jedediah S. Smith (c.1798–1831) that were the first white men to enter California from the East in November 1826; Lazarus was probably one of the eleven killed by the Indians on July 14, 1828 in retaliation for what the Indians considered ill treatment; the Jewish identity of Lazarus, however, has not been unquestionably estab-

lished. (Maurice S. Sullivan, *The Travels of Jedediah Smith,* Santa Ana, California, 1934, pp. 62, 163, 168, and *Jedediah Smith, Trader and Trail Breaker,* New York, 1936, pp. 69, 157, 184; Harrison Clifford Dale, *The Ashley-Smith Explorations and the Discovery of a Central Route to the Pacific 1822–1829 . . .,* Cleveland, 1918, pp. 187, 218, 237, 265; one of the members of the expedition was Peter Ranne, a Negro; Allan Nevins, *Fremont, Pathmarker of the West,* New York and London, 1939, pp. 408–420; Frederick S. Dellenbaugh, *Fremont and '49,* New York, 1914, pp. 432–455; Charles Macnamara, "The First Official Photographer," *The Scientific Monthly,* January, 1936, pp. 68–74.

4. Carvalho, *op. cit.,* 91–92, describes how a few days before this one of the ten Delaware Indians accompanying the Fremont expedition had killed a horse that Utah Indians asserted belonged to one of the squaws; Fremont had ordered she be compensated.

5. The conquest of California from Mexico was achieved by the armed forces of Fremont and others between July 5, 1846 and January 13, 1847, when the treaty of victory was signed. On September 9, 1850, when California was admitted to the Union, Fremont became one of its first United States Senators, failing of re-election, however, because of his anti-slavery views.

6. For his description of his first buffalo hunt, October 25, 1853, see *ibid.,* 50–56.

7. The heavy daguerreotype equipment was buried when it became too burdensome for the weakened company to transport it further (*ibid.,* 124), and it seems never to have been recovered (Macnamara, *op. cit.,* 74).

8. Egloffstein was the topographical engineer of the expedition.

9. Carvalho married Sarah Solis of Philadelphia; his first son, David Nunes, was born in 1848 (died 1925); Jacob S. Carvalho, his second son, was born in October, 1852, before Carvalho left on the expedition. Another son, Solomon Solis, was born in 1856. At the end of the journey, Carvalho went on to Los Angeles and San Francisco. In the former, he enjoyed the hospitality of two Jewish merchants, Samuel and Joseph Labatt, to whom, he says, "I am indebted for many acts of kindness; men who anticipate the necessities of their fellow-man, and spontaneously offer *money advances* to a perfect stranger, I have not often met with, 'but when found, I make a note of it.'" (Carvalho, *op. cit.,* 250). From California, Carvalho went to Baltimore, where he was active in the Jewish community on the Swiss Treaty agitation, the Mortara Case, and similar affairs. By 1861, he settled permanently in New York, working as an artist and photographer, inventing heat treatments and processes that led to his establishing the Steam Super-Heater Co. in 1867 and to his becoming president of the Carvalho Heating and Super-Heating Co. about 1880; in 1889 he was in the lumber business; in 1892 and 1893 he was listed as an inventor; he died May 21, 1897, aged 82. (Rosenbach Collection, Swiss Treaty Folder, A. J. H. S., Carvalho to Mendes I. Cohen, November 1, 1857; *The Israelite,* February 4, 1859, p. 244, col. 4 and September 3, 1858, p. 70, cols. 3–4; *The Occident,* October 18, 1860, p. 180, cols. 1–3 and November 1, 1860, p. 2; *Trow's New York City Directories,* 1863–1894. *Allgemeine Zeitung des Judenthums,* Berlin, July 23, 1897, App. p. 4.)

119. First New York Russian-Jewish Congregation

1. *The Occident,* XIV, March, 1857, pp. 599–601. Isaac Leeser's introductory note explained that this congregation had as its objects "the promotion of Talmudical knowledge and meetings for prayer."

2. The twelve founders were: Benjamin Lichtenstein, Judah Middleman, Abraham Benjamin (of Hamburg), Abraham Joseph Ash, Israel Cohen, Abba Baum, David Lasky, Leib Cohen, Baruch Solomon Rothschild, Joshua Rothstein, Eliah Greenstein, Feibel Philips. (Eisenstein, *AJHSP,* IX, 1901, pp. 64–65.) Because they were recent immigrants, the New York city directories from 1852 to 1858 contain almost no data about these persons, with the following exceptions: in 1853, Abraham Benjamin is listed as in "segars" on Delancey Street, and by 1855 he has become a "plater"; David Lasky in 1856 is named as a manufacturer, and in 1857 his product is defined as "caps." Rabbi Ash (1821–1887), born in Semyatch, Russia, came to the United States in 1851.

3. Grinstein, *op. cit.,* 14, 93, 263, 412.

4. *Arba Turim* (The Four Rows), was a popular codification of Jewish laws and regulations, compiled by Jacob ben Asher (c. 1269–c. 1340).

   The *Rambam* is Moses ben Maimon or Maimonides (1135–1204), the great Spanish Talmudist, philosopher and physician. The name is formed from the initials of Rabbi Moses ben Maimon. His *Code of Jewish Law* is meant here.

   The *Rif* is formed from the initials of Rabbi Isaac Fasi (of Fez, North Africa) (1013–1103), famous for his codification of Talmudic law.

   The *Shulchan Aruch* (Prepared Table) is the code of Jewish ritual, based on Sephardic practise and first printed in Venice, 1565; by the middle of the seventeenth century, the work had gained general recognition, with Joseph Caro's original supplemented by Moses Isserles, who added the Ashkenzic practise.

   The *Midrashim* are biblical expositions.

   The *Kabbalah* (Cabala) is a system of Jewish mysticism and secret lore, best represented by the *Zohar,* probably a 13th century Spanish work.

   The *Sepharim* in the Hechal are the Holy Scrolls kept in the Ark.

5. When Sampson Simson died in 1857, he left $2,000 to the *Beth Hamidrash* (as well as $3,000 to Shearith Israel, of which he was a member, and $1,000 to Columbia College, of which he was an alumnus). (*Ibid.,* 449.) Simson had already donated $3,000 to the *Beth Hamidrash,* thereby helping it to purchase the Welsh Chapel at 78 Allen Street to convert it into a synagogue, which was dedicated June 8, 1856. (Eisenstein, *op. cit.,* 66.) The fact that this appeal speaks as if the congregation still had no permanent home suggests that the text may have been written some time before Leeser published it.

120. Naval Hero Vindicated

1. Pp. 11–13, 15–16, 86–89. The *Defence,* with *An Abstract of the Proceedings and Testimony, and an Appendix Containing the Documents Referred to in the Defence,* was published in New York, 1858, and was prepared and read to the court by Benjamin F. Butler, Levy's Senior Counsel. Butler (1795–1858) had served as attorney-general in Jackson's cabinet, 1833–1837, had organized and been professor in the Law Department of New York University, distinguished himself as a codifier of the New York legal code, and was generally one of the leaders of the bar. He undertook the case "after full investigation of the facts and the law, made up his mind that Levy had been unjustly dealt with, and was entitled to be reinstated in the navy and compensated for the illegal and cruel treatment he had received"; Butler's son regards the victory as "one of the most notable achievements" of his father's career (William Allen Butler, *A Retrospect of Forty years 1825–1865,* New York, 1911, pp. 317–318).

2. James Morris Morgan, *The Century,* September, 1899, pp. 796–800; facts about the USS Levy were provided this editor in a letter from the Office of Public Information, Navy Department, May 23, 1947.

3. No accurate, satisfactory account of Levy's life is available, but the following are useful, although erring in details: *DAB,* XI, 203–204, by John C. Wyllie; *UJE,* VII, 17–18, by Clarence I. Freed; Simon Wolf, *AJYB,* 5663, 1902–1903, pp. 42–45; Morais, *op. cit.,* 469–470.

4. In the *United States Naval Institute Proceedings,* March, 1929, pp. 270–273, Professor Herman F. Krafft, curator at the Naval Academy, describes the important part played by Levy in abolishing flogging in the Navy, although most histories of the Navy ignore the subject. Interesting material on the methods Levy used instead of flogging is contained in editorials in 1839 and 1840 published in *A Brief Review of the Trials of Commander U. P. Levy, United States Navy,* a unique copy of which is in *Lyons Pamphlets, I,* at the American Jewish Historical Society.

5. For a summary of these courts-martial, see Kanof, *AJHSP,* XXXIX, Part 1 (September, 1949), 16, 18ff.

6. B. W. Blandford, "Commodore Uriah P. Levy," *The American Hebrew,* April 24, May 1 and 8, 1925, pp. 787, 823, 835. Levy, an admirer of Thomas Jefferson, had in 1834 presented to the Government a bronze statue he had commissioned from Pierre Jean David, France's leading sculptor. In 1836, Levy bought Jefferson's Monticello for $2,700; his will bequeathing this estate to the Government was broken by one of his heirs (Kanof, *op. cit.,* 11). Levy's fortune seems to have been made chiefly in New York real estate, of which it was estimated in 1846 he owned about $250,000 worth (Moses Y. Beach, *Wealth and Biography of the Wealthy Citizens of New York City,* New York, 10th ed., 1846, p. 19). About 1858 Levy married the young daughter of Abraham Lopez of Jamaica, Virginia Lopez (c. 1833–1925). In the Civil War, he offered his fortune to the Union cause. Levy was a charter member of the Washington Hebrew Congregation, organized April 25, 1852.

7. Levy commanded the corvette *Vandalia* for one year, 1838–1839.

8. George Bancroft (1800–1891) is the famous historian and diplomat who served as Secretary of the Navy in Polk's cabinet, March, 1845 to September, 1846.

9. Lord John Russell (1792–1878) was a leader in the Parliamentary reform movement in the 1820s.

121. The Mortara Case

1. Reprinted in *The Occident,* XVI, No. 10, January 1859, pp. 481–487. Leeser also reprinted the letter by "Plures in Unum" which evoked his reply.

2. Rev. A. F. Day, S. J., *The Mortara Mystery,* London, 1930, p. 4; A. Zacher, *Der Raub des Judenknaben Mortara,* Frankfurt am Main, 1908, pp. 5ff; Joseph Meisl, "Beiträge zum Fall Mortara (1858)," *Monatsschrift für Geschichte und Wissenschaft des Judenthums,* Frankfurt a. M., September–October 1933, pp. 323ff; R. De Cesare, *The Last Days of Papal Rome 1850–1870,* tr. by Helen Zimmern, London, 1909, p. 176. The facts are also given, often inaccurately, in *JE, UJE, Encyclopedia Britannica, The Encyclopedia Americana, La Grande Encyclopédie (Paris), Enciclopedia Universal Ilustrada Europeo-Americana* (Madrid), *The Harmsworth Encyclopaedia* (London), and *The New International Encyclopaedia.* The works by Day, Zacher and Meisl are rich in new

material. For similar instances, see Cecil Roth, "Forced Baptisms in Italy," *The Jewish Quarterly Review*, October 1936, pp. 117–136.

3. For the course of protest in Europe, see *Allgemeine Zeitung des Judenthums*, Leipzig, January 1, 1859, pp. 24–27 and the succeeding numbers; Meisl, *op. cit.; The Jewish Messenger*, December 10, 1858, pp. 132–133, which quotes the *St. Petersburg News* in Russia; N. M. Gelber, *Aus Zwei Jahrhunderten*, Wien und Leipzig, 1924, pp. 169–172 and Israel Levi Kohn, ed., *Beitrag zur Geschichte jüdischer Tartuffe*, Leipzig, 1864, both of which deal with the conduct of Ignaz Deutsch, Viennese Jewish banker and leader of the Jewish Orthodox Party, who denounced the Jews that protested the abduction as reformers and revolutionaries to the Austrian government.

4. For American interest, see Howard R. Marraro, *American Opinion on the Unification of Italy, 1846–1861*, New York, 1932, pp. 150–153; *The Israelite, The Jewish Messenger, The Occident*, and *Sinai* report the meetings and many newspaper comments.

5. New York, Series IV, April, 1859, pp. 227, 233, 236, 237. In Switzerland, the Catholic *Schwyzer-Gazette* condemned the abduction (*The Israelite*, December 24, 1858, p. 198, col. 2). In Paris, the Abbe André Vincent Delacouture published a pamphlet in 1858, *Le Droit Canon et Le Droit Naturel Dans L'Affaire Mortara*, disagreeing with the Papal view. Rev. Dr. Max Lilienthal in Cincinnati several times appealed to the American Catholic Clergy to "petition the Pope in behalf of the abducted child of Bologna" (*The Israelite*, November 5, 1858, p. 143). *The Catholic Encyclopaedia*, New York, 1907, has a passing reference to the Mortara Case in its article, "Baptism," (II, 271). The many volumes of the *Researches* and *Records* of the American Catholic Historical Society of Philadelphia have no mention of the case. *Der Israelitische Volkslehrer*, Frankfurt a. M., April 1859, pp. 117–118, carries an interesting set of documents showing that a young Jewish woman was allowed to revert to Judaism although she had once been voluntarily baptised.

6. On January 10, 1859, a delegation of Philadelphia Jews headed by Isaac Leeser was presented to President Buchanan and Secretary of State Lewis Cass, both of whom had already publicly declared their policy of non-intervention in the matter. When the delegation reminded them that President Van Buren had intervened in the Damascus case in 1840, Buchanan replied, "It happened when I was not President." According to the delegation's printed report, Buchanan said that this was a case with so much merit that if the government took no action in this instance it "would present a ready answer to any attempt to intermeddle by other countries in the affairs of this." (*The Occident*, February 1859, pp. 536–539.) Rev. David Einhorn of Baltimore, an opponent of slavery, pointed out that it was in a sense consistent for a government that supports slavery to refuse to act in the Swiss Treaty and Mortara Cases (*Sinai*, January 1859, pp. 1147–1151; February 1859, p. 3). Isaac M. Wise in Cincinnati, however, taking the state's rights position on slavery, had "to object, the federal government has nothing in the world to do with slavery in the south. The United States are positively not responsible for a domestic institution of Georgia or Texas. . . . A protest of a foreign government against the institution of slavery could not be recognized by the federal government at all, and must be entered in South Carolina, Georgia, &c. Hence we do not understand General Cass." (*The Israelite*, January 7, 1859, pp. 212–213.) Einhorn, who opposed both slavery and the forced baptism of Jewish children, seems the more consistent. Rev. Sabato Morais of Mickveh Israel in Philadelphia ceased praying for the government in November 1858 in protest against Buchanan's

policy (Moshe Davis, "Sabato Morais: A Selected and Annotated Bibliography of his Writings," in *AJHSP,* XXXVII, 1947, p. 83). The Catholic *New York Tablet,* incidentally, rebuked the Protestant weekly, *The Independent,* for criticising the Pope while it made no objection to abduction of slaves by abolitionists! (Grinstein, *op. cit.,* 432.)

7. On January 10, 1859, when a resolution on the Mortara Case was offered to the House of Representatives, it was presented by the Baltimore Know-Nothing American Party leader, Representative James Morrison Harris (1817–1898). Since he had failed to give notice of the introduction of the resolution, it was ruled out of order; his promise to introduce it next day was not kept (*The Congressional Globe,* 35 Cong., 2 Sess., pt. 1, pp. 290–291). In Albany, N. Y., the Know-Nothing Americans passed a resolution on December 20, 1858, participated with the Jews in a joint meeting on December 23, but, not being satisfied with the resolutions and speeches, held their own meeting on December 28, in which they gave their nativism full rein and boosted the American party. Public officials and some Jewish leaders took part in this meeting. (*The Jewish Messenger,* December 24, 1858, p. 149, *The Occident,* March, 1859, pp. 568–571, *The Israelite,* December 31, 1858, p. 202.) In the New York State Legislature, Senator Osmer B. Wheeler on January 12, 1859 introduced a resolution calling on the President to help release the Mortara child from Papal custody, but it was tabled and forgotten; in the Assembly, Samuel A. Law of Delaware Country introduced the same resolution on January 18, but it was not reported out of committee until April 19, 1859, when the Assembly was ready to adjourn.

8. It was the appeal of the 21 Sardinian Jewish Congregations to the London Board of Deputies of British Jews and the Paris Consistory of French Jews, dated August 19, 1858, that stimulated the first actions by European Jews (London *Times,* September 9, 1858, has the text of the appeal, which was widely reprinted; *Lyons Scrapbook* II, item 44, is a circular reprint of the *Times* article).

9. John Nepomucene Neumann (1811–1860), born in Bohemia, was consecrated Bishop of Philadelphia March 28, 1852 (*The Catholic Encyclopaedia,* X, 773–774).

10. This was one of a chain of meetings started by the arrival in this country of a circular letter from the London Board of Jewish Deputies signed by Sir Moses Montefiore, dated late in October, 1858, calling for protest action. (For detailed accounts of the role of Montefiore in this matter, his vain attempt to obtain an audience from Pius IX, and the public clamor in England that culminated in a resolution of British Christians signed by "more than two thousand names of persons of rank and influence," see L. Loewe, ed., *Diaries of Sir Moses and Lady Montefiore,* London, 1890, II, 82–103, and Lucien Wolf, *Sir Moses Montefiore, a Centennial Biography,* New York, 1885, pp. 153–159.) News of the Mortara abduction had appeared in *The Jewish Messenger* as early as August 13, 1858; by September 10, that weekly was urging emigration of Italian Jews to the United States; by October 15, it was contenting itself with proposing that American Jewish mothers nurse their own children instead of leaving them with "Bridget and Mary." On October 22, 1858, however, Lilienthal in *The Israelite* issued the first call for protest action, and the first meeting in response to that call was held in Cincinnati on October 30. When Montefiore's letter arrived, other groups readily responded.

11. Isaac Leeser (1806–1868) had been educated at the Gymnasium in Münster (*JE,* VII, 662).

12. The nurse, Anna Morisi, was born November 28, 1833, and was therefore really nineteen years old when she secretly baptised Edgar (Zacher, *op. cit.,* 21).

13. Piux IX (1792–1878) held the longest pontificate in papal history from 1846 to 1878. Beginning his career as a political liberal, he was, by 1850, a conservative, and by Catholic writers is highly regarded in part for his "unmasking the false liberalism which had begun to insinuate its subtle poison into the very marrow of Catholicism" (*The Catholic Encyclopaedia,* XII, 134–135).

14. In one sense, the international agitation around the Mortara Case was ineffectual: the boy was never returned to his parents. The case, however, contributed to the tide of Italian liberalism which finally led to the restriction of the Papal temporal power to the Vatican City in 1870 (De Cesare, *op. cit.,* 179; Zacher, *op. cit.,* 24); but even before then, the Inquisition in Bologna was disestablished by the new democratic government on November 14, 1859 (Day, *op. cit.,* 27). Pius IX himself is reported to have said to Edgar Mortara, "You are very dear to me, my son, because I acquired you for Christ at a very great price. . . . I do not wish to remember the outrages, the calumnies and the maledictions pronounced by an innumerable crowd of simple, private persons, who appeared indignant that God had conferred the gift of his true faith on you in drawing you from the shadows of death in which your family is still plunged. . . . And nobody, however, pities me, the father of all the faithful, from whom schism snatches thousands of children in Poland, or seeks to corrupt them by its pernicious teaching. . . ." (London *Daily News,* May 4, 1867, reprinted in clipping, May 16, 1867, no source, *Moss Scrapbook I,* p. 4a, in American Jewish Historical Society; in slightly different translation the anecdote appears in *The Hebrew Leader,* New York, June 21, 1867, pp. 1–2.)

Edgar Mortara, at 15, became "a novice in the order of the Canons Regular of the Lateran," and in 1873, "although under the canonical age, he was by special dispensation ordained priest." He visited England and the United States on missions to convert Jews (Day, *op. cit.,* 6, 8, 9; but L. Bamberger, commenting on Mortara's visit to the United States in 1898, mentions only missions among the Italians, and not to convert Jews—*The Jewish Times and Observer,* New York, January 21, 1898, in Mortara Clippings Folder, American Jewish Historical Society). Several plays were produced on the Mortara Case in Naples, Turin, Paris, and Rome; in the latter, in 1870, the performances aroused such anti-clerical demonstrations that they were halted (Zacher, *op. cit.,* 25). In Cincinnati, Bloch & Co., published *Mortara: Or The Pope and His Inquisitors* by Herman M. Moos (1860), but there is no record of a stage production. More lasting consequences were the stimuli to the central organization of Jewish communities for more effective action in such matters. In France the Alliance Israelite Universelle and in the United States the Board of Delegates of American Israelites were established directly as an outcome of the belief that scattered efforts were bound to be unavailing in offsetting such factors as the reliance of the regnant Democratic Party on the Catholic vote, to which Jewish organs attributed the failure of Buchanan to act (*The Israelite,* April 15, 1859, p. 326, col. 1, *The Jewish Messenger,* December 31, 1858, p. 158).

That the relation of the Catholic Church to non-Catholic children is still a problem in American life can be seen from the case of Hampoortzoon Choolakian against the Mission of the Immaculate Virgin and the New York Foundling Hospital in the Supreme Court, New York County (Morris U. Schappes, "Whose Children?" in *Morning Freiheit,* January 17, 1948, p. 8; court records and briefs *amicus curiae* by Armenian Apostolic Orthodox Church, the Human Relations Commission of the Protestant Council of the City of New York, and the American Civil Liberties Union).

The State Courts ruled that a Catholic institution need not surrender to its parents a child which the parents wished to take with them when they were repatriated to Soviet Armenia. The United States Supreme Court in March 1950 refused to review the case.

122. Keeping the Sabbath

1. *The Israelite,* November 4, 1859, p. 140. The meeting had been called by Dr. Isaac Mayer Wise. The Chairman was Henry Mack (of Mack & Brothers, Wholesale Clothiers), who was then President of Wise's Congregation Bene Yeshurun, and also a member of the Cincinnati City Council. The Secretary was Lewis Heinsheimer (of J. H. Heinsheimer & Co., Wholesale Clothing and Dry Goods), and an active member of Bene Yeshurun.

2. Grinstein concludes that in New York by 1860, Sabbath observance "was rapidly falling into neglect or being entirely abandoned by many Jews" (*op. cit.,* 14). It is a curiosity to note that in 1845 a Cincinnati magistrate fined several Jews three dollars each for keeping their stores open on Saturday (*Archives Israelites,* January, 1846, p. 82). In 1864, *The Jewish Record* of New York lamented that in Brooklyn, with "a few thousand Israelites," only three Jewish-owned stores are closed on Saturday, and the editor charged that "there is not a congregation in New-York the majority of whose members are not Sabbath-breakers" (February 26, 1864, p. 2, col. 5 and May 13, 1864, p. 2, col. 1). In San Francisco in 1865 twenty-two firms pledged to keep their businesses closed on the Sabbath (*The Occident,* January, 1866, pp. 479–80), and in 1868 there was a flurry of activity in New York, Baltimore, and elsewhere (*The Sabbath; An Appeal to the Israelites of New York,* New York, 1868; *The Jewish Messenger,* January 24, 1868, p. 1). In 1880, a *Shomre Shabbat* group was organized to agitate for Sabbath observance (*Hazefirah,* Warsaw, VII, No. 16, May 4, 1880, p. 128).

3. *The Occident,* November 17, 1859, p. 199.

4. In the wholesale clothing business, for instance, more than 80% of the firms listed were Jewish (*Williams' Cincinnati Directory,* 1859, pp. 320–321). The clothing industry was the largest in the city, employing 7080 seamstresses working by machine and 7500 sewing by hand at home, and producing commodities valued at $15,000,000 to constitute "the largest market for ready made clothing in the country, east or west" (Charles Cist, *Sketches and Statistics of Cincinnati in 1859,* Cincinnati, 1859, p. 271).

5. According to *Williams' Cincinnati Directory,* 1859 and 1860, and advertisements in *The Israelite,* October 7, 1859, p. 111, col. 4, the following are the lines of business of the 32 firms represented on the list of signatories: wholesale clothiers, 12; clothiers, 11; wholesale gents' furnishings, 3; gents' furnishings, 2; dry goods, 1; wholesale dry goods, 1; wholesale boots and shoes, 1; liquor store, 1; wholesale jewelry, 1. Of the 87 persons comprising these firms, 38 were members of Bene Yshurun, and 13 of Bene Israel, of which Dr. Max Lilienthal was then the minister. There were in 1859, however, five other congregations to which the others may have belonged, or they may have been among the 1500 estimated as not connected with any congregation; there were approximately 8000 Jews in Cincinnati then in a total population of about 200,000 (Cist, *op. cit.,* 197–198).

6. In an editorial note on the resolution, I. M. Wise observes, "Eight additional houses were closed last Sabbath, and the rest we hope and expect will follow." (*The Israelite,* November 4, 1859, p. 140.) Resenting a sneer at the movement in *The Jewish Messenger,* Wise later declared that ten wholesale houses had closed on Saturday because of the "Sabbath movement" and remarked: "The

fact furthermore is, that the most houses from the reform congregations observe the Sabbath. . . . The Sabbath in Cincinnati is observed much stricter (not in Isaac Leeser's Quaker sense,) than among all the orthodox congregations in the United States; this may be said with certainty. . . ." (*Ibid.*, January 20, 1860, p. 227.)

123. Helping Elect Lincoln

1. New York and London, 1916, pp. 1–5, 62–64. For other material on the same subject, see Markens, *AJHSP,* XVII, 1909, pp. 109–166.
2. For a sketch of the relationship of the Jews to the new party, see Schappes, *Jewish Life,* New York, October, 1948, pp. 13–16.
3. *Who's Who in America,* I, 1899–1900, p. 192; obituary, *The New York Times,* February 24, 1919, p. 13, col. 2, where the date of his birth, however, is incorrectly given.
4. For a penetrating scholarly description of this relationship between New York and the south, see Philip Foner, *Business and Slavery,* Chapel Hill, N. C., 1941, *passim.*
5. He graduated at the head of his class in 1856 (*The New York Times, loc. cit.*).
6. The firm consisted of Jesse W. Benedict and Andrew Boardman (1813–1881) and had its offices at 2 Dey Street (*Trow's New York City Directory,* 1856–57, pp. 66, 83; David McAdam et al., eds., *History of the Bench and Bar of New York,* New York, 1897, I, 264).

   John Edward Parsons (1829–1915) had been admitted to the bar in 1852; later he was counsel for the City Bar Association when it moved against the Tweed Ring; still later he used his talents as a lawyer, as Dittenhoefer also did, to defend the sugar trust against federal action. (*DAB,* XIV, 267, by Edward Conrad Smith.)

   O'Conor (1804–1884) had already been the unsuccessful Democratic candidate for Lieutenant-Governor of New York in 1848; a supporter of slavery, he was very popular with southern Democrats; in 1872 he was the candidate for president on the "Straight-out" Democratic ticket.
7. Benjamin's speech on the Kansas question was delivered on March 11, 1858. On March 13, Wade (1800–1878), toward the end of a long and powerful address, made the following observation about the Northern men with Southern principles: "Your allies, the doughfaces of the North, in my judgment, are the most despicable of men. The modern doughface is not a character peculiar to the age in which we live, but you find traces of him at every period of the world's history. . . . Why, sir, when old Moses, under the immediate inspiration of God Almighty, enticed a whole nation of slaves, and ran away, not to Canada, but to old Canaan, I suppose that Pharoah and all the chivalry of old Egypt denounced him as a most furious Abolitionist . . . there were not wanting those who loved Egypt better than they loved liberty; . . . They were not exactly northern men with southern principles; but they were Israelites with Egyptian principles." (*Congressional Globe,* 35 Cong., 1 Sess., p. 1115.) Although this was originally only an oblique reference to Benjamin, the press promptly applied it pointedly to him and made it stick (*New-York Tribune,* March 20, 1858, "Judah Benjamin.")
8. Isaac Dittenhoefer (c. 1812–1860) had arrived in Baltimore from Germany in 1834, and had moved to Charleston and then New York, where he prospered as a drygoods merchant. He was one of the founders of B'nai Brith and active

in the German Hebrew Benevolent Society. (Obituary, *The Israelite,* December 7, 1860, p. 181, cols. 1–2; Grinstein, *op. cit.,* 109, 552.)

9. Hannibal Hamlin (1809–1891), a strong abolitionist, was elected Vice-President on the Lincoln ticket. Isaac Dittenhoefer died on November 21, 1860, only a few weeks after the election.
10. William Marcy Tweed (1823–1878) was already a Tammany power in 1859 and practically dominated the State by 1868.
11. Lee began his retreat to the Potomac on July 4, 1863.
12. The best and most accessible description of the riots is in Carl Sandburg, *Abraham Lincoln, The War Years,* New York, 1939, II, 360–364. Thirty Negroes were killed, 400 other persons killed or wounded, and about $5,000,000 worth of property destroyed. The Colored Orphan Asylum that was burned down was at Lexington Avenue and 43 Street. "So definite were the slogans and purposes of some of the mobs that they would be more correctly termed crowds, or units of mass action, operating an insurrection." It was not until August 19th that the draft was able to proceed peacefully.
13. Writing a half century after the events, Dittenhoefer here errs in several respects. Mrs. Carson was Caroline Petigru Carson (1820–1892), daughter of James Louis Petigru (1789–1863). Not compelled to leave Charleston, she did come to New York in June 1861 because her health was very bad and her Union views had made her women friends malevolent. Her father, however, refused to follow his daughter, and stayed on in Charleston until his death, serving incidentally all the time as a Commissioner elected by the legislature to codify the Statutes of South Carolina at $5,000 a year. As a Union man in South Carolina, furthermore, Petigru was not alone: Benjamin F. Perry was more prominent and vigorous. (James Petigru Carson, *Life, Letters and Speeches of James Louis Petigru, The Union Man of South Carolina,* Washington, D. C., 1920, pp. 381–82, 425, 429, 442, 488. I am indebted to A. S. Salley, State Historian of South Carolina, for identifying Mrs. Carson for me.)
14. Samuel Blatchford (1820–1893), an expert in international and maritime law, after serving as federal judge from 1867, was appointed to the United States Supreme Court in 1882.
15. In 1858, Dittenhoefer had married Miss Sophie Englehart of Cleveland (*AJYB,* 5665, p. 82, McAdam, *op. cit.,* II, 137–38).

124. Propaganda for Slavery

1. *Three Letters from a South Carolinian Relating to Secession, Slavery, and the Trent Case,* London, 1862, pp. 5–7.
2. Frank Lawrence Owsley, *King Cotton Diplomacy,* Chicago, 1931, pp. 176, 178, 182.
3. Dispatch by De Leon to Confederate Secretary of State Judah P. Benjamin, from Paris, June 19, 1863, quoted in John Bigelow, "The Confederate Diplomatists and their Shirt of Nessus," *The Century,* May, 1891, pp. 118–119.
4. Dispatch from De Leon to Jefferson Davis, from Paris, October 1, 1863; the interception of this and other dispatches and their publication in *The New-York Times,* November 16, 1863, page 1, ended De Leon's usefulness as a secret Confederate agent abroad. In his letter of June 19, 1863, however, De Leon had already recognized that anti-slavery sentiment in Europe made attempts to win recognition for the Confederacy futile.
5. For these and other facts not otherwise ascribed, I am indebted to Mrs. Julian (Helen Kohn) Hennig of Columbia, S. C., who kindly lent me a manuscript

copy of her unpublished Master's Thesis, *Edwin De Leon,* University of South Carolina, 1928; Edwin De Leon, *The Duties and Position of Young America,* Charleston, 1845; Siert F. Riepma, *"Young America": A Study in American Nationalism before the Civil War,* unpublished Doctoral Dissertation, Western Reserve University, 1939, pp. 56–59; Merle E. Curti, "'Young America,'" *American Historical Review,* XXXII, 1926, pp. 34, 54; *The New York Times,* December 8, 1891; Mrs. Hennig, *op. cit.,* 110; MS Letter, Isabel Burton to Mrs. De Leon, from Trieste, October 7, 1890, with comment by Abbot Low Moffat, June 23, 1932, *De Leon Papers,* University of South Carolina.

6. The President of the Institute was the Duc de Montmorency. Scanty records show that Jews of various European countries were members of it (*Annales de L'Institut d'Afrique,* IV–VII, 1844–1847).
7. In his preface to the pamphlet, De Leon states that he "was one of the earliest advocates in the United States of Southern Rights, including the Right of Secession."
8. The Negro uprising in San Domingo began August 23, 1791, and even British naval assistance to the French government could not prevent the Island from achieving its independence; in the other West Indian Islands, emancipation of the slaves was accomplished 1834–1838.

   To provide cheap and permanent labor for the planters in tropical colonies, Britain began to import coolies from India about 1834 and from China about 1845. Although formally the coolies were indentured servants, their treatment was wanton and shocking.
9. At the Constitutional Convention in Philadelphia in 1787, it was the threat of South Carolina and Georgia that they would not join the Union that made the majority of delegates compromise their anti-slavery sentiments by providing (Article I, Section 2, Paragraph 3) that three-fifths of the slaves in each state shall be added to the total population in computing the number of representatives the state was to elect to the House of Representatives. This provision was abolished in 1868 by the adoption of the Fourteenth Amendment. Most of the founding fathers, however, like Washington, Franklin, Madison, Hamilton, and Patrick Henry, disapproved of slavery, and Jefferson declared, "I tremble for my country when I reflect that God is just."
10. The United States Congress prohibited the importation of slaves from Africa on March 2, 1807; before then, a Danish royal decree of May 16, 1792 had ordered the slave trade in the Danish West Indies to cease by 1803.
11. Only the impact of politics upon "Southern chivalry" can explain this sneer at Harriet Beecher Stowe (1811–1896), author of *Uncle Tom's Cabin.* She had made triumphant visits to Europe in 1853, 1856–1857, and 1859–1860, stimulating anti-slavery sentiment wherever she went (Catherine Gilbertson, *Harriet Beecher Stowe,* New York and London, 1937, pp. 183, 216, 259, 268).
12. Frederick Douglass (1817–1895), a slave until his twenty-eighth year, had become a great abolitionist leader, orator and journalist. He had lectured in England in 1846–1847 and again from December 1859 to May 1860, on both occasions contributing hugely to the understanding of the status of the slave in the United States. (*Life and Times of Frederick Douglass, Written by Himself,* Centenary Edition, New York, 1941, pp. 259ff, 354–356.)

125. Summary, 1860

1. *The Journal of Commerce,* a daily, was edited by Charles and Gerard Hallock and David A. Hale.

2. *The Israelite,* October 26, 1860, p. 130. The only other published Jewish reaction to this editorial was in a letter by G. M. J., *The Jewish Messenger,* October 26, 1860, p. 123, objecting to "the patronising and somewhat illiberal remarks of the writer." But the editor of the periodical made no comment.

3. In 1860, Jews held professorships or other positions at the Universities of Pisa, Königsberg, Vienna, Munich, Leyden, Breslaw, Zurich, Kiel, Bern, Berlin and University College, London. The first professing Jew to be appointed to a professorship seems to have been Gabriel Gustav Valentin (1810–1883), who assumed the chair of physiology at Bern, Switzerland in 1836. (*UJE,* X, 364–371, by Hugo Bieber.)

4. The Rothschild family was of course internationally famous; the one referred to probably here and certainly at the end of the article was Baron James (Jacob) Mayer de Rothschild (1792–1868), the head of the largest bank in Paris, and a power in French economy and politics.

   Benjamin Disraeli (1804–1881) was already well known as a novelist and British Tory political leader, although he was not to achieve his pinnacle as Prime Minister until 1868 and 1874. G. M. J., cited in Note 2 above, objected to the inclusion of Disraeli as a Jew on the ground that he had been baptized a Christian.

   There is no evidence that Beethoven, or either of his parents or any of his grandparents, was Jewish. It is remarkable that non-Jews in 1860 carelessly assumed he was.

   Felix Mendelssohn-Bartholdy (1809–1847) was a composer.

   The renowned actress, Rachel (1821–1858), whose real name was Elizabeth Felix, had been born in the canton of Aargau, Switzerland; in 1858 she had toured the United States after triumphs in Paris and London.

5. For some reason G. M. J. resented this observation, but, not being able or willing to deny it, he contented himself with the retort that "the Jews of this City are certainly not more 'indigent' in proportion to their numbers than other creeds, and certainly less flamingly so, for the Jew is never found publicly soliciting that charity in the streets which so many other creeds do."

6. What is meant by "distinct literary institutions of their own" is not clear, since there were well known Jewish periodicals and schools. However, Grinstein, estimating the period up to 1860, concluded: "the ideal of learning was sadly neglected. . . . No Jewish scholars were trained in New York prior to the Civil War. Even the transfer from religious to secular studies, which marked the period of the Enlightenment in Europe, did not occur on any large scale in America" (*op. cit.,* 14). But this judgment has to be understood as applying to a period in American intellectual history when scholarship as a whole was being criticized for its backwardness.

7. *Trow's New York City Directory* for the year lists 16 synagogues, while Grinstein gives us the names of 23 (*ibid.,* 472–474).

8. The reference is to the Shearith Israel congregation, which moved to Crosby Street in 1834 and to West Nineteenth Street in 1860.

9. The Jews' Hospital, founded in 1852 and opened in 1855, has been known as Mount Sinai Hospital since 1866. The banquet and ball referred to was held on October 28, 1858 at Niblo's, and was attended by a large gathering that included Mayor Daniel F. Tiemann (*The Jewish Messenger,* November 5, 1858, pp. 92–93).

10. In 1859, when Spain attacked Morocco, several thousand Jews fled to Gibraltar;

funds to aid them were raised by Jewish communities in Europe and the United States (*The Israelite,* July 26, 1861, p. 29, and January 20, 1860, p. 228).

11. *McElroy's Philadelphia City Directory* for 1860 lists seven congregations (p. 1411) and eleven philanthropic societies (p. 1415), but one of the latter is the Hebrew Education Society, which this editorial counts separately. The Jewish Publication Society had been founded November 9, 1845, but most of its stock was destroyed by fire on December 27, 1851, and it is not listed in the 1860 Directory (Morais, *op. cit.,* 175–176).

12. I. M. Wise, in commenting on this editorial, also reprinted a letter from the Rev. Simon Tuska that was published in the Memphis, Tenn., *Daily Appeal* of October 14, 1860, challenging a judgment in *The Jewish Messenger* that "the ancient strength and vigor of Israel are unmistakably decaying." Replying to an article in the *Daily Appeal* that based itself on this estimate, Rev. Tuska contended that while *The Jewish Messenger's* "ultra-orthodox party of Judaism" may be declining, Judaism is not.

13. In 1854 and 1855, a small expedition, financed by the Jewish Society of London, went from Shanghai to Kai-fung-fu to investigate a group of Chinese Jews the existence of which had been reported by Jesuit missionaries, and brought back eight Hebrew manuscripts (*The Israelite,* April 13, 1855, pp. 318–319).

14. Gabriel Riesser (1806–1863), whose campaigns for equal rights for Jews in Germany since 1830 had made an international impression and who had visited the United States in 1856, had recently been appointed judge of a new higher court in Hamburg. He connected the defense of the Jews with the cause of the middle classes oppressed by the nobility and of Negroes enslaved by white masters (*JE,* X, 410–11, by Frederick T. Haneman). Both *The New-York Times* and *North American and United States Gazette* (Philadelphia) on March 16, 1860 carried the following item: "An extraordinary event in the history of the German Jews has just taken place. In the free City of Hamburg, where a Jew, ten years ago, was not even eligible for a night constable, a Jew, by the free suffrages of the citizens, has lately been chosen a chief magistrate, next in station to the highest dignity in that Republic. The gentleman elected is a distinguished juris-consult and writer, Dr. Gabriel Riesser, who was Vice-President of the German Parliament that sat at Frankfort in 1848."

15. The Alliance Israélite Universelle had been launched in May, 1860, partially as a consequence of the Mortara Case, to which it devoted its first energies. Although there was some opposition to the idea of such an organization, it was encouraged by the Board of Delegates of American Israelites and *The Jewish Messenger* (October 26, 1860, p. 124).

16. The occupations of the Jews down the ages and in various countries derive not from any innate characteristics so much as from the opportunities offered and the social conditions that prevail. Yet the Jews were then sensitive to the notion herein expressed; I. M. Wise, for instance, very shortly thereafter published a leading editorial, "Turn your children's attention from Commerce," in *The Israelite,* November 9, 1860, p. 148.

126. The Slaveholders' Bible

1. Pamphlet published in New York by Rudd & Carleton, with a preface by Raphall dated January 15, 1861.

2. William Sumner Jenkins, *Pro-Slavery Thought in the Old South,* Chapel Hill, N. C., 1935, pp. 4–6, 206–07.

3. Charles S. Sydnor, "The Southerner and the Laws," VI, 1940, pp. 5–6.

4. Gilbert Hobbs Barnes, reviewing Arthur Young Lloyd, *The Slavery Controversy 1831–1860,* Chapel Hill, N. C., 1939, in *The Journal of Southern History,* VI, 1940, p. 272. It should be noted that the same text from Jonah iii that Raphall used was taken by the Rev. Dr. B. L. Konreuther of the Congregation Rodeph Sholom in New York on the same National Fast Day as the point of departure for a German discourse that reached conclusions "just the reverse of the former" (*The Israelite,* January 25, 1861, p. 236, col. 4; *The New York Herald,* January 5, 1861). Unfortunately the text of this sermon is not in the congregational archives.

5. Isaac Mendelsohn, *Slavery in the Ancient Near East,* New York, 1949, pp. 1–33, 92–123; Frederick Engels, *Herr Eugen Duehring's Revolution in Science,* New York, n. d., pp. 206–08.

6. *Review of Rev. Dr. Raphael's Disco'rse on "American Slavery as being Consistent with the Hebrew Servitude of the Old Testament," A Sermon Preached (by request) in the Baptist Church, Shushan, on Wednesday, March 27th, 1861, by Rev Hugh Brown, Pastor of the United Presbyterian Church, East Salem, Washington County, N. Y.,* North White Creek, N. Y., 1861, p. 3.

7. Raphall repeated his sermon not on the following day or before the New York Historical Society, as has frequently been stated, but on January 17, 1861 and at the Historical Society *rooms,* which were rented for meetings (*The New York Herald,* January 17, 1861, p. 5, col. 4 and January 19, 1861, p. 5, col. 2; *The Evening Post,* New York, January 17, 1861, p. 2, col. 2, editorial, "Moses and the Prophets.") The meeting was presided over by Professor Samuel F. B. Morse, with Cornelius Dubois as secretary. The chamber was only two-thirds filled. After Raphall's discourse, the merchant Hiram Ketchum "read a speech" and collected funds with which to issue Raphall's sermon in pamphlet form. (*New-York Daily Tribune,* January 18, 1861, p. 8, col. 5.) Dubois and Ketchum were resident members of the New York Historical Society, and Morse was an Honorary Member (MS Membership Rolls, at N. Y. H. S.). They were also leading figures in the American Society for Promoting National Unity, among the 145 honorary members of which there were the following Jews: Raphall and August Belmont of New York; Hon. B. Mordecai of Charleston, S. C.; Rev. Mr. Jacobs of Richmond, Va., Hon. Solomon Cohen of Savannah, Ga.; Rev. James K. Gutheim of New Orleans, La.; Rev. J. Blumenthal of Montgomery, Ala.; and Max Meyer, Esq., of Lynchburg, Va. (*American Society for Promoting National Unity,* New York, 1861). That the Bible sanctioned slavery was an important principle of this Society. After its delivery on January 4, Raphall's sermon was published in full in *The New York Herald,* January 5, 1861, p. 1f, *The New York Daily News,* p. 5, cols. 1–3, and the New York *Evening Express;* there was a long summary in *The New-York Times,* and a shorter one in the *Tribune;* extracts appeared in the *New York Weekly Journal of Commerce,* January 10, 1861, p. 6, cols. 3–4; in some cases this was the only Fast Day sermon reproduced or quoted. It also was published in pamphlet form in Baltimore, and was included in *Fast Day Sermons,* New York, 1861.

8. *The New York Daily News,* January 4, 1861, p. 4, col. 1, *The New York Herald,* January 5, 1861.

9. Apparently some of the extreme slaveholders, however, did not approve of Raphall's very mild statement that Southern slavery was different from Biblical servitude, for when he repeated his sermon on January 17, he stated that some had "required him to withdraw his remarks on the character of Southern slavery." (*The New York Herald,* January 19, 1861, p. 5, col. 2.)

10. *Richmond Daily Dispatch,* January 7 and 29, 1861, quoted in Bertram Wallace Korn, *American Jewry and the Civil War,* Cincinnati, Experimental Edition, 1949, pp. 37–38. Rabbi Korn also cites a letter from a Memphis rabbi, Simon Tuska, in the *Memphis Daily Appeal,* January 23, 1861, defending the loyalty of the Jews partially on the ground that Raphall had refuted "the rabid, abolition views of Henry Ward Beecher" by delivering "the most forceful arguments in justification of the slavery of the African race."

11. Morris Jacob Raphall (1798–1868) had been born in Stockholm, Sweden, educated in Denmark and Germany, and spent twenty-five years in England as rabbi, preacher, lecturer, editor and writer before he came to New York in 1849 "on a life contract" with B'nai Jeshurun at an annual salary of $2,000, "then said to be the highest paid to any clergyman in the country" (*DAB,* XV, 382–383, by David de Sola Pool). He brought with him letters of introduction to the New York literary leader, Evert A. Duyckink (*Duyckink Papers, Literary Correspondence, Eliza Moore Folder,* MSS Div., N. Y. P. L.), with whom Raphall became so friendly that he could invite him to "a cup of tea, a dish of chat and a game of whist en famila" (Letter, Raphall to Duyckink, February 24, 1851, *ibid., Raphall Folder*). Shortly after his arrival, Raphall delivered "A Course of Six Popular Lectures on the Poetry of the Hebrews" in December, 1849 that were widely noticed. For Raphall's support of the Union, and his son's career, see Goldstein, *op. cit.,* 125–126; Markens, *op. cit.,* 135.

12. President James Buchanan (1791–1868) had issued the call on December 14, 1860.

13. Appearing first as the title of a volume by David Christy in 1855, the phrase, "Cotton is King," had become a slogan of the slaveowners. Thus Senator James H. Hammond of South Carolina declared in the Senate on March 4, 1858, "You dare not make war upon cotton! No power on earth dares make war upon it. Cotton is king."

14. In a speech opposing the fugitive slave law in the Senate on March 11, 1850, New York Senator William Henry Seward (1801–1872) had invoked what he called "a higher law than the Constitution" and urged the Senate to bear in mind moral as well as constitutional principles. Opponents of slavery used the concept of the higher law to justify their disobedience of pro-slavery legislation.

15. Raphall did not know that there was "a great civilization in Arabia for nearly, or more than, a thousand years before the Christian era" (*The Encyclopedia Britannica,* 11th edition, 1911, II, 264).

16. Mahomet sought to unite the Arabs to free them from control by Abyssinia, Persia and Rome, and he had almost succeeded when he died in 632.

17. "The idea of the 'barbarous Negro' is a European invention which has consequently prevailed in Europe until the beginning of this century," Leo Frobenius, *Histoire de la Civilisation Africaine,* Paris, 1936, 6th ed., p. 56, cited by W. E. Burghardt Du Bois, *The World and Africa,* New York, 1947, p. 79.

18. King Gezo of Dahomey, who had died in 1858, "had greatly reduced the custom of human sacrifice, and left instructions that after his death there was to be no general sacrifice of the palace women." His successor, King Gléglé, got into difficulties with France and Great Britain by encouraging the slave trade, persecuting native Christians and attacking neighboring states. (*The Encyclopedia Britannica,* 1947 ed., VI, p. 978.) Of Savagery in Dahomey, William Harrison Woodward declared: "It was sorrowfully recognized that the degradation of the Negro peoples of the nearer African interior was the direct result of European slave dealing. The savagery of Dahomey and Benin was the survival of the

ferocity by which native chiefs, a century earlier, had supplied the demands of English and Dutch traders for victims for the plantations." (*A Short History of the Expansion of the British Empire, 1500–1930,* London, 1931, 6th ed., p. 308.)

19. Rational Biblical criticism began in 1753 and proceeded on the principle that "the development of the religious conceptions and institutions of ancient Israel can be traced in a rational order and illustrated by similar phenomena elsewhere." (J. Frederick McCurdy, *JE,* III, pp. 176f.)

20. Raphall is here again reflecting the common European and American chauvinism and ignorance with reference to the Negro people. At least one American Negro, Frederick Douglass (1817–1895), had already achieved an international reputation as an abolitionist writer and orator despite the fact that he had been born into slavery. Du Bois, *op. cit., passim,* sets forth brilliantly the grandeur of African civilization before the European slave trade destroyed it.

21. Rev. Henry Ward Beecher of Brooklyn delivered this sermon; the quotation seems to be from *The New York Herald,* December 31, 1860. That slavery was a national sin was his constant challenge.

22. Molière (1622–1673), in *Le Medecin Malgre Lui* (1666), has Sganarelle, a wood-chopper posing as a doctor, present this new theory (Act. 2, Sc. 6).

23. *The Babylonian Talmud, Seder Nashim. Kiddushin,* London, 1936, p. 22a. For an unflinching study by a rabbi of "the mutilation of the humane Biblical laws of slavery by the Rabbis of the Talmud," see Solomon Zucrow, *Women, Slaves and the Ignorant in Rabbinic Literature,* Boston, 1932, pp. 177–204.

24. This "Deuteronomic ordinance . . . stands unparalleled in the slave-legislation of the Ancient Near East." (Mendelsohn, *op. cit.,* 63.)

25. Canada, "the promised land" of slave songs, was the terminus of the underground railroad on which thousands of slaves rode to freedom.

127. Abolitionists' Bible

1. Page 5, cols. 4–6.
2. January 7, 1861, p. 4, January 9, 1861, p. 4.
3. Page 4, col. 1.
4. The first American rabbi who squarely and publicly took issue with Raphall was David Einhorn (1809–1879), the Reform leader then in Baltimore, whose answer in German appeared in his monthly magazine, *Sinai,* February, 1861, pp. 2–22 (see also March, 1861, pp. 45–50, 60–61 and April, 1861, pp. 99–100); a hitherto unnoted English translation appeared in pamphlet form in New York, *The Rev. Dr. M. J. Raphall's Bible View of Slavery Reviewed by the Rev. D. Einhorn, D.D.,* issued by three Jewish booksellers, Meyer Thalmessinger, Joseph Cahn and Sarony Benedicks; on the day that Raphall repeated his sermon, *The Evening Post,* New York, January 17, 1861, p. 2, col. 2, called attention to Einhorn's answer as evidence that there was disagreement among Jewish rabbis on the question of slavery and the Bible. The text is available in English translation in Ella McKenna Friend Mielziner, *Moses Mielziner 1828–1903,* New York, 1931, pp. 234–50. Another reply to Raphall was published in pamphlet form in San Francisco in 1863: J. L. Stone, *Slavery and the Bible Or Slavery as Seen in its Punishment* (pp. 9 and 25 indicate clearly that it is Raphall he is criticizing). In Manchester, England, the Rev. Dr. Gustav Gottheil (1827–1903) delivered two sermons in opposition to Raphall's thesis on January 26 and

February 2, 1861, which were then published "by Special Request of the Congregation" as a pamphlet: *Moses versus Slavery: Being Two Discourses on the Slave Question,* Manchester and London, 1861. Unavailing have been efforts to locate the answer reportedly made by the physician, Dr. Morris Eisler (1818–1890), in the *New Yorker Demokrat* (Kohler, *AJHSP,* V, 1897, p. 155). Agreeing with Raphall's position, however, was the National Fast Day sermon preached by the Rev. Dr. Bernard Illowy (1814–1871) on January 4, 1861 before the Baltimore Hebrew Congregation (text in *The Occident,* XVIII, January 24, 1861, pp. 267–68).

5. January 18, 1861, p. 21.

6. First applied to Judah P. Benjamin, "the reproach of Egypt" was commonly made against Jewish supporters of slavery. Thus R. S. H., in a poem, *Rabbi Raphall,* asked:

 He that unto thy fathers freedom gave—
 Hath he not taught thee pity for the slave?

 (*The Independent,* New York, February 21, 1861, p. 8, col. 2.)

7. Preston Smith Brooks (1819–1857), South Carolina Congressman, had gained national notoriety when, on May 22, 1856, he clubbed the abolitionist Senator Charles Sumner of Massachusetts "over the head repeatedly with a gutta percha cane, which was broken by the blows, and left him apparently insensible on the floor" of the Senate (*DAB,* III, 88).

 Robert Barnwell Rhett (1800–1876), South Carolina plantation and slave owner and statesman, had resigned from the United States Senate in 1852 because South Carolina did not then secede; convinced that secession would follow a Republican victory in 1860, he secretly worked for such a victory; he felt "secession must be accomplished immediately after the election [of Lincoln] before popular feeling had a chance to cool off" (*DAB,* XV, 526–28).

8. In January 1861, South Carolina adopted the Palmetto Flag as its symbol.

9. The controversy about the proper translation of the Hebrew word had begun as far back as 1836 and become a staple source of dispute in the great debate (Jenkins, *op. cit.,* 219; Arthur Young Lloyd, *The Slavery Controversy 1831–1860,* Chapel Hill, N. C., 1939, pp. 189–90). Isaac Leeser, in a generally very favorable comment on Raphall's sermon, gave it as his judgment that the Jews in antiquity had "perpetual servants (the word *slave* not existing in the Hebrew by any fair construction) . . ." (*The Occident,* January 31, 1861, p. 274, cols. 1–2.)

10. This translation by Mendelssohn (1729–1786) appeared in 1783; the Orthodox rabbis, however, placed it under a ban, because of his unorthodox commentaries on the text.

11. Leopold Zunz (1794–1886) had edited a translation of the Old Testament into German which had been published in 1837 and been often reprinted; he himself translated only the Chronicles, the other books being translated by Heimann Arnheim, Michael Sachs and Julius Fürst.

12. Senator William Bigler (1814–1880), Pennsylvania Democrat; Alfred Iverson (1798–1873), Democratic Senator from Georgia, was an extreme "Southern rights" advocate; Senator Charles Sumner (1811—1874), Massachusetts Republican, was a leader in the anti-slavery and emancipationist movement; Jefferson Davis (1808–1889), Senator from Mississippi, became President of the Confederacy; Senator Henry Wilson (1812–1875), Massachusetts Republican, was an abolitionist; Robert Augustus Toombs (1810–1885), Georgia plantation and slave owner and Senator, was an advocate of secession as early as 1850.

13. Isaac Samuel Reggio (1784–1855), Austro-Italian scholar, rabbi, mathematician and painter, was a liberal in religion and became the Mendelssohn of the Italian Jews of the nineteenth century.

14. Even some who agreed with Raphall on everything else he wrote in his sermon took issue with him on the point that the Negro was meant in the Bible passage cited: Isaac Mayer Wise wrote, "The idea that the Negroes are descendants of Ham is without any foundation either biblical or scientific." (*The Israelite,* January 18, 1861, p. 230, col. 1.) Isaac Leeser could not "coincide with him [Raphall] in consigning the Negro race to bondage through Noah's cursing Canaan, who can hardly be regarded as the progenitor of the black race in Africa." (*The Occident, loc. cit.*) Among non-Jews, an especially effective retort was made in an editorial in Rev. Henry Ward Beecher's organ, *The Independent,* which amply refuted Raphall's argument about Noah's curse by quoting Rashi's commentary on Genesis, ix, 18, another commentary by Ibn Ezra, and opinions by Dr. Ludwig Philippson, Moses Mendelssohn, Rev. Dr. M. M. Kalisch of London, and *Raphall* himself in a commentary on Genesis published in 1844! (January 31, 1861, p. 4, cols. 1–2, "Rabbi Against Rabbi.")

15. Admah and Zeboim were towns destroyed together with Sodom and Gomorrah (Genesis, x, 19, Deuteronomy xxix, 23, and Hosea xi, 8).

16. The story that Plato was sold as a slave at Aegina is now regarded as very improbable. However, Cervantes (1547–1616) was a slave from 1575 to 1580 after being captured by Barbary corsairs near Marseilles and taken to Algiers; he was ransomed in September 1580 for 500 gold ducats. Dominique Francois Jean Arago (1786–1853), French physicist, was captured on August 16, 1808 by Spanish pirates who attacked the French vessel on which he was going from Algiers to Marseilles; he was taken to Rosas and imprisoned until that seaport was captured by the French.

17. It is interesting to compare the approach to the problem used by the Republican Party in the 1860 elections: "But let justice be done the Mosaic code, as regards Slavery. It aimed to soften its fierceness among the rude tribes, among a people so ignorant, being just delivered from Egyptian bondage, that they prostrated themselves in swinish idolatry even at the moment their great lawgiver was uttering the Tables of the Law. . . . It is, therefore, the opposite of the American system, which pronounces Slavery hopeless and perpetual, and is without a peer for its cruelty. . . ." (William Henry Fry, *Republican "Campaign" Text-Book,* New York, 1860, pp. 10–11.)

128. Farewell to the United States

1. *The Congressional Globe,* 36 Congress, 2 Session, I, 721–722.

2. Robert Douthat Meade, *Judah P. Benjamin: Confederate Stateman,* New York, 1943, p. 139.

3. Willie Malvin Caskey, *Secession and Restoration of Louisiana,* University, La., 1938, p. 30; Roy Franklin Nichols, *The Disruption of American Democracy,* New York, 1948, p. 442.

4. Roger W. Shugg, *Origins of Class Struggle in Louisiana,* University, La., 1939, p. 155; contradictions in Benjamin's career are often made clear when seen in the light of his relation to these contradictory forces; Meade, *op. cit.,* 151, 155; serious biographical studies of Benjamin have been made by Kohler, *AJHSP,* XII, 1904, pp. 63–85; Pierce Butler, *Judah P. Benjamin,* Philadelphia, 1907; Louis Gruss, "Judah P. Benjamin," *The Louisiana Historical Quarterly,* XIX,

1936, pp. 964–1068. For a review of various conflicting attitudes to Benjamin, see Schappes, *Jewish Life,* November, 1948, pp. 15–18. For his relation to the Jewish community, see Korn, *AJHSP,* XXXVIII, 1949, Part 3, 153–171.

5. In the elections to the Louisiana convention, with the issue immediate secession or delay, the vote was 20,448 for secession and 17,296 for delay. The total vote was also very much less than had been cast in the presidential election. In New Orleans, only 8,000 of 17,000 voters went to the polls, and the majority for secession was only 300. At the convention itself, a proposal to submit the secession ordinance to a referendum of the electorate was defeated, 84 to 43; the vote on the ordinance itself was 113 to 17. (James Ford Rhodes, *History of the United States from the Compromise of 1850,* New York, 1902, III, 273–274.) Meade concludes that "the result . . . had been accomplished by a determined minority" (*op. cit.,* 142).

6. Replying the following day, Senator Andrew Johnson of Tennessee noted that Benjamin had quoted only article 3 of the treaty, omitting articles 1 and 2 that speak of the "full sovereignty" the United States acquired to the Louisiana Territory; Johnson properly called this lawyer's argument "special pleading." (*Cong. Globe, loc. cit.,* pp. 744–45.) James G. Blaine points to the history of the Louisiana Purchase to nullify Benjamin's distinction, and adds that "the United States, sixteen years after it bought Louisiana from France, actually sold or exchanged a large part of that province to the King of Spain as part of the consideration in the purchase of the Floridas." In fact, Senator David L. Yulee of Florida had unsuccessfully used the same argument in favor of his state. (*Twenty Years of Congress,* Norwich, Conn., 1884, I, 249–251.)

7. The Missouri Compromise of 1820 admitted Maine as a free state and Missouri as a slave state, thereby maintaining the relationship of forces in the legislature, but forbade the introduction of slavery into the territory north of 36° 30′.

8. The majority of the United States Supreme Court in the Dred Scott case (1857) went out of its way to declare the Missouri Compromise unconstitutional. Justice John Catron of Tennessee (c. 1786–1865) had asserted that it was no more constitutional to forbid a southerner to take his slaves north of 36° 30′ than to forbid a northerner to take his "cattle or horses" south of that line. (*Report of the Decision of the Supreme Court of the United States . . . in the case of Dred Scott . . . ,* New York, 1857, pp. 524–28.) Catron, incidentally, improperly "exchanged secret communications" with Buchanan in which he gave the President-elect advance information of the Court decision in order that Buchanan might guide his Inauguration address by that knowledge (Edmund C. Gass, "The Constitutional Opinions of Justice John Catron," *The East Tennessee Historical Society's Publications,* VIII, 1936, pp. 71–72). For the drastic constitutional implications of the Dred Scott decision, see Louis B. Boudin, *Government by Judiciary,* New York, 1932, II, 1–31. It was in replying to a speech by Benjamin defending the Dred Scott decision that Senator Benjamin F. Wade of Ohio first used the expression, "Israelites with Egyptian principles," which at once came to be applied to Benjamin (*Cong. Globe,* 35 Cong., 1 Sess., March 13, 1858, p. 1115).

9. From Dec. 15, 1814 to Jan. 5, 1815 a secret convention met in Hartford, Conn., called at the invitation of the Massachusetts legislature; 26 New England federalists from Massachusetts, Connecticut, Rhode Island, Vermont and New Hampshire there broached and discussed the threat of secession because of their opposition to the War of 1812. From 1836 on, Massachusetts vigorously fought the annexation of Texas and "declared the process unconstitutional and not legally binding upon the State," but there seems to have been no such

official talk of secession as Benjamin mentions (Albert Bushnell Hart, ed., *Commonwealth History of Massachusetts,* New York, 1930, IV, 295).

10. The seceding states had seized various Federal custom houses, arsenals, forts, and a navy yard in South Carolina, Georgia, Florida, Alabama, and Louisiana. The Louisiana convention that voted to secede also "took over an aggregate of $418,311.52 in the United States mint in New Orleans, [and] transferred $141,519.66 of Custom House funds to the Confederacy" (Caskey, *op. cit.,* 33).
11. John Hampden (1594–1643), a cousin of Oliver Cromwell, refused in 1636 to pay King Charles's demand for a ship-money levy.
12. Lord North's speech on the Boston Port Bill was delivered in Parliament on March 14, 1774 (Peter Force, *American Archives,* Washington, 1837, Fourth Series, I, 38).
13. On July 6–8, 1774, a meeting of the people of Charleston denounced the Boston Port Bill as "most cruel and oppressive," approved a Continental Congress and elected a committee of correspondence.
14. William Pitt, Lord Chatham, spoke in Parliament in opposition to enforcing the Stamp Act, on January 16, 1766; quoting from memory, Benjamin is not entirely accurate, although his substance is correct (*Political Debates,* Paris, 1766, pp. 5, 12, 18; *Celebrated Speeches of Chatham, Burke, and Erskine,* Philadelphia, 1835, 1840, 1845, 1851; in the 1840 edition, pp. 11, 12, and 16 contain most of the passages quoted by Benjamin).
15. The term *force bills* harks back to the Act of March 2, 1833 that authorized President Andrew Jackson to use the army and navy to collect custom duties after South Carolina had passed its nullification ordinance.
16. On January 18, 1861, Mr. Pendleton (1825–1889), Democrat from Cincinnati, had delivered a speech urging the House to "remove every cause of agitation and irritation, however unfounded you may deem it," and, if that failed to keep the southern states in the Union, to let them "depart in peace" (*Cong. Globe,* 36 Cong., 2 Sess., App. p. 71). Later he opposed the vigorous measures of Lincoln in conducting the war.
17. Meade writes: "To modern readers this peroration may seem a collection of trite phrases and clichés. But we must remember that Benjamin, his pistol at his side, was speaking on a burning question and to a country on the verge of sectional war. And his style, grandiloquent as it was, suited the taste of his audience, even though one Northern opponent said that 'he drew from his spectators many plaudits for his rhetoric which he could not evoke for his logic.'" (*Op. cit.,* 154.) When the Confederacy collapsed, Benjamin made a daring escape, reached England, and in a few years won recognition as one of the ablest and most successful lawyers in the country. He maintained some contact with Confederate circles in exile and in the United States, and raised funds to help equip the Ku Klux Klan (Susan Lawrence Davis, *Authentic History, Ku Klux Klan, 1865–1877,* New York, 1924, pp. 45–47). He never returned to the United States.

129. Standing by the Union

1. *The Independent,* New York, May 23, 1861, p. 5, in an editorial, "Neither Jew nor Greek," commenting specifically on *The Jewish Messenger's* editorial, "Our Course," May 17, 1861.
2. Simon Wolf lists the names of 1996 Jews who served in the Union armed forces from the state of New York (*The American Jew as Patriot, Soldier and Citizen,*

Philadelphia, 1895, pp. 236–301, 423). This is a minimal figure, since he has 834 names unclassified as to commands; 142 are from New York State. The total from New York is twice as large as that from the next state, Ohio. Unfortunately no more recent and exhaustive study of the statistics of Jewish participation in the armed forces in the Civil War has been made.

130. The Confederate "Holy Cause"

1. *The Jewish Messenger,* June 7, 1861, p. 172, col. 3.
2. Shugg, *op. cit.,* 42–43.
3. *The Jewish Messenger,* May 17, 1861, "Our Course."
4. In introducing his publication of this resolution, the editor had said mockingly: "we have only one subscriber in Shreveport, and he has not paid for two years . . ."

131. Jewish Business Interests in California

1. Reprinted in *The Jewish Messenger,* July 12, 1861, p. 5, cols. 2–3. The *True Pacific Messenger* was a Jewish weekly published in San Francisco in 1860–1861, and edited and owned by the Rev. Herman Bien (1831–1895). In the late 1850's, Rev. Bien was the minister of Temple Emanu-El, San Francisco, during which period Henry J. Labatt several times held the post of Secretary of the Congregation (*The Chronicles of Emanu-El,* San Francisco, 1900, pp. 37, 48; *The Occident,* November 24, 1859, p. 210, col. 1).
2. *Daily Alta California,* San Francisco, February 2, 1861, p. 1, col. 8, "Shipment of Treasure."
3. *The Jewish Record,* New York, April 21, 1865, p. 1, cols. 3–4, quoting the San Francisco *Hebrew; The San Francisco Directory, 1864–65, passim.*
4. From Christmas Eve, 1849 to June 22, 1851, seven huge fires broke out in San Francisco, causing more than $22,000,000 in losses, and destroying almost 2,000 houses. After these fires, the city was practically rebuilt, with brick and stone houses predominating. (J. M. Guinn, *History of the State of California,* Chicago, 1904, pp. 181–182.)
5. In March, 1855, Henry J. Labatt had sharply criticized, in a letter to a San Francisco newspaper, an attack on the Jews made by the Speaker of the State Legislature in Sacramento on March 16, 1855. (*The Occident,* June, 1855, pp. 124–132, "Intolerance in California.") Stowe had advocated taxing the Jews so heavily that they would leave the State.

132. Abolitionist Forced to Flee

1. *Sinai,* VI, No. 5, June, 1861, pp. 135–142 (the first issue published in Philadelphia, and dated May 20, 1861). This article was reprinted in the *Allgemeine Zeitung des Judenthums,* Leipzig, XXV, No. 27, July 2, 1861, pp. 386–388. I am indebted for the translation to Professor John Bridge.
2. *The Jewish Chronicle,* London, November 2, 1849; David de Sola Pool, *DAB,* VI, 65; *Sinai,* I, No. 9, October, 1856, "Review of the Preceding Year," pp. 258–259; Charles Branch Clark, "Politics in Maryland during the Civil War," *The Maryland Historical Magazine,* XXXVI, 1941, p. 252n.

3. *The Evening Post,* January 17, 1861, p. 2, col. 2, published an editorial on Raphall's pro-slavery address, entitled "Moses and the Prophets." The editorial ends with this paragraph: "At the same time, we perceive that all the Hebrews do not put the same interpretation on Moses that Rabbi Raphall has done. A sermon now before us, delivered some weeks ago by Dr. Einhorn, an eminent Jewish divine in Baltimore, says: 'Man—thus reads the doctrine of Sinai—is created in the image of God, and, as such, born free and destined to be king of creation; he may belong to this or that race, or descend from Shem, from Japhet or from Ham; he is God's servant, God's property, but never the 'slave' or the property of man.' " The full text appears in *Sinai,* January, 1861, pp. 365–373; the sentence translated is on p. 369. *The Evening Post* seems to have been interested in Einhorn's views from the very first weeks of his stay in Baltimore, for on December 21, 1855, it carried a long article, "Religious Dissensions Among the Jews," in which it discussed the Cleveland Conference to establish a religious union, and printed the full text of Einhorn's protest against the plan, which he opposed as an attempt to impose an unwanted ecclesiastical authority upon Jewish congregations.
4. *Sinai,* VI, No. 1, pp. 2–22, see Note 4 to Doc. No. 127.
5. Maryland was one of the Border States that did not secede and join the Confederacy (Kentucky, Missouri and Delaware were the others). Only in a few tobacco-plantation counties was secession sentiment strong. Union sentiment, which prevailed, was based on the dependence of manufacturing and merchant interests on raw materials from the Northwest, on fear that the three railroads crossing Baltimore would be ruined by secession, on the fear that the slaves would escape across the State border to the North, on the belief that the Confederacy, if successful, would revive the slave-trade, which would ruin the Maryland slave markets, on the fear of civil war right within Maryland, and on the moral judgment of some abolitionist spokesmen who denounced the evils of slavery (Carl M. Frasure, "Union Sentiment in Maryland, 1859–1861," *The Maryland Historical Magazine,* XXIV, 1929, pp. 214–221; Clark, *op. cit.,* 240, 247, 260).
6. April 19, 1861, a pro-slavery mob attacked the Sixth Massachusetts Regiment, which had arrived from Philadelphia and was moving along Pratt Street to the Camden Station of the Baltimore and Ohio to entrain for Washington. Among the soldiers, four were killed and 36 wounded; the soldiers, returning fire, killed 12 civilians, and wounded an unnamed number. The mob continued its rioting after the troops left. Einhorn had real reason to fear for his safety at the hands of the mob. His friend Wilhelm Rapp, editor of the German abolitionist daily, *Der Wecker,* was forced to leave the city when the office and press of the newspaper were partially wrecked on April 20th. A few days later, a leading member of Einhorn's congregation, Leopold Blumenberg (1827–1876), a prosperous merchant who had come to Baltimore from Germany in 1854 and was a staunch Union man, escaped lynching when his house was attacked by secessionists at night only by having a police guard stationed there for several nights. Blumenberg helped organize the Fifth Maryland Regiment that fought in the Union army and was in command of the regiment as Major at Antietam, when he was badly wounded in the thigh. (Kohler, *AJHSP,* V, 1897, p. 150; *Baltimore, Seine Vergangenheit und Gegenwart,* Baltimore, 1887, pp. 303–304; J. Thomas Scharf, *The Chronicles of Baltimore,* Baltimore, 1874, pp. 600–601; Dieter Cunz, "The Maryland Germans in the Civil War," *The Maryland Historical Magazine,* XXXVI, 1941, pp. 412–413; Wolf, *AJHSP,* III, 1895, pp. 37–38; George William Brown, *Baltimore and the 19th of April,* Baltimore, 1887, p. 53.) Complete order was not restored until May 13, 1861,

when General Benjamin F. Butler marched soldiers in from Annapolis and established martial law.

7. *Sinai* was being printed on the press of C. W. Schneidereith, at 67 S. Sharp Street, near Pratt Street, from which the riot fanned out.

8. The President of Har Sinai was Samuel Dellevie, a tobacconist with a shop on Pratt Street (*Wood's Baltimore City Directory, 1860,* p. 101; *Souvenir, Jubilee Year, Har Sinai Congregation, Baltimore, 1842–1892,* Baltimore, 1892, p. 24).

9. In 1861, *Shevuoth* began on the evening of May 14.

10. The Keneseth Israel Congregation, founded in 1847, engaged Dr. Einhorn for twelve years, at a salary of $1200 for the first year and $1500 thereafter. (*The Israelite,* May 31, 1861, p. 382, cols. 3–4, Philadelphia correspondence, anonymous, dated May 24, 1861.) Another correspondent, A. Kaufman, in the issue of June 7, p. 390, col. 4, writes that at the same time that the call to Keneseth Israel came, there arrived an invitation from another "well-known congregation." Einhorn stayed with Keneseth Israel only until 1866, when he took a post in New York with the Congregation Adath Jeshurun.

11. In *The Jewish Messenger,* May 3, 1861, p. 133, col. 2, there appeared this petty and vindictive item, expressing a hostility of the Orthodox to a Reform rabbi that in this instance transcended the unity of their opposition to the Confederacy: ". . . It seems that he [Einhorn] has been mistaking his vocation, and making the pulpit the vehicle for political invective. The citizens of Baltimore, not regarding this as part of the Dr's duty, politely informed him, that 12 hours' safe residence was about all that they could guarantee him, in *that* place. Accordingly, taking the hint, the political Rabbi left, and at last accounts, was in the neighborhood of Philadelphia. We wonder whether our Baltimore co-religionists grieve over his departure? At the same time, we commend his fate to others, who feel inclined to pursue a similar course. . . . Let Dr. E's fate be a warning." Whether this was written by the editor, Rev. Myer S. Isaacs, is not certain, although it is suggested by the opening reference to Einhorn's opposition to the Board of Delegates, of which Isaacs was a leading spirit. On February 5, 1860, Einhorn and his entire congregation had issued a protest against forming the Board of Delegates, which Einhorn feared, incorrectly it should be added, would become an ecclesiastical authority instead of an instrument of Jewish defense.

12. By "incestuous marriage" Einhorn may be referring to the marriage of cousins and of uncle and niece, both of which are sanctioned by Jewish orthodoxy. (Solomon B. Freehof, *Reform Jewish Practice and its Rabbinic Background,* Cincinnati, 1944, pp. 58, 60; *JE,* VI, 571–575, article on "Incest.")
    The "Jekum-Purkan-heroes" refers to two Aramaic prayers in the Ashkenazic Orthodox ritual recited on the Sabbath after the reading of the Torah. The first, which originated in Babylonia, prays for the teachers and rabbis in Palestine, Babylonia, and elsewhere, for the heads of academies and the judges, for their disciples and the disciples of the disciples. The Reform prayer-book eliminated these prayers as antiquated and meaningless for the contemporary Jew. Those insisting on these prayers were the "heroes."

133. Aiding Soldiers' Families

1. *The Jewish Messenger,* June 28, 1861, p. 196, col. 3.

2. Simon Wolf, *op. cit.,* 128, lists only three Jews as serving in the Union Army from Washington, D. C., but this letter suggests there were many more.

3. William Addleman Ganoe, *The History of the United States Army,* New York and London, 1924, pp. 260, 262.

4. *The Jewish Messenger,* December 4, 1861, p. 36, col. 1. The same communication reports that the newly elected Mayor of Washington was Richard Wallach, a Jew. For instances of other Jewish soldier relief activities, see Korn, *American Jewry and the Civil War,* 202ff, for apathy in response to need, pp. 212–219, 224.

134. Influencing British Opinion

1. August Belmont, *A Few Letters and Speeches of the Late Civil War,* New York, 1870, pp. 32–35.

2. *DAB,* II, 170, by Allan L. Churchill.

3. Moses Yale Beach, *Wealth and Biography of the Wealthy Citizens of New York City,* New York, 5th ed., 1845, p. 6, 12th ed., 1855, p. 10; data about Belmont's service as Austrian Consul General and in The Hague supplied by Mr. Roscoe R. Hill, Chief, Division of State Department Archives of the National Archives, in letter to this editor, August 13, 1946; Roy Franklin Nichols, *The Disruption of American Democracy,* New York, 1948, p. 227; Justin H. Smith, *The War With Mexico,* New York, 1919, II, 266, 481–482, 488.

4. In 1843, Belmont appeared on the list of contributors to the Hebrew Assistance Society of New York with a donation of $20 (*Constitution* of the Society, *Lyons Scrapbook II* item 19f., p. 10). In the 1850s, Isaac Mayer Wise obtained a $10 contribution to his Reform Synagogue in Albany (*Reminiscences,* Cincinnati, 1901, p. 177). *The New-York Daily Tribune,* June 2, 1853, reprinted an article from the Washington *Union* defending Belmont from a nativist Whig attack; *The Asmonean,* February 16, 1855, p. 140, cols. 1–2, editorial, "Nationality of the Jews," "question[ed] the honor of the association" of Belmont's name with the Jews in view of his marriage; but *The Jewish Record,* June 26, 1863, p. 2, col. 2, reprinted a brief item from the *Home Journal,* reporting that a Confederate agent had failed to get a loan from the Paris Rothschilds because of the contrary advice of Belmont, and added: "Will our cotemporaries, who are so fond of quoting Jewish sympathy with rebels, please note."

5. Baron Lionel de Rothschild (1806–1879) had been elected to Parliament in 1847, 1849 and 1852, but was not seated until 1858, when the Jews' Disabilities Bill was passed allowing him to be sworn in on the Old Testament instead of "on the faith of a Christian." He was influential in government circles, having negotiated a £16,000,000 loan to help finance the Crimean War, and having provided funds to buy the shares of the Suez Canal. He was an intimate friend of Lord John Russell.

   It is interesting but hitherto unnoted that on August 6, 1834 Forsyth appointed N. M. Rothschild of London as "Banker of the United States in Europe," replacing Messrs. Baring, Brothers & Co., (Letter, Rothschild to Forsyth, Sept. 29, 1834, *Record Group No. 59, General Records of the Department of State. Records of the Bureau of Accounts.* The National Archives.)

6. Lord John Russell (1792–1878), British Foreign Secretary, had on May 6, 1861 announced in Parliament that the Government would not treat Confederate privateers as pirates, but as the vessels of a belligerent. This act appeared to be a step in the direction of recognition of the Confederate government and was as such resented in the Union, but this was the closest the Confederacy got to recognition by England.

7. The blockade of Southern ports had been proclaimed by Lincoln on April 19,

1861. Although not very effective at first, the blockade later became a major factor in the defeat of the Confederacy.

8. The Confederacy had claimed Forts Sumter and Pickens, which governed the harbors of Charleston, S. C. and Pensacola, Fla., as well as Federal arsenals, post-offices, custom-houses, and other property. In his inaugural address, March 4, 1861, Lincoln had promised to "hold, occupy, and possess the property and places belonging to the government."

9. The Vice-President of the Confederacy, Alexander Hamilton Stephens (1812–1883) of Georgia, had on March 21, 1861 delivered a notorious speech in Savannah in which he challenged Jefferson's theory of the equality of races and declared: "Our new government is founded upon exactly the opposite idea; its foundations are laid, its corner-stone rests upon the great truth that the Negro is not equal to the white man; that slavery—subordination to the superior race—is his natural and normal condition. . . . We are now the nucleus of a growing power, which if we are true to ourselves, our destiny, and high mission, will become the controlling power on this continent." Stephens had also in 1859 approved a proposal to reopen the African slave trade so as to get more slaves for more slave states.

10. Although the foundation of the Confederate "foreign policy" was that cotton is king and will bring the Confederacy the recognition of European powers, no formal, official embargo on the export of cotton was ever proclaimed. However, the theory of the embargo was so widespread among the planters, cotton factors, merchants, newspapers and Confederate legislators, that local organizations of these elements enforced a virtual embargo (Owsley, *op. cit.*, 38–39).

11. As recently as February, 1861, at a special state convention in Albany, the New York Democratic Party had passed a resolution in favor of allowing the Confederacy peaceably to secede. Belmont was one of the prominent delegates. (Sidney David Brummer, *Political History of New York State during the Period of the Civil War,* New York, 1911, pp. 114, 122.)

12. Virginia had on April 4, 1861 voted 88 to 45 *against* secession; but it refused to heed Lincoln's call for volunteers on April 15, and on April 17, the Virginia legislature voted 88 to 55 *for* secession; however, so widespread was popular opposition, that West Virginia, which was Unionist, was admitted to the Union in 1863 as a separate state. In Tennessee, the people had rejected, by a vote of 69,675 to 57,798, the legislature's call, issued January 19, 1861, for a convention at which secession would be on the agenda; yet on May 7, 1861, the legislature had ratified a league with the Confederacy, which was endorsed on June 8, 1861 by a popular vote of 104,913 to 47,238; the Unionist movement in Tennessee was strong, but did not succeed, as it had in Virginia, in dividing the state.

12a. On April 20, 1861, the Confederate Congress had authorized a $50,000,000 loan, to be raised in part by a sale of 8% bonds and in part by the issuance of non-interest bearing treasury notes. Financing was one of the weakest links in the Confederacy, which was longer on cotton than on capital.

13. MS, *Chase Papers,* The Historical Society of Pennsylvania.

14. Belmont to Chase, July 3, 1861, *ibid.;* Belmont to Seward, July 30, 1861, *Letters, Speeches and Addresses of August Belmont,* New York, 1890, pp. 76–78; Chase to Belmont, September 13, 1861, *ibid.,* 110–111.

15. Napoleon III privately encouraged the Confederacy to believe he would grant it recognition, while he publicly professed his sympathy for the Union, waiting for the British government to agree to joint action in support of the Con-

federacy. In May, 1861, he went so far as to urge the Union to recognize the secession as an accomplished fact. But as in England, the antagonism of the people to slavery, and the progressive clarification of the fact that slavery was at stake in the Civil War, prevented Napoleon and the French industrialists from recognizing the Confederacy.

16. The Morrill Tariff, which had passed the House of Representatives on May 10, 1860, did not pass in the Senate until the secession had begun, and became law on March 2, 1861. The Southern planters, who depended upon the export of their raw materials, opposed a high tariff, while the manufacturing capitalists in the North wanted tariffs to protect their manufactures in cotton and woollen fabrics, metal products, glass, and other articles. Industrialists in England and France of course opposed a tariff that reduced their exports to the United States.

17. *The New York Herald*, July 22, 1861, p. 4, cols. 3–4, had in an editorial, "The Entangled State of Our Foreign Relations," climaxed a series of bragging, jingoistic statements with the promise of "just retribution" to England for the Queen's proclamation of neutrality of May 13, 1861, and to Spain for the invasion of San Domingo. As soon as the Civil War was over, the United States was to "possess itself of Canada," and seize Cuba. "Our armies never will consent to lay down their arms while a vestige of European domination remains in the Western hemisphere. Causes of war we have enough, and they will not cool for keeping." In London *The Times*, August 7, 1861, p. 8, cols. 5–6, had a long editorial on the defeat at Bull Run, in the course of which it quoted at length the passage above as coming from "the organ of New York moderation" (without naming *The Herald*), and added: "If this is what we are to receive from the supremacy of the North, the North can scarcely expect that we should put up very ardent vows for their conquest of the South."

18. The New York *Daily News* had been bought in 1860 by Benjamin Wood (1820–1900), younger brother of the notorious Fernando Wood, Mayor of New York. The *Daily News* hampered the Union war effort from the beginning and became a Copperhead organ; in 1864, the Lincoln administration suppressed the paper for several days for its irresponsibility. Another New York newspaper similarly suppressed on that occasion was *The World*, which had been bought in 1862 by Belmont and other Democrats, and in 1863 became the leading Copperhead newspaper in New York! (John F. Heaton, *The Story of a Page*, New York, 1913, pp. 2–3.) As the anti-slavery aspect of the War became clearer, the bankers and merchants of New York, whom Belmont represented, changed their policy into one of "peace without victory" and appeasement of the slaveholders.

19. In his letter to Seward, July 30, 1861, Belmont had written: ". . . I am more than ever convinced that we have nothing to hope from the sympathy of the English Government and people in our struggle. Because this war is not carried on for the abolition of slavery in the Southern States, they try to maintain that the war has nothing to do with slavery." (*Loc. cit.*, 77.) The anti-slavery sentiments of the English masses were decisive in preventing the English ruling class and government from aiding the Confederacy. Even the Confederate agents recognized the depth of anti-slavery sentiment as soon as they landed in England in May, 1861 (Donaldson Jordan and Edwin J. Pratt, *Europe and the American Civil War*, Boston and New York, 1931, p. 10). For the special role of the British working class in preventing Palmerston from intervening on the side of the Confederacy, see Karl Marx and Frederick Engels, *The Civil War in the United States*, New York, 1937, pp. xv–xvi, 130–133, 279–283.

20. In Germany, only the Prussian nobility and army officers sympathized with

the Confederacy. The German people were solidly anti-slavery and in favor of the Union. ". . . the Frankfurt bankers, by purchasing Federal bonds in great quantities at low rates, had a stake in the restoration of the Union." (Jordan and Pratt, *op. cit.,* 196.) Joseph Seligman (1819–1880), the American Jewish clothing merchant turned banker, personally organized the Frankfurt house of Seligman and Stettheimer, which seems to have been largely responsible for the sale of some $200,000,000 worth of United States bonds during the Civil War. (*DAB,* XVI, 571–572, by Max James Kohler; see also Seligman papers, *Kohler Collection,* American Jewish Historical Society.)

21. In this letter of July 3, 1861, Belmont had proposed this plan: "an issue of £ Bonds, payable in London, under the auspices of some of the leading European Banking-Houses, who by taking a portion of the loan out & out would get the Balance from our Government on commission to be subscribed for on lists opened in their different Banking Establishments in England & on the Continent. This is the way Russia, Austria, Brazil & other governments have of late negociated large loans." (*Chase Papers.*)
22. The new Italian government had been recognized by the French in June, 1861. Belmont was a supporter of Italian unification, and sponsored a public meeting in New York on February 17, 1860 to express sympathy with the Italian revolution (Howard R. Marraro, *American Opinion on the Unification of Italy, 1846–1861,* New York, 1932, p. 288).
23. The defeat at Bull Run, July 21–23, 1861, had had its repercussions in Europe.
24. Baron James de Rothschild (1792–1868), born in Frankfurt, had established the French branch of the family and the banking network in Paris in 1812. On June 18, 1861, one month after he had written to the London Rothschilds, Belmont had sent a similar letter to the Paris branch (Belmont, *op. cit.,* 53–54).

135. Aid to the Poor

1. *Sinai,* VI, No. 12, January, 1862, pp. 381–384. The same text, with minor variations in paragraphing, phrasing, and one fact to be noted below, also appeared in *The Occident,* XIX, January, 1862, pp. 459–462. It is interesting that the Recording Secretary of this women's society should be a man; Isaac M. Long is listed in the Philadelphia City Directory for 1862 as a clerk employed at 132 North 3d Street; perhaps his employer was Hyman Gunsenhauser, a merchant at that address, whose wife was one of the Managers of the Society and who was himself one of its Board of Advisers.
2. This Society was organized as a result of a split in the Ladies' Sewing Society founded in 1838. By a majority of only one, at a meeting on October 28, 1860, the members had decided to change their time of meeting from the evening to the day. Those who seceded were unable "on account of domestic duties" to attend day meetings, and on December 25, 1860 they founded the new society, calling it originally the German Ladies' Relief Sewing Society, but later changing the name. The old society had met in the synagogue of Beth-El-Emeth, of which Rev. Isaac Leeser was the minister; the new one, consisting chiefly of German-Jewish women, met at the Congregation Rodeph Shalom, with which most of its founders were connected. The inability to meet during the day also suggests a possible difference in the financial status of the members. (*The Occident,* XVIII, No. 41, January 3, 1861, p. 249.)
3. At the meeting to which this report was delivered, with 67 members in attendance, a resolution was introduced proposing a reduction in dues because "the times being at present in a precarious condition," many find "it difficult

to gain a sustenance." The resolution was referred "to the proper source"! (*ibid.*, XIX, 459.)

4. For the year 1861, the officers had been the following: President, Mrs. Simon Sternberger (wife of a shirt manufacturer); Vice-President, Mrs. Alexander Reinstine (wife of a boot and shoe merchant); Mrs. Lazarus Shloss (wife of a clothier); Secretary, Miss L. Thanhauser; Managers: Mrs. G. Isaacs, Mrs. Levi Mayer (wife of a clothing merchant); Mrs. Hyman Gunsenhauser; Mrs. E. W. Williams (wife either of a tailor or a fancy goods storekeeper, both of whom are listed in the Philadelphia directory); Mrs. L. Walker; Miss Henrietta Frank; and Miss Eliza Weiler. The Board of Advisers consisted of David Teller (tobacco importer), Hyman Gunsenhauser, Alexander Reinstine, Henry Mayer (clothing merchant), and Isaac Lang. (*Ibid.*, XVIII, 249–250.) The officers for 1862 were: President, Henrietta Blum; Vice-President, Henrietta Frank; Treasurer, Mrs. Shloss; Secretary, Josephine Simpson; Board of Managers: Mrs. Joseph Einstein (wife of the jeweller and president of Rodeph Shalom); Miss Eliza Wiler, Mrs. Williams, Mrs. Isaacs, Mrs. P. Pollock, Mrs. Levi Mayer, and Mrs. Siegmund Feinberg (the widow Rachel Feinberg). The Board of Advisers remained the same, with the name of Isaac Lang appearing now as Isaac M. Long (*Sinai, loc. cit.*, 381; *McElroy's Philadelphia City Directory*, 1862, *passim.*)
5. The text in *The Occident, loc. cit.*, gives the number as 95.
6. Dr. Jacob Da Silva Solis-Cohen (1838–1927), who later became a famous laryngologist, had but just been graduated from the University of Pennsylvania as a doctor of medicine in 1860. Sometime in 1861 he enlisted in the Union Army, and was quickly appointed assistant surgeon in the 26th Regiment of Pennsylvania Volunteers.

136. Jewish Chaplains in the Union Army

1. *The Jewish Messenger*, X, No. 13, December 27, 1861, p. 101, col. 1. The exact date of presentation of the Statement is not given, but it must have been between December 16 and 25, 1861. Fischel later reported that he also held conversations on the subject with "the members of the Military Committee" of the Senate, with "a majority of the Senators and . . . a large number of influential members of the House . . ." (Isaacs, *AJHSP*, XII, 1904, pp. 134–135.)
2. Korn, *American Jewish Archives*, I, No. 1, June, 1948, p. 7.
3. *Ibid.*, pp. 7–8.
4. Rabbi Bertram W. Korn, *ibid.*, is carried so far into error by his piece-meal approach to the Civil War and the Confederacy as to conclude that "in this instance the Confederate Congress was more liberal and tolerant than its Washington counterpart"! While Attorney General Judah P. Benjamin, who at that time generally drafted the legislation for the Confederate Congress, may have excluded any formal discrimination from the text of the law, the fact still remains that no Jewish chaplains were ever appointed. Nor does Rabbi Korn appreciate the fact that while opponents of the war were ready to make political capital of the issue, it was the supporters of the war that effected the desired change in the law.
5. *Ibid.*, 11–12. Dr. Fischel's contract as lecturer at the Congregation Shearith Israel in New York expired October 31, 1861, and was not renewed, making him available either for a chaplaincy or similar work.
6. Isaacs, *op. cit.*, 131–133.

7. *The Congressional Globe,* 37 Cong., 2 Sess., Part 1, pp. 25, 67, 88, 157; *ibid.,* Part 2, p. 1181; Korn, *American Jewry and the Civil War,* 136ff.
8. The Chairman of the Senate Committee was Henry Wilson (1812–1875), a leading Massachusetts abolitionist and at that time a Radical Republican, whose conduct of the complicated and pressing affairs of the Committee has won high praise.
9. It was not noticed by Fischel then nor by historians of the incident since then that the request to appoint Chaplains who are to be paid by the government is in itself a violation of a strict interpretation of the concept of the separation of Church and State. Actually, the Jews were then asking for *equality* of treatment of Judaism by the State, and not for separation of all religions from the State.
10. The following Jews were appointed as military chaplains by the Federal government: Rabbi Jacob Frankel (1808–1887) of Philadelphia, on September 18, 1862; Rev. Bernhard H. Gotthelf (1819–1878) of Louisville, Ky., on May 6, 1863; and Rev. Ferdinand L. Sarner (1820–1878) of Rochester and New York, elected chaplain of the 54th N. Y. Volunteers on April 10, 1863. (Markens, *AJHSP,* XVII, 1909, p. 116; Korn, *op. cit.,* 14, 17, 19–21.) Rev. Arnold Fischel himself, however, was never appointed a chaplain. From December, 1861 to April, 1862, as long as the petty funds allotted to him held out, he visited the hospitals in the Potomac area as a representative of the Board of Delegates. On October 6, 1862, the Board petitioned Lincoln to appoint Fischel a chaplain; Lincoln had the petition referred to the Surgeon-General to judge whether there was need for a Jewish chaplain, and there the matter seems to have ended. Shortly thereafter, Fischel left for Holland, and did not return to the United States. (*Ibid.,* 16.)

137. Union Soldier's Correspondence

1. *The Jewish Messenger,* February 7, 1862, p. 41, cols. 1–3. This is the fourth in a series of nine letters which appeared weekly from January 17 through March 14, 1862, and were discontinued when the soldier-correspondent was moved southward. (*Ibid.,* March 21, 1862, p. 88, col. 2.)
2. William Howard Russell (1820–1907), the first professional war correspondent, had already covered the war between Schleswig-Holstein and Denmark, the British invasion of the Crimea, and the British suppression of the Indian mutiny in 1858, before he was assigned by the London *Times* in March, 1861 to the Civil War. When he had come back in 1856 from the Crimea, Trinity College, Dublin, had awarded him an Honorary LL. D. for his description of the miserable condition of the British rank-and-file and the officers' indifference to this situation. As a supporter of the Confederacy, the London *Times* used Russell's correspondence to bolster its position, although Russell himself professed to be opposed to slavery, as he saw it for himself on his trip to the South, and regarded the Union cause as just. Nevertheless his "neutral" dispatches, and his conviction that the Union could not be saved, were helpful to the Confederacy. When he was refused permission to accompany McClellan in the Peninsular campaign, he returned to England in April, 1862. (Donaldson Jordan and Edwin J. Pratt, *Europe and the American Civil War,* Boston and New York, 1931, pp. 80–82; Rupert Furneaux, *The First War Correspondent, William Howard Russell of THE TIMES,* London, 1944; *DNB,* XXIII, 241–243.)
3. *The Times,* London, November 20, 1861, p. 8, col. 4 carried Russell's dispatch dated Washington, November 2, with these observations: ". . . All nationalities

are represented in this army, as well as all religions. The Jews have rushed into the field; but, less fortunate than the members of other religious bodies, they cannot have their chaplains, apparently because it never entered into the contemplation of the lawmakers that a sprinkling of Israelites, like those in the Cameron Dragoons, would come forward, sword in hand, for the Union; and the Secretary of War was accordingly obliged to refuse the application of a rabbi for a chaplaincy, which there is some reason to think was intended as a hoax of no very perceptible fun or tendency. . . ." Of course this was no hoax but a serious attempt to test the discriminatory law by Colonel Max Friedman and his fellow-officers of Cameron's Dragoons (65th Regiment, 5th Pennsylvania Cavalry), who, finding that their Jewish chaplain, Michael M. Allen, was not qualified because he was not a properly ordained rabbi, elected Rev. Arnold Fischel as their chaplain-designate, only to have his application for the commission rejected. (Korn, *op. cit.,* 8–11.)

4. Russell's father, John Russell, of Dublin, was "a large-limbed, solid, joyous man," an agent for a Sheffield firm (Furneaux, *op. cit.,* 8).

5. Jefferson Brick was the pseudonym of Alexander Black of the *Brooklyn Times* (William Cushing, *Initials and Pseudonyms,* New York, 1885, p. 39).

6. No official statistics are available, nor has any systematic attempt been made in the past half century to gather all the available data in official archives, the Jewish press, and other sources. The most extensive count, therefore, is still that of Simon Wolf, *The American Jew as Patriot, Soldier and Citizen,* Philadelphia, 1895, pp. 98ff, from whose listings is derivable the fact that there were more than 6,000 Jewish soldiers in the Union Army, and about 1,200 to 1,500 in the Confederate forces.

7. It is noteworthy that this Jewish correspondent, who is properly quick to resent insults against the Jews, himself lapses into the formula of national insult by linking drunkenness with Scottishness.

8. The highest rank apparently achieved by a Jew in the Union Army was attained by the Hungarian Jew, Frederick Knefler (1833–1901), who rose from the ranks as a private to become the Colonel of the 79th Indiana Infantry; on March 13, 1865, he was brevetted a brigadier-general for gallant and meritorious service, and was mustered out June 7, 1865. (Heitman, *op. cit.,* I, 605–606; a breveted officer was one who nominally was awarded by Congress a higher rank than that for which he continued to receive pay, but who did not exercise that rank in actual command.) Other commanding officers were Colonel Henry Boernstein, 2d Missouri Infantry (*ibid.,* II, 81); Colonel Max Friedman, 5th Pennsylvania Cavalry (*ibid.,* II, 102); Colonel Marcus M. Spiegel, 120th Ohio Infantry, who died of battle wounds in 1864 (*ibid.,* II, 149); Colonel Max Einstein, 27th Pennsylvania Infantry (*ibid.,* II, 98); Lieutenant Colonel Leopold C. Newman (1836–1863), 31st New York Infantry, a lawyer who died of wounds received in the battle at Chancellorsville (*ibid.,* II, 133; *The Jewish Record,* New York, June 12, 1863, p. 2, cols. 2–3, 5; Wolf, *op. cit.,* 285); Lt. Col. Philip J. Joachimsen (1817–1890), 59th New York Infantry (Heitman, *op. cit.,* II, 115); Colonel Simon Levy of the New York Infantry Regiment, "les enfans perdus," (*ibid.,* II, 121; *The Jewish Record,* June 12, 1863, p. 2, col. 3; Wolf, *op. cit.,* 275); Lt. Col. Edward Selig Salomon, 82d Illinois Infantry (Heitman, *op. cit.,* II, 143), also breveted colonel and brigadier general on March 13, 1865 for distinguished, gallant and meritorious service (*ibid.,* I, 857); Lt. Col. Isaac Moses of New York, an adjutant-general with the Army of the Potomac (*ibid.,* I, 731).

9. See 2 Samuel, 8:5ff for the account of David's smiting Hadadezer, son of Rehob, king of Zobah, and then the Aramaeans of Damascus.

10. Four Congressional Medals of Honor were awarded to Jews in the ranks: Leopold Karpeles, color sergeant of the 57th Massachusetts Infantry, for exceptional conduct at the Battle of North Anna; Benjamin B. Levy of the 1st New York Infantry, who enlisted at 16; Sergeant-Major Abraham Cohn of the 6th New Hampshire Infantry; Private David Orbansky of the 58th Ohio Infantry. (Sylvan M. Dubrow, "Identifying the Jewish Servicemen in the Civil War: A Re-appraisal of Simon Wolf's *The American Jew as Patriot, Soldier and Citizen," AJHQ,* LIX, No. 3 [March, 1970], 368–369, correcting Wolf, *op. cit.,* 106–108.)

11. In 1809, since various units of the Dutch Army refused to admit Jews into their ranks, two Jewish infantry battalions, with 883 men in each, were formed, and were staffed with Jewish officers. But in 1810 these units were disbanded when Holland was incorporated into the French kingdom, and the men were distributed among the French regiments. (Simon Dubnow, *Weltgeschichte des jüdischen Volkes,* Berlin, 1928, VIII, 178.)

12. This story about a Jewish regiment in the English army at Waterloo is not verifiable. In 1833, Wellington did state in the House of Lords that fifteen Jewish officers were under his command at Waterloo. Also, 52 Jewish French soldiers were killed at Waterloo. (*UJE,* IX, 600.)

13. Baron David Hendrick Chassé (1765–1840), of Dutch birth, joined the French army in 1793, but as lieutenant-general of the Dutch forces fought against the French at Waterloo.

14. In August, 1861, shortly after the Battle of Manassas Plain, the *Richmond Enquirer* published an editorial giving virtually this version of the origin of the name, which has since passed into the folk-lore of the region, and has been accepted as such by scholars (Isaack Markens, "Manassas, an Israelite of Colonial Days," *The American Jewish Chronicle,* January 26, 1917, pp. 362, 367).

138. Company C, 82nd Illinois Infantry

1. *Sinai,* VII, No. 8, September, 1862, pp. 228–229. The Chicago *Tribune,* August 14, 1862, headlined its story of the same meeting thus: "The Israelites Aroused—Enthusiastic War Meeting—Strong Resolutions and Splendid Liberality." (Meites, *op. cit.,* 89.)

2. *Ibid.,* 91.

3. August 16, 1862 (*Ibid.,* 89). About the same time, a Jewish company was formed in Syracuse, N. Y. and similar companies were recruited for the Confederacy in Macon and West Point, Ga., in 1861 and 1863 (Korn, *op. cit.,* 221, 223).

4. For the Regimental service record, see *Illinois in the War for the Union,* Springfield and Chicago, 1887, pp. 495–499; T. M. Eddy, *The Patriotism of Illinois,* Chicago, 1865, II, 327–330; John Moses and F. Kirkland, *History of Chicago, Illinois,* Chicago and New York, 1895, I, 172, 181, 187.

5. Joseph Gottlob was promoted to the captaincy from the rank of lieutenant (Wolf, *op. cit.,* 143).

   Joseph B. Greenhut was the second Chicagoan to enlist as a private when the call came in April, 1861; in August, 1861, he became a Sergeant in the 12th Illinois Infantry under Colonel Ulysses S. Grant; wounded in February, 1862, in the Battle of Fort Donaldson, he retired, but reenlisted in August, 1862, to become Captain of Company K. For a while he served as Assistant Adjutant-General of the Third Brigade under Hecker (Third Division, Eleventh Corps), and resigned when Hecker did. (*Ibid.,* 143–144.)

Edward S. Salomon, who had come to the United States from his birthplace, Schleswig-Holstein, was commissioned a first lieutenant in Hecker's first regiment, the 24th Illinois, on July 8, 1861, and was mustered out in December, 1861, at about the time that Hecker, disagreeing with some of his officers, resigned. When Hecker began to form his second Regiment, the 82nd Illinois, Salomon became his Lieutenant-Colonel. Generals Carl Schurz, O. O. Howard, and others publicly commended his gallantry and bravery at the battles of Gettysburg, Missionary Ridge, Bentonville, Atlanta, etc. (Heitman, *op. cit.*, I, 857; Wolf, *op. cit.*, 165ff.)

6. The Concordia Club had been organized early in 1862, with Henry Greenebaum as President (Meites, *op. cit.*, 88).

The occupations of the leading figures at this meeting are in part derivable from *Gager's Chicago City Directory*, 1857, *Halpin's Chicago City Directory*, 1858, and *John C. W. Bailey's Chicago City Directory*, 1864/65:

Maximiliam M. Gerstley, "late clothier," 1858.

Benjamin Shoeneman headed a company dealing in "tallow, lard, etc." in 1864; in April, 1861, he had helped organize and became the first president of the Sinai Congregation (Reform).

Jacob Rosenberg, a founder of the first Chicago Jewish congregation (Kehilath Anshe Maariv) in November, 1847, was a partner in a dry goods firm in 1857 and 1858; by 1864 the firm was wholesaling.

Max A. Meyer in 1864 was a partner with Joseph Frank and Moses Lindheim of New York in the firm, Lindheim, Frank & Meyer, dealing in "foreign and domestic dry goods." Joseph Frank had been in the dry goods business since 1858.

Henry Greenebaum was part of the banking firm of Greenebaum Brothers in 1857 and thereafter; in 1856–1857 he had served as Alderman from the Sixth Ward.

Simon Hyman was part of the firm, Hyman and Brother, butchers, in 1858.

I. L. Stettheimer may be an error for Jacob Stettheimer, of the fancy woolens firm of Stettheimer & Friedman in 1864.

Simon Florsheim was an insurance agent in 1864.

F. Greenebaum may be an error for E. (Elias) Greenebaum of the banking family.

Morris Selz was part of the clothing firm of Selz & Cohen in 1857 and 1858, but in 1864 he was a member of the clothing and woolens wholesale house of J. Stettheimer & Co., consisting of Jacob and Joseph S. Stettheimer of New York, and Selz and Hugo Goodman in Chicago.

Gabriel Shoyer was head of Shoyer & Co., wholesale hat, caps, and furs, in 1864.

Samuel Cole, see Index.

7. Frederick Hecker (1811–1881) was very popular among the German-Americans both for his democratic struggles in Baden, Germany up to 1848, when he was forced to emigrate, and for his anti-slavery activities in Illinois. The Jews also remembered his efforts in behalf of Jewish emancipation in the Baden Diet (Wilhelm Kaufman, *Die Deutschen im amerikanischen Bürgerkriege,* Munich and Berlin, 1911, p. 189).

8. Nathan Eisendraht in 1857 was in "soaps and candles" as part of Eisendraht & Hugg; in 1858 he was a broker; and in 1864 he was a member of the wholesale fruit house of W. T. Shufeldt, Kraefft & Co.

Solomon Harris was a clothier in 1857, 1858 and 1864. In May 1852 he had helped organize and became the first president of the Kehilath B'nai Sholom, which followed the Polish *Minhag*.

9. From July 21 to July 23, 1862, $15,000 was raised in bounty money by the Chicago Board of Trade for the Board of Trade Battery, in which 180 men enrolled in two days. (*Illinois in the War for the Union,* 749.)

10. Captain Jacob Lasalle was for a time in command of the regiment when both Colonel Hecker and Major Ferdinand Rolshausen were wounded at the battle of Chancellorsville, May 2, 1863; Lasalle resigned on May 27, 1863 (Moses and Kirkland, *op. cit.,* I, 187, 172.)

    1st Lt. Mayer Frank was promoted to the Captaincy of Company C when Lasalle resigned, and served until he resigned on February 29, 1864 (*ibid.*). Wolf names only 23 of the 96 to 100 that were in the Company (he names an equal number in other companies in the same Regiment). There were many non-Jews in the company too. (*Report of the Adjutant General of the State of Illinois, . . . 1861–1866, Revised,* Springfield, 1886, pp. 104–106.)

139. Revoking General Grant's Order No. 11

1. a) *The War of the Rebellion: . . . Official Records,* Ser. I, Vol. 17, Pt. 2, Washington, 1887, p. 506; a similar text appears in Markens, *AJHSP,* XVII, 1909, p. 117. *The Jewish Record,* New York, January 9, 1863, p. 2, contains a letter from C. J. Kaskel dated December 30, 1862, from on board a ship on which he had begun his journey to Washington. b) *The Israelite,* January 16, 1863, p. 218, cols. 2–3.

2. P. C. Headley, *The Life and Campaigns of General U. S. Grant,* New York, 1869, pp. 188, 197; J. W. Schuckers, *The Life and Public Services of Salmon Portland Chase,* New York, 1874, pp. 322, 325; James Wilford Garner, *Reconstruction in Mississippi,* New York, 1901, p. 31.

3. Lebowich, *AJHSP,* XVII, 1909, pp. 71–72.

4. *The War of the Rebellion, loc. cit.,* 421–422, 424; *The Occident,* January, 1869, pp. 440–441. For additional evidence that it was a comunication from Washington that stimulated this specific order of Grant's, see *The Israelite,* January 30, 1863, p. 236, cols. 3–4; February 6, 1863, p. 244, col. 4; *The Jewish Record,* January 30, 1863, p. 2, col. 2; Philadelphia *Press,* July 26, 1885, reprint from the *New York Dispatch.* Simon Wolf maintains it was Sherman and not Grant who actually wrote out the order (*The American Hebrew,* November 24, 1905, p. 880; *The Presidents I have Known from 1860–1918,* Washington, 1918, pp. 70–71), but the evidence is inconclusive. It should be noted that on December 8, 1862, a similar order had been issued independently by Col. J. V. Du Bois at Holly Springs, Miss., requiring the expulsion from the town in 24 hours of "all cotton speculators, Jews and other vagrants having no honest means of support, except trading on the miseries of their country" (Lebowich, *op. cit.,* 77). Yet on September 29, 1868, Du Bois wrote from Santa Fe, N. M. to the Washington, D. C. *Morning Chronicle,* "This order was revoked by Gen Grant and I was relieved from command on account of it." (MS, Caleb Morgan Papers, Minnesota Historical Society; I am indebted to Miss Bertha L. Heilbron for calling this item to my attention.) See Korn, *op. cit.,* 261–270 for an analysis of evidence on the authorship of Order No. 11.

5. *The Jewish Record,* January 9, 1863, p. 2, col. 5; January 23, 1863, p. 2, col. 4; March 20, 1863, p. 2, col. 3; April 17, 1863, p. 2, col. 2.

6. *The Jewish Messenger,* January 16, 1863, p. 20; January 23, 1863, p. 28.

7. *The Israelite,* January 9, 1863, p. 212, cols. 3–4.

    The *Washington Republican* and the *Washington Chronicle,* the latter published by John W. Forney, secretary of the Senate, editorially supported the

Order, and of course the entire Republican press resisted the effort of the Democrats to censure Grant after the Order was withdrawn (Korn, *op. cit.*, 241–242).

8. A number of Jews had settled in Paducah before 1851; the Paducah directory for 1859 lists some eleven Jewish business firms; Grant's order led to the expulsion of about thirty Jews from the city (Isaac W. Bernheim, *History of the Settlement of Jews in Paducah and the Lower Ohio Valley,* Paducah, 1912, pp. 22–25). Grant, with a force of 5,000 men, had occupied Paducah as far back as September 6, 1861, when most of its citizens were apparently sympathetic to the secessionists, and established military rule in the city, with the military authorities controlling the flow of all merchandise into and out of the area (Fred G. Neuman, *The Story of Paducah, Kentucky,* Paducah, 1927, pp. 128–134).

9. D. Wolff & Brothers was composed of the brothers Daniel, Marcus and Alexander Wolff; Caesar F. Kaskel (1832–1892) was the partner of Solomon Greenbaum in the firm, Greenbaum & Kaskel; J. W. Kaskel was his brother. The Wolff brothers "returned to Germany soon after the close of the war"; Caesar Kaskel left Paducah during the war, moved to New York, and became a haberdasher, founding the firm still in existence as Kaskel & Kaskel; at the time, he was Vice-President of the Union League Club in Paducah; J. W. Kaskel stayed on in Paducah after the war. (Bernheim, *op. cit.*, 24–25, 51–52; Markens, *op. cit.*, 118–123; New York City directories.) It should be noted that the printed source of this document misspells Kaskel as Kaskell, and misprints the name of J. W. Kaskel as J. W. Kaswell.

10. John A. Gurley (1813–1863) was a lame-duck Republican Congressman from Cincinnati who had just been defeated for re-election after serving three terms. Without indicating his source, Markens reports the following colloquy:

"And so the children of Israel were driven from the happy land of Canaan?

"Yes, replied Kaskel, and that is why we have come unto Father Abraham's bosom, asking protection.

"And this protection they shall have at once, said Lincoln." Henry W. Halleck (1815–1872) was then military adviser to Lincoln, with the title of General-in-Chief.

11. The rescinding order was issued from Holly Springs, Miss., on January 7, 1863. (*The War of the Rebellion, loc. cit.*, 544.) In justifying his order to Grant, Halleck felt it necessary to write, on January 21, 1863, a statement offensive in itself: "It may be proper to give you some explanation of the revocation of your order expelling all Jews from your department. The President has no objection to your expelling traitors and Jew peddlers, which, I suppose, was the object of your order; but, as it in terms proscribed an entire religious class, some of whom are fighting in our ranks, the President deemed it necessary to revoke it." (*The War of the Rebellion,* Ser. 1, Vol. 24, Pt. 1, Washington, 1902, p. 9.)

12. The Louisville delegation was appointed on January 1, 1863, after Abraham Goldsmith of Paducah had explained the plight of the Jews there. Martin Bijur was delegated to accompany Goldsmith to Cincinnati. There, on January 4, 1863, at a large meeting, a Cincinnati delegation was selected, consisting of Rev. Dr. Max Lilienthal, Rev. Dr. I. M. Wise, and the lawyer Edgar M. Johnston. Both delegations started for Washington on January 5, 1863 (after Kaskel had already seen Lincoln); near Philadelphia, they learned from the local newspapers that Lincoln had already revoked the order, but decided to verify the report. (*The Israelite,* January 23, 1863, pp. 228–229.)

13. This appreciation of Lincoln's democratic manner contrasts pleasingly with Wise's contemptuous attitude to Lincoln expressed shortly after his election, when he derided Lincoln for looking "like a country squire for the first time in the city" and predicted that Lincoln "will look queer, in the white house, with his primitive manner." (*Ibid.*, February 15, 1861, p. 262, col. 2.) Rev. Lilienthal, who unlike Wise was an abolitionist, in two sermons on Lincoln after his assassination, also commented at length on Lincoln's simplicity and cordiality (David Philipson, *Max Lilienthal, American Rabbi,* New York, 1915, pp. 420, 424).
14. While the Democratic party sought to exploit the incident further, the Republican majority in the Houses of Congress refused to allow a continuation of the merely political attack on a general then actively investing Vicksburg. Senator Lazarus W. Powell, former Governor of Kentucky, was a Democrat; Rep. Pendleton of Ohio later was the vice-presidential candidate on McClellan's ticket, running against Lincoln.
15. Rep. Elihu B. Washburne (1816–1887), a radical Republican from Galena, Ill., and therefore a neighbor of Grant's, was serving his tenth year in Congress; he was a personal and political friend of Lincoln and a sponsor of Grant, with whom he corresponded throughout the war. Wise's is a summary of the congressional resolution and the action taken; the full text and account are in the *Cong. Globe,* 37 Cong., 3 Sess., Pt. 1, p. 222.
16. Lincoln had but just issued the Emancipation Proclamation, but Wise lacked the historic sense to understand its importance and made no comment upon it in his magazine; in this report, by contrasting the "favored" position of the Negro with that of the Jew, Wise reveals how narrowly nationalist was his concern for civil liberties, and how little he understood that slavery and the Negro question were at the bottom of the war, while the position of the Jews in the United States, while not of *central* importance, was itself to be favorably affected by the abolition of chattel slavery. The copperhead press constantly harped on the theme of the "special privileges" and "special attention" the Negroes were getting. *The Jewish Record,* January 23, 1863, p. 2, col. 4, echoes Wise's inept point.
17. Wise followed this report with an editorial, "The Last of General Grant's Order," *The Israelite,* January 23, 1863, pp. 228–229, in which he summarizes the entire story. On January 24, a meeting of the Committee on Resolutions about Grant's order heard Wise's report as printed herein and accepted it. (*Ibid.,* January 30, 1863, p. 234, cols. 1–2.) When Grant ran for President in 1868, the issue of the Order No. 11 was injected into the campaign by his political opponents but his later public record with regard to Jews was unexceptionable (Wolf, *op. cit.; UJE,* V, 3–84; Korn, *op. cit.*, 248–260, who summarizes the attitude of Jews in the 1868 campaign, but does so from a Jewish nationalist point of view).

140. Missouri Emancipationist

1. *Proceedings of the Missouri State Convention, Held in Jefferson City, June, 1863,* St. Louis, 1863, pp. 326–329.

   On September 1–2, 1863, Bush was also a delegate to a convention in Jefferson City, Mo., which thanked Lincoln "for his action in arming and organizing the colored citizens of African descent for the purpose of killing rebels" (*Proceedings of the Missouri State Radical Emancipation Convention,* pp. 10, 41).
2. Virgil C. Blum, "The Political and Military Activities of the German Element in St. Louis, 1859–1861," *Missouri Historical Review,* XLII, 1948, p. 106; Robert J. Rombauer, *The Union Cause in St. Louis in 1861,* St. Louis, 1909, pp. 135–290.

3. Sceva Bright Laughlin, *Missouri Politics During the Civil War,* Salem, Oregon, 1930, p. 42; text in *Journal and Proceedings of the Missouri State Convention . . . March, 1861,* St. Louis, 1861, p. 244. In the decade before the Civil War, Bush had been a merchant, wholesale grocer and small banker in St. Louis and its environs. From September 16 to November 12, 1861 he had served as a Captain on the Staff of Major-General John C. Fremont, being dismissed with Fremont's entire staff when the General was relieved of his command of the Western Department. (Letter to this editor, Adjutant General's Office, Washington, D. C., June 25, 1947.) On May 21, 1862, Bush was appointed a clerk at $1200 per annum in the office of the Second Comptroller of the Treasury, although a plan he had submitted to the Treasury Department for floating a government loan of $100,000,000 was rejected by Secretary Chase. (Benjamin F. Peixotto, "Isidor Bush," *The Menorah,* October, 1890, p. 195; The National Archives, *Treasury Department Records, Personnel Folder on Bush;* letter to this editor from the Director, General Records Office, June 10, 1947.)
4. *Proceedings . . . 1863,* pp. 135–136.
5. On June 23, 1863, Governor Hamilton R. Gamble, chairman of the convention Committee on Emancipation, reported for the majority, and the debate took place on June 24 (when Bush briefly took the floor), 25, 27, and 29, when Bush spoke. (*Ibid.,* 160ff.)
6. In 1860, Missouri had had a large pro-slavery base of 24,320 families that owned one or more slaves. By the summer of 1863, the emancipationist forces estimated that even many of these, especially the small slaveowners, had undergone a change of sentiment, largely owing to Lincoln's proposal to compensate those slaveowners who had been loyal to the Union for whatever slaves they lost by emancipation. (Harrison Anthony Trexler, *Slavery in Missouri 1804–1865,* Baltimore, 1914, p. 234; Blum, *op. cit.,* 106.)
7. The members of the Convention had been elected on February 18, 1861, primarily on the issue of Union or Secession. At its session in June, 1862, the Convention had voted 37 to 23 to forward to Lincoln a statement declining his offer of compensation for emancipation and a resolution declaring that "a majority of this Convention have not felt authorized" to act on emancipation. (Trexler, *op. cit.,* 233–234.) The new state legislature, meeting in January, 1863, had passed resolutions asking Congress for $25,000,000 with which to pay the owners of slaves who might be emancipated. (*Ibid.,* 235.)
8. The convention Call opened thus: "The subject of Emancipation has now for some time engaged the public mind, and it is of the highest importance to the interest of the State that some scheme of Emancipation should be adopted." (*Journal of the Missouri State Convention . . . 1863,* St. Louis, 1863, p. 3.)
9. When in 1857 the Baltimore and Ohio Railroad provided St. Louis with direct rail communication with the Atlantic coast, a decisive link was forged that kept Missouri in the Union and made far-sighted business men look to the Union rather than to the south for their welfare (Blum, *op. cit.,* 106). Bush was himself a director of the St. Louis & Iron Mountain Railroad, as well as, until 1866, its General Freight and Passenger Agent (Peixotto, *op. cit.,* 195–196).
10. Bush's minority report and substitute ordinance called for the abolition of slavery in Missouri as of January 1, 1864, but also provided that slaves and their issue should continue to serve their former owners as "indentured apprentices" until July 4, 1870.
11. United States Senator John B. Henderson (1826–1913), who represented Pike County in the Missouri convention and opposed immediate emancipation, had

in fact pointed out that by 1860 Illinois, though much smaller than Missouri, had farm property that was $200,000,000 more valuable than that of Missouri; if the same rate of increase continued to 1870, Henderson estimated that Illinois property would outvalue Missouri's by $2,664,000,000. Henderson attributed this differential to the fact that Illinois used free, not slave, labor. (*Proceedings . . . 1863,* p. 203.) In the Senate, Henderson was the introducer of the Thirteenth Amendment. May 9, 1862 he recommended Bush to Secretary Chase for a clerkship in the Treasury Department (*Personnel folder, loc. cit.*).

12. In the debate on the proposal that emancipation begin January 1, 1864, Alexander M. Woolfolk had on June 24 voiced his opposition on the ground that such an early date would not give slaveowners a chance to sell their slaves to southern states, and had charged the advocates of immediate emancipation with also being "in favor of marauding, theft, arson, murder, and all the catalogue of crime." He denounced the state law enforcement agencies for not preventing slaves from escaping, and predicted that free Negroes, refusing to work, would ravage the country, as they allegedly had done in Jamaica and the West Indies. (*Proceedings . . . 1863,* pp. 177, 183, 187.) Many of Bush's points in this address seem to be directed against Woolfolk's rant.

13. In 1860, there were 114,931 slaves in Missouri (9.7% of the total population); in the fall of 1862, it was estimated the figure had dropped to 40,000. (Blum, *op. cit.,* 106; B. Gratz Brown, *Missouri Should be Included in the Proclamation,* St. Louis, October 16, 1862, p. 1.) Slaveowners were finding it very difficult to keep their slaves from escaping.

14. The majority report proposed emancipation on July 4, 1876. The vote on the proposal that it begin January 1, 1864 was 19 in favor, 65 against; for January 1, 1866, 27 in favor, 48 against; for January 1, 1868, 29 in favor, 57 against. Bush voted for the dates 1864 and 1866, but against 1868. The proposal to put the date to a popular referendum in November, 1863 was defeated by a vote of 47 to 38. (*Journal . . . 1863,* pp. 28, 30, 43, 38; *Proceedings . . . 1863,* p. 257.)

15. On June 27, Robert M. Stewart of Buchanan had moved adjournment of the convention *sine die,* and been defeated by a vote of 68 to 18. Bush's motion to adjourn was defeated by the same vote. (*Ibid.,* 259; *Journal . . . 1863,* p. 38.) On July 1, the final vote setting the date of emancipation as 1870 (but providing for continued service to the former owners varying from 12 years to a lifetime!) was 51 to 30. Bush of course voted against this ordinance, declaring, "I would have been willing to be the pallbearer at the burial of the corpse of slavery, but I am not willing to be the guard, to stand watch over the gibbet in which the corpse hangs suspended for twenty more years." (*Proceedings . . . 1863,* pp. 367–368, 363.) The triumph of the movement for immediate emancipation of which Bush was a part finally came shortly after a Republican sweep in the 1864 elections, at the reassembled convention on January 11, 1865, with a vote of 60 to 4, one month before the state legislature ratified the Thirteenth Amendment. (*Journal of the Missouri State Convention . . . 1865,* St. Louis, 1865, pp. 26, 281.) At this Convention, Bush was one of only three members who had served in the 1861–1863 Convention, and he played an especially active and distinguished part both on the floor and in several key committees. (Thomas S. Barclay, *The Liberal Republican Movement in Missouri 1865–1871,* Columbia, Mo., 1926, p. 11.) After the Civil War, Bush developed a grape-growing and wine-making enterprise that brought him both financial prosperity and an international reputation as a viticulturist, with his "Bushberg catalog" of American grapes being translated into French, Italian, and German. He continued to be active in political affairs, serving as an Alderman (Repub-

lican) in St. Louis in 1866, as Secretary (without pay) of the State Board of Immigration from 1865 to 1877, and as a member of the St. Louis Board of Education from 1881 to 1884. He was continually active in Temple B'ne El, and also a national leader of the B'nai B'rith, serving as Treasurer from 1874 to 1890, and initiating its fraternal endowment plan. When he died in 1898 at 76, he was widely honored. (Peixotto, *op. cit.*, 198–200; Wax, *op. cit.*, 187–190.)

141. Confederate Diary

1. L. Leon, *Diary of a Tar Heel Confederate Soldier,* Charlotte, N. C., 1913, pp. 1–2, 4–5, 7–14, 16–17, 19–22, 25, 27–29, 34–41, 44–49, 58–67, 69–70. This volume was obtained for use through the courtesy of the North Carolina State Library, Raleigh, N. C. Colonel James T. Morehead, the last commander of Leon's regiment, used the manuscript of the Diary in compiling his regimental history (Walter Clark, ed., *Histories of the Several Regiments and Battalions from North Carolina in the Great War 1861–'65,* Goldsboro, N. C., 1901, III, 264–265).
2. E. Merton Coulter, *Travels in the Confederate States, A Bibliography,* Norman, Okla., 1948, p. 161.
3. The Charlotte Grays was organized early in April, 1861. The Company had one Jewish officer, First Lieutenant E. B. Cohen, and the following privates beside Leon who may be Jewish: S. Hymans, Jack R. Israel, Jacob Katz, J. C. Levi, Jacob Leopold, and S. Oppenheim. The Grays left Charlotte on April 16. In June, "the 'Jewess ladies' of the town raised $150 to assist the volunteers," as part of similar activity by other women in Charlotte. The entire Regiment, its six-month enlistment having expired, was mustered out on October 12, 1861, and many of its men were reorganized into the 11th Regiment on March 31, 1862. (D. A. Tompkins, *History of Mecklenburg County and the City of Charlotte from 1740 to 1903,* Charlotte, N. C., 1903, I, 139–140, II, 144–145; Clark, *op. cit.,* I, 583.) E. B. Cohen may be the author of the letter to the Charlotte *Bulletin* against the anti-Semitic remarks of a North Carolina legislator, reprinted in *The Jewish Messenger,* March 22, 1861, p. 93; Mr. Cohen there promised that, despite North Carolina's constitutional discriminations against Jews, if war came, the Jews would fight for North Carolina's "rights and institutions."
4. Captain J. Harvey White, commissioned March 1, 1862, was killed at the Spottsylvania Court House, May, 1864. There were four Samples in the Company with Leon: H. B., David, John W., and J. M., with the latter perhaps being known as "Mack"; John W. and David had served with Leon in the Charlotte Grays. The Katz mentioned is Aaron, and not the Jacob of the Charlotte Grays; Aaron Katz was promoted to Sergeant Major. (John W. Moore, *Roster of North Carolina Troops in the War Between the States,* Raleigh, 1882, III, 505, 507; Clark, *op. cit.,* III, 261.) There is no Henry Wortheim or Wertheim in the official Roster, but Wolf lists an H. Wertheimer of this Company and Regiment as having died in the service, and Leon is undoubtedly referring to him (*op. cit.,* 305). Colonel William A. Owens was wounded at the Spottsylvania Court House and killed in August, 1864, at Snicker's Ford (Clark, *op. cit.,* III, 250).
5. Second Lieutenant William M. Matthews (not McMatthews) had been promoted from First Sergeant; he was later wounded at Gettysburg. W. B. Harry was captured, like Leon, in 1864. First Lieutenant Samuel E. Belk was also wounded at Gettysburg. (Moore, *op. cit.,* III, 505, 506; Clark, *op. cit.,* III, 261.)
6. Sam Oppenheim is not listed in the official Roster, but he is listed incorrectly

as Oppenheimer in Wolf (*op. cit.,* 304). Lewis Leon's brother, Morris, had enlisted as a private in Company I, 44th Regiment Georgia Infantry on March 4, 1862, at Madison, Ga. He was captured at Spottsylvania Court House, May 10, 1864, imprisoned at Fort Delaware, where he took the oath of allegiance to the Union on February 13, 1865, and was released. He then went to live in Augusta, Ga. (Confederate Pension and Record Department, Atlanta, Ga., Henry W. Thomas, *History of the Doles-Cook Brigade, Army of Northern Virginia, C. S. A.,* Atlanta, 1903, p. 580; *Pughe's City Directory,* Augusta, Ga., 1865/66, p. 32, 1867, p. 34.)

7. Leon erred in the date of Rosh Hashana, which in 1862 began Wednesday evening, September 24 and extended to sundown on Friday, September 26.

8. The official Roster does not list a Donau, but it does have a Jacob Demon, who was discharged for disability; this "Demon" may be a misreading for Jacob Danane, listed by Wolf as belonging to this Company, but not contained in the Roster. (Moore, *op. cit.,* III, 506; Wolf, *op. cit.,* 301.)

9. S. W. Wilson was later captured. An I. Eigenbrun had been a member of the Charlotte Grays (*ibid.,* 302); perhaps he is the same person whose name appears to be misread as J. Engenbrun on the Roster of Leon's Company (Moore, *op. cit.,* III, 506). The W. Engle mentioned by Leon may be the Jonas Engel who was a member of the Charlotte Grays and then of Leon's Company, on the Roster of which he is inaccurately listed as Jones Engel (Wolf, *op. cit.,* 302; Moore, *op. cit.,* III, 506).

10. Probably a misprint for Thomas Trotter, who is listed in the Roster while a Notter is not (*ibid.,* III, 507).

11. By the spring of 1863, desertion was already a major problem in the entire Confederate army, but it was particularly acute in the North Carolina regiments. During the war, about 104,000 deserted the Confederate armies; of this number, 23,694 men and 428 officers deserted from North Carolina regiments. The North Carolina press and many public officials, who were less than enthusiastic about the war, were blamed for the high rate of desertions in North Carolina regiments. In August, 1863, Jefferson Davis proclaimed an amnesty for all deserters who would return to their posts within twenty days after learning of the proclamation, but this did not solve the problem. The mass of desertions prevented the enforcement of death penalties on any extensive scale; therefore resort was had to "truly cruel and unusual modes of punishment," including flogging, branding, gagging, wearing barrel-shirts, and shaving the head. With the proportion of desertions in the Confederacy standing at about one to nine enlistments, the rate in the Union army was even higher, one to seven. But while in the Union army, the problem was being controlled later in the war, in the Confederacy the desertions accelerated towards the end. (Ella Lonn, *Desertion during the Civil War,* New York, 1928, pp. 231–232, 32, 19, 114, 48–49, 57–58.)

12. The "Norman" who fell dead at Leon's side must have been the A. A. Norment listed in the Roster as killed that day at Gettysburg (Moore, *op. cit.,* III, 507). M. E. Alexander was the Second Lieutenant (*ibid.,* III, 505).

13. The regimental historian reports that "Company B lost at Gettysburg out of about 65 men, 8 killed and 22 wounded, and of the four officers, three were wounded." (Clark, *op. cit.,* 264.) The discrepancy with Leon's statement that only 16 men reported after the fighting at Culp's Hill may be due to the fact that the regimental historian omitted the number "missing." John M. Cochrane was later promoted to Second Lieutenant and transferred to the 37th Regiment (Moore, *op. cit.,* III, 506).

14. At Gettysburg, the Confederacy had 70,000 troops to 93,000 of the Union. The Union losses totaled 23,049: 3,155 killed, 14,529 wounded, 5,365 missing. The Confederate losses were 20,451: 2,592 killed, 12,709 wounded, 5,150 missing. The Union army captured 12,227. (J. Franklin Jameson, *Dictionary of United States History,* rev. ed., Philadelphia, 1931, p. 199.) The names of 25 "Jewish Killed and Wounded at the Battle of Gettysburg" appear in *The Jewish Record,* July 10, 1863, p. 2, col. 5, but need verification.
15. "Si Wolf" appears in the Roster as Cyrus H. Wolfe, and is listed as a "Musician" (Moore, *op. cit.,* III, 501, 507).
16. This general offer of a furlough for the Jewish holidays was exceptional, for on August 22, 1861, April 2, 1863, and September 20, 1864 Lee wrote to Rabbi Maximilian J. Michelbacher (c. 1810–1879) of Richmond, Va., denying the practicability of such general furloughs, but offering to have individual applications for furloughs examined by the commanding officers in relation to the military needs of the detachment (texts in Ezekiel and Lichtenstein, *op. cit.,* 161–163; for a letter from Confederate Assistant Attorney General Thomas Jordan to Michelbacher, dated September 1, 1861, and hitherto unnoted but conveying the same denial, see *The Jewish Record,* February 13, 1863, p. 2, col. 2). Leon's is the first and only record of such a general furlough.
17. The text of this advertisement, which appeared in the New York *Daily News,* read thus: "To A. Leon or any of my relatives: Let me hear from you all through Richmond Enquirer, and let me know your address. Have not heard from you since August, 1862. Morris and myself are both well. Lewis Leon." (Ezekiel and Lichtenstein, *op. cit.,* 161.) Abraham Leon, who had been a "pedlar" living on Norfolk Street, had recently worked himself up to operating a "varieties" store at 93 Suffolk Street; later he turned to selling "papers" and then "candy" (*Trow's New York City Directories,* 1858 to 1869).
18. The regimental history reports this incident: "On 5 or 6 May, 1864, the sharpshooters of this regiment were much annoyed by one of the Federal sharpshooters who had a long range rifle and who had climbed up a tall tree from which he could pick off our men, though sheltered by stump and stones, himself out of range of our guns. Private Leon, of Company B (Mecklenburg), concluded that 'this thing had to be stopped,' and taking advantage of every knoll, hollow and stump, he crawled near enough for his rifle to reach, took a 'pop' at this disturber of the peace and he came tumbling down. Upon running up to his victim, Leon discovered him to be a Canadian Indian, and clutching his scalp-lock, dragged him to our line of sharpshooters." (Clark, *op. cit.,* 258.)
19. Wolf gives the names of ten Jews who died at Elmira Prison and are buried in the Woodlawn Cemetery in that city (*op. cit.,* 30).

142. Women Aid the Soldiers

1. *United States Sanitary Commission Papers, Box 640,* New York Public Library. The Commission had been organized June 9, 1861, by order of Secretary of War Simon Cameron, chiefly on the initiative of Rev. Henry Whitney Bellows (1814–1882), minister of the First Unitarian Church in New York.

   I am indebted to Mr. William Maxwell of New York for calling this manuscript to my attention.
2. The gross proceeds of this huge bazaar, held from April 4 to August 1, 1864, were $1,340,050.37, of which $163,378.47 went for expenses, leaving a net income of $1,176,671.90.
3. Moses Lazarus (1813–1885), distiller and sugar refiner (and father of Emma

Lazarus), was on the Executive Committee of 45 of the Gentlemen's Association running the Fair; Mrs. Benjamin Nathan, wife of the financial broker and a sister-in-law of Moses Lazarus, was on the Executive Committee of 25 of the Ladies' Association; on the Clothing Committee of 19, aiming to solicit funds and merchandise from the garment trade, there were David L. Einstein of the shirt-manufacturing firm of Lewis Einstein & Co., William Seligman of the clothing firm of William Seligman & Co., and Simon Bernheimer of the importing and clothiers' firm of Bernheimer Brothers; on the Dress Making Committee of 6 there was Mrs. Benjamin Nathan; chairman of the Florists' Committee of 13 was August Belmont, the banker and Democratic Party politician; the Finance Committee of 28 included Moses Lazarus; and on the Furs, Hats and Caps Committee of 11 there was Lewis J. Phillips, of the cap and fur house of L. J. and I[saac]. Phillips. (*The Jewish Messenger,* December 13, 1863, p. 209, col. 2; February 26, 1864, p. 58, cols. 2–3; *Metropolitan Fair, in Aid of the United States Sanitary Commission,* New York, 1864, pp. 6–7, 12, 13, 14, 15; *Trow's New York City Directory,* 1863/64, *passim.*)

In addition to those on official committees, there were also active Moses Schloss, of the umbrella firm of Schloss Brothers, and Lewis May (1823–1897), hat merchant, both of them leading members of Temple Emanuel, who issued a circular to the Jewish community asking that contributions in money or merchandise be made through them (*The Jewish Messenger,* February 26, 1864, *loc. cit.*). They turned over to the Treasurer $3,162.18, listed as from "Jewish Churches," the contributions being chiefly from members of Temple Emanuel, with $82 coming from the Cong. Shaarey Hashomayim on Attorney St. Scanning the Treasurer's Report for contributions made by persons whose names are, or seem to be, Jewish has produced a total of at least $16,000 (*Report of the Treasurer of the Metropolitan Fair* . . . New York, n. d., pp. 4, 12, 13, 19, 20–21, 26, 28, 35, 41, 42, 46, 48, 49, 50, 56, 66, 68, 69, 71). In addition there was a large number of donations of salable materials, ranging from 32 boxes of fancy goods worth $793.28 from Messrs. Schloss & May to a dirk from Samuel Cohen, a Portrait of General Fremont by S. N. Carvalho, a painting of a scene from Falstaff by Jacob H. Lazarus (brother of Moses Lazarus), an "infant's afghan" by Mrs. Isaac Levy and "1 silver coin bearing date 1652" from Moses Solomon (*Spirit of the Fair,* April 5 to 23, 1864, pp. 118, 130, 154, 166, 46, 10).

4. *The Jewish Messenger,* February 26, 1864, *loc. cit.,* March 4, 1864, p. 66, col. 3; *The Jewish Record,* March 18, 1864, p. 2, col. 2; *A Record of the Metropolitan Fair* . . . New York, 1867, pp. 20, 159. In Rochester, N. Y., Sigmund Stettheimer, dry-goods merchant and President of the Hebrew Congregation there, responded to an invitation that "the Hebrew ladies . . . represent the Jewish nationality in the Bazaar" in Rochester, with the explanation that "the only national character in which they wished to appear would be under the Star Spangled Banner" and they would therefore offer their services "individually" and not as a group, but he enclosed a check for $400 presented "in the name of the Jewish Ladies of Rochester" (*The Jewish Record,* January 8, 1864, p. 1, col. 5).

5. The Shaaray Tefila Ladies' Relief Association's founding on May 1, 1861 was reported in *The Jewish Messenger,* May 3, 1861, p. 133; Mrs. Samuel Myer Isaacs, mother of the Myer S. Isaacs writing the letter, was the Treasurer. At Shearith Israel, the Ladies' Army Relief society was also founded in 1861 (*AJHSP,* XXVII, 1920, p. 124; Korn, *American Jewry and the Civil War,* 189ff).

6. Myer Samuel Isaacs (1841–1904), after being graduated from New York University, had been admitted to the bar in 1862. His father, Rev. Samuel Myer Isaacs (1804–1878), had founded *The Jewish Messenger* in 1857, and the young son was now one of the chief editors. Cooperation of Jews with Sanitary Com-

missions was not confined to New York, but was notable also in Chicago, Pittsburgh, Buffalo, Philadelphia, and Cincinnati. (*The Jewish Record,* May 8, December 25, 1863, January 8, 1864; *The Jewish Messenger,* January 15, 1864.)

143. Anti-Semitism in the Ranks

1. This manuscript was generously loaned to me by Mr. Louis Cohen of the Argosy Book Stores, New York, N. Y., but was subsequently purchased by the American Jewish Archives, Cincinnati, O.

2. Benjamin Franklin Butler (1818–1893) of Massachusetts had been the vigorous military governor of New Orleans from May 1 to December 16, 1862, and then was transferred to command the Districts of eastern Virginia and North Carolina. Originally a Democrat, he became during the course of the war a Radical Republican, and later took a prominent part in the effort to impeach President Andrew Johnson. Shortly before he received this letter from Max Glass (on April 21, 1864), Butler had engaged in a correspondence on the nature and merits of the Jewish people with Myer S. Isaacs, who had initiated the exchange of letters by objecting to Butler's having mentioned in a dispatch that several Jews had been caught running the blockade (Texts, dated Feb. 4 to April 9, in *AJHSP,* XXIX, 1925, pp. 117–128). Butler had also been visited by Simon Wolf, to whom he expressed his regret over the incident (*ibid.,* 117n). Perhaps this background made Butler more receptive to Max Glass's complaints about anti-Semitic mistreatment. The Democratic partisan weekly, *The Jewish Record,* abused Butler unrestrainedly throughout this period (February 5, March 11, July 8, 1864 and January 13, 1865), accusing him of keeping Jews in the military prison without charges or trial.

3. The Office of the Adjutant General, in a letter of September 1, 1949, supplied the following data about Max Glass from its files: he was enrolled on August 18, 1863 at Norwich, Conn., as a private in Company H, 8th Regiment Connecticut Infantry. March 28, 1864, he deserted at Deep Creek, Va.; he was arrested and incarcerated in the Hard Labor Prison, Norfolk, Va., on April 1, 1864. He was pardoned and released May 24 and sent back to his regiment on May 26, 1864. At the time of enrolment, his residence is given as East Lyme, Conn. (*Record of Service of Connecticut Men in the Army and Navy of the United States during the War of the Rebellion,* Hartford, 1889, p. 352.) Here he is also listed as having deserted December 2, 1864, although an earlier, and frequently incorrect tabulation, had listed him as mustered out on December 12, 1865, at City Point, Va. (*Catalogue of Connecticut Volunteer Organizations,* Hartford, 1869, p. 387.)

4 While on an ill-timed and insufficiently prepared march designed to liberate Rome from Napoleon III and unite it to Italy, Garibaldi was wounded and his small band and he were taken captive on August 29, 1862 at Aspromonte, the heavily forested mountain in Calabria; popular clamor effected a royal amnesty of Garibaldi on October 5, 1862, exculpating him from the capital charge of treason. (David Larg, *Giuseppe Garibaldi, A Biography,* London, 1934, pp. 309–310.)

5. The Draft Act of March 3, 1863 provided for a commutation fee of $300 or the hiring of substitutes! As a result, in two years, the draft brought into the service 50,000 conscripts and 120,000 substitutes. Glass's account here tallies with the record, which shows he was mustered in as a substitute in Norwich on August 18, six days after he arrived in this country!

6. Brigadier General Charles Adams Heckman had his headquarters near Portsmouth, Va.

7. John A. Rathbun was then First Lieutenant of Company E. Captain Henry M. Hoyt, of Company A, was then commanding the regiment, in the temporary absence of Colonel J. Edward Ward.

8. The system of offering bounties for volunteers induced the enlistment of six times the number of men obtained through conscription, with the localities, states and federal government paying out about $750,000,000 in bounties. However, bounty-brokers began to work a "racket" that encouraged frequent desertion and re-enlistment to secure the bounties.

9. The obverse of the manuscript contains a record of the persons to whom General Butler referred the letter in his investigation: General Heckman, Colonel Ward and Captain Hoyt were asked for their version of the facts. Their replies are not extant, but General Butler's pardon suggests they did not convincingly contradict Max Glass's story.

144. Georgia Recollections

1. Capt. I. Hermann, *Memoirs of a Veteran, Who Served as a Private in the 60's in the War between the States, Personal Incidents, Experiences and Observations,* Atlanta, Ga., 1911, pp. 8, 14, 69–71, 233, 235–236, 248–249.

2. Ella Mitchell, *History of Washington County,* Atlanta, Ga., 1924, pp. 135–136.

3. Hermann, *op. cit.,* 260.

4. The Georgia Confederate Pension and Record Department records his enlistment in Company E, 1st Regiment Georgia Infantry on June 30, 1861, his discharge from that regiment on January 25, 1862, and his re-enlistment May 10, 1862 in Martin's Battery, Georgia Light Artillery, in which he was appointed a Musician. He was wounded at Jackson, Miss., May 14, 1863, admitted to the Macon, Ga., hospital December 17, 1863, and returned to duty on April 23, 1864.

5. The Freedmen's Bureau, created by Congressional action March 3, 1865, operated until June 30, 1872, as an agency of the War Department under General Oliver O. Howard as Commissioner. It helped the 4,000,000 freed Negroes in many ways, establishing schools and hospitals, trying to provide jobs and homesteads, furnishing food and clothing, and in general seeking to protect the civil rights of the freedmen from being rendered null by both the terror and deception of the southern ruling classes.

6. The terroristic Ku Klux Klan was organized early in 1866 and spread rapidly. The "normalcy" it re-established has plagued the South and the remainder of the country ever since.

7. The firm of Einstein & Eckman, consisting of Abraham Einstein and S. H. Eckman, had been established in Savannah since 1845, and continued there after the war (F. D. Lee and J. L. Agnew, *Historical Record of the City of Savannah,* Savannah, 1869, p. 16 of Advertisements). The *Savannah City Directory for 1867* also lists, in addition to the drygoods firm of Einstein & Eckman, a boot and shoe mercantile house, Einstein, Eckman & Co.

8. The war having been won and slavery disestablished, the northern capitalists and merchants eagerly went south to open up new markets to capitalist enterprise. The identity of this Mr. Cohen of New York is undefinable any further, the city directories of Augusta for 1865–1866 listing no fewer than ten Cohens, while the directory for 1867 lists six (*Pughe's City Directory,* 1865/66, p. 14;

Calvin's *Augusta and Business Directory,* 1865/66, p. 14; *Pughe's Directory for the City of Augusta and Vicinity,* 1867, p. 15–16).

145. On the Assassination of Lincoln

1. *The Israelite,* XI, No. 45, May 5, 1865, pp. 356–357. The text is also reproduced with minor errors in David Philipson, *Max Lilienthal, American Rabbi, Life and Writings,* New York, 1915, pp. 415–429 and in Emanuel Hertz, ed., *Abraham Lincoln, The Tribute of the Synagogue,* New York, 1927, pp. 110–121. Both editors assign the date as April 22, 1865, but the date of April 19 is given in *The Israelite,* April 21, 1865, p. 341, col. 3, and April 28, 1865, p. 348, where it is noted that the text is taken from the *Cincinnati Commercial* of April 20, 1865.

   Lilienthal's reputation for abolitionism having reached New Orleans, Jacob A. Cohen of that city demonstratively removed a portrait of Lilienthal from a wall in his home, and wrote a letter to Lilienthal explaining that he "should be happy to rid Israel of the disgrace of your life" (Sophie Lilienthal, *The Lilienthal Family Record,* San Francisco, 1930, p. 57). Cohen was killed in action in the Confederate army at Manassas, August 30, 1862 (Wolf, *op. cit.,* 191).
2. A representative but not complete collection is to be found in Hertz, *op. cit.*
3. Shortly after this the Republican *Cincinnati Commercial* wrote an editorial accepting as in good faith the expressions of mourning of Copperhead and Democratic organs, but added, "Let us take care neither to gush with forgiveness for rebels before they have repented and done works meet for repentance, nor to involve the innocent with the guilty in the punishment of crimes." (Cited in Carl Sandburg, *Abraham Lincoln, The War Years,* New York, 1939, IV, 409–410.)
4. Brickner, *op. cit.,* 351. Dr. Lilienthal had come to New York from Munich, his birthplace, in November, 1845.
5. Booth, after shooting Lincoln in the back of the head, dropped the pistol, pulled a knife, slashed the arm of a restraining army officer, jumped from the box to the stage, breaking his leg, rose, brandished his knife, shouted "sic semper tyrannis!" and fled.
6. On December 8, 1863, Lincoln had proclaimed that, with certain exceptions, he would pardon all Confederate soldiers who would swear allegiance to the Union. In his speech on April 11, 1865, Lincoln had appealed for restoration of the seceded states to the Union without the general enfranchisement of the Negro people. (Sandburg, *op. cit.,* IV, 220–224.)
7. This description of Lincoln's personality may be based in part on Lilienthal's own contact with him when Lilienthal was on the delegation that went from Cincinnati to Washington in connection with the revocation of Grant's Order No. 11 (see Index).
8. The last sentence of Lincoln's Second Inaugural Address, March 4, 1865, contained the famous words, "With malice toward none, with charity for all, let us strive on to finish the work we are in . . ."
9. John Hampden (1594–1643) had helped spark the English revolution by his resistance to the imposition of the ship money tax.
10. In 1860, Lincoln had won as a minority candidate in a three-cornered race, but in 1864 he had a popular majority of over 400,000 and obtained the electoral college votes of all the states in the Union except Kentucky, Delaware, and New Jersey.

11. Robert Ould (1820–1881), formerly District of Columbia prosecuting attorney in Buchanan's administration, had seceded with Virginia, had been appointed assistant secretary of war by Davis, and in 1862 became Confederate Commissioner for the exchange of prisoners. (*The National Cyclopaedia of American Biography,* New York, 1926, XIX, 275.)

12. On February 23, 1861 Lincoln passed through Baltimore, Md. in a special car late at night, having been informed from various sources that there would be an attempt to assassinate him the following afternoon if he stopped in Baltimore as announced.

13. On Lincoln's advice that the surrender terms be as "honorable" as possible, Grant had generously allowed the officers of Lee's surrendered Army of Northern Virginia to retain their side arms and to return immediately to their homes without imprisonment; privates, however, were disarmed entirely, although cavalry and artillery-men who owned their own horses were permitted to take them home for the ploughing.

14. Andrew Johnson (1808–1875) of Tennessee, Vice-President, had been sworn in as President within a couple of hours after Lincoln expired. On March 4, 1865, when Johnson had taken the oath of office as Vice-President, he marred the occasion by a superfluous and belligerent speech in which "he ranted, bellowed, and shook his fists." The cause of this behavior was that Johnson, weakened from a siege of typhoid and exhausted by the arduous election campaign, had come to Washington to be sworn in only at Lincoln's insistence, and, feeling it necessary to fortify himself with whiskey, he had lost his sense of tact. Enemies of the administration were still making much of this slip when he became, suddenly, President. (Sandburg, *op. cit.,* IV, 88–91; St. George L. Sioussat, *DAB,* X, 84.)

146. Workers, Jew and Gentile

1. John R. Commons and Associates, editors, *A Documentary History of American Industrial Society,* Cleveland, 1910, IX, 158–159. Drafted by Cameron, the text was also signed by the other members of his Committee: Thomas A. Armstrong, a printer from Pittsburgh, Pa., William B. Iles of the Iron Moulders' Union of Augusta and Savannah, Ga., Gilman Rand of the Bookbinders' Union, Boston, Mass., and J. R. Bolan of the Ship Carpenters' Union in Boston (*ibid.,* 168, 128).

2. Philip S. Foner, *History of the Labor Movement in the United States,* New York, 1947, pp. 371–372; Charlotte Todes, *William H. Sylvis and the National Labor Union,* New York, 1942, pp. 59f; John R. Commons and Associates, *History of Labour in the United States,* New York, 1918, II, 110–113. None of the delegates to the National Labor Congress of 1866 was Jewish, nor have any of the delegates to subsequent conventions of the National Labor Union, which lasted only until 1872, been identified as Jewish.

   In *The Israelite,* August 7, 1868, p. 6, col. 2, there was a cordial paragraph calling attention to Cameron's labor weekly, *Working Man's Advocate,* published in Chicago, and wishing him "success."

147. Excluding Jews from Insurance

1. The *Sunday Dispatch* was published by [John] Lawlor, [Robert] Everett. & [Elias J.] Hincken.

2. *Banking and Insurance Chronicle,* Chicago, March 7, 1867, p. 74. This trade weekly, which was vigorous and consistent in its defense of the rights of Jews

to equal insurance treatment, was owned and edited by John J. W. O'Donoghue. *The Jewish Messenger,* May 17, 1867, p. 4, col. 2, summed up the reason for the anti-Semitic attack thus: "The losses by country risks had been unusually severe, and the Directors of the Companies, to justify themselves with their stockholders, were compelled to make some class of insurers the scapegoats, and they hit upon the Jews. It is now a fact that the 'Underwriters' Agency' will not issue a policy to Jew or Gentile covering a 'Southern risk.' The country business of these and other companies has been greatly curtailed."

3. *Banking and Insurance Chronicle, loc. cit.*

4. The attention of *The Israelite* to the "Special Circular" was called by a communication signed by fifteen Jewish merchants of Port Gibson, Miss., dated February 5, 1867, and published February 22. The circular had been sent out on October 20, 1866.

5. Advertisement in *The Insurance Monitor,* March, 1867, p. 137. These four companies were among the ten largest in New York. (Reports on their income for the year, *Banking and Insurance Chronicle,* June 20, 1867, p. 194, col. 4.)

6. For notice of action in these cities, see Brickner, *op. cit.,* 317; *The Israelite,* February 8, April 5, 12, 19, May 3, 17, 31, 1867; *The Hebrew Leader,* New York, April 19, May 3, 17, 31, 1867; *The Jewish Messenger,* May 31, 1867. When the Board of American Delegates met on May 24, 1867, it decided no further action was necessary (*ibid.,* June 6, 1867).

7. Suggestions for a Jewish insurance company were made in *ibid.,* March 8, 22, May 3, 1867; the *New-York Tribune,* March 19, 1867; *The Hebrew Leader,* April 19, 1867. Proposals for boycott and cancellations appeared in *The Jewish Messenger,* March 8, 15, 29, April 5, May 3, 1867; *The Hebrew Leader,* March 8, April 19, May 31, 1867; *The Israelite,* February 22, April 5, 12, 19, 1867. It is noteworthy that among the hundreds of directors of fire insurance companies in New York, only two Jews have been identified: Barrow Benrimo, one of thirty Directors of the Astor Fire Insurance Company (*The Insurance Monitor,* March, 1867, p. 187), and William Seligman, one of forty-six Directors of the Importers and Traders Insurance Company (*Ibid.,* February, 1867, p. 66). Jonas N. Phillips was also the Surveyor for the Astor company, (*The Hebrew Leader,* October 12, 1866). Both companies were among the smaller ones in New York. Later, and perhaps because of the public discussion, the Mechanics' and Traders' Fire Insurance Company added to its Board of Directors "Gottlieb Rosenblatt, Esq., who is already an officer of prominent financial institutions" (*The Jewish Messenger,* June 21, 1867, p. 4, col. 3).

8. For notice of support for the anti-Semitic position, see *ibid.,* March 22, April 19, 1867; New York *Herald,* April 9, 17, 1867; *The Nation,* May 23, 1867; *The Insurance Monitor,* March, April, May, 1867; *The New York Times,* May 27, 1867. For opposition, see *The Jewish Messenger,* March 22, 29, May 3, 1867, *New-York Tribune,* March 19, 1867; *The Israelite,* April 26, 1867, the Philadelphia *Evening Telegraph,* March 26, 1867; *Banking and Insurance Chronicle,* March 28, April 17, May 2, June 6, 1867.

9. *Merry and Wise,* reproduced in *The Insurance Monitor,* May, 1867, p. 293.

10. This preliminary meeting was held March 11, 1867. The circular to the insurance companies was dated March 18, and was signed by Benjamin Nathan (stock broker), chairman, Samuel A. Lewis, secretary, B. L. Solomon (importer), Isaac Bernheimer (clothing manufacturer), S. De Cordova (merchant), Lewis May (milliner), William Seligman (clothing merchant and banker), Emanuel B. Hart (stock broker), Lewis Stix (dry goods), S. M. Cohen (dry

goods), B. F. Peixotto (cloths), Alfred Tobias, J. S. Abecasis (stock broker) and Joseph Fatman (tobacco merchant) (*The Israelite,* April 5, 1867, p. 39, col. 1; text in *The Hebrew Leader,* March 29, 1867, p. 4, col. 3 and in *The Insurance Monitor,* April, 1867, p. 225; *Trow's New York City Directory,* 1866–67). At least the following Congregations were represented on this Committee: Beth Cholim (Nathan and Lewis), Shaarai Tephila (Solomon), Temple Emanuel (May), Shearith Israel (Abecasis) and B'nai Jeshurun (Fatman).

11. The Home and Metropolitan companies were then the insurance giants in New York. Texts of their replies are in *The Insurance Monitor,* April, 1867, p. 225; both companies maintained they did not discriminate, but went on to argue that Jews, especially of German origin, had been bad risks for fifteen years. The letter from the first company was particularly offensive in tone. They were sent to all the newspapers that published the resolutions of the meeting of Jews.

12. The meeting was held April 15, 1867 in the synagogue of the Congregation Shearith Israel, and was attended by leaders of "our various Congregations" (*The Hebrew Leader,* April 19, 1867, p. 4, col. 4). The Directory lists 26 congregations for that year.

13. The Peter Cooper Fire Insurance Company on April 17 wrote to *The Jewish Messenger* explaining it had not received the circular of the Jewish committee and declaring that "*Integrity,* and not Religion or Nationality" is its only criterion in judging insurance risks. (April 19, 1867, p. 7, col. 4.)

14. *The Jewish Messenger* considered these resolutions as disappointing and unsatisfactory and assured Jews in other parts of the country that it would continue to advocate a boycott of the Underwriters' Agency and other companies whose "explanations" did not correspond to their discriminatory practice (*ibid.*). *The Hebrew Leader,* describing the four hour meeting, indicated that there was considerable sentiment for stronger resolutions, but amendments were defeated, "many fearing to incur the hostility of these powerful companies" (April 19, 1867, p. 4, cols. 4–5). The failure to mention the companies of the Underwriters' Agency is conspicuous.

15. Morris Jacob Raphall's *Post-Biblical History of the Jews* was published in two volumes in Philadelphia by Moss & Brother in 1855, and reprinted in 1866 in New York by D. Appleton and Co.

16. One such testimonial was given by Mayor Mayo of Richmond, Va. at a local meeting on the subject. Himself in the insurance business, he declared that "He had had most of his dealings with the Jewish people, and could bear testimony to the uprightness and honesty of their conduct." (*Banking and Insurance Chronicle,* April 17, 1867, pp. 114–115.)

17. The outcome of the public discussion was indefinite, although undoubtedly the affirmation by part of the press of sound democratic principles was healthful. Stoddart's own "defense" was extraordinary. In a letter published in the New York *Herald,* March 23, 1867 (after it had been refused publication in the *Tribune*), he first attempted to explain the term "Jew Risks" as applying to unstable, itinerant peddlers and small merchants of all nationalities and religons! But then he insisted that "the truth of the matter is that the Jews, as a class, have blistered and swindled the Insurance Companies most unmercifully, and doubtless will continue to do so, as long as unrestricted insurance is granted them." Then he cited the Instructions to Agents, some of them dating back to 1852, of the Aetna, Merchants', City Fire and Phoenix companies of Hartford, and the North American and International companies of New York

as justification for his own anti-Semitic instructions. A challenge by the *Banking and Insurance Chronicle* of Chicago on May 2, 1867 that it would gladly publish any figures that would *prove* that Jews as a whole were bad risks of course was never taken up. In reporting cases of arson, this periodical selected instances of both Jewish and non-Jewish arsonists, while *The Insurance Monitor* concentrated exclusively on a couple of cases of Jewish arsonists.

148. Double-Lynching of a Jew and a Negro

1. *The Israelite,* XV, No. 8, August 28, 1868, p. 6, cols. 2–3. No mention of this incident was made in *The Jewish Messenger, The Hebrew Leader,* or *The Occident.*
2. James Welch Patton, *Unionism and Reconstruction in Tennessee, 1860–1869,* Chapel Hill, N. C., 1934, pp. 162–163, 171ff.
3. The name also appears variously as Bierstein, Bearfield, and Bierfeld, but it is given fully as S. A. Bierfield in the *New-York Daily Tribune,* August 19, 1868, p. 4, col. 6 and in the official report of the investigation made by George E. Judd, sub-assistant commissioner, stationed in Pulaski, Tenn., of the Freedmen's Bureau, to Brevet Major-General W. P. Carlin (*Senate Journal of the Extra Session of the Thirty-Fifth General Assembly of the State of Tennessee, . . .* Nashville, 1868, pp. 158–160). This report is especially valuable because it incorporates the eye-witness testimony of Henry Morton. Essentially similar accounts, with variations only in details, appeared in the *Tribune,* August 20, 1868, and in *The New-York Times,* August 19, 1868. The *Tribune,* August 28, 1868, reprinted an item from the *Memphis Post* which mentioned the murder of Bierfield as one of many terroristic acts of southern Democrats.
4. The official report stated "that Mr. Bierfield was an uncommon good business man . . . and was establishing an unprecedented trade." (*Loc. cit.,* 160.) His friendliness toward the Negro was undoubtedly a factor in this success. Anti-Negro·southerners then and to this day resented this democratic approach. Thus Professor E. Merton Coulter says of the Jews in the Reconstruction period, "Sticking to their business and treating the freedman as an important businessman, not eschewing to call him 'Mister,' they secured . . . a great amount of the Negro's trade." (*The South During Reconstruction, 1865–1877,* Louisiana State University, 1947, p. 202.)
5. President Andrew Johnson's weak reconstruction policy, for which he barely later escaped impeachment by one vote, required nothing more of the seceded states than the ratification of the Fourteenth Amendment and the taking of the oath of allegiance to the Union. Tennessee, however, under Radical Republican leadership, had gone further and enfranchised the Negroes. It should be noted that after Union forces occupied most of Tennessee in 1862, eight Negro regiments of soldiers had been raised in that state. (W. E. Burghardt Du Bois, *Black Reconstruction,* New York, 1935, pp. 572, 575; James S. Allen, *Reconstruction, The Battle for Democracy, 1865–1876,* New York, 1937, pp. 40–42.)
6. Late in August, a young man named Ezell had taken part in the kidnaping of a Negro from a Franklin jail and in lynching him, presumably on the charge of "rape." A few days later, Negroes had shot Ezell. Bierfield, it was claimed, had encouraged the Negroes and even sold them ammunition. (*New-York Daily Tribune,* August 20, 1868.) But the official report by Judd found that a letter published in a Nashville newspaper that was the basis of the allegation had been forged (*loc. cit.,* 159).
7. The *Nashville Daily Press and Times* was a Republican newspaper.

8. The official report states that Bierfield, after shouting that he surrendered, made a break for the stable as soon as he was confronted with the mob; he was then caught, "tortured," and shot with the pistol so close that his clothes and skin were burned. Bowman, the Negro clerk, told the doctor before he died that he had been shot in the street. The investigator complains that the civic authorities made no attempt to get further details from Bowman before he became unconscious. (*Ibid.*)
9. Pulaski, Tenn., fifty miles south of Franklin, was the city in which the Ku Klux Klan had first been organized.
10. Nashville, less than twenty miles from Franklin, was the nearest city that had a Jewish congregation (formed the same year by the merger of two congregations, one Orthodox, the other Reform).

149. "The Jews Have It"

1. *The Jewish Messenger,* XXV, No. 10, March 5, 1869, Supplement. *The Los Angeles Daily News,* published by A. J. King and R. H. Offutt, with the former as editor, had become a daily on January 1, 1869, after some eight years as a semi-weekly and tri-weekly. It supported the Democratic Party. (J. M. Guinn, *A History of California and an Extended History of Los Angeles and Environs,* Los Angeles, 1915, Vol. I, p. 410.)
2. It is interesting that this non-Jewish journalist recognizes the harm being done by the stereotypes in *The Merchant of Venice, Ivanhoe,* and *Oliver Twist.* The production in England in 1948 of a film based on *Oliver Twist* provoked international protest in Europe and the Western Hemisphere, and the film was not shown in several countries, including the United States. For an attempt to assess the meaning and influence of such stereotypes, see Montagu Frank Modder, *The Jew in the Literature of England,* Philadelphia, 1939. Modder and others tend to discount the ill effects of Scott's portrayal of Isaac of York (*ibid.,* 138; M. J. Woddis, "Sir Walter Scott and the Jews," *Views,* London, June, 1932, p. 220).
3. Joseph Newmark (1799–1881) had come to this country from West Prussia in 1824, had lived in Somerset, Conn., New York, St. Louis, Dubuque, Iowa, and San Francisco before settling in Los Angeles in 1854 with his wife and six children, all of them born in New York. By 1869, the four daughters were married: Matilda (d. 1907) to Maurice Kremer (1824–1907), a merchant and Democratic politician who had been County Treasurer from 1860 to 1865, on the Board of Supervisors from 1865 to 1867, on the Board of Education from 1866, and was then beginning to serve as Clerk of the City Council (1869–1875); Sarah (1841–1910) to Harris Newmark (1834–1916), who in 1865, hearing a threat by a business man "to drive every Jew in Los Angeles out of business," had challengingly established H. Newmark & Co., wholesale grocers, which in 1915 was still called the "oldest important business house" in Los Angeles; Caroline (d. 1920) to Solomon Lazard (1826–1916), who in 1867 had built one of Los Angeles' first brick stores, known as the "City of Paris"; and Harriet (d. 1922) to Eugene Meyer (c. 1843–1925), in 1867 the partner of Solomon Lazard in a dry-goods firm. The successful marriages of Newmark's daughters appear to have been of continual interest to the Los Angeles press, for when Joseph Newmark died, the obituaries in the *Los Angeles Herald* (October 20, 1881) and *Los Angeles Express* (October 19, 1881) both noted that they were married to "some of our most enterprising citizens" and "to prominent business men of this city." (Harris Newmark, *Sixty Years in Southern California, 1853–*

1913, Boston and New York, 3d ed., 1930, pp. 121–122, 666–667, 191, 224, 290, 347, 504, 636, 660, 661; J. M. Guinn, *Historical and Biographical Record of Los Angeles and Vicinity,* Chicago, 1901, pp. 876, 796–797, 290, 659; Martin A. Meyer, *Western Jewry,* San Francisco, 1916, pp. 62, 130.)

4. The paragraph that follows is an editorial comment by the editor of *The Jewish Messenger.*

150. Separating Religion from Public Schools

1. *The Bible in the Public Schools. Arguments in the Case of John D. Minor et al. Versus The Board of Education of the City of Cincinnati et al. Superior Court of Cincinnati. With the Opinions and Decision of the Court.* Cincinnati, 1870, pp. 12–15. Harper's wished to publish this volume in New York, for the case had aroused national attention, but Robert Clarke & Co. of Cincinnati beat that firm to the arrangements (Max Lilienthal, letter to *The Jewish Times,* New York, December 17, 1869, quoted in David Philipson, *Max Lilienthal, American Rabbi, Life and Writings,* New York, 1915, p. 487). The bibliography of materials on the question of the Bible in the schools is tremendous. Helpful are the following: *Why the Bible Should Not Be Read in the Public Schools,* published by the Committee on Church and State, Central Conference of American Rabbis, 1906 (pamphlet); similar pamphlet, of the same title by the same body, 1922; Max J. Kohler, *The Illegality of Bible-Reading in New York City's Public Schools,* New York, 1930; Alvin W. Johnson, *The Legal Status of Church-State Relationships in the United States with Special Reference to the Public Schools,* Minneapolis, 1934; V. T. Thayer, *Religion in Public Education,* New York, 1947; Nathan Schachner, "Church, State and Education," *American Jewish Year Book,* Vol. 49, 1947–1948; William George Torpey, *Judicial Doctrines of Religious Rights in America,* Chapel Hill, 1948; William Addison Blakely, *American State Papers and Related Documents on Freedom in Religion,* 4th rev. ed., Washington, D. C., R. Freeman Butts, *The American Tradition in Religion and Education,* Boston, 1950; Anson Phelps Stokes, *Church and State in the United States,* 3 vols., New York, 1950.

2. Johnson, *op. cit.*, 25, 300, 301; Schachner, *op. cit.*, 22; Torpey, *op. cit.*, 244.

3. *The Bible in the Public Schools. Proceedings and Addresses at the Mass Meeting, Pike's Music Hall, Cincinnati . . . September 28, 1869,* Cincinnati, 1869, p. 1; Lilienthal, *loc. cit.*, 475.

4. *Proceedings . . . Pike's Music Hall,* 2–8.

5. Edgar M. Johnson (1836–1893) had been on the Board of Education since 1867. It is reported that the Board's decision was reached and the case successfully prosecuted, "largely through his efforts" (Fabian Linden, "Johnson," *UJE,* VI, 170). Johnson was then a member of the law firm, Hoadly, Jackson & Johnson, of which the senior member, George Hoadly (1826–1902), was one of the three lawyers retained by the Board as its counsel; Johnson may therefore have had a good deal to do with the briefs and the argument made by Hoadly.

   Henry Mack (1820–1896) had served in the Cincinnati City Council from 1860 to 1862 and had been a member of the Governor's Military Commission during the Civil War. He served on the Board of Education for fourteen years and later was elected to the State Assembly and Senate. He was also a founder of the Talmid Yelodim Institute. (Charles Theodore Greve, *Centennial History of Cincinnati and Representative Citizens,* Chicago, 1904, II, 232–233.)

   Although Johnson and Mack divided on the issue, the Cincinnati Jewish community in general, and *The Israelite* and Isaac Mayer Wise and Max

Lilienthal in particular, supported the stand of the majority of the Board against the reading of the Bible in the schools (Max B. May, *Isaac Mayer Wise,* New York, 1916, pp. 247–248; Philipson, *op. cit.,* 120–123). Lilienthal had been on the Board of Education, 1866–1867.

6. From *Williams' Cincinnati Directories* for 1866 and 1867, the following are the occupations of the members of the Board: J. H. Brunsman, flour dealer and commission merchant; Joseph P. Carbery, grocer; Herman Eckel, drugs; J. W. B. Kelley, china; Joseph Kramer, tailor; Samuel A. Miller (who made the historic motion), attorney; William J. O'Neil, book-keeper; Henry W. Poor, wholesale grocer and commission merchant; F. W. Rauch, cordial manufacturer; Benjamin J. Ricking, wholesale grocer and liquor dealer; H. P. Seibel, book-keeper; John P. Story, clerk; George D. Temple, insurance agent; A. Theurkauf, foreign books and stationery; Thomas Vickers, minister of the First Congregational (Unitarian) Church; Stephen Wagner, importer and wholesale dealer in fancy goods, toys and French china; Henry L. Wehmer, clerk; John F. Wisnewski, chemist; Bruckner, Macke, Mullaney, and Sweeney are not otherwise identifiable. John D. Minor, the chief Plaintiff, was a wholesale grocer and commission merchant. In the public discussions in the interval while the case was on appeal, Rev. Thomas Vickers was one of the leaders in the debate; see his three addresses, *The Bible in the Public Schools,* in debate against Rev. A. D. Mayo (a member of the minority on the Board), published in New York, May, 1870; also Vickers' controversy with Archbishop J. B. Purcell, *The Roman Catholic Church and Free Thought,* Cincinnati, 1868. Vickers was minister of his Church in Cincinati from 1867 to 1874; the Judge, Alphonso Taft, whose dissenting opinion was later upheld by the Supreme Court, was a member of Vickers' congregation (George Augustine Thayer, *The First Congregational Church of Cincinnati, Unitarian, A History,* Cincinnati, 1947, pp. 34–35.)

7. The first resolution prohibited religious instruction and the reading of religious books, including the Bible, in the public schools; the second repealed a regulation, adopted in 1852, requiring that each school day begin with a reading from the Bible and the singing of hymns. As far back as 1855, *The Israelite* had expressed its disapproval of this regulation (Barnett R. Brickner, *The Jewish Community of Cincinnati . . . 1817–1933,* unpublished dissertation, University of Cincinnati, 1933, p. 307).

8. The Plaintiffs declared that in 1842 the Board had voted that no pupil be required to read or hear reading from the King James version if the parent or guardian objected. This action was supposed to have been taken on the initiative of the Archbishop (Henry A. Ford and Kate B. Ford, *History of Cincinnati, Ohio,* Cincinnati, 1881, p. 191).

9. George Hoadly later became Governor of Ohio; he had already been a judge of the Superior Court of Cincinnati, 1851–1855, 1859–1864, and City Solicitor, 1855 to 1859; he leaned towards Unitarianism. The firm of Stanley and Samuel R. Matthews was headed by Stanley Matthews (1824–1889), who had served on the Superior Court bench from 1863 to 1865, and was to be a justice of the United States Supreme Court from 1881 to 1889. Known as "a devout churchmember," Matthews was held in reserve to make the last argument for the Defendants, and he held the court "entranced" for seven hours, according to Lilienthal (*loc. cit.,* 482). Johann Bernhard Stallo (1823–1900) headed the firm of Stallo and [E. W.] Kittredge.

10. *The Bible in the Schools, loc. cit.,* 70–73. Stallo was not only a lawyer, but a student of and a writer on the philosophy of science, particularly physics, in which his theories anticipated Ernst Mach's. Born in Germany, he had come

to Cincinnati in 1839, had taught in a Catholic school there, and had studied at St. Xavier's College. From 1844 to 1847, he had been professor of physics and chemistry at St. John's College at Fordham, New York. After being admitted to the bar in Cincinnati in 1849, he served on the bench of the Court of Common Pleas of Hamilton County (Cincinnati) from 1853 to 1855. This was one of his most famous cases. (Adolf Edward Zucker, *DAB,* XVII, 496–497.) In January, 1857, Stallo had been the examiner in German at the public examination of the pupils of the Jewish schools (Brickner, *op. cit.,* 141–142). His former connections with Catholic institutions as student and teacher made his advocacy of complete separation of church and state particularly effective. Lilienthal called Stallo's five hour address "an intellectual treat, indeed" and recommended the pamphlet form of it (*loc. cit.,* 479).

11. *The Jewish Record,* New York, December 9 and 23, 1864, February 3 and April 7, 1865; Sidney Warren, *American Freethought, 1860–1914,* New York, 1943, pp. 173, 176.

12. Tertullian (160?–230?): "At every forward step and movement, at every going in and out, when we put on our clothes and shoes, when we bathe, when we sit at table, when we light the lamps, on couch, on seat, in all the ordinary actions of daily life, we trace upon the forehead the sign (of the cross)." *The Writings of Quintus Sept. Flor. Tertullianus,* translated by Rev. S. Thelwall, Edinburgh, 1869, I, 336.

    Cyril (c. 315–386): "But make thou this Sign, when thou eatest and drinkest. sittest or liest down, risest up, speakest, walkest: in a word, on every occasion . . ." *The Catechetical Lectures of S. Cyril, Archibshop of Jerusalem,* translated by R. W. Church, Oxford, 1838, p. 40.

13. Albert Jacob Cardozo (1828–1885), after being elected to the New York Court of Common Pleas in 1863 on the Tammany ticket, was in 1867 elected to the bench of the State Supreme Court. As a Tammany sachem, he was soon to be involved in the Boss Tweed scandals, and on May 1, 1872, when the New York City Bar Association recommended to the State Assembly that Cardozo be impeached, he resigned.

14. Jacob Wolf of Cincinnati sat in the House of Representatives of Ohio in the 58th General Assembly (*Journal of the House of Representatives of the State of Ohio,* 1868/69, Vol. 65). In 1860, Joseph Jonas had served in the same House.

15. On June 30, 1869, the Superior Court had appointed Philip Heidelbach (of Heidelbach, Seasongood & Co., wholesale clothiers and dealers in dry goods) one of five trustees of the Cincinnati Southern Railway, which was planned to run 338 miles from Cincinnati to Chattanooga (Charles G. Hall, *The Cincinnati Southern Railway, A History,* Cincinnati, 1902, p. 36).

16. Joseph Story, *Commentaries on the Constitution of the United States,* first published in 1833, was in its third edition in 1858. Story had been cited by the counsel for the Plaintiff who preceded Stallo in the argument, to the effect that the constitutional provision against a religious establishment was designed merely to "exclude all rivalry among Christian sects" and not to give non-Christian groups equal rights (*The Bible in the Schools, loc. cit.,* 44–45). In the case of Bloom v. Richards, determined in 1853 and cited by Stallo, the Ohio Supreme Court had ruled unanimously that the making of a contract on Sunday is not prohibited by Ohio law. Judge Allen G. Thurman wrote the decision.

17. *The Bible in the Public Schools, loc. cit.,* 390–391, 410–411, 414–417. This opinion

was quoted in 1902 by a Nebraska court, and in 1918 by the Iowa Supreme Court (Johnson, *op. cit.*, 71, 163).

18. Greve, *op. cit.*, 92; *History of Cincinnati and Hamilton County, Ohio . . .* Cincinnati, 1894, p. 106; George Irving Reed, ed., *Bench and Bar of Ohio*, Chicago, 1897, I, 114.

19. Lewis Alexander Leonard, *Life of Alphonso Taft*, New York, 1920, p. 128; George Mortimer Roe, ed., *Cincinnati: The Queen City of the West*, Cincinnati, 1895, pp. 365–366; *Williams' Cincinnati Directory*, 1866, p. 50.

20. John Baptist Purcell (1800–1883), Archbishop of Cincinnati, had in a Pastoral Letter in 1861 declared that the system of common schools, "if carried out according to its alleged intent of abstaining from any definite religious instruction is well calculated to raise up a generation of religious indifferentists, if not of practical infidels," and had then asked for a share of public tax funds for the Catholic parochial schools. (John H. Lamott, *History of the Archdiocese of Cincinnati, 1821–1921*, New York and Cincinnati, 1921, pp. 267–277.) On September 18, 1869, in reply to the invitation by the Board of Education to unite the Catholic parochial schools with the public schools, Archbishop Purcell asserted that "The entire government of public schools in which Catholic youth are educated can not be given over to the civil power.

"We, as Catholics, can not approve of that system of education for youth which is apart from instruction in the Catholic faith and the teaching of the Church." (*Proceedings . . . Pike's Music Hall.* 6.) That this was the official but perhaps not his personal view is suggested by the Archbishop's promise to the Board Committee that consulted him on the subject that he would attempt, when next in Rome, to obtain a modification of the rule that would enable Catholic pupils to attend the public schools. (*Ibid.*, 5.) The *DAB*, XV, 266–267, gives other instances of such divergence on his part, although he always practised the official policy.

21. Roger Williams' well-known parable of the ship was part of a letter written in January, 1655. Judge Taft seems to be straining his interpretation of this passage, for Williams was not here limiting freedom of conscience, but rather explaining to the Town of Providence, R. I., that his views on freedom of conscience were not destructive of civil peace, and that his doctrine of freedom of conscience could not be used to permit the individual to subordinate the rights of society to his own rights or to flout the civil law. (Full texts of the letter in Oscar S. Straus, *Roger Williams, The Pioneer of Religious Liberty*, New York, 1894 ed. reprinted, 1936, p. 110; Emily Easton, *Roger Williams, Prophet and Pioneer*, New York, 1930 pp. 318–319; the same interpretation is given by Samuel Hugh Brockunier, *The Irrepressible Democrat, Roger Williams*, New York, 1940, p. 226.)

22. Thomas McIntyre Cooley (1824–1898), *A Treatise on the Constitutional Limitations which Rest upon the Legislative Power of the States of the American Union*, went into its eighth edition in 1927; the passage quoted is on pp. 468–469 of the second edition, 1871.

23. *Reports of Cases Argued and Determined in the Supreme Court of Ohio*, Cincinnati, 1874 (23 Ohio State Reports), pp. 245–247. The decision was rendered on an unspecified date after April 29, 1873. The five judges were John Welch, who wrote the opinion, William White, Luther Day, George W. McIlvaine, and Walter F. Stone.

24. Johnson, *op. cit.*, 60, 28–29.

In 1949, Bible-reading was required in 12 states, permitted in 26, and prohibited in 8 (National Education Association, *The Status of Religious Education in the Public Schools,* Washington, D.C., 1949, p. 23).

151. Aid to Russian Refugees

1. *New York Herald,* May 2, 1870, p. 8, col. 5. This newspaper had already expressed its approval of Russian-Jewish immigration in its editorial, September 27, 1869, entitled "Hebrew Immigration," which closed with these sentences, "Let our rich Israelites bring their oppressed brethren to this new land of promise. Here at least, they will be free men, and milk and honey will not be found wholly wanting." (Full text quoted in Mark Wischnitzer, *To Dwell in Safety,* Philadelphia, 1949, p. 31.)

2. *The Jewish Times,* New York, April 15, 1870, p. 101. It is also reported that approximately another hundred refugees had already come over between December 21, 1869 and February 13, 1870 (Zoza Szajkowski, *Jewish Social Studies,* IV, 1942, p. 159). *The Jewish Record,* July 21, 1865, p. 2, col. 4, noted that "during the last two weeks over 500 Israelites have landed in New York. They are mostly from Kalvarhie, Lithuania, and, as a matter of course, in indigent circumstances." On August 11, 1865, this weekly returned to the subject and proposed that Polish Jews in New York form a society to aid such newcomers. A similar proposal for an emigrant aid society appeared in *The Hebrew Leader,* March 8, 1867, p. 4, cols. 2–3, in an editorial, "The Condition of Jewish Immigrants."

3. Wischnitzer, *op. cit.,* 29.

4. Letter from the Alliance Israélite Universelle, Paris, December 27, 1869, addressed to Benjamin F. Peixotto, former head of the B'nai B'rith, *The Israelite,* February 11, 1870, p. 7.

5. Final Report of the Board of Delegates, December, 1878, Max J. Kohler, *AJHSP,* XXIX (1925), 101. The Board collected almost $7,000, partly from non-Jews, at first for relief abroad, but then for use to aid those who arrived in New York. For opposition to this immigration, see *The Jewish Messenger,* editorials, January 7 and 14, 1870 and *The Hebrew Leader,* editorials, March 25 and May 6, 1870.

6. Report of the New York City Commissioners of Emigration, *The New-York Times,* April 28, 1870, p. 5, col. 2.

7. That same day an informal meeting of representatives of the Board of Delegates and of the Hebrew Benevolent Society had set up the committee which issued this circular, together with an appeal to the public to provide jobs for coppersmiths, tailors, carpenters, bakers, and domestic workers among the immigrants, but with provision that they can observe the Sabbath. (*The Hebrew Leader,* April 29, 1870, p. 4, col. 4; Wischnitzer, *op. cit.,* 33.)

8. These "urgent remonstrances" of the Board of Delegates were supported editorially in *The Jewish Messenger,* October 15 and 29, 1869 and January 7 and April 29, 1870; *The Hebrew Leader,* April 15, 1870; *The Jewish Times,* March 18 and 25, 1870 (but on April 22, 1870, with the arrival imminent, there was more of a tone of welcome and a promise of aid). *The Israelite,* February 18, 1870, p. 10, col. 4, urged the Polish and Russian Jews already here to organize an "Aid Association," and declared "if they do nothing, we cannot co-operate." Finally, on June 8, 1870, the Board of Delegates wrote to the Alliance offering

to aid, provided groups of able-bodied young men, willing to go West and South, were sent over in groups of about one hundred. (Wischnitzer, *op. cit.*, 34.)

9. The occupations and lines of business of most of the members of the committee may be ascertained from *Trow's New York City Directory,* 1870/71: Myer Stern (1824–1899), a Bavarian Jew who came here in 1849, sold furs and hat and cap trimmings, became a leader of Temple Emanu-El, and in 1872 was to be appointed New York City Commissioner of Charities and Correction; Philip W. Frank was in "gents furnishings"; Seligman Solomon was a Trustee of the Hebrew Benevolent and Orphan Asylum Society; Henry S. Allen was either a book-dealer or a broker, while the Hebrew Relief Society of which he was President had as its Treasurer Emanuel B. Hart, at that time one of the City Commissioners of Emigration; Ephraim Japha dealt in cloths, and was President of Shaarai Zedeck, a Polish congregation; Newman Cowen sold glass on Canal Street, and often helped his fellow-countrymen get a start by staking them to a box of glass to take outside New York; he was a Russian-Polish Jew born in Lipno, whose original name was Nehemiah Lipinski (Philip Cowen, *Memories of An American Jew,* New York, 1932, pp. 23–24); he was President of the Polish congregation, Beth Israel Bikur Cholim, where the founding meeting of the committee was held (*New York Herald,* May 2, 1870); Abraham Baum was a broker and a leader of the Beth Hamidrash, a Russian and Polish congregation; Leopold Cohn was an "agent," and a Vice-President of the Board of Delegates; Alexander S. Saroni dealt in shirts, and was Treasurer of the Board of Delegates; Ellis Joseph, the clothier, was also a leader of Beth Israel Bikur Cholim; Thomas H. Keesing belonged to B'nai Jeshurun since 1852; Myer S. Isaacs was the Secretary of the Board of Delegates.

10. Disregarding the fact that all immigrants tend to stay near the ports in which they land or amidst their kinsmen, the Jews here insisted on scattering the arrivals as much as possible inland. Simon Wolf proposed they be settled in the Shenandoah Valley or in Washington Territory, which then had a Jewish Governor, Edward S. Salomon (*The Jewish Times,* April 15, 1870, p. 101). Rev. Bernhard Felsenthal of Chicago had a year earlier suggested immigrants be located in Iowa, Kansas, and Nebraska, but not in the big cities (E. Lifschitz, *Yorbuch fun Amopteil,* Yearbook, American Division, Yiddish Scientific Institute, 1938, p. 52). Horace Greeley's proposals that young men go west were seized upon as one justification for a program of dispersal that had in mind not so much the needs of the new arrivals as of those whose spokesmen made these plans. Aware of the criticism that Jews were disproportionately concentrated in the urban middle class, this Jewish leadership, not wishing itself to change its own status, thought it could direct the new immigrants into agricultural and other productive labor. Furthermore, by sending them out of the big cities, the established Jewish middle class hoped to prevent the arrivals from becoming either competitors or burdens.

152. What Are the Jews?

1. *The Sun,* September 16, 1870, p. 2, col. 2, and September 19, 1870, p. 2, cols. 2–3. Charles A. Dana (1819–1897) had in 1868 begun to edit *The Sun,* and these editorials have his quality of style.

2. The New York State Republican Party Convention met in Saratoga on September 7 and 8, 1870, nominating Kaufmann on the second day to run as companion to General Stewart L. Woodford, candidate for Governor. On the first vote, Kaufmann was defeated, 196 to 182, by DeWitt C. Littlejohn, but the latter declined the nomination on the ground that as a railroad president he should

not be an office-holder, but also because he believed that the Germans, whom he called "a power in the party," ought to have a candidate of their own. Delegate Morris Ellinger (1830–1907), editor of *The Jewish Times,* assured the convention, as a German, that his fellow-Germans would support the Republican ticket without regard to whether a German was nominated or not, but expressed his enthusiasm for the nomination of Sigismund Kaufmann. (*New-York Daily Tribune,* September 9, 1870, p. 5, col. 2.) Ellinger later accepted nomination as Congressman from the Ninth Congressional District on the Republican ticket (*The Jewish Times,* November 4, 1870, p. 568).

Sigismund Kaufmann (1825–1889), born in Bockenheim, near Frankfort-on-the-Main, after studying in Paris, Frankfort, and Strasbourg, took an active part in the Frankfort uprising in September, 1848, and had to flee to England, from which he came to the United States, settling in Brooklyn. After working in a pocketbook factory and giving lessons in French and German, he studied law and began to practice it successfully in 1852. In 1856, he joined the Republican party, campaigning for Fremont, and in 1860 he was a presidential elector, voting for Lincoln. The Governor of the state appointed him a judge on a draft board in 1863, and Lincoln later offered him the post of Minister to Italy, which Kaufmann declined. In 1869, he was a Republican candidate for the State Senate and, according to the *Tribune* (editorial, "Our Ticket," September 9, 1870), was actually elected, but the "Brooklyn Ring" robbed Kaufmann of the election by fraud and corruption. Active in the German community in the Turn Verein and the Liederkrantz, Kaufmann was also a trustee of the Temple Beth Elohim in Williamsburgh. (*The National Cyclopaedia of American Biography,* II, 413; *The Sun,* September 17, 1870, p. 2, col. 5, "Sketch of Sigismund Kaufmann," by A. Schwab, a letter answering the *Sun's* inquiry as to whether Kaufmann was in fact a Jew.)

In the German-American Turn-Verein movement, Kaufmann was a leader of the left wing which stressed the ideal of socialism and support of the Social-Democratic party rather than the sports-activities. Thus on June 6, 1850, he led a secession of 36 Turners in New York to establish the *Socialistischen Turn-Verein,* which by 1853 had 500 members. (H. Metzner, *Gedenkschrift zur Feier des 25jahrigen Jubiläums des N. Y. Turn-Vereins,* New York, 1875, pp. 2, 6; Heinrich Metzner, *Geschichte des Turner-Bundes,* Indianapolis, 1874, p. 6; *Jahrbücher der Deutsch-Amerikaner Turnerei,* Vol. I, No. 1, November, 1890, pp. 27–30.)

3. Anthropological science has concluded that there is no Aryan "race," and that the term "Aryan" is only "correctly applied to the Sanskrit speaking people who invaded India and to the ancient Persians, inhabitants of Airyana or Iran, both of whom called themselves Aryans." (Frank H. Hankins, "Aryans," *Encyclopedia of the Social Sciences,* New York, 1930, II, 264–265.) At the time these editorials were written, Count Arthur de Gobineau and Houston Stewart Chamberlain had not yet published their works advancing the dangerous theory of Aryan superiority, and the *Sun* editorial writer was using the term loosely as it was being employed by speculative linguistic scholars.

4. Today anthropological science does not acknowledge the existence of Semitic, Aryan, or American Indian "races"; the only distinguishable races are the Negroid, Mongoloid, and Australoid (Franz Boas, "Anthropology," *loc. cit.,* II, 75).

5. In fact, the candidates of the Tweed Ring and political machine did defeat the Republican ticket of Woodford and Kaufmann by 33,096 votes. The Republicans, however, derived some satisfaction from the fact that the Democratic candidates for re-election, John T. Hoffman and Allen C. Beach, obtained

16,000 fewer votes in New York City than they had in 1868. It should be noted that both *The Jewish Times* (September 16, 1870, p. 456 and September 30, 1870, p. 491) and *The Jewish Messenger* (September 16, p. 5, col. 5 and September 23, p. 4, col. 2) resented the editorials in the *Sun*.

153. Roumanian Jews

1. *The Congressional Globe,* 2 Sess., 41 Cong., Part 5, 1869–1870, pp. 4044–4045.
2. *The New-York Times,* June 2, 1870, p. 1, col. 1; *New-York Daily Tribune,* p. 4, col. 1; *New Yorker Staats-Zeitung,* cited in *The Hebrew Leader,* June 3, 1870, p. 4, col. 4; the American Press Association distributed the item throughout the country. The original source was the Paris office of the Alliance Israélite Universelle.
3. In 1866, a synagogue was destroyed in Bucharest. In 1867, Jews were forbidden to own farms, to keep village inns, and to live in rural districts, and hundreds were violently driven across the Danube. The following years brought additional restrictions, so that by 1870, Jews could not own town-houses, practice law, teach in the school-system, be officers in the army, or sell medicines. In December, 1869, they were expelled from the Bacau district. In February, 1870, Jewish doctors and their widows were deprived of their pension-rights, although salary-deductions were still made for their pensions. In April, 1870, there was a pogrom in Tecuciu, with beatings, pillagings, and profanations unchecked by the police. (Saniel Labin, "Roumania," *UJE,* IX, 256; *The Jews in Roumania. Their Recent Persecutions; Measures for Their Protection,* [Board of Delegates of American Israelites] New York, 1872, pp. 5–6; *The Jewish Times,* April 15 and May 27, 1870, pp. 102, 199; *The Jewish Messenger,* February 18, May 20 and 27, 1870; *Papers Relating to the Foreign Relations of the United States,* 1867, Part 2, Washington, 1868, pp. 2–4, 9–11.)
4. Labin, *op. cit.,* 264.
5. *Ibid.,* 248.
6. Senator Oliver H. P. T. Morton (1823–1877) of Indiana, formerly governor of the State, had been elected United States Senator in 1867 on the Union Republican ticket.
7. On this occasion, Jews moved into action with exceptional speed. On June 2, the Jews of Louisville urged all Western congregations to press Congress and the Executive Department for action. That same day, Simon Wolf in Washington presented to the State Department a dozen telegrams he had received, including one from Myer S. Isaacs, secretary of the Board of Delegates, and Henry Greenebaum, the Chicago banker. Wolf lobbied all day, writing to and seeing Congressmen and Senators. Meetings of Jews were also promptly held in Cincinnati, Memphis, Little Rock and Helena, Ark., and elsewhere in the West. (*The New-York Times,* June 3, 1870, p. 1, col. 3; *The Israelite,* June 10, 1870, p. 8, cols. 1–3, and June 24, 1870, pp. 8–9.) As press denials of the reports began to come in, the Board of Delegates in New York "deprecated the precipitate movements of the Jewish societies in the West." (*The New-York Times,* June 8, 1870, p. 1, col. 5.) The resolutions of the Jews of Indianapolis, because they were the first to be effective in Washington, received extensive notice in the press (full text published in the *Pittsburgh Dispatch,* June 3, 1870, clipping in *Philadelphia Scrapbook,* I, 30, at American Jewish Historical Society).
8. Herman Bamberger had come to Indianapolis in 1855 and in 1856 was one of the founders of the Hebrew Congregation; in 1868 he was a merchant of hats,

caps, furs and straw goods. (Jacob Piatt Dunn, *Greater Indianapolis*, Chicago, 1910, p. 628; *Logan's Indianapolis Directory*, 1868, p. 9; *The Israelite*, June 10, 1870, corrected the S. H. Bamberger of the *Cong. Globe* to H. Bamberger.) It has not been possible to identify the other signatories.

9. Senator Charles Sumner was chairman of the Committee on Foreign Relations.

10. On June 8, 1870, President U. S. Grant informed the Senate that Secretary of State Hamilton Fish "has received no official information" on the subject (*Cong. Globe, loc. cit.*, p. 4201).

11. Both *The Hebrew Leader* and *The Jewish Times*, June 3, 1870, were skeptical about the first reports. After the total denials, however, more reliable news was published in the London *Jewish Chronicle* and the Vienna *Neue Freie Presse* about a serious pogrom at Botoshani on May 28 and 29 which, although it caused no deaths, terrorized the Jewish population, destroyed considerable property and wounded many Jews, and about attacks on Jews in Bucharest on May 22, 28 and 30. (*The Jewish Messenger*, June 24, 1870, p. 5, col. 5 and July 8, 1870, pp. 2–3; *The Israelite*, June 24, 1870, pp. 8–9.)

12. Senator William Sprague (1830–1915) of Rhode Island, operator of a textile factory and a locomotive works, was a multi-millionaire who had "fabulously" increased his wealth during the Civil War (*DAB*, XVII, 476; *Biographical Directory of the United States Congress, 1774–1927*, II, 1556–1557). In 1869, however, he had attracted national attention and the support of some labor unions by a series of speeches in the Senate exposing the evil effects of the concentration of capital on our economy, the press, education, and public life in general, and proposing, utopistically, to solve the problem by creating cheap government credit facilities. (*National Affairs. Speeches of William Sprague in the Senate . . . on March 15, 17, 24 and 30, and April 8, 1869*, New York, 1869, *passim*, and *Addenda*, pp. 3, 6.) Sprague's remarks on the Roumanian Jews were roundly denounced not only in the Jewish but in the general press, the New York *Journal of Commerce*, June 7, expressing its shock that Senator Sprague had in effect made "An apology, almost a justification of their wholesale murder!" (*The Jewish Times*, June 10, 1870, p. 233.) Sprague, in a letter to Isaac Rose of Baltimore, explained that his main point had been that wherever the rich grew richer and the poor poorer "there must inevitably occur outbreaks and finally revolutions," whether in Roumania or the United States. (*The Israelite*, June 17, 1870, p. 9.) Isaac M. Wise properly attacked Sprague for having confused the cause of an outbreak with the right to an outbreak, and considered his speech inhuman in its failure to sympathize with the Jews. (*Ibid.*, June 17 and 24, 1870.) *The Nation*, June 9, 1870, pp. 360–361, pointed out acutely that the problems of the Jews in Roumania arose from the "process of transformation" of Roumanian society from a feudal to a capitalist social system, in which some Jews were then the creditors of Christian debtors. Like other liberal capitalist interpreters, however, *The Nation* not only overlooked the masses of poor Jews but failed to realize that capitalism would permanently breed such conflicts, and that they could be abolished only under a non-exploitative, socialist system. When capitalist apologists point to such social cause of anti-Semitism, they always seem to justify the anti-Semitism; only those who oppose capitalism can define this cause without the appearance of lending sanction to anti-Semitism, for they obviously oppose the system that creates the cause.

13. Senator William M. Stewart (1827–1909) of Nevada wittily pointed to this confusion between cause and right.

14. On the same day, Representative Boyd Winchester of Kentucky, under the stimulus of constituents in Louisville, introduced a resolution condemning the

massacre; the matter was referred to the Committee on Foreign Relations for verification. (*Cong. Globe, loc. cit.*, p. 4063.) Press reactions were generally very favorable; the only exception so far noted is an item in the Sandersville, Ga., *Early County News*, which had commented on the reported massacre of Jews with the statement, "We only wish this killing had taken place in Georgia instead of Turkey." The Macon, Ga., *Telegraph and Messenger* blushed for the existence of such a "vile and brutal wretch" as this editor in Georgia. (*The Hebrew Leader*, July 1, 1870, p. 4, col. 4.)

15. This editorial was reprinted without comment in *The Jewish Times*, October 11, 1872, p. 643.

16. The consular correspondence of B. F. Peixotto with our State Department, in which these pogroms are reported, was first presented by President U. S. Grant to the United States Senate on May 14, 1872, in response to its request for information, and printed as *Senate Executive Document No. 75, 42 Congress, 2 Session;* the correspondence appears in expanded form in *Papers Relating to the Foreign Relations of the United States*, 1872, Washington, 1873, pp. 691–706. It is summarized and excerpted in Cyrus Adler and Aaron M. Margalith, *With Firmness in the Right*, New York, 1946, p. 100ff (originally *AJHSP*, XXXVI, 1943, p. 100ff).

17. *The Jewish Times*, August 19, 1870, pp. 390–391. In a letter to his sponsor, Simon Wolf, Peixotto on June 28, 1870 wrote that he wanted to establish schools for the Jews of Roumania for "revolutionizing the social and religious life of our people . . . The salvation of the people of Israel in all countries where despotism rules, lies in the emancipation from the superstitions, forms and ceremonies of the past, their moral, social and religious reform and elevation . . ." (Kohler, *AJHSP*, XXIV, 1916, pp. 9–10.) An incomplete but useful account of Peixotto's work and the trials of the Roumanian Jews is his own "Story of the Roumanian Mission," *The Menorah*, July, 1886 to May, 1888.

18. *The Jewish Times, loc. cit.*

19. See Note 12 above.

20. The editorial writer makes a characteristic mistake when he identifies the conspicuous middle-class among the Jews with the entire Jewish population of Roumania. In a comprehensive report on the social structure and economy of Roumania, Peixotto showed how the Jews as a whole are beaten with the stick of hostility to the middle-class: "The Israelites, who number nearly 250,000 of the population, are, for the most part, devoted to handicraft trades. In all the towns, the carpenters, joiners, glaziers, painters, tinners, tailors, shoe-makers, hat-makers, &c., are principally Hebrews. Not a few are engaged in banking, commerce, and mercantile trade; and it is against this class, in reality, that hatred and jealousy are cherished, (fostered by the Greek and Bulgarian, who are their competitors,) though the poorer classes are made the victims." (*Foreign Relations*, 1872, September 10, p. 706.) The Tsarist Russian Government and its agents were also widely considered to be in part responsible for the pogroms, hoping that the disturbances would lead to the unseating of the Prince Charles (Hohenzollern) government and to the capitulation of Roumania to Tsarist domination (George H. Boker, our Minister to Turkey, to Secretary of State Hamilton Fish, from Constantinople, August 20, 1872, *ibid.*, 679; Kohler, *op. cit.*, 15n; Peixotto, *The Menorah*, January, 1888, p. 60, April, 1888, p. 343).

21. August 2, 1872, Peixotto had inquired of the Roumanian government whether any restrictions existed upon emigration of Jews (Peixotto to Myer S. Isaacs, December 3, 1872, cited by Kohler, *op. cit.*, 27n; Wischnitzer, *op. cit.*, 24). The

Roumanian cabinet promptly offered to issue free passports to Jews from August 18 to the next session of the legislature, and a public discussion in the Roumanian press was initiated, with the implication that either the Jews leave now *en masse* or remain and stop complaining about persecution. (Kohler, *op. cit.*, 26; *The Jewish Times,* October 4, 1872, pp. 628–629.)

22. The Bucharest correspondent of the Vienna *Neue Freie Presse* declared that Roumania could not exist a week without the Jews, because "they pay the largest portion of the taxes. . . . they alone maintain the commercial intercourse, because they are everywhere active as farmers, physicians, teachers, merchants, mechanics, traders, and laborers . . . everybody is more or less in need of them, and nobody is there that could take their place." (Quoted in *ibid.*)

23. *Records of the Office of the Secretary of the Interior. Lands and Railroads Division,* Letters Received (H), No. 10791, The National Archives.

24. Columbus Delano (1809–1896), Ohio Republican and Radical Reconstructionist in Congress, 1865 to 1869, had been Commissioner of Internal Revenue in 1869; he became Secretary of the Interior in 1870.

25. Arthur Wellington Hart, born in Canada, had been an insurance agent in Toronto in 1833, and then lived in England for a while. When he came to the United States, he spent some time in New York and Wisconsin before moving to Scranton, Pa., where in 1861 he was the publisher and editor of *The Scranton Daily News and Hyde Park Advertiser.* In April, 1861, he helped recruit what became Company H of the Eighth Regiment, Pennsylvania Infantry, which enlisted for a three-month term. Later that year he became a clerk in the Ordnance Division of the War Department. January 29, 1863, he was appointed Clerk First Class in the Internal Revenue Service, after passing an examination for that grade; having already advanced to Clerk Fourth Grade, he nevertheless resigned on April 21, 1869 (to take effect June 30, 1869) because of what he alleged to be political pressure. (Benjamin G. Sack, *History of the Jews in Canada,* Montreal, 1945, pp. 112, 115; *Records of the Department of the Army,* Office of the Secretary of the Army, Appointment Division, letter by Hart to Sec. Cameron, September 6, 1861, petition by officers, Company H, May 6, 1861; *Records of the Treasury Department,* Hart's Personnel Record, also *Appointments and Removals, 1861–1869,* Vols. 2, 3, 5, 9; data supplied in letter to this writer, July 9, 1947, by Mr. Lyle J. Holverstott, Acting Head, Fiscal Branch, The National Archives.) There is no basis in the records for the statement, frequently repeated, that he had been a Colonel of a Michigan regiment or of any other regiment. Hart was for many years a prominent figure in Jewish communal affairs, being connected with the Congregation Shearith Israel. He died in Montreal in 1891.

26. *Records of the Office of the Secretary of the Interior. Lands and Railroads Division,* Letters Received (H), The National Archives. A summary of Hart's inquiry and Curtis' reply was published in *The New York Herald,* October 31, 1872, and reprinted therefrom in *The Jewish Times,* November 1, 1872, p. 703, and in *The Israelite,* Cincinnati, November 8, 1872, p. 8, col. 3, where an editorial comment called the original inquiry unauthorized "since no such company, to our knowledge, has been founded."

27. Clipping in *Philadelphia Scrapbook I,* 55b, at A. J. H. S.

28. Kohler, *op. cit.*, 25; Wischnitzer, *op. cit.*, 24–25; *The Jewish Times,* November 15 and 22, 1872, pp. 743, 772–773.

29. *Ibid.*, August 8, 1873, p. 373. Bamberger complained that 90% of the Roumanian immigrants were paupers when they arrived and became a burden, and he

wrote to Peixotto not to send such persons. This Roumanian Emigration Society had been established at a meeting called by a sub-committee of the Board of Delegates of American Israelites for November 19, 1872. The Trustees elected to manage the funds included Barnet L. Solomon, importer of "Furniture, Curtains, Window Shades, Table Linen, and Paper Hangings," Lewis May, broker and president of Temple Emanu-el, Moses Strasburger, jeweler and president of B'nai Jeshurun, Adolph Hallgarten, druggist, and David Greenebaum, banker. (*Ibid.*, November 15 and 22, 1872, pp. 743, 767; *Trow's New York City Directory*, 1870/71 and 1873/74, *passim.*) This Society is not to be confused with the American-Roumanian Society, organized December 11, 1870 at a meeting at the home of Jesse Seligman, called to plan the financial support for Peixotto's mission; the officers of that Society were: Joseph Seligman, president; Barnet L. Solomon, vice-president; Adolph Hallgarten, secretary; Lazarus Rosenfeld, treasurer. (*Ibid.*, December 16, 1870, p. 662; for the Trustees of that Society in Chicago, Philadelphia, Baltimore, Washington, Cincinnati, Cleveland, San Francisco, and Louisville, see *The Jewish Messenger*, December 16, 1870, p. 6, col. 2.)

154. On Behalf of Immigrant Workers

1. *The Hebrew Leader*, New York, January 6, 1871, p. 5, col. 3. Neither *The Jewish Messenger* nor *The Jewish Times* carried any notice of this meeting, although the former, on January 13, 1871, p. 3, col. 1, did print a five-line notice, but without mentioning the date of the meeting!

2. This is the Hebrew Emigration Aid Society already identified as having been organized April 27, 1870.

3. On March 1, 1870, J. K. Buchner had issued the first number of *Di Idishe Zeitung*, a lithographed paper which would be entitled to be regarded as the first Yiddish periodical but for the fact that it appeared irregularly and infrequently, only twelve numbers having been published by November, 1873. (Its English title was: *The New York Hebrew Times*, "a weekly paper of politics, religion, history, science and art.") Buchner seems to have been of Russian-Polish origin, who lived in Germany, England and France before coming to the United States. In 1864–1865, he was the editor in Stuttgart of the *Volks-Kalendar und Jahrbuch für Israeliten*. Here in New York, he seems to have interested himself in the plight of the East-European Jewish immigrant, sometimes using *Di Idishe Zeitung* to back Tammany candidates for office, and in 1872 switching to support of Horace Greeley for the Presidency on the Liberal-Republican ticket, perhaps in the hope that his political connections would be helpful to the immigrants. He made a living by selling sewing-machines on the instalment plan, outfitting peddlers with New Year cards and red woolens, and so forth. As late as 1898, he issued one number of a monthly magazine in Yiddish, *Telefun*, "for tolerant and liberal Israelites." (Kalman Marmor, *The Birth of Yiddish Literature in America, 1870–1890*, New York, 1944, in Yiddish, pp. 10–11, 101n, 126; Moshe Shtarkman, "Vichtige Momentn in der Geschichte fun der Idisher Prese in America," *Yorbuch fun Amopteil*—Yearbook of the American Division of the Yiddish Scientific Institute—New York, 1939, p. 14.)

4. Owing to his illness, Buchner had to postpone the meeting to Saturday afternoon, January 14, 1871. The audience consisted of "about fifty persons, the greater part belonging to the working class, several Christians amongst them." From what sources he drew the non-Jews in his audience is not clear, since

neither the general English nor German press in New York carried announcements or reports of the meeting. Buchner made a long speech in German (not Yiddish), explaining the purpose of the Hebrew Emigrants Working Institution as the teaching of trades to the immigrants, as well as "art and science." The Institution would "plant civilization amongst our brethren, especially amongst the Russian Israelites," against whom, he noted, there was "a predjudice and aversion . . . because they are deficient in education," but "he explained logically, that ignorance is not the fault of the ignorant but of the wise . . ." He remarked on the absence of the "wealthier brethren" and of the Jewish ministers, but expressed the hope they would soon become interested. (*The Hebrew Leader,* January 13, 1871, p. 1, col. 4; and January 20, 1871, p. 8, col. 2, report by M. Davison.)

To help finance the project, Buchner announced "A Course of Humorous Lectures" at Cooper Institute to be given Saturday afternoons from February 18 to March 11. The subjects listed were: "Der Berliner Chasan; Moses Mendelsohn; Israel Baal Schem and Israel Jacobson." Admission was to be $3 for the series, $1 per lecture. Two advertisements appeared in *The Hebrew Leader,* February 10 and 17, 1871. From the absence of further advertisements, it may be inferred that the first lecture was not successful financially, and the series was discontinued. The last mention of the Institution appears in Buchner's letter, *The Hebrew Leader,* March 17, 1871, p. 1, col. 5, in which he reports the receipt of "encouragment" from Dr. Samuel Adler (1809–1891) of Temple Emanu-El and Dr. Adolph Huebsch (1830–1884) of the Bohemian congregation, Ahavath Chesed. Dr. David Einhorn of Adas Jeshurun had promised to raise $300. Several congregations had also promised aid, as had the Tammany Mayor of New York, A. Oakey Hall (1826–1898). Buchner hoped for more editorial support. It is possible, however, that the Institution Buchner planned was not a total failure, for in the February 19, 1873 issue (No. 10) of *Di Idishe Zeitung,* Buchner speaks of a Talmud Torah, the "American Hebrew Institution," in which poor Jewish boys are taught, in addition to Hebrew and English, a trade or a craft, so that they would not have to become beggars or peddlers.

5. Jonas Bondi (1804–1874), editor and owner of *The Hebrew Leader,* had in the very same issue reported that he had just learned, from a German newspaper, of the death of his younger sister, Henriette, in Hanover. Although the meeting was postponed a week, Bondi did not attend.

155. Attempts at Conversion

1. Clipping in *Philadelphia Scrapbook I,* p. 33a, at A.J.H.S. The *Sunday Dispatch* was published by John Lawlor, Robert Everett and Elias J. Hincken.
2. J. de le Roi, "Judentaufen im 19. Jahrhundert," *Nathanael,* Berlin, XV, Nos. 3–4 (1899), p. 97. On the false analogy that in Germany it has been calculated that the church itself is responsible for the conversion of nine Jews to every one converted by special missions to the Jews, de le Roi then proceeds to multiply his figures by nine. It is startling to find Arthur Ruppin, as well as various encyclopedias, accepting this procedure (*Soziologie der Juden,* I, Berlin, 1930, pp. 296–297).
3. June 9, 1871, p. 4, col. 3. On p. 5, col. 1, there is also a brief excerpt from an editorial in the *Sunday Times* (New York, but not to be confused with the Sunday edition of *The New-York Times*) on the folly of attempts to convert the Jews. The *Sunday Times* was published by Elbridge G. Howard.

4. May was the month for religious conventions and annual meetings. On May 11, there had taken place "the great event of the May anniversaries," the 18th Social Reunion of the American Congregational Union (*The Independent,* New York, May 18, 1871, p. 2). May 16, there was the Fourth Annual Convention of the Long Island Episcopal Diocese; May 17, the African Methodist Episcopal Conference, and the Southern Conference of the Evangelical Lutheran Synod of New York; May 18, the 55th Anniversary parade and celebration of the New York Sunday School Missionary Union. (*New-York Daily Tribune,* May 17, 18, 19, 1871.)
5. Little else is known of Rev. Louis C. Newman or his missionary society. In 1863, he was the author of *The Bible View of Slavery Reconsidered. A Letter to the Right Rev. Bishop Hopkins,* published in Philadelphia and New York.
6. This seems to be an exaggeration. *Trow's New York City Directory,* 1871/72, lists only 27 synagogues. *The New-York Times,* May 26, 1871, p. 2, col. 6, in an article on the beginning of "The Pentecost Festival" in the Jewish community, refers to "thirty synagogues and temples."
7. What the editorial writer means is that orthodox Jews believe in the coming of the Messiah, but deny that Jesus is the Messiah. Reform Jews were abandoning the belief in a personal Messiah.
8. In a tract published by the New York Gospel Mission to the Jews and handed to me on the street on the East Side of New York on October 14, 1948 (the day after Yom Kippur), I found the same subjects treated, the Messiah, the Incarnation, and the Trinity.

156. On Rabbinical Education

1. P. 5, cols. 1–2.
2. *The New York Herald,* June 11, 1871, pp. 8–9, had a lengthy editorial, entitled "A Great Jewish Need," probably stimulated by the conference of Reform rabbis in Cincinnati, June 5 to 12, at which it had been decided to establish a rabbinical seminary. This editorial had stressed "the great need of an English ministry for our Jewish congregations . . . if the rising generations of Hebrews are to be kept within the fold of Judaism and obedient to the faith of their fathers," and deplored the fact that "there is not a single American rabbi in this city, and very few such in the country. They are all of foreign importation." *The Jewish Messenger,* June 16, 1871, p. 4, col. 2, in its editorial, "The 'Herald' Aroused," took that newspaper to task for overestimating the importance of the Cincinnati conference, affirmed that the orthodox Jews were aware of the need of English-speaking rabbis and of a seminary in which to train them, and advised the *Herald* to "leave Jewish law to the Rabbis and the Jews."

3 *The Jewish Messenger,* July 19, 1872, editorials, "Hebrew Education" and "The Great Need." The *Herald's* quotations are from the former.

4. The Rev. Dr. James Koppel Gutheim (1817–1886), born in Westphalia, had in 1846 become the rabbi of B'nai Jeshurun in Cincinnati; in 1849, he took the pulpit of Shaare Chesed in New Orleans, and in 1853 that of Nefutzoth Yehuda in the same city. A Confederate supporter, he closed his synagogue in 1862 when New Orleans was in Federal hands and served as Rabbi in Montgomery, Ala. and Columbus, Ga. before returning to New Orleans in 1864. In 1868, he came to Temple Emanu-El in New York as English preacher, resigning in 1872 to return to New Orleans, this time to the new Reform congregation,

Temple Sinai, which he served until his death. He was succeeded at Temple Emanu-El in New York by Rabbi Gustav Gottheil (1827–1903), who came here from a pulpit in Manchester, England.

5. Rabbi Henry Vidaver (1833–1882), born in Poland, had come to the Rodeph Shalom Congregation in Philadelphia in 1859. After serving a congregation in St. Louis for several years, he came to B'nai Jeshurun in New York in January, 1868. But it was not until 1874 that he resigned to go to Sherith Israel in San Francisco; his place was vacant until March 1, 1876, when Henry S. Jacobs was installed in it. (Goldstein, *op. cit.,* 147–148, 160–161.)

6. Rev. Samuel Myer Isaacs (1804–1878), born in Leeuwarden, Holland, had served the Congregation B'nai Jeshurun in New York until 1847, when a group seceded to form Congregation Shaarey Tefila, for which he was still preaching in 1872. He was also the owner of *The Jewish Messenger.*

7. Maimonides College, established by the Hebrew Education Society of Philadelphia and the Board of Delegates of American Israelites as the first American school for rabbinical education, had opened on October 25, 1867, with five students. Before it closed in 1873 for lack of funds, it had graduated three students who took American pulpits: Rev. Dr. Samuel Mendelsohn, at Norfolk, Va. and later at Wilmington, N. C.; Rev. Dr. David Levi, at Beth Elohim, Charleston, S. C.; and Rev. Heyman Saft, one of the English Readers at Shaarey Tefila in New York, 1871–1872. (*UJE,* VII, 296; Morais, *op. cit.,* 188–189; *The Jewish Messenger,* January 10, 1873, p. 5, col. 3; *Trow's New York City Directory,* 1871/72, p. 999.)

   A project for a seminary had been initiated in New York in 1865 by David Einhorn and Samuel Adler, who formed the Emanu-El Theological Seminary Association to help young Jews enter the rabbinate, but it used its funds only to send a couple of students to European institutions to study, among them being Felix Adler and Emil G. Hirsch (1851–1923).

   No lasting rabbinical seminary was established until 1875, when the Hebrew Union College in Cincinnati was founded.

8. Rev. George Jacobs (1834–1884) had been a rabbi in Richmond, Va., before going to Congregation Beth-El in Philadelphia; his brother, Henry S. Jacobs (1827–1893), had served in Richmond, Va., Charleston and Columbia, S. C. and Augusta, Ga. before going to New Orleans in 1866. These brothers, however, were not born in Canada but in another British possession, Kingston, Jamaica.

9. Rev. Dr. Edward B. M. Browne (not George Brown) was Professor of Medical Jurisprudence and Diseases of the Mind at the Evansville Medical College of Indiana (*The Book Jashar,* information on title page, New York, 1876). He had served as rabbi in Montgomery, Ala. and Milwaukee, Wisc. before coming to Evansville (*The Israelite,* July 26, 1872, p. 6, cols. 2–4). In 1873, he edited *The Jewish Independent* in Evansville for a short time (*Ibid.,* January 10, 1873, p. 4, col. 2). November 15, 1881 he became the rabbi of the Reform temple, "Gates of Hope," in New York; in 1904, he was elected Rabbi of Congregation B'nai Sholom in Toledo, Ohio (*AJYB,* 5666, 1905–1906, p. 120).

10. There were of course many more, among them Jacques Judah Lyons (1813–1877) of Congregation Shearith Israel, New York; Sabato Morais (1823–1897) of Mickve Israel and Marcus Jastrow (1829–1903) of Rodeph Shalom, Philadelphia; Maurice Fluegel (1832–1911), at that time in Quincy, Ill., Elkan Cohn of Temple Emanu-El and A. J. Messing of Sherith Israel, San Francisco.

11. Compare the similarity of thought in the editorial, "We Must Have a Semi-

nary," *The Israelite,* July 21, 1871, pp. 8–9, written shortly after the Cincinnati rabbinical conference: "we must have a seminary, to educate for the ministry our American-born sons, (and for our sake also daughters) who know our character and our wants, our feelings and hopes, our claims and expectations, who sympathize with us, feel and think, pray and believe with us, who are ours with heart and soul, speak our language, love our country, respect our feelings, and lead us onward and forward to God and truth, to Israel and humanity. . . ."

12. I. M. Wise's son, Leo Wise (1849–1933), had a law degree but did not practise; he was at that time in South Africa, prospecting the gold fields. I. M. Wise's youngest son, however, Jonah Bondi Wise (1881–1959) did become a well-known New York rabbi.

    Max Lilienthal's four sons, Theodore Max Lilienthal, Jesse W. Lilienthal, Philip Nettre Lilienthal and Albert Lilienthal, were lawyers, merchants, or financiers connected with the Seligman Brothers' banking establishments. At about the time this editorial was written, Rev. Dr. Max Lilienthal was proposing the establishment of a family bank modeled on the Rothschilds and Seligmans, but this "life dream" was never realized (Sophie Lilienthal, *The Lilienthal Family Record,* San Francisco, 1930, pp. 73–74).

    S. M. Isaacs' eldest son, Myer Samuel Isaacs (1841–1904), was a lawyer, but his younger son, Abraham Samuel Isaacs (1852–1920), studied theology in Breslau a couple of years after the date of this editorial, and became a rabbi.

    The Jewish Messenger remarked that the sons of Christian clergymen also eschewed the ministry (July 26, 1872, p. 5, col. 2).

13. Dr. Samuel Adler (1809–1891), born in Worms, Germany, had come to Temple Emanu-El in 1857, and remained there until 1874. His son, Felix Adler (1851–1933), was born in Alzey, Germany (not the United States), and had been brought here in 1857. His European studies were financed by the Emanu-El Theological Seminary Association. In October, 1873, when he accepted an invitation to preach at Temple Emanu-El, his sermon was criticized for its iconoclasm and the omission of any mention of God. In 1876, he founded the New York Society for Ethical Culture.

14. *The New York Herald* on July 28, 1872 published a letter by I. Abarbanel, defending the use of Hebrew in the synagogue because it is "the language which God speaks," a concept derided as naive in *The Jewish Times,* August 2, 1872, p. 448. Later the *Herald* published a letter by A. Deer, "Rabbinical Education—Reasons Why It can not be Had Here," which elicited attacks in *The Israelite,* August 23 and September 13, 1872. *The Jewish Messenger* printed a letter by "C." in Philadelphia blaming the inconsistency and hypocrisy of the rabbinate for the aversion of American Jews to it (August 9, 1872, p. 2, cols. 1–2).

157. In Praise of the Jews

1. Clipping in *Philadelphia Scrapbook I,* p. 60a. *The Evening Telegraph* was owned, published and edited by Charles E. Warburton.
2. At about the same time, for instance, the Chicago *Post* was editorially denouncing Polish Jews as "speculative, carping, ugly, and mean," and thoroughly undesirable as citizens either in this country or any other (*The Israelite,* September 6, 1872, p. 8, col. 3).
3. Morais, *The Jews of Philadelphia,* 116, italics added.
4. The origin of this hospital and home for the aged lay in the fact that in the first half of 1864, three Jews died in "Christian hospitals" in Philadelphia.

Believing that this reflected "the greatest discredit" on the large Jewish community, which had allowed its brethren to die among Christians "without having enjoyed the privilege of hearing the *Shemang Yisrael,*" and after having had to "eat forbidden food," and in view of the danger of dissection after death and of burial among non-Jews (prohibited to orthodox Jews), Lodge No. 8 of B'nai B'rith resolved on August 14, 1864 to form a Jewish Hospital Association to build a hospital. Opened in 1866, the hospital soon outgrew its size by 1870, and a new site was bought; the corner-stone was laid on October 9, 1872, "with Masonic ceremonies" which involved both a rabbi and a Christian clergyman, the chaplain of the Grand Lodge of Masons in Pennsylvania. (Morais, *The Jews of Philadelphia,* 116–118.)

158. Anti-Semitism in the Armed Forces

1. *The New-York Times,* December 15, 1872, p. 3, col. 4, noted that a letter of inquiry had been received from an anxious reader, hoping the regimental colonel would not prolong the investigation until the governor has been replaced and the matter forgotten. *The Jewish Messenger,* December 20, 1872, p. 4, col. 4, replying to another correspondent, declared that "the party aggrieved can alone be heard by the military authorities, and it rests with Mr. Waterman himself to have this wrong righted." The other Jewish periodicals paid no attention to the matter.
2. The Captain of Company A was then R. Kelly Styles (letter from the Adjutant General, Albany, N. Y., January 18, 1950), listed in the City Directory as Richard K. Styles, builder.
3. The writer, N. M. Davis, although he describes himself as a merchant, is not listed in the Memphis directories, and it has not been possible to identify him any further.

159. Capmakers on Strike

1. *The Hat, Cap and Fur Trade Review,* I, Feb. 1874, pp. 118–119, which was also used by J. M. Budish, *Geschichte fun di Cloth Het, Kep un Milineri Arbeiter,* New York, 2nd ed., 1926, pp. 26–31.
2. *Hat . . . Review,* and *New-York Tribune,* Jan. 27, 1874. Very many employers were German Jews, but three were Polish Jews: Adolphus and Samuel Markewitz, Charles H. Petsch & Co. and Yehusha (Harris) Rothstein, the latter a Gabay of the Etz-Haim Yeshiva (E. Tcherikower, *Geschichte fun der Idisher Arbeter-Bavegung in di Fareinikte Shtaten,* New York, 1945, II, 249–250) .
3. Grinstein, *op. cit.,* 111; *The New York Herald,* Jan. 30, Feb. 1, 4, 5; *The Sun,* Jan. 30; *The World,* Feb. 10, 1874.
4. Foner, *op. cit.,* 439; "during the first three months of 1874 about 90,000 homeless workers, two-fifths of whom were women, were lodgers in New York City's police station houses," but the *Nation* disapproved of such hospitality as "thoroughly communistic." (*Ibid.,* 442.) When *The World* printed lists of destitute unemployed, Jewish names appeared (Jan. 30, 31, Feb. 1, 2, 1874) . Efforts to get public relief were denounced by the capitalist press, including Jewish periodicals. *The Jewish Messenger* feared "the utter subversion of society" (Dec. 19, 1873) , and smugly pronounced: "The world is regulated very sensibly, after all . . . The true laborer, who is worthy of his hire, does not find it necessary to cry aloud for help from the public treasury." (Jan. 2, 1874.) But when the editor of the *Herald* financed four soup kitchens, *The Jewish Times* asserted that "it is deeds

like these which truly stamp our century as one of progressive enlightenment; . . . they mean transformation of the religion of dogmas into the religion of practice." (Feb. 20, 1874.) In the next issue, this journal praised the "model soup-house at 100 Mott Street," run by Albert Rosenberg, who stated that "the poverty stricken families of our race in his neighborhood" need much more help.

5. *Herald,* Feb. 5, 1874.
6. *Tribune,* Jan. 27, 1874, reported men averaged $15 a week, women $5 to $10. *Sun,* Jan. 30, noted that families in which man, wife and children worked 12 to 16 hours a day earned $6 to $10 a week. *Herald,* Feb. 3, wrote of wages falling from $18–$20 a week to $8. *Times,* Feb. 7, explained there were two short seasons, totaling five months; workers worked 12 and 14 hours a day, 7 days a week, finishers and blockers earning $10 to $15 a week, while operators with an assistant could net less than $25. *Hat . . . Review* admitted "there can be no doubt that the inconsiderate conduct of certain houses in reducing their wages . . . was the cause of the strike," yet regarded the strikers' demands as "out of all proportion."
7. *Times,* Jan. 11, 1874. There had been earlier attempts to organize. Pres. Ober reminded the workers that in 1869 a strike had failed because they were not well organized (*Herald,* Jan. 30, 1874). There was a Capmakers' Union in 1871 (*Tribune,* Jan. 27, 1874); in 1872 it had some 400 members, led by the cutters (Hertz Burgin, *Di Geschichte fun der Idisher Arbeter Bavegung in Amerika, Rusland un England,* New York, 1915, p. 844). For officers of the Central Union of Capmakers, see *Herald,* Jan. 30, Feb. 4, 5 and *Sun,* Jan. 30, 1874.
8. For shop organization, see *Herald* and *New-Yorker Staats-Zeitung,* Jan. 30; for attendance at meetings, see *Herald,* Jan. 30, *World,* Feb. 2, 10, *Sun,* Feb. 3, 1874.
9. For demands, see *Herald* and *Sun,* Jan. 30, *World,* Feb. 2, and *Hat . . . Review;* for Union rules and regulations see *Staats-Zeitung,* Jan. 21, *Evening Post,* Feb. 4, *Herald,* Feb. 21, 22, and *Arbeiter-Zeitung,* March 7, 1874.
10. The Jewish press did not mention the strike. In addition to the officers, M. Weiner, H. Benjamin and Bromberg, the following Jews were often on Union negotiating committees: Max Lehmann and Abraham, Harris or Moses Cohen (all listed as capmakers, *Trow's New York City Directory,* 1873/1874; *Sun,* Feb. 3, *Herald* and *World,* Feb. 11).
11. *Times* and *World,* Feb. 5, 1874.
12. Marks Bros. & Thompson, employing 150 workers, comprised Abraham and Marcus Marks and George A. Thompson. L. J. Phillips & Co., with over 75 workers, comprised Lewis J. and Henry Phillips. William R. (not J.) Willis & Co. employed some 50 workers. (Moritz) Isidor & (Ferdinand) Hein had 75 workers. Charles Fox's Son & Co., with 150 workers, comprised David Fox and Mrs. Rose Fox, widow of Charles. The Chairman was Samuel Corn, who with brother Julius made up Samuel Corn & Brother, employing some 125 workers. (*Trow's . . . ,* 1873–1874; *Hat . . . Review; Times,* Feb. 5, 1874, where Corn is incorrectly given as Cohen.)
13. After the lockout, the Union began to sign agreements with smaller firms: Samuel Wolff & Co. (including Simon and Sylvester Wolff), with about 60 workers; (Baruch) Cahn & (Sigmund) Bromberg, with 25 workers; Harris Rothstein, with some 50 workers; Henry M. Silverman, etc.
14. Although the Central Union had at least 800 members (*World,* Feb. 2, 1874), it soon disintegrated. Within a half-year, the finishers, the main body, left, the Cutters remaining. The Operators, who had a separate Local within the Central

Union (*World,* Feb. 19), disappear. When a general strike was waged in 1878, organization began anew.

Other noteworthy aspects of the strike are: a) contributions were received from the Old Capmakers' Society, the furriers' and tailors' unions in New York, sections of the International Workingmen's Association, capmakers in Philadelphia, and others, while those whose employers settled assessed themselves weekly sums for the strikers; b) an unsuccessful attempt was made to organize a cooperative shop (*Tribune,* Feb. 6, 9, 10; *Staats-Zeitung,* Feb. 7, 16; *World,* Feb. 7, 8, 13, 14, 15; *Herald,* Feb. 10, 13; *Times,* Feb. 11); c) Feb. 20 the capmakers affiliated with the Workingmen's Union, largest central body in New York, with 30,000 members, which had offered its aid to the capmakers (*Herald,* Feb. 5, 12, 1874).

Corrections and Additional Information: Revised Edition

1. *P. 70, Doc. No. 46, Introduction:* Mr. I. B. Bailin of New York has called my attention to the fact that Isaac Abravanel (1437–1508), Spanish-Portuguese Jewish statesman, theologian and philosopher, had in his commentary on the Bible expressed strong preference for republics like Venice or Florence as against monarchies. Joseph Sarachek, *Don Isaac Abravanel,* New York, 1938, pp. 157–159, confirms this point with a long quotation. Completed in Venice in 1506 and published there in 1579, these commentaries influenced Christian theologians, but to what extent this particular point was influential, and whether it affected the thinking of the American clergy or of American Jews, has not been established.
2. *P. 99, Doc. No. 56, Introduction:* In Virginia, when the law restraining manumissions was repealed in 1782, the number of free Negroes leaped from 3,000 to 12,000 in 1790, to 20,000 in 1800, and to over 30,000 in 1810. In 1849, the constitutional convention prohibited the manumission of slaves. (John Henderson Russell, *The Free Negro in Virginia 1619–1865,* Baltimore, 1913, pp. 43–61.) The condition of the "free" Negro needs to be seen in the light of such data as are given by John Hope Franklin, *From Slavery to Freedom,* New York, 1947, Ch. 14, "Quasi-Free Negroes."
3. *P. 223, Doc. No. 91:* The last sentence of the Introduction, implying that American workers were "moving westward to escape economic difficulties" needs to be corrected in the light of the evidence that few eastern workers went west to become farmers owing to lack of both skill and money; it was eastern *farmers* mostly who went west, and then during periods of prosperity, not depression. (Murray Kane, "Some Considerations on the Safety Valve Doctrine," *The Mississippi Valley Historical Review,* XXIII, 1936, pp. 179–186; Carter Goodrich and Sol Davison, "The Wage-Earner in the Westward Movement II," *Political Science Quarterly,* LI, 1936, pp. 114–116; Sidney L. Jackson, *America's Struggle for Free Schools,* Washington, D. C., 1941, p. 229, note 20.)
4. *P. 279, Doc. No. 98, Introduction:* By a 1929 ordinance, Sabbath-observing Jews in Charleston, S. C. may obtain permission from the Police Commission to keep their stores open Sundays (Charles Reznikoff and Uriah Z. Engelman, *The Jews of Charleston,* Philadelphia, 1950, pp. 215, 322).

5. *P. 439, Doc. No. 130, Introduction:* That Rev. Julius Lewin of Shreveport, La., joined the Confederate Army is asserted by Rabbi Adolf Philippsborn, *UJE,* IX, 519–520. Bertram W. Korn, however, notes that neither the Adjutant General's offices in Washington nor New Orleans can confirm this statement (*American Jewry and the Civil War,* Philadelphia, 1951, p. 258, note 3). Correspondence with Rabbi Philippsborn leads me to conclude that he has confused Rev. Lewin of Shreveport with another person, the merchant Julius Levin of Alexandria, La., who did enlist in the Confederate Army.

6. *P. 576, Doc. No. 32, Note 6:* This 9050 acre tract of land was bought from Croghan in March, 1770, for £1800 (Anita Libman Lebeson, *Pilgrim People,* New York, 1950, pp. 155–156).

7. *P. 603, Doc. No. 69, Note 3:* For an extensive study of the Hep-hep movement, see Eleonore O. Sterling, "Anti-Jewish Riots in Germany in 1819: A Displacement of Social Protest," *Historia Judaica,* October, 1950, pp. 105–142.

8. *P. 603, Doc. No. 70, Note 2:* In his will, Dr. De La Motta left his two slaves and their issue to his sister for life and then to his own children, enjoining them that the slaves "be treated with lenity" (Reznikoff and Engelman, *op. cit.,* 77).

9. *P. 634, Doc. No. 95, Note 1:* This account of the Mexican War was also published as a pamphlet in St. Louis, July, 1903. Jacob Hirshorn died not in 1905, but February 2, 1906 (Bureau of Vital Statistics, St. Louis, Mo.). He was born in Furth, Bavaria, May 19, 1829; arrived in Baltimore in October, 1846; in 1855 he applied for naturalization in Providence, where he was in the dry-goods business. He married Mary Pareira July 5, 1857. They lived for a time in New York. In 1866 he is listed as a partner in a clothing business in St. Louis (*Edwards' Annual Director . . . in the City of St. Louis,* 1866, pp. 456, 711). A daughter, Sadie (Mrs. Max Weil), was in her 91st year in 1951. Except where other sources are cited, I am indebted for the foregoing data to Mr. David C. Adelman of Providence, who is compiling a history of the Jews of Providence, R. I.

10. *P. 637, Note 6:* Altogether, the Relief Committee collected over $170,000 in cash and $70,000 in foodstuffs. The Irish themselves were the main supporters of Irish famine relief, contributing $800,000 in 1846 in New York alone, and in the following decade sending $19,680,000 to Ireland from all over the United States. (Robert Ernst, *Immigrant Life in New York City 1825–1863,* New York, 1949, p. 122.)

11. *P. 638, Doc. No. 98, Note 3:* After the New York State Court of Appeals had upheld the constitutionality of the Sunday laws in the Friedman-Praska case, the American Jewish Congress applied to the United States Supreme Court for a review, but the Court denied the application. *The Harvard Law Review* was critical of the Court's refusal of review (May, 1951, p. 1194).

12. *P. 646, Note 16a:* The New York society of German doctors mentioned on p. 305 was founded in 1846 (Ernst, *op. cit.,* 130).

13. *P. 648, Doc. No. 109, Note 1:* Lyon began to edit the *Mercantile Journal* a few years after he established *The Asmonean.* Before then he was an unsuccessful umbrella manufacturer. (*The Asmonean,* March 12, 1858, p. 172.)

14. *P. 658, Note 19:* Abraham Cohen Labatt, born in Charleston, S. C. in 1802, moved to New Orleans in 1831, to San Francisco in 1849, and was living in Galveston, Texas in 1894 (Cohen, *AJHSP,* II, 1894, p. 139).

15. *P. 678, Note 2:* As early as the 1856 presidential election campaign, an anonymous Jew had written, protesting *The Asmonean's* support of the Democratic candidate Buchanan, "No! the Jew cannot support a party, that would condemn our fellow men for the mere accident of color, to a more than Egyptian bondage in the free soil of the West. . . ." The editor dismissed this position as sophistry. (*The Asmonean,* August 8, 1856, p. 132.)

16. *P. 680, Note 9:* It was the Thirteenth Amendment in 1865 that, by abolishing slavery, cancelled the constitutional provision counting three-fifths of the slaves in computing congressional representation. Furthermore, most of those founding fathers named as disapproving of slavery were themselves slaveowners, and not all of them freed their own slaves.

17. *P. 688, Note 8:* President-elect Buchanan not only improperly ascertained in advance what the Supreme Court decision in the Dred Scott case would be, but actively helped to shape it by his highly irregular correspondence with Justices John Catron and Robert C. Grier (F. H. Hodder, "Some Phases of the Dred Scott Case," *The Mississippi Valley Historical Review,* XVI, 1929, pp. 10–11; Charles Warren, *The Supreme Court in United States History,* Boston, 1923, III, 17–19; Roy F. Nichols, *The Disruption of American Democracy,* New York, 1948, p. 66; Will D. Gilliam, Jr., "Some Textbooks on the Dred Scott Case," *The Negro History Bulletin,* February, 1951, pp. 106–108).

Index

Supplementary Index